COMPLETE PELICAN SHA

THE TRAGEDIES

COMPLETE PELICAN

SHAKESPEARE

THE TRAGEDIES

GENERAL EDITOR ALFRED HARBAGE

PENGUIN BOOKS

Penguin Books Ltd, Harmondsworth, Middlesex, England
Penguin Books, 625 Madison Avenue, New York, New York 10022, U.S.A.
Penguin Books Australia Ltd, Ringwood, Victoria, Australia
Penguin Books Canada Ltd, 2801 John Street, Markham, Ontario, Canada L3R 1B4
Penguin Books (N.Z.) Ltd, 182-190 Wairau Road, Auckland 10, New Zealand

The Pelican text published in thirty-eight volumes between 1956 and 1967
Revised edition first published in one volume by Penguin Books Inc. 1969
Reprinted 1969, 1970 (twice), 1972, 1974, 1975
This three-volume edition first published by Penguin Books 1981

Designed by Hans Schmoller, R.D.I.

Made and printed in Great Britain by Butler & Tanner Ltd,
Frome and London

TABLE OF CONTENTS

THE TRAGEDIES

FOREWORD

No secular works have had wider and more continuous currency than Shakespeare's tragedies, and none have stimulated such persistent efforts of analysis and evaluation. The author himself never defined tragedy, and the definitions and descriptive remarks of such fellow-playwrights as Jonson, Chapman, and Webster are somewhat less comprehensive than Sidney's, written before there were great English tragedies to define: "high and excellent Tragedy, that openeth the greatest wounds, and sheweth forth the Ulcers that are covered with Tissue; that maketh Kinges feare to be Tyrants, and Tyrants manifest their tirranical humors; that, with stirring the affects of admiration and commiseration, teacheth the uncertainty of this world, and upon how weake foundations guilden roofes are builded. . . ." The phrase "stirring the affects of admiration and commiseration" seems an echo of Aristotle's "effecting a purgation of fear and pity" although Sidney's "admiration" means *awe* rather than *fear*. Actually neither Greek tragedy nor Aristotle's commentary upon it had much direct impact upon the Elizabethans. If Shakespearean tragedy shows an affinity with that of Aeschylus, Sophocles, and Euripides (and it does), it is owing to its universality.

Sidney's definition is a useful reminder of the medieval or "Gothic" inheritance of Elizabethan tragedy, transmitted through narrative poetry of the *contemptus mundi* and *de casibus* kinds. The most familiar examples are Chaucer's *Monk's Tale*, and *The Mirror for Magistrates* compiled by William Baldwin and his successors between 1555 and 1587 in continuation of Boccaccio's fourteenth-century *De Casibus Virorum Illustrium* and Lydgate's fifteenth-century *Fall of Princes*. A "tragedy" was a tale of the fall and wretched death of an eminent person. In combination with similar tales, it was designed to demonstrate the treachery of the goddess Fortuna, or the curse upon mankind resulting from Adam's fall, or the wages of particular sins committed by particular men. In this last and most common aspect Gothic tragedy fused with Senecan tragedy of dreadful crime and dreadful retribution, and with the theatrical spawn of novellas of villainous intrigue. One of the mines of the English playwrights was a French compilation by Belleforest leaning heavily upon Italian fiction and called *Histoires Tragiques*. In popular practise, if not in critical theory, a stage tragedy could be based upon a fiction, and could employ devices of intrigue once thought appropriate only in comedy. The usual protagonist was not Aristotle's man "better than ourselves" in most particulars, but a passionate villain superior only in social station. A typical Elizabethan tragedy was a display of transgression and punishment, two parts sensational to one part exemplary.

Shakespeare dramatized the same kinds of material as the other playwrights, although he avoided "domestic" tragedy of middle-class marital infidelity, and, when he turned to historical sources, he tended to focus upon disastrous behavior of a political rather than private kind. In most of his tragedies the intricate action and bloody extravagance of Elizabethan tragedy in general finds a parallel, while the Gothic and Senecan influences are clearly manifest. Yet his tragedies are far from typical. With the exception of *Titus Andronicus*, they transcend both their literary heredity and their theatrical environment. A strain of the heroic had mingled in anterior tragic poetry: there had been tales in honor of famous men who had sacrificed themselves in great causes. And there was, of course, a copious literature and living tradition of religious martyrdom. Shakespeare's sensitiveness to the heroic and self-sacrificial strain, along with his superior endowment as an artist, gives his tragedies their special cast. If we ask what quality his tragic protagonists come nearest to sharing in common, we must answer their *unworldliness*, their incapacity for compromise. They love whatever it is they love not wisely but too well. Macbeth generically is the familiar Elizabethan super-villain, and Antony the very epitome of those mighty ones who fall precipitously from high place, but that is not all they are. Macbeth seems the black shadow of his complete opposite, and Antony lingers in our minds neither as fallen conqueror nor decayed sensualist but as one who valued a personal relationship in heroic excess of its true worth. The term "tragic flaw" is an awkward one in connection with the remaining Shakespearean tragic heroes because the ultimate cause of their suffering is their idealism, which is impractical by definition and yet, in essence, a thing of value. Man owes to aspiration whatever he has that is good, including his human status. But the tragic nature of that status derives from the identical thing which confers it, and in its intimation of this great mystery may lie the symbolic power of Shakespearean tragedy. It treats of imperfect ones torn by their dreams of perfection, mortals with immortal longings in them.

A. H.

TITUS ANDRONICUS

INTRODUCTION

Titus Andronicus is a ridiculous play. This gallimaufry of murders, rape, lopped limbs, and heads baked in a pie, lavishly served with the rich purple sauce of rhetoric, may have been to the taste of the Elizabethans, but what is one to make of it to-day? As long ago as 1614 Ben Jonson bracketed the play with Kyd's *Spanish Tragedy* as representative of the outmoded tragic vein of some twenty-five or thirty years before, and scoffed at those who still admired it. After a brief revival of popularity in the eighteenth century (in Edward Ravenscroft's "improved" version), *Titus Andronicus* became the least performed of all Shakespeare's plays, until in 1955 a production in Stratford-upon-Avon revealed that a modern audience could be moved by it, and that it might have something to say to the twentieth century. Like the Elizabethans, modern man is no stranger to violence, and he could find mirrored in the play the crimes of the concentration camp. Here was stark horror, unrelieved by pity; human agony pitched beyond endurance, until the victim becomes insane. The arbitrariness of the action seemed to symbolize the essential absurdity of modern life: Titus was like a man thrust blindfold into a room full of whirling knives. The play could be seen as Shakespeare's one tragic contribution to the drama of the absurd, or so it seemed at Stratford, under the spell of Sir Laurence Olivier's magnificent interpretation of Titus. Stratford proved that *Titus Andronicus* is still good theatre, and almost succeeded in turning it into a good play, yet reading it again one is tempted to concur with Edward Ravenscroft, who, in the preface to his adaptation of 1678, called it not a "structure," but "a heap of rubbish."

The manifest deficiencies of *Titus Andronicus* have persuaded critics careful of Shakespeare's reputation to dismiss it altogether from the canon as unworthy of his genius. Others, for whom the external evidence pointing to Shakespeare's authorship is not so lightly to be set aside, have sought a compromise by claiming that what we have represents Shakespeare's rather perfunctory reworking of a much older play, in which the hands of Peele, Greene, Kyd, and Marlowe have been variously, but not very convincingly, detected. Others again have argued that *Titus Andronicus* was one of the first plays Shakespeare wrote, and have sought to excuse its imperfections on the grounds of the author's youthfulness and inexperience. More ingeniously, the view has been put forward that the obvious absurdities of plot and diction prove that it was part of Shakespeare's conscious intention to burlesque the conventional excesses of the then popular "tragedy of blood," the formula for which Kyd and others had derived from Seneca's Latin tragedies of revenge. The continuing debate attests to the widespread feeling that the play calls for some sort of apology. The only general agreement so far arrived at is

that in the absence of any conclusive evidence to the contrary the play must be regarded as largely, if not wholly, by Shakespeare, and that the publication of the first quarto in 1594 at least indicates that it was written at a comparatively early date in his dramatic career. An entry in Henslowe's diary records a production of "Titus & Ondronicus" as "ne" (new) by Sussex's Men on January 24, 1594. The entry probably refers to the present play, but there is some doubt as to whether the "ne" means newly written, newly revised, or newly acquired by the company named. Lending some support to the last possibility is the fact that the title page of the quarto of 1594 names Derby's Men and Pembroke's Men as well as Sussex's Men as the companies which had acted it. An original date of 1590 or even earlier is not precluded. It is hard to conceive of *Titus Andronicus* as having been written after *Richard III* and only shortly before the fine plays of Shakespeare's "lyrical period."

The play's failure to arouse any of the emotions usually associated with the tragic experience must be attributed largely to the lack of that frame of moral reference, so clearly and unequivocally established in Shakespeare's major tragedies, which might conceivably have made meaningful its gruesome catalogue

> of murders, rapes, and massacres,
> Acts of black night, abominable deeds,
> Complots of mischief, treason, villainies
> Ruthful to hear, yet piteously performed.
> (V, i, 63–66)

Without this moral framework the play is little more than an horrific entertainment, an empty exercise in revenge tragedy; the barbaric cruelty of the action, the physical shock of Lavinia's entry, "her hands cut off, and her tongue cut out, and ravished," or the monstrous spectacle of Tamora unwittingly eating her dead sons' flesh, can only give rise to feelings of revulsion, or, at best, a curiosity to see where and when the next blow will fall. When T. S. Eliot called *Titus Andronicus* "one of the stupidest and most uninspired plays ever written," it was to the casual irrelevance of these atrocities divorced from moral judgments that he referred.

Symptomatic of this lack of inner significance is the pasteboard-like quality of the protagonists. Lavinia's mutilation cannot move us, for as a character she scarcely begins to exist, while the succession of blows beneath which Titus reels until his mind gives way with grief renders him a pathetic rather than a tragic figure. Titus is no King Lear: his sufferings do not bring increased self-knowledge or greater understanding of the human condition. He is incapable of recognizing that his misfortunes stem from that stern inflexibility which at the beginning of the play caused him to brush aside Tamora's pleadings for her son, and which drove him to kill his own youngest son for venturing to interpose on Lavinia's behalf in a just quarrel. While it is true that Titus is presented initially as the selfless savior of Rome and human embodiment of all the Roman virtues, his ill-considered actions, committed in the empty name of "honor," quickly alienate our sympathies, and he never afterwards succeeds in quite regaining them.

Such wanton violence and inhumanity, unmatched elsewhere in Shakespeare, disqualify the play as a tragedy in the truest sense. Viewed closer, it abounds in minor flaws and inconsistencies such as might have escaped a careless or inexperienced dramatist. No explanation is given for the readiness of the defeated Goths to rally to their former enemy, Lucius, in order to help him free Rome from the tyranny of their queen, Tamora, and her emperor-husband, Saturnine. Tamora herself is given an ambiguous role. When her eloquent plea for mercy goes unheeded, and her son is sacrificed according to the Roman custom, Tamora vows to avenge herself on Titus, yet although she displays her tigerish qualities when the occasion offers, she does not really take an active part in the destruction of the Andronici. Instead, she figures, surprisingly, as the lustful mistress of Aaron the Moor, and it is this image of her that is kept before us while Aaron plans the rape of Lavinia and the deaths of Bassianus, Quintus, and Martius, from no other motive than his sheer delight in doing evil. Again, it is curious, to say the least, that Aaron, the demonic force behind most of the action of the play, should be silent during the entire first act. When Tamora does take a hand in the action it is unclear what she intends to do, and hard to see what dramatic purpose is served by her elaborate masquerade as Revenge in Act V, apart from delivering her sons into Titus' clutches so that he can slit their throats. Other scenes hover on the brink of absurdity: there is an air of grotesque farce about Quintus' fall into the pit from which he is trying to extricate his brother, while the spectacle of Lavinia bearing Titus' severed hand between her teeth must have aroused mixed feelings even in the 1590's.

Despite these glaring faults it must be conceded that *Titus Andronicus* anticipates, in a way which other early tragedies of blood do not, later and better works in the genre, including Shakespeare's own. It has a kind of savage energy and exuberance that carry it successfully over the rough places to its bloody conclusion. Through its imperfections we catch a glimpse of the kind of play it might have been, written ten years later by a more mature and practiced playwright. Titus is the prototype of the Shakespearean tragic hero, a brave and upright warrior, grown old and scarred in his country's service, who holds blindly to honor and justice, thereby setting in motion the forces that will destroy him. His blindness to the consequences of his actions is a condition of life in a corrupt society, where the distinction between good and evil has become blurred. Titus first falls from grace when he puts justice before mercy, and the rapid succession of events that culminate in his murder of his son accomplishes his damnation. His punishment is meted out by an incarnate devil, Aaron, the living symbol of evil itself, who is himself destroyed at the end of the play, thus implying the triumph of goodness and the restoration of true justice to a Rome governed by Titus' sole surviving son. Such an out-

line hints at the far greater plays to come, notably *Macbeth*, while Tamora is an early sketch for Macbeth's fiend-like queen. Titus, the honest soldier, used to the plain dealing of war, suggests Othello; in his anguish he foreshadows the grief-stricken Lear, while his madness, half real, half feigned, points to Hamlet. The liaison between Aaron and Tamora prefigures the intrigue between Edmund and Lear's wicked daughters, yet Aaron is very clearly a cartoon for Iago. Reading *Titus Andronicus* one is constantly reminded of what was to come. None of these tremendous possibilities are realized in the play, yet they are unmistakably there; no other early revenge play has such powerful stuff in it.

The most powerful single ingredient in *Titus Andronicus* is Aaron. Of all the characters he is the most fully developed and the most convincing. He has life and energy; an ingenious contriver of mischief, he is a descendant of the Vice of the old morality play who has learned some new tricks from Kyd's and Marlowe's Machiavellian villains. His aspirations take wing on Marlovian hyperboles:

> I will be bright and shine in pearl and gold,
> To wait upon this new-made empress.
> To wait, said I? to wanton with this queen,
> This goddess, this Semiramis, this nymph,
> This siren that will charm Rome's Saturnine
> And see his shipwreck and his commonweal's.
>
> (II, i, 19–24)

He can display inhuman cruelty, yet he is passionate in defense of the baby that Tamora would have callously had him destroy:

> Now by the burning tapers of the sky,
> That shone so brightly when this boy was got,
> He dies upon my scimitar's sharp point
> That touches this my first-born son and heir!
>
> (IV, ii, 89–92)

When captured he explains that he had no reason for what he did other than the enjoyment he took in the doing of it, and he is sorry only that in a lifetime dedicated to crime he had not time to do more. Like Iago, he is unmoved by the dreadful sentence pronounced upon him, and his last words smack of the devil himself:

> I am no baby, I, that with base prayers
> I should repent the evils I have done;
> Ten thousand worse than ever yet I did
> Would I perform if I might have my will.
> If one good deed in all my life I did,
> I do repent it from my very soul. (V, iii, 185–90)

It took a more assured genius to transfer this whole-hearted and unmotivated malignancy to such an ordinary-seeming soldier as Iago, yet Aaron the Moor is wholly credible as the human agent of the evil forces at work in the world of the play.

It is not the plot, however crudely constructed, nor the characterization that present obstacles to the contemporary reader, but the style of the play. The excessively artificial diction contrasts oddly with the violence of the events we are asked to witness. When Marcus first finds Lavinia with her tongue cut out, his ornate description of her plight is couched in the phrases of a love poet:

Alas, a crimson river of warm blood,
Like to a bubbling fountain stirred with wind,
Doth rise and fall between thy rosèd lips,
Coming and going with thy honey breath.

(II, iv, 22–25)

These are hardly the words of an uncle confronted by a niece savagely assaulted : they seem rather the description of a painting or a tapestry, and this pictorial quality recurs throughout the play. The action halts while speakers deliver themselves of passages of lyrical description, such as Tamora's hymn to nature when she greets her lover :

The birds chaunt melody on every bush,
The snake lies rollèd in the cheerful sun,
The green leaves quiver with the cooling wind,
And make a checkered shadow on the ground.

(II, iii, 12–15)

When Martius peers into the "dark, blood-drinking pit" his description of what he sees lyrically transforms the body of Bassianus :

Upon his bloody finger he doth wear
A precious ring that lightens all this hole,
Which, like a taper in some monument,
Doth shine upon the dead man's earthy cheeks,
And shows the ragged entrails of this pit.
So pale did shine the moon on Pyramus
When he by night lay bathed in maiden blood.

(II, iii, 226–32)

This static, decorative technique belongs to narrative rather than the drama, and forms a link between the play and two early works by Shakespeare which it most resembles, the narrative poems *Venus and Adonis* and *The Rape of Lucrece*, and, through them, with Ovid's *Metamorphoses*.

The immediate source of *Titus Andronicus* was most probably the prose *History of Titus Andronicus*, of which an eighteenth-century chapbook reprint is preserved in the Folger Shakespeare Library, but there can be no doubt that Shakespeare also had in mind the story of Philomela in the *Metamorphoses*, Book VI. The main plot of the play parallels that of Ovid's tale. Philomela was ravished by Tereus, her sister's husband, and her tongue cut out so that she could not inform against him. She reveals the crime to her sister, Procne, by weaving the story into a tapestry, and the pair determine on revenge. Procne kills Itys, her son by Tereus, and the sisters serve him up to his father to eat. Ovid's tale ends not with tragedy, but with wonder : as Tereus is about to kill the sisters he is transformed into a hoopoe, and they into a nightingale and a swallow. There are frequent references to this story in the play, yet more significant is Shakespeare's attempt to capture something of Ovid's manner of telling it. It was Ovid's elegance and luxuriously elaborated imagery that the young dramatist must have thought appropriate for a first tragedy ambitiously cast in the high Roman fashion, but the richly decorative style of the story-teller does not meet the dramatic demand for pace and energy. Often it is as though Shakespeare, like Ovid, were exhibiting his mangled corpses and bleeding victims not as objects of pity and terror, but of wonderment : the florid descriptions ask us to admire the sufferers' wounds as if they were precious stones. Ovid's urbanity and detachment, so admirably reflected in Shakespeare's narrative poems, conflict with the mood of tragic passion : the violence of the play stubbornly refused to be metamorphosed into poetry.

This uncertainty of treatment suggests that *Titus Andronicus* was an experimental play in which the possibilities of the tragic mode were being explored. Ovid proved an unsatisfactory model, and in subsequent tragedies Shakespeare learned to handle horrors more directly and to much more dramatic effect. He learned, moreover, to give a sense of direction to the tragic action, and was able to plumb the depths of man's moral and spiritual being. Alone of the tragedies *Titus Andronicus* does not raise profound questions about the nature of man and his relationship to the universe, nor does it, except in half-hearted fashion, ask us to consider the nature of justice. It is a wholly extrovert play, content simply to show suffering and injustice as empirical facts. A desire for revenge, or a delight in wickedness for its own sake, are sufficient motives to set the plot rolling, and it does not stop until the stage is strewn with corpses. The singleness of purpose with which this is consummated at least proclaims a dramatist who, if uncertain of his ultimate destination, knows what effect he wants to achieve in this play. *Titus Andronicus* is an exercise in woe and wonder, Senecan revenge tragedy pushed to its limits. It is neither subtle nor moving, yet it has tremendous vigor, and it is bursting with promise in a great many different directions. *Titus Andronicus* may be the least satisfactory of Shakespeare's plays, but as the work that marks the beginning of the road that leads to *Macbeth*, *Othello*, and *King Lear* it is by no means the least significant.

University of Newcastle, N.S.W.   GUSTAV CROSS

NOTE ON THE TEXT

The most Lamentable Romaine Tragedie of Titus Andronicus was first published in a quarto of 1594, a unique copy of which was discovered in Sweden in 1904 and is now in the Folger Shakespeare Library. This quarto was almost certainly printed from the author's draft, and the present edition adheres closely to its text. A list of the few departures from it, together with a description of the texts of the two later quartos and of the folio (which supplies one scene, III, ii, omitted from the quartos), is provided in the Appendix. The quarto text is not divided into acts and scenes. The folio text is divided into acts but not into scenes. The folio acts were divided into scenes by later editors, and this traditional division is supplied marginally for reference in the present edition.

TITUS ANDRONICUS

*

I, i   *[Flourish.] Enter the Tribunes and Senators aloft.*
   And then enter [below] Saturninus and his Followers
   at one door ; and Bassianus and his Followers [at the
   other], with Drums and Trumpets.

SATURNINUS
  Noble patricians, patrons of my right,
  Defend the justice of my cause with arms.
  And, countrymen, my loving followers,
4 Plead my successive title with your swords.
5 I am his first-born son that was the last
6 That ware the imperial diadem of Rome,
  Then let my father's honors live in me,
8 Nor wrong mine age with this indignity.

BASSIANUS
  Romans, friends, followers, favorers of my right,
  If ever Bassianus, Caesar's son,
11 Were gracious in the eyes of royal Rome,
12 Keep then this passage to the Capitol;
  And suffer not dishonor to approach
  The imperial seat, to virtue consecrate,
15 To justice, continence, and nobility;
16 But let desert in pure election shine;
  And, Romans, fight for freedom in your choice.
     [Enter] Marcus Andronicus, [aloft,] with the crown.

MARCUS
  Princes that strive by factions and by friends
19 Ambitiously for rule and empery,
  Know that the people of Rome, for whom we stand
  A special party, have by common voice
  In election for the Roman empery
  Chosen Andronicus surnamèd Pius
24 For many good and great deserts to Rome.
  A nobler man, a braver warrior,

Lives not this day within the city walls.
He by the Senate is accited home   27
From weary wars against the barbarous Goths,
That with his sons, a terror to our foes,
Hath yoked a nation strong, trained up in arms.   30
Ten years are spent since first he undertook
This cause of Rome, and chastisèd with arms
Our enemies' pride. Five times he hath returned
Bleeding to Rome, bearing his valiant sons
In coffins from the field, and at this day   35
To the monument of the Andronici
Done sacrifice of expiation,
And slain the noblest prisoner of the Goths.
And now at last, laden with honor's spoils,
Returns the good Andronicus to Rome,
Renownèd Titus, flourishing in arms.
Let us entreat by honor of his name
Whom worthily you would have now succeed,
And in the Capitol and Senate's right,   44
Whom you pretend to honor and adore,   45
That you withdraw you and abate your strength,
Dismiss your followers, and, as suitors should,
Plead your deserts in peace and humbleness.

I, i Before the Capitol in Rome   s.d. *Flourish* trumpet fanfare   **4** *successive title* claim to the succession   **5** *his . . . that* the first-born son of him who   **6** *ware* wore   **8** *age* i.e. seniority   **11** *gracious* acceptable   **12** *Keep* guard   **15** *continence* self-restraint   **16** *let . . . shine* let worth triumph simply in election   **19** *empery* dominion   **24** *deserts* worthy deeds   **27** *accited* summoned   **30** *yoked* subjugated   **35–38** *and . . . Goths* (These three and a half lines occur only in Q1, and are inconsistent with what follows since they imply that Titus has already sacrificed Alarbus. Either they have become misplaced, or Shakespeare omitted to delete them from his manuscript.)   **44** *the Capitol . . . right* the right of the Capitol and of the Senate   **45** *pretend* claim

SATURNINUS

49   How fair the tribune speaks to calm my thoughts.

BASSIANUS

50   Marcus Andronicus, so I do affy
In thy uprightness and integrity,
And so I love and honor thee and thine,
Thy noble brother Titus and his sons,
And her to whom my thoughts are humbled all,
Gracious Lavinia, Rome's rich ornament,
That I will here dismiss my loving friends:
And to my fortune's and the people's favor
Commit my cause in balance to be weighed.
              Exeunt Soldiers [of Bassianus].

SATURNINUS

Friends that have been thus forward in my right,
I thank you all and here dismiss you all,
And to the love and favor of my country

62   Commit myself, my person, and the cause.
              [Exeunt Soldiers of Saturninus.]
Rome, be as just and gracious unto me

64   As I am confident and kind to thee.
Open the gates and let me in.

BASSIANUS

66   Tribunes, and me, a poor competitor.
     [Flourish.] They go up into the Senate House.
     Enter a Captain.

CAPTAIN

Romans, make way. The good Andronicus,

68   Patron of virtue, Rome's best champion,
Successful in the battles that he fights,
With honor and with fortune is returned

71   From where he circumscribèd with his sword
And brought to yoke the enemies of Rome.
     Sound drums and trumpets, and then enter two of
     Titus' sons, [Martius and Mutius;] and then two
     men bearing a coffin covered with black; then
     [Lucius and Quintus,] two other sons; then Titus
     Andronicus; and then Tamora, the Queen of Goths,
     and her two sons, Chiron and Demetrius, with Aaron
     the Moor, and others as many as can be [including
     Tamora's son Alarbus and other Goths, prisoners].
     Then set down the coffin, and Titus speaks.

TITUS

73   Hail, Rome, victorious in thy mourning weeds!

74   Lo, as the bark that hath discharged her fraught
Returns with precious lading to the bay

76   From whence at first she weighed her anchorage,
Cometh Andronicus, bound with laurel boughs,
To re-salute his country with his tears,
Tears of true joy for his return to Rome.

80   Thou great defender of this Capitol,
Stand gracious to the rites that we intend.
Romans, of five and twenty valiant sons,
Half of the number that King Priam had,
Behold the poor remains, alive and dead.

These that survive let Rome reward with love;
These that I bring unto their latest home,   86
With burial amongst their ancestors.
Here Goths have given me leave to sheathe my sword.
Titus, unkind and careless of thine own,   89
Why suffer'st thou thy sons, unburied yet,
To hover on the dreadful shore of Styx?   91
Make way to lay them by their bretheren.
       They open the tomb.
There greet in silence, as the dead are wont,
And sleep in peace, slain in your country's wars.
O sacred receptacle of my joys,
Sweet cell of virtue and nobility,
How many sons hast thou of mine in store
That thou wilt never render to me more!

LUCIUS

Give us the proudest prisoner of the Goths,
That we may hew his limbs and on a pile
Ad manes fratrum sacrifice his flesh   101
Before this earthy prison of their bones,
That so the shadows be not unappeased,
Nor we disturbed with prodigies on earth.   104

TITUS

I give him you, the noblest that survives,
The eldest son of this distressèd queen.

TAMORA

Stay, Roman brethren! Gracious conqueror,
Victorious Titus, rue the tears I shed,
A mother's tears in passion for her son: 109
And if thy sons were ever dear to thee,
O, think my son to be as dear to me.
Sufficeth not that we are brought to Rome
To beautify thy triumphs and return,   113
Captive to thee and to thy Roman yoke;
But must my sons be slaught'red in the streets
For valiant doings in their country's cause?
O, if to fight for king and commonweal
Were piety in thine, it is in these.
Andronicus, stain not thy tomb with blood.
Wilt thou draw near the nature of the gods?
Draw near them then in being merciful.
Sweet mercy is nobility's true badge:
Thrice-noble Titus, spare my first-born son.

TITUS

Patient yourself, madam, and pardon me.   124
These are their brethren whom your Goths beheld
Alive and dead, and for their brethren slain
Religiously they ask a sacrifice:
To this your son is marked, and die he must,
T' appease their groaning shadows that are gone.

LUCIUS

Away with him, and make a fire straight,
And with our swords, upon a pile of wood,
Let's hew his limbs till they be clean consumed.
       Exeunt Titus' sons with Alarbus.

TAMORA

O cruel irreligious piety!

CHIRON

Was never Scythia half so barbarous.   134

DEMETRIUS

Oppose not Scythia to ambitious Rome.   135
Alarbus goes to rest, and we survive
To tremble under Titus' threat'ning look.
Then, madam, stand resolved, but hope withal   138

---

49 *fair* civilly   50 *affy* trust   62 *cause* matter to be decided   64 *confident* trusting; *kind* loving   66 *competitor* rival   68 *Patron* representative   71 *circumscribèd* confined within limits   73 *weeds* apparel   74 *fraught* freight   76 *anchorage* anchors   80 *Thou great defender* i.e. Jupiter   86 *latest* last   89 *unkind* unnatural   91 *Styx* river surrounding Hades   101 *Ad manes fratrum* to the ghosts of our brothers   104 *prodigies* ominous events   109 *passion* grief   113 *triumphs* triumphal processions   124 *Patient* calm   134 *Scythia* ancient name for southern Russia, the inhabitants of which were notorious for their savagery   135 *Oppose* compare   138 *withal* as well

139 The selfsame gods that armed the Queen of Troy
With opportunity of sharp revenge
Upon the Thracian tyrant in his tent
May favor Tamora, the Queen of Goths
(When Goths were Goths, and Tamora was queen),
144 To quit the bloody wrongs upon her foes.
Enter the sons of Andronicus again.

LUCIUS
See, lord and father, how we have performed
Our Roman rites. Alarbus' limbs are lopped
And entrails feed the sacrificing fire,
Whose smoke like incense doth perfume the sky.
Remaineth naught but to inter our brethren
150 And with loud 'larums welcome them to Rome.

TITUS
Let it be so, and let Andronicus
Make this his latest farewell to their souls.
Sound trumpets, and lay the coffin in the tomb.
In peace and honor rest you here, my sons;
Rome's readiest champions, repose you here in rest,
Secure from worldly chances and mishaps.
156 Here lurks no treason, here no envy swells,
157 Here grow no damnèd drugs, here are no storms,
No noise, but silence and eternal sleep.
In peace and honor rest you here, my sons.
Enter Lavinia.

LAVINIA
In peace and honor live Lord Titus long;
My noble lord and father, live in fame.
162 Lo, at this tomb my tributary tears
163 I render for my brethren's obsequies,
And at thy feet I kneel, with tears of joy
Shed on this earth for thy return to Rome.
O, bless me here with thy victorious hand,
Whose fortunes Rome's best citizens applaud.

TITUS
Kind Rome, that hast thus lovingly reserved
169 The cordial of mine age to glad my heart.
Lavinia, live; outlive thy father's days,
And fame's eternal date, for virtue's praise.

MARCUS *[aloft]*
Long live Lord Titus, my belovèd brother,
Gracious triumpher in the eyes of Rome!

TITUS
Thanks, gentle tribune, noble brother Marcus.

MARCUS
And welcome, nephews, from successful wars,
You that survive, and you that sleep in fame.
Fair lords, your fortunes are alike in all
That in your country's service drew your swords;
But safer triumph is this funeral pomp
180 That hath aspired to Solon's happiness
And triumphs over chance in honor's bed.
Titus Andronicus, the people of Rome,
Whose friend in justice thou hast ever been,
Send thee by me, their tribune and their trust,
185 This palliament of white and spotless hue,
186 And name thee in election for the empire,
With these our late-deceasèd emperor's sons.
188 Be candidatus then, and put it on,
And help to set a head on headless Rome.

TITUS
A better head her glorious body fits
Than his that shakes for age and feebleness.

What should I don this robe, and trouble you? 192
Be chosen with proclamations to-day,
To-morrow yield up rule, resign my life,
And set abroad new business for you all?
Rome, I have been thy soldier forty years,
And led my country's strength successfully,
And buried one and twenty valiant sons,
Knighted in field, slain manfully in arms,
In right and service of their noble country.
Give me a staff of honor for mine age,
But not a sceptre to control the world.
Upright he held it, lords, that held it last.

MARCUS
Titus, thou shalt obtain and ask the empery. 204

SATURNINUS
Proud and ambitious tribune, canst thou tell? 205

TITUS
Patience, Prince Saturninus.

SATURNINUS   Romans, do me right.
Patricians, draw your swords, and sheathe them not
Till Saturninus be Rome's emperor.
Andronicus, would thou were shipped to hell
Rather than rob me of the people's hearts!

LUCIUS
Proud Saturnine, interrupter of the good
That noble-minded Titus means to thee!

TITUS
Content thee, prince, I will restore to thee
The people's hearts, and wean them from themselves.

BASSIANUS
Andronicus, I do not flatter thee,
But honor thee, and will do till I die.
My faction if thou strengthen with thy friends,
I will most thankful be, and thanks to men
Of noble minds is honorable meed. 219

TITUS
People of Rome, and people's tribunes here,
I ask your voices and your suffrages.
Will ye bestow them friendly on Andronicus?

TRIBUNES
To gratify the good Andronicus,
And gratulate his safe return to Rome, 224
The people will accept whom he admits.

TITUS
Tribunes, I thank you, and this suit I make,
That you create our emperor's eldest son,
Lord Saturnine; whose virtues will, I hope,
Reflect on Rome as Titan's rays on earth, 229
And ripen justice in this commonweal.
Then, if you will elect by my advice,
Crown him and say 'Long live our emperor!'

MARCUS
With voices and applause of every sort,
Patricians and plebeians, we create

139–41 *Queen . . . tent* (Hecuba, Queen of Troy, revenged herself on Polymnestor, the Thracian tyrant who killed her son, by murdering his sons)   144 *quit* requite   150 *'larums* alarums, trumpet calls   156 *envy* ill will   157 *drugs* poisonous plants   162 *tributary* offered as tribute   163 *obsequies* funeral rites   169 *cordial* comfort   180 *aspired* risen; *Solon's happiness* (refers to Solon's saying, 'Call no man happy until he is dead')   185 *palliament* robe   186 *in election* i.e. as a candidate   188 *candidatus* candidate (in Latin, literally 'white-robed')   192 *What* why   204 *obtain and ask* i.e. obtain if only you ask   205 *canst thou tell* i.e. how can you be certain   219 *meed* reward   224 *gratulate* rejoice at   229 *Titan's* the sun god's

Lord Saturninus Rome's great emperor
And say 'Long live our emperor Saturnine!'
   [A long flourish till they come down.]

SATURNINUS
Titus Andronicus, for thy favors done
238 To us in our election this day
239 I give thee thanks in part of thy deserts,
And will with deeds requite thy gentleness:
241 And for an onset, Titus, to advance
Thy name and honorable family,
Lavinia will I make my emperess,
Rome's royal mistress, mistress of my heart,
245 And in the sacred Pantheon her espouse.
246 Tell me, Andronicus, doth this motion please thee?

TITUS
It doth, my worthy lord, and in this match
I hold me highly honored of your grace;
And here in sight of Rome, to Saturnine,
King and commander of our commonweal,
The wide world's emperor, do I consecrate
My sword, my chariot, and my prisoners,
253 Presents well worthy Rome's imperious lord.
Receive them then, the tribute that I owe,
Mine honor's ensigns humbled at thy feet.

SATURNINUS
Thanks, noble Titus, father of my life.
How proud I am of thee and of thy gifts
Rome shall record, and when I do forget
259 The least of these unspeakable deserts,
260 Romans, forget your fealty to me.

TITUS *[to Tamora]*
Now, madam, are you prisoner to an emperor,
262 To him that for your honor and your state
Will use you nobly and your followers.

SATURNINUS *[aside]*
A goodly lady, trust me, of the hue
That I would choose, were I to choose anew. –
Clear up, fair queen, that cloudy countenance.
267 Though chance of war hath wrought this change of
    cheer,
Thou com'st not to be made a scorn in Rome.
Princely shall be thy usage every way.
Rest on my word, and let not discontent
271 Daunt all your hopes. Madam, he comforts you
Can make you greater than the Queen of Goths.
Lavinia, you are not displeased with this?

LAVINIA
274 Not I, my lord, sith true nobility
275 Warrants these words in princely courtesy.

SATURNINUS
Thanks, sweet Lavinia. Romans, let us go.
Ransomless here we set our prisoners free.
Proclaim our honors, lords, with trump and drum.
    [Flourish. Exeunt Saturninus, Tamora,
    Demetrius, Chiron, and Aaron.]

BASSIANUS
Lord Titus, by your leave, this maid is mine.
   [Seizes Lavinia.]

TITUS
How, sir! Are you in earnest then, my lord?

BASSIANUS
Ay, noble Titus, and resolved withal
To do myself this reason and this right.

MARCUS
'Suum cuique' is our Roman justice: 283
This prince in justice seizeth but his own.

LUCIUS
And that he will, and shall if Lucius live.

TITUS
Traitors, avaunt! Where is the emperor's guard? 286
Treason, my lord! Lavinia is surprised!   287

SATURNINUS *[re-entering]*
Surprised? By whom?

BASSIANUS   By him that justly may
Bear his betrothed from all the world away.
    [Exeunt Bassianus and Marcus with Lavinia.]

MUTIUS
Brothers, help to convey her hence away,
And with my sword I'll keep this door safe.   291
    [Exeunt Lucius, Quintus, and Martius.]

TITUS
Follow, my lord, and I'll soon bring her back.
    [Exit Saturninus.]

MUTIUS
My lord, you pass not here.

TITUS   What, villain boy?
Barr'st me my way in Rome?

MUTIUS   Help, Lucius, help!
   [Titus kills him.]
   [Enter Lucius.]

LUCIUS
My lord, you are unjust, and more than so,
In wrongful quarrel you have slain your son.

TITUS
Nor thou, nor he, are any sons of mine;
My sons would never so dishonor me.
   Enter aloft the Emperor with Tamora and her two
   Sons, and Aaron the Moor.
Traitor, restore Lavinia to the emperor.

LUCIUS
Dead, if you will; but not to be his wife,
That is another's lawful promised love.   *[Exit.]*

SATURNINUS
No, Titus, no. The emperor needs her not,
Nor her, nor thee, nor any of thy stock.
I'll trust by leisure him that mocks me once; 304
Thee never, nor thy traitorous haughty sons,
Confederates all thus to dishonor me.
Was none in Rome to make a stale   307
But Saturnine? Full well, Andronicus,
Agree these deeds with that proud brag of thine
That said'st I begged the empire at thy hands.

TITUS
O monstrous! What reproachful words are these?

SATURNINUS
But go thy ways; go, give that changing piece 312
To him that flourished for her with his sword.
A valiant son-in-law thou shalt enjoy;
One fit to bandy with thy lawless sons,   315

238 *election* (here, as frequently in Shakespeare, the '-ion' is pronounced as a disyllable)   239 *in part of* i.e. as partial reward for   241 *onset* beginning   245 *Pantheon* Roman temple dedicated to all the gods   246 *motion* proposal   253 *imperious* imperial   259 *unspeakable* inexpressible   260 *fealty* loyalty   262 *for* because of   267 *cheer* countenance   271 *he* i.e. the man who   274 *sith* since   275 *Warrants* justifies   283 *Suum cuique* to each his own   286 *avaunt* be off   287 *surprised* taken captive   291 *door* (pronounced as a disyllable)   304 *by leisure* with caution   307 *stale* laughingstock   312 *changing piece* fickle wench   315 *bandy* brawl

316 To ruffle in the commonwealth of Rome.

TITUS
These words are razors to my wounded heart.

SATURNINUS
And therefore, lovely Tamora, Queen of Goths,
319 That like the stately Phoebe 'mongst her nymphs
Dost overshine the gallant'st dames of Rome,
If thou be pleased with this my sudden choice,
Behold, I choose thee, Tamora, for my bride
And will create thee Emperess of Rome.
Speak, Queen of Goths, dost thou applaud my choice?
And here I swear by all the Roman gods,
Sith priest and holy water are so near,
And tapers burn so bright, and everything
328 In readiness for Hymenaeus stand,
I will not re-salute the streets of Rome
Or climb my palace till from forth this place
I lead espoused my bride along with me.

TAMORA
And here in sight of heaven to Rome I swear,
If Saturnine advance the Queen of Goths,
She will a handmaid be to his desires,
A loving nurse, a mother to his youth.

SATURNINUS
Ascend, fair queen, Pantheon. Lords, accompany
Your noble emperor and his lovely bride,
Sent by the heavens for Prince Saturnine,
Whose wisdom hath her fortune conquerèd.
There shall we consummate our spousal rites.
                        Exeunt omnes. [Manet Titus.]

TITUS
341 I am not bid to wait upon this bride.
Titus, when wert thou wont to walk alone,
343 Dishonorèd thus and challengèd of wrongs?
                Enter Marcus and Titus' Sons [Lucius, Quintus,
                and Martius].

MARCUS
O Titus, see, O see what thou hast done,
In a bad quarrel slain a virtuous son.

TITUS
No, foolish tribune, no: no son of mine,
Nor thou, nor these, confederates in the deed
That hath dishonorèd all our family,
Unworthy brother, and unworthy sons!

LUCIUS
350 But let us give him burial as becomes;
Give Mutius burial with our bretheren.

TITUS
Traitors, away! He rests not in this tomb:
This monument five hundred years hath stood,
354 Which I have sumptuously re-edified.
355 Here none but soldiers and Rome's servitors
Repose in fame; none basely slain in brawls.
Bury him where you can, he comes not here.

MARCUS
My lord, this is impiety in you.
My nephew Mutius' deeds do plead for him;
He must be buried with his bretheren.
                Titus' two Sons speak.

[QUINTUS, MARTIUS]
And shall, or him we will accompany.

TITUS
And shall? What villain was it spake that word?
                Titus' Son speaks.

[QUINTUS]
He that would vouch it in any place but here.   363

TITUS
What, would you bury him in my despite?   364

MARCUS
No, noble Titus, but entreat of thee
To pardon Mutius and to bury him.

TITUS
Marcus, even thou hast stroke upon my crest,
And with these boys mine honor thou hast wounded.
My foes I do repute you every one,   369
So trouble me no more, but get you gone.

MARTIUS
He is not with himself, let us withdraw.   371

QUINTUS
Not I, till Mutius' bones be burièd.
                The Brother and the Sons kneel.

MARCUS
Brother, for in that name doth nature plead –

QUINTUS
Father, and in that name doth nature speak –

TITUS
Speak thou no more, if all the rest will speed. 375

MARCUS
Renownèd Titus, more than half my soul –

LUCIUS
Dear father, soul and substance of us all –

MARCUS
Suffer thy brother Marcus to inter   378
His noble nephew here in virtue's nest,
That died in honor and Lavinia's cause.
Thou art a Roman, be not barbarous:
The Greeks upon advice did bury Ajax,   382
That slew himself; and wise Laertes' son   383
Did graciously plead for his funerals.
Let not young Mutius then, that was thy joy,
Be barred his entrance here.

TITUS   Rise, Marcus, rise.
The dismall'st day is this that e'er I saw,
To be dishonorèd by my sons in Rome.
Well, bury him, and bury me the next.
                They put him in the tomb.

LUCIUS
There lie thy bones, sweet Mutius, with thy friends,
Till we with trophies do adorn thy tomb.   391
                They all kneel and say:

[ALL]
No man shed tears for noble Mutius;
He lives in fame that died in virtue's cause.
                Exeunt [i.e. stand aside] all but Marcus and Titus.

MARCUS
My lord, to step out of these dreary dumps,   394
How comes it that the subtle Queen of Goths
Is of a sudden thus advanced in Rome?

TITUS
I know not, Marcus, but I know it is:

---

316 *ruffle* swagger 319 *Phoebe* the moon goddess 328 *Hymenaeus* god
of marriage 341 *bid* asked 343 *challengèd* accused 350 *as becomes* as is
fitting 354 *re-edified* rebuilt 355 *servitors* armed defenders 363 *vouch*
maintain 364 *in my despite* in spite of me 369 *repute* consider 371 *not
with himself* demented 375 *if . . . speed* if everything is to go well 378
Suffer permit 382 *advice* deliberation; *Ajax* (Ajax killed himself in fury
because the armor of Achilles was awarded to Odysseus) 383 *Laertes'
son* Odysseus 391 *trophies* memorial tokens 394 *dumps* i.e. melancholy

398 Whether by device or no, the heavens can tell.
399 Is she not then beholding to the man
That brought her for this high good turn so far ?
[Yes, and will nobly him remunerate.]
    [Flourish.] Enter the Emperor, Tamora and her two
    Sons, with the Moor, at one door. Enter at the other
    door Bassianus and Lavinia, with others.

SATURNINUS
402 So, Bassianus, you have played your prize.
God give you joy, sir, of your gallant bride.

BASSIANUS
And you of yours, my lord. I say no more
Nor wish no less, and so I take my leave.

SATURNINUS
Traitor, if Rome have law or we have power,
Thou and thy faction shall repent this rape.

BASSIANUS
Rape call you it, my lord, to seize my own,
My true betrothèd love, and now my wife ?
But let the laws of Rome determine all ;
411 Meanwhile am I possessed of that is mine.

SATURNINUS
'Tis good, sir. You are very short with us ;
But if we live, we'll be as sharp with you.

BASSIANUS
My lord, what I have done, as best I may
Answer I must, and shall do with my life.
Only thus much I give your grace to know :
By all the duties that I owe to Rome,
This noble gentleman, Lord Titus here,
419 Is in opinion and in honor wronged,
That in the rescue of Lavinia
With his own hand did slay his youngest son,
In zeal to you, and highly moved to wrath
423 To be controlled in that he frankly gave.
Receive him then to favor, Saturnine,
That hath expressed himself in all his deeds
A father and a friend to thee and Rome.

TITUS
427 Prince Bassianus, leave to plead my deeds.
'Tis thou, and those, that have dishonorèd me.
Rome and the righteous heavens be my judge
How I have loved and honored Saturnine.

TAMORA
My worthy lord, if ever Tamora
Were gracious in those princely eyes of thine,
433 Then hear me speak indifferently for all ;
And at my suit, sweet, pardon what is past.

SATURNINUS
What, madam, be dishonorèd openly
436 And basely put it up without revenge ?

TAMORA
437 Not so, my lord ; the gods of Rome forfend
438 I should be author to dishonor you !
439 But on mine honor dare I undertake

398 *device* plan   399 *beholding* indebted   402 *played your prize* won
your contest   411 *that* that which   419 *opinion* reputation   423 *controlled* thwarted; *frankly* freely   427 *leave to plead* refrain from pleading
433 *indifferently* impartially   436 *put it up* submit to it   437 *forfend*
forbid   438 *author* agent   439 *undertake* vouch   441 *Whose . . . griefs*
whose undisguised rage is evidence of his grievances   443 *vain suppose*
idle supposition   452 *at entreats* to entreaty ; *let me alone* leave it to me
454 *race* eradicate   478 *mildly . . . might* as mild as might be (i.e. in the
circumstances)   479 *Tend'ring* having regard for   489 *churl* ill-bred
peasant   491 *part* depart

For good Lord Titus' innocence in all,
Whose fury not dissembled speaks his griefs : 441
Then at my suit look graciously on him.
Lose not so noble a friend on vain suppose, 443
Nor with sour looks afflict his gentle heart.
    [Aside to Saturninus]
My lord, be ruled by me, be won at last ;
Dissemble all your griefs and discontents :
You are but newly planted in your throne ;
Lest, then, the people, and patricians too,
Upon a just survey take Titus' part,
And so supplant you for ingratitude,
Which Rome reputes to be a heinous sin,
Yield at entreats : and then let me alone, 452
I'll find a day to massacre them all
And race their faction and their family, 454
The cruel father, and his traitorous sons,
To whom I suèd for my dear son's life ;
And make them know what 'tis to let a queen
Kneel in the streets and beg for grace in vain.
    [Aloud]
Come, come, sweet emperor – come, Andronicus –
Take up this good old man, and cheer the heart
That dies in tempest of thy angry frown.

SATURNINUS
Rise, Titus, rise, my empress hath prevailed.

TITUS
I thank your majesty, and her, my lord.
These words, these looks, infusè new life in me.

TAMORA
Titus, I am incorporate in Rome,
A Roman now adopted happily,
And must advise the emperor for his good.
This day all quarrels die, Andronicus.
And let it be mine honor, good my lord,
That I have reconciled your friends and you.
For you, Prince Bassianus, I have passed 470
My word and promise to the emperor
That you will be more mild and tractable.
And fear not, lords, and you, Lavinia ;
By my advice, all humbled on your knees
You shall ask pardon of his majesty.
    [They kneel.]

LUCIUS
We do, and vow to heaven and to his highness
That what we did was mildly as we might, 478
Tend'ring our sister's honor and our own. 479

MARCUS
That on mine honor here do I protest.

SATURNINUS
Away, and talk not, trouble us no more.

TAMORA
Nay, nay, sweet emperor, we must all be friends.
The tribune and his nephews kneel for grace.
I will not be denied. Sweet heart, look back.

SATURNINUS
Marcus, for thy sake and thy brother's here,
And at my lovely Tamora's entreats,
I do remit these young men's heinous faults.
Stand up.
    [They rise.]
Lavinia, though you left me like a churl, 489
I found a friend ; and sure as death I swore
I would not part a bachelor from the priest. 491

Come, if the emperor's court can feast two brides,
You are my guest, Lavinia, and your friends.
494 This day shall be a love-day, Tamora.

TITUS

495 To-morrow, an it please your majesty
To hunt the panther and the hart with me,
497 With horn and hound we'll give your grace bonjour.

SATURNINUS

498 Be it so, Titus, and gramercy too.
Exeunt. Sound trumpets. Manet [Aaron the] Moor.

II, i AARON

1 Now climbeth Tamora Olympus' top,
Safe out of fortune's shot, and sits aloft,
3 Secure of thunder's crack or lightning flash,
4 Advanced above pale envy's threat'ning reach.
As when the golden sun salutes the morn,
And having gilt the ocean with his beams,
7 Gallops the zodiac in his glistering coach
8 And overlooks the highest-peering hills,
So Tamora.
Upon her wit doth earthly honor wait,
And virtue stoops and trembles at her frown.
Then, Aaron, arm thy heart and fit thy thoughts
To mount aloft with thy imperial mistress,
14 And mount her pitch whom thou in triumph long
Hast prisoner held, fett'red in amorous chains,
16 And faster bound to Aaron's charming eyes
17 Than is Prometheus tied to Caucasus.
18 Away with slavish weeds and servile thoughts!
I will be bright and shine in pearl and gold,
To wait upon this new-made empress.
To wait, said I? to wanton with this queen,
22 This goddess, this Semiramis, this nymph,
This siren that will charm Rome's Saturnine
And see his shipwrack and his commonweal's.
25 Holla! what storm is this?
Enter Chiron and Demetrius, braving.

DEMETRIUS

26 Chiron, thy years wants wit, thy wits wants edge
27 And manners, to intrude where I am graced
28 And may, for aught thou knowest, affected be.

CHIRON

29 Demetrius, thou dost overween in all,
30 And so in this, to bear me down with braves.
'Tis not the difference of a year or two
Makes me less gracious, or thee more fortunate:
I am as able and as fit as thou
To serve, and to deserve my mistress' grace;
35 And that my sword upon thee shall approve,
And plead my passions for Lavinia's love.

AARON

37 Clubs, clubs! These lovers will not keep the peace.

DEMETRIUS

38 Why, boy, although our mother, unadvised,
39 Gave you a dancing rapier by your side,
Are you so desperate grown to threat your friends?
41 Go to! Have your lath glued within your sheath
Till you know better how to handle it.

CHIRON

Meanwhile, sir, with the little skill I have,
Full well shalt thou perceive how much I dare.

DEMETRIUS

Ay, boy, grow ye so brave?
They draw.

AARON   Why, how now, lords?
So near the emperor's palace dare ye draw
And maintain such a quarrel openly?
Full well I wot the ground of all this grudge: 48
I would not for a million of gold
The cause were known to them it most concerns;
Nor would your noble mother for much more
Be so dishonorèd in the court of Rome.
For shame, put up.   53

DEMETRIUS   Not I, till I have sheathed
My rapier in his bosom, and withal
Thrust those reproachful speeches down his throat
That he hath breathed in my dishonor here.

CHIRON

For that I am prepared and full resolved,
Foul-spoken coward, that thund'rest with thy tongue
And with thy weapon nothing dar'st perform.

AARON

Away, I say!
Now, by the gods that warlike Goths adore,
This petty brabble will undo us all.   62
Why, lords, and think you not how dangerous
It is to jet upon a prince's right?   64
What, is Lavinia then become so loose,
Or Bassianus so degenerate,
That for her love such quarrels may be broached
Without controlment, justice, or revenge?
Young lords, beware! and should the empress know
This discord's ground, the music would not please.   70

CHIRON

I care not, I, knew she and all the world:
I love Lavinia more than all the world.

DEMETRIUS

Youngling, learn thou to make some meaner choice.   73
Lavinia is thine elder brother's hope.

AARON

Why, are ye mad? or know ye not in Rome
How furious and impatient they be,
And cannot brook competitors in love?
I tell you, lords, you do but plot your deaths
By this device.

CHIRON   Aaron, a thousand deaths
Would I propose to achieve her whom I love.   80

AARON

To achieve her! How?

DEMETRIUS   Why makes thou it so strange?   81
She is a woman, therefore may be wooed;

494 *love-day* day appointed to settle disputes (with pun on 'day of love')
495 *an* if   497 *bonjour* good day   498 *gramercy* thanks
II, i (there is clearly no break in the action, since Aaron remains on stage)
1 *Olympus* Mount Olympus (the home of the gods)   3 *of* from   4 *envy's*
hatred's   7 *Gallops* gallops through   8 *overlooks* looks down upon   14
mount her pitch rise to the highest point of her flight (a technical term of
falconry)   16 *charming* casting a magic spell   17 *Prometheus* one of the
Titans of Greek myth who stole fire from heaven and was chained by
Zeus to Mount Caucasus   18 *weeds* garments   22 *Semiramis* legendary
Assyrian queen, renowned for her beauty and sexuality   25 s.d. *braving*
talking arrogantly   26 *wants* (the ending '-s' often occurs with a plural
subject)   27 *graced* favored   28 *affected* loved   29 *overween* presume
too much   30 *braves* threats   35 *approve* prove   37 *Clubs, clubs* (cry to
summon the apprentices to stop a brawl in Elizabethan London)   38
unadvised unwisely   39 *dancing rapier* ornamental sword worn by dancers
41 *lath* wooden stage sword (contemptuous)   48 *wot* know   53 *put up*
sheathe your swords   62 *brabble* brawl   64 *jet* encroach   70 *ground*
reason (with a pun on the musical sense 'bass to a descant')   73 *Youngling*
youngster (contemptuous)   80 *propose* gladly encounter   81 *Why . . .
strange* why do you seem so surprised

She is a woman, therefore may be won ;
She is Lavinia, therefore must be loved.
What, man ! more water glideth by the mill
Than wots the miller of ; and easy it is
87   Of a cut loaf to steal a shive, we know :
Though Bassianus be the emperor's brother,
89   Better than he have worn Vulcan's badge.

AARON *[aside]*
Ay, and as good as Saturninus may.

DEMETRIUS
Then why should he despair that knows to court it
With words, fair looks, and liberality ?
93   What, hast not thou full often stroke a doe,
And borne her cleanly by the keeper's nose ?

AARON
95   Why, then, it seems some certain snatch or so
96   Would serve your turns.

CHIRON   Ay, so the turn were served.

DEMETRIUS
Aaron, thou hast hit it.

AARON   Would you had hit it too !
Then should not we be tired with this ado.
Why, hark ye, hark ye, and are you such fools
100   To square for this ? Would it offend you then
101   That both should speed ?

CHIRON
Faith, not me.

DEMETRIUS   Nor me, so I were one.

AARON
103   For shame, be friends, and join for that you jar.
104   'Tis policy and stratagem must do
105   That you affect ; and so must you resolve,
That what you cannot as you would achieve,
You must perforce accomplish as you may.
108   Take this of me : Lucrece was not more chaste
Than this Lavinia, Bassianus' love.
A speedier course than ling'ring languishment
Must we pursue, and I have found the path.
112   My lords, a solemn hunting is in hand ;
There will the lovely Roman ladies troop :
The forest walks are wide and spacious,
115   And many unfrequented plots there are,
116   Fitted by kind for rape and villainy.
117   Single you thither then this dainty doe,
And strike her home by force, if not by words.
This way, or not at all, stand you in hope.
Come, come, our empress, with her sacred wit
To villainy and vengeance consecrate,
Will we acquaint withal what we intend ;
123   And she shall file our engines with advice,

That will not suffer you to square yourselves,
But to your wishes' height advance you both.
The emperor's court is like the house of fame,   126
The palace full of tongues, of eyes and ears :
The woods are ruthless, dreadful, deaf, and dull.   128
There speak and strike, brave boys, and take your turns,
There serve your lust, shadowed from heaven's eye,
And revel in Lavinia's treasury.

CHIRON
Thy counsel, lad, smells of no cowardice.

DEMETRIUS
'Sit fas aut nefas,' till I find the stream   133
To cool this heat, a charm to calm these fits,
'Per Stygia, per manes vehor.'   *Exeunt.* 135

*

Enter Titus Andronicus and his three Sons, making   II, ii
   a noise with hounds and horns [; and Marcus].

TITUS
The hunt is up, the morn is bright and grey,
The fields are fragrant and the woods are green.
Uncouple here and let us make a bay,   3
And wake the emperor and his lovely bride,
And rouse the prince, and ring a hunter's peal,
That all the court may echo with the noise.
Sons, let it be your charge, as it is ours,
To attend the emperor's person carefully :
I have been troubled in my sleep this night,
But dawning day new comfort hath inspired.   10
    Here a cry of hounds, and wind horns in a peal, then
    enter Saturninus, Tamora, Bassianus, Lavinia,
    Chiron, Demetrius, and their Attendants.
Many good morrows to your majesty !
Madam, to you as many and as good !
I promisèd your grace a hunter's peal.

SATURNINUS
And you have rung it lustily, my lords,
Somewhat too early for new-married ladies.

BASSIANUS
Lavinia, how say you ?

LAVINIA   I say, no :
I have been broad awake two hours and more.

SATURNINUS
Come on then, horse and chariots let us have,
And to our sport. Madam, now shall ye see
Our Roman hunting.

MARCUS   I have dogs, my lord,
Will rouse the proudest panther in the chase,   21
And climb the highest promontory top.

TITUS
And I have horse will follow where the game
Makes way, and runs like swallows o'er the plain.

DEMETRIUS
Chiron, we hunt not, we, with horse nor hound,
But hope to pluck a dainty doe to ground.   *Exeunt.*

*

Enter Aaron alone [with a bag of gold].   II, iii

AARON
He that had wit would think that I had none,
To bury so much gold under a tree,
And never after to inherit it.   3

---

87 *shive* slice   89 *Vulcan's badge* i.e. cuckold's horns (Vulcan, god of fire, was deceived by his wife, Venus)   93 *stroke* struck (with an arrow)   95 *snatch* quick catch (with probable sexual connotation)   96 *turns* purposes (with sexual meaning)   100 *square* quarrel   101 *speed* succeed   103 *join . . . jar* unite to obtain what you are quarrelling over   104 *policy* cunning   105 *affect* desire   108 *Lucrece* chaste Roman matron whose rape by Tarquin and subsequent suicide is the subject of Shakespeare's poem *The Rape of Lucrece*   112 *solemn* ceremonial   115 *plots* spots   116 *kind* nature   117 *Single* single out (a hunting term)   123 *file our engines* sharpen our wits   126 *house of fame* home of rumor (a possible allusion to Chaucer's poem *The House of Fame*)   128 *ruthless* pitiless   133 *Sit . . . nefas* be it right or wrong   135 *Per . . . vehor* I am borne through the Stygian (i.e. infernal) regions
II, ii The grounds of the Emperor's palace   3 *Uncouple* unleash the hounds ; *bay* prolonged barking   10 s.d. *cry* deep barking   21 *chase* hunting ground
II, iii A forest near Rome   3 *inherit* possess

21

Let him that thinks of me so abjectly
5 Know that this gold must coin a stratagem,
Which, cunningly effected, will beget
A very excellent piece of villainy:
8 And so repose, sweet gold, for their unrest
   [Hides the gold.]
That have their alms out of the empress' chest.
   Enter Tamora alone to the Moor.

TAMORA
My lovely Aaron, wherefore look'st thou sad
11 When everything doth make a gleeful boast?
The birds chaunt melody on every bush,
The snake lies rollèd in the cheerful sun,
The green leaves quiver with the cooling wind,
And make a checkered shadow on the ground;
Under their sweet shade, Aaron, let us sit,
And whilst the babbling echo mocks the hounds,
Replying shrilly to the well-tuned horns,
As if a double hunt were heard at once,
20 Let us sit down and mark their yellowing noise;
And after conflict such as was supposed
22 The wand'ring prince and Dido once enjoyed,
When with a happy storm they were surprised,
And curtained with a counsel-keeping cave,
We may, each wreathèd in the other's arms,
Our pastimes done, possess a golden slumber,
Whiles hounds and horns and sweet melodious birds
Be unto us as is as a nurse's song
Of lullaby to bring her babe asleep.

AARON
Madam, though Venus govern your desires,
31 Saturn is dominator over mine.
32 What signifies my deadly-standing eye,
My silence, and my cloudy melancholy,
My fleece of woolly hair that now uncurls
Even as an adder when she doth unroll
To do some fatal execution?
37 No, madam, these are no venereal signs.
Vengeance is in my heart, death in my hand,
Blood and revenge are hammering in my head.
Hark, Tamora, the empress of my soul,
Which never hopes more heaven than rests in thee,
This is the day of doom for Bassianus;
43 His Philomel must lose her tongue to-day,
Thy sons make pillage of her chastity
And wash their hands in Bassianus' blood.
Seest thou this letter? take it up, I pray thee,
And give the king this fatal-plotted scroll.
Now question me no more; we are espied;
49 Here comes a parcel of our hopeful booty,
Which dreads not yet their lives' destruction.
   Enter Bassianus and Lavinia.

TAMORA
Ah, my sweet Moor, sweeter to me than life.

AARON
No more, great empress; Bassianus comes.
Be cross with him, and I'll go fetch thy sons
To back thy quarrels, whatsoe'er they be.   *[Exit.]*

BASSIANUS
Who have we here? Rome's royal emperess,
56 Unfurnished of her well-beseeming troop?
57 Or is it Dian, habited like her,
Who hath abandonèd her holy groves
To see the general hunting in this forest?

TAMORA
Saucy controller of my private steps!   60
Had I the pow'r that some say Dian had,
Thy temples should be planted presently   62
With horns, as was Actaeon's, and the hounds   63
Should drive upon thy new-transformèd limbs,
Unmannerly intruder as thou art!

LAVINIA
Under your patience, gentle emperess,
'Tis thought you have a goodly gift in horning,   67
And to be doubted that your Moor and you   68
Are singled forth to try experiments.
Jove shield your husband from his hounds to-day!
'Tis pity they should take him for a stag.

BASSIANUS
Believe me, queen, your swart Cimmerian   72
Doth make your honor of his body's hue,
Spotted, detested, and abominable.
Why are you sequest'red from all your train,
Dismounted from your snow-white goodly steed,
And wand'red hither to an obscure plot,
Accompanied but with a barbarous Moor,
If foul desire had not conducted you?

LAVINIA
And being intercepted in your sport,
Great reason that my noble lord be rated   81
For sauciness. I pray you let us hence,
And let her joy her raven-colored love;   83
This valley fits the purpose passing well.

BASSIANUS
The king my brother shall have note of this.

LAVINIA
Ay, for these slips have made him noted long.   86
Good king, to be so mightily abused!

TAMORA
Why I have patience to endure all this.
   Enter Chiron and Demetrius.

DEMETRIUS
How now, dear sovereign and our gracious mother,
Why doth your highness look so pale and wan?

TAMORA
Have I not reason, think you, to look pale?
These two have ticed me hither to this place,   92
A barren detested vale you see it is;
The trees, though summer, yet forlorn and lean,
Overcome with moss and baleful mistletoe.
Here never shines the sun; here nothing breeds,
Unless the nightly owl or fatal raven:

---

5 *coin* produce (as in coining money)   8–9 *their unrest . . . chest* the discomfiture of those who find this money belonging to the empress   11 *boast* display   20 *yellowing* loudly bellowing   22 *wand'ring prince* Aeneas, legendary Trojan hero who loved Dido, Queen of Carthage   31 *dominator* the planet that has a dominant place in the horoscope (those dominated by Saturn were reputedly of sluggish, cold, and gloomy temperament)   32 *deadly-standing* fixed in a death-dealing stare (?)   37 *venereal* associated with love (Venus)   43 *Philomel* (in Greek myth Tereus raped Philomel and cut out her tongue, but she revealed his guilt by weaving the story into a tapestry; see also II, iv, 26–27, 38–39; IV, i, 47–48; V, ii, 194)   49 *parcel . . . booty* part of the prize we hope for   56 *Unfurnished of* deprived of   57 *Dian* Diana, goddess of hunting; *habited* dressed   60 *controller* censorious critic   62 *presently* immediately   63 *Actaeon* legendary hunter who spied on Diana bathing and was transformed by her into a stag and killed by his own hounds   67 *horning* (a wife's unfaithfulness was said to give her husband horns)   68 *doubted* suspected   72 *Cimmerian* legendary dweller in darkness   81 *rated* berated   83 *joy* enjoy   86 *noted* notorious   92 *ticed* enticed

And when they showed me this abhorrèd pit,
They told me, here, at dead time of the night,
A thousand fiends, a thousand hissing snakes,
101 Ten thousand swelling toads, as many urchins,
Would make such fearful and confusèd cries
As any mortal body hearing it
Should straight fall mad, or else die suddenly.
No sooner had they told this hellish tale
But straight they told me they would bind me here
Unto the body of a dismal yew
And leave me to this miserable death.
And then they called me foul adulteress,
Lascivious Goth, and all the bitterest terms
That ever ear did hear to such effect;
And had you not by wondrous fortune come,
This vengeance on me had they executed.
Revenge it, as you love your mother's life,
Or be ye not henceforth called my children.

DEMETRIUS
This is a witness that I am thy son.
        Stab him [Bassianus].

CHIRON
And this for me, struck home to show my strength.

LAVINIA
118 Ay, come, Semiramis, nay, barbarous Tamora,
For no name fits thy nature but thy own.

TAMORA
Give me the poniard; you shall know, my boys,
Your mother's hand shall right your mother's wrong.

DEMETRIUS
Stay, madam, here is more belongs to her:
First thrash the corn, then after burn the straw.
124 This minion stood upon her chastity,
Upon her nuptial vow, her loyalty,
126 And with that painted hope braves your mightiness;
And shall she carry this unto her grave?

CHIRON
An if she do, I would I were an eunuch.
Drag hence her husband to some secret hole,
And make his dead trunk pillow to our lust.

TAMORA
But when ye have the honey we desire,
132 Let not this wasp outlive, us both to sting.

CHIRON
I warrant you, madam, we will make that sure.
Come, mistress, now perforce we will enjoy
135 That nice-preservèd honesty of yours.

LAVINIA
O Tamora, thou bearest a woman's face –

TAMORA
I will not hear her speak, away with her!

LAVINIA
Sweet lords, entreat her hear me but a word.

DEMETRIUS
Listen, fair madam: let it be your glory
To see her tears; but be your heart to them
As unrelenting flint to drops of rain.

LAVINIA
When did the tiger's young ones teach the dam?   142
O, do not learn her wrath; she taught it thee;   143
The milk thou suck'dst from her did turn to marble;
Even at thy teat thou hadst thy tyranny.
Yet every mother breeds not sons alike.
        [To Chiron]
Do thou entreat her show a woman's pity.

CHIRON
What, wouldst thou have me prove myself a bastard?

LAVINIA
'Tis true the raven doth not hatch a lark:
Yet have I heard – O, could I find it now! –
The lion, moved with pity, did endure
To have his princely paws pared all away.
Some say that ravens foster forlorn children
The whilst their own birds famish in their nests:
O, be to me, though thy hard heart say no,
Nothing so kind, but something pitiful.   156

TAMORA
I know not what it means, away with her!

LAVINIA
O, let me teach thee for my father's sake,
That gave thee life when well he might have slain thee,
Be not obdurate, open thy deaf ears.

TAMORA
Hadst thou in person ne'er offended me,
Even for his sake am I pitiless.
Remember, boys, I poured forth tears in vain
To save your brother from the sacrifice,
But fierce Andronicus would not relent.
Therefore away with her, and use her as you will;
The worse to her, the better loved of me.

LAVINIA
O Tamora, be called a gentle queen
And with thine own hands kill me in this place,
For 'tis not life that I have begged so long.
Poor I was slain when Bassianus died.

TAMORA
What begg'st thou then? fond woman, let me go.   172

LAVINIA
'Tis present death I beg; and one thing more
That womanhood denies my tongue to tell.   174
O, keep me from their worse than killing lust,
And tumble me into some loathsome pit,
Where never man's eye may behold my body.
Do this, and be a charitable murderer.

TAMORA
So should I rob my sweet sons of their fee.
No, let them satisfice their lust on thee.

DEMETRIUS
Away! for thou hast stayed us here too long.

LAVINIA
No grace? no womanhood? Ah, beastly creature,
The blot and enemy to our general name!   183
Confusion fall –   184

CHIRON
Nay then, I'll stop your mouth. Bring thou her husband.
This is the hole where Aaron bid us hide him.
        *[Demetrius throws the body of Bassianus into the pit;
                then exeunt Demetrius and Chiron,
                        dragging off Lavinia.]*

TAMORA
Farewell, my sons: see that you make her sure.

101 *urchins* hedgehogs   118 *Semiramis* (see II, i, 22n.)   124 *minion* contemptible creature; *stood upon* made much of   126 *painted* unrealistic 132 *outlive* survive   135 *nice-preservèd honesty* carefully guarded chastity 142 *dam* mother   143 *learn* teach   156 *Nothing . . . pitiful* i.e. not so kind as the raven, yet showing some pity   172 *fond* foolish   174 *denies* forbids 183 *our general name* the name of woman   184 *Confusion* destruction

Ne'er let my heart know merry cheer indeed
189 Till all the Andronici be made away.
Now will I hence to seek my lovely Moor
191 And let my spleenful sons this trull deflow'r.   *[Exit.]*
  Enter Aaron, with two of Titus' Sons [Quintus and
  Martius].

AARON
Come on, my lords, the better foot before.
Straight will I bring you to the loathsome pit
Where I espied the panther fast asleep.

QUINTUS
My sight is very dull, whate'er it bodes.

MARTIUS
And mine, I promise you: were it not for shame,
Well could I leave our sport to sleep awhile.
  [Falls into the pit.]

QUINTUS
What, art thou fallen? What subtle hole is this,
Whose mouth is coverèd with rude-growing briers,
Upon whose leaves are drops of new-shed blood
As fresh as morning dew distilled on flowers?
202 A very fatal place it seems to me.
Speak, brother, hast thou hurt thee with the fall?

MARTIUS
O brother, with the dismall'st object hurt
That ever eye with sight made heart lament.

AARON
Now will I fetch the king to find them here,
That he thereby may have a likely guess
How these were they that made away his brother.   *Exit.*

MARTIUS
Why dost not comfort me and help me out
From this unhallowed and bloodstainèd hole?

QUINTUS
211 I am surprisèd with an uncouth fear;
A chilling sweat o'erruns my trembling joints;
My heart suspects more than mine eye can see.

MARTIUS
To prove thou hast a true-divining heart,
Aaron and thou look down into this den
And see a fearful sight of blood and death.

QUINTUS
Aaron is gone, and my compassionate heart
Will not permit mine eyes once to behold
219 The thing whereat it trembles by surmise.
O, tell me who it is, for ne'er till now
Was I a child to fear I know not what.

MARTIUS
222 Lord Bassianus lies berayed in blood,
All on a heap, like to a slaughterèd lamb,
In this detested, dark, blood-drinking pit.

QUINTUS
If it be dark, how dost thou know 'tis he?

MARTIUS
Upon his bloody finger he doth wear
A precious ring that lightens all this hole,
Which, like a taper in some monument,
Doth shine upon the dead man's earthy cheeks,
230 And shows the ragged entrails of this pit.
231 So pale did shine the moon on Pyramus
When he by night lay bathed in maiden blood.
O brother, help me with thy fainting hand,
If fear hath made thee faint, as me it hath,

Out of this fell devouring receptacle,   235
As hateful as Cocytus' misty mouth.   236

QUINTUS
Reach me thy hand, that I may help thee out,
Or, wanting strength to do thee so much good,   238
I may be plucked into the swallowing womb
Of this deep pit, poor Bassianus' grave.
I have no strength to pluck thee to the brink.

MARTIUS
Nor I no strength to climb without thy help.

QUINTUS
Thy hand once more; I will not loose again
Till thou art here aloft, or I below.
Thou canst not come to me: I come to thee.   *[Falls in.]*
  Enter the Emperor and Aaron the Moor.

SATURNINUS
Along with me: I'll see what hole is here,
And what he is that now is leaped into it.
Say, who art thou that lately didst descend
Into this gaping hollow of the earth?

MARTIUS
The unhappy sons of old Andronicus,   250
Brought hither in a most unlucky hour
To find thy brother Bassianus dead.

SATURNINUS
My brother dead? I know thou dost but jest.
He and his lady both are at the lodge
Upon the north side of this pleasant chase;
'Tis not an hour since I left them there.

MARTIUS
We know not where you left them all alive;
But, out alas! here have we found him dead.
  Enter Tamora, Andronicus, and Lucius.

TAMORA
Where is my lord the king?

SATURNINUS
Here, Tamora; though grieved with killing grief.

TAMORA
Where is thy brother Bassianus?

SATURNINUS
Now to the bottom dost thou search my wound: 262
Poor Bassianus here lies murderèd.

TAMORA
Then all too late I bring this fatal writ,
The complot of this timeless tragedy;   265
And wonder greatly that man's face can fold   266
In pleasing smiles such murderous tyranny.
  She giveth Saturnine a letter.

SATURNINUS *(reads the letter)*
'An if we miss to meet him handsomely,   268
Sweet huntsman, Bassianus 'tis we mean,
Do thou so much as dig the grave for him.
Thou know'st our meaning: look for thy reward
Among the nettles at the elder tree
Which overshades the mouth of that same pit
Where we decreed to bury Bassianus.

---

189 *made away* murdered   191 *spleenful* lustful; *trull* harlot   202 *fatal*
ill-omened   211 *surprisèd* overcome; *uncouth* strange   219 *by surmise* to
imagine   222 *berayed* befouled   230 *ragged entrails* rough interior
231 *Pyramus* the lover of Thisbe, who killed himself because he thought
she was dead   235 *fell* savage   236 *Cocytus* a river in Hades   238 *wanting*
lacking   262 *search* probe   265 *complot* plot; *timeless* untimely   266 *fold*
conceal   268 *handsomely* conveniently

Do this, and purchase us thy lasting friends.'
O Tamora, was ever heard the like?
This is the pit, and this the elder tree.
Look, sirs, if you can find the huntsman out
279   That should have murderèd Bassianus here.

AARON
My gracious lord, here is the bag of gold.

SATURNINUS [to Titus]
281   Two of thy whelps, fell curs of bloody kind,
Have here bereft my brother of his life.
Sirs, drag them from the pit unto the prison.
There let them bide until we have devised
Some never-heard-of torturing pain for them.

TAMORA
What, are they in this pit? O wondrous thing!
How easily murder is discoverèd!

TITUS
High emperor, upon my feeble knee
I beg this boon, with tears not lightly shed,
That this fell fault of my accursèd sons,
Accursèd if the fault be proved in them –

SATURNINUS
292   If it be proved? You see it is apparent.
Who found this letter? Tamora, was it you?

TAMORA
Andronicus himself did take it up.

TITUS
I did, my lord, yet let me be their bail;
For by my father's reverent tomb I vow
They shall be ready at your highness' will
298   To answer their suspicion with their lives.

SATURNINUS
Thou shalt not bail them: see thou follow me.
Some bring the murderèd body, some the murderers.
Let them not speak a word; the guilt is plain;
For, by my soul, were there worse end than death,
That end upon them should be executed.

TAMORA
Andronicus, I will entreat the king;
305   Fear not thy sons, they shall do well enough.

TITUS
Come, Lucius, come; stay not to talk with them.
                                   [Exeunt.]

*

II, iv   *Enter the Empress' Sons [Demetrius and Chiron],*
              with Lavinia, her hands cut off, and her tongue cut
              out, and ravished.

DEMETRIUS
So, now go tell, an if thy tongue can speak,
Who 'twas that cut thy tongue and ravished thee.

CHIRON
3   Write down thy mind, bewray thy meaning so,
An if thy stumps will let thee play the scribe.

279 *should* was to   281 *kind* nature   292 *apparent* plainly visible   298 *their suspicion* the suspicion they are under   305 *Fear not* do not be afraid for
II, iv The forest   3 *bewray* reveal   5 *scrowl* scrawl   6 *sweet* perfumed   9 *cause* case   12 *Cousin* (commonly used of a relative more distant than brother or sister)   26 *Tereus* (see II, iii, 43n.)   27 *detect* expose   30 *conduit* fountain   31 *Titan's* (see I, i, 229n.)   38 *Philomel* (see II, iii 43n.)   39 *tedious* laborious; *sampler* tapestry   51 *Cerberus* three-headed dog that guarded the entrance to Hades; *Thracian poet* i.e. Orpheus, whose music lulled Cerberus asleep

DEMETRIUS
See how with signs and tokens she can scrowl.   5

CHIRON
Go home, call for sweet water, wash thy hands.   6

DEMETRIUS
She hath no tongue to call, nor hands to wash;
And so let's leave her to her silent walks.

CHIRON
An 'twere my cause, I should go hang myself.   9

DEMETRIUS
If thou hadst hands to help thee knit the cord.
                    Exeunt [Demetrius and Chiron].
          Enter Marcus, from hunting.

MARCUS
Who is this? my niece, that flies away so fast!
Cousin, a word: where is your husband?   12
If I do dream, would all my wealth would wake me!
If I do wake, some planet strike me down,
That I may slumber an eternal sleep!
Speak, gentle niece, what stern ungentle hand
Hath lopped and hewed and made thy body bare
Of her two branches, those sweet ornaments
Whose circling shadows kings have sought to sleep in,
And might not gain so great a happiness
As half thy love? Why dost not speak to me?
Alas, a crimson river of warm blood,
Like to a bubbling fountain stirred with wind,
Doth rise and fall between thy rosèd lips,
Coming and going with thy honey breath.
But sure some Tereus hath deflow'rèd thee,   26
And, lest thou shouldst detect him, cut thy tongue.   27
Ah, now thou turn'st away thy face for shame,
And, notwithstanding all this loss of blood,
As from a conduit with three issuing spouts,   30
Yet do thy cheeks look red as Titan's face   31
Blushing to be encount'red with a cloud.
Shall I speak for thee? Shall I say 'tis so?
O that I knew thy heart, and knew the beast,
That I might rail at him to ease my mind!
Sorrow concealèd, like an oven stopped,
Doth burn the heart to cinders where it is.
Fair Philomel, why she but lost her tongue,   38
And in a tedious sampler sewed her mind: 39
But, lovely niece, that mean is cut from thee;
A craftier Tereus, cousin, hast thou met,
And he hath cut those pretty fingers off
That could have better sewed than Philomel.
O, had the monster seen those lily hands
Tremble like aspen leaves upon a lute
And make the silken strings delight to kiss them,
He would not then have touched them for his life.
Or had he heard the heavenly harmony
Which that sweet tongue hath made,
He would have dropped his knife, and fell asleep,
As Cerberus at the Thracian poet's feet.   51
Come, let us go and make thy father blind,
For such a sight will blind a father's eye.
One hour's storm will drown the fragrant meads;
What will whole months of tears thy father's eyes?
Do not draw back, for we will mourn with thee:
O, could our mourning ease thy misery!   *Exeunt.*

*

III, i *Enter the Judges and Senators, with Titus' two*
Sons [Martius and Quintus], bound, passing on the
stage to the place of execution, and Titus going
before, pleading.

TITUS

Hear me, grave fathers! noble tribunes, stay,
For pity of mine age, whose youth was spent
In dangerous wars whilst you securely slept;
For all my blood in Rome's great quarrel shed,
For all the frosty nights that I have watched,
And for these bitter tears which now you see
Filling the agèd wrinkles in my cheeks,
Be pitiful to my condemnèd sons,
Whose souls are not corrupted as 'tis thought.
For two and twenty sons I never wept,
Because they died in honor's lofty bed.

Andronicus lieth down, and the Judges pass by him.

For these, tribunes, in the dust I write

13 My heart's deep languor and my soul's sad tears.
14 Let my tears staunch the earth's dry appetite;
My sons' sweet blood will make it shame and blush.
O earth, I will befriend thee more with rain

17 That shall distill from these two ancient urns
Than youthful April shall with all his show'rs.

19 In summer's drought I'll drop upon thee still,
In winter with warm tears I'll melt the snow,
And keep eternal spring-time on thy face,

22 So thou refuse to drink my dear sons' blood.

Enter Lucius, with his weapon drawn.

O reverent tribunes! O gentle agèd men!

24 Unbind my sons, reverse the doom of death;
And let me say, that never wept before,
My tears are now prevailing orators!

LUCIUS

O noble father, you lament in vain,
The tribunes hear you not; no man is by,
And you recount your sorrows to a stone.

TITUS

Ah, Lucius, for thy brothers let me plead.
Grave tribunes, once more I entreat of you –

LUCIUS

My gracious lord, no tribune hears you speak.

TITUS

Why, 'tis no matter, man: if they did hear,
They would not mark me; or if they did mark,
They would not pity me; yet plead I must,

36 And bootless unto them.
Therefore I tell my sorrows to the stones,
Who, though they cannot answer my distress,
Yet in some sort they are better than the tribunes,

40 For that they will not intercept my tale.
When I do weep, they humbly at my feet
Receive my tears and seem to weep with me;

43 And were they but attirèd in grave weeds,
Rome could afford no tribunes like to these.
A stone is soft as wax, tribunes more hard than stones:
A stone is silent and offendeth not,
And tribunes with their tongues doom men to death.

[Rises.]

But wherefore stand'st thou with thy weapon drawn?

LUCIUS

To rescue my two brothers from their death;

50 For which attempt the judges have pronounced
My everlasting doom of banishment.

TITUS

O happy man! they have befriended thee.
Why, foolish Lucius, dost thou not perceive
That Rome is but a wilderness of tigers?
Tigers must prey, and Rome affords no prey
But me and mine: how happy art thou then
From these devourers to be banishèd!
But who comes with our brother Marcus here?

Enter Marcus with Lavinia.

MARCUS

Titus, prepare thy agèd eyes to weep,
Or if not so, thy noble heart to break!
I bring consuming sorrow to thine age.

TITUS

Will it consume me? let me see it then.

MARCUS

This was thy daughter.

TITUS   Why, Marcus, so she is.

LUCIUS

Ay me, this object kills me!   64

TITUS

Faint-hearted boy, arise and look upon her.
Speak, Lavinia, what accursèd hand
Hath made thee handless in thy father's sight?
What fool hath added water to the sea
Or brought a fagot to bright-burning Troy?
My grief was at the height before thou cam'st,
And now like Nilus it disdaineth bounds.   71
Give me a sword: I'll chop off my hands too;
For they have fought for Rome, and all in vain;
And they have nursed this woe in feeding life;
In bootless prayer have they been held up,
And they have served me to effectless use.
Now all the service I require of them
Is that the one will help to cut the other.
'Tis well, Lavinia, that thou hast no hands;
For hands to do Rome service is but vain.

LUCIUS

Speak, gentle sister, who hath martyred thee?   81

MARCUS

O, that delightful engine of her thoughts   82
That blabbed them with such pleasing eloquence   83
Is torn from forth that pretty hollow cage,
Where like a sweet melodious bird it sung
Sweet varied notes, enchanting every ear!

LUCIUS

O, say thou for her, who hath done this deed?

MARCUS

O, thus I found her straying in the park,
Seeking to hide herself, as doth the deer
That hath received some unrecuring wound.   90

TITUS

It was my dear, and he that wounded her
Hath hurt me more than had he killed me dead;
For now I stand as one upon a rock,
Environed with a wilderness of sea,
Who marks the waxing tide grow wave by wave,

III, i A street in Rome 13 *languor* grief 14 *staunch* satisfy 17 *urns*
i.e. his eyes 19 *still* all the time 22 *So* provided that 24 *doom* sentence
36 *bootless* in vain 40 *intercept* interrupt 43 *grave weeds* ceremonial
dress 64 *Ay me* alas; *object* spectacle 71 *Nilus* the Nile 81 *martyred*
mutilated 82 *engine* instrument 83 *blabbed* freely uttered 90 *unrecuring* incurable

96 Expecting ever when some envious surge
    Will in his brinish bowels swallow him.
    This way to death my wretched sons are gone ;
    Here stands my other son, a banished man,
    And here my brother, weeping at my woes :
101 But that which gives my soul the greatest spurn
    Is dear Lavinia, dearer than my soul.
    Had I but seen thy picture in this plight,
    It would have madded me : what shall I do
105 Now I behold thy lively body so ?
    Thou hast no hands to wipe away thy tears,
    Nor tongue to tell me who hath mart'red thee.
    Thy husband he is dead, and for his death
109 Thy brothers are condemned, and dead by this.
    Look, Marcus ! ah, son Lucius, look on her !
    When I did name her brothers, then fresh tears
    Stood on her cheeks, as doth the honeydew
    Upon a gath'red lily almost withered.

MARCUS
    Perchance she weeps because they killed her husband ;
    Perchance because she knows them innocent.

TITUS
    If they did kill thy husband, then be joyful,
    Because the law hath ta'en revenge on them.
    No, no, they would not do so foul a deed ;
    Witness the sorrow that their sister makes.
    Gentle Lavinia, let me kiss thy lips,
121 Or make some sign how I may do thee ease.
    Shall thy good uncle and thy brother Lucius
    And thou and I sit round about some fountain,
    Looking all downwards to behold our cheeks
    How they are stained, like meadows yet not dry
    With miry slime left on them by a flood ?
    And in the fountain shall we gaze so long
128 Till the fresh taste be taken from that clearness,
    And made a brine-pit with our bitter tears ?
    Or shall we cut away our hands like thine ?
131 Or shall we bite our tongues, and in dumb shows
    Pass the remainder of our hateful days ?
    What shall we do ? let us that have our tongues
    Plot some device of further misery,
    To make us wond'red at in time to come.

LUCIUS
    Sweet father, cease your tears ; for at your grief
    See how my wretched sister sobs and weeps.

MARCUS
    Patience, dear niece. Good Titus, dry thine eyes.

TITUS
    Ah, Marcus, Marcus ! brother, well I wot
140 Thy napkin cannot drink a tear of mine,
141 For thou, poor man, hast drowned it with thine own.

LUCIUS
    Ah, my Lavinia, I will wipe thy cheeks.

TITUS
    Mark, Marcus, mark ! I understand her signs :
    Had she a tongue to speak, now would she say
    That to her brother which I said to thee.
    His napkin, with his true tears all bewet,
    Can do no service on her sorrowful cheeks.

    O, what a sympathy of woe is this :   148
    As far from help as Limbo is from bliss !
        Enter Aaron the Moor, alone.

AARON
    Titus Andronicus, my lord the emperor
    Sends thee this word, that, if thou love thy sons,
    Let Marcus, Lucius, or thyself, old Titus,
    Or any one of you, chop off your hand
    And send it to the king : he for the same
    Will send thee hither both thy sons alive ;
    And that shall be the ransom for their fault.

TITUS
    O gracious emperor ! O gentle Aaron !
    Did ever raven sing so like a lark
    That gives sweet tidings of the sun's uprise ?
    With all my heart I'll send the emperor my hand.   160
    Good Aaron, wilt thou help to chop it off ?

LUCIUS
    Stay, father, for that noble hand of thine,
    That hath thrown down so many enemies,
    Shall not be sent : my hand will serve the turn,
    My youth can better spare my blood than you,
    And therefore mine shall save my brothers' lives.

MARCUS
    Which of your hands hath not defended Rome
    And reared aloft the bloody battle-axe,
    Writing destruction on the enemy's castle ?
    O, none of both but are of high desert :   170
    My hand hath been but idle ; let it serve
    To ransom my two nephews from their death ;
    Then have I kept it to a worthy end.

AARON
    Nay, come, agree whose hand shall go along,
    For fear they die before their pardon come.

MARCUS
    My hand shall go.

LUCIUS   By heaven, it shall not go !

TITUS
    Sirs, strive no more. Such withered herbs as these
    Are meet for plucking up, and therefore mine.   178

LUCIUS
    Sweet father, if I shall be thought thy son,
    Let me redeem my brothers both from death.

MARCUS
    And for our father's sake and mother's care,
    Now let me show a brother's love to thee.

TITUS
    Agree between you ; I will spare my hand.

LUCIUS
    Then I'll go fetch an axe.

MARCUS
    But I will use the axe.   *Exeunt [Lucius and Marcus].*

TITUS
    Come hither, Aaron. I'll deceive them both :
    Lend me thy hand, and I will give thee mine.

AARON *[aside]*
    If that be called deceit, I will be honest,
    And never whilst I live deceive men so :
    But I'll deceive you in another sort,
    And that you'll say ere half an hour pass.
        He cuts off Titus' hand.
        Enter Lucius and Marcus again.

TITUS
    Now stay your strife ; what shall be is dispatched.

---

96 *Expecting . . . when* awaiting . . . the time when; *envious* malignant
101 *spurn* stroke   105 *lively* living   109 *by this* by now   121 *do thee ease*
bring you relief   128 *clearness* i.e. clear fountain   131 *dumb shows* mime
140 *napkin* handkerchief   141 *drowned* soaked   148 *sympathy* affinity
178 *meet* fit

Good Aaron, give his majesty my hand :
194 Tell him it was a hand that warded him
From thousand dangers ; bid him bury it ;
More hath it merited, that let it have.
As for my sons, say I account of them
As jewels purchased at an easy price ;
And yet dear too, because I bought mine own.

AARON

I go, Andronicus ; and for thy hand
201 Look by and by to have thy sons with thee.
[Aside]
Their heads, I mean. O, how this villainy
203 Doth fat me with the very thoughts of it !
Let fools do good, and fair men call for grace,
Aaron will have his soul black like his face.   *Exit.*

TITUS

O, here I lift this one hand up to heaven,
And bow this feeble ruin to the earth.
If any power pities wretched tears,
To that I call !
[To Lavinia] What, wouldst thou kneel with me ?
Do then, dear heart ; for heaven shall hear our prayers,
211 Or with our sighs we'll breathe the welkin dim
And stain the sun with fog, as sometime clouds
When they do hug him in their melting bosoms.

MARCUS

O brother, speak with possibility,
And do not break into these deep extremes.

TITUS

Is not my sorrow deep, having no bottom ?
217 Then be my passions bottomless with them !

MARCUS

But yet let reason govern thy lament.

TITUS

If there were reason for these miseries,
220 Then into limits could I bind my woes :
When heaven doth weep, doth not the earth o'erflow ?
If the winds rage, doth not the sea wax mad,
Threat'ning the welkin with his big-swoll'n face ?
224 And wilt thou have a reason for this coil ?
I am the sea ; hark how her sighs doth flow !
She is the weeping welkin, I the earth :
Then must my sea be movèd with her sighs ;
Then must my earth with her continual tears
Become a deluge, overflowed and drowned ;
230 For why my bowels cannot hide her woes,
But like a drunkard must I vomit them.
Then give me leave ; for losers will have leave
233 To ease their stomachs with their bitter tongues.
Enter a Messenger, with two heads and a hand.

MESSENGER

Worthy Andronicus, ill art thou repaid
For that good hand thou sent'st the emperor.
Here are the heads of thy two noble sons,
And here's thy hand, in scorn to thee sent back,
Thy grief their sports, thy resolution mocked,
239 That woe is me to think upon thy woes
More than remembrance of my father's death.   *Exit.*

MARCUS

Now let hot Etna cool in Sicily,
And be my heart an ever-burning hell !
These miseries are more than may be borne.
244 To weep with them that weep doth ease some deal ;
245 But sorrow flouted at is double death.

LUCIUS

Ah, that this sight should make so deep a wound,
And yet detested life not shrink thereat ;   247
That ever death should let life bear his name   248
Where life hath no more interest but to breathe !
[Lavinia kisses Titus.]

MARCUS

Alas, poor heart, that kiss is comfortless
As frozen water to a starvèd snake.   251

TITUS

When will this fearful slumber have an end ?   252

MARCUS

Now farewell, flatt'ry ; die, Andronicus ;
Thou dost not slumber : see thy two sons' heads,
Thy warlike hand, thy mangled daughter here,
Thy other banished son with this dear sight   256
Struck pale and bloodless, and thy brother, I,
Even like a stony image, cold and numb.
Ah, now no more will I control thy griefs :
Rend off thy silver hair, thy other hand
Gnawing with thy teeth ; and be this dismal sight
The closing up of our most wretched eyes.
Now is a time to storm ; why art thou still ?

TITUS Ha, ha, ha !

MARCUS

Why dost thou laugh ? it fits not with this hour.

TITUS

Why, I have not another tear to shed ;
Besides, this sorrow is an enemy,
And would usurp upon my wat'ry eyes
And make them blind with tributary tears.   269
Then which way shall I find Revenge's cave ?
For these two heads do seem to speak to me,
And threat me I shall never come to bliss
Till all these mischiefs be returned again
Even in their throats that hath committed them.
Come, let me see what task I have to do.
You heavy people, circle me about,   276
That I may turn me to each one of you
And swear unto my soul to right your wrongs.
The vow is made. Come, brother, take a head ;
And in this hand the other will I bear.
And, Lavinia, thou shalt be employed in these arms :   281
Bear thou my hand, sweet wench, between thy teeth.
As for thee, boy, go get thee from my sight,
Thou art an exile, and thou must not stay.
Hie to the Goths and raise an army there ;
And if ye love me, as I think you do,
Let's kiss and part, for we have much to do.
Exeunt [all except Lucius].

LUCIUS

Farewell, Andronicus, my noble father,
The woefull'st man that ever lived in Rome.

---

194 *warded* guarded   201 *Look* expect   203 *fat* delight (literally, nourish)
211 *breathe . . . dim* make the heavens cloudy with our breath   217 *passions*
passionate outbursts   220 *bind* confine   224 *coil* disturbance   230 *For
why* because ; *bowels* (formerly associated with compassion)   233 *ease
their stomachs* relieve their feelings   239 *That* so that   244 *some deal*
somewhat   245 *flouted* mocked   247 *shrink* slip away   248 *bear his name*
i.e. still be called 'life'   251 *starvèd* numbed by cold   252 *fearful slumber*
i.e. frightful dream   256 *dear* grievous   269 *tributary* paid as tribute
276 *heavy* sorrowful   281 *employed . . . arms* (clearly corrupt : the word
'arms' may have been intended as a less grotesque substitute for *teeth* in the
following line, mistakenly caught up by the compositor ; the original
reading may have been 'employed in this')

Farewell, proud Rome, till Lucius come again!
He loves his pledges dearer than his life.
Farewell, Lavinia, my noble sister.
293 O, would thou wert as thou tofore hast been!
But now nor Lucius nor Lavinia lives
But in oblivion and hateful griefs.
If Lucius live, he will requite your wrongs
And make proud Saturnine and his empress
298 Beg at the gates like Tarquin and his queen.
Now will I to the Goths and raise a pow'r,
To be revenged on Rome and Saturnine.   *Exit Lucius.*

*

III, ii   *A banquet. Enter Andronicus, Marcus, Lavinia, and*
        the Boy [Lucius].

TITUS

So, so, now sit; and look you eat no more
Than will preserve just so much strength in us
As will revenge these bitter woes of ours.
4 Marcus, unknit that sorrow-wreathen knot:
Thy niece and I, poor creatures, want our hands,
6 And cannot passionate our tenfold grief
With folded arms. This poor right hand of mine
Is left to tyrannize upon my breast;
Who, when my heart, all mad with misery,
Beats in this hollow prison of my flesh,
Then thus I thump it down.
      [To Lavinia]
12 Thou map of woe, that thus dost talk in signs,
When thy poor heart beats with outrageous beating,
Thou canst not strike it thus to make it still.
Wound it with sighing, girl, kill it with groans;
Or get some little knife between thy teeth
And just against thy heart make thou a hole,
That all the tears that thy poor eyes let fall
19 May run into that sink, and soaking in,
20 Drown the lamenting fool in sea-salt tears.

MARCUS

Fie, brother, fie! teach her not thus to lay
Such violent hands upon her tender life.

TITUS

How now! has sorrow made thee dote already?
Why, Marcus, no man should be mad but I.
What violent hands can she lay on her life?
Ah, wherefore dost thou urge the name of hands,
27 To bid Aeneas tell the tale twice o'er,
How Troy was burnt and he made miserable?
O, handle not the theme, to talk of hands,
Lest we remember still that we have none.
31 Fie, fie, how franticly I square my talk,
As if we should forget we had no hands
If Marcus did not name the word of hands!
Come, let's fall to; and, gentle girl, eat this.
Here is no drink! hark, Marcus, what she says.

I can interpret all her martyred signs:
She says she drinks no other drink but tears,
38 Brewed with her sorrow, meshed upon her cheeks.
Speechless complainer, I will learn thy thought.
40 In thy dumb action will I be as perfect
As begging hermits in their holy prayers.
Thou shalt not sigh, nor hold thy stumps to heaven,
43 Nor wink, nor nod, nor kneel, nor make a sign,
But I of these will wrest an alphabet
45 And by still practice learn to know thy meaning.

BOY

Good grandsire, leave these bitter deep laments.
Make my aunt merry with some pleasing tale.

MARCUS

Alas, the tender boy, in passion moved,
Doth weep to see his grandsire's heaviness.

TITUS

Peace, tender sapling, thou art made of tears,
And tears will quickly melt thy life away.
      Marcus strikes the dish with a knife.
What dost thou strike at, Marcus, with thy knife?

MARCUS

At that that I have killed, my lord – a fly.

TITUS

Out on thee, murderer! Thou kill'st my heart;
Mine eyes are cloyed with view of tyranny.
A deed of death done on the innocent
Becomes not Titus' brother. Get thee gone!
I see thou art not for my company.

MARCUS

Alas, my lord, I have but killed a fly.

TITUS

'But'? How if that fly had a father and mother?
How would he hang his slender gilded wings
62 And buzz lamenting doings in the air!
Poor harmless fly,
That, with his pretty buzzing melody,
Came here to make us merry, and thou hast killed him.

MARCUS

Pardon me, sir; it was a black ill-favored fly,
66 Like to the empress' Moor; therefore I killed him.

TITUS

O, O, O!
Then pardon me for reprehending thee,
For thou hast done a charitable deed.
71 Give me thy knife, I will insult on him,
Flattering myself as if it were the Moor
Come hither purposely to poison me.
There's for thyself, and that's for Tamora.
75 Ah, sirrah!
Yet, I think, we are not brought so low
But that between us we can kill a fly
That comes in likeness of a coal-black Moor.

MARCUS

Alas, poor man! Grief has so wrought on him
He takes false shadows for true substances.

TITUS

81 Come, take away. Lavinia, go with me.
82 I'll to thy closet and go read with thee
83 Sad stories chancèd in the times of old.
Come, boy, and go with me. Thy sight is young,
And thou shalt read when mine begin to dazzle.
                     [Exeunt.]

*

293 *tofore* formerly   298 *Tarquin* Roman king, deposed when his son
Tarquin raped Lucrece
III, ii The house of Titus (the quartos omit this scene, but its inclusion in
the folio is sufficient guarantee of its authenticity)   4 *knot* i.e. folded arms,
signifying sorrow   6 *passionate* express with passion   12 *map* symbol
19 *sink* receptacle   20 *fool* (here, as often, a term of affection)   27 *Aeneas*
(see Virgil, *Aeneid* II, 2)   31 *square* regulate   38 *meshed* brewed   40
perfect fully understanding   43 *wink* blink   45 *still* constant   62 *lamenting
doings* lamentations (?)   66 *ill-favored* ugly   71 *insult on* triumph over
75 *sirrah* (contemptuous term of address to inferiors)   81 *take away* clear
the table   82 *closet* private chamber   83 *chancèd* that happened

IV, i *Enter Lucius' Son and Lavinia running after him,*
and the Boy flies from her with his books under his
arm. Enter Titus and Marcus.

BOY

Help, grandsire, help! My aunt Lavinia
Follows me everywhere, I know not why.
Good uncle Marcus, see how swift she comes:
Alas, sweet aunt, I know not what you mean.

MARCUS

Stand by me, Lucius; do not fear thine aunt.

TITUS

She loves thee, boy, too well to do thee harm.

BOY

Ay, when my father was in Rome she did.

MARCUS

What means my niece Lavinia by these signs?

TITUS

Fear her not, Lucius. Somewhat doth she mean.
See, Lucius, see, how much she makes of thee:
Somewhither would she have thee go with her.
12   Ah, boy, Cornelia never with more care
Read to her sons than she hath read to thee
14   Sweet poetry and Tully's Orator.

MARCUS

Canst thou not guess wherefore she plies thee thus?

BOY

My lord, I know not, I, nor can I guess,
Unless some fit or frenzy do possess her;
For I have heard my grandsire say full oft,
Extremity of griefs would make men mad;
And I have read that Hecuba of Troy
Ran mad for sorrow; that made me to fear,
Although, my lord, I know my noble aunt
Loves me as dear as e'er my mother did,
24   And would not, but in fury, fright my youth;
Which made me down to throw my books, and fly,
Causeless, perhaps, but pardon me, sweet aunt;
And, madam, if my uncle Marcus go,
28   I will most willingly attend your ladyship.

MARCUS

Lucius, I will.
    [Lavinia turns over with her stumps the books
    which Lucius has let fall.]

TITUS

How now, Lavinia? Marcus, what means this?
Some book there is that she desires to see.
Which is it, girl, of these? Open them, boy.
But thou art deeper read and better skilled:
Come and take choice of all my library,
And so beguile thy sorrow, till the heavens
Reveal the damned contriver of this deed.
37   Why lifts she up her arms in sequence thus?

MARCUS

I think she means that there were more than one
39   Confederate in the fact. Ay, more there was;
Or else to heaven she heaves them for revenge.

TITUS

41   Lucius, what book is that she tosseth so?

BOY

42   Grandsire, 'tis Ovid's Metamorphosis.
My mother gave it me.

MARCUS   For love of her that's gone
Perhaps she culled it from among the rest.

TITUS

Soft; so busily she turns the leaves!
Help her: what would she find? Lavinia, shall I read?
This is the tragic tale of Philomel   47
And treats of Tereus' treason and his rape;
And rape, I fear, was root of thine annoy.

MARCUS

See, brother, see, note how she quotes the leaves.   50

TITUS

Lavinia, wert thou thus surprised, sweet girl,
Ravished and wronged as Philomela was,
Forced in the ruthless, vast, and gloomy woods?   53
See, see!
Ay, such a place there is where we did hunt
(O had we never, never hunted there!)
Patterned by that the poet here describes,   57
By nature made for murders and for rapes.

MARCUS

O, why should nature build so foul a den,
Unless the gods delight in tragedies?

TITUS

Give signs, sweet girl, for here are none but friends,
What Roman lord it was durst do the deed.
Or slunk not Saturnine, as Tarquin erst,   63
That left the camp to sin in Lucrece' bed?

MARCUS

Sit down, sweet niece: brother, sit down by me.
Apollo, Pallas, Jove, or Mercury,
Inspire me, that I may this treason find.
My lord, look here: look here, Lavinia!
    He writes his name with his staff, and guides it with
    feet and mouth.
This sandy plot is plain; guide, if thou canst,   69
This after me. I have writ my name   70
Without the help of any hand at all.
Cursed be that heart that forced us to this shift!   72
Write thou, good niece, and here display at last
What God will have discoverèd for revenge.   74
Heaven guide thy pen to print thy sorrows plain,
That we may know the traitors and the truth.
    She takes the staff in her mouth and guides it with her
    stumps and writes.

TITUS

O, do ye read, my lord, what she hath writ?
'Stuprum. Chiron. Demetrius.'   78

MARCUS

What, what! the lustful sons of Tamora
Performers of this heinous bloody deed?

TITUS

'Magni dominator poli,   81
Tam lentus audis scelera? tam lentus vides?'

MARCUS

O, calm thee, gentle lord! although I know

IV, i The garden of Titus 12 *Cornelia* mother of the Gracchi, famous
Roman tribunes 14 *Tully's Orator* Cicero's *De Oratore*, or his *ad M.
Brutum Orator* 24 *but in fury* except in madness 28 *attend* accompany
37 *in sequence* one after the other 39 *fact* crime 41 *tosseth* turns the
leaves of 42 *Ovid's Metamorphosis* (the spelling of Golding's translation
of *Metamorphoses*, with which Shakespeare was familiar) 47–48 *Philomel
… Tereus* (see II, iii, 43n.) 50 *quotes* notes 53 *vast* desolate 57 *Patterned
by* on the pattern of 63 *erst* once 69 *plain* level 70 *after me* as I did
72 *shift* stratagem 74 *discoverèd* revealed 78 *Stuprum* rape 81–82
Magni … vides ruler of the great heavens, art thou so slow to hear and to
see crimes (Seneca, *Hippolytus*, ll. 671–72)

There is enough written upon this earth
To stir a mutiny in the mildest thoughts
And arm the minds of infants to exclaims.
My lord, kneel down with me; Lavinia, kneel;
88 And kneel, sweet boy, the Roman Hector's hope;
89 And swear with me, as with the woeful fere
And father of that chaste dishonorèd dame,
91 Lord Junius Brutus sware for Lucrece' rape,
92 That we will prosecute by good advice
Mortal revenge upon these traitorous Goths,
And see their blood or die with this reproach.

TITUS
'Tis sure enough, an you knew how,
But if you hunt these bear-whelps, then beware:
97 The dam will wake, an if she wind ye once;
She's with the lion deeply still in league,
And lulls him whilst she playeth on her back,
100 And when he sleeps will she do what she list.
You are a young huntsman, Marcus; let alone;
And come, I will go get a leaf of brass,
103 And with a gad of steel will write these words,
104 And lay it by: the angry northern wind
105 Will blow these sands like Sibyl's leaves abroad,
And where's our lesson then? Boy, what say you?

BOY
I say, my lord, that if I were a man,
Their mother's bechamber should not be safe
For these base bondmen to the yoke of Rome.

MARCUS
Ay, that's my boy! thy father hath full oft
For his ungrateful country done the like.

BOY
And, uncle, so will I, an if I live.

TITUS
Come, go with me into mine armory:
Lucius, I'll fit thee; and withal my boy
Shall carry from me to the empress' sons
Presents that I intend to send them both.
Come, come; thou'lt do my message, wilt thou not?

BOY
Ay, with my dagger in their bosoms, grandsire.

TITUS
No, boy, not so. I'll teach thee another course.
Lavinia, come. Marcus, look to my house.
121 Lucius and I'll go brave it at the court.
122 Ay, marry, will we, sir; and we'll be waited on.
Exeunt [Titus, Lavinia, and Young Lucius].

MARCUS
O heavens, can you hear a good man groan
And not relent, or not compassion him?
125 Marcus, attend him in his ecstasy,

That hath more scars of sorrow in his heart
Than foemen's marks upon his batt'red shield,
But yet so just that he will not revenge.
Revenge the heavens for old Andronicus! *Exit.* 129

*

Enter Aaron, Chiron, and Demetrius at one door, IV, ii
and at the other door Young Lucius and another,
with a bundle of weapons, and verses writ upon them.

CHIRON
Demetrius, here's the son of Lucius;
He hath some message to deliver us.

AARON
Ay, some mad message from his mad grandfather.

BOY
My lords, with all the humbleness I may,
I greet your honors from Andronicus –
    [Aside]
And pray the Roman gods confound you both. 6

DEMETRIUS
Gramercy, lovely Lucius, what's the news? 7

BOY *[aside]*
That you are both deciphered, that's the news, 8
For villains marked with rape.
    [Aloud]   May it please you,
My grandsire, well-advised, hath sent by me
The goodliest weapons of his armory
To gratify your honorable youth,
The hope of Rome, for so he bid me say;
And so I do, and with his gifts present
Your lordships, that, whenever you have need,
You may be armèd and appointed well. 16
And so I leave you both – *[aside]* like bloody villains.
                              Exit [with Attendant].

DEMETRIUS
What's here? a scroll, and written round about?
Let's see.
'Integer vitae scelerisque purus 20
Non eget Mauri iaculis nec arcu.'

CHIRON
O, 'tis a verse in Horace; I know it well.
I read it in the grammar long ago.

AARON
Ay, just; a verse in Horace; right, you have it.
    [Aside]
Now what a thing it is to be an ass!
Here's no sound jest! the old man hath found their
    guilt,
And sends them weapons wrapped about with lines
That wound, beyond their feeling, to the quick.
But were our witty empress well afoot, 29
She would applaud Andronicus' conceit. 30
But let her rest in her unrest awhile. –
And now, young lords, was't not a happy star
Led us to Rome, strangers, and more than so,
Captives, to be advancèd to this height?
It did me good before the palace gate
To brave the tribune in his brother's hearing.

DEMETRIUS
But me more good to see so great a lord
Basely insinuate and send us gifts. 38

88 *the Roman Hector* i.e. Titus, Roman counterpart of Hector of Troy
89 *fere* husband   91 *Junius Brutus* leader of the revolt against the Tarquins
92 *by good advice* after careful consideration   97 *an . . . ye* if she gets wind
of you   100 *list* please   103 *gad* spike   104 *northern* north   105 *Sibyl's
leaves* (the prophecies of the Sibyl were written on leaves which were
often scattered by the wind)   121 *brave it* act defiantly   122 *marry* (interjection
of affirmation); *waited on* attended to   125 *ecstasy* madness   129 *Revenge
the heavens* let the heavens take vengeance
IV, ii The Emperor's palace   6 *confound* destroy   7 *Gramercy* thanks
8 *deciphered* detected   16 *appointed* equipped   20–21 *Integer . . . arcu* he
who is of upright life and free from crime does not need the javelins or
bow of the Moor (Horace, *Odes*, I, xxii, 1–2)   29 *witty* quick-witted
30 *conceit* device   38 *insinuate* curry favor

AARON
Had he not reason, Lord Demetrius?
Did you not use his daughter very friendly?

DEMETRIUS
I would we had a thousand Roman dames
42 At such a bay, by turn to serve our lust.

CHIRON
A charitable wish and full of love!

AARON
Here lacks but your mother for to say amen.

CHIRON
And that would she for twenty thousand more.

DEMETRIUS
Come, let us go and pray to all the gods
For our belovèd mother in her pains.

AARON [aside]
Pray to the devils; the gods have given us over.
          Trumpets sound.

DEMETRIUS
Why do the emperor's trumpets flourish thus?

CHIRON
50 Belike for joy the emperor hath a son.

DEMETRIUS
Soft, who comes here?
          Enter Nurse, with a blackamoor Child.

NURSE   God morrow, lords.
O, tell me, did you see Aaron the Moor?

AARON
Well, more or less, or ne'er a whit at all,
Here Aaron is; and what with Aaron now?

NURSE
O gentle Aaron, we are all undone!
Now help, or woe betide thee evermore!

AARON
Why, what a caterwauling dost thou keep!
What dost thou wrap and fumble in thine arms?

NURSE
O, that which I would hide from heaven's eye –
Our empress' shame and stately Rome's disgrace!
She is delivered, lords, she is delivered.

AARON
To whom?

NURSE   I mean she is brought a-bed.

AARON
Well, God give her good rest! What hath he sent her?

NURSE
A devil.

64 AARON   Why, then she is the devil's dam:
A joyful issue!

NURSE
A joyless, dismal, black, and sorrowful issue!
Here is the babe, as loathsome as a toad
Amongst the fair-faced breeders of our clime.
The empress sends it thee, thy stamp, thy seal,
And bids thee christen it with thy dagger's point.

AARON
71 Zounds, ye whore! is black so base a hue?
72 Sweet blowse, you are a beauteous blossom sure.

DEMETRIUS
Villain, what hast thou done?

AARON
That which thou canst not undo.

CHIRON
Thou hast undone our mother.

AARON
Villain, I have done thy mother.   76

DEMETRIUS
And therein, hellish dog, thou hast undone her.
Woe to her chance, and damned her loathèd choice!   78
Accursed the offspring of so foul a fiend!

CHIRON
It shall not live.

AARON
It shall not die.

NURSE
Aaron, it must; the mother wills it so.

AARON
What, must it, nurse? then let no man but I
Do execution on my flesh and blood.

DEMETRIUS
I'll broach the tadpole on my rapier's point.
Nurse, give it me; my sword shall soon dispatch it.

AARON
Sooner this sword shall plough thy bowels up.
Stay, murderous villains! will you kill your brother?
Now by the burning tapers of the sky,
That shone so brightly when this boy was got,   90
He dies upon my scimitar's sharp point
That touches this my first-born son and heir!
I tell you, younglings, not Enceladus,   93
With all his threat'ning band of Typhon's brood,
Nor great Alcides, nor the god of war,   95
Shall seize this prey out of his father's hands.
What, what, ye sanguine, shallow-hearted boys!   97
Ye white-limed walls! ye alehouse painted signs!   98
Coal-black is better than another hue
In that it scorns to bear another hue;
For all the water in the ocean
Can never turn the swan's black legs to white,
Although she lave them hourly in the flood.   103
Tell the empress from me I am of age
To keep mine own, excuse it how she can.

DEMETRIUS
Wilt thou betray thy noble mistress thus?

AARON
My mistress is my mistress; this myself,
The vigor and the picture of my youth.
This before all the world do I prefer;
This maugre all the world will I keep safe,   110
Or some of you shall smoke for it in Rome!   111

DEMETRIUS
By this our mother is for ever shamed.

CHIRON
Rome will despise her for this foul escape.   113

NURSE
The emperor in his rage will doom her death.

CHIRON
I blush to think upon this ignomy.   115

AARON
Why, there's the privilege your beauty bears.

42 At . . . bay thus cornered 50 Belike probably 64 dam mother 71
Zounds (an oath; a contraction of 'by God's wounds') 72 blowse red-
cheeked wench (ironical) 76 done had sexual intercourse with 78 chance
luck 90 got begotten 93 Enceladus one of the Titans, sons of Typhon,
who fought the Olympians 95 Alcides Hercules 97 sanguine red-
cheeked 98 white-limed walls i.e. 'whited sepulchres' (Matthew xxiii,
27) 103 lave wash 110 maugre in spite of 111 smoke suffer 113 escape
escapade 115 ignomy ignominy

Fie, treacherous hue, that will betray with blushing
118 The close enacts and counsels of thy heart !
119 Here's a young lad framed of another leer.
Look how the black slave smiles upon the father,
As who should say 'Old lad, I am thine own.'
122 He is your brother, lords, sensibly fed
Of that self blood that first gave life to you ;
And from that womb where you imprisoned were
He is enfranchisèd and come to light.
126 Nay, he is your brother by the surer side,
Although my seal be stampèd in his face.

NURSE
Aaron, what shall I say unto the empress ?

DEMETRIUS
Advise thee, Aaron, what is to be done,
130 And we will all subscribe to thy advice :
Save thou the child, so we may all be safe.

AARON
Then sit we down and let us all consult.
133 My son and I will have the wind of you :
Keep there ; now talk at pleasure of your safety.

DEMETRIUS
How many women saw this child of his ?

AARON
Why, so, brave lords ! when we join in league,
I am a lamb ; but if you brave the Moor,
138 The chafèd boar, the mountain lioness,
The ocean swells not so as Aaron storms.
But say again, how many saw the child ?

NURSE
Cornelia the midwife and myself,
And no one else but the deliverèd empress.

AARON
The emperess, the midwife, and yourself :
Two may keep counsel when the third's away.
Go to the empress, tell her this I said.
He kills her.
Weeke, weeke !
So cries a pig preparèd to the spit.

DEMETRIUS
What mean'st thou, Aaron ? wherefore didst thou this ?

AARON
O Lord, sir, 'tis a deed of policy !
Shall she live to betray this guilt of ours,
A long-tongued babbling gossip ? no, lords, no.
And now be it known to you my full intent.
153 Not far one Muliteus my countryman
His wife but yesternight was brought to bed ;
His child is like to her, fair as you are :
156 Go pack with him, and give the mother gold,
And tell them both the circumstance of all ;
And how by this their child shall be advanced,
And be receivèd for the emperor's heir
And substituted in the place of mine,

To calm this tempest whirling in the court ;
And let the emperor dandle him for his own.
Hark ye, lords : you see I have given her physic, 163
And you must needs bestow her funeral.
The fields are near, and you are gallant grooms. 165
This done, see that you take no longer days, 166
But send the midwife presently to me.
The midwife and the nurse well made away,
Then let the ladies tattle what they please.

CHIRON
Aaron, I see thou wilt not trust the air
With secrets.

DEMETRIUS   For this care of Tamora,
Herself and hers are highly bound to thee.
Exeunt [Demetrius and Chiron,
bearing off the dead Nurse].

AARON
Now to the Goths, as swift as swallow flies,
There to dispose this treasure in mine arms
And secretly to greet the empress' friends.
Come on, you thick-lipped slave, I'll bear you hence ;
For it is you that puts us to our shifts. 177
I'll make you feed on berries and on roots,
And feed on curds and whey, and suck the goat,
And cabin in a cave, and bring you up 180
To be a warrior and command a camp.   *Exit.*

*

Enter Titus, Old Marcus, Young Lucius, and other   IV, iii
Gentlemen, with bows, and Titus bears the arrows
with letters on the ends of them.

TITUS
Come, Marcus, come ; kinsmen, this is the way.
Sir boy, let me see your archery :
Look ye draw home enough, and 'tis there straight. 3
'Terras Astraea reliquit.' 4
Be you remem'bred, Marcus. She's gone, she's fled. 5
Sirs, take you to your tools. You, cousins, shall
Go sound the ocean, and cast your nets ;
Happily you may catch her in the sea. 8
Yet there's as little justice as at land.
No, Publius and Sempronius, you must do it.
'Tis you must dig with mattock and with spade
And pierce the inmost centre of the earth ;
Then, when you come to Pluto's region, 13
I pray you deliver him this petition.
Tell him it is for justice and for aid,
And that it comes from old Andronicus,
Shaken with sorrows in ungrateful Rome.
Ah, Rome ! Well, well, I made thee miserable
What time I threw the people's suffrages
On him that thus doth tyrannize o'er me.
Go, get you gone, and pray be careful all,
And leave you not a man-of-war unsearched :
This wicked emperor may have shipped her hence ;
And, kinsmen, then we may go pipe for justice. 24

MARCUS
O Publius, is not this a heavy case,
To see thy noble uncle thus distract ?

PUBLIUS
Therefore, my lords, it highly us concerns
By day and night t' attend him carefully,
And feed his humor kindly as we may, 29
Till time beget some careful remedy.

118 *close enacts* secret resolutions   119 *leer* complexion   122 *sensibly*
perceptibly to the senses   126 *the surer side* i.e. the mother's side   130
subscribe agree   133 *have the wind of* keep watch upon (as game is watched,
down wind)   138 *chafèd* enraged   153–54 *my countryman His wife* i.e.
my countryman's wife   156 *pack* come to an arrangement   163 *physic*
medicine   165 *grooms* fellows   166 *days* time   177 *puts . . . shifts* makes
us resort to stratagems   180 *cabin* dwell
IV, iii A public place in Rome   3 *home* to the full extent   4 *Terras Astraea*
reliquit Astraea, goddess of justice, has left the earth (Ovid, *Metamorphoses*,
I, 150)   5 *Be you remem'bred* remember   8 *Happily* perhaps   13 *Pluto's*
region Hades   24 *pipe* whistle (i.e. seek vainly)   29 *humor* mood

MARCUS

Kinsmen, his sorrows are past remedy.
Join with the Goths, and with revengeful war
33 Take wreak on Rome for this ingratitude,
And vengeance on the traitor Saturnine.

TITUS

Publius, how now? how now, my masters?
What, have you met with her?

PUBLIUS

No, my good lord; but Pluto sends you word,
If you will have Revenge from hell, you shall.
Marry, for Justice, she is so employed,
He thinks, with Jove in heaven, or somewhere else,
So that perforce you must needs stay a time.

TITUS

He doth me wrong to feed me with delays.
I'll dive into the burning lake below,
44 And pull her out of Acheron by the heels.
Marcus, we are but shrubs, no cedars we,
46 No big-boned men framed of the Cyclops' size;
But metal, Marcus, steel to the very back,
Yet wrung with wrongs more than our backs can bear;
49 And, sith there's no justice in earth nor hell,
We will solicit heaven, and move the gods
51 To send down Justice for to wreak our wrongs.
52 Come, to this gear. You are a good archer, Marcus.
He gives them the arrows.
53 'Ad Jovem,' that's for you: here, 'ad Apollinem.'
'Ad Martem,' that's for myself.
Here, boy, 'to Pallas': here, 'to Mercury.'
'To Saturn,' Caius, not to Saturnine;
57 You were as good to shoot against the wind.
To it, boy! Marcus, loose when I bid.
Of my word, I have written to effect;
There's not a god left unsolicited.

MARCUS

Kinsmen, shoot all your shafts into the court:
We will afflict the emperor in his pride.

TITUS

Now, masters, draw. O, well said, Lucius!
64 Good boy, in Virgo's lap; give it Pallas.

MARCUS

My lord, I aim a mile beyond the moon.
Your letter is with Jupiter by this.

TITUS Ha, ha!

Publius, Publius, what hast thou done?
See, see, thou hast shot off one of Taurus' horns!

MARCUS

This was the sport, my lord: when Publius shot,
The Bull, being galled, gave Aries such a knock
That down fell both the Ram's horns in the court;
And who should find them but the empress' villain?
She laughed, and told the Moor he should not choose
But give them to his master for a present.

TITUS

76 Why, there it goes! God give his lordship joy!
Enter the Clown, with a basket, and two pigeons in it.
News, news from heaven! Marcus, the post is come.
Sirrah, what tidings? Have you any letters?
Shall I have justice? what says Jupiter?

80 **CLOWN** Who? the gibbet-maker? He says that he hath
taken them down again, for the man must not be hanged
till the next week.

TITUS But what says Jupiter I ask thee?

CLOWN Alas, sir, I know not Jubiter; I never drank with
him in all my life.

TITUS Why, villain, art not thou the carrier?

CLOWN Ay, of my pigeons, sir; nothing else.

TITUS Why, didst thou not come from heaven?

CLOWN From heaven? alas, sir, I never came there. God
forbid I should be so bold to press to heaven in my young
days. Why, I am going with my pigeons to the tribunal 91
plebs, to take up a matter of brawl betwixt my uncle and
one of the emperal's men.

MARCUS Why, sir, that is as fit as can be to serve for your
oration; and let him deliver the pigeons to the emperor
from you.

TITUS Tell me, can you deliver an oration to the emperor
with a grace?

CLOWN Nay, truly, sir, I could never say grace in all my
life.

TITUS

Sirrah, come hither: make no more ado,
But give your pigeons to the emperor:
By me thou shalt have justice at his hands.
Hold, hold, meanwhile here's money for thy charges. 103
Give me pen and ink.
Sirrah, can you with a grace deliver a supplication?

CLOWN Ay, sir.

TITUS Then here is a supplication for you. And when you
come to him, at the first approach you must kneel; then
kiss his foot; then deliver up your pigeons; and then look
for your reward. I'll be at hand, sir: see you do it bravely. 110

CLOWN I warrant you, sir, let me alone.

TITUS

Sirrah, hast thou a knife? Come, let me see it.
Here, Marcus, fold it in the oration;
For thou hast made it like an humble suppliant.
And when thou hast given it to the emperor,
Knock at my door and tell me what he says.

CLOWN God be with you, sir; I will.   *Exit.*

TITUS Come, Marcus, let us go. Publius, follow me.
         Exeunt.

*

Enter Emperor and Empress, and her two Sons. The   IV, i
*Emperor brings the arrows in his hand that Titus shot
at him.*

SATURNINUS

Why, lords, what wrongs are these! Was ever seen
An emperor in Rome thus overborne,
Troubled, confronted thus; and, for the extent   3
Of egal justice, used in such contempt?   4
My lords, you know, as know the mightful gods,
However these disturbers of our peace
Buzz in the people's ears, there naught hath passed,
But even with law, against the willful sons   8
Of old Andronicus. And what an if
His sorrows have so overwhelmed his wits?

---

33 *wreak* vengeance   44 *Acheron* river in Hades   46 *Cyclops* giants in
Homer's *Odyssey*, IX   49 *sith* since   51 *wreak* avenge   52 *gear* business
53–54 *Ad Jovem . . . ad Apollinem. Ad Martem* to Jove . . . to Apollo.
To Mars   57 *were . . . shoot* would do as much good by shooting   64 *Virgo*
the Virgin (sign of the Zodiac; *Taurus*, l. 69, is the Bull, and *Aries*, l. 71, the
Ram)   76 s.d. *Clown* yokel   80 *gibbet-maker* (the Clown hears *Jupiter* as
'gibbeter': gibbet-maker)   91–92 *tribunal plebs* (properly '*tribunus plebis*,'
i.e. tribune of the people; *emperal*, l. 93, is another of the Clown's mal-
apropisms)   103 *charges* i.e. pigeons   110 *bravely* well
IV, iv Before the Emperor's palace   3 *extent* exercise   4 *egal* equal
8 *even* in agreement

11 Shall we be thus afflicted in his wreaks,
His fits, his frenzy, and his bitterness?
And now he writes to heaven for his redress.
See, here's 'to Jove,' and this 'to Mercury';
This 'to Apollo'; this 'to the god of war':
Sweet scrolls to fly about the streets of Rome!
What's this but libelling against the Senate
18 And blazoning our unjustice everywhere?
A goodly humor, is it not, my lords?
As who would say, in Rome no justice were.
21 But if I live, his feignèd ecstasies
Shall be no shelter to these outrages;
But he and his shall know that justice lives
In Saturninus' health; whom, if he sleep,
He'll so awake as he in fury shall
Cut off the proud'st conspirator that lives.

TAMORA
My gracious lord, my lovely Saturnine,
Lord of my life, commander of my thoughts,
Calm thee, and bear the faults of Titus' age,
Th' effects of sorrow for his valiant sons,
Whose loss hath pierced him deep and scarred his heart;
And rather comfort his distressèd plight
Than prosecute the meanest or the best
For these contempts. *[aside]* Why, thus it shall become
35 High-witted Tamora to gloze with all.
But, Titus, I have touched thee to the quick;
37 Thy lifeblood out, if Aaron now be wise,
Then is all safe, the anchor in the port.
    Enter Clown.
How now, good fellow? Wouldst thou speak with us?
CLOWN Yea, forsooth, an your mistress-ship be emperial.
TAMORA
Empress I am, but yonder sits the emperor.
42 CLOWN 'Tis he. God and Saint Stephen give you godden.
I have brought you a letter and a couple of pigeons here.
    He [Saturninus] reads the letter.
SATURNINUS
Go take him away, and hang him presently.
CLOWN How much money must I have?
TAMORA Come, sirrah, you must be hanged.
47 CLOWN Hanged? By' lady, then I have brought up a
neck to a fair end.   *Exit.*
SATURNINUS
Despiteful and intolerable wrongs!
Shall I endure this monstrous villainy?
I know from whence this same device proceeds.
May this be borne as if his traitorous sons,
That died by law for murder of our brother,
Have by my means been butcherèd wrongfully?
Go drag the villain hither by the hair;
56 Nor age nor honor shall shape privilege.
For this proud mock I'll be thy slaughterman,
Sly frantic wretch, that holp'st to make me great
59 In hope thyself should govern Rome and me!
    Enter Nuntius Aemilius.
What news with thee, Aemilius?

11 *wreaks* vindictive acts   18 *blazoning* proclaiming   21 *ecstasies* fits of madness   35 *gloze* use fair words   37 *Thy lifeblood out* once thy lifeblood is out   42 *godden* good evening (used at any time after noon)   47 *By' lady* (interjection, from 'by Our Lady')   56 *shape privilege* create immunity   59 s.d. *Nuntius* messenger   62 *gatherèd head* raised an army   64 *conduct* leadership   67 *Coriolanus* Roman hero who led an army against Rome   83 *careful* mindful   85 *stint* stop   90 *honey stalks* clover stalks   104 *stand on* insist upon   108 *temper* work upon   112 *successantly* in succession (?)

AEMILIUS
Arm, my lords! Rome never had more cause.
The Goths have gatherèd head, and with a power   62
Of high-resolvèd men, bent to the spoil,
They hither march amain, under conduct   64
Of Lucius, son to old Andronicus;
Who threats in course of this revenge to do
As much as ever Coriolanus did.   67
SATURNINUS
Is warlike Lucius general of the Goths?
These tidings nip me, and I hang the head
As flowers with frost or grass beat down with storms.
Ay, now begins our sorrows to approach.
'Tis he the common people love so much;
Myself hath often overheard them say,
When I have walkèd like a private man,
That Lucius' banishment was wrongfully,
And they have wished that Lucius were their emperor.
TAMORA
Why should you fear? is not your city strong?
SATURNINUS
Ay, but the citizens favor Lucius
And will revolt from me to succor him.
TAMORA
King, be thy thoughts imperious like thy name.
Is the sun dimmed, that gnats do fly in it?
The eagle suffers little birds to sing,
And is not careful what they mean thereby,   83
Knowing that with the shadow of his wings
He can at pleasure stint their melody: 85
Even so mayest thou the giddy men of Rome.
Then cheer thy spirit; for know thou, emperor,
I will enchant the old Andronicus
With words more sweet, and yet more dangerous,
Than baits to fish or honey stalks to sheep,   90
When as the one is wounded with the bait,
The other rotted with delicious feed.
SATURNINUS
But he will not entreat his son for us.
TAMORA
If Tamora entreat him, then he will;
For I can smooth, and fill his agèd ears
With golden promises, that, were his heart
Almost impregnable, his old ears deaf,
Yet should both ear and heart obey my tongue.
    [To Aemilius]
Go thou before to be our ambassador;
Say that the emperor requests a parley
Of warlike Lucius, and appoint the meeting
Even at his father's house, the old Andronicus.
SATURNINUS
Aemilius, do this message honorably,
And if he stand on hostage for his safety,   104
Bid him demand what pledge will please him best.
AEMILIUS
Your bidding shall I do effectually.   *Exit.*
TAMORA
Now will I to that old Andronicus
And temper him with all the art I have,   108
To pluck proud Lucius from the warlike Goths.
And now, sweet emperor, be blithe again
And bury all thy fear in my devices.
SATURNINUS
Then go successantly, and plead to him.   *Exeunt.* 112

V, i   *Enter Lucius, with an army of Goths, with Drum*
       and Soldiers.

LUCIUS
  Approvèd warriors and my faithful friends,
  I have receivèd letters from great Rome
  Which signifies what hate they bear their emperor
  And how desirous of our sight they are.
  Therefore, great lords, be as your titles witness,
  Imperious, and impatient of your wrongs;
7 And wherein Rome hath done you any scath,
  Let him make treble satisfaction.

1. GOTH
9 Brave slip sprung from the great Andronicus,
  Whose name was once our terror, now our comfort,
  Whose high exploits and honorable deeds
  Ingrateful Rome requites with foul contempt,
13 Be bold in us: we'll follow where thou lead'st,
  Like stinging bees in hottest summer's day,
  Led by their master to the flow'rèd fields,
  And be avenged on cursèd Tamora.

[ALL]
  And as he saith, so say we all with him.

LUCIUS
  I humbly thank him, and I thank you all.
  But who comes here, led by a lusty Goth?
      Enter a Goth, leading of Aaron with his Child in his
      arms.

2. GOTH
  Renownèd Lucius, from our troops I strayed
  To gaze upon a ruinous monastery;
  And as I earnestly did fix mine eye
23 Upon the wasted building, suddenly
  I heard a child cry underneath a wall.
  I made unto the noise, when soon I heard
  The crying babe controlled with this discourse:
27 'Peace, tawny slave, half me and half thy dame.
28 Did not thy hue bewray whose brat thou art,
  Had nature lent thee but thy mother's look,
  Villain, thou mightst have been an emperor:
  But where the bull and cow are both milk-white,
  They never do beget a coal-black calf.
33 Peace, villain, peace!' even thus he rates the babe,
  'For I must bear thee to a trusty Goth,
  Who, when he knows thou art the empress' babe,
  Will hold thee dearly for thy mother's sake.'
  With this, my weapon drawn, I rushed upon him,
  Surprised him suddenly, and brought him hither
  To use as you think needful of the man.

LUCIUS
  O worthy Goth, this is the incarnate devil
  That robbed Andronicus of his good hand:
  This is the pearl that pleased your empress' eye;
  And here's the base fruit of her burning lust.
44 Say, wall-eyed slave, whither wouldst thou convey
  This growing image of thy fiend-like face?
  Why dost not speak? What, deaf? not a word?
  A halter, soldiers! Hang him on this tree,
  And by his side his fruit of bastardy.

AARON
  Touch not the boy, he is of royal blood.

LUCIUS
  Too like the sire for ever being good.
  First hang the child, that he may see it sprawl –
  A sight to vex the father's soul withal.

  Get me a ladder.
      [A ladder brought, which Aaron is made to climb.]

AARON   Lucius, save the child,
  And bear it from me to the emperess.
  If thou do this, I'll show thee wondrous things
  That highly may advantage thee to hear;
  If thou wilt not, befall what may befall,
  I'll speak no more – but vengeance rot you all!

LUCIUS
  Say on; and if it please me which thou speak'st,
  Thy child shall live, and I will see it nourished.   60

AARON
  And if it please thee! why, assure thee, Lucius,
  'Twill vex thy soul to hear what I shall speak:
  For I must talk of murders, rapes, and massacres,
  Acts of black night, abominable deeds,
  Complots of mischief, treason, villainies
  Ruthful to hear, yet piteously performed;   66
  And this shall all be buried in my death
  Unless thou swear to me my child shall live.

LUCIUS
  Tell on thy mind; I say thy child shall live.

AARON
  Swear that he shall, and then I will begin.

LUCIUS
  Who should I swear by? thou believest no god.
  That granted, how canst thou believe an oath?

AARON
  What if I do not? as indeed I do not.
  Yet, for I know thou art religious
  And hast a thing within thee callèd conscience,
  With twenty popish tricks and ceremonies
  Which I have seen thee careful to observe,
  Therefore I urge thy oath; for that I know
  An idiot holds his bauble for a god   79
  And keeps the oath which by that god he swears,
  To that I'll urge him: therefore thou shalt vow
  By that same god, what god soe'er it be,
  That thou adorest and hast in reverence,
  To save my boy, to nourish and bring him up,
  Or else I will discover naught to thee.

LUCIUS
  Even by my god I swear to thee I will.

AARON
  First know thou, I begot him on the empress.

LUCIUS
  O most insatiate and luxurious woman!   88

AARON
  Tut, Lucius, this was but a deed of charity
  To that which thou shalt hear of me anon.   90
  'Twas her two sons that murderèd Bassianus;
  They cut thy sister's tongue, and ravished her,
  And cut her hands, and trimmed her as thou sawest.

LUCIUS
  O detestable villain! call'st thou that trimming?

AARON
  Why, she was washed and cut and trimmed, and 'twas
  Trim sport for them which had the doing of it.

V, i Fields near Rome   7 *scath* harm   9 *slip* offshoot   13 *bold* confident
23 *wasted* devastated   27 *tawny* black; *dame* mother   28 *bewray* make
known; *brat* child   33 *rates* reproves   44 *wall-eyed* glaring (literally, having
a discolored eye)   66 *Ruthful* lamentable; *piteously* so as to arouse pity
79 *bauble* jester's baton   88 *luxurious* lustful   90 *To* compared with

LUCIUS
O barbarous beastly villains like thyself!

AARON
Indeed, I was their tutor to instruct them.
99 That codding spirit had they from their mother,
100 As sure a card as ever won the set;
That bloody mind I think they learned of me,
102 As true a dog as ever fought at head.
Well, let my deeds be witness of my worth.
104 I trained thy brethren to that guileful hole
Where the dead corpse of Bassianus lay.
I wrote the letter that thy father found
And hid the gold within that letter mentioned,
Confederate with the queen and her two sons;
And what not done, that thou hast cause to rue,
Wherein I had no stroke of mischief in it?
111 I played the cheater for thy father's hand,
And when I had it, drew myself apart
And almost broke my heart with extreme laughter.
I pried me through the crevice of a wall
When for his hand he had his two sons' heads,
Beheld his tears, and laughed so heartily
That both mine eyes were rainy like to his;
And when I told the empress of this sport,
119 She sounded almost at my pleasing tale
And for my tidings gave me twenty kisses.

GOTH
What, canst thou say all this and never blush?

AARON
Ay, like a black dog, as the saying is.

LUCIUS
Art thou not sorry for these heinous deeds?

AARON
Ay, that I had not done a thousand more.
Even now I curse the day, and yet I think
Few come within the compass of my curse,
Wherein I did not some notorious ill:
As kill a man, or else devise his death;
Ravish a maid, or plot the way to do it;
130 Accuse some innocent, and forswear myself;
Set deadly enmity between two friends;
Make poor men's cattle break their necks;
133 Set fire on barns and haystalks in the night
And bid the owners quench them with their tears.
Oft have I digged up dead men from their graves
And set them upright at their dear friends' door
Even when their sorrows almost was forgot,
And on their skins, as on the bark of trees,
Have with my knife carvèd in Roman letters
140 'Let not your sorrow die, though I am dead.'
But I have done a thousand dreadful things
As willingly as one would kill a fly,
And nothing grieves me heartily indeed
But that I cannot do ten thousand more.

LUCIUS
Bring down the devil, for he must not die
So sweet a death as hanging presently.

[Aaron is brought down from the ladder.]

AARON
If there be devils, would I were a devil,
To live and burn in everlasting fire,
So I might have your company in hell
But to torment you with my bitter tongue!   150

LUCIUS
Sirs, stop his mouth and let him speak no more.
Enter Aemilius.

GOTH
My lord, there is a messenger from Rome
Desires to be admitted to your presence.

LUCIUS
Let him come near.
Welcome, Aemilius: what's the news from Rome?

AEMILIUS
Lord Lucius, and you princes of the Goths,
The Roman emperor greets you all by me;
And, for he understands you are in arms,
He craves a parley at your father's house,
Willing you to demand your hostages,   160
And they shall be immediately delivered.

GOTH
What says our general?

LUCIUS
Aemilius, let the emperor give his pledges
Unto my father and my uncle Marcus,
And we will come. March, away.   *[Exeunt.]*

*

Enter Tamora and her two Sons, disguised.   V, ii

TAMORA
Thus, in this strange and sad habiliment,   1
I will encounter with Andronicus,
And say I am Revenge, sent from below
To join with him and right his heinous wrongs.
Knock at his study, where they say he keeps   5
To ruminate strange plots of dire revenge.
Tell him Revenge is come to join with him
And work confusion on his enemies.
They knock, and Titus opens his study door.

TITUS
Who doth molest my contemplation?
Is it your trick to make me ope the door,
That so my sad decrees may fly away   11
And all my study be to no effect?
You are deceived; for what I mean to do
See here in bloody lines I have set down;
And what is written shall be executed.

TAMORA
Titus, I am come to talk with thee.

TITUS
No, not a word; how can I grace my talk,
Wanting a hand to give it that accord?   18
Thou hast the odds of me, therefore no more.   19

TAMORA
If thou didst know me, thou wouldst talk with me.

TITUS
I am not mad; I know thee well enough.
Witness this wretched stump, witness these crimson
     lines,
Witness these trenches made by grief and care,
Witness the tiring day and heavy night,

99 *codding* lustful   100 *set* game   102 *at head* (a brave bulldog seized the bull by the nose)   104 *trained* enticed   111 *cheater* officer appointed to look after escheats (property forfeited to the Crown)   119 *sounded* swooned   130 *forswear* perjure   133 *haystalks* haystacks (dialect)
V, ii *Before the house of Titus*   1 *sad habiliment* sombre clothing   5 *keeps* stays   11 *sad decrees* serious resolutions   18 *Wanting ... accord* lacking a hand to make appropriate gestures   19 *odds of* advantage over

Witness all sorrow, that I know thee well
For our proud empress, mighty Tamora.
Is not thy coming for my other hand ?

TAMORA

Know, thou sad man, I am not Tamora ;
She is thy enemy, and I thy friend.
I am Revenge, sent from th' infernal kingdom
To ease the gnawing vulture of thy mind
32 By working wreakful vengeance on thy foes.
Come down and welcome me to this world's light ;
Confer with me of murder and of death.
There's not a hollow cave or lurking place,
No vast obscurity or misty vale,
Where bloody murder or detested rape
38 Can couch for fear, but I will find them out,
And in their ears tell them my dreadful name,
Revenge, which makes the foul offender quake.

TITUS

Art thou Revenge ? and art thou sent to me
To be a torment to mine enemies ?

TAMORA

I am ; therefore come down and welcome me.

TITUS

Do me some service ere I come to thee.
Lo, by thy side where Rape and Murder stands ;
46 Now give some surance that thou art Revenge :
Stab them, or tear them on thy chariot wheels,
And then I'll come and be thy wagoner
And whirl along with thee about the globe.
50 Provide thee two proper palfreys, black as jet,
To hale thy vengeful wagon swift away
And find out murd'rers in their guilty caves ;
53 And when thy car is loaden with their heads,
I will dismount, and by thy wagon wheel
Trot like a servile footman all day long,
56 Even from Hyperion's rising in the east
Until his very downfall in the sea ;
And day by day I'll do this heavy task,
59 So thou destroy Rapine and Murder there.

TAMORA

These are my ministers and come with me.

TITUS

Are they thy ministers ? what are they called ?

TAMORA

Rape and Murder ; therefore callèd so
'Cause they take vengeance of such kind of men.

TITUS

Good Lord, how like the empress' sons they are !
65 And you the empress ! but we worldly men
Have miserable, mad, mistaking eyes.
O sweet Revenge, now do I come to thee ;
And, if one arm's embracement will content thee,
I will embrace thee in it by and by.   [Exit.]

TAMORA

70 This closing with him fits his lunacy.
71 Whate'er I forge to feed his brainsick humors
Do you uphold and maintain in your speeches,
For now he firmly takes me for Revenge ;
And, being credulous in this mad thought,
I'll make him send for Lucius his son,
And whilst I at a banquet hold him sure,
77 I'll find some cunning practice out of hand
To scatter and disperse the giddy Goths,
Or at the least make them his enemies.

See, here he comes, and I must ply my theme.
    [Enter Titus.]

TITUS

Long have I been forlorn, and all for thee.
Welcome, dread Fury, to my woeful house.
Rapine and Murder, you are welcome too.
How like the empress and her sons you are !
Well are you fitted, had you but a Moor.
Could not all hell afford you such a devil ?
For well I wot the empress never wags   87
But in her company there is a Moor ;
And, would you represent our queen aright,
It were convenient you had such a devil.   90
But welcome as you are : what shall we do ?

TAMORA

What wouldst thou have us do, Andronicus ?

DEMETRIUS

Show me a murderer, I'll deal with him.

CHIRON

Show me a villain that hath done a rape,
And I am sent to be revenged on him.

TAMORA

Show me a thousand that hath done thee wrong,
And I will be revengèd on them all.

TITUS

Look round about the wicked streets of Rome,
And when thou find'st a man that's like thyself,
Good Murder, stab him ; he's a murderer.
Go thou with him, and when it is thy hap   101
To find another that is like to thee,
Good Rapine, stab him ; he is a ravisher.
Go thou with them ; and in the emperor's court
There is a queen, attended by a Moor.
Well shalt thou know her by thine own proportion,
For up and down she doth resemble thee.
I pray thee do on them some violent death ;
They have been violent to me and mine.

TAMORA

Well hast thou lessoned us ; this shall we do.   110
But would it please thee, good Andronicus,
To send for Lucius, thy thrice-valiant son,
Who leads towards Rome a band of warlike Goths,
And bid him come and banquet at thy house :
When he is here, even at thy solemn feast,
I will bring in the empress and her sons,
The emperor himself, and all thy foes,
And at thy mercy shall they stoop and kneel,
And on them shalt thou ease thy angry heart.
What says Andronicus to this device ?

TITUS

Marcus, my brother, 'tis sad Titus calls.
    Enter Marcus.
Go, gentle Marcus, to thy nephew Lucius ;
Thou shalt enquire him out among the Goths.
Bid him repair to me and bring with him   124
Some of the chiefest princes of the Goths.
Bid him encamp his soldiers where they are.
Tell him the emperor and the empress too

---

32 *wreakful* avenging   38 *couch* lie hidden   46 *surance* assurance   50 *proper palfreys* handsome horses   53 *car* chariot   56 *Hyperion* the sun god   59 *So* provided that ; *Rapine* rape   65 *worldly* mortal   70 *closing* agreeing   71 *forge* invent   77 *practice* plan of action ; *out of hand* on the spur of the moment   87 *wags* moves   90 *convenient* fitting   101 *hap* chance   110 *lessoned* instructed   124 *repair* come

Feast at my house, and he shall feast with them.
This do thou for my love; and so let him,
As he regards his agèd father's life.

MARCUS
This will I do and soon return again.　　　　　　　　[Exit.]

TAMORA
Now will I hence about thy business
And take my ministers along with me.

TITUS
Nay, nay, let Rape and Murder stay with me,
Or else I'll call my brother back again
And cleave to no revenge but Lucius.

TAMORA [aside to her sons]
What say you, boys? will you abide with him
Whiles I go tell my lord the emperor
139　How I have governed our determined jest?
140　Yield to his humor, smooth and speak him fair,
And tarry with him till I turn again.

TITUS [aside]
I knew them all, though they supposed me mad,
143　And will o'erreach them in their own devices,
A pair of cursèd hellhounds and their dame.

DEMETRIUS
Madam, depart at pleasure; leave us here.

TAMORA
Farewell, Andronicus: Revenge now goes
147　To lay a complot to betray thy foes.

TITUS
I know thou dost; and, sweet Revenge, farewell.
　　　　　　　　　　　　　　　　[Exit Tamora.]

CHIRON
Tell us, old man, how shall we be employed?

TITUS
Tut, I have work enough for you to do.
Publius, come hither, Caius and Valentine.
　　　[Enter Publius, Caius, and Valentine.]

PUBLIUS
What is your will?

TITUS
Know you these two?

PUBLIUS
The empress' sons, I take them, Chiron and Demetrius.

TITUS
Fie, Publius, fie! thou art too much deceived.
The one is Murder, and Rape is the other's name;
And therefore bind them, gentle Publius:
Caius and Valentine, lay hands on them.
Oft have you heard me wish for such an hour,
160　And now I find it. Therefore bind them sure,
And stop their mouths if they begin to cry.　　　[Exit.]

CHIRON
Villains, forbear! we are the empress' sons.

PUBLIUS
And therefore do we what we are commanded.
Stop close their mouths, let them not speak a word.

---

139 governed . . . jest contrived the jest we determined on　140 smooth . . .
fair flatter and humor him　143 o'erreach outwit　147 complot plot　180
martyr kill　188 coffin pie crust　191 increase offspring　194 Philomel
(see II, iii, 43n.)　195 Progne Procne, sister of Philomel and wife of Tereus:
to avenge her sister's rape and mutilation by Tereus, Procne killed her
son Itys and served him to his father Tereus at a meal　199 temper blend
201 officious busy　203 Centaurs' feast (the wedding feast of Pirithous and
Hippodamia, to which the Lapiths invited the Centaurs, ended with the
slaughter of the latter)　205 against by the time that
V, iii The house of Titus　2 repair return

Is he sure bound? look that you bind them fast.
　　Enter Titus Andronicus with a knife, and Lavinia
　　with a basin.

TITUS
Come, come, Lavinia; look, thy foes are bound.
Sirs, stop their mouths, let them not speak to me,
But let them hear what fearful words I utter.
O villains, Chiron and Demetrius!
Here stands the spring whom you have stained with　　170
　　mud,
This goodly summer with your winter mixed.
You killed her husband, and for that vile fault
Two of her brothers were condemned to death,
My hand cut off and made a merry jest;
Both her sweet hands, her tongue, and that more dear
Than hands or tongue, her spotless chastity,
Inhuman traitors, you constrained and forced.
What would you say if I should let you speak?
Villains, for shame you could not beg for grace.
Hark, wretches, how I mean to martyr you.　　　180
This one hand yet is left to cut your throats
Whiles that Lavinia 'tween her stumps doth hold
The basin that receives your guilty blood.
You know your mother means to feast with me,
And calls herself Revenge, and thinks me mad.
Hark, villains, I will grind your bones to dust,
And with your blood and it I'll make a paste,
And of the paste a coffin I will rear,　　　188
And make two pasties of your shameful heads,
And bid that strumpet, your unhallowed dam,
Like to the earth, swallow her own increase.　　　191
This is the feast that I have bid her to,
And this the banquet she shall surfeit on;
For worse than Philomel you used my daughter,　　　194
And worse than Progne I will be revenged.　　　195
And now prepare your throats. Lavinia, come,
Receive the blood; and when that they are dead,
Let me go grind their bones to powder small
And with this hateful liquor temper it;　　　199
And in that paste let their vile heads be baked.
Come, come, be every one officious　　　201
To make this banquet, which I wish may prove
More stern and bloody than the Centaurs' feast.　　　203
　　　He cuts their throats.
So, now bring them in, for I'll play the cook
And see them ready against their mother comes.　　　205
　　　　　　　　　　　　　　　　Exeunt.

*

LUCIUS
Uncle Marcus, since 'tis my father's mind
That I repair to Rome, I am content.　　　2

GOTH
And ours with thine, befall what fortune will.

LUCIUS
Good uncle, take you in this barbarous Moor,
This ravenous tiger, this accursèd devil.
Let him receive no sust'nance, fetter him,
Till he be brought unto the empress' face
For testimony of her foul proceedings.
And see the ambush of our friends be strong;
I fear the emperor means no good to us.

AARON
Some devil whisper curses in mine ear
And prompt me that my tongue may utter forth
The venomous malice of my swelling heart!

LUCIUS
Away, inhuman dog, unhallowèd slave!
Sirs, help our uncle to convey him in.
                              [Exeunt Goths with Aaron.]
The trumpets show the emperor is at hand.
      Sound trumpets. Enter Emperor and Empress, with
      [Aemilius,] Tribunes, and others.

SATURNINUS
17 What, hath the firmament moe suns than one?

LUCIUS
18 What boots it thee to call thyself a sun?

MARCUS
19 Rome's emperor, and nephew, break the parle;
    These quarrels must be quietly debated.

21 The feast is ready which the careful Titus
    Hath ordained to an honorable end,
    For peace, for love, for league, and good to Rome.
    Please you therefore draw nigh and take your places.

SATURNINUS
Marcus, we will.
      [A table brought in.] Trumpets sounding, enter Titus
      like a cook, placing the dishes, and Lavinia with a
      veil over her face.

TITUS
Welcome, my lord; welcome, dread queen;
Welcome, ye warlike Goths; welcome, Lucius;
28 And welcome all: although the cheer be poor,
    'Twill fill your stomachs; please you eat of it.

SATURNINUS
Why art thou thus attired, Andronicus?

TITUS
Because I would be sure to have all well
To entertain your highness and your empress.

TAMORA
We are beholding to you, good Andronicus.

TITUS
An if your highness knew my heart, you were.
35 My lord the emperor, resolve me this:
36 Was it well done of rash Virginius
    To slay his daughter with his own right hand,
38 Because she was enforced, stained, and deflow'red?

SATURNINUS
It was, Andronicus.

TITUS
Your reason, mighty lord?

SATURNINUS
Because the girl should not survive her shame,
And by her presence still renew his sorrows.

TITUS
A reason mighty, strong, and effectual;
44 A pattern, precedent, and lively warrant
    For me, most wretched, to perform the like.
    Die, die, Lavinia, and thy shame with thee,
    And with thy shame thy father's sorrow die!
          [He kills her.]

SATURNINUS
48 What hast thou done, unnatural and unkind?

TITUS
Killed her for whom my tears have made me blind.
I am as woeful as Virginius was,

And have a thousand times more cause than he
To do this outrage; and it now is done.

SATURNINUS
What, was she ravished? tell who did the deed.

TITUS
Will't please you eat? will't please your highness feed?

TAMORA
Why hast thou slain thine only daughter thus?

TITUS
Not I: 'twas Chiron and Demetrius,
They ravished her and cut away her tongue;
And they, 'twas they, that did her all this wrong.

SATURNINUS
Go fetch them hither to us presently.   59

TITUS
Why, there they are, both bakèd in this pie,
Whereof their mother daintily hath fed,
Eating the flesh that she herself hath bred.
'Tis true, 'tis true; witness my knife's sharp point!
      He stabs the Empress.

SATURNINUS
Die, frantic wretch, for this accursèd deed!
      [He stabs Titus.]

LUCIUS
Can the son's eye behold his father bleed?
There's meed for meed, death for a deadly deed!   66
      [He stabs Saturninus.]

MARCUS
You sad-faced men, people and sons of Rome,
By uproar severed, as a flight of fowl
Scattered by winds and high tempestuous gusts,
O, let me teach you how to knit again   70
This scattered corn into one mutual sheaf,
These broken limbs again into one body;
Lest Rome herself be bane unto herself,   73
And she whom mighty kingdoms curtsy to,
Like a forlorn and desperate castaway,
Do shameful execution on herself,
But if my frosty signs and chaps of age,   77
Grave witnesses of true experience,
Cannot induce you to attend my words,
      [To Lucius]
Speak, Rome's dear friend, as erst our ancestor,   80
When with his solemn tongue he did discourse
To lovesick Dido's sad-attending ear   82
The story of that baleful burning night   83
When subtle Greeks surprised King Priam's Troy.
Tell us what Sinon hath bewitched our ears,   85
Or who hath brought the fatal engine in
That gives our Troy, our Rome, the civil wound.   87
My heart is not compact of flint nor steel;   88
Nor can I utter all our bitter grief,
But floods of tears will drown my oratory
And break my utt'rance, even in the time

17 *moe* more 18 *boots* avails 19 *break the parle* break off the dispute
21 *careful* full of cares, sorrowful 28 *cheer* entertainment 35 *resolve*
answer 36 *Virginius* Roman who killed his daughter to save her from rape
38 *enforced* raped 44 *lively* striking 48 *unkind* cruel 59 *presently*
immediately 66 *meed for meed* measure for measure (i.e. fitting reward)
70 *knit* bind together 73 *bane* death 77 *But if* unless; *frosty signs* white
hair; *chaps* wrinkles 80 *erst* formerly; *our ancestor* i.e. Aeneas 82 *sad-attending* seriously listening 83 *baleful* evil 85 *Sinon* cunning Greek
who persuaded the Trojans to admit the wooden horse 87 *civil* incurred
in civil war 88 *compact* composed

When it should move ye to attend me most,
And force you to commiseration.
Here's Rome's young captain, let him tell the tale,
While I stand by and weep to hear him speak.

LUCIUS

96 Then, gracious auditory, be it known to you
That Chiron and the damned Demetrius
Were they that murd'red our emperor's brother,
And they it were that ravishèd our sister.
100 For their fell faults our brothers were beheaded,
101 Our father's tears despised, and basely cozened
Of that true hand that fought Rome's quarrel out
And sent her enemies unto the grave.
104 Lastly, myself unkindly banishèd,
The gates shut on me, and turned weeping out
To beg relief among Rome's enemies;
Who drowned their enmity in my true tears
And oped their arms to embrace me as a friend:
109 I am the turnèd-forth, be it known to you,
That have preserved her welfare in my blood
And from her bosom took the enemy's point,
Sheathing the steel in my advent'rous body.
113 Alas, you know I am no vaunter, I;
My scars can witness, dumb although they are,
That my report is just and full of truth.
116 But soft, methinks I do digress too much,
Citing my worthless praise. O, pardon me!
For when no friends are by, men praise themselves.

MARCUS

Now is my turn to speak. Behold the child:
Of this was Tamora deliverèd,
The issue of an irreligious Moor,
Chief architect and plotter of these woes.
The villain is alive in Titus' house,
And as he is to witness, this is true.
Now judge what cause had Titus to revenge
These wrongs unspeakable, past patience,
Or more than any living man could bear.
Now you have heard the truth, what say you, Romans?
Have we done aught amiss, show us wherein,
And, from the place where you behold us pleading,
The poor remainder of Andronici
Will hand in hand all headlong hurl ourselves
133 And on the ragged stones beat forth our souls,
134 And make a mutual closure of our house.
Speak, Romans, speak, and if you say we shall,
Lo, hand in hand, Lucius and I will fall.

AEMILIUS

Come, come, thou reverent man of Rome,
And bring our emperor gently in thy hand –
Lucius our emperor; for well I know
The common voice do cry it shall be so.

ALL

Lucius, all hail, Rome's royal emperor!

MARCUS

Go, go into old Titus' sorrowful house,
And hither hale that misbelieving Moor
To be adjudged some direful slaught'ring death,

As punishment for his most wicked life.

[Exeunt Attendants.]

ALL

Lucius, all hail, Rome's gracious governor!

LUCIUS

Thanks, gentle Romans: may I govern so
To heal Rome's harms and wipe away her woe.
But, gentle people, give me aim awhile,   149
For nature puts me to a heavy task.
Stand all aloof; but, uncle, draw you near
To shed obsequious tears upon this trunk.   152
O, take this warm kiss on thy pale cold lips,
These sorrowful drops upon thy bloodstained face,
The last true duties of thy noble son!

MARCUS

Tear for tear, and loving kiss for kiss,
Thy brother Marcus tenders on thy lips.
O, were the sum of these that I should pay
Countless and infinite, yet would I pay them.

LUCIUS

Come hither, boy; come, come and learn of us
To melt in showers: thy grandsire loved thee well.
Many a time he danced thee on his knee,
Sung thee asleep, his loving breast thy pillow.
Many a story hath he told to thee,
And bid thee bear his pretty tales in mind
And talk of them when he was dead and gone.

MARCUS

How many thousand times hath these poor lips,
When they were living, warmed themselves on thine!
O, now, sweet boy, give them their latest kiss.   169
Bid him farewell; commit him to the grave;
Do them that kindness, and take leave of them.   171

BOY

O grandsire, grandsire! ev'n with all my heart
Would I were dead, so you did live again!
O Lord, I cannot speak to him for weeping;
My tears will choke me if I ope my mouth.

[Enter Attendants with Aaron.]

ROMAN

You sad Andronici, have done with woes.
Give sentence on this execrable wretch
That hath been breeder of these dire events.

LUCIUS

Set him breast-deep in earth, and famish him.
There let him stand and rave and cry for food.
If any one relieves or pities him,
For the offense he dies. This is our doom.   182
Some stay to see him fast'ned in the earth.

AARON

Ah, why should wrath be mute and fury dumb?
I am no baby, I, that with base prayers
I should repent the evils I have done;
Ten thousand worse than ever yet I did
Would I perform if I might have my will.
If one good deed in all my life I did,
I do repent it from my very soul.

LUCIUS

Some loving friends convey the emperor hence,
And give him burial in his father's grave.
My father and Lavinia shall forthwith
Be closèd in our household's monument.
As for that ravenous tiger, Tamora,
No funeral rite, nor man in mourning weeds,

No mournful bell shall ring her burial;
But throw her forth to beasts and birds to prey.
Her life was beastly and devoid of pity,
200   And being dead, let birds on her take pity!

[See justice done on Aaron, that damned Moor,
By whom our heavy haps had their beginning.
Then, afterwards, to order well the state,
That like events may ne'er it ruinate.]   *Exeunt*.

APPENDIX: THE QUARTO AND FOLIO TEXTS

The only authoritative text of *Titus Andronicus* is that of the first quarto, printed in 1594. Apart from its deficient punctuation and a few obvious errors it provides a remarkably accurate text, and it is moreover the sole source for a number of lines which were omitted or altered in subsequent editions. The wording of some of the stage directions (e.g. I, i, 72, *enter . . . others as many as can be*) and some irregularities in the speech-prefixes (e.g. *Saturninus* is also given as *Emperor* or *King*) suggest that the first quarto was set up from the author's "foul papers" or working manuscript of the play, rather than from a clean copy prepared for use in the theatre.

The second quarto, printed in 1600, was set up from a copy of the first quarto that must have been slightly damaged at the foot of the last three leaves, for six passages towards the end of Act V (including the last four lines of the play) are clearly conjectural. Whoever prepared this copy for the printer also removed the three and a half lines at I, i, 35–38 which are contradicted by the subsequent action, and which may well have been struck out of the original manuscript and printed in the first quarto by mistake. He also made a number of minor corrections and considerably improved the punctuation, but the text incorporated a great many new errors. There is no reason to suppose that the emendations were the work of anyone other than the compositor, and the text therefore has no authority.

A third quarto, printed in 1611, was set up from a copy of the second quarto, and contains far more corruptions than corrections. It would be of little interest but for the fact that it provided the copy for the first folio.

The folio text is even more corrupt than the third quarto, but it adds many new stage directions, as well as an entire new scene, III, ii, which must have derived from a manuscript source. The authenticity of this new scene cannot be disputed, for it is of a piece with the rest of the play. Its most probable source is the playhouse prompt-book, which would also have furnished the additional stage directions, but since the folio does not restore the conjectural readings of the second quarto it must be assumed that the prompt-book used was not the original but a printed copy to which corrections and additions had been made. Only the most perfunctory use can have been made of such new material as the prompt-book made available, for the folio elsewhere follows the text of the third quarto.

The present edition is based on the first quarto, except for III, ii, which is necessarily based on the folio. Speech-prefixes have been regularized throughout, and spelling and punctuation modernized. The act divisions are those introduced by the folio; the scene divisions are those of the later editors.

The following are the only readings in the present edition departing materially from the text of the first quarto (Q1). Corrections of simple literal errors, punctuation, and mislineation of verse are not noted unless the sense is affected. The adopted reading in italics is followed by the Q1 reading in roman. Where the adopted reading derives from the second quarto (Q2), the

third quarto (Q3), or the folio (F), that fact is recorded in parentheses following the reading; where there is no such indication, the reading is an emendation, usually one suggested quite early in the history of Shakespearean scholarship.

I, i, 36 *the Andronici* that Andronicy   58 s.d. *Exeunt* Exit   74 *her* (F4) his   92 *bretheren* (Q3) brethren   101 *manes* (F3) manus   115 *slaught'red* (F) slaughtered   132 s.d. *Exeunt* Exit   229 *Titan's* (Q2) Tytus   243 *emperess* Empresse   245 *Pantheon* (F2) Pathan   267 *chance* (Q2) change   283 *cuique* (F2) cuiqum   319 *Phoebe* (F2) Thebe   360 *bretheren* (Q3) brethren   s.d. *speak* speakes   393 s.d. *Exeunt* Exit   401 *Yes . . . remunerate* (F; omitted in QQ)   477–79 *We do . . . our own* (assigned as in F; printed as part of Tamora's speech in QQ)

II, i, 110 *than* this   130 *shadowed* shadowèd

II, ii, 1 *morn* (Q3) Moone

II, iii, 13 *snake* (Q3) snakes   22 *enjoyed* enjoyèd   55, 66 *emperess* Empresse   69 *try experiments* (Q2) trie thy experimens   72 *swart* swartie   85 *note* notice   110 *Lascivious* (Q3) Lauicious   118 *Ay*, I   132 *outlive, us* out live us   144 *suck'dst* suck'st   160 *ears* (Q3) yeares   198 *What*, (F4) What   210 *unhallowed* unhollow   222 *berayed* bereaud   231 *Pyramus* (Q2) Priamus   236 *Cocytus'* (F2) Ocitus   286 *What*, What   291 *fault* faults   296 *father's* fathers

II, iv, 27 *him* them   30 *three* their   38 *Philomel* Philomela

III, i, 9 *are* (F2) is   17 *urns* ruines   34 *or* (Q2; omitted in Q1)   113 *withered* witherèd   146 *with his* (F4) with her   297 *empress* Emperesse

III, ii (this scene is found only in F)   39 *complainer* complainet   52 *thy* (omitted in F)   53 *fly* Flys   54 *thee*, (F3) the   55 *are* (omitted in F)   72 *myself* my selfes

IV, i, 15 *Marcus* (speech-prefix omitted in Q)   50 *quotes* (Q2) coats   77 *Titus* (F; speech-prefix omitted in QQ)   88 *hope* (Q2) hop (?) I op (?)   91 *sware* (F3) sweare

IV, ii, 95 *Alcides* (Q2) Alciades   104, 143 *emperess* Empresse

IV, iii, 56 *Saturn,' Caius* Saturnine, to Caius   77 *News . . . come* (assigned in Q to Clown)   80 *Who* Ho

IV, iv, 5 *know, as know* know   47 *By' lady* be Lady   59 s.d. *Nuntius* (Q2) Nutius   92 *feed* (Q3) seed   97 *ears* (F) yeares   104 *on* (F4) in

V, i, 16 *avenged* (Q3) adveng'd   53 *Get . . . ladder* (assigned to Aaron in Q)   54 *emperess* Empresse

V, ii, 18 *it* (omitted in QQ; F has 'it action' for QQ 'that accord')   49 *globe* globes   52 *murd'rers* murder   *caves* (F2) cares   56 *Hyperion's* (F2) Epeons   61 *Are they* (F2) Are them   65 *worldly* (Q2) wordlie

V, iii, 73 *Lest* Roman Lord. Let   125 *cause* (F4) course   144 *adjudged* (Q3) adiudge   154 *bloodstained* (F3) blood slaine   163 *Sung* (Q2) Song   201–04 *See . . . ruinate* (not in Q1, but in Q2, Q3, F)   Q concludes "Finis the Tragedy of Titus Andronicus"

ROMEO AND JULIET

INTRODUCTION

Romeo and Juliet is a play of young love. No other conveys so well the impetuous, idealistic passion of youth. The hero and heroine are not remarkable except in the overwhelming strength of their love for each other. Readers who love deeply may find here the idealized utterance of their feelings, and those who do not love deeply are led to wish that they could. The universal longing for a perfect romantic love, for the union of physical desire with selfless self-surrender, finds full expression in this play and makes it what Georg Brandes has called the great typical love-tragedy of the world.

That this appeal to a universal longing in human nature is the true secret of the play's success is witnessed by the great popularity of the balcony scene in Act II, which is not at all the dramatic climax of the play but is usually the scene most clearly remembered. In former centuries the Library of Oxford University kept its folio copy of Shakespeare's works chained to a desk at which students could stand and read. The well-thumbed pages of the balcony scene and of the parting scene in Act III give mute evidence that for young Oxonians these utterances of love were the most popular passages in all of Shakespeare's works.

Indeed, Shakespeare's finest achievement in this play is the successful portrayal of passionate physical love in terms of purity and innocence. The suggestive wink and the salacious leer are present in the jestings of the Nurse and the innuendoes of Mercutio, but these merely serve as contrasts to what Romeo and Juliet feel within themselves. When Juliet, soliloquizing, expresses her eager anticipation of her wedding night, she does not appear immodest but innocent in the best sense. Her passion for Romeo is ennobling, and the same is true of Romeo's love for her. The completeness of their devotion to each other leads them to ironic, untimely death; yet we cannot feel that this is wholly a defeat, for their love has risen superior to the storms of circumstance. In the words of Professor van Kranendonk, late of Amsterdam: "The poet has placed this springtime love in so intense a poetic light that an afterglow still remains over the somber ending. When we hear the names of Romeo and Juliet, we do not think first of all (as with Othello and Desdemona) about their pain, their misery, and their terrible undoing, but about their happiness together."

In style and manner, *Romeo and Juliet* seems nearer to *A Midsummer Night's Dream* than to Shakespeare's other plays. One finds the same intense lyricism, the same dependence upon rhymed couplets, the same enchantment of moonlight scenes, and the same interest in fairy lore. Finally, in *A Midsummer Night's Dream* there occurs a passage which seems to contain the theme enlarged upon in *Romeo and Juliet*. Lysander laments that in stories of the past the "course of true love never did run smooth" and that mutual happiness seldom endured, passing like a sound, a shadow, a dream, a flash of lightning swallowed up in darkness. "So quick bright things come to confusion," Lysander concludes, to which Hermia replies, "If then true lovers have been ever crossed, / It stands as an edict in destiny." These lines anticipate the "star-crossed lovers" of the Prologue to *Romeo and Juliet* and suggest that the evanescence of "bright things," particularly of young love, is a key to the mood in which the later play was written.

For some years scholars have debated the relative dates of these two plays. Internal evidence, while indicating 1594–95 as the date of *A Midsummer Night's Dream*, seemed to place *Romeo and Juliet* in 1591. In the Nurse's first scene, she says, "'Tis since the earthquake now eleven years," a line which has the earmarks of a topical allusion. If she refers to the much-publicized earthquake which shook England on April 6, 1580, then the play should be dated in 1591, a date which on other grounds seems much too early. Recent scholarship, however, has given us a choice of earthquakes, since one occurred in Dorsetshire in 1583 and one in Kent in 1585. A "terrible earthquake" which occurred on the Continent on March 1, 1584, is described in William Covell's *Polimanteia* (1595), a book which also praised "Sweet Shakspeare." It is therefore obvious that the earthquake could date *Romeo and Juliet* in 1594, 1595, or 1596, just as well as in 1591.

Other methods of establishing the date have been attempted. The play opens "a fortnight and odd days" before Lammas Tide (August 1). Calculating the position of the moon as described in the play yields 1596 as the only year that will fit astronomically. The first edition of the play, the quarto of 1597, is described on the title page as having been acted by "Lord Hunsdon's servants." Shakespeare's company was known by this title only from July 1596 to March 1597. A scholar who has compared the type face of this edition with other books issued by its printer, John Danter, concludes that the quarto was printed in February or March of 1597. Since it was a reported edition and was presumably not authorized by Shakespeare, it probably represented an attempt to exploit the popularity of a new play. We may therefore with some confidence assign the composition of the play to the middle of 1596, in which case the earthquake recalled by the Nurse would be the one which occurred in Kent on August 4, 1585. The play followed *A Midsummer Night's Dream* by slightly more than a year.

Shakespeare's source for this play was *The Tragicall Historye of Romeus and Iuliet, written first in Italian by*

Bandell, and now in Englishe by Ar. Br. (1562). This work by Arthur Broke, or Brooke, is a long narrative poem based on the prose of Bandello (1554) through an intermediate French version by Pierre Boaistuau (1559). Before Bandello, elements of the story were used by Luigi da Porto (1525) and Masuccio Salernitano (1476). Brooke's poem apparently created in England a vogue for "tragical histories" translated from Bandello, Boccaccio, and other prose romancers. In the two decades following 1562, extensive collections of these were published in prose by William Painter, Geoffrey Fenton, and George Pettie, and in verse by James Sandford, George Turbervile, Robert Smyth, and Richard Tarleton. Painter's work included a prose translation of the Romeo–Juliet story, but Shakespeare seems not to have used it. Brooke tells us in his preface that he had recently seen a play on the same subject acted on the stage (probably at the Inns of Court), but it seems unlikely that this play came to Shakespeare's attention thirty years later, since no further performances or printings of it are recorded. His obvious source, and probably his only one, was Brooke's poem.

Shakespeare's dramatic genius may be studied in the changes which he has made from Brooke's narrative. He has shortened the duration of the action from nine months to less than a week. Thus the hasty march of events becomes a major cause of the tragedy; there is not time to settle problems which greater leisure would have simplified. He has expanded Mercutio's role from a mere reference in Brooke and has invented the two duels involving Tybalt, thereby enhancing Romeo's dilemma of love against honor; for in Brooke's poem Romeo kills Tybalt accidentally while defending himself in a street brawl. He has taken from Brooke almost every incident involving the Nurse, yet he has created in her affectionate, vulgar, easygoing personality one of his most original characters. Finally, he has portrayed in the Capulet household a remarkable study in family psychology.

In Bandello's story Juliet is eighteen years old, in Brooke's poem she is sixteen, and in Shakespeare's play she is nearing her fourteenth birthday. Since Renaissance physiologists generally considered fourteen to mark the beginning of puberty (cf. *The Winter's Tale*, II, i, 147), Shakespeare apparently intended to picture Juliet's love for Romeo as first love, strengthened by the fact that she is just becoming emotionally aware of the meaning of love itself. (A similar purpose is evident in *The Tempest*, where Miranda is approximately the same age as Juliet.) In her emotions Juliet has suddenly become a woman, while in other respects she is still a child. Neither she nor her parents can quite understand this change; they consider her refusal to marry Paris childish willfulness, and she is too much in awe of them to tell them the truth.

Capulet is an old man married to a young woman. In spite of Lady Capulet's reference to her "old age," she is twenty-eight, only twice the age of her daughter. Capulet, however, had last attended a masquerade more than thirty years before and is now probably in his sixties. Since the earth had "swallowèd all my hopes" but Juliet, and since she is the only child born to Lady Capulet, Capulet must have had children by a former marriage. Lady Capulet has retained something of the awe of the child-bride for her older husband and defers to his judgment – and to his temper – in hastening the marriage with Paris. Her habit of deference to his wishes may have caused her to withhold

from Juliet sympathy which she normally would have given. Capulet assumes the management of the household duties and dearly loves to plan big parties. Even among his laments for Juliet's death is a regret that it should "murder our solemnity," i.e., spoil the feast which he had planned. His domestic ménage is hardly that of a great Italian nobleman and perhaps more nearly resembles that of a wealthy burgher of Stratford, recalled from Shakespeare's youth.

The play also represents an advance in Shakespeare's ability to reproduce the language of young gentlemen. The badinage of Mercutio, Romeo, and Benvolio is a decided improvement over similar conversations in earlier plays. Mercutio's unique blend of critical acumen, delicate fancy, and obscene levity makes him a remarkable character creation. One critic suggests that Shakespeare was forced to kill Mercutio lest he "steal the show" from the major figures of the plot. Like Jaques and Falstaff in later plays, he exists more as a character portrayed for its own innate interest than as an essential participant in the dramatic action.

Unlike Shakespeare's later tragedies, *Romeo and Juliet* is a play of externals, of characters portrayed in their relationships with each other. Their motives and feelings are readily understandable. There is a minimum of introspective brooding, enigmatic utterance, and puzzlement over moral problems; instead, all is quick decision and rapid action. In later tragedies Shakespeare undertook to explore the secret recesses of the soul, but here he shows people in conflict with external circumstance. Their errors of judgment are not errors involving a consciousness of sin but are attributable to impetuous haste and unkind fate. Nothing is withheld from the reader; characters and their motives are revealed as completely as possible. The same lack of reticence is evident in the literary style, which abounds in conceits, plays on words, and luxuriant poetic descriptions. Perhaps it is the quality of complete representations of emotions and moods that has made the play a favorite with musical composers: Gounod, Berlioz, Tchaikovsky, Prokofiev, and Milhaud, among others.

In *Romeo and Juliet* Shakespeare exploits dramatic irony in abrupt reversals of situation. Romeo, despondent, goes unwillingly to Capulet's ball and is quickly raised to joy by his encounter with Juliet, only to find that she is his hereditary enemy. This obstacle overcome, his joy reaches a height with his wedding, but within a half hour he is plunged into despair after his duel with Tybalt. At the beginning of Act V, Romeo is cheerful because of a dream which seems to foretell his reunion with Juliet, but his hopes are quickly dashed by Balthasar's news of her death. The supreme instance of irony comes as he stands beside her in the sepulchre, observing that she looks as though alive, and then drinks the poison to join her in death. The audience knows that she really is alive and will awake in a few minutes. In David Garrick's acting version of the play (as in Bandello's story) Juliet awakes before Romeo dies, and he thus realizes the bitter irony of his situation. The questionable dramatic propriety of this ending has caused considerable debate among students of the play.

Shakespeare makes one other effective use of irony. When Capulet and his wife are scolding Juliet for her refusal to marry Paris, each petulantly expresses a wish for her death. "I would the fool were married to her grave," says Lady Capulet. Capulet says that they have only one child, "But now I see this one is one too much." They do not intend these statements seriously, as Juliet doubtless realizes, but their words are ominous of what is to come. They get what they ask for.

In recent years numerous attempts have been made to state a central theme for the play. One critic views it as a tragedy of unawareness. Capulet and Montague are unaware of the fateful issues which may hang upon their quarrel. Romeo and Juliet fall in love while unaware that they are hereditary enemies. Mercutio and Tybalt are both unaware of the true state of affairs when they fight their duel. In the chain of events leading to the final tragedy, even the servants play a part and are unaware of the results of their actions. The final scene, with Friar Laurence's long explanation, is dramatically justified because it brings Montague, Capulet, Lady Capulet, and the Prince to at least a partial awareness of their responsibility for what has happened. Supplementing this view of the play is one which finds it to be a study of the wholeness and complexity of things in human affairs. The issues of the feud may appear to be simple and clear, but in reality they are highly complex, giving rise to results which are completely unforeseen. The goodness or badness of human actions is relative, not absolute, an idea symbolically set forth in Friar Laurence's opening speech on herbs which are medicinal or poisonous according to the manner of their use.

Other clues to the meaning of the play may be found in the repetitive imagery employed by Shakespeare. The images of haste, of events rushing to a conclusion, are found throughout. When Romeo says, "I stand on sudden haste," Friar Laurence answers, "They stumble that run fast," and thus expresses one moral to be drawn from the play. Romeo and Mercutio symbolize their wit-combat by the wild-goose chase, a reckless cross-country horse race. "Swits and spurs," cries Romeo, using the imagery of speed. Numerous other instances may be found.

Closely allied to the imagery of haste is the violence expressed in the gunpowder image. The Friar warns that too impetuous love is like fire and powder, which, "as they kiss, consume." Romeo desires a poison that will expel life from his body, like powder fired from a cannon. This may identify the Apothecary's poison as aconite, since elsewhere Shakespeare compares the action of aconite with that of "rash gunpowder" (*2 Henry IV*, IV, iv, 48). Violence is also expressed in the image of shipwreck which may end the voyage of life. Capulet compares Juliet weeping to a bark in danger from tempests. Romeo describes his death as the shipwreck of his "seasick weary bark." Earlier, after expressing a premonition that attendance at Capulet's party will cause his death, he resigns himself to him "that hath the steerage of my course," anticipating his later images of the ship and the voyage of life.

Also repeated in the play is the image of Death as the lover of Juliet. She herself uses it, her father uses it beside her bier, and Romeo uses it most effectively in the final scene. The effect of this repeated image is to suggest that Juliet is foredoomed to die, that Death, personified, has claimed her for his own. It thus strengthens the ominous note of fate which is felt throughout the play.

That *Romeo and Juliet* is a tragedy of fate can hardly be doubted. Shakespeare says as much in the Prologue. The lovers are marked for death; their fortunes are "crossed" by the stars. The reason for their doom is likewise given: only the shock of their deaths can force their parents to

end the senseless feud. At the end of the play Capulet calls the lovers "Poor sacrifices of our enmity," and the Prince describes their deaths as Heaven's punishment of their parents' hate. Romeo's premonition of death before going to the party attributes it to some "consequence yet hanging in the stars." The note of fate is struck repeatedly during the play. "A greater power than we can contradict / Hath thwarted our intents," says Friar Laurence to Juliet in the tomb. The numerous mischances experienced by the lovers are not fortuitous bad luck but represent the working out of some hidden design. Critics who attack the play for lacking inevitability have misunderstood Shakespeare's dramatic technique. Like Hamlet's adventure with the pirates, the sequence of mishaps here is deliberately made so improbable that chance alone cannot explain it. Fate, or the will of Heaven, must be invoked.

One finds it difficult to interpret this tragedy in Aristotelian terms, since the parents are really the ones who have the "tragic flaw" and suffer the results of their folly, as Lear does, in the deaths of their children. Yet the children, not the parents, are the major figures of the play. Some critics have named impetuosity as Romeo's "tragic flaw," but Romeo is less impetuous than Tybalt or Mercutio, and one can hardly name as a "flaw" a quality which is pictured as common to youth. It is true that greater placidity of temperament and more deliberate speed might have averted the tragedy under the given circumstances, yet the pattern of circumstances might easily have been different and the will of fate accomplished just the same.

Shakespeare makes it clear that society is partly responsible for the tragedy. The feud between noble families was a matter of social convention. So was the necessity to take personal revenge for an insult to one's honor. Here there seems to be a topical allusion. Prince Escalus represents the view of Queen Elizabeth, whose government decreed that homicide in a duel should be punishable as murder. She was determined to stamp out duelling. Furthermore, the evil arising from any form of civil strife is a constantly reiterated theme in Elizabethan literature. Current social attitudes may be noted both in the Prince's edict against street fighting and in the cavalier disregard of it.

As might be expected, *Romeo and Juliet* has been a popular stage play, never more so than now, when each year sees from ten to twenty new productions by professional and amateur groups. What Hamlet is for the actor, Juliet is for the actress, a role which offers the fullest scope for the display of female histrionics. In past centuries Mrs Betterton and Fanny Kemble made great successes in the part. In the present century Julia Marlowe, Eva Le Gallienne, Jane Cowl, and Katherine Cornell are among those who have played Juliet. The producer of this play always has a problem, for very few great actresses achieve eminence by the age of fourteen, and most of them are recognizably mature women trying to look young. To a lesser extent the same problem exists in casting the masculine roles. The producer must choose between the verisimilitude of a youthful cast and the more sophisticated acting of experienced players. Nevertheless, despite all difficulties, *Romeo and Juliet* is still constantly staged with success, and most of us can recall productions in which it proved as vivid and moving in the theatre as it always proves on the printed page.

University of Maine   JOHN E. HANKINS

NOTE ON THE TEXT

An abridged and inaccurate version of *Romeo and Juliet*, evidently "reporting" the play in performance, was published in quarto in 1597. In 1599 appeared a good quarto, probably printed from Shakespeare's draft with some reference to the earlier quarto. A third quarto was printed from the second in 1609, and this was used as copy for the fourth quarto (1622?) and the text of the first folio, 1623. The present edition follows the quarto of 1599, with faulty readings corrected with caution by reference to the quarto of 1597, and with few emendations. (All material departures from the text of the 1599 quarto are listed in an appendix, with the exception of added stage directions and adjusted cancellations; the two latter classes of departure are noted as they occur.) None of the early texts, including that of the folio, are divided into acts and scenes. The division supplied marginally in the present edition is "editorial" and is for purposes of reference only.

ROMEO AND JULIET

Chorus
Escalus, *Prince of Verona*
Paris, *a young count, kinsman to the Prince*
Montague
Capulet
An old Man, *of the Capulet family*
Romeo, *son to Montague*
Mercutio, *kinsman to the Prince, and friend to Romeo*
Benvolio, *nephew to Montague, and friend to Romeo*
Tybalt, *nephew to Lady Capulet*
Friar Laurence ⎫
Friar John ⎬ *Franciscans*
Balthasar, *servant to Romeo*
Abram, *servant to Montague*

Sampson ⎫
Gregory ⎬ *servants to Capulet*
Peter, *servant to Juliet's nurse*
An Apothecary
Three Musicians
An Officer
Lady Montague, *wife to Montague*
Lady Capulet, *wife to Capulet*
Juliet, *daughter to Capulet*
Nurse *to Juliet*
Citizens *of Verona*, Gentlemen *and* Gentlewomen *of both houses*, Maskers, Torchbearers, Pages, Guards, Watchmen, Servants, *and* Attendants

Scene : *Verona, Mantua*]

*

Pro.   THE PROLOGUE

[Enter] *Chorus.*

CHORUS

Two households, both alike in dignity,
 In fair Verona, where we lay our scene,
3 From ancient grudge break to new mutiny,
4 Where civil blood makes civil hands unclean.
From forth the fatal loins of these two foes
6 A pair of star-crossed lovers take their life ;
Whose misadventured piteous overthrows
 Doth with their death bury their parents' strife.
9 The fearful passage of their death-marked love,
 And the continuance of their parents' rage,
Which, but their children's end, naught could remove,
12 Is now the two hours' traffic of our stage ;
The which if you with patient ears attend,
What here shall miss, our toil shall strive to mend.

[Exit.]

Pro. 3 *mutiny* outbursts of violence 4 *civil . . . civil* citizens' . . . fellow citizens' 6 *star-crossed* thwarted by adverse stars 9 *death-marked* foredoomed to death 12 *two . . . stage* our stage-business for the next two hours
I, i A street in Verona 1 *carry coals* i.e. suffer insults 2 *colliers* coal dealers 3 *an* if ; *choler* anger ; *draw* draw our swords 4 *collar* hangman's noose 11 *take the wall* pass on the inner and cleaner part of the sidewalk 12–13 *the weakest . . . wall* i.e. is pushed from his place (proverbial) 15 *weaker vessels* (cf. 1 Peter iii, 7) 25–26 *sense . . . sense* meaning . . . physical sensation 28, 29 *flesh, fish* (alluding to the proverb 'Neither fish nor flesh') 30 *poor-John* dried hake, the cheapest fish ; *tool* sword (with ribald innuendo)

Enter Sampson and Gregory, with swords and   I, i
bucklers, of the house of Capulet.

SAMPSON Gregory, on my word, we'll not carry coals.   1
GREGORY No, for then we should be colliers.   2
SAMPSON I mean, an we be in choler, we'll draw.   3
GREGORY Ay, while you live, draw your neck out of collar.   4
SAMPSON I strike quickly, being moved.
GREGORY But thou art not quickly moved to strike.
SAMPSON A dog of the house of Montague moves me.
GREGORY To move is to stir, and to be valiant is to stand. Therefore, if thou art moved, thou runn'st away.
SAMPSON A dog of that house shall move me to stand. I will take the wall of any man or maid of Montague's.   11
GREGORY That shows thee a weak slave ; for the weakest   12 goes to the wall.
SAMPSON 'Tis true ; and therefore women, being the weaker vessels, are ever thrust to the wall. Therefore I   15 will push Montague's men from the wall and thrust his maids to the wall.
GREGORY The quarrel is between our masters, and us their men.
SAMPSON 'Tis all one. I will show myself a tyrant. When I have fought with the men, I will be cruel with the maids – I will cut off their heads.
GREGORY The heads of the maids ?
SAMPSON Ay, the heads of the maids, or their maidenheads. Take it in what sense thou wilt.   25
GREGORY They must take it in sense that feel it.
SAMPSON Me they shall feel while I am able to stand ; and 'tis known I am a pretty piece of flesh.   28
GREGORY 'Tis well thou art not fish ; if thou hadst, thou   29 hadst been poor-John. Draw thy tool ! Here comes two   30 of the house of Montagues.

Enter two other Servingmen [Abram and Balthasar].

SAMPSON My naked weapon is out. Quarrel! I will back thee.

GREGORY How? turn thy back and run?

SAMPSON Fear me not.

36 GREGORY No, marry. I fear thee!

37 SAMPSON Let us take the law of our sides; let them begin.

GREGORY I will frown as I pass by, and let them take it as they list.

40 SAMPSON Nay, as they dare. I will bite my thumb at them, which is disgrace to them if they bear it.

ABRAM Do you bite your thumb at us, sir?

SAMPSON I do bite my thumb, sir.

ABRAM Do you bite your thumb at us, sir?

SAMPSON [aside to Gregory] Is the law of our side if I say ay?

GREGORY [aside to Sampson] No.

SAMPSON No, sir, I do not bite my thumb at you, sir; but I bite my thumb, sir.

GREGORY Do you quarrel, sir?

50 ABRAM Quarrel, sir? No, sir.

SAMPSON But if you do, sir, I am for you. I serve as good a man as you.

ABRAM No better.

SAMPSON Well, sir.

Enter Benvolio.

GREGORY [aside to Sampson] Say 'better.' Here comes one of my master's kinsmen.

SAMPSON Yes, better, sir.

ABRAM You lie.

SAMPSON Draw, if you be men. Gregory, remember thy
60 swashing blow.

They fight.

BENVOLIO Part, fools!
Put up your swords. You know not what you do.

Enter Tybalt.

TYBALT
63 What, art thou drawn among these heartless hinds?
Turn thee, Benvolio! look upon thy death.

BENVOLIO
I do but keep the peace. Put up thy sword,
Or manage it to part these men with me.

TYBALT
What, drawn, and talk of peace? I hate the word
As I hate hell, all Montagues, and thee.
Have at thee, coward!

[They fight.]
Enter [an Officer, and] three or four Citizens with clubs or partisans.

70 OFFICER Clubs, bills, and partisans! Strike! beat them down!

CITIZENS Down with the Capulets! Down with the Montagues!

Enter old Capulet in his gown, and his Wife.

CAPULET
What noise is this? Give me my long sword, ho!

WIFE
A crutch, a crutch! Why call you for a sword?

CAPULET
My sword, I say! Old Montague is come
76 And flourishes his blade in spite of me.

Enter old Montague and his Wife.

MONTAGUE
Thou villain Capulet!—Hold me not, let me go.

MONTAGUE'S WIFE
Thou shalt not stir one foot to seek a foe.

Enter Prince Escalus, with his Train.

PRINCE
Rebellious subjects, enemies to peace,
Profaners of this neighbor-stainèd steel—
Will they not hear? What, ho! you men, you beasts,
That quench the fire of your pernicious rage
With purple fountains issuing from your veins!
On pain of torture, from those bloody hands
Throw your mistemp'red weapons to the ground   85
And hear the sentence of your movèd prince.
Three civil brawls, bred of an airy word   87
By thee, old Capulet, and Montague,
Have thrice disturbed the quiet of our streets
And made Verona's ancient citizens   90
Cast by their grave beseeming ornaments   91
To wield old partisans, in hands as old,
Cank'red with peace, to part your cank'red hate.   93
If ever you disturb our streets again,
Your lives shall pay the forfeit of the peace.
For this time all the rest depart away.
You, Capulet, shall go along with me;
And, Montague, come you this afternoon,
To know our farther pleasure in this case,
To old Freetown, our common judgment place.   100
Once more, on pain of death, all men depart.

Exeunt [all but Montague, his Wife, and Benvolio].

MONTAGUE
Who set this ancient quarrel new abroach?   102
Speak, nephew, were you by when it began?

BENVOLIO
Here were the servants of your adversary
And yours, close fighting ere I did approach.
I drew to part them. In the instant came
The fiery Tybalt, with his sword prepared;
Which, as he breathed defiance to my ears,
He swung about his head and cut the winds,
Who, nothing hurt withal, hissed him in scorn.   110
While we were interchanging thrusts and blows,
Came more and more, and fought on part and part,
Till the Prince came, who parted either part.

MONTAGUE'S WIFE
O, where is Romeo? Saw you him to-day?
Right glad I am he was not at this fray.

BENVOLIO
Madam, an hour before the worshipped sun
Peered forth the golden window of the East,
A troubled mind drave me to walk abroad;
Where, underneath the grove of sycamore
That westward rooteth from this city side,
So early walking did I see your son.
Towards him I made, but he was ware of me   122

---

36 *marry* indeed (originally an oath by the Virgin Mary); *I fear thee* to suppose me afraid of you is ridiculous **37** *take . . . of* have the law on **40** *bite my thumb* (an insulting gesture) **60** *swashing* smashing **63** *heartless hinds* cowardly servants **70** *bills, partisans* long-shafted weapons with combined spear-head and cutting-blade **76** *in spite of* in defiance of **85** *mistemp'red* (1) badly made, (2) used for a bad purpose **87** *airy* made with breath **90** *ancient citizens* a volunteer guard of older men **91** *grave beseeming ornaments* staffs and costumes appropriate for the aged **93** *Cank'red . . . cank'red* rusted . . . malignant **100** *Freetown* (Brooke's translation of *Villafranca*) **102** *set . . . abroach* reopened this quarrel of long standing **110** *Who* which; *nothing* not at all; *withal* therewith **122** *ware* aware, wary

And stole into the covert of the wood.
124 I, measuring his affections by my own,
125 Which then most sought where most might not be found,
Being one too many by my weary self,
Pursued my humor, not pursuing his,
And gladly shunned who gladly fled from me.
MONTAGUE
Many a morning hath he there been seen,
With tears augmenting the fresh morning's dew,
Adding to clouds more clouds with his deep sighs ;
But all so soon as the all-cheering sun
Should in the farthest East begin to draw
134 The shady curtains from Aurora's bed,
135 Away from light steals home my heavy son
And private in his chamber pens himself,
Shuts up his windows, locks fair daylight out,
And makes himself an artificial night.
139 Black and portentous must this humor prove
Unless good counsel may the cause remove.
BENVOLIO
My noble uncle, do you know the cause ?
MONTAGUE
I neither know it nor can learn of him.
BENVOLIO
Have you importuned him by any means ?
MONTAGUE
Both by myself and many other friends ;
But he, his own affections' counsellor,
Is to himself – I will not say how true –
But to himself so secret and so close,
148 So far from sounding and discovery,
As is the bud bit with an envious worm
Ere he can spread his sweet leaves to the air
Or dedicate his beauty to the sun.
Could we but learn from whence his sorrows grow,
We would as willingly give cure as know.
            Enter Romeo.
BENVOLIO
See, where he comes. So please you step aside,
I'll know his grievance, or be much denied.
MONTAGUE
I would thou wert so happy by thy stay
157 To hear true shrift. Come, madam, let's away.
            Exeunt [Montague and Wife].
BENVOLIO
158 Good morrow, cousin.
ROMEO   Is the day so young ?
BENVOLIO
But new struck nine.
ROMEO   Ay me ! sad hours seem long.
Was that my father that went hence so fast ?
BENVOLIO
It was. What sadness lengthens Romeo's hours ?

ROMEO
Not having that which having makes them short.
BENVOLIO In love ?
ROMEO Out –
BENVOLIO Of love ?
ROMEO
Out of her favor where I am in love.
BENVOLIO
Alas that love, so gentle in his view,   167
Should be so tyrannous and rough in proof !   168
ROMEO
Alas that love, whose view is muffled still,   169
Should without eyes see pathways to his will !
Where shall we dine ? O me ! What fray was here ?
Yet tell me not, for I have heard it all.
Here's much to do with hate, but more with love.   173
Why then, O brawling love, O loving hate,
O anything, of nothing first create !
O heavy lightness, serious vanity,
Misshapen chaos of well-seeming forms,
Feather of lead, bright smoke, cold fire, sick health,
Still-waking sleep, that is not what it is !
This love feel I, that feel no love in this.
Dost thou not laugh ?
BENVOLIO   No, coz, I rather weep.   181
ROMEO
Good heart, at what ?
BENVOLIO   At thy good heart's oppression.
ROMEO
Why, such is love's transgression.
Griefs of mine own lie heavy in my breast,   184
Which thou wilt propagate, to have it prest
With more of thine. This love that thou hast shown
Doth add more grief to too much of mine own.
Love is a smoke raised with the fume of sighs ;
Being purged, a fire sparkling in lovers' eyes ;
Being vexed, a sea nourished with lovers' tears.
What is it else ? A madness most discreet,
A choking gall, and a preserving sweet.
Farewell, my coz.
BENVOLIO   Soft ! I will go along.
An if you leave me so, you do me wrong.
ROMEO
Tut ! I have lost myself ; I am not here ;   195
This is not Romeo, he's some other where.
BENVOLIO
Tell me in sadness, who is that you love ?   197
ROMEO
What, shall I groan and tell thee ?
BENVOLIO   Groan ? Why, no ;
But sadly tell me who.
ROMEO
Bid a sick man in sadness make his will.
Ah, word ill urged to one that is so ill !
In sadness, cousin, I do love a woman.
BENVOLIO
I aimed so near when I supposed you loved.
ROMEO
A right good markman. And she's fair I love.
BENVOLIO
A right fair mark, fair coz, is soonest hit.   205
ROMEO
Well, in that hit you miss. She'll not be hit
With Cupid's arrow. She hath Dian's wit,   207

124 *affections* inclinations, feelings 125 *most sought . . . found* i.e. desired solitude 134 *Aurora* the dawn 135 *heavy* melancholy 139 *humor* mood 148 *sounding* being measured (as water-depth is measured with a plummet line) 157 *shrift* confession 158 *morrow* morning 167 *view* appearance 168 *in proof* in being experienced 169 *view* sight; *muffled* blindfolded 173–80 *Here's . . . this* (the rhetorical name for such paradoxes is oxymoron ; cf. III, ii, 73–85) 181 *coz* cousin 184–87 *Griefs . . . own* your sorrow for my grief grieves me further to have caused you sorrow 195 *lost* (so both Q2 and Q1, but the emendation 'left,' has been cogently suggested) 197 *in sadness* seriously 205 *fair mark* bright clean target 207 *Dian* Diana, virgin goddess and huntress

208　And, in strong proof of chastity well armed,
209　From Love's weak childish bow she lives unharmed.
210　She will not stay the siege of loving terms,
　　　Nor bide th' encounter of assailing eyes,
　　　Nor ope her lap to saint-seducing gold.
　　　O, she is rich in beauty ; only poor
214　That, when she dies, with beauty dies her store.
　　BENVOLIO
215　Then she hath sworn that she will still live chaste ?
　　ROMEO
216　She hath, and in that sparing makes huge waste ;
　　　For beauty, starved with her severity,
　　　Cuts beauty off from all posterity.
　　　She is too fair, too wise, wisely too fair,
220　To merit bliss by making me despair.
　　　She hath forsworn to love, and in that vow
　　　Do I live dead that live to tell it now.
　　BENVOLIO
　　　Be ruled by me ; forget to think of her.
　　ROMEO
　　　O, teach me how I should forget to think !
　　BENVOLIO
　　　By giving liberty unto thine eyes.
　　　Examine other beauties.
　　ROMEO　　　　　　　　'Tis the way
227　To call hers (exquisite) in question more.
　　　These happy masks that kiss fair ladies' brows,
　　　Being black puts us in mind they hide the fair.
　　　He that is strucken blind cannot forget
　　　The precious treasure of his eyesight lost.
232　Show me a mistress that is passing fair,
　　　What doth her beauty serve but as a note
　　　Where I may read who passed that passing fair ?
　　　Farewell. Thou canst not teach me to forget.
　　BENVOLIO
236　I'll pay that doctrine, or else die in debt.　　　Exeunt.

*

I, ii　　Enter Capulet, County Paris, and the Clown
　　　　[a Servant].
　　CAPULET
1　　But Montague is bound as well as I,
　　　In penalty alike ; and 'tis not hard, I think,
　　　For men so old as we to keep the peace.
　　PARIS
4　　Of honorable reckoning are you both,
　　　And pity 'tis you lived at odds so long.
　　　But now, my lord, what say you to my suit ?
　　CAPULET
　　　But saying o'er what I have said before :
8　　My child is yet a stranger in the world,
　　　She hath not seen the change of fourteen years ;
　　　Let two more summers wither in their pride
　　　Ere we may think her ripe to be a bride.
　　PARIS
　　　Younger than she are happy mothers made.
　　CAPULET
13　And too soon marred are those so early made.
14　Earth hath swallowèd all my hopes but she ;
　　　She is the hopeful lady of my earth.
　　　But woo her, gentle Paris, get her heart ;
　　　My will to her consent is but a part.
18　An she agree, within her scope of choice
19　Lies my consent and fair according voice.

This night I hold an old accustomed feast,　　20
Whereto I have invited many a guest,
Such as I love ; and you among the store,
One more, most welcome, makes my number more.
At my poor house look to behold this night
Earth-treading stars that make dark heaven light.　　25
Such comfort as do lusty young men feel
When well-apparelled April on the heel　　27
Of limping Winter treads, even such delight
Among fresh fennel buds shall you this night　　29
Inherit at my house. Hear all, all see,
And like her most whose merit most shall be ;
Which, on more view of many, mine, being one,　　32
May stand in number, though in reck'ning none.
Come, go with me.
　　　[To Servant, giving him a paper]
　　　　　　　　　　Go, sirrah, trudge about　　34
Through fair Verona ; find those persons out
Whose names are written there, and to them say,
My house and welcome on their pleasure stay.
　　　　　　　　　　　　　Exit [with Paris].
SERVANT　Find them out whose names are written here ?
It is written that the shoemaker should meddle with his
yard and the tailor with his last, the fisher with his pen-　　40
cil and the painter with his nets ; but I am sent to find　　41
those persons whose names are here writ, and can never
find what names the writing person hath here writ. I　　43
must to the learned. In good time !　　44
　　　Enter Benvolio and Romeo.
BENVOLIO
Tut, man, one fire burns out another's burning ;　　45
　　One pain is less'ned by another's anguish ;　　46
Turn giddy, and be holp by backward turning ;　　47
　　One desperate grief cures with another's languish.
Take thou some new infection to thy eye,　　49
And the rank poison of the old will die.
ROMEO
Your plantain leaf is excellent for that.
BENVOLIO
For what, I pray thee ?
ROMEO　　　　　　　　For your broken shin.
BENVOLIO
Why, Romeo, art thou mad ?
ROMEO
Not mad, but bound more than a madman is ;　　54

208 *proof* armor　209 *unharmed* (from Q1 ; Q2 reads 'uncharmed,' perhaps correctly)　210–11 *She . . . eyes* i.e. she gives me no chance to woo her　214 *with . . . store* she will leave no children to perpetuate her beauty　215 *still* always　216 *sparing* miserly economy　220 *bliss* heaven　227 *in question* to my mind　232 *passing* surpassingly　236 *pay that doctrine* convince you otherwise
I, ii A street in Verona　1 *bound* under bond　4 *reckoning* reputation　8 *world* world of society　13 *marred* disfigured by childbirth　14 *hopes* children　18 *scope* range　19 *according* harmoniously agreeing　20 *old accustomed* by custom of long standing　25 *stars* i.e. maidens　27 *April* (Venus' month, the season of lovemaking)　29 *fennel* a flowering herb associated with stimulation and enticement　32–33 *Which . . . none* my daughter will be numerically counted among those present, but possibly not among those you would wish to marry after seeing them all (cf. the common saying 'One is no number')　34 *sirrah* (a familiar form of address, used with servants and sometimes with friends)　40, 41 *yard, last, pencil, nets* (occupational tools humorously reversed)　43 *find* find out (since I cannot read)　44 *In good time* help comes just when I need it　45 *one . . . burning* (proverb used often by Shakespeare)　46 *another's anguish* anguish from another pain　47 *Turn . . . turning* when giddy from whirling around, be helped by reversing direction　49 *infection* (figuratively used, but taken literally by Romeo)　54–56 *bound . . . tormented* (customary treatment of madmen)

Shut up in prison, kept without my food,
56 Whipped and tormented and – God-den, good fellow.
SERVANT God gi' go-den. I pray, sir, can you read ?
ROMEO
Ay, mine own fortune in my misery.
SERVANT Perhaps you have learned it without book. But
I pray, can you read anything you see ?
ROMEO
61 Ay, if I know the letters and the language.
SERVANT Ye say honestly. Rest you merry.
ROMEO Stay, fellow ; I can read.
　　　　He reads the letter.
'Signior Martino and his wife and daughters ;
County Anselmo and his beauteous sisters ;
The lady widow of Vitruvio ;
Signior Placentio and his lovely nieces ;
Mercutio and his brother Valentine ;
Mine uncle Capulet, his wife, and daughters ;
70 My fair niece Rosaline and Livia ;
Signior Valentio and his cousin Tybalt ;
Lucio and the lively Helena.'
A fair assembly. Whither should they come ?
SERVANT Up.
ROMEO Whither ? To supper ?
SERVANT To our house.
ROMEO Whose house ?
SERVANT My master's.
ROMEO
Indeed I should have asked you that before.
SERVANT Now I'll tell you without asking. My master is
the great rich Capulet ; and if you be not of the house of
82 Montagues, I pray come and crush a cup of wine. Rest
you merry.　　　　　　　　　　　　　　　*[Exit.]*
BENVOLIO
At this same ancient feast of Capulet's
Sups the fair Rosaline whom thou so loves ;
With all the admirèd beauties of Verona.
87 Go thither, and with unattainted eye
Compare her face with some that I shall show,
And I will make thee think thy swan a crow.
ROMEO
When the devout religion of mine eye
Maintains such falsehood, then turn tears to fires ;
92 And these, who, often drowned, could never die,
Transparent heretics, be burnt for liars !
One fairer than my love ? The all-seeing sun
Ne'er saw her match since first the world begun.
BENVOLIO
Tut ! you saw her fair, none else being by,
Herself poised with herself in either eye ;
98 But in that crystal scales let there be weighed
Your lady's love against some other maid
That I will show you shining at this feast,
101 And she shall scant show well that now seems best.

56 *God-den* good evening (used after 12 noon; cf. II, iv, 105) 61 *if I know*
(the servant takes this to mean 'only if I have memorized the appearance of')
82 *crush* drink 87 *unattainted* unprejudiced 92 *these* these eyes; *drowned*
i.e. in tears 98 *crystal scales* (Romeo's two eyes are compared to the two
ends of a pair of balances) 101 *scant* scarcely
I, iii Within Capulet's house 7 *give leave* leave us 9 *thou's* thou shalt
13 *teen* sorrow 15 *Lammastide* August 1 23 *earthquake* (see Introduction)
29 *bear a brain* keep my mental powers 32 *tetchy* fretful 33 *Shake . . .
dovehouse* i.e. the dovehouse creaked from the earthquake ; *trow* believe
34 *trudge* run away 36 *high-lone* alone ; *rood* cross 43 *holidam* halidom,
holy relic

ROMEO
I'll go along, no such sight to be shown,
But to rejoice in splendor of my own.　　*[Exeunt.]*

*

　　　　Enter Capulet's Wife, and Nurse.　　　　I, iii
WIFE
Nurse, where's my daughter ? Call her forth to me.
NURSE
Now, by my maidenhead at twelve year old,
I bade her come. What, lamb ! what, ladybird !
God forbid, where's this girl ? What, Juliet !
　　　　Enter Juliet.
JULIET
How now ? Who calls ?
NURSE　　　　　　　　Your mother.
JULIET　　　　　　　　　　Madam, I am here.
What is your will ?
WIFE
This is the matter – Nurse, give leave awhile,　　　7
We must talk in secret. Nurse, come back again ;
I have rememb'red me, thou 's hear our counsel.　　9
Thou knowest my daughter 's of a pretty age.
NURSE
Faith, I can tell her age unto an hour.
WIFE
She's not fourteen.
NURSE　　　　　I'll lay fourteen of my teeth –
And yet, to my teen be it spoken, I have but four –　13
She's not fourteen. How long is it now
To Lammastide ?　　　　　　　　　　　　15
WIFE　　　　　A fortnight and odd days.
NURSE
Even or odd, of all days in the year,
Come Lammas Eve at night shall she be fourteen.
Susan and she (God rest all Christian souls !)
Were of an age. Well, Susan is with God ;
She was too good for me. But, as I said,
On Lammas Eve at night shall she be fourteen ;
That shall she, marry ; I remember it well.
'Tis since the earthquake now eleven years ;　　23
And she was weaned (I never shall forget it),
Of all the days of the year, upon that day ;
For I had then laid wormwood to my dug,
Sitting in the sun under the dovehouse wall.
My lord and you were then at Mantua.
Nay, I do bear a brain. But, as I said,　　　29
When it did taste the wormwood on the nipple
Of my dug and felt it bitter, pretty fool,
To see it tetchy and fall out with the dug !　　32
Shake, quoth the dovehouse ! 'Twas no need, I trow,　33
To bid me trudge.　　　　　　　　　　　34
And since that time it is eleven years,
For then she could stand high-lone ; nay, by th' rood,　36
She could have run and waddled all about ;
For even the day before, she broke her brow ;
And then my husband (God be with his soul !
'A was a merry man) took up the child.
'Yea,' quoth he, 'dost thou fall upon thy face ?
Thou wilt fall backward when thou hast more wit ;
Wilt thou not, Jule ?' and, by my holidam,　　43
The pretty wretch left crying and said 'Ay.'
To see now how a jest shall come about !
I warrant, an I should live a thousand years,

I never should forget it. 'Wilt thou not, Jule?' quoth he,
48   And, pretty fool, it stinted and said 'Ay.'
WIFE
     Enough of this. I pray thee hold thy peace.
NURSE
     Yes, madam. Yet I cannot choose but laugh
     To think it should leave crying and say 'Ay.'
52   And yet, I warrant, it had upon it brow
     A bump as big as a young cock'rel's stone;
     A perilous knock; and it cried bitterly.
     'Yea,' quoth my husband, 'fall'st upon thy face?
     Thou wilt fall backward when thou comest to age;
     Wilt thou not, Jule?' It stinted and said 'Ay.'
JULIET
58   And stint thou too, I pray thee, nurse, say I.
NURSE
     Peace, I have done. God mark thee to his grace!
     Thou wast the prettiest babe that e'er I nursed.
     An I might live to see thee married once,
     I have my wish.
WIFE
     Marry, that 'marry' is the very theme
     I came to talk of. Tell me, daughter Juliet,
     How stands your disposition to be married?
JULIET
     It is an honor that I dream not of.
NURSE
     An honor? Were not I thine only nurse,
     I would say thou hadst sucked wisdom from thy teat.
WIFE
     Well, think of marriage now. Younger than you,
     Here in Verona, ladies of esteem,
     Are made already mothers. By my count,
72   I was your mother much upon these years
     That you are now a maid. Thus then in brief:
     The valiant Paris seeks you for his love.
NURSE
     A man, young lady! lady, such a man
76   As all the world – why he's a man of wax.
WIFE
     Verona's summer hath not such a flower.
NURSE
     Nay, he's a flower, in faith – a very flower.
WIFE
     What say you? Can you love the gentleman?
     This night you shall behold him at our feast.
     Read o'er the volume of young Paris' face,
     And find delight writ there with beauty's pen;
83   Examine every married lineament,
     And see how one another lends content;
85   And what obscured in this fair volume lies
86   Find written in the margent of his eyes.
     This precious book of love, this unbound lover,
88   To beautify him only lacks a cover.
89   The fish lives in the sea, and 'tis much pride
     For fair without the fair within to hide.
     That book in many's eyes doth share the glory,
     That in gold clasps locks in the golden story;
     So shall you share all that he doth possess,
     By having him making yourself no less.
NURSE
95   No less? Nay, bigger! Women grow by men.
WIFE
     Speak briefly, can you like of Paris' love?

JULIET
     I'll look to like, if looking liking move;
     But no more deep will I endart mine eye   98
     Than your consent gives strength to make it fly.
          Enter Servingman.
SERVINGMAN Madam, the guests are come, supper
     served up, you called, my young lady asked for, the
     nurse cursed in the pantry, and everything in extremity. 102
     I must hence to wait. I beseech you follow straight.
WIFE
     We follow thee.   [*Exit Servingman.*]
          Juliet, the County stays.
NURSE
     Go, girl, seek happy nights to happy days.   *Exeunt.*

                          *

          Enter Romeo, Mercutio, Benvolio, with five or six   I, iv
          other Maskers; Torchbearers.
ROMEO
     What, shall this speech be spoke for our excuse?   1
     Or shall we on without apology?
BENVOLIO
     The date is out of such prolixity.   3
     We'll have no Cupid hoodwinked with a scarf,   4
     Bearing a Tartar's painted bow of lath,   5
     Scaring the ladies like a crowkeeper;   6
     [Nor no without-book prologue, faintly spoke   7
     After the prompter, for our entrance;]   8
     But, let them measure us by what they will,
     We'll measure them a measure and be gone.   10
ROMEO
     Give me a torch. I am not for this ambling.
     Being but heavy, I will bear the light.   12
MERCUTIO
     Nay, gentle Romeo, we must have you dance.
ROMEO
     Not I, believe me. You have dancing shoes
     With nimble soles; I have a soul of lead
     So stakes me to the ground I cannot move.
MERCUTIO
     You are a lover. Borrow Cupid's wings
     And soar with them above a common bound.   18
ROMEO
     I am too sore enpiercèd with his shaft
     To soar with his light feathers; and so bound

48 *stinted* stopped   52 *it brow* its brow   58 *say I* (a pun on 'ay' and 'I';
cf. III, ii, 45–50)   72 *much . . . years* at much the same age (indicating that
Lady Capulet's age is now twenty-eight)   76 *a man of wax* handsome,
as a wax model   83 *married lineament* harmonious feature   85 *what . . .
lies* i.e. his concealed inner qualities of character   86 *margent* marginal
gloss   88 *a cover* i.e. a wife   89–94 *The fish . . . no less* i.e. as the sea enfolds the fish and the cover enfolds the book, so you shall enfold Paris
(in your arms), enhancing your good qualities by sharing his   95 *bigger*
i.e. through pregnancy   98 *endart mine eye* shoot my eye-glance (as an
arrow; cf. III, ii, 47)   102 *cursed in the pantry* i.e. the other servants
swear because the Nurse is not helping
I, iv *Before Capulet's house*   1 *this speech* (Romeo has prepared a set
speech, such as customarily introduced visiting maskers)   3 *The date . . .
prolixity* such superfluous speeches are now out of fashion   4 *hoodwinked*
blindfolded   5 *Tartar's . . . lath* (the Tartar's bow, used from horseback,
was much shorter than the English longbow)   6 *crowkeeper* scarecrow
7–8 (added from Q1)   7 *without-book* memorized   8 *entrance* (pronounced
'en-ter-ance'   10 *measure . . . measure* dance one dance   12 *heavy* sad, hence
'weighted down'   18 *bound* a leap, required in some dances

21 I cannot bound a pitch above dull woe.
Under love's heavy burden do I sink.

MERCUTIO
And, to sink in it, should you burden love –
Too great oppression for a tender thing.

ROMEO
Is love a tender thing ? It is too rough,
Too rude, too boist'rous, and it pricks like thorn.

MERCUTIO
If love be rough with you, be rough with love,
Prick love for pricking, and you beat love down.
Give me a case to put my visage in.

30 A visor for a visor ! What care I
31 What curious eye doth quote deformities ?
32 Here are the beetle brows shall blush for me.

BENVOLIO
Come, knock and enter ; and no sooner in
34 But every man betake him to his legs.

ROMEO
A torch for me ! Let wantons light of heart
36 Tickle the senseless rushes with their heels ;
37 For I am proverbed with a grandsire phrase,
38 I'll be a candle-holder and look on ;
39 The game was ne'er so fair, and I am done.

MERCUTIO
40 Tut ! dun 's the mouse, the constable's own word !
41 If thou art Dun, we'll draw thee from the mire
42 Of this sir-reverence love, wherein thou stickest
43 Up to the ears. Come, we burn daylight, ho !

ROMEO
Nay, that's not so.

MERCUTIO   I mean, sir, in delay
We waste our lights in vain, like lamps by day.
Take our good meaning, for our judgments sits
47 Five times in that ere once in our five wits.

ROMEO
And we mean well in going to this masque,
49 But 'tis no wit to go.

MERCUTIO   Why, may one ask ?

ROMEO
I dreamt a dream to-night.

MERCUTIO   And so did I.

ROMEO
Well, what was yours ?

MERCUTIO   That dreamers often lie.

ROMEO
In bed asleep, while they do dream things true.

MERCUTIO
O, then I see Queen Mab hath been with you.   53
She is the fairies' midwife, and she comes
In shape no bigger than an agate stone   55
On the forefinger of an alderman,
Drawn with a team of little atomies   57
Over men's noses as they lie asleep ;
Her wagon spokes made of long spinners' legs,   59
The cover, of the wings of grasshoppers ;
Her traces, of the smallest spider web ;   61
Her collars, of the moonshine's wat'ry beams ;   62
Her whip, of cricket's bone ; the lash, of film ;   63
Her wagoner, a small grey-coated gnat,
Not half so big as a round little worm   65
Pricked from the lazy finger of a maid ;
Her chariot is an empty hazelnut,
Made by the joiner squirrel or old grub,
Time out o' mind the fairies' coachmakers.
And in this state she gallops night by night
Through lovers' brains, and then they dream of love ;
O'er courtiers' knees, that dream on curtsies straight ;
O'er lawyers' fingers, who straight dream on fees ;
O'er ladies' lips, who straight on kisses dream,
Which oft the angry Mab with blisters plagues,
Because their breaths with sweetmeats tainted are.   76
Sometime she gallops o'er a courtier's nose,
And then dreams he of smelling out a suit ;   78
And sometime comes she with a tithe-pig's tail   79
Tickling a parson's nose as 'a lies asleep,
Then dreams he of another benefice.   81
Sometimes she driveth o'er a soldier's neck,
And then dreams he of cutting foreign throats,
Of breaches, ambuscadoes, Spanish blades,
Of healths five fathom deep ; and then anon   85
Drums in his ear, at which he starts and wakes,
And being thus frighted, swears a prayer or two
And sleeps again. This is that very Mab
That plats the manes of horses in the night
And bakes the elflocks in foul sluttish hairs,   90
Which once untangled much misfortune bodes.
This is the hag, when maids lie on their backs,   92
That presses them and learns them first to bear,
Making them women of good carriage.
This is she –

ROMEO   Peace, peace, Mercutio, peace !
Thou talk'st of nothing.   96

MERCUTIO   True, I talk of dreams ;
Which are the children of an idle brain,
Begot of nothing but vain fantasy ;   98
Which is as thin of substance as the air,
And more inconstant than the wind, who woos
Even now the frozen bosom of the North
And, being angered, puffs away from thence,
Turning his side to the dew-dropping South.

BENVOLIO
This wind you talk of blows us from ourselves.
Supper is done, and we shall come too late.

ROMEO
I fear, too early ; for my mind misgives

---

21 *pitch* height (falconry)   30 *A visor . . . visor* a mask for a face ugly
enough to be itself a mask   31 *quote* note   32 *beetle brows* beetling eye-
brows (of the mask)   34 *betake . . . legs* join the dance   36 *rushes* (used
as floor coverings)   37 *grandsire phrase* old saying   38 *candle-holder*
i.e. non-participant   39 *The game . . . done* best quit a game at the height
of enjoyment (proverbial; cf. I, v, 119)   40 *dun 's the mouse* be quiet
as a mouse (proverbial); *constable's own word* i.e. the caution to be quiet
41 *Dun* (stock name for a horse); *mire* (alluding to a winter game, 'Dun is
in the mire,' in which the players lifted a heavy log representing a horse
caught in the mud)   42 *sir-reverence* filthy (literally 'save-your-rever-
ence,' a euphemism associated with physical functions)   43 *burn daylight*
waste time (proverbial)   47 *five wits* mental faculties : common sense (the
perceptive power common to all five physical senses), fantasy, imagination, judgment (reason), memory   49 *no wit* not intelligent   53 *Mab* (a
Celtic folk name for the fairy queen)   55 *agate stone* jewel carved with
figures and set in a ring   57 *atomies* tiny creatures   59 *spinners* spiders
61, 62 *traces, collars* parts of the harness   63 *film* any filament   65–66
worm . . . maid (alluding to the proverbial saying that worms breed in
idle fingers)   76 *with sweetmeats* i.e. as a result of eating sweetmeats
78 *smelling . . . suit* discovering a petitioner who will pay for his influence
with government officials   79 *tithe-pig* the parson's tithe (tenth) of
his parishioner's livestock   81 *another benefice* an additional 'living'
in the church   85 *healths . . . deep* drinking toasts from glasses thirty
feet deep   90 *elflocks* knots of tangled hair   92 *hag* night hag, or nightmare   96 *nothing* no tangible thing   98 *fantasy* (cf. l. 47 and note)

107   Some consequence, yet hanging in the stars,
     Shall bitterly begin his fearful date
     With this night's revels and expire the term
     Of a despisèd life, closed in my breast,
     By some vile forfeit of untimely death.
112   But he that hath the steerage of my course
     Direct my sail! On, lusty gentlemen!

BENVOLIO Strike, drum.

I, v   *They march about the stage, and Servingmen come*
       forth with napkins.

1   1. SERVINGMAN Where's Potpan, that he helps not to
2   take away? He shift a trencher! he scrape a trencher!
3   2. SERVINGMAN When good manners shall lie all in one
     or two men's hands, and they unwashed too, 'tis a foul
     thing.
6   1. SERVINGMAN Away with the joint-stools, remove the
7   court-cupboard, look to the plate. Good thou, save me
8   a piece of marchpane and, as thou loves me, let the
9   porter let in Susan Grindstone and Nell. *[Exit second*
     Servingman.] Anthony, and Potpan!
       [Enter two more Servingmen.]
11   3. SERVINGMAN Ay, boy, ready.
     1. SERVINGMAN You are looked for and called for, asked
     for and sought for, in the great chamber.
14   4. SERVINGMAN We cannot be here and there too.
15   Cheerly, boys! Be brisk awhile, and the longer liver take
     all.   *[Exeunt third and fourth Servingmen.]*
     Enter [Capulet, his Wife, Juliet, Tybalt, Nurse, and]
     all the Guests and Gentlewomen to the Maskers.

CAPULET
     Welcome, gentlemen! Ladies that have their toes
17   Unplagued with corns will walk a bout with you.
     Ah ha, my mistresses! which of you all
19   Will now deny to dance? She that makes dainty,
     She I'll swear hath corns. Am I come near ye now?
     Welcome, gentlemen! I have seen the day
     That I have worn a visor and could tell
     A whispering tale in a fair lady's ear,
     Such as would please. 'Tis gone, 'tis gone, 'tis gone!
     You are welcome, gentlemen! Come, musicians, play.
     Music plays, and they dance.
26   A hall, a hall! give room! and foot it, girls.
     More light, you knaves! and turn the tables up,
     And quench the fire, the room is grown too hot.
29   Ah, sirrah, this unlooked-for sport comes well.
     Nay, sit, nay, sit, good cousin Capulet,
     For you and I are past our dancing days.
     How long is't now since last yourself and I
     Were in a mask?
33   2. CAPULET   By'r Lady, thirty years.
CAPULET
     What, man? 'Tis not so much, 'tis not so much;
     'Tis since the nuptial of Lucentio,
     Come Pentecost as quickly as it will,
     Some five-and-twenty years, and then we masked.
     2. CAPULET
     'Tis more, 'tis more. His son is elder, sir;
     His son is thirty.
CAPULET   Will you tell me that?
40   His son was but a ward two years ago.
ROMEO *[to a Servingman]*
     What lady's that, which doth enrich the hand
     Of yonder knight?
SERVINGMAN I know not, sir.

ROMEO
     O, she doth teach the torches to burn bright!
     It seems she hangs upon the cheek of night
     As a rich jewel in an Ethiop's ear –
     Beauty too rich for use, for earth too dear!
     So shows a snowy dove trooping with crows   48
     As yonder lady o'er her fellows shows.
     The measure done, I'll watch her place of stand
     And, touching hers, make blessèd my rude hand.   51
     Did my heart love till now? Forswear it, sight!
     For I ne'er saw true beauty till this night.
TYBALT
     This, by his voice, should be a Montague.
     Fetch me my rapier, boy. What, dares the slave
     Come hither, covered with an antic face,   56
     To fleer and scorn at our solemnity?   57
     Now, by the stock and honor of my kin,
     To strike him dead I hold it not a sin.
CAPULET
     Why, how now, kinsman? Wherefore storm you so?
TYBALT
     Uncle, this is a Montague, our foe;
     A villain, that is hither come in spite
     To scorn at our solemnity this night.
CAPULET
     Young Romeo is it?
TYBALT   'Tis he, that villain Romeo.
CAPULET
     Content thee, gentle coz, let him alone.
     'A bears him like a portly gentleman,   66
     And, to say truth, Verona brags of him
     To be a virtuous and well-governed youth.
     I would not for the wealth of all this town
     Here in my house do him disparagement.
     Therefore be patient, take no note of him.
     It is my will, the which if thou respect,
     Show a fair presence and put off these frowns,
     An ill-beseeming semblance for a feast.
TYBALT
     It fits when such a villain is a guest.
     I'll not endure him.
CAPULET   He shall be endured.
     What, goodman boy! I say he shall. Go to!
     Am I the master here, or you? Go to!

107 *consequence* future chain of events; *hanging* (in astrology, future events are said to 'hang' – '*dependere*' – from the stars) 112 *he* God
I, v Within Capulet's house   s.d. (Q2 adds 'Enter Romeo,' altered in folio to 'Enter Servant.' It is not certain that the Maskers leave the stage at this point; 'marching about' itself sometimes signalled a change in locale.) 1, 3 *1. Servingman, 2. Servingman* (designated 'Servingman,' '1. Servingman' in Q2) 2 *trencher* wooden platter 3–5 *When . . . thing* (a complaint that household decorum, 'good manners,' is sustained by too few, and too untidy, servants) 6 *joint-stools* stools made by a joiner 7 *court-cupboard* sideboard; *plate* silverware 8 *marchpane* sweetmeat with almonds 9 *Susan . . . Nell* (girls evidently invited for a servants' party in the kitchen after the banquet) 11, 14 *3. Servingman, 4. Servingman* (designated '2.' and '3.' in Q2, but presumably they are Anthony and Potpan, now arrived) 15 *longer . . . all* i.e. the spoils to the survivor (proverbial, but often used in contexts like the above, advocating enjoyment of life) 17 *walk a bout* dance a turn 19 *makes dainty* pretends to hesitate 26 *A hall* clear the hall for dancing 29 *unlooked-for sport* (a dance was not originally planned) 33 *2. Capulet* (an old man of the Capulet family); *thirty years* (indicating Capulet's advanced age) 40 *His son . . . ago* it seems only two years since his son was a minor 48 *with crows* (cf. I, ii, 89) 51 *rude* coarse-skinned 56 *antic face* comic mask 57 *fleer* mock; *solemnity* dignified feast 66 *portly* of good carriage

79 You'll not endure him, God shall mend my soul !
80 You'll make a mutiny among my guests !
81 You will set cock-a-hoop, you'll be the man !

TYBALT
Why, uncle, 'tis a shame.

CAPULET   Go to, go to !
You are a saucy boy. Is't so, indeed ?
84 This trick may chance to scathe you. I know what.
85 You must contrary me ! Marry, 'tis time –
86 Well said, my hearts ! – You are a princox – go !
Be quiet, or – More light, more light ! – For shame !
I'll make you quiet ; what ! – Cheerly, my hearts !

TYBALT
89 Patience perforce with willful choler meeting
Makes my flesh tremble in their different greeting.
I will withdraw ; but this intrusion shall,
Now seeming sweet, convert to bitt'rest gall.   *Exit.*

ROMEO
93 If I profane with my unworthiest hand
94   This holy shrine, the gentle sin is this ;
95 My lips, two blushing pilgrims, ready stand
    To smooth that rough touch with a tender kiss.

JULIET
97 Good pilgrim, you do wrong your hand too much,
    Which mannerly devotion shows in this ;
For saints have hands that pilgrims' hands do touch,
100   And palm to palm is holy palmers' kiss.

ROMEO
Have not saints lips, and holy palmers too ?

JULIET
Ay, pilgrim, lips that they must use in prayer.

ROMEO
103 O, then, dear saint, let lips do what hands do !
    They pray ; grant thou, lest faith turn to despair.

JULIET
105 Saints do not move, though grant for prayers' sake.

ROMEO
Then move not while my prayer's effect I take.
Thus from my lips, by thine my sin is purged.
    [Kisses her.]

JULIET
Then have my lips the sin that they have took.

ROMEO
Sin from my lips ? O trespass sweetly urged !
Give me my sin again.
    [Kisses her.]

110 JULIET   You kiss by th' book.

NURSE
Madam, your mother craves a word with you.

ROMEO
What is her mother ?

NURSE   Marry, bachelor,
Her mother is the lady of the house,
And a good lady, and a wise and virtuous.
I nursed her daughter that you talked withal.   115
I tell you, he that can lay hold of her
Shall have the chinks.   117

ROMEO   Is she a Capulet ?
O dear account ! my life is my foe's debt.   118

BENVOLIO
Away, be gone ; the sport is at the best.   119

ROMEO
Ay, so I fear ; the more is my unrest.

CAPULET
Nay, gentlemen, prepare not to be gone ;
We have a trifling foolish banquet towards.   122
Is it e'en so ? Why then, I thank you all.
I thank you, honest gentlemen. Good night.
More torches here ! Come on then, let's to bed.
Ah, sirrah, by my fay, it waxes late ;   126
I'll to my rest.   *[Exeunt all but Juliet and Nurse.]*

JULIET
Come hither, nurse. What is yond gentleman ?

NURSE
The son and heir of old Tiberio.

JULIET
What's he that now is going out of door ?

NURSE
Marry, that, I think, be young Petruchio.

JULIET
What's he that follows there, that would not dance ?

NURSE
I know not.

JULIET
Go ask his name. – If he be marrièd,
My grave is like to be my wedding bed.

NURSE
His name is Romeo, and a Montague,
The only son of your great enemy.

JULIET
My only love, sprung from my only hate !
Too early seen unknown, and known too late !
Prodigious birth of love it is to me   140
That I must love a loathèd enemy.

NURSE
What's tis ? what's tis ?   142

JULIET   A rhyme I learnt even now
Of one I danced withal.
    One calls within, 'Juliet.'

NURSE   Anon, anon !   143
Come, let's away ; the strangers all are gone.   *Exeunt.*

*

[Enter] Chorus.   II, Cho.

CHORUS
Now old desire doth in his deathbed lie,   1
    And young affection gapes to be his heir ;   2
That fair for which love groaned for and would die,
    With tender Juliet matched, is now not fair.

79 *God . . . soul* (an expression of impatience)   80 *mutiny* violent disturbance   81 *set cock-a-hoop* i.e. take the lead ; *be the man* play the big man   84 *scathe* injure ; *what* what I'm doing   85 *'tis time* it's time you learned your place (?)   86 *said* done ; *my hearts* (addressed to the dancers) ; *princox* saucy boy   89 *Patience perforce* enforced self-restraint ; *choler* anger   93–110 (these lines form an English-style sonnet and the first quatrain of another)   94 *shrine* i.e. Juliet's hand ; *sin* i.e. roughening her soft hand with his coarser one (cf. l. 51)   95 *pilgrims* (so called because pilgrims visit shrines)   97–100 *Good . . . kiss* your touch is not rough, to heal it with a kiss is unnecessary, a handclasp is sufficient greeting   100 *palmers* religious pilgrims   103 *do what hands do* i.e. press each other (in a kiss)   105 *move* take the initiative ; *grant* give permission   110 *book* book of etiquette   115 *withal* with   117 *chinks* money   118 *my foe's debt* owed to my foe   119 *Away . . . best* (cf. I, iv, 39)   122 *banquet* light refreshments ; *towards* in preparation   126 *fay* faith   140 *Prodigious* monstrous   142 *tis* this   143 *Anon* i.e. we are coming right away
II, Cho.   1 *old desire* i.e. Romeo's love of Rosaline   2 *young affection* new love ; *gapes* opens his mouth hungrily

Now Romeo is beloved and loves again,
  Alike bewitchèd by the charm of looks ;
7 But to his foe supposed he must complain,
8   And she steal love's sweet bait from fearful hooks.
  Being held a foe, he may not have access
10   To breathe such vows as lovers use to swear,
  And she as much in love, her means much less
    To meet her new belovèd anywhere ;
  But passion lends them power, time means, to meet,
  Temp'ring extremities with extreme sweet.   *[Exit.]*

II, i   *Enter Romeo alone.*

ROMEO
1 Can I go forward when my heart is here ?
2 Turn back, dull earth, and find thy centre out.
    Enter Benvolio with Mercutio. [Romeo retires.]

BENVOLIO
Romeo ! my cousin Romeo ! Romeo !

MERCUTIO   He is wise,
And, on my life, hath stol'n him home to bed.

BENVOLIO
He ran this way and leapt this orchard wall.
Call, good Mercutio.

6 MERCUTIO   Nay, I'll conjure too.
7 Romeo ! humors ! madman ! passion ! lover !
  Appear thou in the likeness of a sigh ;
  Speak but one rhyme, and I am satisfied !
  Cry but 'Ay me !' pronounce but 'love' and 'dove' ;
11 Speak to my gossip Venus one fair word,
12 One nickname for her purblind son and heir
13 Young Abraham Cupid, he that shot so true
14 When King Cophetua loved the beggar maid !
  He heareth not, he stirreth not, he moveth not ;
16 The ape is dead, and I must conjure him.
  I conjure thee by Rosaline's bright eyes,
  By her high forehead and her scarlet lip,
  By her fine foot, straight leg, and quivering thigh,
20 And the demesnes that there adjacent lie,
  That in thy likeness thou appear to us !

BENVOLIO
An if he hear thee, thou wilt anger him.

MERCUTIO
This cannot anger him. 'Twould anger him
24 To raise a spirit in his mistress' circle
  Of some strange nature, letting it there stand
  Till she had laid it and conjured it down.
  That were some spite ; my invocation
  Is fair and honest : in his mistress' name,
  I conjure only but to raise up him.

BENVOLIO
Come, he hath hid himself among these trees
31 To be consorted with the humorous night.
  Blind is his love and best befits the dark.

MERCUTIO
If love be blind, love cannot hit the mark.
Now will he sit under a medlar tree
And wish his mistress were that kind of fruit
36 As maids call medlars when they laugh alone.
  O, Romeo, that she were, O that she were
38 An open et cetera, thou a pop'rin pear !
39 Romeo, good night. I'll to my truckle-bed ;
  This field-bed is too cold for me to sleep.
  Come, shall we go ?

BENVOLIO   Go then, for 'tis in vain
To seek him here that means not to be found.
              Exit [with Mercutio].

ROMEO *[coming forward]*   II, ii
He jests at scars that never felt a wound.
    [Enter Juliet above at a window.]
But soft ! What light through yonder window breaks ?
It is the East, and Juliet is the sun !
Arise, fair sun, and kill the envious moon,   4
Who is already sick and pale with grief
That thou her maid art far more fair than she. 6
Be not her maid, since she is envious.
Her vestal livery is but sick and green,   8
And none but fools do wear it. Cast it off.
It is my lady ; O, it is my love !
O that she knew she were !
She speaks, yet she says nothing. What of that ?
Her eye discourses ; I will answer it.
I am too bold ; 'tis not to me she speaks.
Two of the fairest stars in all the heaven,
Having some business, do entreat her eyes
To twinkle in their spheres till they return. 17
What if her eyes were there, they in her head ?
The brightness of her cheek would shame those stars
As daylight doth a lamp ; her eyes in heaven
Would through the airy region stream so bright
That birds would sing and think it were not night.
See how she leans her cheek upon her hand !
O that I were a glove upon that hand,
That I might touch that cheek !

JULIET   Ay me !
ROMEO   She speaks.
O, speak again, bright angel ! for thou art
As glorious to this night, being o'er my head,
As is a wingèd messenger of heaven
Unto the white-upturnèd wond'ring eyes   29
Of mortals that fall back to gaze on him
When he bestrides the lazy-pacing clouds
And sails upon the bosom of the air.

JULIET
O Romeo, Romeo ! wherefore art thou Romeo ?
Deny thy father and refuse thy name ;
Or, if thou wilt not, be but sworn my love,
And I'll no longer be a Capulet.

ROMEO *[aside]*
Shall I hear more, or shall I speak at this ?

---

7 *complain* make a lover's plaints 8 *steal . . . hooks* (a popular conceit : the lover 'fishes' for his beloved. For Juliet to be 'caught' is dangerous because of the family feud.) 10 *use* are accustomed
II, i Within Capulet's walled orchard 1 *my heart is here* (the Neo-Platonic fancy that the heart or soul of the lover dwells in the beloved) 2 *earth* i.e. my body ; *centre* i.e. my heart or soul 6 *Nay . . . too* (printed as part of preceding speech in Q2) 7 *humors* whims 11 *gossip* female crony 12 *purblind* dim-sighted 13 *Young Abraham* youthful, yet patriarchal (Cupid, or Love, was both the youngest and the oldest of the gods) 14 *King Cophetua . . . beggar maid* (from a popular ballad) 16 *The ape . . . him* (probably recalling a showman's ape who 'played dead' until called with the right word-formula) 20 *demesnes* domains 24 *circle* the conjurer's circle in which an evoked spirit supposedly appears (Mercutio intends a ribald pun) 31 *humorous* damp ; also, capricious 36, 38 *medlars, pop'rin pear* fruits (used vulgarly in reference to the sex organs) 39 *truckle-bed* trundle bed
II, ii 4 *kill* make invisible by more intense light 6 *her maid* (Diana, moon-goddess, was patroness of virgins) 8 *vestal livery* virginity (after Vesta, another virgin goddess) ; *green* anemic 17 *spheres* orbits 29 *white-upturnèd* (the whites show when the eyes are turned upward)

JULIET
'Tis but thy name that is my enemy.
Thou art thyself, though not a Montague.
What's Montague ? It is nor hand, nor foot,
Nor arm, nor face, nor any other part
Belonging to a man. O, be some other name !
What's in a name ? That which we call a rose
44 By any other name would smell as sweet.
So Romeo would, were he not Romeo called,
46 Retain that dear perfection which he owes
Without that title. Romeo, doff thy name ;
And for thy name, which is no part of thee,
Take all myself.

ROMEO   I take thee at thy word.
Call me but love, and I'll be new baptized ;
Henceforth I never will be Romeo.

JULIET
What man art thou that, thus bescreened in night,
So stumblest on my counsel ?

ROMEO   By a name
I know not how to tell thee who I am.
My name, dear saint, is hateful to myself,
Because it is an enemy to thee.
Had I it written, I would tear the word.

JULIET
My ears have yet not drunk a hundred words
Of thy tongue's uttering, yet I know the sound.
Art thou not Romeo, and a Montague ?

ROMEO
61 Neither, fair maid, if either thee dislike.

JULIET
How camest thou hither, tell me, and wherefore ?
The orchard walls are high and hard to climb,
And the place death, considering who thou art,
If any of my kinsmen find thee here.

ROMEO
66 With love's light wings did I o'erperch these walls ;
For stony limits cannot hold love out,
And what love can do, that dares love attempt.
Therefore thy kinsmen are no stop to me.

JULIET
If they do see thee, they will murder thee.

ROMEO
Alack, there lies more peril in thine eye
Than twenty of their swords ! Look thou but sweet,
73 And I am proof against their enmity.

JULIET
I would not for the world they saw thee here.

ROMEO
I have night's cloak to hide me from their eyes ;
And but thou love me, let them find me here.
My life were better ended by their hate
78 Than death prorogued, wanting of thy love.

JULIET
By whose direction found'st thou out this place ?

ROMEO
By love, that first did prompt me to inquire.
He lent me counsel, and I lent him eyes.

I am no pilot ; yet, wert thou as far
As that vast shore washed with the farthest sea,   83
I should adventure for such merchandise.   84

JULIET
Thou knowest the mask of night is on my face ;
Else would a maiden blush bepaint my cheek
For that which thou hast heard me speak to-night.
Fain would I dwell on form – fain, fain deny
What I have spoke ; but farewell compliment !   89
Dost thou love me ? I know thou wilt say 'Ay' ;
And I will take thy word. Yet, if thou swear'st,
Thou mayst prove false. At lovers' perjuries,
They say Jove laughs. O gentle Romeo,
If thou dost love, pronounce it faithfully.
Or if thou thinkest I am too quickly won,
I'll frown, and be perverse, and say thee nay,
So thou wilt woo ; but else, not for the world.
In truth, fair Montague, I am too fond,
And therefore thou mayst think my havior light ;   99
But trust me, gentleman, I'll prove more true
Than those that have more cunning to be strange.   101
I should have been more strange, I must confess,
But that thou overheard'st, ere I was ware,   103
My true-love passion. Therefore pardon me,
And not impute this yielding to light love,
Which the dark night hath so discoverèd.   106

ROMEO
Lady, by yonder blessèd moon I vow,
That tips with silver all these fruit-tree tops –

JULIET
O, swear not by the moon, th' inconstant moon,
That monthly changes in her circled orb,
Lest that thy love prove likewise variable.

ROMEO
What shall I swear by ?

JULIET   Do not swear at all ;
Or if thou wilt, swear by thy gracious self,
Which is the god of my idolatry,
And I'll believe thee.

ROMEO   If my heart's dear love –

JULIET
Well, do not swear. Although I joy in thee,
I have no joy of this contract to-night.
It is too rash, too unadvised, too sudden ;
Too like the lightning, which doth cease to be
Ere one can say 'It lightens.' Sweet, good night !   120
This bud of love, by summer's ripening breath,
May prove a beauteous flow'r when next we meet.
Good night, good night ! As sweet repose and rest
Come to thy heart as that within my breast !

ROMEO
O, wilt thou leave me so unsatisfied ?

JULIET
What satisfaction canst thou have to-night ?

ROMEO
Th' exchange of thy love's faithful vow for mine.

JULIET
I gave thee mine before thou didst request it ;
And yet I would it were to give again.

ROMEO
Wouldst thou withdraw it ? For what purpose, love ?

JULIET
But to be frank and give it thee again.   131
And yet I wish but for the thing I have.

44 *name* (from Q1 ; Q2 reads 'word,' perhaps correctly)   **46** *owes* owns
61 *dislike* displease   **66** *o'erperch* fly over   **73** *proof* armored   **78** *pro-
roguèd* postponed ; *wanting of* lacking   **83** *farthest sea* the Pacific   **84**
adventure risk a voyage   **89** *compliment* etiquette   **99** *havior* behavior
101 *strange* aloof, distant   **103** *ware* aware of you   **106** *discoverèd* revealed
131 *frank* generous

57

133 My bounty is as boundless as the sea,
My love as deep ; the more I give to thee,
135 The more I have, for both are infinite.
I hear some noise within. Dear love, adieu !
　　　[*Nurse calls within.*]
Anon, good nurse ! Sweet Montague, be true.
Stay but a little, I will come again.　　　　　　*[Exit.]*

ROMEO
O blessèd, blessèd night ! I am afeard,
Being in night, all this is but a dream,
Too flattering-sweet to be substantial.
　　　[*Enter Juliet above.*]

JULIET
Three words, dear Romeo, and good night indeed.
143 If that thy bent of love be honorable,
Thy purpose marriage, send me word to-morrow,
By one that I'll procure to come to thee,
Where and what time thou wilt perform the rite ;
And all my fortunes at thy foot I'll lay
And follow thee my lord throughout the world.

NURSE [*within*] Madam !

JULIET
I come, anon. – But if thou meanest not well,
I do beseech thee –

NURSE [*within*]
Madam !

152 JULIET　　By and by I come. –
To cease thy suit and leave me to my grief.
To-morrow will I send.

ROMEO　　　　　　So thrive my soul –

JULIET
A thousand times good night !　　　　　　*[Exit.]*

ROMEO
A thousand times the worse, to want thy light !
Love goes toward love as schoolboys from their books ;
But love from love, toward school with heavy looks.
　　　Enter Juliet [above] again.

JULIET
Hist ! Romeo, hist ! O for a falc'ner's voice
160 To lure this tassel-gentle back again !
161 Bondage is hoarse and may not speak aloud,
Else would I tear the cave where Echo lies
And make her airy tongue more hoarse than mine
With repetition of 'My Romeo !'

ROMEO
165 It is my soul that calls upon my name.
How silver-sweet sound lovers' tongues by night,
167 Like softest music to attending ears !

JULIET
Romeo !

ROMEO　　My sweet ?

JULIET　　　　　　At what o'clock to-morrow
Shall I send to thee ?

ROMEO　　　　　　By the hour of nine.

JULIET
I will not fail. 'Tis twenty years till then.
I have forgot why I did call thee back.

ROMEO
Let me stand here till thou remember it.

JULIET
I shall forget, to have thee still stand there,
Rememb'ring how I love thy company.

ROMEO
And I'll still stay, to have thee still forget,

Forgetting any other home but this.

JULIET
'Tis almost morning. I would have thee gone –
And yet no farther than a wanton's bird,　　　178
That lets it hop a little from her hand,
Like a poor prisoner in his twisted gyves,　　　180
And with a silken thread plucks it back again,
So loving-jealous of his liberty.

ROMEO
I would I were thy bird.

JULIET　　　　　　Sweet, so would I.
Yet I should kill thee with much cherishing.　　　184
Good night, good night ! Parting is such sweet sorrow
That I shall say good night till it be morrow.　　*[Exit.]* 186

ROMEO
Sleep dwell upon thine eyes, peace in thy breast !　　187
Would I were sleep and peace, so sweet to rest !
Hence will I to my ghostly father's cell,　　　189
His help to crave and my dear hap to tell.　　*Exit.* 190

*

Enter Friar [Laurence] alone, with a basket.　　II, iii

FRIAR
The grey-eyed morn smiles on the frowning night,
Check'ring the Eastern clouds with streaks of light ;
And fleckèd darkness like a drunkard reels　　　3
From forth day's path and Titan's fiery wheels.　　4
Now, ere the sun advance his burning eye
The day to cheer and night's dank dew to dry,
I must up-fill this osier cage of ours　　　7
With baleful weeds and precious-juicèd flowers.
The earth that's nature's mother is her tomb.
What is her burying grave, that is her womb ;
And from her womb children of divers kind
We sucking on her natural bosom find,
Many for many virtues excellent,
None but for some, and yet all different.
O, mickle is the powerful grace that lies　　　15
In plants, herbs, stones, and their true qualities ;
For naught so vile that on the earth doth live
But to the earth some special good doth give ;
Nor aught so good but, strained from that fair use,
Revolts from true birth, stumbling on abuse.　　20
Virtue itself turns vice, being misapplied,
And vice sometime 's by action dignified.　　22
　　　Enter Romeo.
Within the infant rind of this weak flower

---

133 *bounty* wish to give (love)　135 *The more I have* (scholastic theologians debated how love could be given away and yet the giver have more than before ; cf. Dante, *Purgatorio*, XV 61 ff.)　143 *bent* purpose　152 *By and by* immediately　160 *tassel-gentle* tercel-gentle, or male falcon　161 *Bondage* (she feels 'imprisoned' by the nearness of her kinsmen)　165 *my soul* (cf. II, i, 1 and note)　167 *attending* paying attention　178 *wanton* spoiled child　180 *gyves* fetters　184 *cherishing* caressing　186 *morrow* morning　187–90 (In Q2 the speech-prefix 'Juliet' is mistakenly placed before the first of these lines, and they are followed by four lines that are nearly identical with those at II, iii, 1–4. Perhaps Shakespeare decided to let the Friar announce the dawn instead of Romeo, and the cancelled lines in the manuscript were printed in error.)　189 *ghostly* spiritual　190 *dear hap* good luck
II, iii　Before Friar Laurence's cell　3 *fleckèd* spotted, dappled　4 *Titan's fiery wheels* the sun's chariot wheels　7 *osier cage* willow basket　15 *mickle* much　20 *true birth* its true nature　22 *dignified* made worthy ; s.d. (this entrance seems premature, but cf. entrance of Nurse at III, iii, 70)

Poison hath residence, and medicine power ;
25 For this, being smelt, with that part cheers each part ;
Being tasted, slays all senses with the heart.
27 Two such opposèd kings encamp them still
28 In man as well as herbs – grace and rude will ;
And where the worser is predominant,
30 Full soon the canker death eats up that plant.

ROMEO
31 Good morrow, father.

FRIAR   Benedicite !
What early tongue so sweet saluteth me ?
Young son, it argues a distemperèd head
So soon to bid good morrow to thy bed.
Care keeps his watch in every old man's eye,
And where care lodges, sleep will never lie ;
37 But where unbruisèd youth with unstuffed brain
Doth couch his limbs, there golden sleep doth reign.
Therefore thy earliness doth me assure
Thou art uproused with some distemp'rature ;
Or if not so, then here I hit it right –
Our Romeo hath not been in bed to-night.

ROMEO
That last is true – the sweeter rest was mine.

FRIAR
God pardon sin ! Wast thou with Rosaline ?

ROMEO
With Rosaline, my ghostly father ? No.
I have forgot that name and that name's woe.

FRIAR
That's my good son ! But where hast thou been then ?

ROMEO
I'll tell thee ere thou ask it me again.
I have been feasting with mine enemy,
Where on a sudden one hath wounded me
That's by me wounded. Both our remedies
52 Within thy help and holy physic lies.
I bear no hatred, blessèd man, for, lo,
54 My intercession likewise steads my foe.

FRIAR
55 Be plain, good son, and homely in thy drift.
56 Riddling confession finds but riddling shrift.

ROMEO
Then plainly know my heart's dear love is set
On the fair daughter of rich Capulet ;
As mine on hers, so hers is set on mine,
And all combined, save what thou must combine
By holy marriage. When, and where, and how
We met, we wooed, and made exchange of vow,
I'll tell thee as we pass ; but this I pray,
That thou consent to marry us to-day.

FRIAR
Holy Saint Francis ! What a change is here !

Is Rosaline, that thou didst love so dear,
So soon forsaken ? Young men's love then lies
Not truly in their hearts, but in their eyes.
Jesu Maria ! What a deal of brine
Hath washed thy sallow cheeks for Rosaline !
How much salt water thrown away in waste
To season love, that of it doth not taste !   72
The sun not yet thy sighs from heaven clears,
Thy old groans ring yet in mine ancient ears.
Lo, here upon thy cheek the stain doth sit
Of an old tear that is not washed off yet.
If e'er thou wast thyself, and these woes thine,
Thou and these woes were all for Rosaline.
And art thou changed ? Pronounce this sentence then :
Women may fall when there's no strength in men.   80

ROMEO
Thou chid'st me oft for loving Rosaline.

FRIAR
For doting, not for loving, pupil mine.

ROMEO
And bad'st me bury love.

FRIAR   Not in a grave
To lay one in, another out to have.

ROMEO
I pray thee chide not. She whom I love now
Doth grace for grace and love for love allow.   86
The other did not so.

FRIAR   O, she knew well
Thy love did read by rote, that could not spell.   88
But come, young waverer, come go with me.
In one respect I'll thy assistant be ;
For this alliance may so happy prove
To turn your households' rancor to pure love.

ROMEO
O, let us hence ! I stand on sudden haste.   93

FRIAR
Wisely and slow. They stumble that run fast.   *Exeunt.*

*

Enter Benvolio and Mercutio.   II, iv

MERCUTIO
Where the devil should this Romeo be ?
Came he not home to-night ?

BENVOLIO
Not to his father's. I spoke with his man.

MERCUTIO
Why, that same pale hard-hearted wench, that Rosaline,
Torments him so that he will sure run mad.

BENVOLIO
Tybalt, the kinsman to old Capulet,
Hath sent a letter to his father's house.

MERCUTIO A challenge, on my life.

BENVOLIO Romeo will answer it.

MERCUTIO Any man that can write may answer a letter.   10

BENVOLIO Nay, he will answer the letter's master, how
he dares, being dared.

MERCUTIO Alas, poor Romeo, he is already dead !
stabbed with a white wench's black eye ; run through the
ear with a love song ; the very pin of his heart cleft with   15
the blind bow-boy's butt-shaft ; and is he a man to en-   16
counter Tybalt ?

BENVOLIO Why, what is Tybalt ?

MERCUTIO More than Prince of Cats, I can tell you. O,   19

25–26 *being . . . heart* i.e. being smelt, stimulates ; being tasted, kills   27 *still*
always   28 *grace* power of goodness ; *rude will* coarse impulses of the flesh
30 *canker* the worm in the bud   31 *morrow* morning ; *Benedicite* bless you
37 *unstuffed* carefree   52 *physic* medicine   54 *intercession* request ; *steads*
benefits   55 *homely* simple ; *drift* explanation   56 *shrift* absolution   72
season flavor ; *doth not taste* i.e. now has no savor   80 *strength* constancy
86 *grace* favor   88 *by rote . . . spell* like a child repeating words without
understanding them   93 *on* in need of
II, iv A street in Verona   10 *answer* accept   15 *pin* peg in the centre of
a target, bull's eye   16 *bow-boy's butt-shaft* Cupid's arrow (jestingly
identified as a barbless target-arrow)   16–17 *is . . . Tybalt* (Mercutio
has doubts of Romeo's prowess while he is despondent and low-spirited)
19 *Prince of Cats* (Tybalt, or Tybert, is the cat's name in medieval stories
of Reynard the Fox)

20 he's the courageous captain of compliments. He fights as
21 you sing pricksong – keeps time, distance, and propor-
22 tion ; he rests his minim rests, one, two, and the third in
23 your bosom ! the very butcher of a silk button, a duellist,
24 a duellist ! a gentleman of the very first house, of the first
25 and second cause. Ah, the immortal passado ! the punto
26 reverso ! the hay !

BENVOLIO The what ?

28 MERCUTIO The pox of such antic, lisping, affecting fantasticoes – these new tuners of accent ! 'By Jesu, a very
30 good blade ! a very tall man ! a very good whore !' Why,
31 is not this a lamentable thing, grandsir, that we should be
thus afflicted with these strange flies, these fashion-
33 mongers, these pardon-me's, who stand so much on the
34 new form that they cannot sit at ease on the old bench ?
35 O, their bones, their bones !

Enter Romeo.

BENVOLIO Here comes Romeo ! here comes Romeo !

37 MERCUTIO Without his roe, like a dried herring. O flesh,
38 flesh, how art thou fishified ! Now is he for the numbers
39 that Petrarch flowed in. Laura, to his lady, was a
kitchen wench (marry, she had a better love to berhyme
41 her), Dido a dowdy, Cleopatra a gypsy, Helen and Hero
42 hildings and harlots, Thisbe a grey eye or so, but not to
43 the purpose. Signior Romeo, bon jour ! There's a French
44 salutation to your French slop. You gave us the counter-
45 feit fairly last night.

ROMEO Good morrow to you both. What counterfeit did
I give you ?

48 MERCUTIO The slip, sir, the slip. Can you not conceive ?

ROMEO Pardon, good Mercutio. My business was great,
and in such a case as mine a man may strain courtesy.

51 MERCUTIO That's as much as to say, such a case as yours
52 constrains a man to bow in the hams.

ROMEO Meaning, to curtsy.

54 MERCUTIO Thou hast most most kindly hit it.

ROMEO A most courteous exposition.

MERCUTIO Nay, I am the very pink of courtesy.

57 ROMEO Pink for flower.

MERCUTIO Right.

59 ROMEO Why, then is my pump well-flowered.

MERCUTIO Sure wit, follow me this jest now till thou
hast worn out thy pump, that, when the single sole of it
62 is worn, the jest may remain, after the wearing, solely
singular.

64 ROMEO O single-soled jest, solely singular for the singleness !

66 MERCUTIO Come between us, good Benvolio ! My wits
faint.

67 ROMEO Swits and spurs, swits and spurs ! or I'll cry a
match.

68 MERCUTIO Nay, if our wits run the wild-goose chase, I
am done ; for thou hast more of the wild goose in one of
70 thy wits than, I am sure, I have in my whole five. Was I
with you there for the goose ?

72 ROMEO Thou wast never with me for anything when
thou wast not there for the goose.

MERCUTIO I will bite thee by the ear for that jest.

75 ROMEO Nay, good goose, bite not !

76 MERCUTIO Thy wit is a very bitter sweeting ; it is a most
sharp sauce.

78 ROMEO And is it not, then, well served in to a sweet goose ?

79 MERCUTIO O, here's a wit of cheveril, that stretches from
80 an inch narrow to an ell broad !

ROMEO I stretch it out for that word 'broad,' which, added
to the goose, proves thee far and wide a broad goose. 82

MERCUTIO Why, is not this better now than groaning for
love ? Now art thou sociable, now art thou Romeo ; now
art thou what thou art, by art as well as by nature. For
this drivelling love is like a great natural that runs lolling 86
up and down to hide his bauble in a hole. 87

BENVOLIO Stop there, stop there !

MERCUTIO Thou desirest me to stop in my tale against 89
the hair.

BENVOLIO Thou wouldst else have made thy tale large. 91

MERCUTIO O, thou art deceived ! I would have made it
short ; for I was come to the whole depth of my tale, and
meant indeed to occupy the argument no longer. 94

ROMEO Here's goodly gear ! 95

Enter Nurse and her Man [Peter].

MERCUTIO A sail, a sail !

BENVOLIO Two, two ! a shirt and a smock. 97

NURSE Peter !

PETER Anon.

NURSE My fan, Peter.

MERCUTIO Good Peter, to hide her face ; for her fan 's
the fairer face.

NURSE God ye good morrow, gentlemen.

MERCUTIO God ye good-den, fair gentlewoman.

NURSE Is it good-den ? 105

MERCUTIO 'Tis no less, I tell ye ; for the bawdy hand of
the dial is now upon the prick of noon. 107

NURSE Out upon you ! What a man are you !

ROMEO One, gentlewoman, that God hath made for himself to mar.

NURSE By my troth, it is well said. 'For himself to mar,'
quoth 'a ? Gentlemen, can any of you tell me where I 112
may find the young Romeo ?

20 *compliments* etiquette 21 *pricksong* written music 22 *minim rests*
shortest rests (in the old musical notation) ; *third* third rapier thrust 23
button i.e. on his opponent's shirt 24 *first house* finest fencing school
24–25 *first and second cause* causes for a challenge (in the duellist's code)
25 *passado* lunge 25–26 *punto reverso* backhanded stroke 26 *hay* home-
thrust (from 'hai,' 'I have it' ; a new term to Benvolio) 28 *fantasticoes*
coxcombs 30 *tall* brave 31 *grandsir* good sir 33 *pardon-me's* i.e.
sticklers for etiquette 34 *form* (1) fashion, (2) school-bench ; *old bench* i.e.
native manners and learning 35 *bones* Fr. 'good's' : 'bon's' 37 *Without his
roe* i.e. 'shot' 38 *numbers* verses 39 *Laura* Petrarch's beloved ; *to* in
comparison with 41 *Dido* Queen of Carthage who fell in love with Aeneas ;
Helen Helen of Troy ; *Hero* beloved of Leander 42 *hildings* worthless
creatures ; *Thisbe* (Pyramus and Thisbe were young lovers whose story
resembles that of Romeo and Juliet) 42–43 *not to the purpose* not worth
mentioning 43 *bon jour* good day 44 *slop* trousers 45 *fairly* effectively
48 *slip* (1) escape, (2) counterfeit coin 51 *such . . . yours* the pox (implied)
52 *hams* hips 54 *kindly hit it* interpreted it in your own way 57 *flower*
('flower of courtesy' was the usual complimentary form ; cf. II, v, 43)
59 *pump* shoe ; *well-flowered* (because pinked, or punched, with an ornamental design) 62–63 *solely singular* uniquely remarkable 64 *single-soled*
weak ; *singleness* weakness 66 *My wits faint* my mind fails in this
intricate word play 67 *Swits and spurs* switches and spurs, i.e. keep your
horse (wit) running ; *cry a match* claim victory 68 *wild-goose chase* cross-
country horse race of 'follow the leader' 70–71 *Was . . . goose* was I
accurate in calling you a goose 72–73 *Thou . . . goose* you were never
in my company for any purpose when you weren't looking for a prostitute
(goose) 75 *good . . . not* spare me (proverbial) 76 *bitter sweeting* a tart
species of apple 78 *sweet* tasty, tender 79 *cheveril* kid-skin, easily
stretched 80 *ell* forty-five inches (English measure) 82 *broad goose*
possibly, a goose from the Broads, shallow Norfolk lakes (?) 86 *natural*
idiot 87 *bauble* jester's wand, here a phallic symbol 89–90 *against the
hair* with my hair rubbed the wrong way, against my inclination 91 *large*
broad, indecent 94 *occupy the argument* pursue the subject 95 *gear*
stuff 97 *shirt, smock* male and female garments 105 *Is it good-den* is it
already afternoon 107 *prick* (1) indented point on a clock-face or sundial,
(2) phallus 112 *quoth 'a* said he

ROMEO I can tell you; but young Romeo will be older
when you have found him than he was when you sought
116 him. I am the youngest of that name, for fault of a worse.
NURSE You say well.
118 MERCUTIO Yea, is the worst well? Very well took, i'
faith! wisely, wisely.
120 NURSE If you be he, sir, I desire some confidence with you.
121 BENVOLIO She will endite him to some supper.
122 MERCUTIO A bawd, a bawd, a bawd! So ho!
ROMEO What hast thou found?
124 MERCUTIO No hare, sir; unless a hare, sir, in a lenten pie,
125 that is something stale and hoar ere it be spent.
                    [He walks by them and sings.]
                    An old hare hoar,
                    And an old hare hoar,
                Is very good meat in Lent;
                    But a hare that is hoar
                    Is too much for a score
                When it hoars ere it be spent.
Romeo, will you come to your father's? We'll to dinner
thither.
ROMEO I will follow you.
135 MERCUTIO Farewell, ancient lady. Farewell, [sings] lady,
lady, lady.   Exeunt [Mercutio, Benvolio].
NURSE I pray you, sir, what saucy merchant was this that
138 was so full of his ropery?
ROMEO A gentleman, nurse, that loves to hear himself
talk and will speak more in a minute than he will stand
to in a month.
NURSE An 'a speak anything against me, I'll take him
down, an 'a were lustier than he is, and twenty such
Jacks; and if I cannot, I'll find those that shall. Scurvy
145 knave! I am none of his flirt-gills; I am none of his
146 skains-mates. And thou must stand by too, and suffer
every knave to use me at his pleasure!
148 PETER I saw no man use you at his pleasure. If I had, my
weapon should quickly have been out, I warrant you. I
dare draw as soon as another man, if I see occasion in a
good quarrel, and the law on my side.
NURSE Now, afore God, I am so vexed that every part
about me quivers. Scurvy knave! Pray you, sir, a word;
and, as I told you, my young lady bid me inquire you
out. What she bid me say, I will keep to myself; but
156 first let me tell ye, if ye should lead her into a fool's
paradise, as they say, it were a very gross kind of behavior, as they say; for the gentlewoman is young; and
therefore, if you should deal double with her, truly it

were an ill thing to be offered to any gentlewoman, and
very weak dealing.   161
ROMEO Nurse, commend me to thy lady and mistress. I
protest unto thee—
NURSE Good heart, and i' faith I will tell her as much.
Lord, Lord! she will be a joyful woman.
ROMEO What wilt thou tell her, nurse? Thou dost not
mark me.
NURSE I will tell her, sir, that you do protest, which, as I
take it, is a gentlemanlike offer.
ROMEO
Bid her devise
Some means to come to shrift this afternoon;
And there she shall at Friar Laurence' cell
Be shrived and married. Here is for thy pains.
NURSE No, truly, sir; not a penny.
ROMEO Go to! I say you shall.
NURSE This afternoon, sir? Well, she shall be there.
ROMEO
And stay, good nurse, behind the abbey wall.
Within this hour my man shall be with thee
And bring thee cords made like a tackled stair,   178
Which to the high topgallant of my joy   179
Must be my convoy in the secret night.   180
Farewell. Be trusty, and I'll quit thy pains.   181
Farewell. Commend me to thy mistress.
NURSE
Now God in heaven bless thee! Hark you, sir.
ROMEO
What say'st thou, my dear nurse?
NURSE
Is your man secret? Did you ne'er hear say,
Two may keep counsel, putting one away?
ROMEO
I warrant thee my man's as true as steel.
NURSE Well, sir, my mistress is the sweetest lady. Lord,
Lord! when 'twas a little prating thing – O, there is a
nobleman in town, one Paris, that would fain lay knife   190
aboard; but she, good soul, had as lieve see a toad, a   191
very toad, as see him. I anger her sometimes, and tell her
that Paris is the properer man; but I'll warrant you,
when I say so, she looks as pale as any clout in the versal   194
world. Doth not rosemary and Romeo begin both with a
letter?
ROMEO Ay, nurse; what of that? Both with an R.
NURSE Ah, mocker! that's the dog's name. R is for the –   197
No; I know it begins with some other letter; and she
hath the prettiest sententious of it, of you and rosemary,   199
that it would do you good to hear it.
ROMEO Commend me to thy lady.
NURSE Ay, a thousand times. [Exit Romeo.] Peter!
PETER Anon.
NURSE [Peter, take my fan, and go] before, and apace.   204
                                    Exit [after Peter].

                        *

Enter Juliet.   II, v
JULIET
The clock struck nine when I did send the nurse;
In half an hour she promised to return.
Perchance she cannot meet him. That's not so.
O, she is lame! Love's heralds should be thoughts,
Which ten times faster glide than the sun's beams
Driving back shadows over low'ring hills.
Therefore do nimble-pinioned doves draw Love,   7

116 for ... worse (parodying 'for want of a better')   118 took understood
120 confidence conference (malapropism)   121 endite invite (anticipating
a malapropism)   122 So ho (hunter's cry on sighting game)   124 hare
i.e. prostitute; lenten pie meat pie eaten sparingly during Lent   125
hoar (1) grey with mould, (2) grey-haired, with wordplay on 'whore';
s.d. (from Q1)   135–36 lady, lady, lady (ballad refrain from Chaste Susanna)
138 ropery vulgar jesting   145 flirt-gills flirting Jills   146 skains-mates
outlaws, gangster molls   148–49 my weapon ... out (cf. I, i, 30 and n.)
156–57 lead ... paradise seduce her (proverbial)   161 weak unmanly
178 tackled stair rope ladder   179 topgallant mast and sail above the
mainmast   180 convoy conveyance   181 quit thy pains reward your
efforts   190–91 lay knife aboard i.e. partake of this dish   191 lieve willingly
194 clout cloth; versal universal   197 dog's name (R was called 'the dog's
letter,' since the sound 'r-r-r-r' supposedly resembles a dog's growl.
The Nurse thinks it an ugly sound.)   199 sententious sentences   204
Peter ... go (from Q1)
II, v The Capulet orchard   7 nimble-pinioned swift-winged; doves (Venus'
birds, who draw her chariot)

And therefore hath the wind-swift Cupid wings.

9 Now is the sun upon the highmost hill
Of this day's journey, and from nine till twelve
Is three long hours ; yet she is not come.
Had she affections and warm youthful blood,
She would be as swift in motion as a ball ;

14 My words would bandy her to my sweet love,
And his to me.

16 But old folks, many feign as they were dead –
Unwieldy, slow, heavy and pale as lead.

    Enter Nurse [and Peter].

O God, she comes ! O honey nurse, what news ?
Hast thou met with him ? Send thy man away.

NURSE

Peter, stay at the gate.   *[Exit Peter.]*

JULIET

Now, good sweet nurse – O Lord, why lookest thou sad ?
Though news be sad, yet tell them merrily ;
If good, thou shamest the music of sweet news
By playing it to me with so sour a face.

NURSE

25 I am aweary, give me leave awhile.
26 Fie, how my bones ache ! What a jaunce have I had !

JULIET

I would thou hadst my bones, and I thy news.
Nay, come, I pray thee speak. Good, good nurse, speak.

NURSE

29 Jesu, what haste ! Can you not stay awhile ?
Do you not see that I am out of breath ?

JULIET

How art thou out of breath when thou hast breath
To say to me that thou art out of breath ?
The excuse that thou dost make in this delay
Is longer than the tale thou dost excuse.
Is thy news good or bad ? Answer to that.

36 Say either, and I'll stay the circumstance.
Let me be satisfied, is't good or bad ?

38 NURSE Well, you have made a simple choice ; you know
not how to choose a man. Romeo ? No, not he. Though
his face be better than any man's, yet his leg excels all
men's ; and for a hand and a foot, and a body, though
they be not to be talked on, yet they are past compare.
He is not the flower of courtesy, but, I'll warrant him, as
gentle as a lamb. Go thy ways, wench ; serve God. What,
have you dined at home ?

JULIET

No, no. But all this did I know before.
What says he of our marriage ? What of that ?

NURSE

Lord, how my head aches ! What a head have I !
It beats as it would fall in twenty pieces.

50 My back a t' other side – ah, my back, my back !
51 Beshrew your heart for sending me about
To catch my death with jauncing up and down !

JULIET

I' faith, I am sorry that thou art not well.
Sweet, sweet, sweet nurse, tell me, what says my love ?

NURSE Your love says, like an honest gentleman, and a
courteous, and a kind, and a handsome, and, I warrant,
a virtuous – Where is your mother ?

JULIET

Where is my mother ? Why, she is within.
Where should she be ? How oddly thou repliest !
'Your love says, like an honest gentleman,

"Where is your mother ?"'

NURSE   O God's Lady dear !
Are you so hot ? Marry come up, I trow.   62
Is this the poultice for my aching bones ?
Henceforward do your messages yourself.

JULIET

Here's such a coil ! Come, what says Romeo ?   65

NURSE

Have you got leave to go to shrift to-day ?

JULIET

I have.

NURSE

Then hie you hence to Friar Laurence' cell ;
There stays a husband to make you a wife.
Now comes the wanton blood up in your cheeks :
They'll be in scarlet straight at any news.   71
Hie you to church ; I must another way,
To fetch a ladder, by the which your love
Must climb a bird's nest soon when it is dark.   74
I am the drudge, and toil in your delight ;
But you shall bear the burden soon at night.
Go ; I'll to dinner ; hie you to the cell.

JULIET

Hie to high fortune ! Honest nurse, farewell.   *Exeunt.*

*

    Enter Friar [Laurence] and Romeo.   II, vi

FRIAR

So smile the heavens upon this holy act
That after-hours with sorrow chide us not !

ROMEO

Amen, amen ! But come what sorrow can,
It cannot countervail the exchange of joy   4
That one short minute gives me in her sight.
Do thou but close our hands with holy words,
Then love-devouring death do what he dare –
It is enough I may but call her mine.

FRIAR

These violent delights have violent ends
And in their triumph die, like fire and powder,
Which, as they kiss, consume. The sweetest honey
Is loathsome in his own deliciousness   12
And in the taste confounds the appetite.
Therefore love moderately : long love doth so ;
Too swift arrives as tardy as too slow.   15

    Enter Juliet.

Here comes the lady. O, so light a foot
Will ne'er wear out the everlasting flint.   17
A lover may bestride the gossamer   18
That idles in the wanton summer air,
And yet not fall ; so light is vanity.   20

---

9 *upon . . . hill* at the zenith   14 *bandy* speed, as in tennis   16 *old . . . dead*
many persons speak figuratively of old folks as being dead   25 *give me
leave* let me alone   26 *jaunce* jolting   29 *stay* wait   36 *stay the circumstance*
wait for details   38 *simple* foolish   50 *a* on   51 *Beshrew* shame on   62
hot angry ; *Marry come up* by the Virgin Mary, take your come-uppance
(penalty) ; *trow* trust   65 *coil* fuss   71 *in scarlet* (Juliet blushes easily –
cf. II, ii, 86 ; III, ii, 14) ; *straight* straightway   74 *climb . . . nest* i.e. climb
to Juliet's room
II, vi Before Friar Laurence's cell   4 *countervail* outweigh   12 *Is loathsome* i.e. if eaten to excess   15 *Too . . . slow* (proverbial ; cf. II, iii, 94)
17 *wear . . . flint* (suggested by the proverb 'In time small water drops
will wear away the stone')   18 *gossamer* spider's web   20 *vanity* transitory
earthly love (cf. Ecclesiastes ix, 9)

JULIET
21   Good even to my ghostly confessor.

FRIAR
Romeo shall thank thee, daughter, for us both.

JULIET
23   As much to him, else is his thanks too much.

ROMEO
Ah, Juliet, if the measure of thy joy
25   Be heaped like mine, and that thy skill be more
26   To blazon it, then sweeten with thy breath
This neighbor air, and let rich music's tongue
Unfold the imagined happiness that both
Receive in either by this dear encounter.

JULIET
30   Conceit, more rich in matter than in words,
Brags of his substance, not of ornament.
They are but beggars that can count their worth;
33   But my true love is grown to such excess
I cannot sum up sum of half my wealth.

FRIAR
Come, come with me, and we will make short work;
For, by your leaves, you shall not stay alone
Till Holy Church incorporate two in one.   [Exeunt.]

*

III, i   *Enter Mercutio, Benvolio, and Men.*

BENVOLIO
I pray thee, good Mercutio, let's retire.
The day is hot, the Capulets abroad,
And, if we meet, we shall not 'scape a brawl,
For now, these hot days, is the mad blood stirring.

MERCUTIO Thou art like one of these fellows that, when
he enters the confines of a tavern, claps me his sword
upon the table and says 'God send me no need of thee!'
8   and by the operation of the second cup draws him on
the drawer, when indeed there is no need.

BENVOLIO Am I like such a fellow?

MERCUTIO Come, come, thou art as hot a Jack in thy
12   mood as any in Italy; and as soon moved to be moody,
and as soon moody to be moved.

BENVOLIO And what to?

MERCUTIO Nay, an there were two such, we should have
none shortly, for one would kill the other. Thou! why,
thou wilt quarrel with a man that hath a hair more or a
hair less in his beard than thou hast. Thou wilt quarrel
with a man for cracking nuts, having no other reason
but because thou hast hazel eyes. What eye but such an
21   eye would spy out such a quarrel? Thy head is as full of

quarrels as an egg is full of meat; and yet thy head hath
been beaten as addle as an egg for quarrelling. Thou
hast quarrelled with a man for coughing in the street,
because he hath wakened thy dog that hath lain asleep in
the sun. Didst thou not fall out with a tailor for wearing
his new doublet before Easter? with another for tying 27
his new shoes with old riband? And yet thou wilt tutor 28
me from quarrelling!

BENVOLIO An I were so apt to quarrel as thou art, any
man should buy the fee simple of my life for an hour and 31
a quarter.

MERCUTIO The fee simple? O simple!   33
Enter Tybalt and others.

BENVOLIO By my head, here come the Capulets.

MERCUTIO By my heel, I care not.

TYBALT
Follow me close, for I will speak to them.
Gentlemen, good-den. A word with one of you.   37

MERCUTIO
And but one word with one of us?
Couple it with something; make it a word and a blow.

TYBALT You shall find me apt enough to that, sir, an you
will give me occasion.

MERCUTIO Could you not take some occasion without
giving?

TYBALT Mercutio, thou consortest with Romeo.

MERCUTIO Consort? What, dost thou make us minstrels? 45
An thou make minstrels of us, look to hear nothing but
discords. Here's my fiddlestick; here's that shall make 47
you dance. Zounds, consort!   48

BENVOLIO
We talk here in the public haunt of men.
Either withdraw unto some private place,
Or reason coldly of your grievances,
Or else depart. Here all eyes gaze on us.

MERCUTIO
Men's eyes were made to look, and let them gaze.
I will not budge for no man's pleasure, I.
Enter Romeo.

TYBALT
Well, peace be with you, sir. Here comes my man.

MERCUTIO
But I'll be hanged, sir, if he wear your livery.   56
Marry, go before to field, he'll be your follower!   57
Your worship in that sense may call him man.

TYBALT
Romeo, the love I bear thee can afford
No better term than this: thou art a villain.

ROMEO
Tybalt, the reason that I have to love thee
Doth much excuse the appertaining rage   62
To such a greeting. Villain am I none.
Therefore farewell. I see thou knowest me not.

TYBALT
Boy, this shall not excuse the injuries
That thou hast done me; therefore turn and draw.

ROMEO
I do protest I never injured thee,
But love thee better than thou canst devise   68
Till thou shalt know the reason of my love;
And so, good Capulet, which name I tender   70
As dearly as mine own, be satisfied.

MERCUTIO
O calm, dishonorable, vile submission!

21 *ghostly* spiritual 23 *As much* the same greeting 25 *that* if; *thy . . . more*
you sing better than I 26 *blazon* set forth 30–31 *Conceit . . . ornament* my
understanding is fixed upon the reality of my great love, not upon a vocal
expression of it 33 *love . . . excess* (cf. II, ii, 135 and n.)
III, i A public place in Verona 8–9 *by the operation . . . drawer* after drinking
only two cups of wine, draws his sword against the waiter 12 *moody*
angry 21 *spy out* see occasion for 27 *doublet* jacket 28 *riband* ribbon
31 *fee simple* permanent lease 31–32 *hour and a quarter* probable duration
of the lease, i.e. of my life 33 *O simple* O stupid; s.d. (Q2 includes the
name 'Petruchio') 37 *good-den* good afternoon 45 *Consort* (1) associate
with, (2) accompany in vocal or instrumental music; *minstrels* (a more
disreputable title than 'musicians'; cf. IV, v, 111–12) 47 *fiddlestick* i.e.
rapier 48 *Zounds* by God's wounds 56 *livery* servant's uniform (*my
man* could mean 'my manservant') 57 *field* duelling ground 62 *appertaining rage* suitably angry reaction 68 *devise* understand 70 *tender* value

73 Alla stoccata carries it away.
  [Draws.]
 Tybalt, you ratcatcher, will you walk?

TYBALT
 What wouldst thou have with me?

MERCUTIO Good King of Cats, nothing but one of your
77 nine lives. That I mean to make bold withal, and, as you
78 shall use me hereafter, dry-beat the rest of the eight. Will
79 you pluck your sword out of his pilcher by the ears?
 Make haste, lest mine be about your ears ere it be out.

TYBALT I am for you.
  [Draws.]

ROMEO
 Gentle Mercutio, put thy rapier up.

83 MERCUTIO Come, sir, your passado!
  [They fight.]

ROMEO
 Draw, Benvolio; beat down their weapons.
 Gentlemen, for shame! forbear this outrage!
 Tybalt, Mercutio, the Prince expressly hath
 Forbid this bandying in Verona streets.
88 Hold, Tybalt! Good Mercutio!
  [Tybalt under Romeo's arm thrusts Mercutio in,
  and flies with his Followers.]

MERCUTIO   I am hurt.
89 A plague a both your houses! I am sped.
 Is he gone and hath nothing?

BENVOLIO   What, art thou hurt?

MERCUTIO
 Ay, ay, a scratch, a scratch. Marry, 'tis enough.
 Where is my page? Go, villain, fetch a surgeon.
      [Exit Page.]

ROMEO
 Courage, man. The hurt cannot be much.

MERCUTIO No, 'tis not so deep as a well, nor so wide as a
 church door; but 'tis enough, 'twill serve. Ask for me
96 to-morrow, and you shall find me a grave man. I am
 peppered, I warrant, for this world. A plague a both
 your houses! Zounds, a dog, a rat, a mouse, a cat, to
 scratch a man to death! a braggart, a rogue, a villain,
100 that fights by the book of arithmetic! Why the devil
 came you between us? I was hurt under your arm.

ROMEO
 I thought all for the best.

MERCUTIO
 Help me into some house, Benvolio,
 Or I shall faint. A plague a both your houses!
105 They have made worms' meat of me. I have it,
 And soundly too. Your houses!
    Exit [supported by Benvolio].

ROMEO
 This gentleman, the Prince's near ally,
108 My very friend, hath got this mortal hurt
 In my behalf – my reputation stained
 With Tybalt's slander – Tybalt, that an hour
 Hath been my cousin. O sweet Juliet,
 Thy beauty hath made me effeminate
 And in my temper soft'ned valor's steel!
  Enter Benvolio.

BENVOLIO
 O Romeo, Romeo, brave Mercutio is dead!
115 That gallant spirit hath aspired the clouds,
 Which too untimely here did scorn the earth.

ROMEO
 This day's black fate on moe days doth depend; 117
 This but begins the woe others must end.
  [Enter Tybalt.]

BENVOLIO
 Here comes the furious Tybalt back again.

ROMEO
 Alive in triumph, and Mercutio slain?
 Away to heaven respective lenity, 121
 And fire-eyed fury be my conduct now! 122
 Now, Tybalt, take the 'villain' back again
 That late thou gavest me; for Mercutio's soul
 Is but a little way above our heads,
 Staying for thine to keep him company.
 Either thou or I, or both, must go with him.

TYBALT
 Thou, wretched boy, that didst consort him here,
 Shalt with him hence.

ROMEO   This shall determine that.
  They fight. Tybalt falls.

BENVOLIO
 Romeo, away, be gone!
 The citizens are up, and Tybalt slain.
 Stand not amazed. The Prince will doom thee death
 If thou art taken. Hence, be gone, away!

ROMEO
 O, I am fortune's fool! 134

BENVOLIO   Why dost thou stay? *Exit Romeo.*
  Enter Citizens.

CITIZEN
 Which way ran he that killed Mercutio?
 Tybalt, that murderer, which way ran he?

BENVOLIO
 There lies that Tybalt.

CITIZEN   Up, sir, go with me.
 I charge thee in the Prince's name obey.
  Enter Prince [attended], old Montague, Capulet,
  their Wives, and all.

PRINCE
 Where are the vile beginners of this fray?

BENVOLIO
 O noble Prince, I can discover all 140
 The unlucky manage of this fatal brawl. 141
 There lies the man, slain by young Romeo,
 That slew thy kinsman, brave Mercutio.

CAPULET'S WIFE
 Tybalt, my cousin! O my brother's child!
 O Prince! O husband! O, the blood is spilled
 Of my dear kinsman! Prince, as thou art true,
 For blood of ours shed blood of Montague.
 O cousin, cousin!

PRINCE
 Benvolio, who began this bloody fray?

---

73 *Alla stoccata* 'at the thrust'; i.e. Tybalt; *carries it away* triumphs, gets away with it 77 *nine lives* (proverbial: a cat has nine lives) 78 *dry-beat* thrash 79 *pilcher* scabbard 83 *passado* lunge 88 s.d. (from Q1; Q2 reads 'Away Tybalt.') 89 *a* on; *sped* mortally wounded 96 *grave* (1) serious, (2) inhabiting a grave 100 *by . . . arithmetic* by timing his strokes (cf. II, iv, 21) 105 *worms' meat* i.e. a corpse; *I have it* I am wounded 108 *very* true 115 *aspired* climbed toward 117 *moe* more; *depend* hang down over (cf. I, iv, 107 and note) 121 *respective lenity* reasoned gentleness (personified as an angel) 122 *fire-eyed fury* (fury personified); *conduct* guide 134 *fool* dupe, victim 140 *discover* reveal 141 *manage* course

BENVOLIO
Tybalt, here slain, whom Romeo's hand did slay.
Romeo, that spoke him fair, bid him bethink
152 How nice the quarrel was, and urged withal
Your high displeasure. All this – utterèd
With gentle breath, calm look, knees humbly bowed –
155 Could not take truce with the unruly spleen
Of Tybalt deaf to peace, but that he tilts
With piercing steel at bold Mercutio's breast ;
Who, all as hot, turns deadly point to point,
And, with a martial scorn, with one hand beats
Cold death aside and with the other sends
It back to Tybalt, whose dexterity
Retorts it. Romeo, he cries aloud,
'Hold, friends ! friends, part !' and swifter than his
    tongue,
His agile arm beats down their fatal points,
And 'twixt them rushes ; underneath whose arm
166 An envious thrust from Tybalt hit the life
Of stout Mercutio, and then Tybalt fled ;
But by and by comes back to Romeo,
169 Who had but newly entertained revenge,
And to't they go like lightning ; for, ere I
Could draw to part them, was stout Tybalt slain ;
And, as he fell, did Romeo turn and fly.
This is the truth, or let Benvolio die.
CAPULET'S WIFE
He is a kinsman to the Montague ;
Affection makes him false, he speaks not true.
Some twenty of them fought in this black strife,
And all those twenty could but kill one life.
I beg for justice, which thou, Prince, must give.
Romeo slew Tybalt ; Romeo must not live.
PRINCE
Romeo slew him ; he slew Mercutio.
Who now the price of his dear blood doth owe ?
MONTAGUE
Not Romeo, Prince ; he was Mercutio's friend ;
His fault concludes but what the law should end,
The life of Tybalt.
PRINCE   And for that offense
Immediately we do exile him hence.
I have an interest in your hate's proceeding,
My blood for your rude brawls doth lie a-bleeding ;
188 But I'll amerce you with so strong a fine
That you shall all repent the loss of mine.
I will be deaf to pleading and excuses ;
Nor tears nor prayers shall purchase out abuses.
Therefore use none. Let Romeo hence in haste,
Else, when he is found, that hour is his last.

Bear hence this body, and attend our will.   194
Mercy but murders, pardoning those that kill.
                        Exit [with others].

                        *

        Enter Juliet alone.   III, ii
JULIET
Gallop apace, you fiery-footed steeds,   1
Towards Phoebus' lodging ! Such a wagoner   2
As Phaeton would whip you to the west   3
And bring in cloudy night immediately.
Spread thy close curtain, love-performing night,
That runaways' eyes may wink, and Romeo   6
Leap to these arms untalked of and unseen.
Lovers can see to do their amorous rites
By their own beauties ; or, if love be blind,   9
It best agrees with night. Come, civil night,
Thou sober-suited matron, all in black,
And learn me how to lose a winning match,
Played for a pair of stainless maidenhoods.
Hood my unmanned blood, bating in my cheeks,   14
With thy black mantle till strange love grow bold,   15
Think true love acted simple modesty.   16
Come, night ; come, Romeo ; come, thou day in night ;
For thou wilt lie upon the wings of night
Whiter than new snow upon a raven's back.
Come, gentle night ; come, loving, black-browed night ;
Give me my Romeo ; and, when he shall die,
Take him and cut him out in little stars,
And he will make the face of heaven so fine
That all the world will be in love with night
And pay no worship to the garish sun.
O, I have bought the mansion of a love,
But not possessed it ; and though I am sold,
Not yet enjoyed. So tedious is this day
As is the night before some festival
To an impatient child that hath new robes   30
And may not wear them. O, here comes my nurse,
        Enter Nurse, with cords.
And she brings news ; and every tongue that speaks
But Romeo's name speaks heavenly eloquence.
Now, nurse, what news ? What hast thou there, the cords
That Romeo bid thee fetch ?
NURSE   Ay, ay, the cords.
        [Throws them down.]
JULIET
Ay me ! what news ? Why dost thou wring thy hands ?
NURSE
Ah, weraday ! he's dead, he's dead, he's dead !   37
We are undone, lady, we are undone !
Alack the day ! he's gone, he's killed, he's dead !
JULIET
Can heaven be so envious ?   40
NURSE   Romeo can,
Though heaven cannot. O Romeo, Romeo !
Who ever would have thought it ? Romeo !
JULIET
What devil art thou that dost torment me thus ?
This torture should be roared in dismal hell.
Hath Romeo slain himself ? Say thou but 'I,'   45
And that bare vowel 'I' shall poison more
Than the death-darting eye of cockatrice.   47
I am not I, if there be such an 'I'
Or those eyes' shot that makes the answer 'I.'   49

---

152 *nice* trivial 155 *spleen* temper 166 *envious* malicious 169 *entertained* harbored thoughts of 188 *amerce* penalize 194 *attend our will* come to be judged
III, ii Capulet's house 1 *steeds* horses drawing the chariot of the sun 2 *Phoebus* the sun-god; *lodging* (below the western horizon) 3 *Phaeton* Phoebus' son, with whom the horses of the sun ran away 6 *runaways' eyes* eyes of the sun's horses (?); *wink* close 9 *love* Cupid 14 *Hood* cover with a hood (falconry); *unmanned* untamed; *bating* fluttering 15 *strange* unfamiliar 16 *true love acted* the act of true love 37 *weraday* welladay, alas 40 *heaven . . . envious* (cf. III, v, 211) 45–50 *I* (with the alternate meaning 'ay') 47 *cockatrice* basilisk (a fabulous serpent which killed with eye-glances) 49 *those eyes' shot* the Nurse's eye-glance, which may inadvertently reveal her unspoken answer (see supplementary note on page 894)

If he be slain, say 'I' ; or if not, 'no.'
Brief sounds determine of my weal or woe.

NURSE

I saw the wound, I saw it with mine eyes,
53   (God save the mark!) here on his manly breast.
A piteous corse, a bloody piteous corse ;
Pale, pale as ashes, all bedaubed in blood,
56   All in gore-blood. I swounded at the sight.

JULIET

57   O, break, my heart! poor bankrout, break at once!
To prison, eyes ; ne'er look on liberty !
59   Vile earth, to earth resign ; end motion here,
And thou and Romeo press one heavy bier !

NURSE

O Tybalt, Tybalt, the best friend I had !
O courteous Tybalt ! honest gentleman !
That ever I should live to see thee dead !

JULIET

What storm is this that blows so contrary ?
Is Romeo slaught'red, and is Tybalt dead ?
My dearest cousin, and my dearer lord ?
67   Then, dreadful trumpet, sound the general doom !
For who is living, if those two are gone ?

NURSE

Tybalt is gone, and Romeo banishèd ;
Romeo that killed him, he is banishèd.

JULIET

O God ! Did Romeo's hand shed Tybalt's blood ?

NURSE

72   It did, it did ! alas the day, it did !

JULIET

73   O serpent heart, hid with a flow'ring face !
Did ever dragon keep so fair a cave ?
75   Beautiful tyrant ! fiend angelical !
76   Dove-feathered raven ! wolvish-ravening lamb !
Despisèd substance of divinest show !
Just opposite to what thou justly seem'st –
A damnèd saint, an honorable villain !
O nature, what hadst thou to do in hell
81   When thou didst bower the spirit of a fiend
In mortal paradise of such sweet flesh ?
Was ever book containing such vile matter
So fairly bound ? O, that deceit should dwell
In such a gorgeous palace !

NURSE   There's no trust,
No faith, no honesty in men ; all perjured,
All forsworn, all naught, all dissemblers.
88   Ah, where's my man ? Give me some aqua vitae.
These griefs, these woes, these sorrows make me old.
Shame come to Romeo !

JULIET   Blistered be thy tongue
For such a wish ! He was not born to shame.
Upon his brow shame is ashamed to sit ;
For 'tis a throne where honor may be crowned
Sole monarch of the universal earth.
O, what a beast was I to chide at him !

NURSE

Will you speak well of him that killed your cousin ?

JULIET

Shall I speak ill of him that is my husband ?
Ah, poor my lord, what tongue shall smooth thy name
When I, thy three-hours wife, have mangled it ?
But wherefore, villain, didst thou kill my cousin ?
That villain cousin would have killed my husband.

Back, foolish tears, back to your native spring !
Your tributary drops belong to woe,   103
Which you, mistaking, offer up to joy.
My husband lives, that Tybalt would have slain ;
And Tybalt's dead, that would have slain my husband.
All this is comfort ; wherefore weep I then ?
Some word there was, worser than Tybalt's death,
That murd'red me. I would forget it fain ;
But O, it presses to my memory
Like damnèd guilty deeds to sinners' minds !
'Tybalt is dead, and Romeo – banishèd.'
That 'banishèd,' that one word 'banishèd,'
Hath slain ten thousand Tybalts. Tybalt's death
Was woe enough, if it had ended there ;
Or, if sour woe delights in fellowship
And needly will be ranked with other griefs,   117
Why followèd not, when she said 'Tybalt's dead,'
Thy father, or thy mother, nay, or both,
Which modern lamentation might have moved ?   120
But with a rearward following Tybalt's death,   121
'Romeo is banishèd' – to speak that word
Is father, mother, Tybalt, Romeo, Juliet,
All slain, all dead. 'Romeo is banishèd' –
There is no end, no limit, measure, bound,
In that word's death ; no words can that woe sound.
Where is my father and my mother, nurse ?

NURSE

Weeping and wailing over Tybalt's corse.   128
Will you go to them ? I will bring you thither.

JULIET

Wash they his wounds with tears ? Mine shall be spent,
When theirs are dry, for Romeo's banishment.
Take up those cords. Poor ropes, you are beguiled,
Both you and I, for Romeo is exiled.
He made you for a highway to my bed ;
But I, a maid, die maiden-widowèd.
Come, cords ; come, nurse. I'll to my wedding bed ;
And death, not Romeo, take my maidenhead !

NURSE

Hie to your chamber. I'll find Romeo
To comfort you. I wot well where he is.   139
Hark ye, your Romeo will be here at night.
I'll to him ; he is hid at Laurence' cell.

JULIET

O, find him ! give this ring to my true knight
And bid him come to take his last farewell.

Exit [with Nurse].

*

Enter Friar [Laurence].   III, iii

FRIAR

Romeo, come forth ; come forth, thou fearful man.   1
Affliction is enamored of thy parts,   2

53 *God . . . mark* God avert the evil omen   56 *gore-blood* clotted blood;
swounded swooned   57 *bankrout* bankrupt   59 *Vile earth* i.e. my body;
resign return   67 *trumpet* i.e. the 'last trumpet'; *general doom* Judgment
Day   72, 73 (in Q2 l. 72 is mistakenly assigned to Juliet, l. 73 to the Nurse)
73 *flow'ring face* (traditionally, the Serpent in Eden appeared to Eve
with the face of a young girl, wreathed in flowers)   75 *fiend angelical*
(cf. 2 Corinthians xi, 14)   76 *wolvish-ravening lamb* (cf. Matthew vii,
15)   81–82 *spirit . . . paradise* i.e. the Serpent in Eden   88 *aqua vitae*
alcoholic spirits   103 *tributary* tribute-paying   117 *needly* necessarily   120
modern ordinary, conventional   121 *rearward* rearguard   128 *corse* body
139 *wot* know
III, iii Friar Laurence's cell   s.d. (separate entrances in Q1 ; Q2 reads 'Enter
Friar and Romeo.')   1 *fearful* full of fear   2 *parts* qualities

And thou art wedded to calamity.
Enter Romeo.

ROMEO
Father, what news? What is the Prince's doom?
What sorrow craves acquaintance at my hand
That I yet know not?

FRIAR   Too familiar
Is my dear son with such sour company.
8   I bring thee tidings of the Prince's doom.

ROMEO
9   What less than doomsday is the Prince's doom?

FRIAR
10   A gentler judgment vanished from his lips –
Not body's death, but body's banishment.

ROMEO
Ha, banishment? Be merciful, say 'death';
For exile hath more terror in his look,
Much more than death. Do not say 'banishment.'

FRIAR
Hence from Verona art thou banishèd.
Be patient, for the world is broad and wide.

ROMEO
There is no world without Verona walls,
But purgatory, torture, hell itself.
Hence banishèd is banished from the world,
And world's exile is death. Then 'banishèd'
Is death mistermed. Calling death 'banishèd,'
Thou cut'st my head off with a golden axe
And smilest upon the stroke that murders me.

FRIAR
O deadly sin! O rude unthankfulness!
Thy fault our law calls death; but the kind Prince,
26   Taking thy part, hath rushed aside the law,
And turned that black word 'death' to banishment.
This is dear mercy, and thou seest it not.

ROMEO
'Tis torture, and not mercy. Heaven is here,
Where Juliet lives; and every cat and dog
And little mouse, every unworthy thing,
Live here in heaven and may look on her;
33   But Romeo may not. More validity,
34   More honorable state, more courtship lives
In carrion flies than Romeo. They may seize
On the white wonder of dear Juliet's hand
And steal immortal blessing from her lips,
38   Who, even in pure and vestal modesty,
39   Still blush, as thinking their own kisses sin;
40   But Romeo may not, he is banishèd.
Flies may do this but I from this must fly;
They are freemen, but I am banishèd.
And sayest thou yet that exile is not death?
Hadst thou no poison mixed, no sharp-ground knife,
45   No sudden mean of death, though ne'er so mean,
But 'banishèd' to kill me – 'banishèd'?

O friar, the damnèd use that word in hell;
Howling attends it! How hast thou the heart,
Being a divine, a ghostly confessor,
A sin-absolver, and my friend professed,
To mangle me with that word 'banishèd'?

FRIAR
Thou fond mad man, hear me a little speak.   52

ROMEO
O, thou wilt speak again of banishment.

FRIAR
I'll give thee armor to keep off that word;
Adversity's sweet milk, philosophy,
To comfort thee, though thou art banishèd.

ROMEO
Yet 'banishèd'? Hang up philosophy!
Unless philosophy can make a Juliet,
Displant a town, reverse a prince's doom,
It helps not, it prevails not. Talk no more.

FRIAR
O, then I see that madmen have no ears.

ROMEO
How should they, when that wise men have no eyes?

FRIAR
Let me dispute with thee of thy estate.   63

ROMEO
Thou canst not speak of that thou dost not feel.
Wert thou as young as I, Juliet thy love,
An hour but married, Tybalt murderèd,
Doting like me, and like me banishèd,
Then mightst thou speak, then mightst thou tear thy
    hair,
And fall upon the ground, as I do now,
Taking the measure of an unmade grave.   70
Enter Nurse and knock.

FRIAR
Arise; one knocks. Good Romeo, hide thyself.

ROMEO
Not I; unless the breath of heartsick groans
Mist-like infold me from the search of eyes.   73
[Knock.]

FRIAR
Hark, how they knock! Who's there? Romeo, arise;
Thou wilt be taken. – Stay awhile! – Stand up;   75
[Knock.]
Run to my study. – By and by! – God's will,   76
What simpleness is this. – I come, I come!   77
Knock.
Who knocks so hard? Whence come you? What's your
    will?
Enter Nurse.

NURSE
Let me come in, and you shall know my errand.
I come from Lady Juliet.

FRIAR   Welcome then.

NURSE
O holy friar, O, tell me, holy friar,
Where is my lady's lord, where's Romeo?

FRIAR
There on the ground, with his own tears made drunk.

NURSE
O, he is even in my mistress' case,
Just in her case! O woeful sympathy!
Piteous predicament! Even so lies she,
Blubb'ring and weeping, weeping and blubb'ring.

---

8 *Prince's doom* punishment decreed by the Prince   9 *doomsday* i.e. death
10 *vanished* disappeared into air   26 *rushed* pushed   33 *validity* value
34 *courtship* privilege of wooing   38 *vestal* virgin   39 *kisses* (when her
lips touch each other)   40–42 (in Q2 these lines are preceded by 'This
may flies do when I from this must fly' – evidently a cancelled line printed
in error – and by l. 43, evidently misplaced)   45 *mean . . . mean* means
. . . lowly   52 *fond* foolish   63 *dispute* reason; *estate* situation   70 *Taking
the measure* providing the measurements; **s.d.** (so Q2, with another
entrance for Nurse at l. 78)   73 s.d. (Q2 reads 'They knock.')   75 s.d.
(Q2 reads 'Slud knock.')   76 *By and by* in a moment   77 *simpleness*
stupid conduct

Stand up, stand up ! Stand, an you be a man.
For Juliet's sake, for her sake, rise and stand !
90   Why should you fall into so deep an O ?

ROMEO *[rises]* Nurse –

NURSE
Ah sir ! ah sir ! Death 's the end of all.

ROMEO
Spakest thou of Juliet ? How is it with her ?
94   Doth not she think me an old murderer,
Now I have stained the childhood of our joy
With blood removed but little from her own ?
Where is she ? and how doth she ! and what says
98   My concealed lady to our cancelled love ?

NURSE
O, she says nothing, sir, but weeps and weeps ;
And now falls on her bed, and then starts up,
And Tybalt calls ; and then on Romeo cries,
And then down falls again.

ROMEO   As if that name,
103 Shot from the deadly level of a gun,
Did murder her ; as that name's cursèd hand
Murdered her kinsman. O, tell me, friar, tell me,
106 In what vile part of this anatomy
Doth my name lodge ? Tell me, that I may sack
108 The hateful mansion.

*[He offers to stab himself, and Nurse snatches the
dagger away.]*

FRIAR   Hold thy desperate hand.
Art thou a man ? Thy form cries out thou art ;
Thy tears are womanish, thy wild acts denote
111 The unreasonable fury of a beast.
112 Unseemly woman in a seeming man !
113 And ill-beseeming beast in seeming both !
Thou hast amazed me. By my holy order,
I thought thy disposition better tempered.
Hast thou slain Tybalt ? Wilt thou slay thyself ?
117 And slay thy lady that in thy life lives,
By doing damnèd hate upon thyself ?
Why railest thou on thy birth, the heaven, and earth ?
120 Since birth and heaven and earth, all three do meet
In thee at once ; which thou at once wouldst lose.
Fie, fie, thou shamest thy shape, thy love, thy wit,
123 Which, like a usurer, abound'st in all,
124 And usest none in that true use indeed
Which should bedeck thy shape, thy love, thy wit.
126 Thy noble shape is but a form of wax,
Digressing from the valor of a man ;
Thy dear love sworn but hollow perjury,
129 Killing that love which thou hast vowed to cherish ;
130 Thy wit, that ornament to shape and love,
131 Misshapen in the conduct of them both,
132 Like powder in a skilless soldier's flask,
Is set afire by thine own ignorance,
134 And thou dismemb'red with thine own defense.
What, rouse thee, man ! Thy Juliet is alive,
136 For whose dear sake thou wast but lately dead.
137 There art thou happy. Tybalt would kill thee,
But thou slewest Tybalt. There art thou happy too.
The law, that threat'ned death, becomes thy friend
And turns it to exile. There art thou happy.
A pack of blessings light upon thy back ;
Happiness courts thee in her best array ;
But, like a misbehaved and sullen wench,
Thou pout'st upon thy fortune and thy love.

Take heed, take heed, for such die miserable.
Go get thee to thy love, as was decreed,
Ascend her chamber, hence and comfort her.
But look thou stay not till the watch be set,
For then thou canst not pass to Mantua,
Where thou shalt live till we can find a time
To blaze your marriage, reconcile your friends,   151
Beg pardon of the Prince, and call thee back
With twenty hundred thousand times more joy
Than thou went'st forth in lamentation.
Go before, nurse. Commend me to thy lady,
And bid her hasten all the house to bed,
Which heavy sorrow makes them apt unto.
Romeo is coming.

NURSE
O Lord, I could have stayed here all the night
To hear good counsel. O, what learning is !
My lord, I'll tell my lady you will come.

ROMEO
Do so, and bid my sweet prepare to chide.

NURSE
Here is a ring she bid me give you, sir.
Hie you, make haste, for it grows very late.   *[Exit.]*

ROMEO
How well my comfort is revived by this !

FRIAR
Go hence ; good night ; and here stands all your state :   166
Either be gone before the watch be set,
Or by the break of day disguised from hence.
Sojourn in Mantua. I'll find out your man,
And he shall signify from time to time
Every good hap to you that chances here.
Give me thy hand. 'Tis late. Farewell ; good night.

ROMEO
But that a joy past joy calls out on me,
It were a grief so brief to part with thee.
Farewell.   *Exeunt.*

*

Enter old Capulet, his Wife, and Paris.   III, iv

CAPULET
Things have fall'n out, sir, so unluckily
That we have had no time to move our daughter.   2
Look you, she loved her kinsman Tybalt dearly,
And so did I. Well, we were born to die.
'Tis very late ; she'll not come down to-night.
I promise you, but for your company,
I would have been abed an hour ago.

PARIS
These times of woe afford no times to woo.
Madam, good night. Commend me to your daughter.

90 *an O* a fit of groaning 94 *old* hardened 98 *concealed . . . cancelled*
hidden from me . . . invalidated by my act (the two words were given
almost the same pronunciation) 103 *level* aim 106 *anatomy* body
108 s.d. (from Q1) 111 *unreasonable* irrational 112 *Unseemly . . . seeming*
disorderly . . . apparent 113 *ill-beseeming . . . both* inappropriate . . . man
and woman 117 *in . . . lives* (cf. II, i, 1 and n.) 120 *all . . . meet* the soul
comes from heaven, the body from earth ; they unite in man at his birth
123 *Which* (you) who; *all* all capabilities 124 *true use* proper handling
of wealth 126 *form of wax* waxwork, outward appearance 129 *Killing
that love* (cf. l. 117) 130 *wit* intellect 131 *Misshapen* distorted ; *conduct*
guidance 132 *flask* powder horn 134 *defense* i.e. intellect 136 *dead*
as one dead 137 *happy* fortunate 151 *blaze* publish 166 *here . . . state*
here is your situation
III, iv Capulet's house 2 *move* talk with

LADY

    I will, and know her mind early to-morrow;
11   To-night she's mewed up to her heaviness.

CAPULET

12   Sir Paris, I will make a desperate tender
    Of my child's love. I think she will be ruled
    In all respects by me; nay more, I doubt it not.
    Wife, go you to her ere you go to bed;
    Acquaint her here of my son Paris' love
    And bid her (mark you me?) on Wednesday next –
    But soft! what day is this?

PARIS   Monday, my lord.

CAPULET

    Monday! ha, ha! Well, Wednesday is too soon.
20   A Thursday let it be – a Thursday, tell her,
    She shall be married to this noble earl.
    Will you be ready? Do you like this haste?
    We'll keep no great ado – a friend or two;
    For hark you, Tybalt being slain so late,
    It may be thought we held him carelessly,
    Being our kinsman, if we revel much.
    Therefore we'll have some half a dozen friends,
    And there an end. But what say you to Thursday?

PARIS

    My lord, I would that Thursday were to-morrow.

CAPULET

    Well, get you gone. A Thursday be it then.
    Go you to Juliet ere you go to bed;
    Prepare her, wife, against this wedding day.
    Farewell, my lord. – Light to my chamber, ho!
34   Afore me, it is so very very late
35   That we may call it early by and by.
    Good night.   *Exeunt.*

*

III, v   *Enter Romeo and Juliet aloft [at the window].*

JULIET

    Wilt thou be gone? It is not yet near day.
    It was the nightingale, and not the lark,
3   That pierced the fearful hollow of thine ear.
    Nightly she sings on yond pomegranate tree.
    Believe me, love, it was the nightingale.

ROMEO

    It was the lark, the herald of the morn;
    No nightingale. Look, love, what envious streaks
    Do lace the severing clouds in yonder East.
9   Night's candles are burnt out, and jocund day
    Stands tiptoe on the misty mountain tops.
    I must be gone and live, or stay and die.

JULIET

    Yond light is not daylight; I know it, I.
13   It is some meteor that the sun exhales

11 *mewed up* shut up (falconry); *heaviness* grief   12 *desperate tender* risk-taking offer   20 *A* on   34 *Afore me* (a light oath)   35 *by and by* immediately   III, v The Capulet orchard   **s.d.** *at the window* (from Q1)   3 *fearful* apprehensive   9 *Night's candles* the stars   13 *meteor* nocturnal light, such as the will-o'-the-wisp, supposedly of luminous gas given off by the sun or drawn by his power (*exhales*) out of marshy ground   20 *reflex . . . brow* reflection of the moon   25 *my soul* (cf. II, ii, 165)   29 *division* melody   31 *change* exchange (a folk belief)   33 *affray* frighten   34 *hunt's-up* morning song to awaken huntsmen   36 **s.d.** *hastily* (from Q1; Q2 reads 'Enter Madam and Nurse.')   41 *life* (cf. III, iii, 117)   42 **s.d.** (from Q1)   43 *friend* clandestine lover   46 *much* advanced   54 *ill-divining* prophetic of evil   59 *Dry . . . blood* (the presumed effect of grief was to dry up the blood)

    To be to thee this night a torchbearer
    And light thee on thy way to Mantua.
    Therefore stay yet; thou need'st not to be gone.

ROMEO

    Let me be ta'en, let me be put to death.
    I am content, so thou wilt have it so.
    I'll say yon grey is not the morning's eye,
    'Tis but the pale reflex of Cynthia's brow;   20
    Nor that is not the lark whose notes do beat
    The vaulty heaven so high above our heads.
    I have more care to stay than will to go.
    Come, death, and welcome! Juliet wills it so.
    How is't, my soul? Let's talk; it is not day.   25

JULIET

    It is, it is! Hie hence, be gone, away!
    It is the lark that sings so out of tune,
    Straining harsh discords and unpleasing sharps.
    Some say the lark makes sweet division;   29
    This doth not so, for she divideth us.
    Some say the lark and loathèd toad change eyes;   31
    O, now I would they had changed voices too,
    Since arm from arm that voice doth us affray,   33
    Hunting thee hence with hunt's-up to the day.   34
    O, now be gone! More light and light it grows.

ROMEO

    More light and light – more dark and dark our woes.   36
        Enter Nurse [hastily].

NURSE Madam!

JULIET Nurse?

NURSE

    Your lady mother is coming to your chamber.
    The day is broke; be wary, look about.   *[Exit.]*

JULIET

    Then, window, let day in, and let life out.   41

ROMEO

    Farewell, farewell! One kiss, and I'll descend.   42
        [He goeth down.]

JULIET

    Art thou gone so, love-lord, ay husband-friend?   43
    I must hear from thee every day in the hour,
    For in a minute there are many days.
    O, by this count I shall be much in years   46
    Ere I again behold my Romeo!

ROMEO

    Farewell!
    I will omit no opportunity
    That may convey my greetings, love, to thee.

JULIET

    O, think'st thou we shall ever meet again?

ROMEO

    I doubt it not; and all these woes shall serve
    For sweet discourses in our times to come.

JULIET

    O God, I have an ill-divining soul!   54
    Methinks I see thee, now thou art so low,
    As one dead in the bottom of a tomb.
    Either my eyesight fails, or thou lookest pale.

ROMEO

    And trust me, love, in my eye so do you.
    Dry sorrow drinks our blood. Adieu, adieu!   *Exit.* 59

JULIET

    O Fortune, Fortune! all men call thee fickle.
    If thou art fickle, what dost thou with him
    That is renowned for faith? Be fickle, Fortune,

For then I hope thou wilt not keep him long
64   But send him back.
       [She goeth down from the window.]
       Enter Mother.

LADY
Ho, daughter! are you up?

JULIET
Who is't that calls? It is my lady mother.
67   Is she not down so late, or up so early?
What unaccustomed cause procures her hither?

LADY
Why, how now, Juliet?

JULIET   Madam, I am not well.

LADY
Evermore weeping for your cousin's death?
What, wilt thou wash him from his grave with tears?
An if thou couldst, thou couldst not make him live.
Therefore have done. Some grief shows much of love;
But much of grief shows still some want of wit.

JULIET
75   Yet let me weep for such a feeling loss.

LADY
So shall you feel the loss, but not the friend
Which you weep for.

JULIET   Feeling so the loss,
I cannot choose but ever weep the friend.

LADY
Well, girl, thou weep'st not so much for his death
As that the villain lives which slaughtered him.

JULIET
What villain, madam?

LADY   That same villain Romeo.

JULIET *[aside]*
Villain and he be many miles asunder. –
God pardon him! I do, with all my heart;
84   And yet no man like he doth grieve my heart.

LADY
That is because the traitor murderer lives.

JULIET
Ay, madam, from the reach of these my hands.
Would none but I might venge my cousin's death!

LADY
We will have vengeance for it, fear thou not.
Then weep no more. I'll send to one in Mantua,
90   Where that same banished runagate doth live,
Shall give him such an unaccustomed dram
That he shall soon keep Tybalt company;
And then I hope thou wilt be satisfied.

JULIET
Indeed I never shall be satisfied
With Romeo till I behold him – dead –
Is my poor heart so for a kinsman vexed.
Madam, if you could find out but a man
98   To bear a poison, I would temper it;
That Romeo should, upon receipt thereof,
Soon sleep in quiet. O, how my heart abhors
To hear him named and cannot come to him,
To wreak the love I bore my cousin
Upon his body that hath slaughtered him!

LADY
Find thou the means, and I'll find such a man.
But now I'll tell thee joyful tidings, girl.

JULIET
And joy comes well in such a needy time.

What are they, beseech your ladyship?

LADY
Well, well, thou hast a careful father, child;
One who, to put thee from thy heaviness,
Hath sorted out a sudden day of joy   110
That thou expects not nor I looked not for.

JULIET
Madam, in happy time! What day is that?   112

LADY
Marry, my child, early next Thursday morn
The gallant, young, and noble gentleman,
The County Paris, at Saint Peter's Church,
Shall happily make thee there a joyful bride.

JULIET
Now by Saint Peter's Church, and Peter too,
He shall not make me there a joyful bride!
I wonder at this haste, that I must wed
Ere he that should be husband comes to woo.
I pray you tell my lord and father, madam,
I will not marry yet; and when I do, I swear
It shall be Romeo, whom you know I hate,
Rather than Paris. These are news indeed!

LADY
Here comes your father. Tell him so yourself,
And see how he will take it at your hands.
       Enter Capulet and Nurse.

CAPULET
When the sun sets the earth doth drizzle dew,
But for the sunset of my brother's son
It rains downright.
How now? a conduit, girl? What, still in tears?   130
Evermore show'ring? In one little body
Thou counterfeit'st a bark, a sea, a wind:
For still thy eyes, which I may call the sea,
Do ebb and flow with tears; the bark thy body is,
Sailing in this salt flood; the winds, thy sighs,
Who, raging with thy tears and they with them,
Without a sudden calm will overset   137
Thy tempest-tossèd body. How now, wife?
Have you deliverèd to her our decree?

LADY
Ay, sir; but she will none, she gives you thanks.   140
I would the fool were married to her grave!   141

CAPULET
Soft! take me with you, take me with you, wife.   142
How? Will she none? Doth she not give us thanks?
Is she not proud? Doth she not count her blest,
Unworthy as she is, that we have wrought   145
So worthy a gentleman to be her bride?   146

JULIET
Not proud you have, but thankful that you have.
Proud can I never be of what I hate,
But thankful even for hate that is meant love.

---

64 s.d. (from Q1, and so placed that it might apply only to the Nurse; but since the Q1 stage direction immediately following is 'Enter Juliet's Mother, Nurse,' the indications are that the subsequent action takes place below, where Juliet joins her mother; hence the orchard into which Romeo has descended now becomes an interior) 67 *down* abed 75 *feeling* deeply felt 84 *like* so much as 90 *runagate* renegade 98 *temper* prepare or concoct (with play on 'moderate') 110 *sorted* chosen 112 *in happy time* opportunely 130 *conduit* water pipe 137 *sudden* immediate 140 *gives you thanks* says 'No, thank you' 141 *married . . . grave* (a petulant but prophetic comment, like l. 167 below) 142 *take . . . you* let me understand you 145 *wrought* arranged for 146 *bride* bridegroom

CAPULET

150   How, how, how, how, chopped-logic? What is this?
      'Proud' – and 'I thank you' – and 'I thank you not' –
      And yet 'not proud'? Mistress minion you,
      Thank me no thankings, nor proud me no prouds,
154   But fettle your fine joints 'gainst Thursday next
      To go with Paris to Saint Peter's Church,
156   Or I will drag thee on a hurdle thither.
157   Out, you green-sickness carrion! out, you baggage!
158   You tallow-face!

LADY   Fie, fie! what, are you mad?

JULIET

      Good father, I beseech you on my knees,
      Hear me with patience but to speak a word.

CAPULET

      Hang thee, young baggage! disobedient wretch!
162   I tell thee what – get thee to church a Thursday
      Or never after look me in the face.
      Speak not, reply not, do not answer me!
      My fingers itch. Wife, we scarce thought us blest
      That God had lent us but this only child;
      But now I see this one is one too much,
      And that we have a curse in having her.
169   Out on her, hilding!

NURSE   God in heaven bless her!

170   You are to blame, my lord, to rate her so.

CAPULET

      And why, my Lady Wisdom? Hold your tongue,
172   Good Prudence. Smatter with your gossips, go!

NURSE

      I speak no treason.

173   CAPULET   O, God-i-god-en!

NURSE

      May not one speak?

CAPULET   Peace, you mumbling fool!
      Utter your gravity o'er a gossip's bowl,
      For here we need it not.

LADY   You are too hot.

CAPULET

177   God's bread! it makes me mad.
178   Day, night; hour, tide, time; work, play;
      Alone, in company; still my care hath been
      To have her matched; and having now provided
      A gentleman of noble parentage,
182   Of fair demesnes, youthful, and nobly trained,
      Stuffed, as they say, with honorable parts,
      Proportioned as one's thought would wish a man –
185   And then to have a wretched puling fool,
186   A whining mammet, in her fortune's tender,
      To answer 'I'll not wed, I cannot love;

I am too young, I pray you pardon me'!
But, an you will not wed, I'll pardon you!   189
Graze where you will, you shall not house with me.
Look to't, think on't; I do not use to jest.   191
Thursday is near; lay hand on heart, advise: 192
An you be mine, I'll give you to my friend;
An you be not, hang, beg, starve, die in the streets,
For, by my soul, I'll ne'er acknowledge thee,
Nor what is mine shall never do thee good.
Trust to't. Bethink you. I'll not be forsworn.   Exit.

JULIET

Is there no pity sitting in the clouds
That sees into the bottom of my grief?
O sweet my mother, cast me not away!
Delay this marriage for a month, a week;
Or if you do not, make the bridal bed
In that dim monument where Tybalt lies.

LADY

Talk not to me, for I'll not speak a word.
Do as thou wilt, for I have done with thee.   Exit.

JULIET

O God! – O nurse, how shall this be prevented?
My husband is on earth, my faith in heaven.   207
How shall that faith return again to earth   208
Unless that husband send it me from heaven
By leaving earth? Comfort me, counsel me.
Alack, alack, that heaven should practise stratagems
Upon so soft a subject as myself!
What say'st thou? Hast thou not a word of joy?
Some comfort, nurse.

NURSE   Faith, here it is.

Romeo is banished; and all the world to nothing   215
That he dares ne'er come back to challenge you;   216
Or if he do, it needs must be by stealth.
Then, since the case so stands as now it doth,
I think it best you married with the County.
O, he's a lovely gentleman!
Romeo's a dishclout to him. An eagle, madam,   221
Hath not so green, so quick, so fair an eye
As Paris hath. Beshrew my very heart,
I think you are happy in this second match,
For it excels your first; or if it did not,
Your first is dead – or 'twere as good he were
As living here and you no use of him.

JULIET

Speak'st thou from thy heart?

NURSE

And from my soul too; else beshrew them both.   229

JULIET Amen!

NURSE What?

JULIET

Well, thou hast comforted me marvellous much.
Go in; and tell my lady I am gone,
Having displeased my father, to Laurence' cell,
To make confession and to be absolved.

NURSE

Marry, I will; and this is wisely done.   [Exit.]

JULIET

Ancient damnation! O most wicked fiend!   237
Is it more sin to wish me thus forsworn,
Or to dispraise my lord with that same tongue
Which she hath praised him with above compare
So many thousand times? Go, counsellor!
Thou and my bosom henceforth shall be twain.   242

---

150 *chopped-logic* hair-splitting   154 *fettle* prepare   156 *hurdle* sledge on
which criminals were carried to execution   157 *green-sickness* anemic;
baggage worthless woman   158 *tallow-face* pale-face; *are you mad* (addressed
to Capulet)   162 *a* on   169 *hilding* worthless creature   170 *rate* scold
172 *Smatter . . . gossips* chatter with your cronies   173 *God-i-god-en* for
God's sake   177 *bread* bread of the Sacrament   178–79 *Day . . . company*
(in Q1 the equivalent matter occupies two separate lines: 'Day, night; early,
late; at home, abroad: Alone, in company; waking or sleeping;' – more
logical, but irreconcilable with the Q2 passage except by guesswork)
182 *demesnes* domains   185 *puling* whining   186 *mammet* doll; *tender* offer
189 *I'll pardon you* (ironic)   191 *do not use* am not accustomed   192 *advise*
consider   207 *my faith in heaven* my marriage vow is recorded in heaven
208–10 *How . . . earth* how can I marry unless I am first widowed   215 *all
. . . nothing* i.e. it is a safe bet   216 *challenge* demand possession of   221
dishclout dishcloth   229 *beshrew* a curse on   237 *Ancient damnation*
damnable old woman   242 *bosom* confidence; *twain* separated

I'll to the friar to know his remedy.
If all else fail, myself have power to die.   *Exit.*

*

IV, i   *Enter Friar [Laurence] and County Paris.*

FRIAR
On Thursday, sir ? The time is very short.

PARIS
My father Capulet will have it so,
And I am nothing slow to slack his haste.

FRIAR
You say you do not know the lady's mind.
5   Uneven is the course ; I like it not.

PARIS
Immoderately she weeps for Tybalt's death,
And therefore have I little talked of love ;
8   For Venus smiles not in a house of tears.
Now, sir, her father counts it dangerous
That she do give her sorrow so much sway,
And in his wisdom hastes our marriage
To stop the inundation of her tears,
13   Which, too much minded by herself alone,
May be put from her by society.
Now do you know the reason of this haste.

FRIAR *[aside]*
I would I knew not why it should be slowed. –
Look, sir, here comes the lady toward my cell.
       Enter Juliet.

PARIS
Happily met, my lady and my wife !

JULIET
That may be, sir, when I may be a wife.

PARIS
20   That 'may be' must be, love, on Thursday next.

JULIET
What must be shall be.

FRIAR   That's a certain text.

PARIS
Come you to make confession to this father ?

JULIET
To answer that, I should confess to you.

PARIS
Do not deny to him that you love me.

JULIET
I will confess to you that I love him.

PARIS
So will ye, I am sure, that you love me.

JULIET
If I do so, it will be of more price,
Being spoke behind your back, than to your face.

PARIS
Poor soul, thy face is much abused with tears.

JULIET
30   The tears have got small victory by that,
For it was bad enough before their spite.

PARIS
Thou wrong'st it more than tears with that report.

JULIET
That is no slander, sir, which is a truth ;
And what I spake, I spake it to my face.

PARIS
Thy face is mine, and thou hast sland'red it.

JULIET
It may be so, for it is not mine own.
Are you at leisure, holy father, now,
Or shall I come to you at evening mass ?

FRIAR
My leisure serves me, pensive daughter, now.
My lord, we must entreat the time alone.

PARIS
God shield I should disturb devotion !   41
Juliet, on Thursday early will I rouse ye.
Till then, adieu, and keep this holy kiss.   *Exit.*

JULIET
O, shut the door ! and when thou hast done so,
Come weep with me – past hope, past cure, past help !

FRIAR
Ah, Juliet, I already know thy grief ;
It strains me past the compass of my wits.   47
I hear thou must, and nothing may prorogue it,   48
On Thursday next be married to this County.

JULIET
Tell me not, friar, that thou hearest of this,
Unless thou tell me how I may prevent it.
If in thy wisdom thou canst give no help,
Do thou but call my resolution wise
And with this knife I'll help it presently.
God joined my heart and Romeo's, thou our hands ;
And ere this hand, by thee to Romeo's sealed,
Shall be the label to another deed,   57
Or my true heart with treacherous revolt
Turn to another, this shall slay them both.
Therefore, out of thy long-experienced time,   60
Give me some present counsel ; or, behold,
'Twixt my extremes and me this bloody knife   62
Shall play the umpire, arbitrating that
Which the commission of thy years and art   64
Could to no issue of true honor bring.
Be not so long to speak. I long to die
If what thou speak'st speak not of remedy.

FRIAR
Hold, daughter. I do spy a kind of hope,
Which craves as desperate an execution
As that is desperate which we would prevent.
If, rather than to marry County Paris,
Thou hast the strength of will to slay thyself,
Then it is likely thou wilt undertake
A thing like death to chide away this shame,
That cop'st with death himself to scape from it ;   75
And, if thou darest, I'll give thee remedy.

JULIET
O, bid me leap, rather than marry Paris,
From off the battlements of any tower,
Or walk in thievish ways, or bid me lurk   79
Where serpents are ; chain me with roaring bears,
Or hide me nightly in a charnel house,   81

IV, i Friar Laurence's cell   5 *course* i.e. racecourse   8 *Venus . . . tears* the influence of the planet Venus is unfavorable when she appears in the 'house' of a 'moist' constellation, such as Pisces or Aquarius; i.e. one cannot talk of love amidst grief   13 *minded* thought about   41 *shield* forbid   47 *the compass . . . wits* my wit's end   48 *prorogue* postpone   57 *label* i.e. strip of parchment bearing the seal, attached to a deed   60 *time* age   62 *extremes* difficulties   64 *commission . . . art* authority of your age and skill   75 *cop'st* encounterest   79 *thievish ways* roads frequented by robbers   81 *charnel house* depository of human bones

O'ercovered quite with dead men's rattling bones,
83   With reeky shanks and yellow chapless skulls;
Or bid me go into a new-made grave
And hide me with a dead man in his shroud –
Things that, to hear them told, have made me tremble –
And I will do it without fear or doubt,
To live an unstained wife to my sweet love.

FRIAR
Hold, then. Go home, be merry, give consent
To marry Paris. Wednesday is to-morrow.
To-morrow night look that thou lie alone;
Let not the nurse lie with thee in thy chamber.
Take thou this vial, being then in bed,
94   And this distilling liquor drink thou off;
When presently through all thy veins shall run
96   A cold and drowsy humor; for no pulse
97   Shall keep his native progress, but surcease;
No warmth, no breath, shall testify thou livest;
The roses in thy lips and cheeks shall fade
100   To wanny ashes, thy eyes' windows fall
Like death when he shuts up the day of life;
102   Each part, deprived of supple government,
Shall, stiff and stark and cold, appear like death;
And in this borrowèd likeness of shrunk death
Thou shalt continue two-and-forty hours,
And then awake as from a pleasant sleep.
Now, when the bridegroom in the morning comes
To rouse thee from thy bed, there art thou dead.
Then, as the manner of our country is,
In thy best robes uncoverèd on the bier
111   Thou shalt be borne to that same ancient vault
Where all the kindred of the Capulets lie.
113   In the mean time, against thou shalt awake,
114   Shall Romeo by my letters know our drift;
And hither shall he come; and he and I
Will watch thy waking, and that very night
Shall Romeo bear thee hence to Mantua.
And this shall free thee from this present shame,
119   If no inconstant toy nor womanish fear
Abate thy valor in the acting it.

JULIET
Give me, give me! O, tell not me of fear!

FRIAR
Hold! Get you gone, be strong and prosperous
In this resolve. I'll send a friar with speed
To Mantua, with my letters to thy lord.

JULIET
Love give me strength! and strength shall help afford.
Farewell, dear father.   Exit [with Friar].

*

83 reeky smelly; chapless jawless   94 distilling infusing   96 humor moisture
97 surcease cease   100 wanny pale, shrunken; windows i.e. eyelids (the
figure derives from the covering of shop-fronts at the close of the day)
102 supple government the life force that keeps the body supple   111 (in
Q2 this line is preceded by 'Be borne to burial in thy kindred's grave,'
evidently a cancelled version of the line, printed in error)   113 against
. . . awake in preparation for your awaking   114 drift intention   119 toy
whim
IV, ii Capulet's house   5 try test   6–7 'tis . . . fingers it's a poor cook
who doesn't like to taste the food which he prepares (proverbial)   10
unfurnished unprovided   14 harlotry hussy   24 to-morrow morning (i.e.
Wednesday, one day earlier than planned)   32 bound indebted

Enter Father Capulet, Mother, Nurse, and   IV, ii
Servingmen, two or three.

CAPULET
So many guests invite as here are writ.
                              [Exit a Servingman.]
Sirrah, go hire me twenty cunning cooks.

SERVINGMAN You shall have none ill, sir; for I'll try if
they can lick their fingers.

CAPULET
How canst thou try them so?   5

SERVINGMAN Marry, sir, 'tis an ill cook that cannot lick 6
his own fingers. Therefore he that cannot lick his fingers
goes not with me.

CAPULET Go, begone.   [Exit Servingman.]
We shall be much unfurnished for this time.   10
What, is my daughter gone to Friar Laurence?

NURSE Ay, forsooth.

CAPULET
Well, he may chance to do some good on her.
A peevish self-willed harlotry it is.   14
           Enter Juliet.

NURSE
See where she comes from shrift with merry look.

CAPULET
How now, my headstrong? Where have you been gadding?

JULIET
Where I have learnt me to repent the sin
Of disobedient opposition
To you and your behests, and am enjoined
By holy Laurence to fall prostrate here
To beg your pardon. Pardon, I beseech you!
Henceforward I am ever ruled by you.

CAPULET
Send for the County. Go tell him of this.
I'll have this knot knit up to-morrow morning.   24

JULIET
I met the youthful lord at Laurence' cell
And gave him what becomèd love I might,
Not stepping o'er the bounds of modesty.

CAPULET
Why, I am glad on't. This is well. Stand up.
This is as't should be. Let me see the County.
Ay, marry, go, I say, and fetch him hither.
Now, afore God, this reverend holy friar,
All our whole city is much bound to him.   32

JULIET
Nurse, will you go with me into my closet
To help me sort such needful ornaments
As you think fit to furnish me to-morrow?

MOTHER
No, not till Thursday. There is time enough.

CAPULET
Go, nurse, go with her. We'll to church to-morrow.
                      Exeunt [Juliet and Nurse].

MOTHER
We shall be short in our provision.
'Tis now near night.

CAPULET   Tush, I will stir about,
And all things shall be well, I warrant thee, wife.
Go thou to Juliet, help to deck up her.
I'll not to bed to-night; let me alone.
I'll play the housewife for this once. What, ho!
They are all forth; well, I will walk myself

To County Paris, to prepare up him
Against to-morrow. My heart is wondrous light,
Since this same wayward girl is so reclaimed.
                                        Exit [with Mother].

*

IV, iii   *Enter Juliet and Nurse.*
JULIET
   Ay, those attires are best ; but, gentle nurse,
   I pray thee leave me to myself to-night ;
3 For I have need of many orisons
   To move the heavens to smile upon my state,
5 Which, well thou knowest, is cross and full of sin.
            Enter Mother.
MOTHER
   What, are you busy, ho ? Need you my help ?
JULIET
7 No, madam ; we have culled such necessaries
8 As are behoveful for our state to-morrow.
   So please you, let me now be left alone,
   And let the nurse this night sit up with you ;
   For I am sure you have your hands full all
   In this so sudden business.
MOTHER   Good night.
   Get thee to bed, and rest ; for thou hast need.
                     Exeunt [Mother and Nurse].
JULIET
   Farewell ! God knows when we shall meet again.
15 I have a faint cold fear thrills through my veins
   That almost freezes up the heat of life.
   I'll call them back again to comfort me.
   Nurse ! – What should she do here ?
   My dismal scene I needs must act alone.
   Come, vial.
   What if this mixture do not work at all ?
   Shall I be married then to-morrow morning ?
   No, no ! This shall forbid it. Lie thou there.
            [Lays down a dagger.]
   What if it be a poison which the friar
25 Subtly hath minist'red to have me dead,
   Lest in this marriage he should be dishonored
   Because he married me before to Romeo ?
   I fear it is ; and yet methinks it should not,
29 For he hath still been tried a holy man.
   How if, when I am laid into the tomb,
   I wake before the time that Romeo
   Come to redeem me ? There's a fearful point !
   Shall I not then be stifled in the vault,
   To whose foul mouth no healthsome air breathes in,
   And there die strangled ere my Romeo comes ?
   Or, if I live, is it not very like
37 The horrible conceit of death and night,
   Together with the terror of the place –
   As in a vault, an ancient receptacle
   Where for this many hundred years the bones
   Of all my buried ancestors are packed ;
42 Where bloody Tybalt, yet but green in earth,
   Lies fest'ring in his shroud ; where, as they say,
   At some hours in the night spirits resort –
45 Alack, alack, is it not like that I,
   So early waking – what with loathsome smells,
47 And shrieks like mandrakes torn out of the earth,
   That living mortals, hearing them, run mad –
   O, if I wake, shall I not be distraught,

Environèd with all these hideous fears,
And madly play with my forefathers' joints,
And pluck the mangled Tybalt from his shroud,
And, in this rage, with some great kinsman's bone
As with a club dash out my desp'rate brains ?
O, look ! methinks I see my cousin's ghost
Seeking out Romeo, that did spit his body
Upon a rapier's point. Stay, Tybalt, stay !
Romeo, I come ! this do I drink to thee.   58
      [She falls upon her bed within the curtains.]

*

         Enter Lady of the House and Nurse.   IV, iv
LADY
   Hold, take these keys and fetch more spices, nurse.
NURSE
   They call for dates and quinces in the pastry.
         Enter old Capulet.
CAPULET
   Come, stir, stir, stir ! The second cock hath crowed,
   The curfew bell hath rung, 'tis three o'clock.
   Look to the baked meats, good Angelica ;   5
   Spare not for cost.
NURSE   Go, you cot-quean, go,   6
   Get you to bed ! Faith, you'll be sick to-morrow
   For this night's watching.   8
CAPULET
   No, not a whit. What, I have watched ere now
   All night for lesser cause, and ne'er been sick.
LADY
   Ay, you have been a mouse-hunt in your time ;   11
   But I will watch you from such watching now.
                           Exit Lady and Nurse.
CAPULET
   A jealous hood, a jealous hood !   13
         *Enter three or four [Fellows] with
         spits and logs and baskets.*
                              Now, fellow,
   What is there ?
1. FELLOW
   Things for the cook, sir ; but I know not what.   15
CAPULET
   Make haste, make haste.   *[Exit first Fellow.]*
                        Sirrah, fetch drier logs.
   Call Peter ; he will show thee where they are.
2. FELLOW
   I have a head, sir, that will find out logs   18
   And never trouble Peter for the matter.
CAPULET
   Mass, and well said ; a merry whoreson, ha !   20
   Thou shalt be loggerhead.   21
                  [Exit second Fellow, with the others.]
                        Good Father ! 'tis day.

IV, iii *Juliet's chamber* 3 *orisons* prayers 5 *cross* perverse 7 *culled*
picked out 8 *behoveful* fitting ; *state* ceremony 15 *faint* causing faint-
ness 25 *minist'red* administered 29 *tried* proved (after this line, Q1
inserts 'I will not entertain so bad a thought') 37 *conceit* imagination
42 *green* new 45 *like* likely 47 *mandrakes* mandragora (a narcotic plant
with a forked root resembling the human form, supposed to utter maddening shrieks when uprooted) 58 s.d. (from Q1)
IV, iv *Within Capulet's house* 5 *baked meats* meat pies 6 *cot-quean* a man
who plays housewife 8 *watching* staying awake 11 *mouse-hunt* i.e. a nocturnal prowler after women 13 *A jealous hood* you wear the cap (or hood) of
jealousy 15, 18 *1. Fellow, 2. Fellow* (Q2 reads 'Fellow' in both instances)
18 *I . . . logs* i.e. my head is wooden and has an affinity for logs 20 *Mass*
by the Mass ; *whoreson* bastard, rascal 21 *loggerhead* blockhead

The County will be here with music straight,
For so he said he would.
      Play music.   I hear him near.
Nurse ! Wife ! What, ho ! What, nurse, I say !
      Enter Nurse.
25   Go waken Juliet ; go and trim her up.
I'll go and chat with Paris. Hie, make haste,
Make haste ! The bridegroom he is come already :
Make haste, I say.   *[Exit.]*

IV, v   *[Nurse goes to curtains.]*
    NURSE
1   Mistress ! what, mistress ! Juliet ! Fast, I warrant her, she.
2   Why, lamb ! why, lady ! Fie, you slug-abed.
Why, love, I say ! madam ! sweetheart ! Why, bride !
4   What, not a word ? You take your pennyworths now ;
Sleep for a week ; for the next night, I warrant,
6   The County Paris hath set up his rest
That you shall rest but little. God forgive me !
Marry, and amen. How sound is she asleep !
I needs must wake her. Madam, madam, madam !
Ay, let the County take you in your bed ;
He'll fright you up, i' faith. Will it not be ?
      [Draws aside the curtains.]
12   What, dressed, and in your clothes, and down again ?
I must needs wake you. Lady ! lady ! lady !
Alas, alas ! Help, help ! my lady 's dead !
15   O weraday that ever I was born !
16   Some aqua vitae, ho ! My lord ! my lady !
      [Enter Mother.]
    MOTHER
What noise is here ?
    NURSE   O lamentable day !
    MOTHER
What is the matter ?
    NURSE   Look, look ! O heavy day !
    MOTHER
O me, O me ! My child, my only life !
20   Revive, look up, or I will die with thee !
Help, help ! Call help.
      Enter Father.
    FATHER
For shame, bring Juliet forth ; her lord is come.
    NURSE
She's dead, deceased ; she's dead, alack the day !
    MOTHER
Alack the day, she's dead, she's dead, she's dead !
    CAPULET
Ha ! let me see her. Out alas ! she's cold,
Her blood is settled, and her joints are stiff ;
Life and these lips have long been separated.
Death lies on her like an untimely frost
Upon the sweetest flower of all the field.
    NURSE
30   O lamentable day !
    MOTHER   O woeful time !

25 *trim her up* dress her neatly
IV, v 1 *Fast* fast asleep 2 *slug-abed* sleepyhead 4 *pennyworths* small
portions 6 *set . . . rest* i.e. made his firm decision (from primero, a card
game) 12 *down* back to bed 15 *weraday* welladay, alas 16 *aqua vitae*
alcoholic spirits 45 *lasting labor* continuous toil 46 *But one* (cf. III,
v, 166) 61 *To murder . . . solemnity* to spoil our ceremony 69 *Your part*
her mortal body, generated by her parents 70 *his part* her immortal soul,
created directly by God 79 *rosemary* plant symbolizing remembrance 82
fond nature foolish human nature 83 *merriment* cause for optimism

    CAPULET
Death, that hath ta'en her hence to make me wail,
Ties up my tongue and will not let me speak.
      Enter Friar [Laurence] and the County [Paris, with
      Musicians].
    FRIAR
Come, is the bride ready to go to church ?
    CAPULET
Ready to go, but never to return.
O son, the night before thy wedding day
Hath Death lain with thy wife. There she lies,
Flower as she was, deflowerèd by him.
Death is my son-in-law, Death is my heir ;
My daughter he hath wedded. I will die
And leave him all. Life, living, all is Death's.
    PARIS
Have I thought long to see this morning's face,
And doth it give me such a sight as this ?
    MOTHER
Accursed, unhappy, wretched, hateful day !
Most miserable hour that e'er time saw
In lasting labor of his pilgrimage !   45
But one, poor one, one poor and loving child,   46
But one thing to rejoice and solace in,
And cruel Death hath catched it from my sight.
    NURSE
O woe ! O woeful, woeful, woeful day !
Most lamentable day, most woeful day
That ever ever I did yet behold !
O day, O day, O day ! O hateful day !
Never was seen so black a day as this.
O woeful day ! O woeful day !
    PARIS
Beguiled, divorcèd, wrongèd, spited, slain !
Most detestable Death, by thee beguiled,
By cruel cruel thee quite overthrown.
O love ! O life ! not life, but love in death !
    CAPULET
Despised, distressèd, hated, martyred, killed !
Uncomfortable time, why cam'st thou now
To murder, murder our solemnity ?   61
O child, O child ! my soul, and not my child !
Dead art thou – alack, my child is dead,
And with my child my joys are burièd !
    FRIAR
Peace, ho, for shame ! Confusion's cure lives not
In these confusions. Heaven and yourself
Had part in this fair maid – now heaven hath all,
And all the better is it for the maid.
Your part in her you could not keep from death,   69
But heaven keeps his part in eternal life.   70
The most you sought was her promotion,
For 'twas your heaven she should be advanced ;
And weep ye now, seeing she is advanced
Above the clouds, as high as heaven itself ?
O, in this love, you love your child so ill
That you run mad, seeing that she is well.
She's not well married that lives married long,
But she's best married that dies married young.
Dry up your tears and stick your rosemary   79
On this fair corse, and, as the custom is,
In all her best array bear her to church ;
For though fond nature bids us all lament,   82
Yet nature's tears are reason's merriment.   83

CAPULET

  All things that we ordainèd festival
  Turn from their office to black funeral –
  Our instruments to melancholy bells,
  Our wedding cheer to a sad burial feast;
  Our solemn hymns to sullen dirges change;
  Our bridal flowers serve for a buried corse;
  And all things change them to the contrary.

FRIAR

  Sir, go you in; and, madam, go with him;
  And go, Sir Paris. Every one prepare
  To follow this fair corse unto her grave.
94 The heavens do low'r upon you for some ill;
95 Move them no more by crossing their high will.
      Exeunt [casting rosemary on her and shutting the
      curtains]. Manet [the Nurse with Musicians].

1. MUSICIAN

  Faith, we may put up our pipes and be gone.

NURSE

  Honest good fellows, ah, put up, put up!
98 For well you know this is a pitiful case.   *[Exit.]*

1. MUSICIAN

99 Ay, by my troth, the case may be amended.
     Enter Peter.

100 PETER Musicians, O, musicians, 'Heart's ease,' 'Heart's
  ease'! O, an you will have me live, play 'Heart's ease.'

1. MUSICIAN Why 'Heart's ease'?

103 PETER O, musicians, because my heart itself plays 'My
104 heart is full of woe.' O, play me some merry dump to
  comfort me.

1. MUSICIAN Not a dump we! 'Tis no time to play now.

PETER You will not then?

1. MUSICIAN No.

PETER I will then give it you soundly.

1. MUSICIAN What will you give us?

111 PETER No money, on my faith, but the gleek. I will give
  you the minstrel.

1. MUSICIAN Then will I give you the serving-creature.

PETER Then will I lay the serving-creature's dagger on
115 your pate. I will carry no crotchets. I'll re you, I'll fa
  you. Do you note me?

1. MUSICIAN An you re us and fa us, you note us.

118 2. MUSICIAN Pray you put up your dagger, and put out
  your wit.

120 PETER Then have at you with my wit! I will dry-beat you
  with an iron wit, and put up my iron dagger. Answer
  me like men.

123   'When griping grief the heart doth wound,
      And doleful dumps the mind oppress,
     Then music with her silver sound' –
  Why 'silver sound'? Why 'music with her silver sound'?
127 What say you, Simon Catling?

1. MUSICIAN Marry, sir, because silver hath a sweet
  sound.

129 PETER Pretty! What say you, Hugh Rebeck?

2. MUSICIAN I say 'silver sound' because musicians
  sound for silver.

132 PETER Pretty too! What say you, James Soundpost?

3. MUSICIAN Faith, I know not what to say.

134 PETER O, I cry you mercy! you are the singer. I will say
  for you. It is 'music with her silver sound' because
  musicians have no gold for sounding.
    'Then music with her silver sound
      With speedy help doth lend redress.'   *Exit.*

1. MUSICIAN What a pestilent knave is this same!
2. MUSICIAN Hang him, Jack! Come, we'll in here, tarry
  for the mourners, and stay dinner. *Exit [with others].* 14

          *

     Enter Romeo.   V, i

ROMEO

  If I may trust the flattering truth of sleep,   1
  My dreams presage some joyful news at hand.
  My bosom's lord sits lightly in his throne,   3
  And all this day an unaccustomed spirit
  Lifts me above the ground with cheerful thoughts.
  I dreamt my lady came and found me dead
  (Strange dream that gives a dead man leave to think!)
  And breathed such life with kisses in my lips
  That I revived and was an emperor.
  Ah me! how sweet is love itself possessed,
  When but love's shadows are so rich in joy!   11
    Enter Romeo's man [Balthasar, booted].
  News from Verona! How now, Balthasar?
  Dost thou not bring me letters from the friar?
  How doth my lady? Is my father well?
  How fares my Juliet? That I ask again,
  For nothing can be ill if she be well.

MAN

  Then she is well, and nothing can be ill.
  Her body sleeps in Capel's monument,
  And her immortal part with angels lives.
  I saw her laid low in her kindred's vault
  And presently took post to tell it you.   21
  O, pardon me for bringing these ill news,
  Since you did leave it for my office, sir.

ROMEO

  Is it e'en so? Then I defy you, stars!   24
  Thou knowest my lodging. Get me ink and paper
  And hire posthorses. I will hence to-night.

MAN

  I do beseech you, sir, have patience.
  Your looks are pale and wild and do import   28
  Some misadventure.

ROMEO   Tush, thou art deceived.
  Leave me and do the thing I bid thee do.
  Hast thou no letters to me from the friar?

MAN

  No, my good lord.

ROMEO   No matter. Get thee gone
  And hire those horses. I'll be with thee straight.
             Exit [Balthasar].

---

94 *low'r* look angrily; *ill* sin 95 s.d. *casting . . . curtains* (from Q1) 98 s.d. (Q2 reads 'Exit omnes.') 99 *case* instrument case; *amended* repaired; s.d. *Enter Peter* (Q2 has 'Enter Will Kemp,' the actor playing Peter's role) 100, 103–04 *Heart's ease, My heart is full of woe* (old ballad tunes) 104 *dump* slow dance melody 111 *gleek* mock 111–12 *give you* insultingly call you 115 *carry* put up with; *crotchets* (1) whims, (2) quarter notes in music; *re, fa* (musical notes) 118 *put out* display 120 *Then . . . wit* (added to preceding speech in Q2); *dry-beat* thrash 123–25 (The second line is missing in Q2 but appears in Q1. The song is from Richard Edwards' 'In Commendation of Music,' in *The Paradise of Dainty Devices*, 1576.) 127 *Catling* (lutestring) 129 *Rebeck* (three-stringed fiddle) 132 *Soundpost* (wooden peg in a violin, supporting the bridge) 134 *cry you mercy* beg your pardon 141 *stay* await
V, i A street in Mantua 1 *flattering* favorable to me; *truth of sleep* (cf. I, iv, 52) 3 *bosom's lord* heart 11 *shadows* dream-images 21 *presently* at once; *took post* hired posthorses 24 *stars* (cf. I, iv, 107) 28 *import* suggest

Well, Juliet, I will lie with thee to-night.
Let's see for means. O mischief, thou art swift
To enter in the thoughts of desperate men!
I do remember an apothecary,
And hereabouts 'a dwells, which late I noted
39 In tatt'red weeds, with overwhelming brows,
40 Culling of simples. Meagre were his looks,
Sharp misery had worn him to the bones;
And in his needy shop a tortoise hung,
An alligator stuffed, and other skins
Of ill-shaped fishes; and about his shelves
45 A beggarly account of empty boxes,
Green earthen pots, bladders, and musty seeds,
47 Remnants of packthread, and old cakes of roses
Were thinly scattered, to make up a show.
Noting this penury, to myself I said,
'An if a man did need a poison now
Whose sale is present death in Mantua,
52 Here lives a caitiff wretch would sell it him.'
O, this same thought did but forerun my need,
And this same needy man must sell it me.
As I remember, this should be the house.
Being holiday, the beggar's shop is shut.
What, ho! apothecary!
        [Enter Apothecary.]
APOTHECARY   Who calls so loud?
ROMEO
Come hither, man. I see that thou art poor.
Hold, there is forty ducats. Let me have
60 A dram of poison, such soon-speeding gear
As will disperse itself through all the veins
That the life-weary taker may fall dead,
And that the trunk may be discharged of breath
As violently as hasty powder fired
65 Doth hurry from the fatal cannon's womb.
APOTHECARY
66 Such mortal drugs I have; but Mantua's law
67 Is death to any he that utters them.
ROMEO
Art thou so bare and full of wretchedness
And fearest to die? Famine is in thy cheeks,
70 Need and oppression starveth in thy eyes,
Contempt and beggary hangs upon thy back:
The world is not thy friend, nor the world's law;
The world affords no law to make thee rich;
Then be not poor, but break it and take this.
APOTHECARY
My poverty but not my will consents.
ROMEO
I pay thy poverty and not thy will.
APOTHECARY
Put this in any liquid thing you will
And drink it off, and if you had the strength
Of twenty men, it would dispatch you straight.

ROMEO
There is thy gold – worse poison to men's souls,
Doing more murder in this loathsome world,
Than these poor compounds that thou mayst not sell.
I sell thee poison; thou hast sold me none.
Farewell. Buy food and get thyself in flesh.
Come, cordial and not poison, go with me
To Juliet's grave; for there must I use thee.   *Exeunt.*

*

        Enter Friar John to Friar Laurence.   V, ii
JOHN
Holy Franciscan friar, brother, ho!
        Enter [Friar] Laurence.
LAURENCE
This same should be the voice of Friar John.
Welcome from Mantua. What says Romeo?
Or, if his mind be writ, give me his letter.
JOHN
Going to find a barefoot brother out,   5
One of our order, to associate me   6
Here in this city visiting the sick,
And finding him, the searchers of the town,   8
Suspecting that we both were in a house
Where the infectious pestilence did reign,   10
Sealed up the doors, and would not let us forth,
So that my speed to Mantua there was stayed.
LAURENCE
Who bare my letter, then, to Romeo?
JOHN
I could not send it – here it is again –
Nor get a messenger to bring it thee,
So fearful were they of infection.
LAURENCE
Unhappy fortune! By my brotherhood,   17
The letter was not nice, but full of charge,   18
Of dear import; and the neglecting it
May do much danger. Friar John, go hence,
Get me an iron crow and bring it straight   21
Unto my cell.
JOHN   Brother, I'll go and bring it thee.   *Exit.*
LAURENCE
Now must I to the monument alone.
Within this three hours will fair Juliet wake.
She will beshrew me much that Romeo   25
Hath had no notice of these accidents;   26
But I will write again to Mantua,
And keep her at my cell till Romeo come –
Poor living corse, closed in a dead man's tomb!   *Exit.*

*

        Enter Paris and his Page [with flowers and sweet   V, iii
        water].
PARIS
Give me thy torch, boy. Hence, and stand aloof.
Yet put it out, for I would not be seen.
Under yond yew tree lay thee all along,
Holding thy ear close to the hollow ground.   3
So shall no foot upon the churchyard tread
(Being loose, unfirm, with digging up of graves)

39 *weeds* garments; *overwhelming* overhanging 40 *simples* herbs 45 *account* quantity 47 *cakes of roses* compressed rose petals, used for perfume 52 *caitiff* miserable 60 *gear* stuff 65 *womb* i.e. barrel 66 *mortal* deadly 67 *utters* gives out 70 *starveth* are revealed by the starved look
V, ii Friar Laurence's cell 5 *a barefoot brother* another friar 6 *associate* accompany 8 *searchers* health officers 10 *pestilence* plague 17 *brotherhood* order (Franciscans) 18 *nice* trivial; *charge* important matters 21 *crow* crowbar 25 *beshrew* reprove 26 *accidents* occurrences
V, iii A churchyard in Verona s.d. *with . . . water* (from Q1); *sweet* perfumed 3 *all along* at full length

But thou shalt hear it. Whistle then to me,
As signal that thou hearest something approach.
Give me those flowers. Do as I bid thee, go.

PAGE *[aside]*
I am almost afraid to stand alone
Here in the churchyard ; yet I will adventure.   *[Retires.]*

PARIS
Sweet flower, with flowers thy bridal bed I strew
    (O woe ! thy canopy is dust and stones)
Which with sweet water nightly I will dew ;
    Or, wanting that, with tears distillèd by moans.
The obsequies that I for thee will keep
Nightly shall be to strew thy grave and weep.
              Whistle Boy.
The boy gives warning something doth approach.
What cursèd foot wanders this way to-night
20 To cross my obsequies and true love's rite ?
21 What, with a torch ? Muffle me, night, awhile.   *[Retires.]*
      Enter Romeo [and Balthasar with a torch, a mattock,
      and a crow of iron].

ROMEO
Give me that mattock and the wrenching iron.
Hold, take this letter. Early in the morning
See thou deliver it to my lord and father.
Give me the light. Upon thy life I charge thee,
Whate'er thou hearest or seest, stand all aloof
And do not interrupt me in my course.
Why I descend into this bed of death
Is partly to behold my lady's face,
But chiefly to take thence from her dead finger
31 A precious ring – a ring that I must use
In dear employment. Therefore hence, be gone.
33 But if thou, jealous, dost return to pry
In what I farther shall intend to do,
By heaven, I will tear thee joint by joint
And strew this hungry churchyard with thy limbs.
The time and my intents are savage-wild,
More fierce and more inexorable far
Than empty tigers or the roaring sea.

BALTHASAR
I will be gone, sir, and not trouble you.

ROMEO
41 So shalt thou show me friendship. Take thou that.
Live, and be prosperous ; and farewell, good fellow.

BALTHASAR *[aside]*
For all this same, I'll hide me hereabout.
His looks I fear, and his intents I doubt.   *[Retires.]*

ROMEO
Thou detestable maw, thou womb of death,
Gorged with the dearest morsel of the earth,
Thus I enforce thy rotten jaws to open,
48 And in despite I'll cram thee with more food.
      [Romeo opens the tomb.]

PARIS
This is that banished haughty Montague
That murd'red my love's cousin – with which grief
It is supposèd the fair creature died –
And here is come to do some villainous shame
53 To the dead bodies. I will apprehend him.
Stop thy unhallowèd toil, vile Montague !
Can vengeance be pursued further than death ?
Condemnèd villain, I do apprehend thee.
Obey, and go with me ; for thou must die.

ROMEO
I must indeed ; and therefore came I hither.
Good gentle youth, tempt not a desp'rate man.
Fly hence and leave me. Think upon these gone ;   60
Let them affright thee. I beseech thee, youth,
Put not another sin upon my head
By urging me to fury. O, be gone !
By heaven, I love thee better than myself,
For I come hither armed against myself.
Stay not, be gone. Live, and hereafter say
A madman's mercy bid thee run away.

PARIS
I do defy thy conjuration   68
And apprehend thee for a felon here.

ROMEO
Wilt thou provoke me ? Then have at thee, boy !
      [They fight.]

PAGE
O Lord, they fight ! I will go call the watch.
                            [Exit. Paris falls.]

PARIS
O, I am slain ! If thou be merciful,
Open the tomb, lay me with Juliet.
      [Dies.]

ROMEO
In faith, I will. Let me peruse this face.   74
Mercutio's kinsman, noble County Paris !
What said my man when my betossèd soul
Did not attend him as we rode ? I think   77
He told me Paris should have married Juliet.
Said he not so ? or did I dream it so ?
Or am I mad, hearing him talk of Juliet,
To think it was so ? O, give me thy hand,
One writ with me in sour misfortune's book !
I'll bury thee in a triumphant grave.
A grave ? O, no, a lanthorn, slaught'red youth,   84
For here lies Juliet, and her beauty makes
This vault a feasting presence full of light.   86
Death, lie thou there, by a dead man interred.
      [Lays him in the tomb.]
How oft when men are at the point of death
Have they been merry ! which their keepers call   89
A lightning before death. O, how may I   90
Call this lightning ? O my love ! my wife !
Death, that hath sucked the honey of thy breath,
Hath had no power yet upon thy beauty.
Thou are not conquered. Beauty's ensign yet   94
Is crimson in thy lips and in thy cheeks,
And death's pale flag is not advancèd there.
Tybalt, liest thou there in thy bloody sheet ?
O, what more favor can I do to thee
Than with that hand that cut thy youth in twain
To sunder his that was thine enemy ?
Forgive me, cousin ! Ah, dear Juliet,

20 *cross* interfere with   21 s.d. *and Balthasar . . . iron* (from Q1 ; Q2 reads 'Enter Romeo and Peter.') ; *mattock* pickaxe   31 *A precious ring* (a false excuse to assure Balthasar's non-interference)   33 *jealous* curious, jealous of my privacy   41 *that* (a purse)   48 *in despite* to spite you ; s.d. (from Q1)   53 *apprehend* arrest   60 *gone* dead   68 *conjuration* threatening appeal   74 *peruse* read, look at   77 *attend* pay attention to   84 *lanthorn* lantern (a many-windowed turret room)   86 *presence* presence chamber   89 *keepers* jailers   90 *A lightning before death* (a common phrase for the phenomenon described)   94 *ensign* banner

102 Why art thou yet so fair ? Shall I believe
That unsubstantial Death is amorous,
And that the lean abhorrèd monster keeps
Thee here in dark to be his paramour ?
For fear of that I still will stay with thee
And never from this pallet of dim night
108 Depart again. Here, here will I remain
With worms that are thy chambermaids. O, here
110 Will I set up my everlasting rest
111 And shake the yoke of inauspicious stars
From this world-wearied flesh. Eyes, look your last !
Arms, take your last embrace ! and, lips, O you
The doors of breath, seal with a righteous kiss
115 A dateless bargain to engrossing death !
116 Come, bitter conduct ; come, unsavory guide !
117 Thou desperate pilot, now at once run on
118 The dashing rocks thy seasick weary bark !
119 Here's to my love ! *[Drinks.]* O true apothecary !
Thy drugs are quick. Thus with a kiss I die.
    [Falls.]
    Enter Friar [Laurence], with lanthorn, crow, and spade.

FRIAR
121 Saint Francis be my speed ! how oft to-night
122 Have my old feet stumbled at graves ! Who's there ?
BALTHASAR
Here's one, a friend, and one that knows you well.
FRIAR
Bliss be upon you ! Tell me, good my friend,
What torch is yond that vainly lends his light
To grubs and eyeless skulls ? As I discern,
It burneth in the Capels' monument.
BALTHASAR
It doth so, holy sir ; and there's my master,
One that you love.
FRIAR   Who is it ?
BALTHASAR   Romeo.
FRIAR
How long hath he been there ?
BALTHASAR   Full half an hour.
FRIAR
Go with me to the vault.
BALTHASAR   I dare not, sir.
My master knows not but I am gone hence,
And fearfully did menace me with death
If I did stay to look on his intents.
FRIAR
Stay then ; I'll go alone. Fear comes upon me.
136 O, much I fear some ill unthrifty thing.
BALTHASAR
As I did sleep under this yew tree here,

102 *Why . . . fair* (followed in Q2 by a superfluous 'I will believe,' evidently another manuscript cancellation printed in error) 108 *again. Here* (Q2 prints between these words the following material, obviously cancelled in the manuscript because it appears in substance later in the speech : 'come lie thou in my arm. Here's to thy health, where e'er thou tumblest in. O true Apothecary! Thy drugs are quick. Thus with a kiss I die. Depart again.') 110 *set . . . rest* make my decision to stay forever (cf. IV, v, 6) 111 *inauspicious stars* (cf. V, i, 24) 115 *dateless* in perpetuity ; *engrossing* taking everything 116 *conduct* guide, i.e. the poison 117 *pilot* i.e. Romeo's soul 118 *bark* i.e. Romeo's body 119 *Here's to my love* (cf. IV, iii, 58) 121 *speed* aid 122 *stumbled at graves* (a bad omen) 136 *unthrifty* unfortunate 148 *comfortable* comfort-giving 162 *timeless* untimely 166 *restorative* i.e. restoring me to you 169 *happy* opportune 170 *rust* (Q1 'rest') 180 *ground* basis 181 *circumstance* details

I dreamt my master and another fought,
And that my master slew him.
FRIAR   Romeo !
Alack, alack, what blood is this which stains
The stony entrance of this sepulchre ?
What mean these masterless and gory swords
To lie discolored by this place of peace ?
    [Enters the tomb.]
Romeo ! O, pale ! Who else ? What, Paris too ?
And steeped in blood ? Ah, what an unkind hour
Is guilty of this lamentable chance !
The lady stirs.
    [Juliet rises.]
JULIET
O comfortable friar ! where is my lord ?   148
I do remember well where I should be,
And there I am. Where is my Romeo ?
FRIAR
I hear some noise. Lady, come from that nest
Of death, contagion, and unnatural sleep.
A greater power than we can contradict
Hath thwarted our intents. Come, come away.
Thy husband in thy bosom there lies dead ;
And Paris too. Come, I'll dispose of thee
Among a sisterhood of holy nuns.
Stay not to question, for the watch is coming.
Come, go, good Juliet. I dare no longer stay.
JULIET
Go, get thee hence, for I will not away.   *Exit [Friar].*
What's here ? A cup, closed in my true love's hand ?
Poison, I see, hath been his timeless end.   162
O churl ! drunk all, and left no friendly drop
To help me after ? I will kiss thy lips.
Haply some poison yet doth hang on them
To make me die with a restorative.   166
    [Kisses him.]
Thy lips are warm !
CHIEF WATCHMAN *[within]* Lead, boy. Which way ?
JULIET
Yea, noise ? Then I'll be brief. O happy dagger !   169
    [Snatches Romeo's dagger.]
This is thy sheath ; there rust, and let me die.   170
    [She stabs herself and falls.]
    Enter [Paris's] Boy and Watch.
BOY
This is the place. There, where the torch doth burn.
CHIEF WATCHMAN
The ground is bloody. Search about the churchyard.
Go, some of you ; whoe'er you find attach.
    [Exeunt some of the Watch.]
Pitiful sight ! here lies the County slain ;
And Juliet bleeding, warm, and newly dead,
Who here hath lain this two days burièd.
Go, tell the Prince ; run to the Capulets ;
Raise up the Montagues ; some others search.
    [Exeunt others of the Watch.]
We see the ground whereon these woes do lie,
But the true ground of all these piteous woes   180
We cannot without circumstance descry.   181
    Enter [some of the Watch, with] Romeo's Man
    [Balthasar].
2 . WATCHMAN
Here's Romeo's man. We found him in the churchyard.

CHIEF WATCHMAN
Hold him in safety till the Prince come hither.
Enter Friar [Laurence] and another Watchman.

3. WATCHMAN
Here is a friar that trembles, sighs, and weeps.
We took this mattock and this spade from him
As he was coming from this churchyard side.

CHIEF WATCHMAN
A great suspicion ! Stay the friar too.
Enter the Prince [and Attendants].

PRINCE
What misadventure is so early up,
189   That calls our person from our morning rest ?
Enter Capulet and his Wife [with others].

CAPULET
What should it be, that is so shrieked abroad ?

WIFE
O the people in the street cry 'Romeo,'
Some 'Juliet,' and some 'Paris' ; and all run,
With open outcry, toward our monument.

PRINCE
What fear is this which startles in your ears ?

CHIEF WATCHMAN
Sovereign, here lies the County Paris slain ;
And Romeo dead ; and Juliet, dead before,
Warm and new killed.

PRINCE
Search, seek, and know how this foul murder comes.

CHIEF WATCHMAN
Here is a friar, and slaughtered Romeo's man,
With instruments upon them fit to open
These dead men's tombs.

CAPULET
O heavens ! O wife, look how our daughter bleeds !
203   This dagger hath mista'en, for, lo, his house
Is empty on the back of Montague,
And it missheathèd in my daughter's bosom !

WIFE
O me ! this sight of death is as a bell
207   That warns my old age to a sepulchre.
Enter Montague [and others].

PRINCE
Come, Montague ; for thou art early up
To see thy son and heir more early down.

MONTAGUE
Alas, my liege, my wife is dead to-night !
Grief of my son's exile hath stopped her breath.
What further woe conspires against mine age ?

PRINCE
Look, and thou shalt see.

MONTAGUE
O thou untaught ! what manners is in this,
To press before thy father to a grave ?

PRINCE
216   Seal up the mouth of outrage for a while,
Till we can clear these ambiguities
And know their spring, their head, their true descent ;
219   And then will I be general of your woes
220   And lead you even to death. Meantime forbear,
And let mischance be slave to patience.
Bring forth the parties of suspicion.

FRIAR
I am the greatest, able to do least,
Yet most suspected, as the time and place

Doth make against me, of this direful murder ;
And here I stand, both to impeach and purge   226
Myself condemnèd and myself excused.

PRINCE
Then say at once what thou dost know in this.

FRIAR
I will be brief, for my short date of breath   229
Is not so long as is a tedious tale.
Romeo, there dead, was husband to that Juliet ;
And she, there dead, that Romeo's faithful wife.
I married them ; and their stol'n marriage day
Was Tybalt's doomsday, whose untimely death
Banished the new-made bridegroom from this city ;
For whom, and not for Tybalt, Juliet pined.
You, to remove that siege of grief from her,
Betrothed and would have married her perforce   238
To County Paris. Then comes she to me
And with wild looks bid me devise some mean
To rid her from this second marriage,
Or in my cell there would she kill herself.
Then gave I her (so tutored by my art)
A sleeping potion ; which so took effect
As I intended, for it wrought on her
The form of death. Meantime I writ to Romeo
That he should hither come as this dire night   247
To help to take her from her borrowèd grave,
Being the time the potion's force should cease.
But he which bore my letter, Friar John,
Was stayed by accident, and yesternight
Returned my letter back. Then all alone
At the prefixèd hour of her waking
Came I to take her from her kindred's vault ;
Meaning to keep her closely at my cell   255
Till I conveniently could send to Romeo.
But when I came, some minute ere the time
Of her awakening, here untimely lay
The noble Paris and true Romeo dead.
She wakes ; and I entreated her come forth
And bear this work of heaven with patience ;
But then a noise did scare me from the tomb,
And she, too desperate, would not go with me,
But, as it seems, did violence on herself.
All this I know, and to the marriage
Her nurse is privy ; and if aught in this   266
Miscarried by my fault, let my old life
Be sacrificed, some hour before his time,
Unto the rigor of severest law.

PRINCE
We still have known thee for a holy man.   270
Where's Romeo's man ? What can he say in this ?

BALTHASAR
I brought my master news of Juliet's death ;
And then in post he came from Mantua
To this same place, to this same monument.
This letter he early bid me give his father,

---

189 **s.d.** *Enter . . . Wife* (in Q2 'Enter Capels' appears here, with the present stage direction after l. 201) 203 *his house* its sheath 207 *my old age* (she is only twenty-eight – I, iii, 72–73 – but she feels old and ready for death ; cf. III, ii, 89) 216 *mouth of outrage* violent outcries 219 *general . . . woes* your leader in lamentation 220 *even to death* even if grief kills us 226 *impeach and purge* accuse and exonerate 229 *date of breath* life expectancy 238 *perforce* by force 247 *as* on 255 *closely* secretly 266 *privy* in the secret 270 *still* always

And threat'ned me with death, going in the vault,
If I departed not and left him there.

PRINCE
Give me the letter. I will look on it.
Where is the County's page that raised the watch?
280   Sirrah, what made your master in this place?

BOY
He came with flowers to strew his lady's grave;
And bid me stand aloof, and so I did.
283   Anon comes one with light to ope the tomb;
284   And by and by my master drew on him;
And then I ran away to call the watch.

PRINCE
This letter doth make good the friar's words,
Their course of love, the tidings of her death;
And here he writes that he did buy a poison
Of a poor pothecary, and therewithal
Came to this vault to die, and lie with Juliet.
Where be these enemies? Capulet, Montague,

280 *made* did 283 *Anon* soon 284 *by and by* almost at once; *drew* drew his sword 293 *with* by means of 294 *winking at* shutting my eyes to 297 *jointure* marriage portion 301 *rate* value 305 *glooming* cloudy, overcast

See what a scourge is laid upon your hate,
That heaven finds means to kill your joys with love. 293
And I, for winking at your discords too, 294
Have lost a brace of kinsmen. All are punished.

CAPULET
O brother Montague, give me thy hand
This is my daughter's jointure, for no more 297
Can I demand.

MONTAGUE   But I can give thee more;
For I will raise her statue in pure gold,
That whiles Verona by that name is known,
There shall no figure at such rate be set 301
As that of true and faithful Juliet.

CAPULET
As rich shall Romeo's by his lady's lie –
Poor sacrifices of our enmity!

PRINCE
A glooming peace this morning with it brings. 305
  The sun for sorrow will not show his head.
Go hence, to have more talk of these sad things;
  Some shall be pardoned, and some punishèd;
For never was a story of more woe
Than this of Juliet and her Romeo.   *[Exeunt omnes.]*

The only departures from the copy-text (second quarto, 1599) are listed below, except for relineations, corrections of obvious typographical errors, added stage directions (in brackets), and the treatment of cancelled passages (explained in the notes). Variants in speech prefixes within a scene have been regularized without comment. All the listed readings have been adopted from the first quarto, 1597, except those marked Q3 (third quarto, 1609), Q4 (fourth quarto, n.d.), F1 (first folio, 1623), F2 (second folio, 1632), F4 (fourth folio, 1683), and Eds (emendation, usually made quite early in the history of Shakespearean textual study and still generally accepted by modern editors). The adopted reading in italics is followed by the reading of the copy-text in roman.

I, i, 21 *cruel* (Q4) civil   26 *in sense* sense   30 *comes two* comes   60 *swashing* (Q4) washing   85 *mistemp'red* mistemperèd   118 *drave* (F1) drive   151 *sun* (Eds) same   175 *create* created   177 *well-seeming* well-seeing   188 *raised* made   190 *lovers'* loving   200 *Bid a sick* A sick   *make* makes   201 *Ah* A   209 *unharmed* uncharmed   216 *makes* (Q4) make

I, ii, *on more view* (Q4) one more view   70 *and Livia* Livia

I, iii, 66, 67 *honor* hour   99 *make it fly* make fly

I, iv, 39 *done* dum   42 *Of this sir-reverence* Or save your reverence   45 *like lamps* lights lights   47 *five wits* fine wits   66 *maid* man   72 *O'er courtiers'* On courtiers   81 *dreams he* he dreams   113 *sail* suit

I, v, 18 *Ah ha* Ah   95 *ready* did ready

II, i, 10 *pronounce* prouaunt   *dove* day   12 *heir* her   38 *et cetera,* or

II, ii, 31 *pacing* puffing   41 *nor any other part* (omitted in Q2)   44 *name* word   83 *washed* (F2) washeth   99 *havior* behavior   101 *more cunning* coying   110 *circled* circle   153 *suit* (Q4) strife   163 *mine* (omitted in Q2)   168 *sweet* (F2) Neece   *At what* What   179 *her* his   189 *father's* friar's close

II, iii, 4 *fiery* burning   22 *sometime 's* sometime   74 *ring yet* yet ringing   85 *She whom* Her

II, iv, 19 *I can tell you* (omitted in Q2)   28 *fantasticoes* fantasies   96 (spoken by Romeo in Q2)   97 (spoken by Mercutio in Q2)   109 *for* (omitted in Q2)   187 *I warrant* (F2) Warrant   197 *Ah* (Eds) A

II, v, 26 *have I had* (F2) have I

III, i, 106 *soundly too. Your* (Eds) soundly, to your   120 *Alive He gan* 122 *eyed* end   145 *O husband* (Eds) O cousin, husband   164 *agile* aged   186 *hate's* hearts

III, ii, 9 *By* (F2) And by   21 *he* (Q4) I   49 *the* (F2) thee   51 *determine of* (F1) determine   76 *Dove-feathered* (Eds) Ravenous dove-feathered   79 *damnèd* (F2) dimme

III, iii, 15 *Hence* Here   52 *Thou* Then   117 *lives* (F4) lies   138 *happy too* happy   143 *misbehaved* mishavèd   144 *pout'st upon* (Eds) puts up   163 *is* sir

III, iv, 34 *very very* very

III, v, 13 *exhales* exhale   83 *pardon him* (F2) pardon   182 *trained* liand

IV, i, 7 *talked* talk   45 *cure* care   46 *Ah* O   72 *slay* stay   83 *chapless* chapels   85 *his shroud* (Q4) his   98 *breath* breast   100 *wanny* (Eds) many   116 *waking* (Q3) walking

IV, iii, 58 *Romeo . . . thee* Romeo, Romeo, Romeo, here's drink, I drink to thee

IV, v, 41 *long* love   65 *cure* (Eds) care   81 *In all* And in   82 *fond* (F2) some   104 *full of woe* (Q4) full   129, 132 *Pretty* Prates

V, i, 15 *fares my* doth my Lady   24 *defy* deny   76 *pay* pray

V, iii, 3 *yew tree* young trees   68 *conjuration* commiration   137 *yew* (Q3) young   190 *shrieked* (Eds) shrike   209 *more early* now earling   232 *that* that's

SUPPLEMENTARY NOTE

III, ii, 49 *Or those eyes' shot that makes the answer 'I'*

Almost every editor since Capell except H. R. Hoppe (Crofts, 1943) has accepted his emendation *shut* for *shot*, reading "Or those eyes shut that make(s) thee answer 'I' [Ay]." Our copy-text, Q2, reads: "Or those eyes shot, that makes thee answer I." This reading is retained by the later quartos and folios, except that *thee* is emended to *the* in F2, F3, and F4.

I have supplied the apostrophe which makes *eyes* a possessive. Since Q2 regularly omits the apostrophe, as in "eyes windows" (IV, i, 100), supplying it does no violence to the text. *Shot* becomes a noun instead of a past participle. A usage similar to this appears in *Cymbeline*, I, i, 89–90, when Imogen says, "And I shall here abide the hourly shot / Of angry eyes."

If we interpret the passage as emended by Capell, Juliet refers to Romeo's eyes closed in death; or else she refers to the Nurse's eyes which, if shut, will indicate *ay*. If, as I think, the Nurse's eyes are meant, *shot* is the more logical reading. Juliet is studying the Nurse's face and may receive her answer from the Nurse's voice or, failing that, from the Nurse's eyes. Either form of affirmative, the spoken *ay* or the revelatory eye-glance (*eyes' shot*), will slay Juliet, who feels that her life is bound up with that of Romeo. As the eye-glance of the cockatrice (basilisk) darts death, so will the spoken *ay* or the eye-glance of the Nurse. This implies no malice on the part of the Nurse, since it is her message which may be fatal to Juliet.

Involved here is the Elizabethan theory of vision, or the act of seeing. It was believed that the eye darted forth a stream of very fine particles which pierced or fastened upon the beheld object and then relayed impulses back to the sender. The arrow was the appropriate image for such an eye-glance. Thus, Juliet promises her mother to look at Paris, "But no more deep will I endart mine eye" than her mother wishes (I, iii, 98). Such imagery is very common in the works of Shakespeare and his contemporaries.

If one retains *thee* as the correct reading, Juliet's meaning is as follows: "I am not myself if there be such a spoken *ay* or if there be your eye-glance that forces you to answer 'Ay.'" This makes sense after a fashion, but I have adopted the less tortuous reading of the later folios, changing *thee* to *the*. Juliet's meaning then becomes: "I am not myself if there be such a spoken *ay* or if there be your eye-glance that forms the answer 'Ay.'"

In support of the interpretation here given, we may notice that Mercutio pictures Romeo as being "dead," pierced by vision and by sound: "stabbed with a white wench's black eye; run through the ear with a love song" (II, iv, 14–15). So it is with Juliet. The spoken *ay* of the Nurse may slay her through the ear as effectively as the visual eye-dart of the cockatrice. Likewise, the Nurse's "eyes' shot," if it reveals the unspoken *ay*, will kill visually as effectively as her voice would kill through the ear.

JULIUS CAESAR

INTRODUCTION

Despite its apparent simplicity, this play has occasioned opposite interpretations. For some critics, Caesar is, in Antony's words, "the noblest man / That ever livèd in the tide of times" and the assassination a senseless act of criminal folly, while for others Caesar is an ambitious tyrant and the assassination a valiant attempt by patriotic Romans to preserve the Republic. These views of the play correspond to contrasting views of the historical events it dramatizes – the medieval condemnation of Brutus and Cassius, as in Dante and Chaucer, and the Renaissance condemnation of Caesar, as in Machiavelli, Elyot, Montaigne, Sidney, Marlowe, Harington, and Jonson. Shakespeare himself reflects the medieval view in his early trilogy on the reign of Henry VI and the Renaissance view in plays written in the late 1590's and after. As a practical dramatist, however, he was not concerned to teach his audience a particular interpretation of history, as he had to some extent been forced to do in his English chronicle plays; rather, he knew that the more and less educated members of his audience would tend to hold, respectively, the Renaissance and medieval views, and he chose to fashion his play in such a way that it should take advantage of the preconceptions of both sections of his audience. The result is a structure of sustained dramatic ambiguities that are resolved only in the latter part of the play, a method of construction that he was to use with even more brilliant and controversial effect in his next tragedy, *Hamlet*.

Julius Caesar was probably first produced at the new Globe Theatre in the fall of 1599, some months after the appearance of *Henry V*, the last of the nine English histories that Shakespeare wrote in the 1590's, and shortly before the appearance of a comedy with the significant title *As You Like It*. The history and the comedy are culminations of established interests on Shakespeare's part; *The Tragedy of Julius Caesar*, although Shakespeare had already written highly popular tragedies, is a new departure, an important turning-point midway in his career as England's most popular dramatist. He had abandoned English history, was soon to abandon romantic comedy, and was about to undertake his series of great heroic tragedies, to be framed, as it turned out, by four tragedies based on Sir Thomas North's translation of Plutarch's *Lives*, the literary source that Shakespeare seems most to have respected and admired.

With *Julius Caesar* he turned for the first time from Holinshed's *Chronicles* of English history to Plutarch's comparative studies of the careers of great men of Greece and Rome. He was turning from English to Roman history for subject matter, but more significantly he was turning from history to tragedy. His earlier English histories had indeed been tragical, although the later ones must more

aptly be termed comical, and they had finally to take an intensely patriotic view of the civil wars that led to the accession of Henry VII, the first of the Tudors. Even his other tragedies, unlike those drawn from Plutarch, end with the destruction of the forces of evil and the belated victory of the good forces that survive. The Plutarchan tragedies, particularly those concerned with the Roman civil wars, with the decline and fall of the Roman Republic, are more ironic; the forces that prevail at the ends of these tragedies cannot easily be seen as forces of good, and they are, in each case, forces hostile to the tragic heroes. For Brutus is the tragic hero of *Julius Caesar*; Caesar himself, or more properly "the spirit of Caesar" as embodied in Octavius, is the historic victor.

To men of the Renaissance, Republican Rome was the apex of human achievement in civilization and political organization, although without benefit of Christianity. Its heroes, whether legendary or historical, were held in reverence as notable examples of patriotism, military valor, and the pagan virtues. In his popular poem *The Rape of Lucrece* Shakespeare had written of two of the legendary figures, the chaste Lucrece and the patriot Junius Brutus, founder of the Republic and reputed ancestor of Marcus Brutus. In *Julius Caesar* the names of two other admired Romans, Pompey and Cato of Utica, are invoked to lend moral weight to the Republican cause, for both had been destroyed by Caesar as the renowned Cicero was to be destroyed by Caesar's followers.

The play opens with the tribunes of the people, whose function it was to safeguard and maintain popular liberties, using Pompey's memory to dissuade the fickle plebeians from participating in Caesar's triumph over fellow Romans; they express the Republican fear that Caesar seeks to rob the Romans of their ancient liberties. In the next scene, Caesar's ambition to be crowned, a move which if successful would reduce the Republic to a monarchy, is vividly communicated as an off-stage action accompanying Cassius' attempt to persuade Brutus to lead a conspiracy against Caesar. Caesar's scheme to have himself crowned by popular acclaim would surely have reminded many in Shakespeare's audience of the similar scheme used by the usurping tyrant Richard III, as Shakespeare had dramatized it. In both cases, the unwillingness of the people to go along with the scheme frustrates it, and the schemers must resort to other devices to get themselves crowned. The center of interest in this play, however, is not the progress of Caesar and his followers; it is the impact of "the spirit of Caesar" on his fellow Romans, particularly on Brutus, who must choose between his personal friendship for Caesar and his public responsibility, both as a Roman and as a praetor, to prevent the subversion of the Republic. This is his tragic dilemma and Shakespeare's major interest in the first two acts of the play.

Brutus, from the first, is "with himself at war" and deeply concerned for "the general good." His soliloquy at the beginning of Act II, the first of Shakespeare's famous deliberative soliloquies, dramatizes his attempt to resolve his inner conflict. The question is not whether or not Caesar must be killed for the general good – Brutus has already decided that he must be – but how Brutus can reconcile his political decision as a public man with his conscience as a private man: "I know no personal cause to spurn at him, / But for the general." In the rest of the soliloquy, as Coleridge failed to perceive but as Kittredge points out, Brutus considers Caesar as a private man and can find nothing to justify his assassination. By means of the commonplace, however, that absolute power usually corrupts absolutely, he is able to bring his personal feelings into line with his sense of public duty. Yet he is not comfortable with his decision – "all the interim is / Like a phantasma or a hideous dream" – and he continues to distinguish between Caesar the man and Caesar the would-be king and probable tyrant:

> Let's be sacrificers, but not butchers, Caius.
> We all stand up against the spirit of Caesar,
> And in the spirit of men there is no blood.
> O that we then could come by Caesar's spirit
> And not dismember Caesar! But, alas,
> Caesar must bleed for it.

That is what he says privately to the other conspirators; it is an essential part of his public explanation to the plebeians in the Forum: "Not that I loved Caesar less, but that I loved Rome more. . . . As Caesar loved me, I weep for him; . . . as he was ambitious, I slew him."

Cassius and Antony, unlike Brutus, are unscrupulous politicians of the sort that the Elizabethans called Machiavellian. Both place personal gain above the general good. They are, respectively, the dominant villains of the first and second halves of the play. Cassius' soliloquy at the end of Act I, scene ii, is quite as much like the soliloquies of Iago as is Antony's brief soliloquy after he has delivered his masterpiece of demagogic rhetoric: "Now let it work. Mischief, thou art afoot, / Take thou what course thou wilt." Cassius, for all his political shrewdness, must defer to Brutus – as Antony must later defer to Octavius – since Brutus had been chosen to lead the conspiracy just because his known integrity, "like richest alchemy," would make it seem worthy and virtuous. Plutarch analyzes Brutus' failure to preserve the Republic as the result of two major political "mistakes": his refusal to kill Caesar's chief supporters, notably Antony, along with Caesar, and his permission that Antony speak at Caesar's funeral. Some critics find a third "mistake" in Brutus' decision to meet the enemy at Philippi instead of letting them search out the Republican forces. Shakespeare has Cassius propose shrewder alternatives to each of these choices, but in each case Cassius is a foil to Brutus, whose nobility as tragic hero is only the more enhanced by his rejections of Cassius' politic proposals.

The one episode in which Cassius passionately stands up to Brutus, though he is as usual overridden by him, is the famous quarrel scene in Act IV. Here Brutus is most nearly disillusioned about the motives of his fellow conspirators:

> Did not great Julius bleed for justice sake?
> What villain touched his body that did stab
> And not for justice? What, shall one of us,
> That struck the foremost man of all this world
> But for supporting robbers – shall we now
> Contaminate our fingers with base bribes . . . ?

Shakespeare has shown us, at the beginning of Act IV, those robbers, the triumvirate, about their work, with Antony cast in the most villainous role of the three. Many in Shakespeare's audience must have been reminded of the proverbial lack of honor among thieves, which finally, as Shakespeare was to dramatize it in *Antony and Cleopatra*, works to the advantage of Octavius Caesar, the coldest, youngest, and most cunning of the three. In this play, Octavius overrides Antony, much as Brutus overrides Cassius, and the fact that Octavius is given the final speech of the play, generally assigned in both the tragedies and the histories to the highest-ranking of the surviving figures, foreshadows his defeat of Antony.

Antony is at least capable of feeling, and his lamentation over the corpse of Caesar makes him highly sympathetic in Act III, scene i. He and Cassius are opposite types, both of them foils for Brutus, who in some respects stands as a mean between their extremes. Antony is too "gamesome," "a masker and a reveller," and far from having Cassius' "lean and hungry look." Cassius "loves no plays," "hears no music," "reads much," and is envious. They are, respectively, excessive and deficient in their capacities for feeling, for "love," one of the key-words of the play. Brutus loves, and inspires love in others:

> My heart doth joy that yet in all my life
> I found no man but he was true to me.

Like Cassius he reads, like Antony he loves music, but he is not dissolute like the latter, nor envious like the former. His integrity, his honor, contrasts sharply with the conniving of Antony and Cassius. His love for Portia and his concern for the welfare of his servants (notably Lucius, who has no counterpart in Plutarch) heighten our sympathetic admiration of him. Antony's final speech in praise of Brutus directs our proper response to the tragic hero defeated by the spirit of Caesar:

> This was the noblest Roman of them all.
> All the conspirators save only he
> Did that they did in envy of great Caesar;
> He, only in a general honest thought
> And common good to all, made one of them.

Caesar himself is almost enigmatic. Brutus, after the assassination, calls him "the foremost man of all this world," yet Shakespeare presents him in his own person as a pompous, arrogant usurper, and in Cassius' description as a Colossus afflicted with unmanly weaknesses. He sees himself as the polestar and as Mount Olympus, yet he is associated with sterility, epilepsy, and deafness. He insists that he is unshakeable, yet Cassius tells us "How he did shake" and we see how he is shaken. Cassius sees him as a wolf, ferociously carnivorous, Antony as a hart, harmlessly herbivorous. Other images are applied to him, but the concept of Caesar as a diseased statue is the most powerful in the first movement of the play, where he is not so much an active force for evil as a static center of corruption. Even many of the medieval glorifiers of Caesar condemned him for the inordinate ambition that led to his assassination and the ultimate decline of Rome. Even the majority of Renaissance glorifiers of Brutus recognized Caesar's earlier greatness while condemning him for the subversion of the Republic. Shakespeare, while he is careful to disabuse his audience of the vulgar error that Caesar was actually the first of the Roman Emperors, gives the spirit of Caesar its historical due, but he seems to have thought to show Caesar himself as a victim of that blind infatuation, "security," that leads great men to their destruction. Caesar's *hubris* is more extraordinary than that of any other major figure in Shakespeare's plays.

After Brutus, Caesar, Cassius, and Antony, the plebeians are the most important "character" in the play. It is their corruption that defeats the Republican cause from the start. Brutus' major disillusionment, if this had been a history play, should have occurred at the very moment of his greatest apparent success – the moment when, after his plain and honest speech in the Forum, the plebeians shout "Let him be Caesar." "Caesar's better parts / Shall be crowned in Brutus." At this point Shakespeare's audience knew that the Roman mob was no longer capable of Republicanism, that the Romans, like themselves, might best be governed by a king. It is Brutus' nobility as a tragic hero, and his weakness as a political leader, not to have perceived this fact, of which Antony and Octavius will take such advantage. Yet the less politic Brutus is, the more heroic he can be made. Indeed Shakespeare, in transmuting the material he found in Plutarch's lives of Caesar, Antony, and Brutus, selected from and augmented that material in such a way as to make Brutus his centrally admirable figure, the high-minded man in a corrupt world.

Julius Caesar has been widely acclaimed for its essential truth to the spirit of ancient Rome, despite such evident anachronisms as chimney tops, striking clocks, and books with leaves. The contrast between Stoicism and Epicureanism, two of the dominant philosophical systems of the Romans, is clearly brought out. In fact, it is Cassius' shift from Epicureanism (which to the Elizabethans meant atheism) to a belief in portents that helps to make him a sympathetic figure at the end of the play. The anachronisms are not important. To the Elizabethans, excepting such purists as Ben Jonson, the play must have seemed pretty thoroughly Roman. Although there are certain homely references to details of costume that can only have been Elizabethan, there was probably, as we can surmise from a contemporary illustration of the staging of *Titus Andronicus*, an attempt to clothe the major figures in costumes that the Elizabethans thought of as Roman.

Even the style of the play seems to reflect a similar intention. It is unusually straightforward, having neither the lyric floridity of the earlier tragedies nor the condensed metaphoric texture of the later plays. The animal and hunting imagery is as forthright in its application as the frequent use of monosyllabic lines is forceful in its simplicity. Shakespeare subordinated poetry to rhetoric to gain his Roman effects. Rhetoric, the art of persuasion, is structural as well as stylistic in this play: the tribunes persuade the people not to honor Caesar, Cassius persuades Brutus to lead the conspiracy, Brutus persuades himself of the justice of his cause, Portia persuades Brutus to reveal his secret to her, Calphurnia persuades Caesar not to go forth, Decius persuades him to go, Brutus persuades the people to support the Republicans. Antony persuades them to mutiny. This persuasion and counter-persuasion reaches its climax with the speeches in the Forum, the turning-point of the play, after which the spirit of Caesar dominates and the Republic, along with the Republicans, is destroyed.

Shakespeare compresses events of three years into five dramatic "days," the first two of which account for the first three acts of the play, and he compresses the complexities of motives, as Plutarch discussed them, in order to gain momentum for his powerful rhetorical construction. Despite this compression, Shakespeare, following Plutarch, is concerned less with what happens than with why it happens, less with events than with interacting purposes, and this remains his major interest in his later plays. *Julius Caesar* never mounts to the passionate intensity of the greater tragedies that followed it – in this respect it is more stoically Roman than they – but it anticipates their pattern of heroic disillusionment, inner conflict, and the attempt to set right a time which is out of joint. Unlike his legendary ancestor, Junius Brutus, and unlike his immediate successor, Hamlet, Brutus does not accomplish his purpose. Elizabethans may have seen the triumph of Caesarism as Plutarch saw it – "the state of Rome (in my opinion) . . . could not more abide to be governed by many lords, but required one only absolute governor" – or even as an Elizabethan publisher saw it – "an evident demonstration that peoples' rule must give place, and Prince's power prevail." As the play presents it, however, the triumph of Caesarism is a matter of history making tragedy ironic. There is no restoration of a positive moral order to relieve the sense of tragic waste. Only the memory of Brutus' nobility, as his corpse is carried off, transcends the bleak facts of history at the end of the play :

> His life was gentle, and the elements
> So mixed in him that Nature might stand up
> And say to all the world, 'This was a man!'

Columbia University   S. F. JOHNSON

NOTE ON THE TEXT

Julius Caesar was first published in the folio of 1623, evidently from the playhouse prompt-book or a careful transcript of it. The folio text is divided into acts but not into scenes. The act–scene division supplied marginally for reference in the present edition is that of the later editors, and it needlessly indicates a break in the action at IV, iii, 1. The action in V, here printed continuously as in the folio, takes place in various parts of the plains of Philippi. Certain character names have here been normalized in the text as well as in speech-prefixes:

I, i, s.d. *Marullus* (F Murellus)
I, ii, s.d. *Marullus* (F Murellus) 282 *Marullus* (F Murrellus) 3, 4, 6, 190 *Antonius* (F Antonio)
I, iii, 37 *Antonius* (F Antonio)
III, i, 275 s.d. *Octavius* (F Octavio)
IV, iii, 242, 244, 244 s.d., 289 *Claudius* (F Claudio) 244, 244 s.d., 289 *Varro* (F Varrus)

V, ii, 4 *Octavius* (F Octavio)
V, iii, 108 *Labeo, Flavius* (F Labio, Flavio)

Throughout the play Caska is changed to *Casca*, and Lucillius to *Lucilius*. Otherwise the present edition adheres closely to the folio text, and admits only the following emendations in addition to the correction of obvious typographical errors. The adopted reading in italics is followed by the folio reading in roman.

I, iii, 129 *fev'rous* Fauors
II, i, 40 *ides* first
II, ii, 19 *fought* fight 23 *did neigh* do neigh 46 *are* heare
III, i, 113 *states* State 115 *lies* lye 283 *for* from
III, ii, 104 *art* are
V, iii, 104 *Thasos* Tharsus
V, iv, 17 *the news* thee news
V, v, 33 *to thee too, Strato. Countrymen,* to thee, to Strato, Countreymen:

86

JULIUS CAESAR

*

I, i *Enter Flavius, Marullus, and certain Commoners over the stage.*

FLAVIUS
Hence! home, you idle creatures, get you home!
Is this a holiday? What, know you not,
3 Being mechanical, you ought not walk
4 Upon a laboring day without the sign
Of your profession? Speak, what trade art thou?
CARPENTER Why, sir, a carpenter.
MARULLUS
Where is thy leather apron and thy rule?
What dost thou with thy best apparel on?
You, sir, what trade are you?
10 COBBLER Truly, sir, in respect of a fine workman I am
11 but, as you would say, a cobbler.
MARULLUS
12 But what trade art thou? Answer me directly.

COBBLER A trade, sir, that I hope I may use with a safe
conscience, which is indeed, sir, a mender of bad soles. 14
FLAVIUS
What trade, thou knave? Thou naughty knave, what 15
trade?
COBBLER Nay, I beseech you, sir, be not out with me. 16
Yet if you be out, sir, I can mend you. 17
MARULLUS
What mean'st thou by that? Mend me, thou saucy
fellow?
COBBLER Why, sir, cobble you.
FLAVIUS
Thou art a cobbler, art thou?
COBBLER Truly, sir, all that I live by is with the awl. I
meddle with no tradesman's matters nor women's mat- 22
ters; but withal – I am indeed, sir, a surgeon to old shoes. 23
When they are in great danger, I recover them. As proper 24
men as ever trod upon neat's leather have gone upon my 25
handiwork.
FLAVIUS
But wherefore art not in thy shop to-day?
Why dost thou lead these men about the streets?
COBBLER Truly, sir, to wear out their shoes, to get my-
self into more work. But indeed, sir, we make holiday to
see Caesar and to rejoice in his triumph. 31
MARULLUS
Wherefore rejoice? What conquest brings he home?
What tributaries follow him to Rome 33

I, i A street in Rome **s.d.** *over the stage* who cross the stage before halting
3 *mechanical* workers 4 *sign* tools and costume (which indicate a man's
trade) 10 *in . . . workman* as far as skilled work is concerned 11 *cobbler*
(with pun on 'bungler') 12 *directly* plainly 14 *soles* (with pun on
'souls') 15 *naughty* worthless 16 *out* angry 17 *be out* have worn-
out shoes; *mend* (with pun on 'reform') 22 *meddle* (with pun on 'am intimate') 23 *withal* nevertheless (with puns on 'all' and 'awl') 24 *recover*
re-sole (with pun on 'cure'); *proper* handsome 25 *neat's* cattle's (the
phrase is proverbial); *gone* walked 31 *triumph* victory procession 33
tributaries captives

To grace in captive bonds his chariot wheels?
You blocks, you stones, you worse than senseless
    things!
O you hard hearts, you cruel men of Rome.
37 Knew you not Pompey? Many a time and oft
Have you climbed up to walls and battlements,
To tow'rs and windows, yea, to chimney tops,
Your infants in your arms, and there have sat
The livelong day, with patient expectation,
To see great Pompey pass the streets of Rome.
And when you saw his chariot but appear,
Have you not made an universal shout,
45 That Tiber trembled underneath her banks
46 To hear the replication of your sounds
47 Made in her concave shores?
And do you now put on your best attire?
And do you now cull out a holiday?
And do you now strew flowers in his way
51 That comes in triumph over Pompey's blood?
Be gone!
Run to your houses, fall upon your knees,
54 Pray to the gods to intermit the plague
That needs must light on this ingratitude.

FLAVIUS
Go, go, good countrymen, and for this fault
Assemble all the poor men of your sort;
Draw them to Tiber banks, and weep your tears
Into the channel, till the lowest stream
60 Do kiss the most exalted shores of all.
        Exeunt all the Commoners.
61 See, whe'r their basest mettle be not moved.
They vanish tongue-tied in their guiltiness.
Go you down that way towards the Capitol;
64 This way will I. Disrobe the images
65 If you do find them decked with ceremonies.

MARULLUS
May we do so?
67 You know it is the feast of Lupercal.

FLAVIUS
It is no matter. Let no images
69 Be hung with Caesar's trophies. I'll about
70 And drive away the vulgar from the streets.
So do you too, where you perceive them thick.
These growing feathers plucked from Caesar's wing
73 Will make him fly an ordinary pitch,
74 Who else would soar above the view of men
And keep us all in servile fearfulness.   *Exeunt.*

          *

I, ii   *[Music.] Enter Caesar, Antony (for the course),*
Calphurnia, Portia, Decius, Cicero, Brutus,
Cassius, Casca, [a great crowd following, among
them] a Soothsayer; after them, Marullus and
Flavius.

CAESAR
Calphurnia.
CASCA   Peace, ho! Caesar speaks.
  [Music ceases.]
CAESAR   Calphurnia.
CALPHURNIA
Here, my lord.
CAESAR
Stand you directly in Antonius' way
4 When he doth run his course. Antonius.

ANTONY
Caesar, my lord?
CAESAR
Forget not in your speed, Antonius,
To touch Calphurnia; for our elders say
The barren, touchèd in this holy chase,
Shake off their sterile curse.
ANTONY   I shall remember.
When Caesar says 'Do this,' it is performed.
CAESAR
Set on, and leave no ceremony out.
  [Music.]
SOOTHSAYER   Caesar!
CAESAR   Ha! Who calls?
CASCA
Bid every noise be still. Peace yet again!
  [Music ceases.]
CAESAR
Who is it in the press that calls on me?   15
I hear a tongue shriller than all the music
Cry 'Caesar!' Speak. Caesar is turned to hear.
SOOTHSAYER
Beware the ides of March.   18
CAESAR   What man is that?
BRUTUS
A soothsayer bids you beware the ides of March.
CAESAR
Set him before me; let me see his face.
CASSIUS
Fellow, come from the throng; look upon Caesar.
CAESAR
What say'st thou to me now? Speak once again.
SOOTHSAYER
Beware the ides of March.
CAESAR
He is a dreamer. Let us leave him. Pass.   24
  Sennet. Exeunt. Mane[n]t Brutus and Cassius.
CASSIUS
Will you go see the order of the course?   25
BRUTUS   Not I.
CASSIUS   I pray you do.
BRUTUS
I am not gamesome. I do lack some part   28
Of that quick spirit that is in Antony.   29
Let me not hinder, Cassius, your desires.
I'll leave you.
CASSIUS
Brutus, I do observe you now of late;
I have not from your eyes that gentleness   33
And show of love as I was wont to have.   34

37 *Pompey* (defeated by Caesar in 48 B.C., later murdered) 45 *That* such that 46 *replication* reverberation 47 *concave shores* hollowed-out banks 51 *blood* i.e. sons (also the blood of Pompey and his followers) 54 *intermit* withhold 60 *most exalted shores* highest flood level, verge of heavens 61 *whe'r* whether; *their basest* even their very base; *mettle* substance, temperament 64 *images* statues 65 *ceremonies* ornaments 67 *Lupercal* fertility festival held on February 15 69 *trophies* ornaments 70 *vulgar* plebeians, common people 73 *pitch* height 74 *above . . . men* i.e. like the gods
I, ii A public place 4 *run his course* i.e. race naked through the city striking bystanders with a goatskin thong 15 *press* crowd 18 *ides* the half-way point in the month, the fifteenth day in March, May, July, and October 24 s.d. *Sennet* trumpet call 25 *order* events 28 *gamesome* sport-loving 29 *quick spirit* lively nature 33 *gentleness* well-bred politeness 34 *love* friendship; *wont* accustomed

35 You bear too stubborn and too strange a hand
Over your friend that loves you.
  BRUTUS   Cassius,
37 Be not deceived. If I have veiled my look,
I turn the trouble of my countenance
39 Merely upon myself. Vexèd I am
40 Of late with passions of some difference,
41 Conceptions only proper to myself,
42 Which give some soil, perhaps, to my behaviors;
But let not therefore my good friends be grieved
(Among which number, Cassius, be you one)
45 Nor construe any further my neglect
Than that poor Brutus, with himself at war,
47 Forgets the shows of love to other men.
  CASSIUS
48 Then, Brutus, I have much mistook your passion;
49 By means whereof this breast of mine hath buried
Thoughts of great value, worthy cogitations.
Tell me, good Brutus, can you see your face?
  BRUTUS
No, Cassius; for the eye sees not itself
But by reflection, by some other things.
54 CASSIUS 'Tis just.
And it is very much lamented, Brutus,
56 That you have no such mirrors as will turn
57 Your hidden worthiness into your eye,
58 That you might see your shadow. I have heard
59 Where many of the best respect in Rome
(Except immortal Caesar), speaking of Brutus
And groaning underneath this age's yoke,
Have wished that noble Brutus had his eyes.
  BRUTUS
Into what dangers would you lead me, Cassius,
That you would have me seek into myself
For that which is not in me?
  CASSIUS
Therefore, good Brutus, be prepared to hear;
And since you know you cannot see yourself
68 So well as by reflection, I, your glass,
69 Will modestly discover to yourself
That of yourself which you yet know not of.
71 And be not jealous on me, gentle Brutus.
72 Were I a common laughter, or did use
73 To stale with ordinary oaths my love

To every new protester; if you know   74
That I do fawn on men and hug them hard,
And after scandal them; or if you know   76
That I profess myself in banqueting   77
To all the rout, then hold me dangerous.   78
    Flourish and shout.
BRUTUS
What means this shouting? I do fear the people
Choose Caesar for their king.
CASSIUS   Ay, do you fear it?
Then must I think you would not have it so.
BRUTUS
I would not, Cassius; yet I love him well.
But wherefore do you hold me here so long?
What is it that you would impart to me?
If it be aught toward the general good,   85
Set honor in one eye and death i' th' other,
And I will look on both indifferently;   87
For let the gods so speed me as I love   88
The name of honor more than I fear death.
CASSIUS
I know that virtue to be in you, Brutus,
As well as I do know your outward favor.   91
Well, honor is the subject of my story.
I cannot tell what you and other men
Think of this life; but for my single self,   94
I had as lief not be as live to be   95
In awe of such a thing as I myself.   96
I was born free as Caesar; so were you.
We both have fed as well, and we can both
Endure the winter's cold as well as he.
For once, upon a raw and gusty day,
The troubled Tiber chafing with her shores,   101
Caesar said to me, 'Dar'st thou, Cassius, now
Leap in with me into this angry flood
And swim to yonder point?' Upon the word,
Accoutred as I was, I plungèd in   105
And bade him follow. So indeed he did.
The torrent roared, and we did buffet it
With lusty sinews, throwing it aside
And stemming it with hearts of controversy.   109
But ere we could arrive the point proposed,   110
Caesar cried, 'Help me, Cassius, or I sink!'
I, as Aeneas, our great ancestor,   112
Did from the flames of Troy upon his shoulder
The old Anchises bear, so from the waves of Tiber
Did I the tirèd Caesar. And this man
Is now become a god, and Cassius is
A wretched creature and must bend his body
If Caesar carelessly but nod on him.
He had a fever when he was in Spain,
And when the fit was on him, I did mark   120
How he did shake. 'Tis true, this god did shake.
His coward lips did from their color fly,   122
And that same eye whose bend doth awe the world   123
Did lose his luster. I did hear him groan.   124
Ay, and that tongue of his that bade the Romans
Mark him and write his speeches in their books,
'Alas,' it cried, 'give me some drink, Titinius,'
As a sick girl! Ye gods, it doth amaze me
A man of such a feeble temper should   129
So get the start of the majestic world   130
And bear the palm alone.   131
    Shout. Flourish.

35–36 *bear . . . Over* behave roughly and unnaturally to 37 *veiled my look* i.e. concealed my true friendship 39 *Merely* wholly 40 *passions . . . difference* conflicting emotions 41 *proper to* concerning 42 *soil* blemish 45 *construe* interpret (accent on first syllable) 47 *shows* manifestations 48 *passion* feelings 49 *buried* concealed 54 *just* true 56 *turn* reflect 57 *hidden worthiness* true nobility, inner worth 58 *shadow* image 59 *best respect* highest repute 68 *glass* mirror 69 *modestly* without exaggeration 71 *jealous on* suspicious of 72 *laughter* object of ridicule; *did use* were accustomed 73 *stale* cheapen; *ordinary* tavern (?), commonplace (?) 74 *protester* one who easily declares friendship 76 *scandal* slander 77 *profess myself* declare my friendship 78 *rout* rabble s.d. *Flourish* elaborate trumpet call 85 *general good* welfare of the state 87 *indifferently* impartially 88 *speed me* make me prosper 91 *favor* appearance 94 *single* particular 95 *lief . . . as* rather than 96 *such . . . myself* i.e. a mere mortal 101 *chafing with* raging against 105 *Accoutred* fully armed 109 *stemming . . . controversy* making headway with keen competition 110 *arrive* attain 112 *Aeneas* founder of the Roman state and hero of Virgil's *Aeneid*; Anchises was his father 120 *fit* periodic chills; *mark* observe 122 *color* i.e. the color fled from his lips like cowardly soldiers deserting their flag 123 *bend* glance 124 *his* its 129 *temper* constitution 130 *get the start of* outstrip all others in 131 *palm* victor's prize

BRUTUS

Another general shout?
I do believe that these applauses are
For some new honors that are heaped on Caesar.

CASSIUS

Why, man, he doth bestride the narrow world
136 Like a Colossus, and we petty men
Walk under his huge legs and peep about
To find ourselves dishonorable graves.
139 Men at some time are masters of their fates.
The fault, dear Brutus, is not in our stars,
But in ourselves, that we are underlings.
'Brutus,' and 'Caesar.' What should be in that 'Caesar'?
143 Why should that name be sounded more than yours?
Write them together: yours is as fair a name.
Sound them: it doth become the mouth as well.
Weigh them: it is as heavy. Conjure with 'em:
147 'Brutus' will start a spirit as soon as 'Caesar.'
Now in the names of all the gods at once,
Upon what meat doth this our Caesar feed
That he is grown so great? Age, thou art shamed.
Rome, thou hast lost the breed of noble bloods.
152 When went there by an age since the great Flood
But it was famed with more than with one man?
When could they say (till now) that talked of Rome
155 That her wide walks encompassed but one man?
156 Now is it Rome indeed, and room enough,
When there is in it but one only man.
O, you and I have heard our fathers say
159 There was a Brutus once that would have brooked
160 Th' eternal devil to keep his state in Rome
161 As easily as a king.

BRUTUS

162 That you do love me I am nothing jealous.
163 What you would work me to, I have some aim.
How I have thought of this, and of these times,
I shall recount hereafter. For this present,
166 I would not so (with love I might entreat you)
Be any further moved. What you have said
I will consider; what you have to say
I will with patience hear, and find a time
170 Both meet to hear and answer such high things.
171 Till then, my noble friend, chew upon this:
Brutus had rather be a villager
Than to repute himself a son of Rome
174 Under these hard conditions as this time
Is like to lay upon us.

CASSIUS   I am glad
That my weak words have struck but thus much show
177 Of fire from Brutus.

Enter Caesar and his Train.

BRUTUS

The games are done, and Caesar is returning.

CASSIUS

As they pass by, pluck Casca by the sleeve,
180 And he will (after his sour fashion) tell you
What hath proceeded worthy note to-day.

BRUTUS

I will do so. But look you, Cassius,
The angry spot doth glow on Caesar's brow,
And all the rest look like a chidden train.
Calphurnia's cheek is pale, and Cicero
186 Looks with such ferret and such fiery eyes
As we have seen him in the Capitol,

Being crossed in conference by some senators.   188

CASSIUS

Casca will tell us what the matter is.

CAESAR Antonius.

ANTONY Caesar?

CAESAR

Let me have men about me that are fat,   192
Sleek-headed men, and such as sleep a-nights.   193
Yond Cassius has a lean and hungry look.   194
He thinks too much. Such men are dangerous.

ANTONY

Fear him not, Caesar; he's not dangerous.
He is a noble Roman, and well given.   197

CAESAR

Would he were fatter! But I fear him not.
Yet if my name were liable to fear,   199
I do not know the man I should avoid
So soon as that spare Cassius. He reads much,
He is a great observer, and he looks
Quite through the deeds of men. He loves no plays   203
As thou dost, Antony; he hears no music.   204
Seldom he smiles, and smiles in such a sort   205
As if he mocked himself and scorned his spirit
That could be moved to smile at anything.
Such men as he be never at heart's ease
Whiles they behold a greater than themselves,
And therefore are they very dangerous.
I rather tell thee what is to be feared
Than what I fear; for always I am Caesar.
Come on my right hand, for this ear is deaf,
And tell me truly what thou think'st of him.

      Sennet. Exeunt Caesar and his Train.
                   [Manet Casca.]

CASCA

You pulled me by the cloak. Would you speak with me?

BRUTUS

Ay, Casca. Tell us what hath chanced to-day
That Caesar looks so sad.   217

CASCA

Why, you were with him, were you not?

BRUTUS

I should not then ask Casca what had chanced.

CASCA Why, there was a crown offered him; and being
offered him, he put it by with the back of his hand thus;
and then the people fell a-shouting.

BRUTUS What was the second noise for?

CASCA Why, for that too.

---

136 *Colossus* gigantic statue; *petty* inconsiderable   139 *some* a particular
143 *sounded* pronounced (with pun on 'proclaimed')   147 *start* raise up
152 *Flood* Deucalion's flood, the classical analogue to Noah's   155 *walks*
parks and gardens surrounding ancient Rome   156 *Rome, room* (homo-
nyms)   159 *a Brutus* Lucius Junius Brutus, founder of the Roman Republic in 509 B.C.; *brooked* tolerated   160 *eternal* i.e. eternally damned;
devil (pronounced 'deil'); *his* the devil's   161 *As . . . king* as soon as tolerate
a king's doing so   162 *am nothing jealous* have no doubt   163 *work* persuade; *aim* idea   166 *so* that way   170 *meet* fitting; *high* serious   171
chew upon consider   174 *these* such   177 s.d. *Train* followers   180 *sour*
harsh   186 *ferret* like those of a ferret, a weasel-like animal with red eyes
188 *crossed* opposed; *conference* debate   192 *fat* plump (not 'obese')
193 *Sleek-headed* well-groomed   194 *lean* (proverbially associated with
envy)   197 *given* disposed   199 *my name . . . to* I were capable of   203
through . . . men i.e. to the motivations behind men's actions   204 *hears
no music* (cf. *Merchant of Venice*, V, i, 83–88: 'The man that hath no music
in himself . . . Is fit for treasons . . . . Let no such man be trusted.')   205
sort manner   217 *sad* serious

CASSIUS
　They shouted thrice. What was the last cry for?
CASCA　Why, for that too.
BRUTUS　Was the crown offered him thrice?
228 CASCA　Ay, marry, was't! and he put it by thrice, every
　　time gentler than other; and at every putting-by mine
230　honest neighbors shouted.
CASSIUS
　Who offered him the crown?
CASCA　　　　　　　　　　　　Why, Antony.
BRUTUS
233　Tell us the manner of it, gentle Casca.
CASCA　I can as well be hanged as tell the manner of it. It
　　was mere foolery; I did not mark it. I saw Mark Antony
　　offer him a crown – yet 'twas not a crown neither, 'twas
237　one of these coronets – and, as I told you, he put it by
238　once; but for all that, to my thinking, he would fain
　　have had it. Then he offered it to him again; then he put
　　it by again; but to my thinking, he was very loath to lay
　　his fingers off it. And then he offered it the third time.
242　He put it the third time by; and still as he refused it, the
243　rabblement hooted, and clapped their chopt hands, and
244　threw up their sweaty nightcaps, and uttered such a deal
　　of stinking breath because Caesar refused the crown that
246　it had, almost, choked Caesar; for he swounded and fell
　　down at it. And for mine own part, I durst not laugh, for
　　fear of opening my lips and receiving the bad air.
CASSIUS
249　But soft, I pray you. What, did Caesar swound?
CASCA　He fell down in the market place and foamed at
　　mouth and was speechless.
BRUTUS
252　'Tis very like he hath the falling sickness.
CASSIUS
　No, Caesar hath it not; but you, and I,
254　And honest Casca, we have the falling sickness.
CASCA　I know not what you mean by that, but I am sure
256　Caesar fell down. If the tag-rag people did not clap him
　　and hiss him, according as he pleased and displeased
258　them, as they use to do the players in the theatre, I am
　　no true man.
BRUTUS
　What said he when he came unto himself?
CASCA　Marry, before he fell down, when he perceived the
262　common herd was glad he refused the crown, he plucked
263　me ope his doublet and offered them his throat to cut.

228 *marry* indeed (originally an oath by the Virgin Mary)　230 *honest* worthy　233 *gentle* noble　237 *coronets* small crowns wreathed with laurel　238 *fain* willingly　242 *still* each time　243 *chopt* chapped　244 *nightcaps* i.e. the citizens' caps (contemptuous)　246 *swounded* fainted　249 *soft* slowly　252 *like* likely that (Plutarch suggests Caesar feigned an attack); *falling sickness* epilepsy　254 *we . . . sickness* i.e. we are declining (into subjection)　256 *tag-rag people* ragged rabble　258 *use* are accustomed　262–63 *plucked me* i.e. plucked (a colloquialism)　263 *doublet* short jacket　264 *An* if; *man . . . occupation* workingman (also 'man of action'?)　273 *sad* seriously　283 *put to silence* deprived of their tribuneships and exiled (?) or executed (?) (the tribunes were the guardians of the rights of the plebeians)　286 *promised forth* previously engaged　288 *hold* change not　293 *quick mettle* of a lively temperament　296 *tardy form* sluggish pose　297 *wit* intellect　298 *stomach* appetite, disposition; *disgest* digest　302 *come home to* visit　304 *the world* i.e. the times we are experiencing　306–07 *wrought . . . disposed* so worked upon as to change its natural qualities　310 *bear me hard* bear a grudge against me　312 *He* i.e. Brutus; *humor* persuade by flattery　313 *several hands* different handwritings　315 *tending . . . opinion* concerning the high respect　317 *glancèd* hinted　318 *him sure* himself firmly in power　319 *shake him* i.e. from his dominant position

An I had been a man of any occupation, if I would not 264
have taken him at a word I would I might go to hell
among the rogues. And so he fell. When he came to
himself again, he said, if he had done or said anything
amiss, he desired their worships to think it was his
infirmity. Three or four wenches where I stood cried
'Alas, good soul!' and forgave him with all their hearts.
But there's no heed to be taken of them. If Caesar had
stabbed their mothers, they would have done no less.
BRUTUS
　And after that, he came thus sad away?　　　　　　273
CASCA　Ay.
CASSIUS
　Did Cicero say anything?
CASCA　Ay, he spoke Greek.
CASSIUS　To what effect?
CASCA　Nay, an I tell you that, I'll ne'er look you i' th'
face again. But those that understood him smiled at one
another and shook their heads; but for mine own part,
it was Greek to me. I could tell you more news too.
Marullus and Flavius, for pulling scarfs off Caesar's
images, are put to silence. Fare you well. There was more 283
foolery yet, if I could remember it.
CASSIUS　Will you sup with me to-night, Casca?
CASCA　No, I am promised forth.　　　　　　　　　286
CASSIUS　Will you dine with me to-morrow?
CASCA　Ay, if I be alive, and your mind hold, and your 288
dinner worth eating.
CASSIUS　Good. I will expect you.
CASCA　Do so. Farewell both.　　　　　　　*Exit.*
BRUTUS
　What a blunt fellow is this grown to be!
　He was quick mettle when he went to school.　　293
CASSIUS
　So is he now in execution
　Of any bold or noble enterprise,
　However he puts on this tardy form.　　　　　296
　This rudeness is a sauce to his good wit,　　　297
　Which gives men stomach to disgest his words　298
　With better appetite.
BRUTUS
　And so it is. For this time I will leave you.
　To-morrow, if you please to speak with me,
　I will come home to you; or if you will,
　Come home to me, and I will wait for you.　　302
CASSIUS
　I will do so. Till then, think of the world.　*Exit Brutus.* 304
　Well, Brutus, thou art noble; yet I see
　Thy honorable mettle may be wrought　　　306
　From that it is disposed. Therefore it is meet
　That noble minds keep ever with their likes;
　For who so firm that cannot be seduced?
　Caesar doth bear me hard; but he loves Brutus.　310
　If I were Brutus now and he were Cassius,
　He should not humor me. I will this night,　312
　In several hands, in at his windows throw,　313
　As if they came from several citizens,
　Writings, all tending to the great opinion　315
　That Rome holds of his name; wherein obscurely
　Caesar's ambition shall be glancèd at.　　　317
　And after this let Caesar seat him sure,　　318
　For we will shake him, or worse days endure.　*Exit.* 319

*

I, iii

Thunder and lightning. Enter, [from opposite sides,]
Casca, [with his sword drawn,] and Cicero.

CICERO

1 Good even, Casca. Brought you Caesar home?
Why are you breathless? and why stare you so?

CASCA

3 Are not you moved when all the sway of earth
Shakes like a thing unfirm? O Cicero,
I have seen tempests when the scolding winds
6 Have rived the knotty oaks, and I have seen
Th' ambitious ocean swell and rage and foam
8 To be exalted with the threat'ning clouds;
But never till to-night, never till now,
Did I go through a tempest dropping fire.
Either there is a civil strife in heaven,
12 Or else the world, too saucy with the gods,
Incenses them to send destruction.

CICERO

Why, saw you any thing more wonderful?

CASCA

A common slave (you know him well by sight)
Held up his left hand, which did flame and burn
Like twenty torches joined; and yet his hand,
18 Not sensible of fire, remained unscorched.
Besides (I ha' not since put up my sword),
20 Against the Capitol I met a lion,
21 Who glazed upon me, and went surly by
22 Without annoying me. And there were drawn
23 Upon a heap a hundred ghastly women,
Transformèd with their fear, who swore they saw
Men, all in fire, walk up and down the streets.
26 And yesterday the bird of night did sit
Even at noonday upon the market place,
28 Hooting and shrieking. When these prodigies
Do so conjointly meet, let not men say
'These are their reasons – they are natural,'
For I believe they are portentous things
32 Unto the climate that they point upon.

CICERO

Indeed it is a strange-disposèd time.
34 But men may construe things after their fashion,
35 Clean from the purpose of the things themselves.
Comes Caesar to the Capitol to-morrow?

CASCA

He doth; for he did bid Antonius
Send word to you he would be there to-morrow.

CICERO

Good night then, Casca. This disturbèd sky
Is not to walk in.

CASCA   Farewell, Cicero.   *Exit Cicero.*
Enter Cassius.

CASSIUS

Who's there?

CASCA   A Roman.

CASSIUS   Casca, by your voice.

CASCA

Your ear is good. Cassius, what night is this?

CASSIUS

A very pleasing night to honest men.

CASCA

Who ever knew the heavens menace so?

CASSIUS

Those that have known the earth so full of faults.
For my part, I have walked about the streets,

Submitting me unto the perilous night,
And, thus unbracèd, Casca, as you see,   48
Have bared my bosom to the thunder-stone;   49
And when the cross blue lightning seemed to open   50
The breast of heaven, I did present myself
Even in the aim and very flash of it.

CASCA

But wherefore did you so much tempt the heavens?
It is the part of men to fear and tremble   54
When the most mighty gods by tokens send
Such dreadful heralds to astonish us.   56

CASSIUS

You are dull, Casca, and those sparks of life
That should be in a Roman you do want,   58
Or else you use not. You look pale, and gaze,
And put on fear, and cast yourself in wonder;   60
To see the strange impatience of the heavens;
But if you would consider the true cause –
Why all these fires, why all these gliding ghosts,
Why birds and beasts, from quality and kind;   64
Why old men, fools, and children calculate;   65
Why all these things change from their ordinance,   66
Their natures, and preformèd faculties,   67
To monstrous quality – why, you shall find   68
That heaven hath infused them with these spirits   69
To make them instruments of fear and warning
Unto some monstrous state.
Now could I, Casca, name to thee a man
Most like this dreadful night
That thunders, lightens, opens graves, and roars
As doth the lion in the Capitol;
A man no mightier than thyself or me
In personal action, yet prodigious grown
And fearful, as these strange eruptions are.   78

CASCA

'Tis Caesar that you mean. It is not, Cassius?

CASSIUS

Let it be who it is. For Romans now
Have thews and limbs like to their ancestors;
But woe the while, our fathers' minds are dead,   82
And we are governed with our mothers' spirits;
Our yoke and sufferance show us womanish.   84

CASCA

Indeed, they say the senators to-morrow
Mean to establish Caesar as a king,
And he shall wear his crown by sea and land
In every place save here in Italy.   88

I, iii A street 1 *Brought* accompanied, escorted 3 *sway* established
order 6 *rived* split 8 *exalted with* raised to the level of 12 *saucy* insolent
18 *sensible of* feeling 20 *Against* opposite 21 *glazed* stared 22–23
drawn . . . heap crowded together 23 *ghastly* pale as ghosts 26 *bird of
night* screech owl (proverbially ill-omened) 28 *prodigies* monstrous
events 32 *climate* region 34 *construe* (cf. I, ii, 45n.); *after their fashion*
each in his own way 35 *Clean . . . purpose* contrary to the meaning 48
unbracèd with doublet unbuttoned, i.e. exposed 49 *thunder-stone* thunderbolt, lightning 50 *cross* forked 54 *part* appropriate action 56 *heralds*
precursors; *astonish* terrify 58 *want* lack 60 *put on* manifest; *cast . . .
wonder* are astonished 64 *from . . . kind* contrary to their nature (in
behavior) 65 *old men* i.e. in their second childhood; *calculate* compute
future events (proverbially children and fools speak truth, without discourse of reason) 66 *ordinance* established modes of behavior 67 *preformèd faculties* congenital qualities 68 *monstrous* unnatural 69 *spirits*
powers (?), demons (?) 78 *fearful* causing fear; *eruptions* disturbances
of natural and accustomed order 82 *woe the while* alas for the times
84 *yoke and sufferance* i.e. meek endurance of tyranny 88 *every place* all
parts of the Roman Empire

CASSIUS

I know where I will wear this dagger then ;
Cassius from bondage will deliver Cassius.
91 Therein, ye gods, you make the weak most strong ;
Therein, ye gods, you tyrants do defeat.
Nor stony tower, nor walls of beaten brass,
Nor airless dungeon, nor strong links of iron,
95 Can be retentive to the strength of spirit ;
But life, being weary of these worldly bars,
Never lacks power to dismiss itself.
98 If I know this, know all the world besides,
That part of tyranny that I do bear
100 I can shake off at pleasure.
             Thunder still.
CASCA   So can I.
So every bondman in his own hand bears
The power to cancel his captivity.

CASSIUS

And why should Caesar be a tyrant then ?
Poor man ! I know he would not be a wolf
But that he sees the Romans are but sheep ;
106 He were no lion, were not Romans hinds.
Those that with haste will make a mighty fire
Begin it with weak straws. What trash is Rome,
What rubbish and what offal, when it serves
For the base matter to illuminate
So vile a thing as Caesar ! But, O grief,
Where hast thou led me ? I, perhaps, speak this
Before a willing bondman. Then I know
My answer must be made. But I am armed,
115 And dangers are to me indifferent.

CASCA

You speak to Casca, and to such a man
117 That is no fleering telltale. Hold, my hand.
118 Be factious for redress of all these griefs,
And I will set this foot of mine as far
As who goes farthest.
             [They shake hands.]
CASSIUS   There's a bargain made.
Now know you, Casca, I have moved already
Some certain of the noblest-minded Romans
123 To undergo with me an enterprise
124 Of honorable dangerous consequence ;
125 And I do know, by this they stay for me
126 In Pompey's Porch ; for now, this fearful night,
There is no stir or walking in the streets,

And the complexion of the element   128
Is fev'rous, like the work we have in hand,   129
Most bloody, fiery, and most terrible.
             Enter Cinna.
CASCA

Stand close awhile, for here comes one in haste.   131
CASSIUS

'Tis Cinna. I do know him by his gait.
He is a friend. Cinna, where haste you so ?
CINNA

To find out you. Who's that ? Metellus Cimber ?   134
CASSIUS

No, it is Casca, one incorporate   135
To our attempts. Am I not stayed for, Cinna ?
CINNA

I am glad on't. What a fearful night is this !   137
There's two or three of us have seen strange sights.
CASSIUS

Am I not stayed for ? Tell me.
CINNA   Yes, you are.
O Cassius, if you could
But win the noble Brutus to our party –
CASSIUS

Be you content. Good Cinna, take this paper
And look you lay it in the praetor's chair,   143
Where Brutus may but find it. And throw this
In at his window. Set this up with wax
Upon old Brutus' statue. All this done,   146
Repair to Pompey's Porch, where you shall find us.
Is Decius Brutus and Trebonius there ?   148
CINNA

All but Metellus Cimber, and he's gone
To seek you at your house. Well, I will hie   150
And so bestow these papers as you bade me.   151
CASSIUS

That done, repair to Pompey's Theatre.   *Exit Cinna.* 152
Come, Casca, you and I will yet ere day   153
See Brutus at his house. Three parts of him   154
Is ours already, and the man entire
Upon the next encounter yields him ours.   156
CASCA

O, he sits high in all the people's hearts ;
And that which would appear offense in us,
His countenance, like richest alchemy,   159
Will change to virtue and to worthiness.
CASSIUS

Him and his worth and our great need of him
You have right well conceited. Let us go,   162
For it is after midnight ; and ere day
We will awake him and be sure of him.   *Exeunt.*

*

91 *Therein* i.e. in suicide 95 *be retentive to* confine 98 *know all . . . besides* let everyone else know 100 s.d. *still* continually 106 *hinds* does (with pun on 'peasants') 115 *indifferent* a matter of indifference 117 *fleering* mocking, flattering 118 *factious* politically active 123 *undergo* undertake 124 *honorable* honorably 125 *by . . . stay* by this time they are waiting 126 *Pompey's Porch* the colonnade of the great theatre built by Pompey 128 *complexion . . . element* appearance of the sky 129 *fev'rous* feverish (the folio 'Fauors' is sometimes otherwise emended to 'favored,' i.e. featured) 131 *close* concealed 134 *find out* look for 135 *incorporate* closely associated 137 *on't* of it 143 *praetor's chair* official seat of the highest judicial magistrate, at that time Brutus (see II, iv, 35n.) 146 *old Brutus' statue* (see I, ii, 159n.) 148 *Decius Brutus* a kinsman of Marcus Brutus; his name was really Decimus 150 *hie* hasten 151 *bestow* distribute 152 *repair* return 153 *ere* before 154 *Three parts* three-quarters (?), three of the four humours in man (?) (see V, v, 73n.) 156 *yields him ours* i.e. will join our faction 159 *countenance* support ; *alchemy* the proto-science devoted to transmuting base metals into gold 162 *conceited* conceived (with pun on 'expressed in a fanciful simile')
II, i By the house of Brutus **s.d.** *orchard* garden 5 *When* (exclamation of impatience)

             Enter Brutus in his orchard.   II, i
BRUTUS

What, Lucius, ho !
I cannot by the progress of the stars
Give guess how near to day. Lucius, I say !
I would it were my fault to sleep so soundly.
When, Lucius, when ? Awake, I say ! What, Lucius !   5
             Enter Lucius.
LUCIUS Called you, my lord ?

BRUTUS
　　Get me a taper in my study, Lucius.
　　When it is lighted, come and call me here.
LUCIUS I will, my lord.   *Exit.*
BRUTUS
　　It must be by his death ; and for my part,
11　I know no personal cause to spurn at him,
12　But for the general. He would be crowned.
　　How that might change his nature, there's the question.
　　It is the bright day that brings forth the adder,
15　And that craves wary walking. Crown him that,
　　And then I grant we put a sting in him
17　That at his will he may do danger with.
　　Th' abuse of greatness is, when it disjoins
19　Remorse from power. And to speak truth of Caesar,
20　I have not known when his affections swayed
21　More than his reason. But 'tis a common proof
22　That lowliness is young ambition's ladder,
　　Whereto the climber upward turns his face ;
　　But when he once attains the upmost round,
　　He then unto the ladder turns his back,
26　Looks in the clouds, scorning the base degrees
　　By which he did ascend. So Caesar may.
28　Then lest he may, prevent. And since the quarrel
29　Will bear no color for the thing he is,
30　Fashion it thus : that what he is, augmented,
31　Would run to these and these extremities ;
　　And therefore think him as a serpent's egg,
33　Which, hatched, would as his kind grow mischievous,
　　And kill him in the shell.
　　　　Enter Lucius.
LUCIUS
35　The taper burneth in your closet, sir.
　　Searching the window for a flint, I found
　　This paper, thus sealed up ; and I am sure
　　It did not lie there when I went to bed.
　　　　Gives him the letter.
BRUTUS
　　Get you to bed again ; it is not day.
　　Is not to-morrow, boy, the ides of March ?
LUCIUS I know not, sir.
BRUTUS
42　Look in the calendar and bring me word.
LUCIUS I will, sir.   *Exit.*
BRUTUS
44　The exhalations, whizzing in the air,
　　Give so much light that I may read by them.
　　　　Opens the letter and reads.
　　　'Brutus, thou sleep'st. Awake, and see thyself !
47　　　Shall Rome, &c. Speak, strike, redress !'
　　'Brutus, thou sleep'st. Awake !'
　　Such instigations have been often dropped
　　Where I have took them up.
51　'Shall Rome, &c.' Thus must I piece it out :
52　Shall Rome stand under one man's awe ? What, Rome ?
53　My ancestors did from the streets of Rome
　　The Tarquin drive when he was called a king.
　　'Speak, strike, redress !' Am I entreated
　　To speak and strike ? O Rome, I make thee promise,
57　If the redress will follow, thou receivest
58　Thy full petition at the hand of Brutus !
　　　　Enter Lucius.
LUCIUS
59　Sir, March is wasted fifteen days.

Knock within.
BRUTUS
　　'Tis good. Go to the gate ; somebody knocks.
　　　　　　　　　　　　　　　[Exit Lucius.]
　　Since Cassius first did whet me against Caesar,
　　I have not slept.
　　Between the acting of a dreadful thing
　　And the first motion, all the interim is   64
　　Like a phantasma or a hideous dream.   65
　　The genius and the mortal instruments   66
　　Are then in council, and the state of a man,   67
　　Like to a little kingdom, suffers then
　　The nature of an insurrection.
　　　　Enter Lucius.
LUCIUS
　　Sir, 'tis your brother Cassius at the door,   70
　　Who doth desire to see you.
BRUTUS　　　　　　　　　　　　　　Is he alone ?
LUCIUS
　　No, sir, there are moe with him.   72
BRUTUS　　　　　　　　　　Do you know them ?
LUCIUS
　　No, sir. Their hats are plucked about their ears
　　And half their faces buried in their cloaks,
　　That by no means I may discover them   75
　　By any mark of favor.   76
BRUTUS　　　　　　　　Let 'em enter.   *[Exit Lucius.]*
　　They are the faction. O conspiracy,
　　Sham'st thou to show thy dang'rous brow by night,
　　When evils are most free ? O, then by day   79
　　Where wilt thou find a cavern dark enough
　　To mask thy monstrous visage ? Seek none, conspiracy.
　　Hide it in smiles and affability :
　　For if thou path, thy native semblance on,   83
　　Not Erebus itself were dim enough   84
　　To hide thee from prevention.   85
　　　　Enter the Conspirators, Cassius, Casca, Decius,
　　　　Cinna, Metellus [Cimber], and Trebonius.
CASSIUS
　　I think we are too bold upon your rest.   86
　　Good morrow, Brutus. Do we trouble you ?
BRUTUS
　　I have been up this hour, awake all night.
　　Know I these men that come along with you ?

11 *spurn at* kick against 12 *general* public welfare, health of the state
15 *craves* calls for; *Crown him that* i.e. king (a word Brutus here avoids)
17 *danger* harm 19 *Remorse* mercy 20 *affections swayed* passions ruled
21 *common proof* commonplace, conventional observation based on experience 22 *lowliness* apparent humility 26 *base degrees* lower rungs
of the ladder (with pun on 'lower grades of office,' possibly referring to
the Roman *'cursus honorum'*) 28 *prevent* take measures to forestall;
quarrel case (against Caesar) 29 *bear no color* carry no conviction 30
Fashion it put the case 31 *extremities* extremes (of tyranny) 33 *his kind*
its nature is 35 *closet* study 42 *calendar* (the Julian calendar, instituted
by Caesar in 46 B.C.) 44 *exhalations* meteors 47, 51 *&c.* (read '*et
cetera*') 52 *under . . . awe* in fear of one man 53 *ancestors* (see I, ii, 159n.)
57 *redress* i.e. correction of abuses in the Republic 58 *Thy full petition*
all you ask 59 *fifteen* (the Romans counted both the day from which and
the day to which they reckoned) 64 *motion* proposal 65 *phantasma*
hallucination, nightmare 66 *genius* guardian spirit; *mortal instruments*
intellectual and emotional faculties 67 *in council* deliberating; *of a man*
(many editors delete 'a') 70 *brother* i.e. brother-in-law (Cassius was
married to Brutus' sister, Junia) 72 *moe* more 75 *discover* recognize,
identify 76 *favor* appearance 79 *evils . . . free* evil things range abroad
most freely 83 *path* walk; *native semblance* true form 84 *Erebus* region
of primeval darkness between the upper Earth and Hades 85 *prevention*
being forestalled 86 *upon* in intruding on

CASSIUS

    Yes, every man of them; and no man here
    But honors you; and every one doth wish
    You had but that opinion of yourself
    Which every noble Roman bears of you.
    This is Trebonius.

BRUTUS   He is welcome hither.

CASSIUS

    This, Decius Brutus.

BRUTUS   He is welcome too.

CASSIUS

    This, Casca; this, Cinna; and this, Metellus Cimber.

BRUTUS

    They are all welcome.
98   What watchful cares do interpose themselves
    Betwixt your eyes and night?

CASSIUS

    Shall I entreat a word?
       They whisper.

DECIUS

    Here lies the east. Doth not the day break here?

CASCA No.

CINNA

    O, pardon, sir, it doth; and yon grey lines
104 That fret the clouds are messengers of day.

CASCA

    You shall confess that you are both deceived.
    Here, as I point my sword, the sun arises,
107 Which is a great way growing on the south,
108 Weighing the youthful season of the year.
    Some two months hence, up higher toward the north
110 He first presents his fire; and the high east
    Stands as the Capitol, directly here.

BRUTUS

    Give me your hands all over, one by one.

CASSIUS

    And let us swear our resolution.

BRUTUS

114 No, not an oath. If not the face of men,
115 The sufferance of our souls, the time's abuse –
116 If these be motives weak, break off betimes,
117 And every man hence to his idle bed.
118 So let high-sighted tyranny range on
119 Till each man drop by lottery. But if these
120 (As I am sure they do) bear fire enough

To kindle cowards and to steel with valor
The melting spirits of women, then, countrymen,   122
What need we any spur but our own cause   123
To prick us to redress? what other bond   124
Than secret Romans that have spoke the word   125
And will not palter? and what other oath   126
Than honesty to honesty engaged   127
That this shall be, or we will fall for it?
Swear priests and cowards and men cautelous,   129
Old feeble carrions and such suffering souls   130
That welcome wrongs; unto bad causes swear
Such creatures as men doubt; but do not stain
The even virtue of our enterprise,   133
Nor th' insuppressive mettle of our spirits,   134
To think that or our cause or our performance   135
Did need an oath; when every drop of blood
That every Roman bears, and nobly bears,
Is guilty of a several bastardy   138
If he do break the smallest particle
Of any promise that hath passed from him.

CASSIUS

    But what of Cicero? Shall we sound him?   141
    I think he will stand very strong with us.

CASCA

    Let us not leave him out.

CINNA   No, by no means.

METELLUS

    O, let us have him, for his silver hairs
    Will purchase us a good opinion   145
    And buy men's voices to commend our deeds.
    It shall be said his judgment ruled our hands.
    Our youths and wildness shall no whit appear,   148
    But all be buried in his gravity.   149

BRUTUS

    O, name him not. Let us not break with him;   150
    For he will never follow anything
    That other men begin.

CASSIUS   Then leave him out.

CASCA

    Indeed he is not fit.

DECIUS

    Shall no man else be touched but only Caesar?

CASSIUS

    Decius, well urged. I think it is not meet   155
    Mark Antony, so well beloved of Caesar,
    Should outlive Caesar. We shall find of him   157
    A shrewd contriver; and you know, his means,   158
    If he improve them, may well stretch so far   159
    As to annoy us all; which to prevent,   160
    Let Antony and Caesar fall together.

BRUTUS

    Our course will seem too bloody, Caius Cassius,
    To cut the head off and then hack the limbs,
    Like wrath in death and envy afterwards;   164
    For Antony is but a limb of Caesar.   165
    Let's be sacrificers, but not butchers, Caius.
    We all stand up against the spirit of Caesar,   167
    And in the spirit of men there is no blood.
    O that we then could come by Caesar's spirit   169
    And not dismember Caesar! But, alas,
    Caesar must bleed for it. And, gentle friends,   171
    Let's kill him boldly, but not wrathfully;
    Let's carve him as a dish fit for the gods,
    Not hew him as a carcass fit for hounds.

---

98 *watchful cares* concerns that keep you awake 104 *fret* ornamentally interlace 107 *growing on* toward 108 *Weighing* considering 110 *high* due, exact 114 *face* appearance (which should be identical with reality), i.e. the serious manner of the conspirators and the anxious manner of their fellow citizens 115 *sufferance* distress; *time's abuse* corruption of these days (i.e. Caesar's violation of the laws of the Republic) 116 *betimes* at once 117 *idle* unused 118 *high-sighted* looking down from on high (like a falcon), i.e. arrogant 119 *lottery* whim 120 *fire* i.e. spirit, courage 122 *melting* yielding 123 *What* why 124 *prick* spur 125 *secret Romans* the mere fact that we are Romans able to hold our tongues (?), sharing a secret (?); *spoke the word* given one another our word of honor 126 *palter* quibble 127 *honesty* personal honor; *engaged* pledged 129 *Swear* make swear, bind by oath; *cautelous* crafty, deceitful 130 *carrions* physical wrecks, practically corpses 133 *even* uniform, unblemished 134 *insuppressive* indomitable; *mettle* (see I, i, 61n.) 135 *or . . . or* either . . . or 138 *several* separate, individual 141 *sound* feel out 145 *purchase* procure; *opinion* reputation 148 *no whit* not at all 149 *gravity* sobriety and authority of character 150 *break with* put the matter to 155 *urged* recommended 157 *of* in 158 *shrewd contriver* formidable plotter; *means* capacity (to harm us) 159 *improve* exploit 160 *annoy* injure; *prevent* forestall 164 *envy* malice 165 *limb* mere appendage 167 *spirit* principles (i.e. Caesarism) 169 *come by* get at 171 *gentle* noble

175　And let our hearts, as subtle masters do,
　　　Stir up their servants to an act of rage
　　　And after seem to chide 'em. This shall make
178　Our purpose necessary, and not envious ;
　　　Which so appearing to the common eyes,
180　We shall be called purgers, not murderers.
　　　And for Mark Antony, think not of him ;
　　　For he can do no more than Caesar's arm
　　　When Caesar's head is off.
CASSIUS　　　　　　　　　Yet I fear him ;
184　For in the ingrafted love he bears to Caesar –
BRUTUS
　　　Alas, good Cassius, do not think of him !
　　　If he love Caesar, all that he can do
187　Is to himself – take thought, and die for Caesar.
188　And that were much he should ; for he is given
　　　To sports, to wildness, and much company.
TREBONIUS
190　There is no fear in him. Let him not die ;
　　　For he will live, and laugh at this hereafter.
　　　　　　　　　Clock strikes.
BRUTUS
　　　Peace ! Count the clock.
CASSIUS　　　　　　The clock hath stricken three.
TREBONIUS
　　　'Tis time to part.
CASSIUS　　　　　But it is doubtful yet
194　Whether Caesar will come forth to-day or no ;
　　　For he is superstitious grown of late,
196　Quite from the main opinion he held once
197　Of fantasy, of dreams, and ceremonies.
198　It may be these apparent prodigies,
　　　The unaccustomed terror of this night,
200　And the persuasion of his augurers
　　　May hold him from the Capitol to-day.
DECIUS
　　　Never fear that. If he be so resolved,
203　I can o'ersway him ; for he loves to hear
204　That unicorns may be betrayed with trees
205　And bears with glasses, elephants with holes,
206　Lions with toils, and men with flatterers ;
　　　But when I tell him he hates flatterers,
　　　He says he does, being then most flatterèd.
　　　Let me work ;
210　For I can give his humor the true bent
　　　And I will bring him to the Capitol.
CASSIUS
212　Nay, we will all of us be there to fetch him.
BRUTUS
213　By the eight hour. Is that the uttermost ?
CINNA
　　　Be that the uttermost, and fail not then.
METELLUS
215　Caius Ligarius doth bear Caesar hard,
216　Who rated him for speaking well of Pompey.
　　　I wonder none of you have thought of him.
BRUTUS
218　Now, good Metellus, go along by him.
　　　He loves me well, and I have given him reasons.
220　Send him but hither, and I'll fashion him.
CASSIUS
　　　The morning comes upon's. We'll leave you, Brutus.
　　　And, friends, disperse yourselves ; but all remember
　　　What you have said and show yourselves true Romans.

BRUTUS
　　　Good gentlemen, look fresh and merrily.　　　　224
　　　Let not our looks put on our purposes,　　　　225
　　　But bear it as our Roman actors do,　　　　226
　　　With untired spirits and formal constancy.　　　227
　　　And so good morrow to you every one.
　　　　　　　　　　　　Exeunt. Manet Brutus.
　　　Boy ! Lucius ! Fast asleep ? It is no matter.
　　　Enjoy the honey-heavy dew of slumber.　　　　230
　　　Thou hast no figures nor no fantasies　　　　231
　　　Which busy care draws in the brains of men ;
　　　Therefore thou sleep'st so sound.
　　　　　　　Enter Portia.
PORTIA　　　　　　　　　　Brutus, my lord.
BRUTUS
　　　Portia ! What mean you ? Wherefore rise you now ?
　　　It is not for your health thus to commit　　　　235
　　　Your weak condition to the raw cold morning.
PORTIA
　　　Nor for yours neither. Y' have ungently, Brutus,　237
　　　Stole from my bed. And yesternight at supper
　　　You suddenly arose and walked about,
　　　Musing and sighing with your arms across ;　　240
　　　And when I asked you what the matter was,
　　　You stared upon me with ungentle looks.
　　　I urged you further ; then you scratched your head
　　　And too impatiently stamped with your foot.
　　　Yet I insisted ; yet you answered not,
　　　But with an angry wafter of your hand　　　246
　　　Gave sign for me to leave you. So I did,
　　　Fearing to strengthen that impatience
　　　Which seemed too much enkindled, and withal
　　　Hoping it was but an effect of humor,　　　　250
　　　Which sometime hath his hour with every man.　251
　　　It will not let you eat not talk nor sleep,
　　　And could it work so much upon your shape
　　　As it hath much prevailed on your condition,　　254
　　　I should not know you Brutus. Dear my lord,　　255
　　　Make me acquainted with your cause of grief.
BRUTUS
　　　I am not well in health, and that is all.
PORTIA
　　　Brutus is wise and, were he not in health,
　　　He would embrace the means to come by it.　　259
BRUTUS
　　　Why, so I do. Good Portia, go to bed.

175–77 *And . . . chide 'em* i.e. let us not be wrathful in our hearts although our hands must be made to perform this violent act (in order to preserve the Republic) 178 *envious* malicious 180 *purgers* healers 184 *ingrafted* deeply implanted 187 *take thought* fall into a melancholy state 188 *that . . . should* it is unlikely that he would 190 *no fear* nothing to fear 194 *Whether* (pronounced, and often spelled, 'where' or 'whe'r') 196 *from the main* contrary to the strong 197 *fantasy* fancy, i.e. imaginary fears ; *ceremonies* portents 198 *apparent prodigies* manifest signs of disaster 200 *augurers* augurs (priests who interpreted omens) 203 *o'ersway* persuade 204 *betrayed with trees* tricked into running their horns into tree trunks, thence easily captured 205 *glasses* mirrors ; *holes* pits 206 *toils* snares 210 *humor* disposition ; *bent* direction 212 *fetch* escort 213 *eight* eighth ; *uttermost* latest 215 *bear Caesar hard* (see I, ii, 310n.) 216 *rated* upbraided 218 *him* his house 220 *fashion* shape (to our purposes) 224 *fresh* brightly 225 *put on* display 226 *bear it* play your roles 227 *untired* alert ; *formal constancy* proper self-possession 230 *honey-heavy dew* i.e. sweetly drowsy refreshment 231 *figures* figments of imagination 235 *commit* expose 237 *ungently* ignobly, discourteously 240 *across* folded across your chest (a sign of melancholy) 246 *wafter* wafture, gesture 250 *effect of humor* symptom of a temporary mood 251 *his* its 254 *condition* disposition 255 *know you* recognize you as 259 *embrace* adopt ; *come by* regain

PORTIA

261 Is Brutus sick, and is it physical
262 To walk unbracèd and suck up the humors
Of the dank morning? What, is Brutus sick,
And will he steal out of his wholesome bed
265 To dare the vile contagion of the night,
266 And tempt the rheumy and unpurgèd air,
To add unto his sickness? No, my Brutus.
268 You have some sick offense within your mind,
269 Which by the right and virtue of my place
[Kneels.]
I ought to know of; and upon my knees
271 I charm you, by my once commended beauty,
By all your vows of love, and that great vow
273 Which did incorporate and make us one,
274 That you unfold to me, your self, your half,
275 Why you are heavy – and what men to-night
Have had resort to you; for here have been
Some six or seven, who did hide their faces
Even from darkness.

BRUTUS   Kneel not, gentle Portia.
[Raises her.]

PORTIA

I should not need if you were gentle Brutus.
Within the bond of marriage, tell me, Brutus,
281 Is it excepted I should know no secrets
That appertain to you? Am I your self
283 But, as it were, in sort or limitation?
284 To keep with you at meals, comfort your bed,
285 And talk to you sometimes? Dwell I but in the suburbs
Of your good pleasure? If it be no more,
Portia is Brutus' harlot, not his wife.

BRUTUS

You are my true and honorable wife,
As dear to me as are the ruddy drops
That visit my sad heart.

PORTIA

If this were true, then should I know this secret.
I grant I am a woman; but withal
A woman that Lord Brutus took to wife.
I grant I am a woman; but withal
295 A woman well-reputed, Cato's daughter.
Think you I am no stronger than my sex,
Being so fathered and so husbanded?
298 Tell me your counsels; I will not disclose 'em.
299 I have made strong proof of my constancy,

Giving myself a voluntary wound
Here, in the thigh. Can I bear that with patience,
And not my husband's secrets?

BRUTUS   O ye gods,
Render me worthy of this noble wife!
Knock.
Hark, hark! One knocks. Portia, go in awhile,
And by and by thy bosom shall partake
The secrets of my heart.
All my engagements I will construe to thee,   307
All the charactery of my sad brows.   308
Leave me with haste.   *Exit Portia.*
Lucius, who's that knocks?
Enter Lucius and [Caius] Ligarius.

LUCIUS

Here is a sick man that would speak with you.

BRUTUS

Caius Ligarius, that Metellus spake of.
Boy, stand aside. Caius Ligarius, how?   312

CAIUS

Vouchsafe good morrow from a feeble tongue.   313

BRUTUS

O, what a time have you chose out, brave Caius,   314
To wear a kerchief! Would you were not sick.   315

CAIUS

I am not sick if Brutus have in hand
Any exploit worthy the name of honor.

BRUTUS

Such an exploit have I in hand, Ligarius,
Had you a healthful ear to hear of it.

CAIUS

By all the gods that Romans bow before,
I here discard my sickness.
[Throws off his kerchief.]   Soul of Rome,
Brave son derived from honorable loins,   322
Thou like an exorcist hast conjured up   323
My mortifièd spirit. Now bid me run,   324
And I will strive with things impossible;
Yea, get the better of them. What's to do?

BRUTUS

A piece of work that will make sick men whole.   327

CAIUS

But are not some whole that we must make sick?   328

BRUTUS

That must we also. What it is, my Caius,
I shall unfold to thee as we are going   330
To whom it must be done.   331

CAIUS   Set on your foot,
And with a heart new-fired I follow you,
To do I know not what; but it sufficeth
That Brutus leads me on.
Thunder.

BRUTUS   Follow me then.   *Exeunt.*

*

Thunder and lightning. Enter Julius Caesar, in his   **II, ii**
nightgown.

CAESAR

Nor heaven nor eath have been at peace to-night.   1
Thrice hath Calphurnia in her sleep cried out
'Help, ho! They murder Caesar!' Who's within?   3
Enter a Servant.

SERVANT My lord?

---

261 *physical* healthful   262 *unbracèd* (see I, iii, 48n.); *humors* mists, dews   265 *vile . . . night* (night air was thought to be poisonous)   266 *tempt* risk; *rheumy* moist; *unpurgèd* not purified (by the sun)   268 *sick offense* harmful illness   269 *virtue* power; *place* (as your wife)   271 *charm* solemnly entreat   273 *incorporate* make us one flesh   274 *unfold* disclose; *self* other self; *half* i.e. wife   275 *heavy* sad   281 *excepted* made an exception that   283 *in . . . limitation* after a fashion or under restriction (a legalism)   284 *keep* keep company   285 *suburbs* outlying districts (notorious for their brothels and other disreputable haunts)   295 *Cato* (Cato of Utica, famous for absolute moral integrity, fought with Pompey against Caesar and killed himself to avoid capture in 46 B.C.; he was Brutus' uncle as well as father-in-law)   298 *counsels* secrets   299 *proof* trial; *constancy* fortitude   307 *engagements* commitments; *construe* explain fully   308 *the charactery of* that which is written in shorthand upon (accent 'charàctery')   312 *how* how are you   313 *Vouchsafe* deign to accept   314 *brave* noble   315 *To . . . kerchief* i.e. to be sick   322 *derived . . . loins* (see I, ii, 159n.)   323 *exorcist* conjurer   324 *mortifièd* deadened, as if dead   327 *whole* healthy   328 *make sick* i.e. kill   330 *unfold* disclose   331 *To whom* to the house of him to whom; *Set on* advance
II, ii Within the house of Caesar   s.d. *nightgown* dressing gown   1 *Nor . . . nor* neither . . . nor   3 *Who's within* which of the servants is about

CAESAR

5 Go bid the priests do present sacrifice,
6 And bring me their opinions of success.

SERVANT I will, my lord.   Exit.

Enter Calphurnia.

CALPHURNIA

What mean you, Caesar? Think you to walk forth?
You shall not stir out of your house to-day.

CAESAR

Caesar shall forth. The things that threatened me
Ne'er looked but on my back. When they shall see
The face of Caesar, they are vanishèd.

CALPHURNIA

13 Caesar, I never stood on ceremonies,
Yet now they fright me. There is one within,
Besides the things that we have heard and seen,
16 Recounts most horrid sights seen by the watch.
A lioness hath whelpèd in the streets,
And graves have yawned and yielded up their dead.
Fierce fiery warriors fought upon the clouds
20 In ranks and squadrons and right form of war,
Which drizzled blood upon the Capitol.
22 The noise of battle hurtled in the air,
Horses did neigh, and dying men did groan,
And ghosts did shriek and squeal about the streets.
25 O Caesar, these things are beyond all use,
And I do fear them.

CAESAR   What can be avoided
Whose end is purposed by the mighty gods?
Yet Caesar shall go forth; for these predictions
29 Are to the world in general as to Caesar.

CALPHURNIA

When beggars die there are no comets seen;
31 The heavens themselves blaze forth the death of princes.

CAESAR

Cowards die many times before their deaths;
The valiant never taste of death but once.
Of all the wonders that I yet have heard,
It seems to me most strange that men should fear,
Seeing that death, a necessary end,
Will come when it will come.

Enter a Servant.   What say the augurers?

SERVANT

They would not have you to stir forth to-day.
Plucking the entrails of an offering forth,
They could not find a heart within the beast.

CAESAR

The gods do this in shame of cowardice.
42 Caesar should be a beast without a heart
If he should stay at home to-day for fear.
No, Caesar shall not. Danger knows full well
That Caesar is more dangerous than he.
We are two lions littered in one day,
And I the elder and more terrible,
And Caesar shall go forth.

CALPHURNIA   Alas, my lord,
49 Your wisdom is consumed in confidence!
Do not go forth to-day! Call it my fear
That keeps you in the house and not your own.
We'll send Mark Antony to the Senate House,
And he shall say you are not well to-day.
Let me upon my knee prevail in this.

CAESAR

Mark Antony shall say I am not well,

And for thy humor I will stay at home.   56

Enter Decius.

Here's Decius Brutus; he shall tell them so.

DECIUS

Caesar, all hail! Good morrow, worthy Caesar;
I come to fetch you to the Senate House.   59

CAESAR

And you are come in very happy time   60
To bear my greeting to the senators
And tell them that I will not come to-day.
Cannot, is false; and that I dare not, falser:
I will not come to-day. Tell them so, Decius.

CALPHURNIA

Say he is sick.

CAESAR   Shall Caesar send a lie?
Have I in conquest stretched mine arm so far
To be afeard to tell greybeards the truth!
Decius, go tell them Caesar will not come.

DECIUS

Most mighty Caesar, let me know some cause,
Lest I be laughed at when I tell them so.

CAESAR

The cause is in my will: I will not come.
That is enough to satisfy the Senate;
But for your private satisfaction,
Because I love you, I will let you know.
Calphurnia here, my wife, stays me at home.   75
She dreamt to-night she saw my statue,   76
Which, like a fountain with an hundred spouts,
Did run pure blood; and many lusty Romans   78
Came smiling and did bathe their hands in it.
And these does she apply for warnings and portents   80
And evil imminent, and on her knee
Hath begged that I will stay at home to-day.

DECIUS

This dream is all amiss interpreted;
It was a vision fair and fortunate.
Your statue spouting blood in many pipes,
In which so many smiling Romans bathed,
Signifies that from you great Rome shall suck
Reviving blood, and that great men shall press
For tinctures, stains, relics, and cognizance.   89
This by Calphurnia's dream is signified.

CAESAR

And this way have you well expounded it.

DECIUS

I have, when you have heard what I can say;
And know it now. The Senate have concluded   93
To give this day a crown to mighty Caesar.
If you shall send them word you will not come,
Their minds may change. Besides, it were a mock   96
Apt to be rendered, for some one to say

5 *priests* augurs (see II, i, 200n.); *present* immediate   6 *opinions of success* judgments of the success or failure of my plans   13 *stood on ceremonies* heeded portents   16 *watch* nightwatchmen   20 *right form* regular order   22 *hurtled* clashed   25 *use* normal experience   29 *Are to* are as applicable to   31 *blaze forth* i.e. proclaim   42 *should* would indeed   49 *consumed in confidence* destroyed by overconfidence   56 *humor* whim   59 *fetch* escort   60 *in . . . time* at a most opportune moment   75 *stays* keeps   76 *statue* (trisyllabic)   78 *lusty* vigorous, gallant   80 *apply for* interpret as; *portents* (accent 'portènts')   89 *tinctures* stains (with heraldic and alchemical associations); *relics* (as of holy martyrs); *cognizance* an identifying emblem worn by a nobleman's followers   93 *concluded* formally determined   96-97 *mock . . . rendered* sarcastic remark likely to be made

'Break up the Senate till another time,
When Caesar's wife shall meet with better dreams.'
100 If Caesar hide himself, shall they not whisper
'Lo, Caesar is afraid'?
Pardon me, Caesar; for my dear dear love
103 To your proceeding bids me tell you this,
104 And reason to my love is liable.

CAESAR
How foolish do your fears seem now, Calphurnia!
I am ashamèd I did yield to them.
107 Give me my robe, for I will go.
Enter Brutus, Ligarius, Metellus, Casca,
Trebonius, Cinna, and Publius.
And look where Publius is come to fetch me.

PUBLIUS
Good morrow, Caesar.

CAESAR   Welcome, Publius.
What, Brutus, are you stirred so early too?
Good morrow, Casca. Caius Ligarius,
112 Caesar was ne'er so much your enemy
113 As that same ague which hath made you lean.
What is't o'clock?

BRUTUS   Caesar, 'tis strucken eight.

CAESAR
I thank you for your pains and courtesy.
Enter Antony.
See, Antony, that revels long a-nights,
Is notwithstanding up. Good morrow, Antony.

ANTONY
118 So to most noble Caesar.

CAESAR   Bid them prepare within.
I am to blame to be thus waited for.
Now, Cinna. Now, Metellus. What, Trebonius;
I have an hour's talk in store for you;
Remember that you call on me to-day;
Be near me, that I may remember you.

TREBONIUS
124 Caesar, I will. *[aside]* And so near will I be
That your best friends shall wish I had been further.

CAESAR
Good friends, go in and taste some wine with me,
And we (like friends) will straightway go together.

BRUTUS *[aside]*
128 That every like is not the same, O Caesar,
129 The heart of Brutus erns to think upon.   *Exeunt.*

*

100 *shall* will indeed   103 *proceeding* advancement (?), career (?)   104
reason . . . liable i.e. my love outweighs my judgment in speaking thus
freely to you   107 *robe* toga   112 *enemy* (Ligarius, like Brutus, Cassius,
and Cicero, had supported Pompey against Caesar)   113 *lean* (apparently
the same actor took the parts of Cassius and Ligarius)   118 *So* likewise;
prepare i.e. set out the wine   124–25 *And . . . further* (actually Trebonius
lures Antony out of the way before the assassination)   128 *every . . . same*
i.e. appearance is not always the same as reality   129 *erns* grieves
II, iii A street near the Capitol   6 *bent* directed   7 *Security* overconfidence;
way path, opportunity   9 *lover* friend   12 *as a suitor* pretending to be a
petitioner   14 *Out . . . emulation* i.e. beyond the reach of envious rivalry
16 *contrive* conspire
II, iv Before the house of Brutus   6 *constancy* self-control, fortitude
8 *might* strength   9 *counsel* a secret (i.e. Brutus' secret which he has told
her according to his promise; that he has had no opportunity to do so is
irrelevant by the Elizabethan theatrical convention of 'double time')
14 *take good note* observe well   18 *bustling . . . fray* confused noise as in
battle   20 *Sooth* truly   s.d. *Soothsayer* (the same who had warned Caesar
at I, ii, 18)

Enter Artemidorus [reading a paper].   II, iii
[ARTEMIDORUS] 'Caesar, beware of Brutus; take heed
of Cassius; come not near Casca; have an eye to Cinna;.
trust not Trebonius; mark well Metellus Cimber;
Decius Brutus loves thee not; thou hast wronged Caius
Ligarius. There is but one mind in all these men, and it
is bent against Caesar. If thou beest not immortal, look 6
about you. Security gives way to conspiracy. The 7
mighty gods defend thee!
                    'Thy lover, 9
                       'Artemidorus.'
Here will I stand till Caesar pass along
And as a suitor will I give him this.
My heart laments that virtue cannot live   12
Out of the teeth of emulation.
If thou read this, O Caesar, thou mayest live;   14
If not, the Fates with traitors do contrive.   *Exit.* 16

*

Enter Portia and Lucius.   II, iv
PORTIA
I prithee, boy, run to the Senate House.
Stay not to answer me, but get thee gone!
Why dost thou stay?

LUCIUS   To know my errand, madam.

PORTIA
I would have had thee there and here again
Ere I can tell thee what thou shouldst do there.
[Aside]
O constancy, be strong upon my side,   6
Set a huge mountain 'tween my heart and tongue!
I have a man's mind, but a woman's might.   8
How hard it is for women to keep counsel!   9
Art thou here yet?

LUCIUS   Madam, what should I do?
Run to the Capitol and nothing else?
And so return to you and nothing else?

PORTIA
Yes, bring me word, boy, if thy lord look well,
For he went sickly forth; and take good note   14
What Caesar doth, what suitors press to him.
Hark, boy! What noise is that?

LUCIUS
I hear none, madam.

PORTIA   Prithee listen well.
I heard a bustling rumor like a fray,   18
And the wind brings it from the Capitol.

LUCIUS
Sooth, madam, I hear nothing.   20
Enter the Soothsayer.

PORTIA
Come hither, fellow. Which way hast thou been?

SOOTHSAYER
At mine own house, good lady.

PORTIA
What is't o'clock?

SOOTHSAYER   About the ninth hour, lady.

PORTIA
Is Caesar yet gone to the Capitol?

SOOTHSAYER
Madam, not yet. I go to take my stand,
To see him pass on to the Capitol.

PORTIA
Thou hast some suit to Caesar, hast thou not?
SOOTHSAYER
That I have, lady, if it will please Caesar
To be so good to Caesar as to hear me:
I shall beseech him to befriend himself.
PORTIA
Why, know'st thou any harm's intended towards him?
SOOTHSAYER
32 None that I know will be, much that I fear may chance.
Good morrow to you. Here the street is narrow.
The throng that follows Caesar at the heels,
35 Of Senators, of praetors, common suitors,
Will crowd a feeble man almost to death.
37 I'll get me to a place more void and there
Speak to great Caesar as he comes along.   *Exit.*
PORTIA
I must go in. Ay me, how weak a thing
The heart of woman is! O Brutus,
The heavens speed thee in thine enterprise!
Sure the boy heard me. – Brutus hath a suit
That Caesar will not grant. – O, I grow faint. –
44 Run, Lucius, and commend me to my lord;
45 Say I am merry. Come to me again
And bring me word what he doth say to thee.
      Exeunt [severally].

*

III, i   *Flourish. Enter Caesar, Brutus, Cassius, Casca,*
Decius, Metellus, Trebonius, Cinna, Antony,
Lepidus, Artemidorus, [Popilius,] Publius, and the
Soothsayer.
CAESAR
The ides of March are come.
SOOTHSAYER
Ay, Caesar, but not gone.
ARTEMIDORUS
3 Hail, Caesar! Read this schedule.
DECIUS
Trebonius doth desire you to o'erread
(At your best leisure) this his humble suit.
ARTEMIDORUS
O Caesar, read mine first; for mine's a suit
7 That touches Caesar nearer. Read it, great Caesar!
CAESAR
8 What touches us ourself shall be last served.
ARTEMIDORUS
Delay not, Caesar! Read it instantly!
CAESAR
What, is the fellow mad?
10 PUBLIUS   Sirrah, give place.
CASSIUS
What, urge you your petitions in the street?
12 Come to the Capitol.
     [Caesar goes to the Capitol, the rest following.]
POPILIUS
13 I wish your enterprise to-day may thrive.
CASSIUS
What enterprise, Popilius?
POPILIUS   Fare you well.
     [Advances to Caesar.]
BRUTUS
What said Popilius Lena?

CASSIUS
He wished to-day our enterprise might thrive.
I fear our purpose is discoverèd.
BRUTUS
Look how he makes to Caesar. Mark him.   18
CASSIUS
Casca, be sudden, for we fear prevention.   19
Brutus, what shall be done? If this be known,
Cassius or Caesar never shall turn back,   21
For I will slay myself.
BRUTUS   Cassius, be constant.   22
Popilius Lena speaks not of our purposes;
For look, he smiles, and Caesar doth not change.   24
CASSIUS
Trebonius knows his time; for look you, Brutus,
He draws Mark Antony out of the way.
     [Exeunt Antony and Trebonius.]
DECIUS
Where is Metellus Cimber? Let him go
And presently prefer his suit to Caesar.   28
BRUTUS
He is addressed. Press near and second him.   29
CINNA
Casca, you are the first that rears your hand.
CAESAR
Are we all ready? What is now amiss
That Caesar and his Senate must redress?
METELLUS
Most high, most mighty, and most puissant Caesar,
Metellus Cimber throws before thy seat
An humble heart.
     [Kneels.]
CAESAR   I must prevent thee, Cimber.   35
These couchings and these lowly courtesies   36
Might fire the blood of ordinary men
And turn preordinance and first decree   38
Into the lane of children. Be not fond   39
To think that Caesar bears such rebel blood   40
That will be thawed from the true quality   41
With that which melteth fools – I mean, sweet words,
Low-crookèd curtsies, and base spaniel fawning.   43
Thy brother by decree is banishèd.
If thou dost bend and pray and fawn for him,
I spurn thee like a cur out of my way.

32 *chance* happen   35 *praetors* high-ranking judges in the administration of Roman law (Caesar increased their number from eight to sixteen. Brutus, Cassius, and Cinna were praetors in 44 B.C., Brutus being '*praetor urbanus*,' the chief justice of the state and second only in authority to the two consuls – Caesar, who had been appointed Dictator for life, and Antony. Cassius, as '*praetor peregrinus*,' ranked immediately below Brutus.)   37 *void* empty, spacious   44 *commend me* give my best love and wishes   45 *merry* in good spirits
III, i Before the Capitol   3 *schedule* document   7 *touches* concerns   8 *served* attended to   10 *Sirrah* (contemptuous form of address); *give place* get out of the way   12 s.d. *the Capitol* (possibly the 'inner stage,' probably just before it)   13 *enterprise* undertaking   18 *makes to* advances toward   19 *sudden* quick; *prevention* being forestalled   21 *turn back* return alive   22 *constant* unshaken   24 *Caesar . . . change* i.e. his expression does not change   28 *presently* immediately; *prefer* present   29 *addressed* ready   35 *prevent* forestall   36 *couchings* bowings; *courtesies* curtsies, bowings   38 *preordinance . . . decree* the original, time-honored laws by which men organized themselves into societies, i.e. the laws of man in accordance with the laws of nature and of God   39 *lane* path, byway (many editors emend to 'law'); *fond* so foolish as   40 *rebel* untrue to its own nature   41 *thawed* i.e. altered; *true* proper   43 *spaniel* i.e. hypocritically flattering

47 Know, Caesar doth not wrong, nor without cause
Will he be satisfied.

METELLUS
Is there no voice more worthy than my own,
To sound more sweetly in great Caesar's ear
51 For the repealing of my banished brother?

BRUTUS
I kiss thy hand, but not in flattery, Caesar,
Desiring thee that Publius Cimber may
54 Have an immediate freedom of repeal.

CAESAR
What, Brutus?

CASSIUS Pardon, Caesar! Caesar, pardon!
As low as to thy foot doth Cassius fall
To beg enfranchisement for Publius Cimber.

CAESAR
I could be well moved, if I were as you;
If I could pray to move, prayers would move me:
60 But I am constant as the Northern Star,
61 Of whose true-fixed and resting quality
62 There is no fellow in the firmament.
63 The skies are painted with unnumb'red sparks,
They are all fire, and every one doth shine;
65 But there's but one in all doth hold his place.
So in the world: 'tis furnished well with men,
67 And men are flesh and blood, and apprehensive;
Yet in the number I do know but one
69 That unassailable holds on his rank,
Unshaked of motion; and that I am he,
Let me a little show it, even in this –
72 That I was constant Cimber should be banished
And constant do remain to keep him so.

CINNA
O Caesar.

74 CAESAR Hence! Wilt thou lift up Olympus?

DECIUS
Great Caesar.

75 CAESAR Doth not Brutus bootless kneel?

CASCA
Speak hands for me.
They stab Caesar [– Casca first, Brutus last].

CAESAR
77 *Et tu, Brutè?* – Then fall Caesar.
Dies.

CINNA
Liberty! Freedom! Tyranny is dead!

Run hence, proclaim, cry it about the streets!

CASSIUS
Some to the common pulpits and cry out 80
'Liberty, freedom, and enfranchisement!'

BRUTUS
People and senators, be not affrighted.
Fly not; stand still. Ambition's debt is paid. 83

CASCA
Go to the pulpit, Brutus.

DECIUS And Cassius too.

BRUTUS
Where's Publius? 85

CINNA
Here, quite confounded with this mutiny. 86

METELLUS
Stand fast together, lest some friend of Caesar's 87
Should chance –

BRUTUS
Talk not of standing! Publius, good cheer. 89
There is no harm intended to your person
Nor to no Roman else. So tell them, Publius.

CASSIUS
And leave us, Publius, lest that the people,
Rushing on us, should do your age some mischief. 93

BRUTUS
Do so; and let no man abide this deed 94
But we the doers.
Enter Trebonius.

CASSIUS Where is Antony?

TREBONIUS
Fled to his house amazed. 96
Men, wives, and children stare, cry out, and run,
As it were doomsday.

BRUTUS Fates, we will know your pleasures.
That we shall die, we know; 'tis but the time,
And drawing days out, that men stand upon. 100

CASCA
Why, he that cuts off twenty years of life
Cuts off so many years of fearing death.

BRUTUS
Grant that, and then is death a benefit.
So are we Caesar's friends, that have abridged
His time of fearing death. Stoop, Romans, stoop,
And let us bathe our hands in Caesar's blood
Up to the elbows and besmear our swords.
Then walk we forth, even to the market place, 108
And waving our red weapons o'er our heads,
Let's all cry 'Peace, freedom, and liberty!'

CASSIUS
Stoop then and wash. How many ages hence
Shall this our lofty scene be acted over
In states unborn and accents yet unknown!

BRUTUS
How many times shall Caesar bleed in sport, 114
That now on Pompey's basis lies along 115
No worthier than the dust!

CASSIUS So oft as that shall be,
So often shall the knot of us be called 117
The men that gave their country liberty.

DECIUS
What, shall we forth? 119

CASSIUS Ay, every man away.
Brutus shall lead, and we will grace his heels 120
With the most boldest and best hearts of Rome.

47-48 *Know . . . satisfied* (it is possible that Shakespeare first wrote, 'Caesar did never wrong, but with just cause, Nor without cause will he be satisfied,' but altered it out of deference to the criticism of Ben Jonson) 51 *repealing* recalling from banishment 54 *freedom of repeal* permission to be recalled 60 *constant . . . Star* as fixed as the polestar (an ultimate symbol of constancy) 61 *resting* immovable 62 *fellow* equal 63 *painted* adorned 65 *hold* remain fixed in 67 *apprehensive* capable of knowing and reasoning 69 *holds . . . rank* remains fixed in his position 72 *constant* determined (resolutely) 74 *Olympus* a mountain in Greece, the home of the gods 75 *bootless* unavailingly 77 *Et tu, Brutè* and thou, Brutus (cf. Caesar's remark at III, i, 55) 80 *pulpits* platforms for delivering public speeches 83 *Ambition's debt* what was due to Caesar's ambition 85 *Publius* an old senator, too confused to flee 86 *mutiny* tumult 87 *fast* close 89 *standing* organizing resistance 93 *your age* i.e. you as an old man 94 *abide* stand the consequences of, be responsible for 96 *amazed* full of consternation 100 *drawing . . . upon* prolonging life, that men attach importance to 108 *market place* the Roman Forum 114 *in sport* for entertainment, i.e. as plays 115 *basis* pedestal of statue; *along* stretched out prostrate 117 *knot* group (of conspirators) 119 *forth* go out into the city 120 *grace* do honor to

Enter a Servant.

BRUTUS

122   Soft ! who comes here ? A friend of Antony's.

SERVANT

Thus, Brutus, did my master bid me kneel ;
Thus did Mark Antony bid me fall down ;
And being prostrate, thus he bade me say :

126   Brutus is noble, wise, valiant, and honest ;

127   Caesar was mighty, bold, royal, and loving.
Say I love Brutus and I honor him ;
Say I feared Caesar, honored him, and loved him.
If Brutus will vouchsafe that Antony

131   May safely come to him and be resolved
How Caesar hath deserved to lie in death,
Mark Antony shall not love Caesar dead
So well as Brutus living ; but will follow
The fortunes and affairs of noble Brutus

136   Thorough the hazards of this untrod state
With all true faith. So says my master Antony.

BRUTUS

Thy master is a wise and valiant Roman.
I never thought him worse.

140   Tell him, so please him come unto this place,
He shall be satisfied and, by my honor,
Depart untouched.

SERVANT   I'll fetch him presently.   *Exit.*

BRUTUS

143   I know that we shall have him well to friend.

CASSIUS

144   I wish we may. But yet have I a mind

145   That fears him much ; and my misgiving still

146   Falls shrewdly to the purpose.

Enter Antony.

BRUTUS

But here comes Antony. Welcome, Mark Antony.

ANTONY

O mighty Caesar ! dost thou lie so low ?
Are all thy conquests, glories, triumphs, spoils,
Shrunk to this little measure ? Fare thee well.
I know not, gentlemen, what you intend,

152   Who else must be let blood, who else is rank.
If I myself, there is no hour so fit
As Caesar's death's hour ; nor no instrument
Of half that worth as those your swords, made rich
With the most noble blood of all this world.

157   I do beseech ye, if you bear me hard,

158   Now, whilst your purpled hands do reek and smoke,

159   Fulfil your pleasure. Live a thousand years,

160   I shall not find myself so apt to die ;

161   No place will please me so, no mean of death,
As here by Caesar, and by you cut off,
The choice and master spirits of this age.

BRUTUS

O Antony, beg not your death of us !
Though now we must appear bloody and cruel,
As by our hands and this our present act
You see we do, yet see you but our hands
And this the bleeding business they have done.

169   Our hearts you see not. They are pitiful ;
And pity to the general wrong of Rome

171   (As fire drives out fire, so pity pity)
Hath done this deed on Caesar. For your part,
To you our swords have leaden points, Mark Antony.

174   Our arms in strength of malice, and our hearts

Of brothers' temper, do receive you in
With all kind love, good thoughts, and reverence.

CASSIUS

Your voice shall be as strong as any man's   177
In the disposing of new dignities.   178

BRUTUS

Only be patient till we have appeased
The multitude, beside themselves with fear,
And then we will deliver you the cause   181
Why I, that did love Caesar when I struck him,
Have thus proceeded.

ANTONY   I doubt not of your wisdom.
Let each man render me his bloody hand.
First, Marcus Brutus, will I shake with you ;
Next, Caius Cassius, do I take your hand ;
Now, Decius Brutus, yours ; now yours, Metellus ;
Yours, Cinna ; and, my valiant Casca, yours.
Though last, not least in love, yours, good Trebonius.
Gentlemen all – Alas, what shall I say ?
My credit now stands on such slippery ground   191
That one of two bad ways you must conceit me,   192
Either a coward or a flatterer.
That I did love thee, Caesar, O, 'tis true !
If then thy spirit look upon us now,
Shall it not grieve thee dearer than thy death   196
To see thy Antony making his peace,
Shaking the bloody fingers of thy foes,
Most noble ! in the presence of thy corse ?
Had I as many eyes as thou hast wounds,
Weeping as fast as they stream forth thy blood,
It would become me better than to close   202
In terms of friendship with thine enemies.
Pardon me, Julius ! Here wast thou bayed, brave hart ;   204
Here didst thou fall ; and here thy hunters stand,
Signed in thy spoil, and crimsoned in thy lethe.   206
O world, thou wast the forest to this hart ;
And this indeed, O world, the heart of thee !
How like a deer, stroken by many princes,   209
Dost thou here lie !

CASSIUS

Mark Antony –

ANTONY   Pardon me, Caius Cassius.
The enemies of Caesar shall say this ;
Then, in a friend, it is cold modesty.   213

CASSIUS

I blame you not for praising Caesar so ;
But what compact mean you to have with us ?   215

---

122 *Soft* wait a moment, slowly   **126** *honest* honorable   **127** *royal* nobly munificent   **131** *be resolved* have satisfactorily explained to him (?), be fully informed (?)   **136** *Thorough* (common dissyllabic form of 'through'); *untrod state* novel state of affairs (?), uncertain future (?)   **140** *so* if it should   **143** *to* as a   **144** *mind* presentiment   **145** *fears* distrusts; *still* always   **146** *Falls . . . purpose* turns out to be very near the truth   **152** *let blood* i.e. put to death; *rank* diseased (with pun on 'grown too strong')   **157** *bear me hard* bear me a grudge   **158** *purpled* i.e. with blood; *reek and smoke* i.e. steam (with warm blood)   **159** *Live* if I should live   **160** *apt* ready   **161** *so* so well; *mean* manner, means   **169** *pitiful* full of pity   **171** *pity pity* pity for the general wrong drove out pity for Caesar   **174–75** *Our arms . . . temper* both our arms, strong in the appearance of enmity, and our hearts, full of brotherly feeling   **177** *voice* vote   **178** *dignities* offices of state   **181** *deliver* report to   **191** *My credit* my reputation as Caesar's friend (?), trust in me (?)   **192** *conceit* judge   **196** *dearer* more keenly   **202** *close* conclude an agreement   **204** *bayed* brought to bay; *hart* deer (with pun on 'heart')   **206** *Signed . . . spoil* marked with the signs of your slaughter; *lethe* deer's blood, marked on all who were in at the kill (disyllabic)   **209** *stroken* struck down   **213** *modesty* moderation   **215** *compact* agreement (accented on second syllable)

216 Will you be pricked in number of our friends,
    Or shall we on, and not depend on you ?

ANTONY
    Therefore I took your hands, but was indeed
    Swayed from the point by looking down on Caesar.
    Friends am I with you all, and love you all,
    Upon this hope, that you shall give me reasons
    Why and wherein Caesar was dangerous.

BRUTUS
    Or else were this a savage spectacle.
224 Our reasons are so full of good regard
    That were you, Antony, the son of Caesar,
    You should be satisfied.

ANTONY   That's all I seek ;
    And am moreover suitor that I may
228 Produce his body to the market place
    And in the pulpit, as becomes a friend,
230 Speak in the order of his funeral.

BRUTUS
    You shall, Mark Antony.

CASSIUS   Brutus, a word with you.
    [Aside to Brutus]
    You know not what you do. Do not consent
    That Antony speak in his funeral.
    Know you how much the people may be moved
    By that which he will utter ?

BRUTUS *[aside to Cassius]*   By your pardon –
    I will myself into the pulpit first
    And show the reason of our Caesar's death.
238 What Antony shall speak, I will protest
    He speaks by leave and by permission ;
    And that we are contented Caesar shall
241 Have all true rites and lawful ceremonies.
242 It shall advantage more than do us wrong.

CASSIUS *[aside to Brutus]*
243 I know not what may fall. I like it not.

BRUTUS
    Mark Antony, here, take you Caesar's body.
    You shall not in your funeral speech blame us,
    But speak all good you can devise of Caesar ;
    And say you do't by our permission.
    Else shall you not have any hand at all
    About his funeral. And you shall speak
    In the same pulpit whereto I am going,
    After my speech is ended.

ANTONY   Be it so.
    I do desire no more.

BRUTUS
    Prepare the body then, and follow us.
                Exeunt. Manet Antony.

ANTONY
    O, pardon me, thou bleeding piece of earth,

    That I am meek and gentle with these butchers !
    Thou art the ruins of the noblest man
    That ever livèd in the tide of times.   257
    Woe to the hand that shed this costly blood !
    Over thy wounds now do I prophesy
    (Which, like dumb mouths, do ope their ruby lips
    To beg the voice and utterance of my tongue),
    A curse shall light upon the limbs of men ;
    Domestic fury and fierce civil strife
    Shall cumber all the parts of Italy ;   264
    Blood and destruction shall be so in use   265
    And dreadful objects so familiar
    That mothers shall but smile when they behold
    Their infants quarterèd with the hands of war,
    All pity choked with custom of fell deeds ;   269
    And Caesar's spirit, ranging for revenge,   270
    With Atè by his side come hot from hell,   271
    Shall in these confines with a monarch's voice   272
    Cry 'Havoc !' and let slip the dogs of war,   273
    That this foul deed shall smell above the earth   274
    With carrion men, groaning for burial.   275
            Enter Octavius' Servant.
    You serve Octavius Caesar, do you not ?

SERVANT
    I do, Mark Antony.

ANTONY
    Caesar did write for him to come to Rome.

SERVANT
    He did receive his letters and is coming,
    And bid me say to you by word of mouth –
    O Caesar !

ANTONY
    Thy heart is big. Get thee apart and weep.   282
    Passion, I see, is catching ; for mine eyes,   283
    Seeing those beads of sorrow stand in thine,
    Began to water. Is thy master coming ?

SERVANT
    He lies to-night within seven leagues of Rome.

ANTONY
    Post back with speed and tell him what hath chanced.   287
    Here is a mourning Rome, a dangerous Rome,
    No Rome of safety for Octavius yet.   289
    Hie hence and tell him so. Yet stay awhile.   290
    Thou shalt not back till I have borne this corse
    Into the market place. There shall I try   292
    In my oration how the people take
    The cruel issue of these bloody men ;   294
    According to the which thou shalt discourse   295
    To young Octavius of the state of things.
    Lend me your hand.   *Exeunt [with Caesar's body].*

*

216 *pricked* marked down   224 *good regard* sound considerations   228
Produce bring forth   230 *order* ritual, ceremony   238 *protest* proclaim
241 *true* proper   242 *advantage* benefit (us)   243 *fall* happen   257 *tide
of times* course of history   264 *cumber* burden   265 *in use* common   269
custom . . . deeds being accustomed to cruel deeds   270 *ranging* roving (in
search of prey)   271 *Atè* Greek goddess of discord   272 *confines* regions
273 *Havoc* the signal for unlimited slaughter ; *let slip* unleash   274 *That*
so that   275 *carrion* dead and rotting   282 *big* full of grief   283 *Passion*
grief   287 *chanced* happened   289 *Rome* (see I, ii, 156n.)   290 *Hie*
hasten   292 *try* test   294 *cruel issue* result of the cruelty   295 *the which*
the result of my test
III, ii The Forum   1 *will be satisfied* demand a full explanation   2 *audience*
a hearing   4 *part* divide

Enter Brutus and [presently] goes into the pulpit,   III, ii
and Cassius, with the Plebeians.

PLEBEIANS
    We will be satisfied ! Let us be satisfied !   1

BRUTUS
    Then follow me and give me audience, friends.   2
    Cassius, go you into the other street
    And part the numbers.   4
    Those that will hear me speak, let 'em stay here ;
    Those that will follow Cassius, go with him ;

7 And public reasons shall be renderèd
Of Caesar's death.

1. PLEBEIAN   I will hear Brutus speak.

2. PLEBEIAN
I will hear Cassius, and compare their reasons
10 When severally we hear them renderèd.
                    [Exit Cassius, with some of the Plebeians.]

3. PLEBEIAN
The noble Brutus is ascended. Silence!

12 BRUTUS Be patient till the last.

13 Romans, countrymen, and lovers, hear me for my cause,
and be silent, that you may hear. Believe me for mine
15 honor, and have respect to mine honor, that you may
16 believe. Censure me in your wisdom, and awake your
17 senses, that you may the better judge. If there be any in
this assembly, any dear friend of Caesar's, to him I say
that Brutus' love to Caesar was no less than his. If then
that friend demand why Brutus rose against Caesar, this
is my answer: Not that I loved Caesar less, but that I
loved Rome more. Had you rather Caesar were living,
and die all slaves, than that Caesar were dead, to live all
freemen? As Caesar loved me, I weep for him; as he was
fortunate, I rejoice at it; as he was valiant, I honor him;
but – as he was ambitious, I slew him. There is tears for
his love; joy for his fortune; honor for his valor; and
death for his ambition. Who is here so base that would
29 be a bondman? If any, speak; for him have I offended.
30 Who is here so rude that would not be a Roman? If any,
speak; for him have I offended. Who is here so vile that
will not love his country? If any, speak; for him have I
offended. I pause for a reply.

ALL None, Brutus, none!

BRUTUS Then none have I offended. I have done no more
36 to Caesar than you shall do to Brutus. The question of
37 his death is enrolled in the Capitol; his glory not extenu-
38 ated, wherein he was worthy; nor his offenses enforced,
for which he suffered death.
            Enter Mark Antony [and others], with Caesar's
            body.
Here comes his body, mourned by Mark Antony, who,
though he had no hand in his death, shall receive the
42 benefit of his dying, a place in the commonwealth, as
which of you shall not? With this I depart, that, as I slew
44 my best lover for the good of Rome, I have the same
dagger for myself when it shall please my country to
need my death.

ALL Live, Brutus! live, live!

1. PLEBEIAN
Bring him with triumph home unto his house.

2. PLEBEIAN
49 Give him a statue with his ancestors.

3. PLEBEIAN
Let him be Caesar.

4. PLEBEIAN   Caesar's better parts
Shall be crowned in Brutus.

1. PLEBEIAN
We'll bring him to his house with shouts and clamors.

BRUTUS
My countrymen –

2. PLEBEIAN   Peace! silence! Brutus speaks.

1. PLEBEIAN Peace, ho!

BRUTUS
Good countrymen, let me depart alone,
And, for my sake, stay here with Antony.

Do grace to Caesar's corpse, and grace his speech   57
Tending to Caesar's glories which Mark Antony,   58
By our permission, is allowed to make.
I do entreat you, not a man depart,
Save I alone, till Antony have spoke.   Exit.

1. PLEBEIAN
Stay, ho! and let us hear Mark Antony.

3. PLEBEIAN
Let him go up into the public chair.   63
We'll hear him. Noble Antony, go up.

ANTONY
For Brutus' sake I am beholding to you.   65
            [Antony goes into the pulpit.]

4. PLEBEIAN
What does he say of Brutus?

3. PLEBEIAN   He says for Brutus' sake
He finds himself beholding to us all.

4. PLEBEIAN
'Twere best he speak no harm of Brutus here!

1. PLEBEIAN
This Caesar was a tyrant.

3. PLEBEIAN   Nay, that's certain.
We are blest that Rome is rid of him.

2. PLEBEIAN
Peace! Let us hear what Antony can say.

ANTONY
You gentle Romans –

ALL   Peace, ho! Let us hear him.

ANTONY
Friends, Romans, countrymen, lend me your ears;
I come to bury Caesar, not to praise him.
The evil that men do lives after them;
The good is oft interrèd with their bones.
So let it be with Caesar. The noble Brutus
Hath told you Caesar was ambitious.
If it were so, it was a grievous fault,
And grievously hath Caesar answered it.   80
Here under leave of Brutus and the rest
(For Brutus is an honorable man;
So are they all, all honorable men),
Come I to speak in Caesar's funeral.
He was my friend, faithful and just to me;   85
But Brutus says he was ambitious,
And Brutus is an honorable man.
He hath brought many captives home to Rome,
Whose ransoms did the general coffers fill.   89
Did this in Caesar seem ambitious?
When that the poor have cried, Caesar hath wept;
Ambition should be made of sterner stuff.
Yet Brutus says he was ambitious;
And Brutus is an honorable man.
You all did see that on the Lupercal
I thrice presented him a kingly crown,

---

7 *public reasons* reasons having to do with the general good (?), reasons in explanation to the public (?) 10 *severally* separately 12 *last* end of my speech 13 *lovers* dear friends; *my cause* i.e. the cause of freedom 15 *have . . . honor* remember that I am honorable 16 *Censure* judge 17 *senses* reason 29 *bondman* slave 30 *rude* barbarous 36 *shall do* i.e. if Brutus should so offend; *question of* considerations that led to 37 *enrolled in* recorded in the archives of; *extenuated* understated 38 *enforced* overstated 42 *place* i.e. as a free Roman 44 *lover* friend 49 *ancestors* (see I, ii, 159n.) 57 *Do . . . speech* show due respect to Caesar's corpse and listen respectfully to Antony's speech 58 *Tending* relating 63 *chair* pulpit, rostrum 65 *beholding* obliged 80 *answered it* paid the penalty 85 *just* entirely reliable 89 *general coffers* public treasury

Which he did thrice refuse. Was this ambition?
Yet Brutus says he was ambitious;
And sure he is an honorable man.
100 I speak not to disprove what Brutus spoke,
But here I am to speak what I do know.
You all did love him once, not without cause.
What cause withholds you then to mourn for him?
O judgment, thou art fled to brutish beasts,
And men have lost their reason! Bear with me.
My heart is in the coffin there with Caesar,
And I must pause till it come back to me.

1 . PLEBEIAN
Methinks there is much reason in his sayings.

2 . PLEBEIAN
If thou consider rightly of the matter,
Caesar has had great wrong.

3 . PLEBEIAN   Has he, masters?
I fear there will a worse come in his place.

4 . PLEBEIAN
Marked ye his words? He would not take the crown;
Therefore 'tis certain he was not ambitious.

1 . PLEBEIAN
114 If it be found so, some will dear abide it.

2 . PLEBEIAN
Poor soul! his eyes are red as fire with weeping.

3 . PLEBEIAN
There's not a nobler man in Rome than Antony.

4 . PLEBEIAN
Now mark him. He begins again to speak.

ANTONY
But yesterday the word of Caesar might
Have stood against the world. Now lies he there,
120 And none so poor to do him reverence.
O masters! If I were disposed to stir
122 Your hearts and minds to mutiny and rage,
I should do Brutus wrong, and Cassius wrong,
Who, you all know, are honorable men.
I will not do them wrong. I rather choose
To wrong the dead, to wrong myself and you,
Than I will wrong such honorable men.
But here's a parchment with the seal of Caesar.
129 I found it in his closet; 'tis his will.
130 Let but the commons hear this testament,
Which (pardon me) I do not mean to read,
And they would go and kiss dead Caesar's wounds
133 And dip their napkins in his sacred blood;
Yea, beg a hair of him for memory,
And dying, mention it within their wills,
Bequeathing it as a rich legacy
Unto their issue.

4 . PLEBEIAN
We'll hear the will! Read it, Mark Antony.

ALL
The will, the will! We will hear Caesar's will!

114 *dear abide it* pay a heavy penalty for it   120 *so poor* base enough   122
mutiny riot   129 *closet* study (?), cabinet for private papers (?)   130
commons plebeians   133 *napkins* handkerchiefs   141 *meet* fitting that
149 *stay* wait   150 *o'ershot myself* gone further than I intended   165
hearse bier   167 *far* farther   168 *Bear* move   170 *mantle* cloak (here toga)
173 *Nervii* a tribe defeated in 57 B.C. in one of the most decisive victories in
the Gallic Wars   175 *envious* malicious   179 *be resolved* learn for certain
180 *unkindly* unnaturally and cruelly   181 *angel* 'darling,' i.e. favorite
who could do no wrong   183 *most unkindest* cruelest and most unnatural
188 *base* pedestal; *statue* (trisyllabic)   192 *flourished* swaggered and
brandished its sword in triumph

ANTONY
Have patience, gentle friends; I must not read it.
It is not meet you know how Caesar loved you.   141
You are not wood, you are not stones, but men;
And being men, hearing the will of Caesar,
It will inflame you, it will make you mad.
'Tis good you know not that you are his heirs;
For if you should, O, what would come of it?

4 . PLEBEIAN
Read the will! We'll hear it, Antony!
You shall read us the will, Caesar's will!

ANTONY
Will you be patient? Will you stay awhile?   149
I have o'ershot myself to tell you of it.   150
I fear I wrong the honorable men
Whose daggers have stabbed Caesar; I do fear it.

4 . PLEBEIAN
They were traitors. Honorable men!

ALL
The will! the testament!

2 . PLEBEIAN   They were villains,
Murderers! The will! Read the will!

ANTONY
You will compel me then to read the will?
Then make a ring about the corpse of Caesar
And let me show you him that made the will.
Shall I descend? and will you give me leave?

ALL Come down.

2 . PLEBEIAN Descend.

3 . PLEBEIAN You shall have leave.
       [Antony comes down.]

4 . PLEBEIAN A ring! Stand round.

1 . PLEBEIAN
Stand from the hearse! Stand from the body!   165

2 . PLEBEIAN
Room for Antony, most noble Antony!

ANTONY
Nay, press not so upon me. Stand far off.   167

ALL Stand back! Room! Bear back!   168

ANTONY
If you have tears, prepare to shed them now.
You all do know this mantle. I remember   170
The first time ever Caesar put it on.
'Twas on a summer's evening in his tent,
That day he overcame the Nervii.   173
Look, in this place ran Cassius' dagger through.
See what a rent the envious Casca made.   175
Through this the well-belovèd Brutus stabbed;
And as he plucked his cursèd steel away,
Mark how the blood of Caesar followed it,
As rushing out of doors to be resolved   179
If Brutus so unkindly knocked or no;   180
For Brutus, as you know, was Caesar's angel.   181
Judge, O you gods, how dearly Caesar loved him!
This was the most unkindest cut of all;   183
For when the noble Caesar saw him stab,
Ingratitude, more strong than traitors' arms,
Quite vanquished him. Then burst his mighty heart;
And in his mantle muffling up his face,
Even at the base of Pompey's statue   188
(Which all the while ran blood) great Caesar fell.
O, what a fall was there, my countrymen!
Then I, and you, and all of us fell down,
Whilst bloody treason flourished over us.   192

O, now you weep, and I perceive you feel
194 The dint of pity. These are gracious drops.
195 Kind souls, what weep you when you but behold
196 Our Caesar's vesture wounded ? Look you here !
197 Here is himself, marred as you see with traitors.
     1 . PLEBEIAN O piteous spectacle !
     2 . PLEBEIAN O noble Caesar !
     3 . PLEBEIAN O woeful day !
     4 . PLEBEIAN O traitors, villains !
     1 . PLEBEIAN O most bloody sight !
     2 . PLEBEIAN We will be revenged.
204 [ALL] Revenge ! About ! Seek ! Burn ! Fire ! Kill ! Slay !
     Let not a traitor live !
206 ANTONY Stay, countrymen.
     1 . PLEBEIAN Peace there ! Hear the noble Antony.
     2 . PLEBEIAN We'll hear him, we'll follow him, we'll die
     with him !
     ANTONY
     Good friends, sweet friends, let me not stir you up
     To such a sudden flood of mutiny.
     They that have done this deed are honorable.
213 What private griefs they have, alas, I know not,
     That made them do it. They are wise and honorable,
     And will no doubt with reasons answer you.
     I come not, friends, to steal away your hearts.
     I am no orator, as Brutus is,
     But (as you know me all) a plain blunt man
     That love my friend ; and that they know full well
220 That gave me public leave to speak of him.
221 For I have neither writ, nor words, nor worth,
222 Action, nor utterance, nor the power of speech
223 To stir men's blood. I only speak right on.
     I tell you that which you yourselves do know,
     Show you sweet Caesar's wounds, poor poor dumb
         mouths,
     And bid them speak for me. But were I Brutus,
     And Brutus Antony, there were an Antony
228 Would ruffle up your spirits, and put a tongue
     In every wound of Caesar that should move
     The stones of Rome to rise and mutiny.
     ALL
     We'll mutiny.
     1 . PLEBEIAN We'll burn the house of Brutus.
     3 . PLEBEIAN
     Away then ! Come, seek the conspirators.
     ANTONY
     Yet hear me, countrymen. Yet hear me speak.
     ALL
     Peace, ho ! Hear Antony, most noble Antony !
     ANTONY
     Why, friends, you go to do you know not what.
     Wherein hath Caesar thus deserved your loves ?
     Alas, you know not ! I must tell you then.
     You have forgot the will I told you of.
     ALL
     Most true ! The will ! Let's stay and hear the will.
     ANTONY
     Here is the will, and under Caesar's seal.
     To every Roman citizen he gives,
242 To every several man, seventy-five drachmas.
     2 . PLEBEIAN
     Most noble Caesar ! We'll revenge his death !
244 3 . PLEBEIAN O royal Caesar !
     ANTONY Hear me with patience.

ALL Peace, ho !
ANTONY
     Moreover, he hath left you all his walks,   247
     His private arbors, and new-planted orchards,   248
     On this side Tiber ; he hath left them you,
     And to your heirs for ever – common pleasures,   250
     To walk abroad and recreate yourselves.
     Here was a Caesar ! When comes such another ?
     1 . PLEBEIAN
     Never, never ! Come, away, away !
     We'll burn his body in the holy place   254
     And with the brands fire the traitors' houses.
     Take up the body.
     2 . PLEBEIAN Go fetch fire !
     3 . PLEBEIAN Pluck down benches !   258
     4 . PLEBEIAN Pluck down forms, windows, anything !   259
              Exit Plebeians [with the body].
     ANTONY
     Now let it work. Mischief, thou art afoot,   260
     Take thou what course thou wilt.
          Enter Servant.   How now, fellow ?   261
     SERVANT
     Sir, Octavius is already come to Rome.
     ANTONY Where is he ?
     SERVANT
     He and Lepidus are at Caesar's house.
     ANTONY
     And thither will I straight to visit him.   265
     He comes upon a wish. Fortune is merry,   266
     And in this mood will give us anything.
     SERVANT
     I heard him say Brutus and Cassius
     Are rid like madmen through the gates of Rome.   269
     ANTONY
     Belike they had some notice of the people,   270
     How I had moved them. Bring me to Octavius.   *Exeunt.*   271

                 *

       Enter Cinna the Poet, and after him the Plebeians.   III, iii
     CINNA
     I dreamt to-night that I did feast with Caesar,   1
     And things unluckily charge my fantasy.   2
     I have no will to wander forth of doors,
     Yet something leads me forth.   3
     1 . PLEBEIAN What is your name ?

194 *dint* impression ; *gracious* full of grace, becoming   195 *what* why
196 *vesture* i.e. the mantle   197 *marred* mangled ; *with* by   204 *About* to
work   206 *Stay* wait   213 *private griefs* personal grievances   220 *public
. . . speak* permission to speak in public   221 *writ* a written-out speech
(most editors emend to 'wit', i.e. invention, which accords with the rest
of the list of qualities of a good orator that follows) ; *words* fluency ; *worth*
stature as a public figure, authority   222 *Action* skilful use of gesture ;
utterance good delivery   223 *right on* straight out, just as I think it   228
ruffle up stir to rage   242 *several* individual ; *seventy-five drachmas* (at least
£12 to-day)   244 *royal* nobly munificent   247 *walks* (see I, ii, 155n.)
248 *orchards* gardens   250 *common pleasures* public parks   254 *holy place*
where the most sacred temples were in Rome   258 *Pluck down* wrench
loose, tear out   259 *forms* long benches ; *windows* shutters   260 *work*
have its full effect   261 *fellow* (form of address to inferiors)   265 *straight*
at once   266 *upon a wish* exactly as I might have wished ; *merry* in a good
mood (toward us)   269 *Are rid* have ridden   270 *Belike* probably ;
notice of news about   271 *Bring* escort
III, iii A street   1 *to-night* last night   2 *things . . . fantasy* what has happened
gives my dream a bad interpretation   3 *forth* out

2. PLEBEIAN Whither are you going?

3. PLEBEIAN Where do you dwell?

4. PLEBEIAN Are you a married man or a bachelor?

9 **2. PLEBEIAN** Answer every man directly.

1. PLEBEIAN Ay, and briefly.

4. PLEBEIAN Ay, and wisely.

3. PLEBEIAN Ay, and truly, you were best.

CINNA What is my name? Whither am I going? Where
    do I dwell? Am I a married man or a bachelor? Then,
    to answer every man directly and briefly, wisely and
    truly: wisely I say, I am a bachelor.

17 **2. PLEBEIAN** That's as much as to say they are fools that
18   marry. You'll bear me a bang for that, I fear. Proceed
    directly.

CINNA Directly I am going to Caesar's funeral.

1. PLEBEIAN As a friend or an enemy?

CINNA As a friend.

2. PLEBEIAN That matter is answered directly.

4. PLEBEIAN For your dwelling – briefly.

CINNA Briefly, I dwell by the Capitol.

3. PLEBEIAN Your name, sir, truly.

CINNA Truly, my name is Cinna.

1. PLEBEIAN Tear him to pieces! He's a conspirator.

CINNA I am Cinna the poet! I am Cinna the poet!

4. PLEBEIAN Tear him for his bad verses! Tear him for
    his bad verses!

CINNA I am not Cinna the conspirator.

33 **4. PLEBEIAN** It is no matter; his name 's Cinna! Pluck
34   but his name out of his heart, and turn him going.

3. PLEBEIAN Tear him, tear him! *[They kill him.]* Come,
    brands, ho! firebrands! To Brutus', to Cassius'! Burn
    all! Some to Decius' house and some to Casca's; some
    to Ligarius'! Away, go!

              Exeunt all the Plebeians [with the body of Cinna].

*

IV, i   *Enter Antony, Octavius, and Lepidus.*

ANTONY
1   These many, then, shall die; their names are pricked.

OCTAVIUS
  Your brother too must die. Consent you, Lepidus?

LEPIDUS
  I do consent –

OCTAVIUS   Prick him down, Antony.

LEPIDUS
  Upon condition Publius shall not live,
  Who is your sister's son, Mark Antony.

ANTONY
  He shall not live. Look, with a spot I damn him.   6
  But, Lepidus, go you to Caesar's house.
  Fetch the will hither, and we shall determine
  How to cut off some charge in legacies.   9

LEPIDUS
  What? shall I find you here?

OCTAVIUS
  Or here or at the Capitol.   *Exit Lepidus.* 11

ANTONY
  This is a slight unmeritable man,   12
  Meet to be sent on errands. Is it fit,
  The threefold world divided, he should stand   14
  One of the three to share it?

OCTAVIUS   So you thought him,
  And took his voice who should be pricked to die   16
  In our black sentence and proscription.   17

ANTONY
  Octavius, I have seen more days than you;   18
  And though we lay these honors on this man
  To ease ourselves of divers sland'rous loads,   20
  He shall but bear them as the ass bears gold,
  To groan and sweat under the business,   22
  Either led or driven as we point the way;
  And having brought our treasure where we will,
  Then take we down his load, and turn him off   25
  (Like to the empty ass) to shake his ears   26
  And graze in commons.   27

OCTAVIUS   You may do your will;
  But he's a tried and valiant soldier.   28

ANTONY
  So is my horse, Octavius, and for that
  I do appoint him store of provender.   30
  It is a creature that I teach to fight,
  To wind, to stop, to run directly on,   32
  His corporal motion governed by my spirit.   33
  And, in some taste, is Lepidus but so.   34
  He must be taught, and trained, and bid go forth:
  A barren-spirited fellow; one that feeds   36
  On objects, arts, and imitations
  Which, out of use and staled by other men,   38
  Begin his fashion. Do not talk of him   39
  But as a property. And now, Octavius,   40
  Listen great things. Brutus and Cassius   41
  Are levying powers. We must straight make head.   42
  Therefore let our alliance be combined,   43
  Our best friends made, our means stretched;   44
  And let us presently go sit in council
  How covert matters may be best disclosed   46
  And open perils surest answerèd.   47

OCTAVIUS
  Let us do so; for we are at the stake   48
  And bayed about with many enemies;
  And some that smile have in their hearts, I fear,
  Millions of mischiefs.   *Exeunt.* 51

*

9 *directly* plainly   **17–18** *they . . . marry* (proverbial)   **18** *bear me a bang*
get a beating from me   **33** *Pluck* tear   **34** *turn him going* send him
packing
IV, i The house of Antony   **1** *pricked* marked down on a list   **6** *spot* mark;
damn condemn   **9** *cut . . . charge* reduce the outlay of the estate (by altering
the will)   **11** *Or* either   **12** *slight unmeritable* insignificant and unworthy
14 *The . . . divided* the world being divided among the three triumvirs into
three parts (Europe, Africa, and Asia)   **16** *voice* vote   **17** *black* i.e. death;
proscription condemnation to death or exile   **18** *have . . . days* am older,
i.e. more experienced   **20** *ease . . . loads* lighten for ourselves some of the
charges that will be brought against us   **22** *business* work done by beasts
25 *turn him off* send him packing   **26** *empty* unburdened   **27** *commons*
public pasture   **28** *soldier* (trisyllabic)   **30** *appoint* assign; *store* a supply
32 *To wind . . . on* to turn, to stop suddenly, to resume running immediately
33 *corporal* bodily   **34** *taste* degree; *so* the same   **36** *barren-spirited*
without initiative, unoriginal   **36–37** *feeds . . . imitations* nourishes his
spirit with curiosities, artificial contrivances, and following of fashions
38 *staled* cheapened, worn-out   **39** *Begin his fashion* he then adopts as
fashionable   **40** *property* chattel (?), tool (?)   **41** *Listen* hear   **42** *straight
make head* immediately raise an army   **43** *combined* strengthened   **44**
made mustered; *stretched* used to their fullest advantage   **46** *How . . .
disclosed* to determine how hidden dangers may best be discovered   **47**
surest answerèd most safely met   **48** *at the stake* i.e. like a bear at the stake
bayed by dogs   **51** *mischiefs* schemes to harm us

IV, ii   *Drum. Enter Brutus, Lucilius, [Lucius,] and the*
              Army. Titinius and Pindarus meet them.

BRUTUS Stand ho!

LUCILIUS Give the word, ho! and stand!

BRUTUS

What now, Lucilius! Is Cassius near?

LUCILIUS

He is at hand, and Pindarus is come
To do you salutation from his master.

BRUTUS

6   He greets me well. Your master, Pindarus,
7   In his own change, or by ill officers,
8   Hath given me some worthy cause to wish
    Things done undone; but if he be at hand,
10 I shall be satisfied.

PINDARUS   I do not doubt
    But that my noble master will appear
12 Such as he is, full of regard and honor.

BRUTUS

13 He is not doubted. A word, Lucilius,
14 How he received you. Let me be resolved.

LUCILIUS

With courtesy and with respect enough,
16 But not with such familiar instances
17 Nor with such free and friendly conference
    As he hath used of old.

BRUTUS   Thou hast described
19 A hot friend cooling. Ever note, Lucilius,
    When love begins to sicken and decay
21 It useth an enforcèd ceremony.
    There are no tricks in plain and simple faith;
23 But hollow men, like horses hot at hand,
24 Make gallant show and promise of their mettle;
              Low march within.
    But when they should endure the bloody spur,
26 They fall their crests, and like deceitful jades
27 Sink in the trial. Comes his army on?

LUCILIUS

28 They mean this night in Sardis to be quartered.
29 The greater part, the horse in general,
    Are come with Cassius.

BRUTUS   Hark! He is arrived.
31 March gently on to meet him.
              Enter Cassius and his Powers.

CASSIUS Stand, ho!

BRUTUS Stand, ho! Speak the word along.

1. SOLDIER Stand!

2. SOLDIER Stand!

3. SOLDIER Stand!

CASSIUS

Most noble brother, you have done me wrong.

BRUTUS

Judge me, you gods! wrong I mine enemies?
And if not so, how should I wrong a brother.

CASSIUS

40 Brutus, this sober form of yours hides wrongs;
    And when you do them –

41 BRUTUS   Cassius, be content.
42 Speak your griefs softly. I do know you well.
    Before the eyes of both our armies here
    (Which should perceive nothing but love from us)
    Let us not wrangle. Bid them move away.
46 Then in my tent, Cassius, enlarge your griefs,

And I will give you audience.   47

CASSIUS   Pindarus,
Bid our commanders lead their charges off   48
A little from this ground.

BRUTUS

Lucilius, do you the like; and let no man
Come to our tent till we have done our conference.
Let Lucius and Titinius guard our door.   *Exeunt.*
              Mane[n]t Brutus and Cassius.   IV, iii

CASSIUS

That you have wronged me doth appear in this:
You have condemned and noted Lucius Pella   2
For taking bribes here of the Sardians;
Wherein my letters, praying on his side,   4
Because I knew the man, was slighted off.   5

BRUTUS

You wronged yourself to write in such a case.

CASSIUS

In such a time as this it is not meet
That every nice offense should bear his comment.   8

BRUTUS

Let me tell you, Cassius, you yourself
Are much condemned to have an itching palm,   10
To sell and mart your offices for gold   11
To undeservers.

CASSIUS   I an itching palm?
You know that you are Brutus that speaks this,
Or, by the gods, this speech were else your last!

BRUTUS

The name of Cassius honors this corruption,   15
And chastisement doth therefore hide his head.

CASSIUS Chastisement?

BRUTUS

Remember March; the ides of March remember.
Did not great Julius bleed for justice sake?
What villain touched his body that did stab
And not for justice? What, shall one of us,   21
That struck the foremost man of all this world
But for supporting robbers – shall we now   23
Contaminate our fingers with base bribes,
And sell the mighty space of our large honors   25
For so much trash as may be graspèd thus?   26

IV, ii The camp of Brutus (near Sardis)   **6** *greets me well* sends his greetings by a worthy man   **7** *In . . . officers* whether from changed feelings on his part or through the acts of unworthy subordinates   **8** *worthy* justifiable   **10** *be satisfied* receive a full explanation   **12** *Such* exactly; *full . . . honor* regardful (of your interests) and honorable   **13** *A word* i.e. tell me   **14** *resolved* fully informed   **16** *familiar instances* signs of friendship   **17** *conference* conversation   **19** *Ever note* always observe   **21** *enforced* forced   **23** *hollow* insincere; *hot at hand* spirited at the start   **24** *mettle* high spirit   **26** *fall let fall*; *crests* ridges of horses' necks; *jades* horses (contemptuous)   **27** *Sink . . . trial* fail when they are put to the test   **28** *Sardis* (the capital of the ancient kingdom of Lydia, in western Asia Minor; Brutus had requested Cassius to join forces with him there)   **29** *horse in general* all the cavalry   **31** *gently* slowly   **40** *sober form* serious and restrained manner   **41** *content* calm   **42** *griefs* grievances   **46** *enlarge* expound fully   **47** *audience* a hearing   **48** *charges* troops

IV, iii   **2** *noted* publicly disgraced, slandered   **4** *letters* (singular in meaning)   **5** *slighted off* contemptuously dismissed   **8** *nice . . . comment* trivial offense should be criticized   **10** *condemned to have* accused of having; *itching palm* i.e. a covetous disposition   **11** *mart* traffic in   **15** *honors* lends an appearance of honor to   **21** *And not* except   **23** *supporting robbers* i.e. having backed those who desire to rob the Romans of their freedom (see I, ii, 283n.)   **25** *the mighty . . . honors* our great power to confer honorable public offices   **26** *trash* money (contemptuous)

27   I had rather be a dog and bay the moon
      Than such a Roman.
28   CASSIUS   Brutus, bait not me!
      I'll not endure it. You forget yourself
30   To hedge me in. I am a soldier, I,
      Older in practice, abler than yourself
32   To make conditions.
      BRUTUS   Go to! You are not Cassius.
      CASSIUS I am.
      BRUTUS I say you are not.
      CASSIUS
35   Urge me no more! I shall forget myself.
36   Have mind upon your health. Tempt me no farther.
37   BRUTUS Away, slight man!
      CASSIUS
      Is't possible?
      BRUTUS   Hear me, for I will speak.
39   Must I give way and room to your rash choler?
40   Shall I be frighted when a madman stares?
      CASSIUS
      O ye gods, ye gods! Must I endure all this?
      BRUTUS
      All this? Ay, more! Fret till your proud heart break.
      Go show your slaves how choleric you are
44   And make your bondmen tremble. Must I budge?
45   Must I observe you? Must I stand and crouch
46   Under your testy humor? By the gods,
47   You shall digest the venom of your spleen,
      Though it do split you; for from this day forth
49   I'll use you for my mirth, yea, for my laughter,
      When you are waspish.
      CASSIUS   Is it come to this?
      BRUTUS
      You say you are a better soldier.
52   Let it appear so; make your vaunting true,
      And it shall please me well. For mine own part,
54   I shall be glad to learn of noble men.
      CASSIUS
      You wrong me every way! You wrong me, Brutus!
      I said an elder soldier, not a better.
      Did I say 'better'?
      BRUTUS   If you did, I care not.
      CASSIUS
58   When Caesar lived he durst not thus have moved me.
      BRUTUS
59   Peace, peace! You durst not so have tempted him.
      CASSIUS I durst not?
      BRUTUS No.

CASSIUS
What, durst not tempt him?
BRUTUS   For your life you durst not.
CASSIUS
Do not presume too much upon my love.
I may do that I shall be sorry for.
BRUTUS
You have done that you should be sorry for.
There is no terror, Cassius, in your threats;
For I am armed so strong in honesty   67
That they pass by me as the idle wind,
Which I respect not. I did send to you   69
For certain sums of gold, which you denied me;
For I can raise no money by vile means.
By heaven, I had rather coin my heart
And drop my blood for drachmas than to wring
From the hard hands of peasants their vile trash
By any indirection. I did send   75
To you for gold to pay my legions,
Which you denied me. Was that done like Cassius?
Should I have answered Caius Cassius so?
When Marcus Brutus grows so covetous
To lock such rascal counters from his friends,   80
Be ready, gods, with all your thunderbolts,
Dash him to pieces!
CASSIUS   I denied you not.
BRUTUS You did.
CASSIUS
I did not. He was but a fool that brought
My answer back. Brutus hath rived my heart.   85
A friend should bear his friend's infirmities,
But Brutus makes mine greater than they are.
BRUTUS
I do not, till you practise them on me.
CASSIUS
You love me not.
BRUTUS   I do not like your faults.
CASSIUS
A friendly eye could never see such faults.
BRUTUS
A flatterer's would not, though they do appear
As huge as high Olympus.
CASSIUS
Come, Antony, and young Octavius, come!
Revenge yourselves alone on Cassius.   94
For Cassius is aweary of the world:
Hated by one he loves; braved by his brother;   96
Checked like a bondman; all his faults observed,   97
Set in a notebook, learned and conned by rote
To cast into my teeth. O, I could weep   99
My spirit from mine eyes! There is my dagger,
And here my naked breast; within, a heart
Dearer than Pluto's mine, richer than gold.   102
If that thou be'st a Roman, take it forth.
I, that denied thee gold, will give my heart.
Strike as thou didst at Caesar; for I know,
When thou didst hate him worst, thou lovedst him better
Than ever thou lovedst Cassius.
BRUTUS   Sheathe your dagger.
Be angry when you will; it shall have scope.   108
Do what you will; dishonor shall be humor.   109
O Cassius, you are yokèd with a lamb
That carries anger as the flint bears fire;

27 *bay* howl at   28 *bait* harass   30 *hedge me in* i.e. limit my authority   32 *make conditions* manage affairs   35 *Urge* drive   36 *health* safety; *Tempt* provoke   37 *slight* worthless   39 *way . . . choler* course and scope to your rash anger   40 *stares* glares   44 *budge* flinch   45 *observe* wait upon obsequiously; *crouch* bow   46 *testy humor* irritable temper   47 *digest the venom* swallow the poison; *spleen* i.e. hot temper   49 *laughter* object of ridicule   52 *vaunting* boasting   54 *learn of* hear of the existence of (with pun on 'take lessons from')   58 *moved* angered   59 *tempted* provoked   67 *honesty* integrity   69 *respect not* ignore   75 *indirection* irregular means   80 *rascal counters* base coins   85 *rived* split in two   94 *alone* solely   96 *braved* defied   97 *Checked* scolded   99 *cast . . . teeth* i.e. throw up to me   102 *Dearer . . . mine* more precious than the riches within the earth (Pluto, god of the underworld, probably confused with Plutus, god of riches)   108 *it* i.e. your anger; *scope* free play   109 *dishonor . . . humor* I shall take your insults as an effect of your hot temper

112   Who, much enforcèd, shows a hasty spark,
113   And straight is cold again.

CASSIUS   Hath Cassius lived
To be but mirth and laughter to his Brutus
115   When grief and blood ill-tempered vexeth him?

BRUTUS
When I spoke that, I was ill-tempered too.

CASSIUS
Do you confess so much? Give me your hand.

BRUTUS
And my heart too.

CASSIUS   O Brutus!

BRUTUS   What's the matter?

CASSIUS
Have you not love enough to bear with me
120   When that rash humor which my mother gave me
Makes me forgetful?

BRUTUS   Yes, Cassius; and from henceforth,
When you are over-earnest with your Brutus,
123   He'll think your mother chides, and leave you so.

Enter a Poet [followed by Lucilius, Titinius, and Lucius].

POET
Let me go in to see the generals!
125   There is some grudge between 'em. 'Tis not meet
They be alone.

LUCILIUS   You shall not come to them.

POET
Nothing but death shall stay me.

CASSIUS   How now? What's the matter?

POET
For shame, you generals! What do you mean?
Love and be friends, as two such men should be;
For I have seen more years, I'm sure, than ye.

CASSIUS
133   Ha, ha! How vilely doth this cynic rhyme!

BRUTUS
134   Get you hence, sirrah! Saucy fellow, hence!

CASSIUS
Bear with him, Brutus. 'Tis his fashion.

BRUTUS
136   I'll know his humor when he knows his time.
137   What should the wars do with these jigging fools?
138   Companion, hence!

CASSIUS   Away, away, be gone!   *Exit Poet.*

BRUTUS
Lucilius and Titinius, bid the commanders
Prepare to lodge their companies to-night.

CASSIUS
And come yourselves, and bring Messala with you
Immediately to us.   *[Exeunt Lucilius and Titinius.]*

BRUTUS   Lucius, a bowl of wine. *[Exit Lucius.]*

CASSIUS
I did not think you could have been so angry.

BRUTUS
O Cassius, I am sick of many griefs.

CASSIUS
Of your philosophy you make no use
146   If you give place to accidental evils.

BRUTUS
No man bears sorrow better. Portia is dead.

CASSIUS   Ha! Portia?

BRUTUS   She is dead.

CASSIUS
How scaped I killing when I crossed you so?   150
O insupportable and touching loss!   151
Upon what sickness?   152

BRUTUS   Impatient of my absence,
And grief that young Octavius with Mark Antony
Have made themselves so strong; for with her death   154
That tidings came. With this she fell distract,   155
And (her attendants absent) swallowed fire.   156

CASSIUS
And died so?

BRUTUS   Even so.

CASSIUS   O ye immortal gods!

Enter Boy [Lucius], with wine and tapers.

BRUTUS
Speak no more of her. Give me a bowl of wine.
In this I bury all unkindness, Cassius.   159
Drinks.

CASSIUS
My heart is thirsty for that noble pledge.
Fill, Lucius, till the wine o'erswell the cup.
I cannot drink too much of Brutus' love.
            [Drinks. Exit Lucius.]

Enter Titinius and Messala.

BRUTUS
Come in, Titinius! Welcome, good Messala.
Now sit we close about this taper here
And call in question our necessities.   165

CASSIUS
Portia, art thou gone?

BRUTUS   No more, I pray you.
Messala, I have here receivèd letters
That young Octavius and Mark Antony
Come down upon us with a mighty power,   169
Bending their expedition toward Philippi.   170

MESSALA
Myself have letters of the selfsame tenure.   171

BRUTUS
With what addition?

MESSALA
That by proscription and bills of outlawry   173
Octavius, Antony, and Lepidus
Have put to death an hundred senators.

BRUTUS
Therein our letters do not well agree.

---

112 *enforcèd* worked upon   113 *straight* at once   115 *blood ill-tempered* unbalanced disposition   120 *rash humor* choleric or splenetic temperament 123 *mother* i.e. inherited temperament (also hysteria?); *leave you so* leave it at that   125 *grudge* ill-feeling   133 *cynic* boorish fellow   134 *sirrah* (contemptuous form of address); *Saucy* insolent   136 *I'll . . . time* I'll accept his fashion of behavior when he knows the proper time and place for it   137 *jigging* rhyming (contemptuous), doggerel versifying   138 *Companion* fellow (contemptuous)   146 *place* way; *accidental evils* evils caused by chance (i.e. Brutus, as a Stoic, should not be affected by those external adversities caused by Fortune)   150 *killing* being killed by you; *crossed* opposed   151 *touching* grievous   152 *Upon* as a result of; *Impatient of* unable to endure (also desperate at?)   154–55 *for . . . came* for together with the news of her death came the news of their strength   155 *distract* distraught   156 *swallowed fire* (according to Plutarch, as translated by North, she cast 'hot burning coals [from a charcoal brazier] . . . into her mouth, and kept her mouth so close that she choked herself')   159 *In . . . unkindness* in this wine I'll drown all our differences   165 *call in question* deliberate upon   169 *upon* against; *power* army   170 *Bending* directing; *expedition* rapid march   171 *tenure* tenor, purport   173 *proscription* condemnation to death; *bills of outlawry* proscription lists

Mine speak of seventy senators that died
By their proscriptions, Cicero being one.

CASSIUS
Cicero one?

MESSALA   Cicero is dead,
And by that order of proscription.

181   Had you your letters from your wife, my lord?

BRUTUS No, Messala.

MESSALA
Nor nothing in your letters writ of her?

BRUTUS
Nothing, Messala.

MESSALA   That methinks is strange.

BRUTUS
Why ask you? Hear you aught of her in yours?

MESSALA No, my lord.

BRUTUS
Now as you are a Roman, tell me true.

MESSALA
Then like a Roman bear the truth I tell;
For certain she is dead, and by strange manner.

BRUTUS
Why, farewell, Portia. We must die, Messala.
191   With meditating that she must die once,
I have the patience to endure it now.

MESSALA
Even so great men great losses should endure.

CASSIUS
194   I have as much of this in art as you,
195   But yet my nature could not bear it so.

BRUTUS
196   Well, to our work alive. What do you think
Of marching to Philippi presently?

CASSIUS
I do not think it good.

BRUTUS   Your reason?

CASSIUS   This it is:
'Tis better that the enemy seek us.
So shall he waste his means, weary his soldiers,
201   Doing himself offense, whilst we, lying still,
Are full of rest, defense, and nimbleness.

BRUTUS
203   Good reasons must of force give place to better.
The people 'twixt Philippi and this ground
205   Do stand but in a forced affection;
For they have grudged us contribution.
The enemy, marching along by them,
By them shall make a fuller number up,
209   Come on refreshed, new added, and encouraged;
From which advantage shall we cut him off
If at Philippi we do face him there,
These people at our back.

181–95 (some editors, assuming revision, bracket or delete this episode as contradictory and redundant of ll. 143–58 and 166)   191 once at some time   194 this in art i.e. this stoical fortitude in philosophical theory   195 nature natural emotions   196 alive that concerns us as living men   201 offense injury   203 of force of necessity   205 Do . . . affection favor us only by compulsion   209 new added reinforced   220 Omitted not taken   221 bound in confined to   224 ventures investments risked on the high seas; with your will as you wish   228 niggard stint, i.e. sleep only a short time   230 hence go from here   231 gown dressing gown   239 instrument lute or cithern   241 knave lad (affectionate); o'erwatched tired from lack of sleep   247 raise rouse; by and by soon   249 watch your pleasure await your commands   251 otherwise bethink me change my mind

CASSIUS   Hear me, good brother.

BRUTUS
Under your pardon. You must note beside
That we have tried the utmost of our friends,
Our legions are brimful, our cause is ripe.
The enemy increaseth every day;
We, at the height, are ready to decline.
There is a tide in the affairs of men
Which, taken at the flood, leads on to fortune;
220   Omitted, all the voyage of their life
221   Is bound in shallows and in miseries.
On such a full sea are we now afloat,
And we must take the current when it serves
224   Or lose our ventures.

CASSIUS   Then, with your will, go on.
We'll along ourselves and meet them at Philippi.

BRUTUS
The deep of night is crept upon our talk
And nature must obey necessity,
228   Which we will niggard with a little rest.
There is no more to say?

CASSIUS   No more. Good night.
230   Early to-morrow will we rise and hence.

BRUTUS
231   Lucius! (Enter Lucius.) My gown.   [Exit Lucius.]
                Farewell, good Messala.
Good night, Titinius. Noble, noble Cassius,
Good night and good repose.

CASSIUS   O my dear brother,
This was an ill beginning of the night!
Never come such division 'tween our souls!
Let it not, Brutus.
        Enter Lucius, with the gown.

BRUTUS   Everything is well.

CASSIUS
Good night, my lord.

BRUTUS   Good night, good brother.

TITINIUS, MESSALA
Good night, Lord Brutus.

BRUTUS   Farewell every one.
                Exeunt [Cassius, Titinius, and Messala].
239   Give me the gown. Where is thy instrument?

LUCIUS
Here in the tent.

BRUTUS   What, thou speak'st drowsily?
241   Poor knave, I blame thee not; thou art o'erwatched.
Call Claudius and some other of my men;
I'll have them sleep on cushions in my tent.

LUCIUS Varro and Claudius!
        Enter Varro and Claudius.

VARRO Calls my lord?

BRUTUS
I pray you, sirs, lie in my tent and sleep.
247   It may be I shall raise you by and by
On business to my brother Cassius.

VARRO
So please you, we will stand and watch your pleasure.   249

BRUTUS
I will not have it so. Lie down, good sirs.
251   It may be I shall otherwise bethink me.
        [Varro and Claudius lie down.]
Look, Lucius, here's the book I sought for so;
I put it in the pocket of my gown.

LUCIUS
I was sure your lordship did not give it me.
BRUTUS
Bear with me, good boy, I am much forgetful.
Canst thou hold up thy heavy eyes awhile,
257 And touch thy instrument a strain or two?
LUCIUS
258 Ay, my lord, an't please you.
BRUTUS   It does, my boy.
I trouble thee too much, but thou art willing.
LUCIUS It is my duty, sir.
BRUTUS
I should not urge thy duty past thy might.
262 I know young bloods look for a time of rest.
LUCIUS I have slept, my lord, already.
BRUTUS
It was well done; and thou shalt sleep again;
265 I will not hold thee long. If I do live,
266 I will be good to thee.
Music, and a song. [Lucius falls asleep.]
267 This is a sleepy tune. O murd'rous slumber!
268 Layest thou thy leaden mace upon my boy,
That plays thee music? Gentle knave, good night.
I will not do thee so much wrong to wake thee.
If thou dost nod, thou break'st thy instrument;
I'll take it from thee; and, good boy, good night.
Let me see, let me see. Is not the leaf turned down
Where I left reading? Here it is, I think.
[Sits.] Enter the Ghost of Caesar.
275 How ill this taper burns! Ha, who comes here?
276 I think it is the weakness of mine eyes
That shapes this monstrous apparition.
278 It comes upon me. Art thou any thing?
Art thou some god, some angel, or some devil,
280 That mak'st my blood cold and my hair to stare?
Speak to me what thou art.
GHOST
Thy evil spirit, Brutus.
BRUTUS   Why com'st thou?
GHOST
To tell thee thou shalt see me at Philippi.
BRUTUS Well; then I shall see thee again?
GHOST Ay, at Philippi.
BRUTUS
Why, I will see thee at Philippi then.   *[Exit Ghost.]*
Now I have taken heart thou vanishest.
Ill spirit, I would hold more talk with thee.
Boy. Lucius! Varro, Claudius. Sirs! Awake!
Claudius!
291 LUCIUS The strings, my lord, are false.
BRUTUS
He thinks he still is at his instrument.
Lucius, awake!
LUCIUS My lord?
BRUTUS
Didst thou dream, Lucius, that thou so criedst out?
LUCIUS
My lord, I do not know that I did cry.
BRUTUS
Yes, that thou didst. Didst thou see anything?
LUCIUS Nothing, my lord.
BRUTUS
Sleep again, Lucius. Sirrah Claudius!
[To Varro]

Fellow thou, awake!
VARRO My lord?
CLAUDIUS My lord?
BRUTUS
Why did you so cry out, sirs, in your sleep?
BOTH
Did we, my lord?
BRUTUS   Ay. Saw you anything?
VARRO
No, my lord, I saw nothing.
CLAUDIUS   Nor I, my lord.
BRUTUS
Go and commend me to my brother Cassius.   306
Bid him set on his pow'rs betimes before,   307
And we will follow.
BOTH   It shall be done, my lord.   *Exeunt.*

*

Enter Octavius, Antony, and their Army.   V, i
OCTAVIUS
Now, Antony, our hopes are answerèd.
You said the enemy would not come down
But keep the hills and upper regions.
It proves not so. Their battles are at hand;   4
They mean to warn us at Philippi here,   5
Answering before we do demand of them.   6
ANTONY
Tut! I am in their bosoms and I know   7
Wherefore they do it. They could be content   8
To visit other places, and come down
With fearful bravery, thinking by this face   10
To fasten in our thoughts that they have courage.   11
But 'tis not so.
Enter a Messenger.
MESSENGER   Prepare you, generals.
The enemy comes on in gallant show;   13
Their bloody sign of battle is hung out,   14
And something to be done immediately.
ANTONY
Octavius, lead your battle softly on   16
Upon the left hand of the even field.
OCTAVIUS
Upon the right hand I. Keep thou the left.
ANTONY
Why do you cross me in this exigent?   19

257 *touch* play on; *strain* musical composition   258 *an't* if it   262 *young bloods* youthful constitutions   265 *hold* detain   266 s.d. *Music, and a song* (stage tradition prescribes the use of 'Orpheus with his lute,' from *Henry VIII*; more appropriate is 'Come, heavy sleep,' from John Dowland's *First Book of Songs*, 1597)   267 *murd'rous* giving the appearance of death   268 *leaden* heavy (lead was associated with death); *mace* staff of office with which a man was touched on the shoulder when arrested   275 *How . . . burns* (it was commonly held that lights burned dim or blue in the presence of a ghost or spirit)   276 *weakness . . . eyes* i.e. possibly a hallucination   278 *upon* toward   280 *stare* stand on end   291 *false* out of tune   306 *commend me* give my greetings   307 *set on* advance; *betimes before* early in the morning before me
V, i The plains of Philippi   4 *proves* turns out to be; *battles* armies   5 *warn* challenge   6 *Answering . . . them* appearing against us before we call them to combat   7 *in their bosoms* aware of their secrets (i.e. he has spies in their army)   8-9 *could . . . places* would prefer to be elsewhere   10 *fearful bravery* display that inspires (with pun on 'is full of') fear; *face* show   11 *fasten* fix the idea   13 *gallant* splendid   14 *bloody sign* red flag   16 *battle* army; *softly* slowly   19 *cross* oppose; *exigent* critical moment

OCTAVIUS
I do not cross you ; but I will do so.
March. Drum. Enter Brutus, Cassius, and their Army
[; Lucilius, Titinius, Messala, and others].

BRUTUS
They stand and would have parley.

CASSIUS
Stand fast, Titinius. We must out and talk.

OCTAVIUS
Mark Antony, shall we give sign of battle ?

ANTONY
24 No, Caesar, we will answer on their charge.
25 Make forth. The generals would have some words.

OCTAVIUS
Stir not until the signal.

BRUTUS
Words before blows. Is it so, countrymen ?

OCTAVIUS
Not that we love words better, as you do.

BRUTUS
Good words are better than bad strokes, Octavius.

ANTONY
In your bad strokes, Brutus, you give good words ;
Witness the hole you made in Caesar's heart,
Crying 'Long live ! Hail, Caesar !'

CASSIUS   Antony,
33 The posture of your blows are yet unknown ;
34 But for your words, they rob the Hybla bees,
And leave them honeyless.

ANTONY   Not stingless too.

BRUTUS
O yes, and soundless too !
For you have stol'n their buzzing, Antony,
And very wisely threat before you sting.

ANTONY
39 Villains ! you did not so when your vile daggers
Hacked one another in the sides of Caesar.
41 You showed your teeth like apes, and fawned like hounds,
And bowed like bondmen, kissing Caesar's feet ;
Whilst damnèd Casca, like a cur, behind
Struck Caesar on the neck. O you flatterers !

CASSIUS
Flatterers ? Now, Brutus, thank yourself !
This tongue had not offended so to-day
47 If Cassius might have ruled.

OCTAVIUS
48 Come, come, the cause ! If arguing make us sweat,
49 The proof of it will turn to redder drops.

Look,
I draw a sword against conspirators.
When think you that the sword goes up again ?   52
Never, till Caesar's three-and-thirty wounds
Be well avenged, or till another Caesar   54
Have added slaughter to the sword of traitors.   55

BRUTUS
Caesar, thou canst not die by traitors' hands
Unless thou bring'st them with thee.

OCTAVIUS   So I hope.
I was not born to die on Brutus' sword.

BRUTUS
O, if thou wert the noblest of thy strain,   59
Young man, thou couldst not die more honorable.

CASSIUS
A peevish schoolboy, worthless of such honor,   61
Joined with a masker and a reveller !   62

ANTONY
Old Cassius still.

OCTAVIUS   Come, Antony. Away !
Defiance, traitors, hurl we in your teeth.
If you dare fight to-day, come to the field ;
If not, when you have stomachs.   66
        Exit Octavius, [with] Antony, and Army.

CASSIUS
Why, now blow wind, swell billow, and swim bark !
The storm is up, and all is on the hazard.   68

BRUTUS
Ho, Lucilius ! Hark, a word with you.
       Lucilius stands forth.

LUCILIUS   My lord ?
     [Brutus and Lucilius converse apart.]

CASSIUS
Messala.
       Messala stands forth.

MESSALA   What says my general ?

CASSIUS   Messala,
This is my birthday ; as this very day
Was Cassius born. Give me thy hand, Messala.
Be thou my witness that against my will
(As Pompey was) am I compelled to set   74
Upon one battle all our liberties.
You know that I held Epicurus strong   76
And his opinion. Now I change my mind
And partly credit things that do presage.   78
Coming from Sardis, on our former ensign   79
Two mighty eagles fell ; and there they perched,   80
Gorging and feeding from our soldiers' hands,
Who to Philippi here consorted us.   82
This morning are they fled away and gone,
And in their steads do ravens, crows, and kites   84
Fly o'er our heads and downward look on us
As we were sickly prey. Their shadows seem   86
A canopy most fatal, under which   87
Our army lies, ready to give up the ghost.

MESSALA
Believe not so.

CASSIUS   I but believe it partly ;   89
For I am fresh of spirit and resolved
To meet all perils very constantly.   91

BRUTUS
Even so, Lucilius.

CASSIUS   Now, most noble Brutus,
The gods to-day stand friendly, that we may,   93

24 *on their charge* when they attack   25 *Make forth* go forward   33 *posture* fashion, quality   34 *Hybla* a Sicilian town famous for the sweetness of its honey   39 *so* i.e. give warning   41 *showed your teeth* grinned obsequiously   47 *ruled* had his way (at II, i, 155–61)   48 *the cause* to our business   49 *proof* trial   52 *goes up* will be sheathed   54 *another Caesar* i.e. himself   55 *Have . . . to* has also been killed by   59 *strain* line of descent   61 *peevish* childish (Octavius was twenty-one) ; *worthless* unworthy   62 *masker . . . reveller* (see II, i, 189; II, ii, 116)   66 *stomachs* appetite (for battle)   68 *on the hazard* at stake   74 *As Pompey was* (at Pharsalus, where he was persuaded to give battle to Caesar against his will; see I, i, 37n.); *set* stake, gamble   76–77 *held . . . opinion* was a convinced follower of the Epicurean philosophy, i.e. a materialist, who thought it foolishly superstitious to believe in omens (cf. II, i, 193–201)   78 *credit* believe in   79 *former* foremost ; *ensign* standard, banner   80 *fell* swooped down   82 *consorted* accompanied   84 *ravens . . . kites* scavengers which proverbially anticipate death   86 *sickly* dying   87 *fatal* foreboding death   89 *but* only   91 *constantly* resolutely   93 *The . . . friendly* may the gods be well-disposed toward us to-day

94 Lovers in peace, lead on our days to age!
95 But since the affairs of men rests still incertain,
96 Let's reason with the worst that may befall.
    If we do lose this battle, then is this
    The very last time we shall speak together.
99 What are you then determinèd to do?

BRUTUS

100 Even by the rule of that philosophy
101 By which I did blame Cato for the death
    Which he did give himself – I know not how,
    But I do find it cowardly and vile,
104 For fear of what might fall, so to prevent
105 The time of life – arming myself with patience
106 To stay the providence of some high powers
    That govern us below.

CASSIUS   Then, if we lose this battle,

108 You are contented to be led in triumph
    Thorough the streets of Rome.

BRUTUS

    No, Cassius, no. Think not, thou noble Roman,
111 That ever Brutus will go bound to Rome.
    He bears too great a mind. But this same day
    Must end that work the ides of March begun,
    And whether we shall meet again I know not.
    Therefore our everlasting farewell take.
    For ever and for ever farewell, Cassius!
    If we do meet again, why, we shall smile;
    If not, why then this parting was well made.

CASSIUS

    For ever and for ever farewell, Brutus!
    If we do meet again, we'll smile indeed;
    If not, 'tis true this parting was well made.

BRUTUS

    Why then, lead on. O that a man might know
    The end of this day's business ere it come!
    But it sufficeth that the day will end,
    And then the end is known. Come, ho! Away!   *Exeunt.*

V, ii   *Alarum. Enter Brutus and Messala.*

BRUTUS

1 Ride, ride, Messala, ride, and give these bills
2 Unto the legions on the other side.
       Loud alarum.
3 Let them set on at once; for I perceive
4 But cold demeanor in Octavius' wing,
5 And sudden push gives them the overthrow.
6 Ride, ride, Messala! Let them all come down.   *Exeunt.*

V, iii   *Alarums. Enter Cassius and Titinius.*

CASSIUS

1 O, look, Titinius, look! The villains fly!
2 Myself have to mine own turned enemy.
3 This ensign here of mine was turning back;
4 I slew the coward and did take it from him.

TITINIUS

    O Cassius, Brutus gave the word too early,
6 Who, having some advantage on Octavius,
7 Took it too eagerly. His soldiers fell to spoil,
    Whilst we by Antony are all enclosed.
       Enter Pindarus.

PINDARUS

    Fly further off, my lord! fly further off!
10 Mark Antony is in your tents, my lord.
11 Fly, therefore, noble Cassius, fly far off!

CASSIUS

    This hill is far enough. Look, look, Titinius!

    Are those my tents where I perceive the fire?

TITINIUS

    They are, my lord.

CASSIUS   Titinius, if thou lovest me,
    Mount thou my horse and hide thy spurs in him
    Till he have brought thee up to yonder troops
    And here again, that I may rest assured
    Whether yond troops are friend or enemy.

TITINIUS

    I will be here again even with a thought.   *Exit.* 19

CASSIUS

    Go, Pindarus, get higher on that hill.
    My sight was ever thick. Regard Titinius, 21
    And tell me what thou not'st about the field. 22
       [Pindarus goes up.]
    This day I breathèd first. Time is come round,
    And where I did begin, there shall I end.
    My life is run his compass. Sirrah, what news? 25

PINDARUS *(above)* O my lord! 26

CASSIUS What news?

PINDARUS *[above]*
    Titinius is enclosèd round about
    With horsemen that make to him on the spur. 29
    Yet he spurs on. Now they are almost on him.
    Now Titinius. Now some light. O, he lights too! 31
    He's ta'en. *(Shout.)* And hark! They shout for joy. 32

CASSIUS

    Come down; behold no more.
    O coward that I am to live so long
    To see my best friend ta'en before my face!
       Enter Pindarus [from above].
    Come hither, sirrah.
    In Parthia did I take thee prisoner;
    And then I swore thee, saving of thy life, 38
    That whatsoever I did bid thee do,
    Thou shouldst attempt it. Come now, keep thine oath.
    Now be a freeman, and with this good sword,
    That ran through Caesar's bowels, search this bosom. 42
    Stand not to answer. Here, take thou the hilts; 43
    And when my face is covered, as 'tis now,
    Guide thou the sword.
       [Pindarus stabs him.] Caesar, thou art revenged
    Even with the sword that killed thee.
       [Dies.]

PINDARUS

    So, I am free; yet would not so have been, 47

94 *Lovers* dear friends   95 *rests still* remain always   96 *reason . . . befall* consider what to do if the worst should happen   99 *then* i.e. if we should lose   100 *that philosophy* i.e. Stoicism   101 *Cato* (see II, i, 295n.)   104 *fall* happen; *prevent* anticipate   105 *time* natural limit   106 *stay* wait for; *providence* destiny; *some* whatever (i.e. Brutus does not believe in the Roman gods, but he does believe in 'powers' whose nature he cannot exactly define)   108 *in triumph* in a victory procession (as a captive)   111 *bound* in chains (as a captive)

V, ii   s.d. *Alarum* a drum signal calling to arms   1 *bills* written orders   2 *side* wing (of the army), i.e. Cassius' forces   3 *set on* attack   4 *cold demeanor* lack of spirit (in battle)   5 *push* assault; *gives . . . overthrow* will defeat them   6 *them . . . down* the whole army attack

V, iii   1 *villains* i.e. his own troops   2 *mine own* my own men   3 *ensign* standard-bearer   4 *it* i.e. the standard he was bearing   6 *on* over   7 *spoil* ooting   10 *tents* encampment   11 *far* farther   19 *even . . . thought* in the twinkling of an eye   21 *thick* dim, i.e. near-sighted; *Regard* observe   22 *not'st* observe   25 *is . . . compass* has completed its full circuit   26 s.d. *above* (on the 'upper stage')   29 *make to* approach; *on the spur* rapidly   31 *light* dismount   32 *ta'en* captured   38 *swore thee* made you swear; *saving of* when I spared   42 *search* probe, penetrate into   43 *Stand* delay   47 *not so* not in such circumstances

48   Durst I have done my will. O Cassius!
Far from this country Pindarus shall run,
Where never Roman shall take note of him.   *[Exit.]*
      Enter Titinius and Messala.

MESSALA
51   It is but change, Titinius; for Octavius
Is overthrown by noble Brutus' power,
As Cassius' legions are by Antony.

TITINIUS
54   These tidings will well comfort Cassius.

MESSALA
Where did you leave him?

TITINIUS   All disconsolate,
With Pindarus his bondman, on this hill.

MESSALA
Is not that he that lies upon the ground?

TITINIUS
He lies not like the living. O my heart!

MESSALA
Is not that he?

TITINIUS   No, this was he, Messala,
60   But Cassius is no more. O setting sun,
As in thy red rays thou dost sink to night,
So in his red blood Cassius' day is set!
The sun of Rome is set. Our day is gone;
64   Clouds, dews, and dangers come; our deeds are done!
65   Mistrust of my success hath done this deed.

MESSALA
Mistrust of good success hath done this deed.
67   O hateful Error, Melancholy's child,
68   Why dost thou show to the apt thoughts of men
The things that are not? O Error, soon conceived,
Thou never com'st unto a happy birth,
71   But kill'st the mother that engend'red thee!

TITINIUS
What, Pindarus! Where art thou, Pindarus?

MESSALA
Seek him, Titinius, whilst I go to meet
The noble Brutus, thrusting this report
Into his ears. I may say 'thrusting' it;
For piercing steel and darts envenomèd
Shall be as welcome to the ears of Brutus
As tidings of this sight.

78 TITINIUS   Hie you, Messala,
And I will seek for Pindarus the while.   *[Exit Messala.]*
80   Why didst thou send me forth, brave Cassius?
Did I not meet thy friends, and did not they

Put on my brows this wreath of victory
And bid me give it thee? Didst thou not hear their
     shouts?
Alas, thou hast misconstrued everything!   84
But hold thee, take this garland on thy brow.   85
Thy Brutus bid me give it thee, and I
Will do his bidding. Brutus, come apace
And see how I regarded Caius Cassius.   88
By your leave, gods. This is a Roman's part.   89
Come, Cassius' sword, and find Titinius' heart.
      Dies.
      Alarum. Enter Brutus, Messala, Young Cato,
      Strato, Volumnius, and Lucilius.

BRUTUS
Where, where, Messala, doth his body lie?

MESSALA
Lo, yonder, and Titinius mourning it.

BRUTUS
Titinius' face is upward.

CATO   He is slain.

BRUTUS
O Julius Caesar, thou art mighty yet!
Thy spirit walks abroad and turns our swords
In our own proper entrails.   96
      Low alarums.

CATO   Brave Titinius!
Look whe'r he have not crowned dead Cassius.

BRUTUS
Are yet two Romans living such as these?
The last of all the Romans, fare thee well!
It is impossible that ever Rome
Should breed thy fellow. Friends, I owe moe tears   101
To this dead man than you shall see me pay.
I shall find time, Cassius; I shall find time.
Come therefore, and to Thasos send his body.   104
His funerals shall not be in our camp,
Lest it discomfort us. Lucilius, come;   106
And come, young Cato. Let us to the field.
Labeo and Flavius set our battles on.   108
'Tis three o'clock; and, Romans, yet ere night
We shall try fortune in a second fight.
               Exeunt.

      Alarum. Enter Brutus, Messala, [Young] Cato,   V, iv
      Lucilius, and Flavius.

BRUTUS
Yet, countrymen, O, yet hold up your heads!
      [Exit, followed by Messala and Flavius.]

CATO
What bastard doth not? Who will go with me?   2
I will proclaim my name about the field.
I am the son of Marcus Cato, ho!   4
A foe to tyrants, and my country's friend.   5
I am the son of Marcus Cato, ho!
      Enter Soldiers and fight.

LUCILIUS
And I am Brutus, Marcus Brutus I!   7
Brutus, my country's friend! Know me for Brutus!
      [Young Cato falls.]
O young and noble Cato, art thou down?
Why, now thou diest as bravely as Titinius,   10
And mayst be honored, being Cato's son.

[1.] SOLDIER
Yield, or thou diest.

LUCILIUS   Only I yield to die.   12

48 *my will* (rather than Cassius' will, which he was sworn to do)   **51** *change* an exchange, 'quid pro quo'   **54** *comfort* encourage   **60** *setting sun* (a figurative comparison: actually it is mid-afternoon – see l. 109)   **64** *dews* (see II, i, 262n., 265n.)   **65** *Mistrust . . . success* fear as to how I should make out   **67** *Melancholy's child* (melancholy persons fear unreal dangers)   **68** *apt* impressionable   **71** *mother* i.e. the melancholy person who conceived the error   **78** *Hie* hurry   **80** *brave* noble   **84** *misconstrued* (accented on second syllable)   **85** *hold thee* wait a minute   **88** *regarded* respected, honored   **89** *leave* permission; *part* role, function (in such circumstances)   **96** *own proper* very own; *Brave* noble   **101** *moe* more   **104** *Thasos* an island near Philippi where, according to Plutarch, Cassius was buried   **106** *discomfort us* dishearten our army   **108** *battles* forces
V, iv   **2** *What bastard* who is so low-born that he   **4** *Cato* (see II, i, 295n.)   **5** *tyrants* (such as Caesar and his followers)   **7** *Lucilius* (in the folio this speech-prefix appears at l. 9, but Lucilius, as indicated in Plutarch, also speaks ll. 7–8, impersonating Brutus, though some editors give ll. 7–8 to Brutus)   **10** *bravely* nobly   **12** *Only . . . die* I surrender only in order to die

13   There is so much that thou wilt kill me straight.
     Kill Brutus, and be honored in his death.

[1.] SOLDIER
     We must not. A noble prisoner!
        Enter Antony.

2. SOLDIER
     Room ho! Tell Antony Brutus is ta'en.

1. SOLDIER
     I'll tell the news. Here comes the general.
     Brutus is ta'en! Brutus is ta'en, my lord!

ANTONY Where is he?

LUCILIUS
     Safe, Antony; Brutus is safe enough.
     I dare assure thee that no enemy
     Shall ever take alive the noble Brutus.
     The gods defend him from so great a shame!
     When you do find him, or alive or dead,
25   He will be found like Brutus, like himself.

ANTONY
     This is not Brutus, friend; but, I assure you,
     A prize no less in worth. Keep this man safe;
     Give him all kindness. I had rather have
     Such men my friends than enemies. Go on,
     And see whe'r Brutus be alive or dead;
     And bring us word unto Octavius' tent
32   How every thing is chanced.   *Exeunt.*

V, v   *Enter Brutus, Dardanius, Clitus, Strato, and*
       Volumnius.

BRUTUS
1   Come, poor remains of friends, rest on this rock.

CLITUS
2   Statilius showed the torchlight; but, my lord,
     He came not back. He is or ta'en or slain.

BRUTUS
     Sit thee down, Clitus. Slaying is the word.
     It is a deed in fashion. Hark thee, Clitus.
     [Whispers.]

CLITUS
     What, I, my lord? No, not for all the world!

BRUTUS
     Peace then. No words.

CLITUS   I'll rather kill myself.

BRUTUS
     Hark thee, Dardanius.
     [Whispers.]

DARDANIUS   Shall I do such a deed?

CLITUS O Dardanius!

DARDANIUS O Clitus!

CLITUS
     What ill request did Brutus make to thee?

DARDANIUS
     To kill him, Clitus. Look, he meditates.

CLITUS
13   Now is that noble vessel full of grief,
     That it runs over even at his eyes.

BRUTUS
     Come hither, good Volumnius. List a word.

VOLUMNIUS
     What says my lord?

BRUTUS   Why this, Volumnius.
     The ghost of Caesar hath appeared to me
18   Two several times by night – at Sardis once,
     And this last night here in Philippi fields.
     I know my hour is come.

VOLUMNIUS   Not so, my lord.

BRUTUS
     Nay, I am sure it is, Volumnius.
     Thou seest the world, Volumnius, how it goes.
     Our enemies have beat us to the pit.   23
       Low alarums.
     It is more worthy to leap in ourselves   24
     Than tarry till they push us. Good Volumnius,
     Thou know'st that we two went to school together.
     Even for that our love of old, I prithee
     Hold thou my sword-hilts whilst I run on it.

VOLUMNIUS
     That's not an office for a friend, my lord.
       Alarum still.

CLITUS
     Fly, fly, my lord! There is no tarrying here.

BRUTUS
     Farewell to you; and you; and you, Volumnius.
     Strato, thou hast been all this while asleep.
     Farewell to thee too, Strato. Countrymen,
     My heart doth joy that yet in all my life
     I found no man but he was true to me.
     I shall have glory by this losing day
     More than Octavius and Mark Antony
     By this vile conquest shall attain unto.   38
     So fare you well at once; for Brutus' tongue   39
     Hath almost ended his life's history.
     Night hangs upon mine eyes; my bones would rest,
     That have but labored to attain this hour.   42
       Alarum. Cry within: Fly, fly, fly!

CLITUS
     Fly, my lord, fly!

BRUTUS   Hence! I will follow.
       [Exeunt Clitus, Dardanius, and Volumnius.]
     I prithee, Strato, stay thou by thy lord.
     Thou art a fellow of a good respect;   45
     Thy life hath had some smatch of honor in it.   46
     Hold then my sword, and turn away thy face
     While I do run upon it. Wilt thou, Strato?

STRATO
     Give me your hand first. Fare you well, my lord.

BRUTUS
     Farewell, good Strato. Caesar, now be still.
     I killed not thee with half so good a will.
       [He runs on his sword and] dies.
       Alarum. Retreat. Enter Octavius, Antony,
       Messala, Lucilius, and the Army.

OCTAVIUS
     What man is that?

MESSALA
     My master's man. Strato, where is thy master?   53

---

13 *so much* so great an inducement to honor and fame (?), so much that I can be blamed for (?) (some editors suppose an offer of money); *straight* at once   25 *like himself* true to his noble nature   32 *is chanced* has happened

V, v   1 *poor remains* pitiful survivors   2 *Statilius . . . torchlight* i.e. a scout who got as far as Cassius' encampment, occupied by Antony's troops, from which he signalled   13 *noble vessel* completely noble man (also a sacred vessel for holding the tears of devout mourners)   18 *several* different   23 *the pit* (into which a wild animal is driven in order to be captured; with pun on 'the grave')   24 *more worthy* nobler   38 *vile conquest* i.e. the destruction of Republican Rome   39 *at once* all together   42 *but labored* experienced only pain   45 *respect* reputation   46 *smatch* taste   53 *man* servant

STRATO

Free from the bondage you are in, Messala.

55 The conquerors can but make a fire of him ;

56 For Brutus only overcame himself,

And no man else hath honor by his death.

LUCILIUS

So Brutus should be found. I thank thee, Brutus,

59 That thou hast proved Lucilius' saying true.

OCTAVIUS

60 All that served Brutus, I will entertain them.

61 Fellow, wilt thou bestow thy time with me ?

STRATO

62 Ay, if Messala will prefer me to you.

OCTAVIUS

Do so, good Messala.

MESSALA

How died my master, Strato ?

STRATO

I held the sword, and he did run on it.

MESSALA

Octavius, then take him to follow thee,   66

That did the latest service to my master.   67

ANTONY

This was the noblest Roman of them all.

All the conspirators save only he

Did that they did in envy of great Caesar ;

He, only in a general honest thought   71

And common good to all, made one of them.   72

His life was gentle, and the elements   73

So mixed in him that Nature might stand up   74

And say to all the world, 'This was a man !'   75

OCTAVIUS

According to his virtue let us use him,   76

With all respect and rites of burial.

Within my tent his bones to-night shall lie,

Most like a soldier, orderèd honorably.   79

So call the field to rest, and let's away   80

To part the glories of this happy day.   *Exeunt omnes.* 81

55 *make a fire of* cremate   56 *Brutus only overcame* only Brutus defeated   59 *saying* (see V, iv, 21–25)   60 *entertain them* take them into my service   61 *Fellow* (addressed to Strato) ; *bestow* spend   62 *prefer* recommend   66 *follow* serve   67 *latest* last, final   71–72 *general . . . all* honorable purpose to the whole society and for the good of all Romans   72 *made . . . them* joined the conspiracy   73 *gentle* noble ; *elements* the four elements (earth, water, air, fire) of which all matter was thought to be composed, or the four humors (melancholic, phlegmatic, sanguine, choleric)   74 *So mixed* i.e. equally balanced   75 *a man* i.e. an ideal man   76 *use* treat   79 *orderèd* treated   80 *field* army   81 *part* share, divide

HAMLET PRINCE OF DENMARK

INTRODUCTION

Vicissitudes of literary taste and temper in the present age have not weakened the hold of *Hamlet* upon viewer and reader, however much they have changed it. Probably they have made it stronger than ever before, stronger even than it was for the last age of men, in the nineteenth century. This is saying much, for men in the nineteenth century helped mightily to make *Hamlet* the most acted and most written-about of Shakespeare's plays. They earnestly accepted its challenge to understanding.

That from which this challenge issues, stamped with a name in words given by Shakespeare to Hamlet himself – "you would pluck out the heart of my mystery" (III, ii, 351–52) – has come to be called the Hamlet mystery by many. Here and there it has been called so with resignation, sometimes hopelessly, but even in its guise of insolubility it can still command critical statement about its being.

It is already plain that the twentieth century will add perception that will matter to the Hamlet tradition in our culture. What it adds will be, like such an addition by any other age, a characteristic enlargement of Shakespeare's dramatic achievement. After a lapse of centuries an extension of perception for a constantly lived-with and experienced work of art like *Hamlet* is an extension of the original creation much to be reckoned with for its revelation of a complex vitality. The new creation comes about not only because the author has conceived form capable of long-continuing growth but also because a late age of posterity, despite the variety of contributions made by former ages, has conceived form into which growth can proceed.

What we in this age seem bent on giving to *Hamlet* is greatly enlarged scope. We are sure enough of ourselves to think of this as meaning a new breadth, and we may hope that it will mean also a new depth. For a long time after Shakespeare there was no generally recognized Hamlet mystery; Hamlet seems to have been for most men a courageous prince who found it understandably hard to take revenge on a shrewd and powerful king. By the nineteenth century the mystery was well established. It was troublesome enough but it could usually be kept within close bounds – that is, within the outlines of Hamlet the man realistically considered as someone who in all essential qualities, however exceptional they might be, could be judged by common sense as a walking and talking inhabitant of the critic's own age. A further limitation came from much thinking that the key to Hamlet's tragedy was probably some one dominant thing such as unstable nervous quality, or shock from his father's death and his mother's hasty remarriage, or melancholy pessimism, or sensitivity unfitting him for the crass burden of his duty to take revenge, or delight in thought unfitting him for

crucial action. Such ideas were all, of course, well worth the having, and they shook down into a corpus that will be a lasting part of the Hamlet tradition. But they did not offer enough satisfaction to keep critics from hastening on to other searchings.

Our twentieth-century searchings have become less and less confined, even when they have been within the personal creation that is Hamlet. Hamlet psychology, still very much alive in an age that has produced Freud and Jung, is now not content with merely a homely reading of Hamlet's character by everyday use of heart and mind. The field of Elizabethan psychology has been carefully explored for principles applicable to Hamlet, and thus there has been a fitting of his creation into the history of ideas. With the application of modern psychological theories – especially and most inevitably those having to do with the ancient family triad of father, mother, and child – there has been an expansion of his persona to take account of a dark abysm of the human self from which can come to anyone, as is thought, tensely opposed feelings for both father and mother, and from which, we are to understand, there comes to Hamlet so much emotional conflict with regard to his uncle the King as a substitute father image, married to his mother, that his hate cannot achieve the murder of the King before his bringing, by hesitation, of death to both his mother and himself. Hamlet, indeed, may seem to have been shaped to order for psychoanalysis. In modern psychology an extension of the Hamlet creation, truly meaningful whether one responds to it or not, has been made by the coming together with a startling show of affinity of something in us and something in Shakespeare.

Elizabethan, nineteenth-century, and twentieth-century psychologies often invite us to see within Hamlet some severe seizure of the soul which is close to disease, if not actually disease, and is the more easily thought of in these terms because of the dominant disease imagery running through the play. A Hamlet viewed as thus stricken can be found to have the tragic flaw in an extreme form. Frequently enough an idea has been held that Hamlet shows an exceptionally noble nature and that in this there is, and should be, a classic flaw to make his drama a tragedy. Sometimes the flaw has seemed by no means to be disease-like or wholly undesirable but to take a paradoxical coloring of good from the nobility in which it appears. Yet it has been conceived to be no less an explanatory flaw for all that and necessarily to be delimited, even in the face of mounting disagreement as to what it is exactly.

A part of the present releasing of the Hamlet mystery from its former bounds takes Hamlet the created personality into a realm of criticism where the time-honored idea of the tragic flaw suddenly loses validity. Here there is the thought that imperfection in the hero cannot yield even a part of the meaning in his tragedy by providing some show of justice for what happens to him as an individual. But here at the same time a conception of Hamlet's having nobility of nature remains, and it may go so far as to make him into a type of human perfection. The Hamlet mystery may thus turn into something like a mystery of Hamlet's martyrdom, where whatever makes it mystery tends to be found outside the character of an individual Hamlet in the character of man in general and in the character of the universe which produces the common predicament of man. Man must act, but all action involves him in evil. It is a finding in the content of *Hamlet* that our age has perhaps been qualified to make by its rediscovery of some forgotten powers of evil in human life and by its interpretation of these in recent literature. In such an area of criticism the question is bound to rise, and does rise, whether *Hamlet* is after all a tragedy, whether it is not a drama worthy perhaps to stand with the greatest tragedies but of a kind peculiar to itself. Yet most critics still seem not of a mind to release *Hamlet* from an obligation to show tragic form.

It is remarkable that *Hamlet* should so perplex the mind and at the same time work so little confusion in the heart. It has supremely that which can make us forget our questions when we give ourselves over to it. Probably no other tragic hero of Shakespeare's equals Hamlet in drawing from the observer that most profound pity which is really as much admiration as pity, and is perfectly tragic because there is no condescension in it. It seems impossible not to forgive Hamlet his brutalities to Ophelia, Polonius, or Rosencrantz and Guildenstern, for they are washed out in our feeling if not in our thinking. He should not be made, we believe, to suffer fools gladly, he the superior spirit to add that suffering to his load.

Perhaps more strongly than anything else pity senses the terrible loneliness of Hamlet. The idealism which moves him to a life-and-death struggle with imprisoning evil is so complex, including even a composition of low comedy with high seriousness, that his single companion, the good but all too solemn Horatio, must always be alien to it. The way in which Horatio fails him in the grave-diggers' scene – "'Twere to consider too curiously" (V, i, 193) – is a part of the tragedy, and no minor one. Love desired is always falling away from Hamlet – love in father, in mother, in Ophelia. The poetry that circles about him makes us know that the Prince of Denmark goes through darkness and waste places "most dreadfully attended."

A part of the *Hamlet* that troubles the mind's eye seems to come from Shakespeare's absorption, with sympathies not at all narrow, of a story that had already had a development of meaning at different depths in different ages. This development had taken place in some rather widespread folklore, in a sophisticated literary account of "Amlethus" in the twelfth-century *Historia Danica* of Saxo Grammaticus (printed in 1514), in a very free version of Saxo's account in the fifth volume of the *Histoires Tragiques* of François de Belleforest (1576), and in an old play about Hamlet on the English stage. Concerning the pre-Shakespearean *Hamlet* we know little. A not very revelatory passage in Thomas Nashe's epistle to Robert Greene's *Menaphon* contains a reference to "whole Hamlets, I should say handfuls, of tragicall speeches" as being lifted from Seneca, which indicates that a *Hamlet* was on the

stage by 1589, the date of *Menaphon*, and that it was a Senecan tragedy. Some even more tantalizing words of Nashe's in the same passage have led many to believe that Thomas Kyd, the author of the Senecan *Spanish Tragedy*, wrote this old *Hamlet*. A performance of it is recorded for 1594 and a glimpse of a part of its action comes in 1596 in Thomas Lodge's *Wits Miserie* with a description of a countenance "pale as the Visard of yᵉ ghost which cried so miserably at yᵉ Theator like an oister wife, *Hamlet, revenge*." Shakespeare's *Hamlet*, in the present state of our knowledge, may be dated 1600–1601. Mainly its story follows that in Belleforest. An English translation of Belleforest, *The Hystorie of Hamblet*, was published in 1608 and seems to have been affected somewhat by Shakespeare's play. It remains to mention one more Hamlet play, the unpraiseworthy German piece *Der Bestrafte Brudermord*, the origin of which is problematic, but which seems to have derived mainly from an early acting version of Shakespeare's *Hamlet*. The German play was printed as late as 1781 from a manuscript dated 1710.

Some have thought that the Hamlet mystery has been put forever beyond our understanding by the loss of the older English *Hamlet*, the so-called *Ur-Hamlet*. Some have gone so far as to make out that Shakespeare was overwhelmed by matter drawn from the *Ur-Hamlet*, which turned out to be so unmanageable as he built around it that the result was incomprehensibility for his joined whole. That way lies an accusation that *Hamlet* is a failure as a piece of dramatic art, and the accusation has been made more than once. Doubtless Shakespeare found the *Ur-Hamlet* of some avail, and doubtless the *Ur-Hamlet* was a rude play befitting the dramatic immaturity of its time, with a quality very different from the mature Shakespearean. But it would seem probable that when he wrote *Hamlet* Shakespeare was beyond being overwhelmed by an old play he wanted to use. He was almost ready to melt and recast one with complete mastery to make *King Lear*. As for *Hamlet*'s being a dramatic or literary failure, the answer of course is that our western culture has forcefully refused to have it so, and on the contrary has given it esteem of the highest. It is for western man to keep on asking why, as there seems to be no danger of his ceasing to do.

As he asks why, it is for western man to realize that he is posing questions about truth itself, about the glorious but also terrifying lack of simplicity that truth shows – and shows in special ways within his own culture – according to a Shakespearean structure of dramatic and poetic images. Here, I would say, is the Hamlet problem of Hamlet problems, one whose recognition lets us know why, after all, there must be many Hamlet problems and various answers to them, yet a gathering together of these into some containing oneness.

The theme of unsimple truth comes early into the Hamlet story. Saxo's Amlethus pretends madness to protect himself until he can get revenge upon the uncle who has killed his father and married his mother. There is no complication of soul-searching and delay in his taking of revenge. He merely bides his time. But there is complication in his procedure of saying things that will make those around him think he does not have the wit to accomplish his revenge. He has not merely that wit but the greater wit to deceive only by being truthful, by turning toward the simple swordsmen who surround him faces of the truth that they do not recognize. He has compulsion never in deepest consequence to destroy truth and he delights in following truth toward a mastery of its complexity. He mingles "craft and candor" to let no word of his "lack truth." There is in him something of primitive riddling, but that is not all. When his uncle's followers think to have sport with Amlethus on the seashore as with a simpleton and bid him look at the meal, meaning the sand, they fully expect that he will take the sand for meal. He not only takes it so; he makes it so in truth. His reply is that it has "been ground small by hoary tempests of the ocean." Here we suddenly know that we are witnessing in fully acceptable form a demonstration of the wide division between the truth of things and the truth of spirit, and the annihilation of this division in the truth of poetry. Such matter as this is largely replaced in Belleforest by a too simple moralizing but not, certainly, in Shakespeare.

In *Hamlet* the theme of unsimple truth is so abundantly restored and so subtly extended that it is everywhere in the action and the poetry. Hamlet at his first appearance begins a searching of the complexity of truth by means of word play and idea play that is carried on throughout the drama; the craft and candor of his dark rejection of sonship to the King and of royal sun-like favor from him, in the punning words "I am too much in the sun" (I, ii, 67), are right Hamlet substance and right introduction to much of the tragedy that comes later. It is by no means only in words and ideas of the moment that Hamlet stands between truths both to divide and unite them. In the large he stands thus between whole worlds of truths in our culture: between the world of an uncivilized heroic past going back even behind Christianity and that of a civilized present; between the world of medieval faith and other-worldliness and that of modern doubt and this-worldliness. In the same way he stands between the truth of angel-like and god-like man and that of man the quintessence of dust, or, in a realm of complete abstraction, between the truth of love and that of hate. There are, needless to say, countless variations in *Hamlet* on the theme of unsimple truth.

It may be said that *Hamlet* is indeed about the pursuit of revenge but most deeply about the pursuit of truth, and that the two pursuits come together to give form to the action of the tragedy. By meeting and testing his father's ghost Hamlet gains truth that seems adequate. It proves on second thought to be not enough. By testing the King with the play within the play he gains truth "more relative than this." Here is the high point of a rising action. Now comes a testing by circumstance of truth that Hamlet has gained with his own testing. He has the chance to kill the praying King. For some reason (we ourselves never stop

testing to find it) he loses at this moment of opportunity all truth he has won about revenge as a crying *immediate* need. He fails to kill the King and thus makes possible the killing of Polonius, which starts a falling action that carries him to death – and ironically to attainment of his revenge, a revenge that takes being from tragic defeat, not a revenge in simple truth such as the revenger seeks. Just before the end, to sharpen the irony, Hamlet uneasily tests his need for revenge against the King all over again, showing inability to make secure in simplicity whatever of lost truth he has regained:

> ... is't not perfect conscience
> To quit him with this arm? And is't not to be damned
> To let this canker of our nature come
> In further evil?

Hamlet dies on the search for truth that all men die on. But his tragedy has a richness of texture all its own, not only within and around the seeker but also within and around what is sought.

University of California　　　　W ILLARD　F ARNHAM
at Berkeley

NOTE ON THE TEXT

Hamlet is preserved in three distinct but related early texts: first, the corrupt and abbreviated acting version in the "bad" quarto of 1603; second, the version "newly imprinted and enlarged to almost as much again as it was, according to the true and perfect coppie" in the "good" quarto of 1604–05 (now usually regarded, but without complete assurance, as printed from Shakespeare's own draft); and third, the version in the 1623 folio (now usually regarded, but again without complete assurance, as printed from the prompt-book of Shakespeare's acting company or from the good quarto altered after reference to such a prompt-book). The present edition is based on the quarto of 1604–05 with a minimum of emendation, but, in view of the manifest faultiness of the quarto printing, with occasional deference to readings in the folio, and even with an eye on the 1603 quarto. Enclosed in square brackets are all additions to the quarto stage directions, as well as additions of whole lines or more of dialogue from the folio. (The longer passages thus added are II, ii, 237–66, 330–54; IV, v, 161–63; V, i, 32–35; V, ii, 68–80.) The texts of the quartos are undivided, and that of the folio almost so since there is no scene division in the first act after I, iii, 1, and no division of any kind after II, ii, 1. It is a common complaint that the editorial act–scene division superimposed on the text in modern times is mechanical and inorganic, but, as explained in the general foreword, it is supplied in the present edition only for reference purposes. A list of departures from the text of the quarto of 1604–05 is supplied in the Appendix along with a few Supplementary Notes.

HAMLET PRINCE OF DENMARK

*

I, i   *Enter Bernardo and Francisco, two sentinels.*

BERNARDO Who's there?

FRANCISCO
Nay, answer me. Stand and unfold yourself.

BERNARDO Long live the king!

FRANCISCO Bernardo?

BERNARDO He.

FRANCISCO
You come most carefully upon your hour.

BERNARDO
'Tis now struck twelve. Get thee to bed, Francisco.

FRANCISCO
For this relief much thanks. 'Tis bitter cold,
And I am sick at heart.

BERNARDO
Have you had quiet guard?

FRANCISCO   Not a mouse stirring.

BERNARDO
Well, good night.
If you do meet Horatio and Marcellus,
13 The rivals of my watch, bid them make haste.
      Enter Horatio and Marcellus.

FRANCISCO
I think I hear them. Stand, ho! Who is there?

HORATIO
Friends to this ground.

15 MARCELLUS   And liegemen to the Dane.

FRANCISCO
Give you good night.

MARCELLUS   O, farewell, honest soldier.

Who hath relieved you?

FRANCISCO   Bernardo hath my place.
Give you good night.   *Exit Francisco.*

MARCELLUS   Holla, Bernardo!

BERNARDO   Say –
What, is Horatio there?

HORATIO   A piece of him.

BERNARDO
Welcome, Horatio. Welcome, good Marcellus.

HORATIO
What, has this thing appeared again to-night?

BERNARDO
I have seen nothing.

MARCELLUS
Horatio says 'tis but our fantasy,
And will not let belief take hold of him
Touching this dreaded sight twice seen of us.
Therefore I have entreated him along
With us to watch the minutes of this night,
That, if again this apparition come,
He may approve our eyes and speak to it. 29

HORATIO
Tush, tush, 'twill not appear.

BERNARDO   Sit down awhile,
And let us once again assail your ears,
That are so fortified against our story,
What we two nights have seen.

HORATIO   Well, sit we down,
And let us hear Bernardo speak of this.

BERNARDO
Last night of all,
When yond same star that's westward from the pole 36
Had made his course t' illume that part of heaven

I, i Elsinore Castle: a sentry-post **13** *rivals* sharers **15** *Dane* King of
Denmark **29** *approve* confirm **36** *pole* polestar

Where now it burns, Marcellus and myself,
The bell then beating one –
    Enter Ghost.

MARCELLUS
Peace, break thee off. Look where it comes again.

BERNARDO
In the same figure like the king that's dead.

MARCELLUS
Thou art a scholar ; speak to it, Horatio.

BERNARDO
Looks 'a not like the king ? Mark it, Horatio.

HORATIO
Most like. It harrows me with fear and wonder.

BERNARDO
It would be spoke to.

MARCELLUS   Speak to it, Horatio.

HORATIO
What art thou that usurp'st this time of night
Together with that fair and warlike form
48 In which the majesty of buried Denmark
49 Did sometimes march ? By heaven I charge thee, speak.

MARCELLUS
It is offended.

BERNARDO   See, it stalks away.

HORATIO
Stay. Speak, speak. I charge thee, speak.   *Exit Ghost.*

MARCELLUS
'Tis gone and will not answer.

BERNARDO
How now, Horatio ? You tremble and look pale.
Is not this something more than fantasy ?
What think you on't ?

HORATIO
Before my God, I might not this believe
Without the sensible and true avouch
Of mine own eyes.

MARCELLUS   Is it not like the king ?

HORATIO
As thou art to thyself.
Such was the very armor he had on
61 When he th' ambitious Norway combated.
62 So frowned he once when, in an angry parle,
He smote the sledded Polacks on the ice.
'Tis strange.

MARCELLUS
65 Thus twice before, and jump at this dead hour,
With martial stalk hath he gone by our watch.

HORATIO
In what particular thought to work I know not ;
68 But, in the gross and scope of my opinion,
This bodes some strange eruption to our state.

MARCELLUS
Good now, sit down, and tell me he that knows,
Why this same strict and most observant watch
72 So nightly toils the subject of the land,
And why such daily cast of brazen cannon
74 And foreign mart for implements of war,
75 Why such impress of shipwrights, whose sore task
Does not divide the Sunday from the week.
77 What might be toward that this sweaty haste
Doth make the night joint-laborer with the day ?
Who is't that can inform me ?

HORATIO   That can I.
At least the whisper goes so. Our last king,

Whose image even but now appeared to us,
Was as you know by Fortinbras of Norway,
Thereto pricked on by a most emulate pride,   83
Dared to the combat ; in which our valiant Hamlet
(For so this side of our known world esteemed him)
Did slay this Fortinbras ; who, by a sealed compact
Well ratified by law and heraldry,   87
Did forfeit, with his life, all those his lands
Which he stood seized of to the conqueror ;   89
Against the which a moiety competent   90
Was gagèd by our king, which had returned   91
To the inheritance of Fortinbras
Had he been vanquisher, as, by the same comart   93
And carriage of the article designed,   94
His fell to Hamlet. Now, sir, young Fortinbras,
Of unimprovèd mettle hot and full,   96
Hath in the skirts of Norway here and there
Sharked up a list of lawless resolutes   98
For food and diet to some enterprise
That hath a stomach in't ; which is no other,   100
As it doth well appear unto our state,
But to recover of us by strong hand
And terms compulsatory those foresaid lands
So by his father lost ; and this, I take it,
Is the main motive of our preparations,
The source of this our watch, and the chief head   106
Of this posthaste and romage in the land.   107

BERNARDO
I think it be no other but e'en so.
Well may it sort that this portentous figure   109
Comes armèd through our watch so like the king
That was and is the question of these wars.

HORATIO
A mote it is to trouble the mind's eye.   112
In the most high and palmy state of Rome,
A little ere the mightiest Julius fell,
The graves stood tenantless and the sheeted dead   115
Did squeak and gibber in the Roman streets ;
As stars with trains of fire and dews of blood,   117
Disasters in the sun ; and the moist star   118
Upon whose influence Neptune's empire stands
Was sick almost to doomsday with eclipse.
And even the like precurse of feared events,   121
As harbingers preceding still the fates   122
And prologue to the omen coming on,   123
Have heaven and earth together demonstrated
Unto our climatures and countrymen.   125
    Enter Ghost.
But soft, behold, lo where it comes again !
I'll cross it, though it blast me. – Stay, illusion.   127
    He spreads his arms.

48 *buried Denmark* the buried King of Denmark   49 *sometimes* formerly
61 *Norway* King of Norway   62 *parle* parley   65 *jump* just, exactly   68
gross and scope gross scope, general view   72 *toils* makes toil ; *subject* subjects   74 *mart* trading   75 *impress* conscription   77 *toward* in preparation
83 *emulate* jealously rivalling   87 *law and heraldry* law of heralds regulating
combat   89 *seized* possessed   90 *moiety competent* sufficient portion   91
gagèd engaged, staked   93 *comart* joint bargain   94 *carriage* purport
96 *unimprovèd* unused   98 *Sharked* snatched indiscriminately as the shark
takes prey ; *resolutes* desperadoes   100 *stomach* show of venturesomeness
106 *head* fountainhead, source   107 *romage* intense activity   109 *sort*
suit   112 *mote* speck of dust   115 *sheeted* in shrouds   117 *As* (see Appendix : Supplementary Notes)   118 *Disasters* ominous signs ; *moist star*
moon   121 *precurse* foreshadowing   122 *harbingers* forerunners ; *still* constantly   123 *omen* calamity   125 *climatures* regions   127 *cross it* cross its
path

If thou hast any sound or use of voice,
Speak to me.
If there be any good thing to be done
That may to thee do ease and grace to me,
Speak to me.
If thou art privy to thy country's fate,
134 Which happily foreknowing may avoid,
O, speak !
Or if thou hast uphoarded in thy life
Extorted treasure in the womb of earth,
For which, they say, you spirits oft walk in death,
     The cock crows.
Speak of it. Stay and speak. Stop it, Marcellus.

MARCELLUS
140 Shall I strike at it with my partisan ?

HORATIO
Do, if it will not stand.

BERNARDO   'Tis here.

HORATIO   'Tis here.

MARCELLUS
'Tis gone.   *[Exit Ghost.]*
We do it wrong, being so majestical,
To offer it the show of violence,
For it is as the air invulnerable,
And our vain blows malicious mockery.

BERNARDO
It was about to speak when the cock crew.

HORATIO
And then it started, like a guilty thing
Upon a fearful summons. I have heard
The cock, that is the trumpet to the morn,
Doth with his lofty and shrill-sounding throat
Awake the god of day, and at his warning,
Whether in sea or fire, in earth or air,
154 Th' extravagant and erring spirit hies
To his confine ; and of the truth herein
156 This present object made probation.

MARCELLUS
It faded on the crowing of the cock.
158 Some say that ever 'gainst that season comes
Wherein our Saviour's birth is celebrated,
This bird of dawning singeth all night long,
And then, they say, no spirit dare stir abroad,
162 The nights are wholesome, then no planets strike,
163 No fairy takes, nor witch hath power to charm.
So hallowed and so gracious is that time.

HORATIO
So have I heard and do in part believe it.
But look, the morn in russet mantle clad
Walks o'er the dew of yon high eastward hill.
Break we our watch up, and by my advice
Let us impart what we have seen to-night
Unto young Hamlet, for upon my life
This spirit, dumb to us, will speak to him.
Do you consent we shall acquaint him with it,
As needful in our loves, fitting our duty ?

134 *happily* haply, perchance   140 *partisan* pike   154 *extravagant* wandering beyond bounds ; *erring* wandering   156 *probation* proof   158 *'gainst* just before   162 *strike* work evil by influence   163 *takes* bewitches
I, ii Elsinore Castle : a room of state   s.d. *cum aliis* with others   9 *jointress* a woman who has a jointure, or joint tenancy of an estate   14 *barred* excluded   21 *Colleaguèd* united   31 *gait* going   32 *proportions* amounts of forces and supplies   38 *delated* detailed   44 *Dane* King of Denmark   45 *lose your voice* speak in vain   47 *native* joined by nature   48 *instrumental* serviceable

MARCELLUS
Let's do't, I pray, and I this morning know
Where we shall find him most conveniently.   *Exeunt.*

*

Flourish. Enter Claudius, King of Denmark,   I, ii
Gertrude the Queen, Councillors, Polonius and his
son Laertes, Hamlet, cum aliis [including Voltemand
and Cornelius].

KING
Though yet of Hamlet our dear brother's death
The memory be green, and that it us befitted
To bear our hearts in grief, and our whole kingdom
To be contracted in one brow of woe,
Yet so far hath discretion fought with nature
That we with wisest sorrow think on him
Together with remembrance of ourselves.
Therefore our sometime sister, now our queen,
Th' imperial jointress to this warlike state,   9
Have we, as 'twere with a defeated joy,
With an auspicious and a dropping eye,
With mirth in funeral and with dirge in marriage,
In equal scale weighing delight and dole,
Taken to wife. Nor have we herein barred   14
Your better wisdoms, which have freely gone
With this affair along. For all, our thanks.
Now follows, that you know, young Fortinbras,
Holding a weak supposal of our worth,
Or thinking by our late dear brother's death
Our state to be disjoint and out of frame,
Colleaguèd with this dream of his advantage,   21
He hath not failed to pester us with message
Importing the surrender of those lands
Lost by his father, with all bands of law,
To our most valiant brother. So much for him.
Now for ourself and for this time of meeting.
Thus much the business is : we have here writ
To Norway, uncle of young Fortinbras –
Who, impotent and bedrid, scarcely hears
Of this his nephew's purpose – to suppress
His further gait herein, in that the levies,   31
The lists, and full proportions are all made   32
Out of his subject ; and we here dispatch
You, good Cornelius, and you, Voltemand,
For bearers of this greeting to old Norway,
Giving to you no further personal power
To business with the king, more than the scope
Of these delated articles allow.   38
Farewell, and let your haste commend your duty.

CORNELIUS, VOLTEMAND
In that, and all things, will we show our duty.

KING
We doubt it nothing. Heartily farewell.
     [Exeunt Voltemand and Cornelius.]
And now, Laertes, what's the news with you ?
You told us of some suit. What is't, Laertes ?
You cannot speak of reason to the Dane   44
And lose your voice. What wouldst thou beg, Laertes,   45
That shall not be my offer, not thy asking ?
The head is not more native to the heart,   47
The hand more instrumental to the mouth,   48
Than is the throne of Denmark to thy father.
What wouldst thou have, Laertes ?

LAERTES   My dread lord,
Your leave and favor to return to France,
From whence though willingly I came to Denmark
To show my duty in your coronation,
Yet now I must confess, that duty done,
My thoughts and wishes bend again toward France
And bow them to your gracious leave and pardon.

KING
Have you your father's leave? What says Polonius?

POLONIUS
He hath, my lord, wrung from me my slow leave
By laborsome petition, and at last
Upon his will I sealed my hard consent.
I do beseech you give him leave to go.

KING
Take thy fair hour, Laertes. Time be thine,
And thy best graces spend it at thy will.
64 But now, my cousin Hamlet, and my son –

HAMLET [aside]
65 A little more than kin, and less than kind!

KING
How is it that the clouds still hang on you?

HAMLET
67 Not so, my lord. I am too much in the sun.

QUEEN
Good Hamlet, cast thy nighted color off,
And let thine eye look like a friend on Denmark.
70 Do not for ever with thy vailèd lids
Seek for thy noble father in the dust.
Thou know'st 'tis common. All that lives must die,
Passing through nature to eternity.

HAMLET
Ay, madam, it is common.

QUEEN   If it be,
Why seems it so particular with thee?

HAMLET
Seems, madam? Nay, it is. I know not 'seems.'
'Tis not alone my inky cloak, good mother,
Nor customary suits of solemn black,
Nor windy suspiration of forced breath,
80 No, nor the fruitful river in the eye,
Nor the dejected havior of the visage,
Together with all forms, moods, shapes of grief,
That can denote me truly. These indeed seem,
For they are actions that a man might play,
But I have that within which passeth show –
These but the trappings and the suits of woe.

KING
'Tis sweet and commendable in your nature, Hamlet,
To give these mourning duties to your father,
But you must know your father lost a father,
That father lost, lost his, and the survivor bound
In filial obligation for some term
92 To do obsequious sorrow. But to persever
In obstinate condolement is a course
Of impious stubbornness. 'Tis unmanly grief.
It shows a will most incorrect to heaven,
A heart unfortified, a mind impatient,
An understanding simple and unschooled.
For what we know must be and is as common
As any the most vulgar thing to sense,
100 Why should we in our peevish opposition
Take it to heart? Fie, 'tis a fault to heaven,
A fault against the dead, a fault to nature,

To reason most absurd, whose common theme
Is death of fathers, and who still hath cried,
From the first corse till he that died to-day,
'This must be so.' We pray you throw to earth
This unprevailing woe, and think of us
As of a father, for let the world take note
You are the most immediate to our throne,
And with no less nobility of love
Than that which dearest father bears his son
Do I impart toward you. For your intent
In going back to school in Wittenberg,
It is most retrograde to our desire,   114
And we beseech you, bend you to remain
Here in the cheer and comfort of our eye,
Our chiefest courtier, cousin, and our son.

QUEEN
Let not thy mother lose her prayers, Hamlet.
I pray thee stay with us, go not to Wittenberg.

HAMLET
I shall in all my best obey you, madam.

KING
Why, 'tis a loving and a fair reply.
Be as ourself in Denmark. Madam, come.
This gentle and unforced accord of Hamlet
Sits smiling to my heart, in grace whereof
No jocund health that Denmark drinks to-day
But the great cannon to the clouds shall tell,
And the king's rouse the heaven shall bruit again,   127
Respeaking earthly thunder. Come away.
              Flourish. Exeunt all but Hamlet.

HAMLET
O that this too too sullied flesh would melt,   129
Thaw, and resolve itself into a dew,
Or that the Everlasting had not fixed
His canon 'gainst self-slaughter. O God, God,   132
How weary, stale, flat, and unprofitable
Seem to me all the uses of this world!
Fie on't, ah, fie, 'tis an unweeded garden
That grows to seed. Things rank and gross in nature
Possess it merely. That it should come to this,   137
But two months dead, nay, not so much, not two,
So excellent a king, that was to this
Hyperion to a satyr, so loving to my mother   140
That he might not beteem the winds of heaven   141
Visit her face too roughly. Heaven and earth,
Must I remember? Why, she would hang on him
As if increase of appetite had grown
By what it fed on, and yet within a month –
Let me not think on't; frailty, thy name is woman –
A little month, or ere those shoes were old
With which she followed my poor father's body
Like Niobe, all tears, why she, even she –   149

---

64 *cousin* kinsman more distant than parent, child, brother, or sister
65 *kin* related as nephew; *kind* kindly in feeling, as by kind, or nature, a son would be to his father   67 *sun* sunshine of the king's undesired favor (with the punning additional meaning of 'place of a son')   70 *vailèd* downcast   92 *obsequious* proper to obsequies or funerals; *persever* persevere (accented on the second syllable, as always in Shakespeare) 114 *retrograde* contrary   127 *rouse* toast drunk in wine; *bruit* echo   129 *sullied* (see Appendix: Supplementary Notes)   132 *canon* law   137 *merely* completely   140 *Hyperion* the sun god   141 *beteem* allow   149 *Niobe* the proud mother who boasted of having more children than Leto and was punished when they were slain by Apollo and Artemis, children of Leto; the grieving Niobe was changed by Zeus into a stone, which continually dropped tears

150   O God, a beast that wants discourse of reason
Would have mourned longer – married with my uncle,
My father's brother, but no more like my father
Than I to Hercules. Within a month,
Ere yet the salt of most unrighteous tears
155   Had left the flushing in her gallèd eyes,
She married. O, most wicked speed, to post
With such dexterity to incestuous sheets!
It is not nor it cannot come to good.
But break my heart, for I must hold my tongue.
      Enter Horatio, Marcellus, and Bernardo.

HORATIO
Hail to your lordship!
HAMLET   I am glad to see you well.
Horatio – or I do forget myself.
HORATIO
The same, my lord, and your poor servant ever.
HAMLET
163   Sir, my good friend, I'll change that name with you.
164   And what make you from Wittenberg, Horatio?
Marcellus?
MARCELLUS   My good lord!
HAMLET
I am very glad to see you. *[to Bernardo]* Good even, sir.
But what, in faith, make you from Wittenberg?
HORATIO
A truant disposition, good my lord.
HAMLET
I would not hear your enemy say so,
Nor shall you do my ear that violence
To make it truster of your own report
Against yourself. I know you are no truant.
But what is your affair in Elsinore?
We'll teach you to drink deep ere you depart.
HORATIO
My lord, I came to see your father's funeral.
HAMLET
I prithee do not mock me, fellow student.
I think it was to see my mother's wedding.
HORATIO
Indeed, my lord, it followed hard upon.
HAMLET
Thrift, thrift, Horatio. The funeral baked meats
Did coldly furnish forth the marriage tables.
182   Would I had met my dearest foe in heaven
Or ever I had seen that day, Horatio!
My father – methinks I see my father.
HORATIO
Where, my lord?
HAMLET   In my mind's eye, Horatio
HORATIO
I saw him once. 'A was a goodly king.
HAMLET
'A was a man, take him for all in all,
I shall not look upon his like again.
HORATIO
My lord, I think I saw him yesternight.
HAMLET   Saw? who?

HORATIO
My lord, the king your father.
HAMLET   The king my father?
HORATIO
Season your admiration for a while   192
With an attent ear till I may deliver
Upon the witness of these gentlemen
This marvel to you.
HAMLET   For God's love let me hear!
HORATIO
Two nights together had these gentlemen,
Marcellus and Bernardo, on their watch
In the dead waste and middle of the night
Been thus encountered. A figure like your father,
Armèd at point exactly, cap-a-pe,   200
Appears before them and with solemn march
Goes slow and stately by them. Thrice he walked
By their oppressed and fear-surprisèd eyes
Within his truncheon's length, whilst they, distilled   204
Almost to jelly with the act of fear,
Stand dumb and speak not to him. This to me
In dreadful secrecy impart they did,
And I with them the third night kept the watch,
Where, as they had delivered, both in time,
Form of the thing, each word made true and good,
The apparition comes. I knew your father.
These hands are not more like.
HAMLET   But where was this?
MARCELLUS
My lord, upon the platform where we watched.
HAMLET
Did you not speak to it?
HORATIO   My lord, I did,
But answer made it none. Yet once methought
It lifted up it head and did address   216
Itself to motion like as it would speak.
But even then the morning cock crew loud,
And at the sound it shrunk in haste away
And vanished from our sight.
HAMLET   'Tis very strange.
HORATIO
As I do live, my honored lord, 'tis true,
And we did think it writ down in our duty
To let you know of it.
HAMLET
Indeed, indeed, sirs, but this troubles me.
Hold you the watch to-night?
ALL   We do, my lord.
HAMLET   Armed, say you?
ALL   Armed, my lord.
HAMLET
From top to toe?
ALL   My lord, from head to foot.
HAMLET
Then saw you not his face?
HORATIO
O, yes, my lord. He wore his beaver up.   230
HAMLET
What, looked he frowningly?
HORATIO
A countenance more in sorrow than in anger.
HAMLET   Pale or red?
HORATIO
Nay, very pale.

150 *discourse* logical power or process   155 *gallèd* irritated   163 *change* exchange   164 *make* do   182 *dearest* direst, bitterest   192 *Season your admiration* control your wonder   200 *at point* completely; *cap-a-pe* from head to foot   204 *truncheon* military commander's baton   216 *it* its   230 *beaver* visor or movable face-guard of the helmet

HAMLET   And fixed his eyes upon you?

HORATIO
Most constantly.

HAMLET   I would I had been there.

HORATIO
It would have much amazed you.

HAMLET
Very like, very like. Stayed it long?

HORATIO
238 While one with moderate haste might tell a hundred.

BOTH   Longer, longer.

HORATIO
Not when I saw't.

240 HAMLET   His beard was grizzled, no?

HORATIO
It was as I have seen it in his life,

242 A sable silvered.

HAMLET   I will watch to-night.
Perchance 'twill walk again.

HORATIO   I warr'nt it will.

HAMLET
If it assume my noble father's person,
I'll speak to it though hell itself should gape
And bid me hold my peace. I pray you all,
If you have hitherto concealed this sight,
248 Let it be tenable in your silence still,
And whatsomever else shall hap to-night,
Give it an understanding but no tongue.
I will requite your loves. So fare you well.
Upon the platform, 'twixt eleven and twelve
I'll visit you.

ALL   Our duty to your honor.

HAMLET
Your loves, as mine to you. Farewell.
         Exeunt [all but Hamlet].
My father's spirit – in arms? All is not well.
256 I doubt some foul play. Would the night were come!
Till then sit still, my soul. Foul deeds will rise,
Though all the earth o'erwhelm them, to men's eyes.
         Exit.

*

I, iii   *Enter Laertes and Ophelia, his sister.*

LAERTES
My necessaries are embarked. Farewell.
And, sister, as the winds give benefit
3 And convoy is assistant, do not sleep,
But let me hear from you.

OPHELIA   Do you doubt that?

LAERTES
For Hamlet, and the trifling of his favor,
Hold it a fashion and a toy in blood,
7 A violet in the youth of primy nature,
Forward, not permanent, sweet, not lasting,
9 The perfume and suppliance of a minute,
No more.

OPHELIA   No more but so?

LAERTES   Think it no more.
11 For nature crescent does not grow alone
12 In thews and bulk, but as this temple waxes
The inward service of the mind and soul
Grows wide withal. Perhaps he loves you now,
15 And now no soil nor cautel doth besmirch
16 The virtue of his will, but you must fear,

His greatness weighed, his will is not his own.   17
[For he himself is subject to his birth.]
He may not, as unvalued persons do,
Carve for himself, for on his choice depends
The safety and health of this whole state,
And therefore must his choice be circumscribed
Unto the voice and yielding of that body   23
Whereof he is the head. Then if he says he loves you,
It fits your wisdom so far to believe it
As he in his particular act and place
May give his saying deed, which is no further
Than the main voice of Denmark goes withal.
Then weigh what loss your honor may sustain
If with too credent ear you list his songs,
Or lose your heart, or your chaste treasure open   30
To his unmastered importunity.
Fear it, Ophelia, fear it, my dear sister,
And keep you in the rear of your affection,   34
Out of the shot and danger of desire.
The chariest maid is prodigal enough
If she unmask her beauty to the moon.
Virtue itself scapes not calumnious strokes.
The canker galls the infants of the spring   39
Too oft before their buttons be disclosed,   40
And in the morn and liquid dew of youth
Contagious blastments are most imminent.   42
Be wary then; best safety lies in fear.
Youth to itself rebels, though none else near.

OPHELIA
I shall the effect of this good lesson keep
As watchman to my heart, but, good my brother,
Do not as some ungracious pastors do,
Show me the steep and thorny way to heaven,
Whiles like a puffed and reckless libertine
Himself the primrose path of dalliance treads
And recks not his own rede.   51

     Enter Polonius.

LAERTES   O, fear me not.
I stay too long. But here my father comes.
A double blessing is a double grace;
Occasion smiles upon a second leave.

POLONIUS
Yet here, Laertes? Aboard, aboard, for shame!
The wind sits in the shoulder of your sail,
And you are stayed for. There – my blessing with thee,
And these few precepts in thy memory
Look thou character. Give thy thoughts no tongue,   59
Nor any unproportioned thought his act.   60
Be thou familiar, but by no means vulgar.
Those friends thou hast, and their adoption tried,
Grapple them unto thy soul with hoops of steel,
But do not dull thy palm with entertainment
Of each new-hatched, unfledged courage. Beware   65
Of entrance to a quarrel; but being in,

---

238 *tell* count   240 *grizzled* grey   242 *sable silvered* black mixed with white
248 *tenable* held firmly   256 *doubt* suspect, fear
I, iii Elsinore Castle: the chambers of Polonius   3 *convoy* means of transport   7 *primy* of the springtime   9 *perfume and suppliance* filling sweetness   11 *crescent* growing   12 *this temple* the body   15 *cautel* deceit
16 *will* desire   17 *greatness weighed* high position considered   23 *yielding* assent   30 *credent* credulous   34 *affection* feelings, which rashly lead forward into dangers   39 *canker* rose worm; *galls* injures   40 *buttons* buds
42 *blastments* blights   51 *recks* regards; *rede* counsel   59 *character* inscribe
60 *unproportioned* unadjusted to what is right   65 *courage* man of spirit, young blood

Bear't that th' opposèd may beware of thee.
Give every man thine ear, but few thy voice;
69 Take each man's censure, but reserve thy judgment.
Costly thy habit as thy purse can buy,
But not expressed in fancy; rich, not gaudy,
For the apparel oft proclaims the man,
And they in France of the best rank and station
74 Are of a most select and generous chief in that.
Neither a borrower nor a lender be,
For loan oft loses both itself and friend,
77 And borrowing dulleth edge of husbandry.
This above all, to thine own self be true,
And it must follow as the night the day
Thou canst not then be false to any man.
81 Farewell. My blessing season this in thee!

LAERTES
Most humbly do I take my leave, my lord.
POLONIUS
83 The time invites you. Go, your servants tend.
LAERTES
Farewell, Ophelia, and remember well
What I have said to you.
OPHELIA   'Tis in my memory locked,
And you yourself shall keep the key of it.
LAERTES   Farewell.   *Exit Laertes.*
POLONIUS
What is't, Ophelia, he hath said to you?
OPHELIA
So please you, something touching the Lord Hamlet.
POLONIUS
90 Marry, well bethought.
'Tis told me he hath very oft of late
Given private time to you, and you yourself
Have of your audience been most free and bounteous.
If it be so – as so 'tis put on me,
And that in way of caution – I must tell you
You do not understand yourself so clearly
As it behooves my daughter and your honor.
What is between you? Give me up the truth.
OPHELIA
99 He hath, my lord, of late made many tenders
Of his affection to me.
POLONIUS
Affection? Pooh! You speak like a green girl,
102 Unsifted in such perilous circumstance.
Do you believe his tenders, as you call them?
OPHELIA
I do not know, my lord, what I should think.

POLONIUS
Marry, I will teach you. Think yourself a baby
That you have ta'en these tenders for true pay   106
Which are not sterling. Tender yourself more dearly,
Or (not to crack the wind of the poor phrase,   108
Running it thus) you'll tender me a fool.
OPHELIA
My lord, he hath importuned me with love
In honorable fashion.
POLONIUS
Ay, fashion you may call it. Go to, go to.   112
OPHELIA
And hath given countenance to his speech, my lord,
With almost all the holy vows of heaven.
POLONIUS
Ay, springes to catch woodcocks. I do know,   115
When the blood burns, how prodigal the soul
Lends the tongue vows. These blazes, daughter,
Giving more light than heat, extinct in both
Even in their promise, as it is a-making,
You must not take for fire. From this time
Be something scanter of your maiden presence.
Set your entreatments at a higher rate   122
Than a command to parley. For Lord Hamlet,   123
Believe so much in him that he is young,
And with a larger tether may he walk
Than may be given you. In few, Ophelia,
Do not believe his vows, for they are brokers,   127
Not of that dye which their investments show,   128
But mere implorators of unholy suits,
Breathing like sanctified and pious bawds,
The better to beguile. This is for all:
I would not, in plain terms, from this time forth
Have you so slander any moment leisure   133
As to give words or talk with the Lord Hamlet.
Look to't, I charge you. Come your ways.
OPHELIA
I shall obey, my lord.   *Exeunt.*

*

Enter Hamlet, Horatio, and Marcellus.   I, iv
HAMLET
The air bites shrewdly; it is very cold.   1
HORATIO
It is a nipping and an eager air.   2
HAMLET
What hour now?
HORATIO   I think it lacks of twelve.
MARCELLUS No, it is struck.
HORATIO
Indeed? I heard it not. It then draws near the season
Wherein the spirit held his wont to walk.
    A flourish of trumpets, and two pieces goes off.
What does this mean, my lord?
HAMLET
The king doth wake to-night and takes his rouse,   8
Keeps wassail, and the swaggering upspring reels,   9
And as he drains his draughts of Rhenish down   10
The kettledrum and trumpet thus bray out
The triumph of his pledge.   12
HORATIO   Is it a custom?
HAMLET
Ay, marry, is't,
But to my mind, though I am native here

---

69 *censure* judgment   74 *chief* eminence   77 *husbandry* thriftiness   81
season ripen and make fruitful   83 *tend* wait   90 *Marry* by Mary   99
tenders offers   102 *Unsifted* untested   106–09 *tenders . . . Tender . . .*
tender offers . . . hold in regard . . . present (a word play going through three
meanings, the last use of the word yielding further complexity with its
valid implications that she will show herself to him as a fool, will show
him to the world as a fool, and may go so far as to present him with a
baby, which would be a fool because 'fool' was an Elizabethan term of
endearment especially applicable to an infant as a 'little innocent')   108
crack . . . of make wheeze like a horse driven too hard   112 *Go to* go away,
go on (expressing impatience)   115 *springes* snares; *woodcocks* birds
believed foolish   122 *entreatments* military negotiations for surrender
123 *parley* confer with a besieger   127 *brokers* middlemen, panders   128
investments clothes   133 *slander* use disgracefully; *moment* momentary
I, iv The sentry-post   1 *shrewdly* wickedly   2 *eager* sharp   8 *rouse*
carousal   9 *upspring* a German dance   10 *Rhenish* Rhine wine   12 *triumph*
achievement, feat (in downing a cup of wine at one draught)

And to the manner born, it is a custom
16 More honored in the breach than the observance.
This heavy-headed revel east and west
18 Makes us traduced and taxed of other nations.
19 They clepe us drunkards and with swinish phrase
20 Soil our addition, and indeed it takes
From our achievements, though performed at height,
22 The pith and marrow of our attribute.
So oft it chances in particular men
24 That (for some vicious mole of nature in them,
As in their birth, wherein they are not guilty,
26 Since nature cannot choose his origin)
27 By the o'ergrowth of some complexion,
28 Oft breaking down the pales and forts of reason,
29 Or by some habit that too much o'erleavens
30 The form of plausive manners – that (these men
Carrying, I say, the stamp of one defect,
32 Being nature's livery, or fortune's star)
Their virtues else, be they as pure as grace,
As infinite as man may undergo,
Shall in the general censure take corruption
From that particular fault. The dram of evil
37 Doth all the noble substance of a doubt,
To his own scandal.
　　　　Enter Ghost.
HORATIO　　　　　　Look, my lord, it comes.
HAMLET
Angels and ministers of grace defend us!
40 Be thou a spirit of health or goblin damned,
Bring with thee airs from heaven or blasts from hell,
Be thy intents wicked or charitable,
Thou com'st in such a questionable shape
That I will speak to thee. I'll call thee Hamlet,
King, father, royal Dane. O, answer me!
Let me not burst in ignorance, but tell
47 Why thy canonized bones, hearsèd in death,
48 Have burst their cerements, why the sepulchre
Wherein we saw thee quietly interred
Hath oped his ponderous and marble jaws
To cast thee up again. What may this mean
That thou, dead corse, again in complete steel,
Revisits thus the glimpses of the moon,
54 Making night hideous, and we fools of nature
So horridly to shake our disposition
With thoughts beyond the reaches of our souls?
Say, why is this? wherefore? what should we do?
　　　[Ghost] beckons.
HORATIO
It beckons you to go away with it,
As if it some impartment did desire
To you alone.
MARCELLUS　　Look with what courteous action
It waves you to a more removèd ground.
But do not go with it.
HORATIO　　　　　　No, by no means.
HAMLET
It will not speak. Then will I follow it.
HORATIO
Do not, my lord.
HAMLET　　　　Why, what should be the fear?
I do not set my life at a pin's fee,
And for my soul, what can it do to that,
Being a thing immortal as itself?
It waves me forth again. I'll follow it.

HORATIO
What if it tempt you toward the flood, my lord,
Or to the dreadful summit of the cliff
71 That beetles o'er his base into the sea,
And there assume some other horrible form,
73 Which might deprive your sovereignty of reason
And draw you into madness? Think of it.
75 The very place puts toys of desperation,
Without more motive, into every brain
That looks so many fathoms to the sea
And hears it roar beneath.
HAMLET　　　　　It waves me still.
Go on. I'll follow thee.
MARCELLUS
You shall not go, my lord.
HAMLET　　　　　　Hold off your hands.
HORATIO
Be ruled. You shall not go.
HAMLET　　　　My fate cries out
82 And makes each petty artere in this body
83 As hardy as the Nemean lion's nerve.
Still am I called. Unhand me, gentlemen.
85 By heaven, I'll make a ghost of him that lets me!
I say, away! Go on. I'll follow thee.
　　　　　　Exit Ghost, and Hamlet.
HORATIO
He waxes desperate with imagination.
MARCELLUS
Let's follow. 'Tis not fit thus to obey him.
HORATIO
Have after. To what issue will this come?
MARCELLUS
Something is rotten in the state of Denmark.
HORATIO
Heaven will direct it.
MARCELLUS　　　Nay, let's follow him.　　*Exeunt.*

*

　　　Enter Ghost and Hamlet.　　　I, v
HAMLET
Whither wilt thou lead me? Speak. I'll go no further.
GHOST
Mark me.
HAMLET　　I will.
GHOST　　　　My hour is almost come,
When I to sulph'rous and tormenting flames
Must render up myself.
HAMLET　　　　　　Alas, poor ghost!

16 *More . . . observance* better broken than observed　18 *taxed of* censured by　19 *clepe* call　20 *addition* reputation, title added as a distinction　22 *attribute* reputation, what is attributed　24 *mole* blemish, flaw　26 *his* its　27 *complexion* part of the make-up, combination of humors　28 *pales* barriers, fences　29 *o'erleavens* works change throughout, as yeast ferments dough　30 *plausive* pleasing　32 *livery* characteristic equipment or provision; *star* make-up as formed by stellar influence　37 *Doth . . . doubt* (see Appendix: Supplementary Notes)　40 *of health* sound, good; *goblin* fiend　47 *canonized* buried with the established rites of the Church　48 *cerements* waxed grave-cloths　54 *fools of nature* men made conscious of natural limitations by a supernatural manifestation　71 *beetles* juts out　73 *deprive* take away; *sovereignty of reason* state of being ruled by reason　75 *toys* fancies　82 *artere* artery　83 *Nemean lion* a lion slain by Hercules in the performance of one of his twelve labors; *nerve* sinew　85 *lets* hinders
I, v Another part of the fortifications　3 *flames* sufferings in purgatory (not hell)

GHOST
  Pity me not, but lend thy serious hearing
  To what I shall unfold.
HAMLET   Speak. I am bound to hear.
GHOST
  So art thou to revenge, when thou shalt hear.
HAMLET What?
GHOST
  I am thy father's spirit,
  Doomed for a certain term to walk the night,
11 And for the day confined to fast in fires,
  Till the foul crimes done in my days of nature
  Are burnt and purged away. But that I am forbid
  To tell the secrets of my prison house,
  I could a tale unfold whose lightest word
  Would harrow up thy soul, freeze thy young blood,
17 Make thy two eyes like stars start from their spheres,
  Thy knotted and combinèd locks to part,
19 And each particular hair to stand an end
20 Like quills upon the fretful porpentine.
21 But this eternal blazon must not be
  To ears of flesh and blood. List, list, O, list!
  If thou didst ever thy dear father love –
HAMLET O God!
GHOST
  Revenge his foul and most unnatural murder.
HAMLET Murder?
GHOST
  Murder most foul, as in the best it is,
  But this most foul, strange, and unnatural.
HAMLET
  Haste me to know't, that I, with wings as swift
30 As meditation or the thoughts of love,
  May sweep to my revenge.
GHOST   I find thee apt,
  And duller shouldst thou be than the fat weed
33 That roots itself in ease on Lethe wharf,
  Wouldst thou not stir in this. Now, Hamlet, hear.
  'Tis given out that, sleeping in my orchard,
  A serpent stung me. So the whole ear of Denmark
37 Is by a forgèd process of my death
  Rankly abused. But know, thou noble youth,
  The serpent that did sting thy father's life
  Now wears his crown.
HAMLET   O my prophetic soul!
  My uncle?
GHOST
42 Ay, that incestuous, that adulterate beast,
  With witchcraft of his wit, with traitorous gifts –
  O wicked wit and gifts, that have the power
  So to seduce! – won to his shameful lust
  The will of my most seeming-virtuous queen.

O Hamlet, what a falling-off was there,
From me, whose love was of that dignity
That it went hand in hand even with the vow
I made to her in marriage, and to decline
Upon a wretch whose natural gifts were poor
To those of mine!
But virtue, as it never will be moved,
Though lewdness court it in a shape of heaven,   54
So lust, though to a radiant angel linked,
Will sate itself in a celestial bed
And prey on garbage.
But soft, methinks I scent the morning air.
Brief let me be. Sleeping within my orchard,
My custom always of the afternoon,
Upon my secure hour thy uncle stole   61
With juice of cursed hebona in a vial,   62
And in the porches of my ears did pour
The leperous distilment, whose effect
Holds such an enmity with blood of man
That swift as quicksilver it courses through
The natural gates and alleys of the body,
And with a sudden vigor it doth posset   68
And curd, like eager droppings into milk,   69
The thin and wholesome blood. So did it mine,
And a most instant tetter barked about   71
Most lazar-like with vile and loathsome crust   72
All my smooth body.
Thus was I sleeping by a brother's hand
Of life, of crown, of queen at once dispatched,
Cut off even in the blossoms of my sin,
Unhouseled, disappointed, unaneled,   77
No reck'ning made, but sent to my account
With all my imperfections on my head.
O, horrible! O, horrible! most horrible!
If thou hast nature in thee, bear it not.
Let not the royal bed of Denmark be
A couch for luxury and damnèd incest.   83
But howsomever thou pursues this act,
Taint not thy mind, nor let thy soul contrive
Against thy mother aught. Leave her to heaven
And to those thorns that in her bosom lodge
To prick and sting her. Fare thee well at once.
The glowworm shows the matin to be near   89
And gins to pale his uneffectual fire.
Adieu, adieu, adieu. Remember me.   *[Exit.]*
HAMLET
O all you host of heaven! O earth! What else?
And shall I couple hell? O fie! Hold, hold, my heart,
And you, my sinews, grow not instant old,
But bear me stiffly up. Remember thee?
Ay, thou poor ghost, while memory holds a seat
In this distracted globe. Remember thee?   97
Yea, from the table of my memory   98
I'll wipe away all trivial fond records,
All saws of books, all forms, all pressures past   100
That youth and observation copied there,
And thy commandment all alone shall live
Within the book and volume of my brain,
Unmixed with baser matter. Yes, by heaven!
O most pernicious woman!
O villain, villain, smiling, damnèd villain!
My tables – meet it is I set it down
That one may smile, and smile, and be a villain.
At least I am sure it may be so in Denmark.

---

11 *fast* do penance   17 *spheres* transparent revolving shells in each of which, according to the Ptolemaic astronomy, a planet or other heavenly body was placed   19 *an* on   20 *porpentine* porcupine   21 *eternal blazon* revelation of eternity   30 *meditation* thought   33 *Lethe* the river in Hades which brings forgetfulness of past life to a spirit who drinks of it   37 *forgèd process* falsified official report   42 *adulterate* adulterous   54 *shape of heaven* angelic disguise   61 *secure* carefree, unsuspecting   62 *hebona* some poisonous plant   68 *posset* curdle   69 *eager* sour   71 *tetter* eruption; *barked* covered as with a bark   72 *lazar-like* leper-like   77 *Unhouseled* without the Sacrament; *disappointed* unprepared spiritually; *unaneled* without extreme unction   83 *luxury* lust   89 *matin* morning   97 *globe* head   98 *table* writing tablet, record book   100 *saws* wise sayings; *forms* mental images, concepts; *pressures* impressions

[Writes.]
So, uncle, there you are. Now to my word :
It is 'Adieu, adieu, remember me.'
I have sworn't.
Enter Horatio and Marcellus.

HORATIO
My lord, my lord !

MARCELLUS   Lord Hamlet !

HORATIO   Heavens secure him !

HAMLET So be it !

MARCELLUS
115 Illo, ho, ho, my lord !

HAMLET
Hillo, ho, ho, boy ! Come, bird, come.

MARCELLUS
How is't, my noble lord ?

HORATIO   What news, my lord ?

HAMLET O, wonderful !

HORATIO
Good my lord, tell it.

HAMLET   No, you will reveal it.

HORATIO
Not I, my lord, by heaven.

MARCELLUS   Nor I, my lord.

HAMLET
How say you then ? Would heart of man once think it ?
But you'll be secret ?

BOTH   Ay, by heaven, my lord.

HAMLET
There's never a villain dwelling in all Denmark
But he's an arrant knave.

HORATIO
There needs no ghost, my lord, come from the grave
To tell us this.

HAMLET   Why, right, you are in the right,
127 And so, without more circumstance at all,
I hold it fit that we shake hands and part :
You, as your business and desires shall point you,
For every man hath business and desire
Such as it is, and for my own poor part,
Look you, I'll go pray.

HORATIO
These are but wild and whirling words, my lord.

HAMLET
I am sorry they offend you, heartily ;
Yes, faith, heartily.

HORATIO   There's no offense, my lord.

HAMLET
Yes, by Saint Patrick, but there is, Horatio,
And much offense too. Touching this vision here,
138 It is an honest ghost, that let me tell you.
For your desire to know what is between us,
O'ermaster't as you may. And now, good friends,
As you are friends, scholars, and soldiers,
Give me one poor request.

HORATIO
What is't, my lord ? We will.

HAMLET
Never make known what you have seen to-night.

BOTH
My lord, we will not.

HAMLET   Nay, but swear't.

HORATIO   In faith,
My lord, not I.

MARCELLUS   Nor I, my lord – in faith.

HAMLET
Upon my sword.   147

MARCELLUS   We have sworn, my lord, already.

HAMLET
Indeed, upon my sword, indeed.
Ghost cries under the stage.

GHOST Swear.

HAMLET
Ha, ha, boy, say'st thou so ? Art thou there, truepenny ? 150
Come on. You hear this fellow in the cellarage.
Consent to swear.

HORATIO   Propose the oath, my lord.

HAMLET
Never to speak of this that you have seen,
Swear by my sword.

GHOST *[beneath]* Swear.

HAMLET
Hic et ubique ? Then we'll shift our ground.   156
Come hither, gentlemen,
And lay your hands again upon my sword.
Swear by my sword
Never to speak of this that you have heard.

GHOST *[beneath]* Swear by his sword.

HAMLET
Well said, old mole ! Canst work i' th' earth so fast ?
A worthy pioner ! Once more remove, good friends.   163

HORATIO
O day and night, but this is wondrous strange !

HAMLET
And therefore as a stranger give it welcome.
There are more things in heaven and earth, Horatio,
Than are dreamt of in your philosophy.   167
But come :
Here as before, never, so help you mercy,
How strange or odd some'er I bear myself
(As I perchance hereafter shall think meet
To put an antic disposition on),   172
That you, at such times seeing me, never shall,
With arms encumb'red thus, or this head-shake,   174
Or by pronouncing of some doubtful phrase,
As 'Well, well, we know,' or 'We could, an if we would,' 176
Or 'If we list to speak,' or 'There be, an if they might,'
Or such ambiguous giving out, to note
That you know aught of me – this do swear,
So grace and mercy at your most need help you.

GHOST *[beneath]* Swear.
[They swear.]

HAMLET
Rest, rest, perturbèd spirit ! So, gentlemen,
With all my love I do commend me to you,   183
And what so poor a man as Hamlet is
May do t' express his love and friending to you,
God willing, shall not lack. Let us go in together,
And still your fingers on your lips, I pray.   187
The time is out of joint. O cursèd spite
That ever I was born to set it right !
Nay, come, let's go together.   *Exeunt.*

*

115 *Illo, ho, ho* cry of the falconer to summon his hawk   127 *circumstance*
ceremony   138 *honest* genuine (not a disguised demon)   147 *sword* i.e.
upon the cross formed by the sword hilt   150 *truepenny* honest old fellow
156 *Hic et ubique* here and everywhere   163 *pioner* pioneer, miner   167
your philosophy this philosophy one hears about   172 *antic* grotesque, mad
174 *encumb'red* folded   176 *an if* if   183 *commend* entrust   187 *still* always

II, i   *Enter old Polonius, with his man [Reynaldo].*

POLONIUS

Give him this money and these notes, Reynaldo.

REYNALDO

I will, my lord.

POLONIUS

You shall do marvellous wisely, good Reynaldo,
Before you visit him, to make inquire
Of his behavior.

REYNALDO   My lord, I did intend it.

POLONIUS

Marry, well said, very well said. Look you, sir,
7   Enquire me first what Danskers are in Paris,
8   And how, and who, what means, and where they keep,
What company, at what expense; and finding
10   By this encompassment and drift of question
That they do know my son, come you more nearer
12   Than your particular demands will touch it.
Take you as 'twere some distant knowledge of him,
As thus, 'I know his father and his friends,
And in part him' – do you mark this, Reynaldo?

REYNALDO

Ay, very well, my lord.

POLONIUS

'And in part him, but,' you may say, 'not well,
But if't be he I mean, he's very wild
Addicted so and so.' And there put on him
20   What forgeries you please; marry, none so rank
As may dishonor him – take heed of that –
But, sir, such wanton, wild, and usual slips
As are companions noted and most known
To youth and liberty.

REYNALDO   As gaming, my lord.

POLONIUS

Ay, or drinking, fencing, swearing, quarrelling,
26   Drabbing. You may go so far.

REYNALDO

My lord, that would dishonor him.

POLONIUS

28   Faith, no, as you may season it in the charge.
You must not put another scandal on him,
30   That he is open to incontinency.
31   That's not my meaning. But breathe his faults so quaintly
That they may seem the taints of liberty,
The flash and outbreak of a fiery mind,
34   A savageness in unreclaimèd blood,
35   Of general assault.

REYNALDO   But, my good lord –

POLONIUS

Wherefore should you do this?

REYNALDO   Ay, my lord,
I would know that.

POLONIUS   Marry, sir, here's my drift,
And I believe it is a fetch of warrant.   38
You laying these slight sullies on my son
As 'twere a thing a little soiled i' th' working,
Mark you,
Your party in converse, him you would sound,
Having ever seen in the prenominate crimes   43
The youth you breathe of guilty, be assured
He closes with you in this consequence: 45
'Good sir,' or so, or 'friend,' or 'gentleman' –
According to the phrase or the addition   47
Of man and country –

REYNALDO   Very good, my lord.

POLONIUS

And then, sir, does 'a this – 'a does –
What was I about to say? By the mass, I was about to
say something! Where did I leave?

REYNALDO At 'closes in the consequence,' at 'friend or
so,' and 'gentleman.'

POLONIUS

At 'closes in the consequence' – Ay, marry!
He closes thus: 'I know the gentleman;
I saw him yesterday, or t' other day,
Or then, or then, with such or such, and, as you say,
There was 'a gaming, there o'ertook in's rouse,   58
There falling out at tennis'; or perchance,   59
'I saw him enter such a house of sale,'
Videlicet, a brothel, or so forth.   61
See you now –
Your bait of falsehood takes this carp of truth,
And thus do we of wisdom and of reach,   64
With windlasses and with assays of bias,   65
By indirections find directions out.   66
So, by my former lecture and advice,
Shall you my son. You have me, have you not?

REYNALDO

My lord, I have.

POLONIUS   God bye ye, fare ye well.   69

REYNALDO Good my lord.

POLONIUS

Observe his inclination in yourself.

REYNALDO I shall, my lord.

POLONIUS

And let him ply his music.

REYNALDO   Well, my lord.

POLONIUS

Farewell.   *Exit Reynaldo.*
    Enter Ophelia.
    How now, Ophelia, what's the matter?

OPHELIA

O my lord, my lord, I have been so affrighted!

POLONIUS

With what, i' th' name of God?

OPHELIA

My lord, as I was sewing in my closet,   77
Lord Hamlet, with his doublet all unbraced,   78
No hat upon his head, his stockings fouled,
Ungartered, and down-gyvèd to his ankle,   80
Pale as his shirt, his knees knocking each other,
And with a look so piteous in purport
As if he had been loosèd out of hell
To speak of horrors – he comes before me.

POLONIUS

Mad for thy love?

II, i The chambers of Polonius   7 *Danskers* Danes   8 *what means* what their wealth; *keep* dwell   10 *encompassment* circling about   12 *particular demands* definite questions   20 *forgeries* invented wrongdoings   26 *Drabbing* whoring   28 *season* soften   30 *incontinency* extreme sensuality   31 *quaintly* expertly, gracefully   34 *unreclaimèd* untamed   35 *Of general assault* assailing all young men   38 *fetch of warrant* allowable trick   43 *Having ever* if he has ever; *prenominate* aforementioned   45 *closes with you* follows your lead to a conclusion; *consequence* following way   47 *addition* title   58 *o'ertook* overcome with drunkenness; *rouse* carousal   59 *falling out* quarrelling   61 *Videlicet* namely   64 *reach* far-reaching comprehension   65 *windlasses* roundabout courses; *assays of bias* devious attacks   66 *directions* ways of procedure   69 *God bye ye* God be with you, good-bye   77 *closet* private living-room   78 *doublet* jacket; *unbraced* unlaced   80 *down-gyvèd* fallen down like gyves or fetters on a prisoner's legs

OPHELIA   My lord, I do not know,
But truly I do fear it.
POLONIUS   What said he?
OPHELIA
He took me by the wrist and held me hard.
Then goes he to the length of all his arm,
And with his other hand thus o'er his brow
90   He falls to such perusal of my face
As 'a would draw it. Long stayed he so.
At last, a little shaking of mine arm
And thrice his head thus waving up and down,
He raised a sigh so piteous and profound
As it did seem to shatter all his bulk
And end his being. That done, he lets me go,
And with his head over his shoulder turned
He seemed to find his way without his eyes,
For out o' doors he went without their helps
And to the last bended their light on me.
POLONIUS
Come, go with me. I will go seek the king.
102   This is the very ecstasy of love,
103   Whose violent property fordoes itself
And leads the will to desperate undertakings
As oft as any passion under heaven
That does afflict our natures. I am sorry.
What, have you given him any hard words of late?
OPHELIA
No, my good lord; but as you did command
I did repel his letters and denied
His access to me.
POLONIUS   That hath made him mad.
I am sorry that with better heed and judgment
112   I had not quoted him. I feared he did but trifle
113   And meant to wrack thee; but beshrew my jealousy.
By heaven, it is as proper to our age
115   To cast beyond ourselves in our opinions
As it is common for the younger sort
To lack discretion. Come, go we to the king.
118   This must be known, which, being kept close, might
     move
119   More grief to hide than hate to utter love.
Come.   *Exeunt.*

*

II, ii   *Flourish. Enter King and Queen, Rosencrantz, and
Guildenstern [with others].*
KING
Welcome, dear Rosencrantz and Guildenstern.
2   Moreover that we much did long to see you,
The need we have to use you did provoke
Our hasty sending. Something have you heard
Of Hamlet's transformation – so call it,
6   Sith nor th' exterior nor the inward man
Resembles that it was. What it should be,
More than his father's death, that thus hath put him
So much from th' understanding of himself,
I cannot dream of. I entreat you both
That, being of so young days brought up with him,
12   And sith so neighbored to his youth and havior,
That you vouchsafe your rest here in our court
Some little time, so by your companies
To draw him on to pleasures, and to gather
So much as from occasion you may glean,

Whether aught to us unknown afflicts him thus,
That opened lies within our remedy.   18
QUEEN
Good gentlemen, he hath much talked of you,
And sure I am two men there are not living
To whom he more adheres. If it will please you   21
To show us so much gentry and good will   22
As to expend your time with us awhile
For the supply and profit of our hope,
Your visitation shall receive such thanks
As fits a king's remembrance.
ROSENCRANTZ   Both your majesties
Might, by the sovereign power you have of us,
Put your dread pleasures more into command
Than to entreaty.
GUILDENSTERN   But we both obey,
And here give up ourselves in the full bent   30
To lay our service freely at your feet,
To be commanded.
KING
Thanks, Rosencrantz and gentle Guildenstern.
QUEEN
Thanks, Guildenstern and gentle Rosencrantz.
And I beseech you instantly to visit
My too much changèd son. – Go, some of you,
And bring these gentlemen where Hamlet is.
GUILDENSTERN
Heavens make our presence and our practices
Pleasant and helpful to him!
QUEEN   Ay, amen!
     *Exeunt Rosencrantz and Guildenstern
               [with some Attendants].*
    Enter Polonius.
POLONIUS
Th' ambassadors from Norway, my good lord,
Are joyfully returned.
KING
Thou still hast been the father of good news.   42
POLONIUS
Have I, my lord? Assure you, my good liege,
I hold my duty as I hold my soul,
Both to my God and to my gracious king,
And I do think – or else this brain of mine
Hunts not the trail of policy so sure
As it hath used to do – that I have found
The very cause of Hamlet's lunacy.
KING
O, speak of that! That do I long to hear.
POLONIUS
Give first admittance to th' ambassadors.
My news shall be the fruit to that great feast.   52
KING
Thyself do grace to them and bring them in.   53
                   [Exit Polonius.]

---

102 *ecstasy* madness   103 *property* quality; *fordoes* destroys   112 *quoted*
observed   113 *beshrew* curse   115 *cast beyond ourselves* find by calculation
more significance in something than we ought to   118 *close* secret; *move*
cause   119 *to hide . . . love* by such hiding of love than there would be hate
moved by a revelation of it (a violently condensed putting of the case which
is a triumph of special statement for Polonius)
II, ii A chamber in the Castle   2 *Moreover that* besides the fact that   6
Sith since   12 *youth and havior* youthful ways of life   18 *opened* revealed
21 *more adheres* is more attached   22 *gentry* courtesy   30 *in the full bent*
at the limit of bending (of a bow), to full capacity   42 *still* always   52 *fruit*
dessert   53 *grace* honor

He tells me, my dear Gertrude, he hath found
The head and source of all your son's distemper.

QUEEN

56   I doubt it is no other but the main,
His father's death and our o'erhasty marriage.

KING

Well, we shall sift him.
     Enter Ambassadors [Voltemand and Cornelius,
     with Polonius].   Welcome, my good friends.
Say, Voltemand, what from our brother Norway?

VOLTEMAND

Most fair return of greetings and desires.

61   Upon our first, he sent out to suppress
His nephew's levies, which to him appeared
To be a preparation 'gainst the Polack,
But better looked into, he truly found
It was against your highness, whereat grieved,
That so his sickness, age, and impotence

67   Was falsely borne in hand, sends out arrests
On Fortinbras; which he in brief obeys,

69   Receives rebuke from Norway, and in fine
Makes vow before his uncle never more

71   To give th' assay of arms against your majesty.
Whereon old Norway, overcome with joy,
Gives him threescore thousand crowns in annual fee
And his commission to employ those soldiers,
So levied as before, against the Polack,
With an entreaty, herein further shown,
     [Gives a paper.]
That it might please you to give quiet pass
Through your dominions for this enterprise,

79   On such regards of safety and allowance
As therein are set down.

KING   It likes us well;

81   And at our more considered time we'll read,
Answer, and think upon this business.
Meantime we thank you for your well-took labor.
Go to your rest; at night we'll feast together.
Most welcome home!   *Exeunt Ambassadors.*

POLONIUS   This business is well ended.

86   My liege and madam, to expostulate
What majesty should be, what duty is,
Why day is day, night night, and time is time,
Were nothing but to waste night, day, and time.

90   Therefore, since brevity is the soul of wit,
And tediousness the limbs and outward flourishes,
I will be brief. Your noble son is mad.
Mad call I it, for, to define true madness,
What is't but to be nothing else but mad?
But let that go.

QUEEN   More matter, with less art.

POLONIUS

Madam, I swear I use no art at all.
That he is mad, 'tis true: 'tis true 'tis pity,

98   And pity 'tis 'tis true – a foolish figure.

But farewell it, for I will use no art.
Mad let us grant him then, and now remains
That we find out the cause of this effect –
Or rather say, the cause of this defect,
For this effect defective comes by cause.
Thus it remains, and the remainder thus.
Perpend.   105
I have a daughter (have while she is mine),
Who in her duty and obedience, mark,
Hath given me this. Now gather, and surmise.
     [Reads the] letter.
'To the celestial, and my soul's idol, the most beautified
Ophelia,' –
That's an ill phrase, a vile phrase; 'beautified' is a vile
phrase. But you shall hear. Thus:
     [Reads.]
'In her excellent white bosom, these, &c.'

QUEEN

Came this from Hamlet to her?

POLONIUS

Good madam, stay awhile. I will be faithful.
     [Reads.]
     'Doubt thou the stars are fire;
        Doubt that the sun doth move;
        Doubt truth to be a liar;   118
        But never doubt I love.
'O dear Ophelia, I am ill at these numbers. I have not 120
art to reckon my groans, but that I love thee best, O
most best, believe it. Adieu.
     'Thine evermore, most dear lady,
        whilst this machine is to him, Hamlet.'   124

This in obedience hath my daughter shown me,
And more above hath his solicitings,   126
As they fell out by time, by means, and place,
All given to mine ear.

KING   But how hath she
Received his love?

POLONIUS   What do you think of me?

KING

As of a man faithful and honorable.

POLONIUS

I would fain prove so. But what might you think,
When I had seen this hot love on the wing
(As I perceived it, I must tell you that,
Before my daughter told me), what might you,
Or my dear majesty your queen here, think,
If I had played the desk or table book,   136
Or given my heart a winking, mute and dumb,   137
Or looked upon this love with idle sight?
What might you think? No, I went round to work-   139
And my young mistress thus I did bespeak:
'Lord Hamlet is a prince, out of thy star.   141
This must not be.' And then I prescripts gave her,   142
That she should lock herself from his resort,
Admit no messengers, receive no tokens.
Which done, she took the fruits of my advice,
And he, repellèd, a short tale to make,
Fell into a sadness, then into a fast,
Thence to a watch, thence into a weakness,   148
Thence to a lightness, and, by this declension,   149
Into the madness wherein now he raves,
And all we mourn for.

KING   Do you think 'tis this?

---

56 *doubt* suspect   61 *our first* our first words about the matter   67 *borne in hand* deceived   69 *in fine* in the end   71 *assay* trial   79 *regards* terms   81 *considered time* convenient time for consideration   86 *expostulate* discuss   90 *wit* understanding   98 *figure* figure in rhetoric   105 *Perpend* ponder   118 *Doubt* suspect   120 *numbers* verses   124 *machine* body; *to* attached to   126 *above* besides   136 *desk or table book* i.e. silent receiver   137 *winking* closing of the eyes   139 *round* roundly, plainly   141 *star* condition determined by stellar influence   142 *prescripts* instructions   148 *watch* sleepless state   149 *lightness* lightheadedness

QUEEN
It may be, very like.

POLONIUS
Hath there been such a time – I would fain know that –
That I have positively said ' 'Tis so,'
When it proved otherwise ?

KING   Not that I know.

POLONIUS [pointing to his head and shoulder]
Take this from this, if this be otherwise.
If circumstances lead me, I will find
Where truth is hid, though it were hid indeed
159   Within the center.

KING   How may we try it further ?

POLONIUS
You know sometimes he walks four hours together
Here in the lobby.

QUEEN   So he does indeed.

POLONIUS
At such a time I'll loose my daughter to him.
163   Be you and I behind an arras then.
Mark the encounter. If he love her not,
165   And be not from his reason fallen thereon,
Let me be no assistant for a state
But keep a farm and carters.

KING   We will try it.
          Enter Hamlet [reading on a book].

QUEEN
But look where sadly the poor wretch comes reading.

POLONIUS
Away, I do beseech you both, away.
          Exit King and Queen [with Attendants].
170   I'll board him presently. O, give me leave.
How does my good Lord Hamlet ?

172   HAMLET Well, God-a-mercy.

POLONIUS Do you know me, my lord ?

174   HAMLET Excellent well. You are a fishmonger.

POLONIUS Not I, my lord.

HAMLET Then I would you were so honest a man.

POLONIUS Honest, my lord ?

HAMLET Ay, sir. To be honest, as this world goes, is to be
one man picked out of ten thousand.

POLONIUS That's very true, my lord.

HAMLET For if the sun breed maggots in a dead dog,
182   being a good kissing carrion – Have you a daughter ?

POLONIUS I have, my lord.

HAMLET Let her not walk i' th' sun. Conception is a
blessing, but as your daughter may conceive, friend,
look to't.

POLONIUS [aside] How say you by that ? Still harping on
my daughter. Yet he knew me not at first. 'A said I was a
fishmonger. 'A is far gone, far gone. And truly in my
youth I suffered much extremity for love, very near this.
I'll speak to him again. – What do you read, my lord ?

HAMLET Words, words, words.

POLONIUS What is the matter, my lord ?

193   HAMLET Between who ?

POLONIUS I mean the matter that you read, my lord.

HAMLET Slanders, sir, for the satirical rogue says here
that old men have grey beards, that their faces are
wrinkled, their eyes purging thick amber and plum-tree
gum, and that they have a plentiful lack of wit, together
with most weak hams. All which, sir, though I most
powerfully and potently believe, yet I hold it not
honesty to have it thus set down, for you yourself, sir,

should be old as I am if, like a crab, you could go backward.

POLONIUS [aside] Though this be madness, yet there is
method in't. – Will you walk out of the air, my lord ?

HAMLET Into my grave ?

POLONIUS Indeed, that's out of the air. [aside] How preg- 206
nant sometimes his replies are ! a happiness that often 207
madness hits on, which reason and sanity could not so
prosperously be delivered of. I will leave him and suddenly contrive the means of meeting between him and
my daughter. – My honorable lord, I will most humbly
take my leave of you.

HAMLET You cannot, sir, take from me anything that I
will more willingly part withal – except my life, except 214
my life, except my life.

          Enter Guildenstern and Rosencrantz.

POLONIUS Fare you well, my lord.

HAMLET These tedious old fools !

POLONIUS You go to seek the Lord Hamlet. There he is.

ROSENCRANTZ [to Polonius] God save you, sir !
          [Exit Polonius.]

GUILDENSTERN My honored lord !

ROSENCRANTZ My most dear lord !

HAMLET My excellent good friends ! How dost thou,
Guildenstern ? Ah, Rosencrantz ! Good lads, how do ye
both ?

ROSENCRANTZ
As the indifferent children of the earth.   224

GUILDENSTERN
Happy in that we are not over-happy.
On Fortune's cap we are not the very button.

HAMLET Nor the soles of her shoe ?

ROSENCRANTZ Neither, my lord.

HAMLET Then you live about her waist, or in the middle
of her favors ?

GUILDENSTERN Faith, her privates we.   231

HAMLET In the secret parts of Fortune ? O, most true !
she is a strumpet. What news ?

ROSENCRANTZ None, my lord, but that the world 's
grown honest.

HAMLET Then is doomsday near. But your news is not
true. [Let me question more in particular. What have
you, my good friends, deserved at the hands of Fortune
that she sends you to prison hither ?

GUILDENSTERN Prison, my lord ?

HAMLET Denmark 's a prison.

ROSENCRANTZ Then is the world one.

HAMLET A goodly one ; in which there are many con- 243
fines, wards, and dungeons, Denmark being one o' th' 244
worst.

ROSENCRANTZ We think not so, my lord.

HAMLET Why, then 'tis none to you, for there is nothing
either good or bad but thinking makes it so. To me it is a
prison.

159 *center* center of the earth and also of the Ptolemaic universe   163 *arras*
hanging tapestry   165 *thereon* on that account   170 *board* accost; *presently*
at once   172 *God-a-mercy* thank you (literally, 'God have mercy !')   174
fishmonger seller of harlots, procurer (a cant term used here with a glance at
the fishing Polonius is doing when he offers Ophelia as bait)   182 *good
kissing carrion* good bit of flesh for kissing   193 *Between who* matter for a
quarrel between what persons (Hamlet's willful misunderstanding)   206
pregnant full of meaning   207 *happiness* aptness of expression   214 *withal*
with   224 *indifferent* average   231 *privates* ordinary men in private, not
public, life (with obvious play upon the sexual term 'private parts')   243
confines places of imprisonment   244 *wards* cells

ROSENCRANTZ Why, then your ambition makes it one. 'Tis too narrow for your mind.

HAMLET O God, I could be bounded in a nutshell and count myself a king of infinite space, were it not that I have bad dreams.

GUILDENSTERN Which dreams indeed are ambition, for the very substance of the ambitious is merely the shadow of a dream.

HAMLET A dream itself is but a shadow.

ROSENCRANTZ Truly, and I hold ambition of so airy and light a quality that it is but a shadow's shadow.

260 HAMLET Then are our beggars bodies, and our monarchs
261 and outstretched heroes the beggars' shadows. Shall we
262 to th' court? for, by my fay, I cannot reason.

263 BOTH We'll wait upon you.

HAMLET No such matter. I will not sort you with the rest of my servants, for, to speak to you like an honest man, I am most dreadfully attended.] But in the beaten way of
267 friendship, what make you at Elsinore?

ROSENCRANTZ To visit you, my lord; no other occasion.

HAMLET Beggar that I am, I am even poor in thanks, but I thank you; and sure, dear friends, my thanks are too
271 dear a halfpenny. Were you not sent for? Is it your own inclining? Is it a free visitation? Come, come, deal justly with me. Come, come. Nay, speak.

GUILDENSTERN What should we say, my lord?

HAMLET Why, anything – but to th' purpose. You were sent for, and there is a kind of confession in your looks, which your modesties have not craft enough to color. I know the good king and queen have sent for you.

ROSENCRANTZ To what end, my lord?

HAMLET That you must teach me. But let me conjure you
281 by the rights of our fellowship, by the consonancy of our youth, by the obligation of our ever-preserved love, and
283 by what more dear a better proposer can charge you
284 withal, be even and direct with me whether you were sent for or no.

ROSENCRANTZ [aside to Guildenstern] What say you?

HAMLET [aside] Nay then, I have an eye of you. – If you love me, hold not off.

GUILDENSTERN My lord, we were sent for.

290 HAMLET I will tell you why. So shall my anticipation pre-
291 vent your discovery, and your secrecy to the king and queen moult no feather. I have of late – but wherefore I 292 know not – lost all my mirth, forgone all custom of exercises; and indeed, it goes so heavily with my disposition that this goodly frame the earth seems to me a sterile promontory; this most excellent canopy, the air, look you, this brave o'erhanging firmament, this majestical 297 roof fretted with golden fire – why, it appeareth nothing 298 to me but a foul and pestilent congregation of vapors. What a piece of work is a man, how noble in reason, how infinite in faculties; in form and moving how ex- 301 press and admirable, in action how like an angel, in apprehension how like a god: the beauty of the world, the paragon of animals! And yet to me what is this quint- 304 essence of dust? Man delights not me – nor woman neither, though by your smiling you seem to say so.

ROSENCRANTZ My lord, there was no such stuff in my thoughts.

HAMLET Why did ye laugh then, when I said 'Man delights not me'?

ROSENCRANTZ To think, my lord, if you delight not in man, what lenten entertainment the players shall re- 311 ceive from you. We coted them on the way, and hither 312 are they coming to offer you service.

HAMLET He that plays the king shall be welcome – his majesty shall have tribute of me –, the adventurous knight shall use his foil and target, the lover shall not 316 sigh gratis, the humorous man shall end his part in 317 peace, the clown shall make those laugh whose lungs are tickle o' th' sere, and the lady shall say her mind freely, 319 or the blank verse shall halt for't. What players are 320 they?

ROSENCRANTZ Even those you were wont to take such delight in, the tragedians of the city.

HAMLET How chances it they travel? Their residence, 323 both in reputation and profit, was better both ways.

ROSENCRANTZ I think their inhibition comes by the 325 means of the late innovation. 326

HAMLET Do they hold the same estimation they did when I was in the city? Are they so followed?

ROSENCRANTZ No indeed, are they not.

[HAMLET How comes it? Do they grow rusty?

ROSENCRANTZ Nay, their endeavor keeps in the wonted pace, but there is, sir, an eyrie of children, little eyases, 332 that cry out on the top of question and are most tyran- 333 nically clapped for't. These are now the fashion, and so berattle the common stages (so they call them) that 335 many wearing rapiers are afraid of goosequills and dare 336 scarce come thither.

HAMLET What, are they children? Who maintains 'em? How are they escoted? Will they pursue the quality no 339 longer than they can sing? Will they not say afterwards, 340 if they should grow themselves to common players (as it is most like, if their means are no better), their writers do them wrong to make them exclaim against their own succession?

ROSENCRANTZ Faith, there has been much to do on both sides, and the nation holds it no sin to tarre them to con- 346 troversy. There was, for a while, no money bid for argu- 347 ment unless the poet and the player went to cuffs in the question.

HAMLET Is't possible?

GUILDENSTERN O, there has been much throwing about of brains.

HAMLET Do the boys carry it away?

---

260 *bodies* solid substances, not shadows (because beggars lack ambition) 261 *outstretched* elongated as shadows (with a corollary implication of far-reaching with respect to the ambitions that make both heroes and monarchs into shadows) 262 *fay* faith 263 *wait upon* attend 267 *make* do 271 *a halfpenny* at a halfpenny 281 *consonancy* accord (in sameness of age) 283 *proposer* propounder 284 *withal* with; *even* straight 290 *prevent* forestall 291 *discovery* disclosure 292 *moult no feather* be left whole 297 *firmament* sky 298 *fretted* decorated with fretwork 301 *express* well framed 304 *quintessence* fifth or last and finest essence (an alchemical term) 311 *lenten* scanty 312 *coted* overtook 316 *foil and target* sword and shield 317 *humorous man* eccentric character dominated by one of the humours 319 *tickle o' th' sere* hair-triggered for the discharge of laughter ('sere': part of a gunlock) 320 *halt* go lame 323 *residence* residing at the capital 325 *inhibition* impediment to acting in residence (formal prohibition?) 326 *innovation* new fashion of having companies of boy actors play on the 'private' stage (?), political upheaval (?) 332 *eyrie* nest; *eyases* nestling hawks 333 *on the top of question* above others on matter of dispute 335 *berattle* berate; *common stages* 'public' theatres of the 'common' players, who were organized in companies mainly composed of adult actors (allusion being made to the 'War of the Theatres' in Shakespeare's London) 336 *goosequills* pens (of satirists who made out that the London public stage showed low taste) 339 *escoted* supported; *quality* profession of acting 340 *sing* i.e. with unchanged voices 346 *tarre* incite 347 *argument* matter of a play

ROSENCRANTZ Ay, that they do, my lord – Hercules and
354 his load too.]

HAMLET It is not very strange, for my uncle is King of
356 Denmark, and those that would make mows at him
while my father lived give twenty, forty, fifty, a hundred
358 ducats apiece for his picture in little. 'Sblood, there is
something in this more than natural, if philosophy
could find it out.
A flourish.

GUILDENSTERN There are the players.

HAMLET Gentlemen, you are welcome to Elsinore. Your
hands, come then. Th' appurtenance of welcome is
fashion and ceremony. Let me comply with you in this
364 garb, lest my extent to the players (which I tell you must
show fairly outwards) should more appear like entertainment than yours. You are welcome. But my uncle-
father and aunt-mother are deceived.

GUILDENSTERN In what, my dear lord?

HAMLET I am but mad north-north-west. When the
370 wind is southerly I know a hawk from a handsaw.
Enter Polonius.

POLONIUS Well be with you, gentlemen.

HAMLET Hark you, Guildenstern – and you too – at each
ear a hearer. That great baby you see there is not yet out
374 of his swaddling clouts.

375 ROSENCRANTZ Happily he is the second time come to
them, for they say an old man is twice a child.

HAMLET I will prophesy he comes to tell me of the
players. Mark it. – You say right, sir; a Monday morning, 'twas then indeed.

POLONIUS My lord, I have news to tell you.

381 HAMLET My lord, I have news to tell you. When Roscius
was an actor in Rome –

POLONIUS The actors are come hither, my lord.

HAMLET Buzz, buzz.

POLONIUS Upon my honor –

HAMLET Then came each actor on his ass –

POLONIUS The best actors in the world, either for tragedy, comedy, history, pastoral, pastoral-comical, historical-pastoral, tragical-historical, tragical-comical-
390 historical-pastoral; scene individable, or poem unlimi-
391 ted. Seneca cannot be too heavy, nor Plautus too light.
392 For the law of writ and the liberty, these are the only men.

393 HAMLET O Jephthah, judge of Israel, what a treasure
hadst thou!

POLONIUS What treasure had he, my lord?

HAMLET Why,
    'One fair daughter, and no more,
398   The which he lovèd passing well.'

POLONIUS *[aside]* Still on my daughter.

HAMLET Am I not i' th' right, old Jephthah?

POLONIUS If you call me Jephthah, my lord, I have a
daughter that I love passing well.

HAMLET Nay, that follows not.

POLONIUS What follows then, my lord?

HAMLET Why,
    'As by lot, God wot,'
and then, you know,
    'It came to pass, as most like it was.'
409 The first row of the pious chanson will show you more,
410 for look where my abridgment comes.
Enter the Players.
You are welcome, masters, welcome, all. – I am glad to
see thee well. – Welcome, good friends. – O, old friend,

why, thy face is valanced since I saw thee last. Com'st 413
thou to beard me in Denmark? – What, my young lady 414
and mistress? By'r Lady, your ladyship is nearer to
heaven than when I saw you last by the altitude of a
chopine. Pray God your voice, like a piece of uncurrent 417
gold, be not cracked within the ring. – Masters, you are 418
all welcome. We'll e'en to't like French falconers, fly at
anything we see. We'll have a speech straight. Come,
give us a taste of your quality. Come, a passionate speech.

PLAYER What speech, my good lord?

HAMLET I heard thee speak me a speech once, but it was
never acted, or if it was, not above once, for the play, I
remember, pleased not the million; 'twas caviary to the 425
general, but it was (as I received it, and others, whose 426
judgments in such matters cried in the top of mine) an 427
excellent play, well digested in the scenes, set down with
as much modesty as cunning. I remember one said there
were no sallets in the lines to make the matter savory, 430
nor no matter in the phrase that might indict the author
of affectation, but called it an honest method, as wholesome as sweet, and by very much more handsome than
fine. One speech in't I chiefly loved. 'Twas Aeneas' tale
to Dido, and thereabout of it especially where he speaks
of Priam's slaughter. If it live in your memory, begin at 436
this line – let me see, let me see:
    'The rugged Pyrrhus, like th' Hyrcanian beast –'   438
'Tis not so; it begins with Pyrrhus:
    'The rugged Pyrrhus, he whose sable arms,   440
    Black as his purpose, did the night resemble
    When he lay couchèd in the ominous horse,   442
    Hath now this dread and black complexion smeared
    With heraldry more dismal. Head to foot   444
    Now is he total gules, horridly tricked   445
    With blood of fathers, mothers, daughters, sons,
    Baked and impasted with the parching streets,   447
    That lend a tyrannous and a damnèd light
    To their lord's murder. Roasted in wrath and fire,
    And thus o'ersizèd with coagulate gore,   450
    With eyes like carbuncles, the hellish Pyrrhus
    Old grandsire Priam seeks.'
So, proceed you.

354 *load* i.e. the whole world (with a topical reference to the sign of the
Globe Theatre, a representation of Hercules bearing the world on his
shoulders) 356 *mows* grimaces 358 *'Sblood* by God's blood 364 *garb*
fashion; *extent* showing of welcome 370 *hawk* mattock or pickaxe (also
called 'hack'; here used apparently with a play on 'hawk': a bird); *handsaw*
carpenter's tool (apparently with a play on some corrupt form of 'hern-
shaw'; heron, a bird often hunted with the hawk) 374 *clouts* clothes 375
Happily haply, perhaps 381 *Roscius* the greatest of Roman comic actors
390 *scene individable* drama observing the unities; *poem unlimited* drama not
observing the unities 391 *Seneca* Roman writer of tragedies; *Plautus*
Roman writer of comedies 392 *law of writ* orthodoxy determined by
critical rules of the drama; *liberty* freedom from such orthodoxy 393
Jephthah the compelled sacrificer of a dearly beloved daughter (Judges xi)
398 *passing* surpassingly (verses are from a ballad on Jephthah) 409 *row*
stanza; *chanson* song 410 *my abridgment* that which shortens my talk 413
valanced fringed (with a beard) 414 *young lady* boy who plays women's
parts 417 *chopine* women's thick-soled shoe; *uncurrent* not legal tender
418 *within the ring* from the edge through the line circling the design on the
coin (with a play on 'ring': a sound) 425 *caviary* caviare 426 *general*
multitude 427 *in the top of* more authoritatively than 430 *sallets* salads,
highly seasoned passages 436 *Priam's slaughter* i.e. at the fall of Troy
(Aeneid II, 506 ff.) 438 *Hyrcanian beast* tiger 440 *sable* black 442
ominous horse the wooden horse by which the Greeks gained entrance to Troy 444 *dismal* ill-omened 445 *gules* red (heraldic term);
tricked decorated in color (heraldic term) 447 *parching* i.e. because Troy
was burning 450 *o'ersizèd* covered as with size, a glutinous material used
for filling pores of plaster, etc.; *coagulate* clotted

POLONIUS Fore God, my lord, well spoken, with good accent and good discretion.

PLAYER   'Anon he finds him,
    Striking too short at Greeks. His antique sword,
    Rebellious to his arms, lies where it falls,
    Repugnant to command. Unequal matched,
    Pyrrhus at Priam drives, in rage strikes wide,
461   But with the whiff and wind of his fell sword
462   Th' unnervèd father falls. Then senseless Ilium,
    Seeming to feel this blow, with flaming top
464   Stoops to his base, and with a hideous crash
    Takes prisoner Pyrrhus' ear. For lo! his sword,
    Which was declining on the milky head
    Of reverend Priam, seemed i' th' air to stick.
468   So as a painted tyrant Pyrrhus stood,
469   And like a neutral to his will and matter
    Did nothing.
471   But as we often see, against some storm,
472   A silence in the heavens, the rack stand still,
    The bold winds speechless, and the orb below
    As hush as death, anon the dreadful thunder
475   Doth rend the region, so after Pyrrhus' pause,
    Arousèd vengeance sets him new a-work,
477   And never did the Cyclops' hammers fall
478   On Mars' armor, forged for proof eterne,
    With less remorse than Pyrrhus' bleeding sword
    Now falls on Priam.
    Out, out, thou strumpet Fortune! All you gods,
    In general synod take away her power,
483   Break all the spokes and fellies from her wheel,
484   And bowl the round nave down the hill of heaven,
    As low as to the fiends.'

POLONIUS This is too long.

HAMLET It shall to the barber's, with your beard. –
488   Prithee say on. He's for a jig or a tale of bawdry, or he sleeps. Say on; come to Hecuba.

PLAYER
490   'But who (ah woe!) had seen the mobled queen –'

HAMLET 'The mobled queen'?

POLONIUS That's good. 'Mobled queen' is good.

PLAYER
    'Run barefoot up and down, threat'ning the flames
494   With bisson rheum; a clout upon that head
    Where late the diadem stood, and for a robe,
496   About her lank and all o'erteemèd loins,
    A blanket in the alarm of fear caught up –
    Who this had seen, with tongue in venom steeped
499   'Gainst Fortune's state would treason have pronounced.
    But if the gods themselves did see her then,
    When she saw Pyrrhus make malicious sport

    In mincing with his sword her husband's limbs,
    The instant burst of clamor that she made
    (Unless things mortal move them not at all)
    Would have made milch the burning eyes of heaven 505
    And passion in the gods.'

POLONIUS Look, whe'r he has not turned his color, and 507 has tears in's eyes. Prithee no more.

HAMLET 'Tis well. I'll have thee speak out the rest of this soon. – Good my lord, will you see the players well be- 510 stowed? Do you hear? Let them be well used, for they are the abstract and brief chronicles of the time. After your death you were better have a bad epitaph than their ill report while you live.

POLONIUS My lord, I will use them according to their desert.

HAMLET God's bodkin, man, much better! Use every 516 man after his desert, and who shall scape whipping? Use them after your own honor and dignity. The less they deserve, the more merit is in your bounty. Take them in.

POLONIUS Come, sirs.

HAMLET Follow him, friends. We'll hear a play tomorrow. *[aside to Player]* Dost thou hear me, old friend? Can you play 'The Murder of Gonzago'?

PLAYER Ay, my lord.

HAMLET We'll ha't to-morrow night. You could for a need study a speech of some dozen or sixteen lines which I would set down and insert in't, could you not?

PLAYER Ay, my lord.

HAMLET Very well. Follow that lord, and look you mock him not. – My good friends, I'll leave you till night. You 530 are welcome to Elsinore.   *Exeunt Polonius and Players.*

ROSENCRANTZ Good my lord.
                Exeunt [Rosencrantz and Guildenstern].

HAMLET
    Ay, so, God bye to you. – Now I am alone.
    O, what a rogue and peasant slave am I!
    Is it not monstrous that this player here,
    But in a fiction, in a dream of passion,
    Could force his soul so to his own conceit   537
    That from her working all his visage wanned,
    Tears in his eyes, distraction in his aspect,
    A broken voice, and his whole function suiting   540
    With forms to his conceit? And all for nothing,
    For Hecuba!
    What's Hecuba to him, or he to Hecuba,
    That he should weep for her? What would he do
    Had he the motive and the cue for passion
    That I have? He would drown the stage with tears
    And cleave the general ear with horrid speech,
    Make mad the guilty and appal the free,
    Confound the ignorant, and amaze indeed
    The very faculties of eyes and ears.
    Yet I,
    A dull and muddy-mettled rascal, peak   552
    Like John-a-dreams, unpregnant of my cause,   553
    And can say nothing. No, not for a king,
    Upon whose property and most dear life
    A damned defeat was made. Am I a coward?
    Who calls me villain? breaks my pate across?
    Plucks off my beard and blows it in my face?
    Tweaks me by the nose? gives me the lie i' th' throat
    As deep as to the lungs? Who does me this?
    Ha, 'swounds, I should take it, for it cannot be   561

461 *fell* cruel 462 *senseless* without feeling 464 *his* its 468 *painted* pictured 469 *will and matter* purpose and its realization (between which he stands motionless) 471 *against* just before 472 *rack* clouds 475 *region* sky 477 *Cyclops* giant workmen who made armor in the smithy of Vulcan 478 *proof eterne* eternal protection 483 *fellies* segments of the rim 484 *nave* hub 488 *jig* short comic piece with singing and dancing often presented after a play 490 *mobled* muffled 494 *bisson rheum* blinding tears; *clout* cloth 496 *o'erteemèd* overproductive of children 499 *state* government of worldly events 505 *milch* tearful (milk-giving); *eyes* i.e. stars 507 *whe'r* whether 510 *bestowed* lodged 516 *God's bodkin* by God's little body 537 *conceit* conception, idea 540 *function* action of bodily powers 552 *muddy-mettled* dull-spirited; *peak* mope 553 *John-a-dreams* a sleepy dawdler; *unpregnant* barren of realization 561 *'swounds* by God's wounds

562 But I am pigeon-livered and lack gall
To make oppression bitter, or ere this
564 I should ha' fatted all the region kites
565 With this slave's offal. Bloody, bawdy villain!
566 Remorseless, treacherous, lecherous, kindless villain!
O, vengeance!
Why, what an ass am I! This is most brave,
That I, the son of a dear father murdered,
Prompted to my revenge by heaven and hell,
Must like a whore unpack my heart with words
And fall a-cursing like a very drab,
573 A stallion! Fie upon't, foh! About, my brains.
Hum –
I have heard that guilty creatures sitting at a play
Have by the very cunning of the scene
577 Been struck so to the soul that presently
They have proclaimed their malefactions.
For murder, though it have no tongue, will speak
With most miraculous organ. I'll have these players
Play something like the murder of my father
Before mine uncle. I'll observe his looks.
583 I'll tent him to the quick. If 'a do blench,
I know my course. The spirit that I have seen
May be a devil, and the devil hath power
T' assume a pleasing shape, yea, and perhaps
Out of my weakness and my melancholy,
As he is very potent with such spirits,
589 Abuses me to damn me. I'll have grounds
590 More relative than this. The play 's the thing
Wherein I'll catch the conscience of the king.   *Exit.*

*

III, i   *Enter King, Queen, Polonius, Ophelia, Rosencrantz,*
          Guildenstern, Lords.

KING
1 And can you by no drift of conference
Get from him why he puts on this confusion,
Grating so harshly all his days of quiet
With turbulent and dangerous lunacy?
ROSENCRANTZ
He does confess he feels himself distracted,
But from what cause 'a will by no means speak.
GUILDENSTERN
Nor do we find him forward to be sounded,
But with a crafty madness keeps aloof
When we would bring him on to some confession
Of his true state.
QUEEN   Did he receive you well?
ROSENCRANTZ
Most like a gentleman.
GUILDENSTERN
But with much forcing of his disposition.
ROSENCRANTZ
Niggard of question, but of our demands
Most free in his reply.
14 QUEEN   Did you assay him
To any pastime?
ROSENCRANTZ
Madam, it so fell out that certain players
17 We o'erraught on the way. Of these we told him,
And there did seem in him a kind of joy
To hear of it. They are here about the court,
And, as I think, they have already order

This night to play before him.
POLONIUS   'Tis most true,
And he beseeched me to entreat your majesties
To hear and see the matter.
KING
With all my heart, and it doth much content me
To hear him so inclined.
Good gentlemen, give him a further edge   26
And drive his purpose into these delights.
ROSENCRANTZ
We shall, my lord. *Exeunt Rosencrantz and Guildenstern.*
KING   Sweet Gertrude, leave us too,
For we have closely sent for Hamlet hither,   29
That he, as 'twere by accident, may here
Affront Ophelia.   31
Her father and myself (lawful espials)   32
Will so bestow ourselves that, seeing unseen,
We may of their encounter frankly judge
And gather by him, as he is behaved,
If 't be th' affliction of his love or no
That thus he suffers for.
QUEEN   I shall obey you. –
And for your part, Ophelia, I do wish
That your good beauties be the happy cause
Of Hamlet's wildness. So shall I hope your virtues
Will bring him to his wonted way again,
To both your honors.
OPHELIA   Madam, I wish it may. *[Exit Queen.]*
POLONIUS
Ophelia, walk you here. – Gracious, so please you,
We will bestow ourselves. –
     [To Ophelia]   Read on this book,
That show of such an exercise may color   45
Your loneliness. We are oft to blame in this,
'Tis too much proved, that with devotion's visage
And pious action we do sugar o'er
The devil himself.
KING *[aside]*   O, 'tis too true.
How smart a lash that speech doth give my conscience!
The harlot's cheek, beautied with plast'ring art,
Is not more ugly to the thing that helps it   52
Than is my deed to my most painted word.
O heavy burthen!
POLONIUS
I hear him coming. Let's withdraw, my lord.
                    [Exeunt King and Polonius.]
     Enter Hamlet.
HAMLET
To be, or not to be – that is the question:
Whether 'tis nobler in the mind to suffer
The slings and arrows of outrageous fortune
Or to take arms against a sea of troubles
And by opposing end them. To die, to sleep –
No more – and by a sleep to say we end

---

562 *pigeon-livered* of dove-like gentleness   564 *region kites* kites of the air
565 *offal* guts   566 *kindless* unnatural   573 *stallion* prostitute (male or
female)   577 *presently* immediately   583 *tent* probe; *blench* flinch   589
Abuses deludes   590 *relative* pertinent
III, i A chamber in the Castle   1 *drift of conference* direction of conversation   14 *assay* try to win   17 *o'erraught* overtook   26 *edge* keenness
of desire   29 *closely* privately   31 *Affront* come face to face with   32
espials spies   45 *exercise* religious exercise (the book being obviously one
of devotion); *color* give an appearance of naturalness to   52 *to* compared
to

The heartache, and the thousand natural shocks
That flesh is heir to. 'Tis a consummation
Devoutly to be wished. To die, to sleep –
65   To sleep – perchance to dream : ay, there's the rub,
For in that sleep of death what dreams may come
67   When we have shuffled off this mortal coil,
68   Must give us pause. There's the respect
69   That makes calamity of so long life.
For who would bear the whips and scorns of time,
Th' oppressor's wrong, the proud man's contumely
The pangs of despised love, the law's delay,
The insolence of office, and the spurns
That patient merit of th' unworthy takes,
75   When he himself might his quietus make
76   With a bare bodkin ? Who would fardels bear,
To grunt and sweat under a weary life,
But that the dread of something after death,
79   The undiscovered country, from whose bourn
No traveller returns, puzzles the will,
And makes us rather bear those ills we have
Than fly to others that we know not of ?
Thus conscience does make cowards of us all,
And thus the native hue of resolution
Is sicklied o'er with the pale cast of thought,
86   And enterprises of great pitch and moment
87   With this regard their currents turn awry
And lose the name of action. – Soft you now,
89   The fair Ophelia ! – Nymph, in thy orisons
Be all my sins remembered.

OPHELIA   Good my lord,
How does your honor for this many a day ?

HAMLET
I humbly thank you, well, well, well.

OPHELIA
My lord, I have remembrances of yours
That I have longèd long to re-deliver.
I pray you, now receive them.

HAMLET   No, not I,
I never gave you aught.

OPHELIA
My honored lord, you know right well you did,
And with them words of so sweet breath composed
As made the things more rich. Their perfume lost,
Take these again, for to the noble mind
Rich gifts wax poor when givers prove unkind.
There, my lord.

103 HAMLET   Ha, ha ! Are you honest ?

OPHELIA   My lord ?

HAMLET   Are you fair ?

OPHELIA   What means your lordship ?

HAMLET   That if you be honest and fair, your honesty
should admit no discourse to your beauty.

OPHELIA   Could beauty, my lord, have better commerce 109
than with honesty ?

HAMLET   Ay, truly ; for the power of beauty will sooner
transform honesty from what it is to a bawd than the
force of honesty can translate beauty into his likeness.
This was sometime a paradox, but now the time gives it 114
proof. I did love you once.

OPHELIA   Indeed, my lord, you made me believe so.

HAMLET   You should not have believed me, for virtue
cannot so inoculate our old stock but we shall relish of it. 118
I loved you not.

OPHELIA   I was the more deceived.

HAMLET   Get thee to a nunnery. Why wouldst thou be a
breeder of sinners ? I am myself indifferent honest, but 122
yet I could accuse me of such things that it were better
my mother had not borne me : I am very proud,
revengeful, ambitious, with more offenses at my beck
than I have thoughts to put them in, imagination to give
them shape, or time to act them in. What should such
fellows as I do crawling between earth and heaven ? We
are arrant knaves all ; believe none of us. Go thy ways to
a nunnery. Where's your father ?

OPHELIA   At home, my lord.

HAMLET   Let the doors be shut upon him, that he may
play the fool nowhere but in's own house. Farewell.

OPHELIA   O, help him, you sweet heavens !

HAMLET   If thou dost marry, I'll give thee this plague for
thy dowry : be thou as chaste as ice, as pure as snow, thou
shalt not escape calumny. Get thee to a nunnery. Go,
farewell. Or if thou wilt needs marry, marry a fool, for
wise men know well enough what monsters you make 139
of them. To a nunnery, go, and quickly too. Farewell.

OPHELIA   O heavenly powers, restore him !

HAMLET   I have heard of your paintings too, well enough.
God hath given you one face, and you make yourselves
another. You jig, you amble, and you lisp ; you nickname
God's creatures and make your wantonness your igno- 145
rance. Go to, I'll no more on't ; it hath made me mad.
I say we will have no more marriage. Those that are
married already – all but one – shall live. The rest shall
keep as they are. To a nunnery, go.   *Exit.*

OPHELIA
O, what a noble mind is here o'erthrown !
The courtier's, soldier's, scholar's, eye, tongue, sword,
Th' expectancy and rose of the fair state,   152
The glass of fashion and the mould of form,   153
Th' observed of all observers, quite, quite down !
And I, of ladies most deject and wretched,
That sucked the honey of his music vows,
Now see that noble and most sovereign reason
Like sweet bells jangled, out of time and harsh,
That unmatched form and feature of blown youth
Blasted with ecstasy. O, woe is me   160
T' have seen what I have seen, see what I see !
     Enter King and Polonius.

KING
Love ? his affections do not that way tend,   162
Nor what he spake, though it lacked form a little,
Was not like madness. There's something in his soul
O'er which his melancholy sits on brood,
And I do doubt the hatch and the disclose   166
Will be some danger ; which for to prevent,
I have in quick determination
Thus set it down : he shall with speed to England

---

65 *rub* obstacle (literally, obstruction encountered by a bowler's ball)
67 *shuffled off* cast off as an encumbrance ; *coil* to-do, turmoil   68 *respect*
consideration   69 *of so long life* so long-lived   75 *quietus* settlement
(literally, release from debt)   76 *bodkin* dagger ; *fardels* burdens   79
bourn confine, region   86 *pitch* height (of a soaring falcon's flight)   87
regard consideration   89 *orisons* prayers (because of the book of devotion
she reads)   103 *honest* chaste   109 *commerce* intercourse   114 *paradox*
idea contrary to common opinion   118 *inoculate* graft ; *relish* have a flavor
(because of original sin)   122 *indifferent honest* moderately respectable
139 *monsters* i.e. unnatural combinations of wisdom and uxorious folly
145 *wantonness* affectation ; *your ignorance* a matter for which you offer
the excuse that you don't know any better   152 *expectancy and rose* fair
hope   153 *glass* mirror   160 *ecstasy* madness   162 *affections* emotions
166 *doubt* fear

For the demand of our neglected tribute.
Haply the seas, and countries different,
With variable objects, shall expel
173 This something-settled matter in his heart,
Whereon his brains still beating puts him thus
From fashion of himself. What think you on't?

POLONIUS
It shall do well. But yet do I believe
The origin and commencement of his grief
Sprung from neglected love. – How now, Ophelia?
You need not tell us what Lord Hamlet said.
We heard it all. – My lord, do as you please,
But if you hold it fit, after the play
Let his queen mother all alone entreat him
183 To show his grief. Let her be round with him,
And I'll be placed, so please you, in the ear
Of all their conference. If she find him not,
To England send him, or confine him where
Your wisdom best shall think.

KING   It shall be so.
Madness in great ones must not unwatched go. *Exeunt.*

*

III, ii   *Enter Hamlet and three of the Players.*

HAMLET Speak the speech, I pray you, as I pronounced it
2 to you, trippingly on the tongue. But if you mouth it, as
many of our players do, I had as lief the town crier spoke
my lines. Nor do not saw the air too much with your
hand, thus, but use all gently, for in the very torrent,
tempest, and (as I may say) whirlwind of your passion,
you must acquire and beget a temperance that may give
8 it smoothness. O, it offends me to the soul to hear a ro-
9 bustious periwig-pated fellow tear a passion to tatters,
10 to very rags, to split the ears of the groundlings, who for
the most part are capable of nothing but inexplicable
12 dumb shows and noise. I would have such a fellow
13 whipped for o'erdoing Termagant. It out-herods Herod.
Pray you avoid it.

PLAYER I warrant your honor.

HAMLET Be not too tame neither, but let your own discretion be your tutor. Suit the action to the word, the
word to the action, with this special observance, that you
o'erstep not the modesty of nature. For anything so over-
19 done is from the purpose of playing, whose end, both at
the first and now, was and is, to hold, as 'twere, the mirror
up to nature, to show virtue her own feature, scorn her
own image, and the very age and body of the time his
23 form and pressure. Now this overdone, or come tardy off,
though it make the unskillful laugh, cannot but make
25 the judicious grieve, the censure of the which one must
in your allowance o'erweigh a whole theatre of others.
O, there be players that I have seen play, and heard others
praise, and that highly (not to speak it profanely), that
neither having th' accent of Christians, nor the gait of
Christian, pagan, nor man, have so strutted and bellowed
31 that I have thought some of Nature's journeymen had
made men, and not made them well, they imitated humanity so abominably.

34 **PLAYER** I hope we have reformed that indifferently with
us, sir.

HAMLET O, reform it altogether! And let those that play
your clowns speak no more than is set down for them, for
38 there be of them that will themselves laugh, to set on

some quantity of barren spectators to laugh too, though
in the mean time some necessary question of the play be
then to be considered. That's villainous and shows a
most pitiful ambition in the fool that uses it. Go make
you ready.   *[Exeunt Players.]*
Enter Polonius, Guildenstern, and Rosencrantz.
How now, my lord? Will the king hear this piece of
work?

POLONIUS And the queen too, and that presently.   45

HAMLET Bid the players make haste.   *[Exit Polonius.]*
Will you two help to hasten them?

ROSENCRANTZ Ay, my lord.   *Exeunt they two.*

HAMLET What, ho, Horatio!
Enter Horatio.

HORATIO
Here, sweet lord, at your service.

HAMLET
Horatio, thou art e'en as just a man
As e'er my conversation coped withal.   52

HORATIO
O, my dear lord –

HAMLET   Nay, do not think I flatter.
For what advancement may I hope from thee,
That no revenue hast but thy good spirits
To feed and clothe thee? Why should the poor be
    flattered?
No, let the candied tongue lick absurd pomp,
And crook the pregnant hinges of the knee   58
Where thrift may follow fawning. Dost thou hear?   59
Since my dear soul was mistress of her choice
And could of men distinguish her election,
S' hath sealed thee for herself, for thou hast been   62
As one in suff'ring all that suffers nothing,
A man that Fortune's buffets and rewards
Hast ta'en with equal thanks; and blest are those
Whose blood and judgment are so well commeddled   66
That they are not a pipe for Fortune's finger
To sound what stop she please. Give me that man
That is not passion's slave, and I will wear him
In my heart's core, ay, in my heart of heart,
As I do thee. Something too much of this –
There is a play to-night before the king.
One scene of it comes near the circumstance
Which I have told thee, of my father's death.
I prithee, when thou seest that act afoot,
Even with the very comment of thy soul   76
Observe my uncle. If his occulted guilt   77
Do not itself unkennel in one speech,
It is a damnèd ghost that we have seen,   79

---

173 *something-settled* somewhat settled   183 *round* plain-spoken
III, ii The hall of the Castle   2 *trippingly* easily   8 *robustious* boisterous
9 *periwig-pated* wig-wearing (after the custom of actors)   10 *groundlings*
spectators who paid least and stood on the ground in the pit or yard of
the theatre   12 *dumb shows* brief actions without words, forecasting dramatic matter to follow (the play presented later in this scene giving an old-
fashioned example)   13 *Termagant* a Saracen 'god' in medieval romance
and drama; *Herod* the raging tyrant of old Biblical plays   19 *from* apart
from   23 *pressure* impressed or printed character; *come tardy off* brought
off slowly and badly   25 *the censure of the which one* the judgment of even
one of whom   31 *journeymen* workmen not yet masters of their trade
34 *indifferently* fairly well   38 *of them* some of them   45 *presently* at once
52 *conversation coped withal* intercourse with men encountered   58 *pregnant* quick to move   59 *thrift* profit   62 *sealed* marked   66 *blood* passion;
commeddled mixed together   76 *the very . . . soul* thy deepest sagacity   77
occulted hidden   79 *damnèd ghost* evil spirit, devil (as thought of in II, ii,
584 ff.)

And my imaginations are as foul
81 As Vulcan's stithy. Give him heedful note,
For I mine eyes will rivet to his face,
And after we will both our judgments join
84 In censure of his seeming.

HORATIO   Well, my lord.
If 'a steal aught the while this play is playing,
And scape detecting, I will pay the theft.

*Enter Trumpets and Kettledrums, King, Queen,
Polonius, Ophelia [, Rosencrantz, Guildenstern, and
other Lords attendant].*

87 HAMLET They are coming to the play. I must be idle.
Get you a place.

89 KING How fares our cousin Hamlet?

90 HAMLET Excellent, i' faith, of the chameleon's dish. I eat
the air, promise-crammed. You cannot feed capons so.

KING I have nothing with this answer, Hamlet. These
93 words are not mine.

HAMLET No, nor mine now. *[to Polonius]* My lord, you
played once i' th' university, you say?

POLONIUS That did I, my lord, and was accounted a
good actor.

HAMLET What did you enact?

POLONIUS I did enact Julius Caesar. I was killed i' th'
Capitol; Brutus killed me.

HAMLET It was a brute part of him to kill so capital a calf
there. Be the players ready?

103 ROSENCRANTZ Ay, my lord. They stay upon your
patience.

QUEEN Come hither, my dear Hamlet, sit by me.

HAMLET No, good mother. Here's metal more attractive.

POLONIUS *[to the King]* O ho! do you mark that?

HAMLET Lady, shall I lie in your lap?
[He lies at Ophelia's feet.]

OPHELIA No, my lord.

HAMLET I mean, my head upon your lap?

OPHELIA Ay, my lord.

111 HAMLET Do you think I meant country matters?

OPHELIA I think nothing, my lord.

HAMLET That's a fair thought to lie between maids' legs.

OPHELIA What is, my lord?

HAMLET Nothing.

OPHELIA You are merry, my lord.

HAMLET Who, I?

OPHELIA Ay, my lord.

119 HAMLET O God, your only jig-maker! What should a
man do but be merry? For look you how cheerfully my
mother looks, and my father died within's two hours.

OPHELIA Nay, 'tis twice two months, my lord.

HAMLET So long? Nay then, let the devil wear black, for
124 I'll have a suit of sables. O heavens! die two months

ago, and not forgotten yet? Then there's hope a great
man's memory may outlive his life half a year. But, by'r
Lady, 'a must build churches then, or else shall 'a
suffer not thinking on, with the hobby-horse, whose 128
epitaph is 'For O, for O, the hobby-horse is forgot!'

*The trumpets sound. Dumb show follows:
Enter a King and a Queen [very lovingly], the Queen embracing him, and he her. [She kneels; and makes show of
protestation unto him.] He takes her up, and declines his head
upon her neck. He lies him down upon a bank of flowers. She,
seeing him asleep, leaves him. Anon come in another man:
takes off his crown, kisses it, pours poison in the sleeper's ears,
and leaves him. The Queen returns, finds the King dead,
makes passionate action. The poisoner, with some three or
four, come in again, seem to condole with her. The dead body
is carried away. The poisoner woos the Queen with gifts; she
seems harsh awhile, but in the end accepts love.*   *[Exeunt.]*

OPHELIA What means this, my lord?

HAMLET Marry, this is miching mallecho; it means mis- 131
chief.

OPHELIA Belike this show imports the argument of the
play.
Enter Prologue.

HAMLET We shall know by this fellow. The players cannot keep counsel; they'll tell all.

OPHELIA Will 'a tell us what this show meant?

HAMLET Ay, or any show that you'll show him. Be not
you ashamed to show, he'll not shame to tell you what it
means.

OPHELIA You are naught, you are naught. I'll mark the 139
play.

PROLOGUE For us and for our tragedy,
Here stooping to your clemency,
We beg your hearing patiently.   *[Exit.]*

HAMLET Is this a prologue, or the posy of a ring?   143

OPHELIA 'Tis brief, my lord.

HAMLET As woman's love.

Enter [two Players as] King and Queen.

KING
Full thirty times hath Phoebus' cart gone round   146
Neptune's salt wash and Tellus' orbèd ground,   147
And thirty dozen moons with borrowed sheen   148
About the world have times twelve thirties been,
Since love our hearts, and Hymen did our hands,   150
Unite commutual in most sacred bands.   151

QUEEN
So many journeys may the sun and moon
Make us again count o'er ere love be done!
But woe is me, you are so sick of late,
So far from cheer and from your former state,
That I distrust you. Yet, though I distrust,   156
Discomfort you, my lord, it nothing must.
For women fear too much, even as they love,
And women's fear and love hold quantity,   159
In neither aught, or in extremity.
Now what my love is, proof hath made you know,
And as my love is sized, my fear is so.
Where love is great, the littlest doubts are fear;
Where little fears grow great, great love grows there.

KING
Faith, I must leave thee, love, and shortly too;
My operant powers their functions leave to do.   166

And thou shalt live in this fair world behind,
Honored, beloved, and haply one as kind
For husband shalt thou –

QUEEN   O, confound the rest!
Such love must needs be treason in my breast.
In second husband let me be accurst!
None wed the second but who killed the first.

173 HAMLET [aside] That's wormwood.

QUEEN
174 The instances that second marriage move
Are base respects of thrift, but none of love.
A second time I kill my husband dead
When second husband kisses me in bed.

KING
I do believe you think what now you speak,
But what we do determine oft we break.
180 Purpose is but the slave to memory,
181 Of violent birth, but poor validity,
Which now like fruit unripe sticks on the tree,
But fall unshaken when they mellow be.
Most necessary 'tis that we forget
To pay ourselves what to ourselves is debt.
What to ourselves in passion we propose,
The passion ending, doth the purpose lose.
The violence of either grief or joy
189 Their own enactures with themselves destroy.
Where joy most revels, grief doth most lament;
Grief joys, joy grieves, on slender accident.
This world is not for aye, nor 'tis not strange
That even our loves should with our fortunes change,
For 'tis a question left us yet to prove,
Whether love lead fortune, or else fortune love.
The great man down, you mark his favorite flies,
The poor advanced makes friends of enemies;
And hitherto doth love on fortune tend,
For who not needs shall never lack a friend,
And who in want a hollow friend doth try,
201 Directly seasons him his enemy.
But, orderly to end where I begun,
Our wills and fates do so contrary run
204 That our devices still are overthrown;
Our thoughts are ours, their ends none of our own.
So think thou wilt no second husband wed,
But die thy thoughts when thy first lord is dead.

QUEEN
Nor earth to me give food, nor heaven light,
Sport and repose lock from me day and night,
To desperation turn my trust and hope,
211 An anchor's cheer in prison be my scope,
212 Each opposite that blanks the face of joy
Meet what I would have well, and it destroy,
214 Both here and hence pursue me lasting strife,
If, once a widow, ever I be wife!

HAMLET If she should break it now!

KING
'Tis deeply sworn. Sweet, leave me here awhile.
My spirits grow dull, and fain I would beguile
The tedious day with sleep.

QUEEN   Sleep rock thy brain,   [He sleeps.]
And never come mischance between us twain!   Exit.

HAMLET Madam, how like you this play?
QUEEN The lady doth protest too much, methinks.

HAMLET O, but she'll keep her word.
KING Have you heard the argument? Is there no offense 224
in 't?
HAMLET No, no, they do but jest, poison in jest; no
offense i' th' world.
KING What do you call the play?
HAMLET 'The Mousetrap.' Marry, how? Tropically. 229
This play is the image of a murder done in Vienna. Gon-
zago is the duke's name; his wife, Baptista. You shall see
anon. 'Tis a knavish piece of work, but what o' that?
Your majesty, and we that have free souls, it touches us 233
not. Let the galled jade winch; our withers are unwrung. 234
        Enter Lucianus.
This is one Lucianus, nephew to the king.
OPHELIA You are as good as a chorus, my lord.   236
HAMLET I could interpret between you and your love, if I
could see the puppets dallying.   238
OPHELIA You are keen, my lord, you are keen.
HAMLET It would cost you a groaning to take off my edge.
OPHELIA Still better, and worse.
HAMLET So you must take your husbands. – Begin, mur-
derer. Leave thy damnable faces and begin. Come, the
croaking raven doth bellow for revenge.

LUCIANUS
Thoughts black, hands apt, drugs fit, and time agreeing,
Confederate season, else no creature seeing,   246
Thou mixture rank, of midnight weeds collected,
With Hecate's ban thrice blasted, thrice infected,   248
Thy natural magic and dire property
On wholesome life usurps immediately.
        [Pours the poison in his ears.]

HAMLET 'A poisons him i' th' garden for his estate. His
name 's Gonzago. The story is extant, and written in
very choice Italian. You shall see anon how the mur-
derer gets the love of Gonzago's wife.
OPHELIA The king rises.
HAMLET What, frighted with false fire?   256
QUEEN How fares my lord?
POLONIUS Give o'er the play.
KING Give me some light. Away!
POLONIUS Lights, lights, lights!
                    Exeunt all but Hamlet and Horatio.
HAMLET Why, let the strucken deer go weep,
        The hart ungallèd play.
For some must watch, while some must sleep;
        Thus runs the world away.
Would not this, sir, and a forest of feathers – if the rest of 265
my fortunes turn Turk with me – with two Provincial 266
roses on my razed shoes, get me a fellowship in a cry of 267
players, sir?

173 *wormwood* a bitter herb 174 *instances* motives 180 *slave to* i.e.
dependent upon for life 181 *validity* strength 189 *enactures* fulfillments
201 *seasons him* ripens him into 204 *still* always 211 *anchor's* hermit's
212 *blanks* blanches, makes pale 214 *hence* in the next world 224 *argument* plot summary 229 *Tropically* in the way of a trope or figure (with
a play on 'trapically') 233 *free* guiltless 234 *galled* sore-backed; *jade*
horse; *winch* wince; *withers* shoulders 236 *chorus* one in a play who
explains the action 238 *puppets* i.e. you and your lover as in a puppet
show 246 *Confederate season* the occasion being my ally 248 *Hecate*
goddess of witchcraft and black magic; *ban* curse 256 *false fire* a firing
of a gun charged with powder but no shot, a blank-discharge 265 *feathers*
plumes for actors' costumes 266 *turn Turk* turn renegade, like a Christian
turning Mohammedan 266–67 *Provincial roses* ribbon rosettes 267
razed decorated with cut patterns; *cry* pack

HORATIO Half a share.

HAMLET A whole one, I.
       For thou dost know, O Damon dear,
         This realm dismantled was
       Of Jove himself; and now reigns here
         A very, very – peacock.

HORATIO You might have rhymed.

HAMLET O good Horatio, I'll take the ghost's word for a thousand pound. Didst perceive?

HORATIO Very well, my lord.

HAMLET Upon the talk of the poisoning?

HORATIO I did very well note him.

281 HAMLET Aha! Come, some music! Come, the recorders!
       For if the king like not the comedy,
283   Why then, belike he likes it not, perdy.
Come, some music!

Enter Rosencrantz and Guildenstern.

GUILDENSTERN Good my lord, vouchsafe me a word with you.

HAMLET Sir, a whole history.

GUILDENSTERN The king, sir –

HAMLET Ay, sir, what of him?

289 GUILDENSTERN Is in his retirement marvellous distempered.

HAMLET With drink, sir?

291 GUILDENSTERN No, my lord, with choler.

HAMLET Your wisdom should show itself more richer to signify this to the doctor, for for me to put him to his purgation would perhaps plunge him into more choler.

GUILDENSTERN Good my lord, put your discourse into
296 some frame, and start not so wildly from my affair.

HAMLET I am tame, sir; pronounce.

GUILDENSTERN The queen, your mother, in most great affliction of spirit hath sent me to you.

HAMLET You are welcome.

GUILDENSTERN Nay, good my lord, this courtesy is not of the right breed. If it shall please you to make me a wholesome answer, I will do your mother's commandment. If not, your pardon and my return shall be the end of my business.

HAMLET Sir, I cannot.

ROSENCRANTZ What, my lord?

HAMLET Make you a wholesome answer; my wit 's diseased. But, sir, such answer as I can make, you shall command, or rather, as you say, my mother. Therefore no more, but to the matter. My mother, you say –

ROSENCRANTZ Then thus she says: your behavior hath
313 struck her into amazement and admiration.

HAMLET O wonderful son, that can so stonish a mother! But is there no sequel at the heels of this mother's admiration? Impart.

317 ROSENCRANTZ She desires to speak with you in her closet ere you go to bed.

HAMLET We shall obey, were she ten times our mother. Have you any further trade with us?

ROSENCRANTZ My lord, you once did love me.

HAMLET And do still, by these pickers and stealers.   322

ROSENCRANTZ Good my lord, what is your cause of distemper? You do surely bar the door upon your own liberty, if you deny your griefs to your friend.

HAMLET Sir, I lack advancement.

ROSENCRANTZ How can that be, when you have the voice of the king himself for your succession in Denmark?

HAMLET Ay, sir, but 'while the grass grows' – the proverb   329 is something musty.

Enter the Player with recorders.

O, the recorders. Let me see one. To withdraw with   331 you – why do you go about to recover the wind of me, as   332 if you would drive me into a toil?   333

GUILDENSTERN O my lord, if my duty be too bold, my love is too unmannerly.   335

HAMLET I do not well understand that. Will you play upon this pipe?

GUILDENSTERN My lord, I cannot.

HAMLET I pray you.

GUILDENSTERN Believe me, I cannot.

HAMLET I do beseech you.

GUILDENSTERN I know no touch of it, my lord.

HAMLET It is as easy as lying. Govern these ventages   343 with your fingers and thumb, give it breath with your mouth, and it will discourse most eloquent music. Look you, these are the stops.

GUILDENSTERN But these cannot I command to any utt'rance of harmony. I have not the skill.

HAMLET Why, look you now, how unworthy a thing you make of me! You would play upon me, you would seem to know my stops, you would pluck out the heart of my mystery, you would sound me from my lowest note to the top of my compass; and there is much music, excellent voice, in this little organ, yet cannot you make it speak. 'Sblood, do you think I am easier to be played on than a pipe? Call me what instrument you will, though you can fret me, you cannot play upon me.   357

Enter Polonius.

God bless you, sir!

POLONIUS My lord, the queen would speak with you, and presently.   360

HAMLET Do you see yonder cloud that's almost in shape of a camel?

POLONIUS By th' mass and 'tis, like a camel indeed.

HAMLET Methinks it is like a weasel.

POLONIUS It is backed like a weasel.

HAMLET Or like a whale.

POLONIUS Very like a whale.

HAMLET Then I will come to my mother by and by.   368
[aside] They fool me to the top of my bent. – I will come   369 by and by.

POLONIUS I will say so.   *[Exit.]*

HAMLET 'By and by' is easily said. Leave me, friends.
                       [Exeunt all but Hamlet.]
'Tis now the very witching time of night,
When churchyards yawn, and hell itself breathes out
Contagion to this world. Now could I drink hot blood
And do such bitter business as the day
Would quake to look on. Soft, now to my mother.
O heart, lose not thy nature; let not ever
The soul of Nero enter this firm bosom.   379

---

281 *recorders* musical instruments of the flute class   283 *perdy* by God ('*par dieu*')   289 *distempered* out of temper, vexed (twisted by Hamlet into 'deranged')   291 *choler* anger (twisted by Hamlet into 'biliousness')   296 *frame* logical order   313 *admiration* wonder   317 *closet* private room   322 *pickers and stealers* i.e. hands   329 *while the grass grows* (a proverb, ending: 'the horse starves')   331 *recorders* (see III, ii, 281n.); *withdraw* step aside   332 *recover the wind* come up to windward like a hunter   333 *toil* snare   335 *is too unmannerly* leads me beyond the restraint of good manners   343 *ventages* holes, vents   357 *fret* irritate (with a play on the fret-fingering of certain stringed musical instruments)   360 *presently* at once   368 *by and by* immediately   369 *bent* (see II, ii, 30n.)   379 *Nero* murderer of his mother

Let me be cruel, not unnatural ;
I will speak daggers to her, but use none.
My tongue and soul in this be hypocrites :
383   How in my words somever she be shent,
384   To give them seals never, my soul, consent !   *Exit.*

*

III, iii   *Enter King, Rosencrantz, and Guildenstern.*

KING
I like him not, nor stands it safe with us
To let his madness range. Therefore prepare you.
I your commission will forthwith dispatch,
And he to England shall along with you.
5   The terms of our estate may not endure
Hazard so near 's as doth hourly grow
7   Out of his brows.
GUILDENSTERN   We will ourselves provide.
Most holy and religious fear it is
To keep those many many bodies safe
That live and feed upon your majesty.
ROSENCRANTZ
11   The single and peculiar life is bound
With all the strength and armor of the mind
13   To keep itself from noyance, but much more
That spirit upon whose weal depends and rests
15   The lives of many. The cess of majesty
16   Dies not alone, but like a gulf doth draw
What's near it with it ; or 'tis a massy wheel
Fixed on the summit of the highest mount,
To whose huge spokes ten thousand lesser things
Are mortised and adjoined, which when it falls,
Each small annexment, petty consequence,
22   Attends the boist'rous ruin. Never alone
Did the king sigh, but with a general groan.
KING
24   Arm you, I pray you, to this speedy voyage,
For we will fetters put upon this fear,
Which now goes too free-footed.
ROSENCRANTZ   We will haste us. *Exeunt Gentlemen.*
    Enter Polonius.
POLONIUS
My lord, he's going to his mother's closet.
Behind the arras I'll convey myself
29   To hear the process. I'll warrant she'll tax him home,
And, as you said, and wisely was it said,
'Tis meet that some more audience than a mother,
Since nature makes them partial, should o'erhear
33   The speech, of vantage. Fare you well, my liege.
I'll call upon you ere you go to bed
And tell you what I know.
KING   Thanks, dear my lord. *Exit* [*Polonius*].
O, my offense is rank, it smells to heaven ;
37   It hath the primal eldest curse upon 't,
A brother's murder. Pray can I not,
Though inclination be as sharp as will.
My stronger guilt defeats my strong intent,
And like a man to double business bound
I stand in pause where I shall first begin,
And both neglect. What if this cursèd hand
Were thicker than itself with brother's blood,
Is there not rain enough in the sweet heavens
To wash it white as snow ? Whereto serves mercy
47   But to confront the visage of offense ?

And what's in prayer but this twofold force,
To be forestallèd ere we come to fall,
Or pardoned being down ? Then I'll look up.
My fault is past. But, O, what form of prayer
Can serve my turn ? 'Forgive me my foul murder' ?
That cannot be, since I am still possessed
Of those effects for which I did the murder,   54
My crown, mine own ambition, and my queen.
May one be pardoned and retain th' offense ?
In the corrupted currents of this world
Offense's gilded hand may shove by justice,   58
And oft 'tis seen the wicked prize itself
Buys out the law. But 'tis not so above.
There is no shuffling ; there the action lies   61
In his true nature, and we ourselves compelled,
Even to the teeth and forehead of our faults,   63
To give in evidence. What then ? What rests ?
Try what repentance can. What can it not ?
Yet what can it when one cannot repent ?
O wretched state ! O bosom black as death !
O limèd soul, that struggling to be free   68
Art more engaged ! Help, angels ! Make assay.   69
Bow, stubborn knees, and, heart with strings of steel,
Be soft as sinews of the new-born babe.
All may be well.
    [*He kneels.*]
    Enter Hamlet.
HAMLET
Now might I do it pat, now 'a is a-praying,   73
And now I'll do 't. And so 'a goes to heaven,
And so am I revenged. That would be scanned.
A villain kills my father, and for that
I, his sole son, do this same villain send
To heaven.
Why, this is hire and salary, not revenge.
'A took my father grossly, full of bread,   80
With all his crimes broad blown, as flush as May ;   81
And how his audit stands, who knows save heaven ?   82
But in our circumstance and course of thought,
'Tis heavy with him ; and am I then revenged,
To take him in the purging of his soul,
When he is fit and seasoned for his passage ?
No.
Up, sword, and know thou a more horrid hent.   88
When he is drunk asleep, or in his rage,
Or in th' incestuous pleasure of his bed,
At game a-swearing, or about some act
That has no relish of salvation in 't –   92
Then trip him, that his heels may kick at heaven,
And that his soul may be as damned and black

---

383 *shent* reproved   384 *seals* authentications in actions
III, iii A chamber in the Castle   5 *terms* circumstances ; *estate* royal
position   7 *brows* effronteries (apparently with an implication of knitted
brows)   11 *peculiar* individual   13 *noyance* harm   15 *cess* cessation,
decease   16 *gulf* whirlpool   22 *Attends* joins in (like a royal attendant)
24 *Arm* prepare   29 *process* proceedings ; *tax him home* thrust home in
reprimanding him   33 *of vantage* from an advantageous position   37
primal eldest curse that of Cain, who also murdered a brother   47 *offense* sin
54 *effects* things acquired   58 *gilded* gold-laden   61 *shuffling* sharp practice, double-dealing ; *action* legal proceeding (in heaven's court)   63 *teeth
and forehead* face-to-face recognition   68 *limèd* caught in birdlime, a gluey
material spread as a bird-snare   69 *engaged* embedded ; *assay* an attempt
73 *pat* opportunely   80 *grossly* in a state of gross unpreparedness ; *bread*
i.e. worldly sense gratification   81 *broad blown* fully blossomed ; *flush*
vigorous   82 *audit* account   88 *more horrid hent* grasping by me on a more
horrid occasion   92 *relish* flavor

As hell, whereto it goes. My mother stays.
This physic but prolongs thy sickly days.   *Exit.*
KING [*rises*]
My words fly up, my thoughts remain below.
Words without thoughts never to heaven go.   *Exit.*

*

III, iv   *Enter [Queen] Gertrude and Polonius.*
POLONIUS
1   'A will come straight. Look you lay home to him.
2   Tell him his pranks have been too broad to bear with,
And that your grace hath screened and stood between
Much heat and him. I'll silence me even here.
5   Pray you be round with him.
[HAMLET (*within*) Mother, mother, mother!]
QUEEN   I'll warrant you; fear me not. Withdraw; I hear
him coming.   [*Polonius hides behind the arras.*]
Enter Hamlet.
HAMLET
Now, mother, what's the matter?
QUEEN
Hamlet, thou hast thy father much offended.
HAMLET
Mother, you have my father much offended.
QUEEN
12   Come, come, you answer with an idle tongue.
HAMLET
Go, go, you question with a wicked tongue.
QUEEN
Why, how now, Hamlet?
HAMLET   What's the matter now?
QUEEN
Have you forgot me?
15 HAMLET   No, by the rood, not so!
You are the queen, your husband's brother's wife,
And (would it were not so) you are my mother.
QUEEN
Nay, then I'll set those to you that can speak.
HAMLET
Come, come, and sit you down. You shall not budge.
You go not till I set you up a glass
Where you may see the inmost part of you.
QUEEN
What wilt thou do? Thou wilt not murder me?
Help, ho!
POLONIUS [*behind*] What, ho! help!
HAMLET [*draws*]
How now? a rat? Dead for a ducat, dead!
[*Makes a pass through the arras and kills Polonius.*]
POLONIUS [*behind*]
O, I am slain!
QUEEN   O me, what hast thou done?

HAMLET
Nay, I know not. Is it the king?
QUEEN
O, what a rash and bloody deed is this!
HAMLET
A bloody deed – almost as bad, good mother,
As kill a king, and marry with his brother.   *30*
QUEEN
As kill a king?
HAMLET   Ay, lady, it was my word.
[*Lifts up the arras and sees Polonius.*]
Thou wretched, rash, intruding fool, farewell!
I took thee for thy better. Take thy fortune.
Thou find'st to be too busy is some danger. –
Leave wringing of your hands. Peace, sit you down
And let me wring your heart, for so I shall
If it be made of penetrable stuff,
If damnèd custom have not brazed it so   *38*
That it is proof and bulwark against sense.   *39*
QUEEN
What have I done that thou dar'st wag thy tongue
In noise so rude against me?
HAMLET   Such an act
That blurs the grace and blush of modesty,
Calls virtue hypocrite, takes off the rose
From the fair forehead of an innocent love,
And sets a blister there, makes marriage vows   *45*
As false as dicers' oaths. O, such a deed
As from the body of contraction plucks   *47*
The very soul, and sweet religion makes   *48*
A rhapsody of words! Heaven's face does glow,
And this solidity and compound mass,   *50*
With heated visage, as against the doom,   *51*
Is thought-sick at the act.
QUEEN   Ay me, what act,
That roars so loud and thunders in the index?   *53*
HAMLET
Look here upon this picture, and on this,
The counterfeit presentment of two brothers.   *55*
See what a grace was seated on this brow:
Hyperion's curls, the front of Jove himself,   *57*
An eye like Mars, to threaten and command,
A station like the herald Mercury   *59*
New lighted on a heaven-kissing hill –
A combination and a form indeed
Where every god did seem to set his seal
To give the world assurance of a man.
This was your husband. Look you now what follows.
Here is your husband, like a mildewed ear
Blasting his wholesome brother. Have you eyes?
Could you on this fair mountain leave to feed,
And batten on this moor? Ha! have you eyes?   *68*
You cannot call it love, for at your age
The heyday in the blood is tame, it's humble,   *70*
And waits upon the judgment, and what judgment   *71*
Would step from this to this? Sense sure you have,   *72*
Else could you not have motion, but sure that sense   *73*
Is apoplexed, for madness would not err,   *74*
Nor sense to ecstasy was ne'er so thralled   *75*
But it reserved some quantity of choice
To serve in such a difference. What devil was't
That thus hath cozened you at hoodman-blind?   *78*
Eyes without feeling, feeling without sight,
Ears without hands or eyes, smelling sans all,   *80*

III, iv The private chamber of the Queen   1 *lay* thrust   2 *broad* unrestrained   5 *round* plain-spoken   12 *idle* foolish   15 *rood* cross   38 *custom*
habit; *brazed* hardened like brass   39 *proof* armor; *sense* feeling   45
blister brand (of degradation)   47 *contraction* the marriage contract   48
religion i.e. sacred marriage vows   50 *compound mass* the earth as compounded of the four elements   51 *against* in expectation of; *doom* Day of
Judgment   53 *index* table of contents preceding the body of a book   55
counterfeit presentment portrayed representation   57 *Hyperion* the sun god;
front forehead   59 *station* attitude in standing   68 *batten* feed greedily   70
heyday excitement of passion   71 *waits upon* yields to   72 *Sense* feeling
73 *motion* desire, impulse   74 *apoplexed* paralyzed   75 *ecstasy* madness
78 *cozened* cheated; *hoodman-blind* blindman's buff   80 *sans* without

  Or but a sickly part of one true sense
82 Could not so mope.
  O shame, where is thy blush ? Rebellious hell,
84 If thou canst mutine in a matron's bones,
  To flaming youth let virtue be as wax
  And melt in her own fire. Proclaim no shame
87 When the compulsive ardor gives the charge,
  Since frost itself as actively doth burn,
89 And reason panders will.
  QUEEN   O Hamlet, speak no more.
  Thou turn'st mine eyes into my very soul,
91 And there I see such black and grainèd spots
92 As will not leave their tinct.
  HAMLET   Nay, but to live
93 In the rank sweat of an enseamèd bed,
  Stewed in corruption, honeying and making love
  Over the nasty sty –
  QUEEN   O, speak to me no more.
  These words like daggers enter in mine ears.
  No more, sweet Hamlet.
  HAMLET   A murderer and a villain,
98 A slave that is not twentieth part the tithe
99 Of your precedent lord, a vice of kings,
100 A cutpurse of the empire and the rule,
  That from a shelf the precious diadem stole
  And put it in his pocket –
102 QUEEN   No more.
  Enter [the] Ghost [in his nightgown].
  HAMLET
  A king of shreds and patches –
  Save me and hover o'er me with your wings,
  You heavenly guards ? What would your gracious figure ?
  QUEEN
  Alas, he's mad.
  HAMLET
  Do you not come your tardy son to chide,
108 That, lapsed in time and passion, lets go by
  Th' important acting of your dread command ?
  O, say !
  GHOST
  Do not forget. This visitation
  Is but to whet thy almost blunted purpose.
  But look, amazement on thy mother sits.
  O, step between her and her fighting soul !
115 Conceit in weakest bodies strongest works.
  Speak to her, Hamlet.
  HAMLET   How is it with you, lady ?
  QUEEN
  Alas, how is't with you,
  That you do bend your eye on vacancy,
119 And with th' incorporal air do hold discourse ?
  Forth at your eyes your spirits wildly peep,
  And as the sleeping soldiers in th' alarm
122 Your bedded hairs like life in excrements
123 Start up and stand an end. O gentle son,
124 Upon the heat and flame of thy distemper
  Sprinkle cool patience. Whereon do you look ?
  HAMLET
  On him, on him ! Look you, how pale he glares !
  His form and cause conjoined, preaching to stones,
128 Would make them capable. – Do not look upon me,
  Lest with this piteous action you convert
130 My stern effects. Then what I have to do
  Will want true color – tears perchance for blood.

  QUEEN
  To whom do you speak this ?
  HAMLET   Do you see nothing there ?
  QUEEN
  Nothing at all ; yet all that is I see.
  HAMLET
  Nor did you nothing hear ?
  QUEEN   No, nothing but ourselves.
  HAMLET
  Why, look you there ! Look how it steals away !
  My father, in his habit as he lived !
  Look where he goes even now out at the portal !
           Exit Ghost.
  QUEEN
  This is the very coinage of your brain.
  This bodiless creation ecstasy   139
  Is very cunning in.
  HAMLET   Ecstasy ?
  My pulse as yours doth temperately keep time
  And makes as healthful music. It is not madness
  That I have uttered. Bring me to the test,
  And I the matter will reword, which madness
  Would gambol from. Mother, for love of grace, 145
  Lay not that flattering unction to your soul, 146
  That not your trespass but my madness speaks.
  It will but skin and film the ulcerous place
  Whiles rank corruption, mining all within, 149
  Infects unseen. Confess yourself to heaven,
  Repent what's past, avoid what is to come,
  And do not spread the compost on the weeds 152
  To make them ranker. Forgive me this my virtue.
  For in the fatness of these pursy times 154
  Virtue itself of vice must pardon beg,
  Yea, curb and woo for leave to do him good. 156
  QUEEN
  O Hamlet, thou hast cleft my heart in twain.
  HAMLET
  O, throw away the worser part of it,
  And live the purer with the other half.
  Good night – but go not to my uncle's bed.
  Assume a virtue, if you have it not.
  That monster custom, who all sense doth eat, 162
  Of habits devil, is angel yet in this,
  That to the use of actions fair and good
  He likewise gives a frock or livery   165
  That aptly is put on. Refrain to-night,
  And that shall lend a kind of easiness
  To the next abstinence ; the next more easy ;
  For use almost can change the stamp of nature, 169
  And either . . . the devil, or throw him out 170
  With wondrous potency. Once more, good night,

---

82 *mope* be stupid   84 *mutine* mutiny   87 *compulsive* compelling ; *gives the charge* delivers the attack   89 *panders will* acts as procurer for desire   91 *grainèd* dyed in grain   92 *tinct* color   93 *enseamèd* grease-laden   98 *tithe* tenth part   99 *vice* clownish rogue (like the Vice of the morality plays)   100 *cutpurse* skulking thief   102 s.d. *nightgown* dressing gown   108 *lapsed . . . passion* having let the moment slip and passion cool   115 *Conceit* imagination   119 *incorporal* bodiless   122 *excrements* outgrowths   123 *an* on   124 *distemper* mental disorder   128 *capable* susceptible   130 *effects* manifestations of emotion and purpose   139 *ecstasy* madness   145 *gambol* shy (like a startled horse)   146 *unction* ointment   149 *mining* undermining   152 *compost* fertilizing mixture   154 *fatness* gross slackness ; *pursy* corpulent   156 *curb* bow to   162–63 *all sense . . . devil* (see Appendix : Supplementary Notes)   165 *livery* characteristic dress (accompanying the suggestion of 'garb' in *habits*)   169 *use* habit ; *stamp* impression, form   170 *And . . . out* (see Appendix : Supplementary Notes)

And when you are desirous to be blest,
I'll blessing beg of you. – For this same lord,
I do repent ; but heaven hath pleased it so,
To punish me with this, and this with me,
That I must be their scourge and minister.
177 I will bestow him and will answer well
The death I gave him. So again, good night.
I must be cruel only to be kind.
180 Thus bad begins, and worse remains behind.
One word more, good lady.

QUEEN   What shall I do ?

HAMLET
Not this, by no means, that I bid you do :
183 Let the bloat king tempt you again to bed,
Pinch wanton on your cheek, call you his mouse,
185 And let him, for a pair of reechy kisses,
Or paddling in your neck with his damned fingers,
187 Make you to ravel all this matter out,
That I essentially am not in madness,
But mad in craft. 'Twere good you let him know,
For who that's but a queen, fair, sober, wise,
191 Would from a paddock, from a bat, a gib,
192 Such dear concernings hide ? Who would do so ?
No, in despite of sense and secrecy,
Unpeg the basket on the house's top,
195 Let the birds fly, and like the famous ape,
196 To try conclusions, in the basket creep
And break your own neck down.

QUEEN
Be thou assured, if words be made of breath,
And breath of life, I have no life to breathe
What thou hast said to me.

HAMLET
I must to England ; you know that ?

QUEEN   Alack,
I had forgot. 'Tis so concluded on.

HAMLET
There's letters sealed, and my two schoolfellows,
Whom I will trust as I will adders fanged,
205 They bear the mandate ; they must sweep my way
And marshal me to knavery. Let it work.
207 For 'tis the sport to have the enginer
208 Hoist with his own petar, and 't shall go hard
But I will delve one yard below their mines
And blow them at the moon. O, 'tis most sweet
When in one line two crafts directly meet.
212 This man shall set me packing.
I'll lug the guts into the neighbor room.
Mother, good night. Indeed, this counsellor
Is now most still, most secret, and most grave,
Who was in life a foolish prating knave.

Come, sir, to draw toward an end with you.
Good night, mother.

           [Exit the Queen. Then] exit [Hamlet,
                      tugging in Polonius].

                *

Enter King and Queen, with Rosencrantz and   IV, i
Guildenstern.

KING
There's matter in these sighs. These profound heaves
You must translate ; 'tis fit we understand them.
Where is your son ?

QUEEN
Bestow this place on us a little while.
            [Exeunt Rosencrantz and Guildenstern.]
Ah, mine own lord, what have I seen to-night !

KING
What, Gertrude ? How does Hamlet ?

QUEEN
Mad as the sea and wind when both contend
Which is the mightier. In his lawless fit,
Behind the arras hearing something stir,
Whips out his rapier, cries, 'A rat, a rat !'
And in this brainish apprehension kills   11
The unseen good old man.

KING   O heavy deed !
It had been so with us, had we been there.
His liberty is full of threats to all,
To you yourself, to us, to every one.
Alas, how shall this bloody deed be answered ?
It will be laid to us, whose providence   17
Should have kept short, restrained, and out of haunt   18
This mad young man. But so much was our love
We would not understand what was most fit,
But, like the owner of a foul disease,
To keep it from divulging, let it feed   22
Even on the pith of life. Where is he gone ?

QUEEN
To draw apart the body he hath killed ;
O'er whom his very madness, like some ore   25
Among a mineral of metals base,   26
Shows itself pure. 'A weeps for what is done.

KING
O Gertrude, come away !
The sun no sooner shall the mountains touch
But we will ship him hence, and this vile deed
We must with all our majesty and skill
Both countenance and excuse. Ho, Guildenstern !
Enter Rosencrantz and Guildenstern.
Friends both, go join you with some further aid.
Hamlet in madness hath Polonius slain,
And from his mother's closet hath he dragged him.
Go seek him out ; speak fair, and bring the body
Into the chapel. I pray you haste in this.
          [Exeunt Rosencrantz and Guildenstern.]
Come, Gertrude, we'll call up our wisest friends
And let them know both what we mean to do
And what's untimely done . . .   40
Whose whisper o'er the world's diameter,
As level as the cannon to his blank   42
Transports his poisoned shot, may miss our name
And hit the woundless air. O, come away !
My soul is full of discord and dismay.   *Exeunt.*

                *

---

177 *bestow* stow, hide   180 *behind* to come   183 *bloat* bloated with sense gratification   185 *reechy* filthy   187 *ravel . . . out* disentangle   191 *paddock* toad ; *gib* tomcat   192 *dear concernings* matters of great personal significance   195 *famous ape* (one in a story now unknown)   196 *conclusions* experiments   205 *mandate* order   207 *enginer* engineer, constructor of military engines or works   208 *Hoist* blown up ; *petar* petard, bomb or mine   212 *packing* travelling in a hurry (with a play upon his 'packing' or shouldering of Polonius' body and also upon his 'packing' in the sense of 'plotting' or 'contriving')
IV, i A chamber in the Castle   11 *brainish apprehension* headstrong conception   17 *providence* foresight   18 *haunt* association with others   22 *divulging* becoming known   25 *ore* vein of gold   26 *mineral* mine   40 *And . . . done* (see Appendix : Supplementary Notes)   42 *As level* with as direct aim ; *blank* mark, central white spot on a target

IV, ii   *Enter Hamlet.*

HAMLET Safely stowed.

GENTLEMEN *(within)* Hamlet! Lord Hamlet!

HAMLET But soft, what noise? Who calls on Hamlet? O, here they come.

    [Enter] Rosencrantz, [Guildenstern,] and others.

ROSENCRANTZ
    What have you done, my lord, with the dead body?

HAMLET
    Compounded it with dust, whereto 'tis kin.

ROSENCRANTZ
    Tell us where 'tis, that we may take it thence
    And bear it to the chapel.

HAMLET Do not believe it.

ROSENCRANTZ Believe what?

HAMLET That I can keep your counsel and not mine own.

12 Besides, to be demanded of a sponge, what replication
    should be made by the son of a king?

ROSENCRANTZ Take you me for a sponge, my lord?

15 HAMLET Ay, sir, that soaks up the king's countenance,
    his rewards, his authorities. But such officers do the king
    best service in the end. He keeps them, like an ape, in
    the corner of his jaw, first mouthed, to be last swal-
    lowed. When he needs what you have gleaned, it is but
    squeezing you and, sponge, you shall be dry again.

ROSENCRANTZ I understand you not, my lord.

22 HAMLET I am glad of it. A knavish speech sleeps in a
    foolish ear.

ROSENCRANTZ My lord, you must tell us where the
    body is and go with us to the king.

HAMLET The body is with the king, but the king is not
    with the body. The king is a thing –

GUILDENSTERN A thing, my lord?

29 HAMLET Of nothing. Bring me to him. Hide fox, and all
    after.   *Exeunt.*

*

IV, iii   *Enter King, and two or three.*

KING
    I have sent to seek him and to find the body.
    How dangerous is it that this man goes loose!
    Yet must not we put the strong law on him;
4   He's loved of the distracted multitude,
    Who like him not in their judgment, but their eyes,
6   And where 'tis so, th' offender's scourge is weighed,
    But never the offense. To bear all smooth and even,
    This sudden sending him away must seem
9   Deliberate pause. Diseases desperate grown
    By desperate appliance are relieved,
    Or not at all.

        Enter Rosencrantz, [Guildenstern,] and all the rest.
        How now? What hath befallen?

ROSENCRANTZ
    Where the dead body is bestowed, my lord,
    We cannot get from him.

KING   But where is he?

ROSENCRANTZ
    Without, my lord; guarded, to know your pleasure.

KING
    Bring him before us.

ROSENCRANTZ   Ho! Bring in the lord.
        They enter [with Hamlet].

KING Now, Hamlet, where's Polonius?

HAMLET At supper.

KING At supper? Where?

HAMLET Not where he eats, but where 'a is eaten. A
    certain convocation of politic worms are e'en at him. 20
    Your worm is your only emperor for diet. We fat 21
    all creatures else to fat us, and we fat ourselves for
    maggots. Your fat king and your lean beggar is but
    variable service – two dishes, but to one table. That's 24
    the end.

KING Alas, alas!

HAMLET A man may fish with the worm that hath eat of a
    king, and eat of the fish that hath fed of that worm.

KING What dost thou mean by this?

HAMLET Nothing but to show you how a king may go a
    progress through the guts of a beggar. 31

KING Where is Polonius?

HAMLET In heaven. Send thither to see. If your messen-
    ger find him not there, seek him i' th' other place your-
    self. But if indeed you find him not within this month,
    you shall nose him as you go up the stairs into the lobby.

KING *[to Attendants]* Go seek him there.

HAMLET 'A will stay till you come. *[Exeunt Attendants.]*

KING
    Hamlet, this deed, for thine especial safety,
    Which we do tender as we dearly grieve 40
    For that which thou hast done, must send thee hence
    With fiery quickness. Therefore prepare thyself.
    The bark is ready and the wind at help,
    Th' associates tend, and everything is bent 44
    For England.

HAMLET   For England?

KING   Ay, Hamlet.

HAMLET   Good.

KING
    So is it, if thou knew'st our purposes.

HAMLET I see a cherub that sees them. But come, for 47
    England! Farewell, dear mother.

KING Thy loving father, Hamlet.

HAMLET My mother – father and mother is man and
    wife, man and wife is one flesh, and so, my mother.
    Come, for England!   *Exit.*

KING
    Follow him at foot; tempt him with speed aboard. 53
    Delay it not; I'll have him hence to-night.
    Away! for everything is sealed and done
    That else leans on th' affair. Pray you make haste. 56
        [Exeunt all but the King.]
    And, England, if my love thou hold'st at aught – 57
    As my great power thereof may give thee sense,

IV, ii A passage in the Castle   12 *replication* reply   15 *countenance* favor
22 *sleeps in* means nothing to   29 *Of nothing* (cf. Prayer Book, Psalm
cxliv, 4, 'Man is like a thing of naught: his time passeth away like a shadow')
29–30 *Hide . . . after* (apparently well-known words from some game of
hide-and-seek)
IV, iii A chamber in the Castle   4 *distracted* confused   6 *scourge* punishment   9 *Deliberate pause* something done with much deliberation   20
politic worms political and craftily scheming worms (such as Polonius might
well attract)   21 *diet* food and drink (perhaps with a play upon a famous
'convocation,' the Diet of Worms opened by the Emperor Charles V on
January 28, 1521, before which Luther appeared)   24 *variable service*
different servings of one food   31 *progress* royal journey of state   40
tender hold dear; *dearly* intensely   44 *tend* wait; *bent* set in readiness (like a
bent bow)   47 *cherub* one of the cherubim (angels with a distinctive quality
of knowledge)   53 *at foot* at heel, close   56 *leans on* is connected with
57 *England* King of England

60 Since yet thy cicatrice looks raw and red
    After the Danish sword, and thy free awe
61 Pays homage to us – thou mayst not coldly set
62 Our sovereign process, which imports at full
63 By letters congruing to that effect
64 The present death of Hamlet. Do it, England,
65 For like the hectic in my blood he rages,
    And thou must cure me. Till I know 'tis done,
67 Howe'er my haps, my joys were ne'er begun.   *Exit.*

*

IV, iv   *Enter Fortinbras with his Army over the stage.*

FORTINBRAS
    Go, captain, from me greet the Danish king.
    Tell him that by his license Fortinbras
3 Craves the conveyance of a promised march
    Over his kingdom. You know the rendezvous.
    If that his majesty would aught with us,
6 We shall express our duty in his eye ;
    And let him know so.

CAPTAIN   I will do't, my lord.

FORTINBRAS
8 Go softly on.   *[Exeunt all but the Captain.]*
    Enter Hamlet, Rosencrantz, [Guildenstern,] and
    others.

HAMLET
9 Good sir, whose powers are these ?

CAPTAIN
    They are of Norway, sir.

HAMLET
    How purposed, sir, I pray you ?

CAPTAIN
    Against some part of Poland.

HAMLET
    Who commands them, sir ?

CAPTAIN
    The nephew to old Norway, Fortinbras.

HAMLET
15 Goes it against the main of Poland, sir,
    Or for some frontier ?

CAPTAIN
17 Truly to speak, and with no addition,
    We go to gain a little patch of ground
    That hath in it no profit but the name.
20 To pay five ducats, five, I would not farm it,
    Nor will it yield to Norway or the Pole
22 A ranker rate, should it be sold in fee.

HAMLET
    Why, then the Polack never will defend it.

CAPTAIN
    Yes, it is already garrisoned.

HAMLET
    Two thousand souls and twenty thousand ducats
    Will not debate the question of this straw.
27 This is th' imposthume of much wealth and peace,
    That inward breaks, and shows no cause without
    Why the man dies. I humbly thank you, sir.

CAPTAIN
    God bye you, sir.   *[Exit.]*

ROSENCRANTZ   Will't please you go, my lord ?

HAMLET
    I'll be with you straight. Go a little before.
                [Exeunt all but Hamlet.]
32 How all occasions do inform against me
    And spur my dull revenge ! What is a man,
34 If his chief good and market of his time
    Be but to sleep and feed ? A beast, no more.
36 Sure he that made us with such large discourse,
    Looking before and after, gave us not
    That capability and godlike reason
39 To fust in us unused. Now, whether it be
40 Bestial oblivion, or some craven scruple
41 Of thinking too precisely on th' event –
    A thought which, quartered, hath but one part wisdom
    And ever three parts coward – I do not know
    Why yet I live to say, 'This thing's to do,'
    Sith I have cause, and will, and strength, and means
46 To do't. Examples gross as earth exhort me.
47 Witness this army of such mass and charge,
    Led by a delicate and tender prince,
    Whose spirit, with divine ambition puffed,
50 Makes mouths at the invisible event,
    Exposing what is mortal and unsure
    To all that fortune, death, and danger dare,
    Even for an eggshell. Rightly to be great
    Is not to stir without great argument,
55 But greatly to find quarrel in a straw
    When honor's at the stake. How stand I then,
    That have a father killed, a mother stained,
    Excitements of my reason and my blood,
    And let all sleep, while to my shame I see
    The imminent death of twenty thousand men
61 That for a fantasy and trick of fame
    Go to their graves like beds, fight for a plot
63 Whereon the numbers cannot try the cause,
64 Which is not tomb enough and continent
    To hide the slain ? O, from this time forth,
    My thoughts be bloody, or be nothing worth !   *Exit.*

*

Enter Horatio, [Queen] Gertrude, and a Gentleman.   **IV, v**

QUEEN
    I will not speak with her.

GENTLEMAN
    She is importunate, indeed distract.
2 Her mood will needs be pitied.

QUEEN   What would she have ?

GENTLEMAN
    She speaks much of her father, says she hears
    There's tricks i' th' world, and hems, and beats her heart,
5 Spurns enviously at straws, speaks things in doubt
6 That carry but half sense. Her speech is nothing,

---

60 *free awe* voluntary show of respect   61 *set* esteem   62 *process* formal command   63 *congruing* agreeing   64 *present* instant   65 *hectic* a continuous fever   67 *haps* fortunes
IV, iv A coastal highway   3 *conveyance* escort   6 *eye* presence   8 *softly* slowly   9 *powers* forces   15 *main* main body   17 *addition* exaggeration   20 *To pay* i.e. for a yearly rental of   22 *ranker* more abundant ; *in fee* outright   27 *imposthume* abscess   32 *inform* take shape   34 *market of* compensation for   36 *discourse* power of thought   39 *fust* grow mouldy   40 *oblivion* forgetfulness   41 *event* outcome (as also in l. 50)   46 *gross* large and evident   47 *charge* expense   50 *Makes mouths* makes faces scornfully   55 *greatly . . . straw* to recognize the great argument even in some small matter   61 *fantasy* fanciful image ; *trick* toy   63 *try the cause* find space in which to settle the issue by battle   64 *continent* receptacle
IV, v A chamber in the Castle   2 *distract* insane   5 *tricks* deceits   6 *Spurns enviously* kicks spitefully, takes offense ; *straws* trifles

8   Yet the unshapèd use of it doth move
9   The hearers to collection; they aim at it,
10   And botch the words up fit to their own thoughts,
      Which, as her winks and nods and gestures yield them,
      Indeed would make one think there might be thought,
      Though nothing sure, yet much unhappily.

HORATIO
      'Twere good she were spoken with, for she may strew
      Dangerous conjectures in ill-breeding minds.

QUEEN
      Let her come in.   *[Exit Gentleman.]*
      [Aside]
      To my sick soul (as sin's true nature is)
18   Each toy seems prologue to some great amiss.
19   So full of artless jealousy is guilt
20   It spills itself in fearing to be spilt.
        Enter Ophelia [distracted].

OPHELIA
      Where is the beauteous majesty of Denmark?

QUEEN How now, Ophelia?

OPHELIA
      She sings. How should I your true-love know
                  From another one?
25   By his cockle hat and staff
26   And his sandal shoon.

QUEEN
      Alas, sweet lady, what imports this song?

OPHELIA Say you? Nay, pray you mark.

               Song.
      He is dead and gone, lady,
         He is dead and gone;
      At his head a grass-green turf,
         At his heels a stone.

      O, ho!

QUEEN Nay, but Ophelia –

OPHELIA Pray you mark.
      [Sings] White his shroud as the mountain snow –
         Enter King.

QUEEN Alas, look here, my lord.

OPHELIA   *Song.*
38   Larded all with sweet flowers;
         Which bewept to the grave did not go
           With true-love showers.

KING How do you, pretty lady?

42 OPHELIA Well, God dild you! They say the owl was a
      baker's daughter. Lord, we know what we are, but know
      not what we may be. God be at your table!

45 KING Conceit upon her father.

OPHELIA Pray let's have no words of this, but when they
      ask you what it means, say you this:

             Song.
      To-morrow is Saint Valentine's day.
49   All in the morning betime,
      And I a maid at your window,
         To be your Valentine.
      Then up he rose and donned his clo'es
53   And dupped the chamber door,
      Let in the maid, that out a maid
         Never departed more.

KING Pretty Ophelia!

OPHELIA Indeed, la, without an oath, I'll make an end on't:

      [Sings] By Gis and by Saint Charity,   58
         Alack, and fie for shame!
      Young men will do't if they come to't.
         By Cock, they are to blame.   61
      Quoth she, 'Before you tumbled me,
         You promised me to wed.'

He answers:
      'So would I 'a' done, by yonder sun,
         And thou hadst not come to my bed.'

KING How long hath she been thus?

OPHELIA I hope all will be well. We must be patient, but
      I cannot choose but weep to think they would lay him i'
      th' cold ground. My brother shall know of it; and so I 70
      thank you for your good counsel. Come, my coach!
      Good night, ladies, good night. Sweet ladies, good
      night, good night.   *[Exit.]*

KING
      Follow her close; give her good watch, I pray you.
                           [Exit Horatio.]
      O, this is the poison of deep grief; it springs
      All from her father's death – and now behold!
      O Gertrude, Gertrude,
      When sorrows come, they come not single spies,
      But in battalions: first, her father slain;
      Next, your son gone, and he most violent author
      Of his own just remove; the people muddied,   81
      Thick and unwholesome in their thoughts and whispers
      For good Polonius' death, and we have done but greenly 83
      In hugger-mugger to inter him; poor Ophelia   84
      Divided from herself and her fair judgment,
      Without the which we are pictures or mere beasts;
      Last, and as much containing as all these,
      Her brother is in secret come from France,
      Feeds on his wonder, keeps himself in clouds,   89
      And wants not buzzers to infect his ear   90
      With pestilent speeches of his father's death,
      Wherein necessity, of matter beggared,   92
      Will nothing stick our person to arraign   93
      In ear and ear. O my dear Gertrude, this,
      Like to a murd'ring piece, in many places   95
      Gives me superfluous death.
         A noise within.
         Enter a Messenger.

QUEEN   Alack, what noise is this?

KING
      Attend, where are my Switzers? Let them guard the 97
      door.
      What is the matter?

MESSENGER   Save yourself, my lord.
      The ocean, overpeering of his list,   99

---

8 *unshapèd use* disordered manner   9 *collection* attempts at shaping meaning; *aim* guess   10 *botch* patch   18 *toy* trifle; *amiss* calamity   19 *artless* unskillfully managed; *jealousy* suspicion   20 *spills* destroys   25 *cockle hat* hat bearing a cockle shell, worn by a pilgrim who had been to the shrine of St James of Compostela   26 *shoon* shoes   38 *Larded* garnished   42 *dild* yield, repay; *the owl* an owl into which, according to a folk-tale, a baker's daughter was transformed because of her failure to show wholehearted generosity when Christ asked for bread in the baker's shop   45 *Conceit* thought   49 *betime* early   53 *dupped* opened   58 *Gis* Jesus   61 *Cock* God (with a perversion of the name not uncommon in oaths)   81 *muddied* stirred up and confused   83 *greenly* foolishly   84 *hugger-mugger* secrecy and disorder   89 *clouds* obscurity   90 *wants* lacks; *buzzers* whispering talebearers   92 *of matter beggared* unprovided with facts   93 *nothing stick* in no way hesitate; *arraign* accuse   95 *murd'ring piece* cannon loaded with shot meant to scatter   97 *Switzers* hired Swiss guards   99 *overpeering of his list* rising to look over and pass beyond; *list* boundary

100 Eats not the flats with more impiteous haste
101 Than young Laertes, in a riotous head,
     O'erbears your officers. The rabble call him lord,
     And, as the world were now but to begin,
     Antiquity forgot, custom not known,
105 The ratifiers and props of every word,
     They cry, 'Choose we! Laertes shall be king!'
     Caps, hands, and tongues applaud it to the clouds,
     'Laertes shall be king! Laertes king!'
         A noise within.

QUEEN
     How cheerfully on the false trail they cry!
110 O, this is counter, you false Danish dogs!
KING
     The doors are broke.
         Enter Laertes with others.
LAERTES
     Where is this king? – Sirs, stand you all without.
ALL
     No, let's come in.
LAERTES   I pray you give me leave.
ALL We will, we will.
LAERTES
     I thank you. Keep the door.   *[Exeunt his Followers.]*
         O thou vile king,
     Give me my father.
QUEEN   Calmly, good Laertes.
LAERTES
     That drop of blood that's calm proclaims me bastard,
     Cries cuckold to my father, brands the harlot
     Even here between the chaste unsmirchèd brows
     Of my true mother.
KING   What is the cause, Laertes,
     That thy rebellion looks so giant-like?
122 Let him go, Gertrude. Do not fear our person.
     There's such divinity doth hedge a king
124 That treason can but peep to what it would,
     Acts little of his will. Tell me, Laertes,
     Why thou art thus incensed. Let him go, Gertrude.
     Speak, man.
LAERTES
     Where is my father?
KING   Dead.
QUEEN   But not by him.
KING
     Let him demand his fill.
LAERTES
     How came he dead? I'll not be juggled with.
     To hell allegiance, vows to the blackest devil,
     Conscience and grace to the profoundest pit!
     I dare damnation. To this point I stand,
134 That both the worlds I give to negligence,

     Let come what comes, only I'll be revenged
     Most throughly for my father.
136
KING   Who shall stay you?
LAERTES
     My will, not all the world's.
     And for my means, I'll husband them so well
     They shall go far with little.
KING   Good Laertes,
     If you desire to know the certainty
     Of your dear father, is't writ in your revenge
142
     That swoopstake you will draw both friend and foe,
     Winner and loser?
LAERTES
     None but his enemies.
KING   Will you know them then?
LAERTES
     To his good friends thus wide I'll ope my arms
     And like the kind life-rend'ring pelican
146
     Repast them with my blood.
KING   Why, now you speak
     Like a good child and a true gentleman.
     That I am guiltless of your father's death,
     And am most sensibly in grief for it,
150
     It shall as level to your judgment 'pear
151
     As day does to your eye.
         A noise within : 'Let her come in.'
LAERTES
     How now? What noise is that?
         Enter Ophelia.
     O heat, dry up my brains; tears seven times salt
     Burn out the sense and virtue of mine eye!
     By heaven, thy madness shall be paid by weight
     Till our scale turn the beam. O rose of May,
157
     Dear maid, kind sister, sweet Ophelia!
     O heavens, is't possible a young maid's wits
     Should be as mortal as an old man's life?
     [Nature is fine in love, and where 'tis fine,
161
     It sends some precious instance of itself
162
     After the thing it loves.]

OPHELIA   *Song.*
     They bore him barefaced on the bier
       [Hey non nony, nony, hey nony]
       And in his grave rained many a tear –
     Fare you well, my dove!
LAERTES
     Hadst thou thy wits, and didst persuade revenge,
     It could not move thus.
OPHELIA You must sing 'A-down a-down, and you call
     him a-down-a.' O, how the wheel becomes it! It is the 171
     false steward, that stole his master's daughter.
LAERTES This nothing's more than matter.   173
OPHELIA There's rosemary, that's for remembrance.
     Pray you, love, remember. And there is pansies, that's
     for thoughts.
LAERTES A document in madness, thoughts and re- 177
     membrance fitted.
OPHELIA There's fennel for you, and columbines. 179
     There's rue for you, and here's some for me. We may 180
     call it herb of grace o' Sundays. O, you must wear your
     rue with a difference. There's a daisy. I would give you 182
     some violets, but they withered all when my father died. 183
     They say 'a made a good end.
     [Sings] For bonny sweet Robin is all my joy.

---

100 *impiteous* pitiless 101 *head* armed force 105 *word* promise 110 *counter* hunting backward on the trail 122 *fear* fear for 124 *peep to* i.e. through the barrier 134 *both the worlds* whatever may result in this world or the next; *give to negligence* disregard 136 *throughly* thoroughly 142 *swoopstake* sweepstake, taking all stakes on the gambling table 146 *life-rend'ring* life-yielding (because the mother pelican supposedly took blood from her breast with her bill to feed her young) 150 *sensibly* feelingly 151 *level* plain 157 *beam* bar of a balance 161 *fine* refined to purity 162 *instance* token 171 *wheel* burden, refrain 173 *more than matter* more meaningful than sane speech 177 *document* lesson 179 *fennel* symbol of flattery; *columbines* symbol of thanklessness (?) 180 *rue* symbol of repentance 182 *daisy* symbol of dissembling 183 *violets* symbol of faithfulness

LAERTES
Thought and affliction, passion, hell itself,
187   She turns to favor and to prettiness.

OPHELIA   *Song.*

And will 'a not come again?
And will 'a not come again?
No, no, he is dead;
Go to thy deathbed;
He never will come again.
His beard was as white as snow,
194   All flaxen was his poll.
He is gone, he is gone,
And we cast away moan.
God 'a' mercy on his soul!

198   And of all Christian souls, I pray God. God bye you.
                                                   [Exit.]

LAERTES
Do you see this, O God?

KING
Laertes, I must commune with your grief,
Or you deny me right. Go but apart,
Make choice of whom your wisest friends you will,
And they shall hear and judge 'twixt you and me.
204   If by direct or by collateral hand
205   They find us touched, we will our kingdom give,
Our crown, our life, and all that we call ours,
To you in satisfaction; but if not,
Be you content to lend your patience to us,
And we shall jointly labor with your soul
To give it due content.

LAERTES   Let this be so.
His means of death, his obscure funeral –
212   No trophy, sword, nor hatchment o'er his bones,
213   No noble rite nor formal ostentation –
Cry to be heard, as 'twere from heaven to earth,
215   That I must call 't in question.

KING   So you shall;
And where th' offense is, let the great axe fall.
I pray you go with me.   *Exeunt.*

*

IV, vi   *Enter Horatio and others.*

HORATIO What are they that would speak with me?
GENTLEMAN Seafaring men, sir. They say they have
letters for you.
HORATIO Let them come in.   [Exit Attendant.]
I do not know from what part of the world
I should be greeted, if not from Lord Hamlet.
          Enter Sailors.
SAILOR God bless you, sir.
HORATIO Let him bless thee too.
SAILOR 'A shall, sir, an't please him. There's a letter for
you, sir – it came from th' ambassador that was bound
for England – if your name be Horatio, as I am let to
know it is.
HORATIO [reads the letter] 'Horatio, when thou shalt have
14   overlooked this, give these fellows some means to the
king. They have letters for him. Ere we were two days
16   old at sea, a pirate of very warlike appointment gave us
chase. Finding ourselves too slow of sail, we put on a
compelled valor, and in the grapple I boarded them. On
the instant they got clear of our ship; so I alone became

their prisoner. They have dealt with me like thieves of 20
mercy, but they knew what they did: I am to do a good
turn for them. Let the king have the letters I have sent,
and repair thou to me with as much speed as thou
wouldest fly death. I have words to speak in thine ear will
make thee dumb; yet are they much too light for the bore 25
of the matter. These good fellows will bring thee where I
am. Rosencrantz and Guildenstern hold their course for
England. Of them I have much to tell thee. Farewell.
                    'He that thou knowest thine, Hamlet.'
Come, I will give you way for these your letters,
And do 't the speedier that you may direct me
To him from whom you brought them.   *Exeunt.*

*

          Enter King and Laertes.   IV, vii
KING
Now must your conscience my acquittance seal,
And you must put me in your heart for friend,
Sith you have heard, and with a knowing ear,
That he which hath your noble father slain
Pursued my life.

LAERTES   It well appears. But tell me
Why you proceeded not against these feats   6
So crimeful and so capital in nature,   7
As by your safety, wisdom, all things else,
You mainly were stirred up.   9

KING   O, for two special reasons,
Which may to you perhaps seem much unsinewed,
But yet to me they're strong. The queen his mother
Lives almost by his looks, and for myself –
My virtue or my plague, be it either which –
She is so conjunctive to my life and soul   14
That, as the star moves not but in his sphere,
I could not but by her. The other motive
Why to a public count I might not go   17
Is the great love the general gender bear him,   18
Who, dipping all his faults in their affection,
Would, like the spring that turneth wood to stone,
Convert his gyves to graces; so that my arrows,   21
Too slightly timbered for so loud a wind,
Would have reverted to my bow again,
And not where I had aimed them.

LAERTES
And so have I a noble father lost,
A sister driven into desp'rate terms,   26
Whose worth, if praises may go back again,   27
Stood challenger on mount of all the age   28
For her perfections. But my revenge will come.

KING
Break not your sleeps for that. You must not think
That we are made of stuff so flat and dull
That we can let our beard be shook with danger,

187 *favor* charm 194 *poll* head 198 *of* on 204 *collateral* indirect 205
touched i.e. with the crime 212 *trophy* memorial; *hatchment* coat of arms
213 *ostentation* ceremony 215 *That* so that
IV, vi A chamber in the Castle 14 *overlooked* surveyed, scanned; *means*
i.e. of access 16 *appointment* equipment 20–21 *thieves of mercy* merciful
thieves 25 *bore* caliber (as of a gun)
IV, vii A chamber in the Castle 6 *feats* deeds 7 *capital* punishable by
death 9 *mainly* powerfully 14 *conjunctive* closely united 17 *count* trial,
accounting 18 *general gender* common people 21 *gyves* fetters 26 *terms*
circumstances 27 *back again* i.e. to her better circumstances 28 *on mount*
on a height

And think it pastime. You shortly shall hear more.
I loved your father, and we love ourself,
And that, I hope, will teach you to imagine –
Enter a Messenger with letters.
[How now? What news?]

MESSENGER   [Letters, my lord, from Hamlet:]
These to your majesty, this to the queen.

KING
From Hamlet? Who brought them?

MESSENGER
Sailors, my lord, they say; I saw them not.
They were given me by Claudio; he received them
Of him that brought them.

KING   Laertes, you shall hear them. –
Leave us.   *[Exit Messenger.]*

43   *[Reads]* 'High and mighty, you shall know I am set naked
on your kingdom. To-morrow shall I beg leave to see
your kingly eyes; when I shall (first asking your pardon
thereunto) recount the occasion of my sudden and more
strange return.   Hamlet.'
What should this mean? Are all the rest come back?
49   Or is it some abuse, and no such thing?

LAERTES
Know you the hand?

50 KING   'Tis Hamlet's character. 'Naked'!
And in a postscript here, he says 'alone.'
52   Can you devise me?

LAERTES
I am lost in it, my lord. But let him come.
It warms the very sickness in my heart
That I shall live and tell him to his teeth,
'Thus diddest thou.'

KING   If it be so, Laertes,
(As how should it be so? how otherwise?)
Will you be ruled by me?

LAERTES   Ay, my lord,
So you will not o'errule me to a peace.

KING
To thine own peace. If he be now returned,
61   As checking at his voyage, and that he means
No more to undertake it, I will work him
To an exploit now ripe in my device,
Under the which he shall not choose but fall;
And for his death no wind of blame shall breathe,
66   But even his mother shall uncharge the practice
And call it accident.

LAERTES   My lord, I will be ruled;
The rather if you could devise it so
69   That I might be the organ.

KING   It falls right.
You have been talked of since your travel much,

---

43 *naked* destitute   49 *abuse* imposture   50 *character* handwriting   52 *devise* explain to   61 *checking at* turning aside from (like a falcon turning from its quarry for other prey)   66 *uncharge the practice* acquit the stratagem of being a plot   69 *organ* instrument   75 *siege* seat, rank   76 *riband* decoration   78 *livery* distinctive attire   79 *sables* dignified robes richly furred with sable; *weeds* distinctive garments   80 *health* welfare, prosperity   83 *can well* can perform well   86 *incorpsed* made one body; *demi-natured* made sharer of nature half and half (as man shares with horse in the centaur)   87 *topped* excelled; *thought* imagination of possibilities   88 *forgery* invention   92 *brooch* ornament   94 *made confession* admitted the rival accomplishments   99 *scrimers* fencers   111 *passages of proof* incidents of experience   112 *qualifies* weakens   114 *snuff* unconsumed portion of the burned wick   115 *still* always   116 *plurisy* excess   122 *hurts* i.e. shortens life by drawing blood from the heart (as was believed); *quick* sensitive flesh

---

And that in Hamlet's hearing, for a quality
Wherein they say you shine. Your sum of parts
Did not together pluck such envy from him
As did that one, and that, in my regard,
Of the unworthiest siege.   75

LAERTES   What part is that, my lord?

KING
A very riband in the cap of youth,   76
Yet needful too, for youth no less becomes
The light and careless livery that it wears   78
Than settled age his sables and his weeds,   79
Importing health and graveness. Two months since   80
Here was a gentleman of Normandy.
I have seen myself, and served against, the French,
And they can well on horseback, but this gallant   83
Had witchcraft in't. He grew unto his seat,
And to such wondrous doing brought his horse
As had he been incorpsed and demi-natured   86
With the brave beast. So far he topped my thought   87
That I, in forgery of shapes and tricks,   88
Come short of what he did.

LAERTES   A Norman was't?
KING   A Norman.

LAERTES
Upon my life, Lamord.

KING   The very same.

LAERTES
I know him well. He is the brooch indeed   92
And gem of all the nation.

KING
He made confession of you,   94
And gave you such a masterly report
For art and exercise in your defense,
And for your rapier most especial,
That he cried out 'twould be a sight indeed
If one could match you. The scrimers of their nation   99
He swore had neither motion, guard, nor eye,
If you opposed them. Sir, this report of his
Did Hamlet so envenom with his envy
That he could nothing do but wish and beg
Your sudden coming o'er to play with you.
Now, out of this –

LAERTES   What out of this, my lord?

KING
Laertes, was your father dear to you?
Or are you like the painting of a sorrow,
A face without a heart?

LAERTES   Why ask you this?

KING
Not that I think you did not love your father,
But that I know love is begun by time,
And that I see, in passages of proof,   111
Time qualifies the spark and fire of it.   112
There lives within the very flame of love
A kind of wick or snuff that will abate it,   114
And nothing is at a like goodness still,   115
For goodness, growing to a plurisy,   116
Dies in his own too-much. That we would do
We should do when we would, for this 'would' changes,
And hath abatements and delays as many
As there are tongues, are hands, are accidents,
And then this 'should' is like a spendthrift sigh,
That hurts by easing. But to the quick o' th' ulcer –   122
Hamlet comes back; what would you undertake

To show yourself your father's son in deed
More than in words?

LAERTES   To cut his throat i' th' church!

KING
126 No place indeed should murder sanctuarize;
Revenge should have no bounds. But, good Laertes,
Will you do this? Keep close within your chamber.
Hamlet returned shall know you are come home.
130 We'll put on those shall praise your excellence
And set a double varnish on the fame
132 The Frenchman gave you, bring you in fine together
133 And wager on your heads. He, being remiss,
Most generous, and free from all contriving,
135 Will not peruse the foils, so that with ease,
Or with a little shuffling, you may choose
137 A sword unbated, and, in a pass of practice,
Requite him for your father.

LAERTES   I will do't,
And for that purpose I'll anoint my sword.
140 I bought an unction of a mountebank,
So mortal that, but dip a knife in it,
142 Where it draws blood no cataplasm so rare,
143 Collected from all simples that have virtue
Under the moon, can save the thing from death
145 That is but scratched withal. I'll touch my point
146 With this contagion, that, if I gall him slightly,
It may be death.

KING   Let's further think of this,
Weigh what convenience both of time and means
149 May fit us to our shape. If this should fail,
150 And that our drift look through our bad performance,
'Twere better not assayed. Therefore this project
Should have a back or second, that might hold
153 If this did blast in proof. Soft, let me see.
We'll make a solemn wager on your cunnings –
I ha't!
When in your motion you are hot and dry –
As make your bouts more violent to that end –
158 And that he calls for drink, I'll have preferred him
159 A chalice for the nonce, whereon but sipping,
160 If he by chance escape your venomed stuck,
Our purpose may hold there. – But stay, what noise?

          Enter Queen.

QUEEN
One woe doth tread upon another's heel,
So fast they follow. Your sister's drowned, Laertes.

LAERTES Drowned! O, where?

QUEEN
165 There is a willow grows askant the brook,
166 That shows his hoar leaves in the glassy stream.
Therewith fantastic garlands did she make
Of crowflowers, nettles, daisies, and long purples,
169 That liberal shepherds give a grosser name,
But our cold maids do dead men's fingers call them.
171 There on the pendent boughs her crownet weeds
Clamb'ring to hang, an envious sliver broke,
When down her weedy trophies and herself
Fell in the weeping brook. Her clothes spread wide,
And mermaid-like awhile they bore her up,
176 Which time she chanted snatches of old lauds,
177 As one incapable of her own distress,
178 Or like a creature native and indued
Unto that element. But long it could not be

Till that her garments, heavy with their drink,
Pulled the poor wretch from her melodious lay
To muddy death.

LAERTES   Alas, then she is drowned?

QUEEN Drowned, drowned.

LAERTES
Too much of water hast thou, poor Ophelia,
And therefore I forbid my tears; but yet
It is our trick; nature her custom holds,   186
Let shame say what it will. When these are gone,
The woman will be out. Adieu, my lord.   188
I have a speech o' fire, that fain would blaze
But that this folly drowns it.   *Exit.*

KING   Let's follow, Gertrude.
How much I had to do to calm his rage!
Now fear I this will give it start again;
Therefore let's follow.   *Exeunt.*

          *

          Enter two Clowns.   V, i

CLOWN Is she to be buried in Christian burial when she   1
willfully seeks her own salvation?

OTHER I tell thee she is. Therefore make her grave straight.   3
The crowner hath sate on her, and finds it Christian   4
burial.

CLOWN How can that be, unless she drowned herself in
her own defense?

OTHER Why, 'tis found so.

CLOWN It must be *se offendendo*; it cannot be else. For   8
here lies the point: if I drown myself wittingly, it argues
an act, and an act hath three branches – it is to act, to do,
and to perform. Argal, she drowned herself wittingly.   11

OTHER Nay, but hear you, Goodman Delver.   12

CLOWN Give me leave. Here lies the water – good. Here
stands the man – good. If the man go to this water and
drown himself, it is, will he nill he, he goes, mark you   15
that. But if the water come to him and drown him, he
drowns not himself. Argal, he that is not guilty of his
own death shortens not his own life.

OTHER But is this law?

CLOWN Ay marry, is't – crowner's quest law.   20

OTHER Will you ha' the truth on't? If this had not been a
gentlewoman, she should have been buried out o'
Christian burial.

CLOWN Why, there thou say'st. And the more pity that   24
great folk should have count'nance in this world to   25

---

126 *sanctuarize* protect from punishment, give sanctuary to 130 *put on* instigate 132 *in fine* finally 133 *remiss* negligent 135 *peruse* scan 137 *unbated* not blunted; *pass of practice* thrust made effective by trickery 140 *unction* ointment; *mountebank* quack-doctor 142 *cataplasm* poultice 143 *simples* herbs 145 *withal* with it 146 *gall* scratch 149 *shape* plan 150 *drift* intention; *look* show 153 *blast in proof* burst during trial (like a faulty cannon) 158 *preferred* offered 159 *nonce* occasion 160 *stuck* thrust 165 *askant* alongside 166 *hoar* grey 169 *liberal* free-spoken, licentious 171 *crownet* coronet 176 *lauds* hymns 177 *incapable of* insensible to 178 *indued* endowed 186 *trick* way (i.e. to shed tears when sorrowful) 188 *woman* unmanly part of nature
V, i A churchyard s.d. *Clowns* rustics 1 *in Christian burial* in consecrated ground with the prescribed service of the Church (a burial denied to suicides) 3 *straight* straightway, at once 4 *crowner* coroner 8 *se offendendo* a clownish transformation of '*se defendendo*,' 'in self-defense' 11 *Argal* for 'ergo,' 'therefore' 12 *Delver* Digger 15 *will he nill he* willy-nilly 20 *quest* inquest 24 *thou say'st* you have it right 25 *count'nance* privilege

26 drown or hang themselves more than their even-
Christen. Come, my spade. There is no ancient gentlemen but gard'ners, ditchers, and grave-makers. They
hold up Adam's profession.

OTHER Was he a gentleman?

CLOWN 'A was the first that ever bore arms.

32 [OTHER Why, he had none.

CLOWN What, art a heathen? How dost thou understand
the Scripture? The Scripture says Adam digged. Could
he dig without arms?] I'll put another question to thee.
If thou answerest me not to the purpose, confess thyself—

OTHER Go to.

CLOWN What is he that builds stronger than either the
mason, the shipwright, or the carpenter?

OTHER The gallows-maker, for that frame outlives a
thousand tenants.

CLOWN I like thy wit well, in good faith. The gallows
does well. But how does it well? It does well to those
that do ill. Now thou dost ill to say the gallows is built
stronger than the church. Argal, the gallows may do
well to thee. To't again, come.

OTHER Who builds stronger than a mason, a shipwright,
or a carpenter?

49 CLOWN Ay, tell me that, and unyoke.

OTHER Marry, now I can tell.

CLOWN To't.

52 OTHER Mass, I cannot tell.

CLOWN Cudgel thy brains no more about it, for your dull
ass will not mend his pace with beating. And when you
are asked this question next, say 'a grave-maker.' The
houses he makes last till doomsday. Go, get thee in, and
57 fetch me a stoup of liquor.   [Exit Other Clown.]
Enter Hamlet and Horatio [as Clown digs and sings].

Song.

In youth when I did love, did love,
Methought it was very sweet
60 To contract—O—the time for—a—my behove,
O, methought there—a—was nothing—a—meet.

HAMLET Has this fellow no feeling of his business, that 'a
sings at grave-making?

64 HORATIO Custom hath made it in him a property of easiness.

HAMLET 'Tis e'en so. The hand of little employment
66 hath the daintier sense.

---

26 *even-Christen* fellow Christian 32 *had none* i.e. had no gentleman's
coat of arms 49 *unyoke* i.e. unharness your powers of thought after a
good day's work 52 *Mass* by the Mass 57 *stoup* large mug 60 *behove*
behoof, benefit 64 *property* peculiarity *easiness* easy acceptability 66
daintier sense more delicate feeling (because the hand is less calloused)
69 *intil* into 72 *jowls* hurls 74 *politician* crafty schemer; *o'erreaches* gets
the better of (with a play upon the literal meaning) 82 *chapless* lacking
the lower chap or jaw 83 *mazzard* head 86 *loggets* small pieces of wood
thrown in a game 88 *For and* and 92 *quiddities* subtleties (from scholastic *'quidditas,'* meaning the distinctive nature of anything); *quillities*
nice distinctions 93 *tenures* holdings of property 94 *sconce* head 97
statutes, recognizances legal documents or bonds acknowledging debt
98 *fines, recoveries* modes of converting estate tail into fee simple; *vouchers*
persons vouched or called on to warrant a title; *fine* end (introducing a
word play involving four meanings of 'fine') 102 *pair of indentures*
deed or legal agreement in duplicate; *conveyances* deeds 118 *quick*
living

CLOWN   Song.

But age with his stealing steps
    Hath clawed me in his clutch,
And hath shipped me intil the land,
    As if I had never been such.   69

[Throws up a skull.]

HAMLET That skull had a tongue in it, and could sing
once. How the knave jowls it to the ground, as if 'twere 72
Cain's jawbone, that did the first murder! This might be
the pate of a politician, which this ass now o'erreaches; 74
one that would circumvent God, might it not?

HORATIO It might, my lord.

HAMLET Or of a courtier, which could say 'Good morrow, sweet lord! How dost thou, sweet lord?' This
might be my Lord Such-a-one, that praised my Lord
Such-a-one's horse when 'a meant to beg it, might it
not?

HORATIO Ay, my lord.

HAMLET Why, e'en so, and now my Lady Worm's, chap- 82
less, and knocked about the mazzard with a sexton's 83
spade. Here's fine revolution, an we had the trick to
see't. Did these bones cost no more the breeding but to
play at loggets with 'em? Mine ache to think on't.   86

CLOWN   Song.

A pickaxe and a spade, a spade,
    For and a shrouding sheet;   88
O, a pit of clay for to be made
    For such a guest is meet.

[Throws up another skull.]

HAMLET There's another. Why may not that be the skull
of a lawyer? Where be his quiddities now, his quillities, 92
his cases, his tenures, and his tricks? Why does he suffer 93
this mad knave now to knock him about the sconce with 94
a dirty shovel, and will not tell him of his action of
battery? Hum! This fellow might be in's time a great
buyer of land, with his statutes, his recognizances, his 97
fines, his double vouchers, his recoveries. [Is this the fine 98
of his fines, and the recovery of his recoveries,] to have
his fine pate full of fine dirt? Will his vouchers vouch him
no more of his purchases, and double ones too, than the
length and breadth of a pair of indentures? The very con- 102
veyances of his lands will scarcely lie in this box, and
must th' inheritor himself have no more, ha?

HORATIO Not a jot more, my lord.

HAMLET Is not parchment made of sheepskins?

HORATIO Ay, my lord, and of calveskins too.

HAMLET They are sheep and calves which seek out assurance in that. I will speak to this fellow. Whose grave's
this, sirrah?

CLOWN Mine, sir.

[Sings] O, a pit of clay for to be made
         For such a guest is meet.

HAMLET I think it be thine indeed, for thou liest in't.

CLOWN You lie out on't, sir, and therefore 'tis not yours.
For my part, I do not lie in't, yet it is mine.

HAMLET Thou dost lie in't, to be in't and say it is thine.
'Tis for the dead, not for the quick; therefore thou liest. 118

CLOWN 'Tis a quick lie, sir; 'twill away again from me to
you.

HAMLET What man dost thou dig it for?

CLOWN For no man, sir.

HAMLET What woman then?

CLOWN For none neither.

HAMLET Who is to be buried in't?

CLOWN One that was a woman, sir; but, rest her soul, she's dead.

128 HAMLET How absolute the knave is! We must speak by
129 the card, or equivocation will undo us. By the Lord, Horatio, this three years I have taken note of it, the age
131 is grown so picked that the toe of the peasant comes so
132 near the heel of the courtier he galls his kibe. – How long hast thou been a grave-maker?

CLOWN Of all the days i' th' year, I came to't that day that our last king Hamlet overcame Fortinbras.

HAMLET How long is that since?

CLOWN Cannot you tell that? Every fool can tell that. It was the very day that young Hamlet was born – he that is mad, and sent into England.

140 HAMLET Ay, marry, why was he sent into England?

CLOWN Why, because 'a was mad. 'A shall recover his wits there; or, if 'a do not, 'tis no great matter there.

HAMLET Why?

CLOWN 'Twill not be seen in him there. There the men are as mad as he.

HAMLET How came he mad?

CLOWN Very strangely, they say.

HAMLET How strangely?

CLOWN Faith, e'en with losing his wits.

HAMLET Upon what ground?

CLOWN Why, here in Denmark. I have been sexton here, man and boy, thirty years.

HAMLET How long will a man lie i' th' earth ere he rot?

CLOWN Faith, if 'a be not rotten before 'a die (as we have
155 many pocky corses now-a-days that will scarce hold the laying in), 'a will last you some eight year or nine year. A tanner will last you nine year.

HAMLET Why he more than another?

CLOWN Why, sir, his hide is so tanned with his trade that 'a will keep out water a great while, and your water is a sore decayer of your whoreson dead body. Here's a skull now hath lien you i' th' earth three-and-twenty years.

HAMLET Whose was it?

CLOWN A whoreson mad fellow's it was. Whose do you think it was?

HAMLET Nay, I know not.

CLOWN A pestilence on him for a mad rogue! 'A poured a
168 flagon of Rhenish on my head once. This same skull, sir, was – sir – Yorick's skull, the king's jester.

HAMLET This?

CLOWN E'en that.

HAMLET Let me see. [Takes the skull.] Alas, poor Yorick! I knew him, Horatio, a fellow of infinite jest, of most excellent fancy. He hath borne me on his back a thousand times. And now how abhorred in my imagination it is! My gorge rises at it. Here hung those lips that I have kissed I know not how oft. Where be your gibes now? Your gambols, your songs, your flashes of merriment that were wont to set the table on a roar? Not one now to
180 mock your own grinning? Quite chapfall'n? Now get you to my lady's chamber, and tell her, let her paint an
182 inch thick, to this favor she must come. Make her laugh at that. Prithee, Horatio, tell me one thing.

HORATIO What's that, my lord?

HAMLET Dost thou think Alexander looked o' this fashion i' th' earth?

HORATIO E'en so.

HAMLET And smelt so? Pah!
  [Puts down the skull.]

HORATIO E'en so, my lord.

HAMLET To what base uses we may return, Horatio! Why may not imagination trace the noble dust of Alexander till 'a find it stopping a bunghole?

HORATIO 'Twere to consider too curiously, to consider so.

HAMLET No, faith, not a jot, but to follow him thither with modesty enough, and likelihood to lead it; as thus: 195 Alexander died, Alexander was buried, Alexander returneth to dust; the dust is earth; of earth we make loam; and why of that loam whereto he was converted might they not stop a beer barrel?

Imperious Caesar, dead and turned to clay,   200
Might stop a hole to keep the wind away.
O, that that earth which kept the world in awe
Should patch a wall t' expel the winter's flaw!   203
But soft, but soft awhile! Here comes the king –
  Enter King, Queen, Laertes, and the Corse [with
  Lords attendant and a Doctor of Divinity as Priest].
The queen, the courtiers. Who is this they follow?
And with such maimèd rites? This doth betoken
The corse they follow did with desp'rate hand
Fordo it own life. 'Twas of some estate.   208
Couch we awhile, and mark.   209
  [Retires with Horatio.]

LAERTES
What ceremony else?

HAMLET   That is Laertes,
A very noble youth. Mark.

LAERTES
What ceremony else?

DOCTOR
Her obsequies have been as far enlarged
As we have warranty. Her death was doubtful,
And, but that great command o'ersways the order,
She should in ground unsanctified have lodged
Till the last trumpet. For charitable prayers,
Shards, flints, and pebbles should be thrown on her.   218
Yet here she is allowed her virgin crants,   219
Her maiden strewments, and the bringing home   220
Of bell and burial.

LAERTES
Must there no more be done?

DOCTOR   No more be done.
We should profane the service of the dead
To sing a requiem and such rest to her
As to peace-parted souls.

LAERTES   Lay her i' th' earth,
And from her fair and unpolluted flesh
May violets spring! I tell thee, churlish priest,
A minist'ring angel shall my sister be
When thou liest howling.

HAMLET   What, the fair Ophelia?

128 *absolute* positive   128–29 *by the card* by the card on which the points of the mariner's compass are marked, absolutely to the point   129 *equivocation* ambiguity   131 *picked* refined, spruce   132 *galls* chafes; *kibe* chilblain   155 *pocky* rotten (literally, corrupted by pox, or syphilis)   168 *Rhenish* Rhine wine   180 *chapfall'n* lacking the lower chap, or jaw (with a play on the sense 'down in the mouth,' 'dejected')   182 *favor* countenance, aspect   193 *curiously* minutely   195 *modesty* moderation   200 *Imperious* imperial   203 *flaw* gust of wind   208 *Fordo* destroy; *it* its; *estate* rank   209 *Couch* hide   218 *Shards* broken pieces of pottery   219 *crants* garland   220 *strewments* strewings of the grave with flowers; *bringing home* laying to rest

QUEEN
Sweets to the sweet ! Farewell.
  [Scatters flowers.]
I hoped thou shouldst have been my Hamlet's wife.
I thought thy bride-bed to have decked, sweet maid,
And not have strewed thy grave.
LAERTES   O, treble woe
Fall ten times treble on that cursèd head
235 Whose wicked deed thy most ingenious sense
Deprived thee of ! Hold off the earth awhile,
Till I have caught her once more in mine arms.
  [Leaps in the grave.]
Now pile your dust upon the quick and dead
Till of this flat a mountain you have made
240 T' o'ertop old Pelion or the skyish head
Of blue Olympus.
HAMLET *[coming forward]*   What is he whose grief
Bears such an emphasis ? whose phrase of sorrow
243 Conjures the wand'ring stars, and makes them stand
Like wonder-wounded hearers ? This is I,
Hamlet the Dane.
  [Leaps in after Laertes.]
LAERTES   The devil take thy soul !
  [Grapples with him.]
HAMLET
Thou pray'st not well.
I prithee take thy fingers from my throat,
248 For, though I am not splenitive and rash,
Yet have I in me something dangerous,
Which let thy wisdom fear. Hold off thy hand.
KING
Pluck them asunder.
QUEEN   Hamlet, Hamlet !
ALL
Gentlemen !
HORATIO   Good my lord, be quiet.
  *[Attendants part them, and they come out of the
  grave.]*
HAMLET
Why, I will fight with him upon this theme
Until my eyelids will no longer wag.
QUEEN
O my son, what theme ?
HAMLET
I loved Ophelia. Forty thousand brothers
Could not with all their quantity of love
Make up my sum. What wilt thou do for her ?
KING
O, he is mad, Laertes.
QUEEN
For love of God, forbear him.

HAMLET
'Swounds, show me what thou't do.
Woo't weep ? woo't fight ? woo't fast ? woo't tear thyself ? 262
Woo't drink up esill ? eat a crocodile ?   263
I'll do't. Dost thou come here to whine ?
To outface me with leaping in her grave ?
Be buried quick with her, and so will I.   266
And if thou prate of mountains, let them throw
Millions of acres on us, till our ground,
Singeing his pate against the burning zone,
Make Ossa like a wart ! Nay, an thou'lt mouth,
I'll rant as well as thou.
QUEEN   This is mere madness ;   271
And thus a while the fit will work on him.
Anon, as patient as the female dove
When that her golden couplets are disclosed,   274
His silence will sit drooping.
HAMLET   Hear you, sir.
What is the reason that you use me thus ?
I loved you ever. But it is no matter.
Let Hercules himself do what he may,
The cat will mew, and dog will have his day.
KING
I pray thee, good Horatio, wait upon him.
                    Exit Hamlet and Horatio.
  [To Laertes]
Strengthen your patience in our last night's speech.   281
We'll put the matter to the present push. –   282
Good Gertrude, set some watch over your son. –
This grave shall have a living monument.
An hour of quiet shortly shall we see ;
Till then in patience our proceeding be.   *Exeunt.*

                              *

                    Enter Hamlet and Horatio.   V, ii
HAMLET
So much for this, sir ; now shall you see the other.
You do remember all the circumstance ?
HORATIO
Remember it, my lord !
HAMLET
Sir, in my heart there was a kind of fighting
That would not let me sleep. Methought I lay
Worse than the mutines in the bilboes. Rashly,   6
And praised be rashness for it – let us know,
Our indiscretion sometime serves us well
When our deep plots do pall, and that should learn us   9
There's a divinity that shapes our ends,
Rough-hew them how we will –   11
HORATIO   That is most certain.
HAMLET
Up from my cabin,
My sea-gown scarfed about me, in the dark
Groped I to find out them, had my desire,
Fingered their packet, and in fine withdrew   15
To mine own room again, making so bold,
My fears forgetting manners, to unseal
Their grand commission ; where I found, Horatio –
Ah, royal knavery ! – an exact command,
Larded with many several sorts of reasons,   20
Importing Denmark's health, and England's too,   21
With, ho ! such bugs and goblins in my life,   22
That on the supervise, no leisure bated,   23

---

235 *most ingenious* of quickest apprehension   240 *Pelion* a mountain in
Thessaly, like Olympus and also Ossa (the allusion being to the war in
which the Titans fought the gods and attempted to heap Ossa and Olympus
on Pelion, or Pelion and Ossa on Olympus, in order to scale heaven)   243
Conjures charms, puts a spell upon ; *wand'ring stars* planets   248 *splenitive*
of fiery temper (the spleen being considered the seat of anger)   262
Woo't wilt (thou)   263 *esill* vinegar   266 *quick* alive   271 *mere* absolute
274 *couplets* pair of fledglings ; *disclosed* hatched   281 *in* by calling to mind
282 *present push* immediate trial
V, ii The hall of the Castle   6 *mutines* mutineers ; *bilboes* fetters   9 *pall*
fail   11 *Rough-hew* shape roughly in trial form   15 *Fingered* filched ; *in
fine* finally   20 *Larded* enriched   21 *Importing* relating to   22 *bugs* bug-
bears ; *in my life* to be encountered as dangers if I should be allowed to
live   23 *supervise* perusal ; *bated* deducted, allowed

No, not to stay the grinding of the axe,
My head should be struck off.

HORATIO   Is't possible?

HAMLET
Here's the commission; read it at more leisure.
But wilt thou hear me how I did proceed?

HORATIO I beseech you.

HAMLET
Being thus benetted round with villainies,
30 Or I could make a prologue to my brains,
They had begun the play. I sat me down,
Devised a new commission, wrote it fair.
33 I once did hold it, as our statists do,
34 A baseness to write fair, and labored much
How to forget that learning, but, sir, now
36 It did me yeoman's service. Wilt thou know
37 Th' effect of what I wrote?

HORATIO   Ay, good my lord.

HAMLET
An earnest conjuration from the king,
As England was his faithful tributary,
As love between them like the palm might flourish
41 As peace should still her wheaten garland wear
42 And stand a comma 'tween their amities,
43 And many such-like as's of great charge,
That on the view and knowing of these contents,
Without debatement further, more or less,
He should the bearers put to sudden death,
47 Not shriving time allowed.

HORATIO   How was this sealed?

HAMLET
48 Why, even in that was heaven ordinant.
I had my father's signet in my purse,
50 Which was the model of that Danish seal,
Folded the writ up in the form of th' other,
52 Subscribed it, gave't th' impression, placed it safely,
The changeling never known. Now, the next day
54 Was our sea-fight, and what to this was sequent
Thou know'st already.

HORATIO
So Guildenstern and Rosencrantz go to't.

HAMLET
[Why, man, they did make love to this employment.]
They are not near my conscience; their defeat
59 Does by their own insinuation grow.
'Tis dangerous when the baser nature comes
61 Between the pass and fell incensèd points
Of mighty opposites.

HORATIO   Why, what a king is this!

HAMLET
63 Does it not, think thee, stand me now upon —
He that hath killed my king, and whored my mother,
65 Popped in between th' election and my hopes,
66 Thrown out his angle for my proper life,
67 And with such coz'nage – is't not perfect conscience
68 [To quit him with this arm? And is't not to be damned
69 To let this canker of our nature come
In further evil?

HORATIO
It must be shortly known to him from England
What is the issue of the business there.

HAMLET
It will be short; the interim is mine,
And a man's life 's no more than to say 'one.'

But I am very sorry, good Horatio,
That to Laertes I forgot myself,
For by the image of my cause I see
The portraiture of his. I'll court his favors.
But sure the bravery of his grief did put me   79
Into a tow'ring passion.

HORATIO   Peace, who comes here?]
       Enter [Osric,] a courtier.

OSRIC Your lordship is right welcome back to Denmark.

HAMLET I humbly thank you, sir. [aside to Horatio] Dost know this waterfly?

HORATIO [aside to Hamlet] No, my good lord.

HAMLET [aside to Horatio] Thy state is the more gracious, for 'tis a vice to know him. He hath much land, and fertile. Let a beast be lord of beasts, and his crib shall stand at the king's mess. 'Tis a chough, but, as I say, 88
spacious in the possession of dirt.

OSRIC Sweet lord, if your lordship were at leisure, I should impart a thing to you from his majesty.

HAMLET I will receive it, sir, with all diligence of spirit. Put your bonnet to his right use. 'Tis for the head.

OSRIC I thank your lordship, it is very hot.

HAMLET No, believe me, 'tis very cold; the wind is northerly.

OSRIC It is indifferent cold, my lord, indeed.   97

HAMLET But yet methinks it is very sultry and hot for my complexion.   99

OSRIC Exceedingly, my lord; it is very sultry, as 'twere — I cannot tell how. But, my lord, his majesty bade me signify to you that 'a has laid a great wager on your head. Sir, this is the matter —

HAMLET I beseech you remember.   104
       [Hamlet moves him to put on his hat.]

OSRIC Nay, good my lord; for mine ease, in good faith. 105
Sir, here is newly come to court Laertes – believe me, an absolute gentleman, full of most excellent differences, of 107
very soft society and great showing. Indeed, to speak 108
feelingly of him, he is the card or calendar of gentry; for 109
you shall find in him the continent of what part a 110
gentleman would see.

HAMLET Sir, his definement suffers no perdition in you, 112
though, I know, to divide him inventorially would dozy 113
th' arithmetic of memory, and yet but yaw neither in re- 114

30 *Or ere* 33 *statists* statesmen 34 *fair* with professional clarity (like a clerk or a scrivener, not like a gentleman) 36 *yeoman's service* stout service such as yeomen footsoldiers gave as archers 37 *effect* purport 41 *wheaten garland* adornment of fruitful agriculture 42 *comma* connective (because it indicates continuity of thought in a sentence) 43 *charge* burden (with a double meaning to fit a play that makes *as's* into 'asses') 47 *shriving time* time for confession and absolution 48 *ordinant* controlling 50 *model* counterpart 52 *impression* i.e. of the signet 54 *sequent* subsequent 59 *insinuation* intrusion 61 *pass* thrust; *fell* fierce 63 *stand* rest incumbent 65 *election* i.e. to the kingship (the Danish kingship being elective) 66 *angle* fishing line; *proper* own 67 *coz'nage* cozenage, trickery 68 *quit* repay 69 *canker* cancer, ulcer 79 *bravery* ostentatious display 88 *mess* table; *chough* jackdaw, chatterer 97 *indifferent* somewhat 99 *complexion* temperament 104 *remember* i.e. remember you have done all that courtesy demands 105 *for mine ease* i.e. I keep my hat off just for comfort (a conventional polite phrase) 107 *differences* differentiating characteristics, special qualities 108 *soft society* gentle manners; *great showing* noble appearance 109 *feelingly* appropriately; *card* map; *calendar* guide; *gentry* gentlemanliness 110 *continent* all-containing embodiment (with an implication of geographical continent to go with *card*) 112 *definement* definition; *perdition* loss 113 *dozy* dizzy, stagger 114 *yaw* hold to a course unsteadily like a ship that steers wild; *neither* for all that 114-15 *in respect of* in comparison with

116 spect of his quick sail. But, in the verity of extolment, I
117 take him to be a soul of great article, and his infusion of
118 such dearth and rareness as, to make true diction of him,
119 his semblable is his mirror, and who else would trace
    him, his umbrage, nothing more.

OSRIC Your lordship speaks most infallibly of him.

121 HAMLET The concernancy, sir? Why do we wrap the
122 gentleman in our more rawer breath?

OSRIC Sir?

HORATIO Is't not possible to understand in another
125 tongue? You will to't, sir, really.

126 HAMLET What imports the nomination of this gentle-
    man?

OSRIC Of Laertes?

HORATIO [aside to Hamlet] His purse is empty already.
    All's golden words are spent.

HAMLET Of him, sir.

OSRIC I know you are not ignorant –

HAMLET I would you did, sir; yet, in faith, if you did, it
133 would not much approve me. Well, sir?

OSRIC You are not ignorant of what excellence Laertes is –

135 HAMLET I dare not confess that, lest I should compare
    with him in excellence; but to know a man well were to
    know himself.

OSRIC I mean, sir, for his weapon; but in the imputation
139 laid on him by them, in his meed he's unfellowed.

HAMLET What's his weapon?

OSRIC Rapier and dagger.

HAMLET That's two of his weapons – but well.

OSRIC The king, sir, hath wagered with him six Barbary
144 horses, against the which he has impawned, as I take it,
145 six French rapiers and poniards, with their assigns, as
146 girdle, hangers, and so. Three of the carriages, in faith,
147 are very dear to fancy, very responsive to the hilts, most
148 delicate carriages, and of very liberal conceit.

HAMLET What call you the carriages?

HORATIO [aside to Hamlet] I knew you must be edified by
151 the margent ere you had done.

OSRIC The carriages, sir, are the hangers.

HAMLET The phrase would be more germane to the mat-
    ter if we could carry a cannon by our sides. I would it
    might be hangers till then. But on! Six Barbary horses
    against six French swords, their assigns, and three
    liberal-conceited carriages – that's the French bet
    against the Danish. Why is this all impawned, as you
    call it?

OSRIC The king, sir, hath laid, sir, that in a dozen passes
    between yourself and him he shall not exceed you three
    hits; he hath laid on twelve for nine, and it would come
    to immediate trial if your lordship would vouchsafe
    the answer.

HAMLET How if I answer no?

OSRIC I mean, my lord, the opposition of your person in
    trial.

HAMLET Sir, I will walk here in the hall. If it please his
    majesty, it is the breathing time of day with me. Let the 168
    foils be brought, the gentleman willing, and the king
    hold his purpose, I will win for him an I can; if not, I 170
    will gain nothing but my shame and the odd hits.

OSRIC Shall I redeliver you e'en so?

HAMLET To this effect, sir, after what flourish your
    nature will.

OSRIC I commend my duty to your lordship.

HAMLET Yours, yours. [Exit Osric.] He does well to com-
    mend it himself; there are no tongues else for's turn.

HORATIO This lapwing runs away with the shell on his 178
    head.

HAMLET 'A did comply, sir, with his dug before 'a sucked 179
    it. Thus has he, and many more of the same bevy that I 180
    know the drossy age dotes on, only got the tune of the 181
    time, and, out of an habit of encounter, a kind of yeasty
    collection, which carries them through and through the
    most fanned and winnowed opinions; and do but blow 184
    them to their trial, the bubbles are out.

    Enter a Lord.

LORD My lord, his majesty commended him to you by
    young Osric, who brings back to him that you attend
    him in the hall. He sends to know if your pleasure hold
    to play with Laertes, or that you will take longer time.

HAMLET I am constant to my purposes; they follow the
    king's pleasure. If his fitness speaks, mine is ready; now
    or whensoever, provided I be so able as now.

LORD The king and queen and all are coming down.

HAMLET In happy time. 194

LORD The queen desires you to use some gentle enter- 195
    tainment to Laertes before you fall to play.

HAMLET She well instructs me.   *[Exit Lord.]*

HORATIO You will lose this wager, my lord.

HAMLET I do not think so. Since he went into France I
    have been in continual practice. I shall win at the odds.
    But thou wouldst not think how ill all's here about my
    heart. But it is no matter.

HORATIO Nay, good my lord –

HAMLET It is but foolery, but it is such a kind of gain- 204
    giving as would perhaps trouble a woman.

HORATIO If your mind dislike anything, obey it. I will
    forestall their repair hither and say you are not fit.

HAMLET Not a whit, we defy augury. There is special
    providence in the fall of a sparrow. If it be now, 'tis not
    to come; if it be not to come, it will be now; if it be not
    now, yet it will come. The readiness is all. Since no man 211
    of aught he leaves knows, what is't to leave betimes? Let
    be.

    A table prepared. [Enter] Trumpets, Drums, and
    Officers with cushions; King, Queen, [Osric,] and all
    the State, [with] foils, daggers, [and stoups of wine
    borne in;] and Laertes.

KING
Come, Hamlet, come, and take this hand from me.
    [The King puts Laertes' hand into Hamlet's.]

HAMLET
Give me your pardon, sir. I have done you wrong,
But pardon't, as you are a gentleman.
This presence knows, and you must needs have heard, 217
How I am punished with a sore distraction.

116 *article* scope, importance; *infusion* essence   117 *dearth* scarcity   118 *semblable* likeness (i.e. only true likeness); *trace* follow   119 *umbrage* shadow   121 *concernancy* relevance   122 *rawer breath* cruder speech   125 *to't* i.e. get to an understanding   126 *nomination* mention   133 *approve me* be to my credit   135 *compare* compete   139 *meed* worth   144 *impawned* staked   145 *assigns* appurtenances   146 *hangers* straps by which the sword hangs from the belt   147 *dear to fancy* finely designed; *responsive* corresponding closely   148 *liberal conceit* tasteful design, refined conception   151 *margent* margin (i.e. explanatory notes there printed)   168 *breathing time* exercise hour   170 *an* if   178 *lapwing* a bird reputed to be so precocious as to run as soon as hatched   179 *comply* observe formalities of courtesy; *dug* mother's nipple   180 *bevy* company   181 *drossy* frivolous   184 *fanned and winnowed* select and refined   194 *In happy time* I am happy (a polite response)   195 *entertainment* words of reception or greeting   204 *gaingiving* misgiving   211 *all* all that matters   217 *presence* assembly

What I have done
220 That might your nature, honor, and exception
Roughly awake, I here proclaim was madness.
Was't Hamlet wronged Laertes ? Never Hamlet.
If Hamlet from himself be ta'en away,
And when he's not himself does wrong Laertes,
Then Hamlet does it not, Hamlet denies it.
Who does it then ? His madness. If 't be so,
227 Hamlet is of the faction that is wronged ;
His madness is poor Hamlet's enemy.
Sir, in this audience,
Let my disclaiming from a purposed evil
Free me so far in your most generous thoughts
That I have shot my arrow o'er the house
And hurt my brother.

233 LAERTES　　　　　　I am satisfied in nature,
Whose motive in this case should stir me most
235 To my revenge. But in my terms of honor
I stand aloof, and will no reconcilement
Till by some elder masters of known honor
238 I have a voice and precedent of peace
239 To keep my name ungored. But till that time
I do receive your offered love like love,
And will not wrong it.

HAMLET　　　　　　I embrace it freely,
And will this brother's wager frankly play.
Give us the foils. Come on.

LAERTES　　　　　　Come, one for me.

HAMLET
244 I'll be your foil, Laertes. In mine ignorance
Your skill shall, like a star i' th' darkest night,
246 Stick fiery off indeed.

LAERTES　　　　　　You mock me, sir.

HAMLET
No, by this hand.

KING
Give them the foils, young Osric. Cousin Hamlet,
You know the wager ?

HAMLET　　　　　　Very well, my lord.
Your grace has laid the odds o' th' weaker side.

KING
I do not fear it, I have seen you both ;
But since he is bettered, we have therefore odds.

LAERTES
This is too heavy ; let me see another.

HAMLET
This likes me well. These foils have all a length ?
　　　　　　[Prepare to play.]

OSRIC
Ay, my good lord.

KING
Set me the stoups of wine upon that table.
If Hamlet give the first or second hit,
258 Or quit in answer of the third exchange,
Let all the battlements their ordnance fire.
The king shall drink to Hamlet's better breath,
261 And in the cup an union shall he throw
Richer than that which four successive kings
In Denmark's crown have worn. Give me the cups,
264 And let the kettle to the trumpet speak,
The trumpet to the cannoneer without,
The cannons to the heavens, the heaven to earth,
'Now the king drinks to Hamlet.' Come, begin.
　　　　　　Trumpets the while.

And you, the judges, bear a wary eye.

HAMLET
Come on, sir.

LAERTES　　　　　　Come, my lord.
　　　　　　[They play.]

HAMLET　　　　　　　　　　One.

LAERTES　　　　　　　　　　No.

HAMLET　　　　　　　　　　Judgment ?

OSRIC
A hit, a very palpable hit.
　　　Drum, trumpets, and shot. Flourish ; a piece goes off.

LAERTES　　　　　　Well, again.

KING
Stay, give me drink. Hamlet, this pearl is thine.
Here's to thy health. Give him the cup.

HAMLET
I'll play this bout first ; set it by awhile.
Come. *[They play.]* Another hit. What say you ?

LAERTES
A touch, a touch ; I do confess 't.

KING
Our son shall win.

QUEEN　　　　　　He's fat, and scant of breath.　276
Here, Hamlet, take my napkin, rub thy brows.　277
The queen carouses to thy fortune, Hamlet.　278

HAMLET
Good madam !

KING　　　　　　Gertrude, do not drink.

QUEEN
I will, my lord ; I pray you pardon me.
　　　　　　[Drinks.]

KING *[aside]*
It is the poisoned cup ; it is too late.

HAMLET
I dare not drink yet, madam – by and by.

QUEEN
Come, let me wipe thy face.

LAERTES
My lord, I'll hit him now.

KING　　　　　　　　　　I do not think 't.

LAERTES *[aside]*
And yet it is almost against my conscience.

HAMLET
Come for the third, Laertes. You but dally.
I pray you pass with your best violence ;
I am afeard you make a wanton of me.　288

LAERTES
Say you so ? Come on.
　　　　　　[They play.]

OSRIC
Nothing neither way.

LAERTES
Have at you now !
　　　*[In scuffling they change rapiers, and both are
　　　wounded with the poisoned weapon.]*

KING　　　　　　Part them. They are incensed.

220 *exception* disapproval　227 *faction* body of persons taking a side in a contention　233 *nature* natural feeling as a person　235 *terms of honor* position as a man of honor　238 *voice* authoritative statement　239 *ungored* uninjured　244 *foil* setting that displays a jewel advantageously (with a play upon the meaning 'weapon')　246 *Stick fiery off* show in brilliant relief　258 *quit* repay by a hit　261 *union* pearl　264 *kettle* kettledrum　276 *fat* not physically fit, out of training　277 *napkin* handkerchief　278 *carouses* drinks a toast　288 *wanton* pampered child

HAMLET
Nay, come – again !
[The Queen falls.]

OSRIC   Look to the queen there, ho !

HORATIO
They bleed on both sides. How is it, my lord ?

OSRIC
How is't, Laertes ?

LAERTES
295   Why, as a woodcock to mine own springe, Osric.
I am justly killed with mine own treachery.

HAMLET
How does the queen ?

297 **KING**   She sounds to see them bleed.

QUEEN
No, no, the drink, the drink ! O my dear Hamlet !
The drink, the drink ! I am poisoned.
[Dies.]

HAMLET
O villainy ! Ho ! let the door be locked.
Treachery ! Seek it out.
[Laertes falls.]

LAERTES
It is here, Hamlet. Hamlet, thou art slain ;
No med'cine in the world can do thee good.
In thee there is not half an hour's life.
The treacherous instrument is in thy hand,
306   Unbated and envenomed. The foul practice
Hath turned itself on me. Lo, here I lie,
Never to rise again. Thy mother 's poisoned.
I can no more. The king, the king 's to blame.

HAMLET
The point envenomed too ?
Then venom, to thy work.
[Hurts the King.]

ALL   Treason ! treason !

KING
O, yet defend me, friends. I am but hurt.

HAMLET
Here, thou incestuous, murd'rous, damnèd Dane,
Drink off this potion. Is thy union here ?
Follow my mother.
[King dies.]

LAERTES   He is justly served.
317   It is a poison tempered by himself.
Exchange forgiveness with me, noble Hamlet.
Mine and my father's death come not upon thee,
Nor thine on me !
[Dies.]

HAMLET
Heaven make thee free of it ! I follow thee.
I am dead, Horatio. Wretched queen, adieu !
You that look pale and tremble at this chance,
324   That are but mutes or audience to this act,

Had I but time – as this fell sergeant, Death,   325
Is strict in his arrest – O, I could tell you –
But let it be. Horatio, I am dead ;
Thou livest ; report me and my cause aright
To the unsatisfied.

HORATIO   Never believe it.
I am more an antique Roman than a Dane.
Here's yet some liquor left.

HAMLET   As th' art a man,
Give me the cup. Let go. By heaven, I'll ha't !
O God, Horatio, what a wounded name,
Things standing thus unknown, shall live behind me !
If thou didst ever hold me in thy heart,
Absent thee from felicity awhile,
And in this harsh world draw thy breath in pain,
To tell my story.
A march afar off.
          What warlike noise is this ?

OSRIC
Young Fortinbras, with conquest come from Poland,
To the ambassadors of England gives
This warlike volley.

HAMLET   O, I die, Horatio !
The potent poison quite o'ercrows my spirit.   342
I cannot live to hear the news from England,
But I do prophesy th' election lights   344
On Fortinbras. He has my dying voice.   345
So tell him, with th' occurrents, more and less,   346
Which have solicited – the rest is silence.   347
Dies.

HORATIO
Now cracks a noble heart. Good night, sweet prince,
And flights of angels sing thee to thy rest !
[March within.]
Why does the drum come hither ?
Enter Fortinbras, with the Ambassadors [and with his train of Drum, Colors, and Attendants].

FORTINBRAS
Where is this sight ?

HORATIO   What is it you would see ?
If aught of woe or wonder, cease your search.

FORTINBRAS
This quarry cries on havoc. O proud Death,   353
What feast is toward in thine eternal cell   354
That thou so many princes at a shot
So bloodily hast struck ?

AMBASSADOR   The sight is dismal ;
And our affairs from England come too late.
The ears are senseless that should give us hearing
To tell him his commandment is fulfilled,
That Rosencrantz and Guildenstern are dead.
Where should we have our thanks ?

HORATIO   Not from his mouth,
Had it th' ability of life to thank you.
He never gave commandment for their death.
But since, so jump upon this bloody question,   364
You from the Polack wars, and you from England,
Are here arrived, give order that these bodies
High on a stage be placèd to the view,   367
And let me speak to th' yet unknowing world
How these things came about. So shall you hear
Of carnal, bloody, and unnatural acts,
Of accidental judgments, casual slaughters,   371
Of deaths put on by cunning and forced cause,   372

---

295 *woodcock* a bird reputed to be stupid and easily trapped ; *springe* trap
297 *sounds* swoons   306 *Unbated* unblunted ; *practice* stratagem   317
tempered mixed   324 *mutes* actors in a play who speak no lines   325
sergeant sheriff's officer   342 *o'ercrows* triumphs over (like a victor in a
cockfight)   344 *election* i.e. to the throne   345 *voice* vote   346 *occurrents*
occurrences   347 *solicited* incited, provoked   353 *quarry* pile of dead
(literally, of dead deer gathered after the hunt) ; *cries on* proclaims loudly ;
havoc indiscriminate killing and destruction such as would follow the order
'havoc,' or 'pillage,' given to an army   354 *toward* forthcoming   364 *jump*
precisely   367 *stage* platform   371 *judgments* retributions ; *casual* not
humanly planned (reinforcing *accidental*)   372 *put on* instigated

And, in this upshot, purposes mistook
Fall'n on th' inventors' heads. All this can I
Truly deliver.
  FORTINBRAS   Let us haste to hear it,
And call the noblest to the audience.
For me, with sorrow I embrace my fortune.
378   I have some rights of memory in this kingdom,
379   Which now to claim my vantage doth invite me.
  HORATIO
Of that I shall have also cause to speak,
381   And from his mouth whose voice will draw on more.
382   But let this same be presently performed,
Even while men's minds are wild, lest more mischance
384   On plots and errors happen.
  FORTINBRAS   Let four captains

Bear Hamlet like a soldier to the stage,
For he was likely, had he been put on,   386
To have proved most royal ; and for his passage   387
The soldiers' music and the rites of war
Speak loudly for him.
Take up the bodies. Such a sight as this
Becomes the field, but here shows much amiss.
Go, bid the soldiers shoot.
            Exeunt [marching ; after the which
            a peal of ordinance are shot off].

378 *of memory* traditional and kept in mind   379 *vantage* advantageous opportunity   381 *more* i.e. more voices, or votes, for the kingship   382 *presently* immediately   384 *On* on the basis of   386 *put on* set to perform in office   387 *passage* death

Except for a few corrections of obvious typographical errors, all departures from the text of the 1604–05 quarto (Q2) are listed below, with the adopted reading in italics followed by the rejected Q2 reading in roman. The great majority of the adopted readings are from the 1623 folio (F) and are so designated. When the adopted reading appears also in the "bad" quarto of 1603 (Q1), the fact is indicated. When the adopted reading does not occur in Q1 or F, the name of the first to make the emendation is given in most cases; otherwise (usually when the emendation is of an obvious or minor defect) the abbreviation "Eds" for "editors" is used. Quartos other than Q1 and Q2 are occasionally cited, but only when the adopted reading does not occur in F. (Actually Q4, although not regarded as of substantive value, contains a considerable number of the readings that have been adopted from F.)

I, i, 16 *soldier* (Q1, F) souldiers   33 *two nights have* (F) haue two nights   44 *harrows* (F) horrowes   61 *th' ambitious* (F) the ambitious   63 *sledded* (F) sleaded   *Polacks* (Malone) Pollax   68 *my* (Q1, F) mine   73 *why* (Q1, F) with   *cast* (F) cost   87 *heraldry* (Q1, F) heraldy   88 *those* (Q1, F) these   91 *returned* (F) returne   94 *designed* (Pope) desseigne   108 *e'en so* (Eds) enso   121 *feared* (Collier) feare   127 s.d. *He* (Q '76) It (Q2) s.d. omitted (F)   138 *you* (Q1, F) your   140 *at* (F) omitted   164 *hallowed* (F) hallowèd   175 *conveniently* (Q1, F) conuenient

I, ii, s.d. *Councillors,* (Eds) Counsaile : as   16 *all,* (Johnson) all   58 *He hath* (Q1, Q4) Hath   67 *so* (F) so much   77 *good* (F) coold   82 *shapes* (Q4) chapes (Q2) shewes (F)   85 *passeth* (F) passes   96 *a* (F) or   129 *sullied* (anon.) sallied   132 *self* (F) seale   133 *weary* (F) wary   137 *to this* (F) thus   143 *would* (Q1, F) should   148 *followed* (Rowe) followèd   149 *even she* (F) omitted   175 *to drink deep* (Q1, F) for to drinke   178 *see* (Q1, F) omitted   179 *followed* (Eds) followèd   199 *encountered* (Eds) incountred   209 *Where, as* (Q1) Whereas   *delivered* (Q1, F) deliuerèd   213 *watched* (F) watch   224 *Indeed, indeed* (Q1, F) Indeede   237 *Very like, very like* (Q1, F) Very like   257 *Foul* (Q1, F) fonde

I, iii, 1 *embarked* (F) inbarckt   3 *convoy is* (F) conuay, in   12 *bulk* (F) bulkes   32 *unmastered* (Eds) vnmastred   49 *like* (F) omitted   51 *recks* (Pope) reakes   68 *thine* (F) thy   74 *Are* (F) Or   75 *be* (F) boy   76 *loan* (F) loue   83 *invites* (F) inuests   109 *Running* (Collier) Wrong   125 *tether* (F) tider   129 *implorators* (F) imploratotors   130 *bawds* (Theobald) bonds   131 *beguile* (F) beguide

I, iv, 2 *a* (F) omitted   9 *swaggering* (Q1, F) swaggring   17 *revel* (Q4) reueale (Q2) ll. 17–38 omitted (F)   18 *taxed* (Pope) taxèd   27 *the* (Pope) their   33 *Their* (Theobald) His   36 *evil* (Keightley conjecture, withdrawn) eale   63 *will I* (Q1, F) I will   69 *lord* (Q1, F) omitted   87 *imagination* (Q1, F) imagion

I, v, 20 *fretful* (Q1, F) fearefull   43 *wit* (Pope) wits   47 *a* (F) omitted   53 *moved* (Eds) moouèd   55 *lust* (Q1, F) but   56 *sate* (Q1, F) sort   62 *cursed* (Eds) cursèd   64 *leperous* (F) leaprous   68 *posset* (F) possesse   77 *Unhouseled* (Theobald) Vnhuzled (Q2) Vnhouzzled (F)   95 *stiffly* (F) swiftly   96 *while* (F) whiles   116 *bird* (F) and   122 *my lord* (Q1, F) omitted   129 *desires* (Q1, F) desire   132 *Look you, I'll* (F) I will   170 *some'er* (Eds) so mere

II, i, s.d. *man* (Eds) man or two   3 *marvellous* (Q4) meruiles (Q2) maruels (F)   28 *no* (F) omitted   38 *warrant* (F) wit   39 *sullies* (Q4) sallies (Q2) sulleyes (F)   40 *i' th'* (F) with   52–53 at *'friend . . . gentleman'* (F) omitted   56 *t'other* (Q1, F) th' other   58 *gaming,* (F) gaming   *o'ertook* (F) or tooke   63 *takes* (F) take   79 *fouled* (F) foulèd   80 *Ungartered* (Eds) Vngartred   105 *passion* (F) passions

II, ii, 20 *are* (F) is   43 *Assure you,* (F) I assure   57 *o'erhasty* (F) hastie   76 *shown* (Q1, F) shone   81 *considered* (F) considerèd   90 *since* (F) omitted   97 *he is* (F) hee's   108 s.d. *letter* (placed here as in F ; at line 116 in Q2)   112 *Thus :* (Malone, from Jennens substantially) thus   126 *above* (F) about   137 *winking* (F) working   143 *his* (F) her   146 *repelled* (Eds) repell'd   148 *watch*

(F) wath   149 *a* (F) omitted   151 *'tis* (F) omitted   165 *fallen* (Eds) falne   189 *far gone, far gone* (F) farre gone   190 *suffered* (Eds) suffred   201 *you* (F) omitted   202 *should be* (F) shall grow   208 *sanity* (F) sancity   209–10 *and . . . him* (F) omitted   211 *honorable* (F) omitted   *most humbly* (F) omitted   213 *sir* (F) omitted   214 *will* (F) will not   222 *excellent* (F) extent   223 *ye* (F) you   225 *over-* (F) euer   226 *cap* (F) lap   234 *that* (F) omitted   269 *even* (F) euer   275 *Why, anything – but* (F) Anything but   300 *a piece* (F) peece   301 *moving how* (F) moouing, how   302 *admirable* (F) admirable   *action* (F) action, angel,' Angell   *apprehension* (Eds) apprehension,   305 *woman* (Q1, F) women   315 *of* (F) on   318–19 *the clown . . . sere* (F) omitted   320 *blank* (Q1, F) black   356 *mows* (Q1, F) mouths   364 *lest my* (F) let me   389–90 *tragical-historical . . . -pastoral* (F) omitted   395 *treasure* (Walker) a treasure   415 *By'r* (F) by   419 *e'en to't* (Rowe) ento't (Q2) e'ne to't (F)   *French falconers* (Q1, F) friendly Fankners   432 *affectation* (F) affection   434 *tale* (Q1, F) talke   435 *where* (Q1, F) when   442 *the* (Q1, F) th'   462 *Then . . . Ilium* (F) omitted   469 *And* (F) omitted   483 *fellies* (Eds) follies   492 *Mobled . . . good* (F2) omitted   502 *husband's* (Q1, F) husband   507 *whe'r* (Capell) where   526 *ha't* (F) hate   527 *dozen* (Q1, F) dosen lines   538 *his* (F) the   540 *and* (F) an   543 *to Hecuba* (Q1, F) to her   545 *the cue* (F) that   564 *ha'* (Eds) a   567 *O, vengeance!* (F) omitted   569 *father* (Q1, Q4) omitted (Q2, F)   *murdered* (Eds) murtherèd   573 *About,* (Theobald) About   585 *devil . . . devil* (F) deale . . . deale

III, i, 1 *And* (F) An   28 *too* (F) two   32 *lawful espials* (F) omitted   33 *Will* (F) Wee'le   46 *loneliness* (F) lowlines   55 *Let's* (F) omitted   79 *bourn* (Capell) borne (Q2) bourne (Pope)   83 *of us all* (Q1, F) omitted   85 *sicklied* (F) sickled   90 *remembered* (Eds) remembrd   92 *well, well, well* (F) well   99 *the* (F) these   107 *your honesty* (F) you   121 *to* (F) omitted   121, 130, 137, 140, 149 *nunnery* (Q1, F) Nunry   129 *all* (Q1, F) omitted   137 *Go* (Q1, F) omitted   141 *O* (F) omitted   142 *too* (F) omitted   144 *you amble* (Q1, F) & amble   *lisp* (F) list   145–46 *your ignorance* (F) ignorance   147 *more* (F) mo   152 *expectancy* (F) expectation   156 *music* (F) musickt (Q2)   157 *that* (F) what   159 *feature* (F) stature   161 *see!* (F) see. Exit   188 *unwatched* (F) vnmatcht

III, ii, 9 *tatters* (F) totters   10 *split* (Q1, F) spleet   18 *overdone* (F) ore-doone   21 *own* (F) omitted   24 *make* (F) makes   25 *the which* (F) which   28 *praise* (F) praysd   35 *sir* (F) omitted   49 *ho* (F) howe   86 *detecting* (F) detected   94 *now.* (Johnson) now   110 *I mean . . . lord* (these two lines are present in F, omitted in Q2)   123 *devil* (F) deule   129 s.d. *sound* (Q4) sounds   DUMB SHOW (ll. 8, 10) *poisoner* (F) poysner   131 *is* (Q1, F) omitted   *miching* (Q1, F) munching   136 *counsel* (Q1, F) omitted   138 *you'll* (Q1, F) you will   147 *orbed* (Q1, F) orb'd the   148 *borrowed* (Capell) borrowèd   155 *your* (F) our   160 *In neither* (F) Eyther none, in neither   161 *love* (F) Lord   182 *like* (F) the   191 *joys* (F) ioy   211 *An* (Theobald) And   215 *once a* (F) once I be a   *be* (Q1, F) be a   220 s.d. *Exit* (Q1, F) Exeunt   232 *o'* (Q1, F) of   240 *my* (F) mine   242 *must take* (Q1) mistake   246 *Confederate* (Q1, F) Considerat   248 *infected* (Q1, Q4) inuected   256 (this line is present in F, omitted in Q2)   266 *two* (F) omitted   268 *sir* (F) omitted   274 *peacock* (Pope) paiock (Q2) pecock (Q '95)   279 *poisoning* (F) poysning   289 *distempered* (F) distempred   296 *start* (F) stare   305 *of my* (F) of   330 s.d. *Player* (Eds) Players   344 *and thumb* (F) & the vmber   353 *the top of* (F) omitted   357 *can fret me* (F) fret me not   371–72 *Polonius. I . . . friends.* (F) Leaue me friends. / I will, say so. By and by is easily said,   374 *breathes* (F) breakes   376 *bitter business as the day* (F) busines as the bitter day   381 *daggers* (Q1, F) dagger

III, iii, 17 *'tis* (Dyce ii) it is   19 *huge* (F) hough   22 *ruin* (F) raine   23 *with* (F) omitted   25 *upon* (F) about   50 *pardoned* (F) pardon   58 *shove* (F) showe   69 *engaged* (F) ingagèd   73 *pat* (F) but   75 *revenged* (F) reuendge   79 *hire and salary* (F) base and silly   84 *revenged* (F) reuendgèd   89 *drunk* (F) drunke,

III, iv, 5 *with him* (F) omitted 7 *warrant* (F) wait 21 *inmost* (F) most 23, 24 *ho* (Q1, F) how 39 *is* (F) be 50 *And* (Eds) Ore 54 *Hamlet* (placed as in F ; comes one line earlier in Q2) 60 *heaven-kissing* (F) heaue, a kissing 65 *mildewed* (F) mildewèd 80 *sans* (Eds) sance 89 *panders* (F) pardons 90 *mine* (F) my very *very* (F) omitted (Q2) 91 *grainèd* (F) greeued 92 *not leave* (F) leaue there 94 *Stewed* (F) Stewèd 96 *mine* (F) my 98 *tithe* (F) kyth 122 *hairs* (Rowe) haire 136 *lived* (Eds) liuèd 140 *Ecstasy* (F) omitted 143 *uttered* (Eds) vttred 144 *I* (F) omitted 159 *live* (F) leaue 166 *Refrain to-night* (F) to refraine night 171 *wondrous* (Q5) wonderous (Q2) lines omitted (F) 180 *Thus* (F) This 187 *ravel* (F) rouell 216 *foolish* (F) most foolish

IV, i, 35 *dragged* (F) dreg'd 43 *poisoned* (Eds) poysned

IV, ii, 2 (this line is present in F, omitted in Q2) 6 *Compounded* (F) Compound 17 *ape* (F) apple 29–30 *Hide ... after* (F) omitted

IV, iii, 6 *weighed* (F) wayed 11 *befallen* (Eds) befalne 15 *Ho* (F) Howe 29 *King* (F) King. King. 42 *With fiery quickness* (F) omitted 51 *and so* (F) so 67 *were ne'er begun* (F) will nere begin

IV, v, 9 *aim* (F) yawne 16 *Queen* (Blackstone) omitted 39 *grave* (F) ground 42 *God* (F) good 57 *la*, (F) omitted 82 *their* (F) omitted 89 *his* (F) this 96 *Queen ... this?* (F) omitted 97 *are* (F) is 106 *They* (F) The 119 *brows* (Q '76) browe 152 s.d. *Let her come in* (as in F, given as a speech to Laertes in Q2, at l. 153) 156 *by* (F) with 160 *an old* (Q1, F) a poore 164 *bare-faced* (F) bare-faste 181 *O* (F) omitted *must* (Q1, F) may 186 *affliction* (F) afflictions 194 *All* (F) omitted 198 *Christian* (F) Christians *I pray God* (F) omitted 199 *see* (F) omitted

IV, vi, 21 *good* (F) omitted 25 *bore* (F) bord 29 *He* (F) So 30 *give* (F) omitted

IV, vii, 6 *proceeded* (F) proceede 7 *crimeful* (F) criminall 8 *safety,* (F) safetie, greatnes, 11 *they're* (Q '76) tha'r (Q2) they are (F) 14 *conjunctive* (F) concliue 20 *Would* (F) Worke 22 *loud a wind* (F) loued Arm'd 24 *And* (F) But *had* (F) haue 40 *received* (F) receiuèd 45 *your pardon* (F) you pardon 46–47 *and more strange* (F) omitted 55 *shall* (F) omitted 56 *diddest* (F) didst 60 *returned* (F) returnèd 61 *checking* (F) the King 87 *my* (F) me 114 *wick* (Rowe ii) weeke 121 *spendthrift* (Q '76) spend thrifts (Q2) ll. 113–22 omitted (F) 122 *o'* (Eds) of 124 *yourself ... deed* (F) your selfe indeede your fathers sonne 133 *on* (F) ore 139 *that* (F) omitted 155 *ha't* (F) hate 166 *hoar* (F) horry 170 *cold* (F) cull-cold

V, i, 8 *se offendendo* (F) so offended 10–11 *do, and* (F) doe, 11 *Argal* (F) or all 41 *frame* (F) omitted 56 *last* (Q1, Q4) lasts (Q2, F) 57 *stoup* (Q1, F) soope 62 *that* (F) omitted 63 *at* (F) in 66 *daintier* (F) dintier 68 *clawed* (Pope) clawèd 69 *shipped* (Eds) shippèd *intil* (F) into 80 *meant* (F) went 82 *chapless* (F) Choples 83 *mazzard* (F) massene 84 *an* (Capell) and 85 *'em* (F) them 100 *his vouchers* (F) vouchers 101 *double ones too* (F) doubles 112 *O* (F) or 113 (line is present in F, omitted in Q2) 130 *taken* (F) tooke 133 *a* (F) omitted 134 *all* (F) omitted 138 *the* (F) that 155 *now-a-days* (F) omitted 162 *three-and-twenty* (F) 23. 169 *sir – Yorick's* (Eds) sir Yoricks 172 *Let me see* (F) omitted 174 *borne* (F) bore 181 *chamber* (Q1, F) table 195 *as thus* (Q1, F) omitted 203 *winter's* (F) waters 216 *have* (F) been 218 *Shards* (F) omitted 234 *treble* (F) double 236 *Deprived* (F) Depriuèd 248 *and* (F) omitted 256 *loved* (Q1, F) louèd 264 *thou* (F) omitted 272 *thus* (F) this 274 *disclosed* (F) disclosèd 285 *shortly* (F) thirtie

V, ii, 5 *Methought* (F) my thought 6 *bilboes* (F) bilbo 17 *unseal* (F) vnfold 27 *me* (F) now 29 *villainies* (Capell) villaines 43 *as's* (Eds) as sir 46 *the* (F) those 52 *Subscribed* (F) Subscribe 55 *know'st* (F) knowest 93 *Put* (F) omitted 98 *sultry* (F) sully for (F) or 100 *sultry* (F) soultery 101 *But* (F) omitted 105 *mine* (F) my 109 *feelingly* (Q4) sellingly (Q2) omitted (F) 138 *his* (Q '76) this (Q2) omitted (F) 146 *hangers* (F) hanger 152 *carriages* (F) carriage 155 *might* (F) omitted *Barbary* (F) Barbry (Q2) 158 *impawned, as* (Eds) omitted (Q2) impon'd as (F) 170 *an* (Capell) and 172 *redeliver* (F) deliuer *e'en* (F) omitted 176 *yours. He* (F) omitted 179 *comply* (F) omitted 180 *bevy* (F) breede 182 *yeasty* (F) histy 184 *fanned ... win-nowed* (Warburton) prophane ... trennowed 198 *this wager* (F) omitted 201 *But* (F) omitted 204 *gaingiving* (F) gamgiuing 209 *now* (F) omitted 222 *wronged* (F) wrongèd 227 *wronged* (F) wrongèd 229 (this line is present in F, omitted in Q2) 239 *keep* (F) omitted *till* (F) all 243 *Come on* (F) omitted 252 *bettered* (F) better 261 *union* (F) Vnice 275 *A touch, a touch* (F) omitted 281 *poisoned* (F) poysned 286 *but* (F) doe but 288 *afeard* (F) sure 292 *ho* (F) howe 299 *poisoned* (F) poysned 300 *Ho* (Q4) how (Q2, F) 302 *Hamlet. Hamlet* (F) Hamlet 305 *thy* (Q1, F) my 308 *poisoned* (F) poysned 314 *murd'rous* (F) omitted 315 *thy* (Q1, F) the *union* (Q1, F) Onixe 316 *served* (F) seruèd 332 *ha't* (Capell) hate 334 *live* (F) I leaue 338 (all quartos and folios give a s.d. here : Enter Osrick) 340 *the* (Eds) th' 347 s.d. *Dies* (Q1, F) omitted 366 *arrived* (Eds) arriuèd 368 *th'* (F) omitted 372 *forced* (F) for no 381 *on* (F) no 387 *proved* (Q1, F) proouèd 388 *rites* (F) right

SUPPLEMENTARY NOTES

I, i, 117 *As* Something is obviously wrong with the transition of thought. The conjecture that some preceding matter has been left out of the text is perhaps as good as any.

I, ii, 129 *sullied* Use of this emendation of the 'sallied' of the 1604–05 quarto instead of the widely accepted 'solid' of the 1623 folio is strongly recommended by : (1) the implications of the interestingly corrupt 'too much grieu'd and sallied flesh' of the 1603 quarto, into which the intrusive participle 'grieu'd' cannot be thought to have come at the call of an original 'solid' standing in the place of 'sallied'; (2) the example of the 'sallies' in a later passage of the 1604–05 quarto (II, i, 39), which in its context is most certainly to be taken as 'sullies' and which in the folio appears as 'sulleyes.'

I, iv, 37 *Doth ... doubt* This difficult and often altered line is here printed without emendation. In the famous crux of which it is a key part the intent of what Hamlet is saying had perhaps best be taken as a close rewording of what he has just been saying ; he may be taken to say that the dram of evil imparts a doubtful quality to all the noble human substance, to his (its) own scandal, i.e. to the detriment of the nobility itself because of the general censure that he has mentioned before in developing at involved length what he offers here with the emphasis of brevity.

III, iv, 162 *all sense doth eat* absorbs and lives upon all human sense, not only that made up of the bodily faculties but also the contrasting 'inward' sense made up of the faculties of the mind and soul – all sense, whether low or high and whether bad or good in use (looking forward to completion of the image of custom as a monster of double form, part devil and part angel ; see the *Oxford English Dictionary* under 'Sense,' I, 3 and 7). The crux of which these words make a part has also produced frequent emendation. See the note following.

III, iv, 163 *Of habits devil* being a devil in, or in respect of, habits (with a play on 'habits,' as meaning both settled practices and garments, which by looking forward to 'actions fair and good' and to 'frock or livery' is subtly involved in the opposition and monstrous combination within the passage of devil and angel, and which contributes to an essential poetic image that tends to be destroyed by a finding of need to emend the phrase, especially when 'devil' is changed to 'evil'; see the *Oxford English Dictionary* under 'Of,' XI, 37, for a showing of the use of the preposition in the sense here given, as in the example, dated 1535, 'he y^t is a blabbe of his tonge').

III, iv, 170 *And ... out* This line is usually taken to suffer from an omission after 'either' of some such word as 'master,' 'curb,' or 'quell.'

IV, i, 40 *And ... done* It would seem that after this fragmentary line there is an omission. Capell's insertion of 'So, haply, slander,' a purely conjectural completion of the line, has often been accepted as providing desired clarification of thought.

THE HISTORY OF TROILUS AND CRESSIDA

INTRODUCTION

Troilus and Cressida remains an enigma. Complications surrounded its first publication ; our only clues to its first performance are a puzzle ; the customary dramatic categories will neither explain nor include it ; and its fascination for the intellect cannot conceal its defects as art.

On February 7, 1603, there was entered in the Stationers' Register for copyright "The booke of Troilus and Cresseda as yt is acted by my lord Chamberlens men." There is a second entry in 1609 for different publishers, whose quarto edition shortly appeared under the title "The Historie of Troylus and Cresseida. As it was acted by the Kings Maiesties seruants at the Globe. Written by William Shakespeare." But the same text was immediately reissued with the original title page cut away and two new leaves substituted. The first bore a different title : "The Famous Historie of Troylus and Cresseid. Excellently expressing the beginning of their loues, with the conceited wooing of Pandarus Prince of Licia. Written by William Shakespeare." The second leaf contained the preface, "A Never Writer, to an Ever Reader. News," which heads the present edition. In conjunction with the new title, this preface looks like an attempt to urge as a selling point that the play had never been "clapper-clawed with the palms of the vulgar" – that is, had never been performed in the public theatre. The subsequent sentences also imply that the play, having displeased the witless, is now being offered to its proper patrons, the witty.

Still further complications ensued when the first folio was being prepared. Three pages of the play were actually printed for inclusion among the tragedies after *Romeo and Juliet*. Then, presumably because of copyright difficulties, these were withdrawn and *Timon of Athens* was substituted. Finally the play was printed without pagination, too late for inclusion in the preliminary list of plays, and placed between the histories and the tragedies in the complete folio.

The facts just related provide our best clues to the date and performance of the play. Most critics date it about 1602 on the basis of style and allusions in the text, although dissenters have placed it in the late 1590's. One may perhaps conjecture that, shortly before February 7, 1603, it was performed by Shakespeare's company, then the Lord Chamberlain's Men, but for a special audience rather than before the "vulgar" in the Globe Theatre. The character of the play suggests performance before one of the Inns of Court, where wit might be found, if anywhere. It was not unusual for plays to be performed before special audiences at the time, but it must be conceded that it was quite unusual for plays to be especially written for such performances.

Hence we are dealing here not with an established fact, as is sometimes assumed, but with a hypothesis only, although it comes as near as any to explaining the peculiar characteristics of *Troilus and Cressida* : the play is a unique combination of learned subject matter, all-inclusive satire, and something close to smut ; and it is neither comedy nor tragedy – nor, in fact, well-constructed drama. A subject with the most respectable literary antecedents has been treated disrespectfully enough to appeal to the sophisticated and cynical.

Of the two plot-threads of the play, the story of Troilus and Cressida is drawn from Chaucer's *Troilus and Criseyde*. In the background, though little used in the play, lurks Robert Henryson's *Testament of Cresseid*, a sequel in which Cresseid becomes a leper and a beggar. For the military episodes Shakespeare drew upon Caxton's *Recuyell of the Historyes of Troye*, upon Homer in Chapman's translation, and, for such details as the romantic motive of Hector's challenge, upon his own familiarity with tales of chivalry. But the knightly trappings of the Trojan War are thoroughly in accord with the medieval versions of the Troy story that lay behind all his sources but Homer. The subject was dramatically timely. In 1599 Dekker and Chettle had written a play on Troilus and Cressida for the Admiral's Men, a rival company ; and Chapman's *Sir Giles Goosecap*, a comedy contemporary with Shakespeare's play, adapted some of the story elements to English characters in an English setting. Shakespeare, too, may have been trying to give the story a novel treatment, partly by his dissection of the moral issues involved in the war. For this ethical analysis he may have found precedent in Robert Greene's *Euphues His Censure to Philautus* (1587).

Either the classical subject matter or a learned audience may account for the style of the play. Passages in *Troilus and Cressida* come closer than anything else in Shakespeare to the epic style that Milton developed, on the precedent of Latin epic, for *Paradise Lost*. This is true not only of the Latinate diction but also of the figurative language, extreme even by Elizabethan standards and particularly prone to such devices as personification, hyperbole, or substituting an abstraction for a plural noun :

> But let the ruffian Boreas once enrage
> The gentle Thetis, and anon behold
> The strong-ribbed bark through liquid mountains cut.
>
> (I, iii, 38–40)

> The specialty of rule hath been neglected. (I, iii, 78)

Either the audience or Shakespeare's own preoccupation with philosophic ideas must account for the long passages in the two council scenes that make the play almost a summary of Shakespeare's cosmology and ethics. These will be discussed below.

If Shakespeare finds a grand style appropriate to his re-telling of a great love story and the greatest of all war stories, his treatment nevertheless results in a total deflation of both romance and glory. Troilus is an estimable young man, but he is an erotic gourmet nonetheless:

> I am giddy; expectation whirls me round.
> Th' imaginary relish is so sweet
> That it enchants my sense. What will it be
> When that the wat'ry palates taste indeed
> Love's thrice-repurèd nectar? Death, I fear me,
> Sounding destruction, or some joy too fine,
> Too subtle, potent, tuned too sharp in sweetness
> For the capacity of my ruder powers. (III, ii, 16–23)

This is human enough, but it is not romantic love. As to Cressida, if we have any doubts after her exchange of wit with Pandarus at the end of the second scene, they are immediately dispelled by her own words. She is a practiced "daughter of the game," as Ulysses later calls her. She sums herself up:

> Ah, poor our sex! this fault in us I find,
> The error of our eye directs our mind.
> What error leads must err. O, then conclude
> Minds swayed by eyes are full of turpitude.
> (V, ii, 105–08)

When Troilus discovers his mistake in supposing that the woman he has seduced is proof against other men, he is pathetic in his grief, but he is not tragic.

The Trojan War is even more thoroughly deflated. Thersites sums the matter up in his scurrilous way: "All the argument is a whore and a cuckold, a good quarrel to draw emulous factions and bleed to death upon" (II, iii, 68–70). Helen's own character and the atmosphere that surrounds her are perfectly suggested by Pandarus' long scene with her, and particularly by the tone of the song that concludes it (III, i). Diomedes gets down to cases:

> For every false drop in her bawdy veins
> A Grecian's life hath sunk; for every scruple
> Of her contaminated carrion weight
> A Troyan hath been slain. Since she could speak,
> She hath not given so many good words breath
> As for her Greeks and Troyans suff'red death.
> (IV, i, 69–74)

The Greeks, therefore, are trying to recover what is not worth fighting for; but they quarrel like spoiled and selfish children, and Achilles, their hero, is a vainglorious muscleman. He pouts in his tent with his favorite and, in defiance of Homer's account, has his Myrmidons ambush Hector, who is unarmed. He is, in short, a bully and a coward. The Trojans are very different but equally flawed. They know their cause is wrong. Hector proves all too clearly that

> these moral laws
> Of nature and of nations speak aloud
> To have her [Helen] back returned. (II, ii, 184–86)

He knows that Troilus, in arguing for keeping her, is driven by passion as against judgment:

> Or is your blood
> So madly hot that no discourse of reason,
> Nor fear of bad success in a bad cause,
> Can qualify the same? (II, ii, 115–18)

But, after enunciating the soundest moral principles, he reverses himself and concludes:

> Hector's opinion
> Is this in way of truth; yet ne'ertheless,
> My spritely brethren, I propend to you
> In resolution to keep Helen still;
> For 'tis a cause that hath no mean dependence
> Upon our joint and several dignities.
> (II, ii, 188–93)

As a fighter, he is as reckless in his chivalry as Achilles is cowardly. He is playing foolishly in a foolish war. The rational norm of bravery is not in either man. In this play (though nowhere else in Shakespeare) war is what it is in much modern fiction – a bloody mess from which no one emerges with glory or even integrity.

The intention of the play is therefore ambiguous. Apparently it puzzled Shakespeare's contemporaries. The second entry in the Stationers' Register and the quarto title pages call it a history – that is, a dramatic narrative of historical events which is not definitely tragedy. The folio editors intended to place it among the tragedies and called it "The Tragedie of Troylus and Cressida." Elizabethan literary theory restricted comedy to non-historical subject matter. But the play is simply not tragedy, even though it ends with the death of Troilus' illusions and of Hector himself. Its subject matter, unlike its style, is never heroic, and in Thersites it descends to obscene raillery. The war plot has only the loosest narrative organization, and the two great council scenes have no dramatic function at all proportionate to the pains that Shakespeare lavished upon them. Perhaps the best hypothesis is that he tried to adapt the well-known story to the satiric mood then in fashion in the theatre and to make it especially palatable to a learned and sophisticated audience by seasoning it with large, unassimilated chunks of philosophy and a liberal sprinkling of innuendo or even outright scurrility. But, if so, his attempt to turn what was for his audience a great historical theme into comical satire was unique in the Elizabethan theatre.

What has the play to offer the modern reader? The answer, despite what precedes, is that it is Shakespeare's own key to his greatest plays and that it is a powerful, if unconventional, mirror of human nature.

Shakespeare, like most of his contemporaries, believed that God the Creator had imposed upon all nature a universal and hierarchical order, in accordance with which all things performed their part in achieving His ultimate purposes. This order resulted from the obedience of all creation to laws that governed not only the physical universe but also social and political institutions and man the individual. As a rational being and the highest of created things on earth, man shared with God and the angels the possession of free will. He was free to live rationally – that is, to obey the commands of God and conform to the laws of nature. But he was also free to violate "the moral laws of nature and of nations" and, by so doing, to bring suffering upon himself and disruption to the social and even cosmic order of which he was a part. This view is present throughout the plays; it is fundamental to the great tragedies. Shakespeare's concept of universal order is stated fully and explicitly in Ulysses' great speech to the Greek council (I, iii, 75–137). His explanation of human disorder is summarized, more succinctly, in Hector's parallel argument to the Trojan council in the next act (II, ii, 163–93). The decision of the council and of Hector himself is, moreover, an example of "those raging appetites" that overcome the reason and will, and lead men to corrupt the law of nature. And the play is filled with short passages that echo or clarify the same system of ideas, as the psychology and ethics of love and war are analyzed explicitly and fully. In the tragedies Shakespeare presents in action what here he explains in theoretical terms. Always, as in *Othello* and *Macbeth*, we see man's will "benumbed" in sin; in *Macbeth* and *King Lear* we also see "what discord follows" the destruction of "degree," and in *King Lear* the "appetite" that disrupts nature

> Must make perforce an universal prey
> And last eat up himself.   (I, iii, 123–24)

So evil becomes self-destructive, and order is restored to a suffering world. In short, the lover of Shakespeare must know *Troilus and Cressida* thoroughly, or he does not know Shakespeare at all.

But *Troilus and Cressida* itself portrays a very different world from that of tragedy, the world of all-too-human nature. The satire is sharp, but it is justified. The modern reader of the play does not need to be told that what passes for love is often lust, and that what motivates much patriotism has nothing to do with love of country. Modern literature has made these points in wearisome detail. But Shakespeare has intensified and clarified even this aspect of human nature with all the matchless resources of his imagination. His eye has roved from the councils of the mighty to the backbiting of their hangers-on. Modern fiction has done much better, moreover, at giving us Cres-

sidas, or a Pandarus and Thersites, than at showing us a Hector betraying his intellect under pressure of the moment or a Ulysses expending his wisdom on an intrigue to end a petty broil. And Shakespeare has summarized these insights in unforgettable lines of verse. *Troilus and Cressida* is certainly not his greatest play, but it is in some respects his most modern. We may not like its people, but they are with us everywhere. Shakespeare often tells us what we can be or should be. Here he tells us what, unfortunately, we all too often are.

Stanford University   VIRGIL K. WHITAKER

NOTE ON THE TEXT

The present edition is based on the quarto of 1609, which is believed to have been printed from a private transcript of Shakespeare's own draft made by himself or a scribe. The folio text was printed from the quarto, perhaps collated with the original draft after it had been prepared for performance. A few brief passages supplied by the folio have been included in square brackets, and a number of readings from the folio have been adopted at points where the text of the quarto seems corrupt or obviously inferior. These, and the limited number of emendations, are listed in the Appendix. The stage directions are those of the quarto, with bracketed additions and amplifications suggested usually by the folio. Both the quarto and folio are without act–scene divisions, and those of the later editors have been supplied marginally.

THE HISTORY OF TROILUS AND CRESSIDA

A NEVER WRITER, TO AN EVER READER. NEWS.

Eternal reader, you have here a new play, never staled with the stage, never clapper-clawed with the palms of the vulgar, and yet passing full of the palm comical; for it is a birth of your brain that never undertook anything comical vainly. And were but the vain names of comedies changed for the titles of commodities, or of plays for pleas, you should see all those grand censors, that now style them such vanities, flock to them for the main grace of their gravities, especially this author's comedies, that are so framed to the life that they serve for the most common commentaries of all the actions of our lives, showing such a dexterity and power of wit that the most displeased with plays are pleased with his comedies. And all such dull and heavy-witted worldlings as were never capable of the wit of a comedy, coming by report of them to his representations, have found that wit there that they never found in themselves and have parted better witted than they came, feeling an edge of wit set upon them more than ever they dreamed they had brain to grind it on. So much and such savored salt of wit is in his comedies that they seem, for their height of pleasure, to be born in that sea that brought forth Venus. Amongst all there is none more witty than this: and had I time I would comment upon it, though I know it needs not, for so much as will make you think your testern well bestowed, but for so much worth as even poor I know to be stuffed in it. It deserves such a labor as well as the best comedy in Terence or Plautus. And believe this, that when he is gone and his comedies out of sale, you will scramble for them and set up a new English Inquisition. Take this for a warning, and at the peril of your pleasure's loss, and judgment's, refuse not, nor like this the less for not being sullied with the smoky breath of the multitude; but thank fortune for the 'scape it hath made amongst you, since by the grand possessors' wills I believe you should have prayed for them rather than been prayed. And so I leave all such to be prayed for, for the state of their wits' healths, that will not praise it. Vale.

*

[NAMES OF THE ACTORS

Priam, King of Troy	Ulysses
Hector	Nestor
Troilus	Diomedes } Greek commanders
Paris } his sons	Patroclus
Deiphobus	Thersites, a deformed and scurrilous Greek
Helenus	Alexander, servant to Cressida
Margarelon, a bastard son of Priam	Servant to Troilus
Aeneas	Servant to Paris
Antenor } Trojan commanders	Servant to Diomedes
Calchas, a Trojan priest, taking part with the Greeks	Helen, wife to Menelaus
Pandarus, uncle to Cressida	Andromache, wife to Hector
Agamemnon, the Greek general	Cassandra, daughter to Priam; a prophetess
Menelaus, his brother	Cressida, daughter to Calchas
Achilles	Trojan and Greek Soldiers and Attendants
Ajax } Greek commanders	

Scene: *Troy, and the Greek Camp before it*]

*

[THE PROLOGUE

Pro. In Troy there lies the scene. From isles of Greece
2 The princes orgulous, their high blood chafed,
Have to the port of Athens sent their ships,
Fraught with the ministers and instruments
Of cruel war. Sixty and nine, that wore
Their crownets regal, from th' Athenian bay
7 Put forth toward Phrygia; and their vow is made
8 To ransack Troy, within whose strong immures
The ravished Helen, Menelaus' queen,

With wanton Paris sleeps; and that's the quarrel.
To Tenedos they come,
And the deep-drawing barks do there disgorge
Their warlike fraughtage. Now on Dardan plains   13

Preface 21 *Venus* (the Latin goddess was identified with the Greek Aphrodite, who sprang from the sea foam) 24 *testern* sixpence 33 *grand possessors* (the actor-sharers of the King's Men, who apparently were trying to prevent the publication of their plays)
Pro. 2 *orgulous* proud 7 *Phrygia* western Asia Minor 8 *immures* walls 13 *fraughtage* cargo, i.e. warriors; *Dardan* Trojan, Dardanus being a mythical ancestor

The fresh and yet unbruisèd Greeks do pitch
Their brave pavilions. Priam's six-gated city,
16 Dardan, and Timbria, Helias, Chetas, Troien,
And Antenonidus, with massy staples
18 And corresponsive and fulfilling bolts,
19 Sperr up the sons of Troy.
Now expectation, tickling skittish spirits,
On one and other side, Troyan and Greek,
Sets all on hazard. And hither am I come,
23 A prologue armed, but not in confidence
24 Of author's pen or actor's voice, but suited
25 In like conditions as our argument,
To tell you, fair beholders, that our play
27 Leaps o'er the vaunt and firstlings of those broils,
Beginning in the middle, starting thence away
To what may be digested in a play.
Like or find fault ; do as your pleasures are :
Now good or bad, 'tis but the chance of war.]

I, i   *Enter Pandarus and Troilus.*

TROILUS
1   Call here my varlet, I'll unarm again.
Why should I war without the walls of Troy
That find such cruel battle here within ?
Each Troyan that is master of his heart,
Let him to field ; Troilus, alas, hath none.
PANDARUS
6   Will this gear ne'er be mended ?
TROILUS
7   The Greeks are strong, and skillful to their strength,
Fierce to their skill, and to their fierceness valiant ;
But I am weaker than a woman's tear,
10   Tamer than sleep, fonder than ignorance,
Less valiant than the virgin in the night,
And skilless as unpractised infancy.
PANDARUS Well, I have told you enough of this. For my
part, I'll not meddle nor make no farther. He that will
have a cake out of the wheat must tarry the grinding.
TROILUS Have I not tarried ?
PANDARUS Ay, the grinding ; but you must tarry the
17   bolting.
TROILUS Have I not tarried ?
PANDARUS Ay, the bolting ; but you must tarry the
leavening.
TROILUS Still have I tarried.
PANDARUS Ay, to the leavening ; but here's yet in the
word 'hereafter' the kneading, the making of the cake,
the heating of the oven, and the baking ; nay, you must
stay the cooling too, or you may chance to burn your lips.
TROILUS
Patience herself, what goddess e'er she be,
26   Doth lesser blench at suff'rance than I do.

At Priam's royal table do I sit,
And when fair Cressid comes into my thoughts –
So, traitor, then she comes when she is thence.   29
PANDARUS Well, she looked yesternight fairer than ever
I saw her look, or any woman else.
TROILUS
I was about to tell thee, when my heart,
As wedgèd with a sigh, would rive in twain,   33
Lest Hector or my father should perceive me :
I have, as when the sun doth light a-scorn,   35
Buried this sigh in wrinkle of a smile ;
But sorrow, that is couched in seeming gladness,
Is like that mirth fate turns to sudden sadness.
PANDARUS An her hair were not somewhat darker than   39
Helen's – well, go to – there were no more comparison
between the women : but, for my part, she is my kins-
woman ; I would not, as they term it, praise her, but I
would somebody had heard her talk yesterday, as I did.
I will not dispraise your sister Cassandra's wit, but –
TROILUS
O Pandarus ! I tell thee, Pandarus –
When I do tell thee, there my hopes lie drowned,
Reply not in how many fathoms deep
They lie indrenched. I tell thee I am mad
In Cressid's love ; thou answer'st she is fair ;
Pour'st in the open ulcer of my heart
Her eyes, her hair, her cheek, her gait, her voice ;
Handlest in thy discourse, O, that her hand,   52
In whose comparison all whites are ink,
Writing their own reproach ; to whose soft seizure
The cygnet's down is harsh, and spirit of sense   55
Hard as the palm of ploughman. This thou tell'st me,
As true thou tell'st me, when I say I love her ;
But, saying thus, instead of oil and balm,
Thou lay'st in every gash that love hath given me
The knife that made it.
PANDARUS I speak no more than truth.
TROILUS Thou dost not speak so much.
PANDARUS Faith, I'll not meddle in it. Let her be as she
is. If she be fair, 'tis the better for her ; an she be not, she
has the mends in her own hands.   65
TROILUS Good Pandarus, how now, Pandarus ?
PANDARUS I have had my labor for my travail ; ill-
thought-on of her, and ill-thought-on of you ; gone be-
tween and between, but small thanks for my labor.
TROILUS What, art thou angry, Pandarus ? what, with
me ?
PANDARUS Because she's kin to me, therefore she's not so
fair as Helen. An she were not kin to me, she would be as   72
fair on Friday as Helen is on Sunday. But what care I ?
I care not an she were a blackamoor ; 'tis all one to me.   74
TROILUS Say I she is not fair ?
PANDARUS I do not care whether you do or no. She's a
fool to stay behind her father. Let her to the Greeks, and   77
so I'll tell her the next time I see her. For my part, I'll
meddle nor make no more i' th' matter.
TROILUS Pandarus –
PANDARUS Not I.
TROILUS Sweet Pandarus –
PANDARUS Pray you, speak no more to me. I will leave all
as I found it, and there an end.   *Exit. Sound alarum.*   84
TROILUS
Peace, you ungracious clamors ! Peace, rude sounds !
Fools on both sides ! Helen must needs be fair,

16–17 *Dardan . . . Antenonidus* (i.e. Antenorides) names of the gates
18 *fulfilling* filling full, i.e. tightly   19 *Sperr* shut   23 *armed* in armor
24 *suited* dressed   25 *argument* theme, subject   27 *vaunt* first part
I, i Before the palace of Priam in Troy   1 *varlet* servant   6 *gear* business
7 *to* in addition to   10 *fonder* more foolish   17 *bolting* sifting   26 *blench*
flinch   29 *traitor* (a rebuke for implying that she may ever be absent)
33 *rive* split   35 *a-scorn* grudgingly (?)   39 *An* if   52 *that her hand* that
hand of hers   55 *cygnet's* young swan's ; *spirit* a very thin bodily substance that was believed to transmit sense impressions through the nerves
65 *mends* remedies, i.e. cosmetics   72–73 *as fair . . . Sunday* as fair in
ordinary clothes as Helen in her Sunday best   74 *blackamoor* Negro
77 *father* Calchas, a seer who anticipated the Trojan defeat and deserted
to the Greeks   84 s.d. *alarum* signal to arms

When with your blood you daily paint her thus.
88 I cannot fight upon this argument;
It is too starved a subject for my sword.
But Pandarus – O gods, how do you plague me!
I cannot come to Cressid but by Pandar;
92 And he's as tetchy to be wooed to woo
As she is stubborn, chaste, against all suit.
94 Tell me, Apollo, for thy Daphne's love,
What Cressid is, what Pandar, and what we.
Her bed is India; there she lies, a pearl.
97 Between our Ilium and where she resides
Let it be called the wild and wand'ring flood,
Ourself the merchant, and this sailing Pandar
Our doubtful hope, our convoy and our bark.
     Alarum. Enter Aeneas.

AENEAS
How now, Prince Troilus, wherefore not afield?
TROILUS
Because not there. This woman's answer sorts,
For womanish it is to be from thence.
What news, Aeneas, from the field to-day?
AENEAS
That Paris is returnèd home, and hurt.
TROILUS
By whom, Aeneas?
AENEAS   Troilus, by Menelaus.
TROILUS
Let Paris bleed; 'tis but a scar to scorn.
108 Paris is gored with Menelaus' horn.
     Alarum.
AENEAS
Hark what good sport is out of town to-day!
TROILUS
Better at home, if 'would I might' were 'may.'
But to the sport abroad. Are you bound thither?
AENEAS
In all swift haste.
TROILUS   Come, go we then together.   *Exeunt.*

         *

I, ii   *Enter Cressida and [Alexander,] her man.*
CRESSIDA
Who were those went by?
MAN   Queen Hecuba and Helen.
CRESSIDA
And whither go they?
MAN   Up to the eastern tower,
Whose height commands as subject all the vale,
To see the battle. Hector, whose patience
Is as a virtue fixed, to-day was moved.
He chid Andromache, and struck his armorer,
And, like as there were husbandry in war,
7
8 Before the sun rose he was harnessed light,
And to the field goes he, where every flower
Did, as a prophet, weep what it foresaw
In Hector's wrath.
CRESSIDA   What was his cause of anger?
MAN
The noise goes, this: there is among the Greeks
A lord of Troyan blood, nephew to Hector;
They call him Ajax.
CRESSIDA   Good; and what of him?

MAN
They say he is a very man per se
And stands alone.
CRESSIDA So do all men unless they are drunk, sick, or
have no legs.
MAN This man, lady, hath robbed many beasts of their particular additions: he is as valiant as the lion, churlish as 20
the bear, slow as the elephant; a man into whom nature
hath so crowded humors that his valor is crushed into 22
folly, his folly sauced with discretion. There is no man
hath a virtue that he hath not a glimpse of, nor any man 24
an attaint but he carries some stain of it. He is melan- 25
choly without cause and merry against the hair. He hath 26
the joints of everything, but everything so out of joint
that he is a gouty Briareus, many hands and no use, or 28
purblind Argus, all eyes and no sight. 29
CRESSIDA But how should this man that makes me smile
make Hector angry?
MAN They say he yesterday coped Hector in the battle 32
and struck him down, the disdain and shame whereof
hath ever since kept Hector fasting and waking.
     [Enter Pandarus.]
CRESSIDA Who comes here?
MAN Madam, your uncle Pandarus.
CRESSIDA Hector's a gallant man.
MAN As may be in the world, lady.
PANDARUS What's that? What's that?
CRESSIDA Good morrow, uncle Pandarus.
PANDARUS Good morrow, cousin Cressid. What do you 41
talk of? Good morrow, Alexander. How do you,
cousin? When were you at Ilium?
CRESSIDA This morning, uncle.
PANDARUS What were you talking of when I came? Was
Hector armed and gone ere ye came to Ilium? Helen
was not up, was she?
CRESSIDA Hector was gone, but Helen was not up.
PANDARUS E'en so, Hector was stirring early.
CRESSIDA That were we talking of, and of his anger.
PANDARUS Was he angry?
CRESSIDA So he says here. 52
PANDARUS True, he was so. I know the cause too. He'll
lay about him to-day, I can tell them that; and there's
Troilus will not come far behind him. Let them take
heed of Troilus, I can tell them that too.
CRESSIDA What, is he angry too?
PANDARUS Who, Troilus? Troilus is the better man of
the two.
CRESSIDA O Jupiter! there's no comparison.
PANDARUS What, not between Troilus and Hector? Do
you know a man if you see him?
CRESSIDA Ay, if I ever saw him before and knew him.
PANDARUS Well, I say Troilus is Troilus.
CRESSIDA Then you say as I say, for I am sure he is not
Hector.

88 *argument* subject of contention   92 *tetchy* fretful   94 *Daphne* a nymph
beloved of Apollo, who was changed into a bay tree to escape his pursuit
97 *Ilium* here, Priam's palace   108 *horn* (symbol of a cuckold, a man whose
wife had been unfaithful. Paris had stolen Helen from Menelaus.)
I, ii Before the house of Cressida   7 *husbandry* thrift   8 *harnessed* in
armor   20 *additions* indications of rank or distinction added to a man's
name   22 *humors* bodily fluids the excess of which caused emotional disorders   24 *glimpse* spark   25 *attaint* stain on honor   26 *hair* natural
tendency   28 *Briareus* a hundred-handed giant   29 *Argus* a herdsman
who had eyes all over his body   32 *coped* came to blows with   41 *cousin*
i.e. niece   52 *he* i.e. Alexander

67 PANDARUS No, nor Hector is not Troilus in some degrees.

CRESSIDA 'Tis just to each of them ; he is himself.

69 PANDARUS Himself ? Alas, poor Troilus, I would he were.

CRESSIDA So he is.

71 PANDARUS Condition, I had gone barefoot to India.

CRESSIDA He is not Hector.

PANDARUS Himself ? no, he's not himself. Would 'a were himself! Well, the gods are above ; time must friend or end. Well, Troilus, well, I would my heart were in her body. No, Hector is not a better man than Troilus.

CRESSIDA Excuse me.

PANDARUS He is elder.

CRESSIDA Pardon me, pardon me.

80 PANDARUS Th' other's not come to't ; you shall tell me another tale when th' other's come to't. Hector shall not

82 have his wit this year.

CRESSIDA He shall not need it if he have his own.

PANDARUS Nor his qualities.

CRESSIDA No matter.

PANDARUS Nor his beauty.

CRESSIDA 'Twould not become him ; his own 's better.

PANDARUS You have no judgment, niece. Helen herself

89 swore th' other day that Troilus, for a brown favor – for so 'tis, I must confess, not brown neither –

CRESSIDA No, but brown.

PANDARUS Faith, to say truth, brown and not brown.

CRESSIDA To say the truth, true and not true.

PANDARUS She praised his complexion above Paris.

CRESSIDA Why, Paris hath color enough.

PANDARUS So he has.

CRESSIDA Then Troilus should have too much. If she praised him above, his complexion is higher than his. He having color enough, and the other higher, is too flaming a praise for a good complexion. I had as lief Helen's golden tongue had commended Troilus for a copper nose.

PANDARUS I swear to you, I think Helen loves him better than Paris.

104 CRESSIDA Then she's a merry Greek indeed.

PANDARUS Nay, I am sure she does. She came to him th'

106 other day into the compassed window, and, you know, he has not past three or four hairs on his chin –

CRESSIDA Indeed, a tapster's arithmetic may soon bring his particulars therein to a total.

PANDARUS Why, he is very young ; and yet will he, within three pound, lift as much as his brother Hector.

112 CRESSIDA Is he so young a man, and so old a lifter ?

PANDARUS But to prove to you that Helen loves him, she came and puts me her white hand to his cloven chin –

CRESSIDA Juno have mercy ! how came it cloven ?

PANDARUS Why, you know 'tis dimpled. I think his smiling becomes him better than any man in all Phrygia.

CRESSIDA O, he smiles valiantly.

PANDARUS Does he not ?

CRESSIDA O, yes, an 'twere a cloud in autumn.

PANDARUS Why, go to then. But to prove to you that Helen loves Troilus –

CRESSIDA Troilus will stand to the proof, if you'll prove it so.

PANDARUS Troilus ? Why, he esteems her no more than I esteem an addle egg. 125

CRESSIDA If you love an addle egg as well as you love an idle head, you would eat chickens i' th' shell.

PANDARUS I cannot choose but laugh to think how she tickled his chin. Indeed, she has a marvell's white hand, I must needs confess.

CRESSIDA Without the rack. 131

PANDARUS And she takes upon her to spy a white hair on his chin.

CRESSIDA Alas poor chin, many a wart is richer.

PANDARUS But there was such laughing : Queen Hecuba laughed that her eyes ran o'er.

CRESSIDA With millstones. 137

PANDARUS And Cassandra laughed.

CRESSIDA But there was a more temperate fire under the pot of her eyes. Did her eyes run o'er too ?

PANDARUS And Hector laughed.

CRESSIDA At what was all this laughing ?

PANDARUS Marry, at the white hair that Helen spied on Troilus' chin.

CRESSIDA An't had been a green hair, I should have laughed too.

PANDARUS They laughed not so much at the hair as at his pretty answer.

CRESSIDA What was his answer ?

PANDARUS Quoth she, 'Here's but two-and-fifty hairs 150 on your chin, and one of them is white.'

CRESSIDA This is her question.

PANDARUS That's true ; make no question of that. 'Two-and-fifty hairs,' quoth he, 'and one white. That white hair is my father, and all the rest are his sons.' 'Jupiter !' quoth she, 'which of these hairs is Paris, my husband ?' 'The forked one,' quoth he ; 'pluck't out, and give it 157 him.' But there was such laughing, and Helen so blushed, and Paris so chafed, and all the rest so laughed, that it passed.

CRESSIDA So let it now, for it has been a great while going by.

PANDARUS Well, cousin, I told you a thing yesterday ; think on't.

CRESSIDA So I do.

PANDARUS I'll be sworn 'tis true ; he will weep you, an 164 'twere a man born in April. 165

Sound a retreat.

CRESSIDA And I'll spring up in his tears, an 'twere a nettle against May.

PANDARUS Hark, they are coming from the field. Shall we stand up here and see them as they pass toward Ilium ? Good niece, do ; sweet niece, Cressida.

CRESSIDA At your pleasure.

PANDARUS Here, here, here's an excellent place ; here we may see most bravely. I'll tell you them all by their 173 names as they pass by, but mark Troilus above the rest.

Enter Aeneas [passing across the stage].

CRESSIDA Speak not so loud.

PANDARUS That's Aeneas. Is not that a brave man ? He's one of the flowers of Troy, I can tell you. But mark Troilus ; you shall see anon.

Enter Antenor [passing across the stage].

---

67 *in some degrees* by some distance   69 *I would he were* i.e. himself, and not in love   71 *Condition . . . India* even though it meant my going barefoot to India   80 *come to't* come to manhood   82 *wit* intelligence   89 *favor* complexion   104 *a merry Greek* i.e. light of heart and morals   106 *compassed* bay   112 *lifter* thief   125 *addle* rotten, spoiled   131 *rack* torture   137 *millstones* i.e. obviously not tears   157 *forked* (like a cuckold's horns)   164 *an* as if   165–67 *April . . . May* i.e. April showers bring May flowers   173 *bravely* excellently

CRESSIDA Who's that?

PANDARUS That's Antenor. He has a shrewd wit, I can tell you; and he's a man good enough: he's one o' th' sound-
182 est judgments in Troy whosoever, and a proper man of person. When comes Troilus? I'll show you Troilus anon. If he see me, you shall see him nod at me.

185 CRESSIDA Will he give you the nod?

PANDARUS You shall see.

187 CRESSIDA If he do, the rich shall have more.

Enter Hector [passing across the stage].

PANDARUS That's Hector, that, that, look you, that; there's a fellow! Go thy way, Hector! There's a brave man, niece. O brave Hector! Look how he looks; there's a countenance! Is't not a brave man?

CRESSIDA O, a brave man!

PANDARUS Is 'a not? It does a man's heart good. Look you what hacks are on his helmet. Look you yonder, do you see? Look you there. There's no jesting; there's
196 laying on, take't off who will, as they say. There be hacks!

CRESSIDA Be those with swords?

PANDARUS Swords, anything; he cares not; an the devil come to him, it's all one. By God's lid, it does one's heart good.

Enter Paris [passing across the stage].

Yonder comes Paris, yonder comes Paris. Look ye
202 yonder, niece. Is't not a gallant man too, is't not? Why, this is brave now. Who said he came hurt home to-day? He's not hurt. Why, this will do Helen's heart good now, ha! Would I could see Troilus now. You shall see Troilus anon.

CRESSIDA Who's that?

Enter Helenus [passing across the stage].

PANDARUS That's Helenus. I marvel where Troilus is. That's Helenus. I think he went not forth to-day. That's Helenus.

210 CRESSIDA Can Helenus fight, uncle?

PANDARUS Helenus? No. Yes, he'll fight indifferent well. I marvel where Troilus is. Hark, do you not hear the people cry 'Troilus'? Helenus is a priest.

CRESSIDA What sneaking fellow comes yonder?

Enter Troilus [passing across the stage].

PANDARUS Where? Yonder? That's Deiphobus. 'Tis Troilus! There's a man, niece! Hem! Brave Troilus, the prince of chivalry!

CRESSIDA Peace, for shame, peace!

PANDARUS Mark him, note him. O brave Troilus! Look well upon him, niece. Look you how his sword is blood-ied, and his helm more hacked than Hector's; and how he looks, and how he goes. O admirable youth! he never saw three-and-twenty. Go thy way, Troilus, go thy
224 way! Had I a sister were a grace, or a daughter a god-dess, he should take his choice. O admirable man! Paris? Paris is dirt to him; and I warrant Helen, to change, would give an eye to boot.

[Enter Common Soldiers.]

CRESSIDA Here comes more.

PANDARUS Asses, fools, dolts; chaff and bran, chaff and bran; porridge after meat. I could live and die in the eyes of Troilus. Ne'er look, ne'er look. The eagles are gone; crows and daws, crows and daws. I had rather be such a man as Troilus than Agamemnon and all Greece.

CRESSIDA There is amongst the Greeks Achilles, a better man than Troilus.

PANDARUS Achilles? A drayman, a porter, a very camel.

CRESSIDA Well, well.

PANDARUS 'Well, well'? Why, have you any discretion, have you any eyes, do you know what a man is? Is not birth, beauty, good shape, discourse, manhood, learn-ing, gentleness, virtue, youth, liberality, and such like, the spice and salt that season a man?

CRESSIDA Ay, a minced man; and then to be baked with 243 no date in the pie, for then the man's date is out.

PANDARUS You are such a woman a man knows not at what ward you lie. 246

CRESSIDA Upon my back, to defend my belly; upon my wit, to defend my wiles; upon my secrecy, to defend mine honesty; my mask, to defend my beauty; and you, 249 to defend all these: and at all these wards I lie, at a thousand watches.

PANDARUS Say one of your watches. 252

CRESSIDA Nay, I'll watch you for that; and that's one of the chiefest of them too. If I cannot ward what I would not have hit, I can watch you for telling how I took the 255 blow; unless it swell past hiding, and then it's past watching.

PANDARUS You are such another!

Enter [Troilus'] Boy.

BOY Sir, my lord would instantly speak with you.

PANDARUS Where?

BOY At your own house. There he unarms him.

PANDARUS Good boy, tell him I come. *[Exit Boy.]* I doubt he be hurt. Fare ye well, good niece.

CRESSIDA Adieu, uncle.

PANDARUS I will be with you, niece, by and by.

CRESSIDA To bring, uncle? 265

PANDARUS Ay, a token from Troilus.

CRESSIDA By the same token, you are a bawd.

[Exit Pandarus.]

Words, vows, gifts, tears, and love's full sacrifice
He offers in another's enterprise;
But more in Troilus thousandfold I see
Than in the glass of Pandar's praise may be.
Yet hold I off: women are angels, wooing; 272
Things won are done, joy's soul lies in the doing.
That she beloved knows nought that knows not this:
Men prize the thing ungained more than it is; 275
That she was never yet, that ever knew
Love got so sweet as when desire did sue. 277
Therefore this maxim out of love I teach: 278
Achievement is command; ungained, beseech. 279
Then, though my heart's content firm love doth bear,
Nothing of that shall from mine eyes appear.

Exit.

*

182 *proper* good-looking   185 *nod* (quibble on 'noddy,' simpleton) 187 *the rich . . . more* the simple-minded will become simpler   196 *laying on* fighting; *take't off who will* i.e. regardless of circumstances ('take off' being a proverbial tag to 'lay on')   202 *gallant* (a general epithet of praise) 210 *Can Helenus fight* i.e. being a priest   224 *grace* subordinate and attendant goddess   243 *minced* simpering   246 *ward* posture of defense (fencing term)   249 *honesty* chastity   252 *watches* i.e. at night   255 *watch you* i.e. make sure that you do not tell (this passage fully establishes Cressida's moral level)   265 *bring* get even   272 *wooing* while being wooed   275 *it is* its value   277 *got* i.e. by men   278 *out of love* as taught by love   279 *Achievement . . . beseech* having achieved love, men command; when trying to gain it, they beseech

I, iii   *[Sennet.] Enter Agamemnon, Nestor, Ulysses,*
Diomedes, Menelaus, with others.

AGAMEMNON
    Princes,
    What grief hath set the jaundice on your cheeks ?
    The ample proposition that hope makes
    In all designs begun on earth below
    Fails in the promised largeness. Checks and disasters
    Grow in the veins of actions highest reared,
7   As knots, by the conflux of meeting sap,
    Infects the sound pine and diverts his grain
9   Tortive and errant from his course of growth.
    Nor, princes, is it matter new to us
11 That we come short of our suppose so far
    That after seven years' siege yet Troy walls stand ;
    Sith every action that hath gone before,
    Whereof we have record, trial did draw
15 Bias and thwart, not answering the aim
    And that unbodied figure of the thought
    That gave't surmisèd shape. Why then, you princes,
    Do you with cheeks abashed behold our works
    And call them shames, which are indeed nought else
    But the protractive trials of great Jove
    To find persistive constancy in men ?
    The fineness of which metal is not found
    In Fortune's love ; for then, the bold and coward,
24 The wise and fool, the artist and unread,
25 The hard and soft, seem all affined and kin.
    But, in the wind and tempest of her frown,
    Distinction, with a broad and powerful fan,
    Puffing at all, winnows the light away ;
    And what hath mass or matter by itself
30 Lies rich in virtue and unmingled.

NESTOR
    With due observance of thy godlike seat,
    Great Agamemnon, Nestor shall apply
    Thy latest words. In the reproof of chance
    Lies the true proof of men. The sea being smooth,
    How many shallow bauble boats dare sail
    Upon her patient breast, making their way
    With those of nobler bulk ?
38 But let the ruffian Boreas once enrage
39 The gentle Thetis, and anon behold
    The strong-ribbed bark through liquid mountains cut,
    Bounding between the two moist elements
42 Like Perseus' horse, where's then the saucy boat,
    Whose weak untimbered sides but even now
    Co-rivalled greatness ? Either to harbor fled,
45 Or made a toast for Neptune. Even so
    Doth valor's show and valor's worth divide
    In storms of fortune. For in her ray and brightness

The herd hath more annoyance by the breese   48
Than by the tiger ; but when the splitting wind
Makes flexible the knees of knotted oaks,
And flies fled under shade, why then the thing of courage,
As roused with rage, with rage doth sympathize,
And with an accent tuned in self-same key
Returns to chiding fortune.   54

ULYSSES   Agamemnon,
    Thou great commander, nerves and bone of Greece,   55
    Heart of our numbers, soul and only spirit,
    In whom the tempers and the minds of all
    Should be shut up, hear what Ulysses speaks.   58
    Besides th' applause and approbation
    The which, *[to Agamemnon]* most mighty for thy place
        and sway,
        [To Nestor]
    And thou most reverend for thy stretched-out life,
    I give to both your speeches, which were such
    As Agamemnon and the hand of Greece
    Should hold up high in brass ; and such again
    As venerable Nestor, hatched in silver,   65
    Should with a bond of air, strong as the axle-tree
    On which heaven rides, knit all the Greekish ears
    To his experienced tongue ; yet let it please both,
    Thou great, and wise, to hear Ulysses speak.

[AGAMEMNON
    Speak, Prince of Ithaca ; and be't of less expect
    That matter needless, of importless burden,
    Divide thy lips than we are confident,
    When rank Thersites opes his mastic jaws,   73
    We shall hear music, wit, and oracle.]

ULYSSES
    Troy, yet upon his basis, had been down,
    And the great Hector's sword had lacked a master,
    But for these instances.
    The specialty of rule hath been neglected ;   78
    And look, how many Grecian tents do stand
    Hollow upon this plain, so many hollow factions.
    When that the general is not like the hive
    To whom the foragers shall all repair,
    What honey is expected ? Degree being vizarded,   83
    Th' unworthiest shows as fairly in the mask.
    The heavens themselves, the planets, and this centre
    Observe degree, priority, and place,
    Insisture, course, proportion, season, form,   87
    Office, and custom, in all line of order.
    And therefore is the glorious planet Sol   89
    In noble eminence enthroned and sphered
    Amidst the other ; whose med'cinable eye   91
    Corrects the influence of evil planets,   92
    And posts, like the commandment of a king,
    Sans check to good and bad. But when the planets
    In evil mixture to disorder wander,
    What plagues, and what portents, what mutiny,
    What raging of the sea, shaking of earth,
    Commotion in the winds, frights, changes, horrors,
    Divert and crack, rend and deracinate   99
    The unity and married calm of states
    Quite from their fixure ? O, when degree is shaked,
    Which is the ladder of all high designs,
    The enterprise is sick. How could communities,
    Degrees in schools, and brotherhoods in cities,
    Peaceful commerce from dividable shores,
    The primogenity and due of birth,   106

I, iii The Grecian camp   s.d. *Sennet* a conventional sequence of trumpet
notes to indicate a procession   7 *conflux* flowing together   9 *Tortive
and errant* distorted and wandering   11 *suppose* expectation   15 *Bias and
thwart* to one side and crosswise   24 *artist* scholar in the liberal arts
25 *affined* in affinity   30 *unmingled* unalloyed   38 *Boreas* north wind
39 *Thetis* a Nereid or sea-maiden, mother of Achilles, here personifying
the sea   42 *Perseus' horse* the winged horse Pegasus, which sprang from
Medusa's blood after Perseus beheaded her   45 *toast* a piece of toast put
into liquor   48 *breese* gadfly   54 *Returns* answers back   55 *nerves* sinews
58 *shut up* gathered in   65 *hatched in silver* with silver lines in his hair
73 *mastic* abusive (from Greek 'scourge')   78 *specialty of rule* particular
rights of supreme authority   83 *Degree being vizarded* the hierarchy of
authority being hidden   87 *Insisture* regularity of position   89 *Sol* sun
91 *other* others   92 *influence* astrological effect   99 *deracinate* uproot
106 *primogenity* right of the eldest son to succeed

Prerogative of age, crowns, sceptres, laurels,
But by degree, stand in authentic place?
Take but degree away, untune that string,
And hark what discord follows. Each thing meets
111 In mere oppugnancy. The bounded waters
Should lift their bosoms higher than the shores
113 And make a sop of all this solid globe;
114 Strength should be lord of imbecility,
And the rude son should strike his father dead;
Force should be right, or rather right and wrong,
117 Between whose endless jar justice resides,
Should lose their names, and so should justice too;
119 Then everything include itself in power,
Power into will, will into appetite,
And appetite, an universal wolf,
So doubly seconded with will and power,
Must make perforce an universal prey
And last eat up himself. Great Agamemnon,
125 This chaos, when degree is suffocate,
Follows the choking.
127 And this neglection of degree it is
128 That by a pace goes backward with a purpose
It hath to climb. The general's disdained
By him one step below, he by the next,
That next by him beneath; so every step,
132 Exampled by the first pace that is sick
Of his superior, grows to an envious fever
Of pale and bloodless emulation:
And 'tis this fever that keeps Troy on foot,
Not her own sinews. To end a tale of length,
Troy in our weakness stands, not in her strength.

NESTOR
Most wisely hath Ulysses here discovered
The fever whereof all our power is sick.

AGAMEMNON
The nature of the sickness found, Ulysses,
What is the remedy?

ULYSSES
The great Achilles, whom opinion crowns
The sinew and the forehand of our host,
Having his ear full of his airy fame,
145 Grows dainty of his worth, and in his tent
Lies mocking our designs. With him Patroclus
Upon a lazy bed the livelong day
Breaks scurril jests,
And with ridiculous and silly action
(Which, slanderer, he imitation calls)
151 He pageants us. Sometime, great Agamemnon,
152 Thy topless deputation he puts on
And, like a strutting player, whose conceit
154 Lies in his hamstring, and doth think it rich
To hear the wooden dialogue and sound
156 'Twixt his stretched footing and the scaffoldage,
Such to-be-pitied and o'er-wrested seeming
He acts thy greatness in; and when he speaks,
159 'Tis like a chime a-mending, with terms unsquared,
160 Which, from the tongue of roaring Typhon dropped,
Would seem hyperboles. At this fusty stuff
The large Achilles, on his pressed bed lolling,
From his deep chest laughs out a loud applause,
Cries, 'Excellent! 'tis Agamemnon right.
Now play me Nestor; hem, and stroke thy beard,
As he being drest to some oration.'
That's done, as near as the extremest ends

Of parallels, as like as Vulcan and his wife,   168
Yet god Achilles still cries, 'Excellent!
'Tis Nestor right. Now play him me, Patroclus,
Arming to answer in a night alarm.'
And then, forsooth, the faint defects of age
Must be the scene of mirth; to cough and spit,
And with a palsy fumbling on his gorget,   174
Shake in and out the rivet; and at this sport
Sir Valor dies; cries, 'O! enough, Patroclus,
Or give me ribs of steel; I shall split all
In pleasure of my spleen.' And in this fashion   178
All our abilities, gifts, natures, shapes,
Severals and generals of grace exact,   180
Achievements, plots, orders, preventions,
Excitements to the field or speech for truce,
Success or loss, what is or is not, serves
As stuff for these two to make paradoxes.   184

NESTOR
And in the imitation of these twain,
Who, as Ulysses says, opinion crowns
With an imperial voice, many are infect.
Ajax is grown self-willed, and bears his head
In such a rein, in full as proud a place   189
As broad Achilles; keeps his tent like him;
Makes factious feasts; rails on our state of war,
Bold as an oracle, and sets Thersites,
A slave whose gall coins slanders like a mint,   193
To match us in comparisons with dirt,
To weaken and discredit our exposure,
How rank soever rounded in with danger.   196

ULYSSES
They tax our policy and call it cowardice,
Count wisdom as no member of the war,
Forestall prescience, and esteem no act   199
But that of hand. The still and mental parts
That do contrive how many hands shall strike
When fitness calls them on, and know by measure
Of their observant toil the enemies' weight –
Why, this hath not a finger's dignity.
They call this bed-work, mapp'ry, closet-war;   205
So that the ram that batters down the wall,
For the great swinge and rudeness of his poise,   207
They place before his hand that made the engine,
Or those that with the fineness of their souls
By reason guide his execution.

NESTOR
Let this be granted, and Achilles' horse   211

---

111 *mere oppugnancy* total strife 113 *sop* pulp 114 *imbecility* weakness
117 *jar* collision 119 *include itself in* should confine itself within, i.e.
convert itself into 125 *chaos* raw matter without form or order 127
neglection neglect 128–29 *by a pace . . . climb* step by step goes backward
when it is trying to climb 132–33 *Exampled . . . superior* taking its example
from the first step that someone takes against his superior 145 *dainty of*
particular about 151 *pageants* acts or mimics 152 *topless deputation*
supreme authority 154 *hamstring* tendon at the back of the knee 156
scaffoldage stage 159 *unsquared* unsuited 160 *Typhon* a monster with
serpents' heads and a tremendous voice, overwhelmed by Zeus with
thunderbolts 168 *Vulcan and his wife* (the beautiful Venus cuckolded
Vulcan, who was lame and sooty, with Mars) 174 *gorget* throat armor
178 *spleen* (regarded as the seat of the emotions of anger and hilarity)
180 *Severals and generals* individual and common excellences 184
paradoxes absurdities 189 *In such a rein* so high 193 *gall* source of bile, a
humor conducive to rancor 196 *rank* abundantly 199 *Forestall prescience*
discount foresight 205 *mapp'ry* map-making 207 *swinge* impetus 211
horse (either literally or collectively for his horsemen, i.e. Myrmidons)

212 Makes many Thetis' sons.
Tucket.

AGAMEMNON
What trumpet? Look, Menelaus.

MENELAUS
From Troy.
Enter Aeneas.

AGAMEMNON
What would you 'fore our tent?

AENEAS
Is this great Agamemnon's tent, I pray you?

AGAMEMNON
Even this.

AENEAS
May one that is a herald and a prince
219 Do a fair message to his kingly eyes?

AGAMEMNON
With surety stronger than Achilles' arm
'Fore all the Greekish heads, which with one voice
Call Agamemnon head and general.

AENEAS
Fair leave and large security. How may
A stranger to those most imperial looks
Know them from eyes of other mortals?

AGAMEMNON   How?

AENEAS
Ay.
I ask, that I might waken reverence,
And bid the cheek be ready with a blush
Modest as morning when she coldly eyes
230 The youthful Phoebus,
Which is that god in office, guiding men?
Which is the high and mighty Agamemnon?

AGAMEMNON
This Troyan scorns us, or the men of Troy
Are ceremonious courtiers.

AENEAS
Courtiers as free, as debonair, unarmed,
As bending angels; that's their fame in peace.
But when they would seem soldiers, they have galls,
238 Good arms, strong joints, true swords; and, Jove's
accord,
Nothing so full of heart. But peace, Aeneas;
Peace, Troyan; lay thy finger on thy lips.
The worthiness of praise distains his worth,
If that the praised himself bring the praise forth.
But what the repining enemy commends,
That breath fame blows; that praise, sole pure, trans-
cends.

AGAMEMNON
Sir, you of Troy, call you yourself Aeneas?

AENEAS
Ay, Greek, that is my name.

AGAMEMNON
What's your affair, I pray you?

AENEAS
Sir, pardon; 'tis for Agamemnon's ears.

AGAMEMNON
He hears nought privately that comes from Troy.

AENEAS
Nor I from Troy come not to whisper him:
I bring a trumpet to awake his ear,
To set his seat on the attentive bent,   252
And then to speak.

AGAMEMNON   Speak frankly as the wind;
It is not Agamemnon's sleeping hour.
That thou shalt know, Troyan, he is awake,
He tells thee so himself.

AENEAS   Trumpet, blow loud,
Send thy brass voice through all these lazy tents;
And every Greek of mettle, let him know,
What Troy means fairly shall be spoke aloud.
Sound trumpet.
We have, great Agamemnon, here in Troy
A prince called Hector – Priam is his father –
Who in this dull and long-continued truce
Is rusty grown. He bade me take a trumpet,
And to this purpose speak: Kings, princes, lords,
If there be one among the fair'st of Greece
That holds his honor higher than his ease,
That seeks his praise more than he fears his peril,
That knows his valor and knows not his fear,
That loves his mistress more than in confession   269
With truant vows to her own lips he loves,
And dare avow her beauty and her worth
In other arms than hers – to him this challenge.
Hector, in view of Troyans and of Greeks,
Shall make it good, or do his best to do it,
He hath a lady wiser, fairer, truer,
Than ever Greek did compass in his arms;
And will to-morrow with his trumpet call,
Midway between your tents and walls of Troy,
To rouse a Grecian that is true in love.
If any come, Hector shall honor him;
If none, he'll say in Troy when he retires,
The Grecian dames are sunburnt and not worth   282
The splinter of a lance. Even so much.

AGAMEMNON
This shall be told our lovers, Lord Aeneas;
If none of them have soul in such a kind,
We left them all at home. But we are soldiers;
And may that soldier a mere recreant prove,
That means not, hath not, or is not in love!
If then one is, or hath, or means to be,
That one meets Hector; if none else, I am he.

NESTOR
Tell him of Nestor, one that was a man
When Hector's grandsire sucked. He is old now,
But if there be not in our Grecian host
A noble man that hath one spark of fire
To answer for his love, tell him from me,
I'll hide my silver beard in a gold beaver,   296
And in my vantbrace put this withered brawn,   297
And, meeting him, will tell him that my lady
Was fairer than his grandam, and as chaste
As may be in the world. His youth in flood,
I'll prove this troth with my three drops of blood.

AENEAS
Now heavens forfend such scarcity of youth!

ULYSSES
Amen.

212 s.d. *Tucket* preparatory signal on a trumpet 219 *to . . . eyes* i.e. in his presence 230 *Phoebus* Apollo, the sun god 238 *Jove's accord* if Jove favor them, i.e. with God on their side 252 *To set . . . bent* i.e. to make him sit up and take notice 269–70 *more . . . loves* more than enough to swear false vows that he loves her 282 *sunburnt* dark, i.e. ugly 296 *beaver* face-guard of a helmet 297 *vantbrace* armor for the forearm

AGAMEMNON
  For Lord Aeneas, let me touch your hand;
  To our pavilion shall I lead you first.
  Achilles shall have word of this intent;
  So shall each lord of Greece, from tent to tent.
  Yourself shall feast with us before you go,
  And find the welcome of a noble foe.
             [Exeunt. Manent Ulysses and Nestor.]

ULYSSES
  Nestor.

NESTOR
  What says Ulysses?

ULYSSES
312 I have a young conception in my brain;
  Be you my time to bring it to some shape.

NESTOR
  What is't?

ULYSSES
  [This 'tis:]
  Blunt wedges rive hard knots; the seeded pride
  That hath to this maturity blown up
  In rank Achilles, must or now be cropped
319 Or, shedding, breed a nursery of like evil
  To overbulk us all.

NESTOR   Well, and how?

ULYSSES
  This challenge that the gallant Hector sends,
  However it is spread in general name,
  Relates in purpose only to Achilles.

NESTOR
  True, the purpose is perspicuous as substance
325 Whose grossness little characters sum up;
326 And, in the publication, make no strain
  But that Achilles, were his brain as barren
  As banks of Libya – though, Apollo knows,
  'Tis dry enough – will with great speed of judgment,
  Ay with celerity, find Hector's purpose
  Pointing on him.

ULYSSES
  And wake him to the answer, think you?

NESTOR
  Why, 'tis most meet. Who may you else oppose
  That can from Hector bring his honor off,
  If not Achilles? Though't be a sportful combat,
336 Yet in this trial much opinion dwells;
  For here the Troyans taste our dear'st repute
  With their fin'st palate; and trust to me, Ulysses,
339 Our imputation shall be oddly poised
340 In this vild action. For the success,
341 Although particular, shall give a scantling
342 Of good or bad unto the general;
343 And in such indexes, although small pricks
  To their subsequent volumes, there is seen
  The baby figure of the giant mass
  Of things to come at large. It is supposed
  He that meets Hector issues from our choice;
  And choice, being mutual act of all our souls,
349 Makes merit her election, and doth boil,
  As 'twere from forth us all, a man distilled
  Out of our virtues; who miscarrying,
  What heart receives from hence a conquering part,
  To steel a strong opinion to themselves!
354 [Which entertained, limbs are his instruments,

  In no less working than are swords and bows
  Directive by the limbs.]

ULYSSES
  Give pardon to my speech: therefore 'tis meet
  Achilles meet not Hector. Let us, like merchants,
  First show foul wares, and think perchance they'll sell;
  If not, the lustre of the better shall exceed
  By showing the worse first. Do not consent
  That ever Hector and Achilles meet;
  For both our honor and our shame in this
  Are dogged with two strange followers.   364

NESTOR
  I see them not with my old eyes. What are they?

ULYSSES
  What glory our Achilles shares from Hector,
  Were he not proud, we all should share with him.
  But he already is too insolent,
  And we were better parch in Afric sun
  Than in the pride and salt scorn of his eyes,   370
  Should he 'scape Hector fair. If he were foiled,
  Why then we did our main opinion crush   372
  In taint of our best man. No, make a lott'ry;
  And by device let blockish Ajax draw
  The sort to fight with Hector; among ourselves
  Give him allowance for the better man,
  For that will physic the great Myrmidon   377
  Who broils in loud applause, and make him fall 378
  His crest that prouder than blue Iris bends.   379
  If the dull brainless Ajax comes safe off,
  We'll dress him up in voices; if he fail,
  Yet go we under our opinion still
  That we have better men. But, hit or miss,
  Our project's life this shape of sense assumes:
  Ajax employed plucks down Achilles' plumes.

NESTOR
  Now, Ulysses, I begin to relish thy advice,
  And I will give a taste thereof forthwith
  To Agamemnon. Go we to him straight.
  Two curs shall tame each other; pride alone
  Must tarre the mastiffs on, as 'twere a bone.   *Exeunt.* 390

                         *

              Enter Ajax and Thersites.   II, i

AJAX Thersites!

THERSITES Agamemnon, how if he had biles – full, all 2
  over, generally?

AJAX Thersites!

THERSITES And those biles did run? – say so. Did not 5
  the general run then? Were not that a botchy core? 6

AJAX Dog!

THERSITES Then would come some matter from him. I see none now.

AJAX Thou bitch-wolf's son, canst thou not hear? Feel then.

[Strikes him.]

11 THERSITES The plague of Greece upon thee, thou mongrel beef-witted lord!

13 AJAX Speak then, thou vinewed'st leaven, speak. I will beat thee into handsomeness.

THERSITES I shall sooner rail thee into wit and holiness;
16 but I think thy horse will sooner con an oration than
17 thou learn a prayer without book. Thou canst strike,
18 canst thou? A red murrain o' thy jade's tricks!

19 AJAX Toadstool, learn me the proclamation.

THERSITES Dost thou think I have no sense, thou strikest me thus?

AJAX The proclamation!

THERSITES Thou art proclaimed fool, I think.

24 AJAX Do not, porpentine, do not; my fingers itch.

THERSITES I would thou didst itch from head to foot; an I had the scratching of thee, I would make thee the loathsomest scab in Greece. When thou art forth in the
28 incursions, thou strikest as slow as another.

AJAX I say, the proclamation!

THERSITES Thou grumblest and railest every hour on Achilles, and thou art as full of envy at his greatness as
32 Cerberus is at Proserpina's beauty, ay that thou bark'st at him.

AJAX Mistress Thersites!

THERSITES Thou shouldst strike him.

35 AJAX Cobloaf!

36 THERSITES He would pun thee into shivers with his fist, as a sailor breaks a biscuit.

AJAX You whoreson cur!

[Beating him.]

THERSITES Do, do.

AJAX Thou stool for a witch!

THERSITES Ay, do, do, thou sodden-witted lord! thou
42 hast no more brain than I have in mine elbows; an asinico may tutor thee. Thou scurvy-valiant ass, thou art here
44 but to thrash Troyans, and thou art bought and sold among those of any wit like a barbarian slave. If thou use to beat me, I will begin at thy heel, and tell what thou
47 art by inches, thou thing of no bowels, thou!

AJAX You dog!

THERSITES You scurvy lord!

AJAX You cur!

[Beating him.]

51 THERSITES Mars his idiot! Do, rudeness; do, camel; do, do.

[Enter Achilles and Patroclus.]

ACHILLES Why, how now, Ajax, wherefore do ye thus? How now, Thersites, what's the matter, man?

THERSITES You see him there, do you?

ACHILLES Ay, what's the matter?

THERSITES Nay, look upon him.

ACHILLES So I do. What's the matter?

THERSITES Nay, but regard him well.

ACHILLES 'Well' – why so I do.

THERSITES But yet you look not well upon him; for, whosomever you take him to be, he is Ajax.   61

ACHILLES I know that, fool.

THERSITES Ay, but that fool knows not himself.   63

AJAX Therefore I beat thee.

THERSITES Lo, lo, lo, lo, what modicums of wit he utters! His evasions have ears thus long. I have bobbed 66 his brain more than he has beat my bones. I will buy nine sparrows for a penny, and his pia mater is not 68 worth the ninth part of a sparrow. This lord, Achilles, Ajax, who wears his wit in his belly and his guts in his head, I'll tell you what I say of him.

ACHILLES What?

THERSITES I say, this Ajax –

[Ajax offers to strike him.]

ACHILLES Nay, good Ajax.

THERSITES Has not so much wit –

[Ajax again offers to strike him.]

ACHILLES Nay, I must hold you.

THERSITES As will stop the eye of Helen's needle, for whom he comes to fight.

ACHILLES Peace, fool!

THERSITES I would have peace and quietness, but the fool will not – he there, that he. Look you there.

AJAX O thou damned cur, I shall –

ACHILLES Will you set your wit to a fool's?   83

THERSITES No, I warrant you; the fool's will shame it.

PATROCLUS Good words, Thersites.

ACHILLES What's the quarrel?

AJAX I bade the vile owl go learn me the tenor of the proclamation, and he rails upon me.

THERSITES I serve thee not.

AJAX Well, go to, go to.

THERSITES I serve here voluntary.

ACHILLES Your last service was sufferance, 'twas not voluntary; no man is beaten voluntary. Ajax was here the voluntary, and you as under an impress.   94

THERSITES E'en so. A great deal of your wit, too, lies in your sinews, or else there be liars. Hector shall have a great catch if he knock out either of your brains. 'A were as good crack a fusty nut with no kernel.

ACHILLES What, with me too, Thersites?

THERSITES There's Ulysses and old Nestor, whose wit was mouldy ere your grandsires had nails on their toes, yoke you like draught-oxen and make you plough up the wars.

ACHILLES What, what?

THERSITES Yes, good sooth. To, Achilles; to, Ajax; to – 104

AJAX I shall cut out your tongue.

THERSITES 'Tis no matter; I shall speak as much as thou afterwards.

PATROCLUS No more words, Thersites; peace!

THERSITES I will hold my peace when Achilles' brach 109 bids me, shall I?

ACHILLES There's for you, Patroclus.

112 THERSITES I will see you hanged, like clotpoles, ere I
come any more to your tents. I will keep where there is
wit stirring and leave the faction of fools.   *Exit.*

PATROCLUS A good riddance.

ACHILLES

116 Marry, this, sir, is proclaimed through all our host:

117 That Hector, by the fifth hour of the sun,
Will, with a trumpet, 'twixt our tents and Troy
To-morrow morning call some knight to arms
That hath a stomach, and such a one that dare
Maintain – I know not what; 'tis trash. Farewell.

AJAX
Farewell? Who shall answer him?

ACHILLES
I know not. 'Tis put to lott'ry. Otherwise,
He knew his man.

AJAX
O, meaning you? I will go learn more of it.   *[Exeunt.]*

*

II, ii   *Enter Priam, Hector, Troilus, Paris, and Helenus.*

PRIAM
After so many hours, lives, speeches spent,
Thus once again says Nestor from the Greeks:
'Deliver Helen, and all damage else,
As honor, loss of time, travail, expense,
Wounds, friends, and what else dear that is consumed

6 In hot digestion of this cormorant war,
Shall be struck off.' Hector, what say you to't?

HECTOR
Though no man lesser fears the Greeks than I,

9 As far as toucheth my particular,
Yet, dread Priam,
There is no lady of more softer bowels,
More spongy to suck in the sense of fear,
More ready to cry out, 'Who knows what follows?'

14 Than Hector is. The wound of peace is surety,
Surety secure; but modest doubt is called

16 The beacon of the wise, the tent that searches
To th' bottom of the worst. Let Helen go.
Since the first sword was drawn about this question,

19 Every tithe soul, 'mongst many thousand dismes,
Hath been as dear as Helen; I mean, of ours.
If we have lost so many tenths of ours
To guard a thing not ours nor worth to us,
Had it our name, the value of one ten,
What merit 's in that reason which denies
The yielding of her up?

TROILUS   Fie, fie, my brother!
Weigh you the worth and honor of a king
So great as our dread father in a scale

28 Of common ounces? Will you with counters sum

29 The past proportion of his infinite,
And buckle in a waist most fathomless

31 With spans and inches so diminutive
As fears and reasons? Fie, for godly shame!

HELENUS
No marvel, though you bite so sharp at reasons,
You are so empty of them. Should not our father
Bear the great sway of his affairs with reason,
Because your speech hath none that tell him so?

TROILUS
You are for dreams and slumbers, brother priest;
You fur your gloves with reason. Here are your reasons: 38
You know an enemy intends you harm;
You know a sword employed is perilous,
And reason flies the object of all harm.
Who marvels then, when Helenus beholds
A Grecian and his sword, if he do set
The very wings of reason to his heels
And fly like chidden Mercury from Jove,
Or like a star disorbed? Nay, if we talk of reason,   46
Let's shut our gates and sleep. Manhood and honor
Should have hare-hearts, would they but fat their
    thoughts
With this crammed reason. Reason and respect
Make livers pale and lustihood deject.   50

HECTOR
Brother, she is not worth what she doth cost
The keeping.

TROILUS   What's aught but as 'tis valued?

HECTOR
But value dwells not in particular will;   53
It holds his estimate and dignity   54
As well wherein 'tis precious of itself
As in the prizer. 'Tis mad idolatry   56
To make the service greater than the god;
And the will dotes that is attributive   58
To what infectiously itself affects,   59
Without some image of th' affected merit.

TROILUS
I take to-day a wife, and my election
Is led on in the conduct of my will –
My will enkindled by mine eyes and ears,
Two traded pilots 'twixt the dangerous shores   64
Of will and judgment. How may I avoid,
Although my will distaste what it elected,
The wife I chose? There can be no evasion
To blench from this and to stand firm by honor.   68
We turn not back the silks upon the merchant
When we have soiled them, nor the remainder viands
We do not throw in unrespective sieve   71
Because we now are full. It was thought meet
Paris should do some vengeance on the Greeks.
Your breath with full consent bellied his sails;
The seas and winds, old wranglers, took a truce
And did him service; he touched the ports desired,
And for an old aunt whom the Greeks held captive   77
He brought a Grecian queen, whose youth and freshness
Wrinkles Apollo's and makes stale the morning.

112 *clotpoles* blockheads   116 *Marry* why, indeed (originally an oath by
the Virgin Mary)   117 *fifth hour* i.e. 11 a.m.
II, ii The palace of Priam   6 *cormorant* ravenous   9 *my particular* me
personally   14 *The . . . surety* our sense of security imperils peace   16
tent lint for probing wounds   19 *Every . . . dismes* every soul taken by
war as its tenth among many thousand such tenths   28 *counters* worthless
tokens used for counting   29 *The . . . infinite* his infinite greatness past
comparing by measurement   31 *spans* measures of nine inches   38 *fur . . .
reason* use reason in your speech as fur is used to ornament gloves or to
give them a soft, warm lining   46 *disorbed* thrown from its sphere   50
livers (regarded as seats of the passions)   53 *particular will* the individual's
inclination   54 *dignity* worth   56 *prizer* appraiser   58 *attributive* i.e.
subservient as is one who pays tribute   59–60 *To what . . . merit* to what
it inclines toward, as if diseased, without some idea of the value it is seeking
  64 *traded* experienced   68 *blench* shrink   71 *unrespective sieve* receptacle
which does not care what is put into it   77 *aunt* Hesione, Priam's sister
and mother of Ajax

Why keep we her ? The Grecians keep our aunt.
Is she worth keeping ? Why, she is a pearl
82 Whose price hath launched above a thousand ships
And turned crowned kings to merchants.
If you'll avouch 'twas wisdom Paris went –
As you must needs, for you all cried, 'Go, go' –
If you'll confess he brought home worthy prize –
As you must needs, for you all clapped your hands,
And cried, 'Inestimable !' – why do you now
89 The issue of your proper wisdoms rate,
And do a deed that never Fortune did,
91 Beggar the estimation which you prized
Richer than sea and land ? O theft most base,
That we have stol'n what we do fear to keep !
But thieves unworthy of a thing so stol'n,
95 That in their country did them that disgrace
96 We fear to warrant in our native place.

CASSANDRA [within]
97 Cry, Troyans, cry !
PRIAM   What noise ? what shriek is this ?
TROILUS
'Tis our mad sister. I do know her voice.
CASSANDRA [within] Cry, Troyans !
HECTOR It is Cassandra.
    Enter Cassandra raving [with her hair about her ears].
CASSANDRA
Cry, Troyans, cry ! Lend me ten thousand eyes,
And I will fill them with prophetic tears.
HECTOR
Peace, sister, peace !
CASSANDRA
Virgins and boys, mid-age and wrinkled elders,
Soft infancy, that nothing canst but cry,
Add to my clamors ! Let us pay betimes
107 A moiety of that mass of moan to come.
Cry, Troyans, cry ! Practise your eyes with tears !
Troy must not be, nor goodly Ilion stand ;
110 Our firebrand brother, Paris, burns us all.
Cry, Troyans, cry ! A Helen and a woe !
Cry, cry ! Troy burns, or else let Helen go.   Exit.
HECTOR
Now, youthful Troilus, do not these high strains
Of divination in our sister work
Some touches of remorse ? Or is your blood
So madly hot that no discourse of reason,
Nor fear of bad success in a bad cause,
Can qualify the same ?
TROILUS   Why, brother Hector,
We may not think the justness of each act
120 Such and no other than event doth form it,

Nor once deject the courage of our minds
Because Cassandra 's mad. Her brainsick raptures   122
Cannot distaste the goodness of a quarrel   123
Which hath our several honors all engaged
To make it gracious. For my private part,
I am no more touched than all Priam's sons ;
And Jove forbid there should be done amongst us
Such things as might offend the weakest spleen   128
To fight for and maintain.
PARIS
Else might the world convince of levity   130
As well my undertakings as your counsels ;
But I attest the gods, your full consent
Gave wings to my propension and cut off   133
All fears attending on so dire a project.
For what, alas, can these my single arms ?
What propugnation is in one man's valor   136
To stand the push and enmity of those
This quarrel would excite ? Yet, I protest,
Were I alone to pass the difficulties,   139
And had as ample power as I have will,
Paris should ne'er retract what he hath done
Nor faint in the pursuit.
PRIAM   Paris, you speak
Like one besotted on your sweet delights.
You have the honey still, but these the gall ;
So to be valiant is no praise at all.
PARIS
Sir, I propose not merely to myself
The pleasures such a beauty brings with it ;
But I would have the soil of her fair rape   148
Wiped off in honorable keeping her.
What treason were it to the ransacked queen,   150
Disgrace to your great worths, and shame to me,
Now to deliver her possession up
On terms of base compulsion ! Can it be
That so degenerate a strain as this
Should once set footing in your generous bosoms ? 155
There's not the meanest spirit on our party
Without a heart to dare or sword to draw
When Helen is defended, nor none so noble
Whose life were ill bestowed or death unfamed
Where Helen is the subject. Then, I say,
Well may we fight for her, whom we know well
The world's large spaces cannot parallel.
HECTOR
Paris and Troilus, you have both said well ;
And on the cause and question now in hand
Have glozed, but superficially ; not much   165
Unlike young men, whom Aristotle thought
Unfit to hear moral philosophy.   167
The reasons you allege do more conduce
To the hot passion of distemp'red blood
Than to make up a free determination
'Twixt right and wrong, for pleasure and revenge
Have ears more deaf than adders to the voice   172
Of any true decision. Nature craves
All dues be rend'red to their owners. Now,
What nearer debt in all humanity
Than wife is to the husband ? If this law
Of nature be corrupted through affection,   177
And that great minds, of partial indulgence   178
To their benumbèd wills, resist the same,   179
There is a law in each well-ordered nation

82 Whose . . . ships (cf. Marlowe, 'Was this the face that launched a thousand ships ?') 89 your . . . rate your own wisdom condemn 91 estimation thing esteemed 95 disgrace i.e. the rape of Helen 96 warrant justify by defense 97 Cassandra (when she resisted the love of Apollo, he nullified his former gift of prophecy by causing her never to be believed) 107 moiety part 110 firebrand (his mother dreamed that she was delivered of a firebrand when Paris was born) 120 event outcome 122 raptures prophetic seizures 123 distaste make distasteful 128 spleen temper 130 convince convict 133 propension inclination 136 propugnation defense 139 pass undergo 148 rape carrying off 150 ransacked carried off 155 generous of noble birth, and therefore of noble nature 165 glozed commented, glossed 167 moral (Aristotle wrote 'political,' but Shakespeare's 'moral' is paralleled in contemporary translations of the passage) 172 more deaf than adders (cf. Psalms lviii, 4–5) 177 affection movement of appetite 178 partial favoring 179 benumbèd hypnotized by appetite and insensitive to reason

To curb those raging appetites that are
Most disobedient and refractory.
If Helen, then, be wife to Sparta's king,
As it is known she is, these moral laws
Of nature and of nations speak aloud
To have her back returned. Thus to persist
187 In doing wrong extenuates not wrong,
But makes it much more heavy. Hector's opinion
Is this in way of truth; yet ne'ertheless,
190 My spritely brethren, I propend to you
In resolution to keep Helen still;
For 'tis a cause that hath no mean dependence
Upon our joint and several dignities.

TROILUS
Why, there you touched the life of our design.
Were it not glory that we more affected
196 Than the performance of our heaving spleens,
I would not wish a drop of Troyan blood
Spent more in her defense. But, worthy Hector,
She is a theme of honor and renown,
A spur to valiant and magnanimous deeds,
Whose present courage may beat down our foes
And fame in time to come canonize us;
For I presume brave Hector would not lose
So rich advantage of a promised glory
As smiles upon the forehead of this action
For the wide world's revenue.

HECTOR   I am yours,
You valiant offspring of great Priamus.
208 I have a roisting challenge sent amongst
The dull and factious nobles of the Greeks
Will strike amazement to their drowsy spirits.
211 I was advertised their great general slept
212 Whilst emulation in the army crept.
This, I presume, will wake him.   *Exeunt.*

*

II, iii   *Enter Thersites solus.*
THERSITES How now, Thersites? What, lost in the laby-
2   rinth of thy fury? Shall the elephant Ajax carry it thus?
He beats me, and I rail at him. O worthy satisfaction!
Would it were otherwise – that I could beat him, whilst
5   he railed at me. 'Sfoot, I'll learn to conjure and raise
6   devils, but I'll see some issue of my spiteful execrations.
Then there's Achilles, a rare enginer. If Troy be not
taken till these two undermine it, the walls will stand till
they fall of themselves. O thou great thunder-darter of
Olympus, forget that thou art Jove, the king of gods;
11   and, Mercury, lose all the serpentine craft of thy caduceus, if ye take not that little, little, less than little wit from
them that they have; which short-armed ignorance itself knows is so abundant scarce it will not in circumvention deliver a fly from a spider, without drawing their
massy irons and cutting the web. After this, the ven-
17   geance on the whole camp! or, rather, the Neapolitan
bone-ache, for that, methinks, is the curse depending on
19   those that war for a placket. I have said my prayers, and
devil Envy say 'Amen.' What ho, my Lord Achilles!
Enter Patroclus.
PATROCLUS Who's there? Thersites? Good Thersites,
come in and rail.
THERSITES If I could 'a' remembered a gilt counterfeit,
24   thou wouldst not have slipped out of my contemplation.

But it is no matter; thyself upon thyself! The common
curse of mankind, folly and ignorance, be thine in great
revenue. Heaven bless thee from a tutor, and discipline 27
come not near thee. Let thy blood be thy direction till 28
thy death. Then, if she that lays thee out says thou art a
fair corse, I'll be sworn and sworn upon't she never
shrouded any but lazars. Amen. Where's Achilles? 31
PATROCLUS What, art thou devout? Wast thou in
prayer?
THERSITES Ay; the heavens hear me!
PATROCLUS Amen.
Enter Achilles.
ACHILLES Who's there?
PATROCLUS Thersites, my lord.
ACHILLES Where, where, O, where? Art thou come?
Why, my cheese, my digestion, why hast thou not
served thyself in to my table so many meals? Come,
what's Agamemnon?
THERSITES Thy commander, Achilles. Then tell me,
Patroclus, what's Achilles?
PATROCLUS Thy lord, Thersites. Then tell me, I pray
thee, what's thyself?
THERSITES Thy knower, Patroclus. Then tell me, Pat-
roclus, what art thou?
PATROCLUS Thou must tell that knowest.
ACHILLES O tell, tell.
THERSITES I'll decline the whole question. Agamemnon 49
commands Achilles, Achilles is my lord, I am Patroclus'
knower, and Patroclus is a fool.
[PATROCLUS You rascal!
THERSITES Peace, fool! I have not done.
ACHILLES He is a privileged man. Proceed, Thersites.
THERSITES Agamemnon is a fool, Achilles is a fool, Ther-
sites is a fool, and, as aforesaid, Patroclus is a fool.]
ACHILLES Derive this; come.
THERSITES Agamemnon is a fool to offer to command
Achilles, Achilles is a fool to be commanded of Aga-
memnon, Thersites is a fool to serve such a fool, and
this Patroclus is a fool positive.
PATROCLUS Why am I a fool?
THERSITES Make that demand of the Creator. It suffices
me thou art. Look you, who comes here?
*Enter [at a distance] Agamemnon, Ulysses, Nestor,
Diomedes, Ajax, and Calchas.*
ACHILLES Come, Patroclus, I'll speak with nobody.
Come in with me, Thersites.   *Exit.*
THERSITES Here is such patchery, such juggling, and 67
such knavery. All the argument is a whore and a cuck-
old, a good quarrel to draw emulous factions and bleed
to death upon. [Now, the dry serpigo on the subject, 70
and war and lechery confound all!]   *[Exit.]*
AGAMEMNON Where is Achilles?
PATROCLUS
Within his tent, but ill-disposed, my lord.

187 *extenuates* lessens   190 *spritely* spirited; *propend* incline   196 *heaving
spleens* aroused passions   208 *roisting* roistering   211 *advertised* informed
212 *emulation* quarrelsome rivalry
II, iii Before the tent of Achilles   2 *carry it* carry off the honors   5
'Sfoot God's foot   6 *but I'll see* rather than not see   11 *caduceus* Mercury's
staff of office, twined with snakes   17–18 *Neapolitan bone-ache* syphilis
19 *placket* petticoat, i.e. woman   24 *slipped* (pun on 'slip,' a counterfeit coin of brass covered with silver or gold)   27 *bless* save   28 *blood*
violent passion   31 *lazars* lepers   49 *decline* go through (as in declining
a noun)   67 *patchery* roguery   70 *serpigo* impetigo or similar skin
eruption

AGAMEMNON

Let it be known to him that we are here.

75 He shent our messengers, and we lay by

76 Our appertainings, visiting of him.

Let him be told so, lest perchance he think

78 We dare not move the question of our place

Or know not what we are.

PATROCLUS   I shall so say to him.   *[Exit.]*

ULYSSES We saw him at the opening of his tent. He is not sick.

AJAX Yes, lion-sick, sick of proud heart. You may call it melancholy if you will favor the man ; but, by my head, 'tis pride. But why, why ? Let him show us a cause. [A word, my lord.]

    [Takes Agamemnon aside.]

NESTOR What moves Ajax thus to bay at him ?

ULYSSES Achilles hath inveigled his fool from him.

NESTOR Who, Thersites ?

ULYSSES He.

90 NESTOR Then will Ajax lack matter, if he have lost his argument.

ULYSSES No, you see, he is his argument that has his argument, Achilles.

94 NESTOR All the better ; their fraction is more our wish

95 than their faction. But it was a strong composure a fool could disunite.

ULYSSES The amity that wisdom knits not, folly may easily untie.

    [Enter Patroclus.]

    Here comes Patroclus.

NESTOR No Achilles with him ?

ULYSSES

The elephant hath joints, but none for courtesy.

102 His legs are legs for necessity, not for flexure.

PATROCLUS

Achilles bids me say, he is much sorry

If anything more than your sport and pleasure

105 Did move your greatness and this noble state

To call upon him ; he hopes it is no other

But, for your health and your digestion sake,

108 An after-dinner's breath.

AGAMEMNON   Hear you, Patroclus.

We are too well acquainted with these answers ;

But his evasion, winged thus swift with scorn,

Cannot outfly our apprehensions.

Much attribute he hath, and much the reason

Why we ascribe it to him ; yet all his virtues,

114 Not virtuously on his own part beheld,

Do in our eyes begin to lose their gloss,

Yea, like fair fruit in an unwholesome dish,

Are like to rot untasted. Go and tell him,

We come to speak with him ; and you shall not sin

If you do say we think him over-proud

And under-honest, in self-assumption greater   120

Than in the note of judgment ; and worthier than   121

himself

Here tend the savage strangeness he puts on,   122

Disguise the holy strength of their command,   123

And underwrite in an observing kind

His humorous predominance ; yea, watch

His course and time, his ebbs and flows, as if

The passage and whole carriage of this action

Rode on his tide. Go tell him this, and add

That, if he overhold his price so much,   129

We'll none of him ; but let him, like an engine   130

Not portable, lie under this report :

'Bring action hither, this cannot go to war.'

A stirring dwarf we do allowance give   133

Before a sleeping giant. Tell him so.

PATROCLUS

I shall, and bring his answer presently.   *[Exit.]*

AGAMEMNON

In second voice we'll not be satisfied ;

We come to speak with him. Ulysses, enter you.

    [Exit Ulysses.]

AJAX What is he more than another ?

AGAMEMNON No more than what he thinks he is.

AJAX Is he so much ? Do you not think he thinks himself a better man than I am ?

AGAMEMNON No question.

AJAX Will you subscribe his thought, and say he is ?

AGAMEMNON No, noble Ajax ; you are as strong, as valiant, as wise, no less noble, much more gentle, and altogether more tractable.

AJAX Why should a man be proud ? How doth pride grow ? I know not what pride is.

AGAMEMNON Your mind is the clearer and your virtues the fairer. He that is proud eats up himself. Pride is his own glass, his own trumpet, his own chronicle ; and   151 whatever praises itself but in the deed, devours the deed in the praise.

AJAX I do hate a proud man, as I do hate the engendering of toads.

NESTOR *[aside]* And yet he loves himself. Is't not strange ?

    Enter Ulysses.

ULYSSES

Achilles will not to the field to-morrow.

AGAMEMNON

What's his excuse ?

ULYSSES   He doth rely on none,

But carries on the stream of his dispose   158

Without observance or respect of any,

In will peculiar and in self-admission.   160

AGAMEMNON

Why will he not upon our fair request

Untent his person and share th' air with us ?

ULYSSES

Things small as nothing, for request's sake only,   163

He makes important. Possessed he is with greatness,

And speaks not to himself but with a pride

That quarrels at self-breath. Imagined worth   166

Holds in his blood such swoln and hot discourse

That 'twixt his mental and his active parts

Kingdomed Achilles in commotion rages   169

And batters down himself. What should I say ?

He is so plaguy proud that the death-tokens of it   171

---

75 *shent* reviled   76 *appertainings* rights of rank   78 *move . . . place* raise the question of our authority   90 *argument* subject matter   94 *fraction* break   95 *faction* union; *composure* union   102 *flexure* bending   105 *state* accompanying noblemen   108 *breath* exercise   114 *Not . . . beheld* not modestly borne   120 *under-honest* lacking in open dealing   121 *note of judgment* esteem of men of judgment   122 *tend . . . strangeness* wait upon the rude aloofness   123–25 *Disguise . . . predominance* hide their god-given authority and acquiesce obediently in his eccentric claim to superiority   129 *overhold* overvalue   130 *engine* mechanical contrivance (here military)   133 *allowance* approbation   151 *glass* mirror   158 *dispose* bent of mind   160 *self-admission* self-approval   163 *for . . . only* only because they are requested   166 *That . . . self-breath* that quarrels with itself for speaking   169 *Kingdomed* i.e. Achilles is like a kingdom in civil war   171 *death-tokens* symptoms of the plague on the body

Cry 'No recovery.'

AGAMEMNON   Let Ajax go to him.
Dear lord, go you and greet him in his tent :
'Tis said he holds you well, and will be led
At your request a little from himself.

ULYSSES
O Agamemnon, let it not be so !
We'll consecrate the steps that Ajax makes
When they go from Achilles. Shall the proud lord
179 That bastes his arrogance with his own seam
And never suffers matter of the world
Enter his thoughts, save such as doth revolve
And ruminate himself, shall he be worshipped
Of that we hold an idol more than he ?
No, this thrice-worthy and right valiant lord
185 Shall not so stale his palm, nobly acquired,
186 Nor, by my will, assubjugate his merit,
As amply titled as Achilles' is,
By going to Achilles.
That were to enlard his fat-already pride,
190 And add more coals to Cancer when he burns
191 With entertaining great Hyperion.
This lord go to him ! Jupiter forbid,
And say in thunder, 'Achilles, go to him.'

NESTOR [aside]
194 O, this is well. He rubs the vein of him.

DIOMEDES [aside]
And how his silence drinks up his applause !

AJAX
If I go to him, with my armèd fist
197 I'll pash him o'er the face.

AGAMEMNON
O, no ! you shall not go.

AJAX
199 An he be proud with me, I'll pheese his pride.
Let me go to him.

ULYSSES
Not for the worth that hangs upon our quarrel.

AJAX A paltry, insolent fellow !

NESTOR [aside] How he describes himself !

AJAX Can he not be sociable ?

ULYSSES [aside] The raven chides blackness.

206 AJAX I'll let his humorous blood.

AGAMEMNON [aside] He will be the physician that should
be the patient.

AJAX An all men were of my mind —

ULYSSES [aside] Wit would be out of fashion.

211 AJAX 'A should not bear it so, 'a should eat swords first.
Shall pride carry it ?

NESTOR [aside] An 'twould, you'd carry half.

ULYSSES [aside] 'A would have ten shares.

AJAX I will knead him ; I'll make him supple.

216 NESTOR [aside] He's not yet through warm. Force him
with praises ; pour in, pour in ; his ambition is dry.

ULYSSES [to Agamemnon]
My lord, you feed too much on this dislike.

NESTOR
Our noble general, do not do so.

DIOMEDES
You must prepare to fight without Achilles.

ULYSSES
Why, 'tis this naming of him does him harm.
Here is a man — but 'tis before his face ;
I will be silent.

NESTOR   Wherefore should you so ?
He is not emulous, as Achilles is.   224

ULYSSES
Know the whole world, he is as valiant —

AJAX
A whoreson dog, that shall palter with us thus !   226
Would he were a Troyan !

NESTOR What a vice were it in Ajax now —

ULYSSES If he were proud —

DIOMEDES Or covetous of praise —

ULYSSES Ay, or surly borne —

DIOMEDES Or strange, or self-affected !   232

ULYSSES
Thank the heavens, lord, thou art of sweet composure ;
Praise him that got thee, she that gave thee suck ;
Famed be thy tutor, and thy parts of nature
Thrice-famed beyond all erudition ;   236
But he that disciplined thine arms to fight,
Let Mars divide eternity in twain
And give him half ; and, for thy vigor,
Bull-bearing Milo his addition yield   240
To sinewy Ajax. I will not praise thy wisdom,
Which, like a bourn, a pale, a shore, confines   242
Thy spacious and dilated parts. Here's Nestor,
Instructed by the antiquary times,   244
He must, he is, he cannot but be wise ;
But pardon, father Nestor, were your days
As green as Ajax, and your brain so tempered,
You should not have the eminence of him,
But be as Ajax.

AJAX   Shall I call you father ?

NESTOR
Ay, my good son.

DIOMEDES   Be ruled by him, Lord Ajax.

ULYSSES
There is no tarrying here ; the hart Achilles
Keeps thicket. Please it our great general
To call together all his state of war ;   253
Fresh kings are come to Troy. To-morrow,
We must with all our main of power stand fast.   255
And here's a lord — come knights from east to west,
And cull their flower, Ajax shall cope the best.

AGAMEMNON
Go we to council. Let Achilles sleep :
Light boats sail swift, though greater hulks draw deep.
           Exeunt.

*

[Music sounds within.] Enter Pandarus [and a   III, i
   Servant].

PANDARUS Friend you, pray you a word. Do you not follow the young Lord Paris ?

SERVANT Ay, sir, when he goes before me.

PANDARUS You depend upon him, I mean.   4

---

179 *seam* fat   185 *stale his palm* sully his glory   186 *assubjugate* debase
190 *Cancer* i.e. summer, which begins under this sign of the Zodiac   191
Hyperion the sun   194 *vein* mood   197 *pash* batter   199 *pheese* settle the
matter of   206 *let . . . blood* cure his humors by letting blood   211 *'A* he
216 *through* thoroughly   224 *emulous* envious   226 *palter* dodge   232
strange, or self-affected distant or caring only for himself   236 *erudition*
knowledge   240 *Milo* a famous Greek athlete ; *addition* i.e. his epithet
(*Bull-bearing*)   242 *bourn* boundary ; *pale* fence   244 *antiquary* i.e. studied
by antiquaries   253 *state* nobles in council   255 *main* might of military power
III, i The palace of Priam   4 *depend* are in a position of dependence

SERVANT Sir, I do depend upon the Lord.

PANDARUS You depend upon a noble gentleman; I must needs praise him.

SERVANT The Lord be praised!

PANDARUS You know me, do you not?

SERVANT Faith, sir, superficially.

PANDARUS Friend, know me better. I am the Lord Pandarus.

SERVANT I hope I shall know your honor better.

PANDARUS I do desire it.

14 SERVANT You are in the state of grace.

15 PANDARUS Grace? Not so, friend. Honor and lordship are my titles. What music is this?

SERVANT I do but partly know, sir. It is music in parts.

PANDARUS Know you the musicians?

SERVANT Wholly, sir.

PANDARUS Who play they to?

SERVANT To the hearers, sir.

PANDARUS At whose pleasure, friend?

SERVANT At mine, sir, and theirs that love music.

PANDARUS Command, I mean, friend.

SERVANT Who shall I command, sir?

PANDARUS Friend, we understand not one another. I am too courtly, and thou too cunning. At whose request do these men play?

SERVANT That's to't, indeed, sir. Marry, sir, at the re-
30 quest of Paris, my lord, who is there in person; with him the mortal Venus, the heart-blood of beauty, love's invisible soul.

PANDARUS Who? My cousin Cressida?

SERVANT No, sir, Helen. Could you not find out that by her attributes?

PANDARUS It should seem, fellow, that thou hast not seen the Lady Cressid. I come to speak with Paris from the Prince Troilus. I will make a complimental assault
39 upon him, for my business seethes.

40 SERVANT Sodden business! There's a stewed phrase, indeed.

   Enter Paris and Helen.

PANDARUS Fair be to you, my lord, and to all this fair company. Fair desires in all fair measure fairly guide
43 them. Especially to you, fair queen, fair thoughts be your fair pillow.

HELEN Dear lord, you are full of fair words.

PANDARUS You speak your fair pleasure, sweet queen.
47 Fair prince, here is good broken music.

PARIS You have broke it, cousin; and, by my life, you shall make it whole again; you shall piece it out with a piece of your performance. Nell, he is full of harmony.

PANDARUS Truly, lady, no.

HELEN O, sir!

PANDARUS Rude, in sooth; in good sooth, very rude.

54 PARIS Well said, my lord. Well, you say so in fits.

PANDARUS I have business to my lord, dear queen. My lord, will you vouchsafe me a word?

HELEN Nay, this shall not hedge us out. We'll hear you 57 sing, certainly.

PANDARUS Well, sweet queen, you are pleasant with me. But, marry, thus, my lord: my dear lord and most esteemed friend, your brother Troilus —

HELEN My Lord Pandarus, honey-sweet lord —

PANDARUS Go to, sweet queen, go to — commends himself most affectionately to you.

HELEN You shall not bob us out of our melody. If you do, 65 our melancholy upon your head!

PANDARUS Sweet queen, sweet queen; that's a sweet queen, i' faith.

HELEN And to make a sweet lady sad is a sour offense.

PANDARUS Nay, that shall not serve your turn; that shall it not, in truth, la. Nay, I care not for such words; no, no. And, my lord, he desires you that, if the king call for him at supper, you will make his excuse.

HELEN My Lord Pandarus —

PANDARUS What says my sweet queen, my very, very sweet queen?

PARIS What exploit's in hand? Where sups he to-night?

HELEN Nay, but my lord —

PANDARUS What says my sweet queen? My cousin will fall out with you.

HELEN You must not know where he sups.

PARIS I'll lay my life, with my disposer Cressida.   82

PANDARUS No, no; no such matter; you are wide. Come, 83 your disposer is sick.

PARIS Well, I'll make excuse.

PANDARUS Ay, good my lord. Why should you say Cressida? No, your poor disposer's sick.

PARIS I spy.

PANDARUS You spy? What do you spy? Come, give me an instrument now, sweet queen.

HELEN Why, this is kindly done.

PANDARUS My niece is horribly in love with a thing you have, sweet queen.

HELEN She shall have it, my lord, if it be not my Lord Paris.

PANDARUS He? No, she'll none of him; they two are twain.   95

HELEN Falling in, after falling out, may make them three.

PANDARUS Come, come, I'll hear no more of this. I'll sing you a song now.

HELEN Ay, ay, prithee. Now by my troth, sweet lord, thou hast a fine forehead.

PANDARUS Ay, you may, you may.   101

HELEN Let thy song be love. This love will undo us all. O Cupid, Cupid, Cupid!

PANDARUS Love! ay, that it shall, i' faith.

PARIS Ay, good, now 'Love, love, nothing but love.'

PANDARUS [In good troth, it begins so:]

   [Sings.]

Love, love, nothing but love, still love still more!
For, O, love's bow shoots buck and doe.
The shaft confounds not that it wounds,
But tickles still the sore.   110
These lovers cry, O ho! they die!
Yet that which seems the wound to kill
Doth turn O ho! to Ha, ha, he!
So dying love lives still.
O ho! a while, but Ha, ha, ha!
O ho! groans out for Ha, ha, ha! — Heigh ho!

HELEN In love, i' faith, to the very tip of the nose.

PARIS He eats nothing but doves, love, and that breeds
hot blood, and hot blood begets hot thoughts, and hot
120 thoughts beget hot deeds, and hot deeds is love.

PANDARUS Is this the generation of love – hot blood, hot
thoughts, and hot deeds? Why, they are vipers. Is love a
generation of vipers? Sweet lord, who's a-field to-day?

PARIS Hector, Deiphobus, Helenus, Antenor, and all the
gallantry of Troy. I would fain have armed to-day, but
my Nell would not have it so. How chance my brother
Troilus went not?

HELEN He hangs the lip at something. You know all,
Lord Pandarus.

130 PANDARUS Not I, honey-sweet queen. I long to hear how
they sped to-day. You'll remember your brother's excuse?

PARIS To a hair.

PANDARUS Farewell, sweet queen.

HELEN Commend me to your niece.

PANDARUS I will, sweet queen.   *[Exit.] Sound a retreat.*

PARIS
They're come from the field. Let us to Priam's hall
To greet the warriors. Sweet Helen, I must woo you
To help unarm our Hector. His stubborn buckles,
With these your white enchanting fingers touched,
Shall more obey than to the edge of steel
Or force of Greekish sinews. You shall do more
143 Than all the island kings – disarm great Hector.

HELEN
'Twill make us proud to be his servant, Paris;
Yea, what he shall receive of us in duty
Gives us more palm in beauty than we have,
Yea, overshines ourself.

PARIS
Sweet, above thought I love thee.   *Exeunt.*

*

III, ii   *Enter Pandarus [and] Troilus' Man.*

PANDARUS How now, where's thy master? At my cousin
Cressida's?

MAN No, sir; he stays for you to conduct him thither.
    [Enter Troilus.]

PANDARUS O, here he comes. How now, how now?

TROILUS Sirrah, walk off.   *[Exit Man.]*

PANDARUS Have you seen my cousin?

TROILUS
No, Pandarus. I stalk about her door
8 Like a strange soul upon the Stygian banks
9 Staying for waftage. O, be thou my Charon,
And give me swift transportance to those fields
Where I may wallow in the lily-beds
12 Proposed for the deserver. O gentle Pandar,
From Cupid's shoulder pluck his painted wings,
And fly with me to Cressid.

PANDARUS
15 Walk here i' th' orchard. I'll bring her straight.   *[Exit.]*

TROILUS
I am giddy; expectation whirls me round.
Th' imaginary relish is so sweet
That it enchants my sense. What will it be
19 When that the wat'ry palates taste indeed
Love's thrice-repurèd nectar? Death, I fear me,
21 Sounding destruction, or some joy too fine,
Too subtle, potent, tuned too sharp in sweetness
For the capacity of my ruder powers.

I fear it much; and I do fear besides
That I shall lose distinction in my joys,   25
As doth a battle, when they charge on heaps
The enemy flying.
    [Enter Pandarus.]

PANDARUS She's making her ready; she'll come straight;
you must be witty now. She does so blush, and fetches   29
her wind so short as if she were frayed with a spirit. I'll   30
fetch her. It is the prettiest villain; she fetches her   31
breath as short as a new-ta'en sparrow.   *[Exit.]*

TROILUS
Even such a passion doth embrace my bosom.
My heart beats thicker than a feverous pulse,
And all my powers do their bestowing lose,   35
Like vassalage at unawares encount'ring   36
The eye of majesty.
    Enter Pandarus and Cressida.

PANDARUS Come, come, what need you blush? Shame's
a baby. Here she is now; swear the oaths now to her that
you have sworn to me. What! are you gone again? You
must be watched ere you be made tame, must you?   41
Come your ways, come your ways; an you draw backward, we'll put you i' th' fills. Why do you not speak to   43
her? Come, draw this curtain, and let's see your picture.   44
Alas the day, how loath you are to offend daylight! An
'twere dark, you'd close sooner. So, so; rub on, and kiss   46
the mistress. How now, a kiss in fee-farm! Build there,   47
carpenter; the air is sweet. Nay, you shall fight your
hearts out ere I part you. The falcon as the tercel, for all   49
the ducks i' th' river. Go to, go to.

TROILUS You have bereft me of all words, lady.

PANDARUS Words pay no debts, give her deeds; but
she'll bereave you o' th' deeds too if she call your activity
in question. What, billing again? Here's 'In witness   54
whereof the parties interchangeably' – Come in, come
in. I'll go get a fire.   *[Exit.]*

CRESSIDA Will you walk in, my lord?

TROILUS O Cressid, how often have I wished me thus!

CRESSIDA Wished, my lord? The gods grant – O my lord!

TROILUS What should they grant? What makes this
pretty abruption? What too curious dreg espies my   61
sweet lady in the fountain of our love?

CRESSIDA More dregs than water, if my fears have eyes.

TROILUS Fears make devils of cherubins; they never see
truly.

CRESSIDA Blind fear, that seeing reason leads, finds safer
footing than blind reason stumbling without fear. To
fear the worst oft cures the worse.

TROILUS O, let my lady apprehend no fear. In all Cupid's
pageant there is presented no monster.

---

143 *island* i.e. Greek
III, ii Pandarus' orchard   8 *Stygian* (the Styx was a river of the underworld)   9 *waftage* passage by water; *Charon* ferryman of the dead across the
Styx to Hades   12 *Proposed* promised   15 *orchard* garden   19 *wat'ry*
watering (cf. 'mouth waters')   21 *Sounding* swooning   25 *distinction*
power of distinguishing   29 *be witty* have your wits about you   30 *frayed
with a spirit* frightened by a ghost   31 *villain* (a term of endearment here)
35 *bestowing* proper use   36 *vassalage* vassals   41 *watched* kept awake (a
method used in taming a hawk)   43 *fills* shafts   44 *curtain* i.e. veil
46–47 *rub . . . mistress* (in bowling, 'to rub' was to meet obstacles in the
way of the object-ball or 'mistress')   47 *in fee-farm* in perpetuity   49–50
The falcon . . . river i.e. I will bet on the falcon (female hawk, i.e. Cressida)
against the tercel (male hawk) to bring down any amount of game   54–55
In witness . . . interchangeably (a legal formula completed by the words
'have set their hands and seals')   61 *abruption* breaking off; *curious*
causing care or anxiety

70 CRESSIDA Nor nothing monstrous neither?

TROILUS Nothing but our undertakings when we vow to weep seas, live in fire, eat rocks, tame tigers, thinking it harder for our mistress to devise imposition enough than for us to undergo any difficulty imposed. This is the monstruosity in love, lady, that the will is infinite and the execution confined; that the desire is boundless and the act a slave to limit.

CRESSIDA They say all lovers swear more performance than they are able, and yet reserve an ability that they never perform, vowing more than the perfection of ten and discharging less than the tenth part of one. They that have the voice of lions and the act of hares, are they not monsters?

85
86
TROILUS Are there such? Such are not we. Praise us as we are tasted, allow us as we prove; our head shall go bare till merit crown it. No perfection in reversion shall have a praise in present; we will not name desert before his birth, and, being born, his addition shall be humble. Few words to fair faith. Troilus shall be such to Cressid, 90 as what envy can say worst shall be a mock for his truth, and what truth can speak truest not truer than Troilus.

CRESSIDA Will you walk in, my lord?

Enter Pandarus.

PANDARUS What, blushing still? Have you not done talking yet?

CRESSIDA Well, uncle, what folly I commit, I dedicate to you.

PANDARUS I thank you for that. If my lord get a boy of you, you'll give him me. Be true to my lord; if he flinch, chide me for it.

100 TROILUS You know now your hostages, your uncle's word and my firm faith.

PANDARUS Nay, I'll give my word for her too. Our kindred, though they be long ere they be wooed, they are constant being won. They are burrs, I can tell you; they'll stick where they are thrown.

CRESSIDA
Boldness comes to me now and brings me heart.
Prince Troilus, I have loved you night and day
For many weary months.

TROILUS
Why was my Cressid then so hard to win?

CRESSIDA
110 Hard to seem won; but I was won, my lord,
With the first glance that ever – pardon me:
If I confess much you will play the tyrant.
I love you now, but not, till now, so much
But I might master it. In faith, I lie;
My thoughts were like unbridled children grown
Too headstrong for their mother. See, we fools!
Why have I blabbed? Who shall be true to us
When we are so unsecret to ourselves?
But, though I loved you well, I wooed you not;
120 And yet, good faith, I wished myself a man,

Or that we women had men's privilege
Of speaking first. Sweet, bid me hold my tongue,
For in this rapture I shall surely speak
The thing I shall repent. See, see! your silence,
Cunning in dumbness, from my weakness draws
My very soul of counsel. Stop my mouth.   126

TROILUS
And shall, albeit sweet music issues thence.

PANDARUS Pretty, i' faith.

CRESSIDA
My lord, I do beseech you, pardon me;
'Twas not my purpose thus to beg a kiss.
I am ashamed. O heavens, what have I done?
For this time will I take my leave, my lord.

TROILUS
Your leave, sweet Cressid?

PANDARUS Leave! An you take leave till to-morrow morning –

CRESSIDA
Pray you, content you.

TROILUS   What offends you, lady?

CRESSIDA
Sir, mine own company.

TROILUS
You cannot shun yourself.

CRESSIDA
Let me go and try.
I have a kind of self resides with you;
But an unkind self, that itself will leave
To be another's fool. I would be gone.   142
Where is my wit? I know not what I speak.

TROILUS
Well know they what they speak that speak so wisely.

CRESSIDA
Perchance, my lord, I show more craft than love,
And fell so roundly to a large confession   146
To angle for your thoughts. But you are wise,   147
Or else you love not, for to be wise and love
Exceeds man's might; that dwells with gods above.

TROILUS
O! that I thought it could be in a woman –
As, if it can, I will presume in you –
To feed for aye her lamp and flames of love;
To keep her constancy in plight and youth,   153
Outliving beauty's outward, with a mind
That doth renew swifter than blood decays;
Or that persuasion could but thus convince me
That my integrity and truth to you
Might be affronted with the match and weight   158
Of such a winnowed purity in love;
How were I then uplifted! But, alas,
I am as true as truth's simplicity,
And simpler than the infancy of truth.

CRESSIDA
In that I'll war with you.

TROILUS   O virtuous fight,
When right with right wars who shall be most right!
True swains in love shall in the world to come
Approve their truth by Troilus. When their rhymes,   166
Full of protest, of oath, and big compare,
Wants similes, truth tired with iteration,
'As true as steel, as plantage to the moon,   169
As sun to day, as turtle to her mate,   170
As iron to adamant, as earth to th' centre,'   171

---

85 *tasted* tested; *allow* approve   86 *reversion* right of future possession
90 *as what . . . truth* that malice can say no worse than to sneer at his
constancy   126 *soul of counsel* inmost secrets   142 *fool* dupe   146
roundly straightforwardly; *large* unrestrained   147-49 *But . . . might*
(either the text is corrupt or Cressida contradicts herself)   153 *in plight
and youth* as it was plighted, and as fresh   158 *affronted* confronted
166 *Approve* attest   169 *plantage* vegetation (the moon was supposed
to influence vegetation)   170 *turtle* turtledove (a type of love faithful
to death)   171 *adamant* loadstone (magnetic)

Yet, after all comparisons of truth,
As truth's authentic author to be cited,
'As true as Troilus' shall crown up the verse
175 And sanctify the numbers.   Prophet may you be!
CRESSIDA
If I be false or swerve a hair from truth,
When time is old and hath forgot itself,
When waterdrops have worn the stones of Troy,
And blind oblivion swallowed cities up,
180 And mighty states characterless are grated
To dusty nothing, yet let memory,
From false to false among false maids in love,
Upbraid my falsehood! When th' have said, 'as false
As air, as water, wind or sandy earth,
As fox to lamb, as wolf to heifer's calf,
186 Pard to the hind, or stepdame to her son,'
Yea, let them say, to stick the heart of falsehood,
'As false as Cressid.'
PANDARUS Go to, a bargain made; seal it, seal it; I'll be
the witness. Here I hold your hand, here my cousin's. If
ever you prove false one to another, since I have taken
such pains to bring you together, let all pitiful goers-
between be called to the world's end after my name; call
194 them all Pandars; let all constant men be Troiluses, all
false women Cressids, and all brokers-between Pandars! Say, 'Amen.'
TROILUS Amen.
CRESSIDA Amen.
PANDARUS Amen. Whereupon I will show you a cham-
199 ber which bed, because it shall not speak of your pretty
encounters, press it to death. Away!
                    Exeunt [Troilus and Cressida].
And Cupid grant all tongue-tied maidens here
Bed, chamber, Pandar to provide this gear!   *Exit.*

*

III, iii   *[Flourish of trumpets.] Enter Ulysses, Diomedes,*
            Nestor, Agamemnon, [Menelaus, Ajax, and]
            Calchas.
CALCHAS
Now, princes, for the service I have done,
Th' advantage of the time prompts me aloud
To call for recompense. Appear it to mind
That through the sight I bear in things to love,
5 I have abandoned Troy, left my possession,
Incurred a traitor's name, exposed myself,
From certain and possessed conveniences,
8 To doubtful fortunes, sequest'ring from me all
That time, acquaintance, custom, and condition
10 Made tame and most familiar to my nature;
And here, to do you service, am become
As new into the world, strange, unacquainted.
13 I do beseech you, as in way of taste,
To give me now a little benefit
Out of those many regist'red in promise,
Which, you say, live to come in my behalf.
AGAMEMNON
What wouldst thou of us, Troyan? Make demand.
CALCHAS
You have a Troyan prisoner, called Antenor,
Yesterday took; Troy holds him very dear.
Oft have you – often have you thanks therefor –
21 Desired my Cressid in right great exchange,

Whom Troy hath still denied; but this Antenor
I know is such a wrest in their affairs   23
That their negotiations all must slack,
Wanting his manage; and they will almost
Give us a prince of blood, a son of Priam,
In change of him. Let him be sent, great princes,
And he shall buy my daughter; and her presence
Shall quite strike off all service I have done
In most accepted pain.   30
AGAMEMNON   Let Diomedes bear him,
And bring us Cressid hither. Calchas shall have
What he requests of us. Good Diomed,
Furnish you fairly for his interchange.
Withal bring word if Hector will to-morrow
Be answered in his challenge. Ajax is ready.
DIOMEDES
This shall I undertake, and 'tis a burden
Which I am proud to bear.   *Exit [with Calchas].*
            Achilles and Patroclus stand in their tent.
ULYSSES
Achilles stands i' th' entrance of his tent.
Please it our general to pass strangely by him,
As if he were forgot; and, princes all,
Lay negligent and loose regard upon him.
I will come last. 'Tis like he'll question me
Why such unplausive eyes are bent, why turned, on him. 43
If so, I have derision med'cinable
To use between your strangeness and his pride,
Which his own will shall have desire to drink.
It may do good; pride hath no other glass
To show itself but pride, for supple knees   48
Feed arrogance and are the proud man's fees.
AGAMEMNON
We'll execute your purpose, and put on
A form of strangeness as we pass along.
So do each lord, and either greet him not
Or else disdainfully, which shall shake him more
Than if not looked on. I will lead the way.
ACHILLES
What comes the general to speak with me?
You know my mind; I'll fight no more 'gainst Troy.
AGAMEMNON
What says Achilles? Would he aught with us?
NESTOR
Would you, my lord, aught with the general?
ACHILLES No.
NESTOR Nothing, my lord.   60
AGAMEMNON The better.
ACHILLES Good day, good day.
MENELAUS How do you? How do you?
ACHILLES What, does the cuckold scorn me?
AJAX How now, Patroclus?
ACHILLES Good morrow, Ajax.
AJAX Ha?
ACHILLES Good morrow.

175 *numbers* verses   180 *characterless* without a mark   186 *Pard* panther
or leopard; *hind* doe   194 *constant* (the context demands 'inconstant,'
but the text foretells the outcome of the play)   199 *which bed* in which the
bed; *because* in order that
III, iii The Grecian camp   5 *abandoned* (cf. I, i, 77)   8 *sequest'ring*
putting away   10 *tame* familiar   13 *taste* foretaste   21 *right great exchange* exchange for someone very great   23 *wrest* key for tuning a harp,
i.e. key to harmony in Troy   30 *accepted* cheerfully endured   43 *unplausive* disapproving   48 *show* mirror

AJAX Ay, and good next day too.   *Exeunt.*

ACHILLES

70   What mean these fellows? Know they not Achilles?

PATROCLUS

They pass by strangely. They were used to bend,
To send their smiles before them to Achilles,
To come as humbly as they used to creep
To holy altars.

ACHILLES   What, am I poor of late?
'Tis certain, greatness, once fall'n out with fortune,
Must fall out with men too. What the declined is
He shall as soon read in the eyes of others
As feel in his own fall; for men, like butterflies,
79   Show not their mealy wings but to the summer,
And not a man, for being simply man,
Hath any honor, but honor for those honors
82   That are without him, as place, riches, and favor,
Prizes of accident as oft as merit;
Which when they fall, as being slippery standers,
The love that leaned on them as slippery too,
Doth one pluck down another, and together
Die in the fall. But 'tis not so with me;
Fortune and I are friends. I do enjoy
89   At ample point all that I did possess,
Save these men's looks; who do, methinks, find out
Something not worth in me such rich beholding
As they have often given. Here is Ulysses;
I'll interrupt his reading.
How now, Ulysses.

ULYSSES   Now, great Thetis' son.

ACHILLES

What are you reading?

ULYSSES   A strange fellow here
96   Writes me that man, how dearly ever parted,
97   How much in having, or without or in,
Cannot make boast to have that which he hath,
99   Nor feels not what he owes but by reflection;
As when his virtues aiming upon others
Heat them, and they retort that heat again
To the first giver.

ACHILLES   This is not strange, Ulysses.
The beauty that is borne here in the face
The bearer knows not, but commends itself
To others' eyes; nor doth the eye itself,
That most pure spirit of sense, behold itself,
Not going from itself; but eye to eye opposed
Salutes each other with each other's form;
109   For speculation turns not to itself
Till it hath travelled and is married there
Where it may see itself. This is not strange at all.

ULYSSES

112   I do not strain at the position,
It is familiar, but at the author's drift;

Who in his circumstance expressly proves   114
That no man is the lord of anything –
Though in and of him there be much consisting –   116
Till he communicate his parts to others;
Nor doth he of himself know them for aught
Till he behold them formèd in th' applause
Where th' are extended; who, like an arch, reverb'rate   120
The voice again, or, like a gate of steel
Fronting the sun, receives and renders back
His figure and his heat. I was much rapt in this,
And apprehended here immediately
Th' unknown Ajax.
Heavens, what a man is there! A very horse,
That has he knows not what. Nature, what things there are
Most abject in regard and dear in use!   128
What things again most dear in the esteem
And poor in worth! Now shall we see to-morrow,
An act that very chance doth throw upon him,
Ajax renowned. O heavens, what some men do,
While some men leave to do!
How some men creep in skittish Fortune's hall,   134
Whiles others play the idiots in her eyes!
How one man eats into another's pride,
While pride is fasting in his wantonness!   137
To see these Grecian lords – why, even already
They clap the lubber Ajax on the shoulder,
As if his foot were on brave Hector's breast,
And great Troy shrinking.

ACHILLES

I do believe it; for they passed by me
As misers do by beggars, neither gave to me
Good word nor look. What, are my deeds forgot?

ULYSSES

Time hath, my lord, a wallet at his back,
Wherein he puts alms for oblivion,
A great-sized monster of ingratitudes.
Those scraps are good deeds past, which are devoured
As fast as they are made, forgot as soon
As done. Perseverance, dear my lord,
Keeps honor bright; to have done, is to hang
Quite out of fashion, like a rusty mail   152
In monumental mock'ry. Take the instant way;   153
For honor travels in a strait so narrow
Where one but goes abreast. Keep, then, the path;
For emulation hath a thousand sons
That one by one pursue. If you give way,
Or hedge aside from the direct forthright,   158
Like to an ent'red tide they all rush by
And leave you hindmost;
[Or, like a gallant horse fall'n in first rank,
Lie there for pavement to the abject rear,   162
O'errun and trampled on.] Then what they do in present,
Though less than yours in past, must o'ertop yours;
For time is like a fashionable host,
That slightly shakes his parting guest by th' hand,
And with his arms outstretched, as he would fly,
Grasps in the comer. The welcome ever smiles,
And farewell goes out sighing. Let not virtue seek
Remuneration for the thing it was. For beauty, wit,
High birth, vigor of bone, desert in service,
Love, friendship, charity, are subjects all
To envious and calumniating time.
One touch of nature makes the whole world kin,   174

---

79 *mealy* powdered   82 *without* external to   89 *At ample point* in full measure   96 *how . . . parted* with however valuable parts (i.e. natural endowments)   97 *having* possession; *or . . . in* external or internal   99 *Nor . . . reflection* and perceives what he owns only as it is reflected   109 *speculation* the power of sight   112 *position* i.e. of the writer mentioned above   114 *in his circumstance* in getting down to details   116 *Though . . . consisting* though much exists in him and because of him   120 *Where th'are extended* in which they are noised abroad; *who* which   128 *regard* esteem   134 *in* into   137 *his wantonness* its own wanton self-satisfaction   152 *mail* armor   153 *instant* immediately ahead   158 *forthright* straight ahead   162 *abject rear* miserable specimens in the rear   174 *One touch of nature* one common weakness, namely, praising *new-born gawds*

175 That all with one consent praise new-born gawds,
Though they are made and moulded of things past,
And give to dust that is a little gilt
More laud than gilt o'er-dusted.
The present eye praises the present object.
Then marvel not, thou great and complete man,
That all the Greeks begin to worship Ajax;
Since things in motion sooner catch the eye
183 Than what not stirs. The cry went once on thee,
And still it might, and yet it may again,
If thou wouldst not entomb thyself alive
And case thy reputation in thy tent;
Whose glorious deeds, but in these fields of late,
188 Made emulous missions 'mongst the gods themselves
189 And drave great Mars to faction.

ACHILLES   Of this my privacy
I have strong reasons.

ULYSSES   But 'gainst your privacy
The reasons are more potent and heroical.
'Tis known, Achilles, that you are in love
193 With one of Priam's daughters.

ACHILLES Ha! known!

ULYSSES
Is that a wonder?
196 The providence that's in a watchful state
197 Knows almost every grain of Pluto's gold,
198 Finds bottom in th' uncomprehensive deeps,
Keeps place with thought, and almost, like the gods,
Does thoughts unveil in their dumb cradles.
201 There is a mystery – with whom relation
Durst never meddle – in the soul of state,
Which hath an operation more divine
Than breath or pen can give expressure to.
All the commerce that you have had with Troy
As perfectly is ours as yours, my lord;
And better would it fit Achilles much
To throw down Hector than Polyxena.
209 But it must grieve young Pyrrhus now at home,
When fame shall in our islands sound her trump,
And all the Greekish girls shall tripping sing,
'Great Hector's sister did Achilles win,
But our great Ajax bravely beat down him.'
Farewell, my lord; I as your lover speak;
The fool slides o'er the ice that you should break. *[Exit.]*

PATROCLUS
To this effect, Achilles, have I moved you.
A woman impudent and mannish grown
Is not more loathed than an effeminate man
In time of action. I stand condemned for this.
They think my little stomach to the war
And your great love to me restrains you thus.
Sweet, rouse yourself; and the weak wanton Cupid
Shall from your neck unloose his amorous fold
And, like a dew-drop from the lion's mane,
Be shook to air.

ACHILLES   Shall Ajax fight with Hector?

PATROCLUS
Ay, and perhaps receive much honor by him.

ACHILLES
I see my reputation is at stake;
228 My fame is shrewdly gored.

PATROCLUS   O, then, beware!
Those wounds heal ill that men do give themselves.
Omission to do what is necessary

Seals a commission to a blank of danger;   231
And danger, like an ague, subtly taints
Even then when we sit idly in the sun.

ACHILLES
Go call Thersites hither, sweet Patroclus.
I'll send the fool to Ajax and desire him
T' invite the Troyan lords after the combat
To see us here unarmed. I have a woman's longing,   237
An appetite that I am sick withal,
To see great Hector in his weeds of peace,   239
To talk with him and to behold his visage,
Even to my full of view. A labor saved!
Enter Thersites.

THERSITES A wonder!

ACHILLES What?

THERSITES Ajax goes up and down the field, asking for himself.   245

ACHILLES How so?

THERSITES He must fight singly to-morrow with Hector, and is so prophetically proud of an heroical cudgelling that he raves in saying nothing.

ACHILLES How can that be?

THERSITES Why, 'a stalks up and down like a peacock – a stride and a stand; ruminates like an hostess that hath no arithmetic but her brain to set down her reckoning; bites his lip with a politic regard, as who should say, 'There   254 were wit in this head an 'twould out'; and so there is, but it lies as coldly in him as fire in a flint, which will not show without knocking. The man's undone for ever, for if Hector break not his neck i' th' combat, he'll break't himself in vainglory. He knows not me. I said, 'Good morrow, Ajax'; and he replies, 'Thanks, Agamemnon.' What think you of this man that takes me for the general? He's grown a very land-fish, languageless, a monster. A plague of opinion! A man may wear it on both sides like a leather jerkin.   264

ACHILLES Thou must be my ambassador to him, Thersites.

THERSITES Who, I? Why, he'll answer nobody; he professes not answering. Speaking is for beggars; he wears his tongue in's arms. I will put on his presence; let   268 Patroclus make demands to me, you shall see the pageant of Ajax.

ACHILLES To him, Patroclus. Tell him I humbly desire the valiant Ajax to invite the most valorous Hector to come unarmed to my tent, and to procure safe-conduct for his person of the magnanimous and most illustrious, six-or-seven-times-honored captain-general of the Grecian army, Agamemnon, et caetera. Do this.

PATROCLUS Jove bless great Ajax!

THERSITES Hum!

---

175 *gawds* toys, gewgaws   183 *cry* public acclaim   188 *emulous missions* (the gods joined in the fighting, taking opposing sides)   189 *to faction* to become a partisan   193 *one . . . daughters* Polyxena (with whom, in one legend, Achilles was keeping a tryst when Paris shot him in his vulnerable heel)   196 *providence* (here, timely care rather than foresight)   197 *Pluto's* (Shakespeare confused Pluto, god of the underworld, with Plutus, god of wealth)   198 *uncomprehensive* unfathomable   201 *relation* open statement   209 *Pyrrhus* son of Achilles (also called Neoptolemus), who came to the siege after his father's death   228 *shrewdly gored* seriously wounded   231 *Seals . . . danger* binds one to encounter unknown dangers (royal agents were given blank commissions, already sealed, to use for arrests or exactions)   237 *woman's* i.e. pregnant woman's   239 *weeds* dress   245 *himself* ('Ajax,' i.e. a jakes, was slang for a privy)   254 *politic regard* expression of wisdom   264 *jerkin* close-fitting jacket   268 *put on* imitate

PATROCLUS I come from the worthy Achilles –

THERSITES Ha!

280 PATROCLUS Who most humbly desires you to invite Hector to his tent –

THERSITES Hum!

PATROCLUS And to procure safe-conduct from Aga- memnon.

THERSITES Agamemnon?

PATROCLUS Ay, my lord.

THERSITES Ha!

PATROCLUS What say you to't?

THERSITES God be wi' you, with all my heart.

PATROCLUS Your answer, sir.

290 THERSITES If to-morrow be a fair day, by eleven of the clock it will be one way or other; howsoever, he shall pay for me ere he has me.

PATROCLUS Your answer, sir.

THERSITES Fare ye well, with all my heart.

ACHILLES Why, but he is not in this tune, is he?

THERSITES No, but out of tune thus. What music will be in him when Hector has knocked out his brains, I know not; but I am sure none, unless the fiddler Apollo get

299 his sinews to make catlings on.

ACHILLES Come, thou shalt bear a letter to him straight.

THERSITES Let me bear another to his horse, for that's

302 the more capable creature.

ACHILLES
My mind is troubled, like a fountain stirred;
And I myself see not the bottom of it.
        [Exeunt Achilles and Patroclus.]

THERSITES Would the fountain of your mind were clear again, that I might water an ass at it! I had rather be a tick in a sheep than such a valiant ignorance.   [Exit.]

*

IV, i   Enter, at one door, Aeneas with a torch; at another,
        Paris, Deiphobus, Antenor, Diomed the Grecian,
        [and others,] with torches.

PARIS
    See, ho! who is that there?

DEIPHOBUS   It is the Lord Aeneas.

AENEAS
    Is the prince there in person?
    Had I so good occasion to lie long
    As you, Prince Paris, nothing but heavenly business
    Should rob my bed-mate of my company.

DIOMEDES
    That's my mind too. Good morrow, Lord Aeneas.

PARIS
    A valiant Greek, Aeneas; take his hand.
8   Witness the process of your speech, wherein
9   You told how Diomed, a whole week by days,
    Did haunt you in the field.

AENEAS   Health to you, valiant sir,
11 During all question of the gentle truce;

But when I meet you armed, as black defiance
As heart can think or courage execute.

DIOMEDES
The one and other Diomed embraces.
Our bloods are now in calm, and, so long, health!
But when contention and occasion meet,   16
By Jove, I'll play the hunter for thy life
With all my force, pursuit, and policy.

AENEAS
And thou shalt hunt a lion that will fly
With his face backward. In humane gentleness,
Welcome to Troy! Now, by Anchises' life,   21
Welcome indeed! By Venus' hand I swear,   22
No man alive can love in such a sort
The thing he means to kill more excellently.

DIOMEDES
We sympathize. Jove, let Aeneas live,
If to my sword his fate be not the glory,
A thousand complete courses of the sun!
But, in mine emulous honor, let him die
With every joint a wound, and that to-morrow!

AENEAS
We know each other well.

DIOMEDES
We do, and long to know each other worse.

PARIS
This is the most despiteful gentle greeting,
The noblest hateful love, that e'er I heard of.
What business, lord, so early?

AENEAS
I was sent for to the king; but why, I know not.

PARIS
His purpose meets you; 'twas to bring this Greek
To Calchas' house, and there to render him,
For the enfreed Antenor, the fair Cressid.
Let's have your company; or, if you please,
Haste there before us. I constantly do think –   40
Or rather call my thought a certain knowledge –
My brother Troilus lodges there to-night.
Rouse him and give him note of our approach,
With the whole quality wherefore. I fear   44
We shall be much unwelcome.

AENEAS   That I assure you.
Troilus had rather Troy were borne to Greece
Than Cressid borne from Troy.

PARIS   There is no help.
The bitter disposition of the time
Will have it so. On, lord; we'll follow you.

AENEAS
Good morrow, all.   [Exit Aeneas.]

PARIS
And tell me, noble Diomed; faith, tell me true,
Even in the soul of sound good-fellowship,
Who, in your thoughts, deserves fair Helen best,
Myself or Menelaus?

DIOMEDES   Both alike.
He merits well to have her that doth seek her,
Not making any scruple of her soilure,
With such a hell of pain and world of charge;   57
And you as well to keep her that defend her,
Not palating the taste of her dishonor,   59
With such a costly loss of wealth and friends.
He, like a puling cuckold, would drink up
The lees and dregs of a flat tamèd piece;   62

299 catlings strings of catgut   302 capable intelligent
IV, i Within the gates of Troy   8 process drift, gist   9 by days day by day   11 question . . . truce conversation made possible by the truce   16 occasion opportunity   21 Anchises Aeneas' father   22 By Venus' hand (Diomedes had wounded Venus, mother of Aeneas, in the hand)   40 constantly firmly   44 quality explanation   57 charge cost   59 Not palating insensible of   62 flat tamèd piece cask so long opened that the wine is flat; also piece of flesh

You, like a lecher, out of whorish loins
Are pleased to breed out your inheritors.
65   Both merits poised, each weighs nor less nor more ;
But he as he, the heavier for a whore.

PARIS
You are too bitter to your countrywoman.

DIOMEDES
She's bitter to her country. Hear me, Paris :
For every false drop in her bawdy veins
70   A Grecian's life hath sunk ; for every scruple
Of her contaminated carrion weight
A Troyan hath been slain. Since she could speak,
She hath not given so many good words breath
As for her Greeks and Troyans suff'red death.

PARIS
75   Fair Diomed, you do as chapmen do,
Dispraise the thing that you desire to buy ;
But we in silence hold this virtue well,
We'll not commend what we intend to sell.
Here lies our way.   *Exeunt.*

*

IV, ii   *Enter Troilus and Cressida.*

TROILUS
Dear, trouble not yourself ; the morn is cold.

CRESSIDA
Then, sweet my lord, I'll call mine uncle down ;
He shall unbolt the gates.

TROILUS   Trouble him not ;
4   To bed, to bed. Sleep kill those pretty eyes,
And give as soft attachment to thy senses
As infants' empty of all thought !

CRESSIDA   Good morrow then.

TROILUS
I prithee now, to bed.

CRESSIDA   Are you aweary of me ?

TROILUS
O Cressida, but that the busy day,
Waked by the lark, hath roused the ribald crows,
And dreaming night will hide our joys no longer,
I would not from thee.

CRESSIDA   Night hath been too brief.

TROILUS
12   Beshrew the witch ! with venomous wights she stays
As tediously as hell, but flies the grasps of love
With wings more momentary-swift than thought.
You will catch cold and curse me.

CRESSIDA   Prithee, tarry ;
You men will never tarry.
O foolish Cressid ! I might have still held off,
And then you would have tarried. Hark, there's one up.

PANDARUS *[within]* What's all the doors open here ?

TROILUS   It is your uncle.

CRESSIDA   A pestilence on him ! Now will he be mocking.
I shall have such a life.
      Enter Pandarus.

PANDARUS   How now, how now ! How go maidenheads ?
Here, you maid, where's my cousin Cressid ?

CRESSIDA
Go hang yourself, you naughty mocking uncle.
You bring me to do – and then you flout me too.

PANDARUS   To do what ? To do what ? Let her say what.
What have I brought you to do ?

CRESSIDA
Come, come ; beshrew your heart ! You'll ne'er be good,
Nor suffer others.

PANDARUS   Ha, ha ! Alas, poor wretch ! A poor capoc- 31
chia ! Hast not slept to-night ? Would he not, a naughty
man, let it sleep ? A bugbear take him !

CRESSIDA
Did not I tell you ? Would he were knocked i' th' head !
      One knocks.
Who's that at door ? Good uncle, go and see.
My lord, come you again into my chamber.
You smile and mock me, as if I meant naughtily.

TROILUS   Ha, ha !

CRESSIDA
Come, you are deceived, I think of no such thing.
      Knock.
How earnestly they knock ! Pray you, come in.
I would not for half Troy have you seen here.
         Exeunt [Troilus and Cressida].

PANDARUS   Who's there ? What's the matter ? Will you
beat down the door ? How now, what's the matter ?
      [Enter Aeneas.]

AENEAS
Good morrow, lord, good morrow.

PANDARUS   Who's there ? My Lord Aeneas ! By my troth,
I knew you not. What news with you so early ?

AENEAS
Is not Prince Troilus here ?

PANDARUS   Here ? What should he do here ?

AENEAS
Come, he is here, my lord. Do not deny him.
It doth import him much to speak with me.   50

PANDARUS   Is he here, say you ? 'Tis more than I know,
I'll be sworn. For my own part, I came in late. What
should he do here ?

AENEAS   Who ! nay, then. Come, come, you'll do him
wrong ere you are ware. You'll be so true to him, to be
false to him. Do not you know of him, but yet go fetch
him hither ; go.
      [Enter Troilus.]

TROILUS   How now, what's the matter ?

AENEAS
My lord, I scarce have leisure to salute you,
My matter is so rash. There is at hand   60
Paris your brother, and Deiphobus,
The Grecian Diomed, and our Antenor
Delivered to us ; and for him forthwith,
Ere the first sacrifice, within this hour,
We must give up to Diomedes' hand
The Lady Cressida.

TROILUS   Is it concluded so ?

AENEAS
By Priam, and the general state of Troy.
They are at hand and ready to effect it.

TROILUS
How my achievements mock me !
I will go meet them. And, my Lord Aeneas,   70
We met by chance ; you did not find me here.

---

65 *poised* weighed   70 *scruple* the smallest unit of weight   75 *chapmen*
merchants
IV, ii The house of Pandarus   4 *kill* overpower   12 *venomous* poisonous,
i.e. doing evil   31 *capocchia* simpleton   50 *doth import* is important to
60 *rash* urgent

AENEAS
Good, good, my lord ; the secrets of nature
Have not more gift in taciturnity.
                Exeunt [Troilus and Aeneas].
PANDARUS Is't possible ? No sooner got but lost ? The
devil take Antenor ! The young prince will go mad. A
plague upon Antenor ! I would they had broke 's neck !
     Enter Cressida.
CRESSIDA
How now ? What's the matter ? Who was here ?
PANDARUS Ah, ah !
CRESSIDA
Why sigh you so profoundly ? Where's my lord ?
80 Gone ? Tell me, sweet uncle, what's the matter ?
PANDARUS Would I were as deep under the earth as I am
above !
CRESSIDA O the gods ! what's the matter ?
PANDARUS Pray thee, get thee in. Would thou hadst
ne'er been born ! I knew thou wouldst be his death. O
poor gentleman ! A plague upon Antenor !
CRESSIDA Good uncle, I beseech you on my knees,
what's the matter ?
PANDARUS Thou must be gone, wench, thou must be
gone ; thou art changed for Antenor. Thou must to thy
father and be gone from Troilus. 'Twill be his death ;
92 'twill be his bane ; he cannot bear it.
CRESSIDA
O you immortal gods ! I will not go.
PANDARUS Thou must.
CRESSIDA
I will not, uncle. I have forgot my father ;
I know no touch of consanguinity –
No kin, no love, no blood, no soul so near me
As the sweet Troilus. O you gods divine,
Make Cressid's name the very crown of falsehood
If ever she leave Troilus ! Time, force, and death,
Do to this body what extremes you can ;
But the strong base and building of my love
Is as the very centre of the earth,
Drawing all things to it. I'll go in and weep.
PANDARUS Do, do.
CRESSIDA
Tear my bright hair, and scratch my praisèd cheeks,
Crack my clear voice with sobs, and break my heart
With sounding Troilus. I will not go from Troy.
                       [Exeunt.]

           *

IV, iii   *Enter Paris, Troilus, Aeneas, Deiphobus, Antenor,*
           Diomedes.
PARIS
1   It is great morning, and the hour prefixed
For her delivery to this valiant Greek
Comes fast upon. Good my brother Troilus,
Tell you the lady what she is to do,
And haste her to the purpose.
TROILUS   Walk into her house.

92 *bane* destruction
IV, iii Outside the house of Pandarus   1 *great morning* broad daylight
6 *presently* at once
IV, iv The house of Pandarus   4 *violenteth* rages   7 *palate* taste   13
spectacles (a pun)   23 *strained* filtered, purified   24 *fancy* love   32 *injury
of chance* injurious accident   35 *rejoindure* joining again

I'll bring her to the Grecian presently ;   6
And to his hand when I deliver her,
Think it an altar, and thy brother Troilus
A priest there off'ring to it his own heart.
PARIS
I know what 'tis to love ;
And would, as I shall pity, I could help !
Please you walk in, my lords.   *Exeunt.*

           *

       Enter Pandarus and Cressida.   IV, iv
PANDARUS   Be moderate, be moderate.
CRESSIDA
Why tell you me of moderation ?
The grief is fine, full, perfect, that I taste,
And violenteth in a sense as strong   4
As that which causeth it. How can I moderate it ?
If I could temporize with my affections,
Or brew it to a weak and colder palate,
The like allayment could I give my grief.   7
My love admits no qualifying dross ;
No more my grief, in such a precious loss.
     Enter Troilus.
PANDARUS   Here, here, here he comes. Ah, sweet ducks !
CRESSIDA *[embracing him]*   O Troilus ! Troilus !
PANDARUS   What a pair of spectacles is here ! Let me em-   13
brace too. 'O heart,' as the goodly saying is –
        O heart, heavy heart,
        Why sigh'st thou without breaking ?
where he answers again,
        Because thou canst not ease thy smart
        By friendship nor by speaking.
There was never a truer rhyme. Let us cast away noth-
ing, for we may live to have need of such a verse. We see
it, we see it. How now, lambs !
TROILUS
Cressid, I love thee in so strained a purity,   23
That the blest gods, as angry with my fancy,   24
More bright in zeal than the devotion which
Cold lips blow to their deities, take thee from me.
CRESSIDA   Have the gods envy ?
PANDARUS   Ay, ay, ay, ay ; 'tis too plain a case.
CRESSIDA
And is it true that I must go from Troy ?
TROILUS
A hateful truth.
CRESSIDA   What, and from Troilus too ?
TROILUS
From Troy and Troilus.
CRESSIDA   Is't possible ?
TROILUS
And suddenly, where injury of chance   32
Puts back leave-taking, justles roughly by
All time of pause, rudely beguiles our lips
Of all rejoindure, forcibly prevents   35
Our locked embrasures, strangles our dear vows
Even in the birth of our own laboring breath.
We two, that with so many thousand sighs
Did buy each other, must poorly sell ourselves
With the rude brevity and discharge of one.
Injurious time now with a robber's haste
Crams his rich thiev'ry up, he knows not how.
As many farewells as be stars in heaven,

44 With distinct breath and consigned kisses to them,
45 He fumbles up into a loose adieu,
And scants us with a single famished kiss,
47 Distasted with the salt of broken tears.

AENEAS *(within)* My lord, is the lady ready?

TROILUS

49 Hark! you are called. Some say the Genius
Cries so to him that instantly must die.
Bid them have patience; she shall come anon.

PANDARUS Where are my tears? Rain, to lay this wind,
or my heart will be blown up by the root! *[Exit.]*

CRESSIDA
I must, then, to the Grecians?

TROILUS   No remedy.

CRESSIDA
A woeful Cressid 'mongst the merry Greeks!
When shall we see again?

TROILUS
Hear me, love. Be thou but true of heart –

CRESSIDA
58 I true! How now! What wicked deem is this?

TROILUS
Nay, we must use expostulation kindly,
60 For it is parting from us.
I speak not 'be thou true' as fearing thee,
62 For I will throw my glove to Death himself
63 That there's no maculation in thy heart;
64 But 'be thou true,' say I, to fashion in
My sequent protestation; be thou true,
And I will see thee.

CRESSIDA
O, you shall be exposed, my lord, to dangers
As infinite as imminent; but I'll be true.

TROILUS
And I'll grow friend with danger. Wear this sleeve.

CRESSIDA
And you this glove. When shall I see you?

TROILUS
I will corrupt the Grecian sentinels,
To give thee nightly visitation.
But yet, be true.

CRESSIDA   O heavens! 'be true' again!

TROILUS
Hear why I speak it, love.
75 The Grecian youths are full of quality;
[They're loving, well composed, with gift of nature,]
77 And swelling o'er with arts and exercise.
78 How novelty may move, and parts with person,
Alas! a kind of godly jealousy –
Which, I beseech you, call a virtuous sin –
Makes me afeared.

CRESSIDA   O heavens, you love me not!

TROILUS
Die I a villain, then!
In this I do not call your faith in question
So mainly as my merit. I cannot sing,
85 Nor heel the high lavolt, nor sweeten talk,
Nor play at subtle games – fair virtues all,
87 To which the Grecians are most prompt and pregnant;
But I can tell that in each grace of these
89 There lurks a still and dumb-discoursive devil
That tempts most cunningly. But be not tempted.

CRESSIDA Do you think I will?

TROILUS No.

But something may be done that we will not;
And sometimes we are devils to ourselves
When we will tempt the frailty of our powers,
Presuming on their changeful potency.   96

AENEAS *(within)*
Nay, good my lord!

TROILUS   Come, kiss; and let us part.

PARIS *(within)*
Brother Troilus!

TROILUS   Good brother, come you hither;
And bring Aeneas and the Grecian with you.

CRESSIDA
My lord, will you be true?

TROILUS
Who? I? Alas, it is my vice, my fault.
Whiles others fish with craft for great opinion,   102
I with great truth catch mere simplicity;
Whilst some with cunning gild their copper crowns,
With truth and plainess I do wear mine bare.
Fear not my truth; the moral of my wit   106
Is 'plain and true'; there's all the reach of it.
     [Enter Aeneas, Paris, Antenor, Deiphobus, and
     Diomedes.]
Welcome, Sir Diomed. Here is the lady
Which for Antenor we deliver you.
At the port, lord, I'll give her to thy hand,   110
And by the way possess thee what she is.   111
Entreat her fair; and, by my soul, fair Greek,   112
If e'er thou stand at mercy of my sword,
Name Cressid, and thy life shall be as safe
As Priam is in Ilion.

DIOMEDES   Fair Lady Cressid,
So please you, save the thanks this prince expects.
The lustre in your eye, heaven in your cheek,
Pleads your fair usage; and to Diomed
You shall be mistress, and command him wholly.

TROILUS
Grecian, thou dost not use me courteously,
To shame the seal of my petition to thee   121
In praising her. I tell thee, lord of Greece,
She is as far high-soaring o'er thy praises
As thou unworthy to be called her servant.
I charge thee use her well, even for my charge;   125
For, by the dreadful Pluto, if thou dost not,
Though the great bulk Achilles be thy guard,
I'll cut thy throat.

DIOMEDES   O, be not moved, Prince Troilus.
Let me be privileged by my place and message
To be a speaker free. When I am hence,
I'll answer to my lust; and know you, lord,   131
I'll nothing do on charge. To her own worth
She shall be prized; but that you say 'be't so,'

44 *With . . . them* with the words of farewell and kisses that should ratify each   45 *fumbles* wraps up clumsily   47 *Distasted* tasting bad   49 *Genius* a man's attendant spirit   58 *deem* thought   60 *it . . . us* we are saying good-bye   62 *throw my glove* give a challenge   63 *maculation* taint of disloyalty   64–65 *fashion . . . protestation* furnish a pattern for my own promise that follows   75 *quality* good qualities   77 *arts and exercise* i.e. theory and practice   78 *parts with person* accomplishments with personal charm   85 *lavolt* a lively dance   87 *pregnant* ready   89 *dumb-discoursive* speakingly in silence   96 *changeful potency* power that may change (to failure)   102 *opinion* reputation for wisdom   106 *moral* maxim   110 *port* gate   111 *possess* make known to   112 *Entreat* treat   121 *shame the seal of* treat disdainfully my promise given in exchange for   125 *even for my charge* merely because I tell you to   131 *answer . . . lust* do as I please

I'll speak it in my spirit and honor, 'no.'

TROILUS

Come, to the port. I'll tell thee, Diomed,

136 This brave shall oft make thee to hide thy head.

Lady, give me your hand, and, as we walk,

To our own selves bend we our needful talk.

　　　　　　[Exeunt Troilus, Cressida, and Diomedes.]

　　　　　　Sound trumpet.

PARIS

Hark! Hector's trumpet.

AENEAS　　　　　　How have we spent this morning!

The prince must think me tardy and remiss,

That swore to ride before him to the field.

PARIS

'Tis Troilus' fault. Come, come, to field with him.

[DEIPHOBUS

Let us make ready straight.

AENEAS

Yea, with a bridegroom's fresh alacrity,

Let us address to tend on Hector's heels.

The glory of our Troy doth this day lie

On his fair worth and single chivalry.]　　　　Exeunt.

*

IV, v　　Enter Ajax, armed ; Achilles, Patroclus, Agamem-
　　　　non, Menelaus, Ulysses, Nestor, Calchas, &c.

AGAMEMNON

1　Here art thou in appointment fresh and fair,

2　Anticipating time. With starting courage,

Give with thy trumpet a loud note to Troy,

Thou dreadful Ajax, that the appallèd air

May pierce the head of the great combatant

And hale him hither.

6 AJAX　　　　　Thou, trumpet, there's my purse.

Now crack thy lungs, and split thy brazen pipe.

8　Blow, villain, till thy spherèd bias cheek

9　Outswell the colic of puffed Aquilon.

Come, stretch thy chest, and let thy eyes spout blood ;

Thou blowest for Hector.

　　　　[Trumpet sounds.]

ULYSSES

No trumpet answers.

12 ACHILLES　　　　'Tis but early days.

AGAMEMNON

Is not yond Diomed with Calchas' daughter ?

ULYSSES

'Tis he, I ken the manner of his gait ;

He rises on the toe. That spirit of his

In aspiration lifts him from the earth.

　　　　[Enter Diomedes, with Cressida.]

AGAMEMNON

Is this the Lady Cressid ?

DIOMEDES　　　　　Even she.

AGAMEMNON

Most dearly welcome to the Greeks, sweet lady.

NESTOR

Our general doth salute you with a kiss.

ULYSSES

Yet is the kindness but particular.　　　　20

'Twere better she were kissed in general.　　　　21

NESTOR

And very courtly counsel. I'll begin.

So much for Nestor.

ACHILLES

I'll take that winter from your lips, fair lady.

Achilles bids you welcome.

MENELAUS

I had good argument for kissing once.

PATROCLUS

But that's no argument for kissing now ;

For thus popped Paris in his hardiment,　　　　28

And parted thus you and your argument.　　　　29

ULYSSES

O, deadly gall, and theme of all our scorns !

For which we lose our heads to gild his horns.

PATROCLUS

The first was Menelaus' kiss ; this, mine :

Patroclus kisses you.

MENELAUS　　　　O, this is trim.

PATROCLUS

Paris and I kiss evermore for him.

MENELAUS

I'll have my kiss, sir. Lady, by your leave.

CRESSIDA

In kissing, do you render or receive ?

PATROCLUS

Both take and give.

CRESSIDA　　　　I'll make my match to live,　　　　37

The kiss you take is better than you give ;

Therefore no kiss.

MENELAUS

I'll give you boot ; I'll give you three for one.　　　　40

CRESSIDA

You are an odd man ; give even, or give none.　　　　41

MENELAUS

An odd man, lady ? Every man is odd.

CRESSIDA

No, Paris is not, for you know 'tis true

That you are odd and he is even with you.

MENELAUS

You fillip me o' th' head.　　　　45

CRESSIDA　　　　No, I'll be sworn.

ULYSSES

It were no match, your nail against his horn.　　　　46

May I, sweet lady, beg a kiss of you ?

CRESSIDA

You may.

ULYSSES　I do desire it.

CRESSIDA　　　　Why, beg then.

ULYSSES

Why, then, for Venus' sake, give me a kiss,

When Helen is a maid again, and his—

CRESSIDA

I am your debtor ; claim it when 'tis due.

ULYSSES

Never's my day, and then a kiss of you.

DIOMEDES

Lady, a word. I'll bring you to your father.

　　　　　　[Exeunt Diomedes and Cressida.]

136 brave boast
IV, v The Grecian camp 1 appointment equipment 2 starting active
6 trumpet trumpeter 8 bias puffed-out 9 colic . . . Aquilon the north
wind, personified, distended by colic 12 days in the day 20 particular
single 21 in general (1) by the general, (2) universally 28 hardiment
boldness 29 argument i.e. Helen 37 make . . . live wager my life 40
boot odds 41 odd i.e. singular and single 45 fillip tap 46 It . . . horn
your nail, in tapping, would be no match for his hard horn

NESTOR
A woman of quick sense.

ULYSSES   Fie, fie upon her!
There's language in her eye, her cheek, her lip;
Nay, her foot speaks. Her wanton spirits look out
57 At every joint and motive of her body.
O, these encounterers, so glib of tongue,
59 That give a coasting welcome ere it comes,
60 And wide unclasp the tables of their thoughts
To every ticklish reader, set them down
62 For sluttish spoils of opportunity
And daughters of the game.
    Flourish. Enter all of Troy [Hector, Paris, Aeneas,
    Helenus, Troilus, and Attendants].

ALL
The Troyans' trumpet.

AGAMEMNON   Yonder comes the troop.

AENEAS
Hail, all the state of Greece. What shall be done
To him that victory commands? Or do you purpose
A victor shall be known? Will you the knights
Shall to the edge of all extremity
Pursue each other, or shall they be divided
By any voice or order of the field?
Hector bade ask.

AGAMEMNON   Which way would Hector have it?

AENEAS
He cares not; he'll obey conditions.

ACHILLES
73 'Tis done like Hector; but securely done,
A little proudly, and great deal misprising
The knight opposed.

AENEAS   If not Achilles, sir,
What is your name?

ACHILLES   If not Achilles, nothing.

AENEAS
Therefore Achilles; but, whate'er, know this:
In the extremity of great and little,
Valor and pride excel themselves in Hector:
The one almost as infinite as all,
The other blank as nothing. Weigh him well,
And that which looks like pride is courtesy.
83 This Ajax is half made of Hector's blood,
In love whereof half Hector stays at home;
Half heart, half hand, half Hector comes to seek
This blended knight, half Troyan, and half Greek.

ACHILLES
87 A maiden battle, then? O, I perceive you.
    [Enter Diomedes.]

AGAMEMNON
Here is Sir Diomed. Go, gentle knight,
Stand by our Ajax. As you and Lord Aeneas
90 Consent upon the order of their fight,
So be it; either to the uttermost,
92 Or else a breath. The combatants being kin
Half stints their strife before their strokes begin.
    [Ajax and Hector enter the lists.]

[ULYSSES
They are opposed already.]

AGAMEMNON
95 What Troyan is that same that looks so heavy?

ULYSSES
The youngest son of Priam, a true knight,
Not yet mature, yet matchless, firm of word,

Speaking in deeds and deedless in his tongue,   98
Not soon provoked, nor being provoked soon calmed;
His heart and hand both open and both free,   100
For what he has he gives, what thinks he shows;
Yet gives he not till judgment guide his bounty,
Nor dignifies an impare thought with breath;   103
Manly as Hector, but more dangerous;
For Hector, in his blaze of wrath, subscribes   105
To tender objects, but he in heat of action
Is more vindicative than jealous love.
They call him Troilus, and on him erect
A second hope as fairly built as Hector.
Thus says Aeneas, one that knows the youth
Even to his inches, and with private soul   111
Did in great Ilion thus translate him to me.
        Alarum. [Hector and Ajax fight.]

AGAMEMNON
They are in action.

NESTOR
Now, Ajax, hold thine own!

TROILUS   Hector, thou sleep'st; awake thee!

AGAMEMNON
His blows are well disposed. There, Ajax!

DIOMEDES
You must no more.
        Trumpets cease.

AENEAS   Princes, enough, so please you.

AJAX
I am not warm yet; let us fight again.

DIOMEDES
As Hector pleases.

HECTOR   Why, then will I no more.
Thou art, great lord, my father's sister's son,
A cousin-german to great Priam's seed;
The obligation of our blood forbids
A gory emulation 'twixt us twain.
Were thy commixtion Greek and Troyan so   123
That thou couldst say, 'This hand is Grecian all,
And this is Troyan; the sinews of this leg
All Greek, and this all Troy; my mother's blood
Runs on the dexter cheek, and this sinister   127
Bounds in my father's,' by Jove multipotent,   128
Thou shouldst not bear from me a Greekish member
Wherein my sword had not impressure made
[Of our rank feud.] But the just gods gainsay
That any drop thou borrowedst from thy mother,
My sacred aunt, should by my mortal sword
Be drained! Let me embrace thee, Ajax;
By him that thunders, thou hast lusty arms;   135
Hector would have them fall upon him thus.   136
Cousin, all honor to thee!

AJAX   I thank thee, Hector.
Thou art too gentle and too free a man.
I came to kill thee, cousin, and bear hence
A great addition earnèd in thy death.

---

57 *motive* moving part 59 *coasting* sidelong 60 *tables* tablets 62–63
For . . . game for harlots who yield at every opportunity 73 *securely* over-
confidently 83 *Hector's blood* (cf. II, ii, 77) 87 *maiden* bloodless, like
that of men in training 90 *Consent* agree 92 *a breath* merely exercise
95 *heavy* heavy-hearted 98 *deedless . . . tongue* not boastful 100 *free*
open, generous 103 *impare* unequal to his judgment 105–06 *subscribes
. . . objects* grants terms to the defenseless 111 *Even to his inches* from top
to toe; *with private soul* in confidence 123 *commixtion* composition 127
dexter, sinister right, left 128 *multipotent* of many powers 135 *him that
thunders* Zeus 136 *thus* in an embrace

HECTOR
141 Not Neoptolemus so mirable,
142 On whose bright crest Fame with her loud'st 'Oyes'
 Cries, 'This is he!' could promise to himself
 A thought of added honor torn from Hector.

AENEAS
 There is expectance here from both the sides,
 What further you will do.

HECTOR   We'll answer it;
147 The issue is embracement. Ajax, farewell.

AJAX
 If I might in entreaties find success –
149 As seld I have the chance – I would desire
 My famous cousin to our Grecian tents.

DIOMEDES
 'Tis Agamemnon's wish, and great Achilles
 Doth long to see unarmed the valiant Hector.

HECTOR
 Aeneas, call my brother Troilus to me,
 And signify this loving interview
155 To the expecters of our Troyan part.
156 Desire them home. Give me thy hand, my cousin;
 I will go eat with thee and see your knights.
   [Agamemnon and the rest approach them.]

AJAX
 Great Agamemnon comes to meet us here.

HECTOR
 The worthiest of them tell me name by name;
 But for Achilles, mine own searching eyes
 Shall find him by his large and portly size.

AGAMEMNON
 Worthy all arms [embraces him], as welcome as to one
 That would be rid of such an enemy –
 [But that's no welcome. Understand more clear,
 What's past and what's to come is strewed with husks
 And formless ruin of oblivion;
167 But in this extant moment, faith and troth,
168 Strained purely from all hollow bias-drawing,
 Bids thee, with most divine integrity,]
 From heart of very heart, great Hector, welcome.

HECTOR
 I thank thee, most imperious Agamemnon.

AGAMEMNON [to Troilus]
 My well-famed lord of Troy, no less to you.

MENELAUS
 Let me confirm my princely brother's greeting.
 You brace of warlike brothers, welcome hither.

HECTOR
 Who must we answer?

AENEAS   The noble Menelaus.

HECTOR
 O, you, my lord? By Mars his gauntlet, thanks!
177 Mock not that I affect th' untraded oath;
 Your quondam wife swears still by Venus' glove.
 She's well, but bade me not commend her to you.

MENELAUS
 Name her not now, sir; she's a deadly theme.

HECTOR
 O, pardon! I offend.

NESTOR
 I have, thou gallant Troyan, seen thee oft,
 Laboring for destiny, make cruel way   183
 Through ranks of Greekish youth, and I have seen thee,
 As hot as Perseus, spur thy Phrygian steed,
 Despising many forfeits and subduements, 186
 When thou hast hung thy advancèd sword i' th' air, 187
 Not letting it decline on the declinèd,
 That I have said to some my standers-by,
 'Lo, Jupiter is yonder, dealing life!'   190
 And I have seen thee pause and take thy breath,
 When that a ring of Greeks have shraped thee in, 192
 Like an Olympian wrestling. This have I seen;
 But this thy countenance, still locked in steel, 194
 I never saw till now. I knew thy grandsire, 195
 And once fought with him. He was a soldier good;
 But, by great Mars, the captain of us all,
 Never like thee. Let an old man embrace thee;
 And, worthy warrior, welcome to our tents.

AENEAS
 'Tis the old Nestor.

HECTOR
 Let me embrace thee, good old chronicle,
 That hast so long walked hand in hand with time.
 Most reverend Nestor, I am glad to clasp thee.

NESTOR
 I would my arms could match thee in contention,
 [As they contend with thee in courtesy.]

HECTOR
 I would they could.

NESTOR
 Ha,
 By this white beard, I'd fight with thee to-morrow.
 Well, welcome, welcome. I have seen the time –

ULYSSES
 I wonder now how yonder city stands,
 When we have here her base and pillar by us.

HECTOR
 I know your favor, Lord Ulysses, well.   212
 Ah, sir, there's many a Greek and Troyan dead,
 Since first I saw yourself and Diomed
 In Ilion, on your Greekish embassy.

ULYSSES
 Sir, I foretold you then what would ensue.
 My prophecy is but half his journey yet,
 For yonder walls, that pertly front your town,
 Yon towers, whose wanton tops do buss the clouds,
 Must kiss their own feet.

HECTOR   I must not believe you. 220
 There they stand yet, and modestly I think,
 The fall of every Phrygian stone will cost
 A drop of Grecian blood. The end crowns all,
 And that old common arbitrator, Time,
 Will one day end it.

ULYSSES   So to him we leave it.
 Most gentle and most valiant Hector, welcome.
 After the general, I beseech you next
 To feast with me and see me at my tent.

ACHILLES
 I shall forestall thee, Lord Ulysses, thou!

141 *Neoptolemus* (cf. III, iii, 209n.; but perhaps Achilles is meant here); *mirable* wonderful 142 *Oyes* cry beginning a herald's proclamation 147 *issue* outcome 149 *seld* seldom 155 *expecters . . . part* Trojans waiting for news 156 *Desire them home* ask them to go home 167 *extant* present 168 *bias-drawing* tortuous dealings (like the course given by the bias to the bowl in bowling) 177 *untraded* unused 183 *Laboring for destiny* i.e. causing destined deaths 186 *Despising . . . subduements* ignoring the vanquished whose lives were forfeit 187 *hung* held suspended 190 *dealing life* i.e. by not dealing death 192 *shraped* trapped 194 *still* always 195 *grandsire* Laomedon, who built the walls of Troy 212 *favor* face

Now, Hector, I have fed mine eyes on thee;
I have with exact view perused thee, Hector,
232 And quoted joint by joint.

HECTOR   Is this Achilles?

ACHILLES
I am Achilles.

HECTOR
Stand fair, I prithee; let me look on thee.

ACHILLES
Behold thy fill.

HECTOR   Nay, I have done already.

ACHILLES
Thou art too brief. I will the second time,
As I would buy thee, view thee limb by limb.

HECTOR
O, like a book of sport thou'lt read me o'er;
But there's more in me than thou understand'st.
Why dost thou so oppress me with thine eye?

ACHILLES
Tell me, you heavens, in which part of his body
Shall I destroy him, whether there, or there, or there?
That I may give the local wound a name,
And make distinct the very breach whereout
Hector's great spirit flew. Answer me, heavens!

HECTOR
It would discredit the blessed gods, proud man,
To answer such a question. Stand again.
248 Think'st thou to catch my life so pleasantly
249 As to prenominate in nice conjecture
Where thou wilt hit me dead?

ACHILLES   I tell thee, yea.

HECTOR
Wert thou an oracle to tell me so,
I'd not believe thee. Henceforth guard thee well,
For I'll not kill thee there, nor there, nor there;
254 But, by the forge that stithied Mars his helm,
I'll kill thee everywhere, yea, o'er and o'er.
You wisest Grecians, pardon me this brag.
His insolence draws folly from my lips;
But I'll endeavor deeds to match these words,
Or may I never –

AJAX   Do not chafe thee, cousin;
And you, Achilles, let these threats alone,
Till accident or purpose bring you to't.
You may have every day enough of Hector,
263 If you have stomach. The general state, I fear,
Can scarce entreat you to be odd with him.

HECTOR
I pray you, let us see you in the field.
266 We have had pelting wars since you refused
The Grecians' cause.

ACHILLES   Dost thou entreat me, Hector?
268 To-morrow do I meet thee, fell as death;
To-night all friends.

HECTOR   Thy hand upon that match.

AGAMEMNON
First, all you peers of Greece, go to my tent;
271 There in the full convive we. Afterwards,
As Hector's leisure and your bounties shall
273 Concur together, severally entreat him
To taste your bounties. Let the trumpets blow,
That this great soldier may his welcome know.

         Exeunt [all except Troilus and Ulysses].

TROILUS
My Lord Ulysses, tell me, I beseech you,
In what place of the field doth Calchas keep?   277

ULYSSES
At Menelaus' tent, most princely Troilus.
There Diomed doth feast with him to-night;
Who neither looks upon the heaven nor earth,
But gives all gaze and bent of amorous view
On the fair Cressid.

TROILUS
Shall I, sweet lord, be bound to thee so much,
After we part from Agamemnon's tent,
To bring me thither?

ULYSSES   You shall command me, sir.
As gentle tell me, of what honor was
This Cressida in Troy? Had she no lover there
That wails her absence?

TROILUS
O, sir, to such as boasting show their scars
A mock is due. Will you walk on, my lord?
She was beloved, she loved; she is, and doth:
But still sweet love is food for fortune's tooth.   *Exeunt.*

*

         Enter Achilles and Patroclus.   V, i

ACHILLES
I'll heat his blood with Greekish wine to-night,
Which with my scimitar I'll cool to-morrow.
Patroclus, let us feast him to the height.

PATROCLUS
Here comes Thersites.

         Enter Thersites.

ACHILLES   How now, thou cur of envy!
Thou crusty batch of nature, what's the news?   5

THERSITES Why, thou picture of what thou seemest, and
idol of idiot-worshippers, here's a letter for thee.

ACHILLES From whence, fragment?

THERSITES Why, thou full dish of fool, from Troy.

PATROCLUS Who keeps the tent now?   10

THERSITES The surgeon's box or the patient's wound.   11

PATROCLUS Well said, adversity, and what need these
tricks?

THERSITES Prithee, be silent, boy; I profit not by thy
talk. Thou art said to be Achilles' male varlet.

PATROCLUS Male varlet, you rogue! What's that?

THERSITES Why, his masculine whore. Now, the rotten
diseases of the south, the guts-griping ruptures, catarrhs,
loads o' gravel in the back, lethargies, cold palsies, raw   18
eyes, dirt-rotten livers, wheezing lungs, bladders full of
imposthume, sciaticas, lime-kilns i' th' palm, incurable   20
bone-ache, and the rivelled fee-simple of the tetter, and   21

---

232 *quoted* marked   248 *pleasantly* merrily   249 *prenominate* name
beforehand; *nice* precise   254 *stithied* forged   263 *stomach* inclination
263–64 *The general . . . him* i.e. you will have to do it on private impulse,
since you will not do it when the Greek leaders ask you   266 *pelting*
petty   268 *fell* fierce   271 *convive* feast   273 *severally entreat* individually
invite   277 *keep* dwell
V, i Before the tent of Achilles   5 *batch* bread of the same baking   10
Who . . . now (Thersites can no longer taunt Achilles for keeping to his tent)
11 *surgeon's box . . . wound* (play on *tent* in the sense of a lancet for probing
a wound)   18 *back* kidney; *lethargies* apoplexies; *cold palsies* paralysis
20 *imposthume* abscess; *lime-kilns* burnings   21 *rivelled* wrinkled; *tetter*
possibly chronic ringworm

the like, take and take again such preposterous discoveries!

PATROCLUS Why, thou damnable box of envy, thou, what means thou to curse thus?

THERSITES Do I curse thee?

27 PATROCLUS Why, no, you ruinous butt, you whoreson
28 indistinguishable cur, no.

THERSITES No? Why art thou then exasperate, thou idle
30 immaterial skein of sleave silk, thou green sarcenet flap for a sore eye, thou tassel of a prodigal's purse, thou? Ah, how the poor world is pestered with such water-flies, diminutives of nature.

PATROCLUS Out, gall!

THERSITES Finch egg!

ACHILLES
My sweet Patroclus, I am thwarted quite
From my great purpose in to-morrow's battle.
Here is a letter from Queen Hecuba,
A token from her daughter, my fair love,
40 Both taxing me and gaging me to keep
An oath that I have sworn. I will not break it.
Fall Greeks, fail fame, honor or go or stay,
My major vow lies here; this I'll obey.
Come, come, Thersites, help to trim my tent;
This night in banqueting must all be spent.
Away, Patroclus!   *Exit [with Patroclus].*

THERSITES With too much blood and too little brain, these two may run mad; but if with too much brain and too little blood they do, I'll be a curer of madmen. Here's Agamemnon, an honest fellow enough, and one that
51 loves quails, but he has not so much brain as ear-wax; and
52 the goodly transformation of Jupiter there, his brother,
53 the bull, the primitive statue and oblique memorial of
54 cuckolds; a thrifty shoeing-horn in a chain, hanging at his brother's leg, to what form but that he is should wit
56 larded with malice and malice forced with wit turn him to? To an ass, were nothing; he is both ass and ox: to an ox, were nothing; he is both ox and ass. To be a dog, a
59 mule, a cat, a fitchew, a toad, a lizard, an owl, a puttock, or a herring without a roe, I would not care; but to be Menelaus! I would conspire against destiny. Ask me not
62 what I would be, if I were not Thersites, for I care not to
63 be the louse of a lazar, so I were not Menelaus. Hey-day, spirits and fires!
     Enter Agamemnon, Ulysses, Nestor, [Hector, Ajax, Troilus, Menelaus,] and Diomedes, with lights.

AGAMEMNON
We go wrong, we go wrong.

AJAX   No, yonder 'tis;
There, where we see the lights.

HECTOR   I trouble you.

AJAX
No, not a whit.

ULYSSES   Here comes himself to guide you.
     [Enter Achilles.]

ACHILLES
Welcome, brave Hector; welcome, princes all.

AGAMEMNON
So now, fair prince of Troy, I bid good night.
Ajax commands the guard to tend on you.

HECTOR
Thanks and good night to the Greeks' general.

MENELAUS
Good night, my lord.

HECTOR
Good night, sweet Lord Menelaus.

THERSITES Sweet draught! 'Sweet,' quoth 'a! Sweet 74 sink, sweet sewer.

ACHILLES
Good night and welcome both at once, to those
That go or tarry.

AGAMEMNON   Good night.
     Exeunt Agamemnon [and] Menelaus.

ACHILLES
Old Nestor tarries, and you too, Diomed,
Keep Hector company an hour or two.

DIOMEDES
I cannot, lord; I have important business,
The tide whereof is now. Good night, great Hector. 82

HECTOR
Give me your hand.

ULYSSES *[aside to Troilus]* Follow his torch; he goes
To Calchas' tent. I'll keep you company.

TROILUS
Sweet sir, you honor me.

HECTOR   And so, good night.
     [Exeunt Diomedes, then Ulysses and Troilus.]

ACHILLES
Come, come, enter my tent.
     Exeunt [Achilles, Hector, Ajax, and Nestor].

THERSITES That same Diomed's a false-hearted rogue, a most unjust knave; I will no more trust him when he leers than I will a serpent when he hisses. He will spend his mouth and promise like Brabbler the hound; but when he performs, astronomers foretell it, it is prodigious, there will come some change. The sun borrows of the moon when Diomed keeps his word. I will rather leave to see Hector than not to dog him. They say he 95 keeps a Troyan drab, and uses the traitor Calchas' tent. I'll after – nothing but lechery! All incontinent varlets!
     Exit.

*

     Enter Diomed.   V, ii

DIOMEDES What, are you up here, ho? Speak.

CALCHAS *[within]* Who calls?

DIOMEDES Diomed. Calchas, I think. Where's your daughter?

CALCHAS *[within]* She comes to you.
     Enter Troilus and Ulysses [; after them Thersites].

ULYSSES
Stand where the torch may not discover us.
     Enter Cressid.

TROILUS
Cressid comes forth to him.

DIOMEDES   How now, my charge!

---

27 *ruinous butt* dilapidated cask   28 *indistinguishable* shapeless   30 *sleave silk* silk floss; *sarcenet* silk   40 *taxing* censuring; *gaging* binding to a promise   51 *quails* loose women   52 *Jupiter* (who changed himself into a bull to seduce Europa)   53 *primitive . . . memorial* i.e. in having horns, the symbol of a cuckold   54 *thrifty* stingy   54–55 *hanging . . . leg* (so that he cannot be shaken off)   56 *forced* stuffed   59 *fitchew* polecat; *puttock* kite (opprobrious, as feeding on carrion)   62–63 *I care not to be* I wouldn't mind being   63 *lazar* leper   74 *draught* privy   82 *tide* time   95 *leave to see* miss seeing
V, ii Before the tent of Calchas

CRESSIDA
Now, my sweet guardian ! Hark, a word with you.
[*Whispers.*]
TROILUS Yea, so familiar !
ULYSSES She will sing any man at first sight.
THERSITES And any man may sing her, if he can take her
11   cliff ; she's noted.
DIOMEDES Will you remember ?
CRESSIDA Remember ? Yes.
DIOMEDES Nay, but do, then ;
And let your mind be coupled with your words.
TROILUS What shall she remember ?
ULYSSES List !
CRESSIDA
Sweet honey Greek, tempt me no more to folly.
THERSITES Roguery !
DIOMEDES
Nay, then –
20 CRESSIDA   I'll tell you what –
DIOMEDES
Foh, foh ! come, tell a pin. You are forsworn.
CRESSIDA
In faith, I cannot. What would you have me do ?
THERSITES A juggling trick – to be secretly open.
DIOMEDES
What did you swear you would bestow on me ?
CRESSIDA
I prithee, do not hold me to mine oath ;
Bid me do anything but that, sweet Greek.
DIOMEDES Good night.
TROILUS Hold, patience !
ULYSSES How now, Troyan ?
30 CRESSIDA Diomed –
DIOMEDES
No, no, good night ; I'll be your fool no more.
TROILUS
Thy better must.
CRESSIDA   Hark, a word in your ear.
TROILUS
O plague and madness !
ULYSSES
You are movèd, prince ; let us depart, I pray you,
Lest your displeasure should enlarge itself
To wrathful terms. This place is dangerous ;
The time right deadly. I beseech you, go.
TROILUS
Behold, I pray you !
ULYSSES   Nay, good my lord, go off ;
You flow to great distraction ; come, my lord.
TROILUS
I prithee, stay.
40 ULYSSES   You have not patience ; come.
TROILUS
I pray you, stay. By hell, and all hell's torments,
I will not speak a word !
DIOMEDES   And so, good night.
CRESSIDA
Nay, but you part in anger.
TROILUS   Doth that grieve thee ?
O withered truth !
ULYSSES   How now, my lord !
TROILUS   By Jove,
I will be patient.
CRESSIDA   Guardian ! Why, Greek !

DIOMEDES
Foh, foh ! adieu ; you palter.
CRESSIDA
In faith, I do not. Come hither once again.
ULYSSES
You shake, my lord, at something. Will you go ?
You will break out.
TROILUS   She strokes his cheek !
ULYSSES   Come, come.
TROILUS
Nay, stay ; by Jove, I will not speak a word.
There is between my will and all offenses
A guard of patience. Stay a little while.
THERSITES How the devil Luxury, with his fat rump and   53
potato finger, tickles these together. Fry, lechery, fry !   54
DIOMEDES But will you, then ?
CRESSIDA
In faith, I will, la ; never trust me else.
DIOMEDES
Give me some token for the surety of it.
CRESSIDA
I'll fetch you one.   *Exit.*
ULYSSES
You have sworn patience.
TROILUS   Fear me not, my lord ;
I will not be myself, nor have cognition
Of what I feel. I am all patience.
Enter Cressid.
THERSITES Now the pledge ; now, now, now !
CRESSIDA Here, Diomed, keep this sleeve.
TROILUS
O beauty, where is thy faith ?
ULYSSES   My lord –
[TROILUS
I will be patient ; outwardly I will.]
CRESSIDA
You look upon that sleeve ; behold it well.
He loved me – O false wench ! Give't me again.
DIOMEDES
Whose was't ?
CRESSIDA   It is no matter, now I have't again.
I will not meet with you to-morrow night.
I prithee, Diomed, visit me no more.
THERSITES Now she sharpens. Well said, whetstone !   71
DIOMEDES
I shall have it.   72
CRESSIDA   What, this ?
DIOMEDES   Ay, that.
CRESSIDA
O, all you gods ! O pretty, pretty pledge !
Thy master now lies thinking in his bed
Of thee and me, and sighs, and takes my glove,
And gives memorial dainty kisses to it,   76
As I kiss thee. Nay, do not snatch it from me ;
He that takes that doth take my heart withal.
DIOMEDES
I had your heart before ; this follows it.
TROILUS
I did swear patience.

---

11 *cliff* musical clef; *noted* (pun on notes of music)   53 *Luxury* lechery
54 *potato* (considered to stimulate lechery)   71 *sharpens* whets his desire
72 *shall* am determined to   76 *memorial* i.e. of remembrance

CRESSIDA
You shall not have it, Diomed ; faith, you shall not ;
I'll give you something else.
DIOMEDES
I will have this. Whose was it ?
CRESSIDA It is no matter.
DIOMEDES
Come, tell me whose it was.
CRESSIDA
'Twas one's that loved me better than you will.
But, now you have it, take it.
DIOMEDES Whose was it ?
CRESSIDA
87 By all Diana's waiting-women yond,
And by herself, I will not tell you whose.
DIOMEDES
To-morrow will I wear it on my helm,
And grieve his spirit that dares not challenge it.
TROILUS
Wert thou the devil, and wor'st it on thy horn,
It should be challenged.
CRESSIDA
Well, well, 'tis done, 'tis past. And yet it is not ;
I will not keep my word.
DIOMEDES Why then, farewell ;
Thou never shalt mock Diomed again.
CRESSIDA
You shall not go. One cannot speak a word
97 But it straight starts you.
DIOMEDES I do not like this fooling.
98 THERSITES Nor I, by Pluto ; but that that likes not you
pleases me best.
DIOMEDES
What, shall I come ? The hour ?
CRESSIDA Ay, come – O Jove ! –
101 Do come – I shall be plagued.
DIOMEDES Farewell till then.
CRESSIDA
Good night. I prithee, come. [Exit Diomedes.]
Troilus, farewell. One eye yet looks on thee,
But with my heart the other eye doth see.
105 Ah, poor our sex ! this fault in us I find,
106 The error of our eye directs our mind.
What error leads must err. O, then conclude
Minds swayed by eyes are full of turpitude. Exit.
THERSITES
109 A proof of strength she could not publish more,
Unless she say, 'My mind is now turned whore.'

ULYSSES
All's done, my lord.
TROILUS It is.
ULYSSES Why stay we, then ?
TROILUS
To make a recordation to my soul
Of every syllable that here was spoke.
But if I tell how these two did co-act,
Shall I not lie in publishing a truth ?
Sith yet there is a credence in my heart,
An esperance so obstinately strong, 117
That doth invert th' attest of eyes and ears, 118
As if those organs had deceptious functions, 119
Created only to calumniate.
Was Cressid here ?
ULYSSES I cannot conjure, Troyan. 121
TROILUS
She was not, sure.
ULYSSES Most sure she was.
TROILUS
Why, my negation hath no taste of madness.
ULYSSES
Nor mine, my lord. Cressid was here but now.
TROILUS
Let it not be believed for womanhood ! 125
Think we had mothers ; do not give advantage
To stubborn critics, apt, without a theme,
For depravation, to square the general sex 128
By Cressid's rule. Rather think this not Cressid.
ULYSSES
What hath she done, prince, that can soil our mothers ?
TROILUS
Nothing at all, unless that this were she.
THERSITES Will 'a swagger himself out on's own eyes ? 132
TROILUS
This she ? No, this is Diomed's Cressida.
If beauty have a soul, this is not she ;
If souls guide vows, if vows be sanctimonies,
If sanctimony be the gods' delight,
If there be rule in unity itself, 137
This was not she. O madness of discourse, 138
That cause sets up with and against itself ;
Bi-fold authority, where reason can revolt 140
Without perdition, and loss assume all reason
Without revolt. This is, and is not, Cressid.
Within my soul there doth conduce a fight 143
Of this strange nature that a thing inseparate 144
Divides more wider than the sky and earth ;
And yet the spacious breadth of this division
Admits no orifice for a point as subtle
As Ariachne's broken woof to enter. 148
Instance, O instance, strong as Pluto's gates ; 149
Cressid is mine, tied with the bonds of heaven.
Instance, O instance, strong as heaven itself ;
The bonds of heaven are slipped, dissolved, and loosed ;
And with another knot, five-finger-tied,
The fractions of her faith, orts of her love, 154
The fragments, scraps, the bits, and greasy relics
Of her o'er-eaten faith, are bound to Diomed. 156
ULYSSES
May worthy Troilus be half attachèd 157
With that which here his passion doth express ?
TROILUS
Ay, Greek ; and that shall be divulgèd well

87 *Diana's waiting-women* stars attending the moon 97 *starts you* makes you start off (angry) 98 *likes* pleases 101 *plagued* punished 105 *poor our sex* our poor sex 106 *error* wandering (both physical and moral here) 109 *proof of strength* strong proof ; *publish more* confess more clearly 117 *esperance* hope 118 *attest* witness 119 *deceptious* deceiving 121 *conjure* raise spirits (instead of Cressida) 125 *for* for the sake of 128–29 *square . . . rule* measure all women by Cressida's standard (cf. 'carpenter's rule') 132 *swagger . . . eyes* (cf. 'walk out on his own eyes') 137 *If . . . itself* if it is a principle that Cressida must be one 138 *discourse* reason 140–42 *where reason . . . revolt* where reason can revolt against itself without self-destruction, and destruction can take control of reason without its revolting 143 *conduce* go on 144 *thing inseparate* i.e. Cressida, as herself indivisible 148 *Ariachne* properly Arachne (Minerva tore up her fine-spun web in jealousy and turned her into a spider) 149 *Instance* evidence, argument 154 *orts* scraps (properly of food) 156 *o'er-eaten* i.e. she has swallowed her word 157 *half attachèd* half as much affected (as his passion indicates)

In characters as red as Mars his heart
Inflamed with Venus. Never did young man fancy
With so eternal and so fixed a soul.
Hark, Greek : as much as I do Cressid love,
So much by weight hate I her Diomed ;
That sleeve is mine that he'll bear on his helm ;
Were it a casque composed by Vulcan's skill,
My sword should bite it. Not the dreadful spout
Which shipmen do the hurricano call,
169　Constringed in mass by the almighty sun,
Shall dizzy with more clamor Neptune's ear
In his descent than shall my prompted sword
Falling on Diomed.
173　THERSITES　He'll tickle it for his concupy.
TROILUS
　　O Cressid ! O false Cressid ! false, false, false !
　　Let all untruths stand by thy stainèd name,
　　And they'll seem glorious.
ULYSSES　　　　　　　　　O, contain yourself ;
　　Your passion draws ears hither.
　　　　　　　Enter Aeneas.
AENEAS
　　I have been seeking you this hour, my lord.
　　Hector, by this, is arming him in Troy ;
　　Ajax, your guard, stays to conduct you home.
TROILUS
181　Have with you, prince. My courteous lord, adieu.
　　Farewell, revolted fair ; and Diomed,
　　Stand fast, and wear a castle on thy head !
ULYSSES
　　I'll bring you to the gates.
TROILUS
　　Accept distracted thanks.
　　　　　　Exeunt Troilus, Aeneas, and Ulysses.
THERSITES　Would I could meet that rogue Diomed. I
187　would croak like a raven ; I would bode, I would bode.
Patroclus will give me anything for the intelligence of
this whore. The parrot will not do more for an almond
than he for a commodious drab. Lechery, lechery ; still
wars and lechery ; nothing else holds fashion. A burning
devil take them !　　　　　　　　　　　　　　　Exit.

*

V, iii　　　　Enter Hector and Andromache.
ANDROMACHE
　　When was my lord so much ungently tempered,
　　To stop his ears against admonishment ?
　　Unarm, unarm, and do not fight to-day.
HECTOR
4　You train me to offend you ; get you in.
　　By all the everlasting gods, I'll go.
ANDROMACHE
6　My dreams will, sure, prove ominous to the day.
HECTOR
　　No more, I say.
　　　　　Enter Cassandra.
CASSANDRA　　Where is my brother Hector ?
ANDROMACHE
　　Here, sister ; armed and bloody in intent.
　　Consort with me in loud and dear petition ;
　　Pursue we him on knees, for I have dreamed
　　Of bloody turbulence, and this whole night
　　Hath nothing been but shapes and forms of slaughter.

CASSANDRA
　　O, 'tis true.
HECTOR　　Ho, bid my trumpet sound.
CASSANDRA
　　No notes of sally, for the heavens, sweet brother.
HECTOR
　　Be gone, I say ; the gods have heard me swear.
CASSANDRA
　　The gods are deaf to hot and peevish vows.　　　16
　　They are polluted off'rings, more abhorred
　　Than spotted livers in the sacrifice.
ANDROMACHE
　　O, be persuaded ! Do not count it holy
　　[To hurt by being just. It is as lawful,
　　For we would give much, to use violent thefts,　　21
　　And rob in the behalf of charity.
CASSANDRA]
　　It is the purpose that makes strong the vow ;
　　But vows to every purpose must not hold.
　　Unarm, sweet Hector.
HECTOR　　　　　　Hold you still, I say ;
　　Mine honor keeps the weather of my fate.　　　26
　　Life every man holds dear ; but the dear man　　27
　　Holds honor far more precious-dear than life.
　　　　　Enter Troilus.
　　How now, young man ; mean'st thou to fight to-day ?
ANDROMACHE
　　Cassandra, call my father to persuade.　Exit Cassandra.
HECTOR
　　No, faith, young Troilus ; doff thy harness, youth ;
　　I am to-day i' th' vein of chivalry.
　　Let grow thy sinews till their knots be strong,
　　And tempt not yet the brushes of the war.　　　34
　　Unarm thee, go, and doubt thou not, brave boy,
　　I'll stand to-day for thee and me and Troy.
TROILUS
　　Brother, you have a vice of mercy in you,
　　Which better fits a lion than a man.
HECTOR
　　What vice is that, good Troilus ? Chide me for it.
TROILUS
　　When many times the captive Grecian falls,
　　Even in the fan and wind of your fair sword,
　　You bid them rise and live.
HECTOR
　　O, 'tis fair play.
TROILUS　　　　　Fool's play, by heaven, Hector.
HECTOR
　　How now, how now ?
TROILUS　　　　　　For th' love of all the gods,
　　Let's leave the hermit pity with our mother,
　　And when we have our armors buckled on,
　　The venomed vengeance ride upon our swords,
　　Spur them to ruthful work, rein them from ruth.　　48
HECTOR
　　Fie, savage, fie !

169 *Constringed* drawn together　173 *it* i.e. Diomedes (contemptuous); *concupy* concupiscence, lust　181 *Have with you* come along　187 *bode* portend (like a raven, a bird of ill omen)
V, iii Before the palace of Priam　4 *train* tempt; *offend* injure　6 *ominous to the day* omens of the day's events　16 *peevish* perverse　21 *For* because　26 *keeps the weather* keeps to windward (the position of advantage)　27 *dear man* worthy man　34 *brushes* encounters　48 *ruthful* pitiful ; *ruth* pity

49 TROILUS   Hector, then 'tis wars.

HECTOR
   Troilus, I would not have you fight to-day.

TROILUS
   Who should withhold me?
   Not fate, obedience, nor the hand of Mars
53   Beck'ning with fiery truncheon my retire;
   Not Priamus and Hecuba on knees,
55   Their eyes o'ergallèd with recourse of tears;
   Nor you, my brother, with your true sword drawn,
   Opposed to hinder me, should stop my way,
   [But by my ruin.]
     Enter Priam and Cassandra.

CASSANDRA
   Lay hold upon him, Priam, hold him fast;
60   He is thy crutch. Now if thou lose thy stay,
   Thou on him leaning, and all Troy on thee,
   Fall all together.

PRIAM   Come, Hector, come; go back.
   Thy wife hath dreamed, thy mother hath had visions,
   Cassandra doth foresee, and I myself
   Am like a prophet suddenly enrapt
   To tell thee that this day is ominous:
   Therefore, come back.

HECTOR   Aeneas is a-field;
   And I do stand engaged to many Greeks,
69   Even in the faith of valor, to appear
   This morning to them.

PRIAM   Ay, but thou shalt not go.

HECTOR
   I must not break my faith.
   You know me dutiful; therefore, dear sir,
73   Let me not shame respect, but give me leave
   To take that course by your consent and voice,
   Which you do here forbid me, royal Priam.

CASSANDRA
   O Priam, yield not to him!

ANDROMACHE   Do not, dear father.

HECTOR
   Andromache, I am offended with you.
   Upon the love you bear me, get you in.
     Exit Andromache.

TROILUS
   This foolish, dreaming, superstitious girl
80   Makes all these bodements.

CASSANDRA   O farewell, dear Hector!
   Look, how thou diest; look, how thy eye turns pale;
   Look, how thy wounds do bleed at many vents!
   Hark, how Troy roars, how Hecuba cries out,
   How poor Andromache shrills her dolors forth!
   Behold, distraction, frenzy, and amazement,
86   Like witless antics, one another meet,
   And all cry Hector! Hector's dead! O Hector!

TROILUS
   Away! Away!

CASSANDRA
   Farewell. Yet, soft: Hector, I take my leave.
   Thou dost thyself and all our Troy deceive.   *[Exit.]*

HECTOR
   You are amazed, my liege, at her exclaim.
   Go in and cheer the town. We'll forth and fight;
   Do deeds worth praise and tell you them at night.

PRIAM
   Farewell. The gods with safety stand about thee.
     [Exeunt Priam and Hector.] Alarum.

TROILUS
   They are at it, hark. Proud Diomed, believe,
   I come to lose my arm, or win my sleeve.
     Enter Pandar.

PANDARUS   Do you hear, my lord? Do you hear?

TROILUS   What now?

PANDARUS   Here's a letter come from yond poor girl.

TROILUS   Let me read.

PANDARUS   A whoreson tisick, a whoreson rascally tisick 101 so troubles me, and the foolish fortune of this girl; and what one thing, what another, that I shall leave you one o' these days; and I have a rheum in mine eyes too, and such an ache in my bones that, unless a man were cursed, I cannot tell what to think on't. What says she there?

TROILUS
   Words, words, mere words, no matter from the heart;
   Th' effect doth operate another way.
     [Tearing the letter.]
   Go, wind to wind, there turn and change together.
   My love with words and errors still she feeds,
   But edifies another with her deeds.   *Exeunt.*

*

    [Alarum.] Excursions. Enter Thersites [in excursion]. V, iv

THERSITES   Now they are clapper-clawing one another; I'll go look on. That dissembling abominable varlet, Diomed, has got that same scurvy doting foolish young knave's sleeve of Troy there in his helm. I would fain see them meet, that that same young Troyan ass, that loves the whore there, might send that Greekish whoremasterly villain with the sleeve back to the dissembling luxurious drab, of a sleeveless errand. O' th' t' other 8 side, the policy of those crafty swearing rascals – that 9 stale old mouse-eaten dry cheese, Nestor, and that same dog-fox, Ulysses – is not proved worth a blackberry. They set me up, in policy, that mongrel cur, Ajax, against that dog of as bad a kind, Achilles. And now is the cur Ajax prouder than the cur Achilles, and will not arm to-day. Whereupon the Grecians begin to proclaim 15 barbarism, and policy grows into an ill opinion.
     [Enter Diomedes and Troilus.]
   Soft! here comes sleeve, and t' other.

TROILUS
   Fly not; for shouldst thou take the river Styx,
   I would swim after.

DIOMEDES   Thou dost miscall retire.
   I do not fly, but advantageous care   20
   Withdrew me from the odds of multitude.
   Have at thee!

THERSITES   Hold thy whore, Grecian! Now for thy 23 whore, Troyan! Now the sleeve, now the sleeve!
     [Exeunt Troilus and Diomedes, fighting.]

---

49 *then 'tis wars* war is like that   53 *truncheon* staff used to signal the end of a combat between two champions   55 *o'ergallèd* inflamed; *recourse* coursing down   60 *stay* prop   69 *faith of valor* word of honor of a brave man   73 *shame respect* disgrace the respect due a parent   80 *bodements* ill omens   86 *antics* lunatics   101 *tisick* cough
V, iv Field before the walls of Troy   8 *sleeveless* fruitless   9 *crafty swearing* i.e. crafty to the extent of perjury   15–16 *proclaim barbarism* set up the authority of ignorance   20–21 *advantageous . . . multitude* care for my own advantage led me to avoid facing heavy odds   23–24 *Hold . . . sleeve* (Thersites is urging both men on impartially)

Enter Hector.

HECTOR
What art thou, Greek ? Art thou for Hector's match ?
Art thou of blood and honor ?

THERSITES No, no. I am a rascal, a scurvy railing knave,
a very filthy rogue.

HECTOR
I do believe thee ; live. *[Exit.]*

THERSITES God-a-mercy, that thou wilt believe me ; but
a plague break thy neck – for frighting me. What's become of the wenching rogues ? I think they have swallowed one another. I would laugh at that miracle – yet,
in a sort, lechery eats itself. I'll seek them. *Exit.*

V, v *Enter Diomed and Servant.*

DIOMEDES
Go, go, my servant, take thou Troilus' horse ;
Present the fair steed to my Lady Cressid.
Fellow, commend my service to her beauty ;
Tell her I have chastised the amorous Troyan,
And am her knight by proof.

SERVANT I go, my lord. *[Exit.]*

Enter Agamemnon.

AGAMEMNON
Renew, renew ! The fierce Polydamas
Hath beat down Menon ; bastard Margarelon
Hath Doreus prisoner,
9   And stands colossus-wise, waving his beam,
10 Upon the pashèd corses of the kings
Epistrophus and Cedius ; Polixenes is slain,
Amphimachus and Thoas deadly hurt,
Patroclus ta'en or slain, and Palamedes
14 Sore hurt and bruisèd. The dreadful Sagittary
Appals our numbers. Haste we, Diomed,
To reinforcement, or we perish all.

Enter Nestor.

NESTOR
Go, bear Patroclus' body to Achilles,
And bid the snail-paced Ajax arm for shame.
There is a thousand Hectors in the field.
Now here he fights on Galathe his horse,
And there lacks work ; anon he's there afoot,
22 And there they fly or die, like scalèd sculls
Before the belching whale ; then is he yonder,
24 And there the strawy Greeks, ripe for his edge,
Fall down before him, like a mower's swath.
Here, there, and everywhere, he leaves and takes,
Dexterity so obeying appetite
That what he will he does, and does so much
29 That proof is called impossibility.

Enter Ulysses.

ULYSSES
O, courage, courage, princes ! Great Achilles
Is arming, weeping, cursing, vowing vengeance.
Patroclus' wounds have roused his drowsy blood,
Together with his mangled Myrmidons,
That noseless, handless, hacked and chipped, come to
him,
Crying on Hector. Ajax hath lost a friend,
And foams at mouth, and he is armed and at it,
Roaring for Troilus, who hath done to-day
Mad and fantastic execution,
Engaging and redeeming of himself
With such a careless force and forceless care

As if that luck, in very spite of cunning,
Bade him win all.

Enter Ajax.

AJAX
Troilus, thou coward Troilus ! *Exit.*

DIOMEDES Ay, there, there.

NESTOR
So, so, we draw together. *Exit.*

Enter Achilles.

ACHILLES Where is this Hector ?
Come, come, thou boy-queller, show thy face ;   45
Know what it is to meet Achilles angry.
Hector, where's Hector ? I will none but Hector. *Exit.*

Enter Ajax. V, vi

AJAX
Troilus, thou coward Troilus, show thy head.

Enter Diomedes.

DIOMEDES
Troilus, I say, where's Troilus ?

AJAX What wouldst thou ?

DIOMEDES
I would correct him.

AJAX
Were I the general, thou shouldst have my office
Ere that correction. Troilus, I say ; what, Troilus !   5

Enter Troilus.

TROILUS
O traitor Diomed ! Turn thy false face, thou traitor,
And pay thy life thou owest me for my horse.

DIOMEDES
Ha, art thou there ?

AJAX
I'll fight with him alone. Stand, Diomed.

DIOMEDES
He is my prize ; I will not look upon.   10

TROILUS
Come, both you cogging Greeks ; have at you both !   11

[Exeunt, fighting.]

[Enter Hector.]

HECTOR
Yea, Troilus ? O, well fought, my youngest brother !

Enter Achilles.

ACHILLES
Now do I see thee. Have at thee, Hector !

[They fight.]

HECTOR
Pause, if thou wilt.

ACHILLES
I do disdain thy courtesy, proud Troyan.
Be happy that my arms are out of use.
My rest and negligence befriends thee now,
But thou anon shalt hear of me again ;
Till when, go seek thy fortune. *Exit.*

HECTOR Fare thee well :
I would have been much more a fresher man,
Had I expected thee. How now, my brother !

Enter Troilus.

V, v   9 *beam* lance   10 *pashèd corses* battered corpses   14 *Sagittary* a
Centaur (half man, half horse) who aided the Trojans   22 *scalèd sculls*
scaly schools of fish   24 *strawy* i.e. like straw ripe for the mower's scythe
29 *proof* fact   45 *boy-queller* boy-killer
V, vi   5 *correction* privilege of correcting Troilus   10 *look upon* remain a
bystander   11 *cogging* deceitful

TROILUS

22 Ajax hath ta'en Aeneas ! Shall it be ?
No, by the flame of yonder glorious heaven,
He shall not carry him ; I'll be ta'en too,
Or bring him off. Fate, hear me what I say !
I reck not though thou end my life to-day.   *Exit.*
    Enter one in armor.

HECTOR

Stand, stand, thou Greek ; thou art a goodly mark.
No ? Wilt thou not ? I like thy armor well ;
29 I'll frush it and unlock the rivets all,
But I'll be master of it. Wilt thou not, beast, abide ?
Why then, fly on, I'll hunt thee for thy hide.
    Exit [in pursuit].

V, vii   *Enter Achilles with Myrmidons.*

ACHILLES

Come here about me, you my Myrmidons ;
Mark what I say. Attend me where I wheel ;
Strike not a stroke, but keep yourselves in breath ;
And when I have the bloody Hector found,
5 Empale him with your weapons round about ;
6 In fellest manner execute your arms.
Follow me, sirs, and my proceedings eye.
It is decreed, Hector the great must die.
    Exit [with Myrmidons].
    *Enter Thersites, Menelaus, Paris [the last two
fighting].*

THERSITES The cuckold and the cuckold-maker are at it.
10 Now, bull ! now, dog ! 'Loo, Paris, 'loo ! Now, my
11 double-horned Spartan ! 'Loo, Paris, 'loo ! The bull has
the game ; 'ware horns, ho ! *Exeunt Paris and Menelaus.*
    Enter Bastard [Margarelon].

BASTARD Turn, slave, and fight.

THERSITES What art thou ?

BASTARD A bastard son of Priam's.

THERSITES I am a bastard too ; I love bastards. I am a
bastard begot, bastard instructed, bastard in mind,
bastard in valor, in everything illegitimate. One bear
will not bite another, and wherefore should one bastard ? Take heed, the quarrel 's most ominous to us. If
the son of a whore fight for a whore, he tempts judgment. Farewell, bastard.

BASTARD The devil take thee, coward !   *Exit.*

V, viii   *Enter Hector.*

HECTOR

Most putrefièd core, so fair without,
Thy goodly armor thus hath cost thy life.
Now is my day's work done ; I'll take my breath.
Rest, sword ; thou hast thy fill of blood and death.
    [Puts off his helmet, and hangs his shield behind him.]
    Enter Achilles and his Myrmidons.

ACHILLES

Look, Hector, how the sun begins to set,
How ugly night comes breathing at his heels.
7 Even with the vail and dark'ning of the sun,

To close the day up, Hector's life is done.

HECTOR

I am unarmed ; forgo this vantage, Greek.

ACHILLES

Strike, fellows, strike ; this is the man I seek.
    [Hector falls.]
So, Ilion, fall thou next ! Come, Troy, sink down !
Here lies thy heart, thy sinews, and thy bone.
On, Myrmidons, and cry you all amain,
'Achilles hath the mighty Hector slain !'
    Retreat.
Hark, a retire upon our Grecian part.

GREEK

The Troyan trumpets sound the like, my lord.

ACHILLES

The dragon wing of night o'erspreads the earth,
And, stickler-like, the armies separates.   18
My half-supped sword, that frankly would have fed,   19
Pleased with this dainty bait, thus goes to bed.
    [Sheathes his sword.]
Come, tie his body to my horse's tail ;
Along the field I will the Troyan trail.   *Exeunt.*
    Enter Agamemnon, Ajax, Menelaus, Nestor,   V, ix
    *Diomed, and the rest, marching. [Sound retreat.
Shout.]*

AGAMEMNON

Hark, hark, what shout is that ?

NESTOR   Peace, drums !

SOLDIERS *(within)*   Achilles !
Achilles ! Hector 's slain ! Achilles !

DIOMEDES

The bruit is, Hector 's slain, and by Achilles.   3

AJAX

If it be so, yet bragless let it be ;
Great Hector was as good a man as he.

AGAMEMNON

March patiently along. Let one be sent
To pray Achilles see us at our tent.
If in his death the gods have us befriended,
Great Troy is ours, and our sharp wars are ended.
    Exeunt.
    Enter Aeneas, Paris, Antenor, and Deiphobus.   V, x

AENEAS

Stand, ho ! yet are we masters of the field.
Never go home ; here starve we out the night.
    Enter Troilus.

TROILUS

Hector is slain.

ALL   Hector ! The gods forbid !

TROILUS

He's dead and at the murderer's horse's tail,
In beastly sort, dragged through the shameful field.
Frown on, you heavens, effect your rage with speed ;
Sit, gods, upon your thrones, and smile at Troy.   7
I say, at once let your brief plagues be mercy,   8
And linger not our sure destructions on.

AENEAS

My lord, you do discomfort all the host.

TROILUS

You understand me not that tell me so.
I do not speak of flight, of fear, of death,
But dare all imminence that gods and men   13
Address their dangers in. Hector is gone.

---

22 *ta'en* taken captive   29 *frush* batter
V, vii   5 *Empale him* fence him in   6 *execute* give effect to   10 *'Loo* (a
cry to excite dogs)   11–12 *has the game* wins
V, viii   7 *vail* going down   18 *stickler-like* like umpires parting combatants   19 *frankly* freely
V, ix   3 *bruit* rumor
V, x   7 *smile* i.e. in derision   8 *let . . . mercy* show mercy by letting your
plagues destroy quickly   13–14 *But . . . dangers in* but dare whatever
imminent dangers gods and men may be preparing

Who shall tell Priam so, or Hecuba?
Let him that will a screech-owl aye be called
Go in to Troy, and say there Hector's dead.
There is a word will Priam turn to stone,
19   Make wells and Niobes of the maids and wives,
Cold statues of the youth, and in a word
Scare Troy out of itself. [But march away.
Hector is dead;] there is no more to say.
Stay yet. You vile abominable tents,
24   Thus proudly pight upon our Phrygian plains,
25   Let Titan rise as early as he dare,
26   I'll through and through you! And, thou great-sized
     coward,
No space of earth shall sunder our two hates.
I'll haunt thee like a wicked conscience still,
That mouldeth goblins swift as frenzy's thoughts.
Strike a free march to Troy. With comfort go;
Hope of revenge shall hide our inward woe.
         Enter Pandarus.

PANDARUS
But hear you, hear you!

TROILUS
Hence, broker lackey! Ignomy and shame
Pursue thy life, and live aye with thy name.
         Exeunt all but Pandarus.

PANDARUS   A goodly medicine for my aching bones! O
world, world! thus is the poor agent despised. O traitors
and bawds, how earnestly are you set a-work, and

how ill requited! Why should our endeavor be so
loved, and the performance so loathed? What verse for
it? What instance for it? Let me see.
     Full merrily the humble-bee doth sing,
     Till he hath lost his honey and his sting;
     And being once subdued in armèd tail,
     Sweet honey and sweet notes together fail.
Good traders in the flesh, set this in your painted cloths: 45
'As many as be here of Pandar's hall,
Your eyes, half out, weep out at Pandar's fall;
Or if you cannot weep, yet give some groans,
Though not for me, yet for your aching bones.
Brethren and sisters of the hold-door trade,   50
Some two months hence my will shall here be made.
It should be now, but that my fear is this,
Some gallèd goose of Winchester would hiss.   53
Till then I'll sweat and seek about for eases,   54
And at that time bequeath you my diseases.'   *[Exit.]*

---

19 *Niobes* (Niobe, whose seven sons and seven daughters were slain, wept and was turned into a stone that still wept)   24 *pight* pitched   25 *Titan* (Helios, the sun, was one of the Titans)   26 *coward* i.e. Achilles   45 *painted cloths* painted cloth hangings (used like tapestries, and sometimes to advertise wares)   50 *hold-door trade* prostitution   53 *gallèd goose* irritated prostitute; *Winchester* (the brothels of Southwark had once been under the jurisdiction of the Bishop of Winchester, a prostitute being called a Winchester goose)   54 *sweat* (a treatment for venereal diseases)

APPENDIX: THE QUARTO AND FOLIO TEXTS

As indicated in the "Note on the text", both the quarto and folio texts have substantive value. In addition to the passages bracketed, a number of readings in the present text have been adopted from the folio. These are noted below, along with all other material departures from the quarto text. The adopted reading in italics is followed by the quarto reading in roman.

Preface   17 *witted* wittied   30 *judgment's* Iudgements   36 *state* states
Pro. (supplied from F) 8 *immures* emures   12 *barks* barke   19 *Sperr* Stirre
I, i, 23 *of* (F) Omitted (Q)   25 *you* (F) yea   *to* (F) Omitted (Q)   39 *An* And   50 *Pour'st* (F) Powrest   64 *an* And   67–68 *ill-thought-on* (F) ill thought   72 *An* and   *not* (F) Omitted (Q)   73 *on* (F) a   *care* (F) Omitted (Q)   74 *an* and   92 *tetchy* teachy
I, ii, 17 *they* (F) the   43 *Ilium* (F) Illum   46 *ye* yea   82 *wit* will   111 *lift* (F) liste   120 *an* and   123 *the* thee   145 *An't* And t'   181 *a* (F) Omitted (Q)   193 *man's* (F) man   199 *anything;* anything *an* and   200 s.d. (after l. 198 in Q)   211–12 *indifferent well.* indifferent, well,   275 *prize* (F) price
I, iii, 2 *the jaundice on* the Iaundies on (F) these Iaundies ore (Q)   13 *every* (F) ever   31 *thy* (F) the   36 *patient* (F) ancient   54 *Returns* Retires   56 *spirit* (F) spright   61 *thy* (F) the   72 *lips than* lips; then   75 *basis* (F) bases   87 *Insisture* (F) In sisture   110 *meets* (F) melts   156 *scaffoldage* scoaffollage   157 *o'er-wrested* ore-rested   159 *unsquared* (F) unsquare   176 *natures,* natures   188 *self-willed* (F) selfe-wild   195 *and* (F) our   209 *fineness* (F) finesse   212 s.d. (F) Omitted (Q)   214 s.d. (F) Omitted (Q)   238 *Jove's* (F) great Ioves   247 *affair* (F) affaires   250 *him* (F) with him   252 *the* (F) that   256 *loud* (F) alowd   262 *this* (F) his   263 *rusty* (F) restie   267 *That seeks* (F) And feeds   276 *compass* (F) couple   289 *or means* (F) a meanes   294

one (F) no   297 *vantbrace* (F) vambrace   *this withered brawn* (F) my withered braunes   298 *will* (F) Omitted (Q)   302 *youth* (F) men   304 *Agamemnon* (F) Omitted (Q)   305 *first* (F) sir   327 *Achilles, were* (F) Achilles weare   334 *his honor* (F) those honours   336 *this* (F) the   354 *his in* his   369 *we* (F) it   372 *did* (F) do   390 *tarre* (F) arre
II, i, 13 *vinewed'st* whinid'st (F) unsalted (Q)   16 *oration* (F) oration without booke   17 *a* (F) Omitted (Q)   18 *murrain* murren (F) murrion (Q)   *o'* ath   25 *an* and   36, 38, 39 *Thersites, Ajax, Thersites* (F) Omitted (Q)   43 *Thou* (F) you   67 *I* (F) It   71 *I'll* (F) I   92 *sufferance* (F) suffrance   97 *if he* (F) and *out* (F) at   101 *your* their   *or their toes* (F) Omitted (Q)   109 *brach* brooch   117 *fifth* (F) first
II, ii, 14, 15 *surety* (F) surely   17 *worst.* (F) worst   27 *father* (F) fathers   33 *at* (F) of   47 *Let's* (F) Sets   64 *shores* (F) shore   79 *stale* (F) pale   82 *launched* (F) lansh't   100 s.d. (after l. 96 in Q)   210 *strike* (F) shrike
II, iii, 1 *Thersites* [s.p.] (F) Omitted (Q)   20 s.d. (F) Omitted (Q)   24 *wouldst* (F) couldst   29 *art* (F) art not   30 *corse* course   45 *thyself* (F) Thersites   59 *of Agamemnon* (F) Omitted (Q)   63 *Creator* (F) Prover   66 s.d. (F) Omitted (Q)   75 *shent* sent (F) sate (Q)   79 *so say* (F) say so   110 *winged* wingèd   126 *as* (F) and   127 *carriage of this action* (F) streame of his commencement   137 *enter you* (F) entertaine   156 s.d. (after l. 153 in Q)   187 *titled* (F) liked   197 *pash* (F) push   199 *An* and   206 *let* (F) tell   209, 213 *An* And   214 *Ulysses* (F) Aiax   215 *Ajax* (F) Omitted (Q)   216 *Nestor* (after *warm* in l. 216 in Q)   217 *praises* (F) praiers *pour in, pour in* (F) poure in, poure   234 *got* (F) gat   236 *all* (F) all thy   242 *bourn* (F) boord   243 *Thy* (F) This   257 *cull* (F) call
III, i, 6 *noble* (F) notable   24 *friend* (F) Omitted (Q)   34 *you not* (F) not you   36 *that* (F) Omitted (Q)   87 *poor* (F) Omitted (Q)

99 *lord* (F) lad   109 *shaft confounds* (F) shafts confound   140 *these* (F) this   148 *thee* (F) her

III, ii, 3 *he* (F) Omitted (Q)   8 *a* to a   10 *those* (F) these   42, 45 *an* and   63 *fears* teares   75 *is* (F) Omitted (Q)   86 *crown it. No perfection* (F) lover part no affection   92 s.d. (F) Omitted (Q)   111 *glance that ever –* glance; that ever   113 *not, till now* (F) till now not   125 *Cunning* Comming   134 *An* and   149 *might ; might* 152 *aye* (F) age   159 *winnowed* winnowèd   168 *similes,* (F) simele's   172 *Yet* (F) Omitted (Q)   177 *and* (F) or   185 *as* (F) or   192 *pains* (F) paine

III, iii 33 *his* this   39 *to* (F) Omitted (Q)   44 *med'cinable* medecinable   102 *giver* (F) givers   119 *th'* (F) the   128 *abject* (F) obiect   140 *on* (F) one   141 *shrinking* (F) shriking   155 *one* (F) on   158 *hedge* (F) turne   160 *hindmost ;* (F) him, most,   162 *rear* neere   164 *past* (F) passe   177 *give* goe   197 *grain of Pluto's gold* (F) thing   198 *th'* (F) the   *deeps* (F) depth   200 *Does* Do   224 *a* (F) Omitted (Q)   233 *we* (F) they   255 *an* and   265 *to him* (F) Omitted (Q)   272 *most* (F) Omitted (Q)   276 *Grecian* (F) Omitted (Q)   *et caetera* (F) Omitted (Q)   288 *be wi'* buy

IV, i, s.d. *with a torch* (F) Omitted (Q)   4 *you* (F) your   15 *and, so long,* and so long   16 *But* (F) Lul'd   40 *do think* (F) beleeve   52 *the* (F) Omitted (Q)   56 *soilure* (F) soyle   76 *you* (F) they

IV, ii, 6 *infants'* infants   22 s.d. (F) Omitted (Q)   31 *capocchia* chipochia   51 *'Tis* (F) its   63 *us* (F) him   *for him* (F) Omitted (Q)   66 *concluded so* (F) so concluded   72 *nature* (F) neighbor Pandar   77 *Cressida* (F) Omitted (Q)

IV, iv, 4 *as* (F) is   53 *the root* (F) my throate   63 *there's* (F) there is   76 *They're* Their   78 *person* (F) portion   134 *I'll* (F) I   138 s.d. *Sound trumpet* (F) Omitted (Q)

IV, v, 95 *Agamemnon* (F) Ulisses [not a s.p.]   97 *matchless,* (F) matchlesse   98 *in deeds* (F) deeds   115 *disposed* (F) dispo'd   132 *drop* (F) day   142 *O yes* O yes   160 *mine* (F) my   177 *that I affect th' untraded oath* (F) thy affect, the untraded earth   187 *thy* (F) th'   192 *shraped* shrupd   198 *Let* (F) O let   234 *prithee* (F) pray thee   254 *stithied* (F) stichied   283 *thee* (F) you   286 *As* (F) But   291 *she loved* (F) my Lord

V, i, 12 *need these* (F) needs this   14 *boy* (F) box   17 *catarrhs* (F)

Omitted (Q)   18 *o'* a   19 *wheezing* whissing   20 *lime-kilns* lime-kills   21–22 *and the like* (F) Omitted (Q)   31 *tassel* (F) toslell   32 *pestered* pestred   37 *in to-morrow's* (F) into morrowes   46 s.d. (F) Omitted (Q)   52 *brother* (F) be   54 *hanging* (F) Omitted (Q)   55 *brother's* (F) bare   56 *forced* (F) faced   58 *he is* (F) her's   *dog* (F) day   59 *mule* (F) Moyle   *fitchew* (F) Fichooke   61 *Menelaus !* Menelaus   *not* (F) Omitted (Q)   64 *spirits* (F) sprites   75 *sewer* sure   76 *at once* (F) Omitted (Q)   97 s.d. *Exit* Exeunt (F) Omitted (Q)

V, ii, 5 s.d. (F) Omitted (Q)   13 *Cressida.* Cal.   34 *you* (F) Omitted (Q)   38 *Nay* (F) Now   39 *distraction* (F) distruction   44 *withered* witherèd   45 *Why, Greek !* why Greeke?   46 *adieu* (F) Omitted (Q)   54 *these* (F) Omitted (Q)   55 *But* (F) Omitted (Q)   56 *la* lo   66 *Cressida* (F) Troy   68 *have't* (F) ha't   74 *in* (F) on   77 *Nay* Dio: [s.p.] Nay   78 *He* Cres: [s.p.] He   81 *Cressida* (F) Omitted (Q)   85 *one's* on's   87 *By* (F) And by   100 *Ay,* (F) I   101 *plagued* (F) plaguèd   110 *say* (F) said   114 *co-act* (F) Court   119 *had deceptious* (F) were deceptions   130 *soil* (F) spoile   147 *orifice* orifex   148 *Ariachne's* (F) Ariachna's   153 *five-* (F) finde   156 *bound* (F) given   163 *as I* I

V, iii, 14 *Cassandra* (F) Cres.   21 *give* count give   *use* as   29 *mean'st* (F) meanest   39 *that, good Troilus ?* that? good Troylus   85 *distraction* (F) destruction   104 *o' these* ath's

V, iv, 3 *young* (F) Omitted (Q)   15 *begin* began   25 *art thou* (F) art

V, v, 22 *scaled* (F) scaling   41 *luck* (F) lust   43 *Ajax* (F) Omitted (Q)

V, vi, 1 *Ajax* (F) Omitted (Q)   2 *Diomedes* (F) Omitted (Q)   13 *Achilles* (F) Omitted (Q)   *thee* thee ha   26 *reck* wreake   *thou* (F) I

V, vii, 1 *Achilles* (F) Omitted (Q)   10 *'Loo* lowe   *'loo* lowe   11 *-horned* hen'd   *'Loo, Paris, 'loo* lowe Paris, lowe   12 s.d. *Exeunt* Exit   16 *am a bastard* (F) am bastard

V, viii, 4 s.d. *his* (F) Omitted (Q)   15 *part* (F) prat   16 *Greek* (F) One   *Troyan trumpets* (F) Troyans trumpet

V, ix, 1 *shout is that* (F) is this

V, x, s.d. *and* (F) Omitted (Q)   3 *Troilus* (F) before l. 2 in Q   8 *say, say* 12 *fear, of* (F) feare of   17 *there* (F) their   23 *vile* (F) proud   24 *pight* (F) pitcht   29 *frenzy's* (F) frienzes   33 *broker lackey !* broker, lacky,   *Ignomy and* (F) ignomyny   49 *your* (F) my

OTHELLO THE MOOR OF VENICE

INTRODUCTION

Of the four tragedies commonly thought to be Shakespeare's greatest and the most distinguished examples of this form in the English language – *Hamlet*, *Othello*, *King Lear*, and *Macbeth* – *Othello* is the most tightly constructed and the narrowest in scope. The resultant concentration of emotion and action makes it a play of unusual forcefulness, powerful not only on the stage but in the study, sweeping from the confident and brilliant opening to the tragic close. All four tragedies came within a six- or seven-year span ; *Othello*, the second, was probably written not long before November 1, 1604, when it was performed by the King's Men at Court, and it is interesting that it alone has this tight construction and headlong action.

Shakespeare gains this concentration in several ways. For one thing, here the time of action is condensed so that the events of only two or three nights and days appear to be set forth on the stage, and the only emphasized time-lapse is that required for the voyage from Venice to Cyprus. The other three tragedies span months or even years, and time-consuming events which occur between scenes have to be pointed out to the audience : for example, in *Hamlet* Laertes' trip from Elsinore to Paris and return ; in *King Lear* Cordelia's sojourn in France ; and in *Macbeth* Malcolm and Macduff's flight to England, the recruitment of an army there, and then the march of that army to Dunsinane. The elimination in *Othello* of all but one such emphasized space-breaks and time-breaks helps to give the play its headlong rush from the arrival in Cyprus to Othello's death.

Not only by a limitation of time has Shakespeare intensified the effect of rushing events, but also by an unusual concentration of the action in the three main characters, Othello, Desdemona, and Iago. One or more of these three is on the stage in each of the fifteen scenes of the play except for the brief proclamation scene (II, ii), whereas Macbeth and Lady Macbeth are absent from nine scenes of their play, Lear and his daughters fail to appear in six scenes of *King Lear*, and even in the one-man play of *Hamlet* both the protagonist and Ophelia are off-stage during four scenes totalling nearly five hundred lines. These observations afford, of course, no evidence of the comparative merits of the four tragedies, but they do point to Shakespeare's deviation from his customary practice in achieving the distinctive concentration of *Othello*. He has denied himself the development of any subsidiary interests in order to concentrate on the tragic destruction of Othello and Desdemona through the diabolism of Iago.

To the same end Shakespeare has minimized the number of characters in this play. Not only is the cast of *Othello* smaller than those of the other three tragedies – it has half to two-thirds the number of characters – but in it the secondary characters, Brabantio, Cassio, Roderigo, and Emilia, are undeveloped save for their relations to the plotting of Iago or the downfall of Othello and Desdemona. Even Iago's gulling of Roderigo, which might at first glance seem to be an underplot, is really only an instrument in the destruction of Othello ; Roderigo is given little individuality beyond that of the uncomprehending gull to whom Iago may speak freely (thus further revealing for the audience his own character and plans) and who will carry out Iago's schemes for the disgrace and assassination of Cassio. Roderigo has no unrelated or parallel existence, like that of Lady Macduff in *Macbeth*, or Polonius and Fortinbras in *Hamlet*. All such secondary concerns, which add variety and depth of character-interest to Shakespeare's other major tragedies, and to *Romeo and Juliet*, *Julius Caesar*, *Antony and Cleopatra*, and *Coriolanus* as well, have been sacrificed in this play to give *Othello* that unique concentration and simplicity which make it more like modern tragedies in structure than any of Shakespeare's other tragic masterpieces.

Othello differs again from the usual Shakespearean pattern in the extent to which the power of evil is concentrated in one figure. The conflict of good and evil in an ostensibly Christian world was always a basic element in Elizabethan tragedies, and Shakespeare's presentation of the conflict is everywhere more subtle and complex than that of any of his contemporaries, but in the other Shakespearean tragedies the evil is more dispersed through various characters or even, as in *King Lear*, through the entire world of the play. Here the inherent weaknesses of Desdemona and Othello are made fatal through the maneuvering of Iago, whose cunning of the devil makes the finally disabused Othello look for his cloven hoof (V, ii, 286). This further simplification of the structure of the play not only makes possible the creation of Shakespeare's supreme stage villain – one of the most coveted roles in the history of the theatre – but it provides yet another device for the concentration of emotions in the tragedy. The play's excellence in structure and vividness in characterization seem even more impressive when *Othello* is compared with its source, a mediocre Italian tale by "Cinthio" (Giovanni Baptista Giraldi) told in the *Hecatommithi*, a collection of 1565.

Having planned his scenario to reduce the scope and variety made possible by the Elizabethan stage and familiarly exploited in tragedies like his own *Antony and Cleopatra* and Marlowe's *Doctor Faustus*, Shakespeare could lavish his dramatic and poetic genius on the painful degeneration of the noble and assured Othello of Act I, scenes ii and iii, to the pitiful dupe and the figure of passionate remorse we see in V, ii ; on the battering of the proud and confident Desdemona of I, iii into the childlike and uncomprehending victim of Acts IV and V – all by means of the terrifyingly casual and joyous evil of "honest Iago." All the seeds of these tragic events are displayed to the audience in the first act, but they are so adroitly overlaid by a romantic and optimistic tone that the prosperity of the love of Othello and Desdemona is made to seem superficially possible.

Othello is a man of action whose achievement was immediately obvious to an Elizabethan audience, in spite of his exotic color and background, because of his position as the commanding general for the greatest commercial power of the preceding century. He is first presented in a situation in which his experience and reputation make him easily the dominant figure on the stage. In the second scene of the play, as the drawn swords flash about him, Othello, the object of the attack, stands quietly confident, his weapon still in its scabbard, and speaks to these incensed men like a veteran to excited boys : "Keep up your bright swords, for the dew will rust them."

At Othello's second appearance, in the third scene of the play, he dominates not a mere cluster of street fighters but the Duke and senators of a powerful Renaissance state assembled in formal council. The scene is skillfully contrived at the beginning to draw the audience into the crisis of a national emergency ; then a principal senator arrives who focuses the attention of the council on his just indignation against the unnamed seducer of his daughter. Unhesitatingly the Duke accepts Brabantio's story and unhesitatingly promises him the bloody punishment of the culprit, though the man be the Duke's own son. But when Brabantio explains that the unnamed seducer is their great general, the attitude of Duke and senators changes sharply. Respectfully they listen as the black Othello describes his courtship of the daughter of a great Venetian magnifico ; they watch sympathetically as Desdemona confesses her duty and obedience to the Moor above her duty and obedience to her father ; the Duke in the presence of the other senators advises Brabantio to make the best of his new son-in-law ; and Duke and senators proceed to reiterate their confidence in Othello by assigning him the command at Cyprus as though Brabantio had never spoken. Again, as in scene ii, the assured power of Othello over great men in council as well as over lesser men in action is dramatized before the audience.

Yet under this dominating impression of a commanding and unshakeable personality the weaknesses of Othello have been less vividly suggested. In the second scene he speaks confidentially to Iago as to a trusted friend, and toward the end of the third scene he commits his beloved wife to the protection of Iago, whom he calls a man "of honesty and trust." But the audience had been introduced to Iago before they had been to Othello. In the opening scene of the play Iago was heard to admit his hatred of Othello, to declare his moral code as unscrupulous self-aggrandizement, and to assert his policy of consistent insincerity. And in the council chamber scene, immediately after the exit of Othello, the trusted Iago again declares his principles of calculated self-seeking and closes the act with a soliloquy in which he reasserts his hatred of Othello and plots the general's betrayal. Can Othello's assured mastery of threatening situations be so unshakeable as it has seemed

in the two big dramatic scenes of the act if he is so naive in his judgment of Iago ?

And what of the romantic marriage with Desdemona so touchingly presented ? Othello says of his wife that

> She loved me for the dangers I had passed,
> And I loved her that she did pity them.

The lines are beautifully evocative, but many members of the audience might have an uneasy feeling that Desdemona really knew very little about Othello. And they would feel uneasy again at Brabantio's bitter parting jibe at Othello,

> Look to her, Moor, if thou hast eyes to see :
> She has deceived her father, and may thee,

a jibe made in a spirit of animosity and not of thoughtful analysis, yet reminding us that romantic ignorance often prepares the way for deception. The Elizabethan ideal of respect for parents was much stronger than ours, and this emphatic couplet was calculated to make a sharper impression on an audience than a more elaborately rational statement would have made. Even the phrase "if thou hast eyes to see" has an ominous relevance, for Othello has already shown he has no eyes to see the true character of Iago. Does he know more of Desdemona ?

And so carefully planned concentration on Iago, Othello, and Desdemona in the first act of the play leaves a dominant impression of a resourceful and confident general, triumphant in a seriously threatened love affair, off for new triumphs in the field of his greatest competence, so fortunate that as he sets out to meet the challenge of a military emergency he is not even required to forgo the company of his bride. And yet here, less dominantly presented in this opening movement, are all the seeds of the fifth act. Othello is a proud and confident man, but his experience, as he himself points out, is almost exclusively military ; his appealing new wife knows little of him save for his military honors and adventures, and he knows little of her save for her admiration of his exploits ; his trusted ensign is an unscrupulous opportunist who prides himself on his insincerity. In these terms the play is to develop.

The transfer of the action to Cyprus for the developments of the last four acts is significant. From Desdemona's native world of wealthy, sophisticated, pampered Venice, where Othello is out of his usual campaign environment, the action moves to an outpost under martial law, a setting alien to Desdemona. Here, like most of Shakespeare's tragic heroines, she is isolated from her accustomed friends and supporters, while Othello is in a setting familiar, as he has said, from childhood :

> For since these arms of mine had seven years' pith
> Till now some nine moons wasted, they have used
> Their dearest action in the tented field.

In such an environment one would expect Othello to be even more effortlessly dominant than in worldly Venice, and the first two hundred lines of the Cyprus action suggest that he will be, for all on stage are relieved at his arrival and eager to trust and serve him ; even the fortunate dispersal of the Turkish fleet seems another triumph for lucky Othello. But it only seems so, for Othello's accustomed environment of war is suddenly removed, and in the last hundred lines of II, i Iago establishes the cynical, lecherous, intriguing tone of a decadent

Renaissance court more vividly than it was ever set in the first act at Venice itself. Othello's apparent good fortune in the transfer of the action from sophisticated Venice, where, as he says, "little of this great world can I speak," to the familiar setting of a town at war, with the added good fortune of the company of his bride, is a completely illusory triumph. Cyprus is not really an honest camp but an outpost of Venetian intrigue in which Othello is a helpless child; his new wife is not even a typical Venetian, for she is more naive and imperceptive than Othello, as her actions in the third and fourth acts and her conversation with Emilia in the last part of IV, iii so vividly show; Iago is not the trusty ensign who will fight at his commander's side but a Venetian devil incarnate, adept at hellish insinuations. As in so many Shakespearean tragedies, the great man of the first act enters a new set of circumstances and becomes "no more but such a poor, bare, forked animal as thou art."

It is only Iago who prospers in the new environment. The declared villain satisfies his hatred of his general and his lieutenant by creating for Othello the vivid illusion of Desdemona's infidelity with Cassio, and in the terrifying grip of this illusion Othello destroys his reputation, his happiness, his bride, and himself. Perhaps the most tragically terrifying aspect of this irrational destruction is the fact that Othello, like all mortals who only know in part, dimly realizes what he is doing at each step, but in the grip of the illusion he always misunderstands why he is doing it. As early as the middle of the third act he knows that his suspicious uncertainty of Desdemona has destroyed his peace of mind and his cherished professional career.

O, now for ever
Farewell the tranquil mind! farewell content!
Farewell the plumèd troop, and the big wars
That make ambition virtue! O, farewell!
Farewell the neighing steed and the shrill trump,
The spirit-stirring drum, th' ear-piercing fife,
The royal banner, and all quality,
Pride, pomp, and circumstance of glorious war!
And O you mortal engines whose rude throats
Th' immortal Jove's dread clamors counterfeit,
Farewell! Othello's occupation 's gone!

When he comes in to kill Desdemona he is painfully aware that his love for her is as deep as ever, that he destroys what he loves best. He kisses the sleeping girl.

O balmy breath, that dost almost persuade
Justice to break her sword! One more, one more!
Be thus when thou art dead, and I will kill thee,
And love thee after. One more, and that's the last!
So sweet was ne'er so fatal. I must weep,
But they are cruel tears. This sorrow 's heavenly;
It strikes where it doth love.

And a few lines later when she protests her innocence he partially and confusedly understands what he does:

O perjured woman! thou dost stone my heart,
And mak'st me call what I intend to do
A murder, which I thought a sacrifice.

When, immediately after the stifling of Desdemona, Emilia enters the death chamber with news of the street murder, Othello again vaguely recognizes what he has done in the madness of his illusion, though he speaks in general terms:

It is the very error of the moon.
She comes more nearer earth than she was wont
And makes men mad.

And when Emilia roundly asserts the fidelity of her dead mistress, Othello protests in half-realization of his illusion,

Cassio did top her. Ask thy husband else.
O, I were damned beneath all depth in hell
But that I did proceed upon just grounds
To this extremity. Thy husband knew it all.

Only in the last hundred lines of the play does he clearly begin to see himself and to comprehend what has happened to him:

with this little arm and this good sword
I have made my way through more impediments
Than twenty times your stop. But O vain boast!
Who can control his fate? 'Tis not so now.
Be not afraid, though you do see me weaponed.
Here is my journey's end.

And only in his final speech to the emissaries from the Duke and senators, just before he stabs himself, does the great general of Venice, like the great King Lear, truly know himself:

I pray you, in your letters,
When you shall these unlucky deeds relate,
Speak of me as I am. Nothing extenuate,
Nor set down aught in malice. Then must you speak
Of one that loved not wisely, but too well;
Of one not easily jealous, but, being wrought,
Perplexed in the extreme; of one whose hand,
Like the base Judean, threw a pearl away
Richer than all his tribe.

This is the tragedy, then, of another deluded mortal who destroys what he loves best, so that his own death is only an appropriate corollary. King Lear and Coriolanus and Brutus do likewise, but they destroy themselves in a context of troubled kingdoms and empires, while the little world of Othello's tragedy is his own marriage and his false friend, "honest Iago." This narrowed scope of the tragedy reduces the generalized philosophic comments which characterize plays of more varied situation and looser structure like *King Lear* and *Hamlet*, but it intensifies the emotional impact of blind self-destruction.

Princeton University GERALD EADES BENTLEY

NOTE ON THE TEXT

Two versions of *Othello* have come down to us, one in a quarto of 1622 and another in the folio of 1623. Both are good, although they vary somewhat in details and their precise relationship is still subject to debate. The folio version is the fuller (by about 160 lines) and has been used as the basis of the present text; however, a number of readings from the quarto have been admitted, especially in contractions, oaths, and stage directions, where the corresponding words in the folio suggest editorial intervention. A few lines and brief passages of dialogue (I, iii, 372–75; III, iv, 92–93) omitted from the folio have been added from the quarto in square brackets. The act–scene division supplied marginally for reference is identical with that of the folio except for the indication of a new scene (II, iii) after the reading of the proclamation. (Unlike earlier quartos, that of *Othello* is partially divided into acts, with headings at II, IV, and V.) The extent of the use made of the quarto text is indicated in the Appendix as well as a listing of emendations.

OTHELLO THE MOOR OF VENICE

*

I, i   *Enter Roderigo and Iago.*

RODERIGO
Tush, never tell me ! I take it much unkindly
That thou, Iago, who hast had my purse
3   As if the strings were thine, shouldst know of this.
IAGO
4   'Sblood, but you'll not hear me !
If ever I did dream of such a matter,
Abhor me.
RODERIGO
Thou told'st me thou didst hold him in thy hate.
IAGO
Despise me if I do not. Three great ones of the city,
In personal suit to make me his lieutenant,
10   Off-capped to him ; and, by the faith of man,
I know my price ; I am worth no worse a place.
But he, as loving his own pride and purposes,
13   Evades them with a bombast circumstance.
Horribly stuffed with epithets of war ;
[And, in conclusion,]
16   Nonsuits my mediators ; for, 'Certes,' says he,
'I have already chose my officer.'
And what was he ?
19   Forsooth, a great arithmetician,
One Michael Cassio, a Florentine
21   (A fellow almost damned in a fair wife)
That never set a squadron in the field,
Nor the division of a battle knows
More than a spinster ; unless the bookish theoric,
Wherein the togèd consuls can propose
As masterly as he. Mere prattle without practice

Is all his soldiership. But he, sir, had th' election ;
And I (of whom his eyes had seen the proof
At Rhodes, at Cyprus, and on other grounds
Christian and heathen) must be belee'd and calmed   30
By debitor and creditor ; this counter-caster,   31
He, in good time, must his lieutenant be,
And I – God bless the mark ! – his Moorship's ancient.   33
RODERIGO
By heaven, I rather would have been his hangman.
IAGO
Why, there's no remedy ; 'tis the curse of service.
Preferment goes by letter and affection,   36
And not by old gradation, where each second
Stood heir to th' first. Now, sir, be judge yourself,
Whether I in any just term am affined   39
To love the Moor.
RODERIGO   I would not follow him then.
IAGO
O, sir, content you ;
I follow him to serve my turn upon him.
We cannot all be masters, nor all masters
Cannot be truly followed. You shall mark
Many a duteous and knee-crooking knave
That, doting on his own obsequious bondage,
Wears out his time, much like his master's ass,
For naught but provender ; and when he's old, cashiered.   48
Whip me such honest knaves ! Others there are
Who, trimmed in forms and visages of duty,   50
Keep yet their hearts attending on themselves ;
And, throwing but shows of service on their lords,
Do well thrive by them, and when they have lined their
      coats,
Do themselves homage. These fellows have some soul ;
And such a one do I profess myself. For, sir,
It is as sure as you are Roderigo,
Were I the Moor, I would not be Iago.
In following him, I follow but myself ;
Heaven is my judge, not I for love and duty,

I, i A street in Venice   3 *this* i.e. Desdemona's elopement   4 *'Sblood* by
God's blood   10 *him* i.e. Othello   13 *a bombast circumstance* pompous
circumlocutions   16 *Nonsuits* rejects   19 *arithmetician* theoretician   21
almost . . . wife (an obscure allusion ; Cassio is unmarried, but see IV, i,
123)   30 *belee'd and calmed* left in the lurch   31 *counter-caster* book-
keeper   33 *ancient* ensign   36 *affection* favoritism   39 *affined* obliged
48 *cashiered* turned off   50 *trimmed* dressed up

But seeming so, for my peculiar end;
For when my outward action doth demonstrate
62 The native act and figure of my heart
63 In compliment extern, 'tis not long after
But I will wear my heart upon my sleeve
For daws to peck at; I am not what I am.

RODERIGO
66 What a full fortune does the thick-lips owe
If he can carry't thus!

IAGO   Call up her father,
Rouse him. Make after him, poison his delight,
Proclaim him in the streets. Incense her kinsmen,
And though he in a fertile climate dwell,
Plague him with flies; though that his joy be joy,
Yet throw such changes of vexation on't
As it may lose some color.

RODERIGO
Here is her father's house. I'll call aloud.

IAGO
75 Do, with like timorous accent and dire yell
As when, by night and negligence, the fire
Is spied in populous cities.

RODERIGO
What, ho, Brabantio! Signior Brabantio, ho!

IAGO
Awake! What, ho, Brabantio! Thieves! thieves! thieves!
Look to your house, your daughter, and your bags!
81 Thieves! thieves!
        Brabantio at a window.

BRABANTIO *(above)*
What is the reason of this terrible summons?
What is the matter there?

RODERIGO
Signior, is all your family within?

IAGO
Are your doors locked?

BRABANTIO   Why, wherefore ask you this?

IAGO
Zounds, sir, y' are robbed! For shame, put on your
        gown!
Your heart is burst; you have lost half your soul.
Even now, now, very now, an old black ram
Is tupping your white ewe. Arise, arise!
90 Awake the snorting citizens with the bell,
Or else the devil will make a grandsire of you.
Arise, I say!

BRABANTIO What, have you lost your wits?

RODERIGO
Most reverend signior, do you know my voice?

BRABANTIO
Not I. What are you?

RODERIGO
My name is Roderigo.

BRABANTIO   The worser welcome!
I have charged thee not to haunt about my doors.
In honest plainness thou hast heard me say
My daughter is not for thee; and now, in madness,
Being full of supper and distemp'ring draughts,
Upon malicious knavery dost thou come
To start my quiet.

RODERIGO
Sir, sir, sir—

BRABANTIO But thou must needs be sure
My spirit and my place have in them power

To make this bitter to thee.

RODERIGO   Patience, good sir.

BRABANTIO
What tell'st thou me of robbing? This is Venice;
My house is not a grange.   106

RODERIGO   Most grave Brabantio,
In simple and pure soul I come to you.

IAGO Zounds, sir, you are one of those that will not serve
God if the devil bid you. Because we come to do you
service, and you think we are ruffians, you'll have your
daughter covered with a Barbary horse; you'll have
your nephews neigh to you; you'll have coursers for 112
cousins, and gennets for germans.   113

BRABANTIO
What profane wretch art thou?

IAGO I am one, sir, that comes to tell you your daughter
and the Moor are now making the beast with two backs.

BRABANTIO
Thou art a villain.

IAGO   You are—a senator.

BRABANTIO
This thou shalt answer. I know thee, Roderigo.

RODERIGO
Sir, I will answer anything. But I beseech you,
If't be your pleasure and most wise consent,
As partly I find it is, that your fair daughter,
At this odd-even and dull watch o' th' night,   122
Transported, with no worse nor better guard
But with a knave of common hire, a gondolier,
To the gross clasps of a lascivious Moor—
If this be known to you, and your allowance,   126
We then have done you bold and saucy wrongs;
But if you know not this, my manners tell me
We have your wrong rebuke. Do not believe
That, from the sense of all civility,   130
I thus would play and trifle with your reverence.
Your daughter, if you have not given her leave,
I say again, hath made a gross revolt,
Tying her duty, beauty, wit, and fortunes
In an extravagant and wheeling stranger   135
Of here and everywhere. Straight satisfy yourself.
If she be in her chamber, or your house,
Let loose on me the justice of the state
For thus deluding you.

BRABANTIO   Strike on the tinder, ho!
Give me a taper! Call up all my people!
This accident is not unlike my dream.   141
Belief of it oppresses me already.
Light, I say! light!   *Exit [above].*

IAGO   Farewell, for I must leave you.
It seems not meet, nor wholesome to my place,
To be produced—as, if I stay, I shall—
Against the Moor. For I do know the state,
However this may gall him with some check,   147
Cannot with safety cast him; for he's embarked   148

62 *The . . . heart* what I really believe and intend 63 *compliment extern*
outward appearance 66 *thick-lips* (Elizabethans made no clear distinction
between Moors and Negroes); *owe* own 75 *timorous* terrifying 81 *s.d.*
Brabantio at a window (added from quarto) 90 *snorting* snoring 106
grange isolated farmhouse 112 *nephews* i.e. grandsons 113 *gennets for*
germans Spanish horses for near kinsmen 122 *odd-even* between night
and morning 126 *allowance* approval 130 *from the sense* in violation
135 *extravagant and wheeling* expatriate and roving 141 *accident* occur-
rence 147 *check* reprimand 148 *cast* discharge

With such loud reason to the Cyprus wars,
150 Which even now stand in act, that for their souls
151 Another of his fathom they have none
To lead their business ; in which regard,
Though I do hate him as I do hell-pains,
Yet, for necessity of present life,
I must show out a flag and sign of love,
Which is indeed but sign. That you shall surely find him,
157 Lead to the Sagittary the raisèd search ;
158 And there will I be with him. So farewell.   *Exit.*
*Enter [below] Brabantio in his nightgown, and
Servants with torches.*

BRABANTIO
It is too true an evil. Gone she is ;
And what's to come of my despisèd time
Is naught but bitterness. Now, Roderigo,
Where didst thou see her ? – O unhappy girl ! –
With the Moor, say'st thou ? – Who would be a father ? –
How didst thou know 'twas she ? – O, she deceives me
165 Past thought ! – What said she to you ? – Get moe tapers !
Raise all my kindred ! – Are they married, think you ?

RODERIGO
Truly I think they are.

BRABANTIO
O heaven ! How got she out ? O treason of the blood !
Fathers, from hence trust not your daughters' minds
By what you see them act. Is there not charms
171 By which the property of youth and maidhood
May be abused ? Have you not read, Roderigo,
Of some such thing ?

RODERIGO   Yes, sir, I have indeed.

BRABANTIO
Call up my brother. – O, would you had had her ! –
Some one way, some another. – Do you know
Where we may apprehend her and the Moor ?

RODERIGO
I think I can discover him, if you please
To get good guard and go along with me.

BRABANTIO
Pray you lead on. At every house I'll call ;
I may command at most. – Get weapons, ho !
And raise some special officers of night. –
182 On, good Roderigo ; I'll deserve your pains.   *Exeunt.*

*

I, ii   *Enter Othello, Iago, and Attendants with torches.*

IAGO
Though in the trade of war I have slain men,
Yet do I hold it very stuff o' th' conscience
To do no contrived murther. I lack iniquity
Sometimes to do me service. Nine or ten times
5 I had thought t' have yerked him here under the ribs.

OTHELLO
'Tis better as it is.

IAGO   Nay, but he prated,
And spoke such scurvy and provoking terms
Against your honor
That with the little godliness I have
I did full hard forbear him. But I pray you, sir,
Are you fast married ? Be assured of this,   11
That the magnifico is much beloved,   12
And hath in his effect a voice potential   13
As double as the Duke's. He will divorce you,   14
Or put upon you what restraint and grievance
The law, with all his might to enforce it on,
Will give him cable.

OTHELLO   Let him do his spite.
My services which I have done the signiory   18
Shall out-tongue his complaints. 'Tis yet to know –   19
Which, when I know that boasting is an honor,
I shall promulgate – I fetch my life and being
From men of royal siege ; and my demerits   22
May speak unbonneted to as proud a fortune   23
As this that I have reached. For know, Iago,
But that I love the gentle Desdemona,
I would not my unhousèd free condition   26
Put into circumscription and confine
For the sea's worth. But look, what lights come yond ?

IAGO
Those are the raisèd father and his friends.
You were best go in.

OTHELLO   Not I ; I must be found.
My parts, my title, and my perfect soul   31
Shall manifest me rightly. Is it they ?

IAGO
By Janus, I think no.
Enter Cassio, with torches, Officers.

OTHELLO
The servants of the Duke, and my lieutenant.
The goodness of the night upon you, friends !
What is the news ?

CASSIO   The Duke does greet you, general ;
And he requires your haste-post-haste appearance
Even on the instant.

OTHELLO   What's the matter, think you ?

CASSIO
Something from Cyprus, as I may divine.
It is a business of some heat. The galleys
Have sent a dozen sequent messengers   41
This very night at one another's heels,
And many of the consuls, raised and met,
Are at the Duke's already. You have been hotly called for ;
When, being not at your lodging to be found,
The Senate hath sent about three several quests
To search you out.

OTHELLO   'Tis well I am found by you.
I will but spend a word here in the house,
And go with you.   *[Exit.]*

CASSIO   Ancient, what makes he here ?

IAGO
Faith, he to-night hath boarded a land carack.   50
If it prove lawful prize, he's made for ever.

CASSIO
I do not understand.

IAGO   He's married.

CASSIO   To who ?

150 *stand in act* are going on   151 *fathom* capacity   157 *Sagittary* an
inn   158 s.d. *nightgown* dressing down   165 *moe* more   171 *property*
nature   182 *deserve* show gratitude for
I, ii Before the lodgings of Othello   5 *yerked* stabbed   11 *fast* securely
12 *magnifico* grandee (Brabantio)   13 *potential* powerful   14 *double*
doubly influential   18 *signiory* Venetian government   19 *yet to know* still
not generally known   22 *siege* rank ; *demerits* deserts   23–24 *May speak . . .
reached* are equal, I modestly assert, to those of Desdemona's family
26 *unhousèd* unrestrained   31 *perfect soul* stainless conscience   41 *sequent*
consecutive   50 *carack* treasure ship

[Enter Othello.]

IAGO
Marry, to – Come, captain, will you go?

OTHELLO   Have with you.

CASSIO
Here comes another troop to seek for you.
*Enter Brabantio, Roderigo, and others with lights
and weapons.*

IAGO
It is Brabantio. General, be advised.
He comes to bad intent.

OTHELLO   Holla! stand there!

RODERIGO
Signior, it is the Moor.

BRABANTIO   Down with him, thief!
[They draw on both sides.]

IAGO
You, Roderigo! Come, sir, I am for you.

OTHELLO
59   Keep up your bright swords, for the dew will rust them.
Good signior, you shall more command with years
Than with your weapons.

BRABANTIO
O thou foul thief, where hast thou stowed my daughter?
Damned as thou art, thou hast enchanted her!
For I'll refer me to all things of sense,
If she in chains of magic were not bound,
Whether a maid so tender, fair, and happy,
So opposite to marriage that she shunned
The wealthy curlèd darlings of our nation,
Would ever have, t' incur a general mock,
Run from her guardage to the sooty bosom
Of such a thing as thou – to fear, not to delight.
72   Judge me the world if 'tis not gross in sense
That thou hast practiced on her with foul charms,
Abused her delicate youth with drugs or minerals
75   That weaken motion. I'll have't disputed on;
'Tis probable, and palpable to thinking.
77   I therefore apprehend and do attach thee
For an abuser of the world, a practicer
Of arts inhibited and out of warrant.
Lay hold upon him. If he do resist,
Subdue him at his peril.

OTHELLO   Hold your hands,
Both you of my inclining and the rest.
Were it my cue to fight, I should have known it
Without a prompter. Where will you that I go
To answer this your charge?

BRABANTIO   To prison, till fit time
86   Of law and course of direct session
Call thee to answer.

OTHELLO   What if I do obey?
How may the Duke be therewith satisfied,
Whose messengers are here about my side
Upon some present business of the state
To bring me to him?

OFFICER   'Tis true, most worthy signior.
The Duke 's in council, and your noble self
I am sure is sent for.

BRABANTIO   How? The Duke in council?
In this time of the night? Bring him away.
95   Mine's not an idle cause. The Duke himself,
Or any of my brothers of the state,
Cannot but feel this wrong as 'twere their own;

For if such actions may have passage free,
Bondslaves and pagans shall our statesmen be. *Exeunt.*

*

Enter Duke and Senators, set at a table, with lights   I, iii
and Attendants.

DUKE
There is no composition in these news   1
That gives them credit.

1. SENATOR   Indeed they are disproportionèd.
My letters say a hundred and seven galleys.

DUKE
And mine a hundred forty.

2. SENATOR   And mine two hundred.
But though they jump not on a just account –   5
As in these cases where the aim reports   6
'Tis oft with difference – yet do they all confirm
A Turkish fleet, and bearing up to Cyprus.

DUKE
Nay, it is possible enough to judgment.
I do not so secure me in the error   10
But the main article I do approve   11
In fearful sense.

SAILOR *(within)* What, ho! what, ho! what, ho!

OFFICER
A messenger from the galleys.
Enter Sailor.

DUKE   Now, what's the business?

SAILOR
The Turkish preparation makes for Rhodes.
So was I bid report here to the state
By Signior Angelo.

DUKE
How say you by this change?

1. SENATOR   This cannot be
By no assay of reason. 'Tis a pageant   18
To keep us in false gaze. When we consider   19
Th' importancy of Cyprus to the Turk,
And let ourselves again but understand
That, as it more concerns the Turk than Rhodes,
So may he with more facile question bear it,   23
For that it stands not in such warlike brace,   24
But altogether lacks th' abilities
That Rhodes is dressed in – if we make thought of this,
We must not think the Turk is so unskillful
To leave that latest which concerns him first,
Neglecting an attempt of ease and gain
To wake and wage a danger profitless.   30

DUKE
Nay, in all confidence, he's not for Rhodes.

OFFICER
Here is more news.
Enter a Messenger.

MESSENGER
The Ottomites, reverend and gracious,
Steering with due course toward the isle of Rhodes,

---

59 *Keep up* i.e. sheath   72 *gross in sense* obvious   75 *motion* perception
77 *attach* arrest   86 *direct session* regular trial   95 *idle* trifling
I, iii The Venetian Senate Chamber   1 *composition* consistency   5 *jump*
agree   6 *aim* conjecture   10 *so secure me* take such comfort   11 *article*
substance; *approve* accept   18 *assay* test   19 *in false gaze* looking the
wrong way   23 *with . . . bear* more easily capture   24 *brace* posture of
defense   30 *wake and wage* rouse and risk

Have there injointed them with an after fleet.

1. SENATOR
Ay, so I thought. How many, as you guess?

MESSENGER
37   Of thirty sail; and now they do restem
Their backward course, bearing with frank appearance
Their purposes toward Cyprus. Signior Montano,
Your trusty and most valiant servitor,
With his free duty recommends you thus,
And prays you to believe him.

DUKE
'Tis certain then for Cyprus.
44   Marcus Luccicos, is not he in town?

1. SENATOR
He's now in Florence.

DUKE
Write from us to him; post, post-haste dispatch.

1. SENATOR
Here comes Brabantio and the valiant Moor.
*Enter Brabantio, Othello, Cassio, Iago, Roderigo,
and Officers.*

DUKE
Valiant Othello, we must straight employ you
Against the general enemy Ottoman.
[To Brabantio]
I did not see you. Welcome, gentle signior.
We lacked your counsel and your help to-night.

BRABANTIO
So did I yours. Good your grace, pardon me.
Neither my place, nor aught I heard of business,
Hath raised me from my bed; nor doth the general care
Take hold on me; for my particular grief
56   Is of so floodgate and o'erbearing nature
57   That it engluts and swallows other sorrows,
And it is still itself.

DUKE   Why, what's the matter?

BRABANTIO
My daughter! O, my daughter!

ALL   Dead?

BRABANTIO   Ay, to me.
She is abused, stol'n from me, and corrupted
By spells and medicines bought of mountebanks;
For nature so prepost'rously to err,
63   Being not deficient, blind, or lame of sense,
Sans witchcraft could not.

DUKE
Whoe'er he be that in this foul proceeding
Hath thus beguiled your daughter of herself,
And you of her, the bloody book of law
You shall yourself read in the bitter letter
69   After your own sense; yea, though our proper son
70   Stood in your action.

BRABANTIO   Humbly I thank your grace.
Here is the man – this Moor, whom now, it seems,
Your special mandate for the state affairs
Hath hither brought.

ALL   We are very sorry for 't.

DUKE *[to Othello]*
What, in your own part, can you say to this?

BRABANTIO
Nothing, but this is so.

OTHELLO
Most potent, grave, and reverend signiors,
My very noble, and approved good masters,   77
That I have ta'en away this old man's daughter,
It is most true; true I have married her.
The very head and front of my offending
Hath this extent, no more. Rude am I in my speech,   81
And little blessed with the soft phrase of peace;
For since these arms of mine had seven years' pith   83
Till now some nine moons wasted, they have used
Their dearest action in the tented field;
And little of this great world can I speak
More than pertains to feats of broil and battle;
And therefore little shall I grace my cause
In speaking for myself. Yet, by your gracious patience,
I will a round unvarnished tale deliver   90
Of my whole course of love – what drugs, what charms,
What conjuration, and what mighty magic
(For such proceeding am I charged withal)
I won his daughter.

BRABANTIO   A maiden never bold;
Of spirit so still and quiet that her motion   95
Blushed at herself; and she – in spite of nature,
Of years, of country, credit, everything –
To fall in love with what she feared to look on!
It is a judgment maimed and most imperfect
That will confess perfection so could err
Against all rules of nature, and must be driven
To find out practices of cunning hell   102
Why this should be. I therefore vouch again   103
That with some mixtures pow'rful o'er the blood,   104
Or with some dram, conjured to this effect,
He wrought upon her.

DUKE   To vouch this is no proof,
Without more certain and more overt test
Than these thin habits and poor likelihoods   108
Of modern seeming do prefer against him.   109

1. SENATOR
But, Othello, speak.
Did you by indirect and forcèd courses   111
Subdue and poison this young maid's affections?
Or came it by request, and such fair question   113
As soul to soul affordeth?

OTHELLO   I do beseech you,
Send for the lady to the Sagittary
And let her speak of me before her father.
If you do find me foul in her report,
The trust, the office, I do hold of you
Not only take away, but let your sentence
Even fall upon my life.

DUKE   Fetch Desdemona hither.

OTHELLO
Ancient, conduct them; you best know the place.
Exit [Iago, with] two or three [Attendants].
And till she come, as truly as to heaven
I do confess the vices of my blood,
So justly to your grave ears I'll present
How I did thrive in this fair lady's love,
And she in mine.

---

37 *restem* steer again   44 *Marcus Luccicos* (presumably a Venetian envoy)
56 *floodgate* torrential   57 *engluts* devours   63 *deficient* feeble-minded
69 *our proper* my own   70 *Stood in your action* were accused by you   77
approved tested by experience   81 *Rude* unpolished   83 *pith* strength
90 *round* plain   95–96 *her motion Blushed* her own emotions caused her
to blush   102 *practices* plots   103 *vouch* assert   104 *blood* passions
108 *thin habits* slight appearances   109 *modern seeming* everyday supposition   111 *forcèd* violent   113 *question* conversation

DUKE
Say it, Othello.

OTHELLO
Her father loved me, oft invited me ;
129 Still questioned me the story of my life
From year to year – the battles, sieges, fortunes
That I have passed.
I ran it through, even from my boyish days
To th' very moment that he bade me tell it.
Wherein I spoke of most disastrous chances,
Of moving accidents by flood and field ;
Of hairbreadth scapes i' th' imminent deadly breach ;
Of being taken by the insolent foe
And sold to slavery ; of my redemption thence
139 And portance in my travels' history ;
140 Wherein of anters vast and deserts idle,
Rough quarries, rocks, and hills whose heads touch
   heaven,
142 It was my hint to speak – such was the process ;
And of the Cannibals that each other eat,
144 The Anthropophagi, and men whose heads
Do grow beneath their shoulders. This to hear
Would Desdemona seriously incline ;
But still the house affairs would draw her thence ;
Which ever as she could with haste dispatch,
She'ld come again, and with a greedy ear
Devour up my discourse. Which I observing,
151 Took once a pliant hour, and found good means
To draw from her a prayer of earnest heart
153 That I would all my pilgrimage dilate,
154 Whereof by parcels she had something heard,
155 But not intentively. I did consent,
And often did beguile her of her tears
When I did speak of some distressful stroke
That my youth suffered. My story being done,
She gave me for my pains a world of sighs,
She swore, i' faith, 'twas strange, 'twas passing strange ;
'Twas pitiful, 'twas wondrous pitiful.
She wished she had not heard it ; yet she wished
That heaven had made her such a man. She thanked me ;
And bade me, if I had a friend that loved her,
I should but teach him how to tell my story,
166 And that would woo her. Upon this hint I spake.
She loved me for the dangers I had passed,
And I loved her that she did pity them.
This only is the witchcraft I have used.
Here comes the lady. Let her witness it.
   Enter Desdemona, Iago, Attendants.

DUKE
I think this tale would win my daughter too.
Good Brabantio,
Take up this mangled matter at the best.
Men do their broken weapons rather use
Than their bare hands.

BRABANTIO   I pray you hear her speak.
If she confess that she was half the wooer,
Destruction on my head if my bad blame
Light on the man ! Come hither, gentle mistress.
Do you perceive in all this noble company
Where most you owe obedience ?

DESDEMONA   My noble father,
I do perceive here a divided duty.
182 To you I am bound for life and education ;
My life and education both do learn me

How to respect you : you are the lord of duty ;
I am hitherto your daughter. But here's my husband ;
And so much duty as my mother showed
To you, preferring you before her father,
So much I challenge that I may profess   188
Due to the Moor my lord.

BRABANTIO   God be with you ! I have done.
Please it your grace, on to the state affairs.
I had rather to adopt a child than get it.   191
Come hither, Moor.
I here do give thee that with all my heart
Which, but thou hast already, with all my heart
I would keep from thee. For your sake, jewel,   195
I am glad at soul I have no other child ;
For thy escape would teach me tyranny,   197
To hang clogs on them. I have done, my lord.

DUKE
Let me speak like yourself and lay a sentence   199
Which, as a grise or step, may help these lovers   200
[Into your favor.]
When remedies are past, the griefs are ended
By seeing the worst, which late on hopes depended.
To mourn a mischief that is past and gone
Is the next way to draw new mischief on.
What cannot be preserved when fortune takes,
Patience her injury a mock'ry makes.
The robbed that smiles steals something from the thief ;
He robs himself that spends a bootless grief.

BRABANTIO
So let the Turk of Cyprus us beguile :   210
We lose it not so long as we can smile.
He bears the sentence well that nothing bears
But the free comfort which from thence he hears ;
But he bears both the sentence and the sorrow
That to pay grief must of poor patience borrow.
These sentences, to sugar, or to gall,
Being strong on both sides, are equivocal.
But words are words. I never yet did hear
That the bruisèd heart was piercèd through the ear.
Beseech you, now to the affairs of state.

DUKE The Turk with a most mighty preparation makes
for Cyprus. Othello, the fortitude of the place is best 222
known to you ; and though we have there a substitute
of most allowed sufficiency, yet opinion, a more sover- 224
eign mistress of effects, throws a more safer voice on you.
You must therefore be content to slubber the gloss of 226
your new fortunes with this more stubborn and
boist'rous expedition.

OTHELLO
The tyrant custom, most grave senators,
Hath made the flinty and steel couch of war
My thrice-driven bed of down. I do agnize   231
A natural and prompt alacrity
I find in hardness ; and do undertake
These present wars against the Ottomites.

---

129 *Still* continually   139 *portance* behavior   140 *anters* caves   142 *hint* occasion   144 *Anthropophagi* man-eaters   151 *pliant* propitious   153 *dilate* recount in full   154 *parcels* portions   155 *intentively* with full attention   166 *hint* opportunity   182 *education* upbringing   188 *challenge* claim the right   191 *get* beget   195 *For your sake* because of you   197 *escape* escapade   199 *like yourself* as you should ; *sentence* maxim   200 *grise* step   222 *fortitude* fortification   224 *allowed* acknowledged ; *opinion* public opinion   226 *slubber* sully   231–33 *agnize . . . hardness* recognize in myself a natural and easy response to hardship

Most humbly, therefore, bending to your state,
I crave fit disposition for my wife,
237 Due reference of place, and exhibition,
238 With such accommodation and besort
239 As levels with her breeding.

DUKE   If you please,
Be't at her father's.

BRABANTIO   I will not have it so.

OTHELLO
Nor I.

DESDEMONA   Nor I. I would not there reside,
To put my father in impatient thoughts
By being in his eye. Most gracious Duke,
244 To my unfolding lend your prosperous ear,
And let me find a charter in your voice,
246 T' assist my simpleness.

DUKE
What would you, Desdemona?

DESDEMONA
That I did love the Moor to live with him,
My downright violence, and storm of fortunes,
May trumpet to the world. My heart 's subdued
Even to the very quality of my lord.
I saw Othello's visage in his mind,
And to his honors and his valiant parts
Did I my soul and fortunes consecrate.
So that, dear lords, if I be left behind,
A moth of peace, and he go to the war,
The rites for which I love him are bereft me,
And I a heavy interim shall support
By his dear absence. Let me go with him.

OTHELLO
Let her have your voice.
Vouch with me, heaven, I therefore beg it not
To please the palate of my appetite,
263 Not to comply with heat – the young affects
In me defunct – and proper satisfaction;
But to be free and bounteous to her mind;
And heaven defend your good souls that you think
I will your serious and great business scant
When she is with me. No, when light-winged toys
269 Of feathered Cupid seel with wanton dullness
270 My speculative and officed instruments,
271 That my disports corrupt and taint my business,
Let housewives make a skillet of my helm,
273 And all indign and base adversities
274 Make head against my estimation!

DUKE
Be it as you shall privately determine,
Either for her stay or going. Th' affair cries haste,
And speed must answer it.

1. SENATOR
You must away to-night.

OTHELLO   With all my heart.

DUKE
At nine i' th' morning here we'll meet again.
Othello, leave some officer behind,
And he shall our commission bring to you,
With such things else of quality and respect
283 As doth import you.

OTHELLO   So please your grace, my ancient;
A man he is of honesty and trust.
To his conveyance I assign my wife,
With what else needful your good grace shall think
To be sent after me.

DUKE   Let it be so.
Good night to every one.
     [To Brabantio]   And, noble signior,
If virtue no delighted beauty lack,
289 Your son-in-law is far more fair than black.

1. SENATOR
Adieu, brave Moor. Use Desdemona well.

BRABANTIO
Look to her, Moor, if thou hast eyes to see:
She has deceived her father, and may thee.
         Exeunt [Duke, Senators, Officers, &c.].

OTHELLO
My life upon her faith! – Honest Iago,
My Desdemona must I leave to thee.
I prithee let thy wife attend on her,
And bring them after in the best advantage.
297 Come, Desdemona. I have but an hour
Of love, of worldly matters and direction,
To spend with thee. We must obey the time.
         Exit Moor and Desdemona.

RODERIGO   Iago, –

IAGO   What say'st thou, noble heart?

RODERIGO   What will I do, think'st thou?

IAGO   Why, go to bed and sleep.

RODERIGO   I will incontinently drown myself.

IAGO   If thou dost, I shall never love thee after. Why, thou
silly gentleman!

RODERIGO   It is silliness to live when to live is torment;
and then have we a prescription to die when death is
our physician.

IAGO   O villainous! I have looked upon the world for four
times seven years; and since I could distinguish betwixt a benefit and an injury, I never found man that
knew how to love himself. Ere I would say I would
drown myself for the love of a guinea hen, I would
change my humanity with a baboon.

RODERIGO   What should I do? I confess it is my shame
to be so fond, but it is not in my virtue to amend it.

IAGO   Virtue? a fig! 'Tis in ourselves that we are thus or
thus. Our bodies are our gardens, to the which our wills
are gardeners; so that if we will plant nettles or sow
lettuce, set hyssop and weed up thyme, supply it with
one gender of herbs or distract it with many – either to
have it sterile with idleness or manured with industry –
why, the power and corrigible authority of this lies in
our wills. If the balance of our lives had not one scale
of reason to poise another of sensuality, the blood and
baseness of our natures would conduct us to most
preposterous conclusions. But we have reason to cool our
raging motions, our carnal stings, our unbitted lusts;
whereof I take this that you call love to be a sect or scion.

RODERIGO   It cannot be.

IAGO   It is merely a lust of the blood and a permission of

---

237 *exhibition* allowance of money   238 *besort* suitable company   239
levels corresponds   244 *prosperous* favorable   246 *simpleness* lack of
skill   263 *heat* passions; *young affects* tendencies of youth   269 *seel* blind
270 *My . . . instruments* my perceptive and responsible faculties   271 *That
so that*   273 *indign* unworthy   274 *estimation* reputation   283 *import*
concern   289 *delighted* delightful   297 *in the best advantage* at the best
opportunity   305 *incontinently* forthwith   323 *gender* species   325 *corrigible authority* corrective power   327 *poise* counterbalance   327–28 *blood
and baseness* animal instincts   330 *motions* appetites; *unbitted* uncontrolled
331 *sect or scion* offshoot, cutting

the will. Come, be a man! Drown thyself? Drown cats
and blind puppies! I have professed me thy friend, and I
confess me knit to thy deserving with cables of perdurable
toughness. I could never better stead thee than now. Put
338 money in thy purse. Follow thou the wars; defeat thy
favor with an usurped beard. I say, put money in thy
purse. It cannot be that Desdemona should long continue her love to the Moor – put money in thy purse – nor
he his to her. It was a violent commencement in her, and
343 thou shalt see an answerable sequestration – put but
money in thy purse. These Moors are changeable in their
wills – fill thy purse with money. The food that to him
now is as luscious as locusts shall be to him shortly as bit-
347 ter as coloquintida. She must change for youth: when she
is sated with his body, she will find the error of her choice.
[She must have change, she must.] Therefore put money
in thy purse. If thou wilt needs damn thyself, do it a more
351 delicate way than drowning. Make all the money thou
352 canst. If sanctimony and a frail vow betwixt an erring
barbarian and a supersubtle Venetian be not too hard for
my wits and all the tribe of hell, thou shalt enjoy her.
Therefore make money. A pox of drowning thyself! 'Tis
clean out of the way. Seek thou rather to be hanged in
compassing thy joy than to be drowned and go without
her.

RODERIGO Wilt thou be fast to my hopes, if I depend on
the issue?

IAGO Thou art sure of me. Go, make money. I have told
thee often, and I retell thee again and again, I hate the
362 Moor. My cause is hearted; thine hath no less reason.
Let us be conjunctive in our revenge against him. If
thou canst cuckold him, thou dost thyself a pleasure, me
a sport. There are many events in the womb of time,
366 which will be delivered. Traverse, go, provide thy
money! We will have more of this to-morrow. Adieu.

RODERIGO Where shall we meet i' th' morning?

IAGO At my lodging.

RODERIGO I'll be with thee betimes.

IAGO Go to, farewell. – Do you hear, Roderigo?

[RODERIGO What say you?

IAGO No more of drowning, do you hear?

RODERIGO I am changed.

IAGO Go to, farewell. Put money enough in your purse.]

RODERIGO I'll sell all my land.   *Exit.*

IAGO
Thus do I ever make my fool my purse;
For I mine own gained knowledge should profane
379 If I would time expend with such a snipe
But for my sport and profit. I hate the Moor;
And it is thought abroad that 'twixt my sheets
H'as done my office. I know not if't be true;
But I, for mere suspicion in that kind,
384 Will do as if for surety. He holds me well;
The better shall my purpose work on him.
Cassio's a proper man. Let me see now:
387 To get his place, and to plume up my will
In double knavery – How, how? – Let's see: –
After some time, to abuse Othello's ears
That he is too familiar with his wife.
391 He hath a person and a smooth dispose
To be suspected – framed to make women false.
393 The Moor is of a free and open nature
That thinks men honest that but seem to be so;
And will as tenderly be led by th' nose

As asses are.
I have't! It is engend'red! Hell and night
Must bring this monstrous birth to the world's light.
                                                    Exit.

*

Enter Montano and two Gentlemen.   II, i

MONTANO
What from the cape can you discern at sea?

1. GENTLEMAN
Nothing at all: it is a high-wrought flood.
I cannot 'twixt the heaven and the main
Descry a sail.

MONTANO
Methinks the wind hath spoke aloud at land;
A fuller blast ne'er shook our battlements.
If it hath ruffianed so upon the sea,
What ribs of oak, when mountains melt on them,
Can hold the mortise? What shall we hear of this?   9

2. GENTLEMAN
A segregation of the Turkish fleet.   10
For do but stand upon the foaming shore,
The chidden billow seems to pelt the clouds;
The wind-shaked surge, with high and monstrous mane,
Seems to cast water on the burning Bear
And quench the Guards of th' ever-fixèd pole.   15
I never did like molestation view   16
On the enchafèd flood.

MONTANO   If that the Turkish fleet
Be not ensheltered and embayed, they are drowned;
It is impossible to bear it out.
                    Enter a third Gentleman.

3. GENTLEMAN
News, lads! Our wars are done.
The desperate tempest hath so banged the Turks
That their designment halts. A noble ship of Venice   22
Hath seen a grievous wrack and sufferance   23
On most part of their fleet.

MONTANO
How? Is this true?

3. GENTLEMAN   The ship is here put in,
A Veronesa; Michael Cassio,   26
Lieutenant to the warlike Moor Othello,
Is come on shore; the Moor himself at sea,
And is in full commission here for Cyprus.

MONTANO
I am glad on't. 'Tis a worthy governor.

3. GENTLEMAN
But this same Cassio, though he speak of comfort
Touching the Turkish loss, yet he looks sadly
And prays the Moor be safe, for they were parted
With foul and violent tempest.

MONTANO   Pray heaven he be;
For I have served him, and the man commands

338–39 *defeat thy favor* spoil thy appearance   343 *sequestration* estrange-
ment   347 *coloquintida* a medicine   351 *Make* raise   352 *erring* wandering
362 *My cause is hearted* my heart is in it   366 *Traverse* forward march
379 *snipe* fool   384 *well* in high regard   387 *plume up* gratify   391 *dispose*
manner   393 *free* frank
II, i An open place in Cyprus, near the harbor   9 *hold the mortise* hold
their joints together   10 *segregation* scattering   15 *Guards* stars near
the North Star; *pole* polestar   16 *molestation* tumult   22 *designment halts*
plan is crippled   23 *sufferance* disaster   26 *Veronesa* ship furnished by
Verona

Like a full soldier. Let's to the seaside, ho!
As well to see the vessel that's come in
As to throw out our eyes for brave Othello,
Even till we make the main and th' aerial blue
40 An indistinct regard.

3. GENTLEMAN   Come, let's do so;
For every minute is expectancy
Of more arrivance.
     Enter Cassio.

CASSIO
Thanks, you the valiant of this warlike isle,
That so approve the Moor! O, let the heavens
Give him defense against the elements,
For I have lost him on a dangerous sea!

MONTANO
Is he well shipped?

CASSIO
His bark is stoutly timbered, and his pilot
Of very expert and approved allowance;
50 Therefore my hopes, not surfeited to death,
51 Stand in bold cure.
     (Within) A sail, a sail, a sail!
     Enter a Messenger.

CASSIO
What noise?

MESSENGER
The town is empty; on the brow o' th' sea
Stand ranks of people, and they cry 'A sail!'

CASSIO
My hopes do shape him for the governor.
     A shot.

2. GENTLEMAN
They do discharge their shot of courtesy:
Our friends at least.

CASSIO   I pray you, sir, go forth
And give us truth who 'tis that is arrived.

2. GENTLEMAN
I shall.   *Exit.*

MONTANO
But, good lieutenant, is your general wived?

CASSIO
Most fortunately. He hath achieved a maid
62 That paragons description and wild fame;
63 One that excels the quirks of blazoning pens,
64 And in th' essential vesture of creation
Does tire the ingener.
     Enter Second Gentleman.
            How now? Who has put in?

2. GENTLEMAN
'Tis one Iago, ancient to the general.

CASSIO
H'as had most favorable and happy speed:
Tempests themselves, high seas, and howling winds,
69 The guttered rocks and congregated sands,
70 Traitors ensteeped to clog the guiltless keel,
As having sense of beauty, do omit

Their mortal natures, letting go safely by   72
The divine Desdemona.

MONTANO   What is she?

CASSIO
She that I spake of, our great captain's captain,
Left in the conduct of the bold Iago,
Whose footing here anticipates our thoughts   76
A se'nnight's speed. Great Jove, Othello guard,   77
And swell his sail with thine own pow'rful breath,
That he may bless this bay with his tall ship,
Make love's quick pants in Desdemona's arms,
Give renewed fire to our extincted spirits,
[And bring all Cyprus comfort!]
     Enter Desdemona, Iago, Roderigo, and Emilia [with
        Attendants].   O, behold!
The riches of the ship is come on shore!
You men of Cyprus, let her have your knees.   84
Hail to thee, lady! and the grace of heaven,
Before, behind thee, and on every hand,
Enwheel thee round!

DESDEMONA   I thank you, valiant Cassio.
What tidings can you tell me of my lord?

CASSIO
He is not yet arrived; nor know I aught
But that he's well and will be shortly here.

DESDEMONA
O but I fear! How lost you company?

CASSIO
The great contention of the sea and skies
Parted our fellowship.
     (Within) A sail, a sail! *[A shot.]*
             But hark. A sail!

2. GENTLEMAN
They give their greeting to the citadel;
This likewise is a friend.

CASSIO   See for the news.
                [Exit Gentleman.]
Good ancient, you are welcome.
     [To Emilia]   Welcome, mistress. –
Let it not gall your patience, good Iago,
That I extend my manners. 'Tis my breeding
That gives me this bold show of courtesy.   99
     [Kisses Emilia.]

IAGO
Sir, would she give you so much of her lips
As of her tongue she oft bestows on me,
You would have enough.

DESDEMONA   Alas, she has no speech!

IAGO
In faith, too much.
I find it still when I have list to sleep.
Marry, before your ladyship, I grant,
She puts her tongue a little in her heart
And chides with thinking.

EMILIA
You have little cause to say so.

IAGO
Come on, come on! You are pictures out of doors,
Bells in your parlors, wildcats in your kitchens,
Saints in your injuries, devils being offended,
Players in your housewifery, and housewives in your   112
  beds.

DESDEMONA
O, fie upon thee, slanderer!

40 *An indistinct regard* indistinguishable   50 *surfeited to death* over-indulged   51 *in bold cure* a good chance of fulfillment   62 *paragons* surpasses   63 *quirks* ingenuities; *blazoning* describing   64–65 *And . . . ingener* merely to describe her as God made her exhausts her praiser   69 *guttered* jagged   70 *ensteeped* submerged   72 *mortal* deadly   76 *footing* landing   77 *se'nnight's* week's   84 *knees* i.e. kneeling   99 s.d. *Kisses Emilia* (kissing was a common Elizabethan form of social courtesy)   112 *housewifery* housekeeping; *housewives* hussies

IAGO
Nay, it is true, or else I am a Turk :
You rise to play, and go to bed to work.

EMILIA
You shall not write my praise.

IAGO   No, let me not.

DESDEMONA
What wouldst thou write of me, if thou shouldst praise
me ?

IAGO
O gentle lady, do not put me to't,
For I am nothing if not critical.

DESDEMONA
120   Come on, assay. – There's one gone to the harbor ?

IAGO
Ay, madam.

DESDEMONA
I am not merry ; but I do beguile
The thing I am by seeming otherwise. –
Come, how wouldst thou praise me ?

IAGO
I am about it ; but indeed my invention
126   Comes from my pate as birdlime does from frieze –
It plucks out brains and all. But my Muse labors,
And thus she is delivered :
If she be fair and wise, fairness and wit –
The one 's for use, the other useth it.

DESDEMONA
131   Well praised ! How if she be black and witty ?

IAGO
If she be black, and thereto have a wit,
She'll find a white that shall her blackness fit.

DESDEMONA
Worse and worse !

EMILIA
How if fair and foolish ?

IAGO
She never yet was foolish that was fair,
137   For even her folly helped her to an heir.

138   DESDEMONA These are old fond paradoxes to make fools
laugh i' th' alehouse. What miserable praise hast thou
140   for her that's foul and foolish ?

IAGO
There's none so foul, and foolish thereunto,
But does foul pranks which fair and wise ones do.

DESDEMONA O heavy ignorance ! Thou praisest the
worst best. But what praise couldst thou bestow on a
deserving woman indeed – one that in the authority of
146   her merit did justly put on the vouch of very malice
itself ?

IAGO
She that was ever fair, and never proud ;
Had tongue at will, and yet was never loud ;
Never lacked gold, and yet went never gay ;
Fled from her wish, and yet said 'Now I may' ;
She that, being ang'red, her revenge being nigh,
Bade her wrong stay, and her displeasure fly ;
She that in wisdom never was so frail
154   To change the cod's head for the salmon's tail ;
She that could think, and ne'er disclose her mind ;
See suitors following, and not look behind :
She was a wight (if ever such wight were) –

DESDEMONA To do what ?

IAGO
To suckle fools and chronicle small beer.   159

DESDEMONA O most lame and impotent conclusion ! Do
not learn of him, Emilia, though he be thy husband.
How say you, Cassio ? Is he not a most profane and   162
liberal counsellor ?

CASSIO He speaks home, madam. You may relish him   164
more in the soldier than in the scholar.

IAGO [aside] He takes her by the palm. Ay, well said,
whisper ! With as little a web as this will I ensnare as
great a fly as Cassio. Ay, smile upon her, do ! I will gyve 168
thee in thine own courtship. – You say true ; 'tis so, indeed ! – If such tricks as these strip you out of your lieutenantry, it had been better you had not kissed your
three fingers so oft – which now again you are most apt
to play the sir in. Very good ! well kissed ! an excellent   173
courtesy ! 'Tis so, indeed. Yet again your fingers to your
lips ? Would they were clyster pipes for your sake !   175
(Trumpet within.) The Moor ! I know his trumpet.

CASSIO 'Tis truly so.

DESDEMONA Let's meet him and receive him.

CASSIO Lo, where he comes.
            Enter Othello and Attendants.

OTHELLO
O my fair warrior !

DESDEMONA   My dear Othello !

OTHELLO
It gives me wonder great as my content
To see you here before me. O my soul's joy !
If after every tempest come such calms,
May the winds blow till they have wakened death !
And let the laboring bark climb hills of seas
Olympus-high, and duck again as low
As hell 's from heaven ! If it were now to die,
'Twere now to be most happy ; for I fear   188
My soul hath her content so absolute
That not another comfort like to this
Succeeds in unknown fate.

DESDEMONA   The heavens forbid
But that our loves and comforts should increase
Even as our days do grow.

OTHELLO   Amen to that, sweet powers !
I cannot speak enough of this content ;
It stops me here ; it is too much of joy.
And this, and this, the greatest discords be
        They kiss.
That e'er our hearts shall make !

IAGO [aside]   O, you are well tuned now !
But I'll set down the pegs that make this music,   198
As honest as I am.

OTHELLO   Come, let us to the castle.
News, friends ! Our wars are done ; the Turks are
drowned.
How does my old acquaintance of this isle ? –
Honey, you shall be well desired in Cyprus ;   202

120 *assay* try   126 *birdlime* a sticky paste; *frieze* rough cloth   131 *black*
brunette   137 *folly* wantonness   138 *fond* foolish   140 *foul* ugly   146 *put
on the vouch* compel the approval   154 *To . . . tail* i.e. to exchange the good
for the poor but expensive   159 *chronicle small beer* keep petty household
accounts   162–63 *profane and liberal* worldly and licentious   164 *home*
bluntly   168–69 *gyve . . . courtship* manacle you by means of your courtly
manners   173 *sir* courtly gentleman   175 *clyster pipes* syringes   188
happy fortunate   198 *set down* loosen   202 *well desired* warmly welcomed

I have found great love amongst them. O my sweet,
I prattle out of fashion, and I dote
In mine own comforts. I prithee, good Iago,
Go to the bay and disembark my coffers.
207 Bring thou the master to the citadel;
He is a good one, and his worthiness
209 Does challenge much respect. – Come, Desdemona,
Once more well met at Cyprus.

      Exit Othello [with all but Iago and Roderigo].

IAGO *[to an Attendant, who goes out]* Do thou meet me
presently at the harbor. *[to Roderigo]* Come hither. If
thou be'st valiant (as they say base men being in love
have then a nobility in their natures more than is native
to them), list me. The lieutenant to-night watches on
216 the court of guard. First, I must tell thee this: Desdemona is directly in love with him.

RODERIGO With him? Why, 'tis not possible.

219 IAGO Lay thy finger thus, and let thy soul be instructed.
Mark me with what violence she first loved the Moor,
but for bragging and telling her fantastical lies; and will
she love him still for prating? Let not thy discreet heart
think it. Her eye must be fed; and what delight shall she
have to look on the devil? When the blood is made dull
with the act of sport, there should be, again to inflame it
and to give satiety a fresh appetite, loveliness in favor,
sympathy in years, manners, and beauties; all which the
Moor is defective in. Now for want of these required
229 conveniences, her delicate tenderness will find itself
230 abused, begin to heave the gorge, disrelish and abhor the
Moor. Very nature will instruct her in it and compel her
to some second choice. Now sir, this granted – as it is a
233 most pregnant and unforced position – who stands so
eminent in the degree of this fortune as Cassio does? A
235 knave very voluble; no further conscionable than in put-
236 ting on the mere form of civil and humane seeming for
237 the better compassing of his salt and most hidden loose
238 affection? Why, none! why, none! A slipper and subtle
knave; a finder-out of occasions; that has an eye can
stamp and counterfeit advantages, though true advantage never present itself; a devilish knave! Besides, the
knave is handsome, young, and hath all those requisites
in him that folly and green minds look after. A pestilent
complete knave! and the woman hath found him already.

RODERIGO I cannot believe that in her; she's full of most
246 blessed condition.

IAGO Blessed fig's-end! The wine she drinks is made of
grapes. If she had been blessed, she would never have
loved the Moor. Blessed pudding! Didst thou not see
her paddle with the palm of his hand? Didst not mark
that?

RODERIGO Yes, that I did; but that was but courtesy.

IAGO Lechery, by this hand! an index and obscure prologue to the history of lust and foul thoughts. They met
so near with their lips that their breaths embraced together. Villainous thoughts, Roderigo! When these mu- 255
tualities so marshal the way, hard at hand comes the
master and main exercise, th' incorporate conclusion. 257
Pish! But, sir, be you ruled by me: I have brought you
from Venice. Watch you to-night; for the command,
I'll lay't upon you. Cassio knows you not. I'll not be far
from you: do you find some occasion to anger Cassio,
either by speaking too loud, or tainting his discipline, or 262
from what other course you please which the time shall
more favorably minister.

RODERIGO Well.

IAGO Sir, he's rash and very sudden in choler, and haply 266
with his truncheon may strike at you. Provoke him that
he may; for even out of that will I cause these of Cyprus
to mutiny; whose qualification shall come into no true 269
taste again but by the displanting of Cassio. So shall you
have a shorter journey to your desires by the means I
shall then have to prefer them; and the impediment 272
most profitably removed without the which there were
no expectation of our prosperity.

RODERIGO I will do this if you can bring it to any opportunity.

IAGO I warrant thee. Meet me by and by at the citadel; I
must fetch his necessaries ashore. Farewell.

RODERIGO Adieu.   *Exit.*

IAGO
That Cassio loves her, I do well believe't;
That she loves him, 'tis apt and of great credit.   281
The Moor, howbeit that I endure him not,
Is of a constant, loving, noble nature,
And I dare think he'll prove to Desdemona
A most dear husband. Now I do love her too;
Not out of absolute lust, though peradventure
I stand accountant for as great a sin,   287
But partly led to diet my revenge,   288
For that I do suspect the lusty Moor
Hath leaped into my seat; the thought whereof
Doth, like a poisonous mineral, gnaw my inwards;
And nothing can or shall content my soul
Till I am evened with him, wife for wife;
Or failing so, yet that I put the Moor
At least into a jealousy so strong
That judgment cannot cure. Which thing to do,
If this poor trash of Venice, whom I trash   297
For his quick hunting, stand the putting on,   298
I'll have our Michael Cassio on the hip,   299
Abuse him to the Moor in the rank garb   300
(For I fear Cassio with my nightcap too),
Make the Moor thank me, love me, and reward me
For making him egregiously an ass
And practicing upon his peace and quiet   304
Even to madness. 'Tis here, but yet confused:
Knavery's plain face is never seen till used.   *Exit.*

*

207 *master* ship captain 209 *challenge* deserve 216 *court of guard* head-
quarters 219 *thus* i.e. on your lips 229 *conveniences* compatibilities
230 *heave the gorge* be nauseated 233 *pregnant* evident 235 *conscionable*
conscientious 236 *humane* polite 237 *salt* lecherous 238 *slipper* slippery
246 *condition* character 255 *mutualities* exchanges 257 *incorporate*
carnal 262 *tainting* discrediting 266 *sudden in choler* violent in anger
269 *qualification* appeasement 269–70 *true taste* satisfactory state 272
prefer advance 281 *apt* probable 287 *accountant* accountable 288 *diet*
feed 297 *I trash* I weight down (in order to keep under control) 298
For in order to develop; *stand the putting on* responds to my inciting
299 *on the hip* at my mercy 300 *rank garb* gross manner 304 *practicing
upon* plotting against
II, ii A street in Cyprus 3 *mere perdition* complete destruction

Enter Othello's Herald, with a proclamation.   II, ii

HERALD It is Othello's pleasure, our noble and valiant
general, that, upon certain tidings now arrived, importing the mere perdition of the Turkish fleet, every man 3

put himself into triumph; some to dance, some to make bonfires, each man to what sport and revels his addiction leads him. For, besides these beneficial news, it is the celebration of his nuptial. So much was his pleasure
8 should be proclaimed. All offices are open, and there is full liberty of feasting from the present hour of five till the bell have told eleven. Heaven bless the isle of Cyprus and our noble general Othello! *Exit.*

*

II, iii   *Enter Othello, Desdemona, Cassio, and Attendants.*
OTHELLO
Good Michael, look you to the guard to-night.
Let's teach ourselves that honorable stop,
Not to outsport discretion.
CASSIO
Iago hath direction what to do;
But not withstanding, with my personal eye
Will I look to't.
OTHELLO   Iago is most honest.
Michael, good night. To-morrow with your earliest
Let me have speech with you.
    [To Desdemona]   Come, my dear love.
The purchase made, the fruits are to ensue;
That profit's yet to come 'tween me and you. —
Good night.
    Exit [Othello with Desdemona and Attendants].
    Enter Iago.
CASSIO Welcome, Iago. We must to the watch.
IAGO Not this hour, lieutenant; 'tis not yet ten o' th'
14 clock. Our general cast us thus early for the love of his Desdemona; who let us not therefore blame. He hath not yet made wanton the night with her, and she is sport for Jove.
CASSIO She's a most exquisite lady.
IAGO And, I'll warrant her, full of game.
CASSIO Indeed, she's a most fresh and delicate creature.
IAGO What an eye she has! Methinks it sounds a parley to provocation.
CASSIO An inviting eye; and yet methinks right modest.
IAGO And when she speaks, is it not an alarum to love?
CASSIO She is indeed perfection.
IAGO Well, happiness to their sheets! Come, lieutenant, I
27 have a stoup of wine, and here without are a brace of Cyprus gallants that would fain have a measure to the health of black Othello.
CASSIO Not to-night, good Iago. I have very poor and unhappy brains for drinking; I could well wish courtesy would invent some other custom of entertainment.
IAGO O, they are our friends. But one cup! I'll drink for you.
CASSIO I have drunk but one cup to-night, and that was
36 craftily qualified too; and behold what innovation it makes here. I am unfortunate in the infirmity and dare not task my weakness with any more.
IAGO What, man! 'Tis a night of revels: the gallants desire it.
CASSIO Where are they?
IAGO Here at the door; I pray you call them in.
CASSIO I'll do't, but it dislikes me.   *Exit.*
IAGO
If I can fasten but one cup upon him
With that which he hath drunk to-night already,

He'll be as full of quarrel and offense
As my young mistress' dog. Now my sick fool Roderigo,
Whom love hath turned almost the wrong side out,
To Desdemona hath to-night caroused
Potations pottle-deep; and he's to watch.   50
Three lads of Cyprus – noble swelling spirits,
That hold their honors in a wary distance,   52
The very elements of this warlike isle –   53
Have I to-night flustered with flowing cups,
And they watch too. Now, 'mongst this flock of drunkards
Am I to put our Cassio in some action
That may offend the isle.
    Enter Cassio, Montano, and Gentlemen [; Servants following with wine].
                    But here they come.
If consequence do but approve my dream,
My boat sails freely, both with wind and stream.
CASSIO 'Fore God, they have given me a rouse already.   60
MONTANO Good faith, a little one; not past a pint, as I am a soldier.
IAGO Some wine, ho!
    [Sings]   And let me the canakin clink, clink;
             And let me the canakin clink.
                A soldier's a man;
                A life's but a span,
             Why then, let a soldier drink.
Some wine, boys!   70
CASSIO 'Fore God, an excellent song!
IAGO I learned it in England, where indeed they are most potent in potting. Your Dane, your German, and your swag-bellied Hollander – Drink, ho! – are nothing to your English.
CASSIO Is your Englishman so expert in his drinking?
IAGO Why, he drinks you with facility your Dane dead drunk; he sweats not to overthrow your Almain; he gives your Hollander a vomit ere the next pottle can be filled.
CASSIO To the health of our general!
MONTANO I am for it, lieutenant, and I'll do you justice.
IAGO O sweet England!
    [Sings]   King Stephen was a worthy peer;
            His breeches cost him but a crown;
            He held 'em sixpence all too dear,
               With that he called the tailor lown.   87
            He was a wight of high renown,
              And thou art but of low degree.
            'Tis pride that pulls the country down;
              Then take thine auld cloak about thee.
Some wine, ho!
CASSIO 'Fore God, this is a more exquisite song than the other.
IAGO Will you hear't again?
CASSIO No, for I hold him to be unworthy of his place that does those things. Well, God's above all; and there   97 be souls must be saved, and there be souls must not be saved.

---

8 *offices* kitchens and storerooms
II, iii The Cyprian castle   **14** *cast* dismissed   **27** *stoup* two-quart tankard
36 *qualified* diluted; *innovation* disturbance   **50** *pottle-deep* bottoms up
52 *That . . . distance* very sensitive about their honor   **53** *very elements* true representatives   **60** *rouse* bumper   **87** *lown* rascal   **97** *does . . . things* i.e. behaves in this fashion

IAGO It's true, good lieutenant.

CASSIO For mine own part – no offense to the general, nor any man of quality – I hope to be saved.

IAGO And so do I too, lieutenant.

CASSIO Ay, but, by your leave, not before me. The lieutenant is to be saved before the ancient. Let's have no more of this ; let's to our affairs. – God forgive us our sins ! – Gentlemen, let's look to our business. Do not think, gentlemen, I am drunk. This is my ancient ; this is my right hand, and this is my left. I am not drunk now.
110 I can stand well enough, and I speak well enough.

ALL Excellent well !

CASSIO Why, very well then. You must not think then that I am drunk.   *Exit.*

MONTANO
　To th' platform, masters. Come, let's set the watch.

IAGO
　You see this fellow that is gone before.
　He's a soldier fit to stand by Caesar
　And give direction ; and do but see his vice.
118 'Tis to his virtue a just equinox,
　The one as long as th' other. 'Tis pity of him.
　I fear the trust Othello puts him in,
　On some odd time of his infirmity,
　Will shake this island.

MONTANO   But is he often thus ?

IAGO
　'Tis evermore his prologue to his sleep :
124 He'll watch the horologe a double set
　If drink rock not his cradle.

MONTANO   It were well
　The general were put in mind of it.
　Perhaps he sees it not, or his good nature
　Prizes the virtue that appears in Cassio
　And looks not on his evils. Is not this true ?
　　　　　Enter Roderigo.

IAGO *[aside to him]*
　How now, Roderigo ?
　I pray you after the lieutenant, go !   *Exit Roderigo.*

MONTANO
　And 'tis great pity that the noble Moor
　Should hazard such a place as his own second
134 With one of an ingraft infirmity.
　It were an honest action to say
　So to the Moor.

IAGO   Not I, for this fair island !
　I do love Cassio well and would do much
　To cure him of this evil.
　　　　(*Within*) Help ! help !
　　　　　　　　　　But hark ! What noise ?
　　　Enter Cassio, driving in Roderigo.

CASSIO
　Zounds, you rogue ! you rascal !

MONTANO
　What's the matter, lieutenant ?

CASSIO   A knave teach me my duty ?
141 I'll beat the knave into a twiggen bottle.

118 *just equinox* exact equivalent   124 *watch . . . set* stay awake twice around the clock   134 *ingraft* i.e. ingrained   141 *twiggen* wicker-covered   144 *mazzard* head   151 *rise* grow riotous   163 *carve for* indulge   166 *propriety* proper self   170 *quarter* friendliness   175 *peevish odds* childish quarrel   183 *censure* judgment   184 *unlace* undo   185 *rich opinion* high reputation

RODERIGO
　Beat me ?

CASSIO   Dost thou prate, rogue ?
　　　[Strikes him.]

MONTANO   Nay, good lieutenant !
　　　[Stays him.]
　I pray you, sir, hold your hand.

CASSIO   Let me go, sir,
　Or I'll knock you o'er the mazzard.   144

MONTANO   Come, come, you're drunk !

CASSIO Drunk ?
　　　They fight.

IAGO *[aside to Roderigo]*
　Away, I say ! Go out and cry a mutiny !   *Exit Roderigo.*
　Nay, good lieutenant. God's will, gentlemen !
　Help, ho ! – lieutenant – sir – Montano – sir –
　Help, masters ! – Here's a goodly watch indeed !
　　　A bell rung.
　Who's that which rings the bell ? Diablo, ho !
　The town will rise. God's will, lieutenant, hold !   151
　You'll be shamed for ever.
　　　Enter Othello and Gentlemen with weapons.

OTHELLO   What is the matter here ?

MONTANO
　Zounds, I bleed still. I am hurt to th' death.
　He dies !

OTHELLO
　Hold for your lives !

IAGO
　Hold, hold ! Lieutenant – sir – Montano – gentlemen !
　Have you forgot all sense of place and duty ?
　Hold ! The general speaks to you. Hold, for shame !

OTHELLO
　Why, how now, ho ? From whence ariseth this ?
　Are we turned Turks, and to ourselves do that
　Which heaven hath forbid the Ottomites ?
　For Christian shame put by this barbarous brawl !
　He that stirs next to carve for his own rage   163
　Holds his soul light ; he dies upon his motion.
　Silence that dreadful bell ! It frights the isle
　From her propriety. What is the matter, masters ?   166
　Honest Iago, that looks dead with grieving,
　Speak. Who began this ? On thy love, I charge thee.

IAGO
　I do not know. Friends all, but now, even now,
　In quarter, and in terms like bride and groom   170
　Devesting them for bed ; and then, but now –
　As if some planet had unwitted men –
　Swords out, and tilting one at other's breast
　In opposition bloody. I cannot speak
　Any beginning to this peevish odds ;   175
　And would in action glorious I had lost
　Those legs that brought me to a part of it !

OTHELLO
　How comes it, Michael, you are thus forgot ?

CASSIO
　I pray you pardon me ; I cannot speak.

OTHELLO
　Worthy Montano, you were wont to be civil ;
　The gravity and stillness of your youth
　The world hath noted, and your name is great
　In mouths of wisest censure. What's the matter   183
　That you unlace your reputation thus   184
　And spend your rich opinion for the name   185

Of a night-brawler ? Give me answer to it.

MONTANO
Worthy Othello, I am hurt to danger.
Your officer, Iago, can inform you,
189 While I spare speech, which something now offends me,
Of all that I do know ; nor know I aught
By me that's said or done amiss this night,
Unless self-charity be sometimes a vice,
And to defend ourselves it be a sin
When violence assails us.

OTHELLO   Now, by heaven,
195 My blood begins my safer guides to rule,
196 And passion, having my best judgment collied,
197 Assays to lead the way. If I once stir
Or do but lift this arm, the best of you
Shall sink in my rebuke. Give me to know
How this foul rout began, who set it on ;
201 And he that is approved in this offense,
Though he had twinned with me, both at a birth,
Shall lose me. What ! in a town of war,
Yet wild, the people's hearts brimful of fear,
205 To manage private and domestic quarrel ?
In night, and on the court and guard of safety ?
'Tis monstrous. Iago, who began't ?

MONTANO
208 If partially affined, or leagued in office,
Thou dost deliver more or less than truth,
Thou art no soldier.

IAGO   Touch me not so near.
I had rather have this tongue cut from my mouth
Than it should do offense to Michael Cassio ;
Yet I persuade myself, to speak the truth
Shall nothing wrong him. This it is, general.
Montano and myself being in speech,
There comes a fellow crying out for help,
And Cassio following him with determined sword
218 To execute upon him. Sir, this gentleman
Steps in to Cassio and entreats his pause.
Myself the crying fellow did pursue,
Lest by his clamor – as it so fell out –
The town might fall in fright. He, swift of foot,
Outran my purpose ; and I returned then rather
For that I heard the clink and fall of swords,
225 And Cassio high in oath ; which till to-night
I ne'er might say before. When I came back –
For this was brief – I found them close together
At blow and thrust, even as again they were
When you yourself did part them.
More of this matter cannot I report ;
But men are men ; the best sometimes forget.
Though Cassio did some little wrong to him,
As men in rage strike those that wish them best,
Yet surely Cassio I believe received
From him that fled some strange indignity,
236 Which patience could not pass.

OTHELLO   I know, Iago,
Thy honesty and love doth mince this matter,
Making it light to Cassio. Cassio, I love thee ;
But never more be officer of mine.
         Enter Desdemona, attended.
Look if my gentle love be not raised up !
I'll make thee an example.

DESDEMONA   What's the matter ?

OTHELLO
All's well now, sweeting ; come away to bed.
         [To Montano]
Sir, for your hurts, myself will be your surgeon.
Lead him off.
         [Montano is led off.]
Iago, look with care about the town
And silence those whom this vile brawl distracted.   246
Come, Desdemona ; 'tis the soldiers' life
To have their balmy slumbers waked with strife.
                    Exit [with all but Iago and Cassio].

IAGO What, are you hurt, lieutenant ?

CASSIO Ay, past all surgery.

IAGO Marry, God forbid !

CASSIO Reputation, reputation, reputation ! O, I have
lost my reputation ! I have lost the immortal part of
myself, and what remains is bestial. My reputation,
Iago, my reputation !

IAGO As I am an honest man, I thought you had received
some bodily wound. There is more sense in that than in
reputation. Reputation is an idle and most false imposition ; oft got without merit and lost without deserving.
You have lost no reputation at all unless you repute yourself such a loser. What, man ! there are ways to recover 261
the general again. You are but now cast in his mood – a 262
punishment more in policy than in malice, even so as
one would beat his offenseless dog to affright an imperious lion. Sue to him again, and he's yours.

CASSIO I will rather sue to be despised than to deceive so
good a commander with so slight, so drunken, and so
indiscreet an officer. Drunk ! and speak parrot ! and 268
squabble ! swagger ! swear ! and discourse fustian with 269
one's own shadow ! O thou invisible spirit of wine, if
thou hast no name to be known by, let us call thee devil !

IAGO What was he that you followed with your sword ?
What had he done to you ?

CASSIO I know not.

IAGO Is't possible ?

CASSIO I remember a mass of things, but nothing distinctly ; a quarrel, but nothing wherefore. O God, that
men should put an enemy in their mouths to steal away
their brains ! that we should with joy, pleasance, revel,
and applause transform ourselves into beasts !   280

IAGO Why, but you are now well enough. How came you
thus recovered ?

CASSIO It hath pleased the devil drunkenness to give
place to the devil wrath. One unperfectness shows me
another, to make me frankly despise myself.

IAGO Come, you are too severe a moraler. As the time, the
place, and the condition of this country stands, I could
heartily wish this had not so befall'n ; but since it is as it
is, mend it for your own good.

CASSIO I will ask him for my place again : he shall tell me I
am a drunkard ! Had I as many mouths as Hydra, such 291
an answer would stop them all. To be now a sensible

189 *offends* pains 195 *blood* passion 196 *collied* darkened 197 *Assays*
tries 201 *approved in* proved guilty of 205 *manage* carry on 208
partially . . . office prejudiced by comradeship or official relations 218
execute work his will 225 *high in oath* cursing 236 *pass* pass over, ignore
246 *distracted* excited 261 *recover* regain favor with 262 *cast in his
mood* dismissed because of his anger 268 *parrot* meaningless phrases
269 *fustian* bombastic nonsense 280 *applause* desire to please 291
Hydra monster with many heads

man, by and by a fool, and presently a beast ! O strange !
294 Every inordinate cup is unblest, and the ingredient is a
devil.

IAGO Come, come, good wine is a good familiar creature
if it be well used. Exclaim no more against it. And, good
lieutenant, I think you think I love you.

298 CASSIO I have well approved it, sir. I drunk !

IAGO You or any man living may be drunk at some time,
man. I'll tell you what you shall do. Our general's wife is
now the general. I may say so in this respect, for that he
hath devoted and given up himself to the contemplation,
mark, and denotement of her parts and graces. Confess
yourself freely to her ; importune her help to put you in
305 your place again. She is of so free, so kind, so apt, so
blessed a disposition she holds it a vice in her goodness
not to do more than she is requested. This broken joint
308 between you and her husband entreat her to splinter ;
309 and my fortunes against any lay worth naming, this
crack of your love shall grow stronger than it was before.

CASSIO You advise me well.

IAGO I protest, in the sincerity of love and honest kindness.

CASSIO I think it freely ; and betimes in the morning will
I beseech the virtuous Desdemona to undertake for me.
I am desperate of my fortunes if they check me here.

IAGO You are in the right. Good night, lieutenant ; I must
to the watch.

CASSIO Good night, honest Iago.   *Exit Cassio.*

IAGO
And what's he then that says I play the villain,
When this advice is free I give and honest,
321 Probal to thinking, and indeed the course
To win the Moor again ? For 'tis most easy
323 Th' inclining Desdemona to subdue
In any honest suit ; she's framed as fruitful
As the free elements. And then for her
To win the Moor – were't to renounce his baptism,
All seals and symbols of redeemèd sin –
His soul is so enfettered to her love
That she may make, unmake, do what she list,
Even as her appetite shall play the god
With his weak function. How am I then a villain
332 To counsel Cassio to this parallel course,
333 Directly to his good ? Divinity of hell !
334 When devils will the blackest sins put on,
They do suggest at first with heavenly shows,
As I do now. For whiles this honest fool
Plies Desdemona to repair his fortunes,
And she for him pleads strongly to the Moor,
I'll pour this pestilence into his ear,
340 That she repeals him for her body's lust ;
And by how much she strives to do him good,
She shall undo her credit with the Moor.
So will I turn her virtue into pitch,

And out of her own goodness make the net
That shall enmesh them all.

Enter Roderigo.   How, now, Roderigo ?

RODERIGO I do follow here in the chase, not like a hound
that hunts, but one that fills up the cry. My money is al- 347
most spent ; I have been to-night exceedingly well cudg-
elled ; and I think the issue will be – I shall have so
much experience for my pains ; and so, with no money
at all, and a little more wit, return again to Venice.

IAGO
How poor are they that have not patience !
What wound did ever heal but by degrees ?
Thou know'st we work by wit, and not by witchcraft ;
And wit depends on dilatory time.
Does't not go well ? Cassio hath beaten thee,
And thou by that small hurt hast cashiered Cassio.   357
Though other things grow fair against the sun,
Yet fruits that blossom first will first be ripe.
Content thyself awhile. By the mass, 'tis morning !
Pleasure and action make the hours seem short.
Retire thee ; go where thou art billeted.
Away, I say ! Thou shalt know more hereafter.
Nay, get thee gone !   *Exit Roderigo.*
Two things are to be done :
My wife must move for Cassio to her mistress ;
I'll set her on ;
Myself the while to draw the Moor apart
And bring him jump when he may Cassio find   368
Soliciting his wife. Ay, that's the way !
Dull not device by coldness and delay.   *Exit.*

*

Enter Cassio, with Musicians and the Clown.   III, i

CASSIO
Masters, play here, I will content your pains :   1
Something that's brief ; and bid 'Good morrow, general.'
[They play.]

CLOWN Why, masters, ha' your instruments been in
Naples, that they speak i' th' nose thus ?   4

MUSICIAN How, sir, how ?

CLOWN Are these, I pray you, called wind instruments ?

MUSICIAN Ay, marry, are they, sir.

CLOWN O, thereby hangs a tail.

MUSICIAN Whereby hangs a tale, sir ?

CLOWN Marry, sir, by many a wind instrument that I
know. But, masters, here's money for you ; and the
general so likes your music that he desires you, for love's
sake, to make no more noise with it.

MUSICIAN Well, sir, we will not.

CLOWN If you have any music that may not be heard, to't
again : but, as they say, to hear music the general does
not greatly care.

MUSICIAN We have none such, sir.

CLOWN Then put up your pipes in your bag, for I'll away.
Go, vanish into air, away !
Exit Musician [with his fellows].

CASSIO Dost thou hear, my honest friend ?

CLOWN No, I hear not your honest friend. I hear you.

CASSIO Prithee keep up thy quillets. There's a poor piece 23
of gold for thee. If the gentlewoman that attends the
general's wife be stirring, tell her there's one Cassio
entreats her a little favor of speech. Wilt thou do this ?

294 *ingredient* contents   298 *approved* proved   305 *free* bounteous
308 *splinter* bind up with splints   309 *lay* wager   321 *Probal* probable
323 *subdue* persuade   332 *parallel* corresponding   333 *Divinity* theology
334 *put on* incite   340 *repeals him* seeks his recall   347 *cry* pack   357
cashiered Cassio maneuvered Cassio's discharge   368 *jump* at the exact
moment
III, i Before the chamber of Othello and Desdemona   1 *content* reward
4 *Naples* (notorious for its association with venereal disease)   23 *quillets*
quips

CLOWN She is stirring sir. If she will stir hither, I shall
     seem to notify unto her.
CASSIO
     [Do, good my friend.]   *Exit Clown.*
29   *Enter Iago.*   In happy time, Iago.
IAGO
     You have not been abed then ?
CASSIO
     Why, no ; the day had broke
     Before we parted. I have made bold, Iago,
     To send in to your wife : my suit to her
     Is that she will to virtuous Desdemona
     Procure me some access.
IAGO   I'll send her to you presently ;
     And I'll devise a mean to draw the Moor
     Out of the way, that your converse and business
     May be more free.
CASSIO
     I humbly thank you for't.   *Exit [Iago].*
                         I never knew
40   A Florentine more kind and honest.
               Enter Emilia.
EMILIA
     Good morrow, good lieutenant. I am sorry
     For your displeasure ; but all will sure be well.
     The general and his wife are talking of it,
     And she speaks for you stoutly. The Moor replies
     That he you hurt is of great fame in Cyprus
46   And great affinity, and that in wholesome wisdom
     He might not but refuse you ; but he protests he loves
          you,
     And needs no other suitor but his likings
49   [To take the safest occasion by the front]
     To bring you in again.
CASSIO   Yet I beseech you,
     If you think fit, or that it may be done,
     Give me advantage of some brief discourse
     With Desdemona alone.
EMILIA   Pray you come in.
     I will bestow you where you shall have time
55   To speak your bosom freely.
CASSIO   I am much bound to you.
                                                Exeunt.

                         *

III, ii   *Enter Othello, Iago, and Gentlemen.*
OTHELLO
     These letters give, Iago, to the pilot
     And by him do my duties to the Senate.
3   That done, I will be walking on the works ;
     Repair there to me.
IAGO   Well, my good lord, I'll do't.
OTHELLO
     This fortification, gentlemen, shall we see't ?
GENTLEMEN
     We'll wait upon your lordship.   *Exeunt.*

                         *

III, iii   *Enter Desdemona, Cassio, and Emilia.*
DESDEMONA
     Be thou assured, good Cassio, I will do
     All my abilities in thy behalf.

EMILIA
     Good madam, do. I warrant it grieves my husband
     As if the cause were his.
DESDEMONA
     O, that's an honest fellow. Do not doubt, Cassio,
     But I will have my lord and you again
     As friendly as you were.
CASSIO   Bounteous madam,
     Whatever shall become of Michael Cassio,
     He's never anything but your true servant.
DESDEMONA
     I know't ; I thank you. You do love my lord ;
     You have known him long ; and be you well assured
     He shall in strangeness stand no farther off   12
     Than in a politic distance.   13
CASSIO   Ay, but, lady,
     That policy may either last so long,
     Or feed upon such nice and waterish diet,   15
     Or breed itself so out of circumstance,
     That, I being absent, and my place supplied,
     My general will forget my love and service.
DESDEMONA
     Do not doubt that ; before Emilia here   19
     I give thee warrant of thy place. Assure thee,
     If I do vow a friendship, I'll perform it
     To the last article. My lord shall never rest ;
     I'll watch him tame and talk him out of patience ;   23
     His bed shall seem a school, his board a shrift ;   24
     I'll intermingle everything he does
     With Cassio's suit. Therefore be merry, Cassio,
     For thy solicitor shall rather die
     Than give thy cause away.
          Enter Othello and Iago [at a distance].
EMILIA
     Madam, here comes my lord.
CASSIO
     Madam, I'll take my leave.   30
DESDEMONA
     Why, stay, and hear me speak.
CASSIO
     Madam, not now : I am very ill at ease,
     Unfit for mine own purposes.
DESDEMONA
     Well, do your discretion.   *Exit Cassio.*
IAGO
     Ha ! I like not that.
OTHELLO   What dost thou say ?
IAGO
     Nothing, my lord ; or if – I know not what.
OTHELLO
     Was not that Cassio parted from my wife ?
IAGO
     Cassio, my lord ? No, sure, I cannot think it,
     That he would steal away so guilty-like,
     Seeing your coming.
OTHELLO   I do believe 'twas he.   40

---

29 *In happy time* well met   40 *Florentine* i.e. even a Florentine (like
Cassio ; Iago was a Venetian)   46 *affinity* family connections   49 *occasion*
opportunity ; *front* forelock   55 *your bosom* your inmost thoughts
III, ii The castle   3 *works* fortifications
III, iii The castle grounds   12 *strangeness* aloofness   13 *Than . . . distance*
than wise policy requires   15 *Or . . . diet* or be continued for such slight
reasons   19 *doubt* fear   23 *watch him tame* keep him awake until he gives
in   24 *shrift* confessional

DESDEMONA
How now, my lord?
I have been talking with a suitor here,
A man that languishes in your displeasure.

OTHELLO
Who is't you mean?

DESDEMONA
Why, your lieutenant, Cassio. Good my lord,
If I have any grace or power to move you,
47   His present reconciliation take;
For if he be not one that truly loves you,
That errs in ignorance, and not in cunning,
I have no judgment in an honest face.
I prithee call him back.

OTHELLO   Went he hence now?

DESDEMONA
Yes, faith; so humbled
That he hath left part of his grief with me
To suffer with him. Good love, call him back.

OTHELLO
Not now, sweet Desdemon; some other time.

DESDEMONA
But shall't be shortly?

OTHELLO   The sooner, sweet, for you.

DESDEMONA
Shall't be to-night at supper?

OTHELLO   No, not to-night.

DESDEMONA
To-morrow dinner then?

OTHELLO   I shall not dine at home;
I meet the captains at the citadel.

DESDEMONA
Why then, to-morrow night, or Tuesday morn,
On Tuesday noon or night, or Wednesday morn.
I prithee name the time, but let it not
Exceed three days. I' faith, he's penitent;
And yet his trespass, in our common reason
(Save that, they say, the wars must make examples
66   Out of their best), is not almost a fault
67   T' incur a private check. When shall he come?
Tell me, Othello. I wonder in my soul
What you could ask me that I should deny
70   Or stand so mamm'ring on. What? Michael Cassio,
That came a-wooing with you, and so many a time,
When I have spoke of you dispraisingly,
Hath ta'en your part – to have so much to do
To bring him in? By'r Lady, I could do much –

OTHELLO
Prithee no more. Let him come when he will!
I will deny thee nothing.

DESDEMONA   Why, this is not a boon;
'Tis as I should entreat you wear your gloves,
Or feed on nourishing dishes, or keep you warm,
Or sue to you to do a peculiar profit
To your own person. Nay, when I have a suit
Wherein I mean to touch your love indeed,
It shall be full of poise and difficult weight,
83   And fearful to be granted.

OTHELLO   I will deny thee nothing!
Whereon I do beseech thee grant me this,
To leave me but a little to myself.

DESDEMONA
Shall I deny you? No. Farewell, my lord.

OTHELLO
Farewell, my Desdemon: I'll come to thee straight.

DESDEMONA
Emilia, come. – Be as your fancies teach you;
Whate'er you be, I am obedient.   *Exit [with Emilia]*.

OTHELLO
Excellent wretch! Perdition catch my soul   90
But I do love thee! and when I love thee not,
Chaos is come again.

IAGO
My noble lord –

OTHELLO   What dost thou say, Iago?

IAGO
Did Michael Cassio, when you wooed my lady,
Know of your love?

OTHELLO
He did, from first to last. Why dost thou ask?

IAGO
But for a satisfaction of my thought;
No further harm.

OTHELLO   Why of thy thought, Iago?

IAGO
I did not think he had been acquainted with her.

OTHELLO
O, yes, and went between us very oft.   100

IAGO
Indeed?

OTHELLO
Indeed? Ay, indeed! Discern'st thou aught in that?
Is he not honest?

IAGO   Honest, my lord?

OTHELLO   Honest. Ay, honest.

IAGO
My lord, for aught I know.

OTHELLO
What dost thou think?

IAGO   Think, my lord?

OTHELLO   Think, my lord?
By heaven, he echoes me,
As if there were some monster in his thought
Too hideous to be shown. Thou dost mean something:
I heard thee say even now, thou lik'st not that,
When Cassio left my wife. What didst not like?
And when I told thee he was of my counsel
In my whole course of wooing, thou cried'st 'Indeed?'
And didst contract and purse thy brow together,
As if thou then hadst shut up in thy brain
Some horrible conceit. If thou dost love me,   115
Show me thy thought.

IAGO
My lord, you know I love you.

OTHELLO   I think thou dost;
And, for I know thou'rt full of love and honesty
And weigh'st thy words before thou giv'st them breath,
Therefore these stops of thine fright me the more;
For such things in a false disloyal knave
Are tricks of custom; but in a man that's just
They are close dilations, working from the heart   123
That passion cannot rule.

47 *present* immediate 66 *not almost* hardly 67 *a private check* even a
private reprimand 70 *mamm'ring on* hesitating about 83 *fearful* dangerous 90 *wretch* (a term of endearment) 100 *went . . . us* (i.e. as messenger)
115 *conceit* fancy 123–24 *close dilations . . . rule* secret emotions which
well up in spite of restraint

IAGO   For Michael Cassio,
I dare be sworn I think that he is honest.

OTHELLO
I think so too.

IAGO   Men should be what they seem;
127 Or those that be not, would they might seem none!

OTHELLO
Certain, men should be what they seem.

IAGO
Why then, I think Cassio 's an honest man.

OTHELLO
Nay, yet there's more in this.
I prithee speak to me as to thy thinkings,
As thou dost ruminate, and give thy worst of thoughts
The worst of words.

IAGO   Good my lord, pardon me:
Though I am bound to every act of duty,
135 I am not bound to that all slaves are free to.
Utter my thoughts? Why, say they are vile and false,
As where's that palace whereinto foul things
Sometimes intrude not? Who has a breast so pure
But some uncleanly apprehensions
140 Keep leets and law days, and in Sessions sit
With meditations lawful?

OTHELLO
Thou dost conspire against thy friend, Iago,
If thou but think'st him wronged, and mak'st his ear
A stranger to thy thoughts.

IAGO   I do beseech you –
Though I perchance am vicious in my guess
(As I confess it is my nature's plague
147 To spy into abuses, and oft my jealousy
Shapes faults that are not), that your wisdom yet
149 From one that so imperfectly conjects
Would take no notice, nor build yourself a trouble
Out of his scattering and unsure observance.
It were not for your quiet nor your good,
Nor for my manhood, honesty, and wisdom,
To let you know my thoughts.

OTHELLO   What dost thou mean?

IAGO
Good name in man and woman, dear my lord,
156 Is the immediate jewel of their souls.
Who steals my purse steals trash; 'tis something,
  nothing;
'Twas mine, 'tis his, and has been slave to thousands;
But he that filches from me my good name
Robs me of that which not enriches him
And makes me poor indeed.

OTHELLO
By heaven, I'll know thy thoughts!

IAGO
You cannot, if my heart were in your hand;
Nor shall not whilst 'tis in my custody.

OTHELLO
Ha!

IAGO O, beware, my lord, of jealousy!
166 It is the green-eyed monster, which doth mock
The meat it feeds on. That cuckold lives in bliss
Who, certain of his fate, loves not his wronger;
But O, what damnèd minutes tells he o'er
Who dotes, yet doubts – suspects, yet strongly loves!

OTHELLO
O misery!

IAGO
Poor and content is rich, and rich enough;
But riches fineless is as poor as winter   173
To him that ever fears he shall be poor.
Good God, the souls of all my tribe defend
From jealousy!

OTHELLO   Why, why is this?
Think'st thou I'ld make a life of jealousy,
To follow still the changes of the moon
With fresh suspicions? No! To be once in doubt
Is once to be resolved. Exchange me for a goat
When I shall turn the business of my soul
To such exsufflicate and blown surmises, 182
Matching this inference. 'Tis not to make me jealous
To say my wife is fair, feeds well, loves company,
Is free of speech, sings, plays, and dances;
Where virtue is, these are more virtuous.
Nor from mine own weak merits will I draw
The smallest fear or doubt of her revolt, 188
For she had eyes, and chose me. No, Iago;
I'll see before I doubt; when I doubt, prove;
And on the proof there is no more but this –
Away at once with love or jealousy!

IAGO
I am glad of this; for now I shall have reason
To show the love and duty that I bear you
With franker spirit. Therefore, as I am bound,
Receive it from me. I speak not yet of proof.
Look to your wife; observe her well with Cassio;
Wear your eyes thus, not jealous nor secure: 198
I would not have your free and noble nature,
Out of self-bounty, be abused. Look to't. 200
I know our country disposition well:
In Venice they do let God see the pranks
They dare not show their husbands; their best
  conscience
Is not to leave't undone, but keep't unknown.

OTHELLO
Dost thou say so?

IAGO
She did deceive her father, marrying you;
And when she seemed to shake and fear your looks,
She loved them most.

OTHELLO   And so she did.

IAGO   Why, go to then!
She that, so young, could give out such a seeming
To seel her father's eyes up close as oak – 210
He thought 'twas witchcraft – but I am much to blame.
I humbly do beseech you of your pardon
For too much loving you.

OTHELLO   I am bound to thee for ever.

IAGO
I see this hath a little dashed your spirits.

OTHELLO
Not a jot, not a jot.

IAGO   I' faith, I fear it has.

---

127 *seem none* i.e. not pretend to be men when they are really monsters
135 *bound . . . free* to bound to tell that which even slaves are allowed to
keep to themselves 140 *leets and law days* sittings of the courts 147
jealousy suspicion 149 *conjects* conjectures 156 *immediate* nearest the
heart 166 *mock* play with, like a cat with a mouse 173 *fineless* unlimited
182 *exsufflicate and blown* spat out and flyblown 188 *revolt* unfaithfulness
198 *secure* overconfident 200 *self-bounty* natural goodness 210 *seel*
close; *oak* oak grain

I hope you will consider what is spoke
Comes from my love. But I do see y' are moved.
I am to pray you not to strain my speech
219   To grosser issues nor to larger reach
Than to suspicion.

OTHELLO
I will not.

IAGO   Should you do so, my lord,
222   My speech should fall into such vile success
As my thoughts aim not at. Cassio 's my worthy friend –
My lord, I see y' are moved.

OTHELLO   No, not much moved :
225   I do not think but Desdemona 's honest.

IAGO
Long live she so ! and long live you to think so !

OTHELLO
And yet, how nature erring from itself –

IAGO
Ay, there's the point ! as (to be bold with you)
Not to affect many proposèd matches
Of her own clime, complexion, and degree,
Whereto we see in all things nature tends –
Foh ! one may smell in such a will most rank,
Foul disproportions, thoughts unnatural –
234   But pardon me – I do not in position
Distinctly speak of her ; though I may fear
236   Her will, recoiling to her better judgment,
237   May fall to match you with her country forms,
238   And happily repent.

OTHELLO   Farewell, farewell !
If more thou dost perceive, let me know more.
Set on thy wife to observe. Leave me, Iago.

IAGO
My lord, I take my leave.   [Going.]

OTHELLO
Why did I marry ? This honest creature doubtless
Sees and knows more, much more, than he unfolds.

IAGO [returns]
My lord, I would I might entreat your honor
To scan this thing no further : leave it to time.
Although 'tis fit that Cassio have his place,
For sure he fills it up with great ability,
Yet, if you please to hold him off awhile,
You shall by that perceive him and his means.
250   Note if your lady strain his entertainment
With any strong or vehement importunity ;
Much will be seen in that. In the mean time
253   Let me be thought too busy in my fears
(As worthy cause I have to fear I am)
255   And hold her free, I do beseech your honor.

OTHELLO
256   Fear not my government.

IAGO
I once more take my leave.   Exit.

OTHELLO
This fellow 's of exceeding honesty,
And knows all qualities, with a learned spirit   259
Of human dealings. If I do prove her haggard,   260
Though that her jesses were my dear heartstrings,   261
I'd whistle her off and let her down the wind   262
To prey at fortune. Haply, for I am black
And have not those soft parts of conversation   264
That chamberers have, or for I am declined   265
Into the vale of years – yet that's not much –
She's gone. I am abused, and my relief
Must be to loathe her. O curse of marriage,
That we can call these delicate creatures ours,
And not their appetites ! I had rather be a toad
And live upon the vapor of a dungeon
Than keep a corner in the thing I love
For others' uses. Yet 'tis the plague of great ones ;   273
Prerogatived are they less than the base.   274
'Tis destiny unshunnable, like death.
Even then this forkèd plague is fated to us   276
When we do quicken. Look where she comes.   277
                    Enter Desdemona and Emilia.
If she be false, O, then heaven mocks itself !
I'll not believe't.

DESDEMONA   How now, my dear Othello ?
Your dinner, and the generous islanders   280
By you invited, do attend your presence.

OTHELLO
I am to blame.

DESDEMONA   Why do you speak so faintly ?
Are you not well ?

OTHELLO
I have a pain upon my forehead, here.

DESDEMONA
Faith, that's with watching ; 'twill away again.   285
Let me but bind it hard, within this hour
It will be well.

OTHELLO   Your napkin is too little ;   287
        [He pushes the handkerchief from him, and it falls
        unnoticed.]
Let it alone. Come, I'll go in with you.   288

DESDEMONA
I am very sorry that you are not well.   Exit [with Othello].

EMILIA
I am glad I have found this napkin ;
This was her first remembrance from the Moor,
My wayward husband hath a hundred times
Wooed me to steal it ; but she so loves the token
(For he conjured her she should ever keep it)
That she reserves it evermore about her
To kiss and talk to. I'll have the work ta'en out   296
And give't Iago.
What he will do with it heaven knows, not I ;
I nothing but to please his fantasy.   299
                    Enter Iago.

IAGO
How now ? What do you here alone ?

EMILIA
Do not you chide ; I have a thing for you.

IAGO
A thing for me ? It is a common thing –

EMILIA Ha ?

219 *To grosser issues* to mean something more monstrous   222 *vile success* evil outcome   225 *honest* chaste   234 *position* definite assertion   236 *recoiling* reverting   237 *fall to match* happen to compare   238 *happily* haply, perhaps   250 *strain his entertainment* urge his recall   253 *busy* meddlesome   255 *hold her free* consider her guiltless   256 *government* self-control   259 *qualities* natures   259–60 *learned spirit Of* mind informed about   260 *haggard* a wild hawk   261 *jesses* thongs for controlling a hawk   262–63 *whistle . . . fortune* turn her out and let her take care of herself   264 *soft . . . conversation* ingratiating manners   265 *chamberers* courtiers   273 *great ones* prominent men   274 *Prerogatived* privileged   276 *forkèd plague* i.e. horns of a cuckold   277 *do quicken* are born   280 *generous* noble   285 *watching* working late   287 *napkin* handkerchief   288 *it* i.e. his forehead   296 *work ta'en out* pattern copied   299 *fantasy* whim

IAGO
To have a foolish wife.

EMILIA
O, is that all ? What will you give me now
For that same handkerchief ?

IAGO   What handkerchief ?

EMILIA
What handkerchief !
Why, that the Moor first gave to Desdemona ;
That which so often you did bid me steal.

IAGO
Hast stol'n it from her ?

EMILIA
No, faith ; she let it drop by negligence,
312 And to th' advantage, I, being here, took't up.
Look, here it is.

IAGO   A good wench ! Give it me.

EMILIA
What will you do with't, that you have been so earnest
To have me filch it ?

IAGO   Why, what is that to you ?
     [Snatches it.]

EMILIA
316 If it be not for some purpose of import,
Give't me again. Poor lady, she'll run mad
When she shall lack it.

IAGO
319 Be not acknown on't ; I have use for it.
Go, leave me.   *Exit Emilia.*
I will in Cassio's lodgings lose this napkin
And let him find it. Trifles light as air
Are to the jealous confirmations strong
As proofs of holy writ. This may do something.
The Moor already changes with my poison :
326 Dangerous conceits are in their natures poisons,
Which at the first are scarce found to distaste,
But with a little act upon the blood
Burn like the mines of sulphur.
     Enter Othello.   I did say so.
330 Look where he comes ! Not poppy nor mandragora,
Nor all the drowsy syrups of the world,
Shall ever med'cine thee to that sweet sleep
Which thou owedst yesterday.

OTHELLO   Ha ! ha ! false to me ?

IAGO
Why, how now, general ? No more of that !

OTHELLO
Avaunt ! be gone ! Thou hast set me on the rack.
I swear 'tis better to be much abused
Than but to know't a little.

IAGO   How now, my lord ?

OTHELLO
What sense had I of her stol'n hours of lust ?
I saw't not, thought it not, it harmed not me ;
340 I slept the next night well, fed well, was free and merry ;
I found not Cassio's kisses on her lips.
342 He that is robbed, not wanting what is stol'n,
Let him not know't, and he's not robbed at all.

IAGO
I am sorry to hear this.

OTHELLO
I had been happy if the general camp,
346 Pioners and all, had tasted her sweet body,
So I had nothing known. O, now for ever

Farewell the tranquil mind ! farewell content !
Farewell the plumèd troop, and the big wars   349
That make ambition virtue ! O, farewell !
Farewell the neighing steed and the shrill trump,
The spirit-stirring drum, th' ear-piercing fife,
The royal banner, and all quality,
Pride, pomp, and circumstance of glorious war !   354
And O you mortal engines whose rude throats   355
Th' immortal Jove's dread clamors counterfeit,   356
Farewell ! Othello's occupation 's gone !

IAGO
Is't possible, my lord ?

OTHELLO
Villain, be sure thou prove my love a whore !
Be sure of it ; give me the ocular proof ;
Or, by the worth of mine eternal soul,
Thou hadst been better have been born a dog
Than answer my waked wrath !

IAGO   Is't come to this ?

OTHELLO
Make me to see't ; or at the least so prove it
That the probation bear no hinge nor loop
To hang a doubt on – or woe upon thy life !   365

IAGO
My noble lord –

OTHELLO
If thou dost slander her and torture me,
Never pray more ; abandon all remorse ;
On horror's head horrors accumulate ;
Do deeds to make heaven weep, all earth amazed ;
For nothing canst thou to damnation add
Greater than that.

IAGO   O grace ! O heaven forgive me !
Are you a man ? Have you a soul or sense ? –
God b' wi' you ! take mine office. O wretched fool,
That liv'st to make thine honesty a vice !
O monstrous world ! Take note, take note, O world,
To be direct and honest is not safe.
I thank you for this profit ; and from hence   379
I'll love no friend, sith love breeds such offense.

OTHELLO
Nay, stay. Thou shouldst be honest.

IAGO
I should be wise ; for honesty 's a fool
And loses that it works for.

OTHELLO   By the world,
I think my wife be honest, and think she is not ;
I think that thou art just, and think thou art not.
I'll have some proof. Her name, that was as fresh
As Dian's visage, is now begrimed and black
As mine own face. If there be cords, or knives,
Poison, or fire, or suffocating streams,
I'll not endure it. Would I were satisfied !   390

IAGO
I see, sir, you are eaten up with passion :
I do repent me that I put it to you.
You would be satisfied ?

OTHELLO   Would ? Nay, I will.

---

312 *to th' advantage* opportunely   316 *import* importance   319 *Be . . . on't* do not acknowledge it   326 *conceits* ideas   330 *mandragora* a narcotic 340 *free* carefree   342 *wanting* missing   346 *Pioners* sappers, laborers 349 *big* stately   354 *circumstance* pageantry   355 *mortal engines* deadly artillery   356 *counterfeit* imitate   365 *probation* proof   379 *profit* profitable lesson   390 *satisfied* completely informed

IAGO
And may ; but how ? how satisfied, my lord ?
395 Would you, the supervisor, grossly gape on ?
Behold her topped ?
OTHELLO   Death and damnation ! O !
IAGO
It were a tedious difficulty, I think,
To bring them to that prospect. Damn them then,
399 If ever mortal eyes do see them bolster
More than their own ! What then ? How then ?
What shall I say ? Where's satisfaction ?
It is impossible you should see this,
403 Were they as prime as goats, as hot as monkeys,
404 As salt as wolves in pride, and fools as gross
As ignorance made drunk. But yet, I say,
If imputation and strong circumstances
Which lead directly to the door of truth
Will give you satisfaction, you may have't.
OTHELLO
Give me a living reason she's disloyal.
IAGO
410 I do not like the office.
But sith I am ent'red in this cause so far,
Pricked to't by foolish honesty and love,
I will go on. I lay with Cassio lately,
And being troubled with a raging tooth,
I could not sleep.
There are a kind of men so loose of soul
That in their sleeps will mutter their affairs.
One of this kind is Cassio.
In sleep I heard him say, 'Sweet Desdemona,
420 Let us be wary, let us hide our loves !'
And then, sir, would he gripe and wring my hand,
Cry 'O sweet creature !' and then kiss me hard,
As if he plucked up kisses by the roots
That grew upon my lips ; then laid his leg
Over my thigh, and sighed, and kissed, and then
Cried 'Cursèd fate that gave thee to the Moor !'
OTHELLO
O monstrous ! monstrous !
IAGO   Nay, this was but his dream.
OTHELLO
428 But this denoted a foregone conclusion :
429 'Tis a shrewd doubt, though it be but a dream.
IAGO
And this may help to thicken other proofs
That do demonstrate thinly.
OTHELLO   I'll tear her all to pieces !
IAGO
Nay, but be wise. Yet we see nothing done ;
She may be honest yet. Tell me but this –
Have you not sometimes seen a handkerchief
Spotted with strawberries in your wife's hand ?
OTHELLO
I gave her such a one ; 'twas my first gift.
IAGO
I know not that ; but such a handkerchief –

I am sure it was your wife's – did I to-day
See Cassio wipe his beard with.
OTHELLO   If it be that –
IAGO
If it be that, or any that was hers,   440
It speaks against her with the other proofs.
OTHELLO
O, that the slave had forty thousand lives !
One is too poor, too weak for my revenge.
Now do I see 'tis true. Look here, Iago :
All my fond love thus do I blow to heaven.
'Tis gone.
Arise, black vengeance, from the hollow hell !
Yield up, O love, thy crown and hearted throne
To tyrannous hate ! Swell, bosom, with thy fraught,   449
For 'tis of aspics' tongues !   450
IAGO   Yet be content.
OTHELLO
O, blood, blood, blood !
IAGO
Patience, I say. Your mind perhaps may change.
OTHELLO
Never, Iago. Like to the Pontic sea,   453
Whose icy current and compulsive course
Ne'er feels retiring ebb, but keeps due on
To the Propontic and the Hellespont,
Even so my bloody thoughts, with violent pace,
Shall ne'er look back, ne'er ebb to humble love,
Till that a capable and wide revenge   459
Swallow them up.
        He kneels.   Now, by yond marble heaven,
In the due reverence of a sacred vow
I here engage my words.
IAGO   Do not rise yet.
        Iago kneels.
Witness, you ever-burning lights above,
You elements that clip us round about,   464
Witness that here Iago doth give up
The execution of his wit, hands, heart   466
To wronged Othello's service ! Let him command,
And to obey shall be in me remorse,   468
What bloody business ever.
        [They rise.]
OTHELLO   I greet thy love,
Not with vain thanks but with acceptance bounteous,
And will upon the instant put thee to't.
Within these three days let me hear thee say
That Cassio 's not alive.
IAGO
My friend is dead ; 'tis done at your request.
But let her live.
OTHELLO
Damn her, lewd minx ! O, damn her ! damn her !
Come, go with me apart. I will withdraw
To furnish me with some swift means of death
For the fair devil. Now art thou my lieutenant.
IAGO
I am your own for ever.   Exeunt.

*

IAGO
Enter Desdemona, Emilia, and Clown.   III, iv
DESDEMONA Do you know, sirrah, where Lieutenant
Cassio lies ?   2
CLOWN I dare not say he lies anywhere.

---

395 *supervisor* spectator 399 *bolster* lie together 403 *prime* lustful
404 *salt* lecherous ; *pride* heat 428 *foregone conclusion* previous experience
429 *a shrewd doubt* cursedly suspicious 449 *fraught* burden 450 *aspics*
deadly poisonous snakes 453 *Pontic sea* Black Sea 459 *capable* all-
embracing 464 *clip* encompass 466 *execution* activities ; *wit* mind 468
remorse pity
III, iv The environs of the castle 2 *lies* lives, lodges

DESDEMONA Why, man?

CLOWN He's a soldier, and for me to say a soldier lies is
stabbing.

DESDEMONA Go to. Where lodges he?

CLOWN To tell you where he lodges is to tell you where I
lie.

DESDEMONA Can anything be made of this?

CLOWN I know not where he lodges; and for me to devise
a lodging, and say he lies here or he lies there, were to
lie in mine own throat.

DESDEMONA Can you enquire him out, and be edified by
report?

CLOWN I will catechize the world for him; that is, make
questions, and by them answer.

DESDEMONA Seek him, bid him come hither. Tell him I
19   have moved my lord on his behalf and hope all will be
well.

CLOWN To do this is within the compass of man's wit,
and therefore I'll attempt the doing of it.   *Exit.*

DESDEMONA
Where should I lose that handkerchief, Emilia?

EMILIA
I know not, madam.

DESDEMONA
Believe me, I had rather have lost my purse
26   Full of crusadoes; and but my noble Moor
Is true of mind, and made of no such baseness
As jealous creatures are, it were enough
To put him to ill thinking.

EMILIA   Is he not jealous?

DESDEMONA
Who? he? I think the sun where he was born
31   Drew all such humors from him.
        Enter Othello.

EMILIA   Look where he comes.

DESDEMONA
I will not leave him now till Cassio
Be called to him. – How is't with you, my lord?

OTHELLO
Well, my good lady. *[aside]* O, hardness to dissemble! –
How do you, Desdemona?

DESDEMONA   Well, my good lord.

OTHELLO
Give me your hand. This hand is moist, my lady.

DESDEMONA
It yet hath felt no age nor known no sorrow.

OTHELLO
This argues fruitfulness and liberal heart.
Hot, hot, and moist. This hand of yours requires
40   A sequester from liberty, fasting and prayer,
Much castigation, exercise devout;
For here's a young and sweating devil here
That commonly rebels. 'Tis a good hand,
A frank one.

DESDEMONA You may, indeed, say so;
For 'twas that hand that gave away my heart.

OTHELLO
A liberal hand! The hearts of old gave hands;
47   But our new heraldry is hands, not hearts.

DESDEMONA
I cannot speak of this. Come now, your promise!

OTHELLO
What promise, chuck?

DESDEMONA
I have sent to bid Cassio come speak with you.

OTHELLO
I have a salt and sorry rheum offends me.   51
Lend me thy handkerchief.

DESDEMONA   Here, my lord.

OTHELLO
That which I gave you.

DESDEMONA   I have it not about me.

OTHELLO
Not?

DESDEMONA No, faith, my lord.

OTHELLO   That's a fault.
That handkerchief
Did an Egyptian to my mother give.   56
She was a charmer, and could almost read   57
The thoughts of people. She told her, while she kept it,
'Twould make her amiable and subdue my father   59
Entirely to her love; but if she lost it
Or made a gift of it, my father's eye
Should hold her loathèd, and his spirits should hunt
After new fancies. She, dying, gave it me,
And bid me, when my fate would have me wive,
To give it her. I did so; and take heed on't;
Make it a darling like your precious eye.
To lose't or give't away were such perdition   67
As nothing else could match.

DESDEMONA   Is't possible?

OTHELLO
'Tis true. There's magic in the web of it.
A sibyl that had numb'red in the world
The sun to course two hundred compasses,   71
In her prophetic fury sewed the work;
The worms were hallowed that did breed the silk;
And it was dyed in mummy which the skillful
Conserved of maidens' hearts.

DESDEMONA   I' faith? Is't true?

OTHELLO
Most veritable. Therefore look to't well.

DESDEMONA
Then would to God that I had never seen't!

OTHELLO Ha! Wherefore?

DESDEMONA
Why do you speak so startingly and rash?

OTHELLO
Is't lost? Is't gone? Speak, is it out o' th' way?

DESDEMONA Heaven bless us!

OTHELLO Say you?

DESDEMONA
It is not lost. But what an if it were?

OTHELLO How?

DESDEMONA
I say it is not lost.

OTHELLO   Fetch't, let me see't!

DESDEMONA
Why, so I can, sir; but I will not now.
This is a trick to put me from my suit: 87
Pray you let Cassio be received again.

---

19 *moved* made proposals   26 *crusadoes* Portuguese gold coins   31
humors inclinations   40 *sequester* removal   47 *heraldry* heraldic symbolism
51 *salt . . . rheum* distressing head-cold   56 *Egyptian* gypsy   57 *charmer*
sorceress   59 *amiable* lovable   67 *perdition* disaster   71 *compasses* annual
rounds   74 *mummy* a drug made from mummies   87 *put* divert

OTHELLO
   Fetch me the handkerchief! My mind misgives.
DESDEMONA
   Come, come!
   You'll never meet a more sufficient man.
OTHELLO
   The handkerchief!
[DESDEMONA   I pray talk me of Cassio.
OTHELLO
   The handkerchief!]
93 DESDEMONA   A man that all his time
   Hath founded his good fortunes on your love,
   Shared dangers with you –
OTHELLO
   The handkerchief!
DESDEMONA
   I' faith, you are to blame.
OTHELLO Zounds!   *Exit Othello.*
EMILIA Is not this man jealous?
DESDEMONA
   I ne'er saw this before.
   Sure there's some wonder in this handkerchief;
   I am most unhappy in the loss of it.
EMILIA
   'Tis not a year or two shows us a man.
   They are all but stomachs, and we all but food;
   They eat us hungerly, and when they are full,
   They belch us.
     Enter Iago and Cassio.
         Look you – Cassio and my husband!
IAGO
   There is no other way; 'tis she must do't.
108 And lo the happiness! Go and importune her.
DESDEMONA
   How now, good Cassio? What's the news with you?
CASSIO
   Madam, my former suit. I do beseech you
   That by your virtuous means I may again
   Exist, and be a member of his love
   Whom I with all the office of my heart
   Entirely honor. I would not be delayed.
   If my offense be of such mortal kind
   That neither service past, nor present sorrows,
   Nor purposed merit in futurity,
   Can ransom me into his love again,
   But to know so must be my benefit.
   So shall I clothe me in a forced content,
121 And shut myself up in some other course,
   To fortune's alms.
DESDEMONA   Alas, thrice-gentle Cassio!
123 My advocation is not now in tune.
   My lord is not my lord; nor should I know him,
125 Were he in favor as in humor altered.
   So help me every spirit sanctified
   As I have spoken for you all my best
128 And stood within the blank of his displeasure

For my free speech! You must awhile be patient.
   What I can do I will; and more I will
   Than for myself I dare. Let that suffice you.
IAGO
   Is my lord angry?
EMILIA   He went hence but now,
   And certainly in strange unquietness.
IAGO
   Can he be angry? I have seen the cannon
   When it hath blown his ranks into the air
   And, like the devil, from his very arm
   Puffed his own brother – and is he angry?
   Something of moment then. I will go meet him.
   There's matter in't indeed if he be angry.
DESDEMONA
   I prithee do so.   *Exit [Iago].*
       Something sure of state,   140
   Either from Venice or some unhatched practice 141
   Made demonstrable here in Cyprus to him,
   Hath puddled his clear spirit; and in such cases 143
   Men's natures wrangle with inferior things,
   Though great ones are their object. 'Tis even so;
   For let our finger ache, and it endues 146
   Our other, healthful members even to a sense
   Of pain. Nay, we must think men are not gods,
   Nor of them look for such observancy
   As fits the bridal. Beshrew me much, Emilia,
   I was, unhandsome warrior as I am, 151
   Arraigning his unkindness with my soul; 152
   But now I find I had suborned the witness,
   And he's indicted falsely.
EMILIA
   Pray heaven it be state matters, as you think,
   And no conception nor no jealous toy 156
   Concerning you.
DESDEMONA
   Alas the day! I never gave him cause.
EMILIA
   But jealous souls will not be answered so;
   They are not ever jealous for the cause,
   But jealous for they're jealous. 'Tis a monster
   Begot upon itself, born on itself. 162
DESDEMONA
   Heaven keep that monster from Othello's mind!
EMILIA Lady, amen.
DESDEMONA
   I will go seek him. Cassio, walk here about:
   If I do find him fit, I'll move your suit
   And seek to effect it to my uttermost.
CASSIO
   I humbly thank your ladyship.
        Exeunt Desdemona and Emilia.
     Enter Bianca.
BIANCA
   Save you, friend Cassio!
CASSIO   What make you from home?
   How is't with you, my most fair Bianca?
   I' faith, sweet love, I was coming to your house.
BIANCA
   And I was going to your lodging, Cassio.
   What, keep a week away? seven days and nights?
   Eightscore eight hours? and lovers' absent hours,
   More tedious than the dial eightscore times? 175

---

93 *all . . . time* during his whole career 108 *happiness* good luck 121 *shut myself up in* confine myself to 123 *advocation* advocacy 125 *favor* appearance 128 *blank* bull's-eye of the target 140 *state* public affairs 141 *unhatched practice* budding plot 143 *puddled* muddied 146 *endues* brings 151 *unhandsome warrior* inadequate soldier 152 *Arraigning . . . soul* indicting his unkindness before the bar of my soul 156 *toy* fancy 162 *Begot . . . itself* self-engendered 175 *dial* clock

    O weary reck'ning !

CASSIO   Pardon me, Bianca :
    I have this while with leaden thoughts been pressed ;
178   But I shall in a more continuate time
    Strike off this score of absence. Sweet Bianca,
      [Gives her Desdemona's handkerchief.]
180   Take me this work out.

BIANCA   O Cassio, whence came this ?
    This is some token from a newer friend.
    To the felt absence now I feel a cause.
    Is't come to this ? Well, well.

CASSIO   Go to, woman !
    Throw your vile guesses in the devil's teeth,
    From whence you have them. You are jealous now
    That this is from some mistress, some remembrance.
    No, by my faith, Bianca.

BIANCA   Why, whose is it ?

CASSIO
    I know not, sweet ; I found it in my chamber.
189   I like the work well ; ere it be demanded,
    As like enough it will, I'd have it copied.
    Take it and do't, and leave me for this time.

BIANCA
    Leave you ? Wherefore ?

CASSIO
    I do attend here on the general
    And think it no addition, nor my wish,
    To have him see me womaned.

BIANCA   Why, I pray you ?

CASSIO
    Not that I love you not.

BIANCA   But that you do not love me !
    I pray you bring me on the way a little,
    And say if I shall see you soon at night.

CASSIO
    'Tis but a little way that I can bring you,
    For I attend here ; but I'll see you soon.

BIANCA
201   'Tis very good. I must be circumstanced.   *Exeunt.*

*

IV, i   *Enter Othello and Iago.*

IAGO
    Will you think so ?

OTHELLO   Think so, Iago ?

IAGO   What,
    To kiss in private ?

OTHELLO   An unauthorized kiss.

IAGO
    Or to be naked with her friend in bed
    An hour or more, not meaning any harm ?

OTHELLO
    Naked in bed, Iago, and not mean harm ?
6   It is hypocrisy against the devil.
    They that mean virtuously, and yet do so,
    The devil their virtue tempts, and they tempt heaven.

IAGO
    So they do nothing, 'tis a venial slip.
    But if I give my wife a handkerchief –

OTHELLO
    What then ?

IAGO
    Why, then 'tis hers, my lord ; and being hers,
    She may, I think, bestow't on any man.

OTHELLO
    She is protectress of her honor too ;
    May she give that ?

IAGO
    Her honor is an essence that's not seen ;
    They have it very oft that have it not.
    But for the handkerchief –

OTHELLO
    By heaven, I would most gladly have forgot it !
    Thou said'st – O, it comes o'er my memory
    As doth the raven o'er the infected house,   21
    Boding to all ! – he had my handkerchief.

IAGO
    Ay, what of that ?

OTHELLO   That's not so good now.

IAGO   What
    If I had said I had seen him do you wrong ?
    Or heard him say – as knaves be such abroad
    Who having, by their own importunate suit,
    Or voluntary dotage of some mistress,
    Convincèd or supplied them, cannot choose   28
    But they must blab –

OTHELLO   Hath he said anything ?

IAGO
    He hath, my lord ; but be you well assured,
    No more than he'll unswear.

OTHELLO   What hath he said ?

IAGO
    Faith, that he did – I know not what he did.

OTHELLO What ? what ?

IAGO
    Lie –

OTHELLO With her ?

IAGO   With her, on her ; what you will.

OTHELLO Lie with her ? lie on her ? – We say lie on her
    when they belie her. – Lie with her ! Zounds, that's ful-
    some. – Handkerchief – confessions – handkerchief ! –
    To confess, and be hanged for his labor – first to be
    hanged, and then to confess ! I tremble at it. Nature 39
    would not invest herself in such shadowing passion
    without some instruction. It is not words that shakes me
    thus. – Pish ! Noses, ears, and lips ? Is't possible ? – Con-
    fess ? – Handkerchief ? – O devil !
      Falls in a trance.

IAGO Work on,
    My med'cine, work ! Thus credulous fools are caught,
    And many worthy and chaste dames even thus,
    All guiltless, meet reproach. – What, ho ! my lord !
    My lord, I say ! Othello !
      Enter Cassio.   How now, Cassio ?

CASSIO
    What's the matter ?

IAGO
    My lord is fall'n into an epilepsy.
    This is his second fit ; he had one yesterday.

CASSIO
    Rub him about the temples.

---

178 *continuate* uninterrupted 180 *Take . . . out* copy this embroidery for
me 189 *work* needlework 201 *circumstanced* governed by circumstances
IV, i The environs of the castle 6 *hypocrisy . . . devil* i.e. feigned sin
instead of feigned virtue 21 *infected* plague-stricken 28 *Convincèd or
supplied* overcome or gratified 39–41 *Nature . . . instruction* my natural
faculties would not be so overcome by passion without reason

IAGO　　　　　　　　　No, forbear.

53 The lethargy must have his quiet course.
If not, he foams at mouth, and by and by
Breaks out to savage madness. Look, he stirs.
Do you withdraw yourself a little while.
He will recover straight. When he is gone,
I would on great occasion speak with you. *[Exit Cassio.]*
How is it, general? Have you not hurt your head?

OTHELLO
Dost thou mock me?

IAGO　　　　　　　I mock you? No, by heaven.
Would you would bear your fortune like a man!

OTHELLO
62 A hornèd man's a monster and a beast.

IAGO
There's many a beast then in a populous city,
And many a civil monster.

OTHELLO
Did he confess it?

IAGO　　　　　　Good sir, be a man.
Think every bearded fellow that's but yoked
May draw with you. There's millions now alive
68 That nightly lie in those unproper beds
69 Which they dare swear peculiar : your case is better.
O, 'tis the spite of hell, the fiend's arch-mock,
71 To lip a wanton in a secure couch,
And to suppose her chaste! No, let me know;
And knowing what I am, I know what she shall be.

OTHELLO
O, thou art wise! 'Tis certain.

IAGO　　　　　　　　　Stand you awhile apart;
75 Confine yourself but in a patient list.
Whilst you were here, o'erwhelmèd with your grief –
A passion most unsuiting such a man –
Cassio came hither. I shifted him away
79 And laid good 'scuse upon your ecstasy;
Bade him anon return, and here speak with me;
81 The which he promised. Do but encave yourself
And mark the fleers, the gibes, and notable scorns
That dwell in every region of his face;
For I will make him tell the tale anew –
Where, how, how oft, how long ago, and when
86 He hath, and is again to cope your wife.
I say, but mark his gesture. Marry, patience!
88 Or I shall say y'are all in all in spleen,
And nothing of a man.

OTHELLO　　　　　　Dost thou hear, Iago?
I will be found most cunning in my patience;
But – dost thou hear? – most bloody.

IAGO　　　　　　　　　That's not amiss;
But yet keep time in all. Will you withdraw?
　　　　　　　　　　[Othello retires.]
Now will I question Cassio of Bianca,
94 A huswife that by selling her desires
Buys herself bread and clothes. It is a creature
That dotes on Cassio, as 'tis the strumpet's plague

To beguile many and be beguiled by one.
He, when he hears of her, cannot refrain
From the excess of laughter. Here he comes.
　　　Enter Cassio.
As he shall smile, Othello shall go mad;
And his unbookish jealousy must conster　　　101
Poor Cassio's smiles, gestures, and light behavior
Quite in the wrong. How do you now, lieutenant?

CASSIO
The worser that you give me the addition　　　104
Whose want even kills me.

IAGO
Ply Desdemona well, and you are sure on't.
Now, if this suit lay in Bianca's power,
How quickly should you speed!

CASSIO　　　　　　　　　Alas, poor caitiff!　　　108

OTHELLO
Look how he laughs already!

IAGO
I never knew a woman love man so.

CASSIO
Alas, poor rogue! I think, i' faith, she loves me.

OTHELLO
Now he denies it faintly, and laughs it out.

IAGO
Do you hear, Cassio?

OTHELLO　　　　　　Now he importunes him
To tell it o'er. Go to! Well said, well said!

IAGO
She gives it out that you shall marry her.
Do you intend it?

CASSIO Ha, ha, ha!

OTHELLO
Do you triumph, Roman? Do you triumph?

CASSIO I marry her? What, a customer? Prithee bear 119
some charity to my wit; do not think it so unwholesome.
Ha, ha, ha!

OTHELLO So, so, so, so! They laugh that win!

IAGO
Faith, the cry goes that you shall marry her.

CASSIO Prithee say true.

IAGO I am a very villain else.

OTHELLO Have you scored me? Well.　　　126

CASSIO This is the monkey's own giving out. She is persuaded I will marry her out of her own love and flattery,
not out of my promise.

OTHELLO Iago beckons me; now he begins the story. 130

CASSIO She was here even now; she haunts me in every
place. I was t' other day talking on the sea bank with certain Venetians, and thither comes the bauble, and, by 133
this hand, she falls me thus about my neck –

OTHELLO Crying 'O dear Cassio!' as it were. His gesture
imports it.

CASSIO So hangs, and lolls, and weeps upon me; so
shakes and pulls me! Ha, ha, ha!

OTHELLO Now he tells how she plucked him to my
chamber. O, I see that nose of yours, but not that dog I
shall throw it to.

CASSIO Well, I must leave her company.
　　　Enter Bianca.

IAGO Before me! Look where she comes.

CASSIO 'Tis such another fitchew! marry, a perfumed 144
one. What do you mean by this haunting of me?

BIANCA Let the devil and his dam haunt you! What did

53 *lethargy* coma　62 *hornèd man* cuckold　68 *unproper* not exclusively
their own　69 *peculiar* exclusively their own　71 *secure* free from fear of
rivalry　75 *in a patient list* within the limits of self-control　79 *ecstasy*
trance　81 *encave* conceal　86 *cope* meet　88 *all in all in spleen* wholly
overcome by your passion　94 *huswife* hussy　101 *unbookish* uninstructed;
conster construe, interpret　104 *addition* title　108 *caitiff* wretch　119
customer prostitute　126 *scored me* settled my account (?)　130 *beckons*
signals　133 *bauble* plaything　144 *fitchew* polecat (slang for whore)

you mean by that same handkerchief you gave me even now? I was a fine fool to take it. I must take out the whole work? A likely piece of work that you should find it in your chamber and know not who left it there! This is some minx's token, and I must take out the work?

152 There! Give it your hobby-horse. Wheresoever you had it, I'll take out no work on't.

CASSIO How now, my sweet Bianca? How now? how now?

OTHELLO By heaven, that should be my handkerchief!

BIANCA An you'll come to supper to-night, you may; an you will not, come when you are next prepared for. *Exit.*

IAGO After her, after her!

CASSIO Faith, I must; she'll rail in the street else.

IAGO Will you sup there?

CASSIO Yes, I intend so.

IAGO Well, I may chance to see you; for I would very fain speak with you.

CASSIO Prithee come. Will you?

IAGO Go to! say no more.   *Exit Cassio.*

OTHELLO *[comes forward]* How shall I murder him, Iago?

168 IAGO Did you perceive how he laughed at his vice?

OTHELLO O Iago!

IAGO And did you see the handkerchief?

OTHELLO Was that mine?

172 IAGO Yours, by this hand! And to see how he prizes the foolish woman your wife! She gave it him, and he hath giv'n it his whore.

OTHELLO I would have him nine years a-killing!—A fine woman! a fair woman! a sweet woman!

IAGO Nay, you must forget that.

OTHELLO Ay, let her rot, and perish, and be damned to-night; for she shall not live. No, my heart is turned to stone; I strike it, and it hurts my hand. O, the world hath not a sweeter creature! She might lie by an emperor's side and command him tasks.

IAGO Nay, that's not your way.

OTHELLO Hang her! I do but say what she is. So delicate with her needle! an admirable musician! O, she will sing the savageness out of a bear! Of so high and plente-

187 ous wit and invention—

IAGO She's the worse for all this.

OTHELLO O, a thousand thousand times! And then, of so

190 gentle a condition!

IAGO Ay, too gentle.

OTHELLO Nay, that's certain. But yet the pity of it, Iago! O Iago, the pity of it, Iago!

194 IAGO If you are so fond over her iniquity, give her patent to offend; for if it touch not you, it comes near nobody.

OTHELLO I will chop her into messes! Cuckold me!

IAGO O, 'tis foul in her.

OTHELLO With mine officer!

IAGO That's fouler.

OTHELLO Get me some poison, Iago, this night. I'll not

201 expostulate with her, lest her body and beauty unprovide my mind again. This night, Iago!

IAGO Do it not with poison. Strangle her in her bed, even the bed she hath contaminated.

OTHELLO Good, good! The justice of it pleases. Very good!

206 IAGO And for Cassio, let me be his undertaker: you shall hear more by midnight.

OTHELLO
Excellent good!

A trumpet. What trumpet is that same?

IAGO
I warrant something from Venice.
Enter Lodovico, Desdemona, and Attendants.
                                        'Tis Lodovico.
This comes from the Duke; and see, your wife is with 210 him.

LODOVICO
God save you, worthy general!

OTHELLO   With all my heart, sir.

LODOVICO
The Duke and senators of Venice greet you.
[Gives him a letter.]

OTHELLO
I kiss the instrument of their pleasures.
[Opens the letter and reads.]

DESDEMONA
And what's the news, good cousin Lodovico?

IAGO
I am very glad to see you, signior.
Welcome to Cyprus.

LODOVICO
I thank you. How does Lieutenant Cassio?

IAGO   Lives, sir.

DESDEMONA
Cousin, there's fall'n between him and my lord
An unkind breach; but you shall make all well.

OTHELLO Are you sure of that?   220

DESDEMONA My lord?

OTHELLO *[reads]* 'This fail you not to do, as you will—'

LODOVICO
He did not call; he's busy in the paper.
Is there division 'twixt thy lord and Cassio?

DESDEMONA
A most unhappy one. I would do much
T' atone them, for the love I bear to Cassio.   226

OTHELLO
Fire and brimstone!

DESDEMONA   My lord?

OTHELLO   Are you wise?

DESDEMONA
What, is he angry?

LODOVICO   May be the letter moved him;
For, as I think, they do command him home,
Deputing Cassio in his government.

DESDEMONA
By my troth, I am glad on't.

OTHELLO   Indeed?

DESDEMONA   My lord?

OTHELLO
I am glad to see you mad.   232

DESDEMONA   Why, sweet Othello—

OTHELLO Devil!
[Strikes her.]

DESDEMONA I have not deserved this.

LODOVICO
My lord, this would not be believed in Venice,
Though I should swear I saw't. 'Tis very much.
Make her amends; she weeps.

152 *hobby-horse* harlot   168 *vice* i.e. vicious conduct   172 *prizes* values
187 *invention* imagination   190 *condition* disposition   194 *patent* license
201 *unprovide* disarm   206 *be his undertaker* undertake to deal with him
226 *atone* reconcile   232 *mad* i.e. waggish

OTHELLO   O devil, devil !
238 If that the earth could teem with woman's tears,
239 Each drop she falls would prove a crocodile.
     Out of my sight !
DESDEMONA   I will not stay to offend you.   *[Going.]*
LODOVICO
     Truly, an obedient lady.
     I do beseech your lordship call her back.
OTHELLO
     Mistress !
DESDEMONA My lord ?
OTHELLO   What would you with her, sir ?
LODOVICO
     Who ? I, my lord ?
OTHELLO
     Ay ! You did wish that I would make her turn.
     Sir, she can turn, and turn, and yet go on
     And turn again ; and she can weep, sir, weep ;
     And she's obedient ; as you say, obedient,
     Very obedient. – Proceed you in your tears. –
250 Concerning this, sir – O well-painted passion ! –
     I am commanded home. – Get you away ;
     I'll send for you anon. – Sir, I obey the mandate
     And will return to Venice. – Hence, avaunt !
                                    [Exit Desdemona.]
     Cassio shall have my place. And, sir, to-night
     I do entreat that we may sup together.
     You are welcome, sir, to Cyprus. – Goats and monkeys !
                                              Exit.

LODOVICO
     Is this the noble Moor whom our full Senate
     Call all in all sufficient ? Is this the nature
     Whom passion could not shake ? whose solid virtue
     The shot of accident nor dart of chance
     Could neither graze nor pierce ?
IAGO   He is much changed.
LODOVICO
     Are his wits safe ? Is he not light of brain ?
IAGO
     He's that he is ; I may not breathe my censure.
     What he might be – if what he might he is not –
     I would to heaven he were !
LODOVICO   What, strike his wife ?
IAGO
     Faith, that was not so well ; yet would I knew
     That stroke would prove the worst !
267 **LODOVICO**   Is it his use ?
     Or did the letters work upon his blood
     And new-create this fault ?
IAGO   Alas, alas !
     It is not honesty in me to speak
     What I have seen and known. You shall observe him,
     And his own courses will denote him so
     That I may save my speech. Do but go after
     And mark how he continues.
LODOVICO
     I am sorry that I am deceived in him.   *Exeunt.*

                         *

Enter Othello and Emilia.
OTHELLO
     You have seen nothing then ?
EMILIA
     Nor ever heard, nor ever did suspect.
OTHELLO
     Yes, you have seen Cassio and she together.
EMILIA
     But then I saw no harm, and then I heard
     Each syllable that breath made up between them.
OTHELLO
     What, did they never whisper ?
EMILIA   Never, my lord.
OTHELLO
     Nor send you out o' th' way ?
EMILIA Never.
OTHELLO
     To fetch her fan, her gloves, her mask, nor nothing ?
EMILIA Never, my lord.
OTHELLO That's strange.
EMILIA
     I durst, my lord, to wager she is honest,
     Lay down my soul at stake. If you think other,
     Remove your thought ; it doth abuse your bosom.   14
     If any wretch have put this in your head,
     Let heaven requite it with the serpent's curse !   16
     For if she be not honest, chaste, and true,
     There's no man happy ; the purest of their wives
     Is foul as slander.
OTHELLO   Bid her come hither. Go.   *Exit Emilia.*
     She says enough ; yet she's a simple bawd
     That cannot say as much. This is a subtle whore,
     A closet lock and key of villainous secrets ;
     And yet she'll kneel and pray ; I have seen her do't.
          Enter Desdemona and Emilia.
DESDEMONA
     My lord, what is your will ?
OTHELLO   Pray, chuck, come hither.
DESDEMONA
     What is your pleasure ?
OTHELLO   Let me see your eyes.
     Look in my face.
DESDEMONA   What horrible fancy 's this ?
OTHELLO *[to Emilia]*
     Some of your function, mistress.
     Leave procreants alone and shut the door ;   28
     Cough or cry hem if anybody come.
     Your mystery, your mystery ! Nay, dispatch !   30
                                    Exit Emilia.
DESDEMONA
     Upon my knees, what doth your speech import ?
     I understand a fury in your words,
     [But not the words.]
OTHELLO
     Why, what art thou ?
DESDEMONA   Your wife, my lord ; your true
     And loyal wife.
OTHELLO   Come, swear it, damn thyself ;
     Lest, being like one of heaven, the devils themselves   36
     Should fear to seize thee. Therefore be double-damned –
     Swear thou art honest.   38
DESDEMONA   Heaven doth truly know it.
OTHELLO
     Heaven truly knows that thou art false as hell.

238 *teem* breed   239 *crocodile* (crocodiles were supposed to shed hypocritical tears to lure men to destruction)   250 *passion* grief   267 *use* custom
IV, ii Within the castle   14 *abuse . . . bosom* deceive your heart   16 *serpent's
curse* (cf. Genesis iii, 14)   28 *procreants* mating couples   30 *mystery* trade,
occupation   36 *being . . . heaven* looking like an angel   38 *honest* chaste

DESDEMONA
To whom, my lord ? With whom ? How am I false ?
OTHELLO
Ah, Desdemon ! away ! away ! away !
DESDEMONA
Alas the heavy day ! Why do you weep ?
Am I the motive of these tears, my lord ?
If haply you my father do suspect
45 An instrument of this your calling back,
Lay not your blame on me. If you have lost him,
Why, I have lost him too.
OTHELLO   Had it pleased heaven
To try me with affliction, had they rained
All kinds of sores and shames on my bare head,
Steeped me in poverty to the very lips,
Given to captivity me and my utmost hopes,
I should have found in some place of my soul
A drop of patience. But, alas, to make me
54 A fixèd figure for the time of scorn
To point his slow unmoving finger at !
Yet could I bear that too ; well, very well.
But there where I have garnered up my heart,
Where either I must live or bear no life,
The fountain from the which my current runs
Or else dries up – to be discarded thence,
Or keep it as a cistern for foul toads
62 To knot and gender in – turn thy complexion there,
Patience, thou young and rose-lipped cherubin !
Ay, there look grim as hell !
DESDEMONA
I hope my noble lord esteems me honest.
OTHELLO
66 O, ay ; as summer flies are in the shambles,
67 That quicken even with blowing. O thou weed,
Who art so lovely fair, and smell'st so sweet,
That the sense aches at thee, would thou hadst ne'er
     been born !
DESDEMONA
Alas, what ignorant sin have I committed ?
OTHELLO
Was this fair paper, this most goodly book,
Made to write 'whore' upon ? What committed ?
73 Committed ? O thou public commoner !
I should make very forges of my cheeks
That would to cinders burn up modesty,
Did I but speak thy deeds. What committed ?
77 Heaven stops the nose at it, and the moon winks ;
The bawdy wind, that kisses all it meets,
Is hushed within the hollow mine of earth
And will not hear it. What committed ?
Impudent strumpet !
DESDEMONA   By heaven, you do me wrong !
OTHELLO
Are not you a strumpet ?
DESDEMONA   No, as I am a Christian !
If to preserve this vessel for my lord
From any other foul unlawful touch
Be not to be a strumpet, I am none.
OTHELLO
What, not a whore ?
DESDEMONA   No, as I shall be saved !
OTHELLO Is't possible ?
DESDEMONA
O, heaven forgive us !

OTHELLO   I cry you mercy then.   88
I took you for that cunning whore of Venice
That married with Othello. – [calling] You, mistress,
That have the office opposite to Saint Peter
And keep the gate of hell !
     Enter Emilia.   You, you, ay, you !
We have done our course ; there's money for your pains :
I pray you turn the key, and keep our counsel.   Exit.
EMILIA
Alas, what does this gentleman conceive ?
How do you, madam ? How do you, my good lady ?
DESDEMONA Faith, half asleep.   97
EMILIA
Good madam, what's the matter with my lord ?
DESDEMONA With who ?
EMILIA Why, with my lord, madam.
DESDEMONA
Who is thy lord ?
EMILIA   He that is yours, sweet lady.
DESDEMONA
I have none. Do not talk to me, Emilia.
I cannot weep ; nor answers have I none
But what should go by water. Prithee to-night
Lay on my bed my wedding sheets, remember ;
And call thy husband hither.
EMILIA   Here's a change indeed ! Exit.
DESDEMONA
'Tis meet I should be used so, very meet.
How have I been behaved, that he might stick
The small'st opinion on my least misuse ?   109
     Enter Iago and Emilia.
IAGO
What is your pleasure, madam ? How is't with you ?
DESDEMONA
I cannot tell. Those that do teach young babes
Do it with gentle means and easy tasks :
He might have chid me so ; for, in good faith,
I am a child to chiding.
IAGO   What is the matter, lady ?
EMILIA
Alas, Iago, my lord hath so bewhored her,
Thrown such despite and heavy terms upon her
As true hearts cannot bear.
DESDEMONA
Am I that name, Iago ?
IAGO   What name, fair lady ?
DESDEMONA
Such as she said my lord did say I was.
EMILIA
He called her whore. A beggar in his drink
Could not have laid such terms upon his callet.   121
IAGO
Why did he so ?
DESDEMONA
I do not know ; I am sure I am none such.
IAGO
Do not weep, do not weep. Alas the day !

---

45 *An instrument* to be the cause   54 *time of scorn* scornful world   62 *turn thy complexion there* change thy color at that point   66 *shambles* slaughterhouse   67 *quicken* come to life   73 *commoner* harlot   77 *winks* closes her eyes   88 *cry you mercy* beg your pardon   97 *half asleep* i.e. stunned   109 *small'st opinion* least suspicion ; *least misuse* slightest misconduct   121 *callet* whore

EMILIA
Hath she forsook so many noble matches,
Her father and her country, and her friends,
To be called whore? Would it not make one weep?

DESDEMONA
It is my wretched fortune.

IAGO   Beshrew him for't!
129 How comes this trick upon him?

DESDEMONA   Nay, heaven doth know.

EMILIA
I will be hanged if some eternal villain,
Some busy and insinuating rogue,
132 Some cogging, cozening slave, to get some office,
Have not devised this slander. I'll be hanged else.

IAGO
Fie, there is no such man! It is impossible.

DESDEMONA
If any such there be, heaven pardon him!

EMILIA
A halter pardon him! and hell gnaw his bones!
Why should he call her whore? Who keeps her
    company?
What place? what time? what form? what likelihood?
The Moor's abused by some most villainous knave,
Some base notorious knave, some scurvy fellow.
141 O heaven, that such companions thou'dst unfold,
And put in every honest hand a whip
To lash the rascals naked through the world
Even from the east to th' west!

144 IAGO   Speak within door.

EMILIA
O, fie upon them! Some such squire he was
That turned your wit the seamy side without
And made you to suspect me with the Moor.

IAGO
You are a fool. Go to.

DESDEMONA   Alas, Iago,
What shall I do to win my lord again?
Good friend, go to him; for, by this light of heaven,
I know not how I lost him. Here I kneel:
If e'er my will did trespass 'gainst his love
153 Either in discourse of thought or actual deed,
Or that mine eyes, mine ears, or any sense
Delighted them in any other form,
Or that I do not yet, and ever did,
And ever will (though he do shake me off
To beggarly divorcement) love him dearly,
159 Comfort forswear me! Unkindness may do much;
160 And his unkindness may defeat my life,
But never taint my love. I cannot say 'whore.'
It does abhor me now I speak the word;
To do the act that might the addition earn
Not the world's mass of vanity could make me.

IAGO
I pray you be content. 'Tis but his humor.
The business of the state does him offense,

[And he does chide with you.]

DESDEMONA
If 'twere no other –

IAGO   'Tis but so, I warrant.
    [Trumpets within.]
Hark how these instruments summon you to supper.
The messengers of Venice stay the meat:
Go in, and weep not. All things shall be well.
                    Exeunt Desdemona and Emilia.
    Enter Roderigo.
How now, Roderigo?

RODERIGO I do not find that thou deal'st justly with me.

IAGO What in the contrary?

RODERIGO Every day thou daff'st me with some device, 175
Iago, and rather, as it seems to me now, keep'st from me
all conveniency than suppliest me with the least ad- 177
vantage of hope. I will indeed no longer endure it; nor
am I yet persuaded to put up in peace what already I
have foolishly suffered.

IAGO Will you hear me, Roderigo?

RODERIGO Faith, I have heard too much; for your words
and performances are no kin together.

IAGO You charge me most unjustly.

RODERIGO With naught but truth. I have wasted myself
out of my means. The jewels you have had from me to
deliver to Desdemona would half have corrupted a
votarist. You have told me she hath received them, and 188
returned me expectations and comforts of sudden re- 189
spect and acquaintance; but I find none.

IAGO Well, go to; very well.

RODERIGO Very well! go to! I cannot go to, man; nor
'tis not very well. By this hand, I say 'tis very scurvy,
and begin to find myself fopped in it.   194

IAGO Very well.

RODERIGO I tell you 'tis not very well. I will make myself
known to Desdemona. If she will return me my jewels,
I will give over my suit and repent my unlawful solicita-
tion; if not, assure yourself I will seek satisfaction of you.

IAGO You have said now.

RODERIGO Ay, and said nothing but what I protest in-
tendment of doing.

IAGO Why, now I see there's mettle in thee; and even
from this instant do build on thee a better opinion than
ever before. Give me thy hand, Roderigo. Thou hast
taken against me a most just exception; but yet I protest
I have dealt most directly in thy affair.   207

RODERIGO It hath not appeared.

IAGO I grant indeed it hath not appeared, and your suspicion is not without wit and judgment. But, Roderigo, if
thou hast that in thee indeed which I have greater reason
to believe now than ever, I mean purpose, courage, and
valor, this night show it. If thou the next night following
enjoy not Desdemona, take me from this world with
treachery and devise engines for my life.   215

RODERIGO Well, what is it? Is it within reason and compass?

IAGO Sir, there is especial commission come from Venice
to depute Cassio in Othello's place.

RODERIGO Is that true? Why, then Othello and Desdemona return again to Venice.

IAGO O, no; he goes into Mauritania and takes away with
him the fair Desdemona, unless his abode be lingered 222
here by some accident; wherein none can be so deter- 223
minate as the removing of Cassio.

---

129 *trick* freakish behavior 132 *cogging, cozening* cheating, defrauding
141 *companions* rogues; *unfold* expose 144 *within door* with restraint
153 *discourse* course 159 *Comfort forswear* happiness forsake 160 *defeat*
destroy 175 *thou . . . device* you put me off with some trick 177 *conveniency* favorable opportunities 188 *votarist* nun 189 *sudden respect*
immediate notice 194 *fopped* duped 207 *directly* straightforwardly
215 *engines for* plots against 222-23 *abode . . . here* stay here be extended
223 *determinate* effective

RODERIGO How do you mean removing of him?

IAGO Why, by making him uncapable of Othello's place –
knocking out his brains.

RODERIGO And that you would have me to do?

IAGO Ay, if you dare do yourself a profit and a right. He
sups to-night with a harlotry, and thither will I go to
him. He knows not yet of his honorable fortune. If you
will watch his going thence, which I will fashion to fall
out between twelve and one, you may take him at your
pleasure. I will be near to second your attempt, and he
shall fall between us. Come, stand not amazed at it, but
go along with me. I will show you such a necessity in his
death that you shall think yourself bound to put it on
him. It is now high supper time, and the night grows to
waste. About it!

RODERIGO I will hear further reason for this.

IAGO And you shall be satisfied.   *Exeunt.*

*

IV, iii   *Enter Othello, Lodovico, Desdemona, Emilia, and
Attendants.*

LODOVICO
I do beseech you, sir, trouble yourself no further.

OTHELLO
O, pardon me; 'twill do me good to walk.

LODOVICO
Madam, good night. I humbly thank your ladyship.

DESDEMONA
Your honor is most welcome.

OTHELLO   Will you walk, sir?
O, Desdemona –

DESDEMONA My lord?

OTHELLO Get you to bed on th' instant; I will be returned forthwith. Dismiss your attendant there. Look't
be done.

DESDEMONA I will, my lord.
                    Exit [Othello, with Lodovico and Attendants].

EMILIA How goes it now? He looks gentler than he did.

DESDEMONA
11   He says he will return incontinent.
He hath commanded me to go to bed,
And bade me to dismiss you.

EMILIA   Dismiss me?

DESDEMONA
It was his bidding; therefore, good Emilia,
Give me my nightly wearing, and adieu.
We must not now displease him.

EMILIA I would you had never seen him!

DESDEMONA
So would not I. My love doth so approve him
19   That even his stubbornness, his checks, his frowns –
Prithee unpin me – have grace and favor in them.

EMILIA I have laid those sheets you bade me on the bed.

DESDEMONA
All's one. Good faith, how foolish are our minds!
If I do die before thee, prithee shroud me
In one of those same sheets.

EMILIA   Come, come! You talk.

DESDEMONA
My mother had a maid called Barbary.
26   She was in love; and he she loved proved mad
And did forsake her. She had a song of 'Willow';
An old thing 'twas; but it expressed her fortune,

And she died singing it. That song to-night
Will not go from my mind; I have much to do
But to go hang my head all at one side
And sing it like poor Barbary. Prithee dispatch.

EMILIA
Shall I go fetch your nightgown?   33

DESDEMONA   No, unpin me here.
This Lodovico is a proper man.

EMILIA A very handsome man.

DESDEMONA He speaks well.

EMILIA I know a lady in Venice would have walked barefoot to Palestine for a touch of his nether lip.

DESDEMONA *(sings)*
'The poor soul sat sighing by a sycamore tree,
          Sing all a green willow;
Her hand on her bosom, her head on her knee,
          Sing willow, willow, willow.
The fresh streams ran by her and murmured her
          moans;
          Sing willow, willow, willow;
Her salt tears fell from her, and soft'ned the stones' –
Lay by these.
          'Sing willow, willow, willow' –
Prithee hie thee; he'll come anon.   48
          'Sing all a green willow must be my garland.
          Let nobody blame him; his scorn I approve' –
Nay, that's not next. Hark! who is't that knocks?

EMILIA It's the wind.

DESDEMONA *[sings]*
'I called my love false love; but what said he then?
          Sing willow, willow, willow:
          If I court moe women, you'll couch with moe men.'
So, get thee gone; good night. Mine eyes do itch.
Doth that bode weeping?

EMILIA   'Tis neither here nor there.

DESDEMONA
I have heard it said so. O, these men, these men!
Dost thou in conscience think – tell me, Emilia –
That there be women do abuse their husbands   60
In such gross kind?

EMILIA   There be some such, no question.

DESDEMONA
Wouldst thou do such a deed for all the world?

EMILIA
Why, would not you?

DESDEMONA   No, by this heavenly light!

EMILIA
Nor I neither by this heavenly light.
I might do't as well i' th' dark.

DESDEMONA
Wouldst thou do such a deed for all the world?

EMILIA The world's a huge thing; it is a great price for a
small vice.

DESDEMONA
In troth, I think thou wouldst not.

EMILIA In troth, I think I should; and undo't when I
had done it. Marry, I would not do such a thing for a
joint-ring, nor for measures of lawn, nor for gowns,   72
petticoats, nor caps, nor any petty exhibition; but, for   73

IV, iii *Within the castle* 11 *incontinent* at once 19 *stubbornness* roughness; *checks* rebukes 26 *mad* wild, faithless 33 *nightgown* dressing
gown 48 *hie thee* hurry 72 *joint-ring* ring made in separable halves
73 *exhibition* gift

all the whole world – 'Ud's pity ! who would not make
her husband a cuckold to make him a monarch ? I
should venture purgatory for't.

DESDEMONA
Beshrew me if I would do such a wrong
For the whole world.

EMILIA Why, the wrong is but a wrong i' th' world ; and
having the world for your labor, 'tis a wrong in your
own world, and you might quickly make it right.

DESDEMONA I do not think there is any such woman.

83 EMILIA Yes, a dozen ; and as many to th' vantage as
84 would store the world they played for.
But I do think it is their husbands' faults
If wives do fall. Say that they slack their duties
And pour our treasures into foreign laps ;
88 Or else break out in peevish jealousies,
Throwing restraint upon us ; or say they strike us,
90 Or scant our former having in despite –
91 Why, we have galls ; and though we have some grace,
Yet have we some revenge. Let husbands know
Their wives have sense like them. They see, and smell,
And have their palates both for sweet and sour,
As husbands have. What is it that they do
When they change us for others ? Is it sport ?
I think it is. And doth affection breed it ?
I think it doth. Is't frailty that thus errs ?
It is so too. And have not we affections,
Desires for sport, and frailty, as men have ?
Then let them use us well ; else let them know,
The ills we do, their ills instruct us so.

DESDEMONA
103 Good night, good night. God me such usage send,
Not to pick bad from bad, but by bad mend !   *Exeunt.*

*

V, i   *Enter Iago and Roderigo.*

IAGO
1 Here, stand behind this bulk ; straight will he come.
Wear thy good rapier bare, and put it home.
Quick, quick ! Fear nothing ; I'll be at thy elbow.
It makes us, or it mars us – think on that,
And fix most firm thy resolution.

RODERIGO
Be near at hand ; I may miscarry in't.

IAGO
Here, at thy hand. Be bold, and take thy stand.
     [Stands aside.]

RODERIGO
I have no great devotion to the deed,
And yet he hath given me satisfying reasons.
'Tis but a man gone. Forth my sword ! He dies !

IAGO
11 I have rubbed this young quat almost to the sense,
And he grows angry. Now whether he kill Cassio,
Or Cassio him, or each do kill the other,
Every way makes my gain. Live Roderigo,
He calls me to a restitution large

Of gold and jewels that I bobbed from him   16
As gifts to Desdemona.
It must not be. If Cassio do remain,
He hath a daily beauty in his life
That makes me ugly ; and besides, the Moor
May unfold me to him ; there stand I in much peril.
No, he must die. Be't so ! I hear him coming.
     Enter Cassio.

RODERIGO
I know his gait. 'Tis he. Villain, thou diest !
     [Makes a pass at Cassio.]

CASSIO
That thrust had been mine enemy indeed
But that my coat is better than thou know'st.   25
I will make proof of thine.
     [Draws, and wounds Roderigo.]

RODERIGO   O, I am slain !
     [Iago darts from concealment behind Cassio,
             wounds him in the leg, and exit.]

CASSIO
I am maimed for ever. Help, ho ! Murder ! murder !
     [Falls.]
     Enter Othello.

OTHELLO
The voice of Cassio. Iago keeps his word.

RODERIGO
O, villain that I am !

OTHELLO   It is even so.

CASSIO
O, help, ho ! light ! a surgeon !

OTHELLO
'Tis he. O brave Iago, honest and just,
That hast such noble sense of thy friend's wrong !
Thou teachest me. Minion, your dear lies dead,   33
And your unblest fate hies. Strumpet, I come.   34
Forth of my heart those charms, thine eyes, are blotted.
Thy bed, lust-stained, shall with lust's blood be spotted.
     Exit Othello.

     Enter Lodovico and Gratiano.

CASSIO
What, ho ? No watch ? No passage ? Murder ! murder !   37

GRATIANO
'Tis some mischance. The cry is very direful.

CASSIO O, help !

LODOVICO Hark !

RODERIGO O wretched villain !

LODOVICO
Two or three groan. It is a heavy night.   42
These may be counterfeits. Let's think't unsafe
To come in to the cry without more help.

RODERIGO
Nobody come ? Then shall I bleed to death.

LODOVICO Hark !
     Enter Iago, with a light.

GRATIANO
Here's one comes in his shirt, with light and weapons.

IAGO
Who's there ? Whose noise is this that cries on murder ?   48

LODOVICO
We do not know.

IAGO   Did not you hear a cry ?

CASSIO
Here, here ! For heaven's sake, help me !

IAGO   What's the matter ?

83 *to th' vantage* besides   84 *store* populate   88 *peevish* senseless   90
having allowance   91 *galls* spirits to resent   103 *usage* habits
V, i A street in Cyprus   1 *bulk* projecting shop-front   11 *quat* pimple ;
sense quick   16 *bobbed* swindled   25 *coat* under-shirt of mail   33 *Minion*
mistress   34 *hies* hurries on   37 *passage* passers-by   42 *heavy* cloudy,
dark   48 *cries on* raises the cry of

239

GRATIANO
This is Othello's ancient, as I take it.

LODOVICO
The same indeed, a very valiant fellow.

IAGO
What are you here that cry so grievously?

CASSIO
Iago? O, I am spoiled, undone by villains!
Give me some help.

IAGO
O me, lieutenant! What villains have done this?

CASSIO
I think that one of them is hereabout
58   And cannot make away.

IAGO   O treacherous villains!
[To Lodovico and Gratiano]
What are you there? Come in, and give some help.

RODERIGO
O, help me here!

CASSIO
That's one of them.

IAGO   O murd'rous slave! O villain!
[Stabs Roderigo.]

RODERIGO
O damned Iago! O inhuman dog!

IAGO
Kill men i' th' dark? – Where be these bloody thieves? –
How silent is this town! – Ho! murder! murder! –
What may you be? Are you of good or evil?

LODOVICO
As you shall prove us, praise us.

IAGO Signior Lodovico?

LODOVICO He, sir.

IAGO
I cry you mercy. Here's Cassio hurt by villains.

GRATIANO Cassio?

IAGO How is't, brother?

CASSIO
My leg is cut in two.

72 **IAGO**   Marry, heaven forbid!
Light, gentleman. I'll bind it with my shirt.
Enter Bianca.

BIANCA
What is the matter, ho? Who is't that cried?

IAGO
Who is't that cried?

BIANCA
O my dear Cassio! my sweet Cassio!
O Cassio, Cassio, Cassio!

IAGO
O notable strumpet! – Cassio, may you suspect
Who they should be that have thus mangled you?

CASSIO No.

GRATIANO I am sorry to find you thus. I have been to
seek you.

IAGO
82   Lend me a garter. So. O for a chair
To bear him easily hence!

BIANCA
Alas, he faints! O Cassio, Cassio, Cassio!

IAGO
Gentlemen all, I do suspect this trash
To be a party in this injury. –
Patience awhile, good Cassio. – Come, come!

Lend me a light. Know we this face or no?
Alas, my friend and my dear countryman
Roderigo? No. – Yes, sure. – O heaven, Roderigo!

GRATIANO What, of Venice?

IAGO
Even he, sir. Did you know him?

GRATIANO   Know him? Ay.

IAGO
Signior Gratiano? I cry your gentle pardon.
These bloody accidents must excuse my manners
That so neglected you.

GRATIANO   I am glad to see you.

IAGO
How do you, Cassio? – O, a chair, a chair!

GRATIANO Roderigo?

IAGO
He, he, 'tis he!
[A chair brought in.] O, that's well said; the chair.   98
Some good man bear him carefully from hence.
I'll fetch the general's surgeon.
[To Bianca]   For you, mistress,
Save you your labor. – He that lies slain here, Cassio,
Was my dear friend. What malice was between you?

CASSIO
None in the world; nor do I know the man.

IAGO *[to Bianca]*
What, look you pale? – O, bear him out o' th' air.
                    [Cassio and Roderigo are borne off.]
Stay you, good gentlemen. – Look you pale, mistress? –
Do you perceive the gastness of her eye? –   106
Nay, if you stare, we shall hear more anon.
Behold her well; I pray you look upon her.
Do you see, gentlemen? Nay, guiltiness will speak,
Though tongues were out of use.
                    Enter Emilia.

EMILIA
'Las, what's the matter? What's the matter, husband?

IAGO
Cassio hath here been set on in the dark
By Roderigo, and fellows that are scaped.
He's almost slain, and Roderigo dead.

EMILIA
Alas, good gentleman! alas, good Cassio!

IAGO
This is the fruits of whoring. Prithee, Emilia,
Go know of Cassio where he supped to-night.
[To Bianca]
What, do you shake at that?

BIANCA
He supped at my house; but I therefore shake not.

IAGO
O, did he so? I charge you go with me.

EMILIA
Fie, fie upon thee, strumpet!

BIANCA
I am no strumpet, but of life as honest   122
As you that thus abuse me.

EMILIA   As I? Foh! fie upon thee!

IAGO
Kind gentlemen, let's go see poor Cassio dressed.
[To Bianca]

---

58 *make* get   72 *Marry* (from By Mary)   82 *chair* litter   98 *well said*
well done   106 *gastness* terror   122 *honest* chaste

Come, mistress, you must tell's another tale.
Emilia, run you to the citadel
And tell my lord and lady what hath happed.

                     [Exit Emilia.]
Will you go on afore ?   *Exeunt [all but Iago].*
         This is the night

129   That either makes me or fordoes me quite.   *[Exit.]*

                 *

V, ii   *Desdemona [asleep] in her bed. Enter Othello with a light.*

OTHELLO

1   It is the cause, it is the cause, my soul.
Let me not name it to you, you chaste stars !
It is the cause. Yet I'll not shed her blood,
Nor scar that whiter skin of hers than snow,
And smooth as monumental alabaster.
Yet she must die, else she'll betray more men.
Put out the light, and then put out the light.

8   If I quench thee, thou flaming minister,
I can again thy former light restore,
Should I repent me ; but once put out thy light,
Thou cunning'st pattern of excelling nature,

12   I know not where is that Promethean heat

13   That can thy light relume. When I have plucked the rose,
I cannot give it vital growth again ;
It needs must wither. I'll smell thee on the tree.
       He kisses her.
O balmy breath, that dost almost persuade
Justice to break her sword ! One more, one more !
Be thus when thou art dead, and I will kill thee,
And love thee after. One more, and that's the last !
So sweet was ne'er so fatal. I must weep,
But they are cruel tears. This sorrow 's heavenly ;
It strikes where it doth love. She wakes.

DESDEMONA

Who's there ? Othello ?

OTHELLO   Ay, Desdemona.

DESDEMONA

Will you come to bed, my lord ?

OTHELLO

Have you prayed to-night, Desdemon ?

DESDEMONA   Ay, my lord.

OTHELLO

26   If you bethink yourself of any crime
Unreconciled as yet to heaven and grace,
Solicit for it straight.

DESDEMONA

Alack, my lord, what may you mean by that ?

OTHELLO

Well, do it, and be brief ; I will walk by.
I would not kill thy unpreparèd spirit.

32   No, heaven forfend ! I would not kill thy soul.

DESDEMONA

Talk you of killing ?

OTHELLO   Ay, I do.

DESDEMONA   Then heaven
Have mercy on me !

OTHELLO   Amen, with all my heart !

DESDEMONA

If you say so, I hope you will not kill me.

OTHELLO Hum !

DESDEMONA

And yet I fear you ; for you're fatal then
When your eyes roll so. Why I should fear I know not,
Since guiltiness I know not ; but yet I feel I fear.

OTHELLO

Think on thy sins.

DESDEMONA   They are loves I bear to you.

OTHELLO

Ay, and for that thou diest.

DESDEMONA

That death 's unnatural that kills for loving.
Alas, why gnaw you so your nether lip ?
Some bloody passion shakes your very frame.
These are portents ; but yet I hope, I hope,   45
They do not point on me.

OTHELLO   Peace and be still !

DESDEMONA

I will so. What's the matter ?

OTHELLO

That handkerchief which I so loved and gave thee
Thou gav'st to Cassio.

DESDEMONA   No, by my life and soul !
Send for the man and ask him.

OTHELLO   Sweet soul, take heed,
Take heed of perjury ; thou art on thy deathbed.

DESDEMONA

Ay, but not yet to die.

OTHELLO   Yes, presently.   52
Therefore confess thee freely of thy sin ;
For to deny each article with oath
Cannot remove nor choke the strong conception   55
That I do groan withal. Thou art to die.

DESDEMONA

Then Lord have mercy on me !

OTHELLO   I say amen.

DESDEMONA

And have you mercy too ! I never did
Offend you in my life ; never loved Cassio   59
But with such general warranty of heaven
As I might love. I never gave him token.

OTHELLO

By heaven, I saw my handkerchief in's hand !
O perjured woman ! thou dost stone my heart,   63
And mak'st me call what I intend to do
A murder, which I thought a sacrifice.
I saw the handkerchief.

DESDEMONA   He found it then.
I never gave it him. Send for him hither.
Let him confess a truth.

OTHELLO   He hath confessed.

DESDEMONA

What, my lord ?

OTHELLO

That he hath used thee.

DESDEMONA   How ? unlawfully ?

OTHELLO   Ay.

DESDEMONA

He will not say so.

OTHELLO   No, his mouth is stopped.
Honest Iago hath ta'en order for't.   72

---

129 *fordoes* destroys
V, ii A bedchamber in the castle   **1** *cause* cause of justice   **8** *minister*
servant   **12** *Promethean heat* divine fire   **13** *relume* relight   **26** *crime* sin
32 *forfend* forbid   **45** *portents* signs of impending violence   **52** *presently*
at once   **55** *conception* belief   **59** *Offend* wrong   **63** *stone my heart* turn
my heart to stone   **72** *ta'en order* taken measures

DESDEMONA
O, my fear interprets. What, is he dead?
OTHELLO
Had all his hairs been lives, my great revenge
Had stomach for them all.
DESDEMONA
Alas, he is betrayed, and I undone!
OTHELLO
Out, strumpet! Weep'st thou for him to my face?
DESDEMONA
O, banish me, my lord, but kill me not!
OTHELLO
Down, strumpet!
DESDEMONA
80   Kill me to-morrow; let me live to-night!
OTHELLO
Nay, if you strive —
DESDEMONA
But half an hour!
OTHELLO   Being done, there is no pause.
DESDEMONA
But while I say one prayer!
OTHELLO   It is too late.
        Smothers her.
[DESDEMONA   O Lord, Lord, Lord!]
        Emilia at the door.
EMILIA *(calls within)*
My lord, my lord! What, ho! my lord, my lord!
OTHELLO
What noise is this? Not dead? not yet quite dead?
I that am cruel am yet merciful;
I would not have thee linger in thy pain.
So, so.
EMILIA *(within)*
What, ho! my lord, my lord!
OTHELLO   Who's there?
EMILIA *[within]*
O, good my lord, I would speak a word with you!
OTHELLO
92   Yes, 'tis Emilia. — By and by. — She's dead. —
'Tis like she comes to speak of Cassio's death.
The noise was here. Ha! no more moving?
Still as the grave. — Shall she come in? Were't good? —
I think she stirs again. No. — What's best to do?
If she come in, she'll sure speak to my wife.
My wife! my wife! what wife? I have no wife.
O, insupportable! O heavy hour!
Methinks it should be now a huge eclipse
Of sun and moon, and that th' affrighted globe
102 Should yawn at alteration.
EMILIA *[within]*   I do beseech you
That I may speak with you, O good my lord!
OTHELLO
I had forgot thee. O, come in, Emilia.
Soft, by and by. — Let me the curtains draw. —
        [Closes the bed-curtains.]
Where art thou?
        [Opens the door.]
        Enter Emilia.
                        What's the matter with thee now?
EMILIA
O my good lord, yonder's foul murder done!
OTHELLO   What? Now?
EMILIA   But now, my lord.

OTHELLO
It is the very error of the moon.   110
She comes more nearer earth than she was wont
And makes men mad.
EMILIA
Cassio, my lord, hath killed a young Venetian
Called Roderigo.
OTHELLO   Roderigo killed?
And Cassio killed?
EMILIA   No, Cassio is not killed.
OTHELLO
Not Cassio killed? Then murder 's out of tune,
And sweet revenge grows harsh.
DESDEMONA
O, falsely, falsely murdered!
EMILIA   O Lord! what cry is that?
OTHELLO   That? What?
EMILIA
Out and alas! that was my lady's voice.
Help! help, ho! help! O lady, speak again!
Sweet Desdemona! O sweet mistress, speak!
DESDEMONA
A guiltless death I die.
EMILIA
O, who hath done this deed?
DESDEMONA
Nobody — I myself. Farewell.
Commend me to my kind lord. O, farewell!   126
        She dies.
OTHELLO
Why, how should she be murd'red?
EMILIA   Alas, who knows?
OTHELLO
You heard her say herself, it was not I.
EMILIA
She said so. I must needs report the truth.
OTHELLO
She's like a liar gone to burning hell!
'Twas I that killed her.
EMILIA   O, the more angel she,
And you the blacker devil!
OTHELLO
She turned to folly, and she was a whore.
EMILIA
Thou dost belie her, and thou art a devil.
OTHELLO
She was false as water.   135
EMILIA   Thou art rash as fire to say
That she was false. O, she was heavenly true!
OTHELLO
Cassio did top her. Ask thy husband else.
O, I were damned beneath all depth in hell
But that I did proceed upon just grounds
To this extremity. Thy husband knew it all.
EMILIA   My husband?
OTHELLO   Thy husband.
EMILIA
That she was false to wedlock?
OTHELLO
Ay, with Cassio. Nay, had she been true,

92 *By and by* just a moment (addressed to Emilia) 102 *yawn* open, as in
an earthquake 110 *error* straying off course 126 *Commend* remember
135 *water* (which is yielding)

If heaven would make me such another world

146 Of one entire and perfect chrysolite,
I'ld not have sold her for it.

EMILIA
My husband?

OTHELLO   Ay, 'twas he that told me first.
An honest man he is, and hates the slime
That sticks on filthy deeds.

EMILIA   My husband?

OTHELLO
151 What needs this iterance, woman? I say thy husband.

EMILIA
O mistress, villainy hath made mocks with love!
My husband say that she was false?

OTHELLO   He, woman.
I say, thy husband. Dost understand the word?
My friend, thy husband; honest, honest Iago.

EMILIA
If he say so, may his pernicious soul
Rot half a grain a day! he lies to th' heart.
She was too fond of her most filthy bargain.

OTHELLO Ha!

EMILIA Do thy worst.
This deed of thine is no more worthy heaven
Than thou wast worthy her.

OTHELLO   Peace, you were best.

EMILIA
Thou hast not half the power to do me harm
164 As I have to be hurt. O gull! O dolt!
As ignorant as dirt! thou hast done a deed –
I care not for thy sword; I'll make thee known,
Though I lost twenty lives. Help! help! Ho! help!
The Moor hath killed my mistress! Murder! murder!
            Enter Montano, Gratiano, Iago, and others.

MONTANO
What is the matter? How now, general?

EMILIA
170 O, are you come, Iago? You have done well,
That men must lay their murders on your neck.

GRATIANO
What is the matter?

EMILIA
Disprove this villain, if thou be'st a man.
He says thou told'st him that his wife was false.
I know thou didst not; thou'rt not such a villain.
Speak, for my heart is full.

IAGO
I told him what I thought, and told no more
Than what he found himself was apt and true.

EMILIA
But did you ever tell him she was false?

IAGO I did.

EMILIA
You told a lie, an odious damnèd lie!
Upon my soul, a lie! a wicked lie!
She false with Cassio? Did you say with Cassio?

IAGO
184 With Cassio, mistress. Go to, charm your tongue.

146 *chrysolite* (precious topaz) 151 *iterance* repetition 164 *to be hurt*
to endure hurt 184 *charm* cast a spell on 204 *shows* appears 208 *turn*
act 210 *reprobation* rejection by God, damnation 214 *gratify* reward
215 *recognizance* token 221 *liberal as the north* unchecked as the north
wind blows

EMILIA
I will not charm my tongue; I am bound to speak:
My mistress here lies murdered in her bed –

ALL
O heavens forfend!

EMILIA
And your reports have set the murder on.

OTHELLO
Nay, stare not, masters. It is true indeed.

GRATIANO
'Tis a strange truth.   190

MONTANO
O monstrous act!

EMILIA   Villainy, villainy, villainy!
I think upon't – I think I smell't! – O villainy!
I thought so then. – I'll kill myself for grief. –
O villainy, villainy!

IAGO
What, are you mad? I charge you get you home.

EMILIA
Good gentlemen, let me have leave to speak.
'Tis proper I obey him, but not now.
Perchance, Iago, I will ne'er go home.

OTHELLO
O! O! O!
            Falls on the bed.

EMILIA   Nay, lay thee down and roar!
For thou hast killed the sweetest innocent
That e'er did lift up eye.

OTHELLO   O, she was foul!
            [*Rises.*]
I scarce did know you, uncle. There lies your niece,
Whose breath, indeed, these hands have newly stopped.
I know this act shows horrible and grim.   204

GRATIANO
Poor Desdemon! I am glad thy father's dead.
Thy match was mortal to him, and pure grief
Shore his old thread in twain. Did he live now,
This sight would make him do a desperate turn;   208
Yea, curse his better angel from his side,
And fall to reprobation.   210

OTHELLO
'Tis pitiful; but yet Iago knows
That she with Cassio hath the act of shame
A thousand times committed. Cassio confessed it;
And she did gratify his amorous works   214
With that recognizance and pledge of love   215
Which I first gave her. I saw it in his hand.
It was a handkerchief, an antique token
My father gave my mother.

EMILIA
O God! O heavenly God!

IAGO
Zounds, hold your peace!

EMILIA   'Twill out, 'twill out! I peace?
No, I will speak as liberal as the north.   221
Let heaven and men and devils, let them all,
All, all, cry shame against me, yet I'll speak.

IAGO
Be wise, and get you home.

EMILIA   I will not.
            [*Iago draws and threatens Emilia.*]

GRATIANO   Fie!
Your sword upon a woman?

EMILIA
O thou dull Moor, that handkerchief thou speak'st of
I found by fortune, and did give my husband ;
For often with a solemn earnestness –
More than indeed belonged to such a trifle –
He begged of me to steal't.

IAGO   Villainous whore !

EMILIA
She give it Cassio ? No, alas, I found it,
And I did give't my husband.

IAGO   Filth, thou liest !

EMILIA
By heaven, I do not, I do not, gentlemen.
O murd'rous coxcomb ! what should such a fool
Do with so good a wife ?

235 OTHELLO   Are there no stones in heaven
But what serves for the thunder ? Precious villain !
     The Moor runs at Iago [but is disarmed by Montano].
     Iago kills his wife.

GRATIANO
The woman falls. Sure he hath killed his wife.

EMILIA
Ay, ay. O, lay me by my mistress' side.   *Exit Iago.*

GRATIANO
He's gone, but his wife 's killed.

MONTANO
240 'Tis a notorious villain. Take you this weapon,
Which I have here recovered from the Moor.
Come, guard the door without. Let him not pass,
But kill him rather. I'll after that same villain,
For 'tis a damnèd slave.
     Exit [Montano, with all but Othello and Emilia].

OTHELLO   I am not valiant neither ;
245 But every puny whipster gets my sword.
But why should honor outlive honesty ?
Let it go all.

EMILIA   What did thy song bode, lady ?
Hark, canst thou hear me ? I will play the swan,
And die in music. *[Sings]* 'Willow, willow, willow.'
Moor, she was chaste. She loved thee, cruel Moor :
So come my soul to bliss as I speak true.
So speaking as I think, alas, I die.
     She dies.

OTHELLO
I have another weapon in this chamber ;
254 It is a sword of Spain, the ice brook's temper.
O, here it is. – Uncle, I must come forth.

GRATIANO *(within)*
If thou attempt it, it will cost thee dear.
Thou hast no weapon, and perforce must suffer.

OTHELLO
Look in upon me then and speak with me,
259 Or, naked as I am, I will assault thee.
     [Enter Gratiano.]

GRATIANO
What is the matter ?

OTHELLO   Behold, I have a weapon ;
A better never did itself sustain
Upon a soldier's thigh. I have seen the day
That with this little arm and this good sword
I have made my way through more impediments
265 Than twenty times your stop. But O vain boast !
Who can control his fate ? 'Tis not so now.
Be not afraid, though you do see me weaponed.

Here is my journey's end, here is my butt,   268
And very seamark of my utmost sail: 269
Do you go back dismayed ? 'Tis a lost fear.   270
Man but a rush against Othello's breast,   271
And he retires. Where should Othello go ?
Now, how dost thou look now ? O ill-starred wench !
Pale as thy smock ! When we shall meet at compt,   274
This look of thine will hurl my soul from heaven,
And fiends will snatch at it. Cold, cold, my girl ?
Even like thy chastity.
O cursèd, cursèd slave ! Whip me, ye devils,
From the possession of this heavenly sight !
Blow me about in winds ! roast me in sulphur !
Wash me in steep-down gulfs of liquid fire !
Oh Desdemon ! dead Desdemon ! dead ! Oh ! Oh !
     Enter Lodovico, Montano, Iago [as prisoner,] and
     Officers ; Cassio in a chair.

LODOVICO
Where is this rash and most unfortunate man ?

OTHELLO
That's he that was Othello. Here I am.

LODOVICO
Where is that viper ? Bring the villain forth.

OTHELLO
I look down towards his feet – but that's a fable.   286
If that thou be'st a devil, I cannot kill thee.
     [Wounds Iago.]

LODOVICO
Wrench his sword from him.
     [Othello is disarmed.]

IAGO   I bleed, sir, but not killed.

OTHELLO
I am not sorry neither. I'ld have thee live ;
For in my sense, 'tis happiness to die.

LODOVICO
O thou Othello that wert once so good,
Fall'n in the practice of a damnèd slave,   292
What shall be said to thee ?

OTHELLO   Why, anything :
An honorable murderer, if you will ;
For naught did I in hate, but all in honor.

LODOVICO
This wretch hath part confessed his villainy.
Did you and he consent in Cassio's death ?   297

OTHELLO Ay.

CASSIO
Dear general, I never gave you cause.

OTHELLO
I do believe it, and I ask your pardon.
Will you, I pray, demand that demi-devil
Why he hath thus ensnared my soul and body ?

IAGO
Demand me nothing. What you know, you know.
From this time forth I never will speak word.

LODOVICO
What, not to pray ?

GRATIANO   Torments will ope your lips.

---

235 *stones* bolts like those used for thunderbolts   **240** *notorious* notable
245 *puny whipster* top-whipping boy   **254** *ice brook's* i.e. a Spanish blade,
tempered in cold running water   **259** *naked* disarmed   **265** *stop* power
to stop   **268** *butt* limit   **269** *seamark* beacon, destination   **270** *lost*
wasted   **271** *Man but a rush* wield only a reed   **274** *compt* final accounting,
Last Judgment   **286** *I . . . feet* i.e. to see if they are cloven, like the Devil's
292 *practice* plot   **297** *consent in* agree upon

OTHELLO
  Well, thou dost best.

LODOVICO
  Sir, you shall understand what hath befall'n,
  Which, as I think, you know not. Here is a letter
  Found in the pocket of the slain Roderigo ;
310 And here another. The one of them imports
  The death of Cassio to be undertook
  By Roderigo.

OTHELLO
  O villain !

CASSIO   Most heathenish and most gross !

LODOVICO
  Now here's another discontented paper
  Found in his pocket too ; and this, it seems,
  Roderigo meant t' have sent this damnèd villain ;
317 But that, belike, Iago in the nick
  Came in and satisfied him.

OTHELLO   O thou pernicious caitiff ! –
  How came you, Cassio, by that handkerchief
  That was my wife's ?

CASSIO   I found it in my chamber ;
  And he himself confessed but even now
  That there he dropped it for a special purpose
  Which wrought to his desire.

OTHELLO   O fool ! fool ! fool !

CASSIO
  There is besides in Roderigo's letter,
  How he upbraids Iago that he made him
  Brave me upon the watch ; whereon it came
327 That I was cast ; and even but now he spake,
  After long seeming dead – Iago hurt him,
  Iago set him on.

LODOVICO
  You must forsake this room and go with us.
  Your power and your command is taken off,
  And Cassio rules in Cyprus. For this slave,
  If there be any cunning cruelty
  That can torment him much and hold him long,

---

317 *nick* nick of time   327 *cast* dismissed   341 *unlucky* fatal   346 *Perplexed* distracted   347 *Judean* Judas Iscariot (?) (quarto reads 'Indian') 348 *subdued* i.e. conquered by grief   357 *period* ending   362 *fell* cruel 365 *Let it be hid* i.e. draw the bed curtains   366 *seize upon* take legal possession of   368 *censure* judicial sentence

It shall be his. You shall close prisoner rest
Till that the nature of your fault be known
To the Venetian state. Come, bring away.

OTHELLO
  Soft you ! a word or two before you go.
  I have done the state some service, and they know't.
  No more of that. I pray you, in your letters,
  When you shall these unlucky deeds relate,   341
  Speak of me as I am. Nothing extenuate,
  Nor set down aught in malice. Then must you speak
  Of one that loved not wisely, but too well ;
  Of one not easily jealous, but, being wrought,
  Perplexed in the extreme ; of one whose hand,   346
  Like the base Judean, threw a pearl away   347
  Richer than all his tribe ; of one whose subdued eyes,   348
  Albeit unusèd to the melting mood,
  Drop tears as fast as the Arabian trees
  Their med'cinable gum. Set you down this.
  And say besides that in Aleppo once,
  Where a malignant and a turbaned Turk
  Beat a Venetian and traduced the state,
  I took by th' throat the circumcisèd dog
  And smote him – thus.
       He stabs himself.

LODOVICO
  O bloody period !   357

GRATIANO   All that's spoke is marred.

OTHELLO
  I kissed thee ere I killed thee. No way but this,
  Killing myself, to die upon a kiss.
       He [falls upon the bed and] dies.

CASSIO
  This did I fear, but thought he had no weapon ;
  For he was great of heart.

LODOVICO *[to Iago]*   O Spartan dog,
  More fell than anguish, hunger, or the sea !   362
  Look on the tragic loading of this bed.
  This is thy work. The object poisons sight ;
  Let it be hid. Gratiano, keep the house,   365
  And seize upon the fortunes of the Moor,   366
  For they succeed on you. To you, lord governor,
  Remains the censure of this hellish villain,   368
  The time, the place, the torture. O, enforce it !
  Myself will straight aboard, and to the state
  This heavy act with heavy heart relate.   *Exeunt.*

Listed below are all departures from the folio text (F) except for the correction of a few obvious typographical errors and the addition of the bracketed lines mentioned in the "Note on the text." The great majority of these departures represent readings in the quarto (Q), the copy for which may have been a transcript of Shakespeare's draft. Although not printed until 1622, the quarto text remains totally unaffected by the Parliamentary ruling against the use of oaths in stage plays theoretically in force since 1606. On the other hand the folio text, which appears to have derived from the quarto collated with a prompt-book, reveals an unusual scrupulousness in observing this ruling. Perhaps the chief interest in the following list of variants in quarto and folio is the indication of the great variety of expressions which the acting company feared might be considered "oaths." Also of interest is the list of substitutes found for them. The adopted reading in italics is followed by the folio reading in roman.

The Names of the Actors (printed at the end of the play in F)

I, i, 1 *Tush* (Q) Omitted   4 *'Sblood* (Q) Omitted   25 *togèd* (Q) Tongued   30 *Christian* (Q) Christen'd   33 *God* (Q) Omitted   66 *full* (Q) fall   72 *changes* (Q) chances   79 *Thieves! thieves! thieves!* (Q) Theeues, Theeues   81 s.d. *Brabantio at a window* (Q) Omitted   86 *Zounds* (Q) Omitted   103 *spirit* (Q) spirits *them* (Q) their   108 *Zounds* (Q) Omitted   116 *now* (Q) Omitted   122 *odd-even* (Malone) odde Euen   145 *produced* (Q) producted   150 *stand* (Pope) stands   153 *hell-pains* (Dyce) hell apines (F) hells paines (Q)   158 s.d. *and ... with* (Q) with ... and *in his nightgown* (Q) Omitted   181 *night* (Q) might   182 *I'll* (Q) I Will

I, ii, s.d. *and* (Q) Omitted   4 *Sometimes* (Q) Sometime   15 *and* (Q) or   33 s.d. *Officers* (Q) Omitted   34 *Duke* (Q) Dukes   38 *What's* (Q) What is   54 s.d. *and others ... weapons* (Q) with Officers, and Torches   68 *darlings* (Q) Deareling   75 *weaken* (Rowe) weakens   84 *Where* (Q) Whether

I, iii, s.d. *and Senators ... Attendants* (Q) Senators, and Officers   1 *There is* (Q) There's *these* (Q) this   87 *broil* (Q) Broiles   93 *am I* (Q) I am   106 *Duke* (Q) Omitted   107 *certain* (Q) wider   121 s.d. *Exit ... two or three* (Q) Omitted   130 *fortunes* (Q) Fortune   139 *travels'* (Q) Trauellours   141 *and* (Q) Omitted   142 *the* (Q) my   145 *Do grow* (Q) Grew   *This* (Q) These things   147 *thence* (Q) hence   155 *intentively* (Q) instinctiuely   159 *sighs* (Q) kisses   160 *i' faith* (Q) in faith   201 *Into your favor* (Q) Omitted   219 *ear* (Q) eares   220 *Beseech you, now* (Q) I humbly beseech you proceed   *the affairs* (Q) th' Affaires   230 *couch* (Pope) Coach   234 *These* (Malone) This   239–40 *If you please, | Be't at her father's.* (Q) Why at her Fathers?   241 *Nor I. I would not* (Q) Nor would I   248 *did* (Q) Omitted   257 *which* (Q) why   263–64 *heat – the young affects | In me defunct –* (Capell) heat the yong affects | In my defunct,   270 *instruments* (Q) Instrument   293 s.d. *Exeunt* (Q) Exit   299 *matters* (Q) matter   300 s.d. *Moor and Desdemona* (Q) Omitted   322 *thyme* (Pope) Time   326 *balance* (Q) braine   330 *our unbitted* (Q) or vnbitted   340 *be that Desdemona should long continue* (Q) be long that Desdemona should continue   348 *error* (Q) errors   355 *'Tis* (Q) it is   379 *a snipe* (Q) snpe   382 *H'as* (Q) She ha's   398 s.d. *Exit* (Q) Omitted

II, i, 13 *mane* (Knight) Maine   19 s.d. *third* (Q) Omitted   33 *prays* (Q) praye   34 *heaven* (Q) Heauens   42 *arrivance* (Q) arrivancie   43 *this* (Q) the   50 *hopes* (F3) hope's   51 s.d. *Enter a Messenger* (Q) Omitted   53 *Messenger* (Q) Gent.   55 s.d. *A shot* (Q) Omitted   65 *ingener* (Knight) Ingeniuer   s.d. *Second* (Q) Omitted   70 *clog* (Q) enclogge   88 *me* (Q) Omitted   92 *the sea* (Q) Sea   93 *(Within) A sail, a sail! [A shot.] But hark. A sail!* (Collier) But hearke, a Saile. / *Within.* A Saile, a Saile.   94 *their* (Q) this   104 *list* (Q) leaue   117 *thou write* (Q) write   157 *such wight* (Q) such wightes   168 *gyve* (F2) giue   173 *an* (Q) and   174 *courtesy* (Q) curtsy   176 s.d. *Trumpet within* (Q2) Omitted   196 s.d. *They

kiss (Q) Omitted   210 s.d. *Exit Othello* (Eds) Exit Othello and Desdemona   212 *hither* (Q) thither   221–22 *and will she* (Q) To   225 *again* (Q) a game   237 *compassing* (Q) compasse   239 *finder-out* (Q) finder   *occasions* (Q) occasion   *has* (Q) he's   255 *mutualities* (Q) mutabilities   267 *with his truncheon* (Q) Omitted   293 *for wife* (Q) wift   297 *I trash* (Steevens) I trace   300 *rank* (Q) right

II, ii, 5 *addiction* (Q2) addition   10 *Heaven* (Q) Omitted

II, iii (Capell first begins a new scene here)   37 *unfortunate* (Q) infortunate   51 *lads* (Q) else   56 *to put* (Q) put to   60 *God* (Q) heauen   67 *A life's* (Q) Oh, mans life's   71 *God* (Q) Heauen   76 *expert* (Q) exquisite   84 *a* (Q) and-a   86 *'em* (Q) them   91 *Then* (Q) And   *auld* (Q) awl'd   93 *'Fore God* (Q) Why   97 *God's* (Q) heau'ns   106 *God* (Q) Omitted   131 s.d. *Exit Roderigo* (Q) Omitted   138 *(Within) Help! help!* (Q) Omitted   s.d. *driving in* (Q) pursuing   139 *Zounds* (Q) Omitted   145 s.d. *They fight* (Q) Omitted   146 s.d. *Exit Roderigo* (Q2) Omitted   147 *God's will* (Q2) Alas   148 *sir – Montano – sir –* (Capell) Sir Montano (F) Sir, Montano, sir (Q2)   149 s.d. *A bell rung* (Q) Omitted   151 *God's will, lieutenant, hold!* (Q) Fie, fie Lieutenant,   152 *shamed* (Q) asham'd   s.d. *and Gentlemen with weapons* (Q) and Attendants   153 *Zounds* (Q) Omitted   156 *Hold, hold Hold hoa   sir – Montano –* (Rowe) Sir Montano   157 *sense of place* (Hanmer) place of sense   173 *breast* (Q) breastes   208 *leagued* (Pope) league   241 *What's* (Q2) What is   *matter* (Deere?)   242 *now* (Q) Omitted   246 *vile* (Q) vil'd   251 *God* (Q) Heauen   256 *thought* (Q) had thought   261 *ways* (Q) more wayes   277 *God* (Q) Omitted   281 *Why,* (Q) Why?   288 *so* (Q) Omitted   299 *some* (Q) a   300 *I'll* (Q) I   303 *denotement* (Theobald) deuotement   316 *here* (Q) Omitted   326 *were't* (Q) were   337 *fortunes* (Q) Fortune   357 *hast* (Q) hath   360 *By the mass* (Q) Introth   366 *on;* (Q) on   367 *the while* (Theobald) a while

III, i, 3 *ha'* (Q) haue   21 *hear, my* (Capell) heare me, mine (F) hear my (Q)   25 *general's wife* (Q2) Generall   29 *Cassio. Do, good my friend* (Q) Omitted   53 *Desdemona* (Q) Desdemon   55 s.d. *Exeunt* (Q) Omitted

III, ii, 6 *We'll* (F3) well

III, iii, 16 *circumstance* (Q) circumstances   52 *Yes, faith* (Q) I sooth   60 *or* (Q) on   61 *or Wednesday* (Q) on Wensday   63 *I' faith* (Q) Infaith   65 *examples* (Q) example   66 *their* (Rowe) her   69 *could* (Q) would   74 *By'r Lady* (Q) Trust me   87 *Desdemon* (Dyce iii) Desdemona   94 *you* (Q) he   106 *By heaven* (Q) Alas *he echoes* (Q) thou ecchos't   107 *his* (Q) thy   112 *In* (Q) Of   135 *that all* (Q) that: All   *free to* (Q) free   136 *vile* (Q) vild   138 *a* (Q) that   139 *But some* (Q) Wherein   147 *oft* (Q) of   148 *yet* (Q2) Omitted   149 *conjects* (Q) conceits   162 *By heaven* (Q) Omitted   170 *strongly* (Q) soundly   175 *God* (Q) Heauen   180 *once* (Q) Omitted   182 *blown* (Q) blow'd   202 *God* (Q) Heauen   204 *keep't* (Q) kept   215 *I' faith* (Q) Trust me   217 *my* (Q) your   222 *vile* (Q) vilde   223 *As* (Q) Which   *aim not at* (Q) aym'd not   248 *hold* (Q) Omitted   259 *qualities* (Q) Quantities   *learned* (Q) learn'd   262 *I'd* (Q) I'ld   273 *of* (Q) to   278 *O, then* (Q) Omitted   *mocks* (Q) mock'd   285 *Faith* (Q) Why   302 *A thing* (Q) You haue a thing   311 *No, faith; she* (Q) No: but she   313 *it is* (Q) 'tis   332 *med'cine* (Eds) medicine   338 *of her* (Q) in her   349 *troop* (Q) Troopes   375 *b' wi'* (F4) buy   376 *liv'st* (Eds) lou'st (F) liuest (Q)   386 *Her* (Q2) My   391 *sir* (Q) Omitted   393 *I* (Q) and I   395 *supervisor* (Q) supervision   408 *may* (Q) might   422 *and* (Q) Omitted   424 *then* (Q) Omitted   425 *Over* (Q) ore   *sighed* (Eds) sigh   *kissed* (Eds) kisse (F) kissèd (Q)   426 *Cried* (Q) cry   432 *but* (Q) yet   440 *that was* (Malone) it was   452 *perhaps* (Q) Omitted   455 *feels* (Q2) keepes   460 s.d. *He kneels* (Eds) Omitted (F) (in Rowe after l. 461, in Q after l. 450)   462 s.d. *Iago kneels* (Q2) Omitted

III, iv, 5 *is* (Q) 'tis   22 *I'll* (Q) I will   *of* (Q) Omitted   s.d. *Exit* (Q) Exit Clo.   23 *that* (Q) the   37 *yet* (Q) Omitted   48 *Come now, (Capell) Come, now   54 *faith* (Q) indeed   64 *wive* (Q) wiu'd   73 *hallowed* (Capell) hallowèd   75 *I' faith* (Q) Indeed   77 *God* (Q) Heauen   80 *is it* (Q) is't   81 *Heaven* (Q) Omitted   86 *sir* (Q) Omitted   97 *I' faith* (Q) Insooth   98 *Zounds* (Q) Away   116 *neither* (Q) nor my   161 *'Tis* (Q) It is   163 *that* (Q) the   168 s.d. *Exeunt Desdemona and Emilia* (Q) Exit   171 *I' faith* (Q) Indeed   182 *absence now* (Capell) Absence : now   184 *vile* (Q) vilde   187 *by my faith* (Q) in good troth   188 *sweet* neither   190 *I'd* (Q) I would   201 s.d. *Exeunt* (Q) Exeunt omnes

IV, i, 9 *So* (Q) If   21 *infected* (Q) infectious   32 *Faith* (Q) Why   36 *Zounds* (Q) Omitted   45 *med'cine* (Eds) Medicine   *work* (Q) workes   52 *No, forbear* (Q) Omitted   60 *you?* *No* (Q) you not   77 *unsuiting* (Q) resulting   79 *'scuse* (Q) scuses   95 *clothes* (Q) Cloath   98 *refrain* (Q) restraine   101 *conster* (Q) conserue   102 *behavior* (Q) behauiours   103 *now* (Q) Omitted   107 *power* (Q) dowre   110 *a* (Q) Omitted   111 *i' faith* (Q) indeed   118 *you triumph, Roman* (Q) ye triumph, Romaine   119 *her* (Q) Omitted   122 *win* (F4) winnes   123 *Faith* (Q) Why   *shall* (Q) Omitted   130 *beckons* (Q) becomes   133–34 *by this hand, she* (Q) Omitted   149 *whole* (Q) Omitted   157 *An . . . an* (Q) If . . . if   160 *Faith* (Q) Omitted   *street* (Q) streets   166 s.d. *Exit Cassio* (Q) Omitted   189 *thousand thousand* (Q) thousand, a thousand   208 s.d. *A trumpet* (Q) Omitted   210 *and* (Q) Omitted   *wife is* (Q) wife's   211 *God* (Q) Omitted   212 *senators* (Q) the Senators   224 *thy* (Q) my   228 *the letter* (Q) th Letter   231 *By my troth* (Q) Trust me   241 *an* (Q) Omitted   269 *this* (Q) his

IV, ii, 24 *Pray* (Q) Pray you   30 *Nay* (Q) May   31 *knees* (Q) knee   47 *Why* (Q) Omitted   54 *A* (Q) The   55 *unmoving* (Q) and mouing   64 *Ay, there* (Theobald) I heere   69 *ne'er* (Q) neuer   71 *paper,* (Q) Paper ?   80 *hear it* (Steevens) hear't   81 *Impudent strumpet* (Q) Omitted   92 *keep* (Rowe) keepes   117 *As* (Q) That   *bear* (Q) beare it   133 *I'll* (Q) I will   141 *heaven* (Q) heauens   155 *them in* (Q2) them : or   168 *'Tis* (Q) It is   169 *you* (Q) Omitted   170 *stay* (Q) staies   175 *daff'st* (Collier) dafts   180 *suffered* (Q) suffred   182 *Faith* (Q) Omitted   *for* (Q) and   187 *deliver to* (Q) deliuer   193 *By this hand, I say 'tis very* (Q) Nay I think it is   221 *takes* (Q) taketh   222 *lingered* (Q) lingred   225 *of* (Q) Omitted

IV, iii, 12 *He* (Q) And   13 *bade* (Q) bid   20 *in them* (Q) Omitted   22 *faith* (Q) Father   23 *thee* (Q) Omitted   24 *those* (Q) these   39 s.d. *sings* (Q2) Omitted   *sighing* (Q2) singing   46–47 *Lay . . . willow'* (Eds) Sing Willough, &c. (Lay by these)   48–49 *Prithee . . . garland* (Eds) Willough, Willough. (Prythee high thee : he'le come anon)   71 *it* (Q) Omitted   74 *'Ud's pity* (Q) why   103 *God* (Q) Heauen   *usage* (Q) uses

V, i, 1 *bulk* (Q) Barke   22 *Be't* (Q) But   *hear* (Q) heard   35 *Forth* (Q) For   38 *cry* (Q) voyce   42 *It is a* (Q) 'Tis   46 s.d. *with a light* (Q) Omitted   49 *Did* (Q) Do   50 *heaven's* (Q) heauen   60 *here* (Q) there   90 *O heaven* (Q) Yes, 'tis   104 *out* (Q) Omitted   110 s.d. *Enter Emilia* (Q) Omitted   111 *'Las, what's . . . What's* (Q) Alas, what is . . . What is   114 *dead* (Q) quite dead   121 *Fie, fie* (Q) Oh fie   123 *Foh* (Q) Omitted

V, ii, s.d. *Desdemona [asleep] in her bed. Enter Othello with a light* (Eds) Enter Othello, and Desdemona in her bed (F) Enter Othello with a light, and Desdemona in her bed (Q2)   15 s.d. *He kisses her* (Q, after ll. 19–20) Omitted (F) Kisses her (Q2)   32 *heaven* (Q) Heauens   35 *so* (Q) Omitted   41 *diest* (Q) dy'st   52 *Yes* (Q) Omitted   57 *Then Lord* (Q) O Heauen   64 *mak'st* (Q2) makes   85 s.d. *calls within* (Q) Omitted   87 *that am* (Q) am that   94 *here* (Q) high   102 *Should* (Q) Did   107 *murder* (Theobald) murthers   118 *O Lord* (Q) Alas   126 s.d. *She dies* (Q) Omitted   128 *heard* (Q) heare   144 *Nay* (Q) Omitted   148 *me* (Q) me on her   153 *that* (Q2) Omitted   163 *the* (Q) that   168 s.d. *Gratiano, Iago, and others* (Q) Gratiano, and Iago   186 *murdered* (Pope) murtherèd   199 s.d. *Falls on the bed* (Eds) Omitted (F) Oth. fals on the bed (Q)   210 *reprobation* (Q) Reprobance   219 *O God ! O heavenly God* (Q) Oh Heauen ! oh heauenly Powres   220 *Zounds* (Q) Come   236 s.d. *The Moor . . . wife* (Q) Omitted   238 s.d. *Exit Iago* (Q) Omitted   241 *here* (Q) Omitted   252 s.d. *She dies* (Q) Omitted   254 *is* (Q) was   256 s.d. *within* (Q) Omitted   282 s.d. *Enter . . . chair* (Q) Enter Lodouico, Cassio, Montano, and Iago, with Officers   291 *wert* (Q) was   292 *damnèd* (Q) cursed   295 *did I* (Q) I did   317 *nick* (Q) interim   321 *but* (Capell) it but   346 *Perplexed* (Q) Perplexèd   350 *Drop* (Q2) Drops   351 *med'cinable* (Capell) Medicinable   356 s.d. *He stabs himself* (Q) Omitted   357 *that's* (Q) that is   359 s.d. *He . . . dies* (Q) Dyes

KING LEAR

INTRODUCTION

The play begins with a moment of prose "exposition," an idle conversation about the partition of a kingdom and the bastardy of a son. Its tone is casual, jocular, polite. The son responds decorously to a social introduction. The speakers are wearing familiar masks. It is then as if these murmurs by the portal subsided at the opening of some old but half-remembered ceremony. All is ritual – heralding trumpet, formal procession, symbolic objects in coronet and map, a sequence of arbitrary yet strangely predictable acts. What can be made of it? Why should that patriarch who wishes to yield up his power and possessions require of the receivers declarations of love? Why should that maiden who honestly loves him respond only with declarations of her love of honesty? No logical reasons appear – ritual is ritual, its logic its own. Prose is yielding to poetry, "realism" to reality. *King Lear* is not true. It is an allegory of truth.

That its truths are not literal is the first thing about it discerned by the budding critical faculty. Everything is initially *patterned* – this one making obvious errors which he obviously will rue, these others emerging as the good and the evil in almost geometrical symmetry, with the inevitable sisters-three, the two elder chosen though wicked, the younger rejected though virtuous. Surely these are childish things! A defense has been offered by Tolstoy, in his valedictory judgment that the only truths conveyable in literature can be conveyed in the simplest folk-tale. But *King Lear* is not simple, and Tolstoy himself failed to see its relevance to his doctrine. Freud noticed its primitive features, and compared Goneril, Regan, and Cordelia to the caskets of lead, silver, and gold in *The Merchant of Venice*. He identified Cordelia as the benign, though resisted, call of death. Cordelia as the death-wish – *lovely and soothing death* – how suggestive this is! until we recognize that her identification as the life-wish might be equally suggestive. The value of such reflections lies in their reminder that the oldest story-patterns have the greatest power to touch off reverberations. No other framework than this parable-myth could have borne so well the weight of what Shakespeare was compelled to say.

The story of Lear and his three daughters was given written form four centuries before Shakespeare's birth. How much older its components may be we do not know. Cordelia in one guise or another, including Cinderella's, has figured in the folklore of most cultures, perhaps originally expressing what Emerson saw as the conviction of every human being of his worthiness to be loved and chosen, if only his *true* self were truly known. The figure of the ruler asking a question, often a riddle, with disastrous consequences to himself is equally old and dispersed. In his *Historia Regum Britanniae* (1136) Geoffrey of Monmouth converted folklore to history and established Lear and his daughters as rulers of ancient Britain, thus bequeathing them to the chronicles. Raphael Holinshed's (1587) declared that "Leir, the sonne of Baldud," came to the throne "in the yeare of the world 3105, at what time Joas reigned in Juda," but belief in the historicity of such British kings was now beginning to wane, and Shakespeare could deal freely with the record. He read the story also in John Higgins' lamentable verses in *The Firste part of the Mirour for Magistrates* (1574), and in Edmund Spenser's *Faerie Queene*, II, 10, 27–32. He knew, and may even have acted in, a bland dramatic version, *The True Chronicle History of King Leir*, published anonymously in 1605 but staged at least as early as 1594.

The printing of the old play may mark an effort to capitalize upon the staging of Shakespeare's, performed at court on December 26, 1606, and probably first brought out at the Globe playhouse sometime in 1605, although its allusion to "these late eclipses of the sun and moon" was not necessarily suggested by those of September and October of that year. The only certain anterior limit of date is March 16, 1603, when Samuel Harsnett's *Declaration of Egregious Popishe Impostures* was registered for publication. That this excursion in "pseudo-demonology" was available to Shakespeare is evident in various ways, most clearly in the borrowed inventory of devils imbedded in Edgar's jargon as Tom o' Bedlam. It is of small consequence to fix the date of *King Lear* so far as its relation to the older play is concerned, which must be reckoned as analogue rather than source, but if, as seems certain, it was composed in 1605 or early 1606, it belongs to the same season of the poet's growth as *The Tragedy of Macbeth*.

In its pre-Shakespearean forms, both those mentioned above and others, the Lear story remains rudimentary. The emphasis may vary in various recensions, depending upon whether the author was most interested in the inexpedience of subdividing a kingdom, the mutability of fortune, or, as in the older play, the rewards of Christian virtue; but all are alike in that they end happily for Lear, who is reconciled to Cordelia and restored to his throne. The fact that the story was sometimes followed by a sequel in which Cordelia was finally hounded to suicide by the broodlings of her wicked sisters has little bearing on a remarkable fact: Shakespeare alone and in defiance of precedent conducted Lear to ultimate misery. *Enter Lear, with Cordelia in his arms. . . . He dies.* These directions enclose a scene which demonstrates beyond any other in tragic literature the intransigence of poetic art – inventing the inevitable, investing horrifying things with beauty.

Compared with the tragedies of ancient Greece – and it is with these alone that one is tempted to compare it – *King*

Lear suggests the Gothic order. Its form is irregular and organic, determined seemingly by a series of upward thrusts of mounting internal energy. There is even a Gothic element of the grotesque, as when mock-beggar, jester, and king, reduced to common condition, hold their mad juridical proceedings in a storm-lashed shelter, or when crazed king and blinded subject exchange lamentations and puns! In the method of Lear's madness there is often a savage humor, more remarkable when all is said than his companioning with a Fool. It was the Fool, however, who seemed to the next age the unpardonable sin against classical decorum. In the 1680 adaptation by Nahum Tate he was expunged from the play, along with the tragic ending. Tate capped the concluding felicities of the pre-Shakespearean versions by huddling up a marriage between Edgar and Cordelia; yet his work held the stage throughout the eighteenth century. It is always ruefully remarked that the greatest critic of the age approved the adaptation, but in fairness we should add that it was not for literary reasons. The pain of Shakespeare's concluding scenes was simply too much for Dr Johnson; his response is preferable to that of those – fit for treasons, stratagems, and spoils – who can read these scenes unmoved.

The original play, or its approximation, was restored to the stage in the early nineteenth century, after it had begun to receive its critical due from the romantic essayists and poets. It is a poet's play. Keats saw in it the warrant for his conviction that truth and beauty are one, and, more surprisingly, recognized the choral and catalytic function of Lear's jester for the stroke of genius it is. Coleridge, Lamb, and Hazlitt also recorded illuminating judgments, and many critics since, of many different "schools," have said fine things about it.

The question now most frequently debated is whether the play is Christian and affirmative in spirit, or pagan and pessimistic. No work of art could endure the tugs of such a debate without being somewhat torn. "Pessimistic," like "optimistic," is a small word for a small thing, and *King Lear* is not small. It is sad, as all tragedies are sad. It is religious, as all great tragedies are religious. The exclusion of specific Christian reference, more consistent than in any other Shakespearean play of non-Christian setting, is in harmony with its Old Testament atmosphere (when "Joas reigned in Juda"), but it may reflect nothing more than evasion, in the printed text, of a recent Parliamentary ruling, which in effect labelled *God* in stage speech as blasphemy, *gods* as mere classical allusion. Although the play is rather inclusively than exclusively Christian, which can scarcely be deemed a fault, it shows obvious signs of its genesis in a Christian culture. To cite those involving a single character (other than Cordelia, who has often been viewed as a Christ-symbol), there is Edgar's persistence in returning good for evil, his preachments against the sin of despair, and his reluctance to kill except in trial by combat with its implied religious sanctions. Great questions are asked of the unseen powers – "Is there any cause in nature that makes these hard hearts?" – and these questions remain unanswered, but the silence which follows them should be viewed, here as in other contexts, as the substance of faith. On the human level, the implications of the play are more comforting than the data it abstracts. In our actual world, suffering is not always ennobling, evil not always self-consuming. In every scene where there is pain, there is someone who strives to relieve that pain. At the close, the merciless have all perished; the last sound we hear is the choral voices of the merciful.

The workers of evil are stylized in a way not quite typical of Shakespeare. He could not love these characters even as characters, except perhaps Edmund a little. To imitate the dominant animal imagery of the style, Cornwall is less repellent than Goneril and Regan only as the mad bull is less repellent than the hyena, they less repellent than Oswald only as the hyena is less repellent than the jackal. To the latter he failed to give even that engaging touch of the ludicrous he usually reserved for assistant villains. It is useless to speak of their "motivation." Like other aged parents Lear is no gift to good housewifery, and there is something poignantly familiar about such a one's trudging resentfully to the home of a second daughter. "Age is unnecessary." But to see a causal relationship between what he does to Goneril and Regan and what they do to him, or to interpret their aggression as normal revolt against parental domination, is simply to be perverse. The play deals directly, and in both its stories, with one indissoluble bond:

> We'll no more meet, no more see one another.
> But yet thou art my flesh, my blood, my daughter....

Eroded, it leaves no human bond secure. To argue that Edmund's conduct is attributable to humiliating illegitimacy, we must supply him with an "unconscious" and invoke its spectral evidence; there is no sign of sensitivity in his lines. Even that curious product of our times, the liberalism-gone-to-seed which automatically defends anything from treachery to sadism providing it savors of non-conformity, has found little to say for this insatiable quintet.

Shakespeare is not normally associated with hatred, but "a fierce hatred of cruelty and deceitful wickedness" informs *King Lear* – this the opinion of so pure an aesthetician as Benedetto Croce. Hazlitt has said, "It is then the best of all Shakespeare's plays, for it is the one in which he was most in earnest." A non-sequitur may lurk in this assertion, but we cannot deny its relevance. Our inescapable impression of the play is of its overwhelming sincerity. It says everything powerfully and everything twice – and always "what we feel, not what we ought to say." The language varies from the cryptic allusiveness of Lear's "mad" speeches to the biblical plainness of his pleas for forgiveness; and though it is often difficult, it is never ambiguous. Lamb has been much taken to task for declaring that "*Lear* is essentially impossible to be represented on a stage," but more often than not our experiences in the theatre confirm his view. There have been fine productions, but not very many: one touch of insincerity can rot everything away.

Those who now "introduce" this play must wish with Hazlitt, and with much more likelihood of greeting the wish of the reader, that they might resort to silence, since all that can be said will "fall short of the subject, or even what we ourselves conceive of it." Yet an effort must be made to state its theme, and to the present editor there seems no way of doing this except by focussing the gaze directly and continuously upon Lear himself.

"The King is coming." These words announce the first entrance of the tragic hero. Let us see him as he is, no preconceptions or critical rumors spoiling the innocence of our vision. Nothing about him suggests infirmity or decay. His magnitude and force are far greater than one's own. He issues commands with the assurance of instinct and lifelong custom. He holds a map in his hands like a Titan holding a kingdom. The kingdom spreads before us in his spacious utterance :

> Of all these bounds, even from this line to this,
> With shadowy forests and with champains riched,
> With plenteous rivers and wide-skirted meads,
> We make thee lady.

We make thee lady! Thus he disposes of a sector of the earth, this ring-giver, this warrior-leader, this chosen one, his only landlord God! Is it not passing fine . . . ? Here is no soft-brained *Senex*, but the archetypal *King*.

As such Lear symbolizes Mankind, and we will say nothing essential about him by reckoning up his years and growing glib about the symptoms of senile dementia. The king-figure surrogate is an understandable product of the human mind in its early attempts at abstraction, since the most imposing of single men best lends his image to the difficult concept of Man. His vicissitudes best epitomize the vicissitudes of all, since upon the highest altitude the sun shines brightest and the cold snow lies most deep. Early Renaissance drama was steeped in the tradition of this symbolic figure, sometimes still called *King* as well as *Mankind, Everyman, Genus Humanum*, and the like. He is always identifiable by his centrality in the action, and the mixed company he keeps – vices or flatterers on the one hand, virtues or truth-speakers on the other. And there stands Lear – Goneril and Regan to the left, Kent and Cordelia to the right.

But this is also a family gathering. There is the father, and there the servants and children of his house. The central figure is, and seems always more so as the play weaves its spell, not only archetypal King, Man, and Father, but particular king, man, and father. No symbol that remained purely symbol could so touch our emotions. To have children of his flesh and blood, the father must be flesh and blood – such as can be old, grow weary, feel cold and wet.

Only a few days of fictional time elapse, only a few hours in the theatre, so that Lear's first words still echo in our ears as we hear his last.

We make thee lady. . . . Let it be so, thy truth then be thy dower! . . . Peace, Kent! Come not between the dragon and his wrath. . . . The bow is bent and drawn ; make from the shaft. . . . Therefore be gone. . . . Let me not stay a jot for dinner ; go get it ready. . . . Call the clotpoll back.

Such are Lear's accents at the beginning. And at the close –

You must bear with me. . . . I am old and foolish. . . . Her voice was ever soft, gentle, and low. . . . Pray you undo this button. Thank you, sir.

He has learned a new language. We are required to accept this learning as good, but we are forbidden to rejoice.

The play is Lear's gethsemane, its great reality his suffering, which so draws us into itself that our conception of the work as a whole is formed in the crucible of our fear and pity. His anguish is kin with the anguish of Job, Prometheus, Oedipus, and other tragic projections of spirits in agony, but it retains its own peculiar quality. Its cause, its nature, and its meaning will always remain the imperfectly resolved crux of the play ; and one can do no more than explain, with such confidence as one is able to muster, how these things appear to him.

To say that Lear gets what he deserves is to share the opinion of Goneril and Regan. (Some have even implied that Cordelia gets what she deserves, anaesthetizing their heads and hearts with obtuse moralisms suggested by the doctrine of "poetic justice.") What does Lear deserve? He is proud and peremptory, and it is better to be humble and temporizing, but there are occupational hazards in being a king, perhaps even in being a father. Is his charge not true that the world has lied to him, telling him he was wise before he was bearded, returning "yea and nay" to everything he said? His guilt is widely shared, and his "flaw" like that of Oedipus seems mysteriously hereditary. And it is linked inextricably with his virtues. We applaud the resurgence of youthful might that cuts down Cordelia's assassin. We admire the valor of his attempts (and they come quite early) to be patient, to compromise, to hold back womanish tears, to cling to his reason. Nothing is more moving than his bewildered attempts to meet "social" obligations as he kneels by Cordelia's body. We love his *manliness*. Pride has its value too.

Lear's errors stem from no corruption of heart. His rejection of Kent and Cordelia is the reflex of his attachment to them. The errors are not the man. The man is one who has valued and been valued by such as they. The things he wants – fidelity and love – are good things. That he should find them in his servant and his child seems to him an aspect of universal order. In his vocabulary, as distinct from Edmund's, such things are *natural*. His inability to distinguish between the false and the true, and his craving for visible displays, are not failings peculiar to him. "How much do you love me?" – few parents suppress this bullying question, spoken or unspoken, however much they may have felt its burden as children. It seems in the nature of some things that they always are learned too late, that as children we might have offered more, as parents demanded less. To punish a thankless child has the appearance of justice, to withdraw in one's age from the cares of state the appearance of wisdom, to dispose of one's goods by gift instead of testament the appearance of generosity. Plain men in their prime have been similarly deceived. Gloucester shakes his head sadly over Lear's injustice, folly, and selfishness as he duplicates his actions.

In the maimed but agile mind of the Fool faithfully dogging Lear's steps, his errors stand as an *idée fixe* and are harped upon with terrible iteration. We should not imitate the example. We may find more meaning in the excess of expiation. The purely physical suffering – denial of rest, exposure to wind and rain – is real, but it strikes the sufferer himself as little more than a metaphor. We may say that his spiritual suffering is in excess of his actual afflictions, that it is selfish and centrifugal, or a mere symptom of aged petulance, but if we do so, we are stopping our ears to the voice of Shakespeare and all his decent spokesmen. Lear's curse of Goneril is still alienating, like his treatment of Cordelia, but when he stands weeping before his cormorant daughters in whom he has put his faith, and they coolly and relentlessly strip him of every vestige of dignity, our hearts turn over. Humility may be good, but this humiliation is evil.

There is no *need* that this man be attended by a hundred knights, that his messenger be deferentially treated, or that his children offer him more than subsistence. His cause rests upon no more rational grounds than our powers of sympathy and imagination. "O reason not the need." As his every expectation is brutally defeated, and he looks in dazed recognition upon the world as it is instead of what he thought it was, of himself as he is instead of what he thought he was, we defer to his past illusions. He had never identified prestige merely as power, had never imagined that the visages of respect, kindliness, and love could contort into the hideous lines of icy contempt and sour indifference.

Lear's anguish now represents for us Man's horror and sense of helplessness at the discovery of evil – the infiltration of animality in the human world, naked cruelty and appetite. It is a fissure that threatens to widen infinitely, and we see Lear at the center of turbulence as it works its breakage in minds, in families, in nations, in the heavens themselves, interacting in dreadful concatenation.

The significance of Lear's response to his discovery is best seen in the light of Gloucester's. In Sidney's *Arcadia*, II, 10, the "storie of the Paphlagonian unkind King and his kinde sonne" repeats in essence the Lear legend, except that the children, false and true, are sons instead of daughters. By reducing the rank of Sidney's king and interweaving his parallel fate in alternate scenes, Shakespeare is able, amazingly, both further to universalize and further to particularize the experience of Lear. Gloucester also represents Man, but his distinction from Lear suggests the distinction between ordinary and extraordinary men. Gloucester is amiably confused about the tawdriness of his past, of which Edmund is the product, and sentimentally fumbling in the present. What appears in Lear as heroic error appears in him as gullibility. His fine moments are identical with those of a nameless serf of Cornwall's and an ancient tenant of his own – in the presence of cruelty he becomes kind and brave :

GLOUCESTER I am tied to th' stake, and I must stand the course.
REGAN Wherefore to Dover ?
GLOUCESTER Because I would not see thy cruel nails
    Pluck out his poor old eyes.

Like Lear he is incorrupt of heart, and he grows in dignity, but his total response to vicious encroachment is something akin to apathy and surrender; his instinct is to retreat.

Not so with Lear. He batters himself to pieces against the fact of evil. Granted that its disruptive power has been unleashed by his own error, so that error itself partakes of evil, as he is shudderingly aware, yet he remains the great antagonist. Falsity, cruelty, injustice, corruption – their appalling forms swirl about him in phantasmic patterns. His instinct is to rip them from the universe, to annihilate all things if it is the only way to annihilate these things. His charges of universal hypocrisy : "handy-dandy, which is the justice, which is the thief ?" – his denial of human responsibility : "None does offend, none – I say none !" – his indictment of life itself :

Thou know'st, the first time that we smell the air
We wawl and cry –

cancel their own nihilism, because they sound no acquiescence. Lear is the voice of protest. The grandeur of his spirit supplies the impotence of his body as he opposes to evil all that is left him to oppose – his molten indignation, his huge invectives, his capacity for feeling pain.

This quality of Lear seen in retrospect, his hunger after righteousness, gives magnitude to the concluding scenes. His spirit has been doubly lacerated by his own sense of guilt. He has failed "poor naked wretches" no different from himself, and he has wronged Cordelia. His remorse has found expression only in brief occasional utterances, welling up as it were against desperate efforts of containment, but its scalding power is revealed in his acts of abasement when he and Cordelia meet. The final episodes are all vitally linked. When the two are led in captive, we are made to look back upon their reunion, which he dreams of endlessly reenacting :

When thou dost ask me blessing, I'll kneel down
And ask of thee forgiveness ;

then forward to their death :

Upon such sacrifices, my Cordelia,
The gods themselves throw incense.

The words help to effect that perfect coalescence of particular and general tragic experience achieved as he kneels beside her body. This is a father and his child who will come no more, the father remembering his own unkindness and the child's endearing ways. There is no melioration in his dying delusion that she still lives, no mention of an after-life. It is unspeakably sad. But it merges with a larger yet less devastating sadness. This is also a sacrifice, and although the somber tones of the survivors as they take up the burden of survival give it relevance to the future as well as the past, it is such a sacrifice as obliquely vindicates the gods if upon it they throw incense.

We know, not as an item of faith but of simple demonstrable fact, that we are greatly indebted for such wisdom as we have, that it was bought with "sacrifices." In the struggle of our kind against brutality, the great casualties, spiritual and even physical, have always been among those who have been best and those who have cared most. In the world of this play Cordelia has brought us the truest sense of human goodness, her words "No cause, no cause" the truest sense of moral beauty. She is the perfect offering. And so is Lear. She is best. He cares most for what is best. The play ends as it begins in an allegorical grouping, commemorating humanity's long, agonized, and continuing struggle to be human. This larger meaning gives our tears the dignity of an act of ratification and gratitude : to these still figures we have pitied we owe the gift of feeling pity.

Harvard University   ALFRED HARBAGE

NOTE ON THE TEXT

In 1608 a version of *King Lear* appeared in a quarto volume sold by Nathaniel Butter at his shop at the Pied Bull. Its text was reproduced in 1619 in a quarto falsely dated 1608. Various theories have been offered to explain the nature of the Pied Bull text, the most recent being that it represents Shakespeare's rough draft carelessly copied, and corrupted by the faulty memories of actors who were party to the copying. In 1623 a greatly improved though "cut" version of the play appeared in the first folio, evidently printed from the quarto after it had been carefully collated with the official playhouse manuscript. The present edition follows the folio text, and although it adds in square brackets the passages appearing only in the quarto, and accepts fifty-three quarto readings, it follows the chosen text more closely than do most recent editions. However, deference to the quarto is paid in an appendix, where its alternative readings, both those accepted and those rejected, are listed. Few editorial emendations have been retained, but see I, ii, 21 *top* (Q & F 'to'), II, ii, 138 *contemnèd'st* (Q 'temnest'), III, vi, 25 *bourn* (Q 'broom'), III, vi, 67 *lym* (Q & F 'him'), IV, ii, 57 *to threat* (Q 'thereat'), IV, iii, 20 *seemed* (Q 'seeme'), 31 *moistened* (Q 'moistened her'). The quarto text is not divided into acts and scenes. The act and scene division here supplied marginally for reference purposes is that of the folio except that Act II, Scene ii of the latter has been subdivided into Scenes ii, iii, and iv. The continuity of the action here, and at several other misleadingly divided sections of the play, is indicated in the manner explained in the Preface.

KING LEAR

[NAMES OF THE ACTORS

Lear, King of Britain	Edmund, bastard son to Gloucester	A Gentleman attending on Cordelia
King of France	Curan, a courtier	A Herald
Duke of Burgundy	Old Man, tenant to Gloucester	Servants to Cornwall
Duke of Cornwall	Doctor	Goneril
Duke of Albany	Lear's Fool	Regan } daughters to Lear
Earl of Kent	Oswald, steward to Goneril	Cordelia
Earl of Gloucester	A Captain under Edmund's command	Knights attending on Lear, Officers, Messengers,
Edgar, son to Gloucester	Gentlemen loyal to Lear	Soldiers, Attendants

Scene : *Britain*]

*

I, i   *Enter Kent, Gloucester, and Edmund.*

1 KENT I thought the King had more affected the Duke of
2 Albany than Cornwall.

GLOUCESTER It did always seem so to us ; but now, in the
division of the kingdom, it appears not which of the
5 dukes he values most, for equalities are so weighed that
6 curiosity in neither can make choice of either's moiety.

KENT Is not this your son, my lord ?

8 GLOUCESTER His breeding, sir, hath been at my charge.
I have so often blushed to acknowledge him that now I
10 am brazed to't.

11 KENT I cannot conceive you.

GLOUCESTER Sir, this young fellow's mother could ;
whereupon she grew round-wombed, and had indeed,
sir, a son for her cradle ere she had a husband for her
her bed. Do you smell a fault ?

KENT I cannot wish the fault undone, the issue of it being
17 so proper.

GLOUCESTER But I have a son, sir, by order of law, some
19 year elder than this who yet is no dearer in my account :
20 though this knave came something saucily to the world
before he was sent for, yet was his mother fair, there was
22 good sport at his making, and the whoreson must be
acknowledged. Do you know this noble gentleman,
Edmund ?

EDMUND No, my lord.

GLOUCESTER My Lord of Kent. Remember him hereafter as my honorable friend.

EDMUND My services to your lordship.

KENT I must love you, and sue to know you better.

EDMUND Sir, I shall study deserving.

GLOUCESTER He hath been out nine years, and away he 31
shall again. 32
[Sound a] sennet.
The King is coming.
*Enter [one bearing a coronet, then] King Lear, [then
the Dukes of] Cornwall, [and] Albany, [next]
Goneril, Regan, Cordelia, and Attendants.*

LEAR
Attend the lords of France and Burgundy, Gloucester.

GLOUCESTER
I shall, my lord.   *Exit [with Edmund].*

LEAR
Meantime we shall express our darker purpose. 36
Give me the map there. Know that we have divided
In three our kingdom ; and 'tis our fast intent 38
To shake all cares and business from our age,
Conferring them on younger strengths while we
Unburdened crawl toward death. Our son of Cornwall,
And you our no less loving son of Albany,
We have this hour a constant will to publish 43
Our daughters' several dowers, that future strife 44
May be prevented now. The princes, France and
Burgundy,
Great rivals in our youngest daughter's love ;
Long in our court have made their amorous sojourn, 47
And here are to be answered. Tell me, my daughters
(Since now we will divest us both of rule,
Interest of territory, cares of state), 50
Which of you shall we say doth love us most,
That we our largest bounty may extend
Where nature doth with merit challenge. Goneril, 53
Our eldest-born, speak first.

I, i *Room of state within King Lear's palace* 1 *affected* warmly regarded
2 *Albany* i.e. Scotland (once ruled by 'Albanacte') 5 *equalities* . . .
weighed i.e. the portions weigh so equally 6 *curiosity* . . . *moiety* careful
analysis by neither can make him prefer the other's portion 8 *breeding*
rearing 10 *brazed* brazened 11 *conceive* understand (with pun following)
17 *proper* handsome 19 *account* estimation 20 *saucily* (1) impertinently,
(2) bawdily 22 *whoreson* (affectionate abuse, but literally applicable,
like *knave* above) 31 *out* away (for training, or in military service) 32
s.d. *sennet* trumpet flourish (heralding a procession) 36 *darker purpose*
more secret intention (to require declarations of affection) 38 *fast* firm
43 *constant* . . . *publish* fixed intention to announce 44 *several* individual
47 *amorous sojourn* i.e. visit of courtship 50 *Interest* legal possession 53
nature . . . *challenge* natural affection matches other merits

GONERIL

55 Sir, I love you more than word can wield the matter;
56 Dearer than eyesight, space, and liberty;
Beyond what can be valuèd, rich or rare;
No less than life, with grace, health, beauty, honor;
As much as child e'er loved, or father found;
60 A love that makes breath poor, and speech unable.
Beyond all manner of so much I love you.

CORDELIA [aside]

What shall Cordelia speak? Love, and be silent.

LEAR

Of all these bounds, even from this line to this,
64 With shadowy forests and with champains riched,
65 With plenteous rivers and wide-skirted meads,
66 We make thee lady. To thine and Albany's issues
67 Be this perpetual. – What says our second daughter,
Our dearest Regan, wife of Cornwall?

REGAN

I am made of that self mettle as my sister,
70 And prize me at her worth. In my true heart
71 I find she names my very deed of love;
Only she comes too short, that I profess
Myself an enemy to all other joys
74 Which the most precious square of sense possesses,
75 And find I am alone felicitate
In your dear Highness' love.

CORDELIA [aside]   Then poor Cordelia;

And yet not so, since I am sure my love 's
78 More ponderous than my tongue.

LEAR

To thee and thine hereditary ever
Remain this ample third of our fair kingdom,
81 No less in space, validity, and pleasure
Than that conferred on Goneril. – Now, our joy,
83 Although our last and least; to whose young love
84 The vines of France and milk of Burgundy
85 Strive to be interest; what can you say to draw
A third more opulent than your sisters? Speak.

CORDELIA

Nothing, my lord.

LEAR Nothing?

CORDELIA Nothing.

LEAR

Nothing will come of nothing. Speak again.

CORDELIA

Unhappy that I am, I cannot heave
My heart into my mouth. I love your Majesty
93 According to my bond, no more nor less.

LEAR

How, how, Cordelia? Mend your speech a little,
Lest you may mar your fortunes.

CORDELIA   Good my lord,

You have begot me, bred me, loved me. I
97 Return those duties back as are right fit,
Obey you, love you, and most honor you.
Why have my sisters husbands if they say
They love you all? Haply, when I shall wed,
101 That lord whose hand must take my plight shall carry
Half my love with him, half my care and duty.
Sure I shall never marry like my sisters,
[To love my father all.]

LEAR

But goes thy heart with this?

CORDELIA   Ay, my good lord.

LEAR

So young, and so untender?

CORDELIA

So young, my lord, and true.

LEAR

Let it be so, thy truth then be thy dower!
For, by the sacred radiance of the sun,
The mysteries of Hecate and the night, 110
By all the operation of the orbs 111
From whom we do exist and cease to be,
Here I disclaim all my paternal care,
Propinquity and property of blood, 114
And as a stranger to my heart and me
Hold thee from this for ever. The barbarous Scythian, 116
Or he that makes his generation messes 117
To gorge his appetite, shall to my bosom
Be as well neighbored, pitied, and relieved,
As thou my sometime daughter. 120

KENT   Good my liege –

LEAR

Peace, Kent!
Come not between the dragon and his wrath. 122
I loved her most, and thought to set my rest 123
On her kind nursery. – Hence and avoid my sight! – 124
So be my grave my peace as here I give 125
Her father's heart from her! Call France. Who stirs!
Call Burgundy. Cornwall and Albany,
With my two daughters' dowers digest the third;
Let pride, which she calls plainness, marry her.
I do invest you jointly with my power,
Preeminence, and all the large effects 131
That troop with majesty. Ourself, by monthly course, 132
With reservation of an hundred knights,
By you to be sustained, shall our abode
Make with you by due turn. Only we shall retain
The name, and all th' addition to a king. The sway, 136
Revenue, execution of the rest,
Belovèd sons, be yours; which to confirm,
This coronet part between you. 139

KENT   Royal Lear,

Whom I have ever honored as my king,
Loved as my father, as my master followed,
As my great patron thought on in my prayers –

LEAR

The bow is bent and drawn; make from the shaft. 143

KENT

Let it fall rather, though the fork invade 144

---

55 *wield* handle   56 *space* scope (for the exercise of *liberty*)   60 *breath* voice; *unable* inadequate   64 *champains riched* plains enriched   65 *wide-skirted* far spreading   66 *issues* descendants   67 *perpetual* in perpetuity   70 *prize . . . worth* value me at her value   71 *my very deed of* the true fact of my   74 *Which . . . possesses* which the most precise measurement by the senses holds to be most precious   75 *felicitate* made happy   78 *ponderous* weighty   81 *validity* value; *pleasure* pleasing qualities   83 *least* smallest, youngest   84 *vines* vineyards; *milk* pasture-lands (?)   85 *interest* concerned as interested parties   93 *bond* obligation   97 *Return . . . fit* i.e. am fittingly dutiful in return   101 *plight* pledge, troth-plight   110 *Hecate* infernal goddess, patroness of witches   111 *operation . . . orbs* astrological influences   114 *Propinquity* relationship; *property* i.e. common property, something shared   116 *Scythian* (proverbially barbarous)   117 *makes . . . messes* makes meals of his offspring   120 *sometime* former   122 *his* its   123 *set my rest* (1) risk my stake (a term in the card game primero), (2) rely for my repose   124 *nursery* nursing, care   125 *So . . . peace as* let me rest peacefully in my grave only as   131 *effects* tokens   132 *Ourself* I (royal plural)   136 *th' addition* honors and prerogatives   139 *coronet* (symbol of rule; not necessarily the royal crown)   143 *make* make away   144 *fall* strike; *fork* two-pronged head

The region of my heart. Be Kent unmannerly
When Lear is mad. What wouldst thou do, old man?
Think'st thou that duty shall have dread to speak
When power to flattery bows? To plainness honor 's
   bound

149 When majesty falls to folly. Reserve thy state,
150 And in thy best consideration check
151 This hideous rashness. Answer my life my judgment,
Thy youngest daughter does not love thee least,
Nor are those empty-hearted whose low sounds
154 Reverb no hollowness.

LEAR   Kent, on thy life, no more!
KENT
155 My life I never held but as a pawn
156 To wage against thine enemies; ne'er fear to lose it,
157 Thy safety being motive.
LEAR   Out of my sight!
KENT
158 See better, Lear, and let me still remain
159 The true blank of thine eye.
LEAR
Now by Apollo—
KENT   Now by Apollo, King,
Thou swear'st thy gods in vain.
161 LEAR   O vassal! Miscreant!
   [Grasping his sword.]
ALBANY, CORNWALL Dear sir, forbear!
KENT
Kill thy physician, and thy fee bestow
Upon the foul disease. Revoke thy gift,
Or, whilst I can vent clamor from my throat,
I'll tell thee thou dost evil.
166 LEAR   Hear me, recreant,
On thine allegiance, hear me!
168 That thou hast sought to make us break our vows,
169 Which we durst never yet, and with strained pride
170 To come betwixt our sentence and our power,
Which nor our nature nor our place can bear,
172 Our potency made good, take thy reward.
Five days we do allot thee for provision
174 To shield thee from disasters of the world,
And on the sixth to turn thy hated back
Upon our kingdom. If, on the tenth day following,
177 Thy banished trunk be found in our dominions,
The moment is thy death. Away. By Jupiter,
This shall not be revoked.

KENT
Fare thee well, King. Sith thus thou wilt appear,   180
Freedom lives hence, and banishment is here.
   [To Cordelia]
The gods to their dear shelter take thee, maid,
That justly think'st and hast most rightly said.
   [To Regan and Goneril]
And your large speeches may your deeds approve,   184
That good effects may spring from words of love.   185
Thus Kent, O princes, bids you all adieu;
He'll shape his old course in a country new.   Exit. 187
   Flourish. Enter Gloucester, with France and
   Burgundy; Attendants.
GLOUCESTER
Here's France and Burgundy, my noble lord.
LEAR
My Lord of Burgundy,
We first address toward you, who with this king
Hath rivalled for our daughter. What in the least
Will you require in present dower with her,
Or cease your quest of love?
BURGUNDY   Most royal Majesty,
I crave no more than hath your Highness offered,
Nor will you tender less.
LEAR   Right noble Burgundy,
When she was dear to us, we did hold her so;
But now her price is fallen. Sir, there she stands.
If aught within that little seeming substance   198
Or all of it, with our displeasure pieced   199
And nothing more, may fitly like your Grace,
She's there, and she is yours.
BURGUNDY   I know no answer.
LEAR
Will you, with those infirmities she owes,   202
Unfriended, new adopted to our hate,
Dow'red with our curse, and strangered with our oath,   204
Take her, or leave her?
BURGUNDY   Pardon me, royal sir.
Election makes not up on such conditions.   206
LEAR
Then leave her, sir, for by the pow'r that made me
I tell you all her wealth. [to France] For you, great King,
I would not from your love make such a stray   209
To match you where I hate; therefore beseech you
T' avert your liking a more worthier way   211
Than on a wretch whom Nature is ashamed
Almost t' acknowledge hers.
FRANCE   This is most strange,
That she whom even but now was your best object,   214
The argument of your praise, balm of your age,   215
The best, the dearest, should in this trice of time
Commit a thing so monstrous to dismantle   217
So many folds of favor. Sure her offense
Must be of such unnatural degree
That monsters it, or your fore-vouched affection   220
Fall'n into taint; which to believe of her   221
Must be a faith that reason without miracle   222
Should never plant in me.
CORDELIA   I yet beseech your Majesty,
If for I want that glib and oily art
To speak and purpose not since what I well intend   225
I'll do't before I speak, that you make known
It is no vicious blot, murder or foulness,
No unchaste action or dishonorèd step,

---

149 *Reserve thy state* retain your kingly authority   150 *best consideration* most careful deliberation   151 *Answer my life* i.e. I'll stake my life on   154 *Reverb no hollowness* i.e. do not reverberate (like a drum) as a result of hollowness   155 *pawn* stake   156 *wage* wager, pit   157 *motive* the moving cause   158 *still* always   159 *blank* center of the target (to guide your aim truly)   161 *Miscreant* (1) rascal, (2) infidel   166 *recreant* traitor   168 *That* in that, since   169 *strained* excessive   170 *To come . . . power* i.e. to oppose my power to sentence   172 *Our . . . good* if my power is to be demonstrated as real   174 *disasters* accidents   177 *trunk* body   180 *Sith* since   184 *approve* confirm   185 *effects* consequences   187 *shape . . . course* keep to his customary ways (of honesty)   198 *seeming substance* i.e. nothing, mere shell   199 *pieced* joined   202 *owes* owns   204 *strangered* made alien by   206 *Election . . . conditions* no choice is possible on such terms   209 *make . . . stray* stray so far as   211 *avert* turn   214 *best* favorite   215 *argument* theme   217 *to dismantle* so to strip off   220 *That monsters it* as makes it monstrous (i.e. abnormal, freakish); *fore-vouched* previously sworn   221 *taint* decay (with the implication that the affection, and the oath attesting it, were tainted in the first place)   222 *reason . . . miracle* i.e. rational, unaided by miraculous, means of persuasion   225 *purpose not* i.e. without intending to act in accordance with my words

255

That hath deprived me of your grace and favor;
But even for want of that for which I am richer –
231 A still-soliciting eye, and such a tongue
That I am glad I have not, though not to have it
Hath lost me in your liking.

LEAR   Better thou
Hadst not been born than not t' have pleased me better.

FRANCE
235 Is it but this? A tardiness in nature
236 Which often leaves the history unspoke
That it intends to do. My Lord of Burgundy,
What say you to the lady? Love's not love
239 When it is mingled with regards that stands
Aloof from th' entire point. Will you have her?
She is herself a dowry.

BURGUNDY   Royal King,
Give but that portion which yourself proposed,
And here I take Cordelia by the hand,
Duchess of Burgundy.

LEAR
Nothing. I have sworn. I am firm.

BURGUNDY
I am sorry then you have so lost a father
That you must lose a husband.

CORDELIA   Peace be with Burgundy.
248 Since that respects of fortune are his love,
I shall not be his wife.

FRANCE
Fairest Cordelia, that art most rich being poor,
Most choice forsaken, and most loved despised,
Thee and thy virtues here I seize upon.
Be it lawful I take up what's cast away.
Gods, gods! 'Tis strange that from their cold'st neglect
255 My love should kindle to inflamed respect.
Thy dow'rless daughter, King, thrown to my chance,
Is queen of us, of ours, and our fair France.
258 Not all the dukes of wat'rish Burgundy
259 Can buy this unprized precious maid of me.
Bid them farewell, Cordelia, though unkind.
261 Thou losest here, a better where to find.

LEAR
Thou hast her, France; let her be thine, for we
Have no such daughter, nor shall ever see
That face of hers again. Therefore be gone
265 Without our grace, our love, our benison.
Come, noble Burgundy.
        Flourish. Exeunt [Lear, Burgundy, Cornwall,
              Albany, Gloucester, and Attendants].

FRANCE
Bid farewell to your sisters.

CORDELIA
268 The jewels of our father, with washed eyes
Cordelia leaves you. I know you what you are;
270 And, like a sister, am most loath to call
271 Your faults as they are named. Love well our father.
272 To your professèd bosoms I commit him;
But yet, alas, stood I within his grace,
274 I would prefer him to a better place.
So farewell to you both.

REGAN
Prescribe not us our duty.

GONERIL   Let your study
Be to content your lord, who hath received you
278 At fortune's alms. You have obedience scanted,

And well are worth the want that you have wanted.   279
CORDELIA
Time shall unfold what plighted cunning hides,   280
Who covers faults, at last with shame derides.   281
Well may you prosper.

FRANCE   Come, my fair Cordelia.
                              Exit France and Cordelia.

GONERIL Sister, it is not little I have to say of what most
nearly appertains to us both. I think our father will
hence to-night.

REGAN That's most certain, and with you; next month
with us.

GONERIL You see how full of changes his age is. The observation we have made of it hath not been little. He
always loved our sister most, and with what poor judgment he hath now cast her off appears too grossly.   291

REGAN 'Tis the infirmity of his age; yet he hath ever but
slenderly known himself.   293

GONERIL The best and soundest of his time hath been but 294
rash; then must we look from his age to receive not alone
the imperfections of long-ingraffed condition, but there- 296
withal the unruly waywardness that infirm and choleric
years bring with them.

REGAN Such unconstant starts are we like to have from 299
him as this of Kent's banishment.

GONERIL There is further compliment of leave-taking   301
between France and him. Pray you let us hit together; if 302
our father carry authority with such disposition as he
bears, this last surrender of his will but offend us.   304

REGAN We shall further think of it.

GONERIL We must do something, and i' th' heat. Exeunt. 306

                              *

              Enter Bastard [Edmund, solus, with a letter].   I, ii
EDMUND
Thou, Nature, art my goddess; to thy law   1
My services are bound. Wherefore should I
Stand in the plague of custom, and permit   3
The curiosity of nations to deprive me,   4
For that I am some twelve or fourteen moonshines   5
Lag of a brother? Why bastard? Wherefore base,   6
When my dimensions are as well compact,   7
My mind as generous, and my shape as true,   8

231 *still-soliciting* always-begging 235 *tardiness in nature* natural reticence
236 *history unspoke* actions unannounced 239–40 *mingled . . . point*
i.e. mixed with irrelevant considerations 248 *respects* considerations
255 *inflamed respect* ardent regard 258 *wat'rish* (1) watery, weak, (2)
watered, diluted 259 *unprized* unvalued 261 *here* this place; *where*
other place 265 *benison* blessing 268 *jewels* i.e. things held precious
(cf. l. 259); *washed* tear-washed 270 *like a sister* with sisterly loyalty
271 *as . . . named* by their true names 272 *professed* i.e. love-professing
274 *prefer* promote 278 *alms* small offerings 279 *worth . . . wanted*
i.e. deserving no affection since you have shown no affection 280 *plighted*
pleated, enfolded 281 *Who . . . derides* i.e. time at first conceals faults,
then exposes them to shame 291 *grossly* crudely conspicuous 293
known himself i.e. been aware of what he truly is 294 *of his time* period
of his past life 296 *long-ingraffed* ingrown, chronic; *therewithal* along with
that 299 *unconstant starts* impulsive moves 301 *compliment* formality
302 *hit* agree 304 *surrender* i.e. yielding up of authority; *offend* harm
306 *i' th' heat* i.e. while the iron is hot
I, ii Within the Earl of Gloucester's castle 1 *Nature* i.e. the material and
mechanistic as distinct from the spiritual and heaven-ordained 3 *Stand
. . . custom* submit to the affliction of convention 4 *curiosity* nice distinctions 5 *For that* because; *moonshines* months 6 *Lag of* behind (in age)
7 *compact* fitted, matched 8 *generous* befitting the high-born

9   As honest madam's issue? Why brand they us
     With base? with baseness? Bastardy base? Base?
11   Who, in the lusty stealth of nature, take
12   More composition and fierce quality
     Than doth, within a dull, stale, tirèd bed,
14   Go to th' creating a whole tribe of fops
15   Got 'tween asleep and wake? Well then,
     Legitimate Edgar, I must have your land.
     Our father's love is to the bastard Edmund
     As to th' legitimate. Fine word, 'legitimate.'
     Well, my legitimate, if this letter speed,
20   And my invention thrive, Edmund the base
     Shall top th' legitimate. I grow, I prosper.
     Now, gods, stand up for bastards.
          Enter Gloucester.
     GLOUCESTER
     Kent banished thus? and France in choler parted?
24   And the King gone to-night? prescribed his pow'r?
25   Confined to exhibition? All this done
26   Upon the gad? – Edmund, how now? What news?
     EDMUND
     So please your lordship, none.
     GLOUCESTER
28   Why so earnestly seek you to put up that letter?
     EDMUND
     I know no news, my lord.
     GLOUCESTER
     What paper were you reading?
     EDMUND Nothing, my lord.
     GLOUCESTER No? What needed then that terrible dis-
     patch of it into your pocket? The quality of nothing
     hath not such need to hide itself. Let's see. Come, if it
     be nothing, I shall not need spectacles.
     EDMUND I beseech you, sir, pardon me. It is a letter from
     my brother that I have not all o'er-read; and for so much
38   as I have perused, I find it not fit for your o'erlooking.
     GLOUCESTER Give me the letter, sir.
     EDMUND I shall offend, either to detain or give it. The
41   contents, as in part I understand them, are to blame.
     GLOUCESTER Let's see, let's see.
     EDMUND I hope, for my brother's justification, he wrote
44   this but as an essay or taste of my virtue.
45   GLOUCESTER *(reads)* 'This policy and reverence of age
46   makes the world bitter to the best of our times; keeps our

---

9 *honest* chaste 11 *lusty . . . nature* secrecy of natural lust 12 *composition* completeness of constitution, robustness; *fierce* mettlesome,
thoroughbred 14 *fops* fools 15 *Got* begotten 20 *invention thrive* plot
succeed 25 *prescribed* limited 25 *exhibition* an allowance, a pension
26 *gad* spur 28 *put up* put away 38 *o'erlooking* examination 41 *to blame*
blameworthy 44 *essay* trial; *taste* test 45 *policy and reverence* policy
of reverencing 46 *the best of our times* our best years 48 *idle, fond*
foolish (synonyms) 49 *who sways* which rules 50 *suffered* allowed
52 *revenue* income 57 *to this* upon this 59 *casement* window 60 *closet*
room 61 *character* handwriting 62 *matter* contents 63 *in respect of that*
i.e. considering what those contents are; *fain* prefer to 68 *sounded you*
sounded you out 71 *perfect age* prime of life 76 *sirrah* sir (familiar,
or contemptuous, form) 81 *run . . . course* i.e. know where you are going
85 *feel* feel out, test; *affection* attachment, loyalty 86 *pretense of danger*
dangerous intention 88 *judge it meet* consider it fitting 89–90 *by . . .
assurance* i.e. by the proof of your own ears 96 *wind me* worm; *frame*
plan 97–98 *unstate . . . resolution* i.e. give everything to know for certain
99 *presently* at once; *convey* conduct 100 *withal* therewith 101 *late*
recent 102 *wisdom of nature* natural lore, science 102–04 *can . . .
effects* i.e. can supply explanations, yet punitive upheavals in nature
(such as earthquakes) follow 103 *scourged* whipped 104 *sequent* following
105 *mutinies* rebellions 107 *comes . . . prediction* i.e. is included among
these ill-omened things

---

fortunes from us till our oldness cannot relish them. I
begin to find an idle and fond bondage in the oppression 48
of aged tyranny, who sways, not as it hath power, but as 49
it is suffered. Come to me, that of this I may speak more. 50
If our father would sleep till I waked him, you should
enjoy half his revenue for ever, and live the beloved of 52
your brother,   Edgar.'

Hum! Conspiracy? 'Sleep till I waked him, you should
enjoy half his revenue.' My son Edgar! Had he a hand to
write this? A heart and brain to breed it in? When came
you to this? Who brought it?   57
EDMUND It was not brought me, my lord; there's the
cunning of it. I found it thrown in at the casement of my 59
closet.   60
GLOUCESTER You know the character to be your 61
brother's?
EDMUND If the matter were good, my lord, I durst swear 62
it were his; but in respect of that, I would fain think it 63
were not.
GLOUCESTER It is his.
EDMUND It is his hand, my lord; but I hope his heart is
not in the contents.
GLOUCESTER Has he never before sounded you in this 68
business?
EDMUND Never, my lord. But I have heard him oft maintain it to be fit that, sons at perfect age, and fathers 71
declined, the father should be as ward to the son, and
the son manage his revenue.
GLOUCESTER O villain, villain! His very opinion in the
letter. Abhorrèd villain, unnatural, detested, brutish
villain; worse than brutish! Go, sirrah, seek him. I'll 76
apprehend him. Abominable villain! Where is he?
EDMUND I do not well know, my lord. If it shall please
you to suspend your indignation against my brother till
you can derive from him better testimony of his intent,
you should run a certain course; where, if you violently 81
proceed against him, mistaking his purpose, it would
make a great gap in your own honor and shake in pieces
the heart of his obedience. I dare pawn down my life for
him that he hath writ this to feel my affection to your 85
honor, and to no other pretense of danger.   86
GLOUCESTER Think you so?
EDMUND If your honor judge it meet, I will place you 88
where you shall hear us confer of this and by an auri- 89
cular assurance have your satisfaction, and that without
any further delay than this very evening.
GLOUCESTER He cannot be such a monster.
[EDMUND Nor is not, sure.
GLOUCESTER To his father, that so tenderly and entirely
loves him. Heaven and earth!] Edmund, seek him out;
wind me into him, I pray you; frame the business after 96
your own wisdom. I would unstate myself to be in a due 97
resolution.
EDMUND I will seek him, sir, presently; convey the busi- 99
ness as I shall find means, and acquaint you withal. 100
GLOUCESTER These late eclipses in the sun and moon 101
portend no good to us. Though the wisdom of nature can 102
reason it thus and thus, yet nature finds itself scourged by 103
the sequent effects. Love cools, friendship falls off, 104
brothers divide. In cities, mutinies; in countries, dis- 105
cord; in palaces, treason; and the bond cracked 'twixt
son and father. This villain of mine comes under the pre- 107
diction, there's son against father; the King falls from

109 bias of nature, there's father against child. We have seen
the best of our time. Machinations, hollowness, treachery, and all ruinous disorders follow us disquietly to our
112 graves. Find out this villain, Edmund; it shall lose thee
nothing; do it carefully. And the noble and true-hearted
Kent banished; his offense, honesty. 'Tis strange. *Exit.*

115 EDMUND This is the excellent foppery of the world, that
116 when we are sick in fortune, often the surfeits of our own
behavior, we make guilty of our disasters the sun, the
moon, and stars; as if we were villains on necessity; fools
119 by heavenly compulsion; knaves, thieves, and treachers
120 by spherical predominance; drunkards, liars, and adul-
terers by an enforced obedience of planetary influence;
and all that we are evil in, by a divine thrusting on. An
123 admirable evasion of whoremaster man, to lay his goatish
124 disposition on the charge of a star. My father compoun-
125 ded with my mother under the Dragon's Tail, and my
126 nativity was under Ursa Major, so that it follows I am
rough and lecherous. Fut! I should have been that I am,
had the maidenliest star in the firmament twinkled on
my bastardizing. Edgar –
       Enter Edgar.
130 and pat he comes, like the catastrophe of the old comedy.
131 My cue is villainous melancholy, with a sigh like Tom o'
Bedlam. – O, these eclipses do portend these divisions.
Fa, sol, la, mi.
    EDGAR How now, brother Edmund; what serious con-
templation are you in?
    EDMUND I am thinking, brother, of a prediction I read
this other day, what should follow these eclipses.
    EDGAR Do you busy yourself with that?
139 EDMUND I promise you, the effects he writes of succeed
140 unhappily: [as of unnaturalness between the child and
the parent; death, dearth, dissolutions of ancient amities; divisions in state, menaces and maledictions
143 against king and nobles; needless diffidences, banish-
144 ment of friends, dissipation of cohorts, nuptial breaches,
and I know not what.
146 EDGAR How long have you been a sectary astronomical?
    EDMUND Come, come,] when saw you my father last?
    EDGAR The night gone by.
    EDMUND Spake you with him?
    EDGAR Ay, two hours together.
    EDMUND Parted you in good terms? Found you no dis-
152 pleasure in him by word nor countenance?
    EDGAR None at all.
    EDMUND Bethink yourself wherein you may have offen-
ded him; and at my entreaty forbear his presence until
156 some little time hath qualified the heat of his displeasure,
157 which at this instant so rageth in him that with the mis-
158 chief of your person it would scarcely allay.
    EDGAR Some villain hath done me wrong.
160 EDMUND That's my fear. I pray you have a continent forbearance till the speed of his rage goes slower; and, as I
say, retire with me to my lodging, from whence I will
163 fitly bring you to hear my lord speak. Pray ye, go;
there's my key. If you do stir abroad, go armed.
    EDGAR Armed, brother?
    EDMUND Brother, I advise you to the best. Go armed. I
am no honest man if there be any good meaning toward
you. I have told you what I have seen and heard; but
169 faintly, nothing like the image and horror of it. Pray
you, away.
170 EDGAR Shall I hear from you anon?

EDMUND I do serve you in this business.   *Exit [Edgar].*
A credulous father, and a brother noble,
Whose nature is so far from doing harms
That he suspects none; on whose foolish honesty
My practices ride easy. I see the business.   175
Let me, if not by birth, have lands by wit;   176
All with me's meet that I can fashion fit.   *Exit.* 177

             *

     Enter Goneril and Steward [Oswald].   I, iii
GONERIL
Did my father strike my gentleman for chiding of his
    fool?
OSWALD Ay, madam.
GONERIL
By day and night he wrongs me. Every hour
He flashes into one gross crime or other   4
That sets us all at odds. I'll not endure it.
His knights grow riotous, and himself upbraids us   6
On every trifle. When he returns from hunting,
I will not speak with him. Say I am sick.
If you come slack of former services,   9
You shall do well; the fault of it I'll answer.   10
     [Horns within.]
OSWALD He's coming, madam; I hear him.
GONERIL
Put on what weary negligence you please,
You and your fellows. I'd have it come to question.   13
If he distaste it, let him to my sister,   14
Whose mind and mine I know in that are one,
[Not to be overruled. Idle old man,   16
That still would manage those authorities
That he hath given away. Now, by my life,
Old fools are babes again, and must be used
With checks as flatteries, when they are seen abused.]   20
Remember what I have said.
OSWALD   Well, madam.
GONERIL
And let his knights have colder looks among you.
What grows of it, no matter; advise your fellows so.
[I would breed from hence occasions, and I shall,   24
That I may speak.] I'll write straight to my sister
To hold my course. Prepare for dinner.   *Exeunt.*

109 *bias of nature* natural tendency   112–13 *lose thee nothing* i.e. you
will not lose by it   115 *foppery* foolishness   116 *we are sick . . . surfeits*
i.e. our fortunes grow sickly, often from the excesses   119 *treachers*
traitors   120 *spherical predominance* i.e. ascendancy, or rule, of a particular
sphere   123 *goatish* lecherous   124 *compounded* (1) came to terms, (2)
created   125, 126 *Dragon's Tail, Ursa Major* (constellations, cited because of the suggestiveness of their names)   126 *nativity* birthday   130
catastrophe conclusion   131–32 *Tom o' Bedlam* (a type of beggar, mad
or pretending to be, so named from the London madhouse, Bethlehem
or 'Bedlam' Hospital)   139–40 *succeed unhappily* unluckily follow   140
unnaturalness unkindness, enmity   143 *diffidences* instances of distrust
144 *dissipation of cohorts* melting away of supporters   146 *sectary astronomical* of the astrological sect   152 *countenance* expression, look   156
qualified moderated   157 *mischief* injury   158 *allay* be appeased   160
continent forbearance cautious inaccessibility   163 *fitly* conveniently
169 *image and horror* horrible true picture   170 *anon* soon   175 *practices*
plots   176 *wit* intelligence   177 *meet* proper, acceptable; *fashion fit* i.e.
rig up, shape to the purpose
I, iii Within the Duke of Albany's palace   4 *crime* offense   6 *riotous*
boisterous   9 *come . . . services* i.e. serve him less well than formerly
10 *answer* answer for   13 *question* i.e. open issue, a thing discussed
14 *distaste* dislike   16 *Idle* foolish   20 *checks . . . abused* restraints in
place of cajolery when they (they) (the old men) are seen to be deceived (about
their true state)   24–25 *breed . . . speak* i.e. make an issue of it so that I
may speak

I, iv **Enter Kent [disguised].**

KENT

If but as well I other accents borrow

2 That can my speech defuse, my good intent

3 May carry through itself to that full issue

4 For which I razed my likeness. Now, banished Kent,

If thou canst serve where thou dost stand condemned,

So may it come thy master whom thou lov'st

Shall find thee full of labors.

Horns within. Enter Lear, [Knight,] and Attendants.

8 LEAR Let me not stay a jot for dinner; go get it ready. *[Exit an Attendant.]* How now, what art thou?

KENT A man, sir.

11 LEAR What dost thou profess? What wouldst thou with us?

12 KENT I do profess to be no less than I seem, to serve him truly that will put me in trust, to love him that is honest, 14 to converse with him that is wise and says little, to fear 15 judgment, to fight when I cannot choose, and to eat no fish.

LEAR What art thou?

KENT A very honest-hearted fellow, and as poor as the King.

LEAR If thou be'st as poor for a subject as he's for a king, thou art poor enough. What wouldst thou?

KENT Service.

LEAR Who wouldst thou serve?

KENT You.

LEAR Dost thou know me, fellow?

KENT No, sir, but you have that in your countenance 27 which I would fain call master.

LEAR What's that?

KENT Authority.

LEAR What services canst thou do?

31 KENT I can keep honest counsel, ride, run, mar a curious tale in telling it, and deliver a plain message bluntly. That which ordinary men are fit for I am qualified in, and the best of me is diligence.

LEAR How old art thou?

KENT Not so young, sir, to love a woman for singing, nor so old to dote on her for anything. I have years on my back forty-eight.

LEAR Follow me; thou shalt serve me. If I like thee no worse after dinner, I will not part from thee yet. Dinner, 41 ho, dinner! Where's my knave? my fool? Go you and call my fool hither. *[Exit an Attendant.]*

Enter Steward [Oswald].

You, you, sirrah, where's my daughter?

OSWALD So please you –   *Exit.*

I, iv 2 *defuse* disorder, disguise 3 *full issue* perfect result 4 *razed my likeness* erased my natural appearance 8 *stay* wait 11 *profess* do, work at (with pun following) 12 *profess* claim 14 *converse* associate 15 *judgment* i.e. God's judgment 15–16 *eat no fish* be a Protestant (anachronism) (?), avoid unmanly diet (?) 27 *fain* like to 31 *keep honest counsel* keep counsel honestly, i.e. respect confidences; *curious* elaborate, embroidered (as contrasted with *plain*) 41 *knave* boy 45 *clotpoll* clodpoll, dolt 56 *entertained* rendered hospitality 64 *rememb'rest* remind 65 *faint neglect* i.e. the weary negligence of I, iii, 12 66 *jealous curiosity* i.e. suspicious concern about trifles 67 *very pretense* true intention 80 *bandy* volley, exchange 81 *strucken* struck 82 *football* (an impromptu street and field game, held in low esteem) 85 *differences* distinctions in rank 87 *Go to!* . . . *wisdom* i.e. Get along! Do you know what's good for you? 88 *earnest* part payment 90 *coxcomb* (cap of the professional fool, topped with an imitation comb) 95 *smile* . . . *sits* i.e. adapt yourself to prevailing forces 97 *banished* i.e. provided the means for them to become alien to him 99 *nuncle* mine uncle

LEAR What says the fellow there? Call the clotpoll back. 45 *[Exit Knight.]* Where's my fool? Ho, I think the world's asleep. *[Enter Knight.]* How now? Where's that mongrel?

KNIGHT He says, my lord, your daughter is not well.

LEAR Why came not the slave back to me when I called him?

KNIGHT Sir, he answered me in the roundest manner, he would not.

LEAR He would not?

KNIGHT My lord, I know not what the matter is; but to my judgment your Highness is not entertained with 56 that ceremonious affection as you were wont. There's a great abatement of kindness appears as well in the general dependants as in the Duke himself also and your daughter.

LEAR Ha? Say'st thou so?

KNIGHT I beseech you pardon me, my lord, if I be mistaken; for my duty cannot be silent when I think your Highness wronged.

LEAR Thou but rememb'rest me of mine own conception. 64 I have perceived a most faint neglect of late, which I have 65 rather blamed as mine own jealous curiosity than as a 66 very pretense and purpose of unkindness. I will look 67 further into't. But where's my fool? I have not seen him this two days.

KNIGHT Since my young lady's going into France, sir, the fool hath much pined away.

LEAR No more of that; I have noted it well. Go you and tell my daughter I would speak with her. *[Exit Knight.]* Go you, call hither my fool.   *[Exit an Attendant.]*

Enter Steward [Oswald].

O, you, sir, you! Come you hither, sir. Who am I, sir?

OSWALD My lady's father.

LEAR 'My lady's father'? My lord's knave, you whoreson dog, you slave, you cur!

OSWALD I am none of these, my lord; I beseech your pardon.

LEAR Do you bandy looks with me, you rascal?   80 *[Strikes him.]*

OSWALD I'll not be strucken, my lord.   81

KENT Nor tripped neither, you base football player.   82 *[Trips up his heels.]*

LEAR I thank thee, fellow. Thou serv'st me, and I'll love thee.

KENT Come, sir, arise, away. I'll teach you differences. 85 Away, away. If you will measure your lubber's length again, tarry; but away. Go to! Have you wisdom? So. 87 *[Pushes him out.]*

LEAR Now, my friendly knave, I thank thee. There's earnest 88 of thy service.

[Gives money.] Enter Fool.

FOOL Let me hire him too. Here's my coxcomb.   90 *[Offers Kent his cap.]*

LEAR How now, my pretty knave? How dost thou?

FOOL Sirrah, you were best take my coxcomb.

KENT Why, fool?

FOOL Why? For taking one's part that's out of favor. Nay, an thou canst not smile as the wind sits, thou'lt catch 95 cold shortly. There, take my coxcomb. Why, this fellow has banished two on's daughters, and did the third a 97 blessing against his will. If thou follow him, thou must needs wear my coxcomb. – How now, nuncle? Would I 99 had two coxcombs and two daughters.

LEAR Why, my boy?

FOOL If I gave them all my living, I'ld keep my coxcombs myself. There's mine; beg another of thy daughters.

LEAR Take heed, sirrah – the whip.

106 FOOL Truth 's a dog must to kennel; he must be whipped out, when the Lady Brach may stand by th' fire and stink.

108 LEAR A pestilent gall to me.

FOOL Sirrah, I'll teach thee a speech.

LEAR Do.

FOOL Mark it, nuncle.

Have more than thou showest,
Speak less than thou knowest,
114 Lend less than thou owest,
115 Ride more than thou goest,
116 Learn more than thou trowest,
117 Set less than thou throwest;
Leave thy drink and thy whore,
And keep in-a-door,
120 And thou shalt have more
Than two tens to a score.

KENT This is nothing, fool.

123 FOOL Then 'tis like the breath of an unfee'd lawyer – you gave me nothing for't. Can you make no use of nothing, nuncle?

LEAR Why, no, boy. Nothing can be made out of nothing.

127 FOOL [to Kent] Prithee tell him, so much the rent of his land comes to; he will not believe a fool.

LEAR A bitter fool.

FOOL Dost thou know the difference, my boy, between a
131 bitter fool and a sweet one?

LEAR No, lad; teach me.

FOOL   [That lord that counselled thee
To give away thy land,
Come place him here by me –
136 Do thou for him stand.
The sweet and bitter fool
Will presently appear;
The one in motley here,
140 The other found out there.

LEAR Dost thou call me fool, boy?

FOOL All thy other titles thou hast given away; that thou wast born with.

KENT This is not altogether fool, my lord.

145 FOOL No, faith; lords and great men will not let me. If I had a monopoly out, they would have part on't. And ladies too, they will not let me have all the fool to my-
148 self; they'll be snatching.] Nuncle, give me an egg, and I'll give thee two crowns.

LEAR What two crowns shall they be?

FOOL Why, after I have cut the egg i' th' middle and eat up the meat, the two crowns of the egg. When thou clovest thy crown i' th' middle and gav'st away both
154 parts, thou bor'st thine ass on thy back o'er the dirt. Thou hadst little wit in thy bald crown when thou
156 gav'st thy golden one away. If I speak like myself in
157 this, let him be whipped that first finds it so.
158 [Sings] Fools had ne'er less grace in a year,
159 For wise men are grown foppish,
160 And know not how their wits to wear,
Their manners are so apish.

LEAR When were you wont to be so full of songs, sirrah?

163 FOOL I have used it, nuncle, e'er since thou mad'st thy

daughters thy mothers; for when thou gav'st them the rod, and put'st down thine own breeches,

[Sings]   Then they for sudden joy did weep,
And I for sorrow sung,
That such a king should play bo-peep   168
And go the fools among.

Prithee, nuncle, keep a schoolmaster that can teach thy fool to lie. I would fain learn to lie.

LEAR An you lie, sirrah, we'll have you whipped.   172

FOOL I marvel what kin thou and thy daughters are. They'll have me whipped for speaking true; thou'lt have me whipped for lying; and sometimes I am whipped for holding my peace. I had rather be any kind o' thing than a fool, and yet I would not be thee, nuncle: thou hast pared thy wit o' both sides and left nothing i' th' middle.   178 Here comes one o' the parings.

Enter Goneril.

LEAR How now, daughter? What makes that frontlet on?   180 You are too much of late i' th' frown.

FOOL Thou wast a pretty fellow when thou hadst no need to care for her frowning. Now thou art an O without a   183 figure. I am better than thou art now: I am a fool, thou art nothing. [to Goneril] Yes, forsooth, I will hold my tongue. So your face bids me, though you say nothing. Mum, mum,

He that keeps nor crust nor crum,   188
Weary of all, shall want some. –   189
[Points at Lear.]
That's a shealed peascod.   190

GONERIL
Not only, sir, this your all-licensed fool,   191
But other of your insolent retinue
Do hourly carp and quarrel, breaking forth   193
In rank and not-to-be-endurèd riots. Sir,
I had thought by making this well known unto you
To have found a safe redress, but now grow fearful,   196
By what yourself too late have spoke and done,
That you protect this course, and put it on   198
By your allowance; which if you should, the fault   199
Would not 'scape censure, nor the redresses sleep,   200
Which, in the tender of a wholesome weal,   201

106 *Brach* hound bitch 108 *gall* sore, source of irritation 114 *owest* borrow (?), own, keep (?) 115 *goest* walk 116 *Learn* hear, listen to; *trowest* believe 117 *Set . . . throwest* stake less than you throw for (i.e. play for odds) 120–21 *have . . . score* i.e. do better than break even 123 *breath* voice, counsel (reliable only when paid for) 127–28 *rent . . . land* (nothing, since he has no land) 131 *bitter, sweet* satirical, non-satirical 136 *Do . . . stand* (the Fool thus identifying Lear as his own foolish counsellor) 140 *found out* revealed (since Lear is the *born* fool as distinct from himself, the fool in *motley*, professionally satirical) 145 *let me* (i.e. be all fool, since they seek a share of folly) 148 *snatching* (like greedy courtiers seeking shares in royal patents of monopoly) 154 *bor'st . . . dirt* (thus foolishly reversing normal behavior) 156 *like myself* i.e. like a fool 157 *let . . . so* i.e. let him be whipped (as a fool) who mistakes this truth as my typical folly 158 *grace . . . year* favor at any time 159 *foppish* foolish 160 *their wits to wear* i.e. to use their intelligence 163 *used* practiced 168 *play bo-beep* i.e. act like a child 172 *An* if 178 *pared . . . middle* i.e. completely disposed of your wits (in disposing of your power) 180 *frontlet* band worn across the brow; hence, frown 183–84 *O . . . figure* cipher without a digit to give it value 188 *crum* soft bread within the crust 189 *want* need 190 *shealed* shelled, empty; *peascod* pea-pod 191 *all-licensed* all privileged 193 *carp* complain 196 *safe* sure 198 *put it on* instigate it 199 *allowance* approval 200 *redresses sleep* correction lie dormant 201 *tender of* care for; *weal* state

202 Might in their working do you that offense,
Which else were shame, that then necessity
Will call discreet proceeding.
   FOOL   For you know, nuncle,
206   The hedge-sparrow fed the cuckoo so long
207   That it's had it head bit off by it young.
208 So out went the candle, and we were left darkling.
   LEAR   Are you our daughter?
   GONERIL
I would you would make use of your good wisdom
211 (Whereof I know you are fraught) and put away
212 These dispositions which of late transport you
From what you rightly are.
   FOOL   May not an ass know when the cart draws the horse?
215 Whoop, Jug, I love thee!
   LEAR
Does any here know me? This is not Lear.
Does Lear walk thus? speak thus? Where are his eyes?
218 Either his notion weakens, his discernings
219 Are lethargied – Ha! Waking? 'Tis not so.
Who is it that can tell me who I am?
   FOOL   Lear's shadow.
   [LEAR
222 I would learn that; for, by the marks of sovereignty,
Knowledge, and reason, I should be false persuaded
I had daughters.
   FOOL   Which they will make an obedient father.]
   LEAR   Your name, fair gentlewoman?
   GONERIL
227 This admiration, sir, is much o' th' savor
Of other your new pranks. I do beseech you
To understand my purposes aright.
As you are old and reverend, should be wise.
Here do you keep a hundred knights and squires,
232 Men so disordered, so deboshed and bold
That this our court, infected with their manners,
234 Shows like a riotous inn. Epicurism and lust
Makes it more like a tavern or a brothel
236 Than a graced palace. The shame itself doth speak
For instant remedy. Be then desired
By her that else will take the thing she begs
239 A little to disquantity your train,
240 And the remainders that shall still depend

To be such men as may besort your age,   241
Which know themselves, and you.   242
   LEAR   Darkness and devils!
Saddle my horses; call my train together.
Degenerate bastard, I'll not trouble thee: 244
Yet have I left a daughter.
   GONERIL
You strike my people, and your disordered rabble
Make servants of their betters.
     Enter Albany.
   LEAR
Woe that too late repents. – [O, sir, are you come?]
Is it your will? Speak, sir. – Prepare my horses.
Ingratitude! thou marble-hearted fiend,
More hideous when thou show'st thee in a child
Than the sea-monster.
   ALBANY   Pray, sir, be patient.
   LEAR
Detested kite, thou liest.   253
My train are men of choice and rarest parts,   254
That all particulars of duty know
And in the most exact regard support   256
The worships of their name. O most small fault,   257
How ugly didst thou in Cordelia show!
Which, like an engine, wrenched my frame of nature   259
From the fixed place; drew from my heart all love
And added to the gall. O Lear, Lear, Lear!   261
Beat at this gate that let thy folly in
     [Strikes his head.]
And thy dear judgment out. Go, go, my people.
   ALBANY
My lord, I am guiltless, as I am ignorant
Of what hath moved you.
   LEAR   It may be so, my lord.
Hear, Nature, hear; dear goddess, hear:
Suspend thy purpose if thou didst intend
To make this creature fruitful.
Into her womb convey sterility,
Dry up in her the organs of increase,
And from her derogate body never spring   271
A babe to honor her. If she must teem,   272
Create her child of spleen, that it may live   273
And be a thwart disnatured torment to her.   274
Let it stamp wrinkles in her brow of youth,
With cadent tears fret channels in her cheeks,   276
Turn all her mother's pains and benefits   277
To laughter and contempt, that she may feel
How sharper than a serpent's tooth it is
To have a thankless child. Away, away!   *Exit.*
   ALBANY
Now, gods that we adore, whereof comes this?
   GONERIL
Never afflict yourself to know more of it,
But let his disposition have that scope   283
As dotage gives it.
     Enter Lear.
   LEAR
What, fifty of my followers at a clap?
Within a fortnight?
   ALBANY   What's the matter, sir?
   LEAR
I'll tell thee. *[to Goneril]* Life and death, I am ashamed
That thou hast power to shake my manhood thus!

202–04 *Might . . . proceeding* in their operation might be considered humiliating to you but, under the circumstances, are merely prudent 206 *cuckoo* (an image suggesting illegitimacy as well as voraciousness, since the cuckoo lays its eggs in the nests of other birds) 207 *it* its 208 *darkling* in the dark (like the dead hedge-sparrow and the threatened Lear) 211 *fraught* freighted, laden 212 *dispositions* moods 215 *Jug* Joan (evidently part of some catch-phrase) 218 *notion* understanding 219 *Ha! Waking* i.e. so I am really awake (presumably accompanied by the 'business' of pinching himself) 222 *marks of sovereignty* evidences that I am King (and hence the father of the princesses) 227 *admiration* air of wonderment 232 *deboshed* debauched 234 *Epicurism* loose living 236 *graced* honored; *shame* disgrace 239 *disquantity your train* reduce the size of your retinue 240 *depend* be attached 241 *besort* befit 242 *Which know* i.e. who are aware of the status of 244 *Degenerate* unnatural, fallen away from kind 253 *Detested kite* detestable bird of prey 254 *parts* accomplishments 256 *exact regard* careful attention, punctiliousness 257 *worships* honor 259 *engine* destructive contrivance of war 259–60 *wrenched . . . place* set askew my natural structure, distorted my normal self 261 *gall* bitterness 271 *derogate* degraded 272 *teem* increase 273 *spleen* ill-humor, spitefulness 274 *thwart disnatured* perverse unnatural 276 *cadent* falling; *fret* wear 277 *pains and benefits* care and offerings 283 *disposition* mood

289 That these hot tears, which break from me perforce,
Should make thee worth them. Blasts and fogs upon
thee!
291 Th' untented woundings of a father's curse
292 Pierce every sense about thee! Old fond eyes,
293 Beweep this cause again I'll pluck ye out
294 And cast you, with the waters that you loose,
295 To temper clay. [Yea, is it come to this?]
Ha! Let it be so. I have another daughter,
297 Who I am sure is kind and comfortable.
When she shall hear this of thee, with her nails
She'll flay thy wolvish visage. Thou shalt find
300 That I'll resume the shape which thou dost think
I have cast off for ever.
        Exit [Lear with Kent and Attendants].
GONERIL   Do you mark that?
ALBANY
302 I cannot be so partial, Goneril,
To the great love I bear you—
GONERIL
Pray you, content. – What, Oswald, ho!
        [To Fool]
You, sir, more knave than fool, after your master!
306 FOOL Nuncle Lear, nuncle Lear, tarry. Take the fool
with thee.
            A fox, when one has caught her,
            And such a daughter,
310   Should sure to the slaughter,
311   If my cap would buy a halter.
312   So the fool follows after.   *Exit.*
GONERIL
313 This man hath had good counsel – a hundred knights!
314 'Tis politic and safe to let him keep
315 At point a hundred knights – yes, that on every dream,
316 Each buzz, each fancy, each complaint, dislike,
He may enguard his dotage with their pow'rs
318 And hold our lives in mercy. – Oswald, I say!
ALBANY
Well, you may fear too far.
GONERIL   Safer than trust too far.
320 Let me still take away the harms I fear,
321 Not fear still to be taken. I know his heart.
What he hath uttered I have writ my sister.
If she sustain him and his hundred knights,
When I have showed th' unfitness –
        Enter Steward [Oswald].   How now, Oswald?
What, have you writ that letter to my sister?
OSWALD Ay, madam.
GONERIL
327 Take you some company, and away to horse.
328 Inform her full of my particular fear,
And thereto add such reasons of your own
330 As may compact it more. Get you gone,
And hasten your return. *[Exit Oswald.]* No, no, my lord,
332 This milky gentleness and course of yours,
Though I condemn not, yet under pardon,
334 You are much more ataskèd for want of wisdom
335 Than praised for harmful mildness.
ALBANY
How far your eyes may pierce I cannot tell;
Striving to better, oft we mar what's well.
GONERIL Nay then—
339 ALBANY Well, well; th' event.   *Exeunt.*
                          *

        Enter Lear, Kent, and Fool.   I, v
LEAR Go you before to Gloucester with these letters. Ac-
quaint my daughter no further with anything you know
than comes from her demand out of the letter. If your 3
diligence be not speedy, I shall be there afore you.
KENT I will not sleep, my lord, till I have delivered your
letter.   *Exit.*
FOOL If a man's brains were in's heels, were't not in
danger of kibes?   8
LEAR Ay, boy.
FOOL Then I prithee be merry. Thy wit shall not go slip- 10
shod.
LEAR Ha, ha, ha.
FOOL Shalt see thy other daughter will use thee kindly; 12
for though she's as like this as a crab 's like an apple, yet 13
I can tell what I can tell.
LEAR What canst tell, boy?
FOOL She will taste as like this as a crab does to a crab.
Thou canst tell why one's nose stands i' th' middle on's
face?
LEAR No.
FOOL Why, to keep one's eyes of either side 's nose, that
what a man cannot smell out he may spy into.
LEAR I did her wrong.   21
FOOL Canst tell how an oyster makes his shell?
LEAR No.
FOOL Nor I neither; but I can tell why a snail has a house.
LEAR Why?
FOOL Why, to put 's head in; not to give it away to his
daughters, and leave his horns without a case.   27
LEAR I will forget my nature. So kind a father! – Be my 28
horses ready?
FOOL Thy asses are gone about 'em. The reason why the
seven stars are no moe than seven is a pretty reason.   31
LEAR Because they are not eight.
FOOL Yes indeed. Thou wouldst make a good fool.
LEAR To take 't again perforce – Monster ingratitude!   34
FOOL If thou wert my fool, nuncle, I'd have thee beaten
for being old before thy time.
LEAR How's that?
FOOL Thou shouldst not have been old till thou hadst
been wise.

289 *perforce* by force, against my will 291 *untented* untentable, too
deep for treatment by a probe 292 *sense about* faculty possessed by;
fond foolish 293 *Beweep this cause* if you weep over this matter 294
loose let loose 295 *temper* soften 297 *comfortable* ready to comfort
300 *shape* i.e. role of authority 302–03 *partial . . . To* made partial . . .
by 306 *the fool* i.e. both your fool and your folly 310 *slaughter* hanging
and quartering 311, 312 *halter, after* (pronounced 'hauter,' 'auter')
313 *good counsel* i.e. from such company (ironic) 314 *politic* prudent
315 *At point* in arms 316 *buzz* murmur 318 *in mercy* at his mercy
320 *still . . . harms* always eliminate the sources of injury 321 *still . . .
taken* always to be overtaken (by them) 327 *some company* an escort
328 *particular* own 330 *compact it more* substantiate it further 332
milky . . . course mildly gentle way 334 *ataskèd* censured, taken to task
335 *harmful mildness* mildness that proves harmful 339 *th' event* the
outcome, i.e. we shall see what happens

I, v The courtyard of Albany's palace 3 *demand out of* i.e. questioning
provoked by reading 8 *kibes* chilblains 10 *wit . . . slipshod* intelligence
(*brains*) shall not go slippered (because of *kibes*) 12 *Shalt* thou shalt;
kindly after her kind, i.e. in the same way as this daughter 13 *crab* crab
apple 21 *her* i.e. Cordelia (the first of the remarkable intimations of
Lear's inner thoughts in this scene) 27 *horns* i.e. snail's horns (with pun
on cuckold's horns; the legitimacy of Goneril and Regan being, figuratively,
suspect throughout); *case* covering 28 *nature* i.e. fatherly instincts
31 *moe* more 34 *perforce* by force

LEAR
    O, let me not be mad, not mad, sweet heaven!
41   Keep me in temper; I would not be mad!
    [Enter a Gentleman.]
    How now, are the horses ready?
GENTLEMAN Ready, my lord.
LEAR Come, boy.
FOOL
45   She that's a maid now, and laughs at my departure,
    Shall not be a maid long, unless things be cut shorter.
                        Exeunt.

                   *

II, i   *Enter Bastard [Edmund] and Curan severally.*
1 EDMUND Save thee, Curan.
CURAN And you, sir. I have been with your father, and
    given him notice that the Duke of Cornwall and Regan
    his Duchess will be here with him this night.
EDMUND How comes that?
CURAN Nay, I know not. You have heard of the news
    abroad – I mean the whispered ones, for they are yet but
8   ear-kissing arguments?
EDMUND Not I. Pray you, what are they?
10 CURAN Have you heard of no likely wars toward, 'twixt
    the Dukes of Cornwall and Albany?
EDMUND Not a word.
CURAN You may do, then, in time. Fare you well, sir. *Exit.*
EDMUND
14   The Duke be here to-night? The better best!
15   This weaves itself perforce into my business.
    My father hath set guard to take my brother,
17   And I have one thing of a queasy question
18   Which I must act. Briefness and fortune, work!
    Brother, a word: descend. Brother, I say!
          Enter Edgar.
    My father watches. O sir, fly this place.
    Intelligence is given where you are hid.
    You have now the good advantage of the night.
    Have you not spoken 'gainst the Duke of Cornwall?
    He's coming hither; now i' th' night, i' th' haste,
    And Regan with him. Have you nothing said
26   Upon his party 'gainst the Duke of Albany?
27   Advise yourself.
EDGAR   I am sure on't, not a word.
EDMUND
    I hear my father coming. Pardon me:

In cunning I must draw my sword upon you.   29
Draw, seem to defend yourself; now quit you well. –   30
Yield! Come before my father! Light ho, here! –
Fly, brother. – Torches, torches! – So farewell.
                        Exit Edgar.
Some blood drawn on me would beget opinion
Of my more fierce endeavor.
    [Wounds his arm.]   I have seen drunkards
Do more than this in sport. – Father, father!
Stop, stop! No help?
    Enter Gloucester, and Servants with torches.
GLOUCESTER
    Now, Edmund, where's the villain?
EDMUND
    Here stood he in the dark, his sharp sword out,
    Mumbling of wicked charms, conjuring the moon
    To stand auspicious mistress.
GLOUCESTER   But where is he?
EDMUND
    Look, sir, I bleed.
GLOUCESTER   Where is the villain, Edmund?
EDMUND
    Fled this way, sir, when by no means he could –
GLOUCESTER
    Pursue him, ho! Go after.   *[Exeunt some Servants.]*
             By no means what?
EDMUND
    Persuade me to the murder of your lordship;
    But that I told him the revenging gods
    'Gainst parricides did all the thunder bend;   46
    Spoke with how manifold and strong a bond
    The child was bound to th' father – sir, in fine,   48
    Seeing how loathly opposite I stood   49
    To his unnatural purpose, in fell motion   50
    With his preparèd sword he charges home
    My unprovided body, latched mine arm;   52
    And when he saw my best alarumed spirits   53
    Bold in the quarrel's right, roused to th' encounter,   54
    Or whether gasted by the noise I made,   55
    Full suddenly he fled.
GLOUCESTER   Let him fly far.
    Not in this land shall he remain uncaught;
    And found – dispatch. The noble Duke my master,   58
    My worthy arch and patron, comes to-night: 59
    By his authority I will proclaim it
    That he which finds him shall deserve our thanks,
    Bringing the murderous coward to the stake;
    He that conceals him, death.
EDMUND
    When I dissuaded him from his intent
    And found him pight to do it, with curst speech   65
    I threatened to discover him. He replied,   66
    'Thou unpossessing bastard, dost thou think,   67
    If I would stand against thee, would the reposal   68
    Of any trust, virtue, or worth in thee
    Make thy words faithed? No. What I should deny   70
    (As this I would, ay, though thou didst produce
    My very character) I'ld turn it all   72
    To thy suggestion, plot, and damnèd practice;   73
    And thou must make a dullard of the world,   74
    If they not thought the profits of my death   75
    Were very pregnant and potential spirits   76
    To make thee seek it.'
GLOUCESTER   O strange and fast'ned villain!   77

---

41 *in temper* properly balanced   45–46 *She . . . shorter* (an indecent gag addressed to the audience, calculated to embarrass the maids who joined in the laughter)
II, i The Earl of Gloucester's castle   1 *Save* God save   8 *ear-kissing arguments* whispered topics   10 *likely* probable; *toward* impending   14 *better best* (hyperbole)   15 *perforce* of necessity (?), of its own accord (?)   17 *of . . . question* delicately balanced as to outcome, touch-and-go   18 *Briefness and fortune* decisive speed and good luck   26 *Upon his party 'gainst* i.e. reflecting upon his feud against   27 *Advise yourself* take thought; *on't* of it   29 *In cunning* i.e. as a ruse   30 *quit you* acquit yourself   46 *bend* aim   48 *in fine* finally   49 *loathly opposite* in loathing opposition   50 *fell* deadly   52 *unprovided* undefended; *latched* lanced, pierced   53 *best alarumed* fully aroused   54 *Bold . . . right* confident in the justice of the cause   55 *gasted* struck aghast   58 *dispatch* (equivalent to 'death' or 'finis')   59 *arch* superior   65 *pight* determined, set; *curst* angry   66 *discover* expose   67 *unpossessing* having no claim, landless   68 *reposal* placing   70 *faithed* believed   72 *character* written testimony   73 *suggestion* instigation; *practice* devices   74 *make . . . world* i.e. consider everyone stupid   75 *not thought* did not think   76 *pregnant . . . spirits* teeming and powerful spirits, i.e. the devils which 'possess' him   77 *fast'ned* confirmed

78   Would he deny his letter, said he ? [I never got him.]
       Tucket within.
     Hark, the Duke's trumpets. I know not why he comes.
     All ports I'll bar ; the villain shall not 'scape ;
     The Duke must grant me that. Besides, his picture
     I will send far and near, that all the kingdom
     May have due note of him ; and of my land,
     Loyal and natural boy, I'll work the means
85   To make thee capable.
       Enter Cornwall, Regan, and Attendants.

CORNWALL
     How now, my noble friend ? Since I came hither
87   (Which I can call but now) I have heard strange news.

REGAN
     If it be true, all vengeance comes too short
     Which can pursue th' offender. How dost, my lord ?

GLOUCESTER
     O madam, my old heart is cracked, it's cracked.

REGAN
     What, did my father's godson seek your life ?
     He whom my father named, your Edgar ?

GLOUCESTER
     O lady, lady, shame would have it hid.

REGAN
     Was he not companion with the riotous knights
     That tended upon my father ?

GLOUCESTER
     I know not, madam. 'Tis too bad, too bad.

EDMUND
97   Yes, madam, he was of that consort.

REGAN
98   No marvel then though he were ill affected.
99   'Tis they have put him on the old man's death,
100   To have th' expense and waste of his revenues.
     I have this present evening from my sister
     Been well informed of them, and with such cautions
     That, if they come to sojourn at my house,
     I'll not be there.

CORNWALL   Nor I, assure thee, Regan.
     Edmund, I hear that you have shown your father
106   A childlike office.

EDMUND   It was my duty, sir.

GLOUCESTER
107   He did bewray his practice, and received
     This hurt you see, striving to apprehend him.

CORNWALL
     Is he pursued ?

GLOUCESTER   Ay, my good lord.

CORNWALL
     If he be taken, he shall never more
111   Be feared of doing harm. Make your own purpose,
     How in my strength you please. For you, Edmund,
113   Whose virtue and obedience doth this instant
     So much commend itself, you shall be ours.
     Natures of such deep trust we shall much need ;
     You we first seize on.

EDMUND   I shall serve you, sir,
     Truly, however else.

GLOUCESTER   For him I thank your Grace.

CORNWALL
     You know not why we came to visit you ?

REGAN
     Thus out of season, threading dark-eyed night.
120   Occasions, noble Gloucester, of some prize,

Wherein we must have use of your advice.
Our father he hath writ, so hath our sister,
Of differences, which I best thought it fit   123
To answer from our home. The several messengers   124
From hence attend dispatch. Our good old friend,   125
Lay comforts to your bosom, and bestow   126
Your needful counsel to our businesses,   127
Which craves the instant use.   128

GLOUCESTER   I serve you, madam.
Your Graces are right welcome.   *Exeunt. Flourish.*

*

       Enter Kent and Steward [Oswald], severally.   II, ii

OSWALD   Good dawning to thee, friend. Art of this house ?   1
KENT   Ay.
OSWALD   Where may we set our horses ?
KENT   I' th' mire.
OSWALD   Prithee, if thou lov'st me, tell me.
KENT   I love thee not.
OSWALD   Why then, I care not for thee.
KENT   If I had thee in Lipsbury Pinfold, I would make   8
   thee care for me.
OSWALD   Why dost thou use me thus ? I know thee not.
KENT   Fellow, I know thee.
OSWALD   What dost thou know me for ?
KENT   A knave, a rascal, an eater of broken meats ; a base,   13
   proud, shallow, beggarly, three-suited, hundred-pound,   14
   filthy worsted-stocking knave ; a lily-livered, action-   15
   taking, whoreson, glass-gazing, superserviceable, finical   16
   rogue ; one-trunk-inheriting slave ; one that wouldst be a   17
   bawd in way of good service, and art nothing but the
   composition of a knave, beggar, coward, pander, and the   19
   son and heir of a mongrel bitch ; one whom I will beat
   into clamorous whining if thou deny'st the least syllable
   of thy addition.   22
OSWALD   Why, what a monstrous fellow art thou, thus to
   rail on one that is neither known of thee nor knows thee !
KENT   What a brazen-faced varlet art thou to deny thou
   knowest me ! Is it two days ago since I tripped up thy
   heels and beat thee before the King ? [*Draws his sword.*]
   Draw, you rogue, for though it be night, yet the moon
   shines. I'll make a sop o' th' moonshine of you. You   29
   whoreson cullionly barbermonger, draw !   30

---

78 *got* begot ; s.d. *Tucket* (personal signature in trumpet notes)   85 *capable*
i.e. legitimate, able to inherit   87 *call* i.e. say was   97 *consort* company, set
98 *affected* disposed   99 *put* set   100 *expense and waste* wasteful ex-
penditure   106 *childlike* filial   107 *bewray his practice* expose his plot   111
of doing lest he do   111–12 *Make . . . please* i.e. accomplish your purpose,
making free use of my powers   113 *virtue and obedience* virtuous obedience
120 *prize* price, importance   123 *differences* quarrels ; *which* (refers, in-
definitely, to the whole situation)   124 *answer . . . home* cope with away
from home (where she need not receive Lear)   125 *attend dispatch* i.e.
await settlement of the business   126 *Lay . . . bosom* be consoled (about
your own trouble)   127 *needful* needed   128 *craves . . . use* requires immediate transaction (?), requires use of your counsel (?)
II, ii Before Gloucester's castle   1 *dawning* (perhaps indicating that it
is too early for 'good morning') ; *Art . . . house* i.e. do you belong to this
household   8 *Lipsbury Pinfold* i.e. between the teeth (cant term : 'pen in
the region of the lips')   13 *broken meats* scraps   14 *three-suited* with
three suits (the wardrobe allowed serving-men) ; *hundred-pound* (the mini-
mal estate for anyone aspiring to gentility)   15 *worsted-stocking* (servingmen's attire)   15–16 *action-taking* i.e. cowardly (resorting to law instead
of fighting)   16 *glass-gazing, superserviceable, finical* i.e. conceited, toady-
ing, foppish   17 *inheriting* possessing   17–18 *a bawd . . . service* i.e. a
pander, if pleasing your employer required it   19 *composition* composite
22 *addition* titles   29 *sop o' th' moonshine* i.e. something that sops up moonshine through its perforations   30 *cullionly barbermonger* vile fop (i.e.
always dealing with hairdressers)

OSWALD Away, I have nothing to do with thee.

KENT Draw, you rascal. You come with letters against the
33 King, and take Vanity the puppet's part against the
34 royalty of her father. Draw, you rogue, or I'll so car-
35 bonado your shanks. Draw, you rascal. Come your ways!

OSWALD Help, ho! Murder! Help!

37 KENT Strike, you slave! Stand, rogue! Stand, you neat
slave! Strike!
    [Beats him.]

OSWALD Help, ho! Murder, murder!
    Enter Bastard [Edmund, with his rapier drawn],
    Cornwall, Regan, Gloucester, Servants.

EDMUND How now? What's the matter? Part!

41 KENT With you, goodman boy, if you please! Come, I'll
42 flesh ye; come on, young master.

GLOUCESTER Weapons? Arms? What's the matter here?

CORNWALL Keep peace, upon your lives. He dies that
strikes again. What is the matter?

REGAN The messengers from our sister and the King.

CORNWALL What is your difference? Speak.

OSWALD I am scarce in breath, my lord.

49 KENT No marvel, you have so bestirred your valor. You
50 cowardly rascal, Nature disclaims in thee. A tailor made
thee.

CORNWALL Thou art a strange fellow. A tailor make a
man?

53 KENT A tailor, sir. A stonecutter or a painter could not
have made him so ill, though they had been but two
years o' th' trade.

CORNWALL
Speak yet, how grew your quarrel?

OSWALD This ancient ruffian, sir, whose life I have
58 spared at suit of his gray beard –

59 KENT Thou whoreson zed, thou unnecessary letter! My
60 lord, if you will give me leave, I will tread this unbolted
61 villain into mortar and daub the wall of a jakes with him.
62 Spare my gray beard? you wagtail.

CORNWALL
Peace, sirrah!

---

33 *Vanity the puppet* i.e. Goneril (here equated with a stock figure in
morality plays, now dwindled into puppet shows) 34 *carbonado* (cut into
strips or cubes) 35 *your ways* get along 37 *neat* primping 41 *goodman
boy* (doubly contemptuous, since peasants were addressed as 'goodmen')
42 *flesh ye* give you your first taste of blood 49 *bestirred* exercised 50
disclaims claims no part 53 *stonecutter* sculptor 58 *at suit of* on the plea
of, moved to mercy by 59 *zed* (last and least useful of letters) 60 *unbolted*
unsifted, crude 61 *jakes* privy 62 *wagtail* (any of several birds whose
tail-feathers wag or bob, suggesting obsequiousness or effeminacy) 64
beastly beast-like, irrational 69 *holy cords* sacred bonds (between parents
and children, husbands and wives, man and God) 70 *intrinse* intrinsic,
inextricable ; *smooth* flatter, cater to 71 *rebel* (i.e. against reason and
moral restraint) 72 *Being . . . moods* (i.e. feeders of intemperance) 73
Renege deny ; *halcyon beaks* kingfisher beaks (supposedly serving as weather
vanes when the birds were hung up by their necks) 74 *gale and vary*
varying wind 76 *epileptic* contorted in a grin (?) 77 *Smile you* mock
you at, mock you 78 *Sarum Plain* Salisbury Plain (said to have been
associated with geese, but the allusion remains cryptic) 79 *Camelot*
legendary seat of King Arthur, variously sited at Winchester, near Cad-
bury, in Wales, etc. 82 *contraries* opposites 92–93 *constrains . . . nature*
distorts the plain fashion from its true nature, caricatures it 98 *silly-
ducking observants* ludicrously bowing form-servers 99 *nicely* fussily
101 *allowance* approval ; *aspect* (1) appearance, (2) heavenly position 102
influence astrological force 103 *Phoebus' front* sun's forehead (i.e. face)
104 *go . . . dialect* depart from my way of speaking 105 *He* (the type of
plain-speaker Cornwall has condemned) 107–08 *though . . . to't* though I
should persuade your disapproving self to beg me to do so (? with *displeasure* sarcastically substituted for 'grace') 111 *very late* quite recently
112 *misconstruction* misunderstanding

You beastly knave, know you no reverence? 64

KENT
Yes, sir, but anger hath a privilege.

CORNWALL
Why art thou angry?

KENT
That such a slave as this should wear a sword,
Who wears no honesty. Such smiling rogues as these
Like rats oft bite the holy cords atwain 69
Which are too intrinse t' unloose; smooth every passion 70
That in the natures of their lords rebel, 71
Being oil to fire, snow to the colder moods; 72
Renege, affirm, and turn their halcyon beaks 73
With every gale and vary of their masters, 74
Knowing naught, like dogs, but following.
A plague upon your epileptic visage! 76
Smile you my speeches, as I were a fool? 77
Goose, if I had you upon Sarum Plain, 78
I'ld drive ye cackling home to Camelot. 79

CORNWALL
What, art thou mad, old fellow?

GLOUCESTER
How fell you out? Say that.

KENT
No contraries hold more antipathy 82
Than I and such a knave.

CORNWALL
Why dost thou call him knave? What is his fault?

KENT
His countenance likes me not.

CORNWALL
No more perchance does mine, nor his, nor hers.

KENT
Sir, 'tis my occupation to be plain :
I have seen better faces in my time
Than stands on any shoulder that I see
Before me at this instant.

CORNWALL   This is some fellow
Who, having been praised for bluntness, doth affect
A saucy roughness, and constrains the garb 92
Quite from his nature. He cannot flatter, he;
An honest mind and plain – he must speak truth.
An they will take it, so; if not, he's plain.
These kind of knaves I know which in this plainness
Harbor more craft and more corrupter ends
Than twenty silly-ducking observants 98
That stretch their duties nicely. 99

KENT
Sir, in good faith, in sincere verity,
Under th' allowance of your great aspect, 101
Whose influence, like the wreath of radiant fire 102
On flick'ring Phoebus' front – 103

CORNWALL   What mean'st by this?

KENT To go out of my dialect, which you discommend so 104
much. I know, sir, I am no flatterer. He that beguiled 105
you in a plain accent was a plain knave, which, for my
part, I will not be, though I should win your displeasure 107
to entreat me to't.

CORNWALL
What was th' offense you gave him?

OSWALD
I never gave him any.
It pleased the King his master very late 111
To strike at me, upon his misconstruction; 112

113 When he, compact, and flattering his displeasure,
Tripped me behind ; being down, insulted, railed,
115 And put upon him such a deal of man
116 That worthied him, got praises of the King
117 For him attempting who was self-subdued ;
118 And, in the fleshment of this dread exploit,
Drew on me here again.
119 KENT   None of these rogues and cowards
But Ajax is their fool.
CORNWALL   Fetch forth the stocks !
121 You stubborn ancient knave, you reverent braggart,
We'll teach you.
KENT   Sir, I am too old to learn.
Call not your stocks for me, I serve the King –
On whose employment I was sent to you ;
125 You shall do small respect, show too bold malice
126 Against the grace and person of my master,
Stocking his messenger.
CORNWALL
Fetch forth the stocks. As I have life and honor,
There shall he sit till noon.
REGAN
Till noon ? Till night, my lord, and all night too.
KENT
Why, madam, if I were your father's dog,
You should not use me so.
REGAN   Sir, being his knave, I will.
CORNWALL
133 This is a fellow of the selfsame color
134 Our sister speaks of. Come, bring away the stocks.
          Stocks brought out.
GLOUCESTER
Let me beseech your Grace not to do so.
[His fault is much, and the good King his master
137 Will check him for't. Your purposed low correction
138 Is such as basest and contemnèd'st wretches
For pilf'rings and most common trespasses
Are punished with.]
The King his master needs must take it ill
142 That he, so slightly valued in his messenger,
Should have him thus restrained.
143 CORNWALL   I'll answer that.
REGAN
My sister may receive it much more worse,
To have her gentleman abused, assaulted,
[For following her affairs. Put in his legs.]
          [Kent is put in the stocks.]
CORNWALL
Come, my lord, away !
          Exit [with all but Gloucester and Kent].
GLOUCESTER
I am sorry for thee, friend. 'Tis the Duke's pleasure,
149 Whose disposition all the world well knows
150 Will not be rubbed nor stopped. I'll entreat for thee.
KENT
151 Pray do not, sir. I have watched and travelled hard.
Some time I shall sleep out, the rest I'll whistle.
153 A good man's fortune may grow out at heels.
154 Give you good morrow.
GLOUCESTER
155 The Duke's to blame in this. 'Twill be ill taken.   *Exit.*
KENT
156 Good King, that must approve the common saw,
157 Thou out of heaven's benediction com'st

To the warm sun.
Approach, thou beacon to this under globe,   159
That by thy comfortable beams I may
Peruse this letter. Nothing almost sees miracles   161
But misery. I know 'tis from Cordelia,
Who hath most fortunately been informed
Of my obscurèd course. And shall find time   164
From this enormous state, seeking to give   165
Losses their remedies. – All weary and o'erwatched,   166
Take vantage, heavy eyes, not to behold   167
This shameful lodging. Fortune, good night ;   168
Smile once more ; turn thy wheel.   169
          [Sleeps.]
          Enter Edgar.   II, iii
EDGAR
I heard myself proclaimed,
And by the happy hollow of a tree   2
Escaped the hunt. No port is free, no place
That guard and most unusual vigilance
Does not attend my taking. Whiles I may 'scape,   5
I will preserve myself ; and am bethought   6
To take the basest and most poorest shape
That ever penury, in contempt of man,
Brought near to beast : my face I'll grime with filth,
Blanket my loins, elf all my hairs in knots,   10
And with presented nakedness outface   11
The winds and persecutions of the sky.
The country gives me proof and precedent   13
Of Bedlam beggars, who, with roaring voices,   14
Strike in their numbed and mortified bare arms   15
Pins, wooden pricks, nails, sprigs of rosemary ;   16
And with this horrible object, from low farms,   17
Poor pelting villages, sheepcotes, and mills,   18
Sometimes with lunatic bans, sometime with prayers,   19
Enforce their charity. Poor Turlygod, poor Tom,   20
That's something yet : Edgar I nothing am.   21
          Exit.
          Enter Lear, Fool, and Gentleman.   II, iv
LEAR
'Tis strange that they should so depart from home,
And not send back my messenger.

113 *compact* in league with   115 *And put . . . man* i.e. affected such excessive manliness   116 *worthied* enhanced his worth   117 *For him
. . . self-subdued* for assailing him (Oswald) who chose not to resist   118
fleshment of bloodthirstiness induced by   119–20 *None . . . fool* i.e. the
Ajax type, stupidly belligerent, is the favorite butt of cowardly rogues
like Oswald   121 *stubborn* rude ; *reverent* aged   125 *malice* ill will
126 *grace* royal honor   133 *color* kind   134 *away* along   137 *check*
rebuke ; *purposed* intended   138 *contemnèd'st* most harshly sentenced
142 *slightly valued in* i.e. little respected in the person of   143 *answer*
answer for   149 *disposition* inclination   150 *rubbed* deflected (bowling
term)   151 *watched* gone sleepless   153 *A good . . . heels* i.e. it is no
disgrace to decline in fortune   154 *Give* God give   155 *taken* received
156 *approve* demonstrate the truth of ; *saw* saying, proverb   157–58
Thou . . . sun (proverb, meaning from better to worse, i.e. from heavenly
shelter to earthly exposure – 'the heat of the day')   159 *beacon . . . globe*
i.e. the sun (here viewed as benign)   161–62 *Nothing . . . misery* i.e.
miraculous aid is seldom seen (or searched for ?) except by the miserable
164 *obscurèd* disguised   164–66 *And . . . remedies* (incoherent : perhaps
corrupt, or perhaps snatches read from the letter)   165 *enormous state*
monstrous situation   166 *Losses* reverses   167 *vantage* i.e. advantage of
sleep   168 *lodging* (in the stocks)   169 *wheel* (Fortune's wheel was
represented as vertical. Kent is at its bottom.)
II, iii   2 *happy hollow* i.e. lucky hiding-place   5 *attend my taking* contemplate my capture   6 *bethought* in mind   10 *elf* tangle (into 'elf-locks')   11
presented a show of   13 *proof* example   14 *Bedlam* (see I, ii, 131–32n.)   15
Strike stick ; *mortified* deadened to pain   16 *pricks* skewers   17 *object*
picture   18 *pelting* paltry   19 *bans* curses   20 *Turlygod* (unidentified, but
evidently another name for a Tom o' Bedlam)   21 *Edgar* i.e. as Edgar

GENTLEMAN   As I learned,

3   The night before there was no purpose in them

4   Of this remove.

KENT   Hail to thee, noble master.

LEAR Ha!

   Mak'st thou this shame thy pastime?

KENT   No, my lord.

7 FOOL Ha, ha, he wears cruel garters. Horses are tied by
   the heads, dogs and bears by th' neck, monkeys by th'

9   loins, and men by th' legs. When a man 's over-lusty at

10   legs, then he wears wooden nether-stocks.

LEAR

   What's he that hath so much thy place mistook

   To set thee here?

KENT   It is both he and she,

   Your son and daughter.

LEAR No.

KENT Yes.

LEAR No, I say.

KENT I say yea.

[LEAR No, no, they would not.

KENT Yes, they have.]

LEAR

   By Jupiter, I swear no!

KENT

   By Juno, I swear ay!

LEAR   They durst not do't;

   They could not, would not do't. 'Tis worse than murder

23 To do upon respect such violent outrage.

24 Resolve me with all modest haste which way

   Thou mightst deserve or thy impose this usage,

   Coming from us.

KENT   My lord, when at their home

27 I did commend your Highness' letters to them,

   Ere I was risen from the place that showed

   My duty kneeling, came there a reeking post,

30 Stewed in his haste, half breathless, panting forth

   From Goneril his mistress salutations;

32 Delivered letters, spite of intermission,

33 Which presently they read; on whose contents

34 They summoned up their meiny, straight took horse,

   Commanded me to follow and attend

   The leisure of their answer, gave me cold looks;

And meeting here the other messenger,

Whose welcome I perceived had poisoned mine,

Being the very fellow which of late

Displayed so saucily against your Highness,   40

Having more man than wit about me, drew;   41

He raised the house with loud and coward cries.   42

Your son and daughter found this trespass worth

The shame which here it suffers.

FOOL Winter 's not gone yet, if the wild geese fly that way.   45

     Fathers that wear rags

       Do make their children blind,   47

     But fathers that bear bags   48

       Shall see their children kind.

     Fortune, that arrant whore,   50

     Ne'er turns the key to th' poor.   51

But for all this, thou shalt have as many dolors for thy   52

daughters as thou canst tell in a year.   53

LEAR

O, how this mother swells up toward my heart!   54

Hysterica passio, down, thou climbing sorrow;   55

Thy element 's below. Where is this daughter?   56

KENT

With the Earl, sir, here within.

LEAR   Follow me not;

Stay here.   *Exit.*

GENTLEMAN

Made you no more offense but what you speak of?

KENT None.

How chance the King comes with so small a number?

FOOL An thou hadst been set i' th' stocks for that question, thou'dst well deserved it.

KENT Why, fool?

FOOL We'll set thee to school to an ant, to teach thee
   there's no laboring i' th' winter. All that follow their   66
   noses are led by their eyes but blind men, and there's not
   a nose among twenty but can smell him that's stinking.
   Let go thy hold when a great wheel runs down a hill, lest
   it break thy neck with following. But the great one that
   goes upward, let him draw thee after. When a wise man
   gives thee better counsel, give me mine again. I would
   have none but knaves follow it since a fool gives it.   73
     That sir which serves and seeks for gain,
       And follows but for form,   75
     Will pack when it begins to rain   76
       And leave thee in the storm.
     But I will tarry; the fool will stay,
       And let the wise man fly.
     The knave turns fool that runs away;   80
       The fool no knave, perdy.   81

KENT Where learned you this, fool?

FOOL Not i' th' stocks, fool.   83

     Enter Lear and Gloucester.

LEAR

Deny to speak with me? They are sick, they are weary,

They have travelled all the night? Mere fetches,   85

The images of revolt and flying off!   86

Fetch me a better answer.

GLOUCESTER   My dear lord,

You know the fiery quality of the Duke,   88

How unremovable and fixed he is

In his own course.

LEAR   Vengeance, plague, death, confusion!

Fiery? What quality? Why, Gloucester, Gloucester,

I'ld speak with the Duke of Cornwall and his wife.

II, iv   3 *purpose* intention   4 *remove* removal   7 *cruel* painful (with pun on 'crewel,' a yarn used in garters)   9–10 *over-lusty at legs* i.e. too much on the go (?), or too much given to kicking (?)   10 *nether-stocks* stockings (as distinct from 'upper-stocks' or breeches)   23 *To . . . outrage* i.e. to show such outrageous disrespect   24 *Resolve* enlighten; *modest* seemly   27 *commend* entrust   30 *Stewed* steaming   32 *spite of intermission* in disregard of its being an interruption   33 *presently* immediately; *on* on the strength of   34 *meiny* attendants   40 *Displayed* showed off   41 *man* manhood; *wit* sense   42 *raised* aroused   45 *Winter's . . . way* i.e. the ill season continues according to these signs (with Cornwall and Regan equated with *wild geese,* proverbially evasive)   47 *blind* (to their fathers' needs)   48 *bags* (of gold)   50 *Fortune . . . whore* (because so fickle and callous)   51 *turns the key* i.e. opens the door   52 *dolors* sorrows (with pun on 'dollars,' continental coins)   53 *tell* count   54, 55 *mother, Hysterica passio* hysteria (the popular and the medical terms)   56 *element* proper place   66 *no laboring . . . winter* (Lear, accompanied by *so small a number,* is equated with winter bereft of workers, such as ants)   66–68 *All . . . stinking* i.e. almost anyone can smell out a person decayed in fortune   73 *none but knaves* (here and in what follows the Fool repudiates his advice to abandon Lear)   75 *form* show   76 *pack* be off   80 *The knave . . . away* i.e. faithlessness is the true folly   81 *perdy* I swear (from 'par dieu')   83 *fool* (persiflage, but also a term of honor; cf. V, iii, 306n.)   85 *fetches* counterfeit reasons, false likenesses of truth   86 *images* true likenesses; *flying off* revolt   88 *quality* disposition

GLOUCESTER
Well, my good lord, I have informed them so.
LEAR
Informed them ? Dost thou understand me, man ?
GLOUCESTER
Ay, my good lord.
LEAR
The King would speak with Cornwall. The dear father
97 Would with his daughter speak, commands – tends –
     service.
Are they informed of this ? My breath and blood !
Fiery ? The fiery Duke, tell the hot Duke that –
No, but not yet. May be he is not well.
101 Infirmity doth still neglect all office
102 Whereto our health is bound. We are not ourselves
When nature, being oppressed, commands the mind
To suffer with the body. I'll forbear ;
105 And am fallen out with my more headier will
To take the indisposed and sickly fit
For the sound man. – Death on my state ! Wherefore
108 Should he sit here ? This act persuades me
109 That this remotion of the Duke and her
110 Is practice only. Give me my servant forth.
Go tell the Duke and 's wife I'ld speak with them !
112 Now, presently ! Bid them come forth and hear me,
Or at their chamber door I'll beat the drum
114 Till it cry sleep to death.
GLOUCESTER
I would have all well betwixt you.   *Exit.*
LEAR
O me, my heart, my rising heart ! But down !
117 FOOL Cry to it, nuncle, as the cockney did to the eels when
118   she put 'em i' th' paste alive. She knapped 'em o' th' cox-
119   combs with a stick and cried, 'Down, wantons, down !'
     'Twas her brother that, in pure kindness to his horse,
121   buttered his hay.
           Enter Cornwall, Regan, Gloucester, Servants.
LEAR
Good morrow to you both.
CORNWALL   Hail to your Grace.
     Kent here set at liberty.
REGAN
I am glad to see your Highness.
LEAR
Regan, I think you are. I know what reason
I have to think so. If thou shouldst not be glad,
126 I would divorce me from thy mother's tomb,
Sepulchring an adultress. *[to Kent]* O, are you free ?
Some other time for that. – Beloved Regan,
Thy sister 's naught. O Regan, she hath tied
Sharp-toothed unkindness, like a vulture, here.
I can scarce speak to thee. Thou'lt not believe
132 With how depraved a quality – O Regan !
REGAN
133 I pray you, sir, take patience. I have hope
You less know how to value her desert
135 Than she to scant her duty.
LEAR   Say ? How is that ?
REGAN
I cannot think my sister in the least
Would fail her obligation. If, sir, perchance
She have restrained the riots of your followers,
'Tis on such ground, and to such wholesome end,
As clears her from all blame.

LEAR
My curses on her !
REGAN   O, sir, you are old ;
Nature in you stands on the very verge   142
Of his confine. You should be ruled, and led
By some discretion that discerns your state   144
Better than you yourself. Therefore I pray you
That to our sister you do make return ;
Say you have wronged her.
LEAR   Ask her forgiveness ?
Do you but mark how this becomes the house :   148
'Dear daughter, I confess that I am old.
     [Kneels.]
Age is unnecessary. On my knees I beg
That you'll vouchsafe me raiment, bed, and food.'
REGAN
Good sir, no more. These are unsightly tricks.
Return you to my sister.
LEAR *[rises]*   Never, Regan.
She hath abated me of half my train,   154
Looked black upon me, struck me with her tongue
Most serpent-like upon the very heart.
All the stored vengeances of heaven fall
On her ingrateful top ! Strike her young bones,   158
You taking airs, with lameness.   159
CORNWALL   Fie, sir, fie !
LEAR
You nimble lightnings, dart your blinding flames
Into her scornful eyes ! Infect her beauty,
You fen-sucked fogs drawn by the pow'rful sun   162
To fall and blister –   163
REGAN   O the blessed gods !
So will you wish on me when the rash mood is on.
LEAR
No, Regan, thou shalt never have my curse.
Thy tender-hefted nature shall not give   166
Thee o'er to harshness. Her eyes are fierce, but thine
Do comfort, and not burn. 'Tis not in thee
To grudge my pleasures, to cut off my train,
To bandy hasty words, to scant my sizes,   170
And, in conclusion, to oppose the bolt   171
Against my coming in. Thou better know'st
The offices of nature, bond of childhood,   173
Effects of courtesy, dues of gratitude.   174
Thy half o' th' kingdom hast thou not forgot,
Wherein I thee endowed.

97 *tends* attends, awaits (?), tenders, offers (?) 101 *all office* duties 102 *Whereto . . . bound* to which, in health, we are bound 105 *headier* head-strong 108 *he* i.e. Kent 109 *remotion* remaining remote, inaccessible 110 *practice* trickery 112 *presently* immediately 114 *cry* pursue with noise (like a pack or 'cry' of hounds) 117 *cockney* city-dweller 118 *paste* pastry pie ; *knapped* rapped 119 *wantons* i.e. frisky things 121 *buttered his hay* (another example of rustic humor at the expense of cockney inexperience) 126–27 *divorce . . . adultress* i.e. refuse to be buried with your mother since such a child as you must have been conceived in adultery 132 *how . . . quality* i.e. what innate depravity 133 *have hope* i.e. suspect 135 *scant* (in effect, a double negative ; 'do' would be more logical though less emphatic) 142–43 *Nature . . . confine* i.e. your life nears the limit of its tenure 144 *some discretion . . . state* someone discerning enough to recognize your condition 148 *the house* household or family decorum 154 *abated* curtailed 158 *ingrateful top* ungrateful head 159 *taking* infectious 162 *fen-sucked* drawn up from swamps 163 *fall and blister* strike and raise blisters (such as those of smallpox) 166 *tender-hefted* swayed by tenderness, gently disposed 170 *bandy* volley ; *sizes* allowances 171 *oppose the bolt* i.e. bar the door 173 *offices of nature* natural duties 174 *Effects* actions

176 REGAN   Good sir, to th' purpose.
    Tucket within.
LEAR
  Who put my man i' th' stocks?
CORNWALL   What trumpet's that?
REGAN
178   I know't – my sister's. This approves her letter,
  That she would soon be here.
    Enter Steward [Oswald]. Is your lady come?
LEAR
180   This is a slave, whose easy-borrowèd pride
181   Dwells in the fickle grace of her he follows.
182   Out, varlet, from my sight.
CORNWALL   What means your Grace?
LEAR
  Who stocked my servant? Regan, I have good hope
  Thou didst not know on't.
    Enter Goneril.   Who comes here? O heavens!
  If you do love old men, if your sweet sway
186   Allow obedience, if you yourselves are old,
187   Make it your cause. Send down, and take my part.
    [To Goneril]
  Art not ashamed to look upon this beard?
  O Regan, will you take her by the hand?
GONERIL
  Why not by th' hand, sir? How have I offended?
191   All's not offense that indiscretion finds
  And dotage terms so.
192 LEAR   O sides, you are too tough!
  Will you yet hold? How came my man i' th' stocks?
CORNWALL
  I set him there, sir; but his own disorders
195   Deserved much less advancement.
LEAR   You? Did you?
REGAN
196   I pray you, father, being weak, seem so.
  If till the expiration of your month
  You will return and sojourn with my sister,
  Dismissing half your train, come then to me.
  I am now from home, and out of that provision
201   Which shall be needful for your entertainment.
LEAR
  Return to her, and fifty men dismissed?
  No, rather I abjure all roofs, and choose
204   To wage against the emnity o' th' air,
  To be a comrade with the wolf and owl,
206   Necessity's sharp pinch. Return with her?
207   Why, the hot-blooded France, that dowerless took
  Our youngest born, I could as well be brought
209   To knee his throne, and, squire-like, pension beg

To keep base life afoot. Return with her?
  Persuade me rather to be slave and sumpter 211
  To this detested groom. 212
GONERIL   At your choice, sir.
LEAR
  I prithee, daughter, do not make me mad.
  I will not trouble thee, my child; farewell.
  We'll no more meet, no more see one another.
  But yet thou art my flesh, my blood, my daughter;
  Or rather a disease that's in my flesh,
  Which I must needs call mine. Thou art a boil,
  A plague-sore, or embossèd carbuncle 219
  In my corrupted blood. But I'll not chide thee.
  Let shame come when it will, I do not call it.
  I do not bid the thunder-bearer shoot, 222
  Nor tell tales of thee to high-judging Jove. 223
  Mend when thou canst, be better at thy leisure;
  I can be patient, I can stay with Regan,
  I and my hundred knights.
REGAN   Not altogether so.
  I looked not for you yet, nor am provided
  For your fit welcome. Give ear, sir, to my sister;
  For those that mingle reason with your passion 229
  Must be content to think you old and so –
  But she knows what she does.
LEAR   Is this well spoken?
REGAN
  I dare avouch it, sir. What, fifty followers? 232
  Is it not well? What should you need of more?
  Yea, or so many, sith that both charge and danger 234
  Speak 'gainst so great a number? How in one house
  Should many people, under two commands,
  Hold amity? 'Tis hard, almost impossible.
GONERIL
  Why might not you, my lord, receive attendance
  From those that she calls servants, or from mine?
REGAN
  Why not, my lord? If then they chanced to slack ye, 240
  We could control them. If you will come to me
  (For now I spy a danger), I entreat you
  To bring but five-and-twenty. To no more
  Will I give place or notice. 244
LEAR
  I gave you all.
REGAN   And in good time you gave it.
LEAR
  Made you my guardians, my depositaries, 246
  But kept a reservation to be followèd 247
  With such a number. What, must I come to you
  With five-and-twenty? Regan, said you so?
REGAN
  And speak't again, my lord. No more with me.
LEAR
  Those wicked creatures yet do look well-favored 251
  When others are more wicked; not being the worst
  Stands in some rank of praise. 253
    [To Goneril]   I'll go with thee.
  Thy fifty yet doth double five-and-twenty,
  And thou art twice her love. 255
GONERIL   Hear me, my lord.
  What need you five-and-twenty? ten? or five?
  To follow in a house where twice so many
  Have a command to tend you?
REGAN   What need one?

176 *purpose* point   178 *approves* confirms   180 *easy-borrowèd* acquired on small security   181 *grace* favor   low security   182 *varlet* low fellow   186 *Allow* approve   187 *Make . . . cause* i.e. make my cause yours   191 *indiscretion finds* ill judgment detects as such   192 *sides* breast (which should burst with grief)   195 *less advancement* i.e. more abasement   196 *seem so* i.e. act the part   201 *entertainment* lodging   204 *wage* fight   206 *Necessity's sharp pinch* (a summing up of the hardships previously listed)   207 *hot-blooded* choleric (cf. I, ii, 23)   209 *knee* kneel at; *squire-like* like an attendant   211 *sumpter* packhorse   212 *groom* i.e. Oswald   219 *embossèd* risen to a head   222 *thunder-bearer* i.e. Jupiter   223 *high-judging* judging from on high   229 *mingle . . . passion* interpret your passion in the light of reason   232 *avouch* swear by   234 *sith that* since; *charge* expense   240 *slack* neglect   244 *notice* recognition   246 *depositaries* trustees   247 *kept . . . to be* stipulated that I be   251 *well-favored* comely   253 *Stands . . . praise* i.e. is at least relatively praiseworthy   255 *her love* i.e. as loving as she

LEAR

259 O reason not the need ! Our basest beggars
260 Are in the poorest thing superfluous.
261 Allow not nature more than nature needs,
Man's life is cheap as beast's. Thou art a lady :
263 If only to go warm were gorgeous,
Why, nature needs not what thou gorgeous wear'st,
Which scarcely keeps thee warm. But, for true need –
You heavens, give me that patience, patience I need.
You see me here, you gods, a poor old man,
As full of grief as age, wretched in both.
If it be you that stirs these daughters' hearts
270 Against their father, fool me not so much
To bear it tamely ; touch me with noble anger,
And let not women's weapons, water drops,
Stain my man's cheeks. No, you unnatural hags !
I will have such revenges on you both
That all the world shall – I will do such things –
What they are, yet I know not ; but they shall be
The terrors of the earth. You think I'll weep.
No, I'll not weep.
      Storm and tempest.
I have full cause of weeping, but this heart
280 Shall break into a hundred thousand flaws
281 Or ere I'll weep. O fool, I shall go mad !
      Exeunt [Lear, Fool, Kent, and Gloucester].

CORNWALL
Let us withdraw ; 'twill be a storm.

REGAN
This house is little ; the old man and 's people
Cannot be well bestowed.

GONERIL
285 'Tis his own blame ; hath put himself from rest
And must needs taste his folly.

REGAN
287 For his particular, I'll receive him gladly,
But not one follower.

288 **GONERIL**   So am I purposed.
Where is my Lord of Gloucester ?

CORNWALL
Followèd the old man forth.
   [Enter Gloucester.]   He is returned.

GLOUCESTER
The King is in high rage.

CORNWALL   Whither is he going ?

GLOUCESTER
He calls to horse, but will I know not whither.

CORNWALL
'Tis best to give him way ; he leads himself.

GONERIL
My lord, entreat him by no means to stay.

GLOUCESTER
Alack, the night comes on, and the high winds
296 Do sorely ruffle. For many miles about
There's scarce a bush.

REGAN   O, sir, to willful men
The injuries that they themselves procure
Must be their schoolmasters. Shut up your doors.
He is attended with a desperate train,
301 And what they may incense him to, being apt
To have his ear abused, wisdom bids fear.

CORNWALL
Shut up your doors, my lord ; 'tis a wild night.
My Regan counsels well. Come out o' th' storm. *Exeunt.*

Storm still. Enter Kent and a Gentleman severally.   III, i

KENT
Who's there besides foul weather ?

GENTLEMAN
One minded like the weather, most unquietly.   2

KENT
I know you. Where's the King ?

GENTLEMAN
Contending with the fretful elements ;   4
Bids the wind blow the earth into the sea,
Or swell the curlèd waters 'bove the main,   6
That things might change or cease ; [tears his white hair,   7
Which the impetuous blasts, with eyeless rage,   8
Catch in their fury and make nothing of ;
Strives in his little world of man to outscorn   10
The to-and-fro-conflicting wind and rain.
This night, wherein the cub-drawn bear would couch,   12
The lion and the belly-pinchèd wolf   13
Keep their fur dry, unbonneted he runs,
And bids what will take all.]   15

KENT   But who is with him ?

GENTLEMAN
None but the fool, who labors to outjest
His heart-struck injuries.

KENT   Sir, I do know you,
And dare upon the warrant of my note   18
Commend a dear thing to you. There is division,   19
Although as yet the face of it is covered
With mutual cunning, 'twixt Albany and Cornwall ;
Who have – as who have not, that their great stars   22
Throned and set high ? – servants, who seem no less,   23
Which are to France the spies and speculations   24
Intelligent of our state. What hath been seen,   25
Either in snuffs and packings of the Dukes,   26
Or the hard rein which both of them have borne   27
Against the old kind King, or something deeper,
Whereof, perchance, these are but furnishings –   29
[But, true it is, from France there comes a power   30
Into this scatterèd kingdom, who already,   31
Wise in our negligence, have secret feet
In some of our best ports and are at point
To show their open banner. Now to you :
If on my credit you dare build so far   35
To make your speed to Dover, you shall find

---

259 *reason* analyze   260 *Are . . . superfluous* i.e. have some poor possession not utterly indispensable   261 *than nature needs* i.e. than life needs for mere survival   263–65 *If . . . warm* i.e. if to be dressed warmly (i.e. for need) were considered sufficiently gorgeous, you would not need your present attire, which is gorgeous rather than warm   270 *fool* play with, humiliate   280 *flaws* fragments   281 *Or ere* before   285 *hath . . . rest* i.e. he himself is responsible for leaving his resting place with her (?), he is self-afflicted (?)   287 *particular* own person   288 *purposed* determined   296 *ruffle* rage   301–02 *apt . . . abused* i.e. predisposed to listen to ill counsel

III, i *An open heath*   2 *minded . . . unquietly* i.e. in disturbed mood   4 *Contending* quarrelling   6 *main* mainland   7 *change* revert to chaos (?), improve (?)   8 *eyeless* (1) blind, (2) invisible   10 *little world* (the 'microcosm,' which is disturbed like the great world or 'macrocosm')   12 *cub-drawn* cub-sucked (and hence ravenous)   13 *belly-pinchèd* famished   15 *take all* (the cry of the desperate gambler in staking his last)   18 *warrant . . . note* assurance of my knowledge   19 *Commend . . . thing* entrust a precious matter   22 *that* whom; *stars* destinies   23 *Throned* have throned; *no less* i.e. truly so   24 *speculations* spies   25 *Intelligent* supplying intelligence   26 *snuffs* quarrels; *packings* intrigues   27 *hard rein . . . borne* i.e. harsh curbs . . . exercised   29 *furnishings* pretexts   30 *power* army   31 *scatterèd* divided   35 *my credit* trust in me; *build* take constructive action

      Some that will thank you, making just report
38   Of how unnatural and bemadding sorrow
39   The King hath cause to plain.
      I am a gentleman of blood and breeding,
      And from some knowledge and assurance offer
42   This office to you.]

GENTLEMAN
      I will talk further with you.

KENT   No, do not.
      For confirmation that I am much more
45   Than my out-wall, open this purse and take
      What it contains. If you shall see Cordelia,
      As fear not but you shall, show her this ring,
      And she will tell you who that fellow is
      That yet you do not know. Fie on this storm!
      I will go seek the King.

GENTLEMAN
      Give me your hand. Have you no more to say?

KENT
52   Few words, but, to effect, more than all yet:
53   That when we have found the King—in which your pain
      That way, I'll this—he that first lights on him
      Holla the other.   *Exeunt [severally].*

*

III, ii   *Storm still. Enter Lear and Fool.*

    LEAR
      Blow, winds, and crack your cheeks. Rage, blow.
2   You cataracts and hurricanoes, spout
3   Till you have drenched our steeples, drowned the cocks.
4   You sulph'rous and thought-executing fires,
5   Vaunt-couriers of oak-cleaving thunderbolts,
      Singe my white head. And thou, all-shaking thunder,
      Strike flat the thick rotundity o' th' world,
8   Crack Nature's moulds, all germains spill at once,
      That makes ingrateful man.

10 FOOL O nuncle, court holy-water in a dry house is better
      than this rain-water out o' door. Good nuncle, in; ask
      thy daughters blessing. Here's a night pities neither
      wise men nor fools.

38 *bemadding sorrow* maddening grievances 39 *plain* lament 42 *office*
service 45 *out-wall* surface appearance 52 *to effect* in their import
53 *pain* pains, care
III, ii The same 2 *hurricanoes* water-spouts 3 *cocks* weathercocks
4 *thought-executing fires* i.e. flashes of lightning swift as thought (?),
dazing, benumbing the mind (?) 5 *Vaunt-couriers* heralds 8 *moulds* (in
which Nature's creations are formed); *germains* seeds 10 *court holy-water*
flattery (slang) 16 *tax* charge 18 *subscription* deference 19 *pleasure*
will 21 *ministers* agents 23 *high-engendered battles* heavenly battalions
27–30 *The codpiece . . . many* (the moral of the rime is that improvident
cohabitation spells penury) 27 *codpiece* padded gusset at the crotch
of the breeches (slang for penis) 29 *he* it 30 *many* (head-lice and
body-lice, accompanying poverty) 31–34 *The man . . . wake* (a parallel
instance of misery deriving from reckless impulse: to transpose the
tender and precious heart and the tough and base toe is to invite injury;
with *heart* also suggesting Cordelia) 35–36 *made . . . glass* i.e. posed
before a mirror (irrelevant, except as vanity is a form of folly, the
Fool's general theme) 44 *Gallow* frighten 45 *keep their caves* i.e. keep
under cover 46 *horrid* horrible 48 *carry* bear 50 *pudder* turmoil 51
Find . . . enemies i.e. discover sinners (by their show of fear) 54 *simular*
counterfeit 56 *seeming* hypocrisy 57 *practiced on* plotted against; *Close*
secret 58 *Rive* split, break through; *continents* containers, covers 59
summoners arresting officers of ecclesiastical courts; *grace* mercy 61
Gracious my lord my gracious lord 63 *house* household (both building
and occupants) 65 *demanding after* inquiring for 67 *scanted* stinted
70 *art* magic skill (as in alchemy)

LEAR
      Rumble thy bellyful. Spit, fire. Spout, rain.
      Nor rain, wind, thunder, fire are my daughters.
      I tax not you, you elements, with unkindness.   16
      I never gave you kingdom, called you children;
      You owe me no subscription. Then let fall   18
      Your horrible pleasure. Here I stand your slave,   19
      A poor, infirm, weak, and despised old man.
      But yet I call you servile ministers,   21
      That will with two pernicious daughters join
      Your high-engendered battles 'gainst a head   23
      So old and white as this. O, ho! 'tis foul.

FOOL He that has a house to put 's head in has a good
      headpiece.

             The codpiece that will house   27
                Before the head has any,
             The head and he shall louse: 29
                So beggars marry many.   30
             The man that makes his toe   31
                What he his heart should make
             Shall of a corn cry woe,
                And turn his sleep to wake.
      For there was never yet fair woman but she made 35
      mouths in a glass.
        Enter Kent.

LEAR
      No, I will be the pattern of all patience;
      I will say nothing.

KENT Who's there?

FOOL Marry, here's grace and a codpiece; that's a wise
      man and a fool.

KENT
      Alas, sir, are you here? Things that love night
      Love not such nights as these. The wrathful skies
      Gallow the very wanderers of the dark   44
      And make them keep their caves. Since I was man, 45
      Such sheets of fire, such bursts of horrid thunder, 46
      Such groans of roaring wind and rain, I never
      Remember to have heard. Man's nature cannot carry 48
      Th' affliction nor the fear.

LEAR   Let the great gods
      That keep this dreadful pudder o'er our heads   50
      Find out their enemies now. Tremble, thou wretch, 51
      That hast within thee undivulgèd crimes
      Unwhipped of justice. Hide thee, thou bloody hand,
      Thou perjured, and thou simular of virtue   54
      That art incestuous. Caitiff, to pieces shake,
      That under covert and convenient seeming   56
      Has practiced on man's life. Close pent-up guilts, 57
      Rive your concealing continents and cry   58
      These dreadful summoners grace. I am a man   59
      More sinned against than sinning.

KENT   Alack, bareheaded?
      Gracious my lord, hard by here is a hovel;   61
      Some friendship will it lend you 'gainst the tempest.
      Repose you there, while I to this hard house   63
      (More harder than the stones whereof 'tis raised,
      Which even but now, demanding after you,   65
      Denied me to come in) return, and force
      Their scanted courtesy.   67

LEAR   My wits begin to turn.
      Come on, my boy. How dost, my boy? Art cold?
      I am cold myself. Where is this straw, my fellow?
      The art of our necessities is strange,   70

And can make vile things precious. Come, your hovel.
Poor fool and knave, I have one part in my heart
That's sorry yet for thee.

FOOL *[sings]*

    He that has and a little tiny wit,
      With, heigh-ho, the wind and the rain,
76   Must make content with his fortunes fit
      Though the rain it raineth every day.

LEAR True, boy. Come, bring us to this hovel.
                         Exit [with Kent].

79 FOOL This is a brave night to cool a courtesan. I'll speak a
    prophecy ere I go :
81   When priests are more in word than matter ;
82   When brewers mar their malt with water ;
83   When nobles are their tailors' tutors,
84   No heretics burned, but wenches' suitors ;
    When every case in law is right,
    No squire in debt nor no poor knight ;
    When slanders do not live in tongues,
    Nor cutpurses come not to throngs ;
89   When usurers tell their gold i' th' field,
    And bawds and whores do churches build –
91   Then shall the realm of Albion
92   Come to great confusion.
    Then comes the time, who lives to see't,
94   That going shall be used with feet.
95 This prophecy Merlin shall make, for I live before his
    time.   *Exit*.

                 *

III, iii   *Enter Gloucester and Edmund.*

GLOUCESTER Alack, alack, Edmund, I like not this un-
    natural dealing. When I desired their leave that I might
3   pity him, they took from me the use of mine own house,
    charged me on pain of perpetual displeasure neither to
5   speak of him, entreat for him, or any way sustain him.

EDMUND Most savage and unnatural.

7 GLOUCESTER Go to ; say you nothing. There is division
8   between the Dukes, and a worse matter than that. I have
    received a letter this night – 'tis dangerous to be spoken
10   – I have locked the letter in my closet. These injuries
11   King now bears will be revenged home ; there is part of a
12   power already footed ; we must incline to the King. I will
13   look him and privily relieve him. Go you and maintain
    talk with the Duke, that my charity be not of him per-
    ceived. If he ask for me, I am ill and gone to bed. If I die
    for it, as no less is threatened me, the King my old mas-
17   ter must be relieved. There is strange things toward,
    Edmund ; pray you be careful.   *Exit*.

EDMUND
19 This courtesy forbid thee shall the Duke
    Instantly know, and of that letter too.
21 This seems a fair deserving, and must draw me
    That which my father loses – no less than all.
    The younger rises when the old doth fall.   *Exit*.

                 *

III, iv   *Enter Lear, Kent, and Fool.*

KENT
1 Here is the place, my lord. Good my lord, enter.
    The tyranny of the open night 's too rough
    For nature to endure.
           Storm still.

LEAR   Let me alone.

KENT
    Good my lord, enter here.

LEAR   Wilt break my heart ?   4

KENT
    I had rather break mine own. Good my lord, enter.

LEAR
    Thou think'st 'tis much that this contentious storm
    Invades us to the skin. So 'tis to thee,
    But where the greater malady is fixed   8
    The lesser is scarce felt. Thou'dst shun a bear ;
    But if thy flight lay toward the roaring sea,
    Thou'dst meet the bear i' th' mouth. When the mind 's 11
      free,
    The body 's delicate. The tempest in my mind
    Doth from my senses take all feeling else
    Save what beats there. Filial ingratitude,
    Is it not as this mouth should tear this hand
    For lifting food to't ? But I will punish home.   16
    No, I will weep no more. In such a night
    To shut me out ! Pour on ; I will endure.
    In such a night as this ! O Regan, Goneril,
    Your old kind father, whose frank heart gave all –   20
    O, that way madness lies ; let me shun that.
    No more of that.

KENT   Good my lord, enter here.

LEAR
    Prithee go in thyself ; seek thine own ease.
    This tempest will not give me leave to ponder
    On things would hurt me more, but I'll go in.
        [To the Fool]
    In, boy ; go first. You houseless poverty –   26
    Nay, get thee in. I'll pray, and then I'll sleep. *Exit [Fool]*.
    Poor naked wretches, wheresoe'er you are,
    That bide the pelting of this pitiless storm,
    How shall your houseless heads and unfed sides,
    Your looped and windowed raggedness, defend you   31
    From seasons such as these ? O, I have ta'en
    Too little care of this ! Take physic, pomp ;   33
    Expose thyself to feel what wretches feel,
    That thou mayst shake the superflux to them   35
    And show the heavens more just.

EDGAR *[within]* Fathom and half, fathom and half ! Poor 37
    Tom !

76 *make . . . fit* i.e. reconcile himself to his fortunes 79 *brave* fine 81
are . . . matter i.e. can outshine the gospel message (At present their ability
to speak is quite unworthy of their theme.) 82 *mar* i.e. dilute (At present
they dilute water with malt, producing very small beer.) 83 *are . . . tutors*
i.e. are no longer subservient to fashion (Each subsequent line also reverses
the present state of affairs.) 84 *burned* (pun on contracting venereal
disease); *wenches' suitors* i.e. libertines 89 *tell* count; *i' th' field* (instead
of in secret places) 91 *Albion* England 92 *confusion* ruin (ironic : an
edifice of abuses is 'ruined' by reform) 94 *going . . . feet* walking will
be done with feet (the humor of anticlimax, but suggesting a return to
normality) 95 *Merlin* (a legendary magician associated with King Arthur,
who reigned later than King Lear)
III, iii *Within* Gloucester's castle 3 *pity* have mercy upon 5 *entreat*
plead 7 *division* contention 8 *worse* more serious 10 *closet* chamber
11 *home* thoroughly 12 *power* army; *footed* landed; *incline* to side with
13 *look* search for; *privily* secretly 17 *toward* imminent 19 *courtesy* kind
attention (to Lear) 21 *fair deserving* i.e. action that should win favor
III, iv *Before* a hovel on the heath 1 *Good my lord* my good lord 4 *break
my heart* i.e. by removing the distraction of mere physical distress 8
fixed lodged 11 *i' th' mouth* i.e. in the teeth; *free* free of care 16 *home*
i.e. to the hilt 20 *frank* liberal 26 *houseless* unsheltered 31 *looped*
loopholed 33 *Take physic, pomp* i.e. cure yourself, you vainglorious
ones 35 *superflux* superfluities 37 *Fathom and half* (nautical cry in
taking soundings, perhaps suggested by the deluge)

Enter Fool.

FOOL Come not in here, nuncle ; here's a spirit. Help me, help me !

KENT
Give me thy hand. Who's there ?

FOOL A spirit, a spirit. He says his name 's poor Tom.

KENT
What art thou that dost grumble there i' th' straw ? Come forth.

Enter Edgar [as Tom o' Bedlam].

45 **EDGAR** Away ! the foul fiend follows me. Through the
46 sharp hawthorn blow the winds. Humh ! go to thy bed and warm thee.

LEAR Didst thou give all to thy daughters ? And art thou come to this ?

EDGAR Who gives anything to poor Tom ? whom the foul fiend hath led through fire and through flame, through ford and whirlpool, o'er bog and quagmire ; that hath
53 laid knives under his pillow and halters in his pew, set
54 ratsbane by his porridge, made him proud of heart, to
55 ride on a bay trotting horse over four-inched bridges, to
56 course his own shadow for a traitor. Bless thy five wits, Tom 's acold. O, do, de, do, de, do, de. Bless thee from
58 whirlwinds, star-blasting, and taking. Do poor Tom some charity, whom the foul fiend vexes. There could I have him now – and there – and there again – and there –
Storm still.

LEAR
61 Has his daughters brought him to this pass ? Couldst thou save nothing ? Wouldst thou give 'em all ?

63 **FOOL** Nay, he reserved a blanket, else we had been all shamed.

LEAR
65 Now all the plagues that in the pendulous air
66 Hang fated o'er men's faults light on thy daughters !

KENT
He hath no daughters, sir.

LEAR
Death, traitor ! Nothing could have subdued nature
To such a lowness but his unkind daughters.
Is it the fashion that discarded fathers
Should have thus little mercy on their flesh ?   71
Judicious punishment – 'twas this flesh begot
Those pelican daughters.   73

EDGAR Pillicock sat on Pillicock Hill. Alow, alow, loo, loo !   74

FOOL This cold night will turn us all to fools and madmen.

EDGAR Take heed o' th' foul fiend ; obey thy parents ; keep thy words' justice ; swear not ; commit not with   77 man's sworn spouse ; set not thy sweet heart on proud array. Tom 's acold.

LEAR What hast thou been ?

EDGAR A servingman, proud in heart and mind ; that curled my hair, wore gloves in my cap ; served the lust of   82 my mistress' heart, and did the act of darkness with her ; swore as many oaths as I spake words, and broke them in the sweet face of heaven. One that slept in the contriving of lust, and waked to do it. Wine loved I deeply, dice dearly ; and in woman out-paramoured the Turk. False   87 of heart, light of ear, bloody of hand ; hog in sloth, fox in   88 stealth, wolf in greediness, dog in madness, lion in prey. Let not the creaking of shoes nor the rustling of silks be-   90 tray thy poor heart to woman. Keep thy foot out of brothels, thy hand out of plackets, thy pen from lenders'   92 books, and defy the foul fiend. Still through the haw- thorn blows the cold wind ; says suum, mun, nonny.   94 Dolphin my boy, boy, sessa ! let him trot by.   95
Storm still.

LEAR Thou wert better in a grave than to answer with thy   96 uncovered body this extremity of the skies. Is man no more than this ? Consider him well. Thou ow'st the   98 worm no silk, the beast no hide, the sheep no wool, the cat no perfume. Ha ! here's three on's are sophisticated.   100 Thou art the thing itself ; unaccommodated man is no   101 more but such a poor, bare, forked animal as thou art.   102 Off, off, you lendings ! Come, unbutton here.   103
[Begins to disrobe.]

FOOL Prithee, nuncle, be contented ; 'tis a naughty night   104 to swim in. Now a little fire in a wild field were like an   105 old lecher's heart – a small spark, all the rest on's body cold. Look, here comes a walking fire.
Enter Gloucester with a torch.

EDGAR This is the foul Flibbertigibbet. He begins at cur-   108 few, and walks till the first cock. He gives the web and   109 the pin, squints the eye, and makes the harelip ; mildews   110 the white wheat, and hurts the poor creature of earth.   111
     Swithold footed thrice the 'old ;   112
     He met the nightmare, and her nine fold ;   113
       Bid her alight   114
       And her troth plight,   115
     And aroint thee, witch, aroint thee !   116

KENT
How fares your Grace ?

LEAR What's he ?

KENT
Who's there ? What is't you seek ?

GLOUCESTER
What are you there ? Your names ?

EDGAR Poor Tom, that eats the swimming frog, the toad, the todpole, the wall-newt and the water ; that in the fury   122 of his heart, when the foul fiend rages, eats cow-dung for sallets, swallows the old rat and the ditch-dog, drinks   124

45–46 *Through . . . winds* (cf. ll. 93–94 ; a line from a ballad)   46–47 *go . . . thee* (evidently a popular retort ; cf. *Taming of the Shrew*, Ind., i, 7–8)   53, 54 *knives, halters, ratsbane* (temptations to suicide)   53 *pew* a gallery or balcony   55 *ride . . . bridges* i.e. take mad risks   56 *course . . . traitor* chase his own shadow as an enemy   58 *star-blasting* i.e. becoming the victim of malignant stars ; *taking* pestilence   61 *pass* evil condition   63 *blanket* (to cover his nakedness)   65 *pendulous* omin- ously suspended   66 *Hang . . . faults* i.e. destined to chastise sins   71 *have . . . flesh* i.e. torture themselves   73 *pelican* i.e. feeding upon the parent's blood (a supposed habit of this species of bird)   74 *Pillicock . . . Hill* (probably from a nursery rhyme ; 'Pillicock' is a pet name for a child) ; *Alow . . . loo* (hunting cry ?)   77 *justice* i.e. dependability ; *commit not* (i.e. adultery)   82 *gloves . . . cap* (a fashion with Elizabethan gallants)   87 *out-paramoured the Turk* outdid the Sultan in mistress- keeping   88 *light of ear* i.e. attentive to flattery and slander   90 *creaking, rustling* (both considered seductively fashionable sounds)   92 *plackets* slits in skirts   92–93 *pen . . . books* (in signing for loans)   94 *suum . . . nonny* (the refrain of the wind ?)   95 *Dolphin . . . trot by* (variously ex- plained as cant phrases or ballad refrain, equivalent to 'Let it go')   96 *answer* bear the brunt of   98 *ow'st* have borrowed from   100 *cat* civet cat ; *sophisticated* altered by artifice   101 *unaccommodated* unpampered   102 *forked* two-legged   103 *lendings* borrowed coverings   104 *naughty* evil   105 *wild* barren   108 *Flibbertigibbet* (a dancing devil) ; *curfew* (9 p.m.)   109 *first cock* (midnight)   109–10 *web . . . pin* cataract of the eye   110 *squints* crosses   111 *white* ripening   112 *Swithold* St Withold (Anglo-Saxon exorcist) ; *footed* walked over ; *'old* wold, uplands   113 *nightmare* incubus, demon ; *fold* offspring   114 *alight* i.e. from the horse she was afflicting   115 *her troth plight* plight her troth, pledge her good intentions   116 *aroint thee* be gone (a direct command, concluding the charm)   122 *todpole* tadpole ; *water* water-newt ;   124 *sallets* salads ; *ditch- dog* (carcass)

125 the green mantle of the standing pool; who is whipped
126 from tithing to tithing, and stock-punished and imprisoned; who hath had three suits to his back, six
shirts to his body,

     Horse to ride, and weapon to wear,
130   But mice and rats, and such small deer,
     Have been Tom's food for seven long year.

132 Beware my follower! Peace, Smulkin, peace, thou fiend!

GLOUCESTER
What, hath your Grace no better company?

EDGAR
The prince of darkness is a gentleman.
135 Modo he's called, and Mahu.

GLOUCESTER
Our flesh and blood, my lord, is grown so vile
137 That it doth hate what gets it.

EDGAR Poor Tom's acold.

GLOUCESTER
139 Go in with me. My duty cannot suffer
T' obey in all your daughters' hard commands.
Though their injunction be to bar my doors
And let this tyrannous night take hold upon you,
Yet have I ventured to come seek you out
And bring you where both fire and food is ready.

LEAR
First let me talk with this philosopher.
What is the cause of thunder?

KENT
Good my lord, take his offer; go into th' house.

LEAR
148 I'll talk a word with this same learnèd Theban.
149 What is your study?

EDGAR
150 How to prevent the fiend, and to kill vermin.

LEAR
Let me ask you one word in private.

KENT
Importune him once more to go, my lord.
His wits begin t' unsettle.

GLOUCESTER   Canst thou blame him?
     Storm still.
His daughters seek his death. Ah, that good Kent,
He said it would be thus, poor banished man!
Thou sayest the King grows mad – I'll tell thee, friend,
I am almost mad myself. I had a son,
158 Now outlawed from my blood; he sought my life
But lately, very late. I loved him, friend,
No father his son dearer. True to tell thee,
The grief hath crazed my wits. What a night 's this!
I do beseech your Grace –
162 **LEAR**   O, cry you mercy, sir.
Noble philosopher, your company.

EDGAR Tom's acold.

GLOUCESTER
In, fellow, there, into th' hovel; keep thee warm.

LEAR
Come, let's in all.

KENT   This way, my lord.

LEAR   With him!
I will keep still with my philosopher.

KENT
168 Good my lord, soothe him; let him take the fellow.

GLOUCESTER
169 Take him you on.

KENT
Sirrah, come on; go along with us.

LEAR
Come, good Athenian.   171

GLOUCESTER
No words, no words! Hush.

EDGAR   Child Rowland to the dark tower came;   173
     His word was still, 'Fie, foh, and fum,   174
     I smell the blood of a British man.'   *Exeunt.*

*

Enter Cornwall and Edmund.   III, v

CORNWALL I will have my revenge ere I depart his house.

EDMUND How, my lord, I may be censured, that nature 2
thus gives way to loyalty, something fears me to think of. 3

CORNWALL I now perceive it was not altogether your
brother's evil disposition made him seek his death; but a 5
provoking merit, set awork by a reproveable badness in
himself.

EDMUND How malicious is my fortune that I must repent
to be just! This is the letter which he spoke of, which
approves him an intelligent party to the advantages of 10
France. O heavens, that this treason were not! or not I
the detector!

CORNWALL Go with me to the Duchess.

EDMUND If the matter of this paper be certain, you have
mighty business in hand.

CORNWALL True or false, it hath made thee Earl of
Gloucester. Seek out where thy father is, that he may be
ready for our apprehension.

EDMUND *[aside]* If I find him comforting the King, it 19
will stuff his suspicion more fully. – I will persever in 20
my course of loyalty, though the conflict be sore between that and my blood. 22

CORNWALL I will lay trust upon thee, and thou shalt find 23
a dearer father in my love.   *Exeunt.*

*

Enter Kent and Gloucester.   III, vi

GLOUCESTER Here is better than the open air; take it
thankfully. I will piece out the comfort with what addition I can. I will not be long from you.

KENT All the power of his wits have given way to his
impatience. The gods reward your kindness. 5
       Exit [Gloucester].

125 *mantle* scum; *standing* stagnant   126 *tithing* a ten-family district within a parish; *stock-punished* placed in the stocks   130 *deer* game (adapted from lines in the romance *Bevis of Hampton*)   132, 135 *Smulkin, Modo, Mahu* (devils described in Harsnett's *Declaration*, 1603)   137 *gets* begets (a reference to Edgar, Goneril, and Regan)   139 *suffer* permit   148 *Theban* (an unexplained association of Thebes with philosophy, i.e. science)   149 *study* i.e. scientific specialty   150 *prevent* thwart   158 *outlawed . . . blood* proscribed as no child of mine   162 *cry you mercy* I beg your pardon   168 *soothe* humor   169 *you on* along with you   171 *Athenian* i.e. philosopher   173 *Child* (i.e. a candidate for knighthood); *Rowland* Roland of the Charlemagne legends (the line perhaps from a lost ballad)   174 *His word was still* i.e. his repeated word, his motto, was always   174–75 *Fie . . . man* (absurdly heroic)
III, v Within Gloucester's castle   2 *censured* judged   3 *something fears me* frightens me somewhat   5–7 *a provoking . . . himself* i.e. evil justice incited by evil (a case of poison driving out poison)   10 *approves* proves; *intelligent . . . advantages* spying partisan on behalf   19 *comforting* aiding   20 *persever* persevere   22 *blood* natural feelings   23 *lay . . . thee* trust you (?), reward you with a place of trust (?)
III, vi Within a cottage near Gloucester's castle   5 *impatience* rage

Enter Lear, Edgar, and Fool.

6 EDGAR Frateretto calls me, and tells me Nero is an angler
7   in the lake of darkness. Pray, innocent, and beware the
    foul fiend.

FOOL Prithee, nuncle, tell me whether a madman be a
10 gentleman or a yeoman.

LEAR
   A king, a king.

FOOL No, he's a yeoman that has a gentleman to his son;
13 for he's a mad yeoman that sees his son a gentleman
    before him.

LEAR
   To have a thousand with red burning spits
16 Come hizzing in upon 'em –
[EDGAR The foul fiend bites my back.

FOOL He's mad that trusts in the tameness of a wolf, a
    horse's health, a boy's love, or a whore's oath.

LEAR
20 It shall be done; I will arraign them straight.
      [To Edgar]
   Come, sit thou here, most learned justice.
      [To the Fool]
   Thou, sapient sir, sit here. Now, you she-foxes –

23 EDGAR Look, where he stands and glares. Want'st thou
24 eyes at trial, madam?
25   Come o'er the bourn, Bessy, to me.

FOOL   Her boat hath a leak,
       And she must not speak
   Why she dares not come over to thee.

EDGAR The foul fiend haunts poor Tom in the voice of a
30 nightingale. Hoppedance cries in Tom's belly for two
31 white herring. Croak not, black angel; I have no food
    for thee.

KENT
33 How do you, sir? Stand you not so amazed.
   Will you lie down and rest upon the cushions?

LEAR
   I'll see their trial first. Bring in their evidence.
      [To Edgar]
   Thou, robèd man of justice, take thy place.
      [To the Fool]
   And thou, his yokefellow of equity,

6 *Frateretto* (a devil mentioned in Harsnett's *Declaration*); *Nero* (in Rabelais, Trajan was the angler, Nero a fiddler, in Hades) 7 *innocent* hapless victim, plaything 10 *yeoman* a property owner, next in rank to a gentleman (The allusion is to self-penalizing indulgence of one's children.) 13 *sees* i.e. sees to it 16 *hizzing* hissing (Lear is musing on vicious military retaliation) 20 *arraign* bring to trial 23 *he* Lear (?), one of Edgar's 'devils' (?) 24 *eyes* such eyes (?), spectators (?) 25 *bourn* brook (Edgar's line is from a popular song; the Fool's are a ribald improvisation) 30 *nightingale* i.e. the fool; *Hoppedance* (a devil mentioned in Harsnett's *Declaration* as 'Hobberdidance') 31 *white* unsmoked (in contrast with *black angel*, i.e. smoked devil) 33 *amazed* bewildered 38 *commission* those commissioned as King's justices 42 *corn* wheatfield 43 *one . . . mouth* one strain on your delicate shepherd's pipe (?) 45 *gray* (gray cats were among the forms supposedly assumed by devils) 51 *Cry . . . joint-stool* (a cant expression for 'Pardon me for failing to notice you,' but two joint-stools – cf. *warped*, l. 52 – were probably the actual stage objects arraigned as Goneril and Regan) 54 *Corruption . . . place* i.e. bribery in the court 59 *take his part* i.e. fall on his behalf 60 *counterfeiting* i.e. simulating madness 67 *brach* hound bitch; *lym* bloodhound 68 *bobtail . . . trundle-tail* short-tailed cur or long-tailed 71 *hatch* lower half of a 'Dutch door' 72 *Sessa* (interjection, equivalent to 'Away!'); *wakes* parish feasts 73 *Poor . . . dry* (Edgar expresses his exhaustion in his role, by an allusion to the horns proffered by Toms o' Bedlam in begging drink) 78 *Persian* (Persian costume was reputedly gorgeous. Ironically, or in actual delusion, Lear refers thus to Edgar's rags, as he refers to bed curtains in l. 81.)

   Bench by his side. *[to Kent]* You are o' th' commission; 38
   Sit you too.

EDGAR Let us deal justly.
     Sleepest or wakest thou, jolly shepherd?
       Thy sheep be in the corn;   42
     And for one blast of thy minikin mouth   43
       Thy sheep shall take no harm.
   Purr, the cat is gray.   45

LEAR Arraign her first. 'Tis Goneril, I here take my oath
   before this honorable assembly, kicked the poor king
   her father.

FOOL Come hither, mistress. Is your name Goneril?

LEAR She cannot deny it.

FOOL Cry you mercy, I took you for a joint-stool.   51

LEAR
   And here's another, whose warped looks proclaim
   What store her heart is made on. Stop her there!
   Arms, arms, sword, fire! Corruption in the place!   54
   False justicer, why hast thou let her 'scape?]

EDGAR Bless thy five wits!

KENT
   O pity! Sir, where is the patience now
   That you so oft have boasted to retain?

EDGAR *[aside]*
   My tears begin to take his part so much   59
   They mar my counterfeiting.   60

LEAR
   The little dogs and all,
   Tray, Blanch, and Sweetheart – see, they bark at me.

EDGAR Tom will throw his head at them. Avaunt, you curs.
     Be thy mouth or black or white,
     Tooth that poisons if it bite;
     Mastiff, greyhound, mongrel grim,
     Hound or spaniel, brach or lym,   67
     Or bobtail tike, or trundle-tail –   68
     Tom will make him weep and wail;
     For, with throwing thus my head,
     Dogs leaped the hatch, and all are fled.   71
   Do, de, de, de. Sessa! Come, march to wakes and fairs 72
   and market towns. Poor Tom, thy horn is dry.   73

LEAR Then let them anatomize Regan. See what breeds
   about her heart. Is there any cause in nature that makes
   these hard hearts? *[to Edgar]* You, sir, I entertain for
   one of my hundred; only I do not like the fashion of
   your garments. You will say they are Persian; but let 78
   them be changed.

KENT
   Now, good my lord, lie here and rest awhile.

LEAR
   Make no noise, make no noise; draw the curtains.
   So, so. We'll go to supper i' th' morning.

FOOL And I'll go to bed at noon.

Enter Gloucester.

GLOUCESTER
   Come hither, friend. Where is the King my master?

KENT
   Here, sir, but trouble him not; his wits are gone.

GLOUCESTER
   Good friend, I prithee take him in thy arms.
   I have o'erheard a plot of death upon him.
   There is a litter ready; lay him in't
   And drive toward Dover, friend, where thou shalt meet
   Both welcome and protection. Take up thy master.
   If thou shouldst dally half an hour, his life,

    With thine and all that offer to defend him,
    Stand in assurèd loss. Take up, take up,
94 And follow me, that will to some provision
95 Give thee quick conduct.
[KENT   Oppressèd nature sleeps.
96 This rest might yet have balmed thy broken sinews,
97 Which, if convenience will not allow,
98 Stand in hard cure.
      [To the Fool] Come, help to bear thy master.
      Thou must not stay behind.]
GLOUCESTER   Come, come, away!
                 Exeunt [all but Edgar].

[EDGAR
100 When we our betters see bearing our woes,
101 We scarcely think our miseries our foes.
     Who alone suffers suffers most i' th' mind,
103 Leaving free things and happy shows behind;
104 But then the mind much sufferance doth o'erskip
105 When grief hath mates, and bearing fellowship.
106 How light and portable my pain seems now,
     When that which makes me bend makes the King bow.
     He childed as I fatherèd. Tom, away.
109 Mark the high noises, and thyself bewray
110 When false opinion, whose wrong thoughts defile thee,
111 In thy just proof repeals and reconciles thee.
112 What will hap more to-night, safe 'scape the King!
113 Lurk, lurk.]   [Exit.]

                  *

III, vii   Enter Cornwall, Regan, Goneril, Bastard [Edmund],
           and Servants.
CORNWALL [to Goneril] Post speedily to my lord your
     husband; show him this letter. The army of France is
     landed. [to Servants] Seek out the traitor Gloucester.
              [Exeunt some Servants.]
REGAN Hang him instantly.
GONERIL Pluck out his eyes.
CORNWALL Leave him to my displeasure. Edmund, keep
7 you our sister company. The revenges we are bound to
     take upon your traitorous father are not fit for your be-
     holding. Advise the Duke where you are going, to a most
10 festinate preparation. We are bound to the like. Our
11 posts shall be swift and intelligent betwixt us. Farewell,
12 dear sister; farewell, my Lord of Gloucester.
         Enter Steward [Oswald].
     How now? Where's the King?
OSWALD
     My Lord of Gloucester hath conveyed him hence.
     Some five or six and thirty of his knights,
16 Hot questrists after him, met him at gate;
     Who, with some other of the lord's dependants,
     Are gone with him toward Dover, where they boast
     To have well-armèd friends.
CORNWALL   Get horses for your mistress.
                     Exit [Oswald].
GONERIL
     Farewell, sweet lord, and sister.
CORNWALL
     Edmund, farewell.   [Exeunt Goneril and Edmund.]
                Go seek the traitor Gloucester,
     Pinion him like a thief, bring him before us.
                   [Exeunt other Servants.]
23 Though well we may not pass upon his life
     Without the form of justice, yet our power

Shall do a court'sy to our wrath, which men   25
May blame, but not control.
       Enter Gloucester and Servants.
                 Who's there, the traitor?
REGAN
Ingrateful fox, 'tis he.
CORNWALL
Bind fast his corky arms.   28
GLOUCESTER
What means your Graces? Good my friends, consider
You are my guests. Do me no foul play, friends.
CORNWALL
Bind him, I say.
      [Servants bind him.]
REGAN   Hard, hard! O filthy traitor.
GLOUCESTER
Unmerciful lady as you are, I'm none.
CORNWALL
To this chair bind him. Villain, thou shalt find –
      [Regan plucks his beard.]
GLOUCESTER
By the kind gods, 'tis most ignobly done
To pluck me by the beard.
REGAN
So white, and such a traitor?
GLOUCESTER   Naughty lady,   36
These hairs which thou dost ravish from my chin
Will quicken and accuse thee. I am your host.   38
With robber's hands my hospitable favors   39
You should not ruffle thus. What will you do?   40
CORNWALL
Come, sir, what letters had you late from France?   41
REGAN
Be simple-answered, for we know the truth.   42
CORNWALL
And what confederacy have you with the traitors
Late footed in the kingdom?   44
REGAN
To whose hands you have sent the lunatic King.
Speak.
GLOUCESTER
I have a letter guessingly set down,   47
Which came from one that's of a neutral heart,
And not from one opposed.
CORNWALL   Cunning.
REGAN   And false.
CORNWALL
Where hast thou sent the king?

---

94 *provision* supplies   95 *conduct* guidance   96 *balmed* healed; *sinews* nerves   97 *convenience* propitious circumstances   98 *Stand . . . cure* will be hard to cure   100 *our woes* woes like ours   101 *our foes* i.e. our peculiar foes (they seem rather a part of universal misery)   103 *free* carefree; *shows* scenes   104 *sufferance* suffering   105 *bearing fellowship* enduring has company   106 *portable* bearable   109 *Mark . . . noises* i.e. heed the rumors concerning those in power (?); *bewray* reveal   110 *wrong thoughts* misconceptions   111 *In . . . reconciles thee* i.e. upon your vindication recalls you and makes peace with you   112 *What . . . more* whatever more happens   113 *Lurk* i.e. keep covered
III, vii Within Gloucester's castle   7 *bound* required   10 *festinate* speedy   11 *intelligent* informative   12 *Lord of Gloucester* (as now endowed with his father's title and estates)   16 *questrists* seekers   23 *pass upon* issue a sentence against   25 *do a court'sy to* i.e. defer to, act in conformity with   28 *corky* (because aged)   36 *Naughty* evil   38 *quicken* come to life   39 *favors* features   40 *ruffle* tear at   41 *late* of late   42 *Be simple-answered* i.e. give plain answers   44 *footed* landed   47 *guessingly* i.e. tentatively, not stated as an assured fact

GLOUCESTER
To Dover.
REGAN
52   Wherefore to Dover ? Wast thou not charged at peril –
CORNWALL
Wherefore to Dover ? Let him answer that.
GLOUCESTER
54   I am tied to th' stake, and I must stand the course.
REGAN
Wherefore to Dover ?
GLOUCESTER
Because I would not see thy cruel nails
Pluck out his poor old eyes ; nor thy fierce sister
58   In his anointed flesh stick boarish fangs.
The sea, with such a storm as his bare head
60   In hell-black night endured, would have buoyed up
61   And quenched the stellèd fires.
62   Yet, poor old heart, he holp the heavens to rain.
If wolves had at thy gate howled that stern time,
64   Thou shouldst have said, 'Good porter, turn the key.'
65   All cruels else subscribe. But I shall see
66   The wingèd vengeance overtake such children.
CORNWALL
See't shalt thou never. Fellows, hold the chair.
Upon these eyes of thine I'll set my foot.
GLOUCESTER
69   He that will think to live till he be old,
Give me some help. – O cruel ! O you gods !
REGAN
71   One side will mock another. Th' other too.
CORNWALL
If you see vengeance –
1. SERVANT   Hold your hand, my lord !
I have served you ever since I was a child ;
But better service have I never done you
Than now to bid you hold.
REGAN   How now, you dog ?
1. SERVANT
If you did wear a beard upon your chin,
77   I'ld shake it on this quarrel. What do you mean !
CORNWALL
78   My villain !
                [Draw and fight.]

1. SERVANT
Nay, then, come on, and take the chance of anger.
REGAN
Give me thy sword. A peasant stand up thus ?
        [She takes a sword and runs at him behind,] kills him.
1. SERVANT
O, I am slain ! My lord, you have one eye left
To see some mischief on him. O !   82
CORNWALL
Lest it see more, prevent it. Out, vile jelly.
Where is thy lustre now ?
GLOUCESTER
All dark and comfortless. Where's my son Edmund ?
Edmund, enkindle all the sparks of nature   86
To quit this horrid act.   87
REGAN   Out, treacherous villain ;
Thou call'st on him that hates thee. It was he
That made the overture of thy treasons to us ;   89
Who is too good to pity thee.
GLOUCESTER
O my follies ! Then Edgar was abused.   91
Kind gods, forgive me that, and prosper him.
REGAN
Go thrust him out at gates, and let him smell
His way to Dover.   Exit [one] with Gloucester.
                How is't, my lord ? How look you ?   94
CORNWALL
I have received a hurt. Follow me, lady.
Turn out that eyeless villain. Throw this slave
Upon the dunghill. Regan, I bleed apace.
Untimely comes this hurt. Give me your arm.   Exeunt.
[2. SERVANT
I'll never care what wickedness I do,
If this man come to good.
3. SERVANT   If she live long,
And in the end meet the old course of death,   101
Women will all turn monsters.
2. SERVANT
Let's follow the old Earl, and get the bedlam
To lead him where he would. His roguish madness   104
Allows itself to anything.   [Exit.]
3. SERVANT
Go thou. I'll fetch some flax and whites of eggs
To apply to his bleeding face. Now heaven help him.
                                            Exit.]
                        *

52 charged at peril ordered on peril of your life   54 course coursing (as
by a string of dogs baiting a bear or bull tied in the pit)   58 anointed
(as king)   60 buoyed surged   61 stellèd starry   62 holp helped   64
turn the key i.e. let them come in to shelter   65 All . . . subscribe i.e. at
such times all other cruel creatures give way, agree to renounce their
cruelty (?)   66 wingèd heavenly (?), swift (?)   69 will think hopes, expects
71 mock i.e. subject to ridicule (because of the contrast)   77 shake it
(as Regan has done with Gloucester's – an act of extreme defiance) ; on
this quarrel in this cause ; What . . . mean i.e. how dare you (The words
are given to Regan by most editors, but they are no more 'un-servantlike,'
than those which precede them.)   78 My villain i.e. my serf (with play
on its more modern meaning)   82 mischief injury   86 nature natural
feeling   87 quit requite, avenge ; horrid horrible   89 overture disclosure
91 abused wronged   94 How look you i.e. how looks it with you, what is
your condition   101 meet . . . death i.e. die a natural death   104–05
His roguish . . . anything i.e. his being an irresponsible wanderer allows
him to do anything

IV, i A path leading from Gloucester's castle   1 contemned despised   3
dejected cast down, abased   4 esperance hope   6 The worst . . . laughter i.e.
the worst extreme is the point of return to happiness   9 nothing i.e. nothing
good (and hence he is free of debt)   10 poorly poor-like, i.e. like a blind
beggar (?)   11–12 But . . . age i.e. were it not for your hateful mutability,
we would never be reconciled to old age and death

Enter Edgar.   IV, i
EDGAR
Yet better thus, and known to be contemned,   1
Than still contemned and flattered. To be worst,
The lowest and most dejected thing of fortune,   3
Stands still in esperance, lives not in fear.   4
The lamentable change is from the best ;
The worst returns to laughter. Welcome then,   6
Thou unsubstantial air that I embrace :
The wretch that thou hast blown unto the worst
Owes nothing to thy blasts.   9
        Enter Gloucester and an Old Man.
                        But who comes here ?
My father, poorly led ? World, world, O world !   10
But that thy strange mutations make us hate thee, 11
Life would not yield to age.
OLD MAN   O my good lord,
I have been your tenant, and your father's tenant,

These fourscore years.

GLOUCESTER

Away, get thee away. Good friend, be gone.

16 Thy comforts can do me no good at all;

17 Thee they may hurt.

OLD MAN   You cannot see your way.

GLOUCESTER

18 I have no way, and therefore want no eyes;

I stumbled when I saw. Full oft 'tis seen

20 Our means secure us, and our mere defects

Prove our commodities. O dear son Edgar,

22 The food of thy abusèd father's wrath,

23 Might I but live to see thee in my touch

I'ld say I had eyes again!

OLD MAN   How now? Who's there?

EDGAR [aside]

O gods! Who is't can say 'I am at the worst'?

I am worse than e'er I was.

OLD MAN   'Tis poor mad Tom.

EDGAR [aside]

27 And worse I may be yet. The worst is not

So long as we can say 'This is the worst.'

OLD MAN

Fellow, where goest?

GLOUCESTER   Is it a beggarman?

OLD MAN

Madman and beggar too.

GLOUCESTER

31 He has some reason, else he could not beg.

I' th' last night's storm I such a fellow saw,

33 Which made me think a man a worm. My son

Came then into my mind, and yet my mind

Was then scarce friends with him. I have heard more

since.

36 As flies to wanton boys are we to th' gods;

They kill us for their sport.

EDGAR [aside]   How should this be?

Bad is the trade that must play fool to sorrow,

39 Ang'ring itself and others. – Bless thee, master.

GLOUCESTER

Is that the naked fellow?

OLD MAN   Ay, my lord.

GLOUCESTER

Then prithee get thee gone. If for my sake

Thou wilt o'ertake us hence a mile or twain

43 I' th' way toward Dover, do it for ancient love;

And bring some covering for this naked soul,

Which I'll entreat to lead me.

OLD MAN   Alack, sir, he is mad.

GLOUCESTER

46 'Tis the time's plague when madmen lead the blind.

47 Do as I bid thee, or rather do thy pleasure.

Above the rest, be gone.

OLD MAN

49 I'll bring him the best 'parel that I have,

Come on't what will.   Exit.

GLOUCESTER

Sirrah naked fellow –

EDGAR

52 Poor Tom's acold. [aside] I cannot daub it further.

GLOUCESTER

Come hither, fellow.

EDGAR [aside]

And yet I must. – Bless thy sweet eyes, they bleed.

GLOUCESTER

Know'st thou the way to Dover?

EDGAR Both stile and gate, horseway and footpath. Poor

Tom hath been scared out of his good wits. Bless thee,

good man's son, from the foul fiend. [Five fiends have

been in poor Tom at once: of lust, as Obidicut; Hobbi- 59

didence, prince of dumbness; Mahu, of stealing; Modo, 60

of murder; Flibbertigibbet, of mopping and mowing, 61

who since possesses chambermaids and waiting women.

So, bless thee, master.]

GLOUCESTER

Here, take this purse, thou whom the heavens' plagues

Have humbled to all strokes. That I am wretched 65

Makes thee the happier. Heavens, deal so still! 66

Let the superfluous and lust-dieted man, 67

That slaves your ordinance, that will not see 68

Because he does not feel, feel your pow'r quickly;

So distribution should undo excess,

And each man have enough. Dost thou know Dover?

EDGAR Ay, master.

GLOUCESTER

There is a cliff, whose high and bending head 73

Looks fearfully in the confinèd deep. 74

Bring me but to the very brim of it,

And I'll repair the misery thou dost bear

With something rich about me. From that place

I shall no leading need.

EDGAR   Give me thy arm.

Poor Tom shall lead thee.   Exeunt.

*

Enter Goneril, Bastard [Edmund], and Steward   IV, ii
[Oswald].

GONERIL

Welcome, my lord. I marvel our mild husband

Not met us on the way. 2

[To Oswald]   Now, where's your master?

OSWALD

Madam, within, but never man so changed.

I told him of the army that was landed:

He smiled at it. I told him you were coming:

His answer was, 'The worse.' Of Gloucester's treachery

And of the loyal service of his son

When I informed him, then he called me sot 8

And told me I had turned the wrong side out.

16 *comforts* ministrations   17 *hurt* do injury (since they are forbidden)
18 *want* need   20–21 *Our means . . . commodities* i.e. prosperity makes us
rash, and sheer affliction proves a boon   22 *food* i.e. the object fed upon;
abusèd deceived   23 *in* i.e. by means of   27–28 *The worst . . . worst* (because
at the very worst there will be no such comforting thought)   31 *reason*
powers of reason   33–34 *My son . . . mind* (because it was actually he –
a natural touch)   36 *wanton* irresponsibly playful   39 *Ang'ring* offending
43 *ancient love* i.e. such love as formerly bound master and man (nostalgic)
46 *time's plague* i.e. malady characteristic of these times   47 *thy pleasure*
as you please   49 *'parel* apparel   52 *daub it* lay it on, act the part   59
Obidicut Hoberdicut (a devil mentioned in Harsnett's *Declaration*, as are
the four following)   60 *dumbness* muteness (Shakespeare identifies each
devil with some form of possession)   61 *mopping and mowing* grimaces,
affected facial expressions   65 *humbled to* reduced to bearing humbly
66 *happier* i.e. less wretched   67 *superfluous* possessed of superfluities;
lust-dieted i.e. whose desires are feasted   68 *slaves your ordinance* subordinates your injunction (to share)   73 *bending* overhanging   74 *in . . .*
deep i.e. to the sea hemmed in below
IV, ii Before Albany's palace   2 *Not met* has not met   8 *sot* fool

What most he should dislike seems pleasant to him;
11 What like, offensive.
GONERIL *[to Edmund]* Then shall you go no further.
12 It is the cowish terror of his spirit,
13 That dares not undertake. He'll not feel wrongs
14 Which tie him to an answer. Our wishes on the way
May prove effects. Back, Edmund, to my brother.
16 Hasten his musters and conduct his pow'rs.
17 I must change names at home, and give the distaff
Into my husband's hands. This trusty servant
Shall pass between us. Ere long you are like to hear
(If you dare venture in your own behalf)
21 A mistress's command. Wear this. Spare speech.
    [Gives a favor.]
Decline your head. This kiss, if it durst speak,
Would stretch thy spirits up into the air.
24 Conceive, and fare thee well.
    EDMUND
Yours in the ranks of death.   *Exit.*
GONERIL   My most dear Gloucester.
O, the difference of man and man:
To thee a woman's services are due;
28 My fool usurps my body.
    OSWALD   Madam, here comes my lord.
                                        [Exit.]
    Enter Albany.
GONERIL
29 I have been worth the whistle.
    ALBANY   O Goneril,
You are not worth the dust which the rude wind
31 Blows in your face. [I fear your disposition:
That nature which contemns its origin
33 Cannot be borderèd certain in itself.
34 She that herself will sliver and disbranch
35 From her material sap, perforce must wither
And come to deadly use.

GONERIL
No more; the text is foolish.
ALBANY
Wisdom and goodness to the vile seem vile;
Filths savor but themselves. What have you done?   39
Tigers not daughters, what have you performed?
A father, and a gracious agèd man,
Whose reverence even the head-lugged bear would lick, 42
Most barbarous, most degenerate, have you madded.   43
Could my good brother suffer you to do it?
A man, a prince, by him so benefited!
If that the heavens do not their visible spirits   46
Send quickly down to tame these vile offenses,
It will come,   48
Humanity must perforce prey on itself,
Like monsters of the deep.]
GONERIL   Milk-livered man,   50
That bear'st a cheek for blows, a head for wrongs;
Who hast not in thy brows an eye discerning   52
Thine honor from thy suffering; [that not know'st
Fools do those villains pity who are punished   54
Ere they have done their mischief. Where's thy drum? 55
France spreads his banners in our noiseless land,   56
With plumèd helm thy state begins to threat,   57
Whilst thou, a moral fool, sits still and cries   58
'Alack, why does he so?']
ALBANY   See thyself, devil:
Proper deformity seems not in the fiend   60
So horrid as in woman.
GONERIL   O vain fool!
[ALBANY
Thou changèd and self-covered thing, for shame   62
Bemonster not thy feature. Were't my fitness   63
To let these hands obey my blood,   64
They are apt enough to dislocate and tear
Thy flesh and bones. Howe'er thou art a fiend,
A woman's shape doth shield thee.
GONERIL
Marry, your manhood – mew!]   68
    Enter a Messenger.
[ALBANY What news?]
MESSENGER
O, my good lord, the Duke of Cornwall's dead,
Slain by his servant, going to put out   71
The other eye of Gloucester.
ALBANY   Gloucester's eyes?
MESSENGER
A servant that he bred, thrilled with remorse,   73
Opposed against the act, bending his sword
To his great master; who, thereat enraged,
Flew on him, and amongst them felled him dead;   76
But not without that harmful stroke which since
Hath plucked him after.   78
ALBANY   This shows you are above,
You justicers, that these our nether crimes   79
So speedily can venge. But, O poor Gloucester,   80
Lost he his other eye?
MESSENGER   Both, both, my lord.
This letter, madam, craves a speedy answer.   82
'Tis from your sister.
GONERIL *[aside]*   One way I like this well;
But being widow, and my Gloucester with her,
May all the building in my fancy pluck   85
Upon my hateful life. Another way   86

11 *What like* what he should like 12 *cowish* cowardly 13 *undertake* engage 14 *an answer* retaliation 14–15 *Our wishes . . . effects* i.e. our wishes, that you might supplant Albany, may materialize 16 *musters* enlistments; *conduct his pow'rs* lead his army 17 *change names* i.e. exchange the name of 'mistress' for 'master'; *distaff* spinning-staff (symbol of the housewife) 21 *mistress's* (at present she plays the role of master, but, mated with Edmund, she would again *change names*) 24 *Conceive* (1) understand, (2) quicken (with the seed I have planted in you) 28 *usurps* wrongfully occupies 29 *worth the whistle* i.e. valued enough to be welcomed home ('not worth the whistle' applying proverbially to a 'poor dog') 31 *fear your disposition* distrust your nature 33 *borderèd certain* safely contained (it will be unpredictably licentious) 34 *sliver*, *disbranch* cut off 35 *material sap* sustaining stock, nourishing trunk 39 *savor* relish 42 *head-lugged* dragged with a head-chain (hence, surly); *lick* i.e. treat with affection 43 *degenerate* unnatural; *madded* maddened 46 *visible* made visible, material 48 *It* i.e. chaos 50 *Milk-livered* i.e. spiritless 52–53 *discerning . . . suffering* distinguishing between dishonor and tolerance 54 *Fools* i.e. only fools 55 *drum* i.e. military preparation 56 *noiseless* i.e. unaroused 57 *helm* war-helmet 58 *moral* moralizing 60 *Proper* i.e. fair-surfaced 62 *changèd* transformed (diabolically, as in witchcraft); *self-covered* i.e. your natural self overwhelmed by evil (?), devil disguised as woman (?) 63 *Bemonster . . . feature* i.e. do not exchange your human features for a monster's; *my fitness* fit for me 64 *blood* passion 68 *Marry* (oath, derived from 'By Mary'); *your manhood – mew* i.e. 'What a man!' followed by a contemptuous interjection (?), mew up (contain) this display of manliness (?) 71 *going to* about to 73 *bred* reared; *thrilled with remorse* in the throes of pity 76 *amongst them* i.e. aided by the others 78 *plucked him after* drawn him along (to death) 79 *justicers* dispensers of justice; *nether crimes* sins committed here below 80 *venge* avenge 82 *craves* requires 85–86 *May . . . life* i.e. may make my life hateful by destroying my dream-castles 86 *Another way* the other way (alluded to in l. 83, probably the removal of Cornwall as an obstacle to sole reign with Edmund)

87 The news is not so tart. – I'll read, and answer.   *[Exit.]*

ALBANY
Where was his son when they did take his eyes ?

MESSENGER
Come with my lady hither.

ALBANY   He is not here.

MESSENGER
90 No, my good lord ; I met him back again.

ALBANY
Knows he the wickedness ?

MESSENGER
Ay, my good lord. 'Twas he informed against him,
And quit the house on purpose, that their punishment
Might have the freer course.

ALBANY   Gloucester, I live
To thank thee for the love thou show'dst the King,
And to revenge thine eyes. Come hither, friend.
Tell me what more thou know'st.   *Exeunt.*

*

IV, iii   *[Enter Kent and a Gentleman.*

KENT Why the King of France is so suddenly gone back
    know you no reason ?

3 GENTLEMAN Something he left imperfect in the state,
4   which since his coming forth is thought of, which imports
5   to the kingdom so much fear and danger that his per-
6   sonal return was most required and necessary.

KENT
Who hath he left behind him general ?

GENTLEMAN The Marshal of France, Monsieur La Far.

9 KENT Did your letters pierce the Queen to any demon-
    stration of grief ?

GENTLEMAN
Ay, sir. She took them, read them in my presence,
12 And now and then an ample tear trilled down
Her delicate cheek. It seemed she was a queen
14 Over her passion, who, most rebel-like,
Sought to be king o'er her.

KENT   O, then it movèd her ?

GENTLEMAN
Not to a rage. Patience and sorrow strove
17 Who should express her goodliest. You have seen
Sunshine and rain at once – her smiles and tears
19 Were like, a better way : those happy smilets
That played on her ripe lip seemed not to know
What guests were in her eyes, which parted thence
As pearls from diamonds dropped. In brief,
23 Sorrow would be a rarity most belovèd,
If all could so become it.

KENT   Made she no verbal question ?

GENTLEMAN
25 Faith, once or twice she heaved the name of father
Pantingly forth, as if it pressed her heart ;
Cried 'Sisters, sisters, shame of ladies, sisters !
Kent, father, sisters ? What, i' th' storm i' th' night ?
29 Let pity not be believed !' There she shook
The holy water from her heavenly eyes,
31 And clamor moistened ; then away she started
To deal with grief alone.

KENT   It is the stars,
33 The stars above us govern our conditions ;
34 Else one self mate and make could not beget
35 Such different issues. You spoke not with her since ?

GENTLEMAN No.

KENT
Was this before the King returned ?

GENTLEMAN   No, since.

KENT
Well, sir, the poor distressèd Lear 's i' th' town ;
Who sometime, in his better tune, remembers   39
What we are come about, and by no means
Will yield to see his daughter.

GENTLEMAN   Why, good sir ?

KENT
A sovereign shame so elbows him ; his own unkindness,   42
That stripped her from his benediction, turned her   43
To foreign casualties, gave her dear rights   44
To his dog-hearted daughters – these things sting
His mind so venomously that burning shame
Detains him from Cordelia.

GENTLEMAN   Alack, poor gentleman.

KENT
Of Albany's and Cornwall's powers you heard not ?

GENTLEMAN
'Tis so ; they are afoot.   49

KENT
Well, sir, I'll bring you to our master Lear
And leave you to attend him. Some dear cause   51
Will in concealment wrap me up awhile.
When I am known aright, you shall not grieve
Lending me this acquaintance. I pray you go
Along with me.   *Exeunt.]*

*

Enter, with Drum and Colors, Cordelia, Gentleman   IV, iv
[Doctor], and Soldiers.

CORDELIA
Alack, 'tis he ! Why, he was met even now
As mad as the vexed sea, singing aloud,
Crowned with rank fumiter and furrow weeds,   3
With hardocks, hemlock, nettles, cuckoo flow'rs,   4
Darnel, and all the idle weeds that grow   5
In our sustaining corn. A century send forth !   6
Search every acre in the high-grown field
And bring him to our eye.   *[Exit an Officer.]*
                          What can man's wisdom   8
In the restoring his bereavèd sense ?   9
He that helps him take all my outward worth.   10

DOCTOR
There is means, madam.

<hr>

87 *tart* distasteful   90 *back* going back
IV, iii A meeting place at Dover   3 *imperfect . . . state* i.e. rift in affairs
of state   4 *imports* means   5 *fear* uneasiness   6 *most* most urgently
9 *pierce* goad   12 *trilled* trickled   14 *who* which   17 *goodliest* i.e. most
becomingly   19 *Were . . . way* i.e. improved upon that spectacle   23
rarity gem   25–26 *heaved . . . forth* uttered . . . chokingly   29 *Let pity*
let it for pity (?)   31 *clamor moistened* i.e. mixed, and thus muted, lamentation with tears   33 *govern our conditions* determine our characters   34
Else . . . make otherwise the same husband and wife   35 *issues* children
39 *better tune* i.e. more rational state, less jangled   42 *sovereign* over-
ruling ; *elbows* jogs   43 *stripped* cut off (cf. *disbranch*, IV, ii, 34) ; *benediction* blessing   44 *casualties* chances   49 *'Tis so* i.e. I have to this extent
51 *dear cause* important purpose
IV, iv A field near Dover   3 *fumiter* fumitory ; *furrow weeds* (those that
appear after ploughing ?)   4 *hardocks* (variously identified as burdock,
'hoar dock,' 'harlock,' etc.)   5 *Darnel* tares ; *idle* useless   6 *sustaining
corn* life-giving wheat ; *century* troop of a hundred men   8 *can* i.e. can
accomplish   9 *bereavèd* bereft   10 *outward worth* material possessions

12 Our foster nurse of nature is repose,
13 The which he lacks. That to provoke in him
14 Are many simples operative, whose power
   Will close the eye of anguish.
CORDELIA   All blessed secrets,
16 All you unpublished virtues of the earth,
17 Spring with my tears ; be aidant and remediate
   In the good man's distress. Seek, seek for him,
   Lest his ungoverned rage dissolve the life
20 That wants the means to lead it.
       Enter Messenger
MESSENGER   News, madam.
   The British pow'rs are marching hitherward.
CORDELIA
   'Tis known before. Our preparation stands
   In expectation of them. O dear father,
   It is thy business that I go about.
25 Therefore great France
26 My mourning, and importuned tears hath pitied.
27 No blown ambition doth our arms incite,
   But love, dear love, and our aged father's right.
   Soon may I hear and see him !   *Exeunt.*

               *

IV, v   *Enter Regan and Steward [Oswald].*
REGAN
   But are my brother's pow'rs set forth ?
OSWALD   Ay, madam.
REGAN
   Himself in person there ?
2 OSWALD   Madam, with much ado.
   Your sister is the better soldier.
REGAN
   Lord Edmund spake not with your lord at home ?
OSWALD   No, madam.
REGAN
6 What might import my sister's letter to him ?
OSWALD   I know not, lady.
REGAN
8 Faith, he is posted hence on serious matter.
9 It was great ignorance, Gloucester's eyes being out,
   To let him live. Where he arrives he moves
   All hearts against us. Edmund, I think, is gone,
   In pity of his misery, to dispatch
13 His nighted life ; moreover, to descry
   The strength o' th' enemy.
OSWALD
   I must needs after him, madam, with my letter.
REGAN
   Our troops set forth to-morrow. Stay with us.

   The ways are dangerous.
OSWALD   I may not, madam.
   My lady charged my duty in this business.   18
REGAN
   Why should she write to Edmund ? Might not you
   Transport her purposes by word ? Belike,   20
   Some things – I know not what. I'll love thee much,
   Let me unseal the letter.
OSWALD   Madam, I had rather –
REGAN
   I know your lady does not love her husband,
   I am sure of that ; and at her late being here   24
   She gave strange eliads and most speaking looks   25
   To noble Edmund. I know you are of her bosom.   26
OSWALD   I, madam ?
REGAN
   I speak in understanding – y' are, I know't –
   Therefore I do advise you take this note :   29
   My lord is dead ; Edmund and I have talked,
   And more convenient is he for my hand   31
   Than for your lady's. You may gather more.   32
   If you do find him, pray you give him this ;   33
   And when your mistress hears thus much from you,
   I pray desire her call her wisdom to her.   35
   So fare you well.
   If you do chance to hear of that blind traitor,
   Preferment falls on him that cuts him off.   38
OSWALD
   Would I could meet him, madam ! I should show
   What party I do follow.
REGAN   Fare thee well.   *Exeunt.*

               *

      Enter Gloucester and Edgar.   IV, vi
GLOUCESTER
   When shall I come to th' top of that same hill ?
EDGAR
   You do climb up it now. Look how we labor.
GLOUCESTER
   Methinks the ground is even.
EDGAR   Horrible steep.
   Hark, do you hear the sea ?
GLOUCESTER   No, truly.
EDGAR
   Why, then, your other senses grow imperfect
   By your eyes' anguish.   6
GLOUCESTER   So may it be indeed.
   Methinks thy voice is altered, and thou speak'st
   In better phrase and matter than thou didst.
EDGAR
   Y' are much deceived. In nothing am I changed
   But in my garments.
GLOUCESTER   Methinks y' are better spoken.
EDGAR
   Come on, sir ; here's the place. Stand still. How fearful
   And dizzy 'tis to cast one's eyes so low !
   The crows and choughs that wing the midway air   13
   Show scarce so gross as beetles. Halfway down   14
   Hangs one that gathers sampire – dreadful trade ;   15
   Methinks he seems no bigger than his head.
   The fishermen that walk upon the beach
   Appear like mice ; and yond tall anchoring bark,   18

12 *foster* fostering   13 *provoke* induce   14 *simples operative* medicinal herbs, sedatives   16 *unpublished virtues* i.e. little-known benign herbs 17 *Spring* grow ; *remediate* remedial   20 *wants* lacks ; *means* i.e. power of reason ; *lead it* govern it (the rage)   25 *Therefore* therefor, because of that   26 *importuned* importunate   27 *blown* swollen
IV, v At Gloucester's castle   2 *much ado* great bother   6 *import* bear as its message   8 *is posted* has sped   9 *ignorance* error   13 *nighted* benighted, blinded   18 *charged* strictly ordered   20 *Transport her purposes* convey her intentions ; *Belike* probably   24 *late* recently   25 *eliads* amorous glances 26 *of her bosom* in her confidence   29 *take this note* note this   31 *convenient* appropriate   32 *gather more* i.e. draw your own conclusions   33 *this* this word, this reminder   35 *call* recall   38 *Preferment* advancement
IV, vi An open place near Dover   6 *anguish* affliction   13 *choughs* jack-daws ; *midway* i.e. halfway down   14 *gross* large   15 *sampire* samphire (aromatic herb used in relishes)   18 *anchoring* anchored

19 Diminished to her cock; her cock, a buoy
Almost too small for sight. The murmuring surge
21 That on th' unnumb'red idle pebble chafes
Cannot be heard so high. I'll look no more,
23 Lest my brain turn, and the deficient sight
24 Topple down headlong.

GLOUCESTER   Set me where you stand.

EDGAR
Give me your hand. You are now within a foot
Of th' extreme verge. For all beneath the moon
27 Would I not leap upright.

GLOUCESTER   Let go my hand.
Here, friend, 's another purse; in it a jewel
29 Well worth a poor man's taking. Fairies and gods
Prosper it with thee. Go thou further off;
Bid me farewell, and let me hear thee going.

EDGAR
Now fare ye well, good sir.

GLOUCESTER   With all my heart.

EDGAR [aside]
33 Why I do trifle thus with his despair
Is done to cure it.

GLOUCESTER   O you mighty gods!
           [He kneels.]
This world I do renounce, and in your sights
Shake patiently my great affliction off.
37 If I could bear it longer and not fall
38 To quarrel with your great opposeless wills,
39 My snuff and loathèd part of nature should
Burn itself out. If Edgar live, O bless him!
Now, fellow, fare thee well.
           [He falls forward and swoons.]

EDGAR   Gone, sir – farewell.
42 And yet I know not how conceit may rob
The treasury of life when life itself
44 Yields to the theft. Had he been where he thought,
By this had thought been past. Alive or dead?
Ho you, sir! Friend! Hear you, sir? Speak!
Thus might he pass indeed. Yet he revives.
What are you, sir?

GLOUCESTER   Away, and let me die.

EDGAR
Hadst thou been aught but gossamer, feathers, air,
50 So many fathom down precipitating,
Thou'dst shivered like an egg; but thou dost breathe,
Hast heavy substance, bleed'st not, speak'st, art sound.
53 Ten masts at each make not the altitude
Which thou hast perpendicularly fell.
55 Thy life 's a miracle. Speak yet again.

GLOUCESTER
But have I fall'n, or no?

EDGAR
57 From the dread summit of this chalky bourn.
58 Look up a-height. The shrill-gorged lark so far
Cannot be seen or heard. Do but look up.

GLOUCESTER
Alack, I have no eyes.
Is wretchedness deprived that benefit
To end itself by death? 'Twas yet some comfort
63 When misery could beguile the tyrant's rage
And frustrate his proud will.

EDGAR   Give me your arm.
65 Up – so. How is't? Feel you your legs? You stand.

GLOUCESTER
Too well, too well.

EDGAR   This is above all strangeness.
Upon the crown o' th' cliff what thing was that
Which parted from you?

GLOUCESTER   A poor unfortunate beggar.

EDGAR
As I stood here below, methought his eyes
Were two full moons; he had a thousand noses,
Horns whelked and waved like the enridgèd sea.   71
It was some fiend. Therefore, thou happy father,   72
Think that the clearest gods, who make them honors   73
Of men's impossibilities, have preservèd thee.

GLOUCESTER
I do remember now. Henceforth I'll bear
Affliction till it do cry out itself
'Enough, enough, and die.' That thing you speak of,
I took it for a man. Often 'twould say
'The fiend, the fiend' – he led me to that place.

EDGAR
Bear free and patient thoughts.   80
           Enter Lear [mad, bedecked with weeds].
           But who comes here?
The safer sense will ne'er accommodate   81
His master thus.   82

LEAR No, they cannot touch me for coining; I am the   83
King himself.

EDGAR
O thou side-piercing sight!

LEAR Nature 's above art in that respect. There's your   86
press money. That fellow handles his bow like a crow-   87
keeper. Draw me a clothier's yard. Look, look, a mouse!   88
Peace, peace; this piece of toasted cheese will do't.
There's my gauntlet; I'll prove it on a giant. Bring up   90
the brown bills. O, well flown, bird. I' th' clout, i' th'   91
clout – hewgh! Give the word.   92

EDGAR Sweet marjoram.   93

LEAR Pass.

GLOUCESTER
I know that voice.

LEAR Ha! Goneril with a white beard? They flattered me
like a dog, and told me I had the white hairs in my beard   97

19 *Diminished . . . cock* reduced to the size of her cockboat   21 *unnumb'red idle pebble* i.e. barren reach of countless pebbles   23 *the deficient sight* i.e. my dizziness   24 *Topple* topple me   27 *upright* i.e. even upright, let alone forward   29 *Fairies* (the usual wardens of treasure)   33 *Why . . . trifle* i.e. the reason I toy with (*done* in l. 34 being redundant)   37-38 *fall . . . with* i.e. rebel against (irreligiously)   38 *opposeless* not to be opposed   39 *My snuff . . . nature* i.e. the guttering and hateful tag end of my life   42 *conceit* imagination   44 *Yields to* i.e. welcomes   50 *precipitating* falling   53 *at each* end to end   55 *life* survival   57 *bourn* boundary, headland   58 *a-height* on high; *gorged* throated   63 *beguile* outwit   65 *Feel* test   71 *whelked* corrugated; *enridgèd* blown into ridges   72 *happy father* lucky old man   73 *clearest* purest   73-74 *who . . . impossibilities* i.e. whose glory it is to do for man what he cannot do for himself   80 *free* (of despair)   81 *safer* saner; *accommodate* accoutre   82 *His* its   83 *touch* i.e. interfere with; *coining* minting coins (a royal prerogative)   86 *Nature . . . respect* i.e. a born king is above a made king in legal immunity (cf. the coeval debate on the relative merits of poets of nature, i.e. born, and poets of art, i.e. made by self-effort)   87 *press money* i.e. the 'king's shilling' (token payment on military impressment or enlistment)   87-88 *crow-keeper* i.e. farmhand warding off crows   88 *clothier's yard* i.e. arrow (normally a yard long)   90 *gauntlet* armored glove (hurled as challenge); *prove it on* maintain it against   91 *brown bills* varnished halberds; *well flown* (hawking cry); *clout* bull's-eye (archery term)   92 *word* password   93 *Sweet marjoram* (herb, associated with treating madness?)   97 *like a dog* i.e. fawningly; *I . . . beard* i.e. I was wise

98 ere the black ones were there. To say 'ay' and 'no' to
99 everything that I said! 'Ay' and 'no' too was no good
divinity. When the rain came to wet me once, and the
wind to make me chatter; when the thunder would not
peace at my bidding; there I found 'em, there I smelt
'em out. Go to, they are not men o' their words. They
104 told me I was everything. 'Tis a lie – I am not ague-proof.

GLOUCESTER
105 The trick of that voice I do well remember.
Is't not the King?

LEAR   Ay, every inch a king.
When I do stare, see how the subject quakes.
108 I pardon that man's life. What was thy cause?
Adultery?
Thou shalt not die. Die for adultery? No.
The wren goes to't, and the small gilded fly
112 Does lecher in my sight.
Let copulation thrive; for Gloucester's bastard son
Was kinder to his father than my daughters
115 Got 'tween the lawful sheets.
116 To't, luxury, pell-mell, for I lack soldiers.
Behold yond simp'ring dame,
118 Whose face between her forks presages snow,
119 That minces virtue, and does shake the head
120 To hear of pleasure's name.
121 The fitchew nor the soilèd horse goes to't
With a more riotous appetite.
123 Down from the waist they are Centaurs,
Though women all above.
125 But to the girdle do the gods inherit,
Beneath is all the fiend's.
There's hell, there's darkness, there is the sulphurous
pit; burning, scalding, stench, consumption. Fie, fie,
129 fie! pah, pah! Give me an ounce of civet; good apothecary, sweeten my imagination! There's money for thee.

GLOUCESTER
O, let me kiss that hand.
132 LEAR Let me wipe it first; it smells of mortality.

GLOUCESTER
133 O ruined piece of nature; this great world
Shall so wear out to naught. Dost thou know me?

LEAR I remember thine eyes well enough. Dost thou
squiny at me? No, do thy worst, blind Cupid; I'll not 136
love. Read thou this challenge; mark but the penning of it.

GLOUCESTER
Were all thy letters suns, I could not see.

EDGAR [aside]
I would not take this from report – it is,   139
And my heart breaks at it.

LEAR Read.

GLOUCESTER
What, with the case of eyes?   142

LEAR O, ho, are you there with me? No eyes in your head, 143
nor no money in your purse? Your eyes are in a heavy
case, your purse in a light; yet you see how this world 145
goes.

GLOUCESTER
I see it feelingly.   147

LEAR What, art mad? A man may see how this world goes
with no eyes. Look with thine ears. See how yond justice
rails upon yond simple thief. Hark in thine ear: change 150
places and, handy-dandy, which is the justice, which is 151
the thief? Thou hast seen a farmer's dog bark at a beggar?

GLOUCESTER Ay, sir.

LEAR And the creature run from the cur. There thou
mightst behold the great image of authority – a dog's 155
obeyed in office.
Thou rascal beadle, hold thy bloody hand!   157
Why dost thou lash that whore? Strip thy own back.
Thou hotly lusts to use her in that kind   159
For which thou whip'st her. The usurer hangs the 160
cozener.
Through tattered clothes small vices do appear;   161
Robes and furred gowns hide all. Plate sin with gold,
And the strong lance of justice hurtless breaks;   163
Arm it in rags, a pygmy's straw does pierce it.   164
None does offend, none – I say none! I'll able 'em.   165
Take that of me, my friend, who have the power   166
To seal th' accuser's lips. Get thee glass eyes
And, like a scurvy politician, seem   168
To see the things thou dost not. Now, now, now, now!
Pull off my boots. Harder, harder! So.

EDGAR
O, matter and impertinency mixed;   171
Reason in madness.

LEAR
If thou wilt weep my fortunes, take my eyes.
I know thee well enough; thy name is Gloucester.
Thou must be patient. We came crying hither;
Thou know'st, the first time that we smell the air
We wawl and cry. I will preach to thee. Mark.

GLOUCESTER
Alack, alack the day.

LEAR
When we are born, we cry that we are come
To this great stage of fools. – This' a good block.   180
It were a delicate stratagem to shoe   181
A troop of horse with felt. I'll put't in proof,   182
And when I have stol'n upon these son-in-laws,
Then kill, kill, kill, kill, kill, kill!
      Enter a Gentleman [with Attendants].

GENTLEMAN
O, here he is! Lay hand upon him. – Sir,
Your most dear daughter –

---

98 *To say . . . 'no'* i.e. to agree   99–100 *no good divinity* i.e. bad theology
(For 'good divinity' cf. 2 Corinthians i, 18: 'But as God is true, our word
to you was not yea and nay'; also Matthew v, 36–37, James v, 12.)   104
ague-proof proof against chills and fever   105 *trick* peculiarity   108 *cause*
case   112 *lecher* copulate   115 *Got* begotten   116 *luxury* lechery; *for
. . . soldiers* (and therefore a higher birth rate)   118 *Whose . . . snow* i.e.
whose face (mien) presages snow (frigidity) between her forks (legs)
119 *minces* mincingly affects   120 *pleasure's name* i.e. the very name of
sexual indulgence   121 *fitchew* polecat, prostitute; *soilèd* pastured   123
Centaurs (lustful creatures of mythology, half-human and half-beast)
125 *girdle* waist; *inherit* possess   129 *civet* musk perfume   132 *mortality*
death   133–34 *this . . . naught* i.e. the universe (macrocosm) will decay
like this man (microcosm) (cf. III, i, 10n.)   136 *squiny* squint   139 *take*
accept   142 *case* sockets   143 *are . . . me* is that the situation   145 *case*
plight (pun)   147 *feelingly* (1) only by touch, (2) by feeling pain   150
simple mere   151 *handy-dandy* (old formula used in the child's game of
choosing which hand)   155 *great image* universal symbol   155–56 *a dog's
. . . office* i.e. man bows to authority regardless of who exercises it   157
beadle parish constable   159 *lusts* wish (suggestive form of 'lists'); *kind*
i.e. same act   160 *The usurer . . . cozener* i.e. the great cheat, some money-
lending judge, sentences to death the little cheat   161 *appear* show plainly
163 *hurtless* without hurting   164 *Arm . . . rags* i.e. armored (cf. *Plate*,
l. 162) only in rags   165 *able* authorize   166 *that* (i.e. the assurance of
immunity)   168 *scurvy politician* vile opportunist   171 *matter and
impertinency* sense and nonsense   180 *block* felt hat (?)   181 *delicate*
subtle   182 *in proof* to the test

LEAR
No rescue ? What, a prisoner ? I am even
188 The natural fool of fortune. Use me well ;
You shall have ransom. Let me have surgeons ;
190 I am cut to th' brains.
GENTLEMAN   You shall have anything.
LEAR
No seconds ? All myself ?
192 Why, this would make a man a man of salt,
To use his eyes for garden waterpots,
[Ay, and laying autumn's dust.] I will die bravely,
195 Like a smug bridegroom. What, I will be jovial !
Come, come, I am a king ; masters, know you that ?
GENTLEMAN
You are a royal one, and we obey you.
198 LEAR   Then there's life in't. Come, an you get it, you shall
199   get it by running. Sa, sa, sa, sa !
               Exit [running, followed by Attendants].
GENTLEMAN
A sight most pitiful in the meanest wretch,
Past speaking of in a king. Thou hast one daughter
202 Who redeems Nature from the general curse
203 Which twain have brought her to.
EDGAR
Hail, gentle sir.
204 GENTLEMAN   Sir, speed you. What's your will ?
EDGAR
205 Do you hear aught, sir, of a battle toward ?
GENTLEMAN
206 Most sure and vulgar. Every one hears that
Which can distinguish sound.
EDGAR   But, by your favor,
How near's the other army ?
GENTLEMAN
209 Near and on speedy foot. The main descry
Stands on the hourly thought.
EDGAR   I thank you, sir. That's all.
GENTLEMAN
Though that the Queen on special cause is here,
Her army is moved on.
EDGAR   I thank you, sir. *Exit [Gentleman].*
GLOUCESTER
You ever-gentle gods, take my breath from me ;
214 Let not my worser spirit tempt me again
To die before you please.
EDGAR   Well pray you, father.
GLOUCESTER
Now, good sir, what are you ?
EDGAR
217 A most poor man, made tame to fortune's blows,
218 Who, by the art of known and feeling sorrows,
219 Am pregnant to good pity. Give me your hand ;
220 I'll lead you to some biding.
GLOUCESTER   Hearty thanks.
221 The bounty and the benison of heaven
To boot, and boot.
       Enter Steward [Oswald].
222 OSWALD   A proclaimed prize ! Most happy ;
223 That eyeless head of thine was first framed flesh
To raise my fortunes. Thou old unhappy traitor,
225 Briefly thyself remember. The sword is out
That must destroy thee.
226 GLOUCESTER   Now let thy friendly hand
Put strength enough to't.

[Edgar interposes.]
OSWALD   Wherefore, bold peasant,
Dar'st thou support a published traitor ? Hence,   228
Lest that th' infection of his fortune take
Like hold on thee. Let go his arm.
EDGAR
Chill not let go, zir, without vurther 'casion.   231
OSWALD
Let go, slave, or thou diest.
EDGAR   Good gentleman, go your gait, and let poor voke   233
pass. An chud ha' bin zwaggered out of my life, 'twould   234
not ha' bin zo long as 'tis by a vortnight. Nay, come not
near th' old man. Keep out, che vore ye, or Ise try   236
whether your costard or my ballow be the harder. Chill   237
be plain with you.
OSWALD   Out, dunghill !
       [They fight.]
EDGAR   Chill pick your teeth, zir. Come. No matter vor   240
your foins.   241
       [Oswald falls.]
OSWALD
Slave, thou hast slain me. Villain, take my purse.   242
If ever thou wilt thrive, bury my body,
And give the letters which thou find'st about me   244
To Edmund Earl of Gloucester. Seek him out
Upon the English party. O, untimely death !   246
Death !
       [He dies.]
EDGAR
I know thee well. A serviceable villain,   248
As duteous to the vices of thy mistress   249
As badness would desire.
GLOUCESTER   What, is he dead ?
EDGAR
Sit you down, father ; rest you.
Let's see these pockets ; the letters that he speaks of
May be my friends. He's dead ; I am only sorry
He had no other deathsman. Let us see.   254
Leave, gentle wax and manners : blame us not   255
To know our enemies' minds. We rip their hearts ;   256
Their papers is more lawful.   257
       Reads the letter.
'Let our reciprocal vows be remembered. You have
many opportunities to cut him off. If your will want not,   259

---

188 *natural fool* born plaything   190 *cut* wounded   192 *salt* i.e. all tears
195 *smug bridegroom* spruce bridegroom (the image suggested by the
secondary meaning of *bravely*, i.e. handsomely, and the sexual suggestion
of *will die*)   198 *life* (and therefore 'hope')   199 *Sa . . . sa* (hunting and
rallying cry)   202 *general curse* universal condemnation   203 *twain* i.e.
the other two   204 *speed* God speed   205 *toward* impending   206 *sure
and vulgar* commonly known certainty   209 *on speedy foot* rapidly marching   209–10 *main . . . thought* sight of the main body is expected hourly
214 *worser spirit* i.e. bad angel   217 *tame* submissive   218 *art . . . sorrows*
i.e. lesson of sorrows painfully experienced   219 *pregnant* prone   220
biding biding place   221 *benison* blessing   222 *proclaimed prize* i.e. one
with a price on his head ; *happy* lucky   223 *framed flesh* born, created
225 *thyself remember* i.e. pray, think of your soul   226 *friendly* i.e. un-
consciously befriending   228 *published* proclaimed   231 *Chill* I'll (rustic
dialect) ; *vurther 'casion* further occasion   233 *gait* way ; *voke* folk   234
An chud if I could ; *zwaggered* swaggered, bluffed   236 *che vore* I warrant,
assure ; *Ise* I shall   237 *costard* head ; *ballow* cudgel   240 *Chill pick* i.e.
I'll knock out   241 *foins* thrusts   242 *Villain* serf   244 *letters* letter ;
about upon   246 *party* side   248 *serviceable* usable   249 *duteous* ready
to serve   254 *deathsman* executioner   255 *Leave, gentle wax* by your
leave, kind seal (formula used in opening sealed documents)   256 *To
know* i.e. for growing intimate with   257 *Their papers* i.e. to rip their
papers   259 *want not* is not lacking

time and place will be fruitfully offered. There is nothing done, if he return the conqueror. Then am I the
262 prisoner, and his bed my gaol ; from the loathed warmth
whereof deliver me, and supply the place for your labor.
264   'Your (wife, so I would say) affectionate servant,
                                   'Goneril.'
266 O indistinguished space of woman's will –
A plot upon her virtuous husband's life,
268 And the exchange my brother ! Here in the sands
269 Thee I'll rake up, the post unsanctified
270 Of murderous lechers ; and in the mature time
271 With this ungracious paper strike the sight
272 Of the death-practiced Duke. For him 'tis well
That of thy death and business I can tell.
  GLOUCESTER
274 The King is mad. How stiff is my vile sense,
275 That I stand up, and have ingenious feeling
276 Of my huge sorrows ! Better I were distract ;
So should my thoughts be severed from my griefs,
278 And woes by wrong imaginations lose
The knowledge of themselves.
    Drum afar off.
  EDGAR   Give me your hand.
Far off methinks I hear the beaten drum.
281 Come, father, I'll bestow you with a friend.   *Exeunt.*

                                *

IV, vii   *Enter Cordelia, Kent, [Doctor,] and Gentleman.*
  CORDELIA
O thou good Kent, how shall I live and work
To match thy goodness ? My life will be too short
And every measure fail me.
  KENT
To be acknowledged, madam, is o'erpaid.
5 All my reports go with the modest truth ;
6 Nor more nor clipped, but so.
  CORDELIA   Be better suited.
7 These weeds are memories of those worser hours.
I prithee put them off.
  KENT   Pardon, dear madam.
9 Yet to be known shortens my made intent.
10 My boon I make it that you know me not
11 Till time and I think meet.
  CORDELIA
Then be't so, my good lord.
    [To the Doctor]   How does the King ?

  DOCTOR
Madam, sleeps still.
  CORDELIA
O you kind gods,
Cure this great breach in his abusèd nature !   15
Th' untuned and jarring senses, O, wind up   16
Of this child-changèd father !   17
  DOCTOR   So please your Majesty
That we may wake the King ? He hath slept long.
  CORDELIA
Be governed by your knowledge, and proceed
I' th' sway of your own will. Is he arrayed ?   20
    Enter Lear in a chair carried by Servants.
  GENTLEMAN
Ay, madam. In the heaviness of sleep
We put fresh garments on him.
  DOCTOR
Be by, good madam, when we do awake him.
I doubt not of his temperance.
[CORDELIA   Very well.
    [Music.]
  DOCTOR
Please you draw near. Louder the music there.]
  CORDELIA
O my dear father, restoration hang
Thy medicine on my lips, and let this kiss
Repair those violent harms that my two sisters   28
Have in thy reverence made.   29
  KENT   Kind and dear princess.
  CORDELIA
Had you not been their father, these white flakes   30
Did challenge pity of them. Was this a face   31
To be opposed against the jarring winds ?
[To stand against the deep dread-bolted thunder ?   33
In the most terrible and nimble stroke
Of quick cross lightning to watch, poor perdu,   35
With this thin helm ?] Mine enemy's dog,   36
Though he had bit me, should have stood that night
Against my fire ; and wast thou fain, poor father,   38
To hovel thee with swine and rogues forlorn
In short and musty straw ? Alack, alack,   40
'Tis wonder that thy life and wits at once
Had not concluded all. – He wakes. Speak to him.
  DOCTOR
Madam, do you ; 'tis fittest.
  CORDELIA
How does my royal lord ? How fares your Majesty ?
  LEAR
You do me wrong to take me out o' th' grave.
Thou art a soul in bliss ; but I am bound
Upon a wheel of fire, that mine own tears   47
Do scald like molten lead.
  CORDELIA   Sir, do you know me ?
  LEAR
You are a spirit, I know. Where did you die ?
  CORDELIA
Still, still, far wide !   50
  DOCTOR
He's scarce awake. Let him alone awhile.
  LEAR
Where have I been ? Where am I ? Fair daylight ?
I am mightily abused. I should e'en die with pity   53
To see another thus. I know not what to say.
I will not swear these are my hands. Let's see –

262 *gaol* jail 264 *would* wish to 266 *indistinguished* unlimited ; *will*
desire 268 *exchange* substitute 269 *rake up* cover, bury 270 *in the
mature* at the ripe 271 *strike* blast 272 *death-practiced* whose death is
plotted 274 *stiff* obstinate ; *vile sense* i.e. hateful consciousness 275
ingenious feeling i.e. awareness 276 *distract* distracted 278 *wrong
imaginations* i.e. delusions 281 *bestow* lodge
IV, vii The French camp near Dover 5 *go* conform 6 *clipped* i.e. less
(curtailed) ; *suited* attired 7 *weeds* clothes ; *memories* reminders 9 *Yet
. . . intent* i.e. to reveal myself just yet would mar my plan 10 *My boon
. . . it* the reward I ask is 11 *meet* proper 15 *abused* confused, disturbed
16 *jarring* discordant ; *wind up* tune 17 *child-changed* (1) changed to a
child, (2) changed by his children (suggesting 'changeling,' wherein
mental defect is associated with the malignance of witches) 20 *I' th'
sway of* according to 28 *harms* wounds 29 *reverence* reverend person
30 *flakes* strands of hair 31 *challenge* demand 33 *deep dread-bolted*
deep-voiced and full of dreadful bolts 35 *perdu* (1) expendable outpost
(military term), (2) lost one 36 *helm* military helmet ; here, thin hair
38 *fain* glad 40 *short* scanty (?), tramped to fragments (?) 47 *wheel of
fire* (implement combining the tortures of breaking and burning, figuring
in medieval visions of hell) 50 *wide* off the mark 53 *abused* confused

I feel this pin prick. Would I were assured
Of my condition.

CORDELIA   O look upon me, sir,
And hold your hand in benediction o'er me.
You must not kneel.

LEAR   Pray, do not mock me.

60   I am a very foolish fond old man,
Fourscore and upward, not an hour more nor less;
And, to deal plainly,
I fear I am not in my perfect mind.
Methinks I should know you, and know this man;
Yet I am doubtful, for I am mainly ignorant
What place this is; and all the skill I have
Remembers not these garments; nor I know not
Where I did lodge last night. Do not laugh at me;
For, as I am a man, I think this lady
To be my child Cordelia.

70 CORDELIA   And so I am! I am!

LEAR
Be your tears wet? Yes, faith. I pray weep not.
If you have poison for me, I will drink it.
I know you do not love me; for your sisters
Have (as I do remember) done me wrong.
You have some cause, they have not.

CORDELIA   No cause, no cause.

LEAR
Am I in France?

KENT   In your own kingdom, sir.

LEAR
77   Do not abuse me.

DOCTOR
Be comforted, good madam. The great rage
You see is killed in him; [and yet it is danger
80 To make him even o'er the time he has lost.]
Desire him to go in. Trouble him no more
82 Till further settling.

CORDELIA
Will't please your Highness walk?

LEAR   You must bear with me.
Pray you now, forget and forgive. I am old and foolish.
         Exeunt. [Manent Kent and Gentleman.]

[GENTLEMAN Holds it true, sir, that the Duke of Cornwall was so slain?

KENT Most certain, sir.

GENTLEMAN Who is conductor of his people?

KENT As 'tis said, the bastard son of Gloucester.

GENTLEMAN They say Edgar, his banished son, is with
the Earl of Kent in Germany.

KENT Report is changeable. 'Tis time to look about; the
93   powers of the kingdom approach apace.

94 GENTLEMAN The arbitrement is like to be bloody. Fare
you well, sir.   [*Exit.*]

KENT
96 My point and period will be throughly wrought,
97 Or well or ill, as this day's battle 's fought.   *Exit.*]

*

V, i   *Enter, with Drum and Colors, Edmund, Regan,*
          Gentleman, and Soldiers.

EDMUND
1   Know of the Duke if his last purpose hold,
2   Or whether since he is advised by aught
To change the course. He's full of alteration

And self-reproving. Bring his constant pleasure.   4
          [*Exit an Officer.*]

REGAN
Our sister's man is certainly miscarried.   5

EDMUND
'Tis to be doubted, madam.   6

REGAN   Now, sweet lord,
You know the goodness I intend upon you.   7
Tell me, but truly – but then speak the truth –
Do you not love my sister?

EDMUND   In honored love.   9

REGAN
But have you never found my brother's way
To the forfended place?   11

[EDMUND   That thought abuses you.

REGAN
I am doubtful that you have been conjunct   12
And bosomed with her, as far as we call hers.]

EDMUND
No, by mine honor, madam.

REGAN
I never shall endure her. Dear my lord,
Be not familiar with her.

EDMUND   Fear me not.
She and the Duke her husband!
       Enter, with Drum and Colors, Albany, Goneril,
       Soldiers.

[GONERIL [*aside*]
I had rather lose the battle than that sister
Should loosen him and me.]   19

ALBANY
Our very loving sister, well bemet.   20
Sir, this I heard: the King is come to his daughter,
With others whom the rigor of our state   22
Forced to cry out. [Where I could not be honest,   23
I never yet was valiant. For this business,
It touches us as France invades our land,   25
Not bolds the King with others, whom I fear   26
Most just and heavy causes make oppose.

EDMUND
Sir, you speak nobly.]

REGAN   Why is this reasoned?   28

GONERIL
Combine together 'gainst the enemy;
For these domestic and particular broils   30
Are not the question here.   31

ALBANY   Let's then determine
With th' ancient of war on our proceeding.   32

[EDMUND
I shall attend you presently at your tent.]   33

---

77 *abuse* deceive   80 *even o'er* fill in   82 *settling* calming   93 *powers* armies   94 *arbitrement* decisive action   96 *My point . . . wrought* i.e. my destiny will be completely worked out   97 *Or* either
V, i An open place near the British camp   s.d. *Drum and Colors* drummer and standard-bearers   1 *Know* learn; *last purpose hold* most recent intention (i.e. to fight) holds good   2 *advised* induced   4 *constant pleasure* firm decision   5 *miscarried* met with mishap   6 *doubted* feared   7 *goodness I intend* boon I plan to confer   9 *honored* honorable   11 *forfended* forbidden; *abuses* deceives   12–13 *doubtful . . . hers* i.e. fearful you have been intimately linked with her both in mind and body   19 *loosen* separate   20 *bemet* met   22 *rigor* tyranny   23 *honest* honorable   25 *touches us as* concerns me because   26–27 *Not bolds . . . oppose* i.e. but not because he supports the King and others whose truly great grievances arouse them to arms   28 *reasoned* argued   30 *particular broils* private quarrels   31 *question* issue   32 *th' ancient of war* i.e. seasoned officers   33 *presently* immediately

REGAN
    Sister, you'll go with us ?
GONERIL No.
REGAN
36   'Tis most convenient. Pray go with us.
GONERIL
37   O ho, I know the riddle. – I will go.
                       Exeunt both the Armies.
     Enter Edgar.
EDGAR *[to Albany]*
38   If e'er your Grace had speech with man so poor,
    Hear me one word.
ALBANY *[to those departing]*
              I'll overtake you. *[to Edgar]* Speak.
EDGAR
    Before you fight the battle, ope this letter.
41   If you have victory, let the trumpet sound
    For him that brought it. Wretched though I seem,
43   I can produce a champion that will prove
44   What is avouchèd there. If you miscarry,
    Your business of the world hath so an end,
46   And machination ceases. Fortune love you.
ALBANY
    Stay till I have read the letter.
EDGAR   I was forbid it.
    When time shall serve, let but the herald cry,
    And I'll appear again.
ALBANY
50   Why, fare thee well. I will o'erlook thy paper.
                        Exit [Edgar].
     Enter Edmund.
EDMUND
51   The enemy 's in view ; draw up your powers.
52   Here is the guess of their true strength and forces
53   By diligent discovery ; but your haste
    Is now urged on you.
54 ALBANY   We will greet the time.   *Exit.*
EDMUND
    To both these sisters have I sworn my love ;
56   Each jealous of the other, as the stung
    Are of the adder. Which of them shall I take ?
    Both ? One ? Or neither ? Neither can be enjoyed,
    If both remain alive. To take the widow

Exasperates, makes mad her sister Goneril ;
And hardly shall I carry out my side,   61
Her husband being alive. Now then, we'll use
His countenance for the battle, which being done,   63
Let her who would be rid of him devise
His speedy taking off. As for the mercy
Which he intends to Lear and to Cordelia –
The battle done, and they within our power,
Shall never see his pardon ; for my state   68
Stands on me to defend, not to debate.   *Exit.*

                    *

Alarum within. Enter, with Drum and Colors, Lear,   V, ii
*[held by the hand by] Cordelia ; and Soldiers [of
France], over the stage and exeunt.
Enter Edgar and Gloucester.*
EDGAR
    Here, father, take the shadow of this tree
    For your good host. Pray that the right may thrive.
    If ever I return to you again,
    I'll bring you comfort.
GLOUCESTER   Grace go with you, sir.   4
                        Exit [Edgar].
     Alarum and retreat within. Enter Edgar.
EDGAR
    Away, old man ! Give me thy hand. Away !
    King Lear hath lost, he and his daughter ta'en.   6
    Give me thy hand. Come on.
GLOUCESTER
    No further, sir. A man may rot even here.   8
EDGAR
    What, in ill thoughts again ? Men must endure   9
    Their going hence, even as their coming hither ;
    Ripeness is all. Come on.   11
GLOUCESTER   And that's true too.   *Exeunt.*
     Enter, on conquest, with Drum and Colors, Edmund ;   V, iii
     Lear and Cordelia as prisoners ; Soldiers, Captain.
EDMUND
    Some officers take them away. Good guard
    Until their greater pleasures first be known   2
    That are to censure them.   3
CORDELIA   We are not the first
    Who with best meaning have incurred the worst.
    For thee, oppressèd king, I am cast down ;   4
    Myself could else outfrown false Fortune's frown.
    Shall we not see these daughters and these sisters ?
LEAR
    No, no, no, no ! Come, let's away to prison.
    We two alone will sing like birds i' th' cage.
    When thou dost ask me blessing, I'll kneel down   10
    And ask of thee forgiveness. So we'll live,
    And pray, and sing, and tell old tales, and laugh   12
    At gilded butterflies, and hear poor rogues
    Talk of court news ; and we'll talk with them too –
    Who loses and who wins ; who's in, who's out –
    And take upon 's the mystery of things   16
    As if we were God's spies ; and we'll wear out,   17
    In a walled prison, packs and sects of great ones   18
    That ebb and flow by th' moon.
EDMUND   Take them away.
LEAR
    Upon such sacrifices, my Cordelia,   20
    The gods themselves throw incense. Have I caught thee ?

---

36 *convenient* fitting ; *with us* (i.e. with her rather than Edmund as each leads an 'army' from the stage)   **37** *riddle* (i.e. the reason for Regan's strange demand)   **38** *had speech* i.e. has condescended to speak   **41** *sound* sound a summons   **43** *prove* (in trial by combat)   **44** *avouchèd* charged   **46** *machination* i.e. all plots and counterplots   **50** *o'erlook* look over   **51** *powers* troops   **52** *guess* estimate   **53** *discovery* reconnoitering   **54** *greet* i.e. meet the demands of   **56** *jealous* suspicious   **61** *hardly* . . . *side* with difficulty shall I play my part (as Goneril's lover, or as a great power in England?)   **63** *countenance* backing   **68–69** *my state* . . . *debate* i.e. my status depends upon my strength, not my arguments
V, ii An open place near the field of battle   **4** *s.d. Alarum and retreat* (trumpet sounds, signalling the beginning and the ending of a battle)   **6** *ta'en* captured   **8** *rot* i.e. die   **9** *ill* i.e. suicidal ; *endure* put up with, suffer through   **11** *Ripeness* i.e. the time decreed by the gods for the fruit to fall from the branch
V, iii   **2** *greater pleasures* i.e. the desires of those in higher command   **3** *censure* judge   **4** *meaning* intentions   **10–11** *When . . . forgiveness* (cf. IV, vii, 57–59)   **12–14** *laugh . . . news* view with amusement bright ephemera, such as gallants preoccupied with court gossip   **16–17** *take . . . spies* i.e. contemplate the wonder of existence as if with divine insight, seek eternal rather than temporal truths   **17** *wear out* outlast   **18–19** *packs . . . moon* i.e. partisan and intriguing clusters of *great ones* who gain and lose power monthly   **20–21** *Upon . . . incense* i.e. the gods themselves are the the celebrants at such sacrificial offerings to love as we are

22 He that parts us shall bring a brand from heaven
And fire us hence like foxes. Wipe thine eyes.
24 The goodyears shall devour them, flesh and fell,
Ere they shall make us weep ! We'll see 'em starved first.
Come.   *Exeunt [Lear and Cordelia, guarded].*

EDMUND   Come hither, captain ; hark.
Take thou this note.
     [Gives a paper.]   Go follow them to prison.
One step I have advanced thee. If thou dost
As this instructs thee, thou dost make thy way
To noble fortunes. Know thou this, that men
31 Are as the time is. To be tender-minded
32 Does not become a sword. Thy great employment
33 Will not bear question. Either say thou'lt do't,
Or thrive by other means.

CAPTAIN   I'll do't, my lord.

EDMUND
35 About it ; and write happy when th' hast done.
Mark, I say instantly, and carry it so
As I have set it down.
[CAPTAIN
I cannot draw a cart, nor eat dried oats –
If it be man's work, I'll do't.]   *Exit*
    Flourish. Enter Albany, Goneril, Regan, Soldiers.

ALBANY
Sir, you have showed to-day your valiant strain,
And fortune led you well. You have the captives
42 Who were the opposites of this day's strife.
I do require them of you, so to use them
44 As we shall find their merits and our safety
May equally determine.

EDMUND   Sir, I thought it fit
To send the old and miserable King
47 To some retention [and appointed guard] ;
Whose age had charms in it, whose title more,
49 To pluck the common bosom on his side
50 And turn our impressed lances in our eyes
Which do command them. With him I sent the Queen,
My reason all the same ; and they are ready
53 To-morrow, or at further space, t' appear
54 Where you shall hold your session. [At this time
We sweat and bleed, the friend hath lost his friend,
56 And the best quarrels, in the heat, are cursed
57 By those that feel their sharpness.
The question of Cordelia and her father
Requires a fitter place.]

ALBANY   Sir, by your patience,
60 I hold you but a subject of this war,
Not as a brother.

61 REGAN   That's as we list to grace him.
Methinks our pleasure might have been demanded
Ere you had spoke so far. He led our powers,
Bore the commission of my place and person,
65 The which immediacy may well stand up
And call itself your brother.

GONERIL   Not so hot !
In his own grace he doth exalt himself
68 More than in your addition.

REGAN   In my rights
69 By me invested, he compeers the best.

ALBANY
70 That were the most if he should husband you.

REGAN
Jesters do oft prove prophets.

GONERIL   Holla, holla !
That eye that told you so looked but asquint.   72

REGAN
Lady, I am not well ; else I should answer
From a full-flowing stomach. General,   74
Take thou my soldiers, prisoners, patrimony ;   75
Dispose of them, of me ; the walls is thine.   76
Witness the world that I create thee here
My lord and master.

GONERIL   Mean you to enjoy him ?

ALBANY
The let-alone lies not in your good will.   79

EDMUND
Nor in thine, lord.

ALBANY   Half-blooded fellow, yes.   80

REGAN *[to Edmund]*
Let the drum strike, and prove my title thine.   81

ALBANY
Stay yet ; hear reason. Edmund, I arrest thee
On capital treason ; and, in thy attaint,   83
This gilded serpent.
    [Points to Goneril.]   For your claim, fair sister,
I bar it in the interest of my wife.
'Tis she is subcontracted to this lord,   86
And I, her husband, contradict your banes.   87
If you will marry, make your loves to me ;   88
My lady is bespoke.

GONERIL   An interlude !   89

ALBANY
Thou art armed, Gloucester. Let the trumpet sound.
If none appear to prove upon thy person
Thy heinous, manifest, and many treasons,
There is my pledge.
    [Throws down a glove.]   I'll make it on thy heart,   93
Ere I taste bread, thou art in nothing less   94
Than I have here proclaimed thee.

REGAN   Sick, O sick !

GONERIL *[aside]*
If not, I'll ne'er trust medicine.   96

EDMUND
There's my exchange.
    [Throws down a glove.]   What in the world he is

22–23 *He . . . foxes* i.e. to separate us, as foxes are smoked out and scattered, would require not a human but a heavenly torch   **24** *goodyears* (undefined forces of evil); *fell* hide   **31** *as the time is* (i.e. ruthless in war)   **32** *become* befit   **33** *bear question* admit discussion   **35** *write happy* consider yourself fortunate   **42** *opposites of* enemies in   **44** *merits* deserts   **47** *some . . . guard* detention under duly appointed guards   **49** *pluck . . . bosom* draw popular sympathy   **50** *turn . . . eyes* i.e. make our conscripted lancers turn on us   **53** *space* interval   **54** *session* trials   **56** *best quarrels* worthiest causes   **57** *sharpness* i.e. painful effects   **60** *subject of* subordinate in   **61** *list to grace* please to honor   **65** *immediacy* i.e. present status (as my deputy)   **68** *your addition* honors conferred by you   **69** *compeers* equals   **70** *most* i.e. most complete investiture in your rights; *husband* wed   **72** *asquint* cross-eyed, crookedly   **74** *stomach* anger   **75** *patrimony* inheritance   **76** *walls is thine* i.e. you have stormed the citadel (myself)   **79** *let-alone* permission   **80** *Half-blooded* i.e. by birth only half noble   **81** *Let . . . thine* i.e. fight and win for yourself my rights in the kingdom   **83** *in thy attaint* i.e. as party to your corruption (cf. the *serpent* of Eden)   **86** *subcontracted* i.e. engaged, though previously married (sarcastic play on 'precontracted,' a legal term applied to one facing an impediment to marriage because previously engaged to another)   **87** *contradict your banes* forbid your banns, i.e. declare an impediment   **88** *loves* love-suits   **89** *An interlude* a quaint playlet (equivalent to saying 'How dramatic !' or 'How comical !')   **93** *make* prove   **94** *nothing less* i.e. no respect less guilty   **96** *medicine* i.e. poison

That names me traitor, villain-like he lies.
99   Call by the trumpet. He that dares approach,
On him, on you, who not? I will maintain
My truth and honor firmly.

ALBANY
A herald, ho!

[EDMUND   A herald, ho, a herald!]

ALBANY
103   Trust to thy single virtue; for thy soldiers,
All levied in my name, have in my name
Took their discharge.

REGAN   My sickness grows upon me.

ALBANY
She is not well. Convey her to my tent.
                  [Exit Regan, attended.]
     Enter a Herald.
Come hither, herald. Let the trumpet sound,
And read out this.

[CAPTAIN   Sound, trumpet!]
     A trumpet sounds.
110 HERALD *(reads)* 'If any man of quality or degree within
111   the lists of the army will maintain upon Edmund, supposed Earl of Gloucester, that he is a manifold traitor,
let him appear by the third sound of the trumpet. He is
bold in his defense.'

[EDMUND   Sound!]
     First trumpet.
HERALD Again!
     Second trumpet.
Again!
     Third trumpet.
     Trumpet answers within.
     *Enter Edgar, armed [at the third sound, a Trumpeter
before him].*

ALBANY
Ask him his purposes, why he appears
Upon this call o' th' trumpet.

HERALD   What are you?
Your name, your quality, and why you answer
This present summons?

EDGAR   Know my name is lost,
122   By treason's tooth bare-gnawn and canker-bit;
Yet am I noble as the adversary
I come to cope.

ALBANY   Which is that adversary?

EDGAR
What's he that speaks for Edmund Earl of Gloucester?

EDMUND
Himself. What say'st thou to him?

EDGAR   Draw thy sword.
That, if my speech offend a noble heart,
Thy arm may do thee justice. Here is mine.
Behold it is my privilege,   129
The privilege of mine honors,
My oath, and my profession. I protest –
Maugre thy strength, place, youth, and eminence, 132
Despite thy victor sword and fire-new fortune,   133
Thy valor and thy heart – thou art a traitor,   134
False to thy gods, thy brother, and thy father,
Conspirant 'gainst this high illustrious prince,   136
And from th' extremest upward of thy head   137
To the descent and dust below thy foot   138
A most toad-spotted traitor. Say thou 'no,'   139
This sword, this arm, and my best spirits are bent 140
To prove upon thy heart, whereto I speak,
Thou liest.

EDMUND   In wisdom I should ask thy name, 142
But since thy outside looks so fair and warlike,
And that thy tongue some say of breeding breathes, 144
What safe and nicely I might well delay   145
By rule of knighthood I disdain and spurn.
Back do I toss these treasons to thy head,   147
With the hell-hated lie o'erwhelm thy heart,   148
Which – for they yet glance by and scarcely bruise – 149
This sword of mine shall give them instant way
Where they shall rest for ever. Trumpets, speak!
     Alarums. Fight. [Edmund falls.]
ALBANY
Save him, save him.   152
GONERIL   This is practice, Gloucester.
By th' law of war thou wast not bound to answer
An unknown opposite. Thou art not vanquished,
But cozened and beguiled.   155
ALBANY   Shut your mouth, dame,
Or with this paper shall I stop it. – Hold, sir. – 156
     [To Goneril]
Thou worse than any name, read thine own evil.
No tearing, lady! I perceive you know it.
GONERIL
Say if I do – the laws are mine, not thine.   159
Who can arraign me for't?
ALBANY   Most monstrous! O,
Know'st thou this paper?
GONERIL   Ask me not what I know. *Exit.*
ALBANY
Go after her. She's desperate; govern her.   162
                  [Exit an Officer.]
EDMUND
What you have charged me with, that have I done,
And more, much more. The time will bring it out.
'Tis past, and so am I. – But what art thou
That hast this fortune on me? If thou'rt noble, 166
I do forgive thee.
EDGAR   Let's exchange charity.   167
I am no less in blood than thou art, Edmund;
If more, the more th' hast wronged me.   169
My name is Edgar and thy father's son.
The gods are just, and of our pleasant vices   171
Make instruments to plague us.
The dark and vicious place where thee he got   173
Cost him his eyes.

99 *trumpet* trumpeter **103** *single virtue* unaided prowess **110** *degree*
rank **111** *lists* muster **122** *canker-bit* eaten, as by the rose-caterpillar
129–31 *it . . . profession* i.e. wielding this sword is the privilege of my
knightly honor, oath, and function **132** *Maugre* in spite of **133** *fire-
new* brand-new **134** *heart* courage **136** *Conspirant* in conspiracy **137**
extremest upward uppermost extreme **138** *descent and dust* i.e. all that
intervenes from the head to the dust **139** *toad-spotted* i.e. exuding venom
like a toad **140** *bent* directed **142** *wisdom* prudence **144** *some say*
some assay, i.e. proof (?), one might say (?) **145** *safe and nicely* cautiously
and punctiliously **147** *treasons* accusations of treason **148** *hell-hated*
hateful as hell **149–51** *Which . . . ever* i.e. the accusations of treason,
now flying about harmlessly, will be routed into you with my sword-thrust
and lodge there permanently **152** *Save him* spare him (cf. l. 156); *practice*
trickery **155** *cozened* cheated **156** *Hold* wait (If addressed to Edmund,
this suggests a motive for the *Save him* of l. 152: i.e. Albany hopes to
obtain a confession.) **159** *mine* (i.e. as ruler) **162** *govern* control **166**
fortune on i.e. victory over **167** *charity* forgiveness and love **169** *If
more* if greater (since legitimate) **171** *of our pleasant* out of our pleasurable
173 *place* i.e. the bed of adultery; *got* begot

EDMUND   Th' hast spoken right; 'tis true.
175 The wheel is come full circle; I am here.

ALBANY
176 Methought thy very gait did prophesy
A royal nobleness. I must embrace thee.
Let sorrow split my heart if ever I
Did hate thee, or thy father.

EDGAR   Worthy prince, I know't.

ALBANY
Where have you hid yourself?
How have you known the miseries of your father?

EDGAR
By nursing them, my lord. List a brief tale;
And when 'tis told, O that my heart would burst!
The bloody proclamation to escape
185 That followed me so near (O our lives' sweetness,
That we the pain of death would hourly die
Rather than die at once!) taught me to shift
Into a madman's rags, t' assume a semblance
189 That very dogs disdained; and in this habit
190 Met I my father with his bleeding rings,
Their precious stones new lost; became his guide,
Led him, begged for him, saved him from despair;
Never – O fault! – revealed myself unto him
194 Until some half hour past, when I was armed,
Not sure, though hoping of this good success,
I asked his blessing, and from first to last
197 Told him our pilgrimage. But his flawed heart –
Alack, too weak the conflict to support –
'Twixt two extremes of passion, joy and grief,
Burst smilingly.

EDMUND   This speech of yours hath moved me,
And shall perchance do good; but speak you on –
You look as you had something more to say.

ALBANY
If there be more, more woeful, hold it in,
204 For I am almost ready to dissolve,
Hearing of this.

205 [EDGAR   This would have seemed a period
206 To such as love not sorrow; but another,
To amplify too much, would make much more,
And top extremity.
209 Whilst I was big in clamor, came there in a man,
210 Who, having seen me in my worst estate,
Shunned my abhorred society; but then, finding
Who 'twas that so endured, with his strong arms
He fastened on my neck, and bellowed out
As he'd burst heaven, threw him on my father,
Told the most piteous tale of Lear and him
That ever ear received; which in recounting
217 His grief grew puissant, and the strings of life
Began to crack. Twice then the trumpets sounded,
219 And there I left him tranced.

ALBANY   But who was this?

EDGAR
Kent, sir, the banished Kent; who in disguise
221 Followed his enemy king and did him service
Improper for a slave.]

     Enter a Gentleman [with a bloody knife].

GENTLEMAN
Help, help! O, help!

EDGAR   What kind of help?

ALBANY   Speak, man.

EDGAR
What means this bloody knife?

GENTLEMAN   'Tis hot, it smokes. 224
It came even from the heart of – O, she's dead.

ALBANY
Who dead? Speak, man.

GENTLEMAN
Your lady, sir, your lady; and her sister
By her is poisonèd; she confesses it.

EDMUND
I was contracted to them both. All three 229
Now marry in an instant. 230

EDGAR   Here comes Kent.

     Enter Kent.

ALBANY
Produce the bodies, be they alive or dead.

         [Exit Gentleman.]

This judgment of the heavens, that makes us tremble,
Touches us not with pity. – O, is this he?
The time will not allow the compliment 234
Which very manners urges. 235

KENT   I am come
To bid my king and master aye good night.
Is he not here?

ALBANY   Great thing of us forgot! 237
Speak, Edmund, where's the King? and where's
Cordelia?

     Goneril and Regan's bodies brought out.

Seest thou this object, Kent? 239

KENT
Alack, why thus?

EDMUND   Yet Edmund was beloved. 240
The one the other poisoned for my sake,
And after slew herself.

ALBANY
Even so. Cover their faces.

EDMUND
I pant for life. Some good I mean to do, 244
Despite of mine own nature. Quickly send –
Be brief in it – to th' castle, for my writ 246
Is on the life of Lear and on Cordelia.
Nay, send in time.

ALBANY   Run, run, O run!

EDGAR
To who, my lord? Who has the office? Send 249
Thy token of reprieve.

EDMUND
Well thought on. Take my sword;
Give it the captain.

EDGAR   Haste thee for thy life. *[Exit Officer.]*

EDMUND
He hath commission from thy wife and me

---

175 *wheel* (of fortune); *here* (at its bottom)   176 *prophesy* promise   185–86 *O . . . die* i.e. how sweet is life that we would prefer to suffer death-pangs hourly   189 *habit* attire   190 *rings* sockets   194 *armed* in armor   197 *our pilgrimage* of our journey; *flawed* cracked   204 *dissolve* melt into tears   205 *a period* the limit   206–08 *another . . . extremity* i.e. another sorrow, too fully described, would exceed the limit   209 *big in clamor* loud in lamentation   210 *estate* state   217 *puissant* powerful   219 *tranced* insensible   221 *enemy* inimical   224 *smokes* steams   229 *contracted* engaged   230 *marry* (i.e. in death)   234 *compliment* ceremony   235 *very manners* i.e. sheer decency   237 *thing* matter; *of* by   239 *object* sight   240 *Yet* despite all   244 *pant for life* i.e. gasp for life's breath   246 *writ* i.e. order of execution   249 *office* commission

To hang Cordelia in the prison and
To lay the blame upon her own despair
256 That she fordid herself.

ALBANY
The gods defend her! Bear him hence awhile.
         [Edmund is borne off.]
 Enter Lear, with Cordelia in his arms [, Gentleman,
 and others following].

LEAR
Howl, howl, howl! O, you are men of stones.
Had I your tongues and eyes, I'ld use them so
That heaven's vault should crack. She's gone for ever.
I know when one is dead, and when one lives.
She's dead as earth. Lend me a looking glass.
263 If that her breath will mist or stain the stone,
Why then she lives.

264 KENT   Is this the promised end?
EDGAR
265 Or image of that horror?
ALBANY   Fall and cease.
LEAR
This feather stirs; she lives! If it be so,
267 It is a chance which does redeem all sorrows
That ever I have felt.
KENT   O my good master.
LEAR
Prithee away.
EDGAR   'Tis noble Kent, your friend.
LEAR
A plague upon you murderers, traitors all;
I might have saved her; now she's gone for ever.
Cordelia, Cordelia, stay a little. Ha,
What is't thou say'st? Her voice was ever soft,
Gentle, and low – an excellent thing in woman.
I killed the slave that was a-hanging thee.
GENTLEMAN
'Tis true, my lords, he did.
LEAR   Did I not, fellow?
277 I have seen the day, with my good biting falchion
I would have made them skip. I am old now,
279 And these same crosses spoil me. Who are you?
280 Mine eyes are not o' th' best, I'll tell you straight.
KENT
281 If Fortune brag of two she loved and hated,
One of them we behold.

LEAR
This is a dull sight. Are you not Kent? 283
KENT   The same:
Your servant Kent; where is your servant Caius? 284
LEAR
He's a good fellow, I can tell you that.
He'll strike, and quickly too. He's dead and rotten.
KENT
No, my good lord; I am the very man.
LEAR
I'll see that straight. 288
KENT
That from your first of difference and decay 289
Have followed your sad steps.
LEAR   You are welcome hither.
KENT
Nor no man else. All's cheerless, dark, and deadly. 291
Your eldest daughters have fordone themselves, 292
And desperately are dead. 293
LEAR   Ay, so I think.
ALBANY
He knows not what he says; and vain is it
That we present us to him.
EDGAR   Very bootless. 295
 Enter a Messenger.
MESSENGER
Edmund is dead, my lord.
ALBANY   That's but a trifle here.
You lords and noble friends, know our intent.
What comfort to this great decay may come 298
Shall be applied. For us, we will resign,
During the life of this old Majesty,
To him our absolute power; *[to Edgar and Kent]* you to
 your rights,
With boot and such addition as your honors 302
Have more than merited. All friends shall taste
The wages of their virtue, and all foes
The cup of their deservings. – O, see, see!
LEAR
And my poor fool is hanged: no, no, no life? 306
Why should a dog, a horse, a rat, have life,
And thou no breath at all? Thou'lt come no more,
Never, never, never, never, never.
Pray you undo this button. Thank you, sir.
Do you see this? Look on her! Look her lips,
Look there, look there –
 He dies.
EDGAR   He faints. My lord, my lord –
KENT
Break, heart, I prithee break!
EDGAR   Look up, my lord.
KENT
Vex not his ghost. O, let him pass! He hates him 314
That would upon the rack of this tough world 315
Stretch him out longer.
EDGAR   He is gone indeed.
KENT
The wonder is he hath endured so long;
He but usurped his life. 318
ALBANY
Bear them from hence. Our present business
Is general woe.
 [To Kent and Edgar] Friends of my soul, you twain

---

256 *fordid* destroyed 263 *stone* i.e. glass 264 *promised end* i.e. doomsday 265 *image* duplicate; *Fall and cease* i.e. strike once and for all, make an end of things 267 *redeem* atone for 277 *falchion* small sword slightly hooked 279 *crosses* adversities; *spoil me* i.e. sap my strength 280 *tell you straight* admit (?), recognize you in a moment (?) 281 *two* (i.e. Lear, and a hypothetical second extreme example of Fortune's cruelty with whom he may be equated); *loved and hated* i.e. favored, then victimized 283 *sight* eyesight (instinctively Lear shuns the admission that he is dazed and weeping) 284 *Caius* (Kent's alias) 288 *see that straight* understand that in a moment 289 *difference and decay* change and decline in fortune 291 *Nor no man else* i.e. no, nor anyone else 292 *fordone* destroyed 293 *desperately* in a state of despair 295 *bootless* useless 298 *What . . . come* i.e. whatever means of aiding this ruined great one presents itself 302 *boot* good measure; *addition* titles, advancement in rank 306 *fool* i.e. Cordelia ('Fool' was often a term of affection, and sometimes, as in Erasmus and elsewhere in Shakespeare, of praise – an ironic commentary upon self-seeking 'worldly wisdom.') 314 *Vex . . . ghost* do not trouble his departing spirit 315 *rack* instrument of torture 318 *usurped* possessed contrary to (natural) law

Rule in this realm, and the gored state sustain.

KENT

I have a journey, sir, shortly to go.

My master calls me ; I must not say no.

EDGAR

324   The weight of this sad time we must obey,

Speak what we feel, not what we ought to say.

The oldest hath borne most ; we that are young

Shall never see so much, nor live so long.

Exeunt with a dead march.

324 *obey* i.e. accept

APPENDIX : THE QUARTO TEXT

The present edition, as explained in the "Note on the text," adheres closely to the folio version of the play. The quarto version, although inferior in the main, is of great literary interest. The essential material for a comparison of the verbal features of the two versions is here supplied.

Mechanically, the quarto text is very defective : stage directions are often lacking and the speakers are confusingly designated ; the punctuation is bad ; and the verse is often printed as prose, the prose as verse. Omitted from the quarto but included in the folio are passages totalling approximately 100 lines, appearing in the present edition at the following points :

I, i, 40–45 *while . . . now*   49–50 *Since . . . state*   64–65 *and . . . rivers*   83–85 *to whose . . . interest*   88–89 *Nothing . . . Nothing*   162 *Dear sir, forbear*

I, ii 107–12 *This villain . . . graves*   160–65 *I pray . . . brother*

I, iv, 252 *Pray . . . patient*   265 *Of . . . you*   313–24 *This man . . . Oswald*

II, iv, 6 *No, my lord*   21 *By Juno . . . ay*   45–53 *Winter's . . . year*   93–94 *Well . . . man*   98 *Are . . . blood*   135–40 *Say . . . blame*   291–92 *Whither . . . horse*

III, i, 22–29 *Who have . . . furnishings*

III, ii, 79–96 *This . . . time*

III, iv, 17–18 *In . . . endure*   26–27 *In, boy . . . sleep*   37–38 *Fathom . . . Tom*

III, vi, 12–14 *No . . . him*   83 *And . . . noon*

IV, i, 6–9 *Welcome . . . blasts*

IV, ii, 25 *My . . . Gloucester*

IV, vi, 162–67 *Plate . . . lips*

V, ii, 11 *And . . . too*

V, iii, 76 *Dispose . . . thine*   89 *An interlude*   145 *What . . . delay*   223 *Speak, man*   311–12 *Do . . . there*

On the other hand, included in the quarto but omitted from the folio are passages totalling approximately 283 lines – inserted in square brackets in the present edition at the following points :

I, i, 104   I, ii, 93–95, 140–47   I, iii, 16–20, 24–25   I, iv, 133–48, 222–25, 248, 295   II, i, 78   II, ii, 136–40, 146   II, iv, 18–19   III, i, 7–15, 30–42   III, vi, 17–55, 95–99, 100–13   III, vii, 99–107   IV, i, 58–63   IV, ii, 31–50, 53–59, 62–68, 69   IV, iii, 1–55   IV, vi, 194   IV, vii, 24–25, 33–36, 79–80, 85–97   V, i, 11–13, 18–19, 23–28, 33   V, iii, 38–39, 47, 54–59, 102, 109, 115, 205–22.

In addition, the following words in the present edition represent insertions from the quarto : I, i, 214 *best*   289 *not*   I, ii, 127 *Fut* 129 *Edgar*   130 *and*   166 *Go armed*   II, i, 71 *ay*   II, iii, 15 *bare* III, iv, 127 *had*   IV, vii, 24 *not*   V, i, 16 *me*

The wording of the quarto text differs from that of the folio in hundreds of instances. In the present edition a quarto reading has been substituted for a folio reading only when the latter makes poor or obviously inferior sense. The list of such substitutions follows, with the adopted quarto readings in italics followed by the folio readings in roman. (In this appendix the readings of the quarto as well as the folio are given in modern spelling.)

I, i, 5 *equalities* qualities   74 *possesses* professes   170 *sentence* sentences   188 *Gloucester* Cordelia   206 *on* in   221 *Fall'n* Fall 225 *well* will   248 *respects of fortune* respect and fortunes   302 *hit* sit

I, iv, 1 *well* will   93 *Kent. Why, fool* Lear. Why, my boy   163 *e'er* (from ' *euer* ') ere   169 *fools* fool   194 *endurèd* endured   334 *atasked* at task

II, i, 70 *I should* should I   79 *why* where   87 *strange news* strangeness   115 *Natures* Nature's

II, ii, 21 *clamorous* clamors   70 *too* t'   73 *Renege* Revenge   74 *gale* gall   118 *dread* dead   125 *respect* respects

II, iv, 2 *messenger* messengers   30 *panting* painting   33 *whose* those   126 *mother's* mother   181 *fickle* 'fickly'

III, ii, 3 *drowned* drown

III, iv, 52 *ford* sword   86 *deeply* dearly   109 *till the* at   126 *stock-punished* stocked, punished

III, v, 24 *dearer* dear

III, vi, 68 *tike* tight   75 *makes* make

IV, i, 41 *Then prithee get thee gone* Get thee away

IV, ii, 75 *thereat enraged* threat-enraged   79 *justicers* justices

IV, iv, 18 *distress* desires

IV, vi, 17 *walk* walked   71 *enridgèd* enraged   83 *coining* crying 161 *small* great   201 *one* a

V, i, 46 *love* loves

V, iii, 83 *attaint* arrest   84 *sister* sisters   97 *he is* he's   161 *Goneril Bastard (i.e. Edmund)*   278 *them* him

Omitted from the above list are a few instances of variation in which a folio misprint would have been detectable without reference to the quarto. Omitted from the following list are numerous instances of slight variation between quarto and folio in the use of articles, prepositions, elision, number, tense, etc., in which the literary interest is small. In all such instances the folio has been followed in the present edition, as well as in the variations listed below. Here the adopted folio readings are in italics followed by the quarto readings in roman. The great majority of the latter are, by common consent, inferior, but while these cast suspicion upon all, the fact remains that a certain number are not inferior to the folio readings and may represent what Shakespeare actually wrote. Marked with stars are the quarto readings which seem to the present editor best able to compete with the folio readings when judged from a purely literary point of view.

I, i, 20 *to* into   34 *the* my   35 *lord* liege   37 *Give me the map there. Know that we have divided* *The map there. Know we have divided   38 *fast* first   39 *from our age* of our state   40 *Conferring* Confirming   *strengths* years   45 *The princes* The two great princes   53 *Where nature doth with merit challenge* Where merit doth most challenge it   55 *love* do love   62 *speak* do   64 *shadowy* shady   68 *of Cornwall* *to Cornwall ? Speak 69 *of that self mettle as my sister* of the selfsame mettle that my sister is   72 *comes too* came   78 *ponderous* richer   82 *conferred* confirmed   83 *our last and least* the last, not least in our dear love   85 *draw* win   86 *sisters ? Speak* sisters   90 *Nothing will* How ? Nothing can   94 *How, how, Cordelia* Go to, Go to   95 *you* it   108 *Let* Well, let   118 *shall to my bosom* shall   130 *with* in *135 shall* still *149 falls* *stoops *Reserve thy state* *Reverse thy doom *156 ne'er* nor *157 motive* the motive *161 Miscreant* Recreant *163 Kill* Do. Kill *164 gift* doom *166 Hear me, recreant* Hear me *168 That* Since *vows* vow *169 strained* strayed *173 Five* Four *174 disasters* *diseases *175 sixth* fifth *180 Fare* Why, fare *181 Freedom* Friendship *182 dear shelter* protection *190 this* a *193 Most royal* Royal *194 hath* what *200 more* else *202 Will* Sir, will *204 Dow'red* Covered *214 whom* that *216 The best, the dearest* Most best, most dearest *223 Should* Could *226 make known* may know *228 unchaste* *unclean *230 richer* rich *232 That* As *233 Better* Go, to, go to. Better *235 but* no more but *239 regards* respects *241 a dowry* and dower *King* Lear *258 of* in *259 Can* Shall *271 Love* Use *276 duty* duties *280 plighted* pleated *281 with shame* shame them *283 not little* not a little *291 grossly* gross *305 of it* on't

I, ii, *10 With base? with baseness? Bastardy base? Base* With base, base bastardy *15 then* the *18 legitimate. Fine word, 'legitimate'* legitimate *24 prescribed* subscribed *38 o'erlooking* liking *45 policy and reverence* policy *68 before* heretofore *70 heard him oft* often heard him *72 declined* declining *76 sirrah* sir *I'll* I *85 that he hath writ* he hath wrote *86 other* further *100 find* see *103 reason it* reason *118 on* by *120 spherical* spiritual *124 on to a star* stars *129 bastardizing* bastardy *130 pat* out *131 Tom o'* them of *132–33 divisions. Fa, sol, la, mi* divisions *138 with* about *139 writes* writ *148 The night* Why, the night *150 Ay, two* Two

I, iii, *13 fellows* fellow servants *to* in *14 distaste* dislike *18 my* our *21 have said* tell you *Well* Very well *26 course* *very course *Prepare* Go prepare

I, iv, *20 be'st* be *30 canst thou* canst *43 You, you* You *68 my* this *72 noted it well* noted it *75 you, sir, you* you sir, you sir *hither, sir* hither *78–79 your pardon* you pardon me *81 strucken* struck *85 sir, arise, away* sir *87 Go to! Have you wisdom? So* You have wisdom *97 did* done *106 the Lady Brach* Lady o' the Brach *111 nuncle* uncle *122 Kent* Lear *123 'tis like* like *125 nuncle* uncle *131 sweet one* sweet fool *158 grace* wit *160 And* They *to wear* do wear *172 lie, sirrah* lie *181 You* *Methinks you *183 frowning* *frown *188 nor crust* neither crust *204 Will* Must *205 know* trow *210 I would* Come, sir, I would *your* that *212 transport* transform *216 This Why, this* *219 Ha! Waking? 'Tis* Sleeping or waking? Ha! Sure 'tis *227 This admiration, sir* Come, sir, this admiration *229 To understand* Understand *236 graced* great *237 then thou* *248 Woe* We *repents* repent's *261 Lear, Lear, Lear* Lear, Lear *266 Hear* Hark *280 Away, away* Go, go, my people *282 more of it* the cause *294 loose* make *296 Ha! Let it be so. I have another daughter* *Let it be so. Yet have I left a daughter *301 never* ever. Thou shalt, I warrant thee *that* that, my lord *304 Pray you, content. – What, Oswald, ho* Come, sir, no more *306 tarry* tarry and *331 No, no,* Now *333 condemn* dislike

I, v, *4 afore* before *10 not* ne'er *14 can tell what* can what *15 What canst tell, boy* Why, what canst thou tell, my boy *17 canst* canst not *i' th' middle on's* in the middle of his *31 moe* more *33 Yes indeed* Yes *38 till* before *40 O, let me not be mad, not mad, sweet heaven* O, let me not be mad, sweet heaven. I would not be mad *42 How now, are* Are *45 that's a* that is *46 unless* except

II, i, *3–4 Regan his Duchess* his Duchess *4 this* to *7 they* there *8 ear-kissing* *ear-bussing *11 the* the two *13 may do* may *18 I must act. Briefness must ask briefness* work help *23 Cornwall* Cornwall ought *27 yourself* your – *30 Draw, seem* Seem *31 ho* here *32 Fly, brother* Fly, brother, fly *39 Mumbling* Warbling *40 stand* stand's *43 him, ho* him *46 the thunder* *their thunders *52 latched* lanched *56 Full* But *62 coward caitiff* *68 would the reposal* could the reposure *73 practice* pretence *76 spirits* *spurs *77 O strange* *Strong *78 letter, said he* letter *90 O madam* Madam *it's cracked* *is cracked *97 he was of that consort* he was *100 th' expense and waste* the waste and spoil *120 prize* poise

II, ii, *1 dawning* even *5 lov'st* love *15–16 action-taking* action-taking knave. A *16 superserviceable, finical* superfinical *21 deny'st* deny *28 night, yet* night *29 You* Draw, you *32 come with* bring *39 Murder, murder* Murder! help *40 matter? Part* matter *54 they* he *55 years o' th' trade* hours at the trade *64 know you* you have *69 atwain* in twain *72 Being* *Bring *the* *their *79 drive* send *84 fault* offense *90 some* a *94 An honest mind and plain* He must be plain *100 faith* sooth *101 great* grand *103 mean'st* mean'st thou *113 compact* conjunct *120 Fetch* Bring *121 ancient* miscreant *122 Sir, I* I *127 Stocking* Stopping *133 color* nature *141 King his master needs must* King must *142 he* he's *147 Cornwall. Come, my lord, away* *Regan. Come, my good lord, away *152 out* on't *155 taken* took

II, iii, *1 heard* hear *10 hairs in* hair with *19 Sometimes* Sometime

II, iv, *3 purpose in them* purpose *5 Ha* How *7 he* look, he *8 heads* heels *25 impose* purpose *34 meiny* men *57 here within* within *58 here* there *59 but* than *60 None* no *61 number train* *68 twenty* a hundred *70 following* following it *71 upward* up the hill *74 which serves and seeks* that serves *83 stocks, fool* stocks *85 have travelled all the night* travelled hard to-night *91 Fiery? What fiery quality* *97 commands – tends – service* *commands her service *99 Fiery? The fiery Duke* Fiery Duke *that* that Lear *111 Go tell* Tell *116 O me, my heart, my rising heart! But down* O my heart, my heart *118 knapped* rapped *132 With* Of *135 scant* slack *143 his* *her *148 you* but you *153 Never* No *163 blister* blast her pride *164 mood is on* *mood – *186 you yourselves* yourselves *189 will you* wilt thou *217 that's in* that lies within *227 looked* look *230 you* you are *251 look* seem *258 need* needs *267 man* fellow *272 And let* O let *293 best* good *295 high* *bleak *296 ruffle* rustle *297 scarce* not

III, i, s.d. *severally* at several doors *1 Who's there besides* What's there beside *4 elements* element *18 note* art *20 is* be *48 that* *your *53–54 King – in which your pain* That way, I'll this King – I'll this way, you that

III, ii, *5 of* *to *7 Strike* Smite *16 tax* task *18 Then* Now then *22 will* have *join* joined *42 are* sit *49 fear* force *50 pudder* pother *54 simular* simular man *55 to* in *58 concealing continents* concealed centers *64 harder than the stones* hard than is the stone *71 And* *That *73 That's sorry* That sorrows *74 has and* has *77 Though* For *78 boy* my good boy

III, iii, *4 perpetual* their *12 footed* landed *13 look* seek *15 If I Though I* *17 strange things* some strange thing *23 The* Then *doth* do

III, iv, *4 enter here* enter *6 contentious* tempestuous *16 home sure* *22 enter here* enter *29 storm* night *46 blow the winds* *blows the cold wind *Humh! go* Go *bed* *cold bed *48 Didst thou give all to thy two* Hast given all to thy two *54 porridge* pottage *57 acold. O, do, de, do, de, do, de* acold *60 there – and there again – and there* and there again *61 Has his* What, his *62 Wouldst* Didst *66 light* fall *74 Alow, alow, loo, loo* Alo, lo, lo *77 words' justice* *words justly *94 says suum, mun* hay *96 Thou* Why, thou *a* thy *98 more but* *more but *100 Ha! here's* here's *104 contented; 'tis* content; this is *108 foul fiend* *110 squints* *squemes (i.e. squinies?) *132 Smulkin* Snulbug *148 same* most *152 him once more* him *162 mercy, sir* mercy *173 tower came* town come

III, v, *9 letter which* *letter *11 this* his

III, vi, *68 Or bobtail* *Bobtail *69 him* them *71 leaped* *leap *72 Do, de, de, de. Sessa* Loudla doodla *76 these hard hearts* this hardness *78 You will* You'll *Persian* Persian attire *80 here and rest* here *82 So, so. We'll go to supper i' th' morning* So, so, so. We'll go to supper i' th' morning. So, so, so *93 up, take up* up the King

III, vii, *3 traitor* villain *23 Though well* Though *32 I'm none* I am true *42 answered* answerer *53 answer* first answer *58 stick* *rash (meaning 'rip') *59 bare* lowed *62 rain* rage *63 stern* *dearn (meaning 'drear') *65 subscribe* *subscribed *73 served you* served *79 Nay* Why *81 you have* *yet have you *86 enkindle* unbridle *87 treacherous villain* villain

APPENDIX

IV, i, 4 *esperance* experience   9 *But who comes* Who's   10 *poorly led* parti, eyd (sic)   14 *These fourscore years* This fourscore –   17 *You* Alack, sir, you   36 *flies to* flies are to th'   45 *Which* Who   52 *daub* dance   54 *And yet I must. – Bless* Bless   57–58 *thee, good man's son* the good man

IV, ii, 17 *names* *arms   28 *My fool* A fool   *body* bed   29 *whistle* whistling   60 *seems* *shows   73 *thrilled* thralled

IV, iv, 10 *helps* can help   26 *importuned* important

IV, v, 15 *him, madam* him   40 *party* Lady

IV, vi, 1 *I* we   8 *In* With   46 *sir! Friend* sir   51 *Thou'dst* Thou hadst   65 *How is't* How   73 *make them* made their   78 *'twould* would it   89 *this piece of* this   91–92 *I' th' clout, i' th' clout in the air, hah   96 *Goneril with a white beard* Goneril, ha Regan   104 *ague-proof* argue-proof   127 *sulphurous* sulphury   128 *consumption* consummation   130 *sweeten* *to sweeten   132 *Let me* Here   138 *thy* the   *see* see one   148 *this* the   150–51 *change places and, handy-dandy* Handy-dandy   159 *Thou* Thy   blood   161 *clothes* rags   169 *Now, now, now, now* No, now   177 *wawl* wail   *Mark* Mark me   182 *felt. I'll put't in proof* felt   186 *dear daughter* – dear –   192 *a man a man* a man   195 *smug bridegroom* bridegroom   198 *Come* Nay   199 *running. Sa, sa, sa, sa* running   207 *sound* sense   217 *tame to* lame by   224 *old* most   237 *ballow* bat   246 *English* *British   252 *these* his   264 *servant* *servant, and for you her own for venture (sic)   277 *severed* *fencèd

IV, vii, 16 *jarring* hurrying   32 *opposed* exposed   *jarring* *warring   36 *enemy's* injurious   58 *hand* hands   59 *You* No, sir, you   *mock me* mock   61 *upward, not an hour more nor less* upward   70 *I am! I am* I am   79 *killed* cured   84 *Pray you* Pray

V, i, 21 *heard* hear   36 *Pray* Pray you   46 *And machination ceases. Fortune* Fortune   52 *true* great

V, ii, 1 *tree* bush

V, iii, 8 *No, no, no, no* No, no   25 *starved* starve   43 *I* We   62 *might* should   68 *addition* advancement   78 *him* him then   81 *thine* good   90 *Gloucester. Let the trumpet sound* Gloucester   91 *person* head   93 *make* prove   96 *medicine* poison   99 *the* thy   105 *My* This   110–11 *within the lists* in the host   113 *by* at   120 *name, your* name and   124 *cope* *cope withal   129–30 *my privilege, The privilege of mine honors* the privilege of my tongue   136 *Conspirant* Conspicuate   138 *below thy foot* beneath thy feet   144 *tongue* being   146 *rule* right   147 *Back* Here   152 *practice* *mere practice   153 *war* *arms   155 *Shut* *Stop   156 *stop* *stopple   *it. – Hold, sir* it   157 *name* thing   172 *plague* *scourge   174 *right; 'tis true* truth   186 *we* with   191 *Their* The   197 *our* my   223 *help! O, help* help   225 *of* – O, she's dead of   226 *Who dead? Speak, man* Who, man? Speak   228 *poisonèd; she confesses* poisoned; she hath confessed   232 *judgment* justice   233 *is this* 'tis   252 *Edgar* Albany   258 *Howl, howl, howl* Howl, howl, howl, howl   270 *you murderers* your murderous   274 *woman* women   281 *brag* bragged   *and* or   283 *This is a dull sight. Are* Are   289 *first* life   306 *no, no, no* no, no   308 *Thou'lt* O, thou wilt   309 *Never, never, never, never, never* Never, never, never   310 *sir* sir. o, o, o, o   316 *He* O, he   324 *Edgar* Albany   326 *hath* *have

MACBETH

INTRODUCTION

Macbeth is the shortest of Shakespeare's tragedies and the simplest in its statement: *Thou shalt not kill*. In the words of Coleridge, it contains "no reasonings of equivocal morality, . . . no sophistry of self-delusion." With eyes wide open to the hideousness of his offense, a brave, imaginative, and morally sensitive man commits a stealthy murder for gain. His victim is his guest, his benefactor, his kinsman, and his king; and to shield himself from detection he incontinently sacrifices the lives and reputation of two innocent underlings. The retribution is as appalling as the crime – his soul's slow death in self-horror, degradation, loneliness, and despair, then his bloody extermination.

Why should such a man do such evil? That we ask the question instead of dismissing the play as an incredible fiction is our tribute to the poet's vision and artistry. The question reshapes itself on our lips, Why is there evil for men to do? and we realize that there can be no answer. The core of *Macbeth* is a religious mystery, its moral clarity a testament of faith. Evil may be recognized, loathed, and combated without being understood: " . . . in these cases / We still have judgment here."

The earliest mention of the play occurs in notes on a performance at the Globe, April 20, 1611, by the spectator Simon Forman, but the style and a few shreds of literary evidence suggest 1605–06 as the period of composition; hence it followed *Hamlet, Othello*, and possibly also *Lear*, those other tragedies in which destruction is wrought by naked evil, not mere domestic or political strife. *Macbeth* differs from the other three in that the evil works through the protagonist as well as upon him. The one with whom we identify is the one who is possessed; this citadel crumbles from within. The supernatural soliciting of the Weird Sisters, the strenuous persuasions of the wife, do not explain Macbeth's guilt. They enhance its power over our imagination by revealing stages in its course and suggesting forces in perilous balance.

In Holinshed's *Chronicle*, from which Shakespeare drew his material, adding to the sins of the semi-legendary Macbeth those of Donwald, slayer of King Duff, the Weird Sisters are "goddesses of destinie" derived from a heathen fatalism. In the play they are Elizabethan witches, their prescriptive powers subtly curtailed; they predict, abet, and symbolize damnation but do not determine it. Any sense that Macbeth is a helpless victim, his crime predestined, his will bound, is canceled as the play proceeds. We may seem to see in the encounter on the heath the very inception of his lethal designs, but we should ask with Banquo,

> Good sir, why do you start and seem to fear
> Things that do sound so fair?

Nothing in the witches' prophecies would have suggested to an untainted mind that to "be King hereafter" meant to be murderer first. That Macbeth was already tainted would have been apparent to the original audience. In another play of the era, *The Witch of Edmonton*, the black dog appears at her side only when the wish for his presence is wrung from old Mother Sawyer's lips. The stars could influence but could not govern, the devils could come but only upon summons. At some unknown time for some unknown reason Macbeth has corrupted in pride, and has contemplated the sale of his soul as certainly as Faustus. When we later discover through the words of his Lady that plans to murder Duncan had preceded the meeting on the heath, we should not bring charges of inconsistency, speculate about "lost scenes," or complain that we have been tricked.

The prophecies, nevertheless, without explaining or excusing Macbeth's crimes, impress us as mitigation: powerful and wily forces are speeding him on his course. The more earthly influence of his Lady's persuasions impresses us in a similar way. They provide, moreover, an occasion for the display of his aversion for what he is about to do, and convert it, at least in some measure, from utter self-serving into an offering to her. Lady Macbeth's own behavior is not totally alienating. In a perverted way she is doing what all loyal wives are expected to do, urging her husband on to what she deems his good; here, as in the period of danger that follows, she at least is *all for him*. This is one of the marvels of the play, the manner in which this frightful collusion proceeds in an atmosphere of domestic virtue without the effect of irony. If the evil is great it is also limited, even in respect to the malefactors. After the Lady's collapse, her initial ferocity is remembered as something false to her nature, and the solicitude of her wise and kindly physician seems to us not misplaced.

Macbeth himself is as humane in his reflections as he is inhuman in his acts. Like Iago he is a moralizing villain, but his moralizing is not clever aphoristic display. It comes from his heart, sometimes like an echo of ancient folk beliefs,

> It will have blood, they say: blood will have blood.
> Stones have been known to move and trees to speak;
> Augures and understood relations have
> By maggot-pies and choughs and rooks brought forth
> The secret'st man of blood –

sometimes like religious revelation,

>   [Duncan's] virtues
> Will plead like angels, trumpet-tongued against
> The deep damnation of his taking-off;
> And pity, like a naked new-born babe

> Striding the blast, or heaven's cherubin horsed
> Upon the sightless couriers of the air,
> Shall blow the horrid deed in every eye
> That tears shall drown the wind.

No voice in literature has sounded with greater sadness:

> I have lived long enough. My way of life
> Is fall'n into the sear, the yellow leaf,
> And that which should accompany old age,
> As honor, love, obedience, troops of friends,
> I must not look to have; but, in their stead,
> Curses not loud but deep, mouth-honor, breath,
> Which the poor heart would fain deny, and dare not.

To say that no one who has become a bloody tyrant would speak in this way is pointless; he would *feel* in this way, or so we are convinced.

By feeling the pangs that we would feel if we were in his place, and by passing our judgments upon himself, Macbeth attaches us to him and consequently himself to us. We cannot view him with cold objectivity as something strange and apart. The unnaturalness of his acts is always counterpoised by the naturalness of his actions: his hesitant overtures to Banquo, his volubility after Duncan's death, his dazed petulance at the appearance of the ghost,

> The time has been
> That, when the brains were out, the man would die,
> And there an end. But now they rise again,
> With twenty mortal murders on their crowns,
> And push us from our stools.

There is something here both grimly humorous and affecting, this killer's speaking in the accents of a hurt child. We should not ascribe Macbeth's humanity to the automatic working of Shakespeare's sympathetic nature. There is nothing casual about it. If Macbeth were other than he is, less like ourselves, he would be a less powerful symbol of our own worst potentialities and the abyss we have escaped. There is nothing of him in Edmund or Iago for all of Shakespeare's sympathetic nature.

It is hard to believe that so universal a work was calculated to the meridian of any particular person, but there are arguments favoring the possibility. James Stuart, who had ascended the English throne and become the nominal patron of Shakespeare's company a few years before *Macbeth* was written, was supposedly descended from Banquo and was intensely interested in witchcraft; moreover he had assumed in 1605 the prerogative of curing the "king's evil" instituted by Edward the Confessor and mentioned somewhat irrelevantly in the play. On the other hand, one may argue that, had Shakespeare's primary concern been to please the monarch, he might have dramatized more creditable episodes in Scottish history, might have drawn a more flattering portrait of Banquo, and might have seized the opportunity to eulogize James as first holder of the "treble sceptres" mentioned in the show of kings (IV, i). Possibly Shakespeare was responding in his own way to the urgings of his dramatic company; he was in some respects the most reticent writer of his times, and his allusions even to Elizabeth had been few and restrained.

Whether or not *Macbeth* may be considered in a sense "topical" it contains elements that are, or might have been, mere theatrical entertainment. It combines with its great theme the working out of a puzzle, and affords us the pleasure of watching pieces dropping into place. That Macbeth would be king but no father of kings, that he would reign until Birnam Wood marched to Dunsinane, that he would be unconquerable by any man born of woman were riddling prophecies included in Holinshed, but the manner of presenting them through apparitions was Shakespeare's invention: the "Armed Head" instigating the aggression against Macduff probably represents Macbeth himself; the "Child Crowned, with a tree in his hand" certainly represents young Malcolm, deviser of the tactics at Birnam Wood; the "Bloody Child" represents Macduff, who was "from his mother's womb / Untimely ripped." These ingenuities might well have been intrusive in a play so elemental; as handled by Shakespeare they contribute to the master plan by allowing us to watch Macbeth gradually stripped of hope by those "juggling fiends" upon whom he has relied.

The opportunities for spectacularity offered by the play were seized early, and alterations had already been made in the single version that has come down to us, that printed in the folio of 1623. The Hecate scenes (III, v; IV, i, 39–43, 125–32) are interpolations obviously designed in order to introduce songs and dances by the witches. The first words of the songs, "Come away" and "Black spirits," permit us to identify them as having been borrowed from Thomas Middleton's *The Witch*, where their texts appear in full. Who wrote the surrounding matter we do not know, but its quality serves one useful purpose. Such lines as

> O, well done! I commend your pains,
> And every one shall share i' th' gains.
> And now about the cauldron sing
> Like elves and fairies in a ring

make us appreciate the more the magical raucousness of the language that Shakespeare himself gave his witches. The authenticity of the Porter's speech was questioned by Coleridge in one of his critical lapses; this too served a useful purpose, in evoking from De Quincey a gem of literary appreciation. At the Restoration the tradition of spectacular amplification was in full bloom, and on January 7, 1667, Samuel Pepys pronounced a revival as especially excellent "in *divertissement*, though it be a deep tragedy, which is a strange perfection in a tragedy." This "strange perfection" afflicts us still; no other Shakespearean play has provoked more recklessness in the invention of "effects."

Whatever intrudes upon the stark simplicity of this work of art is an offense. It needs no help. Its brevity makes us wonder if there have been cuts as well as additions in the text printed in the folio, but it is hard to imagine any extension that would not have marred its present compact structure. The physical and spiritual terror rises in swift crescendos until Macduff's child is slaughtered at Fife and the universe seems riven in two; then comes the resting place of the scene in England like the still moment at the core of a hurricane; when the blast resumes, it is not to compound chaos but to orchestrate the restoration of moral order. No one who has read the play will ever forget the hardy characters who struggle to readmit light into their murky world, and certainly not that incandescent couple who kill together and die apart. The style has the vigor, condensation, and imaginative splendor of Shakespeare at his greatest, when he seems to be pressing upon the very bounds of the expressible.

Blood and darkness are constantly invoked, and jarring antitheses, violent hyperbole, and chaotic imagery give the lines the quality demanded by the action. But there are also moments of unforgettable hush. Some of the speeches seem to express the agony of all mankind:

> Canst thou not minister to a mind diseased,
> Pluck from the memory a rooted sorrow,
> Raze out the written troubles of the brain,
> And with some sweet oblivious antidote
> Cleanse the stuffed bosom of that perilous stuff
> Which weighs upon the heart?

Over the centuries comes the quiet answer, convincing us, as so often the words of this poet so strangely do, that nothing further can be said,

> Therein the patient
> Must minister to himself.

Harvard University   ALFRED HARBAGE

NOTE ON THE TEXT

The present edition follows closely the only substantive text (folio, 1623), which is mechanically defective but not corrupt in the sense of misrepresenting, in general, Shakespeare's language. The copy was evidently provided by a transcript of a prompt-book. The act–scene division here supplied marginally coincides with the division of the folio text except that V, vii of the latter is subdivided into vii and viii. A more rational point of subdivision comes later (at V, viii, 35) and is marked by some modern editors as scene ix. A stage direction in the folio text indicates that Macbeth was slain in sight of the audience, and this direction is retained in the present text. The body could have been carried offstage by Macduff or another. Except for extensive relineation, the following list of emendations indicates the only material departures from the folio text. The adopted reading in italics is followed by the folio reading in roman.

I, i, 1 *again* again? 9–11 2. *Witch . . . air* (in the folio these lines form a single speech attributed to "All")

I, ii, 13 *gallowglasses* Gallowgrosses 14 *quarrel* Quarry 26 *thunders break* Thunders 56 *point rebellious, arm* point, rebellious arm

I, iii, 32 *weird* weyward 39 *Forres* Soris 98 *Came* Can 109 *borrowed* borrowèd

I, iv, 1 *Are* Or

I, v, 7 *weird* weyward

I, vi, 4 *martlet* Barlet 5 *loved* lovèd 9 *most* must

I, vii, 6 *shoal* Schoole 47 *do* no

II, i, 20 *weird* weyward 55 *strides* sides 56 *sure* sowre 57 *way they* they may

II, ii, 13 s.d. *Enter Macbeth* (appears after line 8 in folio)

III, i, 2 *weird* weyard

III, iv, 78 *time* times 133 *weird* weyard 135 *worst. For* worst, for 144 *in deed* indeed

III, vi, 24 *son* Sonnes 38 *the* their

IV, i, 59 *all together* altogether 93 *Dunsinane* Dunsmane 98 *Birnam* Byrnan 111 s.d. *Kings and Banquo, last* Kings, and Banquo last 119 *eighth* eight 136 *weird* weyard

IV, ii, 22 *none* move 30 s.d. *Exit* Exit Rosse 72 s.d. *Exit* Exit Messenger

IV, iii, 4 *downfall'n* downfall 15 *deserve* discerne 107 *accursed* accust 133 *thy here-approach* they here approach 235 *tune* time

V, i, 1 *two* too

V, ii, 5, 31 *Birnam* Byrnan

V, iii, 2, 60 *Birnam* Byrnan 55 *senna* Cyme

V, iv, 3 *Birnam* Byrnan 11 *gone* given

V, v, 34, 44 *Birnam* Byrnan 39 *shalt* shall

V, vii, 19 *unbattered* unbatterèd

V, viii, 30 *Birnam* Byrnan

MACBETH

[NAMES OF THE ACTORS

Duncan, *King of Scotland*
Malcolm   } *his sons*
Donalbain
Macbeth
Banquo
Macduff
Lennox
Ross   } *noblemen of Scotland*
Menteith
Angus
Caithness
Fleance, *son to Banquo*
Siward, *Earl of Northumberland*
Young Siward, *his son*
Seyton, *an officer attending on Macbeth*

Boy, *son to Macduff*
A Captain
An English Doctor
A Scottish Doctor
A Porter
An Old Man
Three Murderers
Lady Macbeth
Lady Macduff
A Gentlewoman, *attending on Lady Macbeth*
The Weird Sisters
Hecate
The Ghost of Banquo
Apparitions
Lords, Officers, Soldiers, Messengers, Attendants

Scene : *Scotland and England*]

✳

I, i   *Thunder and lightning. Enter three Witches.*

1. WITCH When shall we three meet again
    In thunder, lightning, or in rain ?
2. WITCH When the hurlyburly 's done,
    When the battle 's lost and won.
3. WITCH That will be ere the set of sun.
1. WITCH Where the place ?
2. WITCH   Upon the heath.
3. WITCH There to meet with Macbeth.

8 1. WITCH I come, Graymalkin !
9 2. WITCH Paddock calls.
3. WITCH   Anon !
ALL   Fair is foul, and foul is fair.
    Hover through the fog and filthy air.   *Exeunt.*

✳

I, ii   *Alarum within. Enter King [Duncan], Malcolm,*
    Donalbain, Lennox, with Attendants, meeting a
    bleeding Captain.

KING
    What bloody man is that ? He can report,
    As seemeth by his plight, of the revolt
    The newest state.
3 MALCOLM   This is the sergeant
    Who like a good and hardy soldier fought
    'Gainst my captivity. Hail, brave friend !
    Say to the King the knowledge of the broil
    As thou didst leave it.
CAPTAIN   Doubtful it stood,
    As two spent swimmers that do cling together

    And choke their art. The merciless Macdonwald
    (Worthy to be a rebel, for to that
    The multiplying villainies of nature
    Do swarm upon him) from the Western Isles   12
    Of kerns and gallowglasses is supplied ;   13
    And Fortune, on his damnèd quarrel smiling,
    Showed like a rebel's whore. But all's too weak :
    For brave Macbeth (well he deserves that name),
    Disdaining Fortune, with his brandished steel,
    Which smoked with bloody execution,
    Like valor's minion carved out his passage   19
    Till he faced the slave ;
    Which ne'er shook hands nor bade farewell to him
    Till he unseamed him from the nave to th' chops   22
    And fixed his head upon our battlements.
KING
    O valiant cousin ! worthy gentleman !
CAPTAIN
    As whence the sun 'gins his reflection
    Shipwracking storms and direful thunders break,
    So from that spring whence comfort seemed to come
    Discomfort swells. Mark, King of Scotland, mark.
    No sooner justice had, with valor armed,
    Compelled these skipping kerns to trust their heels

I, i An open place 8 *Graymalkin* her familiar spirit, a gray cat 9 *Paddock*
a toad ; *Anon* at once
I, ii A field near Forres 3 *sergeant* so designated, apparently, as a staff-
officer ; he ranks as a captain 12 *Western Isles* Hebrides (and Ireland ?)
13 *kerns* Irish bush-fighters ; *gallowglasses* Irish regulars, armored infantry-
men 19 *minion* darling 22 *nave* navel

31 But the Norweyan lord, surveying vantage,
   With furbished arms and new supplies of men,
   Began a fresh assault.

KING   Dismayed not this
   Our captains, Macbeth and Banquo?

CAPTAIN   Yes,
   As sparrows eagles, or the hare the lion.
   If I say sooth, I must report they were
37 As cannons overcharged with double cracks,
   So they doubly redoubled strokes upon the foe.
   Except they meant to bathe in reeking wounds,
40 Or memorize another Golgotha,
   I cannot tell –
   But I am faint; my gashes cry for help.

KING
   So well thy words become thee as thy wounds,
   They smack of honor both. Go get him surgeons.
                          [Exit Captain, attended.]
        Enter Ross and Angus.
   Who comes here?

45 MALCOLM   The worthy Thane of Ross.
LENNOX
   What a haste looks through his eyes! So should he look
47 That seems to speak things strange.
ROSS   God save the King!
KING
   Whence cam'st thou, worthy Thane?
ROSS   From Fife, great King,
   Where the Norweyan banners flout the sky
   And fan our people cold.
   Norway himself, with terrible numbers,
   Assisted by that most disloyal traitor
53 The Thane of Cawdor, began a dismal conflict,
54 Till that Bellona's bridegroom, lapped in proof,
55 Confronted him with self-comparisons,
   Point against point rebellious, arm 'gainst arm,
   Curbing his lavish spirit: and to conclude,
   The victory fell on us.
KING   Great happiness!
ROSS   That now
59 Sweno, the Norways' king, craves composition;
   Nor would we deign him burial of his men
61 Till he disbursèd, at Saint Colme's Inch,
62 Ten thousand dollars to our general use.
KING
   No more that Thane of Cawdor shall deceive
64 Our bosom interest. Go pronounce his present death
   And with his former title greet Macbeth.
ROSS
   I'll see it done.
KING
   What he hath lost noble Macbeth hath won.   Exeunt.

                        *

31 *surveying vantage* seeing opportunity   37 *cracks* explosives   40 *memorize
another Golgotha* make memorable as another 'place of the dead'   45 *Thane*
a Scottish lord   47 *seems to* seems about to   53 *dismal* ominous   54 *Bellona*
goddess of war; *lapped in proof* clad in proven armor   55 *self-comparisons*
cancelling powers   59 *composition* terms of surrender   61 *Inch* island   62
dollars Spanish or Dutch coins   64 *bosom interest* heart's trust
I, iii A heath   6 *Aroint thee* get thee gone; *rump-fed ronyon* fat-rumped
scab   15 *very ports they blow* i.e. their power to blow ships to ports   17 *card*
compass card   20 *penthouse lid* eyelid   21 *forbid* accursed   32 *weird* fate-
serving   33 *Posters* swift travellers   43 *question* confer with   44 *choppy*
chapped

Thunder. Enter the three Witches.   I, iii
1. WITCH Where hast thou been, sister?
2. WITCH Killing swine.
3. WITCH Sister, where thou?
1. WITCH A sailor's wife had chestnuts in her lap
          And mounched and mounched and mounched.
          'Give me,' quoth I.
          'Aroint thee, witch!' the rump-fed ronyon   6
          cries.
          Her husband 's to Aleppo gone, master o' th'
          Tiger:
          But in a sieve I'll thither sail
          And, like a rat without a tail,
          I'll do, I'll do, and I'll do.
2. WITCH I'll give thee a wind.
1. WITCH Th' art kind.
3. WITCH And I another.
1. WITCH I myself have all the other,
          And the very ports they blow,   15
          All the quarters that they know
          I' th' shipman's card.   17
          I'll drain him dry as hay.
          Sleep shall neither night nor day
          Hang upon his penthouse lid.   20
          He shall live a man forbid.   21
          Weary sev'nights, nine times nine,
          Shall he dwindle, peak, and pine.
          Though his bark cannot be lost,
          Yet it shall be tempest-tost.
          Look what I have.
2. WITCH Show me, show me.
1. WITCH Here I have a pilot's thumb,
          Wracked as homeward he did come.
          Drum within.
3. WITCH A drum, a drum!
          Macbeth doth come.
ALL   The weird sisters, hand in hand,   32
          Posters of the sea and land,   33
          Thus do go about, about,
          Thrice to thine, and thrice to mine,
          And thrice again, to make up nine.
          Peace! The charm 's wound up.
        Enter Macbeth and Banquo.
MACBETH
   So foul and fair a day I have not seen.
BANQUO
   How far is't called to Forres? What are these,
   So withered and so wild in their attire
   That look not like th' inhabitants o' th' earth
   And yet are on't? Live you, or are you aught
   That man may question? You seem to understand me,   43
   By each at once her choppy finger laying   44
   Upon her skinny lips. You should be women,
   And yet your beards forbid me to interpret
   That you are so.
MACBETH   Speak, if you can. What are you?
1. WITCH
   All hail, Macbeth! Hail to thee, Thane of Glamis!
2. WITCH
   All hail, Macbeth! Hail to thee, Thane of Cawdor!
3. WITCH
   All hail, Macbeth, that shalt be King hereafter!
BANQUO
   Good sir, why do you start and seem to fear

Things that do sound so fair? I' th' name of truth,
53 Are ye fantastical, or that indeed
Which outwardly ye show? My noble partner
55 You greet with present grace and great prediction
Of noble having and of royal hope,
57 That he seems rapt withal. To me you speak not.
58 If you can look into the seeds of time
And say which grain will grow and which will not,
Speak then to me, who neither beg nor fear
Your favors nor your hate.

1. WITCH   Hail!

2. WITCH   Hail!

3. WITCH   Hail!

1. WITCH
Lesser than Macbeth, and greater.

2. WITCH
66 Not so happy, yet much happier.

3. WITCH
67 Thou shalt get kings, though thou be none.
So all hail, Macbeth and Banquo!

1. WITCH
Banquo and Macbeth, all hail!

MACBETH
70 Stay, you imperfect speakers, tell me more:
71 By Sinel's death I know I am Thane of Glamis,
But how of Cawdor? The Thane of Cawdor lives,
A prosperous gentleman; and to be King
Stands not within the prospect of belief,
No more than to be Cawdor. Say from whence
You owe this strange intelligence, or why
Upon this blasted heath you stop our way
With such prophetic greeting. Speak, I charge you.
               Witches vanish.

BANQUO
The earth hath bubbles as the water has,
And these are of them. Whither are they vanished?

MACBETH
81 Into the air, and what seemed corporal melted
As breath into the wind. Would they had stayed!

BANQUO
Were such things here as we do speak about?
84 Or have we eaten on the insane root
That takes the reason prisoner?

MACBETH
Your children shall be kings.

BANQUO   You shall be King.

MACBETH
And Thane of Cawdor too. Went it not so?

BANQUO
To th' selfsame tune and words. Who's here?
      Enter Ross and Angus.

ROSS
The King hath happily received, Macbeth,
90 The news of thy success; and when he reads
Thy personal venture in the rebels' fight,
92 His wonders and his praises do contend
Which should be thine or his. Silenced with that,
In viewing o'er the rest o' th' selfsame day,
He finds thee in the stout Norweyan ranks,
Nothing afeard of what thyself didst make,
97 Strange images of death. As thick as tale
98 Came post with post, and every one did bear
Thy praises in his kingdom's great defense
And poured them down before him.

ANGUS   We are sent
To give thee from our royal master thanks;
Only to herald thee into his sight,
Not pay thee.

ROSS
And for an earnest of a greater honor,
He bade me, from him, call thee Thane of Cawdor;
In which addition, hail, most worthy Thane,   106
For it is thine.

BANQUO   What, can the devil speak true?

MACBETH
The Thane of Cawdor lives. Why do you dress me
In borrowed robes?

ANGUS   Who was the Thane lives yet,
But under heavy judgment bears that life
Which he deserves to lose. Whether he was combined   111
With those of Norway, or did line the rebel   112
With hidden help and vantage, or that with both   113
He labored in his country's wrack, I know not;
But treasons capital, confessed and proved,
Have overthrown him.

MACBETH *[aside]*   Glamis, and Thane of Cawdor —
The greatest is behind!   117
    [To Ross and Angus] Thanks for your pains.
    [Aside to Banquo]
Do you not hope your children shall be kings,
When those that gave the Thane of Cawdor to me
Promised no less to them?

BANQUO *[to Macbeth]*   That, trusted home,   120
Might yet enkindle you unto the crown,
Besides the Thane of Cawdor. But 'tis strange:
And oftentimes, to win us to our harm,
The instruments of darkness tell us truths,
Win us with honest trifles, to betray's
In deepest consequence. —   126
Cousins, a word, I pray you.   127

MACBETH *[aside]*   Two truths are told,
As happy prologues to the swelling act   128
Of the imperial theme. — I thank you, gentlemen. —
    [Aside]
This supernatural soliciting   130
Cannot be ill, cannot be good. If ill,
Why hath it given me earnest of success,
Commencing in a truth? I am Thane of Cawdor.
If good, why do I yield to that suggestion
Whose horrid image doth unfix my hair
And make my seated heart knock at my ribs   136
Against the use of nature? Present fears   137
Are less than horrible imaginings.
My thought, whose murder yet is but fantastical,   139
Shakes so my single state of man that function   140
Is smothered in surmise and nothing is

---

53 *fantastical* creatures of fantasy   55 *grace* honor   57 *rapt withal* spellbound at the thought   58 *seeds of time* genesis of events   66 *happy* fortunate   67 *get* beget   70 *imperfect* incomplete   71 *Sinel* i.e. Macbeth's father   81 *corporal* corporeal   84 *insane* madness-inducing   90 *reads* considers   92–93 *His wonders . . . or his* i.e. dumbstruck admiration makes him keep your praises to himself   97 *thick as tale* i.e. as fast as they can be counted   98 *post with post* messenger after messenger   106 *addition* title   111 *combined* leagued   112 *line* support   113 *vantage* assistance   117 *is behind* is to come   120 *home* all the way   126 *deepest consequence* i.e. in the vital sequel   127 *Cousins* i.e. fellow lords   128–29 *swelling act . . . imperial theme* i.e. stately drama of rise to sovereignty   130 *soliciting* inviting, beckoning   136 *seated* fixed   137 *use* way   139 *fantastical* imaginary   140 *single* unaided, weak; *function* normal powers

But what is not.

142 BANQUO   Look how our partner's rapt.

MACBETH [aside]

If chance will have me King, why chance may crown me
Without my stir.

BANQUO   New honors come upon him,

145 Like our strange garments, cleave not to their mould
But with the aid of use.

MACBETH [aside]   Come what come may,
Time and the hour runs through the roughest day.

BANQUO

Worthy Macbeth, we stay upon your leisure.

MACBETH

149 Give me your favor. My dull brain was wrought
With things forgotten. Kind gentlemen, your pains
Are regist'red where every day I turn
The leaf to read them. Let us toward the King.
     [Aside to Banquo]
Think upon what hath chanced, and at more time,
The interim having weighed it, let us speak

155 Our free hearts each to other.

BANQUO   Very gladly.

MACBETH

Till then, enough. – Come, friends.   *Exeunt.*

*

I, iv   *Flourish. Enter King [Duncan], Lennox, Malcolm,*
     Donalbain, and Attendants.

KING

Is execution done on Cawdor? Are not

2 Those in commission yet returned?

MALCOLM   My liege,
They are not yet come back. But I have spoke
With one that saw him die; who did report
That very frankly he confessed his treasons,
Implored your Highness' pardon, and set forth
A deep repentance. Nothing in his life
Became him like the leaving it. He died

9 As one that had been studied in his death

10 To throw away the dearest thing he owed
As 'twere a careless trifle.

KING   There's no art
To find the mind's construction in the face.
He was a gentleman on whom I built
An absolute trust.

     Enter Macbeth, Banquo, Ross, and Angus.
     O worthiest cousin,
The sin of my ingratitude even now

16 Was heavy on me. Thou art so far before
That swiftest wing of recompense is slow
To overtake thee. Would thou hadst less deserved,

19 That the proportion both of thanks and payment
Might have been mine! Only I have left to say,
More is thy due than more than all can pay.

MACBETH

The service and the loyalty I owe,
In doing it pays itself. Your Highness' part
Is to receive our duties, and our duties
Are to your throne and state children and servants,
Which do but what they should by doing everything
Safe toward your love and honor.
     27

KING   Welcome hither.
I have begun to plant thee and will labor   28
To make thee full of growing. Noble Banquo,
That hast no less deserved nor must be known
No less to have done so, let me enfold thee
And hold thee to my heart.

BANQUO   There if I grow,
The harvest is your own.

KING   My plenteous joys,
Wanton in fullness, seek to hide themselves   34
In drops of sorrow. Sons, kinsmen, thanes,
And you whose places are the nearest, know
We will establish our estate upon
Our eldest, Malcolm, whom we name hereafter
The Prince of Cumberland; which honor must
Not unaccompanied invest him only,
But signs of nobleness, like stars, shall shine
On all deservers. From hence to Inverness,
And bind us further to you.

MACBETH

The rest is labor which is not used for you.
I'll be myself the harbinger, and make joyful
The hearing of my wife with your approach;
So, humbly take my leave.

KING   My worthy Cawdor!

MACBETH [aside]

The Prince of Cumberland – that is a step
On which I must fall down or else o'erleap,
For in my way it lies. Stars, hide your fires;
Let not light see my black and deep desires.
The eye wink at the hand; yet let that be   52
Which the eye fears, when it is done, to see.   *Exit.*

KING

True, worthy Banquo: he is full so valiant,
And in his commendations I am fed;
It is a banquet to me. Let's after him,
Whose care is gone before to bid us welcome.
It is a peerless kinsman.   *Flourish. Exeunt.*

*

Enter Macbeth's Wife, alone, with a letter.   I, v

LADY [reads] 'They met me in the day of success; and I
have learned by the perfect'st report they have more in
them than mortal knowledge. When I burned in desire
to question them further, they made themselves air, into
which they vanished. Whiles I stood rapt in the wonder
of it, came missives from the King, who all-hailed me   6
Thane of Cawdor, by which title, before, these weird
sisters saluted me, and referred me to the coming on of
time with "Hail, King that shalt be!" This have I
thought good to deliver thee, my dearest partner of
greatness, that thou mightst not lose the dues of rejoic-
ing by being ignorant of what greatness is promised
thee. Lay it to thy heart, and farewell.'

Glamis thou art, and Cawdor, and shalt be
What thou art promised. Yet do I fear thy nature.

---

142 *rapt* bemused   145 *strange* new   149 *favor* pardon   155 *Our free
hearts* our thoughts freely
I, iv A field near Forres as before, or a place in the palace itself   2 *in
commission* commissioned to carry out the execution   9 *studied* rehearsed
10 *owed* owned   16 *before* ahead in deserving   19 *proportion* preponder-
ance   27 *Safe* fitting   28 *plant* nurture   34 *Wanton* unrestrained   52
wink at the hand blind itself to what the hand does
I, v Within Macbeth's castle at Inverness   6 *missives* messengers

It is too full o' th' milk of human kindness
To catch the nearest way. Thou wouldst be great,
Art not without ambition, but without
18 The illness should attend it. What thou wouldst highly,
That wouldst thou holily; wouldst not play false,
And yet wouldst wrongly win. Thou'ldst have, great Glamis,
That which cries 'Thus thou must do' if thou have it;
And that which rather thou dost fear to do
Than wishest should be undone. Hie thee hither,
That I may pour my spirits in thine ear
And chastise with the valor of my tongue
26 All that impedes thee from the golden round
27 Which fate and metaphysical aid doth seem
28 To have thee crowned withal.
      Enter Messenger.   What is your tidings?
MESSENGER
The King comes here to-night.
LADY   Thou'rt mad to say it!
Is not thy master with him? who, were't so,
Would have informed for preparation.
MESSENGER
So please you, it is true. Our Thane is coming.
One of my fellows had the speed of him,
34 Who, almost dead for breath, had scarcely more
Than would make up his message.
LADY   Give him tending;
He brings great news.   *Exit Messenger.*
           The raven himself is hoarse
That croaks the fatal entrance of Duncan
Under my battlements. Come, you spirits
39 That tend on mortal thoughts, unsex me here,
And fill me from the crown to the toe top-full
Of direst cruelty. Make thick my blood;
42 Stop up th' access and passage to remorse,
43 That no compunctious visitings of nature
44 Shake my fell purpose nor keep peace between
Th' effect and it. Come to my woman's breasts
46 And take my milk for gall, you murd'ring ministers,
47 Wherever in your sightless substances
48 You wait on nature's mischief. Come, thick night,
49 And pall thee in the dunnest smoke of hell,
That my keen knife see not the wound it makes,
Nor heaven peep through the blanket of the dark
To cry 'Hold, hold!'
     Enter Macbeth. Great Glamis! worthy Cawdor!
Greater than both, by the all-hail hereafter!
Thy letters have transported me beyond
55 This ignorant present, and I feel now
The future in the instant.
MACBETH   My dearest love,
Duncan comes here to-night.
LADY   And when goes hence?
MACBETH
To-morrow, as he purposes.
LADY   O, never
Shall sun that morrow see!
Your face, my Thane, is as a book where men
61 May read strange matters. To beguile the time,
62 Look like the time; bear welcome in your eye,
Your hand, your tongue; look like th' innocent flower,
But be the serpent under't. He that's coming
Must be provided for; and you shall put
66 This night's great business into my dispatch,

Which shall to all our nights and days to come
Give solely sovereign sway and masterdom.
MACBETH
We will speak further.
LADY   Only look up clear.   69
To alter favor ever is to fear.   70
Leave all the rest to me.   *Exeunt.*

*

     Hautboys and torches. Enter King [Duncan],   I, vi
     Malcolm, Donalbain, Banquo, Lennox, Macduff,
     Ross, Angus, and Attendants.
KING
This castle hath a pleasant seat. The air   1
Nimbly and sweetly recommends itself
Unto our gentle senses.   3
BANQUO   This guest of summer,
The temple-haunting martlet, does approve   4
By his loved mansionry that the heaven's breath   5
Smells wooingly here. No jutty, frieze,   6
Buttress, nor coign of vantage, but this bird   7
Hath made his pendent bed and procreant cradle.   8
Where they most breed and haunt, I have observed
The air is delicate.
     Enter Lady [Macbeth].
KING   See, see, our honored hostess!
The love that follows us sometime is our trouble,   11
Which still we thank as love. Herein I teach you
How you shall bid God 'ield us for your pains   13
And thank us for your trouble.
LADY   All our service
In every point twice done, and then done double,
Were poor and single business to contend
Against those honors deep and broad wherewith
Your Majesty loads our house. For those of old,
And the late dignities heaped up to them,
We rest your hermits.   20
KING   Where's the Thane of Cawdor?
We coursed him at the heels and had a purpose
To be his purveyor; but he rides well,   22
And his great love, sharp as his spur, hath holp him
To his home before us. Fair and noble hostess,
We are your guest to-night.
LADY   Your servants ever
Have theirs, themselves, and what is theirs, in compt,   26
To make their audit at your Highness' pleasure,
Still to return your own.   28
KING   Give me your hand.

18 *illness* ruthlessness 26 *round* crown 27 *metaphysical* supernatural 28 *withal* with 34 *breath* want of breath 39 *mortal* deadly 42 *remorse* pity 43 *nature* natural feeling 44 *fell* fierce 44–45 *keep peace . . . and it* i.e. lull it from achieving its end 46 *for gall* in exchange for gall; *ministers* agents 47 *sightless* invisible 48 *wait on* aid 49 *pall thee* shroud thyself; *dunnest* darkest 55 *ignorant* i.e. ordinarily unaware 61 *beguile the time* make sly use of the occasion 62 *Look like the time* play up to the occasion 66 *dispatch* swift management 69 *look up clear* appear untroubled 70 *alter favor* change countenance; *fear* incur risk
I, vi At the portal of Inverness s.d. *Hautboys* oboes 1 *seat* site 3 *gentle* soothed 4 *temple-haunting* nesting in church spires; *martlet* martin, swallow; *approve* prove 5 *loved mansionry* beloved nests 6 *jutty* projection 7 *coign of vantage* convenient corner 8 *procreant* breeding 11–12 *The love . . . as love* the love that sometimes inconveniences us we still hold precious 13 *God 'ield us* God reward me 20 *hermits* beadsmen 22 *purveyor* advance agent of supplies 26 *Have theirs* have their servants; *what is theirs* their possessions; *in compt* in trust 28 *Still* always

Conduct me to mine host ; we love him highly.
And shall continue our graces towards him.
By your leave, hostess.　　　　　　　　　*Exeunt.*

*

I, vii　　　　*Hautboys. Torches. Enter a Sewer, and divers*
　　　　　Servants with dishes and service over the stage. Then
　　　　　enter Macbeth.

MACBETH

1　If it were done when 'tis done, then 'twere well
　It were done quickly. If th' assassination
3　Could trammel up the consequence, and catch
4　With his surcease success, that but this blow
　Might be the be-all and the end-all – ; here,
　But here upon this bank and shoal of time,
7　We'ld jump the life to come. But in these cases
　We still have judgment here, that we but teach
9　Bloody instructions, which, being taught, return
　To plague th' inventor. This even-handed justice
　Commends th' ingredience of our poisoned chalice
　To our own lips. He's here in double trust :
　First, as I am his kinsman and his subject,
　Strong both against the deed ; then, as his host,
　Who should against his murderer shut the door,
　Not bear the knife myself. Besides, this Duncan
17　Hath borne his faculties so meek, hath been
18　So clear in his great office, that his virtues
　Will plead like angels, trumpet-tongued against
　The deep damnation of his taking-off ;
　And pity, like a naked new-born babe
　Striding the blast, or heaven's cherubin horsed
23　Upon the sightless couriers of the air,
　Shall blow the horrid deed in every eye
　That tears shall drown the wind. I have no spur
　To prick the sides of my intent, but only
　Vaulting ambition, which o'erleaps itself
　And falls on th' other –
　　　　Enter Lady [Macbeth].
　　　　　　　　　How now ? What news ?

LADY
He has almost supped. Why have you left the chamber ?

MACBETH
Hath he asked for me ?

LADY　　　　　　　Know you not he has ?

MACBETH
We will proceed no further in this business.
32　He hath honored me of late, and I have bought
　Golden opinions from all sorts of people,
　Which would be worn now in their newest gloss,
　Not cast aside so soon.

LADY　　　　　　　　Was the hope drunk
Wherein you dressed yourself ? Hath it slept since ?
And wakes it now to look so green and pale　　　37
At what it did so freely ? From this time
Such I account thy love. Art thou afeard
To be the same in thine own act and valor
As thou art in desire ? Wouldst thou have that
Which thou esteem'st the ornament of life,
And live a coward in thine own esteem,
Letting 'I dare not' wait upon 'I would,'
Like the poor cat i' th' adage ?　　　　　　45

MACBETH　　　　　　　　Prithee peace !
I dare do all that may become a man ;
Who dares do more is none.

LADY　　　　　　　What beast was't then
That made you break this enterprise to me ?　　48
When you durst do it, then you were a man ;
And to be more than what you were, you would
Be so much more the man. Nor time nor place
Did then adhere, and yet you would make both.　52
They have made themselves, and that their fitness now　53
Does unmake you. I have given suck, and know
How tender 'tis to love the babe that milks me :
I would, while it was smiling in my face,
Have plucked my nipple from his boneless gums
And dashed the brains out, had I so sworn as you
Have done to this.

MACBETH　　　　If we should fail ?

LADY　　　　　　　　We fail ?
But screw your courage to the sticking place　　60
And we'll not fail. When Duncan is asleep
(Whereto the rather shall his day's hard journey
Soundly invite him), his two chamberlains
Will I with wine and wassail so convince　　　64
That memory, the warder of the brain,
Shall be a fume, and the receipt of reason　　66
A limbeck only. When in swinish sleep　　　67
Their drenchèd natures lies as in a death,
What cannot you and I perform upon
Th' unguarded Duncan ? what not put upon
His spongy officers, who shall bear the guilt
Of our great quell ?　　　　　　　　72

MACBETH　　　　Bring forth men-children only ;
For thy undaunted mettle should compose　　73
Nothing but males. Will it not be received,
When we have marked with blood those sleepy two
Of his own chamber and used their very daggers,
That they have done't ?

LADY　　　　　　Who dares receive it other,　77
As we shall make our griefs and clamor roar
Upon his death ?

MACBETH　　　　I am settled, and bend up
Each corporal agent to this terrible feat.
Away, and mock the time with fairest show ;　81
False face must hide what the false heart doth know.
　　　　　　　　　　　　Exeunt.

*

Enter Banquo, and Fleance, with a torch before him.　II, i

BANQUO
How goes the night, boy ?

FLEANCE
The moon is down ; I have not heard the clock.

I, vii The courtyard of Inverness from which open the chambers of the
castle　s.d. *Sewer* chief waiter　1 *done* done with　3 *trammel up the consequence* enclose the consequences in a net　4 *his surcease* its (the assassination's) completion ; *success* all that follows　7 *jump* risk　9 *instructions* lessons　17 *faculties* powers　18 *clear* untainted　23 *sightless couriers* invisible coursers (the winds)　32 *bought* acquired　37 *green* bilious　45 *cat i' th' adage* (who wants the fish but doesn't want to get its paws wet)　48 *break* broach　52 *adhere* lend themselves to the occasion　53 *that their fitness* their very fitness　60 *sticking place* notch (holding the string of a crossbow cranked taut for shooting)　64 *convince* overcome　66 *receipt* container　67 *limbeck* cap of a still (to which the fumes rise)　72 *quell* killing　73 *mettle* vital substance　77 *other* otherwise　81 *mock* delude
II, i The same

BANQUO
And she goes down at twelve.

FLEANCE   I take't, 'tis later, sir.

BANQUO

4   Hold, take my sword. There's husbandry in heaven;
    Their candles are all out. Take thee that too.
6   A heavy summons lies like lead upon me,
    And yet I would not sleep. Merciful powers,
    Restrain in me the cursèd thoughts that nature
    Gives way to in repose.

Enter Macbeth, and a Servant with a torch.
             Give me my sword!
    Who's there?

MACBETH
    A friend.

BANQUO
    What, sir, not yet at rest? The King's abed.
    He hath been in unusual pleasure and
14   Sent forth great largess to your offices.
    This diamond he greets your wife withal
16   By the name of most kind hostess, and shut up
    In measureless content.

MACBETH   Being unprepared,
18   Our will became the servant to defect,
    Which else should free have wrought.

BANQUO   All's well.
    I dreamt last night of the three weird sisters.
    To you they have showed some truth.

MACBETH   I think not of them.
    Yet when we can entreat an hour to serve,
    We would spend it in some words upon that business,
    If you would grant the time.

BANQUO   At your kind'st leisure.

MACBETH
25   If you shall cleave to my consent, when 'tis,
    It shall make honor for you.

BANQUO   So I lose none
    In seeking to augment it, but still keep
28   My bosom franchised and allegiance clear,
29   I shall be counselled.

MACBETH   Good repose the while.

BANQUO
    Thanks, sir. The like to you.

Exeunt Banquo [and Fleance].

MACBETH
    Go bid thy mistress, when my drink is ready,
    She strike upon the bell. Get thee to bed. *Exit [Servant].*
    Is this a dagger which I see before me,
    The handle toward my hand? Come, let me clutch thee!
    I have thee not, and yet I see thee still.
    Art thou not, fatal vision, sensible
    To feeling as to sight? or art thou but
    A dagger of the mind, a false creation
    Proceeding from the heat-oppressèd brain?
    I see thee yet, in form as palpable
    As this which now I draw.
    Thou marshall'st me the way that I was going,
    And such an instrument I was to use.
    Mine eyes are made the fools o' th' other senses,
    Or else worth all the rest. I see thee still,
46   And on thy blade and dudgeon gouts of blood,
    Which was not so before. There's no such thing.
48   It is the bloody business which informs
    Thus to mine eyes. Now o'er the one half-world

Nature seems dead, and wicked dreams abuse   50
The curtained sleep. Witchcraft celebrates
Pale Hecate's offerings; and withered murder,   52
Alarumed by his sentinel, the wolf,   53
Whose howl's his watch, thus with his stealthy pace,
With Tarquin's ravishing strides, towards his design   55
Moves like a ghost. Thou sure and firm-set earth,
Hear not my steps which way they walk, for fear
Thy very stones prate of my whereabout
And take the present horror from the time,   59
Which now suits with it. Whiles I threat, he lives;
Words to the heat of deeds too cold breath gives.
      A bell rings.
I go, and it is done. The bell invites me.
Hear it not, Duncan, for it is a knell
That summons thee to heaven, or to hell.   *Exit.*

Enter Lady [Macbeth].   II, ii

LADY
That which hath made them drunk hath made me bold;
What hath quenched them hath given me fire. Hark!
    Peace!
It was the owl that shrieked, the fatal bellman   3
Which gives the stern'st good-night. He is about it.
The doors are open, and the surfeited grooms
Do mock their charge with snores. I have drugged their   6
    possets,
That death and nature do contend about them
Whether they live or die.

MACBETH *[within]*   Who's there? What, ho?

LADY
Alack, I am afraid they have awaked,
And 'tis not done! Th' attempt, and not the deed,
Confounds us. Hark! I laid their daggers ready –   11
He could not miss 'em. Had he not resembled
My father as he slept, I had done't.

Enter Macbeth.   My husband!

MACBETH
I have done the deed. Didst thou not hear a noise?

LADY
I heard the owl scream and the crickets cry.
Did not you speak?

MACBETH   When?

LADY   Now.

MACBETH   As I descended?

LADY Ay.

MACBETH Hark!
Who lies i' th' second chamber?

LADY   Donalbain.

MACBETH This is a sorry sight.

LADY
A foolish thought, to say a sorry sight.

MACBETH
There's one did laugh in's sleep, and one cried 'Murder!'

---

4 *husbandry* economy   6 *summons* signal to sleep   14 *largess to your offices* gratuities to your household departments   16 *shut up* concluded   18 *will* good will; *defect* deficient means   25 *cleave . . . when 'tis* favor my cause at the proper time   28 *franchised* free from guilt   29 *counselled* open to persuasion   46 *dudgeon* wooden hilt; *gouts* blobs   48 *informs* creates impressions   50 *abuse* deceive   52 *Hecate's offerings* worship of Hecate (Goddess of sorcery)   53 *Alarumed* given the signal   55 *Tarquin* Roman tyrant, ravisher of Lucrece   59–60 *take . . . suits with it* delay, by prating, the commission of the deed at this suitably horrible moment (?), reduce, by breaking the silence, the suitable horror of this moment (?)
II, ii   3–4 *fatal bellman . . . good-night* i.e. like the night-watch cry to felons scheduled for execution in the morning   6 *possets* bedtime drinks   11 *Confounds* ruins

23   That they did wake each other. I stood and heard them.
But they did say their prayers and addressed them
Again to sleep.

LADY   There are two lodged together.

MACBETH
One cried 'God bless us !' and 'Amen !' the other,

27   As they had seen me with these hangman's hands,
List'ning their fear. I could not say 'Amen !'
When they did say 'God bless us !'

LADY   Consider it not so deeply.

MACBETH
But wherefore could not I pronounce 'Amen' ?
I had most need of blessing, and 'Amen'
Stuck in my throat.

LADY   These deeds must not be thought
After these ways ; so, it will make us mad.

MACBETH
Methought I heard a voice cry 'Sleep no more !
Macbeth does murder sleep' – the innocent sleep,

36   Sleep that knits up the ravelled sleave of care,
The death of each day's life, sore labor's bath,

38   Balm of hurt minds, great nature's second course,
Chief nourisher in life's feast.

LADY   What do you mean ?

MACBETH
Still it cried 'Sleep no more !' to all the house ;
'Glamis hath murdered sleep, and therefore Cawdor
Shall sleep no more, Macbeth shall sleep no more.'

LADY
Who was it that thus cried ? Why, worthy Thane,

44   You do unbend your noble strength to think
So brainsickly of things. Go get some water

46   And wash this filthy witness from your hand.
Why did you bring these daggers from the place ?
They must lie there : go carry them and smear
The sleepy grooms with blood.

MACBETH   I'll go no more.
I am afraid to think what I have done ;
Look on 't again I dare not.

LADY   Infirm of purpose !
Give me the daggers. The sleeping and the dead

53   Are but as pictures. 'Tis the eye of childhood
That fears a painted devil. If he do bleed,

55   I'll gild the faces of the grooms withal,
For it must seem their guilt.   *Exit.*
Knock within.

MACBETH
Whence is that knocking ?
How is 't with me when every noise appals me ?
What hands are here ? Ha ! they pluck out mine eyes.
Will all great Neptune's ocean wash this blood
Clean from my hand ? No, this my hand will rather

The multitudinous seas incarnadine,   61
Making the green one red.   62
Enter Lady [Macbeth].

LADY
My hands are of your color, but I shame
To wear a heart so white. *(Knock.)* I hear a knocking
At the south entry. Retire we to our chamber.
A little water clears us of this deed.
How easy is it then ! Your constancy
Hath left you unattended.   68
Knock.   Hark ! more knocking.
Get on your nightgown, lest occasion call us   69
And show us to be watchers. Be not lost   70
So poorly in your thoughts.   71

MACBETH
To know my deed, 'twere best not know myself.
Knock.
Wake Duncan with thy knocking ! I would thou couldst.
         Exeunt.

Enter a Porter. Knocking within.   II, iii

PORTER Here's a knocking indeed ! If a man were porter of
hell gate, he should have old turning the key. *(Knock.)*   2
Knock, knock, knock. Who's there, i' th' name of Belze-
bub ? Here's a farmer that hanged himself on th' expecta-   4
tion of plenty. Come in time ! Have napkins enow about   5
you ; here you'll sweat for 't. *(Knock.)* Knock, knock.
Who's there, in th' other devil's name ? Faith, here's an
equivocator, that could swear in both the scales against   8
either scale ; who committed treason enough for God's
sake, yet could not equivocate to heaven. O come in,
equivocator. *(Knock.)* Knock, knock, knock. Who's
there ? Faith, here's an English tailor come hither for
stealing out of a French hose. Come in, tailor. Here you   13
may roast your goose. *(Knock.)* Knock, knock. Never at   14
quiet ! What are you ? – But this place is too cold for hell.
I'll devil-porter it no further. I had thought to have let
in some of all professions that go the primrose way to th'
everlasting bonfire. *(Knock.)* Anon, anon ! *[Opens the
way.]* I pray you remember the porter.
Enter Macduff and Lennox.

MACDUFF
Was it so late, friend, ere you went to bed,
That you do lie so late ?

PORTER Faith, sir, we were carousing till the second cock ;   22
and drink, sir, is a great provoker of three things.

MACDUFF What three things does drink especially provoke ?

PORTER Marry, sir, nose-painting, sleep, and urine.
Lechery, sir, it provokes, and unprovokes : it provokes
the desire, but it takes away the performance. Therefore
much drink may be said to be an equivocator with lechery : it makes him, and it mars him ; it sets him on, and it
takes him off ; it persuades him, and disheartens him ;
makes him stand to, and not stand to ; in conclusion,   31
equivocates him in a sleep, and, giving him the lie,
leaves him.

MACDUFF I believe drink gave thee the lie last night.   33

PORTER That it did, sir, i' the very throat on me ; but I
requited him for his lie ; and, I think, being too strong
for him, though he took up my legs sometime, yet I
made a shift to cast him.   37

MACDUFF Is thy master stirring ?
Enter Macbeth.
Our knocking has awaked him : here he comes.

---

23 *That* so that   27 *hangman's hands* i.e. bloody, like an executioner's   36
knits up . . . sleave smooths out the tangled skein   38 *second course* i.e. sleep,
after food   44 *unbend* relax   46 *witness* evidence   53 *as pictures* like
pictures (since without motion)   55 *gild* paint   61 *incarnadine* redden
62 *one* uniformly   68 *unattended* deserted   69 *nightgown* dressing gown
70 *watchers* i.e. awake   71 *poorly* weakly
II, iii   2 *old* much   4 *farmer* i.e. one who has hoarded crops   4-5 *expectation of plenty* prospect of a crop surplus (which will lower prices)   5 *enow*
enough   8 *equivocator* (usually considered an allusion to the Jesuits tried
for political conspiracy)   13 *French hose* close-fitting breeches   14 *roast
your goose* heat your pressing-iron   22 *second cock* second cockcrow (3 a.m.)
31 *stand to* stand his guard   33 *gave thee the lie* called you a liar (i.e. unable
to stand)   37 *cast* throw

LENNOX
Good morrow, noble sir.
MACBETH   Good morrow, both.
MACDUFF
Is the King stirring, worthy Thane?
MACBETH   Not yet.
MACDUFF
42   He did command me to call timely on him;
43   I have almost slipped the hour.
MACBETH   I'll bring you to him.
MACDUFF
I know this is a joyful trouble to you;
But yet 'tis one.
MACBETH
46   The labor we delight in physics pain.
This is the door.
MACDUFF   I'll make so bold to call,
48   For 'tis my limited service.   *Exit Macduff.*
LENNOX
Goes the King hence to-day?
MACBETH   He does; he did appoint so.
LENNOX
The night has been unruly. Where we lay,
Our chimneys were blown down; and, as they say,
Lamentings heard i' th' air, strange screams of death,
And prophesying, with accents terrible,
54   Of dire combustion and confused events
55   New hatched to th' woeful time. The obscure bird
Clamored the livelong night. Some say the earth
Was feverous and did shake.
MACBETH   'Twas a rough night.
LENNOX
My young remembrance cannot parallel
A fellow to it.
       Enter Macduff.
MACDUFF
O horror, horror, horror! Tongue nor heart
Cannot conceive nor name thee!
MACBETH AND LENNOX   What's the matter?
MACDUFF
62   Confusion now hath made his masterpiece:
Most sacrilegious murder hath broke ope
The Lord's anointed temple and stole thence
The life o' th' building!
MACBETH   What is't you say? the life?
LENNOX
Mean you his Majesty?
MACDUFF
Approach the chamber and destroy your sight
68   With a new Gorgon. Do not bid me speak.
See, and then speak yourselves.
       Exeunt Macbeth and Lennox.
          Awake, awake!
Ring the alarum bell! Murder and treason!
Banquo and Donalbain! Malcolm, awake!
Shake off this downy sleep, death's counterfeit,
And look on death itself. Up, up, and see
74   The great doom's image. Malcolm! Banquo!
As from your graves rise up and walk like sprites
76   To countenance this horror. Ring the bell!
      Bell rings. Enter Lady [Macbeth].
LADY
What's the business,
That such a hideous trumpet calls to parley

The sleepers of the house? Speak, speak!
MACDUFF   O gentle lady,
'Tis not for you to hear what I can speak:
The repetition in a woman's ear   81
Would murder as it fell.
     Enter Banquo.   O Banquo, Banquo,
Our royal master's murdered!
LADY   Woe, alas!
What, in our house?
BANQUO   Too cruel anywhere.
Dear Duff, I prithee contradict thyself
And say it is not so.
     Enter Macbeth, Lennox, and Ross.
MACBETH
Had I but died an hour before this chance,
I had lived a blessèd time; for from this instant
There's nothing serious in mortality: 89
All is but toys. Renown and grace is dead,   90
The wine of life is drawn, and the mere lees   91
Is left this vault to brag of.   92
     Enter Malcolm and Donalbain.
DONALBAIN
What is amiss?
MACBETH   You are, and do not know't.
The spring, the head, the fountain of your blood
Is stopped, the very source of it is stopped.
MACDUFF
Your royal father's murdered.
MALCOLM   O, by whom?
LENNOX
Those of his chamber, as it seemed, had done't.
Their hands and faces were all badged with blood;   98
So were their daggers, which unwiped we found
Upon their pillows. They stared and were distracted.
No man's life was to be trusted with them.
MACBETH
O, yet I do repent me of my fury
That I did kill them.
MACDUFF   Wherefore did you so?
MACBETH
Who can be wise, amazed, temp'rate and furious,   104
Loyal and neutral, in a moment? No man.
The expedition of my violent love   106
Outrun the pauser, reason. Here lay Duncan,
His silver skin laced with his golden blood;
And his gashed stabs looked like a breach in nature
For ruin's wasteful entrance: there, the murderers,
Steeped in the colors of their trade, their daggers
Unmannerly breeched with gore. Who could refrain   112
That had a heart to love, and in that heart
Courage to make's love known?
LADY   Help me hence, ho!
MACDUFF
Look to the lady.   115
MALCOLM *[aside to Donalbain]*
        Why do we hold our tongues,

42 *timely* early   43 *slipped* let slip   46 *physics pain* cures trouble   48 *limited* appointed   54 *combustion* tumult   55 *obscure bird* i.e. the owl   62 *Confusion* destruction   68 *a new Gorgon* a new Medusa (capable of turning the beholder's eyes to stone)   74 *great doom's image* resemblance of the day of judgment   76 *countenance* appear in keeping with   81 *repetition* recital   89 *serious in mortality* worthwhile in human life   90 *toys* trifles   91 *lees* dregs   92 *vault* wine-vault   98 *badged* marked   104 *amazed* confused   106 *expedition* haste   112 *Unmannerly . . . gore* crudely wearing breeches of blood; *refrain* restrain oneself   115 *Look to* look after

116 That most may claim this argument for ours?
DONALBAIN *[to Malcolm]*
What should be spoken here,
118 Where our fate, hid in an auger hole,
May rush and seize us? Let's away:
Our tears are not yet brewed.
MALCOLM *[to Donalbain]*   Nor our strong sorrow
121 Upon the foot of motion.
BANQUO   Look to the lady.
                [Lady Macbeth is carried out.]
122 And when we have our naked frailties hid,
That suffer in exposure, let us meet
124 And question this most bloody piece of work,
125 To know it further. Fears and scruples shake us.
In the great hand of God I stand, and thence
127 Against the undivulged pretense I fight
Of treasonous malice.
MACDUFF   And so do I.
ALL   So all.
MACBETH
Let's briefly put on manly readiness
And meet i' th' hall together.
ALL   Well contented.
                Exeunt [all but Malcolm and Donalbain].
MALCOLM
What will you do? Let's not consort with them.
To show an unfelt sorrow is an office
Which the false man does easy. I'll to England.
DONALBAIN
To Ireland I. Our separated fortune
Shall keep us both the safer. Where we are
136 There's daggers in men's smiles; the near in blood,
The nearer bloody.
MALCOLM   This murderous shaft that's shot
Hath not yet lighted, and our safest way
Is to avoid the aim. Therefore to horse,
And let us not be dainty of leave-taking
141 But shift away. There's warrant in that theft
Which steals itself when there's no mercy left. *Exeunt.*

*

II, iv   *Enter Ross with an Old Man.*
OLD MAN
Threescore and ten I can remember well;
Within the volume of which time I have seen
Hours dreadful and things strange, but this sore night
4 Hath trifled former knowings.
ROSS   Ha, good father,
5 Thou seest the heavens, as troubled with man's act,
Threatens his bloody stage. By th' clock 'tis day,

And yet dark night strangles the travelling lamp. 7
Is't night's predominance, or the day's shame, 8
That darkness does the face of earth entomb
When living light should kiss it?
OLD MAN   'Tis unnatural,
Even like the deed that's done. On Tuesday last
A falcon, tow'ring in her pride of place, 12
Was by a mousing owl hawked at and killed. 13
ROSS
And Duncan's horses (a thing most strange and certain), 14
Beauteous and swift, the minions of their race, 15
Turned wild in nature, broke their stalls, flung out, 16
Contending 'gainst obedience, as they would make
War with mankind.
OLD MAN   'Tis said they eat each other. 18
ROSS
They did so, to th' amazement of mine eyes
That looked upon't.
                Enter Macduff. Here comes the good Macduff.
How goes the world, sir, now?
MACDUFF   Why, see you not?
ROSS
Is't known who did this more than bloody deed?
MACDUFF
Those that Macbeth hath slain.
ROSS   Alas the day,
What good could they pretend? 24
MACDUFF   They were suborned.
Malcolm and Donalbain, the King's two sons,
Are stol'n away and fled, which puts upon them
Suspicion of the deed.
ROSS   'Gainst nature still.
Thriftless ambition, that will ravin up 28
Thine own live's means! Then 'tis most like
The sovereignty will fall upon Macbeth.
MACDUFF
He is already named, and gone to Scone
To be invested. 32
ROSS   Where is Duncan's body?
MACDUFF
Carried to Colmekill,
The sacred storehouse of his predecessors
And guardian of their bones.
ROSS   Will you to Scone?
MACDUFF
No, cousin, I'll to Fife.
ROSS   Well, I will thither.
MACDUFF
Well, may you see things well done there. Adieu,
Lest our old robes sit easier than our new!
ROSS
Farewell, father.
OLD MAN
God's benison go with you, and with those 40
That would make good of bad, and friends of foes.
                Exeunt omnes.

*

        Enter Banquo.   III, i
BANQUO
Thou hast it now – King, Cawdor, Glamis, all,
As the weird women promised; and I fear
Thou play'dst most foully for't. Yet it was said 3

116 *argument for ours* topic as chiefly our concern 118 *auger hole* i.e. any
tiny cranny 121 *Upon the foot of motion* yet in motion 122 *frailties hid*
bodies clothed 124 *question* discuss 125 *scruples* doubts 127 *undivulged pretense* secret stratagems 136 *near* nearer 141 *warrant* justification
II, iv Outside Inverness castle 4 *trifled former knowings* made former
experiences seem trifling 5 *man's act* the human drama 7 *travelling
lamp* i.e. of Phoebus, the sun 8 *predominance* supernatural ascendancy
12 *tow'ring* soaring 13 *mousing* i.e. ordinarily preying on mice; *hawked
at* swooped upon 14 *certain* significant 15 *minions* darlings 16 *flung
out* lunged about 18 *eat* ate 24 *pretend* expect; *suborned* bribed 28
Thriftless wasteful; *ravin up* bolt, swallow 32 *invested* crowned 40
benison blessing
III, i Within the royal palace (at Forres) 3 *foully* cheatingly

4   It should not stand in thy posterity,
    But that myself should be the root and father
    Of many kings. If there come truth from them
7   (As upon thee, Macbeth, their speeches shine),
    Why, by the verities on thee made good,
    May they not be my oracles as well
10 And set me up in hope ? But hush, no more !
        Sennet sounded. Enter Macbeth as King, Lady
        [Macbeth], Lennox, Ross, Lords, and Attendants.
MACBETH
    Here's our chief guest.
LADY   If he had been forgotten,
    It had been as a gap in our great feast,
13 And all-thing unbecoming.
MACBETH
14 To-night we hold a solemn supper, sir,
    And I'll request your presence.
BANQUO   Let your Highness
    Command upon me, to the which my duties
    Are with a most indissoluble tie
    For ever knit.
MACBETH   Ride you this afternoon ?
BANQUO
    Ay, my good lord.
MACBETH
    We should have else desired your good advice
21 (Which still hath been both grave and prosperous)
    In this day's council ; but we'll take to-morrow.
    Is't far you ride ?
BANQUO
    As far, my lord, as will fill up the time
25 'Twixt this and supper. Go not my horse the better,
26 I must become a borrower of the night
    For a dark hour or twain.
MACBETH   Fail not our feast.
BANQUO
    My lord, I will not.
MACBETH
    We hear our bloody cousins are bestowed
    In England and in Ireland, not confessing
    Their cruel parricide, filling their hearers
32 With strange invention. But of that to-morrow,
33 When therewithal we shall have cause of state
    Craving us jointly. Hie you to horse. Adieu,
    Till you return at night. Goes Fleance with you ?
BANQUO
    Ay, my good lord. Our time does call upon's.
MACBETH
    I wish your horses swift and sure of foot,
    And so I do commend you to their backs.
    Farewell.   *Exit Banquo.*
    Let every man be master of his time
    Till seven at night. To make society
    The sweeter welcome, we will keep ourself
43 Till supper time alone. While then, God be with you !
                            Exeunt Lords [and others].
44 Sirrah, a word with you. Attend those men
    Our pleasure ?
SERVANT
    They are, my lord, without the palace gate.
MACBETH
    Bring them before us.   *Exit Servant.*
48 To be thus is nothing, but to be safely thus –
49 Our fears in Banquo stick deep,

    And in his royalty of nature reigns that
    Which would be feared. 'Tis much he dares ;   51
    And to that dauntless temper of his mind
    He hath a wisdom that doth guide his valor
    To act in safety. There is none but he
    Whose being I do fear ; and under him
    My genius is rebuked, as it is said   56
    Mark Antony's was by Caesar. He chid the sisters
    When first they put the name of King upon me,
    And bade them speak to him. Then, prophet-like,
    They hailed him father to a line of kings.
    Upon my head they placed a fruitless crown
    And put a barren sceptre in my gripe,   62
    Thence to be wrenched with an unlineal hand,
    No son of mine succeeding. If't be so,
    For Banquo's issue have I filed my mind ;   65
    For them the gracious Duncan have I murdered ;
    Put rancors in the vessel of my peace   67
    Only for them, and mine eternal jewel   68
    Given to the common enemy of man   69
    To make them kings – the seeds of Banquo kings.
    Rather than so, come, Fate, into the list,   71
    And champion me to th' utterance ! Who's there ?   72
        Enter Servant and two Murderers.
    Now go to the door and stay there till we call.
                                        Exit Servant.
    Was it not yesterday we spoke together ?
MURDERERS
    It was, so please your Highness.
MACBETH   Well then, now
    Have you considered of my speeches ? Know
    That it was he, in the times past, which held you
    So under fortune, which you thought had been   78
    Our innocent self. This I made good to you
    In our last conference, passed in probation with you 80
    How you were borne in hand, how crossed ; the   81
        instruments ;
    Who wrought with them ; and all things else that might
    To half a soul and to a notion crazed   83
    Say 'Thus did Banquo.'
1. MURDERER   You made it known to us.
MACBETH
    I did so ; and went further, which is now
    Our point of second meeting. Do you find   86
    Your patience so predominant in your nature
    That you can let this go ? Are you so gospelled   88
    To pray for this good man and for his issue,
    Whose heavy hand hath bowed you to the grave
    And beggared yours for ever ?
1. MURDERER   We are men, my liege.

---

4 *stand* continue as a legacy 7 *shine* are brilliantly substantiated 10 s.d.
Sennet trumpet salute 13 *all-thing* altogether 14 *solemn* state 21 *still*
always ; *prosperous* profitable 25 *Go not my horse the better* i.e. unless my
horse goes faster than anticipated 26 *borrower of* i.e. borrower of time from
32 *invention* falsehoods 33–34 *cause . . . jointly* state business requiring
our joint attention 43 *While* until 44 *Sirrah* form used in addressing
inferiors ; *Attend* await 48 *but* unless 49 *in Banquo* about Banquo ; *stick
deep* are deeply imbedded in me 51 *would be* deserves to be 56 *genius is
rebuked* controlling spirit is daunted 62 *gripe* grasp 65 *filed* defiled
67 *rancors* bitter enmities 68 *jewel* soul 69 *common enemy of man* i.e.
Satan 71 *list* lists, field of combat 72 *champion . . . utterance* engage with
me to the death 78 *under fortune* out of favor with fortune 80 *passed in
probation* reviewed the evidence 81 *borne in hand* manipulated ; *crossed*
thwarted ; *instruments* agents 83 *half a soul* a halfwit ; *notion* mind 86
Our point of the point of our 88 *gospelled* tamed by gospel precepts

MACBETH

92 Ay, in the catalogue ye go for men,
As hounds and greyhounds, mongrels, spaniels, curs,
94 Shoughs, water-rugs, and demi-wolves are clept
95 All by the name of dogs. The valued file
Distinguishes the swift, the slow, the subtle,
97 The housekeeper, the hunter, every one
According to the gift which bounteous nature
99 Hath in him closed, whereby he does receive
100 Particular addition, from the bill
That writes them all alike ; and so of men.
Now, if you have a station in the file,
Not i' th' worst rank of manhood, say't ;
104 And I will put that business in your bosoms
Whose execution takes your enemy off,
Grapples you to the heart and love of us,
Who wear our health but sickly in his life,
Which in his death were perfect.

2. MURDERER   I am one, my liege,
Whom the vile blows and buffets of the world
Have so incensed that I am reckless what
I do to spite the world.

1. MURDERER   And I another,
So weary with disasters, tugged with fortune,
113 That I would set my life on any chance
To mend it or be rid on't.

MACBETH   Both of you
Know Banquo was your enemy.

MURDERERS   True, my lord.

MACBETH
116 So is he mine, and in such bloody distance
That every minute of his being thrusts
118 Against my near'st of life ; and though I could
With barefaced power sweep him from my sight
120 And bid my will avouch it, yet I must not,
121 For certain friends that are both his and mine,
122 Whose loves I may not drop, but wail his fall
Who I myself struck down. And thence it is
That I to your assistance do make love,
Masking the business from the common eye
For sundry weighty reasons.

2. MURDERER   We shall, my lord,
Perform what you command us.

1. MURDERER   Though our lives –

MACBETH
Your spirits shine through you. Within this hour at most
I will advise you where to plant yourselves,
130 Acquaint you with the perfect spy o' th' time
The moment on't, for't must be done to-night
132 And something from the palace (always thought
133 That I require a clearness) ; and with him,

To leave no rubs nor botches in the work, 134
Fleance his son, that keeps him company,
Whose absence is no less material to me
Than is his father's, must embrace the fate
Of that dark hour. Resolve yourselves apart ;
I'll come to you anon.

MURDERERS   We are resolved, my lord.

MACBETH
I'll call upon you straight. Abide within.
It is concluded. Banquo, thy soul's flight,
If it find heaven, must find it out to-night.   Exeunt.

*

Enter Macbeth's Lady and a Servant.   III, ii

LADY
Is Banquo gone from court ?

SERVANT
Ay, madam, but returns again to-night.

LADY
Say to the King I would attend his leisure
For a few words.

SERVANT   Madam, I will.   Exit.

LADY   Naught's had, all's spent,
Where our desire is got without content.
'Tis safer to be that which we destroy
Than by destruction dwell in doubtful joy.
Enter Macbeth.
How now, my lord ? Why do you keep alone,
Of sorriest fancies your companions making, 9
Using those thoughts which should indeed have died
With them they think on ? Things without all remedy 11
Should be without regard. What's done is done.

MACBETH
We have scorched the snake, not killed it. 13
She'll close and be herself, whilst our poor malice 14
Remains in danger of her former tooth.
But let the frame of things disjoint, both the worlds 16
suffer,
Ere we will eat our meal in fear, and sleep
In the affliction of these terrible dreams
That shake us nightly. Better be with the dead,
Whom we, to gain our peace, have sent to peace,
Than on the torture of the mind to lie 21
In restless ecstasy. Duncan is in his grave ; 22
After life's fitful fever he sleeps well.
Treason has done his worst : nor steel nor poison,
Malice domestic, foreign levy, nothing, 25
Can touch him further.

LADY   Come on.
Gentle my lord, sleek o'er your rugged looks ;
Be bright and jovial among your guests to-night.

MACBETH
So shall I, love ; and so, I pray, be you.
Let your remembrance apply to Banquo ; 30
Present him eminence both with eye and tongue : 31
Unsafe the while, that we must lave 32
Our honors in these flattering streams
And make our faces vizards to our hearts, 34
Disguising what they are.

LADY   You must leave this.

MACBETH
O, full of scorpions is my mind, dear wife !
Thou know'st that Banquo, and his Fleance, lives.

---

92 *catalogue* inventory, classification   94 *Shoughs* shaggy pet dogs ; *water-rugs* long-haired water-dogs ; *clept* named   95 *valued file* classification according to valuable traits   97 *housekeeper* watchdog   99 *closed* invested   100 *addition, from the bill* distinction, contrary to the listing   104 *in your bosoms* in your trust   113 *set* risk   116 *distance* enmity   118 *near'st of life* vital parts   120 *avouch* justify   121 *For* because of   122 *wail* I must wail   130 *with the perfect spy o' th' time* by means of a perfect look-out (?), with precise timing (?)   132 *thought* borne in mind   133 *clearness* alibi   134 *rubs* defects

III, ii The same   9 *sorriest* most contemptible   11 *all remedy* any form of remedy   13 *scorched* slashed   14 *close* heal ; *poor malice* feeble opposition   16 *frame of things disjoint* structure of the universe collapse ; *both the worlds* i.e. heaven and earth   21 *torture* rack   22 *ecstasy* frenzy   25 *Malice domestic* civil war   30 *remembrance* i.e. awareness of the necessity   31 *Present him eminence* exalt him   32 *lave* dip   34 *vizards* masks

LADY

38 But in them Nature's copy 's not eterne.

MACBETH

There's comfort yet ; they are assailable.
Then be thou jocund. Ere the bat hath flown
His cloistered flight, ere to black Hecate's summons

42 The shard-borne beetle with his drowsy hums
Hath rung night's yawning peal, there shall be done
A deed of dreadful note.

LADY   What's to be done ?

MACBETH

Be innocent of the knowledge, dearest chuck,

46 Till thou applaud the deed. Come, seeling night,

47 Scarf up the tender eye of pitiful day,
And with thy bloody and invisible hand

49 Cancel and tear to pieces that great bond
Which keeps me pale. Light thickens, and the crow

51 Makes wing to th' rooky wood.
Good things of day begin to droop and drowse,
Whiles night's black agents to their preys do rouse.
Thou marvell'st at my words, but hold thee still ;
Things bad begun make strong themselves by ill.
So prithee go with me.   *Exeunt.*

*

III, iii   *Enter three Murderers.*

1 . MURDERER
But who did bid thee join with us ?

3 . MURDERER   Macbeth.

2 . MURDERER

2 He needs not our mistrust, since he delivers

3 Our offices and what we have to do
To the direction just.

1 . MURDERER   Then stand with us.
The west yet glimmers with some streaks of day.

6 Now spurs the lated traveller apace
To gain the timely inn, and near approaches
The subject of our watch.

3 . MURDERER   Hark, I hear horses.

BANQUO *(within)*
Give us a light there, ho !

2 . MURDERER   Then 'tis he : the rest

10 That are within the note of expectation
Already are i' th' court.

1 . MURDERER   His horses go about.

3 . MURDERER
Almost a mile ; but he does usually,
So all men do, from hence to th' palace gate
Make it their walk.
     Enter Banquo and Fleance, with a torch.

2 . MURDERER
A light, a light !

3 . MURDERER   'Tis he.

1 . MURDERER   Stand to't.

BANQUO
It will be rain to-night.

1 . MURDERER   Let it come down !

BANQUO
O, treachery ! Fly, good Fleance, fly, fly, fly !
                              [Exit Fleance.]

Thou mayst revenge – O slave !
     [Banquo slain.]

3 . MURDERER
Who did strike out the light ?

1 . MURDERER   Was't not the way ?   19

3 . MURDERER
There's but one down : the son is fled.

2 . MURDERER
We have lost best half of our affair.

1 . MURDERER
Well, let's away, and say how much is done.   *Exeunt.*

*

Banquet prepared. Enter Macbeth, Lady [Macbeth], **III, iv**
Ross, Lennox, Lords, and Attendants.

MACBETH

You know your own degrees – sit down :   1
At first and last the hearty welcome.

LORDS

Thanks to your Majesty.

MACBETH

Ourself will mingle with society   4
And play the humble host.
Our hostess keeps her state, but in best time   6
We will require her welcome.

LADY

Pronounce it for me, sir, to all our friends,
For my heart speaks they are welcome.
     Enter First Murderer.

MACBETH

See, they encounter thee with their hearts' thanks.   10
Both sides are even. Here I'll sit i' th' midst.
Be large in mirth ; anon we'll drink a measure
The table round.
     [Goes to Murderer.]
There's blood upon thy face.

MURDERER   'Tis Banquo's then.

MACBETH

'Tis better thee without than he within.
Is he dispatched ?

MURDERER   My lord, his throat is cut :
That I did for him.

MACBETH   Thou are the best o' th' cut-throats.
Yet he's good that did the like for Fleance :
If thou didst it, thou art the nonpareil.

MURDERER

Most royal sir, Fleance is 'scaped.

MACBETH *[aside]*

Then comes my fit again. I had else been perfect ;   21
Whole as the marble, founded as the rock,   22
As broad and general as the casing air.   23
But now I am cabined, cribbed, confined, bound in   24
To saucy doubts and fears. – But Banquo 's safe ?   25

38 *Nature's copy* Nature's copyhold, lease on life   **42** *shard-borne* borne on scaly wings   **46** *seeling* sewing together the eyelids (from falconry)   **47** *Scarf up* blindfold   **49** *great bond* i.e. Banquo's lease on life (with suggestion also of the bond of human feeling)   **51** *rooky* harboring rooks
III, iii An approach to the palace   **2** *He needs not our mistrust* i.e. we need not mistrust this man   **3** *offices* duties   **6** *lated* belated   **10** *within the note of expectation* on the list of those expected (invited)   **19** *Was't not the way* i.e. was it not the right thing to do
III, iv The hall of the palace   **1** *degrees* relative rank, order of precedence   **4** *society* the company   **6** *keeps her state* remains seated in her chair of state   **10** *encounter* greet   **21** *perfect* sound of health   **22** *founded* solidly based   **23** *broad and general* unconfined ; *casing* enveloping   **24** *cribbed* boxed in   **25** *saucy* insolent

106 The baby of a girl. Hence, horrible shadow !
Unreal mock'ry, hence !   *[Exit Ghost.]*
      Why, so ; being gone,
I am a man again. Pray you sit still.
   LADY
You have displaced the mirth, broke the good meeting
110 With most admired disorder.
   MACBETH   Can such things be,
111 And overcome us like a summer's cloud
112 Without our special wonder ? You make me strange
Even to the disposition that I owe,
When now I think you can behold such sights
And keep the natural ruby of your cheeks
116 When mine is blanched with fear.
   ROSS   What sights, my lord ?
   LADY
I pray you speak not : he grows worse and worse ;
Question enrages him. At once, good night.
Stand not upon the order of your going,
But go at once.
   LENNOX   Good night and better health
Attend his Majesty.
   LADY   A kind good night to all. *Exeunt Lords.*
   MACBETH
It will have blood, they say : blood will have blood.
Stones have been known to move and trees to speak ;
124 Augures and understood relations have
125 By maggot-pies and choughs and rooks brought forth
The secret'st man of blood. What is the night ?
   LADY
Almost at odds with morning, which is which.
   MACBETH
How say'st thou, that Macduff denies his person
At our great bidding ?
   LADY   Did you send to him, sir ?
   MACBETH
130 I hear it by the way ; but I will send.
There's not a one of them but in his house
132 I keep a servant fee'd. I will to-morrow
133 (And betimes I will) to the weird sisters.
134 More shall they speak, for now I am bent to know
By the worst means the worst. For mine own good
All causes shall give way. I am in blood
Stepped in so far that, should I wade no more,
Returning were as tedious as go o'er.
Strange things I have in head, that will to hand,
140 Which must be acted ere they may be scanned.
   LADY
141 You lack the season of all natures, sleep.
   MACBETH
142 Come, we'll to sleep. My strange and self-abuse
143 Is the initiate fear that wants hard use.
We are yet but young in deed.   *Exeunt.*

*

III, v   *[Thunder. Enter the three Witches, meeting Hecate.*
   I . WITCH
Why, how now, Hecate ? You look angerly.
   HECATE
2 Have I not reason, beldams as you are,
Saucy and overbold ? How did you dare
To trade and traffic with Macbeth
In riddles and affairs of death ;

And I, the mistress of your charms,
The close contriver of all harms,   7
Was never called to bear my part
Or show the glory of our art ?
And, which is worse, all you have done
Hath been but for a wayward son,
Spiteful and wrathful, who, as others do,
Loves for his own ends, not for you.
But make amends now : get you gone
And at the pit of Acheron   15
Meet me i' th' morning. Thither he
Will come to know his destiny.
Your vessels and your spells provide,
Your charms and everything beside.
I am for th' air. This night I'll spend
Unto a dismal and a fatal end.
Great business must be wrought ere noon.
Upon the corner of the moon
There hangs a vap'rous drop profound ;   24
I'll catch it ere it come to ground :
And that, distilled by magic sleights,   26
Shall raise such artificial sprites   27
As by the strength of their illusion
Shall draw him on to his confusion.
He shall spurn fate, scorn death, and bear
His hopes 'bove wisdom, grace, and fear :
And you all know security   32
Is mortals' chiefest enemy.
      Music, and a song.
Hark ! I am called. My little spirit, see,
Sits in a foggy cloud and stays for me.   *[Exit.]*
      Sing within, 'Come away, come away,' &c.
   I . WITCH
Come, let's make haste : she'll soon be back again.
      Exeunt.]

*

Enter Lennox and another Lord.   III, vi
   LENNOX
My former speeches have but hit your thoughts,   1
Which can interpret farther. Only I say   2
Things have been strangely borne. The gracious Duncan
Was pitied of Macbeth. Marry, he was dead.
And the right valiant Banquo walked too late ;
Whom, you may say (if't please you) Fleance killed,
For Fleance fled. Men must not walk too late.
Who cannot want the thought how monstrous   8
It was for Malcolm and for Donalbain
To kill their gracious father ? Damnèd fact,   10
How it did grieve Macbeth ! Did he not straight,

---

106 *The baby of a girl* a baby girl   110 *admired* wondered at   111 *overcome us* come over us   112–13 *You make . . . I owe* you oust me from my proper role (as a brave man)   116 *blanched* made pale   124 *Augures* auguries ; *relations* utterances   125 *maggot-pies* magpies ; *choughs* jackdaws (capable of 'utterances,' as are magpies and rooks)   130 *by the way* casually   132 *fee'd* paid to spy   133 *betimes* speedily   134 *bent* inclined, determined   140 *ere they may be scanned* i.e. without being closely studied   141 *season* seasoning, preservative   142 *self-abuse* delusion   143 *initiate fear* beginner's fear ; *wants hard use* lacks toughening practice
III, v An open place (an interpolated scene, by a different author)   2 *beldams* old crones   7 *close* secret   15 *Acheron* a river of Hades   24 *profound* weighty   26 *sleights* devices   27 *artificial sprites* spirits created by magic arts   32 *security* over-confidence
III, vi Any meeting place in Scotland   1 *My former speeches* what I have just said ; *hit* matched   2 *interpret farther* draw further conclusions   8 *cannot want the thought* can avoid thinking   10 *fact* deed

In pious rage, the two delinquents tear
13 That were the slaves of drink and thralls of sleep?
Was not that nobly done? Ay, and wisely too,
For 'twould have angered any heart alive
To hear the men deny't. So that I say
17 He has borne all things well; and I do think
That, had he Duncan's sons under his key
19 (As, an't please heaven, he shall not), they should find
What 'twere to kill a father. So should Fleance.
21 But peace! for from broad words, and 'cause he failed
His presence at the tyrant's feast, I hear
Macduff lives in disgrace. Sir, can you tell
Where he bestows himself?

LORD   The son of Duncan,
25 From whom this tyrant holds the due of birth,
Lives in the English court, and is received
Of the most pious Edward with such grace
That the malevolence of fortune nothing
29 Takes from his high respect. Thither Macduff
30 Is gone to pray the holy King upon his aid
31 To wake Northumberland and warlike Siward;
That by the help of these (with Him above
To ratify the work) we may again
Give to our tables meat, sleep to our nights,
Free from our feasts and banquets bloody knives,
36 Do faithful homage and receive free honors –
All which we pine for now. And this report
Hath so exasperate the King that he
Prepares for some attempt of war.

LENNOX   Sent he to Macduff?

LORD
He did; and with an absolute 'Sir, not I,'
41 The cloudy messenger turns me his back
And hums, as who should say, 'You'll rue the time
43 That clogs me with this answer.'

LENNOX   And that well might
44 Advise him to a caution t' hold what distance
His wisdom can provide. Some holy angel
Fly to the court of England and unfold
His message ere he come, that a swift blessing
May soon return to this our suffering country
Under a hand accursed!

LORD   I'll send my prayers with him.
           Exeunt.

*

IV, i   *Thunder. Enter the three Witches.*
1 1. WITCH   Thrice the brinded cat hath mewed.
2. WITCH   Thrice, and once the hedge-pig whined.
3 3. WITCH   Harpier cries. – 'Tis time, 'tis time!
1. WITCH   Round about the cauldron go;

13 *thralls* slaves   17 *borne* carried off   19 *an't* if it   21 *from broad words*
through plain speaking   25 *due of birth* birthright   29 *his high respect* high
respect for him   30 *upon his aid* upon Malcolm's behalf   31 *wake* arouse;
Northumberland (English county bordering Scotland)   36 *free* untainted
41 *cloudy* angry   43 *clogs* encumbers   44–45 *Advise him . . . can provide*
warn him to keep at as safe a distance as he can devise
IV, i A *cave* (cf. III, v, 15)   1 *brinded* brindled, striped   3 *Harpier* (name
of familiar spirit, suggestive of harpy)   8 *Swelt'red venom, sleeping got*,
exuded venom formed while sleeping   12 *fenny* swamp   16 *blindworm* a
lizard, popularly supposed poisonous   23 *mummy* mummified flesh; *maw
and gulf* stomach and gullet   24 *ravined* insatiable   31 *drab* harlot   32
slab sticky   33 *chaudron* guts   38 s.d.–43 s.d. (an interpolation)   44 *By*
i.e. I know by   53 *yesty* yeasty, foamy   54 *Confound* destroy   55 *bladed
corn be lodged* ripe grain be beaten to earth   57 *slope* incline   59 *Nature's
germains* seeds of creation   60 *sicken* shall surfeit

In the poisoned entrails throw.
Toad, that under cold stone
Days and nights has thirty-one
Swelt'red venom, sleeping got,   8
Boil thou first i' th' charmèd pot.
ALL   Double, double, toil and trouble,
Fire burn and cauldron bubble.
2. WITCH   Fillet of a fenny snake,   12
In the cauldron boil and bake;
Eye of newt, and toe of frog,
Wool of bat, and tongue of dog,
Adder's fork, and blindworm's sting,   16
Lizard's leg, and howlet's wing –
For a charm of pow'rful trouble
Like a hell-broth boil and bubble.
ALL   Double, double, toil and trouble,
Fire burn and cauldron bubble.
3. WITCH   Scale of dragon, tooth of wolf,
Witch's mummy, maw and gulf   23
Of the ravined salt-sea shark,   24
Root of hemlock digged i' th' dark,
Liver of blaspheming Jew,
Gall of goat, and slips of yew
Slivered in the moon's eclipse,
Nose of Turk, and Tartar's lips,
Finger of birth-strangled babe
Ditch-delivered by a drab   31
Make the gruel thick and slab.   32
Add thereto a tiger's chaudron   33
For th' ingredience of our cauldron.
ALL   Double, double, toil and trouble,
Fire burn and cauldron bubble.
2. WITCH   Cool it with a baboon's blood,
Then the charm is firm and good.   38
    [*Enter Hecate and the other three Witches.*
HECATE   O, well done! I commend your pains,
And every one shall share i' th' gains.
And now about the cauldron sing
Like elves and fairies in a ring,
Enchanting all that you put in.
Music and a song, 'Black spirits,' &c.]
         [*Exeunt Hecate and singers.*]
2. WITCH   By the pricking of my thumbs,   44
Something wicked this way comes.
Open locks,
Whoever knocks!
Enter Macbeth.
MACBETH
How now, you secret, black, and midnight hags,
What is't you do?
ALL   A deed without a name.
MACBETH
I conjure you by that which you profess,
Howe'er you come to know it, answer me.
Though you untie the winds and let them fight
Against the churches, though the yesty waves   53
Confound and swallow navigation up,   54
Though bladed corn be lodged and trees blown down,   55
Though castles topple on their warders' heads,
Though palaces and pyramids do slope   57
Their heads to their foundations, though the treasure
Of Nature's germains tumble all together   59
Even till destruction sicken, answer me   60
To what I ask you.

1 . WITCH   Speak.

2 . WITCH   Demand.

3 . WITCH   We'll answer.

1 . WITCH
Say if th' hadst rather hear it from our mouths
Or from our masters.

MACBETH   Call 'em. Let me see 'em.

1 . WITCH Pour in sow's blood, that hath eaten
65   Her nine farrow ; grease that's sweaten
From the murderer's gibbet throw
Into the flame.

ALL   Come, high or low,
68   Thyself and office deftly show !
Thunder. First Apparition, an Armed Head.

MACBETH
Tell me, thou unknown power –

1 . WITCH   He knows thy thought :
Hear his speech, but say thou naught.

1 . APPARITION
Macbeth, Macbeth, Macbeth, beware Macduff !
Beware the Thane of Fife ! Dismiss me. – Enough.
                 He descends.

MACBETH
Whate'er thou art, for thy good caution thanks :
74   Thou hast harped my fear aright. But one word more –

1 . WITCH
He will not be commanded. Here's another,
More potent than the first.
     Thunder. Second Apparition, a Bloody Child.

2 . APPARITION
Macbeth, Macbeth, Macbeth –

MACBETH
Had I three ears, I'ld hear thee.

2 . APPARITION
Be bloody, bold, and resolute ! Laugh to scorn
The pow'r of man, for none of woman born
Shall harm Macbeth.   *Descends.*

MACBETH
Then live, Macduff, – what need I fear of thee ?
But yet I'll make assurance double sure
84   And take a bond of fate. Thou shalt not live ;
That I may tell pale-hearted fear it lies
And sleep in spite of thunder.
     *Thunder. Third Apparition, a Child Crowned, with
a tree in his hand.*
              What is this
That rises like the issue of a king
88   And wears upon his baby-brow the round
And top of sovereignty ?

ALL   Listen, but speak not to't.

3 . APPARITION
Be lion-mettled, proud, and take no care
Who chafes, who frets, or where conspirers are !
Macbeth shall never vanquished be until
Great Birnam Wood to high Dunsinane Hill
Shall come against him.   *Descends.*

MACBETH   That will never be.
95   Who can impress the forest, bid the tree
96   Unfix his earth-bound root ? Sweet bodements, good !
Rebellious dead rise never till the Wood
Of Birnam rise, and our high-placed Macbeth
99   Shall live the lease of nature, pay his breath
100   To time and mortal custom. Yet my heart
Throbs to know one thing. Tell me, if your art

Can tell so much : Shall Banquo's issue ever   102
Reign in this kingdom ?

ALL   Seek to know no more.

MACBETH
I will be satisfied. Deny me this,
And an eternal curse fall on you ! Let me know.
Why sinks that cauldron ? and what noise is this ?   106
       Hautboys.

1 . WITCH Show !

2 . WITCH Show !

3 . WITCH Show !

ALL   Show his eyes, and grieve his heart !
Come like shadows, so depart !
*A show of eight Kings and Banquo, last [King] with a
glass in his hand.*

MACBETH
Thou art too like the spirit of Banquo. Down !
Thy crown does sear mine eyeballs. And thy hair,
Thou other gold-bound brow, is like the first.
A third is like the former. Filthy hags,
Why do you show me this ? A fourth ? Start, eyes !   116
What, will the line stretch out to th' crack of doom ?
Another yet ? A seventh ? I'll see no more.
And yet the eighth appears, who bears a glass
Which shows me many more ; and some I see
That twofold balls and treble sceptres carry.   121
Horrible sight ! Now I see 'tis true ;
For the blood-boltered Banquo smiles upon me   123
And points at them for his. What ? Is this so ?

[1 . WITCH Ay, sir, all this is so. But why   125
         Stands Macbeth thus amazedly ?
         Come, sisters, cheer we up his sprites   127
         And show the best of our delights.
         I'll charm the air to give a sound
         While you perform your antic round,   130
         That this great king may kindly say
         Our duties did his welcome pay.
     Music. The Witches dance, and vanish.]

MACBETH
Where are they ? Gone ? Let this pernicious hour
Stand aye accursèd in the calendar !
Come in, without there !
     Enter Lennox.

LENNOX   What's your Grace's will ?

MACBETH
Saw you the weird sisters ?

LENNOX   No, my lord.

MACBETH
Came they not by you ?

LENNOX   No indeed, my lord.

MACBETH
Infected be the air whereon they ride,
And damned all those that trust them ! I did hear
The galloping of horse. Who was't came by ?

LENNOX
'Tis two or three, my lord, that bring you word

---

65 *nine farrow* litter of nine   68 *office* function   74 *harped* hit the tune of
84 *take a bond of* secure a guarantee from   88 *round* crown   95 *impress*
conscript   96 *bodements* prophecies   99 *lease of nature* i.e. the full life-
span   100 *mortal custom* normal death   102 *issue* offspring   106 *noise*
music   116 *Start* bulge   121 *twofold balls and treble sceptres* (English
coronation insignia)   123 *blood-boltered* matted with blood   125–32 (an
interpolation)   127 *sprites* spirits   130 *antic round* grotesque circular
dance

Macduff is fled to England.

MACBETH   Fled to England?

LENNOX

Ay, my good lord.

MACBETH [aside]

144   Time, thou anticipat'st my dread exploits.
145   The flighty purpose never is o'ertook
Unless the deed go with it. From this moment
147   The very firstlings of my heart shall be
The firstlings of my hand. And even now,
To crown my thoughts with acts, be it thought and done:
The castle of Macduff I will surprise,
Seize upon Fife, give to th' edge o' th' sword
His wife, his babes, and all unfortunate souls
153   That trace him in his line. No boasting like a fool;
This deed I'll do before this purpose cool.
But no more sights! – Where are these gentlemen?
Come, bring me where they are.   Exeunt.

*

IV, ii   *Enter Macduff's Wife, her Son, and Ross.*

WIFE

What had he done to make him fly the land?

ROSS

2   You must have patience, madam.

WIFE   He had none.

His flight was madness. When our actions do not,
4   Our fears do make us traitors.

ROSS   You know not

Whether it was his wisdom or his fear.

WIFE

Wisdom? To leave his wife, to leave his babes,
His mansion and his titles in a place
From whence himself does fly? He loves us not,
9   He wants the natural touch. For the poor wren
(The most diminutive of birds) will fight,
Her young ones in her nest, against the owl.
All is the fear and nothing is the love,
As little is the wisdom, where the flight
So runs against all reason.

14 ROSS   My dearest coz,

I pray you school yourself. But for your husband,
He is noble, wise, judicious, and best knows
17   The fits o' th' season. I dare not speak much further,
But cruel are the times when we are traitors
19   And do not know ourselves; when we hold rumor
From what we fear, yet know not what we fear
But float upon a wild and violent sea
Each way and none. I take my leave of you.
Shall not be long but I'll be here again.

Things at the worst will cease, or else climb upward   24
To what they were before. – My pretty cousin,
Blessing upon you!

WIFE

Fathered he is, and yet he's fatherless.

ROSS

I am so much a fool, should I stay longer
It would be my disgrace and your discomfort.   29
I take my leave at once.   *Exit.*

WIFE   Sirrah, your father's dead;

And what will you do now? How will you live?

SON

As birds do, mother.

WIFE   What, with worms and flies?

SON

With what I get, I mean; and so do they.

WIFE

Poor bird! thou'dst never fear the net nor lime,   34
The pitfall nor the gin.   35

SON

Why should I, mother? Poor birds they are not set for.
My father is not dead for all your saying.

WIFE

Yes, he is dead. How wilt thou do for a father?

SON Nay, how will you do for a husband?

WIFE Why, I can buy me twenty at any market.

SON Then you'll buy 'em to sell again.   41

WIFE

Thou speak'st with all thy wit; and yet, i' faith,   42
With wit enough for thee.

SON

Was my father a traitor, mother?

WIFE Ay, that he was!

SON What is a traitor?

WIFE Why, one that swears and lies.

SON And be all traitors that do so?

WIFE Every one that does so is a traitor and must be hanged.

SON And must they all be hanged that swear and lie?

WIFE Every one.

SON Who must hang them?

WIFE Why, the honest men.

SON Then the liars and swearers are fools, for there are liars and swearers enow to beat the honest men and   56 hang up them.

WIFE Now God help thee, poor monkey! But how wilt thou do for a father?

SON If he were dead, you'ld weep for him. If you would not, it were a good sign that I should quickly have a new father.

WIFE Poor prattler, how thou talk'st!
        Enter a Messenger.

MESSENGER

Bless you, fair dame! I am not to you known,
Though in your state of honor I am perfect.   65
I doubt some danger does approach you nearly.   66
If you will take a homely man's advice,   67
Be not found here. Hence with your little ones!
To fright you thus methinks I am too savage;
To do worse to you were fell cruelty,   70
Which is too nigh your person. Heaven preserve you!
I dare abide no longer.   *Exit.*

WIFE   Whither should I fly?

I have done no harm. But I remember now

---

144 *anticipat'st* forestall   145 *flighty* fleeting   147-48 *firstlings . . . my hand* i.e. I shall act at the moment I feel the first impulse   153 *trace* follow; *line* family line

IV, ii Within the castle at Fife   2 *patience* self-control   4 *traitors* i.e. traitors to ourselves   9 *wants* lacks   14 *coz* cousin, kinswoman   17 *fits o' th' season* present disorders   19 *know ourselves* know ourselves to be so   19-20 *hold rumor . . . we fear* are credulous in accordance with our fears   24 *will cease* i.e. must cease descending   29 *would be my* would be to my (i.e. his weeping)   34 *lime* birdlime   35 *gin* trap   41 *sell* betray   42-43 *Thou speak'st . . . for thee* i.e. you use all the intelligence you have, and it is quite enough   56 *enow* enough   65 *in your state . . . perfect* I am informed of your noble identity   66 *doubt* fear   67 *homely* plain   70-71 *To do worse . . . your person* i.e. not to frighten you were to do worse, expose you to that fierce cruelty which is impending

I am in this earthly world, where to do harm
Is often laudable, to do good sometime
Accounted dangerous folly. Why then, alas,
Do I put up that womanly defense
To say I have done no harm?
    Enter Murderers.   What are these faces?

MURDERER
Where is your husband?

WIFE
I hope in no place so unsanctified
Where such as thou mayst find him.

MURDERER   He's a traitor.

SON
82   Thou liest, thou shag-eared villain!

MURDERER   What, you egg!
    [Stabs him.]
83   Young fry of treachery!

SON   He has killed me, mother.
Run away, I pray you!
    [Dies.]

        Exit [Wife], crying 'Murder!'
        [pursued by Murderers].

       *

IV, iii   *Enter Malcolm and Macduff.*

MALCOLM
Let us seek out some desolate shade, and there
Weep our sad bosoms empty.

MACDUFF   Let us rather
3   Hold fast the mortal sword and, like good men,
4   Bestride our downfall'n birthdom. Each new morn
New widows howl, new orphans cry, new sorrows
Strike heaven on the face, that it resounds
As if it felt with Scotland and yelled out
8   Like syllable of dolor.

MALCOLM   What I believe, I'll wail;
What know, believe; and what I can redress,
10   As I shall find the time to friend, I will.
What you have spoke, it may be so perchance.
12   This tyrant, whose sole name blisters our tongues,
Was once thought honest; you have loved him well;
14   He hath not touched you yet. I am young; but something
15   You may deserve of him through me, and wisdom
To offer up a weak, poor, innocent lamb
T' appease an angry god.

MACDUFF
I am not treacherous.

MALCOLM   But Macbeth is.
19   A good and virtuous nature may recoil
In an imperial charge. But I shall crave your pardon.
21   That which you are, my thoughts cannot transpose:
22   Angels are bright still though the brightest fell;
Though all things foul would wear the brows of grace,
Yet grace must still look so.

MACDUFF   I have lost my hopes.

MALCOLM
Perchance even there where I did find my doubts.
26   Why in that rawness left you wife and child,
Those precious motives, those strong knots of love,
Without leave-taking? I pray you,
29   Let not my jealousies be your dishonors,
But mine own safeties. You may be rightly just
Whatever I shall think.

MACDUFF   Bleed, bleed, poor country!
Great tyranny, lay thou thy basis sure,   32
For goodness dare not check thee; wear thou thy wrongs,
The title is affeered! Fare thee well, lord.   34
I would not be the villain that thou think'st
For the whole space that's in the tyrant's grasp
And the rich East to boot.

MALCOLM   Be not offended.
I speak not as in absolute fear of you.   38
I think our country sinks beneath the yoke,
It weeps, it bleeds, and each new day a gash
Is added to her wounds. I think withal   41
There would be hands uplifted in my right;
And here from gracious England have I offer
Of goodly thousands. But, for all this,
When I shall tread upon the tyrant's head
Or wear it on my sword, yet my poor country
Shall have more vices than it had before,
More suffer, and more sundry ways than ever,
By him that shall succeed.

MACDUFF   What should he be?

MALCOLM
It is myself I mean, in whom I know
All the particulars of vice so grafted   51
That, when they shall be opened, black Macbeth   52
Will seem as pure as snow, and the poor state
Esteem him as a lamb, being compared
With my confineless harms.   55

MACDUFF   Not in the legions
Of horrid hell can come a devil more damned
In evils to top Macbeth.

MALCOLM   I grant him bloody,
Luxurious, avaricious, false, deceitful,   58
Sudden, malicious, smacking of every sin   59
That has a name. But there's no bottom, none,
In my voluptuousness. Your wives, your daughters,
Your matrons, and your maids could not fill up
The cistern of my lust; and my desire
All continent impediments would o'erbear   64
That did oppose my will. Better Macbeth
Than such an one to reign.

MACDUFF   Boundless intemperance
In nature is a tyranny. It hath been   67
Th' untimely emptying of the happy throne
And fall of many kings. But fear not yet
To take upon you what is yours. You may
Convey your pleasures in a spacious plenty   71
And yet seem cold – the time you may so hoodwink.
We have willing dames enough. There cannot be
That vulture in you to devour so many
As will to greatness dedicate themselves,
Finding it so inclined.

82 *shag-eared* i.e. with shaggy hair falling about the ears 83 *fry* spawn
IV, iii The grounds of the King's palace in England 3 *mortal* deadly
4 *Bestride* i.e. stand over protectively; *birthdom* place of birth 8 *Like
syllable of dolor* a similar cry of pain 10 *time to friend* time propitious
12 *sole name* very name 14 *young* i.e. young and inexperienced 15 *wisdom*
i.e. it may be wise 19–20 *recoil . . . imperial charge* reverse itself under
royal pressure 21 *transpose* alter 22 *the brightest* i.e. Lucifer 26 *rawness* unprotected state 29 *jealousies* suspicions 32 *basis* foundation 34
affeered confirmed by law 38 *absolute* complete 41 *withal* furthermore
51 *particulars* varieties; *grafted* implanted 52 *opened* revealed 55 *confineless harms* unlimited vices 58 *Luxurious* lecherous 59 *Sudden* violent
64 *continent* containing, restraining 67 *In nature* in one's nature 71
Convey obtain by stealth

MURDERER
Ay, my good lord. Safe in a ditch he bides,
27   With twenty trenchèd gashes on his head,
The least a death to nature.

MACBETH   Thanks for that. –
      [Aside]
29   There the grown serpent lies ; the worm that's fled
Hath nature that in time will venom breed,
No teeth for th' present. – Get thee gone. To-morrow
32   We'll hear ourselves again.   Exit Murderer.

LADY   My royal lord,
33   You do not give the cheer. The feast is sold
34   That is not often vouched, while 'tis a-making,
35   'Tis given with welcome. To feed were best at home ;
36   From thence, the sauce to meat is ceremony :
37   Meeting were bare without it.
      Enter the Ghost of Banquo, and sits in Macbeth's
      place.

MACBETH   Sweet remembrancer !
Now good digestion wait on appetite,
And health on both !

LENNOX   May't please your Highness sit.
MACBETH
Here had we now our country's honor roofed
Were the graced person of our Banquo present –
42   Who may I rather challenge for unkindness
Than pity for mischance !

ROSS   His absence, sir,
Lays blame upon his promise. Please't your Highness
To grace us with your royal company ?

MACBETH
The table 's full.
LENNOX   Here is a place reserved, sir.
MACBETH
Where ?
LENNOX
Here, my good lord. What is't that moves your
  Highness ?
MACBETH
Which of you have done this ?
LORDS   What, my good lord ?
MACBETH
Thou canst not say I did it. Never shake
Thy gory locks at me.
ROSS
Gentlemen, rise. His Highness is not well.
LADY
Sit, worthy friends. My lord is often thus,
And hath been from his youth. Pray you keep seat.
The fit is momentary ; upon a thought

He will again be well. If much you note him,
You shall offend him and extend his passion.   57
Feed, and regard him not. – Are you a man ?
MACBETH
Ay, and a bold one, that dare look on that
Which might appal the devil.
LADY   O proper stuff !
This is the very painting of your fear.
This is the air-drawn dagger which you said   62
Led you to Duncan. O, these flaws and starts   63
(Impostors to true fear) would well become   64
A woman's story at a winter's fire,
Authorized by her grandam. Shame itself !   66
Why do you make such faces ? When all's done,
You look but on a stool.
MACBETH   Prithee see there !
Behold ! Look ! Lo ! – How say you ?
Why, what care I ? If thou canst nod, speak too.
If charnel houses and our graves must send
Those that we bury back, our monuments   72
Shall be the maws of kites.   [Exit Ghost.] 73
LADY   What, quite unmanned in folly ?
MACBETH
If I stand here, I saw him.
LADY   Fie, for shame !
MACBETH
Blood hath been shed ere now, i' th' olden time,
Ere humane statute purged the gentle weal ;   76
Ay, and since too, murders have been performed
Too terrible for the ear. The time has been
That, when the brains were out, the man would die,
And there an end. But now they rise again,
With twenty mortal murders on their crowns,   81
And push us from our stools. This is more strange
Than such a murder is.
LADY   My worthy lord,
Your noble friends do lack you.
MACBETH   I do forget.
Do not muse at me, my most worthy friends :
I have a strange infirmity, which is nothing
To those that know me. Come, love and health to all !
Then I'll sit down. Give me some wine, fill full.
      Enter Ghost.
I drink to th' general joy o' th' whole table,
And to our dear friend Banquo, whom we miss.
Would he were here ! To all, and him, we thirst,   91
And all to all.   92
LORDS   Our duties, and the pledge.
MACBETH
Avaunt, and quit my sight ! Let the earth hide thee !
Thy bones are marrowless, thy blood is cold ;
Thou hast no speculation in those eyes   95
Which thou dost glare with !
LADY   Think of this, good peers,
But as a thing of custom. 'Tis no other.
Only it spoils the pleasure of the time.
MACBETH
What man dare, I dare.
Approach thou like the rugged Russian bear,
The armed rhinoceros, or th' Hyrcan tiger ;   101
Take any shape but that, and my firm nerves
Shall never tremble. Or be alive again
And dare me to the desert with thy sword.   104
If trembling I inhabit then, protest me   105

---

27 *trenchèd* deep, trench-like 29 *worm* serpent 32 *hear ourselves* confer 33 *cheer* tokens of convivial hospitality ; *sold* i.e. not freely given 34 *vouched* sworn 35 *To feed . . . home* i.e. mere eating is best done at home 36 *meat* food 37 *bare* barren, pointless ; *remembrancer* prompter 42 *Who may . . . challenge* whom I hope I may reprove 57 *extend his passion* prolong his seizure 62 *air-drawn* fashioned of air 63 *flaws* outbursts 64 *Impostors to true fear* (i.e. because they are authentic signs of false or unjustified fear) 66 *Authorized* sanctioned 72 *monuments* i.e. our only tombs 73 *maws of kites* bellies of ravens 76 *purged the gentle weal* i.e. purged the state of savagery 81 *murders on their crowns* murderous gashes on their heads 91 *thirst* are eager to drink 92 *all to all* let everyone drink to everyone 95 *speculation* intelligence, power of rational observation 101 *Hyrcan* from Hyrcania, anciently a region near the Caspian Sea 104 *the desert* a solitary place 105 *If trembling I inhabit* if I tremble

MALCOLM   With this there grows
77   In my most ill-composed affection such
78   A stanchless avarice that, were I King,
    I should cut off the nobles for their lands,
    Desire his jewels, and this other's house,
    And my more-having would be as a sauce
82   To make me hunger more, that I should forge
    Quarrels unjust against the good and loyal,
    Destroying them for wealth.
MACDUFF   This avarice
    Sticks deeper, grows with more pernicious root
86   Than summer-seeming lust, and it hath been
87   The sword of our slain kings. Yet do not fear.
88   Scotland hath foisons to fill up your will
89   Of your mere own. All these are portable,
    With other graces weighed.
MALCOLM
    But I have none. The king-becoming graces,
    As justice, verity, temp'rance, stableness,
93   Bounty, perseverance, mercy, lowliness,
    Devotion, patience, courage, fortitude,
95   I have no relish of them, but abound
96   In the division of each several crime,
    Acting in many ways. Nay, had I pow'r, I should
    Pour the sweet milk of concord into hell,
99   Uproar the universal peace, confound
    All unity on earth.
MACDUFF   O Scotland, Scotland!
MALCOLM
    If such a one be fit to govern, speak.
    I am as I have spoken.
MACDUFF   Fit to govern?
    No, not to live! O nation miserable,
    With an untitled tyrant bloody-sceptred,
    When shalt thou see thy wholesome days again,
    Since that the truest issue of thy throne
107   By his own interdiction stands accursed
    And does blaspheme his breed? Thy royal father
    Was a most sainted king; the queen that bore thee,
    Oft'ner upon her knees than on her feet,
111   Died every day she lived. Fare thee well.
    These evils thou repeat'st upon thyself
    Hath banished me from Scotland. O my breast,
    Thy hope ends here!
MALCOLM   Macduff, this noble passion,
    Child of integrity, hath from my soul
116   Wiped the black scruples, reconciled my thoughts
    To thy good truth and honor. Devilish Macbeth
118   By many of these trains hath sought to win me
119   Into his power; and modest wisdom plucks me
    From over-credulous haste; but God above

    Deal between thee and me, for even now
    I put myself to thy direction and
    Unspeak mine own detraction, here abjure
    The taints and blames I laid upon myself
    For strangers to my nature. I am yet   125
    Unknown to woman, never was forsworn,
    Scarcely have coveted what was mine own,
    At no time broke my faith, would not betray
    The devil to his fellow, and delight
    No less in truth than life. My first false speaking
    Was this upon myself. What I am truly,   131
    Is thine and my poor country's to command;
    Whither indeed, before thy here-approach,
    Old Siward with ten thousand warlike men
    Already at a point was setting forth.   135
    Now we'll together; and the chance of goodness   136
    Be like our warranted quarrel! Why are you silent?
MACDUFF
    Such welcome and unwelcome things at once
    'Tis hard to reconcile.
      Enter a Doctor.
MALCOLM
    Well, more anon. Comes the King forth, I pray you?   140
DOCTOR
    Ay, sir. There are a crew of wretched souls
    That stay his cure. Their malady convinces   142
    The great assay of art; but at his touch,   143
    Such sanctity hath heaven given his hand,
    They presently amend.
MALCOLM   I thank you, doctor. *Exit [Doctor].*
MACDUFF
    What's the disease he means?
MALCOLM   'Tis called the evil.   146
    A most miraculous work in this good King,
    Which often since my here-remain in England
    I have seen him do: how he solicits heaven
    Himself best knows, but strangely-visited people,   150
    All swol'n and ulcerous, pitiful to the eye,
    The mere despair of surgery, he cures,   152
    Hanging a golden stamp about their necks,   153
    Put on with holy prayers; and 'tis spoken,
    To the succeeding royalty he leaves
    The healing benediction. With this strange virtue,
    He hath a heavenly gift of prophecy,
    And sundry blessings hang about his throne
    That speak him full of grace.
      Enter Ross.
MACDUFF   See who comes here.
MALCOLM
    My countryman; but yet I know him not.
MACDUFF
    My ever gentle cousin, welcome hither.
MALCOLM
    I know him now. Good God betimes remove   162
    The means that makes us strangers!
ROSS   Sir, amen.
MACDUFF
    Stands Scotland where it did?
ROSS   Alas, poor country,
    Almost afraid to know itself. It cannot
    Be called our mother but our grave, where nothing   166
    But who knows nothing is once seen to smile;
    Where sighs and groans, and shrieks that rent the air,
    Are made, not marked; where violent sorrow seems   169

---

77 *ill-composed affection* disordered disposition   78 *stanchless* insatiable
82 *forge* fabricate   86 *summer-seeming* i.e. seasonal, transitory   87 *sword
of our slain* cause of death of our   88–89 *foisons . . . mere own* riches of your
own enough to satisfy you   89 *portable* bearable   93 *lowliness* humility
95 *relish* trace   96 *division* subdivisions   99 *Uproar* blast   107 *interdiction* curse   111 *Died* i.e. turned away from this life   116 *scruples* doubts
118 *trains* plots   119 *modest* cautious; *plucks* holds   125 *For* as   131
upon against   135 *at a point* armed   136–37 *the chance . . . warranted
quarrel* i.e. let the chance of success equal the justice of our cause   140
anon soon   142 *stay* await; *convinces* baffles   143 *assay of art* resources of
medical science   146 *evil* scrofula (king's evil)   150 *strangely-visited*
unusually afflicted   152 *mere* utter   153 *stamp* coin   162 *betimes* quickly
166 *nothing* no one   169 *marked* noticed

170   A modern ecstasy. The dead man's knell
171   Is there scarce asked for who, and good men's lives
      Expire before the flowers in their caps,
      Dying or ere they sicken.
173 MACDUFF   O, relation
174   Too nice, and yet too true!
      MALCOLM   What's the newest grief?
      ROSS
175   That of an hour's age doth hiss the speaker;
176   Each minute teems a new one.
      MACDUFF   How does my wife?
      ROSS
      Why, well.
      MACDUFF   And all my children?
      ROSS   Well too.
      MACDUFF
      The tyrant has not battered at their peace?
      ROSS
      No, they were well at peace when I did leave 'em.
      MACDUFF
      Be not a niggard of your speech. How goes't?
      ROSS
      When I came hither to transport the tidings
182   Which I have heavily borne, there ran a rumor
183   Of many worthy fellows that were out,
184   Which was to my belief witnessed the rather
      For that I saw the tyrant's power afoot.
      Now is the time of help. Your eye in Scotland
      Would create soldiers, make our women fight
      To doff their dire distresses.
      MALCOLM   Be't their comfort
      We are coming thither. Gracious England hath
      Lent us good Siward and ten thousand men,
      An older and a better soldier none
192   That Christendom gives out.
      ROSS   Would I could answer
      This comfort with the like. But I have words
      That would be howled out in the desert air,
195   Where hearing should not latch them.
      MACDUFF   What concern they,
196   The general cause or is it a fee-grief
197   Due to some single breast?
      ROSS   No mind that's honest
      But in it shares some woe, though the main part
      Pertains to you alone.
      MACDUFF   If it be mine,
      Keep it not from me; quickly let me have it.
      ROSS
      Let not your ears despise my tongue for ever,
      Which shall possess them with the heaviest sound
      That ever yet they heard.
      MACDUFF   Humh! I guess at it.
      ROSS
204   Your castle is surprised, your wife and babes
      Savagely slaughtered. To relate the manner
206   Were, on the quarry of these murdered deer,
      To add the death of you.
      MALCOLM   Merciful heaven!
      What, man! Ne'er pull your hat upon your brows.
209   Give sorrow words. The grief that does not speak
210   Whispers the o'erfraught heart and bids it break.
      MACDUFF
      My children too?
      ROSS   Wife, children, servants, all

      That could be found.
      MACDUFF   And I must be from thence?
      My wife killed too?
      ROSS   I have said.
      MALCOLM   Be comforted.
      Let's make us med'cines of our great revenge
      To cure this deadly grief.
      MACDUFF
      He has no children. All my pretty ones?
      Did you say all? O hell-kite! All?
      What, all my pretty chickens and their dam
      At one fell swoop?
      MALCOLM
      Dispute it like a man.   220
      MACDUFF   I shall do so;
      But I must also feel it as a man.
      I cannot but remember such things were
      That were most precious to me. Did heaven look on
      And would not take their part? Sinful Macduff,
      They were all struck for thee! Naught that I am,   225
      Not for their own demerits but for mine
      Fell slaughter on their souls. Heaven rest them now!
      MALCOLM
      Be this the whetstone of your sword. Let grief
      Convert to anger; blunt not the heart, enrage it.
      MACDUFF
      O, I could play the woman with mine eyes
      And braggart with my tongue. But, gentle heavens,
      Cut short all intermission. Front to front   232
      Bring thou this fiend of Scotland and myself.
      Within my sword's length set him. If he scape,
      Heaven forgive him too!
      MALCOLM   This tune goes manly.
      Come, go we to the King. Our power is ready;   236
      Our lack is nothing but our leave. Macbeth   237
      Is ripe for shaking, and the pow'rs above
      Put on their instruments. Receive what cheer you may.   239
      The night is long that never finds the day.   *Exeunt.*

                     *

Enter a Doctor of Physic and a Waiting Gentlewoman.   V, i

DOCTOR   I have two nights watched with you, but can
      perceive no truth in your report. When was it she last
      walked?

GENTLEWOMAN   Since his Majesty went into the field I
      have seen her rise from her bed, throw her nightgown   5
      upon her, unlock her closet, take forth paper, fold it,   6
      write upon't, read it, afterwards seal it, and again return
      to bed; yet all this while in a most fast sleep.

DOCTOR   A great perturbation in nature, to receive at once
      the benefit of sleep and do the effects of watching! In this   10

170 *modern ecstasy* commonplace emotion   171 *Is there . . . for who* scarcely calls forth an inquiry about identity   173 *relation* report   174 *nice* precise 175 *doth hiss the speaker* causes the speaker to be hissed (for stale repetition) 176 *teems* brings forth   182 *heavily borne* sadly carried   183 *out* up in arms   184 *witnessed* attested   192 *gives out* reports   195 *latch* catch hold of   196 *fee-grief* i.e. a grief possessed in private   197 *Due* belonging   204 *surprised* attacked   206 *quarry* heap of game   209 *speak* speak aloud 210 *Whispers* whispers to   220 *Dispute* revenge   225 *Naught* wicked 232 *intermission* interval; *Front to front* face to face   236 *power* army   237 *Our lack . . . our leave* i.e. nothing remains but to say farewell   239 *Put on their instruments* urge on their agents
V, i *Within* Macbeth's castle at Dunsinane   5 *nightgown* dressing gown   6 *closet* a chest, or desk   10 *do the effects of watching* act as if awake

slumb'ry agitation, besides her walking and other actual performances, what (at any time) have you heard her say?

GENTLEWOMAN That, sir, which I will not report after her.

14 DOCTOR You may to me, and 'tis most meet you should.

GENTLEWOMAN Neither to you nor any one, having no witness to confirm my speech.

Enter Lady [Macbeth], with a taper.

17 Lo you, here she comes! This is her very guise, and,
18 upon my life, fast asleep! Observe her; stand close.

DOCTOR How came she by that light?

GENTLEWOMAN Why, it stood by her. She has light by her continually. 'Tis her command.

DOCTOR You see her eyes are open.

23 GENTLEWOMAN Ay, but their sense are shut.

DOCTOR What is it she does now? Look how she rubs her hands.

GENTLEWOMAN It is an accustomed action with her, to seem thus washing her hands. I have known her continue in this a quarter of an hour.

LADY Yet here's a spot.

DOCTOR Hark, she speaks. I will set down what comes from her, to satisfy my remembrance the more strongly.

LADY Out, damned spot! Out, I say! One – two – why then 'tis time to do't. Hell is murky. Fie, my lord, fie! a soldier and afeard? What need we fear who knows it,
35 when none can call our power to accompt? Yet who would have thought the old man to have had so much blood in him?

DOCTOR Do you mark that?

LADY The Thane of Fife had a wife. Where is she now? What, will these hands ne'er be clean? No more o' that, my lord, no more o' that! You mar all with this
42 starting.

DOCTOR Go to, go to! You have known what you should not.

GENTLEWOMAN She has spoke what she should not, I am sure of that. Heaven knows what she has known.

LADY Here's the smell of the blood still. All the perfumes of Arabia will not sweeten this little hand. Oh, oh, oh!

49 DOCTOR What a sigh is there! The heart is sorely charged.

GENTLEWOMAN I would not have such a heart in my bosom for the dignity of the whole body.

DOCTOR Well, well, well.

GENTLEWOMAN Pray God it be, sir.

54 DOCTOR This disease is beyond my practice. Yet I have known those which have walked in their sleep who have died holily in their beds.

LADY Wash your hands, put on your nightgown, look not so pale! I tell you yet again, Banquo 's buried. He cannot come out on's grave.

DOCTOR Even so?

LADY To bed, to bed! There's knocking at the gate.

Come, come, come, come, give me your hand! What's done cannot be undone. To bed, to bed, to bed!   *Exit.*

DOCTOR Will she go now to bed?

GENTLEWOMAN Directly.

DOCTOR
Foul whisp'rings are abroad. Unnatural deeds
Do breed unnatural troubles. Infected minds
To their deaf pillows will discharge their secrets.
More needs she the divine than the physician.
God, God forgive us all! Look after her;
Remove from her the means of all annoyance,   71
And still keep eyes upon her. So good night.
My mind she has mated, and amazed my sight.   73
I think, but dare not speak.

GENTLEWOMAN   Good night, good doctor.
                                                                Exeunt.

*

Drum and Colors. Enter Menteith, Caithness,   V, ii
Angus, Lennox, Soldiers.

MENTEITH
The English pow'r is near, led on by Malcolm,
His uncle Siward, and the good Macduff.
Revenges burn in them; for their dear causes
Would to the bleeding and the grim alarm   4
Excite the mortified man.   5

ANGUS   Near Birnam Wood
Shall we well meet them; that way are they coming.   6

CAITHNESS
Who knows if Donalbain be with his brother?

LENNOX
For certain, sir, he is not. I have a file   8
Of all the gentry. There is Siward's son
And many unrough youths that even now   10
Protest their first of manhood.   11

MENTEITH   What does the tyrant?

CAITHNESS
Great Dunsinane he strongly fortifies.
Some say he's mad; others, that lesser hate him,
Do call it valiant fury; but for certain
He cannot buckle his distempered cause   15
Within the belt of rule.   16

ANGUS   Now does he feel
His secret murders sticking on his hands.
Now minutely revolts upbraid his faith-breach.   18
Those he commands move only in command,
Nothing in love. Now does he feel his title
Hang loose about him, like a giant's robe
Upon a dwarfish thief.

MENTEITH   Who then shall blame
His pestered senses to recoil and start,   23
When all that is within him does condemn
Itself for being there?

CAITHNESS   Well, march we on
To give obedience where 'tis truly owed.
Meet we the med'cine of the sickly weal;   27
And with him pour we in our country's purge
Each drop of us.

LENNOX   Or so much as it needs
To dew the sovereign flower and drown the weeds.   30
Make we our march towards Birnam. *Exeunt, marching.*

14 *meet* fitting   17 *guise* habit   18 *close* concealed   23 *sense* powers of sensation   35 *call our power to accompt* call to account anyone so powerful as we   42 *starting* startled movements   49 *charged* laden   54 *practice* professional competence   71 *annoyance* self-injury   73 *mated* bemused

V, ii Open country near Birnam Wood and Dunsinane   4 *bleeding* blood of battle   5 *Excite* incite; *mortified* dead   6 *well* surely   8 *file* list   10 *unrough* unbearded   11 *Protest* assert   15 *distempered* disease-swollen   16 *rule* reason   18 *minutely* every minute; *revolts* rebellions   23 *pestered* tormented   27 *med'cine* cure (i.e. Malcolm); *weal* commonwealth   30 *dew* water

*

V, iii   *Enter Macbeth, Doctor, and Attendants.*

MACBETH

 Bring me no more reports. Let them fly all !

 Till Birnam Wood remove to Dunsinane,

3 I cannot taint with fear. What's the boy Malcolm ?

 Was he not born of woman ? The spirits that know

5 All mortal consequences have pronounced me thus :

 'Fear not, Macbeth. No man that's born of woman

 Shall e'er have power upon thee.' Then fly, false thanes,

8 And mingle with the English epicures.

9 The mind I sway by and the heart I bear

 Shall never sag with doubt nor shake with fear.

    Enter Servant.

11 The devil damn thee black, thou cream-faced loon !

 Where got'st thou that goose look ?

SERVANT

 There is ten thousand –

MACBETH   Geese, villain ?

SERVANT   Soldiers, sir.

MACBETH

14 Go prick thy face and over-red thy fear,

15 Thou lily-livered boy. What soldiers, patch ?

 Death of thy soul ! those linen cheeks of thine

 Are counsellors to fear. What soldiers, whey-face ?

SERVANT

 The English force, so please you.

MACBETH

 Take thy face hence.   *[Exit Servant.]*

    Seyton ! – I am sick at heart,

20 When I behold – Seyton, I say ! – This push

 Will cheer me ever, or disseat me now.

 I have lived long enough. My way of life

23 Is fall'n into the sear, the yellow leaf,

 And that which should accompany old age,

 As honor, love, obedience, troops of friends,

 I must not look to have ; but, in their stead,

 Curses not loud but deep, mouth-honor, breath,

 Which the poor heart would fain deny, and dare not.

 Seyton !

   Enter Seyton.

SEYTON

 What's your gracious pleasure ?

MACBETH   What news more ?

SEYTON

 All is confirmed, my lord, which was reported.

MACBETH

 I'll fight till from my bones my flesh be hacked.

 Give me my armor.

SEYTON   'Tis not needed yet.

MACBETH

 I'll put it on.

35 Send out moe horses, skirr the country round,

 Hang those that talk of fear. Give me mine armor.

 How does your patient, doctor ?

DOCTOR   Not so sick, my lord,

 As she is troubled with thick-coming fancies

 That keep her from her rest.

MACBETH   Cure her of that !

 Canst thou not minister to a mind diseased,

 Pluck from the memory a rooted sorrow,

42 Raze out the written troubles of the brain,

43 And with some sweet oblivious antidote

44 Cleanse the stuffed bosom of that perilous stuff

 Which weighs upon the heart ?

DOCTOR   Therein the patient

 Must minister to himself.

MACBETH

 Throw physic to the dogs, I'll none of it !   47

 Come, put mine armor on. Give me my staff.

 Seyton, send out. – Doctor, the thanes fly from me. –

 Come, sir, dispatch. – If thou couldst, doctor, cast 50

 The water of my land, find her disease,

 And purge it to a sound and pristine health,

 I would applaud thee to the very echo,

 That should applaud again. – Pull't off, I say. –

 What rhubarb, senna, or what purgative drug

 Would scour these English hence ? Hear'st thou of them ?

DOCTOR

 Ay, my good lord. Your royal preparation

 Makes us hear something.

MACBETH   Bring it after me ! 58

 I will not be afraid of death and bane   59

 Till Birnam Forest come to Dunsinane.

     Exeunt [all but the Doctor].

DOCTOR

 Were I from Dunsinane away and clear,

 Profit again should hardly draw me here. *[Exit.]*

        *

   Drum and Colors. Enter Malcolm, Siward, V, iv

   Macduff, Siward's Son, Menteith, Caithness,

   Angus, [Lennox, Ross,] and Soldiers, marching.

MALCOLM

 Cousins, I hope the days are near at hand

 That chambers will be safe.   2

MENTEITH   We doubt it nothing.

SIWARD

 What wood is this before us ?

MENTEITH   The Wood of Birnam.

MALCOLM

 Let every soldier hew him down a bough

 And bear't before him. Thereby shall we shadow

 The numbers of our host and make discovery 6

 Err in report of us.

SOLDIERS   It shall be done.

SIWARD

 We learn no other but the confident tyrant

 Keeps still in Dunsinane and will endure

 Our setting down before't.

MALCOLM   'Tis his main hope,

 For where there is advantage to be gone   11

 Both more and less have given him the revolt, 12

 And none serve with him but constrainèd things

 Whose hearts are absent too.

MACDUFF   Let our just censures 14

V, iii Within Dunsinane Castle **3** *taint* become tainted **5** *consequences* sequence of events **8** *English epicures* (i.e. as compared with the austerely-living Scots) **9** *sway* direct myself **11** *loon* lout **14** *over-red thy fear* i.e. paint red over your fearful pallor **15** *patch* fool **20** *push* struggle **23** *sear* dry, withered **35** *moe* more; *skirr* scour **42** *Raze* erase **43** *oblivious antidote* opiate, medicine of forgetfulness **44** *stuffed* choked up **47** *physic* medicine **50** *dispatch* hasten **50–51** *cast . . . water* analyze the urine **58** *it* i.e. the remainder of the armor **59** *bane* destruction

V, iv Birnam Wood **2** *That chambers* when sleeping-chambers; *nothing* not at all **6** *discovery* i.e. reports by scouts **11** *advantage* opportunity **12** *more and less* high and low **14** *just censures* impartial judgment

15 Attend the true event, and put we on
    Industrious soldiership.
    SIWARD   The time approaches
    That will with due decision make us know
    What we shall say we have and what we owe.
19 Thoughts speculative their unsure hopes relate,
20 But certain issue strokes must arbitrate –
21 Towards which advance the war.   *Exeunt, marching.*

*

V, v   *Enter Macbeth, Seyton, and Soldiers, with Drum
            and Colors.*
    MACBETH
    Hang out our banners on the outward walls.
2   The cry is still, 'They come !' Our castle's strength
    Will laugh a siege to scorn. Here let them lie
    Till famine and the ague eat them up.
5   Were they not forced with those that should be ours,
    We might have met them dareful, beard to beard,
    And beat them backward home.
        A cry within of women.   What is that noise ?
    SEYTON
    It is the cry of women, my good lord.   *[Exit.]*
    MACBETH
    I have almost forgot the taste of fears.
    The time has been my senses would have cooled
11 To hear a night-shriek, and my fell of hair
12 Would at a dismal treatise rouse and stir
    As life were in't. I have supped full with horrors.
14 Direness, familiar to my slaughterous thoughts,
15 Cannot once start me.
        [Enter Seyton.] Wherefore was that cry ?
    SEYTON
    The Queen, my lord, is dead.
    MACBETH
    She should have died hereafter :
    There would have been a time for such a word.
    To-morrow, and to-morrow, and to-morrow
    Creeps in this petty pace from day to day
    To the last syllable of recorded time,
    And all our yesterdays have lighted fools
    The way to dusty death. Out, out, brief candle !
    Life 's but a walking shadow, a poor player
    That struts and frets his hour upon the stage
    And then is heard no more. It is a tale
    Told by an idiot, full of sound and fury,
    Signifying nothing.
        Enter a Messenger.
    Thou com'st to use thy tongue : thy story quickly !
    MESSENGER
    Gracious my lord,
31 I should report that which I say I saw,
    But know not how to do't.

15 *Attend* await ; *put we on* let us put on   19 *relate* convey   20 *certain issue*
the definite outcome ; *arbitrate* decide   21 *war* army
V, v *Within Dunsinane Castle*   2 *still* always   5 *forced* reinforced   11
fell pelt   12 *treatise* story   14 *Direness* horror   15 *start me* make me start
31 *say* i.e. affirm   40 *cling* shrivel ; *sooth* truth   42 *pull in* curb, check
43 *doubt* suspect ; *equivocation* double-talk   47 *avouches* affirms   52 *harness* armor
V, vi *Fields outside Dunsinane Castle*   4 *battle* battalion   6 *order* battle-
plan   7 *power* forces
V, vii *The same*   2 *course* attack (like a bear tied to a stake and baited by
dogs or men)

    MACBETH   Well, say, sir.
    MESSENGER
    As I did stand my watch upon the hill,
    I looked toward Birnam, and anon methought
    The wood began to move.
    MACBETH   Liar and slave !
    MESSENGER
    Let me endure your wrath if't be not so.
    Within this three mile may you see it coming.
    I say, a moving grove.
    MACBETH   If thou speak'st false,
    Upon the next tree shalt thou hang alive
    Till famine cling thee. If thy speech be sooth,   40
    I care not if thou dost for me as much.
    I pull in resolution, and begin   42
    To doubt th' equivocation of the fiend,   43
    That lies like truth. 'Fear not, till Birnam Wood
    Do come to Dunsinane !' and now a wood
    Comes toward Dunsinane. Arm, arm, and out !
    If this which he avouches does appear,   47
    There is nor flying hence nor tarrying here.
    I 'gin to be aweary of the sun,
    And wish th' estate o' th' world were now undone.
    Ring the alarum bell ! Blow wind, come wrack,
    At least we'll die with harness on our back.   *Exeunt.* 52

*

        Drum and Colors. Enter Malcolm, Siward,   V, vi
        Macduff, and their Army, with boughs.
    MALCOLM
    Now near enough. Your leavy screens throw down
    And show like those you are. You, worthy uncle,
    Shall with my cousin, your right noble son,
    Lead our first battle. Worthy Macduff and we   4
    Shall take upon's what else remains to do,
    According to our order.   6
    SIWARD   Fare you well.
    Do we but find the tyrant's power to-night,   7
    Let us be beaten if we cannot fight.
    MACDUFF
    Make all our trumpets speak, give them all breath,
    Those clamorous harbingers of blood and death.
                    Exeunt. Alarums continued.

*

        Enter Macbeth.   V, vii
    MACBETH
    They have tied me to a stake. I cannot fly,
    But bear-like I must fight the course. What's he   2
    That was not born of woman ? Such a one
    Am I to fear, or none.
        Enter Young Siward.
    YOUNG SIWARD
    What is thy name ?
    MACBETH   Thou'lt be afraid to hear it.
    YOUNG SIWARD
    No, though thou call'st thyself a hotter name
    Than any is in hell.
    MACBETH   My name 's Macbeth.
    YOUNG SIWARD
    The devil himself could not pronounce a title
    More hateful to mine ear.
    MACBETH   No, nor more fearful.

YOUNG SIWARD
Thou liest, abhorrèd tyrant! With my sword
I'll prove the lie thou speak'st.
Fight, and Young Siward slain.
MACBETH   Thou wast born of woman.
But swords I smile at, weapons laugh to scorn,
Brandished by man that's of a woman born.   *Exit.*
Alarums. Enter Macduff.
MACDUFF
That way the noise is. Tyrant, show thy face!
If thou beest slain and with no stroke of mine,
My wife and children's ghosts will haunt me still.
17 I cannot strike at wretched kerns, whose arms
18 Are hired to bear their staves. Either thou, Macbeth,
Or else my sword with an unbattered edge
20 I sheathe again undeeded. There thou shouldst be:
By this great clatter one of greatest note
22 Seems bruited. Let me find him, Fortune,
And more I beg not!   *Exit. Alarums.*
Enter Malcolm and Siward.
SIWARD
24 This way, my lord. The castle's gently rend'red:
The tyrant's people on both sides do fight,
The noble thanes do bravely in the war,
27 The day almost itself professes yours
And little is to do.
MALCOLM   We have met with foes
29 That strike beside us.
SIWARD   Enter, sir, the castle.
Exeunt. Alarum.

V, viii   *Enter Macbeth.*
MACBETH
Why should I play the Roman fool and die
2 On mine own sword? Whiles I see lives, the gashes
Do better upon them.
Enter Macduff.
MACDUFF   Turn, hellhound, turn!
MACBETH
Of all men else I have avoided thee.
5 But get thee back! My soul is too much charged
With blood of thine already.
MACDUFF   I have no words;
My voice is in my sword, thou bloodier villain
Than terms can give thee out!
Fight. Alarum.
MACBETH   Thou losest labor.
9 As easy mayst thou the intrenchant air
10 With thy keen sword impress as make me bleed.
Let fall thy blade on vulnerable crests.
I bear a charmèd life, which must not yield
To one of woman born.
13 MACDUFF   Despair thy charm,
14 And let the angel whom thou still hast served
Tell thee, Macduff was from his mother's womb
Untimely ripped.
MACBETH
Accursèd be that tongue that tells me so,
18 For it hath cowed my better part of man!
And be these juggling fiends no more believed,
20 That palter with us in a double sense,
That keep the word of promise to our ear
And break it to our hope. I'll not fight with thee.
MACDUFF
Then yield thee, coward,

And live to be the show and gaze o' th' time.   24
We'll have thee, as our rarer monsters are,   25
Painted upon a pole, and underwrit   26
'Here may you see the tyrant.'
MACBETH   I will not yield,
To kiss the ground before young Malcolm's feet
And to be baited with the rabble's curse.
Though Birnam Wood be come to Dunsinane,
And thou opposed, being of no woman born,
Yet I will try the last. Before my body
I throw my warlike shield. Lay on, Macduff,
And damned be him that first cries 'Hold, enough!'   34
Exeunt fighting. Alarums.
[Re-]enter fighting, and Macbeth slain.
[Exit Macduff.]

*

*Retreat and flourish. Enter, with Drum and Colors,
Malcolm, Siward, Ross, Thanes, and Soldiers.*
MALCOLM
I would the friends we miss were safe arrived.
SIWARD
Some must go off; and yet, by these I see,   36
So great a day as this is cheaply bought.
MALCOLM
Macduff is missing, and your noble son.
ROSS
Your son, my lord, has paid a soldier's debt.
He only lived but till he was a man,
The which no sooner had his prowess confirmed
In the unshrinking station where he fought   42
But like a man he died.
SIWARD   Then he is dead?
ROSS
Ay, and brought off the field. Your cause of sorrow
Must not be measured by his worth, for then
It hath no end.
SIWARD   Had he his hurts before?
ROSS
Ay, on the front.
SIWARD   Why then, God's soldier be he.
Had I as many sons as I have hairs,
I would not wish them to a fairer death:
And so his knell is knolled.
MALCOLM   He's worth more sorrow,
And that I'll spend for him.
SIWARD   He's worth no more.
They say he parted well and paid his score,   52
And so, God be with him. Here comes newer comfort.
Enter Macduff, with Macbeth's head.
MACDUFF
Hail, King, for so thou art. Behold where stands

---

17 *kerns* soldiers of meanest rank   18 *staves* spears   20 *undeeded* not glorified by deeds   22 *bruited* reported   24 *rend'red* surrendered   27 *itself professes* declares itself   29 *beside us* at our side (?), without trying to hit us (?)
V, viii   2 *lives* living bodies   5 *charged* burdened   9 *intrenchant* incapable of being trenched (gashed)   10 *impress* leave a mark on   13 *Despair* despair of   14 *angel* i.e. of the host of Lucifer; *still* always   18 *better part of man* most manly side   20 *palter* quibble   24 *gaze* sight   25 *monsters* freaks   26 *Painted upon a pole* pictured on a showman's banner   34 s.d. *Exeunt . . . slain* (after this action the scene apparently shifts to within Dunsinane Castle; cf. V, vii, 29)   36 *go off* perish; *these* i.e. these here assembled   42 *unshrinking station* place from which he did not retreat   52 *parted* departed; *score* reckoning

55   Th' usurper's cursèd head. The time is free.
56   I see thee compassed with thy kingdom's pearl,
      That speak my salutation in their minds,
      Whose voices I desire aloud with mine –
      Hail, King of Scotland!

ALL   Hail, King of Scotland!
      Flourish.

MALCOLM
      We shall not spend a large expense of time
61   Before we reckon with your several loves

And make us even with you. My Thanes and kinsmen,   62
Henceforth be Earls, the first that ever Scotland
In such an honor named. What's more to do
Which would be planted newly with the time –   65
As calling home our exiled friends abroad
That fled the snares of watchful tyranny,
Producing forth the cruel ministers   68
Of this dead butcher and his fiend-like queen,
Who (as 'tis thought) by self and violent hands   70
Took off her life – this, and what needful else
That calls upon us, by the grace of Grace
We will perform in measure, time, and place.   73
So thanks to all at once and to each one,
Whom we invite to see us crowned at Scone.
                 Flourish. Exeunt omnes.

55 *free* released from tyranny   56 *compassed* surrounded   61 *reckon* come to an accounting   62 *make us even with you* repay you   65 *would be planted newly with the time* i.e. should be done at the outset of this new era   68 *ministers* agents   70 *self and violent* her own violent   73 *in measure* with decorum; *time, and place* at the proper time and place

THE LIFE OF TIMON OF ATHENS

INTRODUCTION

Critical responses to *Timon of Athens* have been extremely varied, and have not always been characterized by moderation. Commentators seeking in this play exactly the qualities they most value in such undeniable masterpieces as *Macbeth* and *King Lear* have condemned it as an abortive piece of work at best, un-Shakespearean, a failure, not worth the modern reader's serious attention. Other critics, recognizing that not all its differences from these great tragedies need be regarded as weaknesses, and insisting that *Timon* ought, like *Troilus and Cressida,* to be judged by quite different standards, have found it at least as rewarding as that remarkable if also somewhat dissatisfying play. Others still, extravagant admirers indeed, have professed to see in *Timon* one of the final triumphs of the world's dramatic art, an archetypal tragedy so compulsively emotional as to make the voices in *Hamlet, Othello,* and even *Lear* sound childish in comparison. Apparently *Timon* encourages hyperbole. But while in each of these views there is no doubt some measure of truth, it seems folly to regard the play either as one of the very best of Shakespeare's tragedies or as so bad that it cannot even be thought wholly his. The fact is that *Timon,* more strikingly than most other plays, "is of a mingled yarn, good and ill together." From several points of view it must surely be considered less effective than any other of Shakespeare's "mature" tragedies; but at least occasionally, and especially in its last two acts, *Timon* rivals *Lear* in eloquence and power.

In many ways – in tone and temper, in poetic merit, in dramatic technique – the first three acts of *Timon of Athens* differ widely from Acts IV and V. The salient qualities of I–III can best be shown by an examination of the opening scene of the play, which consists of four more or less distinct yet admirably fused parts. In the first of these we hear a conversation in which a poet, a painter, a jeweller, and a merchant discuss the incomparable virtues of Lord Timon, from whose "bounty" it is immediately plain they all hope to profit. The principal speakers are first the painter, who has brought a flattering portrait of Timon to present to him, and then, more important still, the poet. After a momentary interruption which effectively shows the greatest men of Athens, her senators, flocking to the enjoyment of Timon's liberality, the poet describes the instrument with which he hopes to win Timon's favor: an allegorical poem which, while its primary intent is to magnify Timon's glory, is evidently indebted to the old fickleness-of-Fortune tradition and ends by showing the hero betrayed by his erstwhile friends

> When Fortune in her shift and change of mood
> Spurns down her late beloved.

The poet's offering, in short, has a double function. As but the last in a series of gifts which insincere men are pressing on Timon in order to exploit him, it is a principal means of establishing the atmosphere of designing falsehood with which the appearance of Timon is meant to be prefaced; but it has a subtler and more important purpose as well, since it in fact provides the initial statement of the play's theme.

No sooner has the inevitable downfall of the Fortunate Man been thus adumbrated than trumpets sound and Lord Timon, surrounded by admirers and followed by a retinue of servants, makes his grand first entry. The stage direction calls for some ceremony of compliment, and the formality and courtliness of this makes for an effective contrast with what has gone before. But the most essential thing now is the impression we first get of Timon himself, of a man nobly but unwisely generous – though what is emphasized at this point in the play is rather the nobility than the rashness of his bounty. Not a man to desert a friend in his adversity, he redeems Ventidius from prison by paying his heavy debt; and he then endows a mere servant, though an honest one, with a fortune sufficiently large to enable him to marry the girl he truly loves. This is Timon at his best, and there is nothing with which to find fault in these two instances of his goodness, in the very first view we have of him. Cause for dissatisfaction is then at once provided, however, by his behavior toward the poet and his fellows; and it is manifestly the function of the carping Apemantus, who is now introduced, not only to inveigh against the falseness of all such men, whether artists or merchants or great lords, but to insist on the folly of Timon's indiscriminate liberality toward them. Alcibiades, perhaps because he is not meant to be tarred with the same brush, makes his first appearance only very late in the scene – which is then rounded off with a brief colloquy between two Athenian lords about Timon's excessive prodigality. They pay lip service, as it would be out of character for Apemantus to do, to Timon's kindness and nobility; but the chief purpose of their dialogue is to provide choric comment on all that has gone before. The emphasis is again on Timon's folly; and the second lord's "Long may he live / In fortunes" sounds, as the scene ends, the unmistakably ominous note of tragedy to come.

In almost every respect this is an admirable beginning. It is lively, colorful, full of both movement and matter. It has abundant variety, yet its numerous components are coherently interrelated and form a unified whole. The economy with which so much is so quickly imparted is striking: in less than three hundred lines the atmosphere in which the action of the first part of the play is to take place is well established; the theme of this action is both announced and in due course vigorously restated; all the most important characters save one – Timon's steward, Flavius, who is to appear in the next scene – are introduced; the essential qualities of Timon, or at any rate of Timon in his prosperity, are already fairly clear; and the likelihood of future disaster is made plain. Even in *King Lear* (to which *Timon* is so similar as regards the general structure of its opening scene) the exposition, the initial presentation of situation and character, is hardly managed more adroitly.

To point out these virtues is of course not to affirm that there are no defects whatever. On the contrary, the most serious faults with which the play as a whole can be charged (to be noticed more particularly later) are to some extent shared by its initial scene. Alcibiades' part here seems slighted, for example, and the relationship between him and Timon is not made clear; nor is Timon's nobility of soul, though frequently mentioned, made convincing. Notwithstanding these weaknesses, however, the many-faceted excellence of this scene is hardly to be denied; and one may add at once that dramaturgical skill of a high order is evident throughout *Timon*. Still, there are some notable lapses. The passage of approximately seventy lines devoted to the fool and the page (see II, ii, 47–119) is dramatically unnecessary, has small intrinsic merit, and seems at best an infelicitous interruption of the serious business in hand. But this particular kind of artlessness, of which there are instances enough in other Shakespearean plays, is rare, whereas examples of superior craftsmanship abound. The various ingredients that make up the long second scene of Act I are as skillfully combined as those in the first; and what immediately follows, the very short contrasting scene in which the imminence of Timon's fall is made plain (II, i), is equally effective in its very different way. Especially illuminating are the three consecutive scenes at the beginning of Act III which, collectively, provide the play's crucial demonstration of its central figure's betrayal by his fair-weather friends. Here, each of the lords most deeply in Timon's debt is in turn appealed to for help, which he declines to give. The scenes in question are all short, and precisely the same story is told in each. Yet monotony is skillfully avoided. In less than two hundred lines Lords Lucullus, Lucius, and Sempronius become distinct individuals, each loathsome in his own special way; and even Timon's three servants are to some extent individualized. The second, who is much meeker than the other two (one notes that he is called Servilius), is appropriately denied a final speech of passionate denunciation like that given each of his fellows. The vileness of Lord Lucius receives its full share of castigation, however, from the "three strangers" whose presence effectively differentiates the second of these scenes from the first and the third. There is no doubt some artificiality in this, but there is art as well. And there is more art and less trickery later on. It must be acknowledged that the misanthropic tirades of Timon in his latter days (Acts IV and V) are long-drawn-out; but while in aim and mood they are all alike, the virtuosity they nonetheless show as a succession of variations on a single theme is remarkable indeed.

More remarkable still, to be sure, is the poetry in this part of the play. What above all else makes *Timon of Athens* an extraordinary work of art is the magnificence of the language in which its hero, to whom life at its best has become no more than a long disease, pours out his bitterness of soul, his anguished contempt for all humanity, and his longing for the nothingness of death. But the poetic excellence of Acts IV and V has long been recognized, whereas the lesser merits of the play, though both pervasive and real, have tended to be overlooked. Critical interest has usually been directed instead to the reasons for *Timon's* failure to produce at last, despite the eloquence of its concluding scenes, the kind of effect we regard as essential to all really great tragedy. And much attention has also been given to certain peculiarities in the only authoritative text that has come down to us, peculiarities that are without parallel elsewhere. These are especially interesting, and are not without relevance to questions about the play's literary qualities, as indications that Shakespeare left *Timon of Athens* unfinished.

"Unfinished," however, is a misleading term. *Timon* is a whole play. That there is a marked difference between Acts I–III and IV–V does not imply incoherence or betray any lack of plan. What may be called the two movements of the play are evidently intended to produce the very striking before-and-after contrast that we find: the first three acts are a necessary preparation for the last two; progress is systematic throughout; and when the last speech of Alcibiades comes to a close ("Let our drums strike") there can be no more doubt that a conclusion has been reached than when Fortinbras issues a similar command ("Go, bid the soldiers shoot") and *Hamlet* ends.

Emphatically, then, *Timon* is not a mere fragment. It is complete, or at least very nearly so. But the manuscript from which the Folio text was printed was evidently one that still needed a good deal of revision, larded as it was with inconsistencies and irregularities of various kinds. There is one, for instance, in the very first entry direction. The "mercer" who is mentioned here is a "ghost" character. He neither speaks nor is ever referred to again; and the text proper quickly makes it clear (see I, i, 8, where the painter says to the poet, "I know them both") that we cannot even infer his mute presence. What we can infer is an original intention of having five speakers in the opening passage, then the failure to remove all trace of the mercer when only four were actually used. Much more striking anomalies are found in the text proper, however, and the following are but a few of many.

(1) The first fifty-odd lines of the passage which introduces Timon are devoted to two instances of his generosity (see I, i, 94–151). He gives five talents to redeem Ventidius, then settles three talents on Lucilius. A talent being worth, in terms of today's values, something like $2,000, these are impressive gifts – about $10,000 and $6,000 respectively – as of course they were meant to be. However, later in the play (at II, ii, 189–90, 195 and III, i, 17–18) we hear of fifty and a thousand talents: very large sums indeed, especially the latter, since by the same reckoning as before a thousand talents would be equivalent to about $2,000,000. Now there are similar discrepancies in Shakespeare's sources. The play is based mainly on North's translation of Plutarch's *Life of Antony* and, though through precisely what intermediary is uncertain, Lucian's *Timon the Misanthrope*. Relatively small numbers of talents are mentioned in Lucian, much larger ones in Plutarch. Especially interesting, therefore, is what we find in III, ii (lines 12, 23, 35, and 37): three consecutive mentions of no

specific number but only of "so many talents" and then, according to the Folio, of "fifty five hundred Talents" ($11,000,000). Or, as the present text gives it, "fifty – five hundred – talents" – as if the author had set down two alternative sums and had never got around to striking out one or the other. For the repeated use of the manifestly unsatisfactory "so many" in the preceding lines is hardly understandable except as an indication that the writer had become uncertain whether "fifty" or "five hundred" should eventually be used to specify a very large but yet not an altogether preposterous sum.

(2) At IV, iii, 349 the approach of the poet and the painter is announced. Next to appear, however, are first "the Banditti" (after line 394) and then Timon's steward (after line 453). The poet and the painter in due course appear (see V, i), but two major episodes and nearly two hundred lines later than, apparently, they were originally meant to.

(3) There is some inconsistency in Alcibiades' three statements about his knowledge of Timon's misfortunes in IV, iii (compare line 57 with lines 77 and 93–96), but there is grosser inconsistency in the two couplets which Alcibiades later reads out as Timon's epitaph (see V, iv, 70–73). Plutarch gives two epitaphs, first the one he supposes to have been made by Timon himself and, later, one "not his, but made by the poet Callimachus." Though they are quite contradictory ("Seek not my name. . . . Here lie I, Timon"), Shakespeare set down both, one immediately after the other – apparently not yet having decided which to use and which to cancel.

(4) The compositor who set the type for the Folio text of *Timon* was undoubtedly responsible for some misrepresentation of the manuscript from which he worked, but this manuscript must nevertheless have contained a considerable amount of very imperfect verse. In fact it must have contained many passages which, though they represented something nearly complete, something more than rough sketches, could not yet be regarded by Shakespeare as in their final form. For, while there are various kinds of irregularity in the authoritative texts of a number of Shakespeare's plays, the deficiencies of the verse in *Timon* are without parallel elsewhere. Sometimes a single speech is partly in prose, partly in rhymed couplets, and partly in blank verse (as in I, ii, 36–50); and passages wholly in verse often contain some lines with too many stresses and some with too few (as in III, v or IV, ii, 30–50). Examples are to be found throughout the play, even in the great poetic utterances of Acts IV and V (for instance in Timon's soliloquy at IV, iii, 1–48).

There is now pretty general agreement that *Timon of Athens* is not a collaborated work, partly by someone other than Shakespeare. It is consistent in mood and temper; the execution of all its parts seems firmly governed by a single general scheme; the same patterns of image and idea recur throughout; details which all critics have found characteristically if not uniquely Shakespearean are scattered through the very passages which are in other respects so far below the expected standard, and the flaws which mar these are by no means peculiar to them alone. The play is of a piece, and Shakespearean. Yet it undeniably contains hosts of such relatively small anomalies as have been noticed above – metrical irregularities, small inconsistencies of various kinds, signs of false starts and of alterations planned but not made. The simplest and most

satisfactory explanation of these is that the manuscript used by the Folio printers was, in the sense of the word already suggested, unfinished: substantially complete but not yet what could forthwith be made the basis of a prompt-book and so of stage presentation. Parts of this manuscript, indeed, seem to have required transcription before serving as printers' copy (as is suggested in the Note on the Text to the present edition).

Anomalies of the kind we have been considering cannot be said to increase the value of *Timon of Athens* as a work of art. They are not merits but defects, explain them how we may. If we have accounted for them correctly, however, they are matters to which literary criticism can hardly be altogether indifferent. The peculiarities in question may not, it is true, provide a sound basis for generalization about Shakespeare's usual working methods, about the procedures he followed when writing his other plays; but they probably give us the clearest view we are ever likely to get of a Shakespearean manuscript in process of completion. That Shakespeare seldom blotted a line, pious fiction though it essentially is, may not be completely without foundation: much of the time, no doubt, "his mind and his hand went together" and he composed with rapidity and ease – relatively speaking; as compared, say, with Ben Jonson. Yet there are plenty of indications (for instance in *Love's Labor's Lost* and *Romeo and Juliet* and *Julius Caesar*) that the very firstlings of his heart were not invariably the lastlings of his pen as well – as they evidently were not when he was working on *Timon of Athens*.

The imperfections which suggest that Shakespeare left the play unfinished are very numerous but are also relatively trifling. Such faults in *Macbeth* and *King Lear* would not much obscure their essential greatness, and if *Timon* lacks this greatness the reasons must be sought in more serious shortcomings, in weaknesses which nothing short of wholesale rewriting could well obviate. One of these is centered in Alcibiades. Some of the problems associated with his character and function are minor. Though we are given no real opportunity to know him in the first part of the play, what kind of man he is may be sufficiently revealed in the scene which ends in his banishment (III, v) and which in some measure prepares us for the dominant role he will have at the end, where, by sweeping away the old and establishing the new order and by providing the final summary comment on Timon's tragedy, he resolves the action. Again, there is perhaps no absolute need for any more detailed indications than we are given of the nature of the bond between Alcibiades and Timon. But what can be made of their entirely different reactions to Athenian ingratitude? Does this contrast really show that Timon has far greater spiritual worth than his less sensitive but more successful friend, or is this only its imperfectly realized aim? Does it not in fact rather diminish than augment the stature of the protagonist in our eyes? One has only to think of the differing responses of Gloucester and Lear to ingratitude, and of what their tragedy gains from these differences, to appreciate how much less is achieved by the corresponding contrast in *Timon*.

Unless we come to feel that the evils with which a tragedy deals are of the deepest concern to humanity in general, and unless in contending with these evils the protagonist increasingly reveals qualities of mind and spirit which we regard as heroic, the play may fail to produce in us that sense of exaltation which is always evoked by the tragedies we value most. And so it is, for many readers, with this play. For one thing Timon's errors seem more ridiculous than frightening, and it is hard to take very seriously the disaster to which they lead. The crimes of Macbeth and the follies of King Lear precipitate evils which plague all mankind, and are the more terrible because committed by men who have impressive intellectual and spiritual capabilities. The Timon of Acts I–III reveals no such qualities, and his foolishness is of a comparatively trivial kind. Do we really believe that the lure of money is the root of all evil? or that the loss of false friends is a calamity? To be sure there is a certain imaginative grandeur in Timon's vilification, later on, of "Yellow, glittering, precious gold" (IV, iii, 26–48). Evil is generalized here. Indeed a vastly enlarged range of vision and emotion is evident throughout the various indictments of human bestiality that fill Acts IV and V. Yet there are important difficulties here too. One is that, as Apemantus trenchantly observes (IV, iii, 299–300), Timon is now as immoderate in his misanthropy as he was earlier in his bounty. He is foolish still. His transformation, though striking, has not been accompanied by any increase in self-knowledge. His sufferings have not brought him to an awareness of his own imperfections; they have embittered but not magnified him. One of his chief deficiencies as a tragic hero is certainly his incapacity for spiritual growth. Finally, Timon's response to misfortune is not only unheroic but undramatic. He simply withdraws from the world of men. Far from becoming the champion of aspiring humanity in its endless struggle against evil, he rather "slinks out of the race, where that immortal garland is to be run for, not without dust and heat." Dust and heat – involvement and conflict – are the life-blood of drama. As Timon's story is conceived, however, the second half of it must for the most be sustained by other means, by the sheer eloquence of the maledictions with which he belabors a long succession of unwelcome visitors; and, high though the poetic quality of Acts IV and V unquestionably is, it yet fails to make Timon himself an entirely satisfactory protagonist.

There is general agreement that *Timon of Athens* must have been written sometime between 1604 and 1609 (after *Othello* but before the late romances), though whether it is really "the still-born twin of *Lear*" (1605–06) or belongs rather to the period of *Antony and Cleopatra* and *Coriolanus* (1607–08) is by no means clear. It was almost certainly not staged before the Restoration, nor has it ever been successful in the theatre since. Its very survival, by virtue of being printed in 1623, is a little surprising. It is assuredly not one of the great tragedies of a great age. Yet it has rewarding qualities throughout, and parts of it challenge comparison with the supreme manifestations of Shakespeare's maturest art. And if it is also a play which its author never quite finished, as it seems indeed to be, its very imperfections should be of interest to students of Shakespeare.

University of Kansas   CHARLTON HINMAN

NOTE ON THE TEXT

Timon of Athens was first printed in the Folio of 1623, evidently from an author's draft, the peculiar nature of which is discussed below. In the Folio the play is not divided into acts and scenes. The division supplied marginally for reference in the present edition is that given currency by later editors.

In the Folio *Timon* immediately follows *Romeo and Juliet*. Its appearance just here, as the fourth of the Tragedies, was not originally planned. *Troilus and Cressida* had been meant for this position; but difficulties arose (apparently over copyright), the printing of *Troilus* as the next play after *Romeo* was abruptly given over, and *Timon of Athens* was later used to fill the space which had been allotted to the other play. Thus at least the position of *Timon* in the 1623 collection is anomalous; and we cannot even be sure that its inclusion anywhere in the volume was contemplated from the beginning. This much, however, is plain: the "copy" from which the Folio printers were obliged to work was most unusual. It seems to have represented a full but not yet finally revised text, a version antecedent to "foul papers," as an author's last draft of a play is rather misleadingly called. Many of the peculiarities of the copy for *Timon* (including such unnecessarily descriptive details in stage directions as "... *Then comes, drooping after all, Apemantus, discontentedly, like himself.*") are indeed of the kind thought characteristic of foul papers, and much of this copy was very likely in Shakespeare's own handwriting. But numerous oddities in spelling that cannot be attributed to the printers demonstrate the presence of a second hand as well; and perhaps the best explanation that can at present be offered is that various parts of Shakespeare's incompletely revised autograph version were found so untidy and illegible that the services of a scribe had to be enlisted to make them sufficiently "clean" for printing-house use. That in any event the second hand did not belong to a second author but only to a transcriber seems clear enough, since it is sometimes found in the most peculiarly Shakespearean passages in the play.

Except for extensive relineation, the following list shows all the material departures from the Folio text, which is often mani-festly corrupt. The adopted reading in italics is followed by the Folio reading in roman. Most of the corrections first appeared in eighteenth-century editions (along with many other emendations which may now be rejected as unnecessary) and have generally been accepted since.

The Actors' Names (printed at the end of the play in F)

I, i, 21 *gum . . . oozes* Gowne . . . vses   25 *chafes* chases   40 *man* men   87 *hands . . . slip* hand . . . sit   101 *most needs* must neede   166 *satiety* society   210 *cost* cast   221 *feigned* fegin'd   257 *more* most

I, ii, s.d. *drooping* dropping   29 *ever* verie   78 *these* those   99 *joy* ioyes   118 *Th' ear* There   119 *smell, all* all   145 *Lady* Lord   164 *accept* accept it

II, i, 33 *Take* I go sir ? / Take   34 *in compt* in. Come

II, ii, 4 *resumes* resume   38 *broken* debt, broken   72, 99 *mistress'* Masters   125 *proposed* propose   132 *found* sound   152 *of* or   182 *Flaminius* Flauius

III, ii, 37 *fifty – five hundred* – fifty five hundred   64 *spirit* sport

III, iii, 12 *Thrice* Thriue   21 *and I* and

III, iv, 110 *Sempronius* Sempronius Vllorxa   113 *There is* there's

III, v, 4 *him* 'em   14 *this fault* his Fate   17 *An* And   22 *behave* behooue   49 *felon* fellow   63 *I say* say   67 *'em* him   70 *no more* no

III, vi, 19 *here's* heares   78 *foes* fees   79 *lag* legge

IV, i, 6 *steads* steeds   13 *Son* Some

IV, ii, 41 *does* do

IV, iii, 10 *senator* Senators   12 *pasture . . . wether's* Pastour . . . Brothers   13 *lean* leaue   117 *window-bars* window Barne   122, 185 *thy* the   204 *fortune* future   223 *mossed* moyst   283 *my* thy   394 *them* then   430 *villainy* Villaine   470 *grant'st* grunt'st   488 *mild* wilde   505 *A* If not a   521 *Have* Ha's

V, i, 50 *worship* worshipt   69 *men* man   124 *chance* chanc'd   143 *And* Which   145 *sense* since   146 *fail* fall   180 *reverend'st* reuerends   218 *sour* four

V, ii, 8 *had* made

V, iv, 24 *griefs* greefe   44 *all together* altogether   55 *Descend* Defend   62 *rendered* remedied

THE LIFE OF TIMON OF ATHENS

*

I, i *Enter Poet, Painter, Jeweller, Merchant, and*
      Mercer, at several doors.

POET
  Good day, sir.

PAINTER   I am glad y' are well.

POET
2 I have not seen you long ; how goes the world ?

PAINTER
3 It wears, sir, as it grows.

POET   Ay, that's well known.
  But what particular rarity ? What strange,
5 Which manifold record not matches ? See,
6 Magic of bounty, all these spirits thy power
  Hath conjured to attend ! I know the merchant.

PAINTER
  I know them both. Th' other's a jeweller.

MERCHANT
  O, 'tis a worthy lord !

9 JEWELLER   Nay, that's most fixed.

MERCHANT
10 A most incomparable man ; breathed, as it were,
11 To an untirable and continuate goodness.
12 He passes.

JEWELLER I have a jewel here –

MERCHANT
  O, pray let's see't. For the Lord Timon, sir ?

JEWELLER
  If he will touch the estimate ; but for that –   14

POET *[Recites.]*
  'When we for recompense have praised the vile,   15
  It stains the glory in that happy verse
  Which aptly sings the good.'

MERCHANT *[Looks at the jewel.]* 'Tis a good form.

JEWELLER
  And rich. Here is a water, look ye.   18

PAINTER
  You are rapt, sir, in some work, some dedication   19
  To the great lord.

POET   A thing slipped idly from me.
  Our poesy is as a gum which oozes   21
  From whence 'tis nourishèd. The fire i' th' flint
  Shows not till it be struck ; our gentle flame
  Provokes itself and like the current flies   24
  Each bound it chafes. What have you there ?

PAINTER
  A picture, sir. When comes your book forth ?

POET
  Upon the heels of my presentment, sir.   27
  Let's see your piece.

PAINTER   'Tis a good piece.

POET
  So 'tis. This comes off well and excellent.   29

PAINTER
  Indifferent.

POET   Admirable. How this grace
  Speaks his own standing ! What a mental power   31

I, i The house of Timon   s.d. *Mercer* (a ghost character : see Introduction)
2 *long* for a long time   3 *wears . . . grows* wears out as it ages   5 *manifold . . .
matches* is unmatched in all history   6 *bounty* generosity   9 *fixed* certain
10 *breathed* trained (through exercise)   11 *continuate* enduring   12 *passes*
excels   14 *touch the estimate* meet my price   15–17 *When . . . good* i.e. false
praise in real life lowers the value of poetry that praises truly   18 *water*
lustre   19 *rapt* engrossed   21–24 *Our poesy . . . itself* i.e. poetry runs
spontaneously from its source, needing no external stimulus   24–25 *flies
. . . chafes* seeks escape from each riverbank that confines it   27 *presentment*
presentation of it (to Timon)   29 *well and excellent* excellently well   31
Speaks . . . standing expresses the worth of its subject

This eye shoots forth ! How big imagination
33 Moves in this lip ! To th' dumbness of the gesture
One might interpret.

PAINTER
It is a pretty mocking of the life.
Here is a touch ; is't good ?

POET   I will say of it,
37 It tutors nature. Artificial strife
Lives in these touches, livelier than life.
Enter certain Senators [and pass over].

PAINTER
How this lord is followed !

POET
The senators of Athens. Happy man !

PAINTER
41 Look, moe !

POET
You see this confluence, this great flood of visitors :
I have in this rough work shaped out a man
Whom this beneath world doth embrace and hug
45 With amplest entertainment. My free drift
46 Halts not particularly, but moves itself
In a wide sea of wax ; no levelled malice
48 Infects one comma in the course I hold,
49 But flies an eagle flight, bold and forth on,
50 Leaving no tract behind.

PAINTER
How shall I understand you ?

51 POET   I will unbolt to you.
52 You see how all conditions, how all minds,
As well of glib and slipp'ry creatures as
Of grave and austere quality, tender down
Their services to Lord Timon. His large fortune,
Upon his good and gracious nature hanging,
57 Subdues and properties to his love and tendance
All sorts of hearts ; yea, from the glass-faced flatterer
To Apemantus, that few things loves better
Than to abhor himself – even he drops down
The knee before him and returns in peace
Most rich in Timon's nod.

PAINTER   I saw them speak together.

POET
Sir, I have upon a high and pleasant hill
Feigned Fortune to be throned. The base o' th' mount
65 Is ranked with all deserts, all kind of natures
That labor on the bosom of this sphere
67 To propagate their states. Amongst them all
Whose eyes are on this sovereign lady fixed
69 One do I personate of Lord Timon's frame,
Whom Fortune with her ivory hand wafts to her,
71 Whose present grace to present slaves and servants
72 Translates his rivals.

PAINTER   'Tis conceived to scope.
This throne, this Fortune, and this hill, methinks,
With one man beckoned from the rest below,
Bowing his head against the steepy mount
76 To climb his happiness, would be well expressed
In our condition.

POET   Nay, sir, but hear me on.
All those which were his fellows but of late
(Some better than his value) on the moment
Follow his strides, his lobbies fill with tendance,
Rain sacrificial whisperings in his ear,
82 Make sacred even his stirrup, and through him

Drink the free air.

PAINTER   Ay, marry, what of these ?   83

POET
When Fortune in her shift and change of mood
Spurns down her late beloved, all his dependants,
Which labored after him to the mountain's top
Even on their knees and hands, let him slip down,
Not one accompanying his declining foot.

PAINTER
'Tis common.
A thousand moral paintings I can show   90
That shall demonstrate these quick blows of Fortune's
More pregnantly than words. Yet you do well   92
To show Lord Timon that mean eyes have seen   93
The foot above the head.
Trumpets sound. Enter Lord Timon, addressing
himself courteously to every suitor [; a Messenger
from Ventidius talking with him ; Lucilius and other
Servants following].

TIMON   Imprisoned is he, say you ?

MESSENGER
Ay, my good lord. Five talents is his debt,   95
His means most short, his creditors most strait.   96
Your honorable letter he desires
To those have shut him up, which failing
Periods his comfort.   99

TIMON   Noble Ventidius ! Well,
I am not of that feather to shake off
My friend when he most needs me. I do know him
A gentleman that well deserves a help,
Which he shall have. I'll pay the debt and free him.

MESSENGER
Your lordship ever binds him.   104

TIMON
Commend me to him. I will send his ransom ;
And, being enfranchised, bid him come to me.   106
'Tis not enough to help the feeble up,
But to support him after. Fare you well.

MESSENGER
All happiness to your honor !   *Exit.*
Enter an old Athenian.

OLD MAN
Lord Timon, hear me speak.

TIMON   Freely, good father.   110

OLD MAN
Thou hast a servant named Lucilius.

TIMON
I have so. What of him ?

---

33 *Moves in* is suggested by   33–34 *To th' dumbness . . . interpret* i.e. it
'can almost talk'   37 *Artificial strife* the struggle of art to outdo nature
41 *moe* more   45 *entertainment* welcome ; *drift* aim   46 *particularly* on any
individual   46–47 *moves . . . wax* i.e. has great scope (though 'wax' has
not been altogether satisfactorily explained)   48 *comma* i.e. detail   49
flies my course is   50 *tract* trace, track   51 *unbolt* explain   52 *conditions*
social levels   57 *properties* appropriates ; *tendance* care, service   65
ranked . . . deserts filled with men of all degrees of merit   67 *states* fortunes,
estates   69 *personate* represent   71 *to present* immediately to   72 *Trans-*
lates transforms, changes ; *to scope* aptly   76–77 *would . . . condition*
would be closely paralleled by our situation in the real world   82–83
through . . . air act as if indebted to him even for breathing   83 *marry* to
be sure   90 *moral* allegorical   92 *pregnantly* cogently   93 *mean* lowly
95 *talents* sums of silver or gold (each worth about $2,000 by modern
standards)   96 *strait* exacting, strict   99 *Periods* ends   104 *binds* attaches
by ties of gratitude (but with quibble on *free* in l. 103)   106 *enfranchised*
freed   110 *father* (respectful form of address to an old man)

OLD MAN
Most noble Timon, call the man before thee.

TIMON
Attends he here or no? Lucilius!

LUCILIUS
Here, at your lordship's service.

OLD MAN
116   This fellow here, Lord Timon, this thy creature,
By night frequents my house. I am a man
118   That from my first have been inclined to thrift,
And my estate deserves an heir more raised
120   Than one which holds a trencher.

TIMON   Well; what further?

OLD MAN
One only daughter have I, no kin else
On whom I may confer what I have got.
123   The maid is fair, o' th' youngest for a bride,
124   And I have bred her at my dearest cost
125   In qualities of the best. This man of thine
126   Attempts her love. I prithee, noble lord,
127   Join with me to forbid him her resort;
Myself have spoke in vain.

TIMON   The man is honest.

OLD MAN
129   Therefore he will be, Timon.
His honesty rewards him in itself;
131   It must not bear my daughter.

TIMON   Does she love him?

OLD MAN
132   She is young and apt.
Our own precedent passions do instruct us
What levity 's in youth.

TIMON   Love you the maid?

LUCILIUS
Ay, my good lord, and she accepts of it.

OLD MAN
If in her marriage my consent be missing,
I call the gods to witness I will choose
Mine heir from forth the beggars of the world
139   And dispossess her all.

TIMON   How shall she be endowed
If she be mated with an equal husband?

OLD MAN
141   Three talents on the present; in future, all.

TIMON
This gentleman of mine hath served me long;
To build his fortune I will strain a little,
144   For 'tis a bond in men. Give him thy daughter:
What you bestow, in him I'll counterpoise,
And make him weigh with her.

OLD MAN   Most noble lord,

Pawn me to this your honor, she is his.   147

TIMON
My hand to thee; mine honor on my promise.

LUCILIUS
Humbly I thank your lordship. Never may
That state or fortune fall into my keeping
Which is not owed to you!   151

               Exit [Lucilius, with old Athenian].

POET *[Presents his poem.]*
Vouchsafe my labor, and long live your lordship!   152

TIMON
I thank you; you shall hear from me anon.   153
Go not away. – What have you there, my friend?

PAINTER
A piece of painting, which I do beseech
Your lordship to accept.

TIMON   Painting is welcome.
The painting is almost the natural man;   157
For since dishonor traffics with man's nature
He is but outside; these pencilled figures are
Even such as they give out. I like your work,
And you shall find I like it. Wait attendance
Till you hear further from me.

PAINTER   The gods preserve ye!

TIMON
Well fare you, gentleman. Give me your hand;
We must needs dine together. – Sir, your jewel
Hath suffered under praise.   165

JEWELLER   What, my lord? Dispraise?

TIMON
A mere satiety of commendations.
If I should pay you for't as 'tis extolled,
It would unclew me quite.   168

JEWELLER   My lord, 'tis rated
As those which sell would give; but you well know   169
Things of like value, differing in the owners,
Are prizèd by their masters. Believe't, dear lord,   171
You mend the jewel by the wearing it.

TIMON
Well mocked.
     Enter Apemantus.

MERCHANT
No, my good lord; he speaks the common tongue
Which all men speak with him.

TIMON   Look who comes here.
Will you be chid?

JEWELLER   We'll bear, with your lordship.   176

MERCHANT
He'll spare none.

TIMON
Good morrow to thee, gentle Apemantus.

APEMANTUS
Till I be gentle stay thou for thy good morrow –   179
When thou art Timon's dog, and these knaves honest.   180

TIMON
Why dost thou call them knaves? Thou know'st them
    not.

APEMANTUS Are they not Athenians?

TIMON Yes.

APEMANTUS Then I repent not.

JEWELLER You know me, Apemantus?

APEMANTUS Thou know'st I do; I called thee by thy
name.

TIMON Thou art proud, Apemantus.

---

116 *creature* dependent (contemptuous)   118 *first* earliest days, youth
120 *holds a trencher* i.e. waits table   123 *o' th' youngest for* barely old enough
to be   124 *bred* brought up, educated   125 *qualities* accomplishments
126 *Attempts* seeks to win   127 *her resort* access to her   129 *will be* i.e. will
act the part (and stop pursuing my daughter against my wishes?)   131 *bear*
win   132 *apt* impressionable   139 *all* wholly   141 *Three talents* (about
$6,000)   144 *bond* obligation   147 *Pawn . . . honor* if you'll pledge, on your
honor, to do so   151 *owed* (acknowledged as) due to   152 *Vouchsafe* deign
to accept   153 *anon* soon   157-60 *The painting . . . out* i.e. painting can
almost be said to represent what man is instead of what he pretends to be
165 *suffered under* been overwhelmed with (complimentary, but the jeweller
takes it otherwise)   168 *unclew* ruin (undo, as in unwinding a ball of yarn)
169 *As . . . give* i.e. at cost price   171 *by* according to   176 *We'll . . .
lordship* i.e. we can stand it if you can   179 *stay . . . morrow* expect such
greeting from me   180 *When . . . honest* i.e. never

APEMANTUS Of nothing so much as that I am not like
Timon.

TIMON Whither art going?

APEMANTUS To knock out an honest Athenian's brains.

TIMON That's a deed thou'lt die for.

APEMANTUS Right, if doing nothing be death by th' law.

TIMON How lik'st thou this picture, Apemantus?

195 APEMANTUS The best for the innocence.

TIMON Wrought he not well that painted it?

APEMANTUS He wrought better that made the painter,
and yet he's but a filthy piece of work.

PAINTER Y' are a dog.

200 APEMANTUS Thy mother 's of my generation. What's
she, if I be a dog?

TIMON Wilt dine with me, Apemantus?

APEMANTUS No, I eat not lords.

204 TIMON An thou shouldst, thou'dst anger ladies.

APEMANTUS O, they eat lords. So they come by great
bellies.

206 TIMON That's a lascivious apprehension.

APEMANTUS So thou apprehend'st it; take it for thy
labor.

TIMON How dost thou like this jewel, Apemantus?

APEMANTUS Not so well as plain-dealing, which will not
210 cost a man a doit.

TIMON What dost thou think 'tis worth?

APEMANTUS Not worth my thinking. How now, poet?

POET How now, philosopher?

APEMANTUS Thou liest.

POET Art not one?

APEMANTUS Yes.

POET Then I lie not.

APEMANTUS Art not a poet?

POET Yes.

220 APEMANTUS Then thou liest. Look in thy last work,
where thou hast feigned him a worthy fellow.

POET That's not feigned; he is so.

APEMANTUS Yes, he is worthy of thee, and to pay thee
for thy labor. He that loves to be flattered is worthy o'
th' flatterer. Heavens, that I were a lord!

TIMON What wouldst do then, Apemantus?

APEMANTUS E'en as Apemantus does now – hate a lord
with my heart.

TIMON What, thyself?

APEMANTUS Ay.

TIMON Wherefore?

232 APEMANTUS That I had no angry wit to be a lord. Art not
thou a merchant?

MERCHANT Ay, Apemantus.

235 APEMANTUS Traffic confound thee, if the gods will not!

MERCHANT If traffic do it, the gods do it.

APEMANTUS Traffic 's thy god; and thy god confound
thee!

Trumpet sounds. Enter a Messenger.

TIMON
What trumpet 's that?

MESSENGER
'Tis Alcibiades and some twenty horse,
240 All of companionship.

TIMON
Pray entertain them; give them guide to us.

[Exeunt some Attendants.]

You must needs dine with me. Go not you hence
Till I have thanked you. When dinner 's done,

Show me this piece. – I am joyful of your sights.   244
Enter Alcibiades with the rest.
Most welcome, sir!
[They salute.]

APEMANTUS So; so; there!
Aches contract and starve your supple joints!   246
That there should be small love 'mongst these sweet
knaves,
And all this courtesy! The strain of man 's bred out   248
Into baboon and monkey.

ALCIBIADES
Sir, you have saved my longing, and I feed   250
Most hungerly on your sight.

TIMON   Right welcome, sir!
Ere we depart we'll share a bounteous time
In different pleasures. Pray you, let us in.
Exeunt [all but Apemantus].

Enter two Lords.

1. LORD What time o' day is't, Apemantus?

APEMANTUS Time to be honest.

1. LORD That time serves still.   256

APEMANTUS The more accursèd thou that still omit'st it.

2. LORD Thou art going to Lord Timon's feast?

APEMANTUS Ay, to see meat fill knaves and wine heat
fools.

2. LORD Fare thee well, fare thee well.

APEMANTUS Thou art a fool to bid me farewell twice.

2. LORD Why, Apemantus?

APEMANTUS Shouldst have kept one to thyself, for I
mean to give thee none.

1. LORD Hang thyself!

APEMANTUS No, I will do nothing at thy bidding. Make
thy requests to thy friend.

2. LORD Away, unpeaceable dog, or I'll spurn thee
hence!

APEMANTUS I will fly, like a dog, the heels o' th' ass.
[Exit.]

1. LORD
He's opposite to humanity. Come, shall we in   270
And taste Lord Timon's bounty? He outgoes
The very heart of kindness.

2. LORD
He pours it out. Plutus, the god of gold,
Is but his steward. No meed but he repays   274
Sevenfold above itself; no gift to him
But breeds the giver a return exceeding
All use of quittance.   277

1. LORD   The noblest mind he carries
That ever governed man.

2. LORD   Long may he live
In fortunes! Shall we in?   279

1. LORD   I'll keep you company. *Exeunt.*

*

195 *innocence* silliness   200 *generation* breed, species   204 *An* if   206 *apprehension* (1) idea, (2) capture (of men by women)   210 *doit* half a farthing, an eighth of a penny   220 *Then thou liest* (because it is necessary for poets to 'feign,' hence to be liars)   232 *had ... lord* had, in my anger, no more sense than to wish to be a lord (perhaps: the line may be corrupt but has not been convincingly emended)   235 *Traffic* trade   240 *of companionship* of the same party   244 *of your sights* to see you   246 *Aches* (pronounced 'aitches'); *starve* cause to wither   248 *bred out* degenerated   250 *saved my* kept me from further   256 *still* always   270 *opposite* hostile   274 *meed* (1) gift, (2) merit   277 *use of quittance* customary repayment   279 *In fortunes* fortunate, prosperous (but possibly we should read 'In Fortune's,' in the goddess Fortune's mind)

I, ii

Hautboys playing loud music. A great banquet served in [, Flavius the Steward and others attending] ; and then enter Lord Timon, the States, the Athenian Lords, Ventidius (which Timon redeemed from prison). Then comes, drooping after all, Apemantus, discontentedly, like himself.

VENTIDIUS
Most honored Timon,
It hath pleased the gods to remember my father's age
And call him to long peace.
He is gone happy, and has left me rich.
Then, as in grateful virtue I am bound
6 To your free heart, I do return those talents,
Doubled with thanks and service, from whose help
I derived liberty.

TIMON   O, by no means,
Honest Ventidius. You mistake my love:
I gave it freely ever; and there's none
Can truly say he gives, if he receives.
12 If our betters play at that game, we must not dare
13 To imitate them; faults that are rich are fair.

VENTIDIUS
A noble spirit!

TIMON
Nay, my lords, ceremony was but devised at first
To set a gloss on faint deeds, hollow welcomes,
Recanting goodness, sorry ere 'tis shown;
But where there is true friendship, there needs none.
Pray sit. More welcome are ye to my fortunes
Than my fortunes to me.
     [They sit.]

1. LORD
My lord, we always have confessed it.

APEMANTUS
22 Ho, ho, confessed it? Hanged it, have you not?

TIMON
O, Apemantus, you are welcome.

APEMANTUS   No,
You shall not make me welcome;
I come to have thee thrust me out of doors.

TIMON
26 Fie, thou'rt a churl; ye've got a humor there
Does not become a man; 'tis much to blame.
28 They say, my lords, *Ira furor brevis est;* but yon man is
ever angry. Go, let him have a table by himself; for he
30 does neither affect company nor is he fit for't indeed.

31 APEMANTUS Let me stay at thine apperil, Timon. I come
to observe; I give thee warning on't.

TIMON I take no heed of thee. Thou'rt an Athenian,

therefore welcome. I myself would have no power; 34
prithee let my meat make thee silent.

APEMANTUS I scorn thy meat. 'Twould choke me; for I
should ne'er flatter thee. O you gods, what a number of
men eats Timon, and he sees 'em not! It grieves me to
see so many dip their meat in one man's blood; and all
the madness is, he cheers them up too. 40
I wonder men dare trust themselves with men.
Methinks they should invite them without knives: 42
Good for their meat, and safer for their lives.
There's much example for't. The fellow that sits next
him now, parts bread with him, pledges the breath of
him in a divided draft, is the readiest man to kill him. 46
'T has been proved. If I were a huge man, I should fear 47
to drink at meals,
Lest they should spy my windpipe's dangerous notes. 49
Great men should drink with harness on their throats. 50

TIMON *[to a Lord who drinks to him]*
My lord, in heart! and let the health go round. 51

2. LORD
Let it flow this way, my good lord.

APEMANTUS Flow this way? A brave fellow! He keeps
his tides well. Those healths will make thee and thy 54
state look ill, Timon.
Here's that which is too weak to be a sinner:
Honest water, which ne'er left man i' th' mire.
This and my food are equals; there's no odds.
Feasts are too proud to give thanks to the gods. 59

Apemantus' Grace.

Immortal gods, I crave no pelf;
I pray for no man but myself;
Grant I may never prove so fond 62
To trust man on his oath or bond,
Or a harlot for her weeping,
Or a dog that seems a-sleeping,
Or a keeper with my freedom, 66
Or my friends, if I should need 'em.
Amen. So; fall to't;
Rich men sin, and I eat root.

[Eats and drinks.]
Much good dich thy good heart, Apemantus! 70

TIMON Captain Alcibiades, your heart's in the field now.

ALCIBIADES My heart is ever at your service, my lord.

TIMON You had rather be at a breakfast of enemies than a
dinner of friends.

ALCIBIADES So they were bleeding new, my lord, there's
no meat like 'em; I could wish my best friend at such a
feast.

APEMANTUS Would all these flatterers were thine
enemies then, that then thou mightst kill 'em – and bid
me to 'em!

1. LORD Might we but have that happiness, my lord, that
you would once use our hearts, whereby we might ex- 80
press some part of our zeals, we should think ourselves
for ever perfect. 82

TIMON O no doubt, my good friends, but the gods themselves have provided that I shall have much help from
you: how had you been my friends else? Why have you
that charitable title from thousands, did not you chiefly 86
belong to my heart? I have told more of you to myself
than you can with modesty speak in your own behalf;
and thus far I confirm you. O you gods, think I, what 89
need we have any friends if we should ne'er have need

I, ii The hall in Timon's house   s.d. *Hautboys* oboes; *States* rulers of the state; senators   6 *free* generous   12 *If* i.e. even if   13 *that are rich* i.e. in the rich   22 *confessed . . . not* (bitter allusion to proverbial 'confess and be hanged')   26 *humor* mood   28 *Ira . . . est* anger is a brief madness   30 *affect* like, seek   31 *thine apperil* your own risk   34 *power* i.e. to keep you quiet   40 *cheers . . . too* encourages them as well (though possibly 'too' should be 'to't', to do it)   42 *without knives* (Elizabethan if not ancient Athenian guests normally brought their own)   46 *divided draft* shared drink   47 *huge* great (in rank, not physical size)   49 *my . . . notes* indications on my throat of where my windpipe is   50 *harness* armor   51 *in heart* heartily   54 *tides* (1) tides, which *flow*, (2) times, seasons   54–55 *Those healths . . . ill* (cf. proverbial 'to drink healths is to drink sickness')   59 *Feasts* feasters   62 *fond* foolish   66 *keeper* jailer   70 *dich* may it do   80 *use our hearts* put our love to the test   82 *perfect* completely happy   86 *from thousands* i.e. you alone of all the thousands I know   89 *confirm you* vouch for your worthiness

of 'em? They were the most needless creatures living,
should we ne'er have use for 'em; and would most resemble sweet instruments hung up in cases, that keeps
their sounds to themselves. Why, I have often wished
95 myself poorer, that I might come nearer to you. We are
born to do benefits; and what better or properer can we
call our own than the riches of our friends? O what a
precious comfort 'tis to have so many like brothers com-
99 manding one another's fortunes! O joy, e'en made away
100 ere't can be born! Mine eyes cannot hold out water,
methinks. To forget their faults, I drink to you.
APEMANTUS Thou weep'st to make them drink, Timon.
2. LORD
Joy had the like conception in our eyes
And at that instant like a babe sprung up.
APEMANTUS
Ho, ho! I laugh to think that babe a bastard.
3. LORD
I promise you, my lord, you moved me much.
107 APEMANTUS Much!
                    Sound tucket.
TIMON
What means that trump?
                    Enter Servant.   How now?
SERVANT Please you, my lord, there are certain ladies
most desirous of admittance.
TIMON Ladies? What are their wills?
SERVANT There comes with them a forerunner, my lord,
113 which bears that office to signify their pleasures.
TIMON I pray let them be admitted.   [Exit Servant.]
                    Enter Cupid.
CUPID
Hail to thee, worthy Timon, and to all
That of his bounties taste! The five best senses
Acknowledge thee their patron, and come freely
118 To gratulate thy plenteous bosom. Th' ear,
Taste, touch, smell, all, pleased from thy table rise;
They only now come but to feast thine eyes.
TIMON
They're welcome all; let 'em have kind admittance.
Music, make their welcome!   [Exit Cupid.]
1. LORD
You see, my lord, how ample y' are beloved.
                    [Music.] Enter Cupid, with the Masque of Ladies
                    [as] Amazons with lutes in their hands, dancing and
                    playing.
APEMANTUS
Hoy-day!
What a sweep of vanity comes this way!
They dance? They are madwomen.
127 Like madness is the glory of this life
128 As this pomp shows to a little oil and root.
We make ourselves fools to disport ourselves
130 And spend our flatteries to drink those men
131 Upon whose age we void it up again
With poisonous spite and envy.
Who lives that's not depravèd or depraves?
Who dies that bears not one spurn to their graves
135 Of their friends' gift?
I should fear those that dance before me now
Would one day stamp upon me. 'T has been done.
Men shut their doors against a setting sun.
                    The Lords rise from table, with much adoring of
                    Timon, and to show their loves, each single out an

Amazon, and all dance, men with women, a lofty
strain or two to the hautboys, and cease.
TIMON
You have done our pleasures much grace, fair ladies,
Set a fair fashion on our entertainment,
Which was not half so beautiful and kind;   141
You have added worth unto't and lustre,
And entertained me with mine own device.   143
I am to thank you for't.   144
1. LADY
My lord, you take us even at the best.   145
APEMANTUS Faith, for the worst is filthy, and would not
hold taking, I doubt me.   147
TIMON
Ladies, there is an idle banquet attends you;
Please you to dispose yourselves.   149
ALL LADIES
Most thankfully, my lord.   Exeunt [Cupid and Ladies].
TIMON Flavius.
FLAVIUS
My lord?
TIMON   The little casket bring me hither.
FLAVIUS
Yes, my lord. [aside] More jewels yet?
There is no crossing him in's humor;   154
Else I should tell him well, i' faith I should;
When all's spent, he'd be crossed then, an he could. 156
'Tis pity bounty had not eyes behind,
That man might ne'er be wretched for his mind. Exit. 158
1. LORD
Where be our men?
SERVANT
Here, my lord, in readiness.
2. LORD
Our horses!
                    Enter Flavius [with the casket].
TIMON   O my friends, I have one word
To say to you. Look you, my good lord,
I must entreat you honor me so much
As to advance this jewel; accept and wear it,   164
Kind my lord.
1. LORD
I am so far already in your gifts –
ALL
So are we all.
                    Enter a Servant.
SERVANT
My lord, there are certain nobles of the senate
Newly alighted and come to visit you.
TIMON
They are fairly welcome.   [Exit Servant.]

95 come nearer to try 99 made away destroyed, turned to tears 100 cannot . . . water are leaky 107 s.d. tucket trumpet call 113 which . . . office whose function is 118 gratulate . . . bosom greet thy generous heart 118–20 Th' ear . . . eyes i.e. though your feast has gratified all the senses, the masquers can hope to please your sense of sight only 127 Like just such 128 As . . . shows to in the same sense as this lavishness is when compared with; a little . . . root i.e. sane frugality 130 drink drink healths to 131 age old age 135 Of . . . gift given them by their friends 141 was not i.e. before you came 143 mine own device (apparently Timon has himself composed the masque) 144 am to should and do 145 take . . . best i.e. give us most generous praise 147 hold taking bear handling (in an obscene sense) 149 dispose yourselves take your places 154 humor frame of mind 156 crossed (1) freed of debt, (2) thwarted (as in l. 154) 158 for his mind because of his (generosity of) spirit 164 advance add value to (by possessing; cf. I, i, 170–71)

FLAVIUS   I beseech your honor,
171 Vouchsafe me a word; it does concern you near.
TIMON
Near? Why then, another time I'll hear thee. I prithee
Let's be provided to show them entertainment.
FLAVIUS [aside]
I scarce know how.
     Enter another Servant.
SERVANT
May it please your honor, Lord Lucius,
Out of his free love, hath presented to you
177 Four milk-white horses trapped in silver.
TIMON
I shall accept them fairly. Let the presents
179 Be worthily entertained.   *[Exit Servant.]*
     Enter a third Servant.
                How now? What news?
SERVANT Please you, my lord, that honorable gentleman,
Lord Lucullus, entreats your company to-morrow to
hunt with him and has sent your honor two brace of
greyhounds.
TIMON
I'll hunt with him; and let them be received,
Not without fair reward.   *[Exit Servant.]*
FLAVIUS [aside]   What will this come to?
He commands us to provide and give great gifts,
And all out of an empty coffer;
Nor will he know his purse, or yield me this,
To show him what a beggar his heart is,
190 Being of no power to make his wishes good.
191 His promises fly so beyond his state
That what he speaks is all in debt; he owes
For every word. He is so kind that he now
194 Pays interest for't; his land's put to their books.
Well, would I were gently put out of office
Before I were forced out!
Happier is he that has no friend to feed
198 Than such that do e'en enemies exceed.
I bleed inwardly for my lord.   *Exit.*
TIMON   You do yourselves
200 Much wrong; you bate too much of your own merits.
Here, my lord – a trifle of our love.
2. LORD
With more than common thanks I will receive it.
3. LORD
O, he's the very soul of bounty!

171 *Vouchsafe* allow   177 *trapped in silver* in silver-mounted trappings
179 *entertained* taken care of   190 *Being of* (the desires of his heart) having
191 *state* means   194 *put . . . books* mortgaged to them   198 *such . . .
exceed* such (friends) as do more harm than even his enemies   200 *bate . . . of*
reduce, undervalue   204–05 *gave good words* spoke well   207 *pardon . . .
that* i.e. don't ask me to accept such a gift as that   209 *but* anything except;
affect like   211 *call to* visit (?), ask your help in return should I need it (?)
212 *all . . . several* both your joint and separate   217 *It . . . thee* giving to you
is real charity (since you have no property of your own); *living* (1) life, (2)
property   219 *defiled* (1) having, like a battlefield, files of soldiers on it, (2)
contaminated (since 'pitch . . . doth defile'; see *1 Henry IV*, II, iv, 394–95)
222 *All to you* all the obligation is mine, to you   224 *coil* fuss   225 *Serving
of becks* bowing (and scraping)   226 *legs* (1) limbs, (2) bows   234–35 *Thou
. . . shortly* you've so long been squandering your tangible assets that I
fear you'll soon be giving away all that's left of yourself in such unreal
property as promises, mere worthless notes   241 *thy heaven* i.e. my good
counsel
II, i The house of a Senator of Athens   1 *late* recently; *five thousand* (presumably 'crowns' as in III, iv, 29; a very large sum is evidently meant)
3–4 *Still . . . Of* constantly engaged in   5 *steal but* I have only to steal

TIMON And now I remember, my lord, you gave good 204
words the other day of a bay courser I rode on. 'Tis
yours because you liked it.
3. LORD
O, I beseech you pardon me, my lord, in that! 207
TIMON
You may take my word, my lord, I know no man
Can justly praise but what he does affect. 209
I weigh my friends' affection with mine own.
I'll tell you true; I'll call to you. 211
ALL LORDS   O none so welcome!
TIMON
I take all and your several visitations 212
So kind to heart 'tis not enough to give.
Methinks I could deal kingdoms to my friends
And ne'er be weary. Alcibiades,
Thou art a soldier, therefore seldom rich.
It comes in charity to thee; for all thy living 217
Is 'mongst the dead, and all the lands thou hast
Lie in a pitched field.
ALCIBIADES   Ay, defiled land, my lord. 219
1. LORD We are so virtuously bound –
TIMON   And so
Am I to you.
2. LORD   So infinitely endeared –
TIMON
All to you. Lights, more lights! 222
1. LORD   The best of happiness,
Honor, and fortunes keep with you, Lord Timon!
TIMON
Ready for his friends.   *Exeunt Lords [and others.*
              Manent Apemantus and Timon].
APEMANTUS   What a coil's here! 224
Serving of becks and jutting-out of bums! 225
I doubt whether their legs be worth the sums 226
That are given for 'em. Friendship's full of dregs.
Methinks false hearts should never have sound legs.
Thus honest fools lay out their wealth on curtsies.
TIMON
Now, Apemantus, if thou wert not sullen,
I would be good to thee.
APEMANTUS No, I'll nothing; for if I should be bribed
too, there would be none left to rail upon thee, and then
thou wouldst sin the faster. Thou giv'st so long, Timon, 234
I fear me thou wilt give away thyself in paper shortly.
What needs these feasts, pomps, and vainglories?
TIMON Nay, an you begin to rail on society once, I am
sworn not to give regard to you. Farewell, and come
with better music.   *Exit.*
APEMANTUS So. Thou wilt not hear me now; thou shalt
not then. I'll lock thy heaven from thee. 241
O that men's ears should be
To counsel deaf but not to flattery!   *Exit.*

                     *

     Enter a Senator [with papers in his hand].   II, i
SENATOR
And late five thousand. To Varro and to Isidore 1
He owes nine thousand, besides my former sum,
Which makes it five-and-twenty. Still in motion 3
Of raging waste! It cannot hold; it will not.
If I want gold, steal but a beggar's dog 5
And give it Timon – why, the dog coins gold.

If I would sell my horse and buy twenty moe
Better than he – why, give my horse to Timon;
9 Ask nothing, give it him – it foals me straight,
10 And able horses. No porter at his gate,
But rather one that smiles and still invites
12 All that pass by. It cannot hold; no reason
Can sound his state in safety. Caphis, ho!
Caphis, I say!
    Enter Caphis.
CAPHIS   Here, sir. What is your pleasure?
SENATOR
Get on your cloak and haste you to Lord Timon.
16 Importune him for my moneys. Be not ceased
17 With slight denial, nor then silenced when
'Commend me to your master' and the cap
Plays in the right hand, thus; but tell him
My uses cry to me; I must serve my turn
Out of mine own; his days and times are past,
22 And my reliances on his fracted dates
Have smit my credit. I love and honor him,
But must not break my back to heal his finger.
Immediate are my needs, and my relief
Must not be tossed and turned to me in words
But find supply immediate. Get you gone.
Put on a most importunate aspect,
A visage of demand; for I do fear,
30 When every feather sticks in his own wing,
31 Lord Timon will be left a naked gull,
32 Which flashes now a phoenix. Get you gone.
CAPHIS
I go, sir.
SENATOR Take the bonds along with you
34 And have the dates in compt.
CAPHIS   I will, sir.
SENATOR   Go.   *Exeunt.*

                *

II, ii   *Enter [Flavius, Timon's] Steward, with many bills*
        in his hand.
STEWARD
No care, no stop; so senseless of expense
That he will neither know how to maintain it
Nor cease his flow of riot; takes no account
4 How things go from him nor resumes no care
5 Of what is to continue. Never mind
Was to be so unwise to be so kind.
What shall be done? He will not hear till feel.
8 I must be round with him, now he comes from hunting.
Fie, fie, fie, fie!
    Enter Caphis [and the Servants of] Isidore and Varro.
CAPHIS
Good even, Varro. What, you come for money?
VARRO'S SERVANT
Is't not your business too?
CAPHIS
It is; and yours too, Isidore?
ISIDORE'S SERVANT   It is so.
CAPHIS
Would we were all discharged!
13 VARRO'S SERVANT   I fear it.
CAPHIS
Here comes the lord.
    Enter Timon and his Train [with Alcibiades].

TIMON
So soon as dinner's done we'll forth again,
My Alcibiades. – With me? What is your will?
CAPHIS
My lord, here is a note of certain dues.
TIMON
Dues? Whence are you?
CAPHIS   Of Athens here, my lord.
TIMON
Go to my steward.
CAPHIS
Please it your lordship, he hath put me off
To the succession of new days this month.   21
My master is awaked by great occasion   22
To call upon his own, and humbly prays you   23
That with your other noble parts you'll suit   24
In giving him his right.
TIMON   Mine honest friend,
I prithee but repair to me next morning.
CAPHIS
Nay, good my lord –
TIMON   Contain thyself, good friend.
VARRO'S SERVANT
One Varro's servant, my good lord –
ISIDORE'S SERVANT
From Isidore; he humbly prays your speedy payment.
CAPHIS
If you did know, my lord, my master's wants –
VARRO'S SERVANT
'Twas due on forfeiture, my lord, six weeks and past.   31
ISIDORE'S SERVANT
Your steward puts me off, my lord, and I
Am sent expressly to your lordship.
TIMON
Give me breath.
I do beseech you, good my lords, keep on;   35
I'll wait upon you instantly.
        [Exeunt Alcibiades, Lords, etc.]
    [To Flavius]   Come hither. Pray you,
How goes the world that I am thus encount'red
With clamorous demands of broken bonds
And the detention of long-since-due debts,   39
Against my honor?   40
STEWARD   Please you, gentlemen,
The time is unagreeable to this business.
Your importunacy cease till after dinner,
That I may make his lordship understand
Wherefore you are not paid.
TIMON
Do so, my friends – See them well entertained.   *[Exit.]*

9 *straight* forthwith 10 *able* good, strong (as foals are not) 12–13 *no
. . . safety* no reasonable man can investigate his estate and find it financially
secure 16 *ceased* stopped 17–19 *when . . . thus* when with . . . thus (he
tries to put you off) 22 *fracted* broken 30 *every . . . wing* i.e. when all
property is in the hands of its rightful owner 31 *gull* (1) unfledged bird,
(2) dupe 32 *phoenix* i.e. uniquely glorious thing 34 *in compt* noted
down
II, ii Before Timon's house 4 *resumes* takes 5 *what . . . continue* what
will serve future needs 8 *round* blunt 13 *it* i.e. that we won't be 21 *To
. . . days* i.e. from one day to the next 22 *awaked . . . occasion* aroused by
serious need 23 *call . . . own* liquidate his assets (?), ask payment of what
he is owed (?) 24 *suit* be consistent 31 *on forfeiture* under penalty if not
paid 35–36 *keep on . . . instantly* go ahead (without me); I'll be with you
again in no time 39 *the detention* withholding payment 40 *Against my
honor* thus calling my honor into question

STEWARD

46 Pray draw near.   *Exit.*
Enter Apemantus and Fool.

CAPHIS

Stay, stay ; here comes the fool with Apemantus.
Let's ha' some sport with 'em.

VARRO'S SERVANT Hang him, he'll abuse us.

ISIDORE'S SERVANT A plague upon him, dog !

VARRO'S SERVANT How dost, fool ?

APEMANTUS Dost dialogue with thy shadow ?

VARRO'S SERVANT I speak not to thee.

APEMANTUS No, 'tis to thyself. *[to the Fool]* Come
away.

ISIDORE'S SERVANT *[to Varro's Servant]* There's the
56   fool hangs on your back already.

57 APEMANTUS No, thou stand'st single ; thou'rt not on
him yet.

CAPHIS Where's the fool now ?

59 APEMANTUS He last asked the question. Poor rogues and
usurers' men ; bawds between gold and want !

ALL SERVANTS What are we, Apemantus ?

APEMANTUS Asses.

ALL SERVANTS Why ?

APEMANTUS That you ask me what you are, and do not
know yourselves. Speak to 'em, fool.

FOOL How do you, gentlemen ?

67 ALL SERVANTS Gramercies, good fool. How does your
mistress ?

FOOL She's e'en setting on water to scald such chickens
70   as you are. Would we could see you at Corinth !

APEMANTUS Good ! Gramercy.
Enter Page.

FOOL Look you, here comes my mistress' page.

PAGE *[to the Fool]* Why, how now, captain ? What do you
in this wise company ? How dost thou, Apemantus ?

APEMANTUS Would I had a rod in my mouth, that I
might answer thee profitably.

77 PAGE Prithee, Apemantus, read me the superscription of
these letters ; I know not which is which.

APEMANTUS Canst not read ?

PAGE No.

APEMANTUS There will little learning die then that day
thou art hanged. This is to Lord Timon, this to
Alcibiades. Go ; thou wast born a bastard and thou'lt
die a bawd.

PAGE Thou wast whelped a dog and thou shalt famish a
dog's death. Answer not ; I am gone.   *Exit.*

86 APEMANTUS E'en so thou outrun'st grace. Fool, I will go
with you to Lord Timon's.

FOOL Will you leave me there ?

APEMANTUS If Timon stay at home – You three serve 89
three usurers ?

ALL SERVANTS Ay. Would they served us !

APEMANTUS So would I – as good a trick as ever hangman served thief.

FOOL Are you three usurers' men ?

ALL SERVANTS Ay, fool.

FOOL I think no usurer but has a fool to his servant. My
mistress is one, and I am her fool. When men come to
borrow of your masters, they approach sadly and go
away merry ; but they enter my mistress' house merrily
and go away sadly. The reason of this ?

VARRO'S SERVANT I could render one.   101

APEMANTUS Do it then, that we may account thee a
whoremaster and a knave ; which notwithstanding,
thou shalt be no less esteemed.

VARRO'S SERVANT What is a whoremaster, fool ?

FOOL A fool in good clothes, and something like thee. 'Tis
a spirit ; sometime 't appears like a lord, sometime like a
lawyer, sometime like a philosopher, with two stones 108
moe than 's artificial one. He is very often like a knight ; 109
and, generally, in all shapes that man goes up and down
in, from fourscore to thirteen, this spirit walks in.

VARRO'S SERVANT Thou art not altogether a fool.

FOOL Nor thou altogether a wise man. As much foolery
as I have, so much wit thou lack'st.

APEMANTUS That answer might have become Apemantus.

ALL SERVANTS Aside, aside ; here comes Lord Timon.
Enter Timon and [Flavius, his] Steward.

APEMANTUS Come with me, fool, come.

FOOL I do not always follow lover, elder brother, and 118
woman ; sometime the philosopher.
        [Exeunt Apemantus and Fool.]

STEWARD

Pray you walk near ; I'll speak with you anon.
       Exeunt [Servants].

TIMON

You make me marvel wherefore ere this time
Had you not fully laid my state before me,   122
That I might so have rated my expense   123
As I had leave of means.

STEWARD   You would not hear me ;
At many leisures I proposed –

TIMON   Go to !
Perchance some single vantages you took,   126
When my indisposition put you back,
And that unaptness made your minister   128
Thus to excuse yourself.

STEWARD   O my good lord,
At many times I brought in my accounts,
Laid them before you. You would throw them off
And say you found them in mine honesty.   132
When for some trifling present you have bid me
Return so much, I have shook my head and wept ;
Yea, 'gainst th' authority of manners prayed you
To hold your hand more close. I did endure
Not seldom, nor no slight checks, when I have   137
Prompted you in the ebb of your estate   138
And your great flow of debts. My lovèd lord,
Though you hear now too late, yet now's a time :   140
The greatest of your having lacks a half   141
To pay your present debts.

---

46 *draw near* come this way   56 *hangs . . . back* i.e. equated with you
57–58 *thou'rt . . . yet* you haven't yet been identified with *him* (Isidore's
servant)   59–60 *Poor . . . want* (perhaps misplaced, as this characterization
seems to belong after *yourselves* in l. 65)   67 *Gramercies* many thanks   70
Corinth (where the brothels were)   77 *superscription* address   86 *grace* i.e.
the blessing of being chastised by me   89 *If . . . home* i.e. as long as Timon
is there, a fool will be present   101 *one* (for instance that they are now
poorer – and probably diseased as well)   108 *stones* testicles   109 *artificial
one* i.e. the philosophers' stone   118–19 *lover . . . woman* i.e. people likely,
for one reason or another, to prove generous   122 *state* financial position
123–24 *rated . . . means* adjusted my expenditures to my actual wealth
126 *vantages* opportunities   128–29 *And . . . excuse yourself* and made that
indisposition serve you as an excuse thereafter   132 *found . . . honesty* had
all the information you wanted in knowing me to be honest   137 *seldom*
infrequent (an adjective, modifying *checks*)   138 *in* about   140 *now's a
time* i.e. better late than never   141–42 *The greatest . . . debts* what you own
won't, at best, pay half what you owe

TIMON   Let all my land be sold.

STEWARD

143 'Tis all engaged, some forfeited and gone ;
And what remains will hardly stop the mouth
145 Of present dues. The future comes apace ;
146 What shall defend the interim ? and at length
How goes our reck'ning ?

TIMON

148 To Lacedaemon did my land extend.

STEWARD

O my good lord, the world is but a word ;
Were it all yours to give it in a breath,
How quickly were it gone !

TIMON   You tell me true.

STEWARD

152 If you suspect my husbandry of falsehood,
Call me before th' exactest auditors
154 And set me on the proof. So the gods bless me,
155 When all our offices have been oppressed
With riotous feeders, when our vaults have wept
157 With drunken spilth of wine, when every room
Hath blazed with lights and brayed with minstrelsy,
159 I have retired me to a wasteful cock
160 And set mine eyes at flow.

TIMON   Prithee no more.

STEWARD

Heavens, have I said, the bounty of this lord !
162 How many prodigal bits have slaves and peasants
163 This night englutted ! Who is not Timon's ?
What heart, head, sword, force, means, but is Lord
     Timon's ?
Great Timon ; noble, worthy, royal Timon !
Ah, when the means are gone that buy this praise,
The breath is gone whereof this praise is made.
Feast-won, fast-lost : one cloud of winter show'rs,
169 These flies are couched.

TIMON   Come, sermon me no further.
No villainous bounty yet hath passed my heart ;
Unwisely, not ignobly, have I given.
172 Why, dost thou weep ? Canst thou the conscience lack
173 To think I shall lack friends ? Secure thy heart ;
If I would broach the vessels of my love
175 And try the argument of hearts by borrowing,
Men and men's fortunes could I frankly use
As I can bid thee speak.

177 STEWARD   Assurance bless your thoughts !

TIMON

And in some sort these wants of mine are crowned,
179 That I account them blessings ; for by these
Shall I try friends. You shall perceive how you
Mistake my fortunes ; I am wealthy in my friends.
Within there ! Flaminius ! Servilius !

     Enter three Servants [Flaminius, Servilius, and
     another].

SERVANTS My lord ? My lord ?

TIMON I will dispatch you severally – *[to Servilius]* you to
Lord Lucius ; *[to Flaminius]* to Lord Lucullus you ; I
hunted with his honor to-day ; *[to the other]* you to
Sempronius. Commend me to their loves ; and I am
proud, say, that my occasions have found time to use 'em
189 toward a supply of money. Let the request be fifty
talents.

FLAMINIUS As you have said, my lord. *[Exeunt Servants.]*

STEWARD *[aside]* Lord Lucius and Lucullus ? Humh.

TIMON

Go you, sir, to the senators,
Of whom, even to the state's best health, I have   193
Deserved this hearing. Bid 'em send o' th' instant
A thousand talents to me.   195

STEWARD   I have been bold,
For that I knew it the most general way,
To them to use your signet and your name ;
But they do shake their heads, and I am here
No richer in return.

TIMON   Is't true ? Can't be ?

STEWARD

They answer in a joint and corporate voice
That now they are at fall, want treasure, cannot   201
Do what they would, are sorry : you are honorable,
But yet they could have wished – they know not –
Something hath been amiss – a noble nature
May catch a wrench – would all were well – 'tis pity –   205
And so, intending other serious matters,   206
After distasteful looks and these hard fractions,   207
With certain half-caps and cold-moving nods   208
They froze me into silence.

TIMON   You gods, reward them !
Prithee, man, look cheerily. These old fellows
Have their ingratitude in them hereditary.
Their blood is caked, 'tis cold, it seldom flows ;
'Tis lack of kindly warmth they are not kind ;   213
And nature, as it grows again toward earth,   214
Is fashioned for the journey, dull and heavy.
Go to Ventidius. Prithee be not sad ;
Thou art true and honest ; ingeniously I speak,   217
No blame belongs to thee. Ventidius lately
Buried his father, by whose death he's stepped
Into a great estate. When he was poor,
Imprisoned, and in scarcity of friends,
I cleared him with five talents. Greet him from me.
Bid him suppose some good necessity   223
Touches his friend, which craves to be rememb'red   224
With those five talents. That had, give't these fellows
To whom 'tis instant due. Ne'er speak or think
That Timon's fortunes 'mong his friends can sink.

STEWARD

I would I could not think it.
That thought is bounty's foe ;   229
Being free itself, it thinks all others so.   *Exeunt.* 230

*

143 *engaged* mortgaged 145 *present dues* immediate obligations 146–47
What . . . reck'ning what shall we meanwhile use to ward off disaster, and
what will our eventual fate be 148 *Lacedaemon* Sparta 152 *husbandry*
household management 154 *set me on* put me to 155 *offices* kitchens,
pantries, etc. 157 *spilth* spilling 159 *wasteful cock* leaky tap (of a wine
barrel) 160 *set . . . flow* wept 162 *prodigal bits* lavish morsels 163 *englutted* swallowed; *is not* does not profess to be 169 *couched* gone into
hiding 172 *conscience* judgment 173 *Secure* set at ease 175 *try the
argument* test the protestations 177 *Assurance . . . thoughts* may it prove so
179 *That* so that 189–90, 195 *fifty . . . A thousand talents* (large sums
indeed: see I, i, 95n.) 193 *even . . . health* the very soundness of the state's
treasury being due to me 201 *fall* low ebb; *want treasure* lack funds 205
catch a wrench suffer a reverse 206 *intending* giving their attention to 207
hard fractions callous fragments of sentences 208 *half-caps* grudging
salutations 213 *lack* i.e. from lack; *kindly* (1) natural, (2) generous 214
grows . . . earth nears the grave 217 *ingeniously* sincerely 223 *good*
genuine 224–25 *craves . . . talents* i.e. asks that Ventidius recall the gift
which restored his freedom – and reciprocate 229–30 *That thought . . . so*
(obscure, metrically odd ; perhaps corrupt) 230 *free* liberal

III, i *Flaminius waiting to speak with a Lord, [Lucullus,] from his Master ; enters a Servant to him.*

SERVANT I have told my lord of you ; he is coming down to you.

FLAMINIUS I thank you, sir.

Enter Lucullus.

SERVANT Here's my lord.

6 LUCULLUS *[aside]* One of Lord Timon's men? A gift, I warrant. Why, this hits right ; I dreamt of a silver basin
8 and ewer to-night. – Flaminius, honest Flaminius, you are very respectively welcome, sir. Fill me some wine. *[Exit Servant.]* And how does that honorable, complete, freehearted gentleman of Athens, thy very bountiful good lord and master ?

FLAMINIUS His health is well, sir.

LUCULLUS I am right glad that his health is well, sir. And what hast thou there under thy cloak, pretty Flaminius ?

FLAMINIUS Faith, nothing but an empty box, sir, which in my lord's behalf I come to entreat your honor to
17 supply ; who, having great and instant occasion to use fifty talents, hath sent to your lordship to furnish him, nothing doubting your present assistance therein.

LUCULLUS La, la, la, la ! 'Nothing doubting,' says he ? Alas, good lord ! a noble gentleman 'tis, if he would not
22 keep so good a house. Many a time and often I ha' dined with him and told him on't, and come again to supper to him of purpose to have him spend less ; and yet he would embrace no counsel, take no warning by my
26 coming. Every man has his fault, and honesty is his. I ha' told him on't, but I could ne'er get him from't.

Enter Servant with wine.

SERVANT Please your lordship, here is the wine.

LUCULLUS Flaminius, I have noted thee always wise.
30 Here's to thee.

31 FLAMINIUS Your lordship speaks your pleasure.

32 LUCULLUS I have observed thee always for a towardly prompt spirit, give thee thy due, and one that knows what belongs to reason, and canst use the time well if the time use thee well. Good parts in thee ! *[to Servant]* Get you gone, sirrah. *[Exit Servant.]* Draw nearer, honest Flaminius. Thy lord 's a bountiful gentleman ; but thou art wise, and thou know'st well enough, although thou com'st to me, that this is no time to lend money, especially upon bare friendship without security. Here's
41 three solidares for thee. Good boy, wink at me and say thou saw'st me not. Fare thee well.

FLAMINIUS
Is't possible the world should so much differ, 43
And we alive that lived ? Fly, damnèd baseness,
To him that worships thee !
[Throws the money back.]

LUCULLUS Ha ! Now I see thou art a fool, and fit for thy master. *Exit Lucullus.*

FLAMINIUS
May these add to the number that may scald thee !
Let molten coin be thy damnation, 49
Thou disease of a friend, and not himself !
Has friendship such a faint and milky heart
It turns in less than two nights ? O you gods,
I feel my master's passion. This slave unto his honor 53
Has my lord's meat in him.
Why should it thrive and turn to nutriment
When he is turned to poison ?
O may diseases only work upon't ;
And when he's sick to death, let not that part of nature 58
Which my lord paid for be of any power
To expel sickness, but prolong his hour ! *Exit.* 60

*

Enter Lucius with three Strangers. III, ii

LUCIUS Who? the Lord Timon? He is my very good friend and an honorable gentleman.

1. STRANGER We know him for no less, though we are but strangers to him. But I can tell you one thing, my lord, and which I hear from common rumors : now Lord Timon's happy hours are done and past, and his estate shrinks from him.

LUCIUS Fie, no, do not believe it ; he cannot want for money.

2. STRANGER But believe you this, my lord, that not long ago one of his men was with the Lord Lucullus to borrow so many talents ; nay, urged extremely for't, 12 and showed what necessity belonged to't, and yet was denied.

LUCIUS How ?

2. STRANGER I tell you denied, my lord.

LUCIUS What a strange case was that ! Now before the gods, I am ashamed on't. Denied that honorable man ? There was very little honor showed in't. For my own part, I must needs confess, I have received some small kindnesses from him, as money, plate, jewels, and suchlike trifles – nothing comparing to his ; yet had he mis- 21
took him and sent to me, I should ne'er have denied his 22
occasion so many talents. 23

Enter Servilius.

SERVILIUS See, by good hap, yonder's my lord. I have sweat to see his honor. – My honored lord !

LUCIUS Servilius ? You are kindly met, sir. Fare thee well ; commend me to thy honorable virtuous lord, my very exquisite friend.

SERVILIUS May it please your honor, my lord hath sent –

LUCIUS Ha ! What has he sent ? I am so much endeared to that lord ! He's ever sending. How shall I thank him, think'st thou ? And what has he sent now ?

SERVILIUS Has only sent his present occasion now, my 33
lord, requesting your lordship to supply his instant use with so many talents. 35

LUCIUS
I know his lordship is but merry with me ;
He cannot want fifty – five hundred – talents. 37

III, i The house of Lucullus 6 *hits right* is just as it should be 8 *respectively* particularly 17 *supply* fill 22 *keep . . . house* be so hospitable 26 *honesty* generosity 30 *Here's to thee* (drinking the wine originally meant for Flaminius) 31 *speaks your pleasure* is pleased to say so 32–33 *towardly prompt* friendly and well-disposed 41 *solidares* (of Shakespeare's invention but evidently for coins of no great worth) 43–44 *Is't . . . lived* can we possibly have lived long enough to see the world so much changed 49 *Let . . . damnation* i.e. may you be sent to hell by having melted gold poured down your throat 53 *passion* anger (?), suffering (?) (with religious overtones, as in *my lord's meat* in the next line) ; *slave . . . honor* (a better characterization of Sempronius : see III, iii, 26. Many editors follow Pope in emending 'unto his honor' to 'unto this hour' as more suitable to both sense and metre.) 58 *of nature* i.e. of his body 60 *hour* time of suffering

III, ii A public place in Athens 12, 23, 35 *so many* (probably expressions which the author intended to change later to specific numbers : see Introduction) 21–22 *mistook . . . me* made the mistake of sending to me, a man who owed him less 22–23 *denied his occasion* refused him in his need 33 *Has* he has ; *his present occasion* word of his urgent need 37 *fifty – five hundred* (indicating the author's uncertainty as to which number he should use ; see Introduction)

SERVILIUS
But in the mean time he wants less, my lord.
If his occasion were not virtuous,
I should not urge it half so faithfully.

LUCIUS
Dost thou speak seriously, Servilius?

SERVILIUS
Upon my soul, 'tis true, sir.

LUCIUS What a wicked beast was I to disfurnish myself
44   against such a good time, when I might ha' shown
myself honorable! How unluckily it happ'ned that I
46   should purchase the day before for a little part and undo
a great deal of honor! Servilius, now before the gods, I
am not able to do – the more beast, I say – I was sending
49   to use Lord Timon myself, these gentlemen can witness;
but I would not for the wealth of Athens I had done't
now. Commend me bountifully to his good lordship;
and I hope his honor will conceive the fairest of me,
because I have no power to be kind. And tell him this
from me: I count it one of my greatest afflictions, say,
that I cannot pleasure such an honorable gentleman.
Good Servilius, will you befriend me so far as to use
mine own words to him?

SERVILIUS Yes, sir, I shall.

LUCIUS
59   I'll look you out a good turn, Servilius.   *Exit Servilius.*
True, as you said, Timon is shrunk indeed;
61   And he that's once denied will hardly speed.   *Exit.*

1. STRANGER
Do you observe this, Hostilius?

2. STRANGER   Ay, too well.

1. STRANGER
63   Why, this is the world's soul, and just of the same piece
Is every flatterer's spirit. Who can call him
His friend that dips in the same dish? For in
66   My knowing Timon has been this lord's father
67   And kept his credit with his purse,
Supported his estate. Nay, Timon's money
Has paid his men their wages. He ne'er drinks
But Timon's silver treads upon his lip;
And yet – O, see the monstrousness of man
72   When he looks out in an ungrateful shape! –
73   He does deny him, in respect of his,
What charitable men afford to beggars.

3. STRANGER
Religion groans at it.

1. STRANGER   For mine own part,
76   I never tasted Timon in my life,
Nor came any of his bounties over me
To mark me for his friend; yet I protest,
For his right noble mind, illustrious virtue,
80   And honorable carriage,
Had his necessity made use of me,
82   I would have put my wealth into donation
And the best half should have returned to him,
So much I love his heart. But I perceive
Men must learn now with pity to dispense;
For policy sits above conscience.   *Exeunt.*

Enter a third Servant [of Timon's] with Sempronius,   **III, iii**
another of Timon's Friends.

SEMPRONIUS
Must he needs trouble me in't – hum! – 'bove all others?
He might have tried Lord Lucius or Lucullus;
And now Ventidius is wealthy too,
Whom he redeemed from prison. All these
Owes their estates unto him.

SERVANT   My lord,
They have all been touched and found base metal,   6
For they have all denied him.

SEMPRONIUS   How? Have they denied him?   7
Has Ventidius and Lucullus denied him,
And does he send to me? Three? Humh!   9
It shows but little love or judgment in him.
Must I be his last refuge? His friends, like physicians,
Thrice give him over. Must I take th' cure upon me?
Has much disgraced me in't; I'm angry at him,   13
That might have known my place. I see no sense for't
But his occasions might have wooed me first;
For, in my conscience, I was the first man   16
That e'er received gift from him;
And does he think so backwardly of me now
That I'll requite it last? No.
So it may prove an argument of laughter   20
To th' rest, and I 'mongst lords be thought a fool.
I'd rather than the worth of thrice the sum
Had sent to me first, but for my mind's sake;   23
I'd such a courage to do him good. But now return,   24
And with their harsh reply this answer join:
Who bates mine honor shall not know my coin.   *Exit.*   26

SERVANT Excellent! Your lordship 's a goodly villain.
The devil knew not what he did when he made man
politic. He crossed himself by't; and I cannot think but   29
in the end the villainies of man will set him clear. How   30
fairly this lord strives to appear foul! takes virtuous
copies to be wicked, like those that under hot ardent
zeal would set whole realms on fire. Of such a nature is
his politic love.
This was my lord's best hope; now all are fled
Save only the gods. Now his friends are dead.
Doors that were ne'er acquainted with their wards   37
Many a bounteous year must be employed
Now to guard sure their master.   39
And this is all a liberal course allows:
Who cannot keep his wealth must keep his house. *Exit.*   41

*

44 *against . . . time* for dealing with such an opportunity   46–47 *for . . . honor* (probably somewhat corrupt, but Lucius is evidently saying that only his present lack of funds keeps him from treating Timon handsomely)   49 *use* i.e. borrow from   59 *look you out* find a way to do you   61 *speed* prosper   63 *world's soul* essence of this corrupt world   66 *father* sponsor, protector   67 *his . . . his* Lucius' . . . Timon's   72 *looks out in* shows himself as   73–74 *in respect . . . afford* considering his wealth, even the pittance good men give   76 *tasted Timon* i.e. sampled his liberality   80 *carriage* conduct   82 *put . . . donation* treated my wealth as a gift from Timon

III, iii The house of Sempronius   6 *touched* tested (as with a touchstone)   7 *denied* refused   9 *Three* (Lucius as well as Ventidius and Lucullus)   13 *Has* he has   16 *in my conscience* to my knowledge   20 *argument of* subject for   23 *Had* he had   24 *courage* inclination   26 *bates* detracts from   29 *crossed* thwarted (since man thus becomes his superior in evil)   30 *set him clear* make the devil look innocent   37 *wards* locks   39 *guard sure* (lest he be arrested for debt)   41 *keep . . . keep* preserve . . . stay inside

III, iv   *Enter [two of] Varro's Men, meeting [Lucius'*
   Servant and] others, all [being servants of] Timon's
   creditors, to wait for his coming out. Then enter Titus
   and Hortensius.

1. VARRO'S MAN
   Well met ; good morrow, Titus and Hortensius.

TITUS
   The like to you, kind Varro.

HORTENSIUS   Lucius !
   What, do we meet together ?

LUCIUS' SERVANT   Ay, and I think
   One business does command us all, for mine
   Is money.

TITUS
   So is theirs and ours.
   Enter Philotus.

LUCIUS' SERVANT   And Sir Philotus too !

PHILOTUS
7   Good day at once.

LUCIUS' SERVANT   Welcome, good brother.
   What do you think the hour ?

8 PHILOTUS   Laboring for nine.

LUCIUS' SERVANT
   So much ?

PHILOTUS   Is not my lord seen yet ?

LUCIUS' SERVANT   Not yet.

PHILOTUS
   I wonder on't ; he was wont to shine at seven.

LUCIUS' SERVANT
11   Ay, but the days are waxèd shorter with him.
   You must consider that a prodigal course
   Is like the sun's,
14   But not, like his, recoverable. I fear
   'Tis deepest winter in Lord Timon's purse ;
16   That is, one may reach deep enough and yet
   Find little.

PHILOTUS   I am of your fear for that.

TITUS
   I'll show you how t' observe a strange event.
   Your lord sends now for money.

HORTENSIUS   Most true, he does.

TITUS
   And he wears jewels now of Timon's gift,
21   For which I wait for money.

HORTENSIUS
   It is against my heart.

LUCIUS' SERVANT   Mark how strange it shows :
   Timon in this should pay more than he owes,
24   And e'en as if your lord should wear rich jewels
   And send for money for 'em.

HORTENSIUS
   I'm weary of this charge, the gods can witness ;

I know my lord hath spent of Timon's wealth,
And now ingratitude makes it worse than stealth.   28

1. VARRO'S MAN
   Yes, mine's three thousand crowns ; what's yours ?

LUCIUS' SERVANT
   Five thousand mine.

1. VARRO'S MAN
   'Tis much deep ; and it should seem by th' sum   31
   Your master's confidence was above mine,   32
   Else surely his had equalled.   33
   Enter Flaminius.

TITUS One of Lord Timon's men.

LUCIUS' SERVANT Flaminius ? Sir, a word. Pray, is my
   lord ready to come forth ?

FLAMINIUS No, indeed he is not.

TITUS We attend his lordship ; pray signify so much.

FLAMINIUS I need not tell him that ; he knows you are
   too diligent.   *[Exit.]*
   Enter [Timon's] Steward, [Flavius,] in a cloak,
   muffled.

LUCIUS' SERVANT
   Ha, is not that his steward muffled so ?
   He goes away in a cloud. Call him, call him !   42

TITUS Do you hear, sir ?

2. VARRO'S MAN By your leave, sir —

STEWARD
   What do ye ask of me, my friend ?

TITUS
   We wait for certain money here, sir.

STEWARD   Ay,
   If money were as certain as your waiting,
   'Twere sure enough.
   Why then preferred you not your sums and bills   49
   When your false masters ate of my lord's meat ?
   Then they could smile, and fawn upon his debts,
   And take down th' int'rest into their glutt'nous maws.   52
   You do yourselves but wrong to stir me up ;
   Let me pass quietly.
   Believe't, my lord and I have made an end ;
   I have no more to reckon, he to spend.

LUCIUS' SERVANT
   Ay, but this answer will not serve.

STEWARD
   If 'twill not serve, 'tis not so base as you,
   For you serve knaves.   *[Exit.]*

1. VARRO'S MAN How ? What does his cashiered wor- 60
   ship mutter ?

2. VARRO'S MAN No matter what ; he's poor, and that's
   revenge enough. Who can speak broader than he that 63
   has no house to put his head in ? Such may rail against
   great buildings.
   Enter Servilius.

TITUS O, here's Servilius ; now we shall know some
   answer.

SERVILIUS If I might beseech you, gentlemen, to repair 67
   some other hour, I should derive much from't. For
   take't of my soul, my lord leans wondrously to discontent. His comfortable temper has forsook him ; he's
   much out of health and keeps his chamber.

LUCIUS' SERVANT
   Many do keep their chambers are not sick ;   72
   And if it be so far beyond his health,   73
   Methinks he should the sooner pay his debts
   And make a clear way to the gods.   75

III, iv **The house of Timon**   7 *at once* to all of you   8 *Laboring for* slowly
approaching   11 *waxèd* become (not here, as often, 'grown larger')   14
recoverable retraceable (with quibble on idea of financial recovery)   16
reach deep enough (as do animals digging deep in the snow for food)   21
For . . . money for buying which Timon borrowed the money I now seek
from him   24–25 *wear . . . 'em* not only wear the rich jewels given him but
also ask for the money that bought them   28 *stealth* theft   31 *much very*
32 *above mine* greater than my master's   33 *his* my master's loan   42 *in a
cloud* (1) disguised, (2) gloomily   49 *preferred* presented   52 *th' int'rest*
i.e. the food Timon provided was one kind of interest they got on their
loans   60 *cashiered* dismissed   63 *broader* more freely (with quibble on
idea of being abroad)   67 *repair* come back   72 *are* who are   73 *it be . . .
health* his state is so unhealthy   75 *And . . . gods* i.e. and so prepare himself
for death

SERVILIUS   Good gods!

TITUS
We cannot take this for answer, sir.

FLAMINIUS *(within)*
Servilius, help! My lord, my lord!
    Enter Timon, in a rage.

TIMON
What, are my doors opposed against my passage?

79 Have I been ever free, and must my house
Be my retentive enemy, my jail?
The place which I have feasted, does it now,
Like all mankind, show me an iron heart?

LUCIUS' SERVANT Put in now, Titus.

TITUS My lord, here is my bill.

LUCIUS' SERVANT Here's mine.

HORTENSIUS And mine, my lord.

BOTH VARRO'S MEN And ours, my lord.

PHILOTUS All our bills.

TIMON

89 Knock me down with 'em; cleave me to the girdle!

LUCIUS' SERVANT Alas, my lord—

TIMON Cut my heart in sums!

TITUS Mine, fifty talents.

93 TIMON Tell out my blood!

LUCIUS' SERVANT Five thousand crowns, my lord.

TIMON Five thousand drops pays that. What yours? and
yours?

1. VARRO'S MAN My lord—

2. VARRO'S MAN My lord—

TIMON Tear me, take me, and the gods fall upon you!
                        Exit.

99 HORTENSIUS Faith, I perceive our masters may throw
their caps at their money. These debts may well be
called desperate ones, for a madman owes 'em. *Exeunt.*
    Enter Timon [and Flavius, his Steward].

TIMON They have e'en put my breath from me, the
slaves! Creditors? Devils!

STEWARD My dear lord—

105 TIMON What if it should be so?

STEWARD My lord—

TIMON I'll have it so. My steward!

STEWARD Here, my lord.

TIMON

109 So fitly? Go, bid all my friends again,
Lucius, Lucullus, and Sempronius—all.
I'll once more feast the rascals.

STEWARD   O my lord,
You only speak from your distracted soul;

113 There is not so much left to furnish out
A moderate table.

TIMON   Be it not in thy care. Go,
I charge thee, invite them all; let in the tide
Of knaves once more; my cook and I'll provide. *Exeunt.*

            *

III, v   *Enter three Senators at one door, Alcibiades meeting*
         them, with Attendants.

1. SENATOR

1 My lord, you have my voice to't; the fault's
Bloody; 'tis necessary he should die.
Nothing emboldens sin so much as mercy.

2. SENATOR
Most true. The law shall bruise him.

ALCIBIADES
Honor, health, and compassion to the senate!

1. SENATOR
Now, Captain?

ALCIBIADES
I am an humble suitor to your virtues;
For pity is the virtue of the law,   8
And none but tyrants use it cruelly.
It pleases time and fortune to lie heavy
Upon a friend of mine, who in hot blood
Hath stepped into the law, which is past depth   12
To those that without heed do plunge into't.
He is a man, setting this fault aside,
Of comely virtues;
Nor did he soil the fact with cowardice   16
(An honor in him which buys out his fault)
But with a noble fury and fair spirit,
Seeing his reputation touched to death,   19
He did oppose his foe;
And with such sober and unnoted passion   21
He did behave his anger, ere 'twas spent,   22
As if he had but proved an argument.

1. SENATOR
You undergo too strict a paradox,   24
Striving to make an ugly deed look fair.
Your words have took such pains as if they labored
To bring manslaughter into form and set   27
Quarrelling upon the head of valor; which indeed   28
Is valor misbegot, and came into the world
When sects and factions were newly born.
He's truly valiant that can wisely suffer
The worst that man can breathe, and make his wrongs
His outsides, to wear them like his raiment, carelessly,   33
And ne'er prefer his injuries to his heart,   34
To bring it into danger.
If wrongs be evils, and enforce us kill,   36
What folly 'tis to hazard life for ill!

ALCIBIADES
My lord—

1. SENATOR You cannot make gross sins look clear.   38
To revenge is no valor, but to bear.   39

ALCIBIADES
My lords, then, under favor, pardon me
If I speak like a captain.
Why do fond men expose themselves to battle   42
And not endure all threats? sleep upon't,   43
And let the foes quietly cut their throats
Without repugnancy? If there be   45
Such valor in the bearing, what make we

79 *free* (1) at liberty, (2) generous   89 *Knock . . . girdle* (since *bills* also meant weapons which could split a man to his belt)   93 *Tell out* count out drops of 99-100 *throw . . . at* give up hoping for   105 *What . . . so* I wonder if it would work (Timon has just thought of giving his mock banquet: see ll. 109-11; also III, vi)   109 *fitly* opportunely   113 *to* as to

III, v The senate house   1 *my voice to't* my vote for it (the death sentence we are considering)   8 *virtue* chief merit   12 *stepped into* i.e. to some extent violated; *past depth* overwhelming   16 *soil the fact* blemish his deed 19 *touched to death* fatally threatened   21 *sober and unnoted* serious and unmarked by excess   22 *behave* govern   24 *undergo . . . paradox* are trying to maintain too highly strained an argument   27-28 *set . . . head* make duelling the highest manifestation   28 *which* i.e. *Quarrelling*, fighting duels 33 *His outsides* mere externals, nothing vital to him   34 *prefer* present 36-37 *If . . . ill* (some senators are less lucid than sententious)   38 *clear* innocent   39 *bear* put up with wrongs   42 *fond* foolish   43 *sleep* why do they not sleep   45 *repugnancy* resistance

Abroad? Why then, women are more valiant
48 That stay at home, if bearing carry it;
And the ass more captain than the lion; the felon
Loaden with irons wiser than the judge,
If wisdom be in suffering. O my lords,
As you are great, be pitifully good.
Who cannot condemn rashness in cold blood?
54 To kill, I grant, is sin's extremest gust;
55 But in defense, by mercy, 'tis most just.
To be in anger is impiety;
57 But who is man that is not angry?
Weigh but the crime with this.

2. SENATOR
You breathe in vain.

ALCIBIADES   In vain? His service done
At Lacedaemon and Byzantium
Were a sufficient briber for his life.

1. SENATOR
What's that?

ALCIBIADES
Why, I say, my lords, he's done fair service
And slain in fight many of your enemies.
How full of valor did he bear himself
In the last conflict, and made plenteous wounds!

2. SENATOR
He has made too much plenty with 'em.
68 He's a sworn rioter; he has a sin that often
Drowns him and takes his valor prisoner.
70 If there were no more foes, that were enough
To overcome him. In that beastly fury
He has been known to commit outrages
73 And cherish factions. 'Tis inferred to us
His days are foul and his drink dangerous.

1. SENATOR
He dies.

ALCIBIADES Hard fate! He might have died in war.
76 My lords, if not for any parts in him—
77 Though his right arm might purchase his own time,
And be in debt to none — yet, more to move you,
Take my deserts to his and join 'em both;
And, for I know your reverend ages love
81 Security, I'll pawn my victories, all
My honor to you, upon his good returns.
If by this crime he owes the law his life,
84 Why, let the war receive't in valiant gore;
For law is strict, and war is nothing more.

1. SENATOR
We are for law. He dies. Urge it no more,
87 On height of our displeasure. Friend or brother,

He forfeits his own blood that spills another. 88

ALCIBIADES
Must it be so? It must not be. My lords,
I do beseech you know me.

2. SENATOR   How?

ALCIBIADES
Call me to your remembrances.

3. SENATOR   What!

ALCIBIADES
I cannot think but your age has forgot me;
It could not else be I should prove so base,
To sue and be denied such common grace. 94
My wounds ache at you.

1. SENATOR   Do you dare our anger?
'Tis in few words but spacious in effect:
We banish thee for ever.

ALCIBIADES   Banish me?
Banish your dotage, banish usury,
That makes the senate ugly!

1. SENATOR
If after two days' shine Athens contain thee,
Attend our weightier judgment. And, not to swell our 101
    spirit,
He shall be executed presently.   *Exeunt [Senators].* 102

ALCIBIADES
Now the gods keep you old enough that you may live 103
Only in bone, that none may look on you!
I'm worse than mad: I have kept back their foes
While they have told their money and let out 106
Their coin upon large interest, I myself
Rich only in large hurts. All those for this?
Is this the balsam that the usuring senate
Pours into captains' wounds? Banishment!
It comes not ill; I hate not to be banished;
It is a cause worthy my spleen and fury,
That I may strike at Athens. I'll cheer up
My discontented troops and lay for hearts. 114
'Tis honor with most lands to be at odds; 115
Soldiers should brook as little wrongs as gods.   *Exit.* 116

*

[*Music. Tables set out, Servants attending.*] Enter   III, vi
divers Friends [of Timon, being Senators and Lords,]
at several doors.

1. FRIEND The good time of day to you, sir.

2. FRIEND I also wish it to you. I think this honorable
lord did but try us this other day.

1. FRIEND Upon that were my thoughts tiring when we 4
encount'red. I hope it is not so low with him as he made
it seem in the trial of his several friends.

2. FRIEND It should not be, by the persuasion of his new 7
feasting.

1. FRIEND I should think so. He hath sent me an earnest
inviting, which many my near occasions did urge me to 10
put off; but he hath conjured me beyond them, and I 11
must needs appear.

2. FRIEND In like manner was I in debt to my importu- 13
nate business, but he would not hear my excuse. I am
sorry, when he sent to borrow of me, that my provision
was out.

1. FRIEND I am sick of that grief too, as I understand
how all things go.

2. FRIEND Every man here's so. What would he have
borrowed of you?

48 *bearing* enduring (with pun on the meaning 'childbearing')   54 *gust*
indulgence   55 *by mercy* if we but take a merciful view of it   57 *not* never
68 *sworn rioter* confirmed debauchee   70 *that* i.e. the sin of drunkenness
73 *cherish factions* foster dissension; *inferred* alleged   76 *parts* good
qualities   77 *his own time* the right to a natural death when his time comes
81 *Security* (1) safety, (2) collateral (hence *pawn* and *good returns*)   84
let . . . gore i.e. let him give it in battle   87 *On height of our* on pain of our
highest   88 *another* i.e. another's blood   94 *To . . . denied* that I should
ask for and be refused   101 *Attend . . . judgment* expect our more severe
sentence; *spirit* anger   102 *presently* immediately   103–04 *live . . . bone*
be mere skeletons   106 *told* counted   114 *lay for hearts* try to win their
loyalty   115 *most lands* (meaning unclear; probably corrupt)   116 *as gods*
as do gods
III, vi The hall of Timon's house   4 *tiring* feeding (a term in falconry)
7 *persuasion* evidence   10 *my near occasions* pressing interests of mine
11 *put off* decline; *conjured . . . them* enticed me away from them   13–14
was . . . business did my own affairs make urgent demands of me

1 . FRIEND A thousand pieces.

2 . FRIEND A thousand pieces!

1 . FRIEND What of you?

2 . FRIEND He sent to me, sir – Here he comes.
Enter Timon and Attendants.

25 TIMON With all my heart, gentlemen both! And how
fare you?

1 . FRIEND Ever at the best, hearing well of your lordship.

2 . FRIEND The swallow follows not summer more willing
than we your lordship.

TIMON *[aside]* Nor more willingly leaves winter; such
summer birds are men. – Gentlemen, our dinner will
not recompense this long stay. Feast your ears with the
33 music awhile, if they will fare so harshly o' th' trumpets'
sound; we shall to't presently.

35 1 . FRIEND I hope it remains not unkindly with your
lordship that I returned you an empty messenger.

TIMON O sir, let it not trouble you.

2 . FRIEND My noble lord –

TIMON Ah, my good friend, what cheer?

2 . FRIEND My most honorable lord, I am e'en sick of
shame that when your lordship this other day sent to me
42 I was so unfortunate a beggar.

TIMON Think not on't, sir.

2 . FRIEND If you had sent two hours before –

45 TIMON Let it not cumber your better remembrance. *(The
banquet brought in.)* Come, bring in all together.

47 2 . FRIEND All covered dishes!

1 . FRIEND Royal cheer, I warrant you.

3 . FRIEND Doubt not that, if money and the season can
yield it.

1 . FRIEND How do you? What's the news?

3 . FRIEND Alcibiades is banished. Hear you of it?

BOTH Alcibiades banished?

3 . FRIEND 'Tis so, be sure of it.

1 . FRIEND How? how?

56 2 . FRIEND I pray you, upon what?

TIMON My worthy friends, will you draw near?

3 . FRIEND I'll tell you more anon. Here's a noble feast
59 toward.

2 . FRIEND This is the old man still.

61 3 . FRIEND Will't hold? Will't hold?

2 . FRIEND It does; but time will – and so –

63 3 . FRIEND I do conceive.

TIMON Each man to his stool, with that spur as he would
65 to the lip of his mistress. Your diet shall be in all places
alike; make not a City feast of it, to let the meat cool ere
we can agree upon the first place; sit, sit. The gods require our thanks.

You great benefactors, sprinkle our society with
thankfulness. For your own gifts make yourselves
71 praised; but reserve still to give, lest your deities be
despised. Lend to each man enough, that one need not
lend to another; for were your godheads to borrow of
men, men would forsake the gods. Make the meat be
beloved more than the man that gives it. Let no assembly of twenty be without a score of villains. If there sit
twelve women at the table, let a dozen of them be – as they
are. The rest of your foes, O gods – the senators of Athens,
79 together with the common lag of people – what is amiss
80 in them, you gods, make suitable for destruction. For
these my present friends, as they are to me nothing, so
in nothing bless them, and to nothing are they welcome.

Uncover, dogs, and lap.
*[The dishes are uncovered, and seen to be full of
warm water and stones.]*

SOME SPEAK
What does his lordship mean?

SOME OTHER   I know not.

TIMON
May you a better feast never behold,
You knot of mouth-friends! Smoke and lukewarm water 86
Is your perfection. This is Timon's last;   87
Who, stuck and spangled with your flatteries,
Washes it off and sprinkles in your faces
[Throws the water in their faces.]
Your reeking villainy. Live loathed and long,
Most smiling, smooth, detested parasites,
Courteous destroyers, affable wolves, meek bears,
You fools of fortune, trencher-friends, time's flies,   93
Cap-and-knee slaves, vapors, and minute-jacks!   94
Of man and beast the infinite malady   95
Crust you quite o'er! What, dost thou go?
Soft, take thy physic first; thou too, and thou!   97
Stay, I will lend thee money, borrow none.
[Throws stones and drives them out.]
What, all in motion? Henceforth be no feast
Whereat a villain's not a welcome guest.
Burn house! Sink Athens! Henceforth hated be
Of Timon man and all humanity!   *Exit.*
*Enter [the Friends –] the Senators with other Lords
[, returning].*

1 . FRIEND How now, my lords?

2 . FRIEND Know you the quality of Lord Timon's fury?

3 . FRIEND Push! Did you see my cap?   105

4 . FRIEND I have lost my gown.

1 . FRIEND He's but a mad lord and naught but humors 107
sways him. He gave me a jewel th' other day, and now
he has beat it out of my hat. Did you see my jewel?

3 . FRIEND Did you see my cap?

2 . FRIEND Here 'tis.

4 . FRIEND Here lies my gown.

1 . FRIEND Let's make no stay.

2 . FRIEND
Lord Timon's mad.

3 . FRIEND   I feel't upon my bones.

4 . FRIEND
One day he gives us diamonds, next day stones. *Exeunt.*

*

Enter Timon.   IV, i

TIMON
Let me look back upon thee. O thou wall
That girdles in those wolves, dive in the earth

25 *With . . . heart* my cordial greetings   33 *so harshly o'* on such rough
fare as   35–36 *it remains . . . messenger* you don't harbor unkind thoughts
toward me because I sent your man back without any money   42 *so . . .
beggar* so unlucky as to be out of funds   45 *cumber . . . remembrance* trouble
you   47 *covered* (implying especially good food)   56 *upon what* why
59 *toward* in prospect   61 *hold* last   63 *conceive* get your idea   65–67
Your . . . place i.e. let's be informal and not waste time arguing about
who is entitled by rank to sit where, as at an official state dinner   71
reserve still always keep something more   79 *lag* dregs   80 *For* as for
86 *Smoke* steam ('hot air')   87 *Is your perfection* suits you best   93 *time's
flies* fair-weather insects   94 *vapors* creatures without substance; *minute-
jacks* time-servers   95–96 *the infinite . . . o'er* every possible disease cover
you wholly with scabs   97 *physic* medicine   105 *Push* tush   107 *humors*
caprice
IV, i Outside the walls of Athens

And fence not Athens ! Matrons, turn incontinent !
Obedience fail in children ! Slaves and fools,
Pluck the grave wrinkled senate from the bench
6 And minister in their steads ! To general filths
Convert o' th' instant, green virginity !
Do't in your parents' eyes ! Bankrupts, hold fast ;
Rather than render back, out with your knives
And cut your trusters' throats ! Bound servants, steal :
11 Large-handed robbers your grave masters are
12 And pill by law. Maid, to thy master's bed :
Thy mistress is o' th' brothel. Son of sixteen,
14 Pluck the lined crutch from thy old limping sire ;
With it beat out his brains ! Piety and fear,
16 Religion to the gods, peace, justice, truth,
17 Domestic awe, night-rest and neighborhood,
18 Instruction, manners, mysteries and trades,
19 Degrees, observances, customs and laws,
20 Decline to your confounding contraries,
And yet confusion live ! Plagues incident to men,
Your potent and infectious fevers heap
On Athens, ripe for stroke ! Thou cold sciatica,
24 Cripple our senators, that their limbs may halt
25 As lamely as their manners ! Lust and liberty
Creep in the minds and marrows of our youth,
That 'gainst the stream of virtue they may strive
28 And drown themselves in riot ! Itches, blains,
Sow all th' Athenian bosoms, and their crop
Be general leprosy ! Breath infect breath,
That their society, as their friendship, may
32 Be merely poison ! Nothing I'll bear from thee
But nakedness, thou detestable town ;
34 Take thou that too, with multiplying bans ! ·
Timon will to the woods, where he shall find
Th' unkindest beast more kinder than mankind.
The gods confound – hear me, you good gods all –
Th' Athenians both within and out that wall ;
And grant, as Timon grows, his hate may grow
To the whole race of mankind, high and low !
Amen.   *Exit.*

*

IV, ii   *Enter [Flavius the] Steward with two or three*
               Servants.

1 . SERVANT
Hear you, Master Steward, where's our master ?
Are we undone ? cast off ? nothing remaining ?

STEWARD
Alack, my fellows, what should I say to you ?

---

6 *general filths* common whores 11 *Large-handed* i.e. sticky-fingered
12 *pill* rob 14 *lined* padded 16 *Religion to* veneration of 17 *Domestic*
awe respect for parents ; *neighborhood* neighborliness 18 *mysteries* crafts
19 *Degrees* ranks 20–21 *Decline . . . live* degenerate into chaos, and may
confusion then persist 24 *halt* limp 25 *liberty* license 28 *blains* blisters
32 *merely* pure 34 *that too* (another article of clothing) ; *bans* curses
IV, ii The house of Timon 7 *his fortune* i.e. him, in his misfortune 9
From . . . grave from the grave of a newly buried friend 13 *dedicated*
. . . air beggar who has pledged himself to the open air 15 *like contempt*
as if he were contempt itself 20 *dying* i.e. sinking 21–22 *part . . . air*
depart into this expanse of nothingness, death 23 *The latest* what remains
28 *put out all* all of you put out 35 *what state compounds* that splendor
consists of 36 *But only* nothing more than 38 *blood* nature 40 *again*
hereafter 42 *to be* only to be 46–47 *to Supply* what is needed to sustain
47 *that . . . it* i.e. money
IV, iii Before Timon's cave in a wood by the sea 2 *thy sister's* the
moon's

Let me be recorded by the righteous gods,
I am as poor as you.
1 . SERVANT   Such a house broke ?
So noble a master fall'n ; all gone, and not
One friend to take his fortune by the arm
7 And go along with him ?
2 . SERVANT   As we do turn our backs
From our companion thrown into his grave,
9 So his familiars to his buried fortunes
Slink all away ; leave their false vows with him,
Like empty purses picked ; and his poor self,
A dedicated beggar to the air,
13 With his disease of all-shunned poverty,
Walks, like contempt, alone. More of our fellows.
15   *Enter other Servants.*
STEWARD
All broken implements of a ruined house.
3 . SERVANT
Yet do our hearts wear Timon's livery ;
That see I by our faces. We are fellows still,
Serving alike in sorrow. Leaked is our bark ;
20 And we, poor mates, stand on the dying deck,
21 Hearing the surges threat. We must all part
Into this sea of air.
STEWARD   Good fellows all,
23 The latest of my wealth I'll share amongst you.
Wherever we shall meet, for Timon's sake
Let's yet be fellows ; let's shake our heads and say,
As 'twere a knell unto our master's fortunes,
'We have seen better days.' Let each take some.
               [Gives money.]
Nay, put out all your hands. Not one word more ;
28 Thus part we rich in sorrow, parting poor.
               Embrace, and part several ways.
O the fierce wretchedness that glory brings us !
Who would not wish to be from wealth exempt,
Since riches point to misery and contempt ?
Who would be so mocked with glory, or to live
But in a dream of friendship,
To have his pomp and all what state compounds
35 But only painted, like his varnished friends ?
36 Poor honest lord, brought low by his own heart,
Undone by goodness ! Strange, unusual blood,
38 When man's worst sin is he does too much good !
Who then dares to be half so kind again ?
40 For bounty, that makes gods, does still mar men.
My dearest lord, blest to be most accurst,
42 Rich only to be wretched, thy great fortunes
Are made thy chief afflictions. Alas, kind lord,
He's flung in rage from this ingrateful seat
Of monstrous friends ; nor has he with him to
46 Supply his life, or that which can command it.
47 I'll follow and inquire him out.
I'll ever serve his mind with my best will ;
Whilst I have gold, I'll be his steward still.   *Exit.*

*

               Enter Timon in the woods.   IV, iii
TIMON
O blessed breeding sun, draw from the earth
Rotten humidity ; below thy sister's orb
2 Infect the air ! Twinned brothers of one womb –
Whose procreation, residence, and birth

5 Scarce is dividant – touch them with several fortunes,
6 The greater scorns the lesser. Not nature,
To whom all sores lay siege, can bear great fortune
8 But by contempt of nature.
9 Raise me this beggar and deny't that lord ;
10 The senator shall bear contempt hereditary,
The beggar native honor.
12 It is the pasture lards the wether's sides,
The want that makes him lean. Who dares, who dares
In purity of manhood stand upright
And say 'This man's a flatterer' ? If one be,
16 So are they all ; for every grise of fortune
Is smoothed by that below. The learnèd pate
18 Ducks to the golden fool. All's obliquy ;
19 There's nothing level in our cursèd natures
But direct villainy. Therefore be abhorred
All feasts, societies, and throngs of men.
22 His semblable, yea himself, Timon disdains.
23 Destruction fang mankind ! Earth, yield me roots ;
 [Digs.]
Who seeks for better of thee, sauce his palate
25 With thy most operant poison. What is here ?
Gold ? Yellow, glittering, precious gold !
27 No, gods, I am no idle votarist :
28 Roots, you clear heavens ! Thus much of this will make
Black white, foul fair, wrong right,
Base noble, old young, coward valiant.
Ha, you gods, why this ? What this, you gods ? Why, this
Will lug your priests and servants from your sides,
Pluck sick men's pillows from below their heads.
This yellow slave
Will knit and break religions, bless th' accursed,
36 Make the hoar leprosy adored, place thieves
37 And give them title, knee, and approbation
With senators on the bench. This is it
39 That makes the wappened widow wed again ;
40 She whom the spital-house and ulcerous sores
Would cast the gorge at, this embalms and spices
42 To th' April day again. Come, damnèd earth,
43 Thou common whore of mankind, that puts odds
Among the rout of nations, I will make thee
45 Do thy right nature.
 March afar off. Ha ! a drum ? Thou'rt quick ;
46 But yet I'll bury thee. Thou'lt go, strong thief,
When gouty keepers of thee cannot stand.
48 Nay, stay thou out for earnest.
 [Keeps some gold.]
 Enter Alcibiades, with Drum and Fife, in warlike
 manner ; and Phrynia and Timandra.
ALCIBIADES What art thou there ?
 Speak.
TIMON
50 A beast, as thou art. The canker gnaw thy heart
For showing me again the eyes of man !
ALCIBIADES
What is thy name ? Is man so hateful to thee
That art thyself a man ?
TIMON
I am Misanthropos and hate mankind.
For thy part, I do wish thou wert a dog,
56 That I might love thee something.
ALCIBIADES I know thee well,
57 But in thy fortunes am unlearned and strange.

TIMON
I know thee too ; and more than that I know thee
I not desire to know. Follow thy drum ;
60 With man's blood paint the ground, gules, gules !
Religious canons, civil laws are cruel ;
62 Then what should war be ? This fell whore of thine
Hath in her more destruction than thy sword
64 For all her cherubin look.
PHRYNIA Thy lips rot off !
TIMON
I will not kiss thee ; then the rot returns
To thine own lips again.
ALCIBIADES
How came the noble Timon to this change ?
TIMON
68 As the moon does, by wanting light to give.
But then renew I could not, like the moon ;
There were no suns to borrow of.
ALCIBIADES Noble Timon,
What friendship may I do thee ?
TIMON None, but to
Maintain my opinion.
ALCIBIADES What is it, Timon ?
73 TIMON Promise me friendship, but perform none. If thou
wilt not promise, the gods plague thee, for thou art a
man ! if thou dost perform, confound thee, for thou art
a man !
ALCIBIADES
77 I have heard in some sort of thy miseries.
TIMON
Thou saw'st them when I had prosperity.
ALCIBIADES
I see them now ; then was a blessèd time.
TIMON
As thine is now, held with a brace of harlots.
TIMANDRA
81 Is this th' Athenian minion whom the world
82 Voiced so regardfully ?
TIMON Art thou Timandra ?
TIMANDRA Yes.
TIMON
Be a whore still. They love thee not that use thee ;
Give them diseases, leaving with thee their lust.
86 Make use of thy salt hours. Season the slaves

5 *dividant* divisible 6 *The* so that the 6–7 *Not nature . . . can* human nature . . . cannot 8 *nature* natural ties 9 *deny't* withhold such elevation from 10–11 *The senator . . . honor* i.e. let each be treated as if born to what he now merits 12 *lards . . . sides* fattens the sheep 16–17 *every . . . below* each rank is flattered by the next lower one 18 *golden* rich ; *obliquy* indirectness 19 *level* straightforward 22 *His semblable* anything like him 23 *fang* seize 25 *operant* potent 27 *idle votarist* insincere worshipper (I meant it when I asked for roots) 28 *clear* pure 36 *hoar* white (as lepers' skins are) ; *place* give high office to 37 *knee* deference (shown by kneeling to) 39 *wappened* worn out 40–41 *whom . . . gorge at* at the mere sight of whom hospital patients with running sores would vomit 42 *damnèd earth* i.e. gold 43–44 *puts odds Among* sets at each other's throats 45 *thy right nature* your proper work (of corrupting mankind) ; *quick* (1) swift, (2) alive (hence unburied) 46 *go* walk 48 *for earnest* as a token 50 *canker* cancerous disease 56 *something* a little 57 *unlearned and strange* uninformed and ignorant (but cf. ll. 77, 93–96) 60 *gules* red (in heraldry) 62 *fell* deadly 64 *cherubin* angelic 68 *wanting* lacking 73–76 *If . . . man* if you are a man you deserve damnation even if you do not make false promises, and also even if you do what you promise to 77 *in some sort* a little (though even with this qualification the speech seems inconsistent with the statement in l. 57 ; see also ll. 93–96) 81 *minion* darling 82 *Voiced* spoke of 86 *salt* lustful

87 For tubs and baths ; bring down rose-cheekèd youth
To the tub-fast and the diet.

TIMANDRA   Hang thee, monster !

ALCIBIADES

Pardon him, sweet Timandra ; for his wits
Are drowned and lost in his calamities.
I have but little gold of late, brave Timon,
The want whereof doth daily make revolt

93 In my penurious band. I have heard, and grieved,
How cursèd Athens, mindless of thy worth,
Forgetting thy great deeds when neighbor states,
But for thy sword and fortune, trod upon them –

TIMON

I prithee beat thy drum and get thee gone.

ALCIBIADES

I am thy friend and pity thee, dear Timon.

TIMON

How dost thou pity him whom thou dost trouble ?
I had rather be alone.

ALCIBIADES   Why, fare thee well.
Here is some gold for thee.

TIMON   Keep it ; I cannot eat it.

ALCIBIADES

102 When I have laid proud Athens on a heap –

TIMON

Warr'st thou 'gainst Athens ?

ALCIBIADES   Ay, Timon, and have cause.

TIMON

The gods confound them all in thy conquest,
And thee after, when thou hast conquerèd !

ALCIBIADES

Why me, Timon ?

TIMON   That by killing of villains
Thou wast born to conquer my country.
Put up thy gold. Go on. Here's gold. Go on.

109 Be as a planetary plague when Jove
Will o'er some high-viced city hang his poison
In the sick air. Let not thy sword skip one.
Pity not honored age for his white beard ;

113 He is an usurer. Strike me the counterfeit matron ;

114 It is her habit only that is honest,
Herself 's a bawd. Let not the virgin's cheek

Make soft thy trenchant sword ; for those milk paps   116
That through the window-bars bore at men's eyes   117
Are not within the leaf of pity writ,   118
But set them down horrible traitors. Spare not the babe
Whose dimpled smiles from fools exhaust their mercy ;
Think it a bastard whom the oracle
Hath doubtfully pronounced thy throat shall cut,   122
And mince it sans remorse. Swear against objects ;   123
Put armor on thine ears and on thine eyes,
Whose proof nor yells of mothers, maids, nor babes,   125
Nor sight of priests in holy vestments bleeding,
Shall pierce a jot. There's gold to pay thy soldiers ;
Make large confusion ; and, thy fury spent,   128
Confounded be thyself ! Speak not ; be gone.

ALCIBIADES

Hast thou gold yet ? I'll take the gold thou givest me,
Not all thy counsel.

TIMON

Dost thou, or dost thou not, heaven's curse upon thee !

BOTH [WOMEN]

Give us some gold, good Timon. Hast thou more ?

TIMON

Enough to make a whore forswear her trade,
And, to make whores, a bawd. Hold up, you sluts,   135
Your aprons mountant. You are not oathable,   136
Although I know you'll swear, terribly swear,   137
Into strong shudders and to heavenly agues,
Th' immortal gods that hear you. Spare your oaths ;
I'll trust to your conditions. Be whores still ;   140
And he whose pious breath seeks to convert you –
Be strong in whore, allure him, burn him up,
Let your close fire predominate his smoke,   143
And be no turncoats. Yet may your pains six months   144
Be quite contrary ! And thatch your poor thin roofs   145
With burdens of the dead – some that were hanged,
No matter ; wear them, betray with them. Whore still ;
Paint till a horse may mire upon your face.   148
A pox of wrinkles !

BOTH   Well, more gold ! What then ?
Believe 't that we'll do anything for gold.

TIMON

Consumption sow
In hollow bones of man ; strike their sharp shins,
And mar men's spurring. Crack the lawyer's voice,
That he may never more false title plead
Nor sound his quillets shrilly. Hoar the flamen,   155
That scolds against the quality of flesh   156
And not believes himself. Down with the nose –   157
Down with it flat ; take the bridge quite away –
Of him that, his particular to foresee,   159
Smells from the general weal. Make curled-pate
    ruffians bald,
And let the unscarred braggarts of the war
Derive some pain from you. Plague all,
That your activity may defeat and quell   163
The source of all erection. There's more gold.   164
Do you damn others and let this damn you,
And ditches grave you all !   166

BOTH

More counsel with more money, bounteous Timon.

TIMON

More whore, more mischief first ; I have given you
    earnest.   168

---

87 *tubs and baths* (used to treat venereal disease ; cf. in l. 88 *tub-fast*, abstinence during the treatment)   93 *penurious* poverty-stricken   102 *on a heap* in ruins   109 *planetary* (the plagues London suffered were often attributed to the baleful influence of planets 'in opposition')   113 *counterfeit matron* woman pretending married respectability   114 *habit* garb ; *honest* chaste   116 *trenchant* sharp   117 *window-bars* latticework of the bodice (?)   118 *Are . . . writ* have nothing to do with pity   122 *doubtfully* ambiguously ; *thy . . . cut* shall cut thy throat   123 *mince* chop it to bits ; *objects* things that evoke pity   125 *proof* tested strength (the armor's)   128 *large confusion* wholesale ruin   135 *to . . . bawd* to make a bawd give over making whores   136 *mountant* i.e. in such a way as to hold what I am about to give you (with a bawdy quibble on heraldic jargon ; cf. *erection* in l. 164) ; *oathable* believable though on oath   137 *swear* (to do what I shall ask)   140 *your conditions* what you are   143 *Let . . . smoke* let the hidden flames of desire overcome his pious 'hot air' (cf. III, vi, 86)   144–45 *Yet . . . contrary* (obscure and commonly supposed corrupt ; is painful miscarriage being spoken of ?)   145–46 *thatch . . . dead* cover your baldness with hair taken from corpses   148 *mire upon* bog down in   155 *quillets* quibbles ; *Hoar the flamen* whiten (with leprosy) the priest   156 *the . . . flesh* fleshly desire   157–59 *Down . . . Of* i.e. let syphilis afflict   159–60 *his . . . weal* in hunting after private gain loses scent of the common good   163 *quell* destroy   164 *erection* advancement (with an obvious bawdy pun)   166 *grave* entomb   168 *earnest* a token payment

ALCIBIADES
Strike up the drum towards Athens! Farewell, Timon;
If I thrive well, I'll visit thee again.

TIMON
171   If I hope well, I'll never see thee more.

ALCIBIADES
I never did thee harm.

TIMON
Yes, thou spok'st well of me.

ALCIBIADES   Call'st thou that harm?

TIMON
174   Men daily find it. Get thee away and take
Thy beagles with thee.

ALCIBIADES   We but offend him. Strike!
                    [Drum beats.] Exeunt [all but Timon].

TIMON
That nature, being sick of man's unkindness,
Should yet be hungry! Common mother, thou
        [Digs.]
Whose womb unmeasurable and infinite breast
179   Teems and feeds all; whose selfsame mettle
Whereof thy proud child, arrogant man, is puffed
Engenders the black toad and adder blue,
The gilded newt and eyeless venomed worm,
With all th' abhorrèd births below crisp heaven
184   Whereon Hyperion's quick'ning fire doth shine –
Yield him who all thy human sons doth hate,
From forth thy plenteous bosom, one poor root!
187   Ensear thy fertile and conceptious womb;
Let it no more bring out ingrateful man!
189   Go great with tigers, dragons, wolves, and bears;
190   Teem with new monsters whom thy upward face
Hath to the marbled mansion all above
Never presented! – O, a root! Dear thanks! –
Dry up thy marrows, vines, and plough-torn leas,
194   Whereof ingrateful man with liquorish drafts
195   And morsels unctuous greases his pure mind,
196   That from it all consideration slips –
        Enter Apemantus.
More man? Plague, plague!

APEMANTUS
I was directed hither. Men report
199   Thou dost affect my manners and dost use them.

TIMON
'Tis then because thou dost not keep a dog,
Whom I would imitate. Consumption catch thee!

APEMANTUS
This is in thee a nature but infected,
A poor unmanly melancholy sprung
From change of fortune. Why this spade? this place?
205   This slave-like habit and these looks of care?
Thy flatterers yet wear silk, drink wine, lie soft,
207   Hug their diseased perfumes, and have forgot
That ever Timon was. Shame not these woods
209   By putting on the cunning of a carper.
Be thou a flatterer now and seek to thrive
By that which has undone thee; hinge thy knee
212   And let his very breath whom thou'lt observe
Blow off thy cap; praise his most vicious strain
And call it excellent. Thou wast told thus;
Thou gav'st thine ears, like tapsters that bade welcome,
To knaves and all approachers. 'Tis most just
That thou turn rascal; hadst thou wealth again,
Rascals should have't. Do not assume my likeness.

TIMON
Were I like thee, I'd throw away myself.

APEMANTUS
Thou hast cast away thyself, being like thyself;
A madman so long, now a fool. What, think'st
That the bleak air, thy boisterous chamberlain,   222
Will put thy shirt on warm? Will these mossed trees,
That have outlived the eagle, page thy heels   224
And skip when thou point'st out? Will the cold brook,
Candied with ice, caudle thy morning taste   226
To cure thy o'er-night's surfeit? Call the creatures   227
Whose naked natures live in all the spite   228
Of wreakful heaven, whose bare unhousèd trunks,   229
To the conflicting elements exposed,
Answer mere nature; bid them flatter thee.   231
O, thou shalt find –

TIMON   A fool of thee. Depart.   232

APEMANTUS
I love thee better now than e'er I did.

TIMON
I hate thee worse.

APEMANTUS   Why?

TIMON   Thou flatter'st misery.

APEMANTUS
I flatter not, but say thou art a caitiff.

TIMON
Why dost thou seek me out?

APEMANTUS   To vex thee.

TIMON
Always a villain's office or a fool's.
Dost please thyself in't?

APEMANTUS   Ay.

TIMON   What, a knave too?   238

APEMANTUS
If thou didst put this sour cold habit on   239
To castigate thy pride, 'twere well; but thou
Dost it enforcedly. Thou'dst courtier be again
Wert thou not beggar. Willing misery
Outlives incertain pomp, is crowned before;   243
The one is filling still, never complete,   244
The other at high wish; best state, contentless,   245
Hath a distracted and most wretched being,
Worse than the worst, content.   247
Thou shouldst desire to die, being miserable.   248

TIMON
Not by his breath that is more miserable.   249

171 *If . . . well* if my hopes are realized   174 *find it* learn that it is   179 *Teems* prolifically brings forth; *mettle* essence   184 *Hyperion's quick'ning* the sun's life-giving   187 *Ensear* dry up   189 *Go great* be pregnant   190–92 *whom . . . presented* i.e. hitherto unknown   194 *liquorish* appetizing   195 *greases* (1) oils, (2) makes lewd   196 *consideration* ability to think   199 *affect* assume   205 *habit* garb (cf. IV, i, 32–34)   207 *diseased perfumes* perfumed but diseased mistresses   209 *putting on . . . carper* pretending to a cynic's art   212 *observe* court   222–23 *chamberlain . . . warm* valet will warm your shirt before you put it on   224 *eagle* (proverbially long-lived)   224–25 *page . . . out* serve you as a page and jump to do your bidding   226 *Candied* crusted over; *caudle . . . taste* warm your breakfast drink   227 *o'er-night's surfeit* last night's overindulgence   227–31 *creatures . . . nature* (cf. *Lear* III, iv, 28–36, 96–103)   228 *live in* are continually exposed to   229 *wreakful* vengeful   231 *Answer mere nature* must cope with nature in its crudest form   232 *of* in   238 *too* i.e. as well as a fool (see l. 237)   239 *put . . . habit on* adopt . . . manner of living   243 *is crowned before* achieves glory sooner   244 *still* always   245 *at high wish* just as desired; *best state, contentless* pomp, which does not bring content   247 *the worst, content* misery, if it is accepted contentedly   248 *miserable* discontented   249 *Not . . . miserable* i.e. not when you are the one recommending this desire

Thou art a slave whom Fortune's tender arm
251 With favor never clasped, but bred a dog.
252 Hadst thou, like us from our first swath, proceeded
The sweet degrees that this brief world affords
254 To such as may the passive drugs of it
Freely command, thou wouldst have plunged thyself
In general riot, melted down thy youth
In different beds of lust, and never learned
The icy precepts of respect, but followed
The sug'red game before thee. But myself,
Who had the world as my confectionary,
The mouths, the tongues, the eyes, and hearts of men
262 At duty, more than I could frame employment;
That numberless upon me stuck, as leaves
264 Do on the oak, have, with one winter's brush,
265 Fell from their boughs and left me open, bare
266 For every storm that blows – I to bear this,
That never knew but better, is some burden.
268 Thy nature did commence in sufferance; time
Hath made thee hard in't. Why shouldst thou hate men?
They never flattered thee. What hast thou given?
If thou wilt curse, thy father, that poor rag,
Must be thy subject, who in spite put stuff
To some she-beggar and compounded thee
Poor rogue hereditary. Hence; be gone!
If thou hadst not been born the worst of men,
Thou hadst been a knave and flatterer.

APEMANTUS　　　　　　　Art thou proud yet?

TIMON
Ay, that I am not thee.

APEMANTUS　　　　　I, that I was
No prodigal.

TIMON　　　　　I, that I am one now.
Were all the wealth I have shut up in thee,
280 I'd give thee leave to hang it. Get thee gone.
That the whole life of Athens were in this!
Thus would I eat it.
　　　　　[Gnaws a root.]
282 APEMANTUS　　　　　Here! I will mend thy feast.
　　　　　[Offers him food.]

TIMON
First mend my company; take away thyself.

APEMANTUS
So I shall mend mine own, by th' lack of thine.

TIMON
285 'Tis not well mended so; it is but botched.
286 If not, I would it were.

APEMANTUS
What wouldst thou have to Athens?

TIMON
Thee thither in a whirlwind. If thou wilt,

---

251 *bred a dog* have been a dog from birth　252 *swath* swaddling clothes
254 *drugs* drudges, servants　262 *At duty* serving me; *frame* provide with
264 *have* and that have; *winter's brush* onslaught of winter　265 *Fell*
fallen　266 *I* for me　268 *sufferance* suffering　280 *it* i.e. yourself　282
mend improve the quality of　285 *botched* badly patched (since you are
still in your own company)　286 *If not* i.e. if not mended to this extent,
by your leaving　292 *that's* what's　302 *curiosity* fastidiousness　303
medlar small apple, eaten when decayed (often used, as here, in quibbles
on *meddlers* in others' affairs)　306 *like thee* i.e. well decayed　307 *An if*
309 *unthrift* (to be a) spendthrift; *after* in accordance with (?), after the
dissipation of (?)　331 *livedst* would live　334 *unicorn* (supposed captured
by goading it to drive its horn deeply into a tree trunk)　338 *germane* akin
338–39 *spots . . . life* sins that are yours only 'by association' would condemn
you to death　340 *remotion* going elsewhere　342–43 *thy . . . transformation*
what you would lose by the change

Tell them there I have gold. Look, so I have.

APEMANTUS
Here is no use for gold.

TIMON　　　　　　　The best and truest;
For here it sleeps, and does no hirèd harm.

APEMANTUS
Where liest a-nights, Timon?

TIMON　　　　　　　Under that's above me. 292
Where feed'st thou a-days, Apemantus?

APEMANTUS Where my stomach finds meat; or rather,
where I eat it.

TIMON
Would poison were obedient and knew my mind!

APEMANTUS
Where wouldst thou send it?

TIMON
To sauce thy dishes.

APEMANTUS The middle of humanity thou never knew-
est, but the extremity of both ends. When thou wast in
thy gilt and thy perfume, they mocked thee for too much
curiosity; in thy rags thou know'st none, but art de- 302
spised for the contrary. There's a medlar for thee; eat it. 303

TIMON On what I hate I feed not.

APEMANTUS Dost hate a medlar?

TIMON
Ay, though it look like thee. 306

APEMANTUS An thou'dst hated meddlers sooner, thou 307
shouldst have loved thyself better now. What man didst
thou ever know unthrift that was beloved after his 309
means?

TIMON Who, without those means thou talk'st of, didst
thou ever know beloved?

APEMANTUS Myself.

TIMON I understand thee. Thou hadst some means to
keep a dog.

APEMANTUS What things in the world canst thou nearest
compare to thy flatterers?

TIMON Women nearest; but men – men are the things
themselves. What wouldst thou do with the world,
Apemantus, if it lay in thy power? 320

APEMANTUS Give it the beasts, to be rid of the men.

TIMON Wouldst thou have thyself fall in the confusion of
men, and remain a beast with the beasts?

APEMANTUS Ay, Timon.

TIMON A beastly ambition, which the gods grant thee
t' attain to! If thou wert the lion, the fox would beguile
thee; if thou wert the lamb, the fox would eat thee; if
thou wert the fox, the lion would suspect thee when
peradventure thou wert accused by the ass; if thou wert
the ass, thy dullness would torment thee, and still thou
livedst but as a breakfast to the wolf. If thou wert the 331
wolf thy greediness would afflict thee, and oft thou
shouldst hazard thy life for thy dinner. Wert thou the
unicorn, pride and wrath would confound thee and 334
make thine own self the conquest of thy fury; wert thou
a bear, thou wouldst be killed by the horse; wert thou a
horse, thou wouldst be seized by the leopard; wert thou
a leopard, thou wert germane to the lion, and the spots 338
of thy kindred were jurors on thy life: all thy safety were
remotion and thy defense absence. What beast couldst 340
thou be that were not subject to a beast? And what a
beast art thou already, that seest not thy loss in trans- 342
formation!

APEMANTUS If thou couldst please me with speaking to

me, thou mightst have hit upon it here. The commonwealth of Athens is become a forest of beasts.

TIMON How has the ass broke the wall, that thou art out
of the city?

349 APEMANTUS Yonder comes a poet and a painter. The
plague of company light upon thee! I will fear to catch
it, and give way. When I know not what else to do, I'll
see thee again.

TIMON When there is nothing living but thee, thou shalt
be welcome. I had rather be a beggar's dog than
Apemantus.

APEMANTUS

355   Thou art the cap of all the fools alive.

TIMON

Would thou wert clean enough to spit upon!

APEMANTUS

A plague on thee! thou art too bad to curse.

TIMON

358   All villains that do stand, by thee, are pure.

APEMANTUS

There is no leprosy but what thou speak'st.

TIMON

If I name thee.

361   I'll beat thee, but I should infect my hands.

APEMANTUS

I would my tongue could rot them off!

TIMON

Away, thou issue of a mangy dog!
Choler does kill me that thou art alive;
I swoon to see thee.

APEMANTUS   Would thou wouldst burst!

TIMON   Away,
Thou tedious rogue! I am sorry I shall lose
A stone by thee.
        [Throws a stone at him.]

APEMANTUS Beast!

TIMON Slave!

APEMANTUS Toad!

TIMON

Rogue, rogue, rogue!
I am sick of this false world, and will love naught
373   But even the mere necessities upon't.
Then, Timon, presently prepare thy grave.
Lie where the light foam of the sea may beat
Thy gravestone daily. Make thine epitaph,
377   That death in me at others' lives may laugh.
        [To the gold.]
O thou sweet king-killer, and dear divorce
'Twixt natural son and sire; thou bright defiler
380   Of Hymen's purest bed; thou valiant Mars;
Thou ever young, fresh, loved, and delicate wooer,
382   Whose blush doth thaw the consecrated snow
383   That lies on Dian's lap; thou visible god,
384   That sold'rest close impossibilities
And mak'st them kiss; that speak'st with every tongue
386   To every purpose! O thou touch of hearts!
Think thy slave man rebels; and by thy virtue
388   Set them into confounding odds, that beasts
May have the world in empire!

APEMANTUS   Would 'twere so,
But not till I am dead. I'll say thou'st gold.
Thou wilt be thronged to shortly.

TIMON   Thronged to?

APEMANTUS   Ay.

TIMON

Thy back, I prithee.

APEMANTUS   Live, and love thy misery.

TIMON

Long live so, and so die. I am quit.

APEMANTUS

Moe things like men! Eat, Timon, and abhor them.
                                          Exit Apemantus.
    Enter the Banditti.

1. BANDIT Where should he have this gold? It is some 395
poor fragment, some slender ort of his remainder. The 396
mere want of gold and the falling-from of his friends
drove him into this melancholy.

2. BANDIT It is noised he hath a mass of treasure.

3. BANDIT Let us make the assay upon him. If he care not 400
for't, he will supply us easily; if he covetously reserve
it, how shall's get it?   402

2. BANDIT True; for he bears it not about him; 'tis hid.

1. BANDIT Is not this he?

ALL Where?

2. BANDIT 'Tis his description.

3. BANDIT He! I know him.

ALL Save thee, Timon!

TIMON Now, thieves?

ALL

Soldiers, not thieves.

TIMON   Both too, and women's sons.   410

ALL

We are not thieves, but men that much do want.

TIMON

Your greatest want is, you want much of meat.   412
Why should you want? Behold, the earth hath roots;
Within this mile break forth a hundred springs;
The oaks bear mast, the briers scarlet hips;   415
The bounteous housewife Nature on each bush
Lays her full mess before you. Want? Why want?   417

1. BANDIT

We cannot live on grass, on berries, water,
As beasts and birds and fishes.

TIMON

Nor on the beasts themselves, the birds and fishes;
You must eat men. Yet thanks I must you con   421
That you are thieves professed, that you work not
In holier shapes; for there is boundless theft
In limited professions. Rascal thieves,   424
Here's gold. Go, suck the subtle blood o' th' grape
Till the high fever seethe your blood to froth,   426
And so scape hanging. Trust not the physician;
His antidotes are poison, and he slays
Moe than you rob. Take wealth and lives together.
Do villainy, do, since you protest to do't,   430

349 *Yonder . . . painter* (they don't in fact appear until about 190 lines later:
see Introduction)   355 *cap* i.e. top dog   358 *by* compared with   361
I'll I'd   373 *But even* save only; *necessities* (of which death is the chief:
see next line)   377 *death in me* I, though dead   380 *Hymen* the god of
marriage; *Mars* the adulterous god of war   382 *blush* glow (of the gold,
not of Mars)   383 *Dian* a virgin goddess, patroness of chastity   384 *close*
firmly together   386 *touch* touchstone   388 *them* all men   395 *should he*
have can he have got (?), can he be keeping (?)   396 *ort . . . remainder*
scrap of what he had left   400 *make . . . him* try him (in the language of
gold miners)   402 *shall's* shall we   410 *Both too, and* both indeed, and
also   412 *Your . . . meat* what you really need is merely plenty of food
415 *mast* acorns; *hips* fruit of the rose   417 *full mess* complete menu   421
con tender   424 *limited* regular, legal   426 *high fever seethe* drunkenness
boil   430 *protest* profess

431 Like workmen. I'll example you with thievery :
The sun 's a thief, and with his great attraction
Robs the vast sea ; the moon 's an arrant thief,
And her pale fire she snatches from the sun ;
The sea 's a thief, whose liquid surge resolves
The moon into salt tears ; the earth 's a thief,
437 That feeds and breeds by a composture stol'n
From gen'ral excrement. Each thing 's a thief.
The laws, your curb and whip, in their rough power
Has unchecked theft. Love not yourselves : away,
Rob one another. There's more gold. Cut throats.
All that you meet are thieves. To Athens go ;
Break open shops ; nothing can you steal
444 But thieves do lose it. Steal less for this I give you,
445 And gold confound you howsoe'er ! Amen.
   3 . BANDIT Has almost charmed me from my profession
     by persuading me to it.
   1 . BANDIT 'Tis in the malice of mankind that he thus
449 advises us, not to have us thrive in our mystery.
450 2 . BANDIT I'll believe him as an enemy, and give over
     my trade.
452 1 . BANDIT Let us first see peace in Athens ; there is no
     time so miserable but a man may be true.

Exit [with the other] Thieves.
Enter [Flavius] the Steward, to Timon.

STEWARD
   O you gods !
   Is yon despised and ruinous man my lord ?
   Full of decay and failing ? O monument
   And wonder of good deeds evilly bestowed !
   What an alteration of honor has desp'rate want made !
   What viler thing upon the earth than friends,
   Who can bring noblest minds to basest ends !
461 How rarely does it meet with this time's guise
   When man was wished to love his enemies !
   Grant I may ever love, and rather woo
464 Those that would mischief me than those that do !
   Has caught me in his eye ; I will present
   My honest grief unto him, and as my lord
   Still serve him with my life. My dearest master !

TIMON
   Away ! What art thou ?

STEWARD   Have you forgot me, sir ?

TIMON
   Why dost ask that ? I have forgot all men ;
   Then if thou grant'st thou'rt a man, I have forgot thee.

STEWARD
   An honest poor servant of yours.

TIMON
   Then I know thee not.
   I never had honest man about me ; ay, all
   I kept were knaves, to serve in meat to villains.

431 *example you with* give some examples to justify your 437 *composture*
manure 444 *for* because you have 445 *howsoe'er* anyhow 449 *mystery*
profession 450 *as* as I would 452 *peace* (when thievery is less easy) 452–
53 *there . . . true* i.e. since one may reform at any time, let's not make any
radical changes while the pickings are so good 461–62 *rarely . . . wished*
especially apt for to-day's world is the admonition to man 464 *Those . . .
do* professed enemies than those who harm me though pretending friendship 480 *give* yield tears 481 *But thorough* except through 485 *entertain*
employ 487 *comfortable* comforting 491 *exceptless* making no exceptions
505 *as* as what we have when 508 *suspect* suspicion 510 *still* ever 511
merely purely 513 *Care of* concern for 515 *points to* may be indicated for
516 *in . . . present* later or now 519 *singly* (1) uniquely, (2) truly 522 *thus
conditioned* with those provisos ; *from* remote from

STEWARD
   The gods are witness,
   Ne'er did poor steward wear a truer grief
   For his undone lord than mine eyes for you.

TIMON
   What, dost thou weep ? Come nearer then ; I love thee
   Because thou art a woman and disclaim'st
   Flinty mankind, whose eyes do never give   480
   But thorough lust and laughter. Pity 's sleeping.   481
   Strange times, that weep with laughing, not with
     weeping !

STEWARD
   I beg of you to know me, good my lord,
   T' accept my grief, and whilst this poor wealth lasts
   To entertain me as your steward still.   485

TIMON
   Had I a steward
   So true, so just, and now so comfortable ?   487
   It almost turns my dangerous nature mild.
   Let me behold thy face. Surely this man
   Was born of woman.
   Forgive my general and exceptless rashness,   491
   You perpetual-sober gods ! I do proclaim
   One honest man – mistake me not, but one ;
   No more, I pray – and he's a steward.
   How fain would I have hated all mankind,
   And thou redeem'st thyself. But all save thee
   I fell with curses.
   Methinks thou art more honest now than wise ;
   For by oppressing and betraying me
   Thou mightst have sooner got another service ;
   For many so arrive at second masters,
   Upon their first lord's neck. But tell me true –
   For I must ever doubt, though ne'er so sure –
   Is not thy kindness subtle-covetous,
   A usuring kindness, and as rich men deal gifts,   505
   Expecting in return twenty for one ?

STEWARD
   No, my most worthy master, in whose breast
   Doubt and suspect, alas, are placed too late.   508
   You should have feared false times when you did feast.
   Suspect still comes where an estate is least.   510
   That which I show, heaven knows, is merely love,   511
   Duty, and zeal to your unmatchèd mind,
   Care of your food and living ; and believe it,   513
   My most honored lord,
   For any benefit that points to me,   515
   Either in hope or present, I'd exchange   516
   For this one wish, that you had power and wealth
   To requite me by making rich yourself.

TIMON
   Look thee, 'tis so ! Thou singly honest man,   519
   Here, take. The gods out of my misery
   Have sent thee treasure. Go, live rich and happy,
   But thus conditioned : thou shalt build from men,   522
   Hate all, curse all, show charity to none,
   But let the famished flesh slide from the bone
   Ere thou relieve the beggar. Give to dogs
   What thou deniest to men. Let prisons swallow 'em,
   Debts wither 'em to nothing ; be men like blasted
     woods,
   And may diseases lick up their false bloods !
   And so farewell, and thrive.

STEWARD   O let me stay

And comfort you, my master.

TIMON   If thou hat'st curses,
Stay not; fly, whilst thou art blest and free;
Ne'er see thou man, and let me ne'er see thee.
                    [Timon withdraws.] Exit [Flavius].

*

V, i   *Enter Poet and Painter. [Timon watches them from*
             his cave.]

PAINTER As I took note of the place, it cannot be far
where he abides.

POET What's to be thought of him? Does the rumor hold
for true that he's so full of gold?

PAINTER Certain. Alcibiades reports it; Phrynia and
Timandra had gold of him. He likewise enriched poor
straggling soldiers with great quantity. 'Tis said he
gave unto his steward a mighty sum.

9 POET Then this breaking of his has been but a try for his
friends?

PAINTER Nothing else. You shall see him a palm in
Athens again, and flourish with the highest. Therefore
'tis not amiss we tender our loves to him in this sup-
14 posed distress of his; it will show honestly in us and is
15 very likely to load our purposes with what they travail
16 for, if it be a just and true report that goes of his having.

POET What have you now to present unto him?

PAINTER Nothing at this time but my visitation. Only I
will promise him an excellent piece.

20 POET I must serve him so too, tell him of an intent that's
coming toward him.

PAINTER Good as the best. Promising is the very air o'
th' time; it opens the eyes of expectation. Performance
24 is ever the duller for his act; and, but in the plainer and
25 simpler kind of people, the deed of saying is quite out of
use. To promise is most courtly and fashionable; performance is a kind of will or testament which argues a
great sickness in his judgment that makes it.
             Enter Timon from his cave.

TIMON *[aside]* Excellent workman! Thou canst not paint
a man so bad as is thyself.

POET I am thinking what I shall say I have provided for
32 him. It must be a personating of himself; a satire against
33 the softness of prosperity, with a discovery of the infinite flatteries that follow youth and opulency.

35 TIMON *[aside]* Must thou needs stand for a villain in
thine own work? Wilt thou whip thine own faults in
other men? Do so, I have gold for thee.

POET Nay, let's seek him.
Then do we sin against our own estate
When we may profit meet, and come too late.

PAINTER True.
42 When the day serves, before black-cornered night,
Find what thou want'st by free and offered light.
Come.

TIMON *[aside]*
45 I'll meet you at the turn. What a god's gold
That he is worshipped in a baser temple
Than where swine feed!
'Tis thou that rigg'st the bark and plough'st the foam,
49 Settlest admirèd reverence in a slave.
To thee be worship, and thy saints for aye
Be crowned with plagues, that thee alone obey!
52 Fit I meet them.
             [Comes forward.]

POET
Hail, worthy Timon!

PAINTER   Our late noble master!

TIMON
Have I once lived to see two honest men?   54

POET Sir,
Having often of your open bounty tasted,
Hearing you were retired, your friends fall'n off,
Whose thankless natures – O abhorrèd spirits! –
Not all the whips of heaven are large enough –
What, to you,
Whose starlike nobleness gave life and influence
To their whole being? – I am rapt, and cannot cover   62
The monstrous bulk of this ingratitude
With any size of words.   64

TIMON
Let it go naked; men may see't the better.
You that are honest, by being what you are
Make them best seen and known.   67

PAINTER   He and myself
Have travelled in the great show'r of your gifts,   68
And sweetly felt it.

TIMON   Ay, you are honest men.

PAINTER
We are hither come to offer you our service.

TIMON
Most honest men! Why, how shall I requite you?
Can you eat roots and drink cold water? No?

BOTH
What we can do, we'll do, to do you service.

TIMON
Y' are honest men. Ye've heard that I have gold?
I am sure you have. Speak truth; y' are honest men.

PAINTER
So it is said, my noble lord; but therefore   76
Came not my friend, nor I.

TIMON
Good honest men! Thou draw'st a counterfeit   78
Best in all Athens. Thou'rt indeed the best;
Thou counterfeit'st most lively.   80

PAINTER   So so, my lord.

TIMON
E'en so, sir, as I say. *[to the Poet]* And for thy fiction,   81
Why, thy verse swells with stuff so fine and smooth
That thou art even natural in thine art.   83
But for all this, my honest-natured friends,
I must needs say you have a little fault.
Marry, 'tis not monstrous in you; neither wish I
You take much pains to mend.

V, i Before Timon's cave 9 *breaking* going bankrupt; *try* test 14 *show honestly* seem honorable 15 *travail* strive 16 *having* wealth 20–21 *an intent . . . him* what I have in mind for him 24 *for his act* for its being realized; *but* except 25 *deed of saying* fulfillment of promises 32 *a personating of himself* an allegorical representation of his own case 33 *discovery* disclosure 35 *stand* serve as a model 42 *black-cornered* (presumably because night has the attributes of dark corners) 45 *meet . . . turn* i.e. give you a little of your own dishonest game (as he presently does) 49 *Settlest . . . slave* makes slaves admire and revere their masters 52 *Fit I* I'd better 54 *once* actually, after all 62 *rapt* bemused 64 *size* of i.e. adequate 67 *them* i.e. the ingrates you speak of 68 *travelled in* experienced 76–77 *therefore Came not* not for this reason came 78 *counterfeit* (1) portrait, (2) spurious imitation (the verb, as in l. 80, being likewise equivocal) 80 *lively* (1) in lifelike fashion, (2) actively 81 *fiction* imaginative work 83 *thou . . . thine art* the products of your art are like nature itself (but *natural* also meant 'like a born fool')

BOTH   Beseech your honor
To make it known to us.

TIMON   You'll take it ill.

BOTH
Most thankfully, my lord.

TIMON   Will you, indeed?

BOTH
Doubt it not, worthy lord.

TIMON
There's never a one of you but trusts a knave
That mightily deceives you.

BOTH   Do we, my lord?

TIMON
93 Ay, and you hear him cog, see him dissemble,
94 Know his gross patchery, love him, feed him,
95 Keep in your bosom; yet remain assured
96 That he's a made-up villain.

PAINTER
I know none such, my lord.

POET   Nor I.

TIMON
Look you, I love you well; I'll give you gold,
Rid me these villains from your companies.
100 Hang them or stab them, drown them in a draught,
Confound them by some course, and come to me,
I'll give you gold enough.

BOTH
Name them, my lord; let's know them.

TIMON
104 You that way, and you this, but two in company;
Each man apart, all single and alone,
Yet an arch-villain keeps him company.
    [To Painter]
If, where thou art, two villains shall not be,
Come not near him.
    [To Poet]   If thou wouldst not reside
But where one villain is, then him abandon. –
110 Hence, pack! There's gold; you came for gold, ye slaves.
    [To Painter]
111 You have work for me; there's payment.
Hence!
    [To Poet]
112 You are an alchemist; make gold of that. –
Out, rascal dogs!   *Exeunt [both, beaten out by Timon,*
                     who retires to his cave].
    Enter [Flavius the] Steward and two Senators.

STEWARD
It is vain that you would speak with Timon;
115 For he is set so only to himself

That nothing but himself which looks like man
Is friendly with him.

1. SENATOR   Bring us to his cave.
It is our part and promise to th' Athenians   118
To speak with Timon.

2. SENATOR   At all times alike
Men are not still the same. 'Twas time and griefs   120
That framed him thus. Time, with his fairer hand
Offering the fortunes of his former days,
The former man may make him. Bring us to him,
And chance it as it may.

STEWARD   Here is his cave.
Peace and content be here! Lord Timon! Timon!
Look out, and speak to friends. Th' Athenians
By two of their most reverend senate greet thee.
Speak to them, noble Timon.
    Enter Timon out of his cave.

TIMON
Thou sun that comforts, burn! Speak and be hanged!
For each true word a blister, and each false
Be as a cauterizing to the root o' th' tongue,   131
Consuming it with speaking!

1. SENATOR   Worthy Timon –

TIMON
Of none but such as you, and you of Timon.

1. SENATOR
The senators of Athens greet thee, Timon.

TIMON
I thank them; and would send them back the plague,
Could I but catch it for them.

1. SENATOR   O, forget
What we are sorry for ourselves in thee.   137
The senators with one consent of love
Entreat thee back to Athens, who have thought
On special dignities, which vacant lie
For thy best use and wearing.

2. SENATOR   They confess
Toward thee forgetfulness too general-gross;
And now the public body, which doth seldom
Play the recanter, feeling in itself
A lack of Timon's aid, hath sense withal
Of it own fail, restraining aid to Timon,   146
And send forth us to make their sorrowed render,   147
Together with a recompense more fruitful
Than their offense can weigh down by the dram;   149
Ay, even such heaps and sums of love and wealth
As shall to thee blot out what wrongs were theirs   151
And write in thee the figures of their love,   152
Ever to read them thine.   153

TIMON   You witch me in it;
Surprise me to the very brink of tears.
Lend me a fool's heart and a woman's eyes,
And I'll beweep these comforts, worthy senators.

1. SENATOR
Therefore so please thee to return with us   157
And of our Athens, thine and ours, to take
The captainship, thou shalt be met with thanks,
Allowed with absolute power, and thy good name   160
Live with authority. So soon we shall drive back   161
Of Alcibiades th' approaches wild,
Who like a boar too savage doth root up
His country's peace.

2. SENATOR   And shakes his threat'ning sword
Against the walls of Athens.

---

93 *cog* cheat   94 *patchery* roguery   95 *Keep . . . bosom* cherish him   96 *made-up* complete   100 *draught* privy   104–06 *You . . . company* i.e. each of you is a thorough villain (riddlingly spelled out further in ll. 107–09)   110 *pack* be off   111 *there's payment* (since Timon now strikes him)   112 *alchemist* i.e. one who strives by art to improve on nature, out of common things to produce precious; *that* (the blow Timon now gives him as well)   115 *set . . . to* so completely wrapped up in   118 *part and promise* promised part   120 *still the same* 'at all times alike' (as before: senators sometimes repeat themselves)   131 *cauterizing* searing with acid or a hot iron   137 *What . . . thee* the wrongs we are sorry to have done you   146 *it own fail* its own fault   147 *sorrowed render* amends for regretted wrongs   149 *can . . . dram* can, weighed scrupulously, outbalance   151 *were theirs* they did you   152 *write . . . figures* enter you in the ledgers (the imagery is persistently commercial though the subject is love)   153 *Ever . . . thine* thus providing a permanent record of their esteem for you   157 *so* if it   160 *Allowed with* given   161 *Live with authority* shall remain authoritative

1 . SENATOR   Therefore, Timon –

TIMON
Well, sir, I will ; therefore I will, sir, thus :
If Alcibiades kill my countrymen,
Let Alcibiades know this of Timon,
That Timon cares not. But if he sack fair Athens
And take our goodly agèd men by th' beards,
Giving our holy virgins to the stain
172 Of contumelious, beastly, mad-brained war,
Then let him know (and tell him Timon speaks it
In pity of our agèd and our youth)
I cannot choose but tell him that I care not –
And let him take't at worst – for their knives care not,
177 While you have throats to answer. For myself,
178 There's not a whittle in th' unruly camp
179 But I do prize it at my love before
The reverend'st throat in Athens. So I leave you
181 To the protection of the prosperous gods,
182 As thieves to keepers.

STEWARD   Stay not ; all's in vain.

TIMON
Why, I was writing of my epitaph.
It will be seen to-morrow. My long sickness
185 Of health and living now begins to mend,
186 And nothing brings me all things. Go, live still ;
Be Alcibiades your plague, you his,
And last so long enough !

1 . SENATOR   We speak in vain.

TIMON
But yet I love my country and am not
One that rejoices in the common wrack,
191 As common bruit doth put it.

1 . SENATOR   That's well spoke.

TIMON
Commend me to my loving countrymen –

1 . SENATOR
These words become your lips as they pass through
them.

2 . SENATOR
And enter in our ears like great triumphers
In their applauding gates.

TIMON   Commend me to them,
And tell them that, to ease them of their griefs,
Their fears of hostile strokes, their aches, losses,
Their pangs of love, with other incident throes
That nature's fragile vessel doth sustain
In life's uncertain voyage, I will some kindness do
them :
201 I'll teach them to prevent wild Alcibiades' wrath.

1 . SENATOR
I like this well. He will return again.

TIMON
203 I have a tree which grows here in my close
That mine own use invites me to cut down,
And shortly must I fell it. Tell my friends,
Tell Athens, in the sequence of degree
From high to low throughout, that whoso please
To stop affliction, let him take his haste,
Come hither ere my tree hath felt the axe –
And hang himself ! I pray you do my greeting.

STEWARD
Trouble him no further ; thus you still shall find him.

TIMON
Come not to me again ; but say to Athens,
Timon hath made his everlasting mansion
Upon the beachèd verge of the salt flood,   214
Who once a day with his embossèd froth   215
The turbulent surge shall cover. Thither come,
And let my gravestone be your oracle.   217
Lips, let sour words go by and language end.
What is amiss, plague and infection mend !
Graves only be men's works, and death their gain.
Sun, hide thy beams ; Timon hath done his reign.
Exit Timon [into his cave].

1 . SENATOR
His discontents are unremovably
Coupled to nature.   223

2 . SENATOR
Our hope in him is dead. Let us return
And strain what other means is left unto us
In our dear peril.   226

1 . SENATOR   It requires swift foot.   *Exeunt.*

*

Enter two other Senators with a Messenger.   V, ii

3 . SENATOR
Thou hast painfully discovered ; are his files   1
As full as thy report ?

MESSENGER   I have spoke the least.   2
Besides, his expedition promises   3
Present approach.

4 . SENATOR
We stand much hazard if they bring not Timon.   5

MESSENGER
I met a courier, one mine ancient friend ;
Whom, though in general part we were opposed,   7
Yet our old love had a particular force
And made us speak like friends. This man was riding
From Alcibiades to Timon's cave
With letters of entreaty, which imported
His fellowship i' th' cause against your city,
In part for his sake moved.   13

Enter the other Senators [from Timon].

3 . SENATOR   Here come our brothers.

1 . SENATOR
No talk of Timon ; nothing of him expect.
The enemy's drum is heard, and fearful scouring   15
Doth choke the air with dust. In, and prepare.
Ours is the fall, I fear ; our foe's the snare.   *Exeunt.* 17

*

172 *contumelious* insolent   177 *answer* suffer the consequences   178 *whittle* clasp-knife   179 *at* in   181 *prosperous* propitious   182 *keepers* jailers   185 *health and living* healthful life   186 *nothing* oblivion, death   191 *bruit* rumor   201 *prevent* anticipate   203 *in my close* i.e. alongside my cave ('close' ordinarily meaning 'enclosure,' 'yard')   214 *beachèd verge of* beach that edges (is the limit of)   215 *embossèd* foaming   217 *oracle* source of wisdom   223 *Coupled to nature* part and parcel of his being   226 *dear* grievous
V, ii Before the walls of Athens   1 *painfully discovered* reconnoitered with great care (?), revealed distressing facts (?) ; *files* ranks (of Alcibiades' army)   2 *spoke the least* given a conservative estimate   3 *expedition* speed   5 *they* (the senators, designated 1 and 2, sent out for this purpose)   7 *general part* public affairs   13 *moved* undertaken   15 *scouring* scurrying about in preparation for battle   17 *Ours . . . snare* i.e. I fear we are about to fall into our enemy's trap

V, iii   *Enter a Soldier in the woods, seeking Timon for*
            Alcibiades.

SOLDIER

    By all description this should be the place.
    Who's here ? Speak, ho ! No answer ? What is this ?
      [Reads.]
    'Timon is dead, who hath outstretched his span.
4 Some beast read this ; there does not live a man.'
    Dead, sure, and this his grave. What's on this tomb
6 I cannot read ; the character I'll take with wax.
    Our captain hath in every figure skill,
    An aged interpreter, though young in days.
    Before proud Athens he's set down by this,
10 Whose fall the mark of his ambition is.   *Exit.*

           *

V, iv   *Trumpets sound. Enter Alcibiades with his Powers*
            before Athens.

ALCIBIADES

    Sound to this coward and lascivious town
    Our terrible approach.
      Sound a parley. The Senators appear upon the walls.
    Till now you have gone on and filled the time
4 With all licentious measure, making your wills
5 The scope of justice. Till now myself and such
    As slept within the shadow of your power
7 Have wandered with our traversed arms and breathed
8 Our sufferance vainly. Now the time is flush,
9 When crouching marrow in the bearer strong
    Cries, of itself, 'No more !' Now breathless wrong
    Shall sit and pant in your great chairs of ease,
12 And pursy insolence shall break his wind
    With fear and horrid flight.

1. SENATOR   Noble and young,
14 When thy first griefs were but a mere conceit,
    Ere thou hadst power or we had cause of fear,
    We sent to thee, to give thy rages balm,
    To wipe out our ingratitude with loves
    Above their quantity.

2. SENATOR   So did we woo
    Transformèd Timon to our city's love

By humble message and by promised means.
We were not all unkind, nor all deserve   21
The common stroke of war.

1. SENATOR   These walls of ours
Were not erected by their hands from whom
You have received your griefs ; nor are they such   24
That these great tow'rs, trophies, and schools should fall
For private faults in them.   26

2. SENATOR   Nor are they living
Who were the motives that you first went out.   27
Shame, that they wanted cunning, in excess   28
Hath broke their hearts. March, noble lord,
Into our city with thy banners spread.
By decimation and a tithèd death,   31
If thy revenges hunger for that food
Which nature loathes, take thou the destined tenth,
And by the hazard of the spotted die   34
Let die the spotted.   35

1. SENATOR   All have not offended.
For those that were, it is not square to take,   36
On those that are, revenge ; crimes, like lands,
Are not inherited. Then, dear countryman,
Bring in thy ranks, but leave without thy rage ;   39
Spare thy Athenian cradle, and those kin
Which in the bluster of thy wrath must fall
With those that have offended. Like a shepherd
Approach the fold and cull th' infected forth,
But kill not all together.

2. SENATOR   What thou wilt,
Thou rather shalt enforce it with thy smile
Than hew to't with thy sword.

1. SENATOR   Set but thy foot
Against our rampired gates and they shall ope,   47
So thou wilt send thy gentle heart before   48
To say thou'lt enter friendly.

2. SENATOR   Throw thy glove,
Or any token of thine honor else,
That thou wilt use the wars as thy redress
And not as our confusion, all thy powers   52
Shall make their harbor in our town till we
Have sealed thy full desire.   54

ALCIBIADES   Then there's my glove ;
Descend, and open your unchargèd ports.   55
Those enemies of Timon's and mine own
Whom you yourselves shall set out for reproof
Fall, and no more ; and, to atone your fears   58
With my more noble meaning, not a man   59
Shall pass his quarter or offend the stream
Of regular justice in your city's bounds
But shall be rendered to your public laws
At heaviest answer.   63

BOTH   'Tis most nobly spoken.

ALCIBIADES
Descend, and keep your words.
    [The Senators descend and open the gates.]
    Enter [Soldier as] a Messenger.

MESSENGER
My noble general, Timon is dead,
Entombed upon the very hem o' th' sea,
And on his gravestone this insculpture, which   67
With wax I brought away, whose soft impression
Interprets for my poor ignorance.   69

ALCIBIADES *(Reads the epitaph.)*

70 'Here lies a wretched corse, of wretched soul bereft ;
Seek not my name. A plague consume you wicked caitiffs left !
Here lie I, Timon, who alive all living men did hate.
73 Pass by and curse thy fill ; but pass, and stay not here thy gait.'

These well express in thee thy latter spirits.
Though thou abhorred'st in us our human griefs,
76 Scorned'st our brains' flow and those our droplets which
77 From niggard nature fall, yet rich conceit
Taught thee to make vast Neptune weep for aye

On thy low grave, on faults forgiven. Dead
Is noble Timon, of whose memory
Hereafter more. Bring me into your city,
And I will use the olive with my sword, 82
Make war breed peace, make peace stint war, make each 83
Prescribe to other, as each other's leech. 84
Let our drums strike. *Exeunt.*

70–73 *Here . . . gait* (one of these two contradictory couplets was probably meant for cancellation: see Introduction) 73 *gait* steps 76 *brains' flow* tears 77 *niggard* (since our tears are *droplets* indeed when compared with the seas which now wash Timon's grave); *conceit* imagination 82 *use . . . sword* combine peace with war 83 *stint* stop 84 *leech* physician

ANTONY AND CLEOPATRA

INTRODUCTION

Critics have been known to speak of *Macbeth, King Lear*, and *Antony and Cleopatra* as Shakespeare's *Inferno, Purgatorio*, and *Paradiso*. The comparison is misleading if taken as a guide to Shakespeare's states of mind, of which we know nothing, or even as a guide to the order of the three plays, the consensus of modern opinion being that *Macbeth* (ca. 1606) falls between *King Lear* (ca. 1605) and *Antony and Cleopatra* (ca. 1607). But the notion has a certain merit if taken solely as a guide to tone.

Macbeth and *King Lear*, like *Othello* earlier, are dark plays, filled with actions taking place in what can only be called "dramatic" as well as literal night, a dark night of the soul engulfed by evil. *Antony and Cleopatra*, on the other hand, is a bright play. *Macbeth* and *King Lear*, too, are savage – if one fully responds to them, terrifying. There is no savagery in *Antony and Cleopatra*; it is moving, exhilarating, even exalting, but contains nothing that should tear an audience to tatters. The humor of *Macbeth* and *King Lear* is either grim or pitiful: a drunken porter at the gate of hell, a court jester shivering on a stormy heath. The humor of *Antony and Cleopatra* is neither grim nor pitiful, although sometimes acrid enough. Cleopatra is given qualities that make her a very unqueenly queen: she lies, wheedles, sulks, screams, and makes love, all with equal abandon. Antony is given qualities that make him in some senses more like an elderly playboy than a tragic hero. We are encouraged by Shakespeare in this play to disengage ourselves from the protagonists, to feel superior to them, even to laugh at them, as we rarely are with his earlier tragic persons.

Against laughter, however, the playwright poises sympathy and even admiration. Tawdry though he has made these seasoned old campaigners in love and war, he has also magnified and idealized them, to the point at which their mutual passion becomes glorious as well as cheap. Antony, the play tells us, has "infinite virtue," Cleopatra "infinite variety." He is the "triple pillar of the world," she is the "day o' th' world." He seems a "plated Mars," she more beautiful than Venus. His guardian spirit is called "unmatchable," she is called a "lass unparalleled." He descends from the god Hercules, she from the moon-goddess Isis. She sees him as the sun and moon, lighting this "little O, th' earth"; Charmian sees her as the "Eastern star." When Antony cries Ho! "Like boys unto a muss, kings would start forth"; Cleopatra has a hand that "kings Have lipped, and trembled kissing." When Antony will swear an oath, he cries, "Let Rome in Tiber melt and the wide arch Of the ranged empire fall!" When Cleopatra will swear, she cries, "Melt Egypt into Nile! and kindly creatures Turn all to serpents." Antony, about to die, thinks of death as a continuing amour with Cleopatra: "Where souls do couch on flowers, we'll hand in hand, And with our sprightly port make the ghosts gaze." When Cleopatra is about to die, she sees death in the same transcendent terms: "Go fetch My best attires. I am again for Cydnus, To meet Mark Antony."

Traces of Shakespeare's duality of attitude toward his lovers may be found in Plutarch, whose *Lives of the Noble Grecians and Romans Compared Together* he had read in Thomas North's magnificent English rendering (1579) of Jacques Amyot's translation of the original into French (1559). So eloquent was North's prose that in certain instances it could be assumed into blank verse with a minimum of change, as in the following well-known description of Cleopatra going to meet Antony in her barge, which should be compared with the lines of Enobarbus (II, ii, 191–241) in Shakespeare's play.

. . . She went to Antonius at the age when a woman's beauty is at the prime, and she also of best judgment. . . . She disdained to set forward otherwise but to take her barge in the river of Cydnus, the poop whereof was of gold, the sails of purple, and the oars of silver, which kept stroke in rowing after the sound of the music of flutes, hautboys, cithers, viols, and such other instruments as they played upon in the barge. And now for the person of herself: She was laid under a pavilion of cloth-of-gold of tissue, apparelled and attired like the goddess Venus commonly drawn in picture; and hard by her, on either hand of her, pretty fair boys, apparelled as painters do set forth god Cupid, with little fans in their hands, with the which they fanned wind upon her. Her ladies and gentlewomen also, the fairest of them, were apparelled like the nymphs Nereides (which are the mermaids of the waters) and like the Graces, some steering the helm, others tending the tackle and ropes of the barge, out of the which there came a wonderful passing sweet savor of perfumes that perfumed the wharf's side, pestered with innumerable multitudes of people. Some of them followed the barge all alongest the river's side, others also ran out of the city to see her coming in, so that in the end there ran such multitudes of people one after another to see her that Antonius was left post-alone in the market place in his imperial seat to give audience. And there went a rumor in the people's mouths that the goddess Venus was come to play with the god Bacchus for the general good of all Asia.

Shakespeare's play owes to Plutarch's life of Antony many of its incidents, and to North's prose the wording of occasional passages like the lines of Enobarbus referred to above. It precipitates, however, an interpretation of these materials that is spectacularly Shakespeare's own. Plutarch's narrative, for all its stress on the baffling blends of vice and virtue in great minds, is at bottom the relatively familiar story of the Great Man and the Temptress. His Antony loses the world for love, not wisely but too well, and his Cleopatra, though possibly she rises to genuine love before the end (Plutarch leaves this point undecided), is rather the instrument of a great man's downfall than a tragic figure in herself. To understand the distinctiveness of Shakespeare's treatment of her, we have only to return to the passage in Plutarch and the lines of Enobarbus already cited. Plutarch's Cleopatra is all siren, every effect calculated to ensnare the senses of the conquering Roman. Shakespeare's Cleopatra is all siren too, but she is more. The repeated paradoxes in Enobarbus' language serve notice on us that everything about her is impossible, mysteriously contradictory. Her page-boys cool her cheeks only to make them burn, "and what they undid did." Her gentlewomen are seeming mermaids, half human, half sea-creature. The silken tackle swells with a life of its own at "the touches of those flower-soft hands." The wharves come alive and have "sense," quickened by her "strange invisible perfume." The city comes alive, to "cast" its people out upon her. Antony is left sitting in the market place, whistling to the air, and the air itself, except that nature abhors a vacuum, would have "gone to gaze on Cleopatra too" and left a gap behind. She is a creature, says Enobarbus in conclusion, who makes defect perfection, and, when breathless, power breathes forth. Other women cloy the appetites they feed, "but she makes hungry Where most she satisfies." Even the vilest things are so becoming when she does them that "the holy priests Bless her when she is riggish."

This is clearly not a portrait of a mere intriguing woman, but a kind of absolute oxymoron: Cleopatra is glimpsed here as a force like the Lucretian Venus, whose vitality resists both definition and regulation. Yet enveloped as she is by Enobarbus' mocking tones, wise and faintly world-weary, calculating amusedly the effects of his words on these uninitiated Romans, she remains the more a trollop for that. His reliable anti-romanticism undercuts the picture he draws of her, and at the same time confirms it, because it comes from him.

The ambiguity of these lines extends to almost everything in the play. In the world the dramatist has given his lovers, nothing is stable, fixed, or sure, not even ultimate values; all is in motion. Seen from one point of view, the motion may be discerned as process, the inexorable march of causes and effects, exemplified in Antony's fall and epitomized by Caesar in commenting to Octavia on the futility of her efforts to preserve the peace: "But let determined things to destiny Hold unbewailed their way." Seen from another angle, the motion reveals itself as flux, the restless waxing and waning of tides, of moons, of human feeling. Especially of human feeling. Antony pursued Brutus to his death, we are reminded by Enobarbus, yet wept when he found him slain. So within the play itself Caesar weeps, having pursued Antony to his death; and Antony, desiring that Fulvia die, finds her "good, being gone"; and Enobarbus, seeking some way to leave his master, is heart-struck when he succeeds; and the Roman populace, always fickle, "Like to a vagabond flag upon the stream, Goes to and back, lackeying the varying tide, To rot itself with motion."

In such a context, it is not surprising that the lovers' passion is subject to vicissitudes, going to and back in ever more violent oscillations of attraction and recoil. Shakespeare nowhere disguises the unstable and ultimately destructive character of their relationship, and those who, like Shaw, have belabored him for not giving sexual

infatuation the satiric treatment it deserves have read too carelessly. It is likewise not surprising that the play's structure should reflect, in its abrupt and numerous shifts of scene, so marked a quality of its leading characters – their emotional and psychological vacillation. Though these shifts have also met with criticism, some finding in them a serious threat to unity, they are easily seen in the theatre to be among the dramatist's means of conveying to us an awareness of the competing values by which the lovers, and particularly Antony, are torn. "Kingdoms are clay," he declares in Egypt; "The nobleness of life Is to do thus," and embraces Cleopatra. A few hours later, however, he says with equal earnestness, "These strong Egyptian fetters I must break Or lose myself in dotage," and he departs for Rome. Again, he declares to Octavia in Rome, hereafter everything shall "be done by th' rule," yet scarcely thirty lines later, after his interview with the soothsayer, he has added, "I will to Egypt." From this point on follows a succession of fluctuations in both war and love. In war, confidence of victory shifting to despair at loss, then to new confidence, then to new despair. In love, adorings of Cleopatra changing to recriminations, then to renewed adorings, then to fresh disgust. This aspect of the play's rhythm is vividly summed up in two speeches in the third act (III, xi). "I have offended reputation," Antony says after the first sea defeat, "A most unnoble swerving": there is the voice of Rome and the soldier. A few seconds after, he says to Cleopatra, "Fall not a tear, I say: one of them rates All that is won and lost": this is the voice of Egypt and the lover.

"All that is won *and* lost" is of course the crucial ambiguity of this tragedy. Perhaps it is one about which no two readers are likely finally to agree. Much is obviously lost by the lovers in the course of the play, and Shakespeare underscores this fact, as Plutarch had done, by placing their deaths in Cleopatra's monument – that is to say, a tomb. All those imperial ambitions that once mustered the "kings o' th' earth for war" have shrunk now to this narrow stronghold, which is also a waiting grave. Antony had said as he put his arms about Cleopatra in the opening scene, "Here is my space." Now that challenge has been taken up. This is his space indeed.

But what then, if anything, has been won? The answer to this question depends as much on what one brings to *Antony and Cleopatra* as on what one finds there, for the evidence is mixed. Antony does give his life for his love before the play ends, and we observe that there are no recriminations at his final meeting with Cleopatra; only his quiet hope that she will remember him for what was noblest in him, and her acknowledgment that he was, and is, her man of men. But then, too, his death has been precipitated by her duplicity in the false report of hers; it has among its motives a self-interested desire to evade Caesar's triumph; and the suicide is even bungled in the doing: if this is a hero's death, it is a humiliating one. Likewise, Cleopatra seems to give her life for love. As Antony will be a bridegroom in his death, "and run into't As to a lover's bed," so Cleopatra will be a bride in hers, calling, "Husband, I come," receiving darkness as if it were "a lover's pinch, Which hurts, and is desired," and breathing out, in words that could equally be describing the union of life with death or the union of lover with lover, "As sweet as balm, as soft as air, as gentle – O

Antony!" This, however, is the same woman who has long studied "easy ways to die," who ends her life only after becoming convinced that Caesar means to lead her in triumph, and who has cached away with her treasurer Seleucus more than half her valuables in case of need. True, the scene with Seleucus can be so played as to indicate that she is using his confession to dupe Caesar about her intention to die. But that is precisely the point. What the actor or reader makes of her conduct here will be conditioned by what he has made of her elsewhere, by what he makes of the play as a whole, and even, perhaps, by his beliefs about human nature and the depiction of human nature in art.

Are we to take the high-sounding phrases which introduce us to this remarkable love affair in the play's first scene as amorous rant?

CLEOPATRA
    If it be love indeed, tell me how much.
ANTONY
    There's beggary in the love that can be reckoned.
CLEOPATRA
    I'll set a bourn how far to be beloved.
ANTONY
    Then must thou needs find out new heaven, new earth.

Or is there a prophetic resonance in that reference to "new heaven, new earth," which we are meant to remember when Cleopatra, dreaming of a transcendent Antony –

His face was as the heav'ns, and therein stuck
A sun and moon, which kept their course and lighted
The little O, th' earth. . . .
His legs bestrid the ocean : his reared arm
Crested the world : his voice was propertied
As all the tunèd spheres –

consigns her baser elements to "baser life"? Does the passion of these two remain a destructive element to the bitter end, doomed like all the feeling in the play to "rot itself with motion"? Or, as the world slips from them, have they a glimmering of something they could not have earlier understood, of another power besides death "Which shackles accidents and bolts up change"? Is it "paltry to be Caesar," as Cleopatra claims, since "Not being Fortune, he's but Fortune's knave"? Or is it more paltry to be Antony, and, as Caesar sees it, "give a kingdom for a mirth," as well as, eventually, the world?

To such questions, *Antony and Cleopatra*, like life itself, gives no clear-cut answers. Shakespeare holds the balance even, and does not decide for us who finally is the strumpet of the play, Antony's Cleopatra, or Caesar's Fortune, and who, therefore, is the "strumpet's fool." Those who would have it otherwise, who are "hot for certainties in this our life," as Meredith phrased it, should turn to other authors than Shakespeare, and should have been born into some other world than this.

Yale University   MAYNARD MACK

Antony and Cleopatra was first published in the folio of 1623, in a good text with full stage directions, evidently printed from Shakespeare's own draft after it had been prepared for stage production. The folio text is undivided into acts and scenes. The division appearing marginally in the present edition is editorial, and supplied only for reference purposes. The following list of departures from the folio text, amplified from the one supplied by the editor, perhaps errs on the side of inclusiveness; it omits only the most obvious typographical errors, the instances of mislineation, and the variations in speech-prefixes and proper names, including several instances of "Cleopater" which may indicate an alternative pronunciation. The adopted reading in italics is followed by the folio reading in roman.

I, i, 18 *me!* me, 39 *On* One 50 *whose* who

I, ii, 4 *charge* change 37 *fertile* foretell 58 *Charmian* Alexas 76 *Saw* Save 106 *minds* windes 108 s.d. Omitted (in F: Enter another Messenger) 110 *1. Attendant* 1. Mes. 111 *2. Attendant* 2. Mes. 114 *Messenger* 3. Mes. 134 *occasion* an occasion 175 *leave* love 180 *Hath* Have 189 *hair* heire 191 *place is* places *requires* require

I, iii, 20 *What,* What 24 *know –* know. 25 *betrayed* betrayèd 33 *sued* suèd 43 *services* Servicles 51 *thrived* thrivèd 80 *blood: no more.* blood no more ? 82 *my* (not in F)

I, iv, 3 *Our* One 8 *Vouchsafed* vouchsafe 9 *the abstract* th' abstracts 21 *smell* smels 44 *deared* fear'd 46 *lackeying* lacking 49 *Make* Makes 56 *wassails* Vassailes 75 *we* me

I, v, 5 *time* time: 29 *time?* time. 34 s.d. *Alexas* Alexas from Caesar 50 *dumbed* dumbe 61 *man* mans

II, i, 41 *warred* wan'd 43 *greater.* greater, 44 *all,* all :

II, ii, 71–72 *you . . . Alexandria ;* you, . . . Alexandria 107 *soldier* Souldier, 115–16 *staunch, . . . world* staunch . . . world: 120 *so* say 121 *reproof* proofe 122 *deserved* deservèd 146–47 *hand : | Further* hand / Further 171 s.d. *[Exeunt.]* Exit omnes. 195 *lovesick with* Love-sicke. | With 205 *glow* glove 207 *gentlewomen* Gentlewoman 224 *'no'* no *heard* hard 229 *ploughed* ploughèd 233 *And, breathless,* And breathlesse

II, iii, 8 *Octavia* (not in F) 20 *high, unmatchable* high unmatchable 24 *thee, no more but when to thee.* thee no more but : when to thee, 30 *away* alway

II, v, 10–11 *river : there, | My . . . off,* River there | My . . . off. 12 *finned* fine 28 *him,* him. 43 *is* 'tis 96 *face, to me* face to me, 111 *Alexas;* Alexas 115 *not! – Charmian,* not Charmian,

II, vi, 19 *is* his 30 *present)* how you take *present* how you take) 43 *telling,* telling. 52 *gained* gainèd 58 *composition* composion 66 *meanings* meaning 69 *of* (not in F) 81 s.d. *Manent* Manet

II, vii, 91 *is* he is 99 *grows* grow 101 *all four days* all, foure dayes, 110 *bear* beate 119 *off* of 123 *Splits* Spleet's 127 *father's* Father 128–29 *not. | Menas* not Menas

III, i, 3 *body* body, 4 *army.* Army

III, ii, 10 *Agrippa* Ant. 16 *figures* Figure 20 *beetle. [. . .] So –* Beetle, so : 49 *full* the full 59 *wept* weepe

III, iii, 21 *lookedst* look'st

III, iv, 8 *them* then 9 *took't* look't 24 *yours* your 30 *Your* You 38 *has* he's

III, v, 12 *world* would *hast* hadst *chaps,* chaps 14 *the one* (not in F)

III, vi, 13 *he there proclaimed the kings* hither proclaimèd the King 19 *reported,* reported 22 *know* knowes 28 *triumvirate* Triumpherate 29 *being, that* being that, 78 *do* does

III, vii, 4 *it is* it it 5 *Is't not* If not, 23 *Toryne* Troine 35 *muleters* Militers 51 *Actium* Action 72 *Canidius* Ven. 78 *Well* Well,

III, x, s.d. *Enobarbus* Enobarbus and Scarus 14 *June* Inne 28 *he* his

III, xi, 19 *that* them 22 *pray,* pray 44 *He is* Hee's 47 *seize* cease 56 *followed* followèd 58 *tow* stowe 59 *Thy* The

III, xiii, 10 *merèd* meered 55 *Caesar* Caesars 57 *feared* fearèd 60 *deserved* deservèd 74 *this :* this *deputation,* disputation, 90 *me. Of late,* me of late. 103 *again. This* againe, the 112–13 *eyes, | In . . . filth* eyes | In . . . filth, 132 *'a* a 137 *whipped for . . . him.* whipt. For . . . him, 162 *smite* smile 165 *discandying* discandering 168 *sits* sets 178 *sinewed* sinewèd 199 *on* in 201 s.d. *Exit* Exeunt

IV, i, 3 *combat,* combat.

IV, ii, 1 *No.* No ? 12 *And thou* Thou

IV, iii, 8 *4. Soldier* 2 10 *3. Soldier* 1 15 *loved* lovèd 17 *Omnes (speak together)* Speak together. | Omnes.

IV, iv, 5–6 *too. | What's* too, Anthony. | What's 6 *Antony* (not in F) 8 *Cleopatra* (not in F) 24 *Captain* Alex. 32 *thee* thee. 33 *steel.* Steele,

IV, v, 1, 3, 6 *Soldier* Eros 17 *Dispatch.* Dispatch

IV, vi, 20 *more* mote 36 *do't, I feel.* doo't. I feele

IV, vii, 8 s.d. *far off* (in F after 'heads', line 6)

IV, viii, 18 *My* Mine 23 *favoring* savouring 26 *Destroyed* Destroyèd

IV, xii, 4 *augurers* Auguries 9 s.d. *Alarum . . . sea-fight* (in F before line 1) 10 *betrayed* betrayèd 21 *spanieled* pannelled

IV, xiii, 10 *death.* death

IV, xiv, 4 *towered* toward 10 *dislimns* dislimes 19 *Caesar* Caesars 77 *ensued* ensuèd 95 s.d. *Kills himself* (in F after line 93) 104 *ho* how

IV, xv, 54 *lived the* lived. The 76 *e'en* in 86 *What, what !* What, what

V, i, s.d. *Maecenas* Menas 28 *Agrippa* Dol. 31 *Agrippa* Dola. 36 *followed* followèd 48 s.d. *Enter an Egyptian* (in F after 'says', line 51) 53 *all she has,* all, she has 54 *intents desires* intents, desires, 59 *live* leave 68 s.d. *Exit* Exit Proculeius

V, ii, 35 *You* Pro. [s.p.] You 56 *varletry* Varlotarie 66 *me* (not in F) 81 *O,* o' 87 *autumn 'twas* Anthony it was 104 *smites* suites 139 *valued* valewèd 151 *followed* followèd 216 *Ballad us out o'* Ballads us out a 223 *my* mine 317 *awry* away 318 s.d. *in.* in, and Dolabella. 324 *here! Charmian* here Charmian 340 *diadem* diadem ; 341 *mistress ;* Mistris

ANTONY AND CLEOPATRA

*

I, i *Enter Demetrius and Philo.*

PHILO

1 Nay, but this dotage of our general's
O'erflows the measure : those his goodly eyes
That o'er the files and musters of the war
4 Have glowed like plated Mars, now bend, now turn
5 The office and devotion of their view
6 Upon a tawny front. His captain's heart,
Which in the scuffles of great fights hath burst
8 The buckles on his breast, reneges all temper
And is become the bellows and the fan
10 To cool a gypsy's lust.
Flourish. Enter Antony, Cleopatra, her Ladies, the Train, with Eunuchs fanning her.
Look where they come :
Take but good note, and you shall see in him
12 The triple pillar of the world transformed
13 Into a strumpet's fool. Behold and see.

I, i The palace of Cleopatra in Alexandria   1 *dotage* (applicable not only to the aged ; Antony 'dotes' on Cleopatra)   4 *plated* armored   5 *office* service   6 *front* face (with pun on military sense)   8 *reneges* rejects ; *temper* moderation   10 *gypsy* (1) native of Egypt (gypsies were thought to originate thence), (2) slut   12 *The triple . . . world* one of the three 'pillars' of the world (the others being Octavius Caesar and Lepidus)   13 *fool* dupe   16 *bourn* limit   18 *Grates . . . sum* it annoys me ; be brief   20 *Fulvia* Antony's wife   21 *scarce-bearded* hardly grown up (Octavius was twenty-three)   23 *Take* in seize ; *enfranchise* set free   26 *dismission* recall   28 *process* summons   31 *Is Caesar's homager* pays respect to Caesar's authority ; *else* or else

CLEOPATRA
If it be love indeed, tell me how much.
ANTONY
There's beggary in the love that can be reckoned.
CLEOPATRA
I'll set a bourn how far to be beloved.   16
ANTONY
Then must thou needs find out new heaven, new earth.
Enter a Messenger.
MESSENGER
News, my good lord, from Rome.
ANTONY   Grates me ! The sum.   18
CLEOPATRA
Nay, hear them, Antony.
Fulvia perchance is angry ; or who knows   20
If the scarce-bearded Caesar have not sent   21
His pow'rful mandate to you, 'Do this, or this ;
Take in that kingdom, and enfranchise that.   23
Perform't, or else we damn thee.'
ANTONY   How, my love ?
CLEOPATRA
Perchance ? Nay, and most like :
You must not stay here longer, your dismission   26
Is come from Caesar ; therefore hear it, Antony.
Where's Fulvia's process ? Caesar's I would say ? both ?   28
Call in the messengers. As I am Egypt's Queen,
Thou blushest, Antony, and that blood of thine
Is Caesar's homager : else so thy cheek pays shame   31
When shrill-tongued Fulvia scolds. The messengers !

ANTONY
　　Let Rome in Tiber melt and the wide arch
34　Of the ranged empire fall! Here is my space,
　　Kingdoms are clay: our dungy earth alike
　　Feeds beast as man. The nobleness of life
37　Is to do thus; when such a mutual pair
　　And such a twain can do't, in which I bind,
39　On pain of punishment, the world to weet
　　We stand up peerless.
　　CLEOPATRA　　　　　Excellent falsehood!
　　Why did he marry Fulvia, and not love her?
42　I'll seem the fool I am not. Antony
　　Will be himself.
　　ANTONY　　　　But stirred by Cleopatra.
　　Now for the love of Love and her soft hours,
45　Let's not confound the time with conference harsh.
46　There's not a minute of our lives should stretch
　　Without some pleasure now. What sport to-night?
　　CLEOPATRA
　　Hear the ambassadors.
　　ANTONY　　　　　Fie, wrangling queen!
　　Whom every thing becomes – to chide, to laugh,
50　To weep; whose every passion fully strives
　　To make itself, in thee, fair and admired.
　　No messenger but thine, and all alone
　　To-night we'll wander through the streets and note
　　The qualities of people. Come, my queen;
　　Last night you did desire it. – Speak not to us.
　　　　　　　Exeunt [Antony and Cleopatra] with the Train.
　　DEMETRIUS
56　Is Caesar with Antonius prized so slight?
　　PHILO
　　Sir, sometimes when he is not Antony
58　He comes too short of that great property
　　Which still should go with Antony.
　　DEMETRIUS　　　　　I am full sorry
60　That he approves the common liar, who
　　Thus speaks of him at Rome; but I will hope
　　Of better deeds to-morrow. Rest you happy!　　_Exeunt._

*

I, ii　　_Enter Enobarbus, Lamprius, a Soothsayer, Rannius,_
　　　　Lucillius, Charmian, Iras, Mardian the Eunuch, and
　　　　Alexas.
　　CHARMIAN Lord Alexas, sweet Alexas, most anything
2　Alexas, almost most absolute Alexas, where's the sooth-
　　sayer that you praised so to th' Queen? O that I knew
4　this husband which, you say, must charge his horns
　　with garlands!
　　ALEXAS Soothsayer!
　　SOOTHSAYER Your will?
　　CHARMIAN Is this the man? Is't you, sir, that know
　　things?
　　SOOTHSAYER
　　In nature's infinite book of secrecy
　　A little I can read.
　　ALEXAS Show him your hand.
　　ENOBARBUS
　　Bring in the banquet quickly: wine enough
　　Cleopatra's health to drink.
　　CHARMIAN Good sir, give me good fortune.
　　SOOTHSAYER
　　I make not, but foresee.

　　CHARMIAN Pray then, foresee me one.
　　SOOTHSAYER
　　You shall be yet far fairer than you are.
　　CHARMIAN He means in flesh.　　　　　　　　　17
　　IRAS No, you shall paint when you are old.
　　CHARMIAN Wrinkles forbid!
　　ALEXAS Vex not his prescience, be attentive.
　　CHARMIAN Hush!
　　SOOTHSAYER
　　You shall be more beloving than beloved.
　　CHARMIAN I had rather heat my liver with drinking.　23
　　ALEXAS Nay, hear him.
　　CHARMIAN Good now, some excellent fortune. Let me
　　be married to three kings in a forenoon and widow them
　　all. Let me have a child at fifty, to whom Herod of Jewry 27
　　may do homage. Find me to marry me with Octavius
　　Caesar, and companion me with my mistress.　　29
　　SOOTHSAYER
　　You shall outlive the lady whom you serve.
　　CHARMIAN O excellent! I love long life better than figs.
　　SOOTHSAYER
　　You have seen and proved a fairer former fortune　　32
　　Than that which is to approach.
　　CHARMIAN Then belike my children shall have no names. 34
　　Prithee, how many boys and wenches must I have?　35
　　SOOTHSAYER
　　If every of your wishes had a womb,
　　And fertile every wish, a million.
　　CHARMIAN Out, fool! I forgive thee for a witch.　　38
　　ALEXAS You think none but your sheets are privy to your 39
　　wishes.
　　CHARMIAN Nay, come, tell Iras hers.
　　ALEXAS We'll know all our fortunes.
　　ENOBARBUS Mine, and most of our fortunes, to-night,
　　shall be – drunk to bed.
　　IRAS There's a palm presages chastity, if nothing else.
　　CHARMIAN E'en as the o'erflowing Nilus presageth
　　famine.
　　IRAS Go, you wild bedfellow, you cannot soothsay.
　　CHARMIAN Nay, if an oily palm be not a fruitful prog-　48
　　nostication, I cannot scratch mine ear. Prithee tell her
　　but a workyday fortune.　　　　　　　　　　　50
　　SOOTHSAYER Your fortunes are alike.
　　IRAS But how, but how? Give me particulars.
　　SOOTHSAYER I have said.
　　IRAS Am I not an inch of fortune better than she?

34 _ranged_ well-ordered (?), wide-ranging (?)　37 _thus_ (perhaps indicating
an embrace; perhaps a general reference to their way of life)　39 _weet_
know　42 _the fool . . . not_ i.e. foolish enough to believe you　45 _confound_
destroy, waste　46 _stretch_ pass　50 _passion_ mood　56 _prized_ valued
58 _property_ distinction　60 _approves_ confirms
I, ii The chambers of Cleopatra　s.d. _Enter Enobarbus . . . Alexas_ (thus in
folio, but Lamprius, Rannius, and Lucillius do not speak in the scene and
do not appear elsewhere in the play. Possibly Lamprius is the name of the
Soothsayer.)　2 _absolute_ perfect　4–5 _must . . . garlands_ i.e. must be not
only a cuckold and grow horns (as cuckolds – husbands of unfaithful
wives – were humorously said to do) but a champion cuckold, wearing a
winner's garland　17 _He . . . flesh_ he means that you will put on weight
23 _heat . . . drinking_ i.e. rather than with unreciprocated love (the liver
being regarded as love's residence)　27–28 _to . . . homage_ i.e. to whom even
King Herod (who massacred the infants of Judea) would do homage　29
companion me with give me as my servant　32 _proved_ experienced　34
have no names be illegitimate　35 _wenches_ girls　38 _I . . . witch_ i.e. I can
see that you have no prophetic powers　39 _privy to_ in on the secret of
48 _oily palm_ (symptom of sensuality); _fruitful prognostication_ prophetic
sign of fertility　50 _workyday_ ordinary

CHARMIAN Well, if you were but an inch of fortune better than I, where would you choose it?

IRAS Not in my husband's nose.

CHARMIAN Our worser thoughts Heavens mend! Alexas
– come, his fortune, his fortune. O, let him marry a
60 woman that cannot go, sweet Isis, I beseech thee, and
let her die too, and give him a worse, and let worse
follow worse till the worst of all follow him laughing
to his grave, fiftyfold a cuckold. Good Isis, hear me this
prayer, though thou deny me a matter of more weight:
good Isis, I beseech thee.

IRAS Amen, dear goddess, hear that prayer of the people.
67 For, as it is a heartbreaking to see a handsome man loose-
wived, so it is a deadly sorrow to behold a foul knave
69 uncuckolded. Therefore, dear Isis, keep decorum, and
fortune him accordingly.

CHARMIAN Amen.

ALEXAS Lo now, if it lay in their hands to make me a
cuckold, they would make themselves whores but
74 they'ld do't.

Enter Cleopatra.

ENOBARBUS
Hush, here comes Antony.

CHARMIAN   Not he, the Queen.

CLEOPATRA
Saw you my lord?

ENOBARBUS   No, lady.

CLEOPATRA   Was he not here?

CHARMIAN No, madam.

CLEOPATRA
He was disposed to mirth; but on the sudden
A Roman thought hath struck him. Enobarbus!

ENOBARBUS Madam?

CLEOPATRA
Seek him, and bring him hither. Where's Alexas?

ALEXAS
Here at your service. My lord approaches.

Enter Antony with a Messenger [and Attendants].

CLEOPATRA
We will not look upon him. Go with us.

*Exeunt [all but Antony, Messenger,
and Attendants].*

MESSENGER
Fulvia thy wife first came into the field.

ANTONY
Against my brother Lucius?

MESSENGER Ay.
87 But soon that war had end, and the time's state
Made friends of them, jointing their force 'gainst Caesar,

Whose better issue in the war from Italy   89
Upon the first encounter drave them.   90

ANTONY   Well, what worst?

MESSENGER
The nature of bad news infects the teller.

ANTONY
When it concerns the fool or coward. On.
Things that are past are done with me. 'Tis thus:
Who tells me true, though in his tale lie death,
I hear him as he flattered.   95

MESSENGER   Labienus
(This is stiff news) hath with his Parthian force
Extended Asia: from Euphrates,   97
His conquering banner shook, from Syria
To Lydia and to Ionia,
Whilst –

ANTONY Antony, thou wouldst say.

MESSENGER   O, my lord.

ANTONY
Speak to me home, mince not the general tongue,   101
Name Cleopatra as she is called in Rome:
Rail thou in Fulvia's phrase, and taunt my faults
With such full license as both truth and malice   104
Have power to utter. O, then we bring forth weeds
When our quick minds lie still, and our ills told us   106
Is as our earing. Fare thee well awhile.   107

MESSENGER
At your noble pleasure.   *Exit Messenger.*

ANTONY
From Sicyon, how the news? Speak there!

1. ATTENDANT
The man from Sicyon – is there such an one?

2. ATTENDANT
He stays upon your will.   111

ANTONY   Let him appear.
These strong Egyptian fetters I must break
Or lose myself in dotage.

Enter another Messenger, with a letter.
                        What are you?

MESSENGER
Fulvia thy wife is dead.

ANTONY   Where died she?

MESSENGER
In Sicyon.
Her length of sickness, with what else more serious
Importeth thee to know, this bears.   117

[Gives a letter.]

ANTONY   Forbear me. *[Exit Messenger.]*
There's a great spirit gone! Thus did I desire it:
What our contempts doth often hurl from us,
We wish it ours again. The present pleasure,
By revolution low'ring, does become   121
The opposite of itself: she's good, being gone;
The hand could pluck her back that shoved her on.
I must from this enchanting queen break off: 124
Ten thousand harms, more than the ills I know,
My idleness doth hatch.   126

Enter Enobarbus.
How now, Enobarbus!

ENOBARBUS What's your pleasure, sir?

ANTONY I must with haste from hence.

ENOBARBUS Why, then we kill all our women. We see
how mortal an unkindness is to them. If they suffer our
departure, death's the word.

---

60 *go* bear children (?), give – or receive – sexual satisfaction (?); *Isis* Egyptian goddess of earth, fertility, and the moon   **67** *loose-wived* married to a loose woman   **69** *keep decorum* i.e. act as suits his quality   **74** s.d. (this, the folio's, placing of Cleopatra's entrance suggests either that the sound of her approach is heard before she can be seen, thus causing Enobarbus' error, or that his remark is ironical, alluding to her power over Antony's will)   **87** *time's state* conditions of the moment   **89** *issue* success   **90** *drave* drove   **95** *as* as if; *Labienus* Quintus Labienus, who had been sent by Brutus and Cassius to seek aid against Antony and Octavius Caesar from Orodes, King of Parthia, and was now commanding a Parthian army   **97** *Extended* seized   **101** *home* plainly; *mince . . . tongue* don't soften what everybody is saying   **104** *license* freedom   **106** *quick* live, fertile   **107** *earing* being ploughed (to uproot the weeds)   **111** *stays upon* awaits   **117** *Importeth* concerns; *Forbear* leave   **121** *By revolution low'ring* i.e. moving downward on the revolving wheel of our opinions   **124** *enchanting* (Cleopatra is felt by the Romans in the play to have witchlike powers of seduction)   **126** *idleness* trifling

ANTONY I must be gone.

ENOBARBUS Under a compelling occasion let women die.
It were pity to cast them away for nothing, though
between them and a great cause they should be esteemed nothing. Cleopatra, catching but the least noise
of this, dies instantly: I have seen her die twenty times
139   upon far poorer moment. I do think there is mettle in
death, which commits some loving act upon her, she
hath such a celerity in dying.

ANTONY She is cunning past man's thought.

ENOBARBUS Alack, sir, no; her passions are made of
nothing but the finest part of pure love. We cannot call
her winds and waters sighs and tears: they are greater
storms and tempests than almanacs can report. This
147   cannot be cunning in her; if it be, she makes a shower of
148   rain as well as Jove.

ANTONY Would I had never seen her!

ENOBARBUS O, sir, you had then left unseen a wonderful
piece of work, which not to have been blest withal
would have discredited your travel.

ANTONY Fulvia is dead.

ENOBARBUS Sir?

ANTONY Fulvia is dead.

ENOBARBUS Fulvia?

ANTONY Dead.

ENOBARBUS Why, sir, give the gods a thankful sacrifice.
When it pleaseth their deities to take the wife of a man
160   from him, it shows to man the tailors of the earth;
comforting therein, that when old robes are worn out,
there are members to make new. If there were no more
163   women but Fulvia, then had you indeed a cut, and the
164   case to be lamented. This grief is crowned with consola-
tion, your old smock brings forth a new petticoat, and
indeed the tears live in an onion that should water this
sorrow.

ANTONY
167   The business she hath broachèd in the state
Cannot endure my absence.

169 ENOBARBUS And the business you have broached here
cannot be without you; especially that of Cleopatra's,
171   which wholly depends on your abode.

ANTONY
No more light answers. Let our officers
173   Have notice what we purpose. I shall break
174   The cause of our expedience to the Queen
And get her leave to part. For not alone
176   The death of Fulvia, with more urgent touches,
Do strongly speak to us, but the letters too
178   Of many our contriving friends in Rome
179   Petition us at home. Sextus Pompeius
Hath given the dare to Caesar and commands
The empire of the sea. Our slippery people,
Whose love is never linked to the deserver
183   Till his deserts are past, begin to throw
Pompey the Great and all his dignities
Upon his son; who, high in name and power,
186   Higher than both in blood and life, stands up
187   For the main soldier; whose quality, going on,
188   The sides o' th' world may danger. Much is breeding,
189   Which, like the courser's hair, hath yet but life
And not a serpent's poison. Say, our pleasure,
191   To such whose place is under us, requires
Our quick remove from hence.

ENOBARBUS I shall do't.

[Exeunt.]

*

Enter Cleopatra, Charmian, Alexas, and Iras.   I, iii

CLEOPATRA
Where is he?

CHARMIAN I did not see him since.

CLEOPATRA
See where he is, who's with him, what he does:
I did not send you. If you find him sad,   3
Say I am dancing; if in mirth, report
That I am sudden sick. Quick, and return. [Exit Alexas.]

CHARMIAN
Madam, methinks, if you did love him dearly,
You do not hold the method to enforce
The like from him.

CLEOPATRA   What should I do, I do not?   8

CHARMIAN
In each thing give him way, cross him in nothing.

CLEOPATRA
Thou teachest like a fool: the way to lose him!

CHARMIAN
Tempt him not so too far. I wish, forbear.   11
In time we hate that which we often fear.
     Enter Antony.
But here comes Antony.

CLEOPATRA   I am sick and sullen.

ANTONY
I am sorry to give breathing to my purpose —   14

CLEOPATRA
Help me away, dear Charmian! I shall fall.
It cannot be thus long; the sides of nature   16
Will not sustain it.

ANTONY   Now, my dearest queen —

CLEOPATRA
Pray you stand farther from me.

ANTONY   What's the matter?

CLEOPATRA
I know by that same eye there's some good news.
What, says the married woman you may go?   20
Would she had never given you leave to come!
Let her not say 'tis I that keep you here.
I have no power upon you: hers you are.

ANTONY
The gods best know —

CLEOPATRA   O, never was there queen
So mightily betrayed: yet at the first
I saw the treasons planted.

ANTONY   Cleopatra —

CLEOPATRA
Why should I think you can be mine, and true,
(Though you in swearing shake the thronèd gods)
Who have been false to Fulvia? Riotous madness,

139 *moment* cause; *mettle* vigor   147 *makes* manufactures   148 *Jove* i.e.
Jupiter Pluvius, Roman god of rain   160 *the tailors* i.e. that the gods are
the tailors   163, 164, 169 (in *cut, case, business,* and *broached,* Enobarbus
puns bawdily)   167 *broachèd* opened up   171 *abode* staying   173 *break*
tell   174 *expedience* haste   176 *touches* motives   178 *contriving* i.e.
acting in my interest   179 *at home* to return home; *Sextus Pompeius* son
of Pompey the Great, who had been outlawed, but, owing to the division
between Antony and Octavius Caesar, was able to seize Sicily and command
the Roman sea-routes   183 *throw* transfer   186 *blood and life* vital energy
187 *quality* character and position; *going on* evolving   188 *danger* en-
danger   189 *courser's hair* (horse hairs in water were thought to come to
life as small serpents)   191 *place* rank
I, iii The chambers of Cleopatra   3 *sad* serious   8 *I do not* that I am not
doing   11 *Tempt* try; *I wish* I wish you would   14 *breathing* utterance
16 *sides of nature* human body   20 *the married woman* i.e. Fulvia

To be entangled with those mouth-made vows
Which break themselves in swearing.

ANTONY   Most sweet queen –

CLEOPATRA

32 Nay, pray you seek no color for your going,
33 But bid farewell, and go : when you sued staying,
Then was the time for words : no going then,
Eternity was in our lips and eyes,
36 Bliss in our brows' bent : none our parts so poor
37 But was a race of heaven. They are so still,
Or thou, the greatest soldier of the world,
Art turned the greatest liar.

ANTONY   How now, lady ?

CLEOPATRA

I would I had thy inches ; thou shouldst know
41 There were a heart in Egypt.

ANTONY   Hear me, Queen ;
The strong necessity of time commands
Our services awhile, but my full heart
44 Remains in use with you. Our Italy
45 Shines o'er with civil swords ; Sextus Pompeius
Makes his approaches to the port of Rome ;
Equality of two domestic powers
48 Breed scrupulous faction ; the hated, grown to strength,
Are newly grown to love ; the condemned Pompey,
Rich in his father's honor, creeps apace
Into the hearts of such as have not thrived
52 Upon the present state, whose numbers threaten ;
53 And quietness, grown sick of rest, would purge
54 By any desperate change. My more particular,
55 And that which most with you should safe my going,
Is Fulvia's death.

CLEOPATRA

Though age from folly could not give me freedom,
It does from childishness. Can Fulvia die ?

ANTONY

She's dead, my queen.
Look here, and at thy sovereign leisure read
61 The garboils she awaked. At the last, best,
See when and where she died.

CLEOPATRA   O most false love !
63 Where be the sacred vials thou shouldst fill
With sorrowful water ? Now I see, I see,
In Fulvia's death, how mine received shall be.

ANTONY

Quarrel no more, but be prepared to know
The purposes I bear : which are, or cease,
As you shall give th' advice. By the fire   68
That quickens Nilus' slime, I go from hence   69
Thy soldier, servant, making peace or war
As thou affects.   71

CLEOPATRA   Cut my lace, Charmian, come ;
But let it be, I am quickly ill, and well –
So Antony loves.   73

ANTONY   My precious queen, forbear,
And give true evidence to his love, which stands   74
An honorable trial.

CLEOPATRA   So Fulvia told me.   75
I prithee turn aside and weep for her ;
Then bid adieu to me, and say the tears
Belong to Egypt. Good now, play one scene
Of excellent dissembling, and let it look,
Like perfect honor.

ANTONY   You'll heat my blood : no more.

CLEOPATRA

You can do better yet ; but this is meetly.   81

ANTONY

Now by my sword –

CLEOPATRA   And target. Still he mends.   82
But this is not the best. Look, prithee, Charmian,
How this Herculean Roman does become   84
The carriage of his chafe.

ANTONY

I'll leave you, lady.

CLEOPATRA   Courteous lord, one word.
Sir, you and I must part, but that's not it :
Sir, you and I have loved, but there's not it ;
That you know well. Something it is I would –
O, my oblivion is a very Antony,   90
And I am all forgotten.   91

ANTONY   But that your royalty
Holds idleness your subject, I should take you
For idleness itself.

CLEOPATRA   'Tis sweating labor
To bear such idleness so near the heart
As Cleopatra this. But, sir, forgive me,
Since my becomings kill me when they do not   96
Eye well to you. Your honor calls you hence ;   97
Therefore be deaf to my unpitied folly,
And all the gods go with you. Upon your sword
Sit laurel victory, and smooth success
Be strewed before your feet !

ANTONY   Let us go. Come :
Our separation so abides and flies
That thou residing here goes yet with me,
And I hence fleeting here remain with thee.
Away !   *Exeunt.*

*

Enter Octavius [Caesar], reading a letter, Lepidus,   I, iv
and their Train.

CAESAR

You may see, Lepidus, and henceforth know
It is not Caesar's natural vice to hate
Our great competitor. From Alexandria   3
This is the news : he fishes, drinks, and wastes
The lamps of night in revel ; is not more manlike
Than Cleopatra, nor the queen of Ptolemy   6

32 *color* pretext   33 *sued* begged for   36 *bent* curve   37 *a race of heaven* of heavenly origin (?), of heavenly flavor (?)   41 *Egypt* Cleopatra   44 *in . . . you* for you to keep and use   45 *civil swords* i.e. civil war   48 *scrupulous faction* contest over trifles   52 *state* government   53–54 *grown . . . change* i.e. ill through peace, would cure itself by letting blood   54 *particular* personal concern   55 *safe* make safe   61 *garboils* commotions ; *best* best news of all   63–64 *sacred vials . . . water* (a reference to the practice of consecrating bottles of tears to the dead)   68 *fire* i.e. the sun   69 *quickens* vivifies ; *Nilus' slime* fertile mud left by the Nile's annual overflow   71 *affects* choosest ; *lace* i.e. of her bodice   73 *So* provided (?), with sudden changes like my own change now (?) ; *forbear* desist   74 *stands* will sustain   75 *told* taught (through my observing how faithful you were to her)   81 *meetly* well suited to the occasion   82 *target* shield   84–85 *How . . . chafe* i.e. how becomingly he plays his role of angry Hercules (from whom Antony was supposed to be descended)   90 *my . . . Antony* my forgetfulness is like Antony, who is now leaving, i.e. forgetting, me   91 *I . . . forgotten* (1) I have forgotten what I was going to say, (2) I am all forgotten by Antony   91–92 *But . . . subject* if you were not the queen of trifling   96 *my becomings* the emotions that become me (in my situation of abandoned lover)   97 *Eye* look
I, iv The house of Octavius Caesar in Rome   3 *competitor* partner   6 *Ptolemy* Cleopatra's dead husband

7 More womanly than he ; hardly gave audience, or
Vouchsafed to think he had partners. You shall find there
9 A man who is the abstract of all faults
That all men follow.

LEPIDUS   I must not think there are
11 Evils enow to darken all his goodness :
12 His faults, in him, seem as the spots of heaven,
More fiery by night's blackness ; hereditary
14 Rather than purchased, what he cannot change
Than what he chooses.

CAESAR
You are too indulgent. Let's grant it is not
Amiss to tumble on the bed of Ptolemy,
To give a kingdom for a mirth, to sit
19 And keep the turn of tippling with a slave,
20 To reel the streets at noon, and stand the buffet
With knaves that smell of sweat. Say this becomes him
22 (As his composure must be rare indeed
Whom these things cannot blemish), yet must Antony
24 No way excuse his foils when we do bear
So great weight in his lightness. If he filled
26 His vacancy with his voluptuousness,
27 Full surfeits and the dryness of his bones
28 Call on him for't. But to confound such time
29 That drums him from his sport and speaks as loud
As his own state and ours, 'tis to be chid
31 As we rate boys who, being mature in knowledge,
Pawn their experience to their present pleasure
33 And so rebel to judgment.

Enter a Messenger.

LEPIDUS   Here's more news.

MESSENGER
Thy biddings have been done, and every hour,
Most noble Caesar, shalt thou have report
How 'tis abroad. Pompey is strong at sea,
And it appears he is beloved of those
That only have feared Caesar : to the ports
39 The discontents repair, and men's reports
40 Give him much wronged.

CAESAR   I should have known no less.
41 It hath been taught us from the primal state
That he which is was wished until he were ;
And the ebbed man, ne'er loved till ne'er worth love,
44 Comes deared by being lacked. This common body,
45 Like to a vagabond flag upon the stream,
46 Goes to and back, lackeying the varying tide,
To rot itself with motion.

MESSENGER   Caesar, I bring thee word
Menecrates and Menas, famous pirates,
Make the sea serve them, which they ear and wound
With keels of every kind. Many hot inroads
They make in Italy ; the borders maritime
52 Lack blood to think on't, and flush youth revolt.
No vessel can peep forth but 'tis as soon
54 Taken as seen ; for Pompey's name strikes more
Than could his war resisted.

CAESAR   Antony,
56 Leave thy lascivious wassails. When thou once
Was beaten from Modena, where thou slew'st
Hirtius and Pansa, consuls, at thy heel
Did famine follow, whom thou fought'st against
(Though daintily brought up) with patience more
Than savages could suffer. Thou didst drink
62 The stale of horses and the gilded puddle

Which beasts would cough at. Thy palate then did deign
The roughest berry on the rudest hedge.
Yea, like the stag when snow the pasture sheets,
The barks of trees thou browsed. On the Alps
It is reported thou didst eat strange flesh,
Which some did die to look on. And all this
(It wounds thine honor that I speak it now)
Was borne so like a soldier that thy cheek
So much as lanked not.   71

LEPIDUS   'Tis pity of him.

CAESAR
Let his shames quickly
Drive him to Rome. 'Tis time we twain
Did show ourselves i' th' field ; and to that end
Assemble we immediate council. Pompey
Thrives in our idleness.

LEPIDUS   To-morrow, Caesar,
I shall be furnished to inform you rightly
Both what by sea and land I can be able   78
To front this present time.   79

CAESAR   Till which encounter,
It is my business too. Farewell.

LEPIDUS
Farewell, my lord. What you shall know meantime
Of stirs abroad, I shall beseech you, sir,
To let me be partaker.

CAESAR   Doubt not, sir ;
I knew it for my bond.   *Exeunt.* 84

*

Enter Cleopatra, Charmian, Iras, and Mardian.   I, v
CLEOPATRA Charmian !
CHARMIAN Madam ?
CLEOPATRA
Ha, ha.   3
Give me to drink mandragora.   4
CHARMIAN   Why, madam ?
CLEOPATRA
That I might sleep out this great gap of time
My Antony is away.
CHARMIAN   You think of him too much.
CLEOPATRA
O, 'tis treason !
CHARMIAN   Madam, I trust, not so.

---

7 *audience* i.e. to Caesar's messengers (cf. I, i)   9 *is the abstract of* sums up
11 *enow* enough   12–13 *His . . . blackness* i.e. like stars that show the
brighter by night's blackness, Antony's faults stand out the more in the
present dark political situation   14 *purchased* acquired   19 *keep . . . of*
take turns   20 *stand the buffet* trade blows   22 *his composure* that man's
make-up   24 *foils* disgraces   24–25 *when . . . lightness* when his levity
puts so heavy a burden upon us   26 *vacancy* leisure   27–28 *Full . . .
him* i.e. let his own physical symptoms be the reckoning   28 *confound*
destroy, waste   29–30 *speaks . . . ours* calls urgently for decisions affecting
the political futures of all of us   31 *rate* berate ; *mature in knowledge* old
enough to know better   33 *to judgment* against good sense   39 *discontents*
discontented   40 *Give* declare   41 *from . . . state* since government
began   44 *Comes deared* becomes beloved ; *common body* common people
45 *flag* iris   46 *lackeying* following obsequiously   52 *Lack blood* grow
pale ; *flush* vigorous   54–55 *strikes . . . resisted* is more effective than his
forces would be if opposed   56 *wassails* carousings   62 *stale* urine ;
gilded yellow-colored   71 *lanked* thinned   78 *be able* muster   79 *front*
cope with   84 *bond* duty
I, v The chambers of Cleopatra   3 *Ha, ha* (perhaps indicating a yawn)
4 *mandragora* mandrake (a narcotic)

CLEOPATRA
Thou, eunuch Mardian !

MARDIAN   What's your Highness' pleasure ?

CLEOPATRA
Not now to hear thee sing. I take no pleasure
In aught an eunuch has : 'tis well for thee
11   That, being unseminared, thy freer thoughts
May not fly forth of Egypt. Hast thou affections ?

MARDIAN Yes, gracious madam.

CLEOPATRA Indeed ?

MARDIAN
Not in deed, madam ; for I can do nothing
But what indeed is honest to be done :
Yet have I fierce affections, and think
What Venus did with Mars.

CLEOPATRA   O Charmian,
Where think'st thou he is now ? Stands he, or sits he ?
Or does he walk ? or is he on his horse ?
O happy horse, to bear the weight of Antony !
22   Do bravely, horse ! for wot'st thou whom thou mov'st ?
23   The demi-Atlas of this earth, the arm
24   And burgonet of men. He's speaking now,
Or murmuring, 'Where's my serpent of old Nile ?'
(For so he calls me). Now I feed myself
With most delicious poison. Think on me,
28   That am with Phoebus' amorous pinches black
29   And wrinkled deep in time ? Broad-fronted Caesar,
When thou wast here above the ground, I was
A morsel for a monarch ; and great Pompey
Would stand and make his eyes grow in my brow ;
33   There would he anchor his aspect, and die
With looking on his life.
           Enter Alexas.

ALEXAS   Sovereign of Egypt, hail !

CLEOPATRA
How much unlike art thou Mark Antony !
36   Yet, coming from him, that great med'cine hath
With his tinct gilded thee.
38   How goes it with my brave Mark Antony ?

ALEXAS
Last thing he did, dear Queen,
He kissed – the last of many doubled kisses –
41   This orient pearl. His speech sticks in my heart.

CLEOPATRA
Mine ear must pluck it thence.

ALEXAS   'Good friend,' quoth he,
43   'Say the firm Roman to great Egypt sends
This treasure of an oyster ; at whose foot,
To mend the petty present, I will piece
Her opulent throne with kingdoms. All the East
(Say thou) shall call her mistress.' So he nodded,

And soberly did mount an arm-gaunt steed,   48
Who neighed so high that what I would have spoke
Was beastly dumbed by him.   50

CLEOPATRA   What was he, sad or merry ?

ALEXAS
Like to the time o' th' year between the extremes
Of hot and cold, he was nor sad nor merry.

CLEOPATRA
O well-divided disposition ! Note him,
Note him, good Charmian, 'tis the man ; but note him.   54
He was not sad, for he would shine on those
That make their looks by his ; he was not merry,
Which seemed to tell them his remembrance lay
In Egypt with his joy ; but between both.
O heavenly mingle ! Be'st thou sad or merry,
The violence of either thee becomes,
So does it no man else. – Met'st thou my posts ?   61

ALEXAS
Ay, madam, twenty several messengers.
Why do you send so thick ?

CLEOPATRA   Who's born that day
When I forget to send to Antony
Shall die a beggar. Ink and paper, Charmian.
Welcome, my good Alexas. Did I, Charmian,
Ever love Caesar so ?

CHARMIAN   O that brave Caesar !

CLEOPATRA
Be choked with such another emphasis !
Say 'the brave Antony.'

CHARMIAN   The valiant Caesar !

CLEOPATRA
By Isis, I will give thee bloody teeth
If thou with Caesar paragon again   71
My man of men.

CHARMIAN   By your most gracious pardon,
I sing but after you.

CLEOPATRA   My salad days,   73
When I was green in judgment, cold in blood,
To say as I said then. But come, away,
Get me ink and paper.
He shall have every day a several greeting,
Or I'll unpeople Egypt.   *Exeunt.* 78

                         *

Enter Pompey, Menecrates, and Menas, in warlike   II, i
manner.

POMPEY
If the great gods be just, they shall assist
The deeds of justest men.

MENECRATES   Know, worthy Pompey,
That what they do delay, they not deny.

POMPEY
Whiles we are suitors to their throne, decays   4
The thing we sue for.

MENECRATES   We, ignorant of ourselves,
Beg often our own harms, which the wise pow'rs
Deny us for our good : so find we profit
By losing of our prayers.

POMPEY   I shall do well :
The people love me, and the sea is mine ;
My powers are crescent, and my auguring hope   10
Says it will come to th' full. Mark Antony   11
In Egypt sits at dinner, and will make

---

11 *unseminared* unsexed   22 *wot'st* knowest   23 *demi-Atlas* i.e. Antony
and Caesar, like Atlas, support the world between them (Lepidus being
of no importance)   24 *burgonet* helmet   28 *Phoebus'* the sun's   29
Broad-fronted with broad forehead ; *Caesar* Julius Caesar   33 *aspect*
gaze   36–37 *that . . . thee* (Cleopatra playfully compares Antony to the
'great medicine' of the alchemists which turned baser metals to gold :
even Alexas shows some effect)   38 *brave* splendid   41 *orient* i.e. bright
as the east   43 *firm* constant   48 *arm-gaunt* toughened for war (?),
battle-hungry (?)   50 *dumbed* silenced   54 *the man* i.e. the real Antony
61 *posts* messengers   71 *paragon* compare   73 *salad days* green youth
78 *unpeople* i.e. by sending messengers to Antony
II, i Pompey's house in Messina   4–5 *Whiles . . . for* i.e. the thing we pray
for loses its worth even while we pray   10 *crescent* increasing   11 *it* i.e.
my fortunes (imaged as a crescent moon)

No wars without doors. Caesar gets money where
He loses hearts. Lepidus flatters both,
Of both is flattered ; but he neither loves,
Nor either cares for him.

MENAS   Caesar and Lepidus
Are in the field ; a mighty strength they carry.

POMPEY
Where have you this ? 'Tis false.

MENAS   From Silvius, sir.

POMPEY
He dreams : I know they are in Rome together,
Looking for Antony. But all the charms of love,
21   Salt Cleopatra, soften thy waned lip !
Let witchcraft join with beauty, lust with both !
Tie up the libertine in a field of feasts,
Keep his brain fuming. Epicurean cooks
25   Sharpen with cloyless sauce his appetite,
26   That sleep and feeding may prorogue his honor
27   Even till a Lethe'd dulness –
       Enter Varrius.   How now, Varrius ?

VARRIUS
This is most certain that I shall deliver :
Mark Antony is every hour in Rome
Expected. Since he went from Egypt 'tis
31   A space for farther travel.

POMPEY   I could have given less matter
A better ear. Menas, I did not think
33   This amorous surfeiter would have donned his helm
For such a petty war. His soldiership
Is twice the other twain. But let us rear
36   The higher our opinion, that our stirring
Can from the lap of Egypt's widow pluck
The ne'er-lust-wearied Antony.

38 MENAS   I cannot hope
39   Caesar and Antony shall well greet together ;
His wife that's dead did trespasses to Caesar ;
41   His brother warred upon him ; although I think
Not moved by Antony.

POMPEY   I know not, Menas,
How lesser enmities may give way to greater.
Were't not that we stand up against them all,
45   'Twere pregnant they should square between them-
      selves,
For they have entertainèd cause enough
To draw their swords ; but how the fear of us
May cement their divisions and bind up
The petty difference, we yet not know.
50   Be't as our gods will have't ! It only stands
Our lives upon to use our strongest hands.
Come, Menas.   *Exeunt.*

*

II, ii   *Enter Enobarbus and Lepidus.*

LEPIDUS
Good Enobarbus, 'tis a worthy deed,
And shall become you well, to entreat your captain
To soft and gentle speech.

ENOBARBUS   I shall entreat him
4   To answer like himself : if Caesar move him,
Let Antony look over Caesar's head
And speak as loud as Mars. By Jupiter,
Were I the wearer of Antonio's beard,
8   I would not shave't to-day !

LEPIDUS   'Tis not a time
For private stomaching.   9

ENOBARBUS   Every time
Serves for the matter that is then born in't.

LEPIDUS
But small to greater matters must give way.

ENOBARBUS
Not if the small come first.

LEPIDUS   Your speech is passion ;
But pray you stir no embers up. Here comes
The noble Antony.
       Enter Antony and Ventidius.

ENOBARBUS   And yonder, Caesar.
       Enter Caesar, Maecenas, and Agrippa.

ANTONY
If we compose well here, to Parthia.   15
Hark, Ventidius.

CAESAR   I do not know,
Maecenas ; ask Agrippa.

LEPIDUS   Noble friends,
That which combined us was most great, and let not
A leaner action rend us. What's amiss,
May it be gently heard. When we debate
Our trivial difference loud, we do commit
Murder in healing wounds. Then, noble partners,
The rather for I earnestly beseech,   23
Touch you the sourest points with sweetest terms,
Nor curstness grow to th' matter.   25

ANTONY   'Tis spoken well.
Were we before our armies, and to fight,
I should do thus.   27
       Flourish.

CAESAR
Welcome to Rome.

ANTONY   Thank you.

CAESAR   Sit.

ANTONY   Sit, sir.

CAESAR   Nay then.
   [They sit.]

ANTONY
I learn you take things ill which are not so,
Or being, concern you not.

CAESAR   I must be laughed at
If, or for nothing or a little, I   31
Should say myself offended, and with you
Chiefly i' th' world ; more laughed at that I should
Once name you derogately, when to sound your name   34
It not concerned me.

ANTONY   My being in Egypt, Caesar,
What was't to you ?

CAESAR
No more than my residing here at Rome

21 *Salt* lustful ; *waned* faded   25 *cloyless* which never cloys   26 *prorogue* suspend   27 *Lethe'd dulness* i.e. an oblivion as deep as that which comes from drinking of the river Lethe in the underworld   31 *A space . . . travel* time enough for even a longer journey   33 *surfeiter* one who indulges to excess   36 *opinion* i.e. of ourselves   38 *hope* expect   39 *greet* get on   41 *brother* (cf. I, ii, 84–90)   45 *pregnant* likely ; *square* quarrel   50–51 *stands . . . upon* is a matter of life and death
II, ii The house of Lepidus in Rome   4 *like himself* as befits his greatness   8 *I . . . shave't* i.e. I would dare Caesar to pluck it   9 *stomaching* resentment   15 *compose* reach agreement   23 *The rather for* all the more because   25 *Nor . . . matter* and let not ill temper make matters worse   27 *thus* (Antony makes some courteous gesture)   31 *or . . . or* either . . . or   34 *derogately* disparagingly

       Might be to you in Egypt : yet if you there

39   Did practice on my state, your being in Egypt

40   Might be my question.

ANTONY   How intend you ? practiced ?

CAESAR

       You may be pleased to catch at mine intent

       By what did here befall me. Your wife and brother

       Made wars upon me, and their contestation

44   Was theme for you ; you were the word of war.

ANTONY

       You do mistake your business : my brother never

46   Did urge me in his act. I did inquire it

47   And have my learning from some true reports

       That drew their swords with you. Did he not rather

       Discredit my authority with yours,

50   And make the wars alike against my stomach,

51   Having alike your cause ? Of this my letters

52   Before did satisfy you. If you'll patch a quarrel,

       As matter whole you have to make it with,

       It must not be with this.

CAESAR   You praise yourself

       By laying defects of judgment to me, but

       You patched up your excuses.

ANTONY   Not so, not so :

       I know you could not lack, I am certain on't,

       Very necessity of this thought, that I,

       Your partner in the cause 'gainst which he fought,

60   Could not with graceful eyes attend those wars

       Which fronted mine own peace. As for my wife,

       I would you had her spirit in such another ;

63   The third o' th' world is yours, which with a snaffle

64   You may pace easy, but not such a wife.

ENOBARBUS Would we had all such wives, that the men

       might go to wars with the women.

ANTONY

67   So much uncurbable, her garboils, Caesar,

       Made out of her impatience – which not wanted

       Shrewdness of policy too – I grieving grant

       Did you too much disquiet : for that you must

       But say I could not help it.

CAESAR   I wrote to you

       When rioting in Alexandria ; you

       Did pocket up my letters, and with taunts

74   Did gibe my missive out of audience.

ANTONY   Sir,

       He fell upon me, ere admitted, then :

76   Three kings I had newly feasted, and did want

       Of what I was i' th' morning ; but next day

78   I told him of myself, which was as much

       As to have asked him pardon. Let this fellow

       Be nothing of our strife : if we contend,

       Out of our question wipe him.   81

CAESAR   You have broken

       The article of your oath, which you shall never

       Have tongue to charge me with.

LEPIDUS   Soft, Caesar.

ANTONY   No,

       Lepidus ; let him speak.

       The honor is sacred which he talks on now,   85

       Supposing that I lacked it. But on, Caesar,

       The article of my oath –

CAESAR

       To lend me arms and aid when I required them,

       The which you both denied.

ANTONY   Neglected rather :

       And then when poisonèd hours had bound me up   90

       From mine own knowledge. As nearly as I may,

       I'll play the penitent to you. But mine honesty   92

       Shall not make poor my greatness, nor my power

       Work without it. Truth is, that Fulvia,

       To have me out of Egypt, made wars here,

       For which myself, the ignorant motive, do

       So far ask pardon as befits mine honor

       To stoop in such a case.

LEPIDUS   'Tis noble spoken.

MAECENAS

       If it might please you, to enforce no further

       The griefs between ye : to forget them quite

       Were to remember that the present need

       Speaks to atone you.   102

LEPIDUS   Worthily spoken, Maecenas.

ENOBARBUS Or, if you borrow one another's love for the

       instant, you may, when you hear no more words of

       Pompey, return it again : you shall have time to wrangle

       in when you have nothing else to do.

ANTONY

       Thou art a soldier only, speak no more.

ENOBARBUS That truth should be silent I had almost

       forgot.

ANTONY

       You wrong this presence, therefore speak no more.   109

ENOBARBUS Go to, then ; your considerate stone.   110

CAESAR

       I do not much dislike the matter, but

       The manner of his speech ; for't cannot be

       We shall remain in friendship, our conditions

       So diff'ring in their acts. Yet if I knew

       What hoop should hold us staunch, from edge to edge

       O' th' world I would pursue it.

AGRIPPA   Give me leave, Caesar.

CAESAR

       Speak, Agrippa.

AGRIPPA

       Thou hast a sister by the mother's side,

       Admired Octavia : great Mark Antony

       Is now a widower.

CAESAR   Say not so, Agrippa :

       If Cleopatra heard you, your reproof

       Were well deserved of rashness.   122

ANTONY

       I am not married, Caesar : let me hear

       Agrippa further speak.

AGRIPPA

       To hold you in perpetual amity,

39 *practice on* plot against   40 *question* concern   44 *you were . . . war* the war was carried on in your name   46 *urge me* use my name   47 *reports* reporters   50 *stomach* desire   51 *Having . . . cause* i.e. I having as much cause as you to resent it   52–54 *If . . . this* i.e. if you are determined to patch a quarrel out of pieces, when you actually have whole cloth to fashion it from (cf. ll. 81–98), this is not the right piece   60 *with . . . attend* regard with pleasure   63 *snaffle* bridle bit   64 *pace* manage   67 *garboils* commotions   74 *missive* messenger   76–77 *did . . . morning* was not myself   78 *myself* my condition   81 *question* argument   85 *honor* i.e. keeping an oath   90–91 *bound . . . knowledge* i.e. prevented my realizing what I was doing   92–94 *mine . . . it* i.e. my actions will be prompted by my honesty (which makes me willing to apologize) but also by my power (which does not intend to grovel)   102 *atone* reconcile   109 *presence* company   110 *your considerate stone* i.e. I'll be dumb as a stone, but still thinking (considering)   122 *of rashness* because of your rashness (in ignoring Antony's bond to Cleopatra)

To make you brothers, and to knit your hearts
With an unslipping knot, take Antony
Octavia to his wife ; whose beauty claims
No worse a husband than the best of men ;
Whose virtue and whose general graces speak
That which none else can utter. By this marriage
132   All little jealousies, which now seem great,
And all great fears, which now import their dangers,
134   Would then be nothing : truths would be tales,
Where now half-tales be truths : her love to both
Would each to other, and all loves to both,
Draw after her. Pardon what I have spoke ;
For 'tis a studied, not a present thought,
By duty ruminated.

ANTONY   Will Caesar speak ?

CAESAR
Not till he hears how Antony is touched
With what is spoke already.

ANTONY   What power is in Agrippa,
If I would say, 'Agrippa, be it so,'
To make this good ?

CAESAR   The power of Caesar, and
His power unto Octavia.

ANTONY   May I never
145   To this good purpose, that so fairly shows,
Dream of impediment : let me have thy hand :
147   Further this act of grace, and from this hour
The heart of brothers govern in our loves
And sway our great designs.

CAESAR   There's my hand.
A sister I bequeath you, whom no brother
Did ever love so dearly. Let her live
152   To join our kingdoms and our hearts ; and never
Fly off our loves again.

LEPIDUS   Happily, amen.

ANTONY
I did not think to draw my sword 'gainst Pompey,
155   For he hath laid strange courtesies and great
Of late upon me. I must thank him only,
157   Lest my remembrance suffer ill report :
At heel of that, defy him.

LEPIDUS   Time calls upon's.
159   Of us must Pompey presently be sought,
Or else he seeks out us.

ANTONY   Where lies he ?

CAESAR
161   About the Mount Mesena.

ANTONY
What is his strength by land ?

CAESAR
Great and increasing ; but by sea
He is an absolute master.

164 ANTONY   So is the fame.
Would we had spoke together ! Haste we for it,
Yet, ere we put ourselves in arms, dispatch we
The business we have talked of.

CAESAR   With most gladness ;
And do invite you to my sister's view,
Whither straight I'll lead you.

ANTONY   Let us, Lepidus,
Not lack your company.

LEPIDUS   Noble Antony,
Not sickness should detain me.   *Flourish. [Exeunt.]*
Mane[n]t Enobarbus, Agrippa, Maecenas.

MAECENAS   Welcome from Egypt, sir.

ENOBARBUS   Half the heart of Caesar, worthy Maecenas. 173
My honorable friend, Agrippa.

AGRIPPA   Good Enobarbus.

MAECENAS   We have cause to be glad that matters are so
well disgested. You stayed well by't in Egypt.   177

ENOBARBUS   Ay, sir, we did sleep day out of countenance 178
and made the night light with drinking.

MAECENAS   Eight wild boars roasted whole at a breakfast,
and but twelve persons there. Is this true ?

ENOBARBUS   This was but as a fly by an eagle : we had 182
much more monstrous matter of feast, which worthily
deserved noting.

MAECENAS   She's a most triumphant lady, if report be
square to her.   186

ENOBARBUS   When she first met Mark Antony, she pursed 187
up his heart, upon the river of Cydnus.

AGRIPPA   There she appeared indeed ; or my reporter de- 189
vised well for her.

ENOBARBUS
I will tell you.
The barge she sat in, like a burnished throne,
Burned on the water : the poop was beaten gold ;
Purple the sails, and so perfumèd that
The winds were lovesick with them ; the oars were
    silver,
Which to the tune of flutes kept stroke, and made
The water which they beat to follow faster,
As amorous of their strokes. For her own person,
It beggared all description : she did lie
In her pavilion, cloth-of-gold of tissue,   200
O'erpicturing that Venus where we see   201
The fancy outwork nature. On each side her   202
Stood pretty dimpled boys, like smiling Cupids,
With divers-colored fans, whose wind did seem
To glow the delicate cheeks which they did cool,   205
And what they undid did.

AGRIPPA   O, rare for Antony.

ENOBARBUS
Her gentlewomen, like the Nereides,   207
So many mermaids, tended her i' th' eyes,   208
And made their bends adornings. At the helm   209
A seeming mermaid steers : the silken tackle
Swell with the touches of those flower-soft hands,
That yarely frame the office. From the barge   212
A strange invisible perfume hits the sense
Of the adjacent wharfs. The city cast
Her people out upon her ; and Antony,
Enthroned i' th' market place, did sit alone,

---

132 *jealousies* misunderstandings   134-35 *would be . . . be* would be taken
for . . . are taken for   145 *so fairly shows* looks so hopeful   147 *grace*
reconciliation   152-53 *never . . . loves* never may we be estranged   155
strange unusual   157 *remembrance* readiness to acknowledge favors
159 *presently* at once   161 *Mesena* i.e. Misenum, an Italian port   164
fame report   173 *Half* i.e. sharing it with Agrippa   177 *disgested* digested,
arranged ; *stayed . . . by't* kept at it, 'lived it up'   178-79 *we . . . drinking*
i.e. we ruffled the dignity of day (personified) by sleeping through it, and
made night light (i.e. bright, lightheaded, and wanton) with drinking
parties   182 *by* compared to   186 *square* fair   187-88 *pursed up* pocketed
(but with a suggestion of pursed lips for kissing)   189 *appeared* came
before the public ; *devised* invented   200 *cloth-of-gold of tissue* cloth
interwoven with gold threads   201 *O'erpicturing* outdoing the picture of
202 *fancy* i.e. the painter's imagination   205 *glow* make glow (as if heated)
207 *Nereides* sea nymphs   208 *tended . . . eyes* waited on her every glance
209 *made . . . adornings* made their postures of submission decorative
(as in a tableau)   212 *yarely frame* nimbly perform

217 Whistling to th' air; which, but for vacancy,
Had gone to gaze on Cleopatra too,
And made a gap in nature.

AGRIPPA   Rare Egyptian!

ENOBARBUS
Upon her landing, Antony sent to her,
Invited her to supper. She replied,
It should be better he became her guest;
Which she entreated. Our courteous Antony,
Whom ne'er the word of 'no' woman heard speak,
Being barbered ten times o'er, goes to the feast,
226 And for his ordinary pays his heart
For what his eyes eat only.

AGRIPPA   Royal wench!
She made great Caesar lay his sword to bed;
229 He ploughed her, and she cropped.

ENOBARBUS   I saw her once
Hop forty paces through the public street;
And having lost her breath, she spoke, and panted,
232 That she did make defect perfection
And, breathless, pow'r breathe forth.

MAECENAS
Now Antony must leave her utterly.

ENOBARBUS
Never; he will not:
Age cannot wither her, nor custom stale
Her infinite variety: other women cloy
The appetites they feed, but she makes hungry
Where most she satisfies. For vilest things
240 Become themselves in her, that the holy priests
241 Bless her when she is riggish.

MAECENAS
If beauty, wisdom, modesty, can settle
The heart of Antony, Octavia is
244 A blessèd lottery to him.

AGRIPPA   Let us go.
Good Enobarbus, make yourself my guest
Whilst you abide here.

ENOBARBUS   Humbly, sir, I thank you. *Exeunt.*

*

II, iii   *Enter Antony, Caesar, Octavia between them.*

ANTONY
The world and my great office will sometimes
Divide me from your bosom.

OCTAVIA   All which time
Before the gods my knee shall bow my prayers
To them for you.

ANTONY   Good night, sir. My Octavia,
Read not my blemishes in the world's report:
6 I have not kept my square, but that to come
Shall all be done by th' rule. Good night, dear lady.

OCTAVIA Good night, sir.
CAESAR Good night.   *Exit [with Octavia].*
       Enter Soothsayer.

ANTONY
Now, sirrah: you do wish yourself in Egypt?

SOOTHSAYER
Would I had never come from thence, nor you thither.

ANTONY
If you can, your reason?

SOOTHSAYER
I see it in my motion, have it not in my tongue,   14
But yet hie you to Egypt again.

ANTONY   Say to me,
Whose fortunes shall rise higher, Caesar's or mine?

SOOTHSAYER Caesar's.
Therefore, O Antony, stay not by his side.
Thy demon, that thy spirit which keeps thee, is   19
Noble, courageous, high, unmatchable,
Where Caesar's is not. But near him thy angel
Becomes a fear, as being o'erpow'red. Therefore   22
Make space enough between you.

ANTONY   Speak this no more.

SOOTHSAYER
To none but thee, no more but when to thee.
If thou dost play with him at any game,
Thou art sure to lose; and of that natural luck
He beats thee 'gainst the odds. Thy lustre thickens   27
When he shines by: I say again, thy spirit
Is all afraid to govern thee near him;
But he away, 'tis noble.

ANTONY   Get thee gone.
Say to Ventidius I would speak with him.
       Exit [Soothsayer].
He shall to Parthia. – Be it art or hap,   32
He hath spoken true. The very dice obey him,
And in our sports my better cunning faints   34
Under his chance: if we draw lots, he speeds;   35
His cocks do win the battle still of mine   36
When it is all to naught, and his quails ever   37
Beat mine, inhooped, at odds. I will to Egypt: 38
And though I make this marriage for my peace,
I' th' East my pleasure lies.
       Enter Ventidius.   O, come, Ventidius,
You must to Parthia. Your commission 's ready:
Follow me, and receive 't.   *Exeunt.*

*

       Enter Lepidus, Maecenas, and Agrippa.   II, iv

LEPIDUS Trouble yourselves no further: pray you,
hasten your generals after.

AGRIPPA Sir, Mark Antony will e'en but kiss Octavia,
and we'll follow.

LEPIDUS Till I shall see you in your soldier's dress,
which will become you both, farewell.

MAECENAS We shall, as I conceive the journey, be at
Mount before you, Lepidus.   8

LEPIDUS Your way is shorter; my purposes do draw me
much about: you'll win two days upon me.   10

BOTH Sir, good success.

LEPIDUS Farewell.   *Exeunt.*

*

217 *but for vacancy* except that it would have left a vacuum   226 *ordinary*
meal   229 *cropped* bore fruit (i.e. Julius Caesar's son, Caesarion)   232
defect i.e. the resulting breathlessness   240 *Become . . . her* are so becoming
to her   241 *riggish* lewd   244 *lottery* gift of fortune
II, iii The house of Octavius Caesar   6 *square* carpenter's square (i.e. I
have not followed the straight and narrow)   14 *motion* mind   19 *demon*
guardian angel   22 *a fear* i.e. timorous   27 *thickens* dims   32 *art or hap*
skill or chance   34 *cunning* skill   35 *chance* luck; *speeds* wins   36 *still*
always   37 *it . . . naught* i.e. the odds are everything to nothing in my
favor   38 *inhooped* i.e. fighting confined within a hoop
II, iv Before the house of Lepidus   8 *Mount* (cf. II, ii, 161)   10 *about*
roundabout

II, v *Enter Cleopatra, Charmian, Iras, and Alexas.*

CLEOPATRA
Give me some music : music, moody food
Of us that trade in love.

OMNES The music, ho !

Enter Mardian the Eunuch.

CLEOPATRA
Let it alone, let's to billiards : come, Charmian.

CHARMIAN
My arm is sore ; best play with Mardian.

CLEOPATRA
As well a woman with an eunuch played
As with a woman. Come, you'll play with me, sir ?

MARDIAN As well as I can, madam.

CLEOPATRA
And when good will is showed, though't come too short,
The actor may plead pardon. I'll none now.
10 Give me mine angle, we'll to th' river : there,
My music playing far off, I will betray
Tawny-finned fishes. My bended hook shall pierce
Their slimy jaws ; and as I draw them up,
I'll think them every one an Antony,
And say, 'Ah, ha ! y' are caught !'

CHARMIAN 'Twas merry when
You wagered on your angling, when your diver
17 Did hang a salt fish on his hook, which he
With fervency drew up.

CLEOPATRA That time – O times ! –
I laughed him out of patience ; and that night
I laughed him into patience ; and next morn
Ere the ninth hour I drunk him to his bed ;
22 Then put my tires and mantles on him, whilst
23 I wore his sword Philippan.

Enter a Messenger. O, from Italy !
Ram thou thy fruitful tidings in mine ears,
That long time have been barren.

MESSENGER Madam, madam –

CLEOPATRA
Antonio 's dead : if thou say so, villain,
Thou kill'st thy mistress : but well and free,
If thou so yield him, there is gold and here
My bluest veins to kiss, a hand that kings
Have lipped, and trembled kissing.

MESSENGER
First, madam, he is well.

CLEOPATRA Why, there's more gold.
But, sirrah, mark, we use
33 To say the dead are well : bring it to that,
The gold I give thee will I melt and pour
Down thy ill-uttering throat.

MESSENGER
Good madam, hear me.

CLEOPATRA Well, go to, I will :
37 But there's no goodness in thy face if Antony
38 Be free and healthful ; so tart a favor
To trumpet such good tidings ? If not well,
Thou shouldst come like a Fury crowned with snakes,
41 Not like a formal man.

MESSENGER Will't please you hear me ?

CLEOPATRA
I have a mind to strike thee ere thou speak'st :
Yet, if thou say Antony lives, is well,
Or friends with Caesar, or not captive to him,
I'll set thee in a shower of gold, and hail
Rich pearls upon thee.

MESSENGER Madam, he's well.

CLEOPATRA Well said.

MESSENGER
And friends with Caesar.

CLEOPATRA Th' art an honest man.

MESSENGER
Caesar and he are greater friends than ever.

CLEOPATRA
Make thee a fortune from me.

MESSENGER But yet, madam –

CLEOPATRA
I do not like 'but yet,' it does allay 50
The good precedence : fie upon 'but yet,'
'But yet' is as a jailer to bring forth
Some monstrous malefactor. Prithee, friend,
Pour out the pack of matter to mine ear,
The good and bad together : he's friends with Caesar,
In state of health, thou say'st, and thou say'st, free.

MESSENGER
Free, madam, no : I made no such report,
He's bound unto Octavia.

CLEOPATRA For what good turn ?

MESSENGER
For the best turn i' th' bed.

CLEOPATRA I am pale, Charmian.

MESSENGER
Madam, he's married to Octavia.

CLEOPATRA
The most infectious pestilence upon thee !
Strikes him down.

MESSENGER
Good madam, patience.

CLEOPATRA What say you ?
Strikes him. Hence,
Horrible villain ! or I'll spurn thine eyes 63
Like balls before me : I'll unhair thy head, 64
She hales him up and down.
Thou shalt be whipped with wire and stewed in brine,
Smarting in ling'ring pickle. 66

MESSENGER Gracious madam,
I that do bring the news made not the match.

CLEOPATRA
Say 'tis not so, a province I will give thee,
And make thy fortunes proud : the blow thou hadst
Shall make thy peace for moving me to rage,
And I will boot thee with what gift beside 71
Thy modesty can beg. 72

MESSENGER He's married, madam.

CLEOPATRA
Rogue, thou hast lived too long.
Draw a knife.

MESSENGER Nay, then I'll run.
What mean you, madam ? I have made no fault. *Exit.*

II, v The chambers of Cleopatra in her palace at Alexandria 10 *angle* fishing tackle 17 *salt* dried 22 *tires* headdresses 23 *Philippan* (so called because he had beaten Brutus and Cassius with it at Philippi) 33 *well* i.e. in heaven ; *bring . . . that* say that you mean that 37 *goodness* i.e. truth 38 *tart a favor* sour a face 41 *Not . . . man* not in human shape 50–51 *allay . . . precedence* spoil the good that preceded it 63 *spurn* kick 64 s.d. *hales* drags 66 *pickle* pickling solution 71 *boot* benefit 72 *modesty* humble condition

CHARMIAN
Good madam, keep yourself within yourself,
The man is innocent.

CLEOPATRA
Some innocents 'scape not the thunderbolt.
Melt Egypt into Nile ! and kindly creatures
Turn all to serpents ! Call the slave again :
Though I am mad, I will not bite him. Call !

CHARMIAN
He is afeard to come.

CLEOPATRA   I will not hurt him. *[Exit Charmian.]*
These hands do lack nobility, that they strike
A meaner than myself ; since I myself
84 Have given myself the cause.
         Enter [Charmian and] the Messenger again.
                 Come hither, sir.
Though it be honest, it is never good
To bring bad news : give to a gracious message
An host of tongues, but let ill tidings tell
Themselves when they be felt.

MESSENGER   I have done my duty.

CLEOPATRA
Is he married ?
I cannot hate thee worser than I do
If thou again say 'Yes.'

MESSENGER   He's married, madam.

CLEOPATRA
92 The gods confound thee ! Dost thou hold there still ?

MESSENGER
Should I lie, madam ?

CLEOPATRA   O, I would thou didst,
94 So half my Egypt were submerged and made
A cistern for scaled snakes ! Go get thee hence ;
96 Hadst thou Narcissus in thy face, to me
Thou wouldst appear most ugly. He is married ?

MESSENGER
I crave your Highness' pardon.

CLEOPATRA   He is married ?

MESSENGER
99 Take no offense that I would not offend you :
To punish me for what you make me do
101 Seems much unequal : he's married to Octavia.

CLEOPATRA
O, that his fault should make a knave of thee,
103 That art not what th' art sure of ! Get thee hence,
The merchandise which thou hast brought from Rome
105 Are all too dear for me. Lie they upon thy hand,
106 And be undone by 'em !   *[Exit Messenger.]*

CHARMIAN   Good your Highness, patience.

CLEOPATRA
In praising Antony I have dispraised Caesar.

---

84 *cause* i.e. by loving Antony   92 *confound* destroy   94 *So* even though
96 *Hadst . . . face* were you as handsome as Narcissus (in Greek legend,
the youth who fell in love with his image reflected in a stream)   99 *Take
. . . you* don't be angry that I'd rather not anger you (i.e. by answering)
101 *unequal* unjust   103 *That . . . of* i.e. who are not really hateful, like
the news you bring   105 *upon thy hand* i.e. unsold   106 *undone* bankrupt
116 *Gorgon* Medusa (the sight of whose ugly face turned men to stone)
II, vi An open place near Misenum   2 *meet* suitable   7 *tall* bold   10
factors agents   13 *ghosted* haunted   24 *fear* frighten   25 *speak* contest
26 *o'ercount* outnumber   27 *o'ercount* cheat; *house* (Plutarch says that
Antony had bought this house but not paid for it)   28 *cuckoo* (which
never builds its own nest but lays its eggs in the nests of other birds)
29 *as thou mayst* as long as you can   30 *from the present* off the topic   33
embraced if accepted

CHARMIAN
Many times, madam.

CLEOPATRA   I am paid for 't now.
Lead me from hence,
I faint. O Iras, Charmian ! 'Tis no matter.
Go to the fellow, good Alexas ; bid him
Report the feature of Octavia : her years,
Her inclination, let him not leave out
The color of her hair. Bring me word quickly.
                     [Exit Alexas.]
Let him for ever go ! – let him not ! – Charmian,
Though he be painted one way like a Gorgon,   116
The other way 's a Mars. *[to Mardian]* Bid you Alexas
Bring me word how tall she is. – Pity me, Charmian,
But do not speak to me. Lead me to my chamber.
                       Exeunt.

*

Flourish. Enter Pompey at one door, with Drum and   II, vi
*Trumpet : at another, Caesar, Lepidus, Antony,
Enobarbus, Maecenas, Agrippa, Menas, with
Soldiers marching.*

POMPEY
Your hostages I have, so have you mine ;
And we shall talk before we fight.

CAESAR   Most meet   2
That first we come to words, and therefore have we
Our written purposes before us sent ;
Which if thou hast considerèd, let us know
If 'twill tie up thy discontented sword
And carry back to Sicily much tall youth
That else must perish here.   7

POMPEY   To you all three,
The senators alone of this great world,
Chief factors for the gods : I do not know   10
Wherefore my father should revengers want,
Having a son and friends, since Julius Caesar,
Who at Philippi the good Brutus ghosted,   13
There saw you laboring for him. What was 't
That moved pale Cassius to conspire ? And what
Made all-honored, honest, Roman Brutus,
With the armed rest, courtiers of beauteous freedom,
To drench the Capitol, but that they would
Have one man but a man ? And that is it
Hath made me rig my navy, at whose burden
The angered ocean foams ; with which I meant
To scourge th' ingratitude that despiteful Rome
Cast on my noble father.

CAESAR   Take your time.

ANTONY
Thou canst not fear us, Pompey, with thy sails.   24
We'll speak with thee at sea. At land thou know'st   25
How much we do o'ercount thee.   26

POMPEY   At land indeed
Thou dost o'ercount me of my father's house :   27
But since the cuckoo builds not for himself,   28
Remain in 't as thou mayst.   29

LEPIDUS   Be pleased to tell us
(For this is from the present) how you take   30
The offers we have sent you.

CAESAR   There's the point.

ANTONY
Which do not be entreated to, but weigh
What it is worth embraced.
                       33

CAESAR   And what may follow,
34 To try a larger fortune.
POMPEY   You have made me offer
    Of Sicily, Sardinia; and I must
    Rid all the sea of pirates; then, to send
    Measures of wheat to Rome; this 'greed upon,
38 To part with unhacked edges and bear back
39 Our targes undinted.
OMNES   That's our offer.
POMPEY   Know then
    I came before you here a man prepared
    To take this offer; but Mark Antony
    Put me to some impatience. Though I lose
    The praise of it by telling, you must know,
    When Caesar and your brother were at blows,
    Your mother came to Sicily and did find
    Her welcome friendly.
ANTONY   I have heard it, Pompey,
47 And am well studied for a liberal thanks,
    Which I do owe you.
POMPEY   Let me have your hand:
    I did not think, sir, to have met you here.
ANTONY
    The beds i' th' East are soft; and thanks to you,
    That called me timelier than my purpose hither;
    For I have gained by't.
CAESAR   Since I saw you last
    There's a change upon you.
POMPEY   Well, I know not
54 What counts harsh fortune casts upon my face,
    But in my bosom shall she never come
    To make my heart her vassal.
LEPIDUS   Well met here.
POMPEY
    I hope so, Lepidus. Thus we are agreed.
58 I crave our composition may be written,
    And sealed between us.
CAESAR   That's the next to do.
POMPEY
    We'll feast each other ere we part, and let's
    Draw lots who shall begin.
ANTONY   That will I, Pompey.
POMPEY
    No, Antony, take the lot:
    But, first or last, your fine Egyptian cookery
    Shall have the fame. I have heard that Julius Caesar
    Grew fat with feasting there.
ANTONY   You have heard much.
POMPEY
    I have fair meanings, sir.
ANTONY   And fair words to them.
POMPEY
    Then so much have I heard,
    And I have heard Apollodorus carried –
ENOBARBUS
    No more of that: he did so.
POMPEY   What, I pray you?
ENOBARBUS
    A certain queen to Caesar in a mattress.
POMPEY
    I know thee now; how far'st thou, soldier?
ENOBARBUS   Well;
    And well am like to do, for I perceive
73 Four feasts are toward.

POMPEY   Let me shake thy hand,
    I never hated thee: I have seen thee fight
    When I have envied thy behavior.
ENOBARBUS   Sir,
    I never loved you much; but I ha' praised ye
    When you have well deserved ten times as much
    As I have said you did.
POMPEY   Enjoy thy plainness,
    It nothing ill becomes thee.   79
    Aboard my galley I invite you all:
    Will you lead, lords?
ALL   Show's the way, sir.
POMPEY   Come.
    Exeunt. Manent Enobarbus and Menas.
MENAS [aside] Thy father, Pompey, would ne'er have
    made this treaty. – You and I have known, sir.   83
ENOBARBUS At sea, I think.
MENAS We have, sir.
ENOBARBUS You have done well by water.
MENAS And you by land.
ENOBARBUS I will praise any man that will praise me;
    though it cannot be denied what I have done by land.
MENAS Nor what I have done by water.
ENOBARBUS Yes, something you can deny for your own
    safety: you have been a great thief by sea.
MENAS And you by land.
ENOBARBUS There I deny my land service. But give me
    your hand, Menas: if our eyes had authority, here they 95
    might take two thieves kissing.
MENAS All men's faces are true, whatsome'er their hands
    are.
ENOBARBUS But there is never a fair woman has a true 99
    face.
MENAS No slander, they steal hearts.
ENOBARBUS We came hither to fight with you.
MENAS For my part, I am sorry it is turned to a drinking.
    Pompey doth this day laugh away his fortune.
ENOBARBUS If he do, sure he cannot weep't back again.
MENAS Y' have said, sir. We looked not for Mark Antony 105
    here. Pray you, is he married to Cleopatra?
ENOBARBUS Caesar's sister is called Octavia.
MENAS True, sir, she was the wife of Caius Marcellus.
ENOBARBUS But she is now the wife of Marcus Antonius.
MENAS Pray ye, sir?   110
ENOBARBUS 'Tis true.
MENAS Then is Caesar and he for ever knit together.
ENOBARBUS If I were bound to divine of this unity, I
    would not prophesy so.
MENAS I think the policy of that purpose made more in 115
    the marriage than the love of the parties.
ENOBARBUS I think so too. But you shall find the band
    that seems to tie their friendship together will be the
    very strangler of their amity: Octavia is of a holy, cold,
    and still conversation.   120
MENAS Who would not have his wife so?
ENOBARBUS Not he that himself is not so; which is Mark
    Antony. He will to his Egyptian dish again: then shall

---

34 *a larger fortune* i.e. war with the triumvirs 38 *edges* swords 39
targes shields; *Omnes* all (Antony, Caesar, Lepidus) 47 *studied for*
prepared with 54 *counts* tallies (as on a scoring stick) 58 *composition*
agreement 73 *toward* coming up 79 *nothing* not at all 83 *known* met
95 *had* were in 99 *true* honest 105 *Y' have said* i.e. you are quite right
110 *Pray ye* i.e. how's that again 115 *made more* played more part 120
conversation way of life

the sighs of Octavia blow the fire up in Caesar, and, as I
said before, that which is the strength of their amity shall
prove the immediate author of their variance. Antony
127 will use his affection where it is. He married but his
128 occasion here.

MENAS And thus it may be. Come, sir, will you aboard?
I have a health for you.

ENOBARBUS I shall take it, sir: we have used our throats
in Egypt.

MENAS Come, let's away.   *Exeunt.*

*

II, vii   *Music plays. Enter two or three Servants, with a
banquet.*

1 1. SERVANT Here they'll be, man. Some o' their plants
are ill-rooted already; the least wind i' th' world will
blow them down.

2. SERVANT Lepidus is high-colored.

5 1. SERVANT They have made him drink alms-drink.

2. SERVANT As they pinch one another by the disposition, he cries out 'No more,' reconciles them to his entreaty, and himself to th' drink.

1. SERVANT But it raises the greater war between him
and his discretion.

2. SERVANT Why, this it is to have a name in great
12 men's fellowship. I had as live have a reed that will do
13 me no service as a partisan I could not heave.

14 1. SERVANT To be called into a huge sphere and not to
be seen to move in't, are the holes where eyes should be,
16 which pitifully disaster the cheeks.

      *A sennet sounded. Enter Caesar, Antony, Pompey,
Lepidus, Agrippa, Maecenas, Enobarbus, Menas,
with other Captains.*

ANTONY
Thus do they, sir: they take the flow o' th' Nile
18 By certain scales i' th' pyramid. They know
19 By th' height, the lowness, or the mean, if dearth
Or foison follow. The higher Nilus swells,
The more it promises; as it ebbs, the seedsman
Upon the slime and ooze scatters his grain,
And shortly comes to harvest.

LEPIDUS Y' have strange serpents there.

ANTONY Ay, Lepidus.

LEPIDUS Your serpent of Egypt is bred now of your mud
by the operation of your sun: so is your crocodile.

ANTONY They are so.

POMPEY Sit – and some wine! A health to Lepidus!

---

127 *where it is* i.e. in Egypt   128 *occasion* convenience
II, vii Aboard Pompey's galley in the port of Misenum   1 *plants* feet (with
pun on the usual sense: cf. *ill-rooted*)   5 *alms-drink* drink drunk on behalf
of one too far gone to continue his part in a round of toasts (Lepidus
has been tricked into drinking more than the rest)   7 *No more* i.e. no more
quarrelling   12 *live* lief   13 *partisan* spear   14–16 *To . . . cheeks* (Lepidus,
a little man in a part too big for him, is compared first to a heavenly body
that fails to perform its function in its *sphere*, and then to a face without
eyes; *disaster*, carrying the image back on itself, likens the face without
eyes to a heaven without stars)   16 s.d. *sennet* distinctive set of trumpet
notes announcing persons of importance   18 *scales* graduations   19–20
dearth Or foison famine or plenty   30 *ne'er out* never give up   31 *in*
drunk   33 *pyramises* (Lepidus's drunken rendering of 'pyramides,' i.e.
pyramids)   42–43, 46 *it own* its own   44 *transmigrates* i.e. its soul takes
over the body of some other creature (Antony is teasing the drunken
Lepidus)   48 *tears* i.e. its 'crocodile tears'   56 *held . . . off* i.e. been
devoted   62 *But entertain it* only accept the idea   67 *pales* encloses
69 *competitors* partners

LEPIDUS I am not so well as I should be, but I'll ne'er out.   30

ENOBARBUS Not till you have slept. I fear me you'll be in   31
till then.

LEPIDUS Nay, certainly, I have heard the Ptolemies' pyra-   33
mises are very goodly things: without contradiction I
have heard that.

MENAS
Pompey, a word.

POMPEY   Say in mine ear. What is't?

MENAS
Forsake thy seat, I do beseech thee, captain,
And hear me speak a word.

POMPEY   Forbear me till anon.
      [Menas] whispers in's ear.
This wine for Lepidus!

LEPIDUS What manner o' thing is your crocodile?

ANTONY It is shaped, sir, like itself, and it is as broad as it
hath breadth; it is just so high as it is, and moves with it   42
own organs. It lives by that which nourisheth it, and
the elements once out of it, it transmigrates.   44

LEPIDUS What color is it of?   46

ANTONY Of it own color too.

LEPIDUS 'Tis a strange serpent.

ANTONY 'Tis so, and the tears of it are wet.   48

CAESAR Will this description satisfy him?

ANTONY With the health that Pompey gives him; else he
is a very epicure.
      [Menas whispers again.]

POMPEY
Go hang, sir, hang! Tell me of that? Away!
Do as I bid you. – Where's this cup I called for?

MENAS
If for the sake of merit thou wilt hear me,
Rise from thy stool.

POMPEY   I think th' art mad.
      [Rises and walks aside.]   The matter?

MENAS
I have ever held my cap off to thy fortunes.   56

POMPEY
Thou hast served me with much faith. What's else to
say? –
Be jolly, lords.

ANTONY   These quicksands, Lepidus,
Keep off them, for you sink.

MENAS
Wilt thou be lord of all the world?

POMPEY   What say'st thou?

MENAS
Wilt thou be lord of the whole world? That's twice.

POMPEY
How should that be?

MENAS   But entertain it,   62
And though thou think me poor, I am the man
Will give thee all the world.

POMPEY   Hast thou drunk well?

MENAS
No, Pompey, I have kept me from the cup.
Thou art, if thou dar'st be, the earthly Jove:
Whate'er the ocean pales, or sky inclips,   67
Is thine, if thou wilt ha't.

POMPEY   Show me which way.

MENAS
These three world-sharers, these competitors,   69
Are in thy vessel. Let me cut the cable;

And when we are put off, fall to their throats.
All there is thine.

POMPEY   Ah, this thou shouldst have done,
And not have spoke on't. In me 'tis villainy,
In thee't had been good service. Thou must know,
76   Mine honor, it. Repent that e'er thy tongue
Hath so betrayed thine act. Being done unknown,
I should have found it afterwards well done,
But must condemn it now. Desist, and drink.

MENAS [aside]
For this,
81   I'll never follow thy palled fortunes more.
Who seeks, and will not take when once 'tis offered,
Shall never find it more.

POMPEY   This health to Lepidus!

ANTONY
84   Bear him ashore. I'll pledge it for him, Pompey.

ENOBARBUS
Here's to thee, Menas.

MENAS   Enobarbus, welcome.

POMPEY   Fill till the cup be hid.

ENOBARBUS   There's a strong fellow, Menas.
        [Points to the Servant who carries off Lepidus.]

MENAS   Why?

ENOBARBUS   'A bears the third part of the world, man;
    seest not?

MENAS
The third part then is drunk. Would it were all,
92   That it might go on wheels!

ENOBARBUS
93   Drink thou: increase the reels.

MENAS   Come.

POMPEY
This is not yet an Alexandrian feast.

ANTONY
96   It ripens towards it. Strike the vessels, ho!
Here's to Caesar!

97   CAESAR   I could well forbear't.
It's monstrous labor when I wash my brain
And it grows fouler.

ANTONY   Be a child o' th' time.

CAESAR
100   Possess it, I'll make answer;
But I had rather fast from all four days
Than drink so much in one.

ENOBARBUS   Ha, my brave emperor!
Shall we dance now the Egyptian Bacchanals
And celebrate our drink?

POMPEY   Let's ha't, good soldier.

ANTONY
Come, let's all take hands
Till that the conquering wine hath steeped our sense
107   In soft and delicate Lethe.

ENOBARBUS   All take hands:
Make battery to our ears with the loud music;
The while I'll place you; then the boy shall sing.
110   The holding every man shall bear as loud
As his strong sides can volley.
        Music plays. Enobarbus places them hand in hand.

        The Song.

Come, thou monarch of the vine,
Plumpy Bacchus with pink eyne!
113

In thy fats our cares be drowned,   114
With thy grapes our hairs be crowned.
Cup us till the world go round,
Cup us till the world go round!

CAESAR
What would you more? Pompey, good night.
Good brother,
Let me request you off: our graver business   119
Frowns at this levity. Gentle lords, let's part;
You see we have burned our cheeks. Strong Enobarb
Is weaker than the wine, and mine own tongue
Splits what it speaks: the wild disguise hath almost   123
Anticked us all. What needs more words? Good night. 124
Good Antony, your hand.

POMPEY   I'll try you on the shore.   125

ANTONY
And shall, sir. – Give's your hand.

POMPEY   O Antony,
You have my father's house. But what, we are friends!
Come down into the boat.

ENOBARBUS   Take heed you fall not.
        [Exeunt all but Enobarbus and Menas.]
Menas, I'll not on shore.

MENAS   No, to my cabin.
These drums! these trumpets, flutes! what!
Let Neptune hear we bid a loud farewell
To these great fellows. Sound and be hanged, sound
    out!
        Sound a flourish, with drums.

ENOBARBUS
Hoo! says 'a. There's my cap.

MENAS
Hoo! Noble captain, come.   Exeunt.

            *

        Enter Ventidius as it were in triumph, the dead body   III, i
        of Pacorus borne before him [by Romans].

VENTIDIUS
Now, darting Parthia, art thou struck, and now   1
Pleased fortune does of Marcus Crassus' death
Make me revenger. Bear the King's son's body
Before our army. Thy Pacorus, Orodes,
Pays this for Marcus Crassus.   5

ROMAN [SILIUS]   Noble Ventidius,
Whilst yet with Parthian blood thy sword is warm,
The fugitive Parthians follow. Spur through Media,
Mesopotamia, and the shelters whither
The routed fly: so thy grand captain, Antony,
Shall set thee on triumphant chariots and
Put garlands on thy head.

VENTIDIUS   O Silius, Silius,
I have done enough. A lower place, note well,   12
May make too great an act. For learn this, Silius,

76 Mine honor, it i.e. my honor comes before my profit   81 palled decayed
84 I'll . . . him (cf. l. 5: Antony is now taking an alms-drink)   92 go on
wheels whirl smoothly   93 reels whirls   96 Strike the vessels broach the
casks   97 forbear't i.e. pass up this toast   100 Possess it down it   107
Lethe (cf. II, i, 27n.)   110 holding refrain   113 pink half-closed   114
fats vats   119 off to come away   123 disguise dancing and drinking
124 Anticked made fools of   125 try you take you on in a drinking bout
III, i A field in Syria   1 darting i.e. famous for its bowmen   5 Marcus
Crassus (member of the first triumvirate with Pompey the Great and Julius
Caesar, who was killed by the Parthians and who is now avenged by the
death of Pacorus, son to Orodes the Parthian king)   12 A lower place an
underling

Better to leave undone, than by our deed
Acquire too high a fame when him we serve's away.
Caesar and Antony have ever won
More in their officer than person. Sossius,
One of my place in Syria, his lieutenant,
For quick accumulation of renown,
Which he achieved by th' minute, lost his favor.
Who does i' th' wars more than his captain can
Becomes his captain's captain ; and ambition
(The soldier's virtue) rather makes choice of loss
Than gain which darkens him.
I could do more to do Antonius good,
26 But 'twould offend him. And in his offense
Should my performance perish.

27 ROMAN [SILIUS]   Thou hast, Ventidius, that
Without the which a soldier and his sword
Grants scarce distinction. Thou wilt write to Antony ?

VENTIDIUS
I'll humbly signify what in his name,
That magical word of war, we have effected ;
How with his banners and his well-paid ranks
The ne'er-yet-beaten horse of Parthia
34 We have jaded out o' th' field.

ROMAN [SILIUS]   Where is he now ?

VENTIDIUS
He purposeth to Athens ; whither, with what haste
The weight we must convey with's will permit,
We shall appear before him. – On, there, pass along.
                                 Exeunt.

*

III, ii   *Enter Agrippa at one door, Enobarbus at another.*

AGRIPPA
1 What, are the brothers parted ?

ENOBARBUS
They have dispatched with Pompey ; he is gone ;
3 The other three are sealing. Octavia weeps
To part from Rome ; Caesar is sad, and Lepidus
Since Pompey's feast, as Menas says, is troubled
6 With the green-sickness.

AGRIPPA   'Tis a noble Lepidus.

ENOBARBUS
A very fine one. O, how he loves Caesar !

AGRIPPA
Nay, but how dearly he adores Mark Antony !

ENOBARBUS
Caesar ? Why, he's the Jupiter of men.

AGRIPPA
What's Antony ? The god of Jupiter.

ENOBARBUS
Spake you of Caesar ? How ! the nonpareil !

AGRIPPA
12 O Antony ! O thou Arabian bird !

ENOBARBUS
Would you praise Caesar, say 'Caesar' : go no further.

AGRIPPA
Indeed he plied them both with excellent praises.

ENOBARBUS
But he loves Caesar best, yet he loves Antony :
Hoo ! hearts, tongues, figures, scribes, bards, poets, cannot
Think, speak, cast, write, sing, number – hoo ! –
His love to Antony. But as for Caesar,
Kneel down, kneel down, and wonder.

AGRIPPA   Both he loves

ENOBARBUS
They are his shards, and he their beetle.   20
     [*Trumpet within.*]   So –
This is to horse. Adieu, noble Agrippa.

AGRIPPA
Good fortune, worthy soldier, and farewell !
     Enter Caesar, Antony, Lepidus, and Octavia.

ANTONY
No further, sir.

CAESAR
You take from me a great part of myself ;
Use me well in't. Sister, prove such a wife
As my thoughts make thee, and as my farthest band   26
Shall pass on thy approof. Most noble Antony,
Let not the piece of virtue which is set   28
Betwixt us as the cement of our love
To keep it builded, be the ram to batter
The fortress of it : for better might we
Have loved without this mean, if on both parts   32
This be not cherished.

ANTONY   Make me not offended
In your distrust.

CAESAR   I have said.

ANTONY   You shall not find,
Though you be therein curious, the least cause   35
For what you seem to fear. So the gods keep you
And make the hearts of Romans serve your ends !
We will here part.

CAESAR
Farewell, my dearest sister, fare thee well.
The elements be kind to thee, and make
Thy spirits all of comfort : fare thee well.

OCTAVIA
My noble brother !

ANTONY
The April 's in her eyes : it is love's spring,
And these the showers to bring it on. Be cheerful.

OCTAVIA
Sir, look well to my husband's house ; and –

CAESAR   What,
Octavia ?

OCTAVIA   I'll tell you in your ear.

ANTONY
Her tongue will not obey her heart, nor can
Her heart inform her tongue – the swan's down-feather   48
That stands upon the swell at full of tide,
And neither way inclines.

ENOBARBUS
Will Caesar weep ?   51

AGRIPPA   He has a cloud in's face.

ENOBARBUS
He were the worse for that, were he a horse ;   52

---

26 *in his offense* in offending him   27 *that* i.e. discretion   34 *jaded* driven weary
III, ii The house of Octavius Caesar in Rome   1 *parted* departed   3 *sealing* concluding agreements   6 *green-sickness* (traditionally the disease of lovesick girls : Lepidus is likened to one in his relations to Caesar and Antony)   12 *Arabian bird* i.e. unique (like the mythical phoenix, of which only one was supposed to exist at a time)   20 *shards* wings   26–27 *as my farthest . . . approof* such as I will give my uttermost bond that you will prove to be   28 *piece* paragon   32 *mean* intermediary   35 *curious* punctiliously exacting   48–50 *the swan's . . . inclines* i.e. her feelings for husband and brother are evenly balanced   51–59 (Enobarbus and Agrippa talk aside)   52 *horse* (horses without white markings on the face were thought to be ill-tempered)

    So is he, being a man.

AGRIPPA   Why, Enobarbus,
    When Antony found Julius Caesar dead,
    He cried almost to roaring ; and he wept
    When at Philippi he found Brutus slain.

ENOBARBUS
57   That year indeed he was troubled with a rheum.
58   What willingly he did confound he wailed,
    Believe't, till I wept too.

CAESAR   No, sweet Octavia,
60   You shall hear from me still : the time shall not
    Outgo my thinking on you.

ANTONY   Come, sir, come,
    I'll wrestle with you in my strength of love :
    Look, here I have you ; thus I let you go,
    And give you to the gods.

CAESAR   Adieu, be happy !

LEPIDUS
    Let all the number of the stars give light
    To thy fair way !

CAESAR   Farewell, farewell !
      Kisses Octavia.

ANTONY   Farewell !
      Trumpets sound. Exeunt.

                *

III, iii   *Enter Cleopatra, Charmian, Iras, and Alexas.*

CLEOPATRA
    Where is the fellow ?

ALEXAS   Half afeard to come.

CLEOPATRA
    Go to, go to.
      Enter the Messenger as before.
      Come hither, sir.

ALEXAS   Good Majesty,
3   Herod of Jewry dare not look upon you
    But when you are well pleased.

CLEOPATRA   That Herod's head
    I'll have : but how, when Antony is gone
    Through whom I might command it ? Come thou near.

MESSENGER
    Most gracious Majesty !

CLEOPATRA
    Didst thou behold Octavia ?

MESSENGER   Ay, dread Queen.

CLEOPATRA Where.

MESSENGER
    Madam, in Rome.
    I looked her in the face, and saw her led
    Between her brother and Mark Antony.

CLEOPATRA
    Is she as tall as me ?

MESSENGER   She is not, madam.

CLEOPATRA
    Didst hear her speak ? Is she shrill-tongued or low ?

MESSENGER
    Madam, I heard her speak ; she is low-voiced.

CLEOPATRA
17   That's not so good. He cannot like her long.

CHARMIAN
    Like her ? O Isis ! 'tis impossible.

CLEOPATRA
    I think so, Charmian. Dull of tongue, and dwarfish.

    What majesty is in her gait ? Remember,
    If e'er thou lookedst on majesty.

MESSENGER   She creeps :
    Her motion and her station are as one.   22
    She shows a body rather than a life,
    A statue than a breather.

CLEOPATRA   Is this certain ?

MESSENGER
    Or I have no observance.

CHARMIAN   Three in Egypt
    Cannot make better note.

CLEOPATRA   He's very knowing,
    I do perceive't. There's nothing in her yet.
    The fellow has good judgment.

CHARMIAN   Excellent.

CLEOPATRA
    Guess at her years, I prithee.

MESSENGER   Madam,
    She was a widow –

CLEOPATRA   Widow ? Charmian, hark.

MESSENGER
    And I do think she's thirty.

CLEOPATRA
    Bear'st thou her face in mind ? is't long or round ?   32

MESSENGER
    Round even to faultiness.

CLEOPATRA
    For the most part, too, they are foolish that are so.
    Her hair, what color ?

MESSENGER
    Brown, madam ; and her forehead
    As low as she would wish it.

CLEOPATRA   There's gold for thee.
    Thou must not take my former sharpness ill ;
    I will employ thee back again : I find thee
    Most fit for business. Go, make thee ready ;
    Our letters are prepared.   *[Exit Messenger.]*

CHARMIAN   A proper man.   41

CLEOPATRA
    Indeed he is so : I repent me much
    That so I harried him. Why, methinks, by him,   43
    This creature 's no such thing.   44

CHARMIAN   Nothing, madam.

CLEOPATRA
    The man hath seen some majesty, and should know.

CHARMIAN
    Hath he seen majesty ? Isis else defend,
    And serving you so long !

CLEOPATRA
    I have one thing more to ask him yet, good Charmian ;
    But 'tis no matter, thou shalt bring him to me
    Where I will write. All may be well enough.

CHARMIAN
    I warrant you, madam.   *Exeunt.*

                *

---

57 *rheum* running at the eyes   58 *confound* destroy   60–61 *the time . . . you* i.e. my thoughts of you will not be left behind (as in a race) by time
III, iii The chambers of Cleopatra in her palace at Alexandria   3 *Herod* i.e. even Herod (traditionally represented as a tyrant)   17 *good* i.e. as I am   22 *Her . . . one* even in motion she is still   32 *long or round* (thought to be signs, respectively, of prudence and folly)   41 *proper* attractive   43 *harried* mistreated   44 *no such thing* nothing much

III, iv   *Enter Antony and Octavia.*

ANTONY
Nay, nay, Octavia, not only that,
That were excusable, that and thousands more
3   Of semblable import – but he hath waged
4   New wars 'gainst Pompey ; made his will, and read it
To public ear ;
Spoke scantly of me : when perforce he could not
But pay me terms of honor, cold and sickly
8   He vented them, most narrow measure lent me ;
When the best hint was given him, he not took't,
10   Or did it from his teeth.

OCTAVIA   O, my good lord,
Believe not all, or if you must believe,
12   Stomach not all. A more unhappy lady,
If this division chance, ne'er stood between,
Praying for both parts.
15   The good gods will mock me presently
When I shall pray 'O, bless my lord and husband !'
Undo that prayer by crying out as loud
'O, bless my brother !' Husband win, win brother,
Prays, and destroys the prayer ; no midway
'Twixt these extremes at all.

ANTONY   Gentle Octavia,
Let your best love draw to that point which seeks
Best to preserve it. If I lose mine honor,
I lose myself : better I were not yours
24   Than yours so branchless. But as you requested,
Yourself shall go between's : the mean time, lady,
I'll raise the preparation of a war
27   Shall stain your brother. Make your soonest haste ;
So your desires are yours.

OCTAVIA   Thanks to my lord.
The Jove of power make me most weak, most weak,
Your reconciler ! Wars 'twixt you twain would be
As if the world should cleave, and that slain men
Should solder up the rift.

ANTONY
When it appears to you where this begins,
Turn your displeasure that way, for our faults
Can never be so equal that your love
Can equally move with them. Provide your going ;
Choose your own company, and command what cost
Your heart has mind to.   *Exeunt.*

III, v   *Enter Enobarbus and Eros.*

ENOBARBUS How now, friend Eros ?
EROS There's strange news come, sir.
ENOBARBUS What, man ?
EROS Caesar and Lepidus have made wars upon Pompey.
5 **ENOBARBUS** This is old. What is the success ?
6 **EROS** Caesar, having made use of him in the wars 'gainst
7   Pompey, presently denied him rivality, would not let
him partake in the glory of the action ; and not resting

here, accuses him of letters he had formerly wrote to
Pompey ; upon his own appeal, seizes him ; so the poor 10
third is up till death enlarge his confine. 11

ENOBARBUS
Then, world, thou hast a pair of chaps, no more ; 12
And throw between them all the food thou hast,
They'll grind the one the other. Where's Antony ?

EROS
He's walking in the garden – thus, and spurns
The rush that lies before him ; cries 'Fool Lepidus !'
And threats the throat of that his officer 17
That murd'red Pompey.

ENOBARBUS   Our great navy's rigged.

EROS
For Italy and Caesar. More, Domitius :
My lord desires you presently. My news
I might have told hereafter.

ENOBARBUS   'Twill be naught ;
But let it be. Bring me to Antony.

EROS Come, sir.   *Exeunt.*

*

         Enter Agrippa, Maecenas, and Caesar.   III, vi

CAESAR
Contemning Rome, he has done all this and more 1
In Alexandria. Here's the manner of't :
I' th' market place on a tribunal silvered,
Cleopatra and himself in chairs of gold
Were publicly enthroned ; at the feet sat
Caesarion, whom they call my father's son, 6
And all the unlawful issue that their lust
Since then hath made between them. Unto her
He gave the stablishment of Egypt ; made her 9
Of lower Syria, Cyprus, Lydia,
Absolute queen.

MAECENAS   This in the public eye ?

CAESAR
I' th' common show-place, where they exercise.
His sons he there proclaimed the kings of kings :
Great Media, Parthia, and Armenia
He gave to Alexander ; to Ptolemy he assigned
Syria, Cilicia, and Phoenicia. She
In th' habiliments of the goddess Isis 17
That day appeared, and oft before gave audience,
As 'tis reported, so.

MAECENAS   Let Rome be thus
Informed.

AGRIPPA   Who, queasy with his insolence 20
Already, will their good thoughts call from him.

CAESAR
The people know it, and have now received
His accusations.

AGRIPPA   Who does he accuse ?

CAESAR
Caesar, and that, having in Sicily
Sextus Pompeius spoiled, we had not rated him 25
His part o' th' isle. Then does he say he lent me 26
Some shipping unrestored. Lastly, he frets
That Lepidus of the triumvirate
Should be deposed ; and, being, that we detain
All his revenue.

AGRIPPA   Sir, this should be answered.

CAESAR
'Tis done already, and the messenger gone.

I have told him Lepidus was grown too cruel,
That he his high authority abused
And did deserve his change. For what I have conquered,
I grant him part; but then in his Armenia,
And other of his conquered kingdoms, I
Demand the like.

MAECENAS   He'll never yield to that.

CAESAR
Nor must not then be yielded to in this.
    Enter Octavia with her Train.

OCTAVIA
Hail, Caesar, and my lord, hail, most dear Caesar!

CAESAR
40   That ever I should call thee castaway!

OCTAVIA
You have not called me so, nor have you cause.

CAESAR
Why have you stol'n upon us thus? You come not
Like Caesar's sister. The wife of Antony
Should have an army for an usher, and
The neighs of horse to tell of her approach
Long ere she did appear. The trees by th' way
Should have borne men, and expectation fainted,
Longing for what it had not. Nay, the dust
Should have ascended to the roof of heaven,
Raised by your populous troops. But you are come
A market-maid to Rome, and have prevented
The ostentation of our love; which, left unshown,
53   Is often left unloved. We should have met you
By sea and land, supplying every stage
With an augmented greeting.

OCTAVIA   Good my lord,
To come thus was I not constrained, but did it
On my free will. My lord, Mark Antony,
Hearing that you prepared for war, acquainted
My grievèd ear withal; whereon I begged
His pardon for return.

CAESAR   Which soon he granted,
61   Being an abstract 'tween his lust and him.

OCTAVIA
Do not say so, my lord.

CAESAR   I have eyes upon him,
And his affairs come to me on the wind.
Where is he now?

OCTAVIA   My lord, in Athens.

CAESAR
No, my most wrongèd sister, Cleopatra
Hath nodded him to her. He hath given his empire
Up to a whore, who now are levying
The kings o' th' earth for war. He hath assembled
Bocchus, the king of Libya; Archelaus,
Of Cappadocia; Philadelphos, king
Of Paphlagonia; the Thracian king, Adallas;
72   King Mauchus of Arabia; King of Pont;
Herod of Jewry; Mithridates, king
Of Comagene; Polemon and Amyntas,
The kings of Mede and Lycaonia; with a
More larger list of sceptres.

OCTAVIA   Ay me most wretched,
That have my heart parted betwixt two friends
That do afflict each other!

CAESAR   Welcome hither.
Your letters did withhold our breaking forth,
Till we perceived both how you were wrong led

And we in negligent danger. Cheer your heart: 81
Be you not troubled with the time, which drives
O'er your content these strong necessities;
But let determined things to destiny
Hold unbewailed their way. Welcome to Rome,
Nothing more dear to me. You are abused   86
Beyond the mark of thought: and the high gods,   87
To do you justice, makes his ministers   88
Of us and those that love you. Best of comfort,
And ever welcome to us.

AGRIPPA   Welcome, lady.

MAECENAS
Welcome, dear madam.
Each heart in Rome does love and pity you.
Only th' adulterous Antony, most large   93
In his abominations, turns you off
And gives his potent regiment to a trull   95
That noises it against us.

OCTAVIA   Is it so, sir?

CAESAR
Most certain. Sister, welcome. Pray you
Be ever known to patience. My dear'st sister!   *Exeunt.* 98

*

    Enter Cleopatra and Enobarbus.   III, vii

CLEOPATRA
I will be even with thee, doubt it not.

ENOBARBUS
But why, why, why?

CLEOPATRA
Thou hast forspoke my being in these wars,   3
And say'st it is not fit.

ENOBARBUS   Well, is it, is it?

CLEOPATRA
Is't not denounced against us? Why should not we   5
Be there in person?

ENOBARBUS [aside] Well, I could reply:
If we should serve with horse and mares together,
The horse were merely lost; the mares would bear   8
A soldier and his horse.

CLEOPATRA   What is't you say?

ENOBARBUS
Your presence needs must puzzle Antony;   10
Take from his heart, take from his brain, from's time,
What should not then be spared. He is already
Traduced for levity; and 'tis said in Rome
That Photinus an eunuch and your maids
Manage this war.

CLEOPATRA   Sink Rome, and their tongues rot
That speak against us! A charge we bear i' th' war,   16
And as the president of my kingdom will
Appear there for a man. Speak not against it,
I will not stay behind.
    Enter Antony and Canidius.

---

53 *left unloved* thought to be unfelt   61 *abstract* short-cut   72 *Mauchus*
(so spelled in folio; Plutarch reads 'Malchus,' and North's translation
'Manchus')   81 *negligent danger* danger through negligence   86 *abused*
betrayed (by Antony)   87 *mark* reach   88 *makes his* make their   93 *large*
uninhibited   95 *regiment* rule; *trull* harlot   96 *noises it* clamors   98 *Be
. . . patience* be always calm
III, vii Antony's camp near Actium   3 *forspoke* opposed   5 *denounced*
declared   8 *merely* entirely   10 *puzzle* paralyze   16 *charge* responsibility

ENOBARBUS   Nay, I have done.
Here comes the Emperor.
ANTONY   Is it not strange, Canidius,
That from Tarentum and Brundusium
He could so quickly cut the Ionian sea
23   And take in Toryne? – You have heard on't, sweet?
CLEOPATRA
Celerity is never more admired
Than by the negligent.
ANTONY   A good rebuke,
Which might have well becomed the best of men
To taunt at slackness. Canidius, we
Will fight with him by sea.
CLEOPATRA   By sea; what else?
CANIDIUS
Why will my lord do so?
29   ANTONY   For that he dares us to't.
ENOBARBUS
So hath my lord dared him to single fight.
CANIDIUS
Ay, and to wage this battle at Pharsalia,
Where Caesar fought with Pompey. But these offers,
Which serve not for his vantage, he shakes off;
And so should you.
ENOBARBUS   Your ships are not well manned;
35   Your mariners are muleters, reapers, people
36   Ingrossed by swift impress. In Caesar's fleet
Are those that often have 'gainst Pompey fought;
38   Their ships are yare; yours, heavy: no disgrace
39   Shall fall you for refusing him at sea,
Being prepared for land.
ANTONY   By sea, by sea.
ENOBARBUS
Most worthy sir, you therein throw away
The absolute soldiership you have by land,
43   Distract your army, which doth most consist
Of war-marked footmen, leave unexecuted
Your own renownèd knowledge, quite forgo
The way which promises assurance, and
Give up yourself merely to chance and hazard
From firm security.
ANTONY   I'll fight at sea.
CLEOPATRA
I have sixty sails, Caesar none better.
ANTONY
Our overplus of shipping will we burn,
And with the rest full-manned, from th' head of Actium
Beat th' approaching Caesar. But if we fail,
We then can do't at land.
        Enter a Messenger. Thy business?
MESSENGER
The news is true, my lord, he is descried;
Caesar has taken Toryne.
ANTONY
Can he be there in person? 'Tis impossible;

Strange that his power should be. Canidius,   57
Our nineteen legions thou shalt hold by land
And our twelve thousand horse. We'll to our ship.
Away, my Thetis!   60
        Enter a Soldier. How now, worthy soldier?
SOLDIER
O noble Emperor, do not fight by sea,
Trust not to rotten planks. Do you misdoubt
This sword and these my wounds? Let th' Egyptians
And the Phoenicians go a-ducking: we
Have used to conquer standing on the earth
And fighting foot to foot.
ANTONY   Well, well, away!
        Exit Antony [with] Cleopatra and Enobarbus.
SOLDIER
By Hercules, I think I am i' th' right.
CANIDIUS
Soldier, thou art; but his whole action grows   68
Not in the power on't: so our leader's led,
And we are women's men.
SOLDIER   You keep by land
The legions and the horse whole, do you not?
CANIDIUS
Marcus Octavius, Marcus Justeius,
Publicola, and Caelius are for sea;
But we keep whole by land. This speed of Caesar's
Carries beyond belief.   75
SOLDIER   While he was yet in Rome,
His power went out in such distractions as   76
Beguiled all spies.   77
CANIDIUS   Who's his lieutenant, hear you?
SOLDIER
They say, one Taurus.
CANIDIUS   Well I know the man.
        Enter a Messenger.
MESSENGER
The Emperor calls Canidius.
CANIDIUS
With news the time's with labor and throws forth   80
Each minute some.   *Exeunt.*

                        *

        Enter Caesar, with his Army, marching.   III, viii
CAESAR Taurus!
TAURUS My lord?
CAESAR
Strike not by land; keep whole, provoke not battle
Till we have done at sea. Do not exceed
The prescript of this scroll. Our fortune lies
Upon this jump.   *Exit [with Taurus and the Army].* 6
        Enter Antony and Enobarbus.   III, ix
ANTONY
Set we our squadrons on yond side o' th' hill
In eye of Caesar's battle; from which place   2
We may the number of the ships behold,
And so proceed accordingly.   *Exit [with Enobarbus].*
        Canidius marcheth with his land army one way over III, x
        the stage, and Taurus, the lieutenant of Caesar, the
        other way. After their going in is heard the noise of a
        sea-fight. Alarum. Enter Enobarbus.
ENOBARBUS
Naught, naught, all naught! I can behold no longer.   1
Th' Antoniad, the Egyptian admiral,   2

---

23 *take in* seize 29 *For that* because 35 *muleters* mule-drivers, i.e.
peasants 36 *Ingrossed* collected wholesale; *impress* draft 38 *yare* nimble
39 *you* to you 43 *Distract* divide 57 *power* army 60 *Thetis* name of a sea
goddess 68–69 *his . . . on't* his plan of action does not spring from a right
estimate of the nature of his strength 75 *Carries* i.e. like an arrow 76
distractions detachments 77 *Beguiled* deceived 80 *throws* i.e. as an
animal 'throws,' gives birth to, its young
III, viii A field near Actium 6 *jump* chance
III, ix 2 *battle* battle-line
III, x 1 *Naught* i.e. all's come to naught 2 *admiral* flagship

With all their sixty, fly and turn the rudder:
To see't mine eyes are blasted.

Enter Scarus.

SCARUS   Gods and goddesses,
5   All the whole synod of them!

ENOBARBUS   What's thy passion?

SCARUS
6   The greater cantle of the world is lost
With very ignorance; we have kissed away
Kingdoms and provinces.

ENOBARBUS   How appears the fight?

SCARUS
9   On our side like the tokened pestilence
10   Where death is sure. Yon ribaudred nag of Egypt –
Whom leprosy o'ertake! – i' th' midst o' th' fight,
When vantage like a pair of twins appeared,
13   Both as the same, or rather ours the elder,
14   The breese upon her, like a cow in June,
Hoists sails, and flies.

ENOBARBUS   That I beheld:
Mine eyes did sicken at the sight, and could not
Endure a further view.

18 SCARUS   She once being loofed,
The noble ruin of her magic, Antony,
20   Claps on his sea-wing, and (like a doting mallard)
Leaving the fight in heighth, flies after her.
I never saw an action of such shame;
Experience, manhood, honor, ne'er before
Did violate so itself.

ENOBARBUS   Alack, alack!

Enter Canidius.

CANIDIUS
Our fortune on the sea is out of breath,
And sinks most lamentably. Had our general
27   Been what he knew himself, it had gone well.
O, he has given example for our flight
Most grossly by his own.

29 ENOBARBUS   Ay, are you thereabouts?
Why then, good night indeed.

CANIDIUS
Toward Peloponnesus are they fled.

SCARUS
'Tis easy to't; and there I will attend
What further comes.

CANIDIUS   To Caesar will I render
My legions and my horse; six kings already
Show me the way of yielding.

ENOBARBUS   I'll yet follow
36   The wounded chance of Antony, though my reason
37   Sits in the wind against me.   *[Exeunt.]*

*

III, xi   *Enter Antony with Attendants.*

ANTONY
Hark! the land bids me tread no more upon't,
It is ashamed to bear me. Friends, come hither.
3   I am so lated in the world that I
Have lost my way for ever. I have a ship
Laden with gold: take that, divide it. Fly,
And make your peace with Caesar.

OMNES   Fly? Not we.

ANTONY
I have fled myself, and have instructed cowards
To run and show their shoulders. Friends, be gone.
I have myself resolved upon a course
Which has no need of you. Be gone.
My treasure 's in the harbor. Take it! O,
I followed that I blush to look upon.   12
My very hairs do mutiny: for the white
Reprove the brown for rashness, and they them
For fear and doting. Friends, be gone, you shall
Have letters from me to some friends that will
Sweep your way for you. Pray you look not sad   17
Nor make replies of loathness; take the hint
Which my despair proclaims. Let that be left   19
Which leaves itself. To the seaside straightway!
I will possess you of that ship and treasure.
Leave me, I pray, a little: pray you now,
Nay, do so; for indeed I have lost command,   23
Therefore I pray you. I'll see you by and by.

Sits down.

Enter Cleopatra led by Charmian, [Iras,] and Eros.

EROS Nay, gentle madam, to him, comfort him.

IRAS Do, most dear Queen.

CHARMIAN Do? Why, what else?

CLEOPATRA Let me sit down. O Juno!

ANTONY No, no, no, no, no.

EROS See you here, sir?

ANTONY O fie, fie, fie!

CHARMIAN Madam!

IRAS Madam, O good Empress!

EROS Sir, sir!

ANTONY
Yes, my lord, yes. He at Philippi kept   35
His sword e'en like a dancer, while I struck
The lean and wrinkled Cassius; and 'twas I
That the mad Brutus ended: he alone
Dealt on lieutenantry, and no practice had   39
In the brave squares of war: yet now – No matter.   40

CLEOPATRA Ah, stand by.

EROS The Queen, my lord, the Queen.

IRAS
Go to him, madam, speak to him;
He is unqualitied with very shame.   44

CLEOPATRA
Well then, sustain me. O!

EROS
Most noble sir, arise. The Queen approaches.
Her head 's declined, and death will seize her, but   47
Your comfort makes the rescue.

ANTONY
I have offended reputation,
A most unnoble swerving.

---

5 *synod* assembly 6 *cantle* piece 9 *like . . . pestilence* like the plague when its certain symptoms have been seen 10 *ribaudred* foul, obscene (many editors read 'ribald-rid,' but the meaning is the same) 13 *elder* i.e. superior 14 *breese* stinging fly (with pun on 'breeze') 18 *loofed* luffed, turned to the wind to fly (?), disengaged (?) 20 *doting mallard* lovesick wild duck 27 *what . . . himself* his true self (as a great soldier) 29 *are you thereabouts* i.e. is that where your thoughts are 36 *chance* fortunes 37 *Sits . . . me* dissuades me

III, xi The palace of Cleopatra in Alexandria 3 *so . . . world* i.e. like a traveller after nightfall 12 *that* what 17 *Sweep* i.e. with Caesar 19 *that* i.e. himself 23–24 *I . . . pray you* i.e. I have lost the right to order you, so I entreat you 35–36 *kept . . . dancer* i.e. never drew his sword 39 *Dealt on lieutenantry* relied on subordinates 40 *squares* squadrons 44 *unqualitied* unmanned 47 *but* unless

EROS   Sir, the Queen.

ANTONY

O, whither hast thou led me, Egypt? See
How I convey my shame out of thine eyes
53 By looking back what I have left behind
'Stroyed in dishonor.

CLEOPATRA   O my lord, my lord,
Forgive my fearful sails: I little thought
You would have followed.

ANTONY   Egypt, thou knew'st too well
My heart was to thy rudder tied by th' strings,
And thou shouldst tow me after. O'er my spirit
Thy full supremacy thou knew'st, and that
60 Thy beck might from the bidding of the gods
Command me.

CLEOPATRA   O, my pardon!

ANTONY   Now I must
62 To the young man send humble treaties, dodge
63 And palter in the shifts of lowness, who
With half the bulk o' th' world played as I pleased,
Making and marring fortunes. You did know
How much you were my conqueror, and that
My sword, made weak by my affection, would
Obey it on all cause.

CLEOPATRA   Pardon, pardon!

ANTONY

69 Fall not a tear, I say: one of them rates
All that is won and lost. Give me a kiss;
71 Even this repays me. We sent our schoolmaster.
72 Is 'a come back? Love, I am full of lead.
Some wine, within there, and our viands! Fortune
     knows
We scorn her most when most she offers blows. *Exeunt.*

*

     Enter Caesar, Agrippa, Dolabella, [Thidias,]
          with others.

CAESAR

Let him appear that's come from Antony.
Know you him?

DOLABELLA   Caesar, 'tis his schoolmaster:
An argument that he is plucked, when hither
He sends so poor a pinion of his wing,
Which had superfluous kings for messengers
Not many moons gone by.

         Enter Ambassador from Antony.

CAESAR   Approach and speak.

AMBASSADOR

Such as I am, I come from Antony.
I was of late as petty to his ends
As is the morn-dew on the myrtle leaf

To his grand sea.

CAESAR   Be't so. Declare thine office.   10

AMBASSADOR

Lord of his fortunes he salutes thee, and
Requires to live in Egypt; which not granted,   12
He lessons his requests, and to thee sues   13
To let him breathe between the heavens and earth,   14
A private man in Athens: this for him.
Next, Cleopatra does confess thy greatness,
Submits her to thy might, and of thee craves
The circle of the Ptolemies for her heirs,   18
Now hazarded to thy grace.   19

CAESAR   For Antony,
I have no ears to his request. The Queen
Of audience nor desire shall fail, so she   21
From Egypt drive her all-disgracèd friend
Or take his life there. This if she perform,
She shall not sue unheard. So to them both.

AMBASSADOR

Fortune pursue thee!

CAESAR   Bring him through the bands.   25
                [Exit Ambassador.]
     [To Thidias]
To try thy eloquence now 'tis time. Dispatch.
From Antony win Cleopatra: promise,
And in our name, what she requires; add more,
From thine invention, offers. Women are not
In their best fortunes strong, but want will perjure
The ne'er-touched Vestal. Try thy cunning, Thidias;
Make thine own edict for thy pains, which we   32
Will answer as a law.

THIDIAS   Caesar, I go.

CAESAR

Observe how Antony becomes his flaw,   34
And what thou think'st his very action speaks   35
In every power that moves.

THIDIAS   Caesar, I shall.   *Exeunt.*

*

     Enter Cleopatra, Enobarbus, Charmian, and Iras.   III, xiii

CLEOPATRA

What shall we do, Enobarbus?

ENOBARBUS   Think, and die.

CLEOPATRA

Is Antony or we in fault for this?

ENOBARBUS

Antony only, that would make his will
Lord of his reason. What though you fled   3
From that great face of war, whose several ranges
Frighted each other? Why should he follow?   5
The itch of his affection should not then
Have nicked his captainship, at such a point,
When half to half the world opposed, he being   8
The merèd question. 'Twas a shame no less
Than was his loss, to course your flying flags   10
And leave his navy gazing.   11

CLEOPATRA   Prithee peace.
     Enter the Ambassador, with Antony.

ANTONY

Is that his answer?

AMBASSADOR

Ay, my lord.

---

53 *By looking back* i.e. by averting my eyes from yours and looking back at
60 *beck* beckoning   62 *treaties* proposals   63 *palter . . . lowness* i.e. use
the tricks to which a man brought low is reduced   69 *Fall* let fall; *rates*
equals   71 *schoolmaster* i.e. his children's tutor   72 *lead* i.e. grief
III, xii The camp of Octavius Caesar in Egypt   10 *sea* i.e. the ultimate
source of dew   12 *Requires* requests   13 *lessons* disciplines   14 *breathe*
i.e. go on living   18 *circle* crown   19 *hazarded . . . grace* dependent on
your mercy   21 *audience* a hearing; *so* provided   25 *bands* troops   32 *Make*
. . . *edict* name your own price (as reward)   34 *becomes his flaw* takes his
fall   35–36 *And . . . moves* and what you think his every move reveals
III, xiii The palace of Cleopatra   3 *will* desire   5 *ranges* battle-lines
8 *nicked* got the better of   10 *merèd question* sole cause (?), decisive factor
(?)   11 *course* chase

ANTONY
The Queen shall then have courtesy, so she
Will yield us up.

AMBASSADOR   He says so.

ANTONY   Let her know't.
To the boy Caesar send this grizzled head,
And he will fill thy wishes to the brim
With principalities.

CLEOPATRA   That head, my lord?

ANTONY
To him again! Tell him he wears the rose
Of youth upon him; from which the world should note
22   Something particular. His coin, ships, legions
May be a coward's, whose ministers would prevail
Under the service of a child as soon
As i' th' command of Caesar. I dare him therefore
26   To lay his gay comparisons apart
27   And answer me declined, sword against sword,
Ourselves alone. I'll write it: follow me.
       [Exeunt Antony and Ambassador.]

ENOBARBUS *[aside]*
29   Yes, like enough: high-battled Caesar will
30   Unstate his happiness and be staged to th' show
Against a sworder! I see men's judgments are
32   A parcel of their fortunes, and things outward
33   Do draw the inward quality after them
34   To suffer all alike. That he should dream,
35   Knowing all measures, the full Caesar will
Answer his emptiness! Caesar, thou has subdued
His judgment too.
      Enter a Servant.

SERVANT   A messenger from Caesar.

CLEOPATRA
What, no more ceremony? See, my women,
Against the blown rose may they stop their nose
That kneeled unto the buds. Admit him, sir.
         [Exit Servant.]

ENOBARBUS *[aside]*
41   Mine honesty and I begin to square.
The loyalty well held to fools does make
Our faith mere folly: yet he that can endure
To follow with allegiance a fall'n lord
Does conquer him that did his master conquer
And earns a place i' th' story.
      Enter Thidias.

CLEOPATRA   Caesar's will?

THIDIAS
Hear it apart.

CLEOPATRA   None but friends: say boldly.

THIDIAS
48   So, haply, are they friends to Antony.

ENOBARBUS
He needs as many, sir, as Caesar has,
Or needs not us. If Caesar please, our master
Will leap to be his friend; for us, you know,
52   Whose he is we are, and that is Caesar's.

THIDIAS   So.
Thus then, thou most renowned, Caesar entreats
54   Not to consider in what case thou stand'st
Further than he is Caesar.

CLEOPATRA   Go on: right royal.

THIDIAS
He knows that you embrace not Antony
As you did love, but as you feared him.

CLEOPATRA   O!

THIDIAS
The scars upon your honor therefore he
Does pity, as constrainèd blemishes,
Not as deserved.

CLEOPATRA   He is a god, and knows
What is most right. Mine honor was not yielded,
But conquered merely.

ENOBARBUS *[aside]*   To be sure of that,
I will ask Antony. Sir, sir, thou art so leaky
That we must leave thee to thy sinking, for
Thy dearest quit thee.   *Exit Enobarbus.*

THIDIAS   Shall I say to Caesar
What you require of him? For he partly begs   66
To be desired to give. It much would please him
That of his fortunes you should make a staff
To lean upon. But it would warm his spirits
To hear from me you had left Antony,
And put yourself under his shroud,   71
The universal landlord.

CLEOPATRA   What's your name?

THIDIAS
My name is Thidias.

CLEOPATRA   Most kind messenger,
Say to great Caesar this: in deputation   74
I kiss his conqu'ring hand; tell him I am prompt
To lay my crown at's feet, and there to kneel.
Tell him, from his all-obeying breath, I hear   77
The doom of Egypt.

THIDIAS   'Tis your noblest course:
Wisdom and fortune combating together,
If that the former dare but what it can,   80
No chance may shake it. Give me grace to lay
My duty on your hand.   82

CLEOPATRA   Your Caesar's father oft,
When he hath mused of taking kingdoms in,
Bestowed his lips on that unworthy place,
As it rained kisses.
      Enter Antony and Enobarbus.

ANTONY   Favors? by Jove that thunders!
What art thou, fellow?

THIDIAS   One that but performs
The bidding of the fullest man, and worthiest
To have command obeyed.

ENOBARBUS *[aside]*   You will be whipped.

ANTONY
Approach there! Ah, you kite! Now, gods and devils!
Authority melts from me. Of late, when I cried 'Ho!'
Like boys unto a muss, kings would start forth,   91
And cry 'Your will?' Have you no ears? I am
Antony yet.

---

22 *Something particular* i.e. some personal heroism   26 *comparisons* i.e. all things which give him the advantage when he compares his position with mine   27 *declined* i.e. in years and fortune   29 *high-battled* lifted high in strength and mood by successful armies   30 *Unstate* abdicate   30–31 *be . . . sworder* be exposed as a public spectacle in a gladiatorial duel   32 *A parcel* i.e. part and parcel   33 *quality* nature   34 *To . . . alike* so that both decline together   35 *Knowing all measures* being a good judge (of men and things)   41 *square* quarrel   48 *haply* most likely   52 *Whose . . . are* i.e. whomever Antony belongs to, we belong to (?)   54–55 *Not . . . Caesar* i.e. not to think about your situation beyond realizing that you have to do with (a generous conqueror like) Caesar   66 *require* request   71 *shroud* shelter   74 *in deputation* i.e. through you as deputy   77 *all-obeying* that all obey   80 *If . . . can* if discretion confines itself to the possible   82 *My duty* i.e. a kiss   91 *muss* scramble

Enter a Servant.

93   Take hence this Jack and whip him.

ENOBARBUS *[aside]*
'Tis better playing with a lion's whelp
Than with an old one dying.

ANTONY   Moon and stars!
Whip him. Were't twenty of the greatest tributaries
That do acknowledge Caesar, should I find them
98   So saucy with the hand of she here – what's her name
Since she was Cleopatra? Whip him, fellows,
Till like a boy you see him cringe his face
And whine aloud for mercy. Take him hence.

THIDIAS
Mark Antony –

ANTONY   Tug him away. Being whipped,
Bring him again. This Jack of Caesar's shall
Bear us an errand to him. *Exeunt [Servants] with Thidias.*
You were half blasted ere I knew you. Ha!
Have I my pillow left unpressed in Rome,
Forborne the getting of a lawful race,
108 And by a gem of women, to be abused
109 By one that looks on feeders?

CLEOPATRA   Good my lord –
ANTONY
110 You have been a boggler ever:
But when we in our viciousness grow hard
112 (O misery on't!) the wise gods seel our eyes,
In our own filth drop our clear judgments, make us
Adore our errors, laugh at's while we strut
To our confusion.

CLEOPATRA   O, is't come to this?
ANTONY
I found you as a morsel cold upon
117 Dead Caesar's trencher: nay, you were a fragment
Of Gneius Pompey's, besides what hotter hours,
119 Unregist'red in vulgar fame, you have
120 Luxuriously picked out. For I am sure,
Though you can guess what temperance should be,
You know not what it is.

CLEOPATRA   Wherefore is this?
ANTONY
To let a fellow that will take rewards
124 And say 'God quit you!' be familiar with
My playfellow, your hand, this kingly seal
126 And plighter of high hearts. O that I were
Upon the hill of Basan to outroar
The hornèd herd! for I have savage cause,
129 And to proclaim it civilly were like
A haltered neck which does the hangman thank
131 For being yare about him.

---

93 *Jack* conceited upstart   98–99 *what's . . . Cleopatra* (Antony implies that this common trafficker in kisses cannot be the imperial Cleopatra) 108 *abused* betrayed   109 *feeders* menials   110 *boggler* shifty one   112 *seel* sew up   117 *trencher* plate; *fragment* leftover   119 *vulgar fame* common gossip   120 *Luxuriously* lustfully   124 *quit* repay   126–28 *O . . . herd* (Antony thinks of himself as chief among the herd of bulls of Bashan whose roaring is described in Psalms xxii, 12–13 – i.e. as chief cuckold among all the lovers cuckolded by Cleopatra)   129 *like* to act like   131 *yare* nimble 140 *entertainment* reception (here)   146 *orbs* the spheres in which they turn   149 *Hipparchus* (who had earlier revolted to Caesar); *enfranchèd* freed   153 *our . . . moon* i.e. Cleopatra, our terrestrial Isis or moon-goddess 155 *stay his time* wait out his fury   157 *one . . . points* his valet   161 *determines* melts   163 *the memory . . . womb* i.e. my offspring   165 *discandying* melting (as if it were hard candy)   171 *fleet* are afloat   172 *heart* courage 174 *in blood* (1) bloody, (2) with blood up, spirited   175 *our chronicle* our place in history

---

Enter a Servant with Thidias.

                 Is he whipped?

SERVANT
Soundly, my lord.

ANTONY   Cried he? and begged 'a pardon?

SERVANT
He did ask favor.

ANTONY
If that thy father live, let him repent
Thou wast not made his daughter; and be thou sorry
To follow Caesar in his triumph, since
Thou hast been whipped for following him. Henceforth
The white hand of a lady fever thee,
Shake thou to look on't. Get thee back to Caesar,
Tell him thy entertainment: look thou say   140
He makes me angry with him. For he seems
Proud and disdainful, harping on what I am,
Not what he knew I was. He makes me angry,
And at this time most easy 'tis to do't,
When my good stars that were my former guides
Have empty left their orbs and shot their fires   146
Into th' abysm of hell. If he mislike
My speech and what is done, tell him he has
Hipparchus, my enfranchèd bondman, whom   149
He may at pleasure whip, or hang, or torture,
As he shall like, to quit me. Urge it thou.
Hence with thy stripes, be gone!   *Exit Thidias.*

CLEOPATRA
Have you done yet?

ANTONY   Alack, our terrene moon   153
Is now eclipsed, and it portends alone
The fall of Antony.

CLEOPATRA   I must stay his time.   155
ANTONY
To flatter Caesar, would you mingle eyes
With one that ties his points?   157

CLEOPATRA   Not know me yet?
ANTONY
Cold-hearted toward me?

CLEOPATRA   Ah, dear, if I be so,
From my cold heart let heaven engender hail,
And poison it in the source, and the first stone
Drop in my neck: as it determines, so   161
Dissolve my life! The next Caesarion smite,
Till by degrees the memory of my womb,   163
Together with my brave Egyptians all,
By the discandying of this pelleted storm,   165
Lie graveless, till the flies and gnats of Nile
Have buried them for prey!

ANTONY   I am satisfied.
Caesar sits down in Alexandria, where
I will oppose his fate. Our force by land
Hath nobly held; our severed navy too
Have knit again, and fleet, threat'ning most sea-like.   171
Where hast thou been, my heart? Dost thou hear, lady?   172
If from the field I shall return once more
To kiss these lips, I will appear in blood;   174
I and my sword will earn our chronicle.   175
There's hope in't yet.

CLEOPATRA
That's my brave lord!

ANTONY
I will be treble-sinewed, hearted, breathed,
And fight maliciously; for when mine hours

180 Were nice and lucky, men did ransom lives
    Of me for jests ; but now I'll set my teeth
    And send to darkness all that stop me. Come,
183 Let's have one other gaudy night : call to me
    All my sad captains ; fill our bowls once more ;
    Let's mock the midnight bell.

CLEOPATRA   It is my birthday.
    I had thought t' have held it poor. But since my lord
    Is Antony again, I will be Cleopatra.

ANTONY
    We will yet do well.

CLEOPATRA
    Call all his noble captains to my lord.

ANTONY
    Do so, we'll speak to them ; and to-night I'll force
    The wine peep through their scars. Come on, my queen,
192 There's sap in't yet ! The next time I do fight,
    I'll make death love me, for I will contend
    Even with his pestilent scythe.
                              Exeunt [all but Enobarbus].

ENOBARBUS
    Now he'll outstare the lightning. To be furious
    Is to be frighted out of fear, and in that mood
197 The dove will peck the estridge ; and I see still
    A diminution in our captain's brain
    Restores his heart. When valor preys on reason,
    It eats the sword it fights with : I will seek
    Some way to leave him.   *Exit.*

                              *

IV, i   *Enter Caesar, Agrippa, and Maecenas, with his
             Army, Caesar reading a letter.*

CAESAR
    He calls me boy, and chides as he had power
    To beat me out of Egypt. My messenger
    He hath whipped with rods ; dares me to personal
        combat,
    Caesar to Antony. Let the old ruffian know
    I have many other ways to die, meantime
    Laugh at his challenge.

MAECENAS   Caesar must think,
    When one so great begins to rage, he's hunted
    Even to falling. Give him no breath, but now
9   Make boot of his distraction : never anger
    Made good guard for itself.

CAESAR   Let our best heads
    Know that to-morrow the last of many battles
12 We mean to fight. Within our files there are,
    Of those that served Mark Antony but late,
14 Enough to fetch him in. See it done,
    And feast the army ; we have store to do't,
    And they have earned the waste. Poor Antony !
                              Exeunt.

                              *

IV, ii   *Enter Antony, Cleopatra, Enobarbus, Charmian,
             Iras, Alexas, with others.*

ANTONY
    He will not fight with me, Domitius ?

ENOBARBUS   No.

ANTONY
    Why should he not ?

ENOBARBUS
    He thinks, being twenty times of better fortune,
    He is twenty men to one.

ANTONY   To-morrow, soldier,
    By sea and land I'll fight : or I will live,   5
    Or bathe my dying honor in the blood
    Shall make it live again. Woo't thou fight well ?

ENOBARBUS
    I'll strike, and cry 'Take all !'   8

ANTONY   Well said, come on ;
    Call forth my household servants ; let's to-night
    Be bounteous at our meal.
                    Enter three or four Servitors.
                              Give me thy hand,
    Thou hast been rightly honest, so hast thou,
    And thou, and thou, and thou : you have served me well,
    And kings have been your fellows.

CLEOPATRA   What means this ?   13

ENOBARBUS
    'Tis one of those odd tricks which sorrow shoots
    Out of the mind.

ANTONY   And thou art honest too.
    I wish I could be made so many men,   16
    And all of you clapped up together in
    An Antony, that I might do you service
    So good as you have done.

OMNES   The gods forbid !

ANTONY
    Well, my good fellows, wait on me to-night :
    Scant not my cups, and make as much of me
    As when mine empire was your fellow too
    And suffered my command.

CLEOPATRA   What does he mean ?

ENOBARBUS
    To make his followers weep.

ANTONY   Tend me to-night ;
    May be it is the period of your duty.   25
    Haply you shall not see me more ; or if,   26
    A mangled shadow. Perchance to-morrow
    You'll serve another master. I look on you
    As one that takes his leave. Mine honest friends,
    I turn you not away, but like a master
    Married to your good service, stay till death.
    Tend me to-night two hours, I ask no more,
    And the gods yield you for't !   33

ENOBARBUS   What mean you, sir,
    To give them this discomfort ? Look, they weep,
    And I, an ass, am onion-eyed ; for shame !
    Transform us not to women.

ANTONY   Ho, ho, ho !
    Now the witch take me if I meant it thus !
    Grace grow where those drops fall ! My hearty friends, 38
    You take me in too dolorous a sense,
    For I spake to you for your comfort, did desire you
    To burn this night with torches. Know, my hearts,

---

180 *nice* able to be 'choosy'   183 *gaudy* joyous   192 *sap* i.e. life, hope
197 *estridge* species of hawk
IV, i The camp of Octavius Caesar   9 *boot* advantage   12 *files* troops
14 *fetch him in* capture him
IV, ii The palace of Cleopatra   5 *or* either   8 *Take all* winner take all
13-15 (here and in ll. 23-24 Enobarbus and Cleopatra talk aside)   16 *so
many men* i.e. so many men as you are   25 *period* end   26 *Haply* most
likely   33 *yield* repay   38 *Grace grow* may virtues spring up (with a pun on
'grace' as one name for the herb rue)

I hope well of to-morrow, and will lead you
Where rather I'll expect victorious life
Than death and honor. Let's to supper, come,
And drown consideration.   *Exeunt.*

*

IV, iii   *Enter a Company of Soldiers.*

1 . SOLDIER
Brother, good night : to-morrow is the day.

2 . SOLDIER
It will determine one way : fare you well.
Heard you of nothing strange about the streets ?

1 . SOLDIER
Nothing. What news ?

2 . SOLDIER
Belike 'tis but a rumor. Good night to you.

1 . SOLDIER
Well, sir, good night.
         They meet other Soldiers.

2 . SOLDIER   Soldiers, have careful watch.

3 . SOLDIER
And you. Good night, good night.
        They place themselves in every corner of the stage.

4 . SOLDIER
8   Here we ; and if to-morrow
Our navy thrive, I have an absolute hope
Our landmen will stand up.

3 . SOLDIER   'Tis a brave army,
And full of purpose.
        Music of the hautboys is under the stage.

2 . SOLDIER   Peace ! What noise ?

1 . SOLDIER   List, list !

2 . SOLDIER
Hark !

1 . SOLDIER   Music i' th' air.

3 . SOLDIER   Under the earth.

4 . SOLDIER
13   It signs well, does it not ?

3 . SOLDIER   No.

1 . SOLDIER   Peace, I say !
What should this mean ?

2 . SOLDIER
15   'Tis the god Hercules, whom Antony loved,
Now leaves him.

1 . SOLDIER   Walk ; let's see if other watchmen
Do hear what we do.

2 . SOLDIER   How now, masters ?

OMNES *(speak together)*   How now ?
How now ? Do you hear this ?

1 . SOLDIER   Ay. Is't not strange ?

3 . SOLDIER
Do you hear, masters ? do you hear ?

1 . SOLDIER
20   Follow the noise so far as we have quarter.

IV, iii An open place in Alexandria   **8** *Here we* i.e. here is our post   **13** *signs* signifies   **15** *Hercules* (cf. I, iii, 84–85n.)   **20** *as . . . quarter* as our watch extends
IV, iv The palace of Cleopatra   **3** *thine iron* i.e. this armor of mine   **7** *False* wrong   **10** *Briefly* in a moment   **13** *daff't* take it off   **15** *tight* deft   **18** *workman* craftsman, expert   **19** *charge* duty   **20** *betime* early   **22** *riveted trim* armor   **23** *port* gate   **25** *blown* opened (i.e. the morning)   **28** *said* done (spoken to Cleopatra, who is arming him)   **31** *check* reproof   **31–32** *stand . . . compliment* use more elaborate ceremony

Let's see how it will give off.

OMNES
Content. 'Tis strange.   *Exeunt.*

*

      Enter Antony and Cleopatra, with others.   **IV, iv**

ANTONY
Eros ! mine armor, Eros !

CLEOPATRA   Sleep a little.

ANTONY
No, my chuck. Eros, come ; mine armor, Eros.
        Enter Eros [with armor].
Come, good fellow, put thine iron on.   3
If fortune be not ours to-day, it is
Because we brave her. Come.

CLEOPATRA   Nay, I'll help too.
What's this for ?

ANTONY   Ah, let be, let be ! Thou art
The armorer of my heart. False, false ; this, this.   7

CLEOPATRA
Sooth, la, I'll help : thus it must be.

ANTONY   Well, well,
We shall thrive now. Seest thou, my good fellow ?
Go, put on thy defenses.

EROS   Briefly, sir.   10

CLEOPATRA
Is not this buckled well ?

ANTONY   Rarely, rarely :
He that unbuckles this, till we do please
To daff't for our repose, shall hear a storm.   13
Thou fumblest, Eros, and my queen 's a squire
More tight at this than thou. Dispatch. O love,   15
That thou couldst see my wars to-day, and knew'st
The royal occupation : thou shouldst see
A workman in't.   18
        Enter an armed Soldier.
          Good morrow to thee, welcome,
Thou look'st like him that knows a warlike charge.   19
To business that we love we rise betime   20
And go to't with delight.

SOLDIER   A thousand, sir,
Early though't be, have on their riveted trim,   22
And at the port expect you.   23
        Shout. Trumpets flourish. Enter Captains and
        Soldiers.

CAPTAIN
The morn is fair. Good morrow, General.

ALL
Good morrow, General.

ANTONY   'Tis well blown, lads.   25
This morning, like the spirit of a youth
That means to be of note, begins betimes.
So, so. Come, give me that : this way. Well said.   28
Fare thee well, dame ; whate'er becomes of me,
This is a soldier's kiss. Rebukable
And worthy shameful check it were to stand   31
On more mechanic compliment. I'll leave thee
Now like a man of steel. You that will fight,
Follow me close ; I'll bring you to't. Adieu.
        Exeunt [Antony, Eros, Captains, and Soldiers].

CHARMIAN
Please you retire to your chamber ?

CLEOPATRA   Lead me.

He goes forth gallantly. That he and Caesar might
Determine this great war in single fight!
Then Antony – but now – Well, on.   *Exeunt.*

*

IV, v   *Trumpets sound. Enter Antony and Eros [, a Soldier*
              meeting them].

SOLDIER
The gods make this a happy day to Antony!
ANTONY
Would thou and those thy scars had once prevailed
To make me fight at land!
SOLDIER   Hadst thou done so,
The kings that have revolted and the soldier
That has this morning left thee would have still
Followèd thy heels.
ANTONY   Who's gone this morning?
SOLDIER   Who?
One ever near thee: call for Enobarbus,
He shall not hear thee, or from Caesar's camp
Say 'I am none of thine.'
ANTONY   What sayest thou?
SOLDIER   Sir,
He is with Caesar.
EROS   Sir, his chests and treasure
He has not with him.
ANTONY   Is he gone?
SOLDIER   Most certain.
ANTONY
Go, Eros, send his treasure after; do it;
Detain no jot, I charge thee. Write to him
14   (I will subscribe) gentle adieus and greetings;
Say that I wish he never find more cause
To change a master. O, my fortunes have
Corrupted honest men! Dispatch. Enobarbus!
                    Exit [with Eros and Soldier].

*

IV, vi   *Flourish. Enter Agrippa, Caesar, with Enobarbus,*
               and Dolabella.

CAESAR
Go forth, Agrippa, and begin the fight.
Our will is Antony be took alive:
Make it so known.
AGRIPPA
Caesar, I shall.   *[Exit.]*
CAESAR
The time of universal peace is near.
6   Prove this a prosp'rous day, the three-nooked world
Shall bear the olive freely.
               Enter a Messenger.
MESSENGER   Antony
Is come into the field.
CAESAR   Go charge Agrippa
9   Plant those that have revolted in the vant,
That Antony may seem to spend his fury
11 Upon himself.   *Exeunt [all but Enobarbus].*
ENOBARBUS
Alexas did revolt and went to Jewry on
13 Affairs of Antony; there did dissuade
Great Herod to incline himself to Caesar

And leave his master Antony. For this pains
Caesar hath hanged him. Canidius and the rest
That fell away have entertainment, but   17
No honorable trust. I have done ill,
Of which I do accuse myself so sorely
That I will joy no more.
               Enter a Soldier of Caesar's.
SOLDIER   Enobarbus, Antony
Hath after thee sent all thy treasure, with
His bounty overplus. The messenger
Came on my guard, and at thy tent is now
Unloading of his mules.
ENOBARBUS   I give it you.
SOLDIER
Mock not, Enobarbus.
I tell you true. Best you safed the bringer   26
Out of the host; I must attend mine office
Or would have done't myself. Your emperor
Continues still a Jove.   *Exit.*
ENOBARBUS
I am alone the villain of the earth,
And feel I am so most. O Antony,
Thou mine of bounty, how wouldst thou have paid
My better service, when my turpitude
Thou dost so crown with gold! This blows my heart. 34
If swift thought break it not, a swifter mean   35
Shall outstrike thought; but thought will do't, I feel.
I fight against thee? No, I will go seek
Some ditch wherein to die: the foul'st best fits
My latter part of life.   *Exit.*

*

          Alarum. Drums and Trumpets. Enter Agrippa   IV, vii
          [and Soldiers].
AGRIPPA
Retire. We have engaged ourselves too far.   1
Caesar himself has work, and our oppression   2
Exceeds what we expected.   *Exit [with Soldiers].*
               Alarums. Enter Antony, and Scarus wounded.
SCARUS
O my brave Emperor, this is fought indeed!
Had we done so at first, we had driven them home
With clouts about their heads.   6
ANTONY   Thou bleed'st apace.
SCARUS
I had a wound here that was like a T,
But now 'tis made an H.   8
               [Sound retreat] far off.
ANTONY   They do retire.
SCARUS
We'll beat 'em into bench-holes. I have yet   9
Room for six scotches more.   10
               Enter Eros.

IV, v An open place in Alexandria   14 *subscribe* sign
IV, vi The camp of Octavius Caesar   6 *three-nooked* three-cornered
(Africa, Asia, Europe)   9 *vant* front lines   11 *himself* i.e. his own former
soldiers   13 *dissuade* i.e. from Antony   17 *entertainment* employment
26 *safed* gave safe conduct to   34 *blows* makes swell   35 *thought* grief
IV, vii A field near Alexandria   1 *engaged* entangled (with the enemy)
2 *our oppression* the pressure on us   6 *clouts* bandages   8 *H* (pun on
'ache,' which was pronounced 'aitch')   9 *bench-holes* privy holes   10
scotches gashes

EROS
They are beaten, sir, and our advantage serves
For a fair victory.

12 **SCARUS**   Let us score their backs
And snatch 'em up, as we take hares, behind :
'Tis sport to maul a runner.

ANTONY   I will reward thee
Once for thy sprightly comfort, and tenfold
For thy good valor. Come thee on.

16 **SCARUS**   I'll halt after.
                                Exeunt.

IV, viii   *Alarum. Enter Antony again in a march ; Scarus,*
           with others.

ANTONY
We have beat him to his camp. Run one before

2 And let the Queen know of our gests. To-morrow,
Before the sun shall see 's, we'll spill the blood
That has to-day escaped. I thank you all,
For doughty-handed are you, and have fought
Not as you served the cause, but as 't had been

7 Each man's like mine : you have shown all Hectors.

8 Enter the city, clip your wives, your friends,
Tell them your feats, whilst they with joyful tears
Wash the congealment from your wounds, and kiss
The honored gashes whole.
       Enter Cleopatra.
       [To Scarus]   Give me thy hand ;

12 To this great fairy I'll commend thy acts,
Make her thanks bless thee. – O thou day o' th' world,
Chain mine armed neck ; leap thou, attire and all,

15 Through proof of harness to my heart, and there

16 Ride on the pants triumphing.

CLEOPATRA   Lord of lords !

17 O infinite virtue, com'st thou smiling from

18 The world's great snare uncaught ?

ANTONY   My nightingale,
We have beat them to their beds. What, girl ! though
    gray
Do something mingle with our younger brown, yet ha'
    we
A brain that nourishes our nerves, and can

22 Get goal for goal of youth. Behold this man :
Commend unto his lips thy favoring hand. –
Kiss it, my warrior. – He hath fought to-day
As if a god in hate of mankind had
Destroyed in such a shape.

CLEOPATRA   I'll give thee, friend,
An armor all of gold ; it was a king's.

ANTONY

28 He has deserved it, were it carbuncled

29 Like holy Phoebus' car. Give me thy hand.

12 *score* mark   16 *halt* limp
IV, viii Before the gates of Alexandria   2 *gests* deeds   7 *shown* proved
8 *clip* hug   12 *fairy* enchantress   15 *proof of harness* i.e. impenetrable
armor   16 *Ride . . . pants* i.e. as if his heart were a panting steed   17
virtue valor   18 *snare* i.e. death in war   22 *Get . . . of* hold our own with
28 *carbuncled* jewelled   29 *holy Phoebus' car* the sun-god's chariot   31
targets shields ; *owe* own
IV, ix The camp of Octavius Caesar   5 *shrewd* wicked   8–9 *When . . .*
memory when traitors go down in history shamed   12 *mistress* i.e. the moon
13 *disponge* squeeze (as from a sponge)   17 *Which* (refers to *heart*) ; *dried*
(sorrow was thought to dry up the blood)   20 *in . . . particular* i.e. yourself
21 *in register* in its records   22 *master leaver* (1) runaway servant, (2) outstanding traitor   26 *Swoonds* faints   27 *for sleep* conducive to sleep   29
raught reached   30 *Demurely* softly

Through Alexandria make a jolly march ;
Bear our hacked targets like the men that owe them.   31
Had our great palace the capacity
To camp this host, we all would sup together
And drink carouses to the next day's fate,
Which promises royal peril. Trumpeters,
With brazen din blast you the city's ear,
Make mingle with our rattling tabourines,
That heaven and earth may strike their sounds together,
Applauding our approach.   *Exeunt.*

                    *

       Enter a Sentry and his Company. Enobarbus   **IV, ix**
       follows.

SENTRY
If we be not relieved within this hour,
We must return to th' court of guard. The night
Is shiny, and they say we shall embattle
By th' second hour i' th' morn.

1 . **WATCHMAN**   This last day was
A shrewd one to's.   5

ENOBARBUS   O, bear me witness, night –

2 . **WATCHMAN**
What man is this ?

1 . **WATCHMAN**   Stand close, and list him.

ENOBARBUS
Be witness to me, O thou blessèd moon,
When men revolted shall upon record   8
Bear hateful memory, poor Enobarbus did
Before thy face repent !

SENTRY   Enobarbus ?

2 . **WATCHMAN**   Peace :
Hark further.

ENOBARBUS
O sovereign mistress of true melancholy,   12
The poisonous damp of night disponge upon me,   13
That life, a very rebel to my will,
May hang no longer on me. Throw my heart
Against the flint and hardness of my fault,
Which, being dried with grief, will break to powder,   17
And finish all foul thoughts. O Antony,
Nobler than my revolt is infamous,
Forgive me in thine own particular,   20
But let the world rank me in register   21
A master leaver and a fugitive.   22
O Antony ! O Antony !
       [Dies.]

1 . **WATCHMAN**   Let's speak
To him.

SENTRY Let's hear him, for the things he speaks
May concern Caesar.

2 . **WATCHMAN**   Let's do so. But he sleeps.

SENTRY
Swoonds rather, for so bad a prayer as his   26
Was never yet for sleep.   27

1 . **WATCHMAN**   Go we to him.

2 . **WATCHMAN**
Awake, sir, awake, speak to us.

1 . **WATCHMAN**   Hear you, sir ?

SENTRY
The hand of death hath raught him.   29
       Drums afar off.   Hark ! The drums
Demurely wake the sleepers. Let us bear him   30

To th' court of guard : he is of note. Our hour
Is fully out.

2 . WATCHMAN
Come on then,
He may recover yet.   *Exeunt [with the body].*

*

IV, x   *Enter Antony and Scarus, with their Army.*

ANTONY
Their preparation is to-day by sea ;
We please them not by land.

SCARUS   For both, my lord.

ANTONY
I would they'ld fight i' th' fire or i' th' air ;

4   We'ld fight there too. But this it is, our foot
Upon the hills adjoining to the city
Shall stay with us – Order for sea is given ;
They have put forth the haven –

8   Where their appointment we may best discover
And look on their endeavor.   *Exeunt.*

IV, xi   *Enter Caesar and his Army.*

CAESAR
1   But being charged, we will be still by land,
Which, as I take't, we shall ; for his best force
Is forth to man his galleys. To the vales,
And hold our best advantage.   *Exeunt.*

IV, xii   *Enter Antony and Scarus.*

ANTONY
Yet they are not joined. Where yond pine does stand
I shall discover all. I'll bring thee word
Straight how 'tis like to go.   *Exit.*

SCARUS   Swallows have built
In Cleopatra's sails their nests. The augurers
Say they know not, they cannot tell, look grimly,
And dare not speak their knowledge. Antony
Is valiant, and dejected, and by starts

8   His fretted fortunes give him hope and fear
Of what he has, and has not.
       Alarum afar off, as at a sea-fight.
       Enter Antony.

ANTONY   All is lost !
This foul Egyptian hath betrayed me :
My fleet hath yielded to the foe, and yonder
They cast their caps up and carouse together

13   Like friends long lost. Triple-turned whore ! 'tis thou
Hast sold me to this novice, and my heart
Makes only wars on thee. Bid them all fly ;

16   For when I am revenged upon my charm,
I have done all. Bid them all fly, be gone. *[Exit Scarus.]*
O sun, thy uprise shall I see no more.
Fortune and Antony part here, even here
Do we shake hands. All come to this ? The hearts
That spanieled me at heels, to whom I gave

22   Their wishes, do discandy, melt their sweets

23   On blossoming Caesar ; and this pine is barked,
That overtopped them all. Betrayed I am.

25   O this false soul of Egypt ! this grave charm,
Whose eye becked forth my wars, and called them home,

27   Whose bosom was my crownet, my chief end,

28   Like a right gypsy hath at fast and loose
Beguiled me to the very heart of loss.
What, Eros, Eros !
       Enter Cleopatra.

30   Ah, thou spell ! Avaunt !

CLEOPATRA
Why is my lord enraged against his love ?

ANTONY
Vanish, or I shall give thee thy deserving
And blemish Caesar's triumph. Let him take thee   33
And hoist thee up to the shouting plebeians ;
Follow his chariot, like the greatest spot
Of all thy sex. Most monster-like be shown
For poor'st diminitives, for dolts, and let   37
Patient Octavia plough thy visage up
With her preparèd nails.   *Exit Cleopatra.*
            'Tis well th' art gone,
If it be well to live ; but better 'twere
Thou fell'st into my fury, for one death
Might have prevented many. Eros, ho !
The shirt of Nessus is upon me ; teach me,   43
Alcides, thou mine ancestor, thy rage.   44
Let me lodge Lichas on the horns o' th' moon
And with those hands that grasped the heaviest club
Subdue my worthiest self. The witch shall die.
To the young Roman boy she hath sold me, and I fall
Under this plot : she dies for't. Eros, ho !   *Exit.*

*

       Enter Cleopatra, Charmian, Iras, Mardian.   IV, xiii

CLEOPATRA
Help me, my women : O, he's more mad
Than Telamon for his shield ; the boar of Thessaly   2
Was never so embossed.   3

CHARMIAN   To th' monument !
There lock yourself, and send him word you are dead.
The soul and body rive not more in parting   5
Than greatness going off.

CLEOPATRA   To th' monument !
Mardian, go tell him I have slain myself :
Say that the last I spoke was 'Antony'
And word it, prithee, piteously. Hence, Mardian,
And bring me how he takes my death. To th' monument !
           Exeunt.

*

       Enter Antony and Eros.   IV, xiv

ANTONY
Eros, thou yet behold'st me ?

EROS   Ay, noble lord.

IV, x A field near Alexandria   4 *foot* infantry   8 *appointment* arrangement
IV, xi   1 *But being* unless we are
IV, xii   8 *fretted* shifting   13 *Triple-turned* i.e. from Pompey, from
Julius Caesar, and now from himself   16 *charm* enchantress   22 *discandy*
melt   23 *barked* stripped   25 *grave* deadly   27 *my crownet . . . end* the
crown and purpose of my life   28 *right* true ; *fast and loose* (a game)   30
Avaunt be gone   33 *triumph* triumphal procession (in Rome)   37 *diminitives* little people, i.e. the populace   43 *Nessus* (Fatally wounded by
Hercules with a poisoned arrow, the centaur Nessus persuaded Hercules'
wife to give his blood-stained shirt to her husband, telling her it would
assure his love for her. The shirt so poisoned Hercules that in his agony
he threw his page Lichas, who had brought it, to the skies and set about
destroying himself.)   44 *Alcides* Hercules
IV, xiii The palace of Cleopatra   2 *Telamon* Ajax Telamon, who went mad
when Achilles' shield was not given to him but to his rival, Ulysses ; *boar of
Thessaly* (sent by Artemis to ravage Thessaly in punishment for omitted
sacrifices)   3 *embossed* infuriated ; *monument* tomb (which like other
Egyptian rulers Cleopatra had prepared in advance)   5 *rive* rend
IV, xiv Near the palace of Cleopatra

ANTONY
Sometime we see a cloud that's dragonish;
A vapor sometime like a bear or lion,
A towered citadel, a pendant rock,
A forkèd mountain, or blue promontory
With trees upon't that nod unto the world
And mock our eyes with air. Thou hast seen these signs;
8 They are black Vesper's pageants.

EROS   Ay, my lord.

ANTONY
That which is now a horse, even with a thought
10 The rack dislimns, and makes it indistinct
As water is in water.

EROS   It does, my lord.

ANTONY
My good knave Eros, now thy captain is
Even such a body: here I am Antony,
Yet cannot hold this visible shape, my knave.
15 I made these wars for Egypt, and the Queen,
Whose heart I thought I had, for she had mine,
Which, whilst it was mine, had annexed unto't
18 A million moe, now lost – she, Eros, has
19 Packed cards with Caesar, and false-played my glory
20 Unto an enemy's triumph.
Nay, weep not, gentle Eros, there is left us
Ourselves to end ourselves.
    Enter Mardian.   O, thy vile lady!
23 She has robbed me of my sword.

MARDIAN   No, Antony.
My mistress loved thee and her fortunes mingled
With thine entirely.

ANTONY   Hence, saucy eunuch, peace!
She hath betrayed me and shall die the death.

MARDIAN
Death of one person can be paid but once,
And that she has discharged. What thou wouldst do
Is done unto thy hand. The last she spake
Was 'Antony! most noble Antony!'
Then in the midst a tearing groan did break
The name of Antony; it was divided
Between her heart and lips: she rend'red life,
Thy name so buried in her.

ANTONY   Dead, then?

MARDIAN   Dead.

ANTONY
Unarm, Eros. The long day's task is done,
And we must sleep.
    [To Mardian] That thou depart'st hence safe
Does pay thy labor richly: go.   *Exit Mardian.*
    Off, pluck off:

The sevenfold shield of Ajax cannot keep   38
The battery from my heart. O, cleave, my sides!   39
Heart, once be stronger than thy continent,   40
Crack thy frail case! Apace, Eros, apace.
No more a soldier. Bruisèd pieces, go;
You have been nobly borne. – From me awhile. *Exit Eros.*
I will o'ertake thee, Cleopatra, and
Weep for my pardon. So it must be, for now
All length is torture: since the torch is out,   46
Lie down, and stray no farther. Now all labor   47
Mars what it does; yea, very force entangles
Itself with strength: seal then, and all is done.   49
Eros! – I come, my queen. – Eros! – Stay for me.
Where souls do couch on flowers, we'll hand in hand,   51
And with our sprightly port make the ghosts gaze: 52
Dido and her Aeneas shall want troops,   53
And all the haunt be ours. – Come, Eros, Eros!
    Enter Eros.

EROS
What would my lord?

ANTONY   Since Cleopatra died
I have lived in such dishonor that the gods
Detest my baseness. I, that with my sword
Quartered the world and o'er green Neptune's back
With ships made cities, condemn myself to lack   59
The courage of a woman – less noble mind
Than she which by her death our Caesar tells
'I am conqueror of myself.' Thou art sworn, Eros,
That, when the exigent should come, which now   63
Is come indeed, when I should see behind me
Th' inevitable prosecution of   65
Disgrace and horror, that on my command
Thou then wouldst kill me. Do't, the time is come.
Thou strik'st not me, 'tis Caesar thou defeat'st.
Put color in thy cheek.

EROS   The gods withhold me!
Shall I do that which all the Parthian darts,
Though enemy, lost aim and could not?

ANTONY   Eros,
Wouldst thou be windowed in great Rome and see   72
Thy master thus with pleached arms, bending down   73
His corrigible neck, his face subdued   74
To penetrative shame, whilst the wheeled seat   75
Of fortunate Caesar, drawn before him, branded
His baseness that ensued?   77

EROS   I would not see't.

ANTONY
Come then: for with a wound I must be cured.
Draw thou thy honest sword, which thou hast worn
Most useful for thy country.

EROS   O sir, pardon me.

ANTONY
When I did make thee free, swor'st thou not then
To do this when I bade thee? Do it at once,
Or thy precedent services are all   83
But accidents unpurposed. Draw, and come.

EROS
Turn from me then that noble countenance
Wherein the worship of the whole world lies.

ANTONY
Lo thee!
    [Turns from him.]

EROS
My sword is drawn.

---

8 *black Vesper's pageants* i.e. shows heralding the coming of night (as pageants used to herald the coming of a king or queen)   10 *rack* cloud; *dislimns* unshapes   15 *Egypt* i.e. Cleopatra   18 *moe* more   19 *Packed* i.e. stacked the deck; *false-played* falsely played away   20 *triumph* (1) victory, (2) trump   23 *sword* manhood and soldiership   38 *sevenfold* having seven thicknesses   39 *battery* the battering (of grief)   40 *continent* i.e. that which contains thee   46 *length* i.e. of life   47–49 *labor . . . strength* i.e. force is defeated by its own strength, labor by its own effort   49 *seal* bring all to a close (as in sealing a document or will)   51 *Where . . . flowers* i.e. in the Elysian fields   52 *port* behavior   53 *want troops* lack admirers (i.e. in comparison with us as faithful lovers – since Aeneas deserted Dido for Roman greatness whereas Antony is deserting Roman greatness for Cleopatra)   59 *to lack* for lacking   63 *exigent* need   65 *prosecution* pursuit   72 *windowed* i.e. watching from a window   73 *pleached* folded   74 *corrigible* submissive   75 *penetrative* penetrating   77 *His . . . ensued* the baseness of him that followed   83 *precedent* former

ANTONY   Then let it do at once
The thing why thou hast drawn it.
EROS   My dear master,
My captain, and my emperor, let me say,
Before I strike this bloody stroke, farewell.
ANTONY
'Tis said, man, and farewell.
EROS
Farewell, great chief. Shall I strike now?
ANTONY   Now, Eros.
EROS
Why, there then! Thus I do escape the sorrow
Of Antony's death.
  Kills himself.
ANTONY   Thrice-nobler than myself!
Thou teachest me, O valiant Eros, what
I should, and thou couldst not. My queen and Eros

98 Have by their brave instruction got upon me
A nobleness in record. But I will be
A bridegroom in my death, and run into't
As to a lover's bed. Come then; and, Eros,
Thy master dies thy scholar. To do thus
  [Falls on his sword.]
I learned of thee. How? not dead? not dead?

104 The guard, ho! O, dispatch me!
  Enter [Decretas and] a [Company of the] Guard.
1. GUARDSMAN   What's the noise?
ANTONY
I have done my work ill, friends. O, make an end
Of what I have begun.
2. GUARDSMAN   The star is fall'n.
1. GUARDSMAN

107 And time is at his period.
ALL   Alas, and woe!
ANTONY
Let him that loves me strike me dead.
1. GUARDSMAN
Not I.
2. GUARDSMAN Nor I.
3. GUARDSMAN Nor any one.
  Exeunt [the Guardsmen].
DECRETAS
Thy death and fortunes bid thy followers fly.
This sword but shown to Caesar, with this tidings,

113 Shall enter me with him.
  Enter Diomedes.
DIOMEDES
Where's Antony?
DECRETAS   There, Diomed, there.
DIOMEDES   Lives he?
Wilt thou not answer, man? *[Exit Decretas.]*
ANTONY
Art thou there, Diomed? Draw thy sword, and give me
Sufficing strokes for death.
DIOMEDES   Most absolute lord,
My mistress Cleopatra sent me to thee.
ANTONY
When did she send thee?
DIOMEDES   Now, my lord.
ANTONY   Where is she?
DIOMEDES
Locked in her monument. She had a prophesying fear
Of what hath come to pass; for when she saw
(Which never shall be found) you did suspect

She had disposed with Caesar, and that your rage 123
Would not be purged, she sent you word she was dead; 124
But, fearing since how it might work, hath sent
Me to proclaim the truth, and I am come,
I dread, too late.
ANTONY
Too late, good Diomed. Call my guard, I prithee.
DIOMEDES
What ho! the Emperor's guard! the guard, what ho!
Come, your lord calls!
  Enter four or five of the Guard of Antony.
ANTONY
Bear me, good friends, where Cleopatra bides;
'Tis the last service that I shall command you.
1. GUARDSMAN
Woe, woe are we, sir, you may not live to wear
All your true followers out.
ALL   Most heavy day!
ANTONY
Nay, good my fellows, do not please sharp fate
To grace it with your sorrows. Bid that welcome
Which comes to punish us, and we punish it,
Seeming to bear it lightly. Take me up:
I have led you oft; carry me now, good friends,
And have my thanks for all.
  Exit [the Guard,] bearing Antony.

      *

  Enter Cleopatra and her Maids aloft, with Charmian IV, xv
  and Iras.
CLEOPATRA
O Charmian, I will never go from hence.
CHARMIAN
Be comforted, dear madam.
CLEOPATRA   No, I will not.
All strange and terrible events are welcome,
But comforts we despise. Our size of sorrow,
Proportioned to our cause, must be as great
As that which makes it.
  Enter Diomed [below].
     How now? Is he dead?
DIOMEDES
His death's upon him, but not dead.
Look out o' th' other side your monument;
His guard have brought him thither.
  Enter [below,] Antony, and the Guard [bearing
  him].
CLEOPATRA   O sun,
Burn the great sphere thou mov'st in, darkling stand 10
The varying shore o' th' world! O Antony,
Antony, Antony! Help, Charmian, help, Iras, help:
Help, friends below, let's draw him hither.
ANTONY   Peace!
Not Caesar's valor hath o'erthrown Antony,
But Antony's hath triumphed on itself.
CLEOPATRA
So it should be, that none but Antony
Should conquer Antony, but woe 'tis so!

98–99 *got . . . record* beaten me to a noble name in history 104 s.d. *Decretas*
(the usual folio spelling of a name which also appears in the folio as 'Der-
cetus' and is sometimes revised by editors to 'Dercetas') 107 *period* end
113 *enter* recommend 123 *disposed* made terms 124 *purged* expelled
IV, xv Before the monument of Cleopatra 10 *darkling* darkened

ANTONY
    I am dying, Egypt, dying; only
19   I here importune death awhile, until
    Of many thousand kisses the poor last
    I lay upon thy lips.
21 CLEOPATRA   I dare not, dear;
    Dear my lord, pardon : I dare not,
    Lest I be taken. Not th' imperious show
    Of the full-fortuned Caesar ever shall
25   Be brooched with me, if knife, drugs, serpents have
    Edge, sting, or operation. I am safe :
    Your wife Octavia, with her modest eyes
28   And still conclusion, shall acquire no honor
29   Demuring upon me. But come, come, Antony !
    Help me, my women, we must draw thee up :
    Assist, good friends.
ANTONY   O, quick, or I am gone.
CLEOPATRA
    Here's sport indeed ! How heavy weighs my lord !
33   Our strength is all gone into heaviness :
    That makes the weight. Had I great Juno's power,
    The strong-winged Mercury should fetch thee up
    And set thee by Jove's side. Yet come a little,
    Wishers were ever fools. O, come, come, come.
        They heave Antony aloft to Cleopatra.
    And welcome, welcome ! Die when thou hast lived,
39   Quicken with kissing. Had my lips that power,
    Thus would I wear them out.
ALL   A heavy sight !
ANTONY
    I am dying, Egypt, dying.
    Give me some wine, and let me speak a little
CLEOPATRA
    No, let me speak, and let me rail so high
44   That the false huswife Fortune break her wheel,
    Provoked by my offense.
ANTONY   One word, sweet queen.
    Of Caesar seek your honor, with your safety. O !
CLEOPATRA
    They do not go together.
ANTONY   Gentle, hear me :
    None about Caesar trust but Proculeius.
CLEOPATRA
    My resolution and my hands I'll trust,
    None about Caesar.
ANTONY
    The miserable change now at my end
    Lament nor sorrow at ; but please your thoughts
    In feeding them with those my former fortunes,
    Wherein I lived the greatest prince o' th' world,
    The noblest : and do now not basely die,
    Not cowardly put off my helmet to
    My countryman. A Roman, by a Roman
    Valiantly vanquished. Now my spirit is going,
    I can no more.

CLEOPATRA   Noblest of men, woo't die ?   59
    Hast thou no care of me ? Shall I abide
    In this dull world, which in thy absence is
    No better than a sty ? O, see, my women,
        [Antony dies.]
    The crown o' th' earth doth melt. My lord !
    O, withered is the garland of the war,   64
    The soldier's pole is fall'n : young boys and girls   65
    Are level now with men. The odds is gone,   66
    And there is nothing left remarkable
    Beneath the visiting moon.
        [Swoons.]
CHARMIAN   O, quietness, lady !
IRAS   She's dead too, our sovereign.
CHARMIAN   Lady !
IRAS   Madam !
CHARMIAN   O madam, madam, madam !
IRAS   Royal Egypt ! Empress !
CHARMIAN   Peace, peace, Iras !
CLEOPATRA
    No more but e'en a woman, and commanded
    By such poor passion as the maid that milks
    And does the meanest chares. It were for me   78
    To throw my sceptre at the injurious gods,
    To tell them that this world did equal theirs
    Till they had stol'n our jewel. All's but naught.
    Patience is sottish, and impatience does   82
    Become a dog that's mad : then is it sin
    To rush into the secret house of death
    Ere death dare come to us ? How do you, women ?
    What, what ! good cheer ! Why, how now, Charmian ?
    My noble girls ! Ah, women, women, look !
    Our lamp is spent, it's out ! Good sirs, take heart :   88
    We'll bury him ; and then, what's brave, what's noble,
    Let's do't after the high Roman fashion,
    And make death proud to take us. Come away.
    This case of that huge spirit now is cold.
    Ah, women, women ! Come ; we have no friend
    But resolution, and the briefest end.
        Exeunt, bearing off Antony's body.

            *

    Enter Caesar, Agrippa, Dolabella, Maecenas,   V, i
    [Gallus, Proculeius,] with his Council of War.
CAESAR
    Go to him, Dolabella, bid him yield :
    Being so frustrate, tell him he mocks   2
    The pauses that he makes.
DOLABELLA   Caesar, I shall.   *[Exit.]*
    Enter Decretas, with the sword of Antony.
CAESAR
    Wherefore is that ? And what art thou that dar'st
    Appear thus to us ?
DECRETAS   I am called Decretas.
    Mark Antony I served, who best was worthy
    Best to be served. Whilst he stood up and spoke,
    He was my master, and I wore my life
    To spend upon his haters. If thou please
    To take me to thee, as I was to him
    I'll be to Caesar ; if thou pleasest not,
    I yield thee up my life.
CAESAR   What is't thou say'st ?

19 *importune* beg to delay   21 *dare not* i.e. dare not descend to Antony's side
25 *brooched* adorned   28 *still conclusion* wordless censure   29 *Demuring*
looking demurely   33 *heaviness* (with pun on 'grief')   39 *Quicken* come
back to life   44 *huswife* jilt   59 *woo't* wilt thou   64 *garland . . . war* flower
of all soldiers   65 *pole* North Star (?)   66 *odds* standard of measurement
78 *chares* chores   82–83 *Patience . . . mad* both patience and sorrow are now
beside the point   88 *sirs* i.e. Cleopatra's women
V, i The camp of Octavius Caesar   2 *frustrate* helpless   2–3 *he mocks . . .
makes* i.e. to delay surrendering is ridiculous

DECRETAS
    I say, O Caesar, Antony is dead.
CAESAR
    The breaking of so great a thing should make
    A greater crack. The round world
16 Should have shook lions into civil streets
    And citizens to their dens. The death of Antony
    Is not a single doom, in the name lay
19 A moiety of the world.
DECRETAS   He is dead, Caesar,
    Not by a public minister of justice
21 Nor by a hirèd knife; but that self hand
    Which writ his honor in the acts it did
    Hath, with the courage which the heart did lend it,
    Splitted the heart. This is his sword,
    I robbed his wound of it: behold it stained
    With his most noble blood.
CAESAR   Look you sad, friends?
    The gods rebuke me, but it is tidings
    To wash the eyes of kings.
AGRIPPA   And strange it is
    That nature must compel us to lament
30 Our most persisted deeds.
MAECENAS   His taints and honors
31 Waged equal with him.
AGRIPPA   A rarer spirit never
    Did steer humanity; but you, gods, will give us
    Some faults to make us men. Caesar is touched.
MAECENAS
    When such a spacious mirror's set before him,
    He needs must see himself.
CAESAR   O Antony,
36 I have followed thee to this. But we do launch
    Diseases in our bodies. I must perforce
    Have shown to thee such a declining day
39 Or look on thine: we could not stall together
    In the whole world. But yet let me lament
41 With tears as sovereign as the blood of hearts
42 That thou, my brother, my competitor
43 In top of all design, my mate in empire,
    Friend and companion in the front of war,
    The arm of mine own body, and the heart
46 Where mine his thoughts did kindle – that our stars,
    Unreconciliable, should divide
    Our equalness to this. Hear me, good friends –
        Enter an Egyptian.
    But I will tell you at some meeter season.
50 The business of this man looks out of him;
    We'll hear him what he says. Whence are you?
EGYPTIAN
    A poor Egyptian yet. The Queen my mistress,
    Confined in all she has, her monument,
    Of thy intents desires instruction,
    That she preparèdly may frame herself
    To th' way she's forced to.
CAESAR   Bid her have good heart:
    She soon shall know of us, by some of ours,
    How honorable and how kindly we
    Determine for her. For Caesar cannot live
    To be ungentle.
EGYPTIAN   So the gods preserve thee!   Exit.
CAESAR
    Come hither, Proculeius. Go and say
    We purpose her no shame: give her what comforts

The quality of her passion shall require,   63
Lest, in her greatness, by some mortal stroke
She do defeat us. For her life in Rome
Would be eternal in our triumph. Go,   66
And with your speediest bring us what she says
And how you find of her.
PROCULEIUS   Caesar, I shall.   Exit.
CAESAR
    Gallus, go you along. [Exit Gallus.] Where's Dolabella,
    To second Proculeius?
ALL   Dolabella!
CAESAR
    Let him alone, for I remember now
    How he's employed. He shall in time be ready.
    Go with me to my tent, where you shall see
    How hardly I was drawn into this war,
    How calm and gentle I proceeded still
    In all my writings. Go with me, and see   76
    What I can show in this.   Exeunt.

*

Enter Cleopatra, Charmian, Iras, and Mardian.   V, ii
CLEOPATRA
    My desolation does begin to make
    A better life. 'Tis paltry to be Caesar: 2
    Not being Fortune, he's but Fortune's knave,   3
    A minister of her will. And it is great
    To do that thing that ends all other deeds,
    Which shackles accidents and bolts up change;
    Which sleeps, and never palates more the dung,   7
    The beggar's nurse and Caesar's.
        Enter [to the gates of the monument] Proculeius.
PROCULEIUS
    Caesar sends greeting to the Queen of Egypt,
    And bids thee study on what fair demands
    Thou mean'st to have him grant thee.
CLEOPATRA   What's thy name?
PROCULEIUS
    My name is Proculeius.
CLEOPATRA   Antony
    Did tell me of you, bade me trust you, but
    I do not greatly care to be deceived,   14
    That have no use for trusting. If your master
    Would have a queen his beggar, you must tell him
    That majesty, to keep decorum, must
    No less beg than a kingdom: if he please
    To give me conquered Egypt for my son,
    He gives me so much of mine own as I   20
    Will kneel to him with thanks.
PROCULEIUS   Be of good cheer:
    Y' are fall'n into a princely hand, fear nothing.
    Make your full reference freely to my lord,   23
    Who is so full of grace that it flows over

---

16 *civil* city   19 *moiety* half   21 *self* same   30 *persisted* i.e. persisted in
31 *Waged equal with* were evenly balanced in   36 *launch* lance   39 *stall*
dwell   41 *sovereign* potent   42 *competitor* partner   43 *In . . . design* in
every lofty enterprise   46 *his* its   50 *looks . . . him* shows in his eyes   63
passion grief   66 *eternal* eternally memorable   76 *writings* dispatches (to
Antony)
V, ii Before the monument of Cleopatra   2 *A better life* i.e. a truer estimate
of values   3 *knave* servant   7 *dung* i.e. the fruits of earth, which is everybody's nurse   14 *to be deceived* whether I am deceived or not   20 *as* that
23 *Make . . . reference* entrust your case

On all that need. Let me report to him
Your sweet dependency, and you shall find
27   A conqueror that will pray in aid for kindness,
Where he for grace is kneeled to.

CLEOPATRA   Pray you, tell him
I am his fortune's vassal, and I send him
30   The greatness he has got. I hourly learn
A doctrine of obedience, and would gladly
Look him i' th' face.

PROCULEIUS   This I'll report, dear lady.
Have comfort, for I know your plight is pitied
Of him that caused it.
    [Enter Roman Soldiers into the monument.]
You see how easily she may be surprised.
    [They seize Cleopatra.]
Guard her till Caesar come.

IRAS   Royal Queen!

CHARMIAN   O Cleopatra! thou art taken, Queen.

CLEOPATRA
Quick, quick, good hands!
    [Draws a dagger.]

PROCULEIUS   Hold, worthy lady, hold!
    [Disarms her.]
Do not yourself such wrong, who are in this
41   Relieved, but not betrayed.

CLEOPATRA   What, of death too,
42   That rids our dogs of languish?

PROCULEIUS   Cleopatra,
Do not abuse my master's bounty by
Th' undoing of yourself: let the world see
45   His nobleness well acted, which your death
Will never let come forth.

CLEOPATRA   Where art thou, death?
Come hither, come: come, come, and take a queen
Worth many babes and beggars!

PROCULEIUS   O, temperance, lady!

CLEOPATRA
Sir, I will eat no meat, I'll not drink, sir—
50   If idle talk will once be necessary—
I'll not sleep neither. This mortal house I'll ruin,
Do Caesar what he can. Know, sir, that I
Will not wait pinioned at your master's court
Nor once be chastised with the sober eye
Of dull Octavia. Shall they hoist me up
56   And show me to the shouting varletry
Of censuring Rome? Rather a ditch in Egypt
Be gentle grave unto me! Rather on Nilus' mud
Lay me stark-nak'd and let the waterflies
60   Blow me into abhorring! Rather make
My country's high pyramides my gibbet
And hang me up in chains!

PROCULEIUS   You do extend
These thoughts of horror further than you shall
Find cause in Caesar.
    Enter Dolabella.

DOLABELLA   Proculeius,
What thou hast done thy master Caesar knows,
And he hath sent me for thee. For the Queen,
I'll take her to my guard.

PROCULEIUS   So, Dolabella,
It shall content me best: be gentle to her.
    [To Cleopatra]
To Caesar I will speak what you shall please,
If you'll employ me to him.

CLEOPATRA   Say, I would die.   70
    Exit Proculeius [with Soldiers].

DOLABELLA
Most noble Empress, you have heard of me?

CLEOPATRA
I cannot tell.

DOLABELLA   Assuredly you know me.

CLEOPATRA
No matter, sir, what I have heard or known.
You laugh when boys or women tell their dreams;
Is't not your trick?

DOLABELLA   I understand not, madam.

CLEOPATRA
I dreamt there was an Emperor Antony.
O, such another sleep, that I might see
But such another man.

DOLABELLA   If it might please ye—

CLEOPATRA
His face was as the heav'ns, and therein stuck
A sun and moon, which kept their course and lighted
The little O, th' earth.   81

DOLABELLA   Most sovereign creature—

CLEOPATRA
His legs bestrid the ocean: his reared arm
Crested the world: his voice was propertied   83
As all the tunèd spheres, and that to friends;
But when he meant to quail and shake the orb,   85
He was as rattling thunder. For his bounty,
There was no winter in't: an autumn 'twas
That grew the more by reaping: his delights   88
Were dolphin-like, thy showed his back above
The element they lived in: in his livery
Walked crowns and crownets: realms and islands were   91
As plates dropped from his pocket.   92

DOLABELLA   Cleopatra—

CLEOPATRA
Think you there was or might be such a man
As this I dreamt of?

DOLABELLA   Gentle madam, no.

CLEOPATRA
You lie, up to the hearing of the gods.
But if there be nor ever were one such,
It's past the size of dreaming: nature wants stuff   97
To vie strange forms with fancy, yet t' imagine
An Antony were nature's piece 'gainst fancy,
Condemning shadows quite.

DOLABELLA   Hear me, good madam.
Your loss is as yourself, great; and you bear it
As answering to the weight. Would I might never   102
O'ertake pursued success but I do feel,
By the rebound of yours, a grief that smites

---

27 *pray . . . kindness* ask your aid in naming kindnesses he can do for you
30 *got* i.e. won from me   41 *Relieved* rescued   42 *languish* pain   45 *acted*
put into effect   50 *If . . . necessary* even if I must for the present moment
resort to words, not acts   56 *varletry* mob   60 *Blow me* make me swell
81 *Th' . . . earth* (the generally accepted rendering of a folio reading which
may possibly mean something quite different: 'The little o' th' earth')
83–84 *was propertied As* i.e. made music like   85 *quail* cow; *orb* earth
88–90 *his . . . lived in* i.e. he rose above the pleasures that he lived in as the
dolphin rises above the surface of the sea   91 *crowns and crownets* i.e.
kings and princes   92 *plates* coins   97–100 *nature . . . quite* i.e. nature
rarely can compete with man's imagination in creating outstanding forms of
excellence, but if she created an Antony, he would be her masterpiece,
outdoing the unreal images of imagination altogether   102–03 *Would . . . do*
i.e. may I never have success if I do not

My very heart at root.

CLEOPATRA   I thank you, sir.
Know you what Caesar means to do with me?

DOLABELLA
I am loath to tell you what I would you knew.

CLEOPATRA
Nay, pray you, sir.

DOLABELLA   Though he be honorable –

CLEOPATRA
He'll lead me, then, in triumph?

DOLABELLA
Madam, he will. I know't.
      Flourish. Enter Proculeius, Caesar, Gallus,
      Maecenas, [Seleucus,] and others of his Train.

ALL
Make way there! Caesar!

CAESAR
Which is the Queen of Egypt?

DOLABELLA
It is the Emperor, madam.
      Cleopatra kneels.

CAESAR
Arise! You shall not kneel:
I pray you rise, rise, Egypt.

CLEOPATRA   Sir, the gods
Will have it thus. My master and my lord
I must obey.

CAESAR   Take to you no hard thoughts.
The record of what injuries you did us,
Though written in our flesh, we shall remember
As things but done by chance.

CLEOPATRA   Sole sir o' th' world,
121   I cannot project mine own cause so well
To make it clear, but do confess I have
Been laden with like frailties which before
Have often shamed our sex.

CAESAR   Cleopatra, know,
125   We will extenuate rather than enforce.
126   If you apply yourself to our intents,
Which towards you are most gentle, you shall find
A benefit in this change; but if you seek
To lay on me a cruelty by taking
Antony's course, you shall bereave yourself
Of my good purposes, and put your children
To that destruction which I'll guard them from
If thereon you rely. I'll take my leave.

CLEOPATRA
And may, through all the world: 'tis yours, and we,
135   Your scutcheons and your signs of conquest, shall
Hang in what place you please. Here, my good lord.
      [Offering a scroll.]

CAESAR
You shall advise me in all for Cleopatra.

CLEOPATRA
138   This is the brief of money, plate, and jewels
I am possessed of. 'Tis exactly valued,
Not petty things admitted. Where's Seleucus?

SELEUCUS
Here, madam.

CLEOPATRA
This is my treasurer; let him speak, my lord,
Upon his peril, that I have reserved
To myself nothing. Speak the truth, Seleucus.

SELEUCUS
Madam,
I had rather seel my lips than to my peril   146
Speak that which is not.

CLEOPATRA   What have I kept back?

SELEUCUS
Enough to purchase what you have made known.

CAESAR
Nay, blush not, Cleopatra, I approve
Your wisdom in the deed.

CLEOPATRA   See, Caesar: O, behold,
How pomp is followed! Mine will now be yours,   151
And should we shift estates, yours would be mine.   152
The ingratitude of this Seleucus does
Even make me wild. O slave, of no more trust
Than love that's hired! What, goest thou back? Thou
   shalt
Go back, I warrant thee; but I'll catch thine eyes,
Though they had wings. Slave, soulless villain, dog!
O rarely base!

CAESAR   Good Queen, let us entreat you.

CLEOPATRA
O Caesar, what a wounding shame is this,
That thou vouchsafing here to visit me,
Doing the honor of thy lordliness
To one so meek, that mine own servant should
Parcel the sum of my disgraces by   163
Addition of his envy. Say, good Caesar,
That I some lady trifles have reserved,   165
Immoment toys, things of such dignity   166
As we greet modern friends withal; and say   167
Some nobler token I have kept apart
For Livia and Octavia, to induce
Their mediation – must I be unfolded
With one that I have bred? The gods! It smites me   171
Beneath the fall I have. *[to Seleucus]* Prithee go hence,
Or I shall show the cinders of my spirits   173
Through th' ashes of my chance. Wert thou a man,   174
Thou wouldst have mercy on me.

CAESAR   Forbear, Seleucus.
      [Exit Seleucus.]

CLEOPATRA
Be it known that we, the greatest, are misthought   176
For things that others do; and, when we fall,
We answer others' merits in our name,   178
Are therefore to be pitied.

CAESAR   Cleopatra,
Not what you have reserved, nor what acknowledged,
Put we i' th' roll of conquest: still be't yours,
Bestow it at your pleasure, and believe   182
Caesar's no merchant, to make prize with you   183
Of things that merchants sold. Therefore be cheered,
Make not your thoughts your prisons: no, dear Queen,   185
For we intend so to dispose you as   186

---

121 *project* set forth   125 *enforce* emphasize (them)   126 *apply* conform
135 *scutcheons* victor's trappings   138 *brief* résumé   146 *seel* sew up   151
Mine i.e. my followers   152 *estates* positions   163 *Parcel* piece out further
165 *lady* feminine   166 *Immoment* of no moment   167 *modern* common
171 *With* by   173 *cinders* burning coals   174 *chance* fortune   176 *misthought* misjudged   178 *merits . . . name* misdeeds done in our name (as if
Seleucus had falsified the inventory for his own gain)   182 *Bestow* use
183 *make prize* haggle   185 *Make . . . prisons* i.e. only in your own conception are you a prisoner   186 *you* of you

Yourself shall give us counsel. Feed and sleep :
Our care and pity is so much upon you
That we remain your friend ; and so adieu.

CLEOPATRA
My master, and my lord !

CAESAR   Not so. Adieu.
Flourish. Exeunt Caesar, and his Train.

CLEOPATRA
191 He words me, girls, he words me, that I should not
192 Be noble to myself ! But hark thee, Charmian.
[Whispers Charmian.]

IRAS
Finish, good lady, the bright day is done,
And we are for the dark.

CLEOPATRA   Hie thee again :
I have spoke already, and it is provided ;
Go put it to the haste.

CHARMIAN   Madam, I will.
Enter Dolabella.

DOLABELLA
Where's the Queen ?

CHARMIAN   Behold, sir.   *[Exit.]*

CLEOPATRA   Dolabella !

DOLABELLA
Madam, as thereto sworn, by your command
(Which my love makes religion to obey)
200 I tell you this : Caesar through Syria
Intends his journey, and within three days
You with your children will he send before.
Make your best use of this. I have performed
Your pleasure, and my promise.

CLEOPATRA   Dolabella,
I shall remain your debtor.

DOLABELLA   I your servant.
Adieu, good Queen ; I must attend on Caesar.

CLEOPATRA
Farewell, and thanks.   *Exit [Dolabella].*
                    Now, Iras, what think'st thou ?
Thou, an Egyptian puppet, shall be shown
In Rome as well as I : mechanic slaves
With greasy aprons, rules, and hammers shall
Uplift us to the view. In their thick breaths,
212 Rank of gross diet, shall we be enclouded,
And forced to drink their vapor.

IRAS   The gods forbid !

CLEOPATRA
214 Nay, 'tis most certain, Iras. Saucy lictors
215 Will catch at us like strumpets, and scald rhymers
Ballad us out o' tune. The quick comedians
Extemporally will stage us, and present
Our Alexandrian revels : Antony
Shall be brought drunken forth, and I shall see
220 Some squeaking Cleopatra boy my greatness
I' th' posture of a whore.

IRAS   O the good gods !

191 *words* deceives with words 192 *noble* i.e. by suicide 212 *Rank of* offensive because of 214 *lictors* officers 215 *scald* scabby 220 *squeaking* i.e. because women's parts were acted by young boys ; *boy* satirize 231 *chare* chore 238 *placed* fixed 241 s.d. *Clown* rustic 242 *Avoid* go 243 *worm* serpent (asp) 247 *immortal* mortal, i.e. deadly (the rustic blunders in speech here and below) 251 *honest* respectable 257 *falliable* (an error for 'infallible') 262 *his kind* i.e. what may be expected from his species

CLEOPATRA
Nay, that's certain.

IRAS
I'll never see't ! for I am sure my nails
Are stronger than mine eyes.

CLEOPATRA   Why, that's the way
To fool their preparation, and to conquer
Their most absurd intents.
          Enter Charmian.   Now, Charmian !
Show me, my women, like a queen : go fetch
My best attires. I am again for Cydnus,
To meet Mark Antony. Sirrah Iras, go.
Now, noble Charmian, we'll dispatch indeed,
And when thou hast done this chare, I'll give thee leave 231
To play till doomsday. – Bring our crown and all.
                    [Exit Iras.] A noise within.
Wherefore's this noise ?
          Enter a Guardsman.

GUARDSMAN   Here is a rural fellow
That will not be denied your Highness' presence :
He brings you figs.

CLEOPATRA
Let him come in.   *Exit Guardsman.*
                    What poor an instrument
May do a noble deed ! He brings me liberty.
My resolution 's placed, and I have nothing   238
Of woman in me : now from head to foot
I am marble-constant : now the fleeting moon
No planet is of mine.   241
          Enter Guardsman and Clown [with basket].

GUARDSMAN   This is the man.

CLEOPATRA
Avoid, and leave him.   *Exit Guardsman.* 242
Hast thou the pretty worm of Nilus there,   243
That kills and pains not ?

CLOWN Truly I have him ; but I would not be the party
that should desire you to touch him, for his biting is
immortal : those that do die of it do seldom or never 247
recover.

CLEOPATRA Remember'st thou any that have died on't ?

CLOWN Very many, men and women too. I heard of one
of them no longer than yesterday ; a very honest woman, 251
but something given to lie, as a woman should not do
but in the way of honesty – how she died of the biting
of it, what pain she felt. Truly, she makes a very good
report o' th' worm ; but he that will believe all that they
say shall never be saved by half that they do ; but this is
most falliable, the worm 's an odd worm.   257

CLEOPATRA Get thee hence, farewell.

CLOWN I wish you all joy of the worm.
          [Sets down his basket.]

CLEOPATRA Farewell.

CLOWN You must think this, look you, that the worm
will do his kind.   262

CLEOPATRA Ay, ay ; farewell.

CLOWN Look you, the worm is not to be trusted but in the
keeping of wise people : for indeed there is no goodness
in the worm.

CLEOPATRA Take thou no care, it shall be heeded.

CLOWN Very good. Give it nothing, I pray you, for it is
not worth the feeding.

CLEOPATRA Will it eat me ?

CLOWN You must not think I am so simple but I know the

devil himself will not eat a woman : I know that a
273 woman is a dish for the gods, if the devil dress her not.
But truly, these same whoreson devils do the gods great
harm in their women ; for in every ten that they make,
the devils mar five.

CLEOPATRA Well, get thee gone, farewell.

CLOWN Yes, forsooth. I wish you joy o' th' worm.   *Exit.*
    [Enter Iras with a robe, crown, etc.]

CLEOPATRA
Give me my robe, put on my crown, I have
Immortal longings in me. Now no more
The juice of Egypt's grape shall moist this lip.
282 Yare, yare, good Iras ; quick. Methinks I hear
Antony call : I see him rouse himself
To praise my noble act. I hear him mock
The luck of Caesar, which the gods give men
To excuse their after wrath. Husband, I come :
Now to that name my courage prove my title !
288 I am fire, and air ; my other elements
I give to baser life. So, have you done ?
Come then, and take the last warmth of my lips.
Farewell, kind Charmian, Iras, long farewell.
    [Kisses them. Iras falls and dies.]
292 Have I the aspic in my lips ? Dost fall ?
If thou and nature can so gently part,
The stroke of death is as a lover's pinch,
Which hurts, and is desired. Dost thou lie still ?
If thus thou vanishest, thou tell'st the world
It is not worth leave-taking.

CHARMIAN
Dissolve, thick cloud, and rain, that I may say
The gods themselves do weep.

CLEOPATRA   This proves me base :
If she first meet the curlèd Antony,
He'll make demand of her, and spend that kiss
Which is my heaven to have. Come, thou mortal wretch,
    [To an asp, which she applies to her breast.]
303 With thy sharp teeth this knot intrinsicate
Of life at once untie. Poor venomous fool,
305 Be angry, and dispatch. O, couldst thou speak,
That I might hear thee call great Caesar ass
307 Unpolicied !

CHARMIAN   O Eastern star !

CLEOPATRA   Peace, peace !
Dost thou not see my baby at my breast,
That sucks the nurse asleep ?

CHARMIAN   O, break ! O, break !

CLEOPATRA
As sweet as balm, as soft as air, as gentle –
O Antony ! Nay, I will take thee too :
    [Applies another asp to her arm.]
What should I stay –
    Dies.

CHARMIAN
In this wild world ? So, fare thee well.
Now boast thee, death, in thy possession lies
A lass unparalleled. Downy windows, close ;
And golden Phoebus never be beheld
Of eyes again so royal ! Your crown 's awry ;
I'll mend it, and then play –
    Enter the Guard, rustling in.

1 . GUARDSMAN
Where's the Queen ?

CHARMIAN   Speak softly, wake her not.

1 . GUARDSMAN
Caesar hath sent –

CHARMIAN   Too slow a messenger.
    [Applies an asp.]
O, come apace, dispatch, I partly feel thee.

1 . GUARDSMAN
Approach, ho ! All's not well : Caesar 's beguiled.   322

2 . GUARDSMAN
There's Dolabella sent from Caesar. Call him.

1 . GUARDSMAN
What work is here ! Charmian, is this well done ?

CHARMIAN
It is well done, and fitting for a princess
Descended of so many royal kings.
Ah, soldier !
    Charmian dies.
    Enter Dolabella.

DOLABELLA
How goes it here ?

2 . GUARDSMAN   All dead.

DOLABELLA   Caesar, thy thoughts
Touch their effects in this : thyself art coming   329
To see performed the dreaded act which thou
So sought'st to hinder.
    Enter Caesar and all his Train, marching.

ALL   A way there, a way for Caesar !

DOLABELLA
O sir, you are too sure an augurer :
That you did fear is done.

CAESAR   Bravest at the last,
She levelled at our purposes, and being royal,   334
Took her own way. The manner of their deaths ?
I do not see them bleed.

DOLABELLA   Who was last with them ?

1 . GUARDSMAN
A simple countryman, that brought her figs.
This was his basket.

CAESAR   Poisoned, then.

1 . GUARDSMAN   O Caesar,
This Charmian lived but now, she stood and spake ;
I found her trimming up the diadem
On her dead mistress ; tremblingly she stood,
And on the sudden dropped.

CAESAR   O noble weakness !
If they had swallowed poison, 'twould appear
By external swelling ; but she looks like sleep,
As she would catch another Antony
In her strong toil of grace.   346

DOLABELLA   Here on her breast
There is a vent of blood, and something blown ;   347
The like is on her arm.

1 . GUARDSMAN
This is an aspic's trail, and these fig leaves
Have slime upon them, such as th' aspic leaves
Upon the caves of Nile.

---

273 *dress* (with pun on the culinary sense)   282 *Yare* nimbly   288 *fire, and air* (the lighter of the four elements, thought of as belonging to immortality); *other elements* i.e. water and earth, the heavier elements, bequeathed by Cleopatra to mortality   292 *aspic* asp   303 *intrinsicate* intricate   305 *dispatch* make haste   307 *Unpolicied* outwitted   322 *beguiled* tricked   329 *Touch their effects* meet fulfillment   334 *levelled at* guessed   346 *toil* net   347 *vent* discharge ; *blown* swelled

CAESAR   Most probable
That so she died : for her physician tells me
353   She hath pursued conclusions infinite
Of easy ways to die. Take up her bed,
And bear her women from the monument.
She shall be buried by her Antony.

353 *conclusions* experiments   357 *clip* clasp   359 *Strike* touch

No grave upon the earth shall clip in it   357
A pair so famous. High events as these
Strike those that make them ; and their story is   359
No less in pity than his glory which
Brought them to be lamented. Our army shall
In solemn show attend this funeral,
And then to Rome. Come, Dolabella, see
High order in this great solemnity.   *Exeunt omnes.*

CORIOLANUS

INTRODUCTION

This play, which must have seen its first performance in 1608 or thereabouts, may be the last of Shakespeare's tragedies as we define them to-day. Criticism has tended to range it beside his greatest for its power, its amplitude, and its craftsmanship. But it has never been so popular as the others; and that is by no means surprising, since it so expressly calls into question the equivocal values of popularity. On an elementary human basis, Shakespeare's appeal has always been exerted through his characters, and through the bonds of sympathy that ally them with the spectator or the reader. From the outset of *Coriolanus,* however, such an identification is harshly repelled; and modern ideology, which disposes us to sympathize less readily with the hero than with the viewpoint of his antagonists, has slanted and colored our understanding of both. Yet recent history, by grimly reviving the very issues that Shakespeare dramatized, has greatly increased the importance and the impressiveness of his dramatization. *Coriolanus* has been found, on revival, to be more fraught with significance for our time than any other drama in the Shakespearean repertory. Max Reinhardt's production in Germany was turbulently prophetic. French crowds rioted when, in the years between the wars, it was performed at the Comédie Française.

Shakespeare's audiences, on occasion, could be quite as explosive. His England must often have seemed to be rifted internally, as well as externally menaced. Even while he was writing *Coriolanus,* outcries over the scarcity of grain were daily reaching London from the Midlands. A Stuart monarch, recently enthroned, claimed more and wielded less authority than his Tudor predecessors had done. Strong-willed men could make spectacular bids for power; Sir Walter Ralegh was being held in the Tower on charges of conspiracy; the Earl of Essex had incited Londoners to fight in the streets a few years before; and for that insurrection *Richard II* had been utilized as propaganda. Such, of course, had not been Shakespeare's purpose. His mounting sequence of histories had made England's coming-of-age coincide with his own, and had subsumed – along with the English past – the most triumphant decade of the first Elizabeth's reign. Therefore his chronicle plays had been somewhat controlled by considerations of patriotism, royal prerogative, and the relative familiarity of the facts. Seeking a freer field of political observation, pushing toward profounder formulations of statecraft, shifting his concern from the ruler's duties and rights to those of the citizen, Shakespeare was inevitably led to a point where more distant roads converge: the archetype of city-states, the keystone of western traditions, Rome.

At the beginning of his tragic period – the opening years of the seventeenth century – he essayed this republican theme in *Julius Caesar.* He resumed it with an even grander sequel, *Antony and Cleopatra,* but not until after completing his exhaustive explorations of personality in *Hamlet, Othello, Macbeth,* and *King Lear.* Thus *Coriolanus* rounds out a trilogy, though it stands somewhat apart from the other two Roman plays, possibly nearer to *Antony and Cleopatra* in scope and to *Julius Caesar* in subject. All three, taken together, constitute a great debate on ethics, in which the statement of private interests is balanced against the counter-statement of public responsibilities. *Julius Caesar* lays the dialectical groundwork by showing a group of individuals in conflict over the state. *Antony and Cleopatra* shows its individualistic hero and heroine rejecting their obligations to their respective states and behaving as if they were laws unto themselves. *Coriolanus* explores the extreme situation of the individual who pits himself against the state. Here Julius Caesar might have proved a monumental counterpart; but Shakespeare's portrait was brief and enigmatic, registering the impact of Caesarism on others, notably on the conscience of Marcus Brutus; and Brutus, acting in the "common good to all," presented the obverse of the Roman coin whereon Coriolanus is stamped incisively.

The historical Caius Marcius Coriolanus, figuring in the earliest annals of the Republic, had won his victory at Corioli in 493 B.C. He may indeed have been a half-legendary embodiment of patrician resistance to the increasing demands of the plebeians and especially their newly appointed spokesmen, the tribunes. Hence, instead of being elected to the consulate, he was banished, and went over to the enemy as the hero does in the play. In the end, as the historian Mommsen sums it up, "he expiated his first treason by a second, and both by death." Poetic justice was better served than either side. Shakespeare drew his version of these episodes from Plutarch's *Lives,* the source that inspired him most, that treasury of ancient biography which comprises a series of comparative studies in heroic citizenship. Plutarch, the Greek moralist, saw Coriolanus as an outstanding example of the peculiarly Roman conception of virtue: *virtus,* which is translated "valiantness." The vice that attended and finally defeated this salient quality was "willfulness." Plutarch's contrasting parallel is the career of Alcibiades, whose ingratiating suppleness – like Antony's – throws the intransigent arrogance of Coriolanus into bold relief. That the latter was brought up by his widowed mother, and was chiefly animated by the desire to please her, Plutarch is at pains to emphasize.

Shakespeare follows Plutarch so very closely that he often echoes the phraseology of the magnificent Elizabethan translation by Sir Thomas North. Volumnia's plea to her son in Act V, eloquently massive as it is, is scarcely more than a metrical adaptation of North's prose. On the other hand, her appeal to him in Act III is Shakespeare's interpolation; he has reserved his right to modify and augment his material in the interests of psychological motivation and dramatic equilibrium; and those two interventions of Volumnia, in each case changing the mind of Coriolanus, are the turning-points of the plot. Rhetoric, the art of persuasion, determined not only the style but also the structure of *Julius Caesar*: Cassius persuades Brutus, Brutus persuades the people, Mark Antony persuades them otherwise. *Coriolanus* is not less Roman in its recourse to public speech; and speech-making triumphs ironically over war-mongering; but now the forensic mode is that of dissuasion. The candidate actually dissuades the people from voting for him; the general at length is dissuaded from pursuing his revenge. His vein is negation: curses, threats, and invectives from first to last. Once he rallies his men; many times he scolds them. When he girds the gods, his rant sounds more like the misanthropic Timon than the iconoclastic Tamburlaine. Yet how narrowly it misses the tone of Hotspur!

Coriolanus to the contrary, the word is not "mildly." The language of the play reverberates with the dissonance of its subject-matter and the thunder-like percussion of its protagonist. The words are so tensely involved in the situation that they do not lend themselves much to purple passages or quotations out of context. Reflecting a stylistic transition, they seem to combine the serried diction of Shakespeare's middle period with the flowing rhythm of his later plays. The speeches frequently begin and break off in the middle of a line; but the cadence of the blank verse persists through occasional setbacks; and sometimes the overlapping pentameters are more evident to the ear than on the page. This has been a problem for editors, many of whom have regarded the difficulties of the text as invitations to change it. The present edition assumes that the unique redaction of *Coriolanus*, which has come down to us through the folios, is more or less authoritative; and that, except for some obvious readjustments and a few unavoidable emendations, it simply needs to be modernized in spelling and punctuation. The original stage directions, which are unusually explicit, convey a suggestion of pageantry commanding the full resources of the resplendent Globe. And from a contemporary sketch of *Titus Andronicus*, we know that the Elizabethans could approximate Roman dress.

Though the scenes march by in swift continuity, moving from camp to camp and faction to faction, the acts are sharply divided, as if to stress the division among the characters. Act I presents the hero in his proper field of action, the battlefield, where heroism can be demonstrated in its simplest terms as valiantness. Act II brings him reluctantly home to his triumph, and even more grudgingly into the electoral campaign. This goes against him in Act III and leads, after another disastrous attempt at propitiation, to the decree of banishment. Act IV pursues the exiled Coriolanus traversing the distance between Rome and Antium, and betraying himself and his fellow Romans to the Volscian general, Aufidius. Act V witnesses his capitulation and consummates his tragedy: military commitment, resisting civic pressure, yields to domestic. Throughout these vicissitudes he sustains his predomi-

nating role, the central figure when he is on stage, the topic of discussion when he is not. His monolithic character is measured by no single foil of comparable stature – least of all by his rival, Aufidius, who has failed to square accounts with him honorably, and vowed to do so through dishonorable means if necessary – but by his dynamic relations with all the others, on the diverging levels of family, city, and enemy.

The one is accordingly weighed against the many; and the tendency toward monodrama is counterpoised by an unusual number of choric roles – citizens, officers, soldiers, servants, other ranks of society. The scales tip during the roadside interview between a Roman and a Volscian, with its implication that Coriolanus is taking the same road to espionage and betrayal. As for the populace, the tribunes can hardly speak for it because it is so vocal on its own behalf; the mistake of Coriolanus is to believe that its "voices" are merely votes. Generalization soon breaks down into Hob and Dick, and the types are individualized, loudly insisting upon their individuality. There are some ugly mob-scenes and one violent outbreak of street-fighting, but mother-wit is the characteristic weapon. The humorous mediator, Menenius Agrippa, can handle this pithy prose idiom. The crowd in turn can rise to the pitch of blank verse, while their shrewd heckling enlivens his tale of the belly and the members. The First Citizen, "great toe" though he may be, accepts the question-begging metaphor that identifies the organ of digestion with the deliberation of the Senate. But, logically enough, he presses the claims of the other parts, including the soldierly arm. The parable will apply to the choleric hero as much as to the angry mob.

In a subsequent argument, when Coriolanus is compared to a disease, Menenius retorts that he is rather a diseased limb which can be cured. By this time many sores and wounds have been metaphorically and literally probed, thereby revealing other aspects of the body politic. The age-old fable expounded by Menenius, appeasing the uproar of the introductory scene, has served to establish an ideal of social order – the concept of commonweal, *res publica* – more honored in the breach than the observance. It has also concretely grounded the imagery of the play in the matter at hand, the dearth of corn, the fundamental problem of nourishment. The struggling classes seek to feed on each other; Menenius is a self-confessed epicure; the poor justify themselves by hungry proverbs; and Coriolanus finds himself in their desperate position when he appears at the feast of Aufidius. In close association with these images of food, battle is described as if it were harvest, with the swords of destruction figuratively turning into the ploughshares of fertility. Another associated train of thought runs to animals, always an inspiration for name-calling. The hero is introduced as a dog to the people, who are curs to him then and crucially later. The prevailing code is dog-eat-dog.

Menenius points the moral succinctly when he demands: "On both sides more respect." Since both sides indulge in such embittered polemics, interpretation has varied between the extremes of left and right, now underlining the dangers of dictatorship and now the weaknesses of democracy, according to the political adherence of the interpreters. Nothing could better attest what Coleridge, in this connection, called "the wonderful philosophic impartiality in Shakespeare's politics." His portrayal of the multitude, whose sedition he arms with a grievance, is anti-demagogic rather than anti-democratic. The demagogues are the tribunes, portrayed in unequivocal cynicism, dissuading the plebs from the suffrage they have already pledged to Coriolanus. Coriolanus, on his side, is no friend of the people; and it is to the credit of his integrity that he cannot act a part he does not feel. He earns, with an authoritarian vengeance, the title that Ibsen would bestow in irony upon his humanitarian Dr Stockmann – *An Enemy of the People*. All men are enemies, rivals if not foes, to Coriolanus. His aggressive temperament could never be happy until it had lurched all other swords of the garland. His fight against the world is not for booty nor praise nor office, but for acknowledged superiority; he does not want to dominate but to excel; and he cannot bear the thought of subordination.

We need not look far afield for the school that nurtured that spirit of single-minded competitiveness. The Roman matron, the masculine dowager, the statuesque Volumnia, is both father and mother to her son; and she has taught him aristocratic scorn along with martial courage. His wife, the gracious Virgilia, in contrast is sheer femininity; and her main attribute, like Cordelia's, is silence. His young son chases butterflies with congenital resolution; subsequently Coriolanus commands a Volscian army as eager as boys chasing butterflies. No man can withstand him and only one woman can plead with him. In yielding to her, in feeling this ultimate modicum of feminine tenderness, the strong man becomes again – as it were – a child. Thence the sting in the last taunt of Aufidius. Under the epithet "traitor" Coriolanus has slightly flinched. But "boy!" "Thou boy of tears!" In significant contradistinction, we are reminded continually that the tribunes are elderly men. Leadership, as Volumnia's boy had learned it in the wars, was largely an individual matter of athletic prowess, having little to do with the sort of maturity that peaceful civilian government requires. Perhaps the trouble, as analyzed by Aufidius, lay in a soldier's inability to move "from th' casque to th' cushion." The virtues of war may well be the vices of peace; the man on horseback, dismounted, a sorry creature.

T. S. Eliot's modernized *Coriolan* consists of two poems: "Triumphal March" and "Difficulties of a Statesman." These headings suggest the dilemma of Shakespeare's protagonist. His is not an internal struggle; so far as his two short soliloquies indicate, the treason causes him less mental anguish than the election; and, what is even worse, at Antium he employs the flatteries he has despised at Rome. Rather it is the external manifestation of his colossal pride that exalts him, all but deifies him, and renders the slippery turns of fortune more precipitous than the Tarpeian Rock. "Rome or I! One or the other must fall!" Such is the climax, verbalized by Wagner, to Beethoven's orchestration of this theme. "The note of banishment," the note that James Joyce kept hearing in Shakespeare's plays, is never more plangently sounded than in the parting denunciation of Coriolanus to the Romans: "I banish you!" Never was man more alienated than he, as the gates of Rome close behind him and he is forced to seek "a world elsewhere." The scene reverses his initial triumph, when the gates of Corioli shut him in alone of all the Romans. The ironic pattern is completed, on his return to the hostile town, by his fatal words to its citizens. And note the emphatic position of the first personal pronoun:

> If you have writ your annals true, 'tis there
> That, like an eagle in a dovecote, I
> Fluttered your Volscians in Corioles.
> Alone I did it.

Othello, at a similar moment, had the satisfaction of recalling his services to the state. Caius Marcius – Coriolanus no longer – can only glory in his isolation. The word "alone" is repeated more than in any other Shakespearean work; and, from the welter of similes, the most memorable is "a lonely dragon." We end by realizing the ambiguity of the foreign name this Roman has proudly flaunted. How can he expect it to be anything but a target of hatred for the orphans and widows and comrades-in-arms of men he has killed? After the combat in which he gained it, he had generously tried to befriend a certain Volscian, and had characteristically forgotten the poor man's name – a touch which Shakespeare added to Plutarch's anecdote. Shakespeare's insight, detailed as it is, confirms an observation cited from Plato by Plutarch: that such overriding egoism can only terminate in "desolation." This must be that desolation of solitude which the American imagination has paralleled in the career of another tragic captain, Melville's Ahab.

Harvard University   HARRY LEVIN

NOTE ON THE TEXT

Coriolanus was first published in the folio of 1623, evidently from the author's own manuscript. The present edition follows the folio text, with emendation confined as a rule to the most generally recognized instances of misprinting and mislineation. The folio text is divided into acts but not into scenes. The division provided marginally for reference in the present edition represents the folio acts as divided into scenes by later editors. This play is exceptional in the large number of speakers given only generic names in the speech-prefixes. These have been spelled out *First Citizen* etc. instead of *1. Citizen* etc. as in the other plays of the present edition. All material departures from the folio text are listed below, with the adopted reading in italics followed by the folio reading in roman.

I, i, 60 *First Citizen* 2 Cit. (and so through rest of scene) 62 *you.
For* you for 105 *tauntingly* taintingly 110 *crownèd* crown'd 179 *vile* vilde 209 *Shouting* Shooting 221 s.d. *Junius* Annius 234 *Lartius* Lucius 239, 243 *First Senator* Sen.

I, ii, 4 *on* one

I, iii, 34 *that's* that 81 *Ithaca* Athica 108 s.d. *Exeunt* Exeunt Ladies

I, iv, 42 *Follow me* followes 45 s.d. *gates* Gati 57 *Cato's* Calues

I, v, 3 s.d. *Alarum* exeunt. Alarum *Titus Lartius* Titus

I, vi, 24 s.d. *Enter Marcius* (at l. 21 in F) 32 *burned* burnt 53 *Antiates* Antients 70 *Lesser* Lessen 81 *select* select from all

I, vii, 7 s.d. *Exeunt* Exit

I, ix, s.d. *Flourish* (not in F) 46 *coverture* Ouerture 49 *shout* shoot 66 *All* Omnes *Caius Marcius* Marcus Caius 67, 78, 81, 89 *Coriolanus* Martius

I, x, 2, 16, 29, 33 *First Soldier* Sould 22 *Embargements* Embarquements

II, i, 16 *with all* withall 52 *cannot* can 57 *you* you you 59 *bisson* beesome 155 *Coriolanus* Martius Caius Coriolanus 179 *relish* Rallish 193 s.d. *Brutus . . . forward* Enter Brutus and Sicinius 244 *touch* teach 249 *to th'* to the

II, ii, 44 *Caius Marcius* Martius Caius 65, 121, 128 *First Senator* Senat 79 *one on's* on ones 89 *chin* Shinne 90 *bristled* brizled 106 *took. From face to foot* tooke from face to foote : 136 *suffrage* sufferage 152 *Senators* Senat s.d. *Manent* Manet

II, iii, 26 *wedged* wadg'd 35 *it. I say, if* it, I say. If 39 *all together* altogether 59 s.d. *Enter . . . Citizens* (at l. 58 in F) 65 *not* but 84, 87, 101 *Fourth Citizen* 1. 100 *Fifth Citizen* 2. 109 *hire* higher 110 *toge* tongue 113 *do't,* doo't? 116 *t' o'erpeer* to o'epeere 121, 125 *voices!* voyces? 221 *th'* the 238 *And Censorinus nobly* And nobly *namèd* nam'd 239 *being by the people chosen* being chosen

III, i, s.d. *Lartius* Latius 10 *vilely* vildly 63, 75 *First Senator* Senat. 91 *O good* O God! 143 *Where one* Whereon 172 s.d. *Enter an Aedile* (at l. 171 in F) 185 *All* (at l. 187 in F) 198, 233, 335 *First Senator* Sena. 231 *Coriolanus* Com. 237 *Cominius* Corio. 238 *Coriolanus* Mene. 287 *our* one 305 *Sicinius* Menen. 323 *bring him* bring him in peace

III, ii, 13 s.d. *Enter Volumnia* (at l. 6 in F) 25 *taxings* things 26 *First Senator* Sen. 32 *th' herd* th' heart 101 *bear? Well, I beare Well? I 115 *lulls* lull

III, iii, 32 *for th'* fourth 36 *Throng* Through 55 *accents* Actions 99 *i' th' name* In the Name 110 *for* from 136 s.d. *Menenius Cumalijs 138 *Hoo! hoo!* Hoo, oo.

IV, i, 34 *wilt* will

IV, ii, 9 s.d. *Enter . . . Menenius* (at l. 7 in F) 36 *let us* let's 44 s.d. *Exeunt* Exit 53 *Exeunt* (at end of preceding speech in F, with *Exit* here)

IV, iii, 31 *will* well

IV, iv, 23 *hate* haue

IV, v, 108 *thy* that 151 *strucken* strocken 164 *on* one 178 *lief* liue 203 *sowl* sole 225 *sprightly, waking* spightly walking 227 *sleepy* sleepe 229 *war* warres

IV, vi, 10 s.d. *Enter Menenius* (at l. 9 in F) 25 *Citizens* All

IV, vii, 15 *Had* haue 37 *'twas* 'was 49 *virtues* Vertue 55 *founder* fouler

V, i, 41 *toward* towards

V, ii, s.d. *on* or 16 *haply* happely 56 s.d. *and* with 58 *errand* arrant 61 *by my* my 72 *our* your 83 *pity note* pitty : Note 90 s.d. *Manent* Manet

V, iii, 48 *prate* pray 56 *What is* What's 63 *holp* hope 79 *you'd* youl'd 149 *fine* fiue 154 *noble man* Nobleman 163 *clucked* clock'd 169 *him* him with him 179 *this* his

V, v, 4 *Unshout* Unshoot

V, vi, 48 s.d. *sound* sounds 72 *That* Then, 99 *other* others 114 *Fluttered* Flatter'd 115 *it. Boy?* it, Boy. 129 s.d. *Draw* Draw both *kill* kils 153 s.d. *Coriolanus* Martius

CORIOLANUS

*

I, i *Enter a company of mutinous Citizens, with staves, clubs, and other weapons.*

FIRST CITIZEN Before we proceed any further, hear me speak.

ALL Speak, speak.

FIRST CITIZEN You are all resolved rather to die than to famish?

ALL Resolved, resolved.

FIRST CITIZEN First, you know Caius Marcius is chief enemy to the people.

ALL We know't, we know't.

FIRST CITIZEN Let us kill him, and we'll have corn at
10 our own price. Is't a verdict?

11 ALL No more talking on't! Let it be done! Away, away!

SECOND CITIZEN One word, good citizens.

FIRST CITIZEN We are accounted poor citizens, the
14 patricians good. What authority surfeits on would re-
15 lieve us. If they would yield us but the superfluity while it were wholesome, we might guess they relieved us
17 humanely; but they think we are too dear. The leanness
18 that afflicts us, the object of our misery, is as an in-
19 ventory to particularize their abundance; our sufferance
20 is a gain to them. Let us revenge this with our pikes ere
21 we become rakes; for the gods know I speak this in hunger for bread, not in thirst for revenge.

SECOND CITIZEN Would you proceed especially against Caius Marcius?

FIRST CITIZEN Against him first. He's a very dog to the
26 commonalty.

SECOND CITIZEN Consider you what services he has done for his country?

FIRST CITIZEN Very well, and could be content to give him good report for't, but that he pays himself with being proud.

SECOND CITIZEN Nay, but speak not maliciously.

FIRST CITIZEN I say unto you, what he hath done
34 famously, he did it to that end. Though soft-conscienced men can be content to say it was for his country, he did it to please his mother and to be partly proud, which he
37 is, even to the altitude of his virtue.

SECOND CITIZEN What he cannot help in his nature, you account a vice in him. You must in no way say he is covetous.

FIRST CITIZEN If I must not, I need not be barren of accusations. He hath faults, with surplus, to tire in repetition.

Shouts within.

What shouts are these? The other side o' th' city is risen.
Why stay we prating here? To th' Capitol! 44

ALL Come, come!

FIRST CITIZEN Soft! who comes here? 46

Enter Menenius Agrippa.

SECOND CITIZEN Worthy Menenius Agrippa, one that hath always loved the people.

FIRST CITIZEN He's one honest enough. Would all the rest were so!

I, i A street in Rome   10 *verdict* agreement   11 *on't* about it   14 *patricians* aristocrats; *good* substantial; *authority* the ruling class   15 *superfluity* surplus   17 *dear* expensive   18 *object* spectacle   19 *sufferance* suffering   20 *pikes* pitchforks   21 *rakes* lean as rakes   26 *commonalty* common people   34 *to that end* i.e. to achieve fame   37 *altitude of his virtue* height of his valor   44 *Capitol* Temple of Jupiter, Capitoline Hill   46 *Soft* stay

MENENIUS
What work 's, my countrymen, in hand? Where go you
With bats and clubs? The matter? Speak, I pray you.

FIRST CITIZEN Our business is not unknown to th'
Senate. They have had inkling this fortnight what we
intend to do, which now we'll show 'em in deeds. They
56 say poor suitors have strong breaths; they shall know
we have strong arms too.

MENENIUS
Why, masters, my good friends, mine honest neighbors,
Will you undo yourselves?

FIRST CITIZEN We cannot, sir, we are undone already.

MENENIUS
I tell you, friends, most charitable care
62 Have the patricians of you. For your wants,
63 Your suffering in this dearth, you may as well
Strike at the heaven with your staves as lift them
65 Against the Roman state, whose course will on
The way it takes, cracking ten thousand curbs
Of more strong link asunder than can ever
68 Appear in your impediment. For the dearth,
The gods, not the patricians, make it, and
Your knees to them, not arms, must help. Alack,
71 You are transported by calamity
Thither where more attends you, and you slander
73 The helms o' th' state, who care for you like fathers,
When you curse them as enemies.

FIRST CITIZEN Care for us? True, indeed! They ne'er
cared for us yet: suffer us to famish, and their store-
houses crammed with grain; make edicts for usury, to
support usurers; repeal daily any wholesome act estab-
79 lished against the rich, and provide more piercing
statutes daily to chain up and restrain the poor. If the
wars eat us not up, they will; and there's all the love
they bear us.

MENENIUS
Either you must
83 Confess yourselves wondrous malicious,
Or be accused of folly. I shall tell you
A pretty tale. It may be you have heard it;
But, since it serves my purpose, I will venture
87 To stale't a little more.

FIRST CITIZEN Well, I'll hear it, sir; yet you must not
89 think to fob off our disgrace with a tale. But, an't please
you, deliver.

MENENIUS
There was a time when all the body's members
Rebelled against the belly, thus accused it:
That only like a gulf it did remain
I' th' midst o' th' body, idle and unactive,
95 Still cupboarding the viand, never bearing
96 Like labor with the rest, where th' other instruments
Did see and hear, devise, instruct, walk, feel,

And mutually participate, did minister   98
Unto the appetite and affection common   99
Of the whole body. The belly answered—

FIRST CITIZEN Well, sir, what answer made the belly?

MENENIUS
Sir, I shall tell you. With a kind of smile,
Which ne'er came from the lungs, but even thus—   103
For, look you, I may make the belly smile
As well as speak—it tauntingly replied
To th' discontented members, the mutinous parts
That envied his receipt; even so most fitly   107
As you malign our senators, for that   108
They are not such as you.

FIRST CITIZEN   Your belly's answer? What?
The kingly crownèd head, the vigilant eye,
The counsellor heart, the arm our soldier,
Our steed the leg, the tongue our trumpeter,
With other muniments and petty helps   113
In this our fabric, if that they—

MENENIUS   What then?
'Fore me, this fellow speaks! What then? what then?   115

FIRST CITIZEN
Should by the cormorant belly be restrained,
Who is the sink o' th' body—

MENENIUS   Well, what then?

FIRST CITIZEN
The former agents, if they did complain,
What could the belly answer?

MENENIUS   I will tell you;
If you'll bestow a small—of what you have little—
Patience awhile, you'st hear the belly's answer.   121

FIRST CITIZEN
Y' are long about it.   122

MENENIUS   Note me this, good friend;
Your most grave belly was deliberate,   123
Not rash like his accusers, and thus answered:
'True is it, my incorporate friends,' quoth he,
'That I receive the general food at first,
Which you do live upon; and fit it is,
Because I am the storehouse and the shop   128
Of the whole body. But, if you do remember,
I send it through the rivers of your blood
Even to the court, the heart, to th' seat o' th' brain;
And, through the cranks and offices of man,   132
The strongest nerves and small inferior veins
From me receive that natural competency   134
Whereby they live. And though that all at once'—
You, my good friends! This says the belly. Mark me.

FIRST CITIZEN
Ay, sir, well, well.

MENENIUS   'Though all at once cannot
See what I do deliver out to each,
Yet I can make my audit up, that all
From me do back receive the flour of all,
And leave me but the bran.' What say you to't?

FIRST CITIZEN
It was an answer. How apply you this?

MENENIUS
The senators of Rome are this good belly,
And you the mutinous members. For examine
Their counsels and their cares, disgest things rightly   145
Touching the weal o' th' common, you shall find   146
No public benefit which you receive
But it proceeds or comes from them to you,

56 *suitors* petitioners   62 *For* as for   63 *dearth* famine   65 *on* go on   68 *your impediment* the obstruction you raise   71 *transported* carried away   73 *helms* pilots   79 *piercing* far-reaching   83 *wondrous* extra-ordinarily   87 *stale't* make it stale   89 *fob off* elude; *disgrace* hardship; *an't* if it   95 *Still* always   96 *Like* similar; *instruments* organs   98 *partici-pate* taking part   99 *affection* inclination   103 *lungs* i.e. organ of laughter   107 *his receipt* what he received   108 *for that* because   113 *muniments* furnishings   115 *'Fore me* upon my soul   121 *you'st* you'll (provincial)   122 *Y'* are you're   123 *Your* this   128 *shop* workshop   132 *cranks* windings; *offices* servants' quarters   134 *competency* sufficiency   145 *disgest* digest   146 *weal o' th' common* public welfare

And no way from yourselves. What do you think,
You, the great toe of this assembly?

FIRST CITIZEN
I the great toe! Why the great toe?

MENENIUS
For that, being one o' th' lowest, basest, poorest
Of this most wise rebellion, thou goest foremost.

154 Thou rascal, that art worst in blood to run,
155 Lead'st first to win some vantage.
But make you ready your stiff bats and clubs.
Rome and her rats are at the point of battle;
158 The one side must have bale.
     Enter Caius Marcius.   Hail, noble Marcius!

MARCIUS
159 Thanks. What's the matter, you dissentious rogues,
That, rubbing the poor itch of your opinion,
Make yourselves scabs?

FIRST CITIZEN   We have ever your good word.

MARCIUS
He that will give good words to thee will flatter
Beneath abhorring. What would you have, you curs,
164 That like nor peace nor war? The one affrights you,
165 The other makes you proud. He that trusts to you,
Where he should find you lions, finds you hares;
Where foxes, geese. You are no surer, no,
Than is the coal of fire upon the ice,
Or hailstone in the sun. Your virtue is
170 To make him worthy whose offense subdues him
171 And curse that justice did it. Who deserves greatness
Deserves your hate; and your affections are
A sick man's appetite, who desires most that
Which would increase his evil. He that depends
Upon your favors swims with fins of lead
And hews down oaks with rushes. Hang ye! Trust ye?
With every minute you do change a mind,
And call him noble that was now your hate,
Him vile that was your garland. What's the matter,
That in these several places of the city
You cry against the noble Senate, who,
Under the gods, keep you in awe, which else
183 Would feed on one another? What's their seeking?

MENENIUS
For corn at their own rates, whereof they say
The city is well stored.

MARCIUS   Hang 'em! They say?
They'll sit by th' fire and presume to know
What's done i' th' Capitol, who's like to rise,
188 Who thrives and who declines; side factions and give
out
Conjectural marriages, making parties strong
190 And feebling such as stand not in their liking
191 Below their cobbled shoes. They say there's grain
enough?
192 Would the nobility lay aside their ruth,
193 And let me use my sword, I'd make a quarry
194 With thousands of these quartered slaves as high
195 As I could pick my lance.

MENENIUS
Nay, these are almost thoroughly persuaded;
For though abundantly they lack discretion,
198 Yet are they passing cowardly. But, I beseech you,
What says the other troop?

MARCIUS   They are dissolved. Hang 'em!
200 They said they were anhungry, sighed forth proverbs –

That hunger broke stone walls, that dogs must eat,
That meat was made for mouths, that the gods sent not
Corn for the rich men only. With these shreds
They vented their complainings, which being answered
And a petition granted them, a strange one,
To break the heart of generosity,   206
And make bold power look pale, they threw their caps
As they would hang them on the horns o' th' moon,
Shouting their emulation.   209

MENENIUS   What is granted them?

MARCIUS
Five tribunes to defend their vulgar wisdoms,   210
Of their own choice. One's Junius Brutus,
Sicinius Velutus, and I know not – 'Sdeath!   212
The rabble should have first unroofed the city
Ere so prevailed with me; it will in time
Win upon power, and throw forth greater themes   215
For insurrection's arguing.   216

MENENIUS   This is strange.

MARCIUS
Go, get you home, you fragments!
     Enter a Messenger hastily.

MESSENGER
Where's Caius Marcius?

MARCIUS   Here. What's the matter?

MESSENGER
The news is, sir, the Volsces are in arms.

MARCIUS
I am glad on't. Then we shall ha' means to vent   220
Our musty superfluity. See, our best elders.
     Enter Sicinius Velutus, Junius Brutus, Cominius,
     Titus Lartius, with other Senators.

FIRST SENATOR
Marcius, 'tis true that you have lately told us:
The Volsces are in arms.

MARCIUS   They have a leader,
Tullus Aufidius, that will put you to't.   224
I sin in envying his nobility;
And were I any thing but what I am,
I would wish me only he.

COMINIUS   You have fought together?   227

MARCIUS
Were half to half the world by th' ears and he
Upon my party, I'd revolt, to make   229
Only my wars with him. He is a lion
That I am proud to hunt.

FIRST SENATOR   Then, worthy Marcius,
Attend upon Cominius to these wars.

COMINIUS
It is your former promise.

MARCIUS   Sir, it is,
And I am constant. Titus Lartius, thou
Shalt see me once more strike at Tullus' face.

---

154 *rascal* worthless deer; *blood* condition   155 *vantage* advantage   158 *bale* destruction   159 *dissentious* seditious   164 *nor . . . nor* neither . . . nor; *The one* i.e. war   165 *The other* i.e. peace   170 *make him worthy* glorify that man; *subdues* degrades   171 *that justice* that justice which   183 *seeking* petition 188 *side* take sides with   190 *feebling* making weak   191 *cobbled* mended   192 *ruth* pity   193 *quarry* heap of slaughtered   194 *quartered* cut in four like criminals   195 *pick* pitch   198 *passing* extremely   200 *anhungry* hungry   206 *generosity* aristocracy   209 *emulation* envy   210 *tribunes* official protectors of the people's interests   212 *'Sdeath* (modified oath)   215 *Win upon power* gain authority   216 *For insurrection's arguing* for revolution to fight over 220 *vent* get rid of   224 *to't* to the test   227 *together* one another   229 *party* side

236   What, art thou stiff? Stand'st out?

TITUS   No, Caius Marcius,
I'll lean upon one crutch and fight with t' other,
Ere stay behind this business.

MENENIUS   O, true-bred!

FIRST SENATOR
Your company to th' Capitol, where I know
240   Our greatest friends attend us.

TITUS *[to Cominius]*   Lead you on.
        [To Marcius]
Follow Cominius. We must follow you.
242   Right worthy you priority.

COMINIUS   Noble Marcius!

FIRST SENATOR *[to the Citizens]*
Hence to your homes, be gone!

MARCIUS   Nay, let them follow.
The Volsces have much corn. Take these rats thither
To gnaw their garners. Worshipful mutineers,
246   Your valor puts well forth. Pray follow.
              Exeunt. Citizens steal away.
              Manent Sicinius and Brutus.

SICINIUS
Was ever man so proud as is this Marcius?

BRUTUS
He has no equal.

SICINIUS
When we were chosen tribunes for the people –

BRUTUS
Marked you his lip and eyes?

SICINIUS   Nay, but his taunts.

BRUTUS
251   Being moved, he will not spare to gird the gods.

SICINIUS
Bemock the modest moon.

BRUTUS
The present wars devour him. He is grown
Too proud to be so valiant.

SICINIUS   Such a nature,
Tickled with good success, disdains the shadow
Which he treads on at noon. But I do wonder
His insolence can brook to be commanded
Under Cominius.

BRUTUS   Fame, at the which he aims,
259   In whom already he's well graced, cannot
Better be held nor more attained than by
A place below the first; for what miscarries
Shall be the general's fault, though he perform
To th' utmost of a man, and giddy censure
Will then cry out of Marcius, 'O, if he
Had borne the business!'

SICINIUS   Besides, if things go well,
266   Opinion, that so sticks on Marcius, shall
267   Of his demerits rob Cominius.

BRUTUS   Come.
268   Half all Cominius' honors are to Marcius,

Though Marcius earned them not; and all his faults
To Marcius shall be honors, though indeed
In aught he merit not.

SICINIUS   Let's hence and hear
How the dispatch is made, and in what fashion,   272
More than his singularity, he goes   273
Upon this present action.

BRUTUS   Let's along.   *Exeunt.*

*

       Enter Tullus Aufidius, with Senators of Corioles.   I, ii

FIRST SENATOR
So, your opinion is, Aufidius,
That they of Rome are entered in our counsels   2
And know how we proceed.

AUFIDIUS   Is it not yours?
What ever have been thought on in this state,   4
That could be brought to bodily act ere Rome
Had circumvention? 'Tis not four days gone   6
Since I heard thence. These are the words. I think
I have the letter here. Yes, here it is:
'They have pressed a power, but it is not known   9
Whether for east or west. The dearth is great,
The people mutinous; and it is rumored,
Cominius, Marcius your old enemy,
Who is of Rome worse hated than of you,
And Titus Lartius, a most valiant Roman,
These three lead on this preparation
Whither 'tis bent. Most likely 'tis for you.
Consider of it.'

FIRST SENATOR   Our army's in the field.
We never yet made doubt but Rome was ready
To answer us.

AUFIDIUS   Nor did you think it folly
To keep your great pretenses veiled till when   20
They needs must show themselves, which in the
     hatching,
It seemed, appeared to Rome. By the discovery   22
We shall be shortened in our aim, which was   23
To take in many towns ere almost Rome   24
Should know we were afoot.

SECOND SENATOR   Noble Aufidius,
Take your commission; hie you to your bands;
Let us alone to guard Corioles.
If they set down before's, for the remove   28
Bring up your army; but, I think, you'll find
Th' have not prepared for us.   30

AUFIDIUS   O, doubt not that,
I speak from certainties. Nay more,
Some parcels of their power are forth already,   32
And only hitherward. I leave your honors.
If we and Caius Marcius chance to meet,
'Tis sworn between us we shall ever strike
Till one can do no more.

ALL   The gods assist you!

AUFIDIUS
And keep your honors safe!

FIRST SENATOR   Farewell.

SECOND SENATOR   Farewell.

ALL
Farewell.   *Exeunt omnes.*

*

---

236 *Stand'st out* do you keep aloof   240 *attend* await   242 *worthy you priority* you are worthy of precedence   246 *puts . . . forth* blossoms   251 *spare to gird* desist from taunting   259 *whom* which   266 *so sticks* is so set   267 *demerits* merits   268 *are to* belong to   272 *dispatch* completion 273 *More than his singularity* personal considerations aside
I, ii The senate house in Corioli   2 *entered in* initiated into   4 *What* what counsels   6 *circumvention* means of foiling   9 *pressed a power* raised an army   20 *pretenses* designs   22 *appeared* became visible   23 *shortened* reduced   24 *take in* capture   28 *for the remove* to force their departure 30 *Th'* they   32 *parcels* parts

I, iii   *Enter Volumnia and Virgilia, mother and wife to*
             Marcius. They set them down on two low stools and sew.

VOLUMNIA I pray you, daughter, sing, or express your-
2   self in a more comfortable sort. If my son were my
       husband, I should freelier rejoice in that absence where-
       in he won honor than in the embracements of his bed
       where he would show most love. When yet he was but
       tender-bodied and the only son of my womb, when
7   youth with comeliness plucked all gaze his way, when
       for a day of kings' entreaties a mother should not sell
9   him an hour from her beholding, I, considering how
10   honor would become such a person, that it was no better
       than picture-like to hang by th' wall, if renown made it
       not stir, was pleased to let him seek danger where he
       was like to find fame. To a cruel war I sent him, from
14   whence he returned, his brows bound with oak. I tell
       thee, daughter, I sprang not more in joy at first hearing
       he was a man-child than now in first seeing he had
       proved himself a man.

VIRGILIA But had he died in the business, madam, how
       then?

VOLUMNIA Then his good report should have been my
       son; I therein would have found issue. Hear me profess
       sincerely: had I a dozen sons, each in my love alike, and
       none less dear than thine and my good Marcius, I had
       rather had eleven die nobly for their country than one
23   voluptuously surfeit out of action.

             Enter a Gentlewoman.

GENTLEWOMAN
       Madam, the Lady Valeria is come to visit you.

VIRGILIA
25   Beseech you, give me leave to retire myself.

VOLUMNIA
       Indeed, you shall not.
       Methinks I hear hither your husband's drum;
       See him pluck Aufidius down by th' hair;
       As children from a bear, the Volsces shunning him.
       Methinks I see him stamp thus, and call thus:
31   'Come on, you cowards! You were got in fear,
       Though you were born in Rome.' His bloody brow
       With his mailed hand then wiping, forth he goes,
34   Like to a harvest-man that's tasked to mow
35   Or all or lose his hire.

VIRGILIA
       His bloody brow? O Jupiter, no blood!

VOLUMNIA
       Away, you fool! it more becomes a man
38   Than gilt his trophy. The breasts of Hecuba,
39   When she did suckle Hector, looked not lovelier
       Than Hector's forehead when it spit forth blood
41   At Grecian sword, contemning. Tell Valeria,
       We are fit to bid her welcome.   *Exit Gentlewoman.*

VIRGILIA
43   Heavens bless my lord from fell Aufidius!

VOLUMNIA
       He'll beat Aufidius' head below his knee
       And tread upon his neck.

             Enter Valeria, with an Usher and a Gentlewoman.

VALERIA My ladies both, good day to you.

VOLUMNIA Sweet madam.

VIRGILIA I am glad to see your ladyship.

49   VALERIA How do you both? You are manifest house-
50   keepers. What are you sewing here? A fine spot, in good
       faith. How does your little son?

VIRGILIA I thank your ladyship; well, good madam.

VOLUMNIA He had rather see the swords and hear a drum
       than look upon his schoolmaster.

VALERIA O' my word, the father's son! I'll swear 'tis a   55
       very pretty boy. O' my troth, I looked upon him o'
       Wednesday half an hour together. 'Has such a con-   57
       firmed countenance! I saw him run after a gilded
       butterfly, and when he caught it, he let it go again, and
       after it again, and over and over he comes, and up
       again; catched it again; or whether his fall enraged him,
       or how 'twas, he did so set his teeth and tear it! O, I
       I warrant, how he mammocked it!   62

VOLUMNIA One on's father's moods.

VALERIA Indeed, la, 'tis a noble child.

VIRGILIA A crack, madam.   65

VALERIA Come, lay aside your stitchery. I must have you
       play the idle housewife with me this afternoon.

VIRGILIA No, good madam, I will not out of doors.

VALERIA Not out of doors?

VOLUMNIA She shall, she shall.

VIRGILIA Indeed, no, by your patience. I'll not over the
       threshold till my lord return from the wars.

VALERIA Fie, you confine yourself most unreasonably.
       Come, you must go visit the good lady that lies in.   74

VIRGILIA I will wish her speedy strength and visit her
       with my prayers, but I cannot go thither.

VOLUMNIA Why, I pray you?

VIRGILIA 'Tis not to save labor, nor that I want love.   78

VALERIA You would be another Penelope; yet they say   79
       all the yarn she spun in Ulysses' absence did but fill
       Ithaca full of moths. Come; I would your cambric were
       sensible as your finger, that you might leave pricking it 82
       for pity. Come, you shall go with us.

VIRGILIA No, good madam, pardon me; indeed I will
       not forth.

VALERIA In truth, la, go with me, and I'll tell you ex-
       cellent news of your husband.

VIRGILIA O, good madam, there can be none yet.

VALERIA Verily, I do not jest with you. There came news
       from him last night.

VIRGILIA Indeed, madam?

VALERIA In earnest, it's true; I heard a senator speak it.
       Thus it is: the Volsces have an army forth, against
       whom Cominius the general is gone, with one part of
       our Roman power. Your lord and Titus Lartius are set
       down before their city Corioles. They nothing doubt
       prevailing and to make it brief wars. This is true, on
       mine honor; and so, I pray, go with us.

VIRGILIA Give me excuse, good madam. I will obey you   99
       in everything hereafter.

VOLUMNIA Let her alone, lady. As she is now, she will
       but disease our better mirth.   102

I, iii Within the house of Marcius   2 *comfortable sort* cheerful manner   7
plucked all gaze attracted the attention of all   9 *from her beholding* out of
her sight   10 *person* body   14 *bound with oak* crowned for saving a Roman
citizen in battle   23 *surfeit* overindulge himself   25 *Beseech* I beseech
31 *got* begotten   34 *tasked* employed   35 *Or . . . or* either . . . or   38 *gilt
his trophy* gilding becomes his monument; *Hecuba* queen of Troy   39
Hector Trojan champion   41 *contemning* despising   43 *bless* protect
49–50 *manifest house-keepers* well known for staying at home   50 *spot* embroidered figure   55 *O'* on   57 *confirmed* resolute   62 *mammocked* tore to
pieces   65 *crack* imp   74 *lies in* expects a child   78 *want* am lacking in   79
Penelope faithful wife of Ulysses, who put off suitors by weaving   82 *sensible*
capable of sensation; *leave* stop   99 *Give me excuse* excuse me   102 *disease*
make uneasy; *better mirth* enjoyment which will be greater without her

VALERIA In troth, I think she would. Fare you well, then.
  Come, good sweet lady. Prithee, Virgilia, turn thy
  solemnness out o' door and go along with us.
VIRGILIA No, at a word, madam. Indeed, I must not. I
  wish you much mirth.
VALERIA Well, then, farewell.   *Exeunt.*

*

I, iv   *Enter Marcius, Titus Lartius, with Drum and
        Colors, with Captains and Soldiers, as before the city
        Corioles. To them a Messenger.*
MARCIUS
  Yonder comes news. A wager they have met.
LARTIUS
  My horse to yours, no.
MARCIUS   'Tis done.
LARTIUS   Agreed.
MARCIUS
  Say, has our general met the enemy?
MESSENGER
4 They lie in view, but have not spoke as yet.
LARTIUS |
  So, the good horse is mine.
MARCIUS   I'll buy him of you.
LARTIUS
  No, I'll nor sell nor give him. Lend you him I will
  For half a hundred years. Summon the town.
MARCIUS
  How far off lie these armies?
MESSENGER   Within this mile and half.
MARCIUS
9 Then shall we hear their 'larum, and they ours.
  Now, Mars, I prithee, make us quick in work,
  That we with smoking swords may march from hence,
12 To help our fielded friends! Come, blow thy blast.
        *They sound a parley.
        Enter two Senators, with others, on the walls of
        Corioles.*
  Tullus Aufidius, is he within your walls?
FIRST SENATOR
  No, nor a man that fears you less than he:
15 That's lesser than a little.
        Drum afar off.   Hark! our drums
  Are bringing forth our youth. We'll break our walls
17 Rather than they shall pound us up. Our gates,
  Which yet seem shut, we have but pinned with rushes;
  They'll open of themselves.
        Alarum afar off.   Hark you, far off!
  There is Aufidius. List what work he makes
21 Amongst your cloven army.
MARCIUS   O, they are at it!
LARTIUS
22 Their noise be our instruction. Ladders, ho!
        Enter the army of the Volsces.

I, iv Before the gates of Corioli   4 *spoke* encountered   9 *'larum* call to
arms   12 *fielded* in the battlefield   15 *lesser than a little* next to nothing
17 *pound* pen   21 *cloven* split   22 *our instruction* a lesson to us   25 *proof*
impenetrable   29 *edge* sword   38 *agued* trembling; *home* to the utmost
43 *ope* open; *seconds* supporters   44 *followers* pursuers   45 *fliers* pursued
47 *To th' pot* to destruction   53 *sensibly* feelingly; *senseless* insensate
57 *Cato* the Censor, exponent of Roman ethics   61 *feverous* feverish
62 *make remain alike* stay there similarly

MARCIUS
  They fear us not, but issue forth their city.
  Now put your shields before your hearts, and fight
  With hearts more proof than shields. Advance, brave   25
  Titus.
  They do disdain us much beyond our thoughts,
  Which makes me sweat with wrath. Come on, my
  fellows.
  He that retires, I'll take him for a Volsce,
  And he shall feel mine edge.   29
      *Alarum. The Romans are beat back to their trenches.
      Enter Marcius, cursing.*
MARCIUS
  All the contagion of the south light on you,
  You shames of Rome! you herd of – Boils and plagues
  Plaster you o'er, that you may be abhorred
  Farther than seen, and one infect another
  Against the wind a mile! You souls of geese,
  That bear the shapes of men, how have you run
  From slaves that apes would beat! Pluto and hell!
  All hurt behind! backs red, and faces pale
  With flight and agued fear! Mend and charge home,   38
  Or, by the fires of heaven, I'll leave the foe
  And make my wars on you! Look to't. Come on!
  If you'll stand fast, we'll beat them to their wives,
  As they us to our trenches. Follow me!
      *Another alarum and Marcius follows them to gates
      and is shut in.*
  So, now the gates are ope. Now prove good seconds.   43
  'Tis for the followers fortune widens them,   44
  Not for the fliers. Mark me, and do the like.   45
      Enter the gates.
FIRST SOLDIER
  Foolhardiness, not I.
SECOND SOLDIER   Nor I.
FIRST SOLDIER
  See, they have shut him in.
      Alarum continues.
ALL   To th' pot, I warrant him.   47
      Enter Titus Lartius.
LARTIUS
  What is become of Marcius?
ALL   Slain, sir, doubtless.
FIRST SOLDIER
  Following the fliers at the very heels,
  With them he enters, who upon the sudden
  Clapped to their gates; he is himself alone,
  To answer all the city.
LARTIUS   O noble fellow!
  Who sensibly outdares his senseless sword,   53
  And, when it bows, stand'st up. Thou art left, Marcius.
  A carbuncle entire, as big as thou art,
  Were not so rich a jewel. Thou wast a soldier
  Even to Cato's wish, not fierce and terrible   57
  Only in strokes; but with thy grim looks and
  The thunder-like percussion of thy sounds,
  Thou mad'st thine enemies shake, as if the world
  Were feverous and did tremble.   61
      Enter Marcius, bleeding, assaulted by the Enemy.
FIRST SOLDIER   Look, sir.
LARTIUS   O, 'tis Marcius!
  Let's fetch him off, or make remain alike.   62
      They fight, and all enter the City.

*

I, v   *Enter certain Romans, with spoils.*

FIRST ROMAN   This will I carry to Rome.

SECOND ROMAN   And I this.

3 THIRD ROMAN   A murrain on't! I took this for silver.
           Alarum continues still afar off.
           Enter Marcius and Titus Lartius, with a Trumpet.

MARCIUS

4   See here these movers that do prize their hours
5   At a cracked drachma! Cushions, leaden spoons,
6   Irons of a doit, doublets that hangmen would
    Bury with those that wore them, these base slaves,
    Ere yet the fight be done, pack up. Down with them!
    And hark, what noise the general makes! To him!
    There is the man of my soul's hate, Aufidius,
    Piercing our Romans. Then, valiant Titus, take
    Convenient numbers to make good the city;
    Whilst I, with those that have the spirit, will haste
    To help Cominius.

LARTIUS   Worthy sir, thou bleed'st.
    Thy exercise hath been too violent
16 For a second course of fight.

MARCIUS   Sir, praise me not.
    My work hath yet not warmed me. Fare you well.
18 The blood I drop is rather physical
    Than dangerous to me. To Aufidius thus
    I will appear and fight.

LARTIUS   Now the fair goddess Fortune
    Fall deep in love with thee, and her great charms
    Misguide thy opposers' swords! Bold gentleman,
    Prosperity be thy page!

MARCIUS   Thy friend no less
24 Than those she placeth highest. So, farewell.

LARTIUS
    Thou worthiest Marcius!   *[Exit Marcius.]*
    Go sound thy trumpet in the market-place.
    Call thither all the officers o' th' town,
    Where they shall know our mind. Away!   *Exeunt.*

                        *

I, vi   *Enter Cominius, as it were in retire, with Soldiers.*

COMINIUS
    Breathe you, my friends. Well fought! We are come off
    Like Romans, neither foolish in our stands
3   Nor cowardly in retire. Believe me, sirs,
    We shall be charged again. Whiles we have struck,
5   By interims and conveying gusts we have heard
    The charges of our friends. The Roman gods
7   Lead their successes as we wish our own,
    That both our powers, with smiling fronts encount'ring,
    May give you thankful sacrifice.
           Enter a Messenger.   Thy news?

MESSENGER
10 The citizens of Corioles have issued,
    And given to Lartius and to Marcius battle.
    I saw our party to their trenches driven,
    And then I came away.

COMINIUS   Though thou speakest truth,
    Methinks thou speak'st not well. How long is't since?

MESSENGER
    Above an hour, my lord.

COMINIUS
16 'Tis not a mile; briefly we heard their drums.
17 How couldst thou in a mile confound an hour,

And bring thy news so late?

MESSENGER   Spies of the Volsces
Held me in chase, that I was forced to wheel   19
Three or four miles about; else had I, sir,
Half an hour since brought my report.

COMINIUS   Who's yonder,
That does appear as he were flayed? O gods!
He has the stamp of Marcius, and I have
Beforetime seen him thus.   24
      Enter Marcius.

MARCIUS   Come I too late?

COMINIUS
The shepherd knows not thunder from a tabor   25
More than I know the sound of Marcius' tongue
From every meaner man.

MARCIUS   Come I too late?

COMINIUS
Ay, if you come not in the blood of others,
But mantled in your own.

MARCIUS   O, let me clip ye   29
In arms as sound as when I wooed, in heart
As merry as when our nuptial day was done,
And tapers burned to bedward!   32

COMINIUS   Flower of warriors!
How is't with Titus Lartius?

MARCIUS
As with a man busied about decrees:
Condemning some to death, and some to exile;
Ransoming him or pitying, threatening th' other;   36
Holding Corioles in the name of Rome,
Even like a fawning greyhound in the leash,
To let him slip at will.   39

COMINIUS   Where is that slave
Which told me they had beat you to your trenches?
Where is he? Call him hither.

MARCIUS   Let him alone.
He did inform the truth. But for our gentlemen,
The common file, — a plague! tribunes for them! —   43
The mouse ne'er shunned the cat as they did budge
From rascals worse than they.

COMINIUS   But how prevailed you?

MARCIUS
Will the time serve to tell? I do not think.
Where is the enemy? Are you lords o' th' field?
If not, why cease you till you are so?

COMINIUS   Marcius,
We have at disadvantage fought and did
Retire to win our purpose.

MARCIUS
How lies their battle? Know you on which side
They have placed their men of trust?

COMINIUS   As I guess, Marcius,
Their bands i' th' vaward are the Antiates,   53

I, v A street in Corioli 3 *murrain* cattle plague; **s.d.** *Trumpet* trumpeter
4 *movers* active men; *prize their hours* value their time 5 *drachma* Greek
coin 6 *of a doit* worth the smallest sum; *hangmen* (whose perquisites
included the clothes of the hanged) 16 *course* round; *praise* appraise
18 *physical* curative 24 *those* friend to those
I, vi An open place near the Roman camp 3 *retire* withdrawal 5 *conveying*
carrying the noise of battle 7 *successes* fortunes 10 *issued* sallied forth
16 *briefly* a short while ago 17 *confound* waste 19 *that* so that 24
Beforetime in former time 25 *tabor* small drum 29 *clip* embrace 32
tapers burned to bedward candles indicated bedtime 36 *Ransoming* releasing 39 *let him slip* unleash him 43 *common file* rank and file 53
vaward vanguard

Of their best trust; o'er them Aufidius,
Their very heart of hope.

MARCIUS   I do beseech you
By all the battles wherein we have fought,
By th' blood we have shed together, by th' vows
58   We have made to endure friends, that you directly
Set me against Aufidius and his Antiates;
And that you not delay the present, but,
Filling the air with swords advanced and darts,
62   We prove this very hour.

COMINIUS   Though I could wish
You were conducted to a gentle bath
And balms applied to you, yet dare I never
Deny your asking. Take your choice of those
That best can aid your action.

MARCIUS   Those are they
That most are willing. If any such be here –
As it were sin to doubt – that love this painting
69   Wherein you see me smeared; if any fear
Lesser his person than an ill report;
If any think brave death outweighs bad life,
And that his country's dearer than himself;
Let him alone, or so many so minded,
Wave thus, to express his disposition,
And follow Marcius.

     They all shout and wave their swords, take him up in
     their arms, and cast up their caps.

O, me alone! Make you a sword of me?
77   If these shows be not outward, which of you
But is four Volsces? None of you but is
Able to bear against the great Aufidius
A shield as hard as his. A certain number,
Though thanks to all, must I select. The rest
Shall bear the business in some other fight,
83   As cause will be obeyed. Please you to march;
And four shall quickly draw out my command,
Which men are best inclined.

COMINIUS   March on, my fellows.
86   Make good this ostentation, and you shall
Divide in all with us.   *Exeunt.*

        *

I, vii   *Titus Lartius, having set a guard upon Corioles,*
        going with Drum and Trumpet toward Cominius and
        Caius Marcius, enters with a Lieutenant, other
        Soldiers, and a Scout.

LARTIUS
1   So, let the ports be guarded. Keep your duties,
As I have set them down. If I do send, dispatch
3   Those centuries to our aid; the rest will serve
For a short holding. If we lose the field,
We cannot keep the town.

LIEUTENANT   Fear not our care, sir.   5
LARTIUS
Hence, and shut your gates upon's.
Our guider, come; to th' Roman camp conduct us.   7
                        Exeunt.

        *

    Alarum, as in battle. Enter Marcius and Aufidius at   I, viii
    several doors.

MARCIUS
I'll fight with none but thee, for I do hate thee
Worse than a promise-breaker.
AUFIDIUS   We hate alike.
Not Afric owns a serpent I abhor   3
More than thy fame and envy. Fix thy foot.   4
MARCIUS
Let the first budger die the other's slave,
And the gods doom him after!
AUFIDIUS   If I fly, Marcius,
Hollo me like a hare.   7
MARCIUS   Within these three hours, Tullus,
Alone I fought in your Corioles walls,
And made what work I pleased. 'Tis not my blood
Wherein thou seest me masked. For thy revenge
Wrench up thy power to th' highest.
AUFIDIUS   Wert thou the Hector
That was the whip of your bragged progeny,   12
Thou shouldst not scape me here.   13
    Here they fight, and certain Volsces come in the aid of
    Aufidius. Marcius fights till they be driven in
    breathless.
Officious and not valiant, you have shamed me   14
In your condemnèd seconds.   15
                   [Exeunt.]
    Flourish. Alarum. A retreat is sounded. Flourish.   I, ix
    Enter, at one door, Cominius, with the Romans; at
    another door, Marcius, with his arm in a scarf.
COMINIUS
If I should tell thee o'er this thy day's work,
Thou't not believe thy deeds. But I'll report it   2
Where senators shall mingle tears with smiles;
Where great patricians shall attend and shrug,
I' th' end admire; where ladies shall be frighted,
And, gladly quaked, hear more; where the dull tribunes,   6
That with the fusty plebeians hate thine honors,   7
Shall say against their hearts, 'We thank the gods
Our Rome hath such a soldier.'
Yet camest thou to a morsel of this feast,   10
Having fully dined before.
    Enter Titus [Lartius], with his Power, from the
    pursuit.
LARTIUS   O general,
Here is the steed, we the caparison.   12
Hadst thou beheld –
MARCIUS   Pray now, no more. My mother,
Who has a charter to extol her blood,   14
When she does praise me grieves me. I have done
As you have done – that's what I can; induced
As you have been – that's for my country.
He that has but effected his good will   18
Hath overta'en mine act.
COMINIUS   You shall not be   19
The grave of your deserving. Rome must know
The value of her own. 'Twere a concealment

---

58 *endure* remain   62 *prove* test   69–70 *fear Lesser* fear less for   77 *shows* gestures   83 *cause will be obeyed* circumstances require   86 *ostentation* showing
I, vii Before the gates of Corioli   1 *ports* gates   3 *centuries* companies of a hundred   5 *Fear not* do not worry about   7 *guider* guide
I, viii An open place near the Roman camp   s.d. *at several doors* from different entrances   3 *Afric* Africa   4 *fame and envy* enviable fame   7 *Hollo* hunt down   12 *whip* champion; *bragged progeny* boasted progenitors   13 *scape* escape   14 *Officious* meddling   15 *condemnèd seconds* ineffectual aid
I, ix   2 *Thou't* thou wouldst   6 *quaked* made to tremble   7 *fusty* mouldy; *plebeians* lowest class   10 *of* in   12 *caparison* trappings   14 *charter* privilege   18 *effected his good will* accomplished his intention   19–20 *You . . . deserving* you shall not bury your merit

22 Worse than a theft, no less than a traducement,
    To hide your doings and to silence that
24 Which, to the spire and top of praises vouched,
25 Would seem but modest. Therefore, I beseech you –
26 In sign of what you are, not to reward
    What you have done – before our army hear me.

MARCIUS
    I have some wounds upon me, and they smart
    To hear themselves rememb'red.

COMINIUS   Should they not,
30 Well might they fester 'gainst ingratitude
31 And tent themselves with death. Of all the horses,
32 Whereof we have ta'en good and good store, of all
    The treasure in this field achieved and city,
    We render you the tenth, to be ta'en forth
    Before the common distribution at
    Your only choice.

MARCIUS   I thank you, general,
    But cannot make my heart consent to take
    A bribe to pay my sword. I do refuse it,
    And stand upon my common part with those
    That have beheld the doing.

A long flourish. They all cry, 'Marcius! Marcius!',
cast up their caps and lances. Cominius and Lartius
stand bare.

MARCIUS
    May these same instruments which you profane
    Never sound more! When drums and trumpets shall
    I' th' field prove flatterers, let courts and cities be
44 Made all of false-faced soothing! When steel grows
45 Soft as the parasite's silk, let him be made
46 A coverture for th' wars. No more, I say!
    For that I have not washed my nose that bled,
48 Or foiled some debile wretch, which without note
    Here's many else have done, you shout me forth
    In acclamations hyperbolical,
51 As if I loved my little should be dieted
    In praises sauced with lies.

COMINIUS   Too modest are you,
    More cruel to your good report than grateful
54 To us that give you truly. By your patience,
    If 'gainst yourself you be incensed, we'll put you,
56 Like one that means his proper harm, in manacles,
    Then reason safely with you. Therefore be it known,
    As to us, to all the world, that Caius Marcius
    Wears this war's garland; in token of the which,
    My noble steed, known to the camp, I give him,
61 With all his trim belonging; and from this time,
    For what he did before Corioles, call him,
    With all th' applause and clamor of the host,
    Caius Marcius Coriolanus. Bear
65 Th' addition nobly ever!
Flourish. Trumpets sound, and drums.

ALL
    Caius Marcius Coriolanus!

CORIOLANUS
    I will go wash;
    And when my face is fair, you shall perceive
    Whether I blush or no. Howbeit, I thank you.
    I mean to stride your steed, and at all times
71 To undercrest your good addition
72 To th' fairness of my power.

COMINIUS   So, to our tent,
    Where, ere we do repose us, we will write

To Rome of our success. You, Titus Lartius,
Must to Corioles back. Send us to Rome
The best, with whom we may articulate,   76
For their own good and ours.

LARTIUS   I shall, my lord.

CORIOLANUS
The gods begin to mock me. I, that now
Refused most princely gifts, am bound to beg
Of my lord general.

COMINIUS   Take't, 'tis yours. What is't?

CORIOLANUS
I sometime lay here in Corioles   81
At a poor man's house; he used me kindly.   82
He cried to me; I saw him prisoner;   83
But then Aufidius was within my view,
And wrath o'erwhelmed my pity. I request you
To give my poor host freedom.

COMINIUS   O, well begged!
Were he the butcher of my son, he should
Be free as is the wind. Deliver him, Titus.

LARTIUS
Marcius, his name?

CORIOLANUS   By Jupiter, forgot!
I am weary; yea, my memory is tired.
Have we no wine here?

COMINIUS   Go we to our tent.
The blood upon your visage dries; 'tis time
It should be looked to. Come.   *Exeunt.*

*

A flourish. Cornets. Enter Tullus Aufidius, bloody,   I, x
with two or three Soldiers.

AUFIDIUS
The town is ta'en.

FIRST SOLDIER
'Twill be delivered back on good condition.   2

AUFIDIUS
Condition?
I would I were a Roman; for I cannot,
Being a Volsce, be that I am. Condition?
What good condition can a treaty find
I' th' part that is at mercy? Five times, Marcius,   7
I have fought with thee; so often hast thou beat me,
And wouldst do so, I think, should we encounter
As often as we eat. By th' elements,
If e'er again I meet him beard to beard,
He's mine or I am his. Mine emulation   12
Hath not that honor in't it had; for where
I thought to crush him in an equal force,
True sword to sword, I'll potch at him some way;   15
Or wrath or craft may get him.

22 *traducement* slander 24 *vouched* attested 25 *modest* moderate 26 *sign* token 30 *'gainst* exposed to 31 *tent* cure by probing 32 *good and good store* good in quality and quantity 44 *false-faced soothing* hypocritical flattery 45 *him* i.e. the silk 46 *coverture* covering 48 *foiled* have defeated; *debile* weak; *without note* unnoticed 51 *little* small share; *dieted* fed 54 *give* represent 56 *means* intends; *proper* own 61 *trim belonging* appertaining equipment 65 *addition* title 71 *undercrest* adopt and justify (heraldic) 72 *To . . . power* as fairly as I can 76 *articulate* come to terms 81 *sometime lay* once lodged 82 *used* treated 83 *cried* cried out
I, x The camp of the Volsces 2 *good condition* favorable terms 7 *I' th' part* for the side; *at mercy* in the victor's power 12 *emulation* rivalry 15 *potch* make a stab

FIRST SOLDIER   He's the devil.

AUFIDIUS

Bolder, though not so subtle. My valor 's poisoned
With only suffering stain by him; for him
19 Shall fly out of itself. Nor sleep nor sanctuary,
20 Being naked, sick, nor fane nor capitol,
The prayers of priests nor times of sacrifice,
22 Embargements all of fury, shall lift up
Their rotten privilege and custom 'gainst
My hate to Marcius. Where I find him, were it
25 At home, upon my brother's guard, even there,
26 Against the hospitable canon, would I
Wash my fierce hand in's heart. Go you to th' city.
Learn how 'tis held, and what they are that must
Be hostages for Rome.

FIRST SOLDIER   Will not you go?

AUFIDIUS

I am attended at the cypress grove: I pray you –
'Tis south the city mills – bring me word thither
How the world goes, that to the pace of it
I may spur on my journey.

FIRST SOLDIER   I shall, sir.   *[Exeunt.]*

*

II, i   *Enter Menenius, with the two Tribunes of the People,*
Sicinius and Brutus.

1 MENENIUS The augurer tells me we shall have news to-
night.

BRUTUS Good or bad?

MENENIUS Not according to the prayer of the people, for
they love not Marcius.

SICINIUS Nature teaches beasts to know their friends.

MENENIUS Pray you, who does the wolf love?

SICINIUS The lamb.

MENENIUS Ay, to devour him, as the hungry plebeians
would the noble Marcius.

BRUTUS He's a lamb indeed, that baas like a bear.

MENENIUS He's a bear indeed, that lives like a lamb. You
two are old men: tell me one thing that I shall ask you.

BOTH Well, sir.

14 MENENIUS In what enormity is Marcius poor in, that you
two have not in abundance?

BRUTUS He's poor in no one fault, but stored with all.

SICINIUS Especially in pride.

BRUTUS And topping all others in boasting.

MENENIUS This is strange now. Do you two know how
20 you are censured here in the city, I mean of us o' th'
21 right-hand file? Do you?

BOTH Why, how are we censured?

MENENIUS Because you talk of pride now – will you not
be angry?

BOTH Well, well, sir, well.

MENENIUS Why, 'tis no great matter; for a very little 26
thief of occasion will rob you of a great deal of patience.
Give your dispositions the reins and be angry at your
pleasures – at the least, if you take it as a pleasure to you
in being so. You blame Marcius for being proud?

BRUTUS We do it not alone, sir.

MENENIUS I know you can do very little alone; for your
helps are many, or else your actions would grow wondrous single. Your abilities are too infant-like for doing 33
much alone. You talk of pride: O that you could turn
your eyes toward the napes of your necks, and make but
an interior survey of your good selves! O that you could!

BRUTUS What then, sir?

MENENIUS Why, then you should discover a brace of un-
meriting, proud, violent, testy magistrates, alias fools,
as any in Rome.

SICINIUS Menenius, you are known well enough too.

MENENIUS I am known to be a humorous patrician, and 43
one that loves a cup of hot wine with not a drop of allay- 44
ing Tiber in't; said to be something imperfect in favor- 45
ing the first complaint; hasty and tinder-like upon too
trivial motion; one that converses more with the buttock 47
of the night than with the forehead of the morning.
What I think, I utter, and spend my malice in my
breath. Meeting two such wealsmen as you are, – I can- 50
not call you Lycurguses – if the drink you give me touch 51
my palate adversely, I make a crooked face at it. I cannot
say your worships have delivered the matter well, when
I find the ass in compound with the major part of your 54
syllables; and though I must be content to bear with
those that say you are reverend grave men, yet they lie
deadly that tell you you have good faces. If you see this
in the map of my microcosm, follows it that I am known 58
well enough too? What harm can your bisson conspec- 59
tuities glean out of this character, if I be known well
enough too?

BRUTUS Come, sir, come, we know you well enough.

MENENIUS You know neither me, yourselves, nor anything. You are ambitious for poor knaves' caps and legs. 63
You wear out a good wholesome forenoon in hearing a
cause between an orange-wife and a forset-seller, and 65
then rejourn the controversy of threepence to a second 66
day of audience. When you are hearing a matter between party and party, if you chance to be pinched with
the colic, you make faces like mummers; set up the 69
bloody flag against all patience; and, in roaring for a
chamber-pot, dismiss the controversy bleeding, the 71
more entangled by your hearing. All the peace you
make in their cause is, calling both the parties knaves.
You are a pair of strange ones.

BRUTUS Come, come, you are well understood to be a 74
perfecter giber for the table than a necessary bencher in
the Capitol.

MENENIUS Our very priests must become mockers, if
they shall encounter such ridiculous subjects as you are.
When you speak best unto the purpose, it is not worth
the wagging of your beards; and your beards deserve
not so honorable a grave as to stuff a botcher's cushion 81
or to be entombed in an ass's pack-saddle. Yet you
must be saying Marcius is proud; who, in a cheap estimation, is worth all your predecessors since Deucalion, 84

though peradventure some of the best of 'em were hereditary hangmen. Good-e'en to your worships.

87 More of your conversation would infect my brain, being the herdsmen of the beastly plebeians. I will be bold to take my leave of you.

Brutus and Sicinius aside.
Enter Volumnia, Virgilia, and Valeria.

How now, my as fair as noble ladies, – and the moon, were she earthly, no nobler – whither do you follow your eyes so fast?

VOLUMNIA Honorable Menenius, my boy Marcius approaches. For the love of Juno, let's go.

MENENIUS Ha? Marcius coming home?

VOLUMNIA Ay, worthy Menenius, and with most prosperous approbation.

97 MENENIUS Take my cap, Jupiter, and I thank thee. Hoo! Marcius coming home!

TWO LADIES Nay, 'tis true.

VOLUMNIA Look, here's a letter from him. The state hath another, his wife another; and, I think, there's one at home for you.

MENENIUS I will make my very house reel to-night. A letter for me!

VIRGILIA Yes, certain, there's a letter for you; I saw't.

MENENIUS A letter for me! It gives me an estate of seven
107 years' health, in which time I will make a lip at the
108 physician. The most sovereign prescription in Galen is
109 but empiricutic and, to this preservative, of no better
110 report than a horse-drench. Is he not wounded? He was wont to come home wounded.

VIRGILIA O, no, no, no.

VOLUMNIA O, he is wounded; I thank the gods for't.

114 MENENIUS So do I too, if it be not too much. Brings 'a victory in his pocket? The wounds become him.

VOLUMNIA On's brows. Menenius, he comes the third time home with the oaken garland.

MENENIUS Has he disciplined Aufidius soundly?

VOLUMNIA Titus Lartius writes they fought together, but Aufidius got off.

MENENIUS And 'twas time for him too, I'll warrant him that. An he had stayed by him, I would not have been so
123 fidiused for all the chests in Corioles and the gold that's
124 in them. Is the Senate possessed of this?

VOLUMNIA Good ladies, let's go. Yes, yes, yes! The Senate has letters from the general, wherein he gives my
127 son the whole name of the war. He hath in this action outdone his former deeds doubly.

129 VALERIA In troth, there's wondrous things spoke of him.

MENENIUS Wondrous? Ay, I warrant you, and not with-
131 out his true purchasing.

VIRGILIA The gods grant them true!

133 VOLUMNIA True? pow waw!

MENENIUS True? I'll be sworn they are true. Where is he wounded? *[to the Tribunes]* God save your good worships! Marcius is coming home. He has more cause to be proud. – Where is he wounded?

VOLUMNIA I' th' shoulder and i' th' left arm. There will be
139 large cicatrices to show the people, when he shall stand
140 for his place. He received in the repulse of Tarquin seven hurts i' th' body.

MENENIUS One i' th' neck and two i' th' thigh – there's nine that I know.

VOLUMNIA He had, before this last expedition, twenty-five wounds upon him.

MENENIUS Now it's twenty-seven. Every gash was an enemy's grave. *(A shout and flourish.)* Hark! the trumpets.

VOLUMNIA These are the ushers of Marcius. Before him he carries noise, and behind him he leaves tears.
Death, that dark spirit, in's nervy arm doth lie; 150
Which, being advanced, declines, and then men die. 151

A sennet. Trumpets sound. Enter Cominius the General and Titus Lartius; between them, Coriolanus, crowned with an oaken garland; with Captains and Soldiers and a Herald.

HERALD
Know, Rome, that all alone Marcius did fight
Within Corioles gates, where he hath won,
With fame, a name to Caius Marcius. These 154
In honor follows Coriolanus.
Welcome to Rome, renownèd Coriolanus!
Sound. Flourish.

ALL
Welcome to Rome, renownèd Coriolanus!

CORIOLANUS
No more of this; it does offend my heart.
Pray now, no more.

COMINIUS   Look, sir, your mother!

CORIOLANUS   O,
You have, I know, petitioned all the gods
For my prosperity!
Kneels.

VOLUMNIA   Nay, my good soldier, up.
My gentle Marcius, worthy Caius, and
By deed-achieving honor newly named – 163
What is it? – Coriolanus must I call thee? –
But, O, thy wife!

CORIOLANUS   My gracious silence, hail!
Wouldst thou have laughed had I come coffined home,
That weep'st to see me triumph? Ah, my dear,
Such eyes the widows in Corioles wear,
And mothers that lack sons.

MENENIUS   Now, the gods crown thee!

CORIOLANUS
And live you yet? *[to Valeria]* O my sweet lady, pardon.

VOLUMNIA
I know not where to turn. O, welcome home!
And welcome, General! and y' are welcome all!

MENENIUS
A hundred thousand welcomes! I could weep
And I could laugh; I am light and heavy. Welcome. 174
A curse begin at very root on's heart 175
That is not glad to see thee! You are three
That Rome should dote on; yet, by the faith of men,
We have some old crab-trees here at home that will not
Be grafted to your relish. Yet welcome, warriors! 179
We call a nettle but a nettle and
The faults of fools but folly.

87 *being* since you are 97 *Take . . . Jupiter* I throw my cap in the air 107 *make a lip at* mock 108 *sovereign* efficacious; *Galen* Greek medical authority 109 *empiricutic* quackish; *to* compared to 110 *drench* dose 114 *'a* he (familiar) 123 *fidiused* treated like Aufidius 124 *possessed* fully informed 127 *name* credit 129 *troth* truth 131 *purchasing* winning 133 *pow waw* pooh 139 *cicatrices* scars; *stand* be a candidate 140 *Tarquin* deposed Roman tyrant 150 *nervy* sinewy 151 *declines* sinks down; s.d. *sennet* trumpet signal 154 *With* along with; *to* in addition to 163 *deed-achieving* achieved by deeds 174 *light* joyful; *heavy* sad 175 *begin at* penetrate to; *on's* of his 179 *grafted to your relish* implanted with a liking for you

COMINIUS   Ever right.
CORIOLANUS
182   Menenius, ever, ever.
HERALD
       Give way there, and go on!
CORIOLANUS [to Volumnia and Virgilia]
                              Your hand, and yours.
       Ere in our own house I do shade my head,
       The good patricians must be visited;
       From whom I have received not only greetings,
187   But with them change of honors.
VOLUMNIA   I have lived
188   To see inherited my very wishes
       And the buildings of my fancy. Only
       There's one thing wanting, which I doubt not but
       Our Rome will cast upon thee.
CORIOLANUS   Know, good mother,
       I had rather be their servant in my way,
193   Than sway with them in theirs.
COMINIUS   On, to the Capitol!
       Flourish. Cornets. Exeunt in state, as before. Brutus
       and Sicinius [come forward].
BRUTUS
194   All tongues speak of him, and the blearèd sights
       Are spectacled to see him. Your prattling nurse
196   Into a rapture lets her baby cry,
197   While she chats him; the kitchen malkin pins
198   Her richest lockram 'bout her reechy neck,
199   Clamb'ring the walls to eye him. Stalls, bulks, windows
200   Are smothered up, leads filled, and ridges horsed
201   With variable complexions, all agreeing
202   In earnestness to see him. Seld-shown flamens
       Do press among the popular throngs, and puff
204   To win a vulgar station. Our veiled dames
205   Commit the war of white and damask in
206   Their nicely-gawded cheeks to th' wanton spoil
207   Of Phoebus' burning kisses – such a pother
       As if that whatsoever god who leads him
       Were slily crept into his human powers
       And gave him graceful posture.
SICINIUS   On the sudden,
211   I warrant him consul.
BRUTUS   Then our office may,
       During his power, go sleep.
SICINIUS
       He cannot temp'rately transport his honors
214   From where he should begin and end, but will
       Lose those he hath won.
BRUTUS   In that there's comfort.
SICINIUS   Doubt not

The commoners, for whom we stand, but they
Upon their ancient malice will forget   217
With the least cause these his new honors, which
That he will give them make I as little question
As he is proud to do't.   220
BRUTUS   I heard him swear,
Were he to stand for consul, never would he
Appear i' th' market-place nor on him put
The napless vesture of humility;   223
Nor, showing, as the manner is, his wounds
To th' people, beg their stinking breaths.
SICINIUS   'Tis right.
BRUTUS
It was his word: O, he would miss it rather
Than carry it but by the suit of the gentry to him   227
And the desire of the nobles.
SICINIUS   I wish no better
Than have him hold that purpose and to put it
In execution.
BRUTUS   'Tis most like he will.   230
SICINIUS
It shall be to him then as our good wills,   231
A sure destruction.
BRUTUS   So it must fall out
To him or our authorities for an end.
We must suggest the people in what hatred   234
He still hath held them; that to's power he would
Have made them mules, silenced their pleaders, and
Dispropertied their freedoms, holding them,   237
In human action and capacity,
Of no more soul nor fitness for the world
Than camels in their war, who have their provand   240
Only for bearing burthens, and sore blows   241
For sinking under them.
SICINIUS   This, as you say, suggested
At some time when his soaring insolence
Shall touch the people – which time shall not want,   244
If he be put upon't, and that's as easy   245
As to set dogs on sheep – will be his fire
To kindle their dry stubble; and their blaze
Shall darken him for ever.
       Enter a Messenger.
BRUTUS   What's the matter?
MESSENGER
You are sent for to th' Capitol. 'Tis thought
That Marcius shall be consul.
I have seen the dumb men throng to see him, and
The blind to hear him speak. Matrons flung gloves,
Ladies and maids their scarfs and handkerchers,
Upon him as he passed. The nobles bended,
As to Jove's statue, and the commons made
A shower and thunder with their caps and shouts.
I never saw the like.
BRUTUS   Let's to the Capitol,
And carry with us ears and eyes for th' time,   258
But hearts for the event.   259
SICINIUS   Have with you.   Exeunt.

*

Enter two Officers, to lay cushions, as it were in the   II, ii
Capitol.
FIRST OFFICER Come, come, they are almost here. How
many stand for consulships?

182 ever still the same   187 change of honors promotion   188 inherited realized   193 sway rule   194 sights eyesights   196 rapture fit   197 chats gossips about; malkin slattern   198 lockram coarse linen; reechy grimy   199 bulks shop-fronts   200 leads leaden roofs; ridges horsed roof-tops bestridden   201 variable complexions different types   202 Seld-shown flamens priests who rarely appear   204 vulgar station place in the crowd   205 damask red   206 nicely-gawded daintily adorned   207 Phoebus the sun; pother turmoil   211 consul one of Rome's two chief magistrates   214 and end to where he should end   217 Upon . . . malice because of their longstanding hostility   220 As as that   223 napless threadbare   227 carry win   230 like likely   231 good wills advantage requires   234 suggest insinuate to   237 Dispropertied dispossessed   240 provand provender   241 burthens burdens   244 which . . . want and that time will come   245 put upon't provoked   258 time situation   259 event outcome
II, ii The Roman senate house in the Capitol   s.d. cushions used on stage for seats

3 SECOND OFFICER Three, they say; but 'tis thought of every one Coriolanus will carry it.

5 FIRST OFFICER That's a brave fellow; but he's vengeance proud, and loves not the common people.

SECOND OFFICER Faith, there hath been many great men that have flattered the people, who ne'er loved them; and there be many that they have loved, they know not wherefore; so that, if they love they know not why, they hate upon no better a ground. Therefore, for Coriolanus neither to care whether they love or hate

13 him manifests the true knowledge he has in their dis-
14 position, and out of his noble carelessness lets them plainly see't.

FIRST OFFICER If he did not care whether he had their
16 love or no, he waved indifferently 'twixt doing them neither good nor harm; but he seeks their hate with greater devotion than they can render it him, and leaves
19 nothing undone that may fully discover him their
20 opposite. Now to seem to affect the malice and displeasure of the people is as bad as that which he dislikes – to flatter them for their love.

SECOND OFFICER He hath deserved worthily of his country; and his ascent is not by such easy degrees as those who, having been supple and courteous to the
26 people, bonneted, without any further deed to have them at all into their estimation and report. But he hath so planted his honors in their eyes and his actions in their hearts for their tongues to be silent and not confess so much were a kind of ingrateful injury; to report otherwise were a malice that, giving itself the lie, would pluck reproof and rebuke from every ear that heard it.

FIRST OFFICER No more of him; he's a worthy man.
34 Make way, they are coming.

A sennet. Enter the Patricians and the Tribunes of the People, Lictors before them : Coriolanus, Menenius, Cominius the Consul. Sicinius and Brutus take their places by themselves. Coriolanus stands.

MENENIUS
35 Having determined of the Volsces and
To send for Titus Lartius, it remains,
37 As the main point of this our after-meeting,
38 To gratify his noble service that
Hath thus stood for his country. Therefore, please you,
Most reverend and grave elders, to desire
The present consul, and last general
42 In our well-found successes, to report
A little of that worthy work performed
By Caius Marcius Coriolanus, whom
We met here both to thank and to remember
With honors like himself.

FIRST SENATOR   Speak, good Cominius.
Leave nothing out for length, and make us think
48 Rather our state 's defective for requital
49 Than we to stretch it out.
           [To the Tribunes]   Masters o' th' people,
We do request your kindest ears, and after,
51 Your loving motion toward the common body
52 To yield what passes here.

SICINIUS   We are convented
53 Upon a pleasing treaty, and have hearts
Inclinable to honor and advance
The theme of our assembly.

BRUTUS   Which the rather   55
We shall be blest to do, if he remember   56
A kinder value of the people than
He hath hereto prized them at.

MENENIUS   That's off, that's off!   58
I would you rather had been silent. Please you
To hear Cominius speak ?

BRUTUS   Most willingly ;
But yet my caution was more pertinent
Than the rebuke you give it.

MENENIUS   He loves your people ;
But tie him not to be their bedfellow.
Worthy Cominius, speak.
       Coriolanus rises, and offers to go away.
                          Nay, keep your place.

FIRST SENATOR
Sit, Coriolanus. Never shame to hear
What you have nobly done.

CORIOLANUS   Your honors' pardon.
I had rather have my wounds to heal again
Than hear say how I got them.

BRUTUS   Sir, I hope
My words disbenched you not.   69

CORIOLANUS   No, sir. Yet oft,
When blows have made me stay, I fled from words.
You soothed not, therefore hurt not : but your people,   71
I love them as they weigh –

MENENIUS   Pray now, sit down.

CORIOLANUS
I had rather have one scratch my head i' th' sun   73
When the alarum were struck than idly sit
To hear my nothings monstered.   *Exit Coriolanus.* 75

MENENIUS   Masters of the people,
Your multiplying spawn how can he flatter –
That's thousand to one good one – when you now see
He'd rather venture all his limbs for honor
Than one on's ears to hear it ? Proceed, Cominius.   79

COMINIUS
I shall lack voice. The deeds of Coriolanus
Should not be uttered feebly. It is held
That valor is the chiefest virtue, and
Most dignifies the haver. If it be,
The man I speak of cannot in the world
Be singly counterpoised. At sixteen years,   85
When Tarquin made a head for Rome, he fought   86
Beyond the mark of others. Our then dictator,   87
Whom with all praise I point at, saw him fight,
When with his Amazonian chin he drove   89
The bristled lips before him ; he bestrid   90
An o'erpressed Roman and i' th' consul's view   91

3 *of* by   5 *vengeance* terribly   13 *in* of   14 *carelessness* indifference   16 *waved* wavered   19–20 *discover . . . opposite* show that he is opposed to them   20 *affect* cultivate   26–27 *bonneted . . . report* did nothing but doff their hats to attain popularity   34 s.d. *Lictors* magistrates' attendants   35 *of* concerning   37 *after-meeting* later meeting   38 *gratify* requite   42 *well-found* fortunately encountered   48 *defective for requital* unable to reward adequately   49 *stretch it out* extend it   51 *Your . . . body* your kind mediation with the people   52 *yield* grant; *convented* summoned   53 *Upon* to consider   55 *rather* sooner   56 *blest* happy   58 *off* beside the point   69 *disbenched you* made you get up   71 *soothed* flattered   73–74 *have . . . struck* be idle during battle   75 *monstered* made marvels of   79 *Than . . . hear it* than venture one of his ears to hear about it   85 *singly counterpoised* equalled by another individual   86 *made . . . for* raised an army to reconquer   87 *dictator* wartime leader   89 *Amazonian* unbearded (like a female warrior)   90 *bestrid* protected   91 *o'erpressed* overwhelmed

Slew three opposers ; Tarquin's self he met,
93 And struck him on his knee. In that day's feats,
When he might act the woman in the scene,
He proved best man i' th' field, and for his meed
Was brow-bound with the oak. His pupil age
97 Man-entered thus, he waxèd like a sea,
And in the brunt of seventeen battles since
99 He lurched all swords of the garland. For this last,
Before and in Corioles, let me say,
101 I cannot speak him home. He stopped the fliers,
And by his rare example made the coward
Turn terror into sport. As weeds before
A vessel under sail, so men obeyed
105 And fell below his stem ; his sword, death's stamp,
Where it did mark, it took. From face to foot
He was a thing of blood, whose every motion
108 Was timed with dying cries. Alone he entered
109 The mortal gate of th' city, which he painted
110 With shunless destiny ; aidless came off,
And with a sudden reinforcement struck
Corioles like a planet. Now all's his,
113 When by and by the din of war gan pierce
114 His ready sense ; then straight his doubled spirit
115 Requickened what in flesh was fatigate,
And to the battle came he ; where he did
117 Run reeking o'er the lives of men, as if
'Twere a perpetual spoil, and till we called
119 Both field and city ours, he never stood
To ease his breast with panting.
MENENIUS   Worthy man !
FIRST SENATOR
121 He cannot but with measure fit the honors
Which we devise him.
COMINIUS   Our spoils he kicked at,
And looked upon things precious as they were
The common muck of the world. He covets less
125 Than misery itself would give ; rewards
His deeds with doing them ; and is content
127 To spend the time to end it.
MENENIUS   He's right noble.
Let him be called for.
FIRST SENATOR   Call Coriolanus.
OFFICER
He doth appear.
      Enter Coriolanus.
MENENIUS
The Senate, Coriolanus, are well pleased
To make thee consul.
CORIOLANUS   I do owe them still
My life and services.
MENENIUS   It then remains
That you do speak to the people.

CORIOLANUS   I do beseech you,
Let me o'erleap that custom ; for I cannot
Put on the gown, stand naked, and entreat them   135
For my wounds' sake to give their suffrage. Please you
That I may pass this doing.
SICINIUS   Sir, the people
Must have their voices ; neither will they bate   138
One jot of ceremony.
MENENIUS   Put them not to 't.
Pray you, go fit you to the custom and
Take to you, as your predecessors have,
Your honor with your form.   142
CORIOLANUS   It is a part
That I shall blush in acting, and might well
Be taken from the people.
BRUTUS *[to Sicinius]*   Mark you that ?
CORIOLANUS
To brag unto them, 'Thus I did, and thus !'
Show them th' unaching scars which I should hide,
As if I had received them for the hire
Of their breath only !
MENENIUS   Do not stand upon 't.   148
We recommend to you, tribunes of the people,
Our purpose to them ; and to our noble consul
Wish we all joy and honor.
SENATORS
To Coriolanus come all joy and honor !
       Flourish. Cornets. Then exeunt.
       Manent Sicinius and Brutus.
BRUTUS
You see how he intends to use the people.
SICINIUS
May they perceive's intent ! He will require them   154
As if he did contemn what he requested   155
Should be in them to give.   156
BRUTUS   Come, we'll inform them
Of our proceedings here. On th' market-place   157
I know they do attend us.   *[Exeunt.]*

                  *

      Enter seven or eight Citizens.   II, iii
FIRST CITIZEN Once if he do require our voices, we
ought not to deny him.
SECOND CITIZEN We may, sir, if we will.
THIRD CITIZEN We have power in ourselves to do it, but   4
it is a power that we have no power to do ; for if he show   5
us his wounds and tell us his deeds, we are to put our
tongues into those wounds and speak for them. So, if he
tell us his noble deeds, we must also tell him our noble
acceptance of them. Ingratitude is monstrous ; and for
the multitude to be ingrateful were to make a monster
of the multitude ; of the which we being members,
should bring ourselves to be monstrous members.
FIRST CITIZEN And to make us no better thought of, a   13
little help will serve ; for once we stood up about the corn,   14
he himself stuck not to call us the many-headed multi-   15
tude.
THIRD CITIZEN We have been called so of many ; not   16
that our heads are some brown, some black, some abram,   17
some bald, but that our wits are so diversely colored ;
and truly I think if all our wits were to issue out of one
skull, they would fly east, west, north, south, and their

---

93 *on* to 97 *Man-entered* initiated into manhood ; *waxèd* grew 99
lurched robbed 101 *home* sufficiently 105 *stem* bow 108 *timed* rhyth-
mically accompanied 109 *mortal* fatal 110 *shunless* inevitable 113 *gan*
began to 114 *ready* alert ; *doubled* strengthened 115 *fatigate* weary 117
reeking steaming 119 *stood* stopped 121 *with measure* in proportion
125 *misery* poverty 127 *spend* . . . *it* pass his time in killing time 135
naked exposed 138 *voices* votes ; *bate* abate 142 *form* formality 148
stand insist 154 *require* ask 155 *contemn* despise 156 *Should* . . . *give*
that they should be willing to give 157 *market-place* the Forum
II, iii The Roman Forum 4 *power* authority 5 *no power* no right 13-14
a little . . . *serve* not much is needed 14 *once* when 15 *stuck not* did not
hesitate 16 *of* by 17 *abram* auburn

21 consent of one direct way should be at once to all the points o' th' compass.

SECOND CITIZEN Think you so? Which way do you judge my wit would fly?

THIRD CITIZEN Nay, your wit will not so soon out as another man's will; 'tis strongly wedged up in a block-head; but if it were at liberty, 'twould, sure, southward.

SECOND CITIZEN Why that way?

THIRD CITIZEN To lose itself in a fog; where being three
30 parts melted away with rotten dews, the fourth would return for conscience sake, to help to get thee a wife.

SECOND CITIZEN You are never without your tricks.
33 You may, you may!

THIRD CITIZEN Are you all resolved to give your voices?
35 But that's no matter, the greater part carries it. I say, if he would incline to the people, there was never a worthier man.

Enter Coriolanus in a gown of humility, with Menenius.

Here he comes, and in the gown of humility. Mark his behavior. We are not to stay all together, but to come by him where he stands, by ones, by twos, and by threes.
41 He's to make his requests by particulars; wherein every one of us has a single honor, in giving him our own voices with our own tongues. Therefore follow me, and I'll direct you how you shall go by him.

ALL Content, content. *[Exeunt Citizens.]*

MENENIUS
O sir, you are not right. Have you not known
The worthiest men have done't?

CORIOLANUS   What must I say?
'I pray, sir'–Plague upon't! I cannot bring
My tongue to such a pace. 'Look, sir, my wounds!
I got them in my country's service, when
Some certain of your brethren roared and ran
From th' noise of our own drums.'

MENENIUS   O me, the gods!
You must not speak of that. You must desire them
To think upon you.

CORIOLANUS   Think upon me? Hang 'em!
I would they would forget me, like the virtues
56 Which our divines lose by 'em.

MENENIUS   You'll mar all.
I'll leave you. Pray you, speak to 'em, I pray you,
58 In wholesome manner.   *Exit.*

CORIOLANUS   Bid them wash their faces
And keep their teeth clean.

Enter three of the Citizens.

59   So, here comes a brace.
You know the cause, sir, of my standing here.

THIRD CITIZEN We do, sir. Tell us what hath brought you to't.

CORIOLANUS Mine own desert.

SECOND CITIZEN Your own desert?

CORIOLANUS Ay, not mine own desire.

THIRD CITIZEN How not your own desire?

CORIOLANUS No, sir, 'twas never my desire yet to trouble the poor with begging.

THIRD CITIZEN You must think, if we give you any-thing, we hope to gain by you.

CORIOLANUS Well then, I pray, your price o' th' consul-ship?

FIRST CITIZEN The price is to ask it kindly.

CORIOLANUS Kindly, sir, I pray, let me ha't. I have wounds to show you, which shall be yours in private. 74 Your good voice, sir. What say you?

SECOND CITIZEN You shall ha't, worthy sir.

CORIOLANUS A match, sir. There's in all two worthy 77 voices begged. I have your alms. Adieu.

THIRD CITIZEN But this is something odd.

SECOND CITIZEN An 'twere to give again – but 'tis no matter.   *Exeunt.*
                Enter two other Citizens.

CORIOLANUS Pray you now, if it may stand with the tune 81 of your voices that I may be consul, I have here the cus-tomary gown.

FOURTH CITIZEN You have deserved nobly of your country, and you have not deserved nobly.

CORIOLANUS Your enigma?

FOURTH CITIZEN You have been a scourge to her enemies; you have been a rod to her friends. You have not indeed loved the common people.

CORIOLANUS You should account me the more virtuous that I have not been common in my love. I will, sir, flat-ter my sworn brother, the people, to earn a dearer esti- 92 mation of them. 'Tis a condition they account gentle; 93 and since the wisdom of their choice is rather to have my hat than my heart, I will practice the insinuating nod and be off to them most counterfeitly: that is, sir, I will 96 counterfeit the bewitchment of some popular man and 97 give it bountiful to the desirers. Therefore, beseech you, I may be consul.

FIFTH CITIZEN We hope to find you our friend, and therefore give you our voices heartily.

FOURTH CITIZEN You have received many wounds for your country.

CORIOLANUS I will not seal your knowledge with show- 103 ing them. I will make much of your voices, and so trouble you no farther.

BOTH The gods give you joy, sir, heartily!   *[Exeunt.]*

CORIOLANUS
Most sweet voices!
Better it is to die, better to starve,
Than crave the hire which first we do deserve.   109
Why in this wolvish toge should I stand here,   110
To beg of Hob and Dick that does appear   111
Their needless vouches? Custom calls me to't.   112
What custom wills, in all things should we do't,
The dust on antique time would lie unswept
And mountainous error be too highly heaped
For truth t' o'erpeer. Rather than fool it so,   116
Let the high office and the honor go
To one that would do thus. I am half through;
The one part suffered, the other will I do.

Enter three Citizens more.

Here come moe voices.   120

---

21 *consent . . . way* agreement to go straight   30 *rotten* unwholesome
33 *You may* go on   35 *greater part* majority   41 *by particulars* to individuals
56 *lose by* fail to inculcate in   58 *wholesome* decent   59 *brace* pair   74 *yours* available to you   77 *match* agreement   81 *stand* accord   92–93 *dearer estimation of* higher opinion from   93 *condition* quality; *gentle* amiable
96 *be off* take my hat off   97 *bewitchment* witchery; *popular man* man of the people   103 *seal* confirm   109 *hire* reward; *first* beforehand   110 *toge* toga   111 *Hob* rustic nickname for Robert; *that does appear* as they come by
112 *vouches* attestations   116 *o'erpeer* overtop; *fool it* play the fool   120 *moe* more

Your voices! For your voices I have fought;
122 Watched for your voices; for your voices bear
Of wounds two dozen odd; battles thrice six
I have seen and heard of; for your voices have
Done many things, some less, some more. Your voices!
Indeed, I would be consul.

FIRST CITIZEN He has done nobly, and cannot go without any honest man's voice.

SECOND CITIZEN Therefore let him be consul. The gods
give him joy, and make him good friend to the people!

ALL Amen, amen. God save thee, noble consul! *[Exeunt.]*

CORIOLANUS Worthy voices!

Enter Menenius, with Brutus and Sicinius.

MENENIUS
133 You have stood your limitation, and the tribunes
134 Endue you with the people's voice. Remains
135 That, in th' official marks invested, you
Anon do meet the Senate.

CORIOLANUS   Is this done?

SICINIUS
The custom of request you have discharged.
The people do admit you, and are summoned
139 To meet anon upon your approbation.

CORIOLANUS
Where? at the Senate House?

SICINIUS   There, Coriolanus.

CORIOLANUS
May I change these garments?

SICINIUS   You may, sir.

CORIOLANUS
That I'll straight do; and, knowing myself again,
Repair to th' Senate House.

MENENIUS
144 I'll keep you company. Will you along?

BRUTUS
We stay here for the people.

SICINIUS   Fare you well.

Exeunt Coriolanus and Menenius.

He has it now; and by his looks, methinks,
'Tis warm at's heart.

BRUTUS
With a proud heart he wore his humble weeds.
Will you dismiss the people?

Enter the Plebeians.

SICINIUS
150 How now, my masters! Have you chose this man?

FIRST CITIZEN
He has our voices, sir.

BRUTUS
We pray the gods he may deserve your loves.

SECOND CITIZEN
Amen, sir. To my poor unworthy notice,

He mocked us when he begged our voices.

THIRD CITIZEN   Certainly
He flouted us downright.

FIRST CITIZEN
No, 'tis his kind of speech; he did not mock us.

SECOND CITIZEN
Not one amongst us, save yourself, but says
He used us scornfully. He should have showed us
His marks of merit, wounds received for's country. 159

SICINIUS
Why, so he did, I am sure.

ALL   No, no! No man saw 'em.

THIRD CITIZEN
He said he had wounds, which he could show in private;
And with his hat, thus waving it in scorn,
'I would be consul,' says he. 'Aged custom, 163
But by your voices, will not so permit me.
Your voices therefore.' When we granted that,
Here was 'I thank you for your voices, thank you!
Your most sweet voices! Now you have left your voices,
I have no further with you.' Was not this mockery? 168

SICINIUS
Why either were you ignorant to see it, 169
Or, seeing it, of such childish friendliness
To yield your voices?

BRUTUS   Could you not have told him
As you were lessoned? When he had no power, 172
But was a petty servant to the state,
He was your enemy, ever spake against
Your liberties and the charters that you bear 175
I' th' body of the weal; and now, arriving 176
A place of potency and sway o' th' state,
If he should still malignantly remain
Fast foe to th' plebeii, your voices might 179
Be curses to yourselves. You should have said
That as his worthy deeds did claim no less
Than what he stood for, so his gracious nature
Would think upon you for your voices and 183
Translate his malice towards you into love, 184
Standing your friendly lord.

SICINIUS   Thus to have said,
As you were fore-advised, had touched his spirit 186
And tried his inclination; from him plucked
Either his gracious promise, which you might,
As cause had called you up, have held him to; 189
Or else it would have galled his surly nature,
Which easily endures not article 191
Tying him to aught; so putting him to rage,
You should have ta'en the advantage of his choler
And passed him unelected.

BRUTUS   Did you perceive
He did solicit you in free contempt 195
When he did need your loves, and do you think
That his contempt shall not be bruising to you
When he hath power to crush? Why, had your bodies
No heart among you? Or had you tongues to cry 199
Against the rectorship of judgment? 200

SICINIUS   Have you,
Ere now, denied the asker? And now again,
Of him that did not ask but mock, bestow 202
Your sued-for tongues! 203

THIRD CITIZEN
He's not confirmed; we may deny him yet.

122 *Watched* stayed awake   133 *limitation* appointed time   134 *Endue* endow; *Remains* it remains   135 *official marks* insignia   139 *upon your approbation* to confirm your election   144 *along* come along   150 *my masters* gentlemen   159 *for's* for his   163 *Aged* ancient   168 *no further* nothing further to do   169 *ignorant* too unobservant   172 *lessoned* taught   175 *charters* rights   176 *body of the weal* commonwealth; *arriving* attaining   179 *plebeii* plebeians (Latin)   183 *Would think upon* should remember   184 *Translate* change   186 *fore-advised* previously advised; *had* would have   189 *As . . . up* as occasion aroused you   191–92 *article . . . aught* any conditions   195 *free* open   199 *heart* courage; *cry* protest   200 *rectorship* rule   202 *bestow* to bestow   203 *sued-for* solicited

SECOND CITIZEN
And will deny him.
I'll have five hundred voices of that sound.

FIRST CITIZEN

207 I twice five hundred, and their friends to piece 'em.

BRUTUS
Get you hence instantly, and tell those friends
They have chose a consul that will from them take
Their liberties ; make them of no more voice
Than dogs, that are as often beat for barking

212 As therefore kept to do so.

SICINIUS   Let them assemble,
And on a safer judgment all revoke

214 Your ignorant election. Enforce his pride,

215 And his old hate unto you. Besides, forget not
With what contempt he wore the humble weed,
How in his suit he scorned you ; but your loves,
Thinking upon his services, took from you

219 Th' apprehension of his present portance,
Which most gibingly, ungravely, he did fashion
After th' inveterate hate he bears you.

221 BRUTUS   Lay
A fault on us, your tribunes : that we labored,

223 No impediment between, but that you must
Cast your election on him.

SICINIUS   Say you chose him

225 More after our commandment than as guided
By your own true affections, and that your minds,
Preoccupied with what you rather must do
Than what you should, made you against the grain

229 To voice him consul. Lay the fault on us.

BRUTUS
Ay, spare us not. Say we read lectures to you,
How youngly he began to serve his country,
How long continued, and what stock he springs of,
The noble house o' th' Marcians, from whence came

234 That Ancus Marcius, Numa's daughter's son,
Who after great Hostilius here was king ;
Of the same house Publius and Quintus were,

237 That our best water brought by conduits hither ;
And [Censorinus,] nobly namèd so,

239 Twice being [by the people chosen] censor,
Was his great ancestor.

SICINIUS   One thus descended,
That hath beside well in his person wrought
To be set high in place, we did commend
To your remembrances ; but you have found,

244 Scaling his present bearing with his past,
That he's your fixèd enemy, and revoke
Your sudden approbation.

BRUTUS   Say, you ne'er had done 't –

247 Harp on that still – but by our putting on ;

248 And presently, when you have drawn your number,
Repair to th' Capitol.

ALL   We will so : almost all
Repent in their election.   Exeunt Plebeians.

BRUTUS   Let them go on.

251 This mutiny were better put in hazard

252 Than stay past doubt, for greater. If,
as his nature is, he fall in rage

254 With their refusal, both observe and answer
The vantage of his anger.

SICINIUS   To th' Capitol, come.
We will be there before the stream o' th' people ;

And this shall seem, as partly 'tis, their own,
Which we have goaded onward.   Exeunt.

*

*Cornets. Enter Coriolanus, Menenius, all the
Gentry, Cominius, Titus Lartius, and other
Senators.*

III, i

CORIOLANUS
Tullus Aufidius then had made new head ?   1

LARTIUS
He had, my lord, and that it was which caused
Our swifter composition.   3

CORIOLANUS
So then the Volsces stand but as at first,
Ready, when time shall prompt them, to make road   5
Upon's again.

COMINIUS   They are worn, lord consul, so,
That we shall hardly in our ages see
Their banners wave again.

CORIOLANUS   Saw you Aufidius ?

LARTIUS
On safeguard he came to me ; and did curse   9
Against the Volsces, for they had so vilely   10
Yielded the town. He is retired to Antium.   11

CORIOLANUS
Spoke he of me ?

LARTIUS   He did, my lord.

CORIOLANUS   How ? what ?

LARTIUS
How often he had met you, sword to sword ;
That of all things upon the earth he hated
Your person most ; that he would pawn his fortunes
To hopeless restitution, so he might   16
Be called your vanquisher.

CORIOLANUS   At Antium lives he ?

LARTIUS
At Antium.

CORIOLANUS
I wish I had a cause to seek him there,
To oppose his hatred fully. Welcome home.
Enter Sicinius and Brutus.
Behold, these are the tribunes of the people,
The tongues o' th' common mouth. I do despise them ;
For they do prank them in authority   23
Against all noble sufferance.   24

SICINIUS   Pass no further.

CORIOLANUS
Ha ! What is that ?

BRUTUS
It will be dangerous to go on. No further.

207 *piece* supplement   212 *therefore* for that reason   214 *Enforce* emphasize
215 *forget not* do not ignore   219 *apprehension* observation ; *portance*
bearing   221–22 *Lay . . . on* blame   223 *No impediment between* that
there should be no obstacle   225 *after* according to   229 *voice* vote
234 *Numa* second king of Rome   237 *conduits* aqueducts   239 *censor*
keeper of public records   244 *Scaling* weighing   247 *putting on* instigation
248 *presently* immediately ; *drawn your number* gathered a crowd   251
put in hazard risked   252 *for greater* and run a greater risk   254–55 *answer
The vantage* take advantage
III, i A Roman street   1 *made new head* raised another army   3 *swifter
composition* coming to terms the more speedily   5 *road* inroads   9 *safeguard*
safe-conduct   10 *for* because   11 *Antium* Volscian capital   16 *To hopeless
restitution* beyond hope of recovery   23 *prank* dress up   24 *noble sufferance*
patrician endurance

CORIOLANUS
What makes this change?

MENENIUS
The matter?

COMINIUS
29 Hath he not passed the noble and the common?

BRUTUS
Cominius, no.

CORIOLANUS   Have I had children's voices?

FIRST SENATOR
Tribunes, give way. He shall to th' market-place.

BRUTUS
The people are incensed against him.

SICINIUS   Stop,
Or all will fall in broil.

CORIOLANUS   Are these your herd?
Must these have voices, that can yield them now
And straight disclaim their tongues? What are your
    offices?
36 You being their mouths, why rule you not their teeth?
Have you not set them on?

MENENIUS   Be calm, be calm.

CORIOLANUS
It is a purposed thing, and grows by plot,
To curb the will of the nobility.
40 Suffer't, and live with such as cannot rule
Nor ever will be ruled.

BRUTUS   Call't not a plot:
The people cry you mocked them; and of late,
43 When corn was given them gratis, you repined;
44 Scandaled the suppliants for the people, called them
45 Time-pleasers, flatterers, foes to nobleness.

CORIOLANUS
Why, this was known before.

BRUTUS   Not to them all.

CORIOLANUS
47 Have you informed them sithence?

BRUTUS   How! I inform them!

CORIOLANUS
You are like to do such business.

BRUTUS   Not unlike,
49 Each way, to better yours.

CORIOLANUS
Why then should I be consul? By yond clouds,
Let me deserve so ill as you, and make me
Your fellow tribune.

SICINIUS   You show too much of that
53 For which the people stir. If you will pass
To where you are bound, you must inquire your way,
55 Which you are out of, with a gentler spirit,
Or never be so noble as a consul,
57 Nor yoke with him for tribune.

MENENIUS   Let's be calm.

29 *passed* been approved by   36 *rule* control   40 *live* you will live   43
repined expressed regret   44 *Scandaled* defamed   45 *nobleness* aristocracy
47 *sithence* since   49 *better yours* do better than you would do as consul
53 *For . . . stir* which disturbs the people   55 *are out of* have strayed from
57 *yoke* cooperate   58 *abused* deceived; *paltering* equivocating   60
dishonored rub shameful obstacle   66 *For* as for; *meiny* multitude   70
cockle weed   78 *those measles* that leprosy   79 *tetter* break out in; *sought*
have sought   89 *Triton* god who calms the waves   90 *from the canon*
contrary to rule   93 *Given* allowed; *Hydra* many-headed monster   95
horn (attribute of Triton)   98 *vail your ignorance* let your negligence bow
down   99 *lenity* mildness   101 *have cushions by you* sit with you in the
Senate   103 *great'st taste* taste of the greatest   104 *palates* smacks of

COMINIUS
The people are abused, set on. This paltering   58
Becomes not Rome, nor has Coriolanus
Deserved this so dishonored rub, laid falsely   60
I' th' plain way of his merit.

CORIOLANUS   Tell me of corn!
This was my speech, and I will speak't again—

MENENIUS
Not now, not now.

FIRST SENATOR   Not in this heat, sir, now.

CORIOLANUS
Now, as I live, I will. My nobler friends,
I crave their pardons.
For the mutable, rank-scented meiny, let them   66
Regard me as I do not flatter, and
Therein behold themselves. I say again,
In soothing them we nourish 'gainst our Senate
The cockle of rebellion, insolence, sedition,   70
Which we ourselves have ploughed for, sowed, and
    scattered
By mingling them with us, the honored number,
Who lack not virtue, no, nor power, but that
Which they have given to beggars.

MENENIUS   Well, no more.

FIRST SENATOR
No more words, we beseech you.

CORIOLANUS   How? no more?
As for my country I have shed my blood,
Not fearing outward force, so shall my lungs
Coin words till their decay against those measles   78
Which we disdain should tetter us, yet sought   79
The very way to catch them.

BRUTUS   You speak o' th' people
As if you were a god to punish, not
A man of their infirmity.

SICINIUS   'Twere well
We let the people know't.

MENENIUS   What, what? His choler?

CORIOLANUS
Choler!
Were I as patient as the midnight sleep,
By Jove, 'twould be my mind!

SICINIUS   It is a mind
That shall remain a poison where it is,
Not poison any further.

CORIOLANUS   Shall remain!
Hear you this Triton of the minnows? Mark you   89
His absolute 'shall'?

COMINIUS   'Twas from the canon.   90

CORIOLANUS   'Shall'?
O good but most unwise patricians! Why,
You grave but reckless senators, have you thus
Given Hydra here to choose an officer,   93
That with his peremptory 'shall,' being but
The horn and noise o' th' monster's, wants not spirit   95
To say he'll turn your current in a ditch,
And make your channel his? If he have power,
Then vail your ignorance; if none, awake   98
Your dangerous lenity. If you are learned,   99
Be not as common fools; if you are not,
Let them have cushions by you. You are plebeians   101
If they be senators; and they are no less
When, both your voices blended, the great'st taste   103
Most palates theirs. They choose their magistrate;   104

And such a one as he, who puts his 'shall,'
His popular 'shall,' against a graver bench
Than ever frowned in Greece. By Jove himself,
It makes the consuls base ! and my soul aches
109 To know, when two authorities are up,
Neither supreme, how soon confusion
May enter 'twixt the gap of both and take
The one by th' other.

COMINIUS   Well, on to th' market-place.

CORIOLANUS
Whoever gave that counsel, to give forth
The corn o' th' storehouse gratis, as 'twas used
Sometime in Greece –

MENENIUS   Well, well, no more of that.

CORIOLANUS
Though there the people had more absolute power –
I say they nourished disobedience, fed
The ruin of the state.

BRUTUS   Why, shall the people give
One that speaks thus their voice ?

CORIOLANUS   I'll give my reasons,
More worthier than their voices. They know the corn
121 Was not our recompense, resting well assured
122 They ne'er did service for't. Being pressed to th' war,
123 Even when the navel of the state was touched,
124 They would not thread the gates. This kind of service
Did not deserve corn gratis. Being i' th' war,
Their mutinies and revolts, wherein they showed
Most valor, spoke not for them. Th' accusation
Which they have often made against the Senate,
129 All cause unborn, could never be the native
130 Of our so frank donation. Well, what then ?
131 How shall this bosom multiplied digest
The Senate's courtesy ? Let deeds express
What's like to be their words : 'We did request it ;
134 We are the greater poll, and in true fear
They gave us our demands.' Thus we debase
The nature of our seats, and make the rabble
Call our cares fears ; which will in time
Break ope the locks o' th' Senate, and bring in
The crows to peck the eagles.

MENENIUS   Come, enough.

BRUTUS
Enough, with over-measure.

CORIOLANUS   No, take more !
What may be sworn by, both divine and human,
142 Seal what I end withal ! This double worship,
Where one part does disdain with cause, the other
144 Insult without all reason ; where gentry, title, wisdom,
Cannot conclude but by the yea and no
146 Of general ignorance – it must omit
Real necessities, and give way the while
148 To unstable slightness. Purpose so barred, it follows,
Nothing is done to purpose. Therefore, beseech you, –
150 You that will be less fearful than discreet ;
That love the fundamental part of state
152 More than you doubt the change on't ; that prefer
A noble life before a long, and wish
154 To jump a body with a dangerous physic
That's sure of death without it – at once pluck out
The multitudinous tongue ; let them not lick
157 The sweet which is their poison. Your dishonor
Mangles true judgment, and bereaves the state
159 Of that integrity which should become't,

Not having the power to do the good it would
For th' ill which doth control't.

BRUTUS   'Has said enough.   161

SICINIUS
'Has spoken like a traitor, and shall answer
As traitors do.

CORIOLANUS   Thou wretch, despite o'erwhelm thee !   163
What should the people do with these bald tribunes ?
On whom depending, their obedience fails
To th' greater bench. In a rebellion,   166
When what's not meet, but what must be, was law,
Then were they chosen. In a better hour,
Let what is meet be said it must be meet,   169
And throw their power i' th' dust.

BRUTUS
Manifest treason !

SICINIUS   This a consul ? No.

BRUTUS
The aediles, ho !   172

Enter an Aedile.
      Let him be apprehended.

SICINIUS
Go, call the people ; *[exit Aedile]* in whose name myself
Attach thee as a traitorous innovator,   174
A foe to th' public weal. Obey, I charge thee,
And follow to thine answer.   176

CORIOLANUS   Hence, old goat !

ALL [PATRICIANS]
We'll surety him.   177

COMINIUS   Ag'd sir, hands off.

CORIOLANUS
Hence, rotten thing ! or I shall shake thy bones
Out of thy garments.

SICINIUS   Help, ye citizens !

Enter a rabble of Plebeians, with the Aediles.

MENENIUS
On both sides more respect.

SICINIUS
Here's he that would take from you all your power.

BRUTUS
Seize him, aediles !

ALL [PLEBEIANS]
Down with him ! down with him !

SECOND SENATOR
Weapons, weapons, weapons !

They all bustle about Coriolanus.

ALL
Tribunes ! – Patricians ! – Citizens ! – What, ho !
Sicinius ! – Brutus ! – Coriolanus ! – Citizens !
Peace, peace, peace ! – Stay, hold, peace !

MENENIUS
What is about to be ? I am out of breath ;
Confusion's near ; I cannot speak. You, tribunes   189
To th' people ! – Coriolanus, patience ! –

---

109 *up* in action   121 *recompense* reward to them   122 *pressed* conscripted
123 *navel* center   124 *thread* pass through   129 *All cause unborn* without
justification ; *native* origin   130 *frank* free   131 *bosom multiplied* many-
breasted crowd   134 *greater poll* majority   142 *Seal* confirm ; *withal* with ;
double worship divided authority   144 *without* beyond   146 *omit* neglect
148 *Purpose so barred* when planning thus becomes impossible   150 *discreet*
wise   152 *doubt* fear   154 *jump* risk   157 *sweet* flattery   159 *integrity*
wholeness ; *become't* befit it   161 *'Has* he has   163 *despite* scorn   166
greater bench Senate   169 *Let . . . be meet* let it be said that what is proper
should be done   172 *aediles* police officers   174 *Attach* arrest   176 *answer*
interrogation   177 *surety* stand pledged for   189 *Confusion* ruin

Speak, good Sicinius.

SICINIUS   Hear me, people. Peace!

ALL [PLEBEIANS] Let's hear our tribune. Peace! Speak,
speak, speak!

SICINIUS

194   You are at point to lose your liberties.
Marcius would have all from you, Marcius,
Whom late you have named for consul.

MENENIUS   Fie, fie, fie!
This is the way to kindle, not to quench.

FIRST SENATOR
To unbuild the city and to lay all flat.

SICINIUS
What is the city but the people?

ALL [PLEBEIANS]   True,
The people are the city.

BRUTUS
By the consent of all we were established
The people's magistrates.

ALL [PLEBEIANS]   You so remain.

MENENIUS
And so are like to do.

COMINIUS
That is the way to lay the city flat,
To bring the roof to the foundation,
206   And bury all, which yet distinctly ranges,
In heaps and piles of ruin.

SICINIUS   This deserves death.

BRUTUS
Or let us stand to our authority,
Or let us lose it. We do here pronounce,
Upon the part o' th' people, in whose power
We were elected theirs, Marcius is worthy
212   Of present death.

SICINIUS   Therefore lay hold of him;
213   Bear him to th' Rock Tarpeian, and from thence
Into destruction cast him.

BRUTUS   Aediles, seize him!

ALL [PLEBEIANS]
Yield, Marcius, yield!

MENENIUS   Hear me one word.
Beseech you, tribunes, hear me but a word.

AEDILES
Peace, peace!

MENENIUS [to Brutus]
Be that you seem, truly your country's friend,
And temp'rately proceed to what you would
Thus violently redress.

BRUTUS   Sir, those cold ways,
That seem like prudent helps, are very poisonous
Where the disease is violent. Lay hands upon him,
And bear him to the Rock.
        Coriolanus draws his sword.

CORIOLANUS   No, I'll die here.
There's some among you have beheld me fighting:
Come, try upon yourselves what you have seen me.

MENENIUS
Down with that sword! Tribunes, withdraw awhile.

BRUTUS
Lay hands upon him.

MENENIUS   Help Marcius, help!
You that be noble, help him, young and old!

ALL [PLEBEIANS]
Down with him! down with him!   *Exeunt.*
        *In this mutiny the Tribunes, the Aediles, and the
        People are beat in.*

MENENIUS
Go, get you to your house! be gone, away!
All will be naught else.   231

SECOND SENATOR   Get you gone.

CORIOLANUS   Stand fast!
We have as many friends as enemies.

MENENIUS
Shall it be put to that?

FIRST SENATOR   The gods forbid!
I prithee, noble friend, home to thy house;
Leave us to cure this cause.

MENENIUS   For 'tis a sore upon us
You cannot tent yourself. Be gone, beseech you.   236

COMINIUS
Come, sir, along with us.

CORIOLANUS
I would they were barbarians, as they are,
Though in Rome littered; not Romans, as they are not,
Though calvèd i' th' porch o' th' Capitol —

MENENIUS   Be gone;
Put not your worthy rage into your tongue.
One time will owe another.   242

CORIOLANUS   On fair ground
I could beat forty of them.

MENENIUS   I could myself
Take up a brace o' th' best of them; yea, the two tribunes. 244

COMINIUS
But now 'tis odds beyond arithmetic,
And manhood is called foolery when it stands
Against a falling fabric. Will you hence   247
Before the tag return? whose rage doth rend   248
Like interrupted waters, and o'erbear   249
What they are used to bear.

MENENIUS   Pray you, be gone.
I'll try whether my old wit be in request   251
With those that have but little. This must be patched
With cloth of any color.

COMINIUS   Nay, come away.
        Exeunt Coriolanus and Cominius [with others].

PATRICIAN
This man has marred his fortune.

MENENIUS
His nature is too noble for the world.
He would not flatter Neptune for his trident,   256
Or Jove for's power to thunder. His heart's his mouth. 257
What his breast forges, that his tongue must vent;
And, being angry, does forget that ever
He heard the name of death.   260
        A noise within.
Here's goodly work!

PATRICIAN   I would they were abed!

MENENIUS
I would they were in Tiber! What the vengeance!
Could he not speak 'em fair?   263

---

194 *at point to lose* on the point of losing   206 *distinctly ranges* is ranked
separately   212 *present* immediate   213 *Rock Tarpeian* Capitoline cliff
from which state criminals were hurled   231 *naught* ruined   236 *tent* treat
242 *One . . . another* another time will make up for this   244 *Take up* cope
with   247 *fabric* building   248 *tag* rabble   249 *o'erbear* overpower   251
request demand   256 *trident* three-pronged fork symbolizing sea-power
257 *His . . . mouth* he speaks what he feels   260 s.d. *within* backstage
263 *speak 'em fair* address them graciously

Enter Brutus and Sicinius, with the Rabble again.

SICINIUS   Where is this viper
That would depopulate the city and
265 Be every man himself?
MENENIUS   You worthy tribunes—
SICINIUS
He shall be thrown down the Tarpeian Rock
With rigorous hands. He hath resisted law;
And therefore law shall scorn him further trial
Than the severity of the public power,
Which he so sets at nought.
FIRST CITIZEN   He shall well know
The noble tribunes are the people's mouths,
And we their hands.
272 ALL [PLEBEIANS]   He shall, sure on't.
MENENIUS   Sir, sir,—
SICINIUS
Peace!
MENENIUS
274 Do not cry havoc, where you should but hunt
275 With modest warrant.
SICINIUS   Sir, how comes't that you
276 Have holp to make this rescue?
MENENIUS   Hear me speak:
As I do know the consul's worthiness,
So can I name his faults—
SICINIUS   Consul! what consul?
MENENIUS
The consul Coriolanus.
BRUTUS   He consul!
ALL [PLEBEIANS]
No, no, no, no, no!
MENENIUS
If, by the tribunes' leave, and yours, good people,
I may be heard, I would crave a word or two;
283 The which shall turn you to no further harm
Than so much loss of time.
SICINIUS   Speak briefly then;
285 For we are peremptory to dispatch
This viperous traitor. To eject him hence
Were but our danger, and to keep him here
Our certain death. Therefore it is decreed
He dies to-night.
MENENIUS   Now the good gods forbid
That our renownèd Rome, whose gratitude
291 Towards her deservèd children is enrolled
In Jove's own book, like an unnatural dam
Should now eat up her own!
SICINIUS
He's a disease that must be cut away.
MENENIUS
O, he's a limb that has but a disease:
Mortal, to cut it off; to cure it, easy.
297 What has he done to Rome that's worthy death?
Killing our enemies, the blood he hath lost—
Which, I dare vouch, is more than that he hath,
By many an ounce—he dropped it for his country;
And what is left, to lose it by his country
Were to us all that do't and suffer it
A brand to th' end o' th' world.
303 SICINIUS   This is clean kam.
BRUTUS
304 Merely awry. When he did love his country,
It honored him.

SICINIUS   The service of the foot,
Being once gangrened, is not then respected
For what before it was.
BRUTUS   We'll hear no more.
Pursue him to his house and pluck him thence,
Lest his infection, being of catching nature,
Spread further.
MENENIUS   One word more, one word.
This tiger-footed rage, when it shall find
The harm of unscanned swiftness, will too late   312
Tie leaden pounds to's heels. Proceed by process,   313
Lest parties, as he is beloved, break out
And sack great Rome with Romans.
BRUTUS   If it were so—
SICINIUS
What do ye talk?
Have we not had a taste of his obedience?
Our aediles smote? ourselves resisted? Come.   318
MENENIUS
Consider this: he has been bred i' th' wars
Since 'a could draw a sword, and is ill schooled
In bolted language; meal and bran together   321
He throws without distinction. Give me leave,
I'll go to him and undertake to bring him
Where he shall answer by a lawful form,   324
In peace, to his utmost peril.
FIRST SENATOR   Noble tribunes,
It is the humane way. The other course
Will prove too bloody, and the end of it
Unknown to the beginning.
SICINIUS   Noble Menenius,
Be you then as the people's officer.
Masters, lay down your weapons.
BRUTUS   Go not home.
SICINIUS
Meet on the market-place. We'll attend you there;   331
Where, if you bring not Marcius, we'll proceed
In our first way.
MENENIUS   I'll bring him to you.
[To the Senators]
Let me desire your company. He must come,
Or what is worst will follow.
FIRST SENATOR   Pray you, let's to him.   335
                      Exeunt omnes.

*

Enter Coriolanus, with Nobles.   III, ii
CORIOLANUS
Let them pull all about mine ears, present me
Death on the wheel or at wild horses' heels,   2
Or pile ten hills on the Tarpeian Rock,
That the precipitation might down stretch   4
Below the beam of sight, yet will I still   5

265 *Be . . . himself* constitute himself the whole population   272 *sure on't* for certain   274 *cry havoc* call for slaughter   275 *modest* moderate   276 *holp* helped   283 *turn you to* cause you   285 *peremptory* resolved   291 *deservèd* meritorious   291–92 *enrolled . . . book* recorded in the Capitol   297 *worthy* deserving of   303 *clean kam* quite wrong   304 *Merely awry* completely twisted   312 *unscanned swiftness* thoughtless haste   313 *to's* to its; *process* course of law   318 *smote* smitten   321 *bolted* sifted   324–25 *answer . . . peril* peacefully face judgment, however severe   331 *attend* await   335 *to* go to
III, ii The house of Coriolanus   2 *wheel* instrument of torture   4 *precipitation* precipitousness   5 *Below . . . sight* beyond eyesight

Be thus to them.

NOBLE   You do the nobler.

CORIOLANUS

7   I muse my mother
Does not approve me further, who was wont
To call them woollen vassals, things created
10 To buy and sell with groats, to show bare heads
11 In congregations, to yawn, be still and wonder,
12 When one but of my ordinance stood up
To speak of peace or war.
     Enter Volumnia.   I talk of you :
Why did you wish me milder ? Would you have me
False to my nature ? Rather say I play
The man I am.

VOLUMNIA   O, sir, sir, sir,
I would have had you put your power well on,
Before you had worn it out.

18 CORIOLANUS   Let go.

VOLUMNIA
You might have been enough the man you are
With striving less to be so. Lesser had been
21 The taxings of your dispositions, if
You had not showed them how ye were disposed
23 Ere they lacked power to cross you.

CORIOLANUS   Let them hang !

VOLUMNIA
Ay, and burn too !
     Enter Menenius, with the Senators.

MENENIUS
25 Come, come, you have been too rough, something too
    rough.
You must return and mend it.

FIRST SENATOR   There's no remedy,
Unless, by not so doing, our good city
28 Cleave in the midst, and perish.

VOLUMNIA   Pray, be counselled.

29 I have a heart as little apt as yours,
But yet a brain that leads my use of anger
31 To better vantage.

MENENIUS   Well said, noble woman !
Before he should thus stoop to th' herd, but that
33 The violent fit o' th' time craves it as physic
For the whole state, I would put mine armor on,
Which I can scarcely bear.

CORIOLANUS   What must I do ?

MENENIUS
Return to th' tribunes.

CORIOLANUS   Well, what then ? what then ?

MENENIUS
Repent what you have spoke.

CORIOLANUS
For them ? I cannot do it to the gods.
Must I then do't to them ?

VOLUMNIA   You are too absolute ;
Though therein you can never be too noble,
But when extremities speak. I have heard you say,   41
Honor and policy, like unsevered friends,   42
I' th' war do grow together. Grant that, and tell me,
In peace what each of them by th' other lose,
That they combine not there.

CORIOLANUS   Tush, tush !

MENENIUS   A good demand.

VOLUMNIA
If it be honor in your wars to seem
The same you are not, – which, for your best ends,
You adopt your policy – how is it less or worse,   48
That it shall hold companionship in peace
With honor, as in war ; since that to both   50
It stands in like request ?

CORIOLANUS   Why force you this ?   51

VOLUMNIA
Because that now it lies you on to speak   52
To th' people, not by your own instruction,
Nor by th' matter which your heart prompts you,
But with such words that are but roted in   55
Your tongue, though but bastards and syllables
Of no allowance to your bosom's truth.   57
Now, this no more dishonors you at all
Than to take in a town with gentle words,   59
Which else would put you to your fortune and
The hazard of much blood.
I would dissemble with my nature where
My fortunes and my friends at stake required
I should do so in honor. I am in this   64
Your wife, your son, these senators, the nobles ;
And you will rather show our general louts   66
How you can frown than spend a fawn upon 'em,   67
For the inheritance of their loves and safeguard   68
Of what that want might ruin.   69

MENENIUS   Noble lady ! –
Come, go with us. Speak fair. You may salve so,
Not what is dangerous present, but the loss   71
Of what is past.

VOLUMNIA   I prithee now, my son,
Go to them, with this bonnet in thy hand ;
And thus far having stretched it, – here be with them –   74
Thy knee bussing the stones, – for in such business   75
Action is eloquence, and the eyes of th' ignorant
More learned than the ears – waving thy head,   77
Which, often thus correcting thy stout heart,   78
Now humble as the ripest mulberry   79
That will not hold the handling ; or say to them
Thou art their soldier, and being bred in broils
Hast not the soft way which, thou dost confess,
Were fit for thee to use as they to claim,
In asking their good loves ; but thou wilt frame
Thyself, forsooth, hereafter theirs, so far   85
As thou hast power and person.

MENENIUS   This but done,
Even as she speaks, why, their hearts were yours ;   87
For they have pardons, being asked, as free
As words to little purpose.   89

VOLUMNIA   Prithee now,
Go, and be ruled ; although I know thou hadst rather   90

---

7 *muse* wonder that   10 *groats* fourpenny pieces   11 *congregations* assemblies   12 *ordinance* rank   18 *Let go* desist   21 *dispositions* inclinations   23 *Ere they lacked* before they lost   25 *something* somewhat   28 *Cleave . . . midst* divide in the middle   29 *apt* compliant   31 *vantage* advantage   33 *physic* medicine   41 *extremities speak* necessity prompts   42 *policy* strategy ; *unsevered* inseparable   48 *adopt* adopt as   50–51 *since . . . request* since it is equally necessary to both   51 *force* urge   52 *lies you on* is incumbent upon you   55 *roted* memorized   57 *Of . . . truth* unsanctioned by your real feelings   59 *take in* capture   64 *am* speak for   66 *general* common   67 *fawn* flattering appeal   68 *inheritance* obtainment   69 *that want* the lack of their loves   71–72 *Not . . . past* not only immediate danger but past loss   74 *here . . . them* treat them thus   75 *bussing* kissing (vulgar)   77 *waving* bowing   78 *correcting* chastening   79 *humble* abase   85 *theirs* to suit them   87 *were* would be   89 *words . . . purpose* a trifling concession   90 *ruled* advised

91   Follow thine enemy in a fiery gulf
92   Than flatter him in a bower.
         Enter Cominius.   Here is Cominius.
COMINIUS
     I have been i' th' market-place ; and, sir, 'tis fit
     You make strong party, or defend yourself
     By calmness or by absence. All's in anger.
MENENIUS
     Only fair speech.
COMINIUS   I think 'twill serve, if he
     Can thereto frame his spirit.
VOLUMNIA   He must, and will.
     Prithee now, say you will, and go about it.
CORIOLANUS
99   Must I go show them my unbarbed sconce ? Must I
     With my base tongue give to my noble heart
     A lie that it must bear ? Well, I will do't.
102 Yet, were there but this single plot to lose,
103 This mould of Marcius, they to dust should grind it
     And throw't against the wind. To th' market-place !
     You have put me now to such a part which never
106 I shall discharge to th' life.
COMINIUS   Come, come, we'll prompt you.
VOLUMNIA
     I prithee now, sweet son, as thou hast said
     My praises made thee first a soldier, so,
     To have my praise for this, perform a part
     Thou hast not done before.
CORIOLANUS   Well, I must do't.
     Away, my disposition, and possess me
     Some harlot's spirit ! My throat of war be turned,
113 Which quired with my drum, into a pipe
     Small as an eunuch, or the virgin voice
115 That babies lulls asleep ! The smiles of knaves
116 Tent in my cheeks, and schoolboys' tears take up
117 The glasses of my sight ! A beggar's tongue
     Make motion through my lips, and my armed knees,
     Who bowed but in my stirrup, bend like his
     That hath received an alms ! I will not do't,
121 Lest I surcease to honor mine own truth
     And by my body's action teach my mind
123 A most inherent baseness.
VOLUMNIA   At thy choice, then.
     To beg of thee, it is my more dishonor
     Than thou of them. Come all to ruin ! Let
     Thy mother rather feel thy pride than fear
127 Thy dangerous stoutness ; for I mock at death
128 With as big heart as thou. Do as thou list.
     Thy valiantness was mine, thou suck'st it from me ;
130 But owe thy pride thyself.
CORIOLANUS   Pray, be content.
     Mother, I am going to the market-place.
132 Chide me no more. I'll mountebank their loves,
133 Cog their hearts from them, and come home beloved
     Of all the trades in Rome. Look, I am going.
     Commend me to my wife. I'll return consul,
     Or never trust to what my tongue can do
     I' th' way of flattery further.
VOLUMNIA   Do your will. *Exit Volumnia.*
COMINIUS
     Away ! The tribunes do attend you. Arm yourself
     To answer mildly ; for they are prepared
     With accusations, as I hear, more strong
     Than are upon you yet.

CORIOLANUS
     The word is 'mildly.' Pray you, let us go.   142
     Let them accuse me by invention, I   143
     Will answer in mine honor.   144
MENENIUS   Ay, but mildly.
CORIOLANUS
     Well, mildly be't then. Mildly !   *Exeunt.*

                        *

         Enter Sicinius and Brutus.   III, iii
BRUTUS
     In this point charge him home, that he affects   1
     Tyrannical power. If he evade us there,
     Enforce him with his envy to the people,   3
     And that the spoil got on the Antiates
     Was ne'er distributed.
         Enter an Aedile.   What, will he come ?
AEDILE
     He's coming.
BRUTUS   How accompanied ?
AEDILE
     With old Menenius, and those senators
     That always favored him.
SICINIUS   Have you a catalogue
     Of all the voices that we have procured
     Set down by th' poll ?   10
AEDILE   I have ; 'tis ready.
SICINIUS
     Have you collected them by tribes ?
AEDILE   I have.
SICINIUS
     Assemble presently the people hither ;
     And when they hear me say, 'It shall be so
     I' th' right and strength o' th' commons,' be it either
     For death, for fine, or banishment, then let them,
     If I say fine, cry 'Fine !' – if death, cry 'Death !',
     Insisting on the old prerogative
     And power i' th' truth o' th' cause.   18
AEDILE   I shall inform them.
BRUTUS
     And when such time they have begun to cry,   19
     Let them not cease, but with a din confused
     Enforce the present execution
     Of what we chance to sentence.
AEDILE   Very well.
SICINIUS
     Make them be strong, and ready for this hint   23
     When we shall hap to give't them.   24
BRUTUS   Go about it. *[Exit Aedile.]*
     Put him to choler straight. He hath been used
     Ever to conquer, and to have his worth   26

91 *in* into 92 *bower* boudoir 99 *unbarbed sconce* uncovered head 102
plot piece of earth 103 *mould* form 106 *discharge . . . life* enact convincingly 113 *quired* sang in chorus 115 *babies lulls* lulls dolls 116
Tent encamp ; *take up* occupy 117 *glasses . . . sight* eyeballs 121 *surcease*
cease 123 *inherent* irremovable 127 *dangerous stoutness* danger provoked
by your obstinacy 128 *thou list* you please 130 *owe* you own 132
mountebank gain by artful speeches 133 *Cog* cheat 142 *word* watchword
143 *accuse . . . invention* invent accusations against me 144 *in* according to
III, iii The Roman Forum 1 *charge him home* press the charge against
him ; *affects* aims at 3 *Enforce* confront ; *envy to* ill-will toward 10 *poll*
registry of voters 18 *truth . . . cause* justice of the case 19 *when such
time* in such time as ; *cry* shout 23 *hint* occasion 24 *hap* chance 26
worth pennyworth

Of contradiction. Being once chafed, he cannot
Be reined again to temperance; then he speaks
29 What's in his heart, and that is there which looks
With us to break his neck.

*Enter Coriolanus, Menenius, and Cominius, with
others.*

SICINIUS   Well, here he comes.
MENENIUS
Calmly, I do beseech you.
CORIOLANUS
32 Ay, as an ostler, that for th' poorest piece
33 Will bear the knave by th' volume. Th' honored gods
Keep Rome in safety, and the chairs of justice
Supplied with worthy men! plant love among's!
36 Throng our large temples with the shows of peace,
And not our streets with war!
FIRST SENATOR   Amen, amen.
MENENIUS
A noble wish.

Enter the Aedile, with the Plebeians.

SICINIUS
Draw near, ye people.
AEDILE
40 List to your tribunes. Audience! Peace, I say!
CORIOLANUS
First hear me speak.
BOTH TRIBUNES   Well, say. Peace, ho!
CORIOLANUS
42 Shall I be charged no further than this present?
43 Must all determine here?
SICINIUS   I do demand,
If you submit you to the people's voices,
45 Allow their officers, and are content
To suffer lawful censure for such faults
As shall be proved upon you?
CORIOLANUS   I am content.
MENENIUS
Lo, citizens, he says he is content.
The warlike service he has done, consider; think
50 Upon the wounds his body bears, which show
Like graves i' th' holy churchyard.
CORIOLANUS   Scratches with briars,
· Scars to move laughter only.
MENENIUS   Consider further,
That when he speaks not like a citizen,
You find him like a soldier. Do not take
His rougher accents for malicious sounds,
But, as I say, such as become a soldier,
57 Rather than envy you.
COMINIUS   Well, well, no more.
CORIOLANUS
What is the matter
That being passed for consul with full voice,
I am so dishonored that the very hour
You take it off again?

SICINIUS   Answer to us.   61
CORIOLANUS
Say, then. 'Tis true, I ought so.   62
SICINIUS
We charge you that you have contrived to take
From Rome all seasoned office, and to wind   64
Yourself into a power tyrannical,
For which you are a traitor to the people.
CORIOLANUS
How? traitor?
MENENIUS   Nay, temperately! your promise.
CORIOLANUS
The fires i' th' lowest hell fold in the people!   68
Call me their traitor, thou injurious tribune!   69
Within thine eyes sat twenty thousand deaths,   70
In thy hands clutched as many millions, in
Thy lying tongue both numbers, I would say
'Thou liest' unto thee with a voice as free
As I do pray the gods.
SICINIUS   Mark you this, people?
ALL
To th' Rock, to th' Rock with him!
SICINIUS   Peace!
We need not put new matter to his charge.
What you have seen him do and heard him speak,
Beating your officers, cursing yourselves,
Opposing laws with strokes, and here defying
Those whose great power must try him – even this,
So criminal and in such capital kind,   81
Deserves th' extremest death.
BRUTUS   But since he hath
Served well for Rome –
CORIOLANUS   What do you prate of service?
BRUTUS
I talk of that, that know it.
CORIOLANUS
You?
MENENIUS
Is this the promise that you made your mother?
COMINIUS
Know, I pray you –
CORIOLANUS   I'll know no further.
Let them pronounce the steep Tarpeian death,
Vagabond exile, flaying, pent to linger   89
But with a grain a day – I would not buy
Their mercy at the price of one fair word;
Nor check my courage for what they can give,   92
To have't with saying 'Good morrow.'
SICINIUS   For that he has,   93
As much as in him lies, from time to time   94
Envied against the people, seeking means   95
To pluck away their power; as now at last   96
Given hostile strokes, and that not in the presence
Of dreaded justice, but on the ministers
That doth distribute it: i' th' name o' th' people
And in the power of us the tribunes, we,
Even from this instant, banish him our city,
In peril of precipitation   102
From off the Rock Tarpeian, never more
To enter our Rome gates. I' th' people's name,
I say it shall be so.
ALL
It shall be so! it shall be so! Let him away!
He's banished, and it shall be so!

29 *looks* tends 32 *piece* coin 33 *bear . . . volume* allow himself to be
called knave repeatedly 36 *shows* ceremonies 40 *List* listen; *Audience*
hearing 42 *this present* the moment 43 *determine* end 45 *Allow*
acknowledge 50 *Upon* about 57 *envy* show malice toward 61 *Answer to
us* i.e. we will ask the questions 62 *so* to do so 64 *seasoned* established
68 *fold in* enfold 69 *injurious* insulting 70 *Within* if within 81 *capital*
punishable by death 89 *pent* were I confined 92 *check* restrain 93 *For
that* because 94 *in him lies* he could 95 *Envied against* shown ill-will
toward 96 *as* and because he has 102 *precipitation* being thrown

COMINIUS
Hear me, my masters, and my common friends –
SICINIUS
He's sentenced. No more hearing.
COMINIUS   Let me speak.
I have been consul, and can show for Rome
Her enemies' marks upon me. I do love
My country's good with a respect more tender,
More holy and profound, than mine own life,
114   My dear wife's estimate, her womb's increase,
And treasure of my loins. Then if I would
Speak that –
    SICINIUS   We know your drift. Speak what?
BRUTUS
117   There's no more to be said, but he is banished
As enemy to the people and his country.
It shall be so.
    ALL
It shall be so! it shall be so!
CORIOLANUS
121   You common cry of curs, whose breath I hate
122   As reek o' th' rotten fens, whose loves I prize
As the dead carcasses of unburied men
That do corrupt my air, I banish you!
And here remain with your uncertainty.
Let every feeble rumor shake your hearts!
Your enemies, with nodding of their plumes,
Fan you into despair! Have the power still
To banish your defenders, till at length
130   Your ignorance – which finds not till it feels,
131   Making but reservation of yourselves,
Still your own foes – deliver you as most
133   Abated captives to some nation
That won you without blows! Despising,
135   For you, the city, thus I turn my back.
There is a world elsewhere.
       Exeunt Coriolanus, Cominius, with Menenius
           [and the other Senators].
    AEDILE
The people's enemy is gone, is gone!
    ALL
Our enemy is banished! he is gone!
       They all shout, and throw up their caps.
           Hoo! hoo!
    SICINIUS
Go, see him out at gates, and follow him
As he hath followed you, with all despite;
141   Give him deserved vexation. Let a guard
Attend us through the city.
    ALL
Come, come, let's see him out at gates! Come.
The gods preserve our noble tribunes! Come.   *Exeunt.*

*

IV, i   *Enter Coriolanus, Volumnia, Virgilia, Menenius,*
       Cominius, with the young Nobility of Rome.
    CORIOLANUS
Come, leave your tears. A brief farewell. The beast
With many heads butts me away. Nay, mother,
3   Where is your ancient courage? You were used
To say extremities was the trier of spirits;
That common chances common men could bear;
That when the sea was calm all boats alike

Showed mastership in floating; fortune's blows
When most struck home, being gentle wounded craves   8
A noble cunning. You were used to load me
With precepts that would make invincible
The heart that conned them.   11
VIRGILIA
O heavens! O heavens!
CORIOLANUS   Nay, I prithee, woman –
VOLUMNIA
Now the red pestilence strike all trades in Rome,
And occupations perish!
CORIOLANUS   What, what, what!
I shall be loved when I am lacked. Nay, mother,   15
Resume that spirit when you were wont to say,
If you had been the wife of Hercules,
Six of his labors you'd have done, and saved
Your husband so much sweat. Cominius,
Droop not; adieu. Farewell, my wife, my mother.
I'll do well yet. Thou old and true Menenius,
Thy tears are salter than a younger man's,   22
And venomous to thine eyes. My sometime general,   23
I have seen thee stern, and thou hast oft beheld
Heart-hard'ning spectacles. Tell these sad women
'Tis fond to wail inevitable strokes,   26
As 'tis to laugh at 'em. My mother, you wot well   27
My hazards still have been your solace; and   28
Believe't not lightly – though I go alone,
Like to a lonely dragon, that his fen   30
Makes feared and talked of more than seen – your son
Will or exceed the common or be caught   32
With cautelous baits and practice.   33
VOLUMNIA   My first son,
Whither wilt thou go? Take good Cominius
With thee awhile. Determine on some course,
More than a wild exposture to each chance   36
That starts i' th' way before thee.
CORIOLANUS   O the gods!
COMINIUS
I'll follow thee a month, devise with thee
Where thou shalt rest, that thou mayst hear of us
And we of thee. So, if the time thrust forth
A cause for thy repeal, we shall not send   41
O'er the vast world to seek a single man,
And lose advantage, which doth ever cool
I' th' absence of the needer.
CORIOLANUS   Fare ye well.
Thou hast years upon thee, and thou art too full
Of the wars' surfeits to go rove with one   46
That's yet unbruised. Bring me but out at gate.   47
Come, my sweet wife, my dearest mother, and
My friends of noble touch. When I am forth,   49
Bid me farewell, and smile. I pray you, come.
While I remain above the ground, you shall
Hear from me still, and never of me aught

114 *estimate* value   117 *but* except that   121 *cry* pack   122 *reek* vapor
130 *finds . . . feels* learns only through experience   131 *Making . . . of*
seeking to preserve only   133 *Abated* humbled   135 *For* because of
141 *vexation* mortification
IV, i Before a gate of Rome   3 *ancient* earlier   8 *being . . . craves* to bear
one's wounds like a gentleman requires   11 *conned* studied   15 *lacked*
missed   22 *salter* saltier   23 *sometime* former   26 *fond* foolish   27 *wot*
know   28 *still* always   30 *fen* marsh   32 *or . . . common* either be exceptional   33 *cautelous* crafty; *practice* stratagem   36 *exposture* exposure   41
repeal recall   46 *surfeits* excesses   47 *Bring . . . gate* just accompany me
to the gate   49 *noble touch* tested nobility

But what is like me formerly.

MENENIUS   That's worthily
As any ear can hear. Come, let's not weep.
If I could shake off but one seven-years
From these old arms and legs, by the good gods,
I'd with thee every foot.

CORIOLANUS   Give me thy hand.
Come.   *Exeunt.*

*

IV, ii   *Enter the two Tribunes, Sicinius and Brutus, with
              the Aedile.*

SICINIUS
1   Bid them all home. He's gone, and we'll no further.
     The nobility are vexed, whom we see have sided
     In his behalf.

BRUTUS   Now we have shown our power,
     Let us seem humbler after it is done
5   Than when it was a-doing.

SICINIUS   Bid them home.
     Say their great enemy is gone, and they
7   Stand in their ancient strength.

BRUTUS   Dismiss them home. *[Exit Aedile.]*
     Here comes his mother.

SICINIUS   Let's not meet her.

BRUTUS   Why?

SICINIUS
     They say she's mad.
              Enter Volumnia, Virgilia, and Menenius.

BRUTUS
     They have ta'en note of us. Keep on your way.

VOLUMNIA
11   O, y' are well met. The hoarded plague o' th' gods
     Requite your love!

MENENIUS   Peace, peace. Be not so loud.

VOLUMNIA
     If that I could for weeping, you should hear –
     Nay, and you shall hear some.
              [To Brutus]   Will you be gone?

VIRGILIA *[to Sicinius]*
     You shall stay too. I would I had the power
     To say so to my husband.

16 SICINIUS   Are you mankind?

VOLUMNIA
     Ay, fool, is that a shame? Note but this fool.
18   Was not a man my father? Hadst thou foxship
     To banish him that struck more blows for Rome
     Than thou hast spoken words?

SICINIUS   O blessed heavens!

VOLUMNIA
21   Moe noble blows than ever thou wise words,
     And for Rome's good. I'll tell thee what – Yet go.
     Nay, but thou shalt stay too. I would my son
24   Were in Arabia, and thy tribe before him,
     His good sword in his hand.

SICINIUS   What then?

VIRGILIA   What then?

He'ld make an end of thy posterity.

VOLUMNIA
Bastards and all.
Good man, the wounds that he does bear for Rome!

MENENIUS
Come, come, peace.

SICINIUS
I would he had continued to his country
As he began, and not unknit himself   31
The noble knot he made.

BRUTUS   I would he had.

VOLUMNIA
'I would he had'?'Twas you incensed the rabble.
Cats, that can judge as fitly of his worth
As I can of those mysteries which heaven
Will not have earth to know!

BRUTUS   Pray, let us go.

VOLUMNIA
Now, pray, sir, get you gone.
You have done a brave deed. Ere you go, hear this :
As far as doth the Capitol exceed
The meanest house in Rome, so far my son, –
This lady's husband here, this, do you see? –
Whom you have banished, does exceed you all.

BRUTUS
Well, well, we'll leave you.

SICINIUS   Why stay we to be baited
With one that wants her wits?   *Exeunt Tribunes.*   44

VOLUMNIA   Take my prayers with you.
I would the gods had nothing else to do
But to confirm my curses. Could I meet 'em
But once a day, it would unclog my heart
Of what lies heavy to 't.

MENENIUS   You have told them home ;   48
And, by my troth, you have cause. You'll sup with me?

VOLUMNIA
Anger 's my meat. I sup upon myself,
And so shall starve with feeding. Come, let's go.
Leave this faint puling, and lament as I do,   52
In anger, Juno-like. Come, come, come.

MENENIUS   Fie, fie, fie! *Exeunt.*

*

              Enter a Roman and a Volsce.   IV, iii

ROMAN I know you well, sir, and you know me. Your
     name, I think, is Adrian.

VOLSCE It is so, sir. Truly, I have forgot you.

ROMAN I am a Roman ; and my services are, as you are,
     against 'em. Know you me yet?

VOLSCE Nicanor, no?

ROMAN The same, sir.

VOLSCE You had more beard when I last saw you ; but
     your favor is well appeared by your tongue. What's the   9
     news in Rome? I have a note from the Volscian state to
     find you out there. You have well saved me a day's
     journey.

ROMAN There hath been in Rome strange insurrections :
     the people against the senators, patricians, and nobles.

VOLSCE Hath been? is it ended then? Our state thinks
     not so. They are in a most warlike preparation, and hope
     to come upon them in the heat of their division.

ROMAN The main blaze of it is past, but a small thing
     would make it flame again ; for the nobles receive so to

IV, ii A street in Rome   1 *home* go home   5 *a-doing* being done   7 *ancient*
previous   11 *hoarded* accumulated   16 *mankind* masculine, human   18
foxship animal cunning   21 *Moe* more   24 *Arabia* the desert   31–32
unknit . . . knot himself undone the patriotic ties   44 *wants* lacks   48 *home*
off   52 *puling* whimpering
IV, iii The highway to Antium   9 *favor* face ; *appeared* made apparent

heart the banishment of that worthy Coriolanus that they are in a ripe aptness to take all power from the people and to pluck from them their tribunes for ever. This lies glowing, I can tell you, and is almost mature for the violent breaking out.

VOLSCE Coriolanus banished?

ROMAN Banished, sir.

VOLSCE You will be welcome with this intelligence, Nicanor.

28 ROMAN The day serves well for them now. I have heard it said, the fittest time to corrupt a man's wife is when she's fall'n out with her husband. Your noble Tullus Aufidius will appear well in these wars, his great opposer, Coriolanus, being now in no request of his country.

33 VOLSCE He cannot choose. I am most fortunate, thus accidentally to encounter you. You have ended my business, and I will merrily accompany you home.

36 ROMAN I shall, between this and supper, tell you most strange things from Rome, all tending to the good of their adversaries. Have you an army ready, say you?

39 VOLSCE A most royal one: the centurions and their
40 charges, distinctly billeted, already in th' entertainment, and to be on foot at an hour's warning.

ROMAN I am joyful to hear of their readiness, and am the man, I think, that shall set them in present action. So, sir, heartily well met, and most glad of your company.

VOLSCE You take my part from me, sir. I have the most cause to be glad of yours.

ROMAN Well, let us go together.   *Exeunt.*

*

IV, iv   *Enter Coriolanus in mean apparel, disguised and muffled.*

CORIOLANUS
A goodly city is this Antium. City,
'Tis I that made thy widows. Many an heir
3 Of these fair edifices 'fore my wars
Have I heard groan and drop. Then know me not,
Lest that thy wives with spits and boys with stones
6 In puny battle slay me.
     Enter a Citizen.   Save you, sir.

CITIZEN
And you.

CORIOLANUS Direct me, if it be your will,
8 Where great Aufidius lies. Is he in Antium?

CITIZEN
He is, and feasts the nobles of the state
At his house this night.

CORIOLANUS   Which is his house, beseech you?

CITIZEN
This, here before you.

CORIOLANUS   Thank you, sir. Farewell.
     Exit Citizen.
O world, thy slippery turns! Friends now fast sworn,
Whose double bosoms seems to wear one heart,
Whose hours, whose bed, whose meal and exercise
15 Are still together; who twin, as 'twere, in love
Unseparable, shall within this hour,
17 On a dissension of a doit, break out
18 To bitterest enmity. So, fellest foes,
Whose passions and whose plots have broke their sleep
To take the one the other, by some chance,
21 Some trick not worth an egg, shall grow dear friends

And interjoin their issues. So with me.   22
My birthplace hate I, and my love's upon
This enemy town. I'll enter. If he slay me,
He does fair justice; if he give me way,   25
I'll do his country service.   *Exit.*

*

Music plays. Enter a Servingman.   IV, v

FIRST SERVINGMAN Wine, wine, wine! What service is here? I think our fellows are asleep.   *[Exit.]* 2
     Enter another Servingman.

SECOND SERVINGMAN Where's Cotus? My master calls for him. Cotus!   *Exit.*
     Enter Coriolanus.

CORIOLANUS
A goodly house. The feast smells well, but I
Appear not like a guest.
     Enter the first Servingman.

FIRST SERVINGMAN What would you have, friend? Whence are you? Here's no place for you. Pray, go to the door.   *Exit.*

CORIOLANUS
I have deserved no better entertainment,
In being Coriolanus.
     Enter second Servant.

SECOND SERVINGMAN Whence are you, sir? Has the porter his eyes in his head, that he gives entrance to such companions? Pray, get you out.

CORIOLANUS Away!

SECOND SERVINGMAN Away? get you away!

CORIOLANUS Now th' art troublesome.

SECOND SERVINGMAN Are you so brave? I'll have you talked with anon.   18
     Enter third Servingman; the first meets him.

THIRD SERVINGMAN What fellow's this?

FIRST SERVINGMAN A strange one as ever I looked on. I cannot get him out o' th' house. Prithee, call my master to him.

THIRD SERVINGMAN What have you to do here, fellow? Pray you, avoid the house.   23

CORIOLANUS Let me but stand; I will not hurt your hearth.

THIRD SERVINGMAN What are you?

CORIOLANUS A gentleman.

THIRD SERVINGMAN A marv'llous poor one.   27

CORIOLANUS True, so I am.

THIRD SERVINGMAN Pray you, poor gentleman, take up some other station. Here's no place for you. Pray you, avoid. Come.

CORIOLANUS Follow your function, go, and batten on 32 cold bits.
     Pushes him away from him.

THIRD SERVINGMAN What, you will not? Prithee, tell my master what a strange guest he has here.

---

28 *them* the Volscians   33 *choose* help appearing well   36 *this* now   39 *centurions* officers each commanding a century, i.e. a hundred men   40 *distinctly* separately; *entertainment* service
IV, iv Before the house of Aufidius in Antium   3 *'fore* before   6 *puny* petty; *Save* God save   8 *lies* lodges   15 *still* always   17 *dissension . . . doit* trivial dispute   18 *fellest* fiercest   21 *trick* trifle   22 *interjoin their issues* join fortunes   25 *give me way* grant my request
IV, v Within the house of Aufidius   2 *fellows* companions   18 *anon* at once   23 *avoid* leave   27 *marv'llous* curiously   32 *batten* grow fat

SECOND SERVINGMAN And I shall.

                 Exit second Servingman.

THIRD SERVINGMAN Where dwell'st thou?

38 CORIOLANUS Under the canopy.

THIRD SERVINGMAN Under the canopy?

CORIOLANUS Ay.

THIRD SERVINGMAN Where's that?

42 CORIOLANUS I' th' city of kites and crows.

THIRD SERVINGMAN I' th' city of kites and crows?

44   What an ass it is! Then thou dwell'st with daws too?

CORIOLANUS No, I serve not thy master.

THIRD SERVINGMAN How, sir? Do you meddle with my master?

CORIOLANUS Ay, 'tis an honester service than to meddle with thy mistress.

50   Thou prat'st, and prat'st. Serve with thy trencher. Hence!

        Beats him away.

        Enter Aufidius with the [second] Servingman.

AUFIDIUS Where is this fellow?

SECOND SERVINGMAN Here, sir. I'd have beaten him like a dog, but for disturbing the lords within.

AUFIDIUS

Whence com'st thou? What wouldst thou? Thy name?
Why speak'st not? Speak, man. What's thy name?

CORIOLANUS   If, Tullus,

Not yet thou know'st me, and, seeing me, dost not

57   Think me for the man I am, necessity

58   Commands me name myself.

AUFIDIUS   What is thy name?

CORIOLANUS

A name unmusical to the Volscians' ears,
And harsh in sound to thine.

AUFIDIUS   Say, what's thy name?

Thou hast a grim appearance, and thy face
Bears a command in't; though thy tackle's torn,
Thou show'st a noble vessel. What's thy name?

CORIOLANUS

Prepare thy brow to frown. Know'st thou me yet?

AUFIDIUS

I know thee not. Thy name?

CORIOLANUS

My name is Caius Marcius, who hath done
To thee particularly and to all the Volsces
Great hurt and mischief; thereto witness may

69   My surname, Coriolanus. The painful service,
The extreme dangers, and the drops of blood
Shed for my thankless country are requited

72   But with that surname—a good memory,
And witness of the malice and displeasure
Which thou shouldst bear me. Only that name remains.

75   The cruelty and envy of the people,
Permitted by our dastard nobles, who
Have all forsook me, hath devoured the rest;

38 *canopy* sky (metaphorical)   42 *kites and crows* birds of prey   44 *daws* foolish birds   50 *trencher* plate; *Hence* get away   57 *Think* take   58 *name* to name   69 *painful* laborious   72 *memory* memorial   75 *cruelty and envy* envious cruelty   79 *Whooped* shouted   83 *mere* pure   84 *full quit of* completely even with   86 *heart of wreak* vengeful heart; *that wilt* so that thou wilt   92 *cank'red* corrupted; *spleen* anger   93 *under* infernal   94 *prove* try   108 *whereagainst* against which   109 *grainèd ash* wooden lance   110 *clip* embrace   117 *rapt* enraptured   119 *Bestride* step over   121 *target* shield; *brawn* muscular arm   122 *out* thoroughly   123 *several* different   127 *waked* I have awakened   128 *to* against   132 *o'erbeat* overflow violently   137 *absolute* perfect

And suffered me by th' voice of slaves to be
Whooped out of Rome. Now this extremity   79
Hath brought me to thy hearth, not out of hope—
Mistake me not—to save my life; for if
I had feared death, of all the men i' th' world
I would have 'voided thee; but in mere spite,   83
To be full quit of those my banishers,   84
Stand I before thee here. Then if thou hast
A heart of wreak in thee, that wilt revenge   86
Thine own particular wrongs, and stop those maims
Of shame seen through thy country, speed thee straight,
And make my misery serve thy turn. So use it
That my revengeful services may prove
As benefits to thee; for I will fight
Against my cank'red country with the spleen   92
Of all the under fiends. But if so be   93
Thou dar'st not this, and that to prove more fortunes   94
Th' art tired, then, in a word, I also am
Longer to live most weary; and present
My throat to thee and to thy ancient malice;
Which not to cut would show thee but a fool,
Since I have ever followed thee with hate,
Drawn tuns of blood out of thy country's breast,
And cannot live but to thy shame, unless
It be to do thee service.

AUFIDIUS   O Marcius, Marcius!

Each word thou hast spoke hath weeded from my heart
A root of ancient envy. If Jupiter
Should from yond cloud speak divine things,
And say ''Tis true,' I'd not believe them more
Than thee, all-noble Marcius. Let me twine
Mine arms about thy body, whereagainst   108
My grainèd ash an hundred times hath broke,   109
And scarred the moon with splinters. Here I clip   110
The anvil of my sword, and do contest
As hotly and as nobly with thy love
As ever in ambitious strength I did
Contend against thy valor. Know thou first,
I loved the maid I married; never man
Sighed truer breath. But that I see thee here,
Thou noble thing, more dances my rapt heart   117
Than when I first my wedded mistress saw
Bestride my threshold. Why, thou Mars, I tell thee,   119
We have a power on foot; and I had purpose
Once more to hew thy target from thy brawn,   121
Or lose mine arm for't. Thou hast beat me out   122
Twelve several times, and I have nightly since   123
Dreamt of encounters 'twixt thyself and me.
We have been down together in my sleep,
Unbuckling helms, fisting each other's throat,
And waked half dead with nothing. Worthy Marcius,   127
Had we no other quarrel else to Rome, but that   128
Thou art thence banished, we would muster all
From twelve to seventy, and, pouring war
Into the bowels of ungrateful Rome,
Like a bold flood o'erbeat. O, come, go in,   132
And take our friendly senators by th' hands,
Who now are here, taking their leaves of me,
Who am prepared against your territories,
Though not for Rome itself.

CORIOLANUS   You bless me, gods!

AUFIDIUS

Therefore, most absolute sir, if thou wilt have   137
The leading of thine own revenges, take

139 Th' one half of my commission; and set down –
As best thou art experienced, since thou know'st
Thy country's strength and weakness – thine own ways,
Whether to knock against the gates of Rome,
Or rudely visit them in parts remote,
144 To fright them ere destroy. But come in.
Let me commend thee first to those that shall
Say yea to thy desires. A thousand welcomes!
And more a friend than e'er an enemy;
Yet, Marcius, that was much. Your hand. Most wel-
come!   *Exeunt.*

Enter two of the Servingmen.

FIRST SERVINGMAN Here's a strange alteration!

SECOND SERVINGMAN By my hand, I had thought to
151 have strucken him with a cudgel; and yet my mind gave
me his clothes made a false report of him.

FIRST SERVINGMAN What an arm he has! He turned
me about with his finger and his thumb as one would set
up a top.

SECOND SERVINGMAN Nay, I knew by his face that
there was something in him. He had, sir, a kind of face,
methought – I cannot tell how to term it.

FIRST SERVINGMAN He had so, looking as it were –
Would I were hanged, but I thought there was more in
him than I could think.

SECOND SERVINGMAN So did I, I'll be sworn. He is
simply the rarest man i' th' world.

FIRST SERVINGMAN I think he is. But a greater soldier
164 than he you wot on.

SECOND SERVINGMAN Who, my master?

166 FIRST SERVINGMAN Nay, it's no matter for that.

SECOND SERVINGMAN Worth six on him.

FIRST SERVINGMAN Nay, not so neither. But I take him
to be the greater soldier.

SECOND SERVINGMAN Faith, look you, one cannot tell
how to say that. For the defense of a town, our general is
excellent.

FIRST SERVINGMAN Ay, and for an assault too.

Enter the third Servingman.

THIRD SERVINGMAN O slaves, I can tell you news.
News, you rascals!

BOTH [FIRST AND SECOND] What, what, what? Let's
partake.

THIRD SERVINGMAN I would not be a Roman, of all
nations. I had as lief be a condemned man.

BOTH Wherefore? Wherefore?

180 THIRD SERVINGMAN Why, here's he that was wont to
thwack our general, Caius Marcius.

FIRST SERVINGMAN Why do you say, 'thwack our
general'?

THIRD SERVINGMAN I do not say, 'thwack our general,'
but he was always good enough for him.

SECOND SERVINGMAN Come, we are fellows and friends.
He was ever too hard for him; I have heard him say so
himself.

FIRST SERVINGMAN He was too hard for him directly,
189 to say the troth on't. Before Corioles he scotched him
190 and notched him like a carbonado.

191 SECOND SERVINGMAN An he had been cannibally given,
he might have boiled and eaten him too.

FIRST SERVINGMAN But more of thy news?

194 THIRD SERVINGMAN Why, he is so made on here within,
as if he were son and heir to Mars; set at upper end o' th'
196 table; no question asked him by any of the senators, but

they stand bald before him. Our general himself makes a 197
mistress of him; sanctifies himself with's hand, and 198
turns up the white o' th' eye to his discourse. But the
bottom of the news is, our genera: is cut i' th' middle
and but one half of what he was yesterday; for the other
has half, by the entreaty and grant of the whole table.
He'll go, he says, and sowl the porter of Rome gates by 203
th' ears. He will mow all down before him, and leave
his passage polled. 205

SECOND SERVINGMAN And he's as like to do't as any
man I can imagine.

THIRD SERVINGMAN Do't? he will do't! for, look you,
sir, he has as many friends as enemies; which friends,
sir, as it were, durst not, look you, sir, show themselves,
as we term it, his friends whilst he's in directitude. 211

FIRST SERVINGMAN Directitude? what's that?

THIRD SERVINGMAN But when they shall see, sir, his
crest up again, and the man in blood, they will out of
their burrows like conies after rain, and revel all with him. 215

FIRST SERVINGMAN But when goes this forward?

THIRD SERVINGMAN To-morrow, to-day, presently. 217
You shall have the drum struck up this afternoon. 'Tis,
as it were, a parcel of their feast, and to be executed ere 219
they wipe their lips.

SECOND SERVINGMAN Why, then we shall have a stirring world again. This peace is nothing but to rust iron,
increase tailors, and breed ballad-makers.

FIRST SERVINGMAN Let me have war, say I. It exceeds
peace as far as day does night. It's sprightly, waking,
audible, and full of vent. Peace is a very apoplexy, 226
lethargy; mulled, deaf, sleepy, insensible; a getter of 227
more bastard children than war's a destroyer of men.

SECOND SERVINGMAN 'Tis so; and as war, in some sort,
may be said to be a ravisher, so it cannot be denied but
peace is a great maker of cuckolds.

FIRST SERVINGMAN Ay, and it makes men hate one another.

THIRD SERVINGMAN Reason: because they then less
need one another. The wars for my money. I hope to see
Romans as cheap as Volscians. They are rising, they are
rising.

BOTH [FIRST AND SECOND] In, in, in, in!   *Exeunt.*

*

Enter the two Tribunes, Sicinius and Brutus.   IV, vi

SICINIUS
We hear not of him, neither need we fear him;
His remedies are tame: the present peace 2
And quietness of the people, which before
Were in wild hurry. Here do we make his friends
Blush that the world goes well, who rather had,
Though they themselves did suffer by't, behold 6
Dissentious numbers pest'ring streets than see 7

139 *commission* command; *set down* decide   144 *ere destroy* before destroying them   151 *gave* suggested to   164 *wot on* know of   166 *it's . . . that*
never mind about names   189 *troth* truth; *scotched* slashed   190 *carbonado*
meat cut for broiling   191 *An* if   194 *made on* made much of   196 *but*
unless   197 *bald* bareheaded   198 *sanctifies . . . hand* touches his hand
as if it were a sacred relic   203 *sowl* pull roughly   205 *polled* stripped bare
211 *directitude* discredit (verbal blunder)   215 *conies* rabbits   217 *presently*
immediately   219 *parcel* part   226 *audible* capable of hearing; *apoplexy*
paralysis   227 *mulled* stupefied; *getter* begetter
IV, vi A public place in Rome   2 *His remedies* the remedies against him;
tame mild   6 *behold* beheld   7 *pest'ring* crowding

Our tradesmen singing in their shops and going
About their functions friendly.

BRUTUS

10 We stood to't in good time.

Enter Menenius. Is this Menenius?

SICINIUS

'Tis he, 'tis he! O, he is grown most kind of late.–
Hail, sir!

MENENIUS Hail to you both!

SICINIUS Your Coriolanus
Is not much missed, but with his friends.
The commonwealth doth stand, and so would do,
Were he more angry at it.

MENENIUS

All's well; and might have been much better, if
17 He could have temporized.

SICINIUS Where is he, hear you?

MENENIUS

Nay, I hear nothing. His mother and his wife
Hear nothing from him.

Enter three or four Citizens.

ALL

The gods preserve you both!

20 **SICINIUS** Good-e'en, our neighbors.

BRUTUS

Good-e'en to you all, good-e'en to you all.

FIRST CITIZEN

Ourselves, our wives, and children, on our knees,
Are bound to pray for you both.

SICINIUS Live, and thrive!

BRUTUS

Farewell, kind neighbors. We wished Coriolanus
Had loved you as we did.

CITIZENS Now the gods keep you!

BOTH TRIBUNES

Farewell, farewell. *Exeunt Citizens.*

SICINIUS

27 This is a happier and more comely time
Than when these fellows ran about the streets,
Crying confusion.

BRUTUS Caius Marcius was
A worthy officer i' th' war, but insolent,
O'ercome with pride, ambitious past all thinking,
Self-loving–

SICINIUS And affecting one sole throne
33 Without assistance.

MENENIUS I think not so.

SICINIUS

34 We should by this, to all our lamentation,
If he had gone forth consul, found it so.

BRUTUS

The gods have well prevented it, and Rome
Sits safe and still without him.

Enter an Aedile.

AEDILE Worthy tribunes,
There is a slave whom we have put in prison

Reports the Volsces with two several powers
Are ent'red in the Roman territories, 39
And with the deepest malice of the war
Destroy what lies before 'em.

MENENIUS 'Tis Aufidius,
Who, hearing of our Marcius' banishment,
Thrusts forth his horns again into the world;
Which were inshelled when Marcius stood for Rome, 45
And durst not once peep out.

SICINIUS Come, what talk you
Of Marcius?

BRUTUS

Go see this rumorer whipped. It cannot be
The Volsces dare break with us.

MENENIUS Cannot be!
We have record that very well it can,
And three examples of the like hath been
Within my age. But reason with the fellow, 52
Before you punish him, where he heard this,
Lest you shall chance to whip your information 54
And beat the messenger who bids beware
Of what is to be dreaded.

SICINIUS Tell not me.
I know this cannot be.

BRUTUS Not possible.

Enter a Messenger.

MESSENGER

The nobles in great earnestness are going
All to the Senate House. Some news is coming
That turns their countenances. 60

SICINIUS 'Tis this slave–
Go whip him 'fore the people's eyes – his raising, 61
Nothing but his report.

MESSENGER Yes, worthy sir.
The slave's report is seconded; and more, 63
More fearful, is delivered. 64

SICINIUS What more fearful?

MESSENGER

It is spoke freely out of many mouths–
How probable I do not know – that Marcius,
Joined with Aufidius, leads a power 'gainst Rome,
And vows revenge as spacious as between 68
The young'st and oldest thing.

SICINIUS This is most likely!

BRUTUS

Raised only, that the weaker sort may wish 70
Good Marcius home again.

SICINIUS The very trick on't.

MENENIUS

This is unlikely.
He and Aufidius can no more atone 73
Than violent'st contrariety. 74

Enter [another] Messenger.

MESSENGER

You are sent for to the Senate.
A fearful army, led by Caius Marcius
Associated with Aufidius, rages
Upon our territories; and have already
O'erborne their way, consumed with fire, and took 79
What lay before them.

Enter Cominius.

COMINIUS O, you have made good work!

MENENIUS

What news? What news?

10 *stood to't* took a stand 17 *temporized* compromised 20 *Good-e'en*
good evening 27 *comely* decent 33 *assistance* partners 34 *this* this
time 39 *several* separate 45 *inshelled* drawn in; *stood* stood up 52
reason discuss 54 *information* source of information 60 *turns* changes
61 *raising* incitement 63 *seconded* confirmed 64 *delivered* reported
68–69 *as spacious . . . thing* embracing all 70 *Raised* set going 73 *atone*
be reconciled 74 *violent'st contrariety* opposite extremes 79 *O'erborne*
crushed down

433

COMINIUS

82   You have holp to ravish your own daughters and

83   To melt the city leads upon your pates,
     To see your wives dishonored to your noses, –

MENENIUS
     What's the news? What's the news?

COMINIUS
     Your temples burnèd in their cement, and

87   Your franchises, whereon you stood, confined

88   Into an auger's bore.

MENENIUS   Pray now, your news? –
     You have made fair work, I fear me. – Pray, your news? –
     If Marcius should be joined with Volscians –

COMINIUS   If?
     He is their god. He leads them like a thing
     Made by some other deity than nature,
     That shapes man better; and they follow him
     Against us brats with no less confidence
     Than boys pursuing summer butterflies
     Or butchers killing flies.

MENENIUS   You have made good work,
     You and your apron-men! you that stood so much

98   Upon the voice of occupation and
     The breath of garlic-eaters!

COMINIUS   He'll shake
     Your Rome about your ears.

MENENIUS   As Hercules

101   Did shake down mellow fruit. You have made fair work!

BRUTUS
     But is this true, sir?

COMINIUS   Ay, and you'll look pale
     Before you find it other. All the regions

104   Do smilingly revolt; and who resists
     Are mocked for valiant ignorance,

106   And perish constant fools. Who is't can blame him?
     Your enemies and his find something in him.

MENENIUS
     We are all undone, unless
     The noble man have mercy.

COMINIUS   Who shall ask it?
     The tribunes cannot do't for shame; the people
     Deserve such pity of him as the wolf
     Does of the shepherds. For his best friends, if they

113   Should say, 'Be good to Rome,' they charged him even
     As those should do that had deserved his hate,

115   And therein showed like enemies.

MENENIUS   'Tis true.
     If he were putting to my house the brand
     That should consume it, I have not the face

118   To say, 'Beseech you, cease.' You have made fair hands,

119   You and your crafts! You have crafted fair!

COMINIUS   You have brought
     A trembling upon Rome, such as was never
     S' incapable of help.

TRIBUNES   Say not we brought it.

MENENIUS
     How? Was't we? We loved him; but, like beasts

123   And cowardly nobles, gave way unto your clusters,
     Who did hoot him out o' th' city.

COMINIUS   But I fear
     They'll roar him in again. Tullus Aufidius,

126   The second name of men, obeys his points
     As if he were his officer. Desperation
     Is all the policy, strength, and defense

That Rome can make against them.
     Enter a troop of Citizens.

MENENIUS   Here come the clusters.
     And is Aufidius with him? – You are they
     That made the air unwholesome, when you cast
     Your stinking greasy caps in hooting at
     Coriolanus' exile. Now he's coming;
     And not a hair upon a soldier's head
     Which will not prove a whip. As many coxcombs   135
     As you threw caps up will he tumble down,
     And pay you for your voices. 'Tis no matter.
     If he could burn us all into one coal,
     We have deserved it.

OMNES
     Faith, we hear fearful news.

FIRST CITIZEN   For mine own part,   140
     When I said banish him, I said 'twas pity.

SECOND CITIZEN   And so did I.

THIRD CITIZEN   And so did I; and, to say the truth, so
     did very many of us. That we did, we did for the best;
     and though we willingly consented to his banishment,
     yet it was against our will.

COMINIUS
     Y' are goodly things, you voices!

MENENIUS   You have made
     Good work, you and your cry! Shall's to the Capitol?   148

COMINIUS
     O, ay, what else?   *Exeunt both.*

SICINIUS
     Go, masters, get you home; be not dismayed.
     These are a side that would be glad to have
     This true, which they so seem to fear. Go home,
     And show no sign of fear.

FIRST CITIZEN   The gods be good to us! Come, masters,
     let's home. I ever said we were i' th' wrong when we
     banished him.

SECOND CITIZEN   So did we all. But come, let's home.
                              Exeunt Citizens.

BRUTUS
     I do not like this news.

SICINIUS   Nor I.

BRUTUS
     Let's to the Capitol. Would half my wealth   160
     Would buy this for a lie!

SICINIUS   Pray, let us go.
                              Exeunt Tribunes.

*

Enter Aufidius, with his Lieutenant.   IV, vii

AUFIDIUS
     Do they still fly to th' Roman?

LIEUTENANT
     I do not know what witchcraft 's in him, but
     Your soldiers use him as the grace 'fore meat,

---

82 *holp* helped   83 *leads* leaden roofs   87 *franchises* political rights; *whereon you stood* on which you insisted   88 *auger's bore* smallest aperture   98 *voice of occupation* mechanics' suffrage   101 *fruit* apples of Hesperides   104 *who* whoever   196 *constant* loyal   113 *charged* would enjoin   115 *showed* would appear   118 *made fair hands* done a fine job (ironic)   119 *crafted fair* intrigued beautifully   123 *clusters* crowds   126 *of* among; *points* directions   135 *coxcombs* fool's caps   140 *For . . . part* speaking for myself   148 *cry* pack; *Shall's* shall us   160–61 *Would . . . lie* I would give half my fortune if this were untrue
IV, vii A camp near Rome

Their talk at table, and their thanks at end;
5 And you are dark'ned in this action, sir,
Even by your own.

AUFIDIUS   I cannot help it now,
7 Unless by using means I lame the foot
Of our design. He bears himself more proudlier,
Even to my person, than I thought he would
When first I did embrace him. Yet his nature
11 In that's no changeling, and I must excuse
What cannot be amended.

LIEUTENANT   Yet I wish, sir, –
13 I mean for your particular – you had not
Joined in commission with him; but either
Had borne the action of yourself, or else
To him had left it solely.

AUFIDIUS
I understand thee well; and be thou sure,
When he shall come to his account, he knows not
What I can urge against him. Although it seems,
And so he thinks, and is no less apparent
To th' vulgar eye, that he bears all things fairly,
22 And shows good husbandry for the Volscian state,
23 Fights dragon-like, and does achieve as soon
As draw his sword: yet he hath left undone
That which shall break his neck or hazard mine,
Whene'er we come to our account.

LIEUTENANT
27 Sir, I beseech you, think you he'll carry Rome?

AUFIDIUS
28 All places yield to him ere he sits down,
And the nobility of Rome are his;
The senators and patricians love him too.
The tribunes are no soldiers, and their people
Will be as rash in the repeal as hasty
To expel him thence. I think he'll be to Rome
34 As is the osprey to the fish, who takes it
35 By sovereignty of nature. First he was
A noble servant to them, but he could not
37 Carry his honors even. Whether 'twas pride,
38 Which out of daily fortune ever taints
The happy man; whether defect of judgment,
40 To fail in the disposing of those chances
41 Which he was lord of; or whether nature,
Not to be other than one thing, not moving
43 From th' casque to th' cushion, but commanding peace
Even with the same austerity and garb
As he controlled the war; but one of these,
46 As he hath spices of them all, – not all,
47 For I dare so far free him – made him feared,

So hated, and so banished. But he has a merit,
To choke it in the utt'rance. So our virtues
Lie in th' interpretation of the time;   49
And power, unto itself most commendable,   50
Hath not a tomb so evident as a chair
T' extol what it hath done.   52
One fire drives out one fire; one nail, one nail;
Rights by rights founder, strengths by strengths do fail.
Come, let's away. When, Caius, Rome is thine,
Thou art poor'st of all; then shortly art thou mine.   57

                                        Exeunt.

                        *

Enter Menenius, Cominius; Sicinius, Brutus, the   V, i
two Tribunes; with others.

MENENIUS
No, I'll not go. You hear what he hath said
Which was sometime his general, who loved him   2
In a most dear particular. He called me father.   3
But what o' that? Go, you that banished him;
A mile before his tent fall down, and knee   5
The way into his mercy. Nay, if he coyed   6
To hear Cominius speak, I'll keep at home.   7

COMINIUS
He would not seem to know me.   8

MENENIUS   Do you hear?

COMINIUS
Yet one time he did call me by my name.
I urged our old acquaintance, and the drops
That we have bled together. Coriolanus
He would not answer to; forbade all names.
He was a kind of nothing, titleless,
Till he had forged himself a name o' th' fire   14
Of burning Rome.

MENENIUS   Why, so. – You have made good work!
A pair of tribunes that have racked for Rome,
To make coals cheap! A noble memory!   16

COMINIUS
I minded him how royal 'twas to pardon   18
When it was less expected. He replied,
It was a bare petition of a state   20
To one whom they had punished.

MENENIUS   Very well.
Could he say less?

COMINIUS
I offered to awaken his regard   23
For's private friends. His answer to me was,
He could not stay to pick them in a pile   25
Of noisome musty chaff. He said 'twas folly,
For one poor grain or two, to leave unburnt
And still to nose th' offense.   28

MENENIUS   For one poor grain or two?
I am one of those! His mother, wife, his child,
And this brave fellow too, we are the grains;
You are the musty chaff, and you are smelt
Above the moon. We must be burnt for you.

SICINIUS
Nay, pray, be patient. If you refuse your aid
In this so-never-needed help, yet do not
Upbraid's with our distress. But, sure, if you   34
Would be your country's pleader, your good tongue,
More than the instant army we can make,
Might stop our countryman.

MENENIUS   No, I'll not meddle.

5 dark'ned eclipsed   7 means means whereby   11 In . . . changeling is
not inconstant in that respect   13 for your particular in your own interests
22 husbandry management   23 achieve carry out his intention   27 carry
win   28 ere . . . down before he lays siege   34 osprey fish-hawk   35
sovereignty predominance   37 even without losing his equilibrium   38
daily fortune uninterrupted success; taints corrupts   40 disposing making
good use of   41 nature character   43 casque general's helmet; cushion
senator's seat   46 spices . . all a tincture of each   47 free absolve   49
To . . . utt'rance enough to suppress the recital of his faults   50 the time
our contemporaries   52 not . . . chair no memorial so certain as a public
rostrum   57 shortly soon
V, i A public place in Rome   2 Which who; sometime formerly   3 In . . .
particular with warmest personal affection   5 knee crawl   6 coyed disdained   7 keep stay   8 would not seem pretended not   14 o' out of   16
racked striven   18 minded reminded   20 bare mere   23 offered attempted
25 stay . . . them stop to pick them out   28 nose smell; offense offensive
matter   34 so-never-needed never so much needed

SICINIUS
Pray you, go to him.

MENENIUS   What should I do?

BRUTUS
Only make trial what your love can do
For Rome toward Marcius.

MENENIUS   Well, and say that Marcius

42 Return me, as Cominius is returned,
Unheard – what then?

44 But as a discontented friend, grief-shot
With his unkindness? Say't be so?

SICINIUS   Yet your good will

46 Must have that thanks from Rome, after the measure
As you intended well.

MENENIUS   I'll undertake't:
I think he'll hear me. Yet, to bite his lip

49 And hum at good Cominius much unhearts me.

50 He was not taken well; he had not dined.
The veins unfilled, our blood is cold, and then
We pout upon the morning, are unapt
To give or to forgive; but when we have stuffed

54 These pipes and these conveyances of our blood
With wine and feeding, we have suppler souls

56 Than in our priest-like fasts. Therefore I'll watch him

57 Till he be dieted to my request,
And then I'll set upon him.

BRUTUS
You know the very road into his kindness,
And cannot lose your way.

MENENIUS   Good faith, I'll prove him,
Speed how it will. I shall ere long have knowledge

62 Of my success.   *Exit.*

COMINIUS   He'll never hear him.

SICINIUS   Not?

COMINIUS

63 I tell you, he does sit in gold, his eye

64 Red as 'twould burn Rome, and his injury
The jailer to his pity. I kneeled before him.
'Twas very faintly he said, 'Rise'; dismissed me
Thus, with his speechless hand. What he would do
He sent in writing after me; what he would not

69 Bound with an oath to yield to his conditions;
So that all hope is vain

71 Unless his noble mother and his wife,
Who, as I hear, mean to solicit him
For mercy to his country. Therefore let's hence,

74 And with our fair entreaties haste them on.   *Exeunt.*

*

V, ii   *Enter Menenius to the Watch on guard.*

FIRST WATCH
Stay. Whence are you?

SECOND WATCH   Stand, and go back.

MENENIUS
You guard like men; 'tis well. But, by your leave,
I am an officer of state, and come
To speak with Coriolanus.

FIRST WATCH   From whence?

MENENIUS   From Rome.

FIRST WATCH
You may not pass; you must return. Our general
Will no more hear from thence.

SECOND WATCH
You'll see your Rome embraced with fire before
You'll speak with Coriolanus.

MENENIUS   Good my friends,   8
If you have heard your general talk of Rome
And of his friends there, it is lots to blanks   10
My name hath touched your ears. It is Menenius.

FIRST WATCH
Be't so; go back. The virtue of your name
Is not here passable.

MENENIUS   I tell thee, fellow,
Thy general is my lover. I have been   14
The book of his good acts, whence men have read
His fame unparalleled, haply amplified;   16
For I have ever verified my friends,   17
Of whom he's chief, with all the size that verity
Would without lapsing suffer. Nay, sometimes,
Like to a bowl upon a subtle ground,   20
I have tumbled past the throw; and in his praise
Have almost stamped the leasing. Therefore, fellow,   22
I must have leave to pass.

FIRST WATCH Faith, sir, if you had told as many lies in
his behalf as you have uttered words in your own, you
should not pass here; no, though it were as virtuous to
lie as to live chastely. Therefore go back.   27

MENENIUS Prithee, fellow, remember my name is
Menenius, always factionary on the party of your   29
general.

SECOND WATCH Howsoever you have been his liar, as
you say you have, I am one that, telling true under him,
must say you cannot pass. Therefore go back.

MENENIUS Has he dined, canst thou tell? For I would
not speak with him till after dinner.

FIRST WATCH You are a Roman, are you?

MENENIUS I am, as thy general is.

FIRST WATCH Then you should hate Rome, as he does.
Can you, when you have pushed out your gates the very   38
defender of them, and in a violent popular ignorance
given your enemy your shield, think to front his re-   40
venges with the easy groans of old women, the virginal
palms of your daughters, or with the palsied intercession
of such a decayed dotant as you seem to be? Can you   43
think to blow out the intended fire your city is ready to
flame in, with such weak breath as this? No, you are
deceived; therefore back to Rome, and prepare for your
execution. You are condemned; our general has sworn
you out of reprieve and pardon.   48

MENENIUS Sirrah, if thy captain knew I were here, he
would use me with estimation.   50

FIRST WATCH Come, my captain knows you not.

MENENIUS I mean thy general.

FIRST WATCH My general cares not for you. Back, I say,

42 *Return* send away   **44** *grief-shot* sorrow-stricken   **46–47** *after . . . As*
to the extent that   **49** *unhearts* disheartens   **50** *taken well* approached
opportunely   **54** *conveyances* channels   **56** *watch* wait for   **57** *dieted to*
fed to the point of entertaining   **62** *success* result   **63** *does . . . gold* is
enthroned   **64** *injury* sense of injury   **69** *Bound* he bound; *to yield* that
we should yield   **71** *Unless* except for   **74** *fair* courteous
V, ii The Volscian camp before Rome   **8** *Good my friends* my good friends
10 *lots* prizes; *blanks* lottery tickets without value   **14** *lover* well-wisher
16 *haply* possibly   **17** *verified* supported the credit of   **20** *bowl* wooden
ball; *subtle* deceptive   **22** *stamped* attested; *leasing* falsehood   **27** *chastely*
honestly   **29** *factionary* partisan   **38** *out* out of   **40** *front* meet   **43** *dotant*
dotard   **48** *out of* beyond   **50** *use* treat; *estimation* esteem

go! lest I let forth your half-pint of blood, – back! –
55 that's the utmost of your having. Back!
MENENIUS Nay, but, fellow, fellow –
Enter Coriolanus and Aufidius.
CORIOLANUS What's the matter?
MENENIUS Now, you companion, I'll say an errand for
you. You shall know now that I am in estimation; you
60 shall perceive that a Jack guardant cannot office me
61 from my son Coriolanus. Guess but by my entertainment with him. If thou stand'st not i' th' state of hang-
63 ing, or of some death more long in spectatorship and
crueler in suffering, behold now presently, and swound
for what's to come upon thee. *[to Coriolanus]* The
glorious gods sit in hourly synod about thy particular
prosperity, and love thee no worse than thy old father
Menenius does! O my son, my son! Thou art preparing
fire for us. Look thee, here's water to quench it. I was
70 hardly moved to come to thee; but being assured none
but myself could move thee, I have been blown out of
our gates with sighs; and conjure thee to pardon Rome
73 and thy petitionary countrymen. The good gods assuage
thy wrath, and turn the dregs of it upon this varlet here
75 – this, who, like a block, hath denied my access to thee.
CORIOLANUS Away!
MENENIUS How? away?
CORIOLANUS
Wife, mother, child, I know not. My affairs
79 Are servanted to others. Though I owe
80 My revenge properly, my remission lies
In Volscian breasts. That we have been familiar,
82 Ingrate forgetfulness shall poison, rather
Than pity note how much. Therefore be gone.
Mine ears against your suits are stronger than
85 Your gates against my force. Yet, for I loved thee,
Take this along. I writ it for thy sake,
[Gives a letter.]
And would have sent it. Another word, Menenius,
I will not hear thee speak. This man, Aufidius,
Was my beloved in Rome; yet thou behold'st!
AUFIDIUS
You keep a constant temper.
Exeunt. Manent the Guard and Menenius.
FIRST WATCH Now, sir, is your name Menenius?
SECOND WATCH 'Tis a spell, you see, of much power.
You know the way home again.
94 FIRST WATCH Do you hear how we are shent for keeping
your greatness back?
SECOND WATCH What cause do you think I have to
swound?
MENENIUS I neither care for th' world nor your general.
For such things as you, I can scarce think there's any,
99 y' are so slight. He that hath a will to die by himself fears

it not from another. Let your general do his worst. For
you, be that you are, long; and your misery increase 101
with your age! I say to you, as I was said to, 'Away!'
Exit.
FIRST WATCH A noble fellow, I warrant him.
SECOND WATCH The worthy fellow is our general. He's
the rock, the oak not to be wind-shaken. *Exit Watch.*

*

Enter Coriolanus and Aufidius [with others].   V, iii
CORIOLANUS
We will before the walls of Rome to-morrow
Set down our host. My partner in this action, 2
You must report to th' Volscian lords how plainly
I have borne this business. 3
AUFIDIUS   Only their ends
You have respected; stopped your ears against
The general suit of Rome; never admitted
A private whisper, no, not with such friends
That thought them sure of you.
CORIOLANUS   This last old man,
Whom with a cracked heart I have sent to Rome,
Loved me above the measure of a father;
Nay, godded me indeed. Their latest refuge 11
Was to send him; for whose old love I have –
Though I showed sourly to him – once more offered 13
The first conditions, which they did refuse
And cannot now accept. To grace him only, 15
That thought he could do more, a very little
I have yielded to. Fresh embassies and suits, 17
Nor from the state nor private friends, hereafter
Will I lend ear to.
Shout within. Ha! What shout is this?
Shall I be tempted to infringe my vow
In the same time 'tis made? I will not.
Enter Virgilia, Volumnia, Valeria, young Marcius,
with Attendants.
My wife comes foremost; then the honored mould 22
Wherein this trunk was framed, and in her hand 23
The grandchild to her blood. But out, affection!
All bond and privilege of nature, break!
Let it be virtuous to be obstinate.
What is that curt'sy worth? or those doves' eyes,
Which can make gods forsworn? I melt, and am not
Of stronger earth than others. My mother bows,
As if Olympus to a molehill should
In supplication nod; and my young boy 30
Hath an aspect of intercession which
Great nature cries, 'Deny not!' Let the Volsces
Plough Rome and harrow Italy! I'll never
Be such a gosling to obey instinct, but stand
As if a man were author of himself
And knew no other kin.
VIRGILIA   My lord and husband!
CORIOLANUS
These eyes are not the same I wore in Rome.
VIRGILIA
The sorrow that delivers us thus changed
Makes you think so. 39
CORIOLANUS   Like a dull actor now,
I have forgot my part, and I am out,
Even to a full disgrace. Best of my flesh, 41

---

55 *the . . . having* as much as you have   60 *Jack guardant* knave on guard;
office officiously keep   61 *entertainment* reception   63 *spectatorship* watching   70 *hardly* with difficulty   73 *petitionary* entreating   75 *block*
obstruction, blockhead   79 *servanted* made subservient; *owe* possess
80 *properly* as my own; *remission* power to pardon   82 *Ingrate forgetfulness*
your ingratitude in failing to defend me   85 *for* because   94 *shent* taken
to task   99 *by himself* at his own hands   101 *long* tedious, long-lived
V, iii Before the tent of Coriolanus   2 *host* army   3 *plainly* straightforwardly   11 *godded* idolized; *latest* last   13 *showed* acted   15 *grace*
gratify   17–18 *Fresh . . . friends* neither fresh embassies from the state nor
suits from private friends   22 *mould* matrix   23 *trunk* body   30 *Olympus*
sacred mountain   39 *delivers* shows   41 *out* at fault

Forgive my tyranny ; but do not say
For that, 'Forgive our Romans.' O, a kiss
Long as my exile, sweet as my revenge !
46 Now, by the jealous queen of heaven, that kiss
47 I carried from thee dear ; and my true lip
48 Hath virgined it e'er since. You gods ! I prate,
And the most noble mother of the world
Leave unsaluted. Sink, my knee, i' th' earth ;
     Kneels.
Of thy deep duty more impression show
Than that of common sons.

VOLUMNIA   O, stand up blest !
Whilst with no softer cushion than the flint
I kneel before thee, and unproperly
Show duty as mistaken all this while
Between the child and parent.

CORIOLANUS   What is this ?
57 Your knees to me ? to your corrected son ?
58 Then let the pebbles on the hungry beach
59 Fillip the stars ! Then let the mutinous winds
Strike the proud cedars 'gainst the fiery sun,
61 Murd'ring impossibility, to make
What cannot be, slight work.

VOLUMNIA   Thou art my warrior ;
63 I holp to frame thee. Do you know this lady ?

CORIOLANUS
64 The noble sister of Publicola,
The moon of Rome, chaste as the icicle
66 That's curded by the frost from purest snow
67 And hangs on Dian's temple – dear Valeria !

VOLUMNIA
68 This is a poor epitome of yours,
Which by th' interpretation of full time
70 May show like all yourself.

CORIOLANUS   The god of soldiers,
With the consent of supreme Jove, inform
Thy thoughts with nobleness, that thou mayst prove
73 To shame unvulnerable, and stick i' th' wars
74 Like a great sea-mark, standing every flaw
And saving those that eye thee !

75 VOLUMNIA   Your knee, sirrah.

CORIOLANUS
That's my brave boy !

VOLUMNIA
Even he, your wife, this lady, and myself,
Are suitors to you.

CORIOLANUS   I beseech you, peace !
Or, if you'd ask, remember this before :
80 The thing I have forsworn to grant may never
Be held by you denials. Do not bid me
82 Dismiss my soldiers, or capitulate
Again with Rome's mechanics. Tell me not
Wherein I seem unnatural. Desire not
T' allay my rages and revenges with
Your colder reasons.

VOLUMNIA   O, no more, no more !
You have said you will not grant us anything ;
For we have nothing else to ask but that
Which you deny already ; yet we will ask,
90 That, if you fail in our request, the blame
May hang upon your hardness. Therefore hear us.

CORIOLANUS
Aufidius, and you Volsces, mark ; for we'll
Hear naught from Rome in private. – Your request ?

VOLUMNIA
Should we be silent and not speak, our raiment
And state of bodies would bewray what life
We have led since thy exile. Think with thyself
How more unfortunate than all living women
Are we come hither ; since that thy sight, which should
Make our eyes flow with joy, hearts dance with comforts,
100 Constrains them weep and shake with fear and sorrow,
Making the mother, wife, and child to see
The son, the husband, and the father tearing
103 His country's bowels out. And to poor we
104 Thine enmity 's most capital. Thou barr'st us
Our prayers to the gods, which is a comfort
That all but we enjoy. For how can we,
Alas, how can we for our country pray,
Whereto we are bound, together with thy victory,
109 Whereto we are bound ? Alack, or we must lose
The country, our dear nurse, or else thy person,
Our comfort in the country. We must find
112 An evident calamity, though we had
Our wish which side should win. For either thou
114 Must as a foreign recreant be led
With manacles through our streets, or else
Triumphantly tread on thy country's ruin,
117 And bear the palm for having bravely shed
Thy wife and children's blood. For myself, son,
I purpose not to wait on fortune till
120 These wars determine. If I cannot persuade thee
121 Rather to show a noble grace to both parts
Than seek the end of one, thou shalt no sooner
March to assault thy country than to tread –
Trust to't, thou shalt not – on thy mother's womb
That brought thee to this world.

VIRGILIA   Ay, and mine,
That brought you forth this boy, to keep your name
Living to time.

BOY   A' shall not tread on me !
127 I'll run away till I am bigger, but then I'll fight.

CORIOLANUS
Not of a woman's tenderness to be
Requires nor child nor woman's face to see.
I have sat too long.
     [Rises.]

VOLUMNIA   Nay, go not from us thus.
If it were so that our request did tend
To save the Romans, thereby to destroy
The Volsces whom you serve, you might condemn us
As poisonous of your honor. No, our suit
Is, that you reconcile them while the Volsces
May say, 'This mercy we have showed,' the Romans,
'This we received,' and each in either side
Give the all-hail to thee and cry, 'Be blest 139
For making up this peace !' Thou know'st, great son,

46 *queen of heaven* Juno 47 *dear* cherished 48 *virgined it* kept it intact 57 *corrected* chastised 58 *hungry* barren 59 *Fillip* snap with a finger 61 *Murd'ring impossibility* making nothing seem impossible 63 *holp* helped 64 *Publicola* a famous consul 66 *curded* congealed 67 *Dian* virgin goddess 68 *epitome* miniature 70 *show* appear 73 *To shame unvulnerable* incapable of disgrace ; *stick* be fixed 74 *sea-mark* point serving as guide for navigators ; *flaw* gust 75 *sirrah* sir 80 *forsworn* sworn not 82 *capitulate* come to terms 90 *fail* fail to grant 100 *weep* to weep 103 *poor we* our poor selves 104 *capital* deadly ; *barr'st us* keep us from 109 *or* either 112 *evident* certain 114 *recreant* traitor 117 *palm* emblem of triumph 120 *determine* end 121 *grace* mercy ; *parts* sides 127 *'A* he (familiar) 139 *all-hail* salutation of honor

438

The end of war's uncertain, but this certain,
That, if thou conquer Rome, the benefit
Which thou shalt thereby reap is such a name
Whose repetition will be dogged with curses,
145 Whose chronicle thus writ: 'The man was noble,
146 But with his last attempt he wiped it out,
Destroyed his country; and his name remains
To th' ensuing age abhorred,' Speak to me, son.
149 Thou hast affected the fine strains of honor,
To imitate the graces of the gods;
To tear with thunder the wide cheeks o' th' air,
152 And yet to change thy sulphur with a bolt
153 That should but rive an oak. Why dost not speak?
Think'st thou it honorable for a noble man
Still to remember wrongs? Daughter, speak you.
He cares not for your weeping. Speak thou, boy.
Perhaps thy childishness will move him more
Than can our reasons. There's no man in the world
More bound to's mother; yet here he lets me prate
160 Like one i' th' stocks. Thou hast never in thy life
161 Showed thy dear mother any courtesy,
162 When she, poor hen, fond of no second brood,
Has clucked thee to the wars, and safely home
Loaden with honor. Say my request's unjust,
And spurn me back; but if it be not so,
166 Thou art not honest, and the gods will plague thee
167 That thou restrain'st from me the duty which
To a mother's part belongs. He turns away.
Down, ladies! Let us shame him with our knees.
170 To his surname Coriolanus 'longs more pride
Than pity to our prayers. Down! An end!
This is the last. So, we will home to Rome,
173 And die among our neighbors. Nay, behold's!
This boy, that cannot tell what he would have
But kneels and holds up hands for fellowship,
176 Does reason our petition with more strength
Than thou hast to deny't. Come, let us go.
178 This fellow had a Volscian to his mother;
His wife is in Corioles, and this child
Like him by chance. Yet give us our dispatch.
I am hushed until our city be afire,
182 And then I'll speak a little.
    [Coriolanus] holds her by the hand, silent.
CORIOLANUS   O mother, mother!
183 What have you done? Behold, the heavens do ope,
The gods look down, and this unnatural scene
They laugh at. O my mother, mother! O!
You have won a happy victory to Rome;
But for your son – believe it, O believe it! –
Most dangerously you have with him prevailed,
189 If not most mortal to him. But let it come.

Aufidius, though I cannot make true wars,
I'll frame convenient peace. Now, good Aufidius, 191
Were you in my stead, would you have heard
A mother less? or granted less, Aufidius?
AUFIDIUS
I was moved withal.
CORIOLANUS   I dare be sworn you were! 194
And, sir, it is no little thing to make
Mine eyes to sweat compassion. But, good sir,
What peace you'll make, advise me. For my part,
I'll not to Rome, I'll back with you; and pray you,
Stand to me in this cause. O mother! wife! 199
AUFIDIUS *[aside]*
I am glad thou hast set thy mercy and thy honor
At difference in thee. Out of that I'll work
Myself a former fortune. 202
CORIOLANUS *[to Volumnia]*
     Ay, by and by.
But we will drink together; and you shall bear
A better witness back than words, which we, 204
On like conditions, will have counter-sealed.
Come, enter with us. Ladies, you deserve
To have a temple built you. All the swords 207
In Italy, and her confederate arms, 208
Could not have made this peace.   *Exeunt.*

*

Enter Menenius and Sicinius.   V, iv
MENENIUS See you yond coign o' th' Capitol, yond 1
cornerstone?
SICINIUS Why, what of that?
MENENIUS If it be possible for you to displace it with
your little finger, there is some hope the ladies of Rome,
especially his mother, may prevail with him. But I say
there is no hope in't; our throats are sentenced and stay 7
upon execution.
SICINIUS Is't possible that so short a time can alter the
condition of a man?
MENENIUS There is difference between a grub and a 11
butterfly; yet your butterfly was a grub. This Marcius
is grown from man to dragon. He has wings; he's more
than a creeping thing.
SICINIUS He loved his mother dearly.
MENENIUS So did he me; and he no more remembers his
mother now than an eight-year-old horse. The tartness
of his face sours ripe grapes. When he walks, he moves
like an engine, and the ground shrinks before his tread- 19
ing. He is able to pierce a corslet with his eye; talks like 20
a knell and his hum is a battery. He sits in his state, as a 21
thing made for Alexander. What he bids be done is 22
finished with his bidding. He wants nothing of a god but 23
eternity, and a heaven to throne in.
SICINIUS Yes, mercy, if you report him truly.
MENENIUS I paint him in the character. Mark what 26
mercy his mother shall bring from him. There is no
more mercy in him than there is milk in a male tiger.
That shall our poor city find; and all this is long of you. 29
SICINIUS The gods be good unto us!
MENENIUS No, in such a case the gods will not be good
unto us. When we banished him, we respected not
them; and, he returning to break our necks, they respect
not us.
     Enter a Messenger.

MESSENGER
Sir, if you'd save your life, fly to your house.
The plebeians have got your fellow-tribune,
36 And hale him up and down ; all swearing, if
The Roman ladies bring not comfort home,
They'll give him death by inches.
     Enter another Messenger.
SICINIUS   What's the news ?
MESSENGER
Good news, good news ! The ladies have prevailed,
40 The Volscians are dislodged, and Marcius gone.
A merrier day did never yet greet Rome,
42 No, not th' expulsion of the Tarquins.
SICINIUS   Friend,
Art thou certain this is true ? is't most certain ?
MESSENGER
As certain as I know the sun is fire.
45 Where have you lurked that you make doubt of it ?
46 Ne'er through an arch so hurried the blown tide
47 As the recomforted through th' gates. Why, hark you !
     Trumpets, hautboys ; drums beat ; all together.
48 The trumpets, sackbuts, psalteries, and fifes,
49 Tabors and cymbals and the shouting Romans
Make the sun dance. Hark you !
     A shout within.
MENENIUS   This is good news.
I will go meet the ladies. This Volumnia
Is worth of consuls, senators, patricians,
A city full ; of tribunes, such as you,
A sea and land full. You have prayed well to-day.
This morning for ten thousand of your throats
56 I'd not have given a doit. Hark, how they joy !
     Sound still, with the shouts.
SICINIUS
First, the gods bless you for your tidings ; next,
Accept my thankfulness.
MESSENGER   Sir, we have all
Great cause to give great thanks.
SICINIUS   They are near the city ?
MESSENGER
60 Almost at point to enter.
SICINIUS   We will meet them,
And help the joy.   *Exeunt.*
V, v   *Enter two Senators with Ladies [Volumnia, Virgilia,*
     Valeria] passing over the stage, with other Lords.
SENATOR
Behold our patroness, the life of Rome !
Call all your tribes together, praise the gods,
And make triumphant fires ; strew flowers before them.
Unshout the noise that banished Marcius ;
5 Repeal him with the welcome of his mother.
Cry, 'Welcome, ladies, welcome !'
ALL   Welcome, ladies,
Welcome !
     A flourish with drums and trumpets. [Exeunt.]

         *

V, vi   *Enter Tullus Aufidius, with Attendants.*
AUFIDIUS
Go tell the lords o' th' city I am here.
2 Deliver them this paper. Having read it,
Bid them repair to th' market-place, where I,
4 Even in theirs and in the commons' ears,

Will vouch the truth of it. Him I accuse 5
The city ports by this hath entered and
Intends t' appear before the people, hoping
To purge himself with words. Dispatch.
     [Exeunt Attendants.]
   Enter three or four Conspirators of Aufidius' faction.
            Most welcome !
FIRST CONSPIRATOR
How is it with our general ?
AUFIDIUS   Even so
As with a man by his own alms empoisoned
And with his charity slain.
SECOND CONSPIRATOR   Most noble sir,
If you do hold the same intent wherein
You wished us parties, we'll deliver you 13
Of your great danger.
AUFIDIUS   Sir, I cannot tell.
We must proceed as we do find the people.
THIRD CONSPIRATOR
The people will remain uncertain whilst
'Twixt you there's difference ; but the fall of either
Makes the survivor heir of all.
AUFIDIUS   I know it ;
And my pretext to strike at him admits
A good construction. I raised him, and I pawned 20
Mine honor for his truth ; who being so heightened, 21
He watered his new plants with dews of flattery,
Seducing so my friends ; and to this end
He bowed his nature, never known before
But to be rough, unswayable, and free.
THIRD CONSPIRATOR
Sir, his stoutness 26
When he did stand for consul, which he lost
By lack of stooping –
AUFIDIUS   That I would have spoke of.
Being banished for't, he came unto my hearth ;
Presented to my knife his throat. I took him ;
Made him joint-servant with me ; gave him way 31
In all his own desires ; nay, let him choose
Out of my files, his projects to accomplish, 33
My best and freshest men ; served his designments 34
In mine own person ; holp to reap the fame 35
Which he did end all his ; and took some pride 36
To do myself this wrong ; till at the last
I seemed his follower, not partner, and
He waged me with his countenance as if 39
I had been mercenary.
FIRST CONSPIRATOR   So he did, my lord.
The army marvelled at it ; and in the last,
When he had carried Rome and that we looked
For no less spoil than glory –
AUFIDIUS   There was it ! 43
For which my sinews shall be stretched upon him. 44

---

36 *hale* pull   40 *dislodged* retired   42 *Tarquins* dynasty of tyrants   45 *lurked* been hiding   46 *blown* swollen   47 s.d. *hautboys* oboes   48 *sackbuts* trombones ; *psalteries* stringed instruments   49 *Tabors* small drums   56 *doit* smallest possible sum   60 *at . . . enter* on the point of entering   V, v   5 *Repeal him* recall him from exile   V, vi A public place in Corioli   2 *them* to them   4 *theirs* their ears   5 *Him* he whom   13 *parties* to be allies   20 *construction* interpretation   21 *truth* loyalty ; *heightened* exalted   26 *stoutness* obstinacy   31 *joint-servant* colleague ; *gave him way* gave way to him   33 *files* ranks   34 *designments* enterprises   35 *holp* help   36 *end* gather in as a harvest   39 *waged* remunerated ; *countenance* patronage   43 *There* that   44 *sinews . . . upon* strength shall be exerted against

45 At a few drops of women's rheum, which are
46 As cheap as lies, he sold the blood and labor
    Of our great action; therefore shall he die,
48 And I'll renew me in his fall. But, hark!
       *Drums and trumpets sound, with great shouts of the
       People.*

FIRST CONSPIRATOR
49 Your native town you entered like a post,
    And had no welcomes home; but he returns,
    Splitting the air with noise.

SECOND CONSPIRATOR   And patient fools,
    Whose children he hath slain, their base throats tear
    With giving him glory.

53 THIRD CONSPIRATOR Therefore, at your vantage,
    Ere he express himself or move the people
    With what he would say, let him feel your sword,
56 Which we will second. When he lies along,
57 After your way his tale pronounced shall bury
58 His reasons with his body.

AUFIDIUS   Say no more.
    Here come the lords.
       Enter the Lords of the city.

ALL LORDS
    You are most welcome home.

AUFIDIUS   I have not deserved it.
    But, worthy lords, have you with heed perused
    What I have written to you?

ALL   We have.
FIRST LORD   And grieve to hear't.
63 What faults he made before the last, I think
64 Might have found easy fines; but there to end
    Where he was to begin, and give away
66 The benefit of our levies, answering us
67 With our own charge, making a treaty where
    There was a yielding – this admits no excuse.

AUFIDIUS
    He approaches. You shall hear him.
       *Enter Coriolanus, marching with Drum and Colors,
       the Commoners being with him.*

CORIOLANUS
    Hail, lords! I am returned your soldier;
    No more infected with my country's love
    That when I parted hence, but still subsisting
    Under your great command. You are to know
74 That prosperously I have attempted, and
75 With bloody passage led your wars even to
76 The gates of Rome. Our spoils we have brought home
77 Do more than counterpoise a full third part
    The charges of the action. We have made peace
    With no less honor to the Antiates
    Than shame to th' Romans; and we here deliver,
    Subscribed by th' consuls and patricians,
    Together with the seal o' th' Senate, what
83 We have compounded on.

45 *rheum* tears 46 *blood and labor* bloody labor 48 *renew me* be restored
49 *post* messenger 53 *at your vantage* seizing your opportunity 56
along prone 57 *After . . . pronounced* your own version of the affair 58
reasons justification 63 *made* committed 64 *fines* punishments 66 *levies*
forces raised; *answering* repaying 67 *charge* expenses 74 *prosperously
. . . attempted* my endeavors have been fortunate 75 *passage* course 76
spoils plunder *which* 77 *Do . . . counterpoise* outweigh 83 *compounded*
reached an agreement 98 *That* so that; *heart* courage 102 *Too . . . it* too
swollen for my breast 105 *notion* understanding 111 *edges* swords 112
there recorded there 116 *blind fortune* mere luck 119 *presently* at once
123 *folds in* enfolds 125 *judicious* judicial

AUFIDIUS   Read it not, noble lords;
    But tell the traitor in the highest degree
    He hath abused your powers.

CORIOLANUS
    Traitor? how now?

AUFIDIUS   Ay, traitor, Marcius!

CORIOLANUS   Marcius?

AUFIDIUS
    Ay, Marcius, Caius Marcius! Dost thou think
    I'll grace thee with that robbery, thy stol'n name
    Coriolanus in Corioles?
    You lords and heads o' th' state, perfidiously
    He has betrayed your business and given up,
    For certain drops of salt, your city Rome –
    I say 'your city' – to his wife and mother;
    Breaking his oath and resolution like
    A twist of rotten silk; never admitting
    Counsel o' th' war; but at his nurse's tears
    He whined and roared away your victory,
    That pages blushed at him and men of heart
    Looked wond'ring each at other.   98

CORIOLANUS   Hear'st thou, Mars?

AUFIDIUS
    Name not the god, thou boy of tears!

CORIOLANUS   Ha!

AUFIDIUS   No more.

CORIOLANUS
    Measureless liar, thou hast made my heart
    Too great for what contains it. Boy? O slave!   102
    Pardon me, lords, 'tis the first time that ever
    I was forced to scold. Your judgments, my grave lords,
    Must give this cur the lie; and his own notion – 105
    Who wears my stripes impressed upon him, that
    Must bear my beating to his grave – shall join
    To thrust the lie unto him.

FIRST LORD
    Peace, both, and hear me speak.

CORIOLANUS
    Cut me to pieces, Volsces. Men and lads,
    Stain all your edges on me. Boy? False hound!   111
    If you have writ your annals true, 'tis there   112
    That, like an eagle in a dovecote, I
    Fluttered your Volscians in Corioles.
    Alone I did it. Boy?

AUFIDIUS   Why, noble lords,
    Will you be put in mind of his blind fortune,   116
    Which was your shame, by this unholy braggart,
    'Fore your own eyes and ears?

ALL CONSPIRATORS   Let him die for't.

ALL PEOPLE Tear him to pieces! – Do it presently! – 119
    He killed my son! – My daughter! – He killed my
    cousin Marcus! He killed my father!

SECOND LORD
    Peace, ho! No outrage. Peace!
    The man is noble and his fame folds in   123
    This orb o' th' earth. His last offenses to us
    Shall have judicious hearing. Stand, Aufidius,   125
    And trouble not the peace.

CORIOLANUS   O that I had him,
    With six Aufidiuses, or more, his tribe,
    To use my lawful sword!

AUFIDIUS   Insolent villain!

ALL CONSPIRATORS
    Kill, kill, kill, kill, kill him!

Draw the Conspirators, and kill Marcius, who falls.
Aufidius stands on him.

LORDS   Hold, hold, hold, hold!

AUFIDIUS
My noble masters, hear me speak.

FIRST LORD   O Tullus –

SECOND LORD
Thou hast done a deed whereat valor will weep.

THIRD LORD
Tread not upon him. Masters all, be quiet!
Put up your swords.

AUFIDIUS
My lords, when you shall know – as in this rage
Provoked by him you cannot – the great danger
136 Which this man's life did owe you, you'll rejoice
137 That he is thus cut off. Please it your honors
To call me to your Senate. I'll deliver
Myself your loyal servant, or endure
Your heaviest censure.

FIRST LORD   Bear from hence his body,

And mourn you for him. Let him be regarded
As the most noble corse that ever herald   142
Did follow to his urn.

SECOND LORD   His own impatience
Takes from Aufidius a great part of blame.
Let's make the best of it.

AUFIDIUS   My rage is gone,
And I am struck with sorrow. Take him up.
Help, three o' th' chiefest soldiers; I'll be one.
Beat thou the drum, that it speak mournfully.
Trail your steel pikes. Though in this city he
Hath widowed and unchilded many a one,   150
Which to this hour bewail the injury,
Yet he shall have a noble memory.   152
Assist.   *Exeunt, bearing the body of Coriolanus.*
             A dead march sounded.

---

136 *did owe you* possessed for you   137 *Please it* may it please   142 *corse*
corpse   150 *unchilded* deprived of children   152 *memory* memorial